PRAISE FOR
CHRISTOPHER ISHERWOOD INSIDE OUT

"A masterly biography of the author of *Goodbye to Berlin* and *A Single Man*, this book captures the intricacies of a fascinating, often contradictory character. Isherwood was an upper-class Englishman (he gained American citizenship in his forties) who genuinely loved people from all walks of life; a libertine turned Vedanta monk; a gay literary icon who didn't come out publicly until his sixties. But, above all, as Bucknell shows, he was a tireless observer and recorder of people, places, and historical moments... Isherwood, she writes, 'imagined a world in which he might be able to live differently'; through his work, he helped usher that world into being." —*The New Yorker*

"Katherine Bucknell, who has edited four huge volumes of Isherwood's diaries and a collection of his letters, knows the man as no other scholar ever will... Bucknell is indefatigable, leading us expertly through every detail of his early years in England, his time in Weimar Germany, his travels everywhere from China to Western Samoa. Beneath the carnival of his social life, she never loses sight of the fact that even his spiky friend Gore Vidal named Isherwood 'the best prose writer in English.'" —Pico Iyer, *Air Mail*

"Bucknell brings scholarly acumen and bravura storytelling to her stunning biography of novelist and playwright Christopher Isherwood ... [Her] background as a novelist shows in her elegant lyricism. The sharp analysis sheds light on how Isherwood's life influenced his work. This is a monumental achievement." —*Publishers Weekly* (starred review)

"It was Nabokov's notion that the only biography of a writer that matters is the biography of their style, and Bucknell is better on this, in relation to Isherwood, than anybody has ever been—the editing of his diaries and letters has made her an authority. With this biography, we end up with an electrifying portrait of an entire period in British letters, yet the focus is where it should be, on the question of what made Isherwood the stylist he was." —Andrew O'Hagan, *London Review of Books*

"Two features in particular mark the biography as new: the close attention it pays to the influence of Isherwood's childhood and family background on his life and work; and the equally close attention it pays to the life Isherwood made for himself in California ... The book is meticulously documented, drawing on material unavailable to previous biographers ... As a critic or interpreter, Bucknell is clever, sometimes daring, and mostly convincing." —Zachary Leader, *The Times Literary Supplement*

"A penetrating exploration of the life and work of the acclaimed novelist, memoirist, and pioneering figure in gay culture. While Christopher Isherwood (1904–1986) may be best known for *Goodbye to Berlin*, which drew on his experiences in Weimar-era Berlin and inspired the musical *Cabaret*, this new biography by Bucknell, director of the Christopher Isherwood Foundation, astutely highlights the considerable merits of his other novels and candid autobiographical works. The author renders a sweeping portrait of Isherwood's remarkable life journey, during which he forged indelible connections with many of the era's preeminent literary and artistic figures." —*Kirkus Reviews* (starred review)

"Bucknell goes beyond the diaries, gathering up the many strands of the writer's personal and public lives to create a nuanced, masterful portrait of a brilliant, insecure, charismatic seeker of artistic truth and personal freedom ... Bucknell's book homes in on the conflict between Isherwood's thirst for public recognition and social climbing and the cultivation of his inner life ... As Bucknell's definitive wide-screen biography shows us, Isherwood's struggles were transmuted into lyrical

fiction that never stopped questioning what it meant to be a man in the twentieth century, and thus his art became our gift."
—Marc Weingarten, *The Boston Globe*

"Katherine Bucknell's remarkable *Christopher Isherwood Inside Out* displays an unmatched familiarity with the enormous range of Isherwood's writings, published and unpublished, while simultaneously offering a striking portrait of an extremely complicated, self-contesting and not always winning personality. His work is such a strange and compelling mixture of self-exposure and self-invention, and Bucknell gets that brilliantly, tracing his unlikely path from English squire-in-the-making to Californian Vedantist with exemplary sympathy and wit."
—Seamus Perry, *The Times Literary Supplement*

"Isherwood, the diarist and fiction writer whose work inspired the musical *Cabaret*, lived one of the twentieth century's great literary lives. He pushed to make homosexuality a mainstream subject and a pursuit seen as beautiful, like any love. Bucknell sensed that no other biography (and there have been several) had quite managed to illuminate Isherwood's 'inner life.'"
—Casey Schwartz, *The Washington Post*

"It's hard to imagine a better qualified candidate for this task than Katherine Bucknell, who has spent many years carefully untangling fact from fiction as the editor of Isherwood's diaries and letters. While she notes Isherwood's famous charm—the schoolboy grin, floppy fringe and ice-blue eyes that crinkled invitingly when he turned them on you—she is plainly keen not to be seduced. Instead, she lays out the facts in meticulous detail . . . Bucknell is scrupulously non-judgmental, and because she has all the facts at her fingertips, she is good at noticing hidden patterns in Isherwood's life."
—Robert Douglas-Fairhurst, *The Times* (London)

"Bucknell knows Isherwood like no one else—indeed, as her title has it, inside out. Here he is, in all his grippingly messed up splendour . . . Her account is utterly moving, right to the end, where she describes Isherwood on his deathbed 'occasionally calling for Nanny.'"
—Valentine Cunningham, *Literary Review*

"This absorbing biography burrows deeply into each stage of Isherwood's continuous intellectual and spiritual evolutions. Bucknell closely examines his bourgeois English childhood, marked by family tragedies, and his famous lifelong friendships with poets W. H. Auden and Stephen Spender and their interwoven influences on each other's work as well as Isherwood's successive literary triumphs . . . Bucknell's marvelously knowledgeable portrait reveals the full dimensions of his richly contemplative life." —Raúl Niño, *Booklist* (starred review)

"Bucknell's considerable sourcework—so much writing from all fronts, so many interviews from the golden age of newspapers, magazines, Cavett—is more than synthesis; it is photosynthesis. Her big blue book breathes and glistens. Her subject, who regularly meditated as a convert with Aldous Huxley to the Hindu philosophy Vedanta, is reincarnated . . . Stone by stone, she's built up a gritty, gorgeous monument to a curiously indelible twentieth-century figure."
—Alexandra Jacobs, *The New York Times Book Review*

"Immensely thorough . . . to a depth never reached before . . . A triumph of sympathetic understanding. [Bucknell] has carved her subject a place in the pantheon, and the benefits of her work, to general readers as well as to scholars, will last for a very long time."
—Andrew Motion, *New Statesman*

"A deeply penetrating psychological study written in direct, lucid, and graceful prose worthy of its subject."
—Daniel A. Burr, *The Gay and Lesbian Review*

"A first-rate biography of the man, the writer, and the lover."
—David Hockney

"*Christopher Isherwood Inside Out* is the best biography I've ever read. The subject, Christopher Isherwood, was a mindful, moral man, an example for all, and a wonderfully talented writer. Katherine Bucknell explores every moment of his life—English, German, American—and links them all to the vast ongoing project of his life and work. The book is long, but every page is full of surprises." —Edmund White

"This book—profoundly sympathetic to its subject, lucidly and excitingly written—is both a fast-paced story of an extraordinary life and a broadly illuminating history of vast cultural changes across eight decades and four continents. Katherine Bucknell, having edited four volumes of

Christopher Isherwood's diaries, has distilled her expertise into the finest literary biography of its century."

—Edward Mendelson, author of
Early Auden, Later Auden: A Critical Biography

"A roller-coaster ride through a genuinely remarkable life. Katherine Bucknell has had full access to all the primary sources—and it shows. Her Christopher Isherwood is both fascinating and dangerous, as reckless in his relationships as he was scrupulous in his art. His virtues shine, and his faults are documented with admirable candor."

—Neil Bartlett, author of *Address Book*

"Magnificent . . . This is the Isherwood book we've been waiting for. While Christopher Isherwood is rightly celebrated as a courageous forefather of the gay liberation movement, he should be equally celebrated as a fearless early practitioner and writer on Hinduism (Vedanta), again pulling the rest of the country with him. By telling the truth through his writing and through his life, Isherwood achieved greatness in his art and in his spiritual quest, and that will continue to move us and change us long after we, and all those who knew him, are gone."

—Pravrajika Vrajaprana, Vedanta Society of Southern California

"The best biographies make the reader feel they are looking over the subject's shoulder, watching them grow up and into life. Katherine Bucknell does exactly this, marshaling an enormous range of scholarship with insight, empathy, and humor. Her long immersion in Christopher Isherwood's work and life is lightly worn, she writes beautifully, and whether she is invoking declining English country-house life, Weimar Berlin, midcentury Hollywood, or the alternative cultures of California, one trusts her judgment implicitly. *Christopher Isherwood Inside Out* matches its subject's narrative skill and psychological insight, and brilliantly illuminates his search for a new way to live."

—Roy F. Foster, author of *W. B. Yeats: A Life*

KATHERINE BUCKNELL

CHRISTOPHER ISHERWOOD INSIDE OUT

Katherine Bucknell is the editor of four volumes of diaries by Christopher Isherwood; *The Animals*, a volume of letters between Isherwood and his longtime partner, Don Bachardy; and W. H. Auden's *Juvenilia: Poems, 1922–1928*. She is the director of the Christopher Isherwood Foundation as well as a founder of the W. H. Auden Society and coeditor of *Auden Studies*. Bucknell is also the author of four novels: *Canarino*, *Leninsky Prospekt*, *What You Will*, and *+1*. She lives in London.

ALSO BY KATHERINE BUCKNELL

FICTION

Canarino

Leninsky Prospekt

What You Will

+1

AS EDITOR

"*The Map of All My Youth*": *Early Works, Friends, and Influences*
(Auden Studies 1) (with Nicholas Jenkins)

"*The Language of Learning and the Language of Love*":
Uncollected Writings, New Interpretations
(Auden Studies 2) (with Nicholas Jenkins)

"*In Solitude, For Company*": *W. H. Auden after 1960*
(Auden Studies 3) (with Nicholas Jenkins)

Juvenilia: Poems, 1922–1928 by W. H. Auden
(with Nicholas Jenkins)

Diaries by Christopher Isherwood

Lost Years: A Memoir 1945–1951 by Christopher Isherwood

The Sixties: Diaries, 1960–1969 by Christopher Isherwood

Liberation: Diaries, 1970–1983 by Christopher Isherwood

The Animals:
Love Letters Between Christopher Isherwood and Don Bachardy

CHRISTOPHER ISHERWOOD INSIDE OUT

CHRISTOPHER ISHERWOOD INSIDE OUT

KATHERINE BUCKNELL

Picador
Farrar, Straus and Giroux
New York

Picador
120 Broadway, New York 10271

EU Representative: Macmillan Publishers Ireland Ltd, 1st Floor, The Liffey Trust Centre, 117–126 Sheriff Street Upper, Dublin 1, D01 YC43

Copyright © 2024 by Katherine Bucknell
All rights reserved
Printed in the United States of America
Originally published in 2024 by Chatto & Windus, Great Britain
Published in the United States in 2024 by Farrar, Straus and Giroux
First paperback edition, 2025

Illustration credits can be found on pages 851–852.

The Library of Congress has cataloged the Farrar, Straus and Giroux hardcover edition as follows:
Names: Bucknell, Katherine, author.
Title: Christopher Isherwood inside out / Katherine Bucknell.
Description: First American edition. | New York : Farrar, Straus and Giroux, 2024. | Includes bibliographical references and index.
Identifiers: LCCN 2023059580 | ISBN 9780374119362 (hardcover)
Subjects: LCSH: Isherwood, Christopher, 1904–1986. | Authors, English—20th century—Biography. | Gay authors—Great Britain—Biography.
Classification: LCC PR6017.S5 Z6286 2024 | DDC 823/.912dc23/eng/20240216
LC record available at https://lccn.loc.gov/2023059580

Paperback ISBN: 978-1-250-39057-8

The publisher of this book does not authorize the use or reproduction of any part of this book in any manner for the purpose of training artificial intelligence technologies or systems. The publisher of this book expressly reserves this book from the Text and Data Mining exception in accordance with Article 4(3) of the European Union Digital Single Market Directive 2019/790.

Our books may be purchased in bulk for specialty retail/wholesale, literacy, corporate/premium, educational, and subscription box use. Please contact MacmillanSpecialMarkets@macmillan.com.

Picador® is a US registered trademark and is used by Macmillan Publishing Group, LLC, under license from Pan Books Limited.

picadorusa.com • Follow us on social media at @picador or @picadorusa

10 9 8 7 6 5 4 3 2 1

For the Animals and the Others

Sri Krishna:

You and I, Arjuna,
Have lived many lives.
I remember them all:
You do not remember.

> *Bhagavad Gita IV,*
>
> *"Renunciation Through Knowledge"*

Contents

PROLOGUE	1
1. SON OF THE BRITISH ARMY, HEIR TO THE ESTATE (1904–1915)	11
2. SACRED ORPHAN (1915–1923)	89
3. FAILED HISTORY SCHOLAR, PUBLISHED NOVELIST (1923–1929)	158
4. BERLIN, SEX, POLITICS, AND FAME (1929–1939)	203
5. HOLLYWOOD SCREENWRITER AND HINDU MONK (1939–1945)	298
6. AMERICAN APOSTATE (1945–1953)	370
7. THE IDEAL COMPANION: DON BACHARDY (1953–1961)	445
8. EXISTENTIAL ISHERWOOD: THE OUTSIDER (1961–1964)	550
9. THE ANIMALS' GOLDEN AGE (1964–1986)	639

ACKNOWLEDGMENTS	731
NOTES	735
INDEX	813

A photographic insert follows page 444.

CHRISTOPHER ISHERWOOD INSIDE OUT

Prologue

THE SS *CHAMPLAIN* AND THE SS *AMERICAN TRADER*

Christopher Isherwood was looking for a permanent loving union as he steamed across the North Atlantic toward America in January 1939. "Off the coast of Newfoundland," he wrote in his diary, "we ran into a blizzard. The ship entered New York harbour looking like a wedding cake."

A fair-haired American rent boy waited for him on the pier, "pinched and scarlet with the cold."[1] An English dancer waited for him back in London, hoping, after a tearful farewell in a taxi, to be sent a ticket to join Isherwood in New York. Another young Englishman was completing his undergraduate degree at Cambridge University, dejected that Isherwood had ended their romance just a few months before. In Germany, a young man of twenty-three was serving a sentence of hard labor for illegal sexual acts and draft evasion after a five-year love affair with Isherwood spent partly on the run from the Gestapo. Accompanying Isherwood aboard the *Champlain* was an old friend, a poet, who had fallen unrequitedly in love with him back in 1926.

There had been and would be more—many more—boys, as he romantically called them. Younger boys who needed protection; taller boys who offered it; boys with whom Isherwood felt mentally or physically matched and energetically rivalrous. He charmed them all; his charisma was legendary. Something stopped him from caring. In his 1945 novel, the overlooked gem *Prater Violet*, he was to write in the voice of the narrator based on himself:

> Love, at the moment, was J. [. . .] After J, there would be K., and L., and M., right down the alphabet. [. . .] J. isn't really what I want. J. has only the value of being now. J. will pass, the need will remain. The need to

get back into the dark, into the bed, into the warm naked embrace, where J. is no more J. than K., L., or M.

Such a need—impervious to the individual personality of the beloved—was fed in Isherwood by fears that had haunted him since childhood. Fears that had been intensified by the death of his father in World War I and by the consequent shattering of his childhood world—the decline of his father's landed family, the hopeless grief of his mother, the developmental backwardness of his younger brother, the forced parting from his German boyfriend, his growing certainty of the coming of World War II. Isherwood summarized these fears in a passage of internal monologue in *Prater Violet* that conveys, as fiction, his intense and continuous feeling of imminent annihilation, of the approaching end of his world and himself:

> Death, the desired, the feared. The longed-for sleep. The terror of the coming of sleep. Death. War. The vast sleeping city, doomed for the bombs. The roar of oncoming engines. The gunfire. The screams. The houses shattered. Death universal. My own death. Death of the seen and known and tasted and tangible world. Death with its army of fears. Not the acknowledged fears, the fears that are advertised. More dreadful than those: the private fears of childhood. Fear of the height of the high-dive, fear of the farmer's dog and the vicar's pony, fear of cupboards, fear of the dark passage, fear of splitting your finger-nail with a chisel. And behind them, most unspeakably terrible of all, the arch-fear: the fear of being afraid.[2]

Isherwood had been on the run from fear ever since he could remember. He ran from his schoolmates in childhood. He ran from Cambridge University and a proposed academic career. He ran from Hitler's Berlin. In 1939, at the height of the fame he shared with his lifelong friend, the poet W.H. Auden, he ran west, from New York to Hollywood, where he found work writing for the movie studios and where he unexpectedly—and to some implausibly—embraced pacifism and a new religion, Vedanta. Vedanta was personified for him in a surrogate father, a Hindu guru, who offered unconditional personal love and trained him in devotional techniques that helped control his debilitating anxiety.

Isherwood was seeking a new way of life. As he and Auden had both recognized, their writing had failed to prevent the rise of fascism and could not change the world; Isherwood resolved to change himself. As the hopes of the thirties expired and old orders and conventions collapsed around him, he turned inward, to self-examination. In the near term, this would bring accusations of escapism; in the long term, it would place him in the vanguard of a new civil society which was to prize, with evolving vocabulary and emphasis, self-understanding, self-realization, non-attachment, consciousness-raising, civil rights, equal opportunity, social justice, mindfulness, wokeness.

For more than two years during World War II, February 1943 to August 1945, Isherwood lived as a monk in the Vedanta monastery in Hollywood and considered taking preliminary vows. He managed six months of chastity before reverting to a life of spiritually illuminated promiscuity, running again—through countless new love affairs. The most important of these was a serious though ultimately self-destructive six-year relationship with a charming and belligerent Irish-Catholic-Cherokee alcoholic from Kentucky, Bill Caskey.

At last, in the spring of 1953, Isherwood fell in love with a boy who was in some ways just like all the other boys, and in other ways, completely different. Don Bachardy, Isherwood eventually wrote in his diary, "has mattered and does matter more than any of the others. Because he imposes himself more, demands more, cares more—about everything he does and encounters. He is so desperately alive."[3] With Bachardy, who became a portrait painter, Isherwood was to live the life he had long imagined—physical and domestic intimacy, shared games and disciplines, daydreaming and art. As the years unfolded, Bachardy's passionate vitality was to carry them off Isherwood's life script with reckless and invigorating genius and to make real, despite betrayals and separations, the storyteller's cliché of happily ever after.

A DAY BEHIND the French liner SS *Champlain* that carried Isherwood across the Atlantic in 1939 steamed another boat, the SS *American Trader*. In boxes in the hold of the *American Trader* were 550 sets of printed pages for *Goodbye to Berlin*, the collection of fictionalized diary passages and stories based on Isherwood's real-life experiences in Berlin from 1929 to 1933 when Hitler was rising to power. Leonard and Virginia Woolf were about to publish the book at the Hogarth Press and Bennett Cerf at Random House had bought the printed pages to bind in his own cover for the U.S. market. The pieces had already appeared individually in the U.K., mostly in the magazine *New Writing*, attracting widespread praise.

When reviews of *Goodbye to Berlin* began appearing in March, the British papers were almost uniformly positive about Isherwood's portrait of the Berlin that had vanished six years earlier. In the U.S., recognition took until May, when the leading literary journalist Edmund Wilson published a knockout review in the *New Republic*. Wilson called Isherwood "a master" of social observation whose eye was free "from national or social bias." He compared the "transparency" of Isherwood's prose to Pushkin's—"You seem to look right through Isherwood and to see what he sees." Moreover, Wilson recognized Isherwood's discipline in keeping his writing "accurate, lucid and cool" in the mounting historical crisis. The novel "never gives way to sentimentality or melodrama," Wilson wrote. "To have done this is in itself to have scored a kind of victory at a moment when such victories count even more than they always do."[4]

Goodbye to Berlin secured Isherwood's fame. It trademarked his view of the city in ways that made it impossible for him ever to say goodbye, really, to Berlin. Berlin followed him across the Atlantic in the pages of his book and made him the center of continuing public attention that shaped his life both from the inside and from the outside. In 1951, one of the stories, "Sally Bowles," was adapted for the stage and became a hit Broadway play, *I Am a Camera*. In 1955, the play became a film. In 1966, it was transformed again into *Cabaret*, one of the most successful musicals of all time. In 1972, *Cabaret* was adapted for the screen, launching Liza Minnelli to superstardom as Sally Bowles, the sexual renegade and would-be showbiz star created by Isherwood. More than half a century later, *Cabaret* is still being staged somewhere in the world every day.

Isherwood had also made himself into a character in his Berlin stories. This character—named by him Chris, Christoph, Isherwood, Herr Issyvoo—reappeared on stage and screen with new names invented by adapters—Clifford Bradshaw, Brian Roberts. None of these characters was really Isherwood, partly for literary reasons and partly because Isherwood was a gay man writing at a time when his sexuality made him an outlaw. As an outlaw, he had to disguise himself. All the while, in real life, Isherwood was fighting for space in which to live and grow.

In the 1930s, his writing about Berlin, with its concern for the destiny of the workers and the poor as well as its enthusiasm for the sexually freewheeling night life, set up an expectation among his readers that Isherwood was a leader of the literary left. This expectation was greatly enhanced by the leftist plays and a travel book about China on which he collaborated with Auden. When the two emigrated together to the U.S., their followers, friends, fans and foes, felt abandoned and even betrayed. As World War II began, voices of the Left piled in with voices of the Right to attack them both as cowards for leaving their country in wartime, notwithstanding the fact that they made their departure eight months before the war started and that Isherwood had already lived abroad for most of the 1930s.

Much of Isherwood's writing aims to explain in one way or another to those he left behind why he could not stay and live among them. Why he had to run. Much of it presents the better life he sought for himself. For he always sought a better life and a better self. His spiritual journey, a journey that began with healing through devotional acts and personal love, lasted his whole adult life, and it channeled but did not quench his restlessness. His habit of harsh and public self-criticism, part of his process of change, often provided ammunition for his critics whether or not they ever subjected themselves to the same scrutiny.

Isherwood also always sought a new and larger audience, eventually this meant an American audience. For this, he worked to transform his writing as well as himself. The novel he came to consider his worst, *The World in the Evening* (1954), is in some ways his most revealing since it exposes his struggles over a period of eight years to analyse and reformulate his English literary self in a new American one; writing the novel, he retook some of the very first steps he had taken as a young writer, in order, mid-career and mid-century, to find his way as if from the beginning. His next novel, *Down There on a Visit* (1962), returns to stories and drafts abandoned in the 1930s in order to reexamine the whole idea of the self and the metamorphosing personality that found its only real home in California and in mysticism.

Isherwood worked on the boundary of fiction and nonfiction. He kept diaries most of his adult life and drew on them for his published writing, creating narratives more vivid, more revealing, more entertaining than what he documented. He altered the truth in order to make the truth more compelling, and his subtle and mysterious reworking accounts, more than anything else, for the lasting appeal of his writing. Arguably, many of his alterations get closer to the truth than mere documentation ever could; still, he put his reader on notice that fiction was at work. He combined many threads to spin his simple, seemingly light narrative line, and this gave his delicate work extraordinary strength and potency. Applying his literary skills to what he observed happening around him allowed him to intimate the flow of historical and cultural change beneath the surface of day-to-day events.

In this biography, I highlight connections between Isherwood's real-life experiences and his writing. I take you inside his imagination, where time is malleable and identity is changeable. I tell what happened to Isherwood and what Isherwood made from what happened to him. "What happened" includes the events of the imagination and the spirit—books he read, movies he saw, music he heard, rituals he practiced, fears, dreams or visions he had—as well as love affairs, toothaches, house fires, deaths of near ones, early fame, bad reviews. The differences between actual events, in so far as I can objectively establish them, and what Isherwood wrote about them may sometimes appear slight, but these differences reveal Isherwood's artistic intentions and his underlying political and spiritual agenda. They show Isherwood to be fruitfully conversing, both overtly and obliquely, with his literary forebears and contemporaries. They tend, also, to unmask a man who seemed to be hidden behind many masks—christened Christopher William Bradshaw Isherwood, published under the name Christopher Isherwood, fictionalised in his work as William Bradshaw as well as the various versions of Christopher Isherwood, known to his British friends by countless nicknames, and eventually to his American friends as, simply, Chris. They also show that Isherwood changed and grew through the practice of writing. The narratives he published began as private adventures in his imagination. He drafted and redrafted his work, traveling routes that sometimes had no outlet, retracing his steps, trying again, until he made his way into new country. His surviving drafts and workbooks offer glimpses of these secret adventures. Even false starts expanded his interior life, revealing how he continued to evolve through his work, often with a collaborator, into his eighties. (In this book, I use "Christopher" for his childhood and fictional selves and "Isherwood" from the time he arrived at Cambridge at nineteen. He referred to himself in the third person in much of his work, indicating his detachment and the constant changing of the self over time.)

His mother's diaries, crammed with detail about his infancy and childhood, allow us to recognize how early and how deeply Isherwood began absorbing the experiences that were to shape his writing. The personalities and relationships among the adults in his childhood world—marital difficulties, sibling rivalries, tensions among servants and neighbors—washed over him constantly and shaped his psychological bedrock. They erupt again and again in his mature writing along with richly resounding echoes of his earliest fears and earliest friendships. When he wrote about Germany in the 1930s, Isherwood was also writing symbolically or covertly about Britain and all that he experienced during the years his imagination was forming. His first reading, his first trips to the theater and movies, his playing, his religious education, like his circle of family and friends, have outsize importance in his adult work and way of life. He often dismissed his mother and the past she treasured, but they make a meaningful contribution to every book he wrote. He found his narrative voice through her, and he often took women writers as his literary models and spoke through his women characters. The acts of self-criticism which engendered his lifelong process of personal growth began as criticisms of his mother and then of the parts of himself which once identified with her.

Perhaps because I am an American, I am eager to show you more of Isherwood's American life and work than earlier biographies have done. I commend those biographies to you; I build on them. None so far has addressed Isherwood's inner world, and his life project of coming to understand his own feelings. Perhaps because I am settled in London, I am also eager to show you the continuity between Isherwood's English and American selves, and his unexpected resuscitation in maturity of some of the best aspects of his boyhood and youth. The life he made for himself in California shared a surprising amount with his childhood world crushed by history, albeit with crucial differences. Moreover, the liberal atmosphere of Weimar bloomed again in southern California as the New Age experiments of the 1940s—to which so many European refugees were party—gave way to the counterculture of the 1960s and the open rebellion of civil rights movements for all minority groups.

I have spent several decades editing Isherwood's diaries and studying his writing. The books he left unpublished and unwritten at his death—in particular the million-plus words of his American diaries—tip the scales toward his adopted country. I focus new attention on his California life, in which he supported himself by writing for the movies and worshipped as a Hindu at the Hollywood Vedanta Society, because this is the life Isherwood chose when he was already famous and for which he gave up his public position in England and the approval of his circle there. Isherwood and Auden with their close friends Stephen Spender and Edward Upward and a wider circle including Cecil Day Lewis and Louis MacNeice changed English literature so boldly and completely in the 1930s that they became identified as a movement, even though some of them hardly knew each other and they were seldom all together in the same place. It is less recognized that Isherwood later had a varied and significant influence on American cultural life, especially in the cosmopolitan and anti-Establishment milieu that grew out of the dislocations and relocations of World War II and the jet-set excitement of the 1960s, and in particular through his close friendships with Aldous Huxley, Lincoln Kirstein, Tennessee Williams, Truman Capote, Gore Vidal, Tony Richardson, and David Hockney.

I focus, also, on the life partner Isherwood singled out as the most important among many partners, Don Bachardy. This was the romantic relationship with which he publicly and professionally identified himself when he came out in the early days of gay liberation. I am lucky to have had unlimited access to Bachardy, who arguably knew Isherwood better than anyone else.

I often enter Isherwood's life through his work because it is the work which first made him worthy of public attention. His diaries offer wide-ranging and keen observations of the second half of the twentieth century, and I urge readers to explore them; in this book, I use them primarily for what they reveal about Isherwood himself.

Many of the books Isherwood wrote in the U.S. drew on ideas and drafts promulgated during his English and European lives, reimagining their themes and material in his new world. He returned to some themes and experiences again and again, addressing them differently in different times and different places. By reimagining them in his American writing, he honored the achievements of British modernism and the Bloomsbury Group, in particular his immediate forebears E.M. Forster and Virginia Woolf. His engagement with French and Russian writers was more clandestine but no less important.

He revealed his sexuality obliquely and gradually to a public whose prejudices were fickle at best and often hostile. His 1976 memoir about his sexual liberation in Berlin, *Christopher and His Kind*, took the lid off his earlier works set there, *Mr. Norris Changes Trains* and *Goodbye to Berlin*, and reclaimed the identity sanitized and flattened for stage and screen. But he never told as much about earlier struggles, during his school and university years, to understand his sexuality and decide what to do about it. He had searched for models to emulate, finding important ones he did not want to copy, such as Oscar Wilde. Meantime, his imagination was a haven in a world that sometimes felt threatening, even terrifying, and it offered an outlet for intense feelings of anger and revenge. At Cambridge with Upward, he had created a fantasy world, Mortmere, energized by anti-Establishment violence, sexual abuse, and black humor. Letting go in fantasy freed him to positive actions he might otherwise never have taken, a pattern which recurred throughout his creative life.

EVERY WORD ISHERWOOD wrote, apart from letters and his early diaries, was intended for the mainstream, a stream whose direction he was determined to alter while never to be seen doing so. The more time you spend with Isherwood, the more clearly you will see that his lightly connected episodic stories, his memoirs that compartmentalize a standout decade or key relationship, most of his novels—in particular his lyrical masterpiece about a day in the life of a homosexual, expatriate professor living in southern California, *A Single Man* (1964)—are part of an overarching imaginative endeavor to make sense of the twentieth century from a point of view that, when the century began, was outside the pale or at best on the margins, and by the time the century ended, had moved closer to the center. Isherwood's contribution to gay liberation, the watershed change in Western culture that strikingly overtook related and analogous movements for civil rights and social justice, was significant, subtle, and hidden away in many tiny rivulets both strategic and sentimental. His genius as a prose stylist and literary artist empowered him to engage his readers again and again until all his truths were told, even the truths that some of his readers did not like. He saw from the outset of his career that he must make homosexuality attractive to mainstream audiences if he was to change their view of it, and he worked to do this in all his writing in different ways.

I call this book *Christopher Isherwood Inside Out* because I hope it will reveal his powerful imagination and rich inner world, and also because as a gay man he came out to different audiences in different places at different historical moments to different degrees and in different ways—indirectly, implicitly, silently, comically, cautiously—but never completely until he explicitly announced his political commitment to gay liberation in the 1970s. Among writers, he was one of the first.

The gay world that lay hidden in plain sight through the first three-quarters of the twentieth century can hardly be imagined in today's Western culture—the difficulty, the danger, the pain, the excitement, the fun, the complexity and nuance of this secret community before liberation, before AIDS, before gay marriage. Isherwood's work and his life story allow us to return there in imagination, an urgent matter if we are to understand and progress from or even hold fast to where we are now. His contribution to the sexual openness of our culture in the twenty-first century is as great as his contribution to the literature of the twentieth century and cannot be separated from it. For how he lived as well as for what he wrote, he is worthy of our closest attention.

1

Son of the British Army, Heir to the Estate (1904–1915)

WYBERSLEGH HALL, HIGH LANE, CHESHIRE, 1904

Christopher Isherwood was never without an audience. He was born under the spotlight of a full August moon in a medieval manor house on his grandfather's estate in the north of England. His mother, Kathleen Bradshaw Isherwood, had sat out in the garden all morning, as she had sat out through many long, bright days that summer of 1904 with her own mother, Emily Machell-Smith, or with her husband, Isherwood's father, Captain Francis (Frank) Bradshaw Isherwood of the York and Lancaster Regiment, watching and waiting for an entrance which they could neither schedule nor control. "What a lovely year it was," Kathleen wrote in her diary many years later, "& I always associate it with harebells and heather & ripening corn . . ."¹

The baby arrived just before midnight, August 26. To his mother, August 27 seemed more desirable because it was his grandfather's birthday. Thus, throughout his childhood Isherwood celebrated his birthday one day late, playing his part in his mother's family script—for the time being.

The isolated stone manor house was poised high on a chain of hills between two villages called Disley and Marple. The front view swept southwest over the flat Cheshire plain, the back rose toward rugged moorland and the Derbyshire border. "Never outside a novel or dreams was there such an absolutely perfect house and garden with such a wonderful charm about it all," wrote Kathleen in her diary. Isherwood was later to say that it looked "like a miniature castle" because the parapet along the top was ornamented with a local design called crow-step that looked like small battlements.²

Wyberslegh Hall had been built in the fifteenth century. It was an ancestral home of Isherwood's Bradshaw forebears, purchased in 1606 by a branch of the Bradshaws of Derbyshire and Lancashire, who also purchased other local property around the same time. The Bradshaws were thereby "landed" gentry as Isherwood explained to an American lecture audience in 1960, "families that have no title and are not ennobled, but who have lived in the same place with a certain amount of money, naturally, for two or three hundred years." Family snobbery "breathed into" Isherwood that this was "the real aristocracy of England."

In the later eighteenth century, the last Miss Bradshaw married a Mr. Isherwood, a timber merchant whose family later went into shipping—"commercial" and "democratic," as Isherwood noted.[3] The prized older name was joined with the new one, though there was no hyphen, and Isherwood's father and uncles were christened with Bradshaw as a given name to guarantee against becoming merely Isherwood.

Wyberslegh was comfortable and prettily decorated. Hallways and staircase were lined with dark pink paper; pink silk curtains draped the floor-to-ceiling windows in the drawing room where sofas and easy chairs were covered in pink and white flowered material. The blue-and-white dining room was crowded with mahogany furniture. The pale blue "stone" parlor had a floor of stone blocks and a fireplace reaching to the wood-beamed ceiling with tightly packed bookshelves around it.

Zulu weapons and shields from South Africa, where Frank served in the Second Boer War, hung in the upstairs hall. Small oriental carpets were thrown down on wood floors and layered on top of larger carpets. Ornaments brought back from southern Europe decorated mantels and shelves. In the main bedroom, cut-glass perfume bottles and silver-backed hairbrushes lay on a linen runner on the dressing table. Three big drawers of Kathleen's old drop-front desk were stuffed with sketchbooks, diaries, letters, pencils, pens. There was one large bathroom with a fireplace, the nursery, a spare bedroom, Frank's dressing room, a servant's room, and a tiny back staircase leading to the kitchen and scullery with cellars underneath for coal and wine.

At the back of the house, toward the east, was a working farmyard—threshing barns, cowsheds, a dairy. The farmers lived in the rear wing walled off from the main house and worked the surrounding fields. The outbuildings included a nineteenth-century carriage house and stables forming a substantial compound. At the front of the house, sloping down to a central carriage drive, were lawns shaded by a few big trees. The garden was "gay with wallflowers and forgetmenots and orange and tawny tulips."[4]

Kathleen had sparkling gray eyes and heavy brown hair that fell waving to her waist or which she piled on her head with pins or a dark narrow ribbon. Her brows were thick and widely arched and, like her nose and her mouth, they had a kink midway along, lending her face an intriguing beakiness and point. She was highly intelligent and vivacious, unevenly educated and liked to have fun. She once recorded in her diary that a family friend reminded her how in girlhood she had had "all the boys in love with me!"[5] She was an only child, pampered and put upon by her parents, who relied on her as companion and confidante, helpmeet and nurse. She was dutiful, cautious, and correct but also energetic and curious, and she sometimes longed for experiences that lay just beyond her grasp.

The pregnancy had seemed to her like the end of youth and possibility. Two months before the arrival of this first child, Kathleen had told Frank that her life was a failure. Her slim five-foot figure—102 pounds when she married—had swelled into "a perfect mountain,"[6] and she had felt too ill to drive out visiting in a carriage over the bumpy local roads let alone travel to London or to summer house parties. In July, she had signed her will, suggesting the mortal fear of childbirth underlying her self-pity.

Nevertheless, by the time the baby was a few hours old, Kathleen began to feel a new sense of purpose. Frank was only a second son, but she had produced the first male in the next generation, making her the mother of the presumptive heir to the family estate. Frank rode with the news down the hills to his parents at Marple Hall, an Elizabethan mansion with mullioned windows and a cloak of ivy that stood inside a walled garden surrounded by trees and half buried in a hollow at the end of a long drive. "The greatest delight and pleasure at its being a grandson. Flag flying in honour . . . Felt so proud and happy and thankful. [. . .] Many wires of congratulations."[7] It was a cause for relief and celebration, this flattering birthday gift for the squire of Marple Hall, John Bradshaw Isherwood, a newborn future squire to secure the family line and the Bradshaw Isherwood name.

The future squire, the family line, the continuation of the Bradshaw Isherwood name were not to be. The baby was to grow into a young man who could not accept any prescribed place in history, and a cascade of real and metaphorical bombs was to explode the world in which that prescribed place had seemed to exist. But until he reached university, the baby did what was expected of him, and even when he turned against upbringing and background, he carried them inside him.

WHEN CHRISTOPHER WAS born, his parents were both already thirty-five years old. Only a few members of the family worked for a living. Their houses were run by servants, their affairs by lawyers.[8] They were expert at entertaining themselves. They read, they painted, they traveled, they played and listened to music, performed in amateur theatricals, went to the theater and museums, took courses on literature, on church architecture, on archaeology, on bookbinding. They attended church with solemn regularity, sometimes twice on a Sunday. They pursued close and complicated relationships with their wide circle of family and friends.

In this group of busy adults, Christopher was a curiosity. On the night of his birth, his mother observed, "He screamed loudly but is the most delightful creature with amusing long slitty eyes like a Japanese baby but lovely skin." The eyes that looked concerningly foreign to her were the chief physical feature of the charm that the baby learned to exercise upon his family circle and eventually upon the wider world. At nine months old, the eyes turned a piercing gray-blue with a small tawny patch in the right one, and much later they were overhung by romantically shaggy brows.

Christopher was adored by both his parents, and he was also looked to for diversion. "Frank is delightful with the Baby & they are most amusing together," wrote Kathleen. For two weeks, she breastfed her son between the maternity nurse's bottles, to her evident surprise: "light refreshment from me!"[9] Christopher recognized from a very early age that there was competition for the attention of his mother and father. Sometimes the Bradshaw Isherwoods made him the center of their lives, sometimes they did not.

FRANCIS BRADSHAW ISHERWOOD, educated at Cambridge and Sandhurst, the royal military academy, served as an officer in the British army for nearly twenty-three years during the period when the British Empire, the largest empire in history, covering a quarter of the Earth's land mass, was at the height of its power. An 1899 photograph shows Frank with four fellow officers in dress uniform—spiked helmets, gold-braided epaulettes, tasseled sashes, swords.[10] Frank's dark, snugly tailored jacket sets off his lean physique. His thick blond moustache flows luxuriously from nose to upper lip. Underneath the helmet, his hair was much sparser than his moustache; he wore it close-cropped. He had a broad, open face, and his blue eyes were big, contributing to a stillness and candor that contrasts with Kathleen's moody mystery and flirtatiousness.

In mid-December 1899, thirty-year-old Frank had voyaged to Durban as part of the largest contingent of British troops ever sent abroad, to quell the two-month-old rebellion of the Boers, Dutch-Afrikaans farmers, against British rule. He wrote to Kathleen, then his sweetheart, of the beauty of the landscape, of the colors he would use to paint it, of his longing for music and art galleries. Nearly eighty men were killed and wounded around him the first time he advanced under enemy artillery fire. He wasn't frightened when they were on the move, he said, but found it "demoralizing" when they had to sit in the hot sun being shelled. "Even at my worst, I always carry my knitting," he wrote. "It's such a resource." He was "making a pair of socks to march into Ladysmith," where he helped to liberate a besieged British garrison in February 1900.[11]

Then he caught typhoid and spent nearly three months in hospitals in South Africa before being invalided home. Once recovered, he served briefly in Ireland before a second South African tour, maintaining security in the newly annexed Boer republics. A month before the peace treaty was signed on May 31, 1902, he was released to sail home for good.

At the time of Christopher's birth in 1904, Frank was serving in Stockport, outside the northern industrial city of Manchester, as assistant to the commanding officer of the Fourth Volunteer Battalion of the Cheshire Regiment. He had secured this post near Wyberslegh so he could marry and settle down with Kathleen, even though it had meant leaving his own regiment.

The wedding took place on March 12, 1903, in Thurston, Suffolk, near Bury St. Edmunds, 165 miles southeast, where Kathleen grew up. Her maternal uncle, Sir Walter Greene, a wealthy brewer and the local Conservative Member of Parliament, hosted the wedding party at his large country house, Nether Hall, scene of the house parties, balls, hunt breakfasts and shoots Kathleen had attended throughout her girlhood.

The marriage was harmonious and close, but the courtship had been long and difficult because Kathleen's parents were reluctant to part with her, as Isherwood was to show in *Kathleen and Frank*, the poignant, widely acclaimed, and massive narrative about his family that he was to assemble in the late 1960s in California, a project of rediscovery and reconciliation with his rejected English past.

Kathleen's father, Frederick Machell-Smith, spurned Frank for being too poor and for courting Kathleen in secret. He held Kathleen hostage only through her guilt and fear since she was old enough to marry without his permission. By contrast, Kathleen's mother Emily insinuated herself into the lovers' relationship to claim them as her longterm companions. Emily and Kathleen both liked to talk and write endlessly about every detail of finer feeling, every nicety of dress, decor, and behavior, and whenever Kathleen's attention focused too closely on Frank, Emily became dramatically ill, inspired by her heroine, the celebrated French actress Sarah Bernhardt. Isherwood later recalled that Emily "was no imaginary invalid, but a great psychosomatic virtuoso who could produce high fevers, large swellings and mysterious rashes within the hour; her ailments were roles into which she threw herself with abandon."

Emily was a classic beauty and imposed herself like an empress. On arriving at one of the many hotels and lodgings to which she was constantly on the move, she would have the landlady "move all the furniture around, perhaps turning the bedroom into the sitting-room and vice versa. She always settled in as if she were staying forever—a characteristically royal mode of behavior." In letters, Emily referred to Kathleen as "my Mama" and signed herself "Baby-Mama."[12] Through this role reversal, Kathleen's maternal instincts were already thoroughly engaged before Christopher was born.

Frank's family was far less showy emotionally, yet the family dynamic lying below the surface was complicated and intense. Frank's father, John, had a stroke very young, forcing him to leave the army; he limped, and his speech was unclear. He was "cheerful, generous, careless and indeed wildly extravagant with his money."[13]

Frank's mother, Elizabeth, née Luce, was the daughter of Thomas Luce, banker, brewer, and Member of Parliament for Malmesbury, Wiltshire. She was the ninth of ten children and had lost two elder brothers to the empire, one serving in the navy, one in the army. She was gentle and devout, "very quiet, very undemonstrative" and "very self-sacrificing" as Frank told Kathleen.[14] She loved her children and was attentive to their needs even in adulthood,

Drama in the Bradshaw Isherwood family emanated from Henry, Frank's handsome, blond, blue-eyed elder brother, the heir apparent, who instinctively attracted attention to himself and always got his way. Henry took a B.A. at Cambridge then qualified as a barrister though evidently did not practice; he was consulted by his father on financial and estate matters, giving him power over his four siblings which Frank, only a year younger, especially resented. He was homosexual, and for this the family seemed to dismiss him, despite his privileged position. His style was camp; he "lisped slightly and dropped his final g's, as in huntin' and shootin'; otherwise his enunciation was so precise that it seemed affected."[15] The family also dismissed Henry's spiritual struggles, which were clearly linked to his sexuality. As a young man, Henry converted from Anglicanism to Roman Catholicism and entered a monastery "intending to give up the world," then he got rheumatic fever and decided—as Isherwood decided decades later in Hollywood—not to become a monk.[16] Instead, he regularly confessed "to an understanding priest," as Isherwood later recalled, "for, in his own way, he had remained sincerely devout."[17] In some respects, Uncle Henry offered Isherwood an example for his own life, but Isherwood was not prepared to be dismissed as a lightweight like his uncle nor to be indulged as overly dramatic. He wanted to be respected as a man, like his father. These contrasting father figures set up a conflict in Isherwood from an early age, especially because Henry and Frank were often in conflict with each other.

By going into the army, Frank achieved some autonomy and a life with wider vistas, but he always had to work long hours for modest pay. Even so, he was never superficial in his intellectual, artistic, and sporting pursuits. He cycled to Manchester for weekly piano lessons, attended the Hallé concerts there with his German piano teacher, and was accomplished enough to invite other musicians to play with him at Wyberslegh.[18] He worked hard at his painting, too, taking classes and studying paintings in galleries, often with Kathleen who had also studied painting and could discuss it in a more sophisticated way than she could discuss music.

Jack Bradshaw Isherwood, the third brother, christened John after their father, was seven years younger than Frank and an even better pianist. He trained as a lawyer and entered the Civil Service, dealing with death duties and property deeds in a government legal department at Somerset House in London. In his youth, Jack lived a bohemian life in London, sharing lodgings with the late-Romantic composer and poet Cyril Scott with whom he followed a series of avant-garde wellness therapies that foreshadowed the experiments of the Huxley–Isherwood circle in California in the early 1940s. Scott even met a visiting swami and attempted to form a Vedanta society.[19]

There were two sisters. Mary (Moey) Bradshaw Isherwood, two years younger than Frank, was a tomboy golfer, always outdoors, until her lungs were severely damaged by rheumatic fever and she was forced to move to the coast for the sea air as a semi-invalid. Her piety and her evident unhappiness were expressed, like her brother Henry's, in her conversion to Roman Catholicism. She never married, and her most intimate companions were women.

Esther, the youngest child, a beauty, married against the family's wishes a clergyman called Joseph Hooker Toogood, a brilliant mathematician and gifted woodcarver, viewed by the family, according to Isherwood, as "a nearly penniless nobody with a funny lower-class accent."[20]

Frank's father favored the marriage between Frank and Kathleen and offered to let them live for free at Wyberslegh. He increased Frank's allowance and guaranteed that Kathleen would continue to receive this allowance if she were widowed. The marriage settlement had to be agreed by Henry, requiring much correspondence and discussion during which Henry extracted his own promises about the estate. Kathleen grew impatient, and her resentment toward Henry was to grow and to contribute to future conflict in the family.

Incredibly, Kathleen's father gave away the bride without ever speaking to Frank at the time of the engagement or the wedding. In private, he threatened and bullied Emily and Kathleen, greatly distressing them both. In fact, Frederick was seriously ill and underwent surgery that probably removed his prostate and perhaps castrated him. He ignored Christopher's birth just as he had ignored Christopher's father. His final act of cruelty, committed in secret, was to disinherit Kathleen.[21] She later received money from Emily's side of the family, the income from a trust set up for Christopher and his brother Richard by her favorite cousin and Christopher's godmother, Agatha Greene Trevor, one of Uncle Walter Greene's daughters with whom Kathleen had grown up at Nether Hall.

By the time Frederick died, Christopher was fifteen months old and Kathleen and Frank blissfully happy. Denied her own patrimony, Kathleen was to grow increasingly focused on Christopher's future as heir to Marple Hall.

IN THE LATE 1960s, as he worked on his big book about his parents, Isherwood—by then a connoisseur of sexual matters—scoured their papers for details of physical and sexual interaction. He imagined an "unsatisfactory" kiss when Frank first proposed, and another perhaps more passionate kiss a year and a half later before Frank gave Kathleen an engagement ring. He felt certain that "Kathleen wasn't capable of encouraging him by making a passionate response."[22] This was only conjecture based on his later knowledge of her and reflecting what he wished to believe; in her diary Kathleen usually omitted or relied on euphemism for matters of sex and passion.

Frank relied on Emily to address some of the unquenchable need for emotional intimacy he had detected in Kathleen. He referred to "the *trio* of friends" arriving together at Wyberslegh after the wedding, warning "I own to having felt in the past that you did expect and want more than the close friendship we originally made our ideal . . ." Moreover, he encouraged Kathleen to invite her mother to join their honeymoon in Cambridge, where the newlyweds had only two nights at the University Arms before Emily arrived. "We slept with our window wide open all night," wrote Kathleen after her first night alone with Frank—the only hint of abandon.[23] Kathleen's intense emotional needs were to crack through Isherwood's youth like a bolt of lightning.

Frank evidently approached Kathleen sexually in a way that suited her, for she wrote again and again in her diary that she could not believe how happy she was, beginning on the day after her wedding, and seven months into the marriage she became pregnant. Isherwood thought she was shy about physical love, but Kathleen was certainly practical about fertility. Her diaries came with a yearly calendar printed in the front pages, and she marked these with ink dots, counting out when to expect her periods. Isherwood left no comment on these records and possibly overlooked them. For 1904, Kathleen put an X over August 26, when Christopher was born, and made a note, "275 days from Nov 17." On November 17, 1903, she had seen a new kind of flower, "a wonderful bright rose crimson carnation," then read some poetry and a novel Conrad and Ford Madox Ford wrote together, *Romance*. She believed her son was conceived that night. D.H. Lawrence could not have supplied better symbols.

The baby was christened Christopher William Bradshaw Isherwood at Disley Church on September 27, 1904. He wore his mother's christening robe; none of the godparents was present. The infant cross-dressing was perfectly conventional, but, like the absence of the key witnesses, right away sounded a theme that was to be repeated.

The baby's father generally called him William; his mother called him Christopher William, or Christopher, or William. Already he had more than one identity. "William" commemorated Captain William Bradshaw of the York and Lancasters, "one of Frank's few close army friends," killed in South Africa in 1899, just a few weeks before Frank arrived there. Frank admired Bradshaw as an example of the true soldier—more mannish, more soldierly, more likable than himself. Isherwood said they were not related,[24] yet their surnames linked them. The choice of "William" was in any case supported by family history because a William Bradshaw had been the father of the Henry Bradshaw who originally purchased Wyberslegh Hall. Christopher William was to be even less like Captain William Bradshaw than Frank.

"Christopher" was justified by Kathleen as having belonged to at least two distant relatives, but really, it was personal whimsy: "she chose Christopher because she liked the name," Isherwood later wrote. She wanted him to be heir, but somewhere inside her was a defiant spark wanting him to be himself. Isherwood, writing about himself in the third person, agreed with Kathleen about his name: "It has always seemed to him to be *his* name, the only one which really describes him."[25]

The day after the christening, Christopher William, not yet five weeks old, traveled by train to London with his mother and nurse. They were met on board by Emily and her maid. Emily took Kathleen into her first-class compartment, relegating the baby to second class with nurse and maid. "Christopher William behaved with astonishing dignity," wrote Kathleen in her diary, "looking most impressive & important in his best clothes—"[26]

So began the first of countless journeys he was to make throughout his life. Already, he was the central character in a story. At present, it was Kathleen telling the story; in just a few years, he would begin to tell it with her in narratives they devised together. His authorial voice was to be rooted in hers, to grow from it, at first in collaboration and later in opposition. The conversation between mother and son was so intimate that even when he was not in her presence, Isherwood was to speak to her in his thoughts and in his writing. As he grew older, he sometimes experienced Kathleen as a rival with whom he competed unconsciously. Perhaps this is one reason he never read her diaries until after her death and why, in telling his own life story, he was to mock or to omit the infant details recorded by his mother. Yet many of these details illuminate his mature personality and his work.

Kathleen and nurse settled in rented rooms in Wimbledon, just outside London, where they walked or relaxed on the common with Christopher William. Kathleen loved her baby, but she had never been led to believe that she could care for him alone, and she could not sleep for worrying who would succeed the maternity nurse. After several missteps, she hired a temporary nanny called Davis. Then she packed and left her six-week-old son with a woman she had known for two days. She didn't see the baby again for three weeks, and she never went back to Wimbledon.

Frank took Kathleen to the Norfolk coast, driving, walking, and sketching. She interviewed another nanny, Anne Avis, at Liverpool Street Station in London, before catching the Norfolk train; she followed up a single reference, then sent Anne Avis to Wimbledon to meet Christopher William "before he was finally handed over to her." The rhyming pair of nurses, Davis and Avis, brought their charge to London on October 29, and Nurse Avis traveled on with Christopher William and his mother to Stockport and Wyberslegh Hall, where they arrived by carriage to find everything prepared by invisible hands: "The house looked so fresh & clean & the nursery very nice—and quite big with the smaller bed in it."[27]

The smaller bed was for Nurse Avis. She slept in it for the next three and a half years at Wyberslegh, and thereafter in Christopher's other nurseries for a decade in total. She was to create for him a simple, steady routine that ballasted him against the mania for movement and diversion that so often possessed his parents and which he himself came to love.

ANNE AVIS WAS about thirty when she began working for the Bradshaw Isherwoods, perhaps only five years younger than Kathleen. Like Kathleen she had been born near Bury St. Edmunds. She came from a big family and was raised by an aunt and uncle. She had once been engaged but her fiancé died.

In *Kathleen and Frank*, Isherwood described Anne Avis as "small and sturdily built. She was quite pretty when young."[28] In a photo taken when

Isherwood was five, she grips the reins of his pony as he sits astride at the front door of Marple Hall. Her posture is erect, her complexion well washed and weathered with a strong nose and bony jaw. Wavy dark hair covers her ears and is neatly pulled up underneath a straight brimmed little hat. She wears a tweed jacket and skirt, a high-necked white blouse and white fingerless gloves.

Anne Avis had no acquaintances or attachments in Cheshire. She sometimes went to the servants' supper at Marple Hall, and she grew friendly with the housekeepers there and at Wyberslegh. She was in contact with other neighborhood nannies once Christopher was old enough for playmates. She never missed church on Sundays.

As was the custom of the time, she devoted herself entirely to the baby, giving up her name for her new role; Kathleen called her Nurse, and Christopher was to call her Nanny. Every morning and every afternoon, Nanny took him out for several hours in his pram. Later, she took him in a stroller designed after a Victorian postal cart, which allowed him to sit up facing her. Kathleen recorded that Christopher's mail cart, a lavish gift from a friend, was "such a pretty white one"[29]—more suited to fairyland than to the wilds of Cheshire. Once a week, Nanny pushed Christopher the three miles to Marple Hall for lunch with his grandparents, then home again afterwards. The going was hilly, rough, and wet, and sometimes so muddy that the wheels would come off whichever vehicle she was pushing.

When Nanny was off or busy with chores like laundry, Kathleen herself looked after Christopher. She reveled in his robust health and infectious happiness, and their time together was given special importance by her natural sense of ceremony and by the fact that she reported it all to her diary. Everything she did was part of a performance for an invisible audience. She made a little book about Christopher William called *The Baby's Progress*, in which she recorded with excitement the milestones of his thriving baby life, underlining and supplementing in later years anything that seemed to prophesy literary talent.

To Christopher, Kathleen was glamorous and exciting. "I went in to see him in a jetted dress before going out to dinner," she noted in her diary in July 1906 when he was nearly two, "& he at once sat up in bed & said, 'Oh smart, pretty.'"[30] It was the usual intoxicating love affair between mother and child.

But Kathleen was often away for weeks at a time, a torment for Christopher, who would wave her off on the train, his infant yearning to be aboard fulfilled in his lifelong addiction to departures and arrivals.[31] In *Kathleen and Frank*, Isherwood looked kindly on this traditional British upper-middle-class arrangement. Kathleen "had to be wife and daughter first, a mother second," he wrote. "Under the circumstances she was wise to leave Nanny supreme in her own sphere, instead of competing with her as a nurse and inviting comparisons."[32] In fact, competition and jealousy lay just beneath the surface. Baby, for his part, was in love on both sides of the covert power struggle between mother and nanny that unfolded over the years.

Though Nanny took Kathleen's authority seriously and thirsted for her approval, she had a subversive streak. Baby's was the only authority she liked to acknowledge. She signed her letters to Kathleen "Yours obediently" but celebrated a spirit of anarchy and independence in her charge: "I wish you could see the mischief Baby gets into, now he can get about the floor. Yesterday he got under the table & pulled the table cloth off. His jug was on the table with his milk in of course that broke he thought it was grand to see a little stream of milk running down the nursery." She was careful to assuage Kathleen's jealousy, adding that "he says, air Mama"[33]—where is Mama? Probably she knew that family and close friends reported on her and Baby by letter when Kathleen was away.

Nanny's absence was a greater torment than Kathleen's. When Nanny went on her annual holiday in July 1906, she and Christopher were "both in tears." When she returned, after two weeks away, he "Simply yelled,"[34] evidently punishing Nanny for leaving him. Triangles were to shape Isherwood's adult friendships, and they were introduced at an early age, along with the emotional principle that intimate companions should be interchangeable.

Christopher William's clothes were impossibly elaborate. One photograph shows him at sixteen months old lovingly slung on his mother's hip in the doorway at Wyberslegh in a snow-white dress, long-sleeved, reaching to his feet which are shod in tiny white shoes. A frilled white bonnet is tied under his chin with ribbon. Nanny made him a protective overall: "I can just slip that off if any one calls & he is beautifully clean," she assured Kathleen.[35] It was his first disguise, permitting him to descend to the freedom and pleasure of playing on the floor and to return fresh and pure in appearance to the eyes of his admirers. He was to play just as freely in the slums of Berlin and to return to the drawing rooms of polite society with no outward stain.

Isherwood later described Kathleen's parents Frederick and Emily as "star personalities, demanding complete cooperation from their supporting cast."[36] He presented Henry Bradshaw Isherwood as another star personality, with ostentatiously handsome features suitable for the stage. In this galaxy of stars, Kathleen and Nanny were like stage mothers, training Christopher William, the next generation of talent, to make himself a center of attention wherever he went and launching him into the limelight. On his first Christmas at Marple Hall: "Baby was established in Moey's room,"

Kathleen recorded, "& receiving much attention—he was very good & looked so rosy & well His grandfather sent for him down to the dining room to have his health drunk—"[37]

Nanny created an offstage, where Christopher could retire from the demands of his first public and the pressure of his position as heir. In *Kathleen and Frank*, Isherwood wrote that "he loved Nanny dearly. He bullied her and ordered her around but rewarded her by telling her his secrets ... He treated her as a familiar with whom he could be shameless and at ease, as a servant with whom he could league himself against his own class."[38]

On his first birthday, Nanny gave Christopher a toy horse, a dobbin. In later years, Isherwood was to take Dobbin as his pet identity, and this pet identity formed the heart of a private world he shared with Don Bachardy, who took the identity of a kitten. Secretly, Isherwood and Bachardy referred to themselves as The Animals, and they evolved an alternative Animal world that afforded them the freedom and security that Isherwood first felt in his nursery. When Christopher was six, his parents brought back from Banja Luka in Bosnia and Herzegovina a crockery whistle in the shape of a horse which he kept all his life.

FRANK AND KATHLEEN themselves sometimes privately adopted alternative identities and engaged in quasi-literary role-playing. For instance, in his letters during their courtship, Frank had addressed Kathleen as Elizabeth for Elizabeth Barrett whom he, as Robert Browning, must rescue from her father and marry. From South Africa, he had portrayed himself as a gypsy, longing "to have a little cart and a little tent beside it and wander about from countryside to countryside at your own sweet will, not with a train of soldiers."[39]

Kathleen had an unconventional friendship with a woman about ten years younger than she, Mable Tristram, known as Mamie, who also liked to act out her feelings through role-playing. Mamie met and fell in love with Kathleen soon after Kathleen settled at Wyberslegh. There is no suggestion of a sexual relationship, but Mamie's letters are sensual. She told Kathleen that she wanted to sleep with an umbrella Kathleen had given her and that she was captivated by Kathleen's appearance, for instance on a walk: "When we were 'stuck up' and you were standing on the path I thought you were lovelier than I'd ever seen you."[40]

Sometimes Kathleen expressed impatience with the intensity of Mamie's feelings, but she encouraged the friendship, and she evidently enjoyed the role-playing. She sent Mamie a copy of John Ruskin's *Sesame and Lilies*, in which Ruskin proposed a chivalric order to instill kingly power in a man and queenly power in a woman. Thereafter, Mamie referred to Kathleen as her Queen, casting herself as Kathleen's handmaiden, writing to her on parchment in illuminated handwriting and sketching yearning figures in medieval dress. She referred to Frank and her own husband, Harold, as mystical personages and as Arthurian knights, alluding to her jealousy of Frank through these fantasy roles.

Mamie had another fantasy in which she and Kathleen were the Ladies of Llangollen, Eleanor Butler and Sarah Ponsonby, the educated, upper-class women who in 1778 had eloped from their family homes in Ireland and settled at Llangollen in Wales where they created a Gothic house and garden and attracted the attention of the Romantic poets and their circle.

Sometimes Mamie assigned roles from the novels of Robert Louis Stevenson, a favorite author of Frank and a cousin of Kathleen through the Greenes. Thus, Christopher was born into games of pretend already being played around him with great flair—camps of courtly love, Gothic girl love, adventuring love. He was to become a master of this kind of game.

Eventually, the friendship with Mamie shifted into a more conventional emotional register, but Kathleen saved Mamie's letters, and later showed them off to her grown-up sons who laughed excitedly over them. Meantime, Christopher was to follow Mamie's infatuations with glee. At eleven years old, as Kathleen recorded, he baited one crush, a Mrs. Seeley, who had taken control of the Tristram household. Christopher, "knowing all, asked her 'innocently' where she lived, & if she had no home of her own!!"[41]

Christopher was often thrown together with Mamie's son, Leonard Tristram, three years older than he, who was to follow a spiritual path strikingly similar to his own. Leonard Tristram became a disciple of Krishnamurti, the one-time messiah of Theosophy, and settled in California. Isherwood was to draw on Leonard Tristram's life story for his final novel, *A Meeting by the River*.

MOST AUGUSTS, KATHLEEN and Frank spent a week or two in Oxford attending university extension lectures with Emily. Sketching trips abroad took place in October—to Spain in 1905 and 1907; to Italy in 1906 and 1909. It was in 1910 that they ventured to Bosnia and Herzegovina and Dalmatia.

During their absences, Christopher spent more time with his Isherwood grandparents at Marple Hall. Marple "had the self-assured charm of a 'country-seat,'" he recalled in *Kathleen and Frank*. "Coming into the house, you felt at once that you were in a showplace." Indeed, it was ranked "second to none among the old manor houses of Cheshire" in a lavishly illustrated article published in *Country Life* in the spring of 1919.[42]

The house was E-shaped, to honor Elizabeth, monarch at the time of construction, built of local red sandstone and much remodeled over the centuries. The original low-ceilinged entrance hall still ran all the way through the ground floor, with five or six doors leading off it, a white stone floor set with black marble lozenges and a huge fireplace. There were weapons and suits of armor on display, dower chests, pewter dishes, family portraits, stag heads. The massive black oak staircase mounted from the right side. Upstairs were tall canopy beds, initricately carved and draped; one bedroom included a minstrels' gallery.

The library, with perhaps fifteen hundred books, many behind glass doors in a massive oak bookcase, opened onto "a Victorian Gothic conservatory." The dining room could seat twenty. A Gobelins tapestry, "Winter," covered one wall, and Isherwood recalled, "Over the sideboard was a portrait of Queen Elizabeth in ruff and jeweled stomacher." Over the mantel was a unique double portrait of John Donne and his wife Anne More, harbinger of Isherwood's life theme, the writer and his soulmate, partners despite the opposition of their world.[43]

The drawing room, reached by its own staircase, had more recent formal furniture, another Gobelins tapestry, "Autumn," on the chimney wall,[44] and a massive pink marble fireplace brought back from Venice by Uncle Henry. Two caryatids as tall as a man supported the mantel.

Marple Hall was dark and shadowy, and being set in a hollow, "was apt to make you feel shut in." The interior was mostly paneled in dark oak, some panels decorated with gilded edges and coats of arms, and many of the windows were stained glass, dimming the light. The air was smoky from the chimneys of the nearby mills. "And there was so much furniture," wrote Isherwood.[45]

A shrine to King Charles I, known as King Charles's Closet, faced the foot of the drawing-room stairs in a tiny, dark, oak-paneled room. Here, as Christopher learned growing up, a great-aunt had prayed for forgiveness to an effigy of the martyr king kneeling as he read his death warrant which was signed by Christopher's most notorious forebear, John Bradshaw, the Puritan revolutionary judge appointed by Oliver Cromwell to preside over King Charles's trial. As Christopher also learned, there was a schism in the family between those descendants eager for expiation and those proud of the regicide. Isherwood was to proclaim his pride in the Puritan revolutionary, but over the years, he was to take both sides, and to devise a private myth about heroism that permitted him to reconcile them, as we shall see.

The setting of Marple Hall afforded a dramatic surprise. There was a spectacular drop concealed behind the house. From the terrace, wooded sandstone cliffs fell two hundred feet into a narrow valley where there was a pond, complete with an island and grotto. The pond had once filled the valley and formed part of the River Goyt which feeds the Mersey, "rapid and foaming yellow with chemicals from the mills" in Isherwood's memory of his childhood. The pond was called the Mere Pool, hence the name Marple.[46]

In 1907, the year Christopher turned three, he and Nanny stayed at Marple Hall in August and again in October and November, and Isherwood later remembered that he had liked to accompany the housemaids on their daily cleaning rounds. "Since Marple had many visitors in those days, some of them unexpected, its show-rooms had to be kept dusted and polished—" Like Christopher in Nanny's overall, Marple Hall had to be kept ready for its public. Christopher liked to be among those putting on the show, the servants: "But when the curtain finally went up, and some of the maids put on starched aprons and became actresses who served lunch in the Dining-Room, then Christopher was excluded. He had to sit still at the table and be waited on. He was just a member of the audience."[47]

Frank oversaw the electrification of Marple Hall, completed in 1904, but what Isherwood recalled in adulthood was "the thrill of visiting the engine-room to watch Coyne, the gardener, start the engine" which powered up the house from the ground floor to the attics. "This always seemed exciting and dangerous, because Coyne, who was muscular but small and light, had to climb onto the great flywheel and use his whole weight to get it moving, leaping off again before it kicked back."[48]

The suits of armor, the Flemish tapestries, the portrait of Elizabeth I, silver tankards, salvers, ancient leather books had all been placed there by previous generations. Christopher's paternal grandparents were mere passengers in a historical trajectory which took little note of them as individual personalities and which did not even permit them to decide what became of the house at their death. Their sons had the same names as their predecessors—Henry, Francis, John. Only a handful of Bradshaw Isherwoods had stood out in a long repetitious tale. During meals, Christopher was trapped in a Jacobean dining chair staring at a tapestry of winter and a painting of a dead virgin queen.

On top of this forced passivity, Marple Hall literally spooked him. He devoted many pages in *Kathleen and Frank* to the Marple ghosts, and one in particular that haunted both him and his younger brother. This ghost was a woman from nearby Brabyns Hall who had married into the Bradshaw Isherwood family, failed to produce an heir, and been sent back to Brabyns. She was known as Moll of Brabyns. "Moll was supposed to have resented the loss of Marple so passionately that her ghost came back to haunt it, looking for her wedding ring ... Moll was also supposed to hate children, as being usurpers of 'her' property. So she wanted to scare them off the premises."[49]

While his parents were away, Nanny reported to Kathleen that Moll of Brabyns haunted Christopher every night between midnight and 2 a.m. "How she must have reveled in the telling of it and in the knowledge that she was forcing her mistrustful mistress to believe her!" Isherwood wrote. Kathleen recorded it all in her diary. And what a grip it gave Nanny on her infant charge, for as Kathleen noted, "Christopher is naturally a nervous child, and if he ever does wake and find himself alone, shrieks almost hysterically for 'Nanny.'"[50]

In October, the hauntings took a fantastic turn when Christopher was removed from bed in his nursery while Nanny was at servants' supper. "A strange noise" was heard on the terrace outside the servants' hall, and then Christopher appeared inside, calling for Nanny. He reported that his father—more than a thousand miles away in Spain—had carried him downstairs. When Christopher was taken back up to bed, Uncle Jack had to force open the nursery door which was blocked from inside by a chair jammed against a chest of drawers. Isherwood methodically analysed the episode in *Kathleen and Frank* without arriving at the most likely explanation—that the servants were pranking Nanny for making so much of Moll of Brabyns. Perhaps he preferred not to address the loneliness and unease that might have driven Nanny to such behavior.[51]

It was the servants at Marple Hall who evinced vigor and purpose. The maids seemed to have control of the house; Coyne could start the generator; the coachman, Robert Dobson, drove Isherwood's grandfather through the village each day in the family brougham, often with Christopher accompanying, "fetching the papers & ordering the fish & going to bank"; Anne Pott, the housekeeper, assigned bedrooms and finalized menus. The family, like Christopher without Nanny, was helpless alone. The hauntings reflected attitudes and aspirations that could be expressed only in fleeting, indirect snatches, in servants' hall gossip, in grumblings, in jokes and tricks. They were part of the evidence that Marple Hall, and the hierarchical social structure on which it depended, was doomed: "After the First World War it was already obsolete, because it was too big. You couldn't maintain it without a large staff of servants, and servants had now become prohibitively expensive—"[52]

In *Kathleen and Frank*, Isherwood recalled a sensation of relief when he could flip roles and join the haunters:

> Once or twice, when his schoolfriends came to stay, he played "ghosts" with them. They put on sheets and ran around the pitch-black passages or peered in through the kitchen windows from the darkness outside, wailing to scare the maids. From Christopher's point of view the

curious thing was that, as long as he was playing this game, he lost all his fear of the psychic menace; indeed, he felt that *he was part of it.*⁵³

Going over to the other side—be it the dark side or the light side—was a strategy Isherwood used throughout his life to address fear or disillusionment, to negotiate confrontation, to break an impasse, to reach higher ground.⁵⁴

THE MESSAGE FROM Moll of Brabyns to the occupant of the nursery was, essentially, "You do not belong here, you are a usurper," reflecting emotions within the Bradshaw Isherwood family, as well as among the broader household. Matters of precedence and sibling rivalry created intense resentment in all the adults around Christopher. He absorbed it, and it was to inform his mature fiction, particularly in the 1930s, something he never explicitly acknowledged.

In addition to resenting Uncle Henry, Kathleen—unused to siblings—took against her beautiful sister-in-law Esther Toogood and Esther's children, Christopher's first cousins, Joan and Timothy, born 1902 and 1905. To Kathleen, Esther's children ranked below Christopher, because Christopher was the heir and also because Esther had married beneath her. But Esther was a daughter of the house, and whenever the Toogood children stayed at Marple, Kathleen felt crowded out. On more than one occasion, Christopher's overnight visits were canceled. Nanny identified with Kathleen in all of this, on behalf of her charge, and in childhood, Christopher, too, adopted his mother's attitude. Even in *Kathleen and Frank*, Isherwood did not mention Joan and Timothy Toogood by name.

The fraught relationship between Frank and his brother Henry was made worse in October 1907, when Henry surprised the whole family by becoming engaged to an heiress, Beatrice Muriel Bagshawe. Both Muriel's parents were dead, and Muriel possessed two estates—the grander being The Oakes, near Sheffield, a seventeenth-century mansion with Georgian renovations. She had agreed that children could be raised Roman Catholic. "Poor C. W. his nose already seemed out of joint & his charms to have grown less, in view of his Bagshawe cousins to be!" wrote Kathleen.

Henry and Muriel's wedding was in London in November. Frank and Kathleen were in Spain and so did not attend. In the new year, Henry and Muriel, who adopted the joined surname Bradshaw Isherwood Bagshawe, gave celebratory dinners for their tenants at The Oakes and at Marple Hall. Again, Frank and Kathleen did not attend. Henry was indignant and wrote Frank a stinging letter. A full-fledged feud was breaking out. To Kathleen,

1: Son of the British Army, Heir to the Estate (1904–1915) / 29

Frank observed, "If he is suffering so badly from a swelled head, the less we see of him in the future, the better. He writes as if we were in some way his dependants. . . . His tone most high and mighty."[55]

The unexpected marriage was not the first time Henry had toyed with Frank's expectations. Isherwood recalled in his draft for *Kathleen and Frank* that when Henry had entered the Roman Catholic monastery, he "wrote to Frank saying that, having given up the world and its goods, he was glad to think that Frank would be the one to inherit the family property."[56] Frank had looked on Henry as a dynastic cul de sac while seeing himself as the carrier of the true hereditary line of the Bradshaw Isherwood family, the virile, masculine line which had produced a male heir.

Frank was even angrier when he learned eight months after the wedding that Muriel and Henry's lawyers had changed the Bradshaw Isherwood entail to match Muriel's, so that the Marple Estate could be inherited through the female line, doubling the chance that Frank and Christopher might be pushed aside. Henry insisted the change had been forced on them by Muriel's lawyers but acknowledged he had been in a rush to marry. Indeed, he had extravagant habits, and he was happy to sign whatever his rich bride required. Whether or not he deliberately tricked his father, double-crossed his brother, and sold up his nephew, it certainly seemed that way to Frank and Kathleen. Henry's greed and manipulativeness entered family lore, and Isherwood was to build the first of his reputation-making Berlin novels, *Mr. Norris Changes Trains* (1935), on behavior like Henry's, using different characters and a German setting to act out the unscrupulous use of nearest and dearest that had electrified his childhood.

WYBERSLEGH HALL WAS not haunted, not fought over. It was bright with sunlight, and in *Kathleen and Frank,* Isherwood depicted it as belonging to the natural world of landscape and weather rather than to social history, politics, and power. This wild world, in which Kathleen and Frank had been blissfully happy for five years, closed to them in the winter of 1908 when Christopher was three and a half. Frank had to return to his own regiment which was stationed about eighty miles away at York—just the sort of reality that Henry Bradshaw Isherwood never had to face.

They took a tiny cottage in a village called Strensall where Frank taught signaling and his students, junior officers, regularly visited for tea and supper. Christopher's grandfather took him into the soaring Gothic interior of York Minster "to see the old regimental colours that he used to carry,"[57] and Christopher watched the soldiers parade in on Military Sunday.

Frank and Kathleen never lived together at Wyberslegh Hall again. The slow Edenic time into which Christopher had been born became a kind of golden age which Kathleen remembered and referred to as a lost, perfect happiness. Kathleen, Christopher and Nanny became camp followers. They were to move with the regiment twice more over the next six years before breaking up the household altogether when World War I started in 1914.

Their later homes were buffeted less by the Bradshaw Isherwood family dynamic, and they had many additional happy, domestic hours. Still, the hauntings—and the emotional turmoil they embodied—presaged a permanent exile. "I feel like the Israelites journeying across the desert," Kathleen wrote in her diary, "I suppose one gets used to wandering."[58]

The fight with Henry over the entail went on through 1908. Frank was called to London for meetings with the family lawyer, and he and Kathleen were already hunting for another new house at his next posting. Frank broke down under the strain. In September, he had a severe relapse of the typhoid he had caught during the Boer War, "almost as if he had eaten something of a poisonous nature," Kathleen wrote. The doctor prescribed a "mild diet—Tapioca pudding, toast & milk—"[59] The plainest eating would never rid Frank of the germ living in his gut, nor of the family ghosts haunting them all.

FRIMLEY AND ALDERSHOT, 1908

After nine months at York, the Bradshaw Isherwood family relocated more than two hundred miles south, to Aldershot, established in 1854 as the first purpose-built British army camp. There were thousands of soldiers living in the area, along with everything required for housing, feeding, training, arming and transporting them: brick barracks, dining halls, parade grounds, a hospital for the wounded, and a graveyard for the dead. The camp, divided into North Camp and South Camp by the Basingstoke Canal, had its own schools, reservoir, gasworks, power station, and sewage. It was the heart of the British army, and it was still growing.

The Bradshaw Isherwoods settled three miles from camp at Frimley Green, surrounded by woods and ponds. The new house, Frimley Lodge, was bigger and much more to Kathleen's taste than the cottage at Strensall, and it was only forty miles from Emily and the delights of Edwardian London. Here they were to stay for three years, marked by Christopher's first attendance at school and culminating with the birth of his only sibling, Richard, in 1911.

The constant movement to Marple Hall, Bury St. Edmunds, London, abroad, and even to stay with Henry and Muriel at The Oakes never stopped. Christopher often came along. In April 1909, there was a two-week holiday with Granny Emily in Lyme Regis on the Dorset coast, where he played on the beach every morning, "intensely happy."[60] It was not his first seaside holiday. He had visited Penmaenmawr in Wales when he was just ten months old, and since then Kathleen had taken him to various seaside resorts nearly every year, and sometimes twice. Again and again, she described in her diary his complete physical abandon when he played on the sand by the water's edge, waded, and swam.

Sensitive as he was to the dark threat of Marple Hall, Christopher had an instinct for the light. His earliest summers were a daydream of innocent sensual intoxication. At Frimley, he helped his parents in the garden, planting and tending flowers, vegetables, and fruit for their own table. He and Kathleen took special hedonistic pleasure in the greenhouse, alive with baby fir trees or tomatoes or grapes: "It really is delicious there—quite 'summerland' as Christopher says, & we have long chairs, & get all the sun."[61]

The timeless garden world in which he played at home with his parents was matched by the seaside world where he lost himself with Nanny or all alone, free of fear, and which he sought to recapture in his adult life. For him, these outdoor worlds of garden and shore tapped the transcendent.

But set against these joys were shocks of fear that affected him with growing power. In June 1909, he suffered an extreme fright when he went with his mother and grandparents to see an exhibition of war games. The scale and realism—complete with gigantic mechanized artillery—terrified both him and Kathleen. Until now, Christopher had been thrilled by military shows, but suddenly Frank's army world of parade and flag-draped rituals exploded with chaotic troop movement and overwhelming noise:

> We found ourselves in the midst of a terrific battle, Aldershot supposed to be evacuating & the other side attacking. We looked down over a big valley & miles of country & the big cannons booming off all round us, were awful. C & I hated them & the guns in the trenches made a horribly fearful noise too.[62]

Of course, they did not know this game presaged horrible realities to come in a half-decade.

That October, when Frank and Kathleen returned to Marple Hall from one of their European trips, five-year-old Christopher collaborated with Kathleen on a story she called "The Adventures of Daddie & Mummie, chiefly about himself!"[63] Two versions survive, showcasing his joys and fears. One reports factually on Christopher's life at this time—his grandparents, the pony hired so he could learn to ride, the dog that walked with them, Old Dash, and the letters and postcards exchanged with his parents abroad. A vivid image is borrowed from a letter describing Florence, "in the garden they wrote and said the peaches hung ripe upon the trees."

In this embryo autobiography, Christopher and Kathleen addressed themes to which Isherwood was to return throughout his career. Already, letters played a role, joining present and absent; already "abroad" was the realm of safety and adventure where an exotic southern garden lured with its fruit. The climax was the return of the travelers just in time for Guy Fawkes Night and Christopher's excitement at being the center of attention when he disguised himself as the Roman Catholic rebel, who was hanged, drawn and quartered for trying to blow up the Houses of Parliament: "when Anne came to the door she saw the little boy dressed up as Guy Fawkes, and lots of other people came to see him, Even the cook, and some of the Maids."[64]

The other version focuses on the frightening backstage area in the attics at Marple Hall, where

> there was a little dark place called the Glory Hole rather like a Dungeon and there was a kind of little low archway with a nasty little hole in the floor, and if you looked down that hole you could see the foundation of the house—It is supposed that in olden days when people were troublesome they threw them down that hole—[65]

That dark hole sucked at Christopher, down into the past, into nothingness. His story announced to his maternal collaborator his determination not to be lost at Marple and not to be forgotten.

ONE OF CHRISTOPHER'S Frimley playmates, Arthur Forbes, made a particularly strong impression on him, and Arthur's mother, Agnes, made a strong impression on Kathleen, who pushed the friendship by allowing Christopher to accept spur-of-the-moment invitations from Arthur and accompanying him herself rather than sending Nanny. The Bradshaw Isherwoods and the Forbeses occasionally dined together in the evening. Major Forbes was descended from the 1st Earl of Granard, founder of his regiment; Agnes was pretty and played the violin. Frank accompanied her at home and in public, and Kathleen was evidently jealous. Her emotions around the friendship seem to have intensified Christopher's emotions toward Arthur, making Christopher feel that the friendship must succeed for his mother's pleasure if not for his own.

As Christopher approached six years old, he was proving increasingly highly strung. Thunder and lightning upset him, playing with friends in new mown-hay made him ill (possibly he was allergic), and he was in tears again when Nanny left for her summer holiday in 1910. While Nanny was away, he experienced another extreme fright, this time on a funfair ride, "the Flying Ostriches, which went up & down & round, & round to sickly music." Humiliatingly, he had to be removed in front of Arthur, who "never turned a hair." Nanny returned that very day, and off went Frank and Kathleen to Oxford, up and down and round and round. By the time they got home again, they found "Poor C looking very pale—" His teeth were aching. Kathleen called in a doctor, who offered a range of worrying advice including circumcision ("a sword to my heart"), consulting an eye doctor, and "drilling to develop chest." The doctor prescribed both a sedative and a tonic.[66]

Kathleen's dentist advised that six-year-old Christopher's molars might be the cause of his misery. The eruptions in his mouth seemed to exacerbate something brewing in his psyche, making him afraid of things previously enjoyed, as Kathleen noted at Marple during August when "Even going on the pony seems to frighten him."[67]

It was decided that Christopher should give up riding the pony, which was sent back to the farmer. The Marple doctor agreed with the dentist, prescribed a tonic plus beef tea every night, and then Virol, a mixture of bone marrow, eggs, malt extract, and lemon syrup. Christopher seemed "brighter" on his return to Frimley, but when Kathleen and Agnes Forbes took him to play in the woods with Arthur, he panicked: "C. all on wires & all nerves terrified if the dog came near him & easily excited & up-set, changing colours quickly."[68]

These were the fears Isherwood evoked half a century later in his first novel written in California, *Prater Violet*, set on the cusp of fascist triumph in Germany and Austria, fears that had made him turn to the spiritual life: "the private fears of childhood ... fear of the farmer's dog and the vicar's pony, fear of cupboards, fear of the dark passage ... And behind them, most unspeakably terrible of all, the arch-fear: the fear of being afraid."

Frank supervised calisthenics and gymnastics as advised by the doctor to build up Christopher's chest, drilling Christopher with a friend. He also began to teach Christopher French. A year later, he began teaching him piano, even though it was agreed that Christopher "does not seem to have any particular ear for it."[69]

For Christopher, Frank was a dynamic presence, both in his public role as a soldier and in private as a playmate, storyteller, and teacher. In January 1909, Frank took the lead in an amateur production of John Lenville Hillcox's humorous dialogue, *In Chancery, or, Browne with an E*. Christopher sensed the excitement, but he was not allowed to see the show. This prohibition launched a tremor of anticipation so intense that Isherwood could summon it again all his life. In *Kathleen and Frank*, he wrote: "they let him peep into the hall just before the performance began and see the audience and the lighted curtain. What he so vividly remembers is the thrill this curtain gave him, with its infinite promise of what it would reveal when it rose."[70] In some of his other mature writing, Isherwood was to use the curtain image to mark the threshold of sexual fantasy at the entrances to bars that were staging areas for life-changing romances—the Cosy Corner, his first ever boy bar in Berlin, and the fictional Starboard Side, based on a real bar, the Friendship, in Santa Monica.

Toward the end of 1910, to help Christopher with his reading, Frank began making a little newspaper, *The Toy-Drawer Times*: "He could draw very fast and also write in block capitals (which were easier for Christopher to read) as quickly as most people could write long hand. He told Christopher the story as he did this. The stories were mostly adaptations from Dumas, Henty, Stevenson, Conan Doyle, H.G. Wells." They kept the newspaper going until Christopher went away to boarding school in 1914, and the authors Frank adapted became favorites of Isherwood in adolescence. Isherwood explained that the newspaper "evolved into a kind of comic strip,"[71] and it also foretold the moving pictures—silent, captioned—that Christopher was soon to see and fall in love with.

―――

FRANK'S PAINTING WAS going well, engendering a crisis. Could he advance to a new level as an artist, perhaps make it the center of his life and turn professional? In February 1910, two of his watercolors were chosen for a show at the Old Dudley Art Society in Mayfair, and he considered retiring from active duty. When he heard that one of the pictures had sold for four guineas—enough to keep a working-class family for a month—he had a relapse of typhoid. He applied for a job in the Cheshire police force but didn't get it. Kathleen hated being an army wife; she wanted a settled home. That November, the Dudley showed three more of Frank's watercolors, and Kathleen recorded that "one was actually sold while he was there!"[72]

In December, Frank was bowled over by the epoch-making exhibition, "Manet and the Post-Impressionists," organized by the art critic Roger Fry to show London audiences what had been happening in French painting. It included work by Cezanne, Van Gogh, Gauguin, Matisse, Picasso, and marked a cultural watershed, when European ideas broke into the English Edwardian consciousness. Virginia Woolf, a friend of Roger Fry, was to identify the time of the exhibition as a turning point in human relations and the moment at which the techniques for writing novels, like those for making paintings, had to be made new; "in or about December, 1910, human character changed," she wrote.[73]

Kathleen went with Frank to the exhibition and recorded his enthusiasm, though she like many Londoners did not appreciate the show: "the select few see marvels, & the others jeer! [...] Frank liked them enormously & stayed on to gloat!"[74] The newspapers attacked the paintings for rejecting the skills accumulated by artistic tradition in favor of a spurious simplicity. It was pointed out that several of the artists were mad. Frank's own watercolors were not avant-garde, but he could not get enough of the post-impressionists and went back a second time with Emily.

His taste for the new also drew him, solo, to Covent Garden on December 8 to see Strauss's *Salome* performed for the first time in London after a ban by the Lord Chamberlain. The opera was based on a German translation of Oscar Wilde's play written in French (also banned). It had premiered in Dresden in 1905 and attracted controversy for its heavy blend of religion, eroticism, and violence, in particular Salome's Dance of the Seven Veils before her stepfather Herod and her lustful kissing of the severed head of John the Baptist. The version permitted at Covent Garden was not allowed to show the severed head.

Frank liked *Salome* so much that he persuaded Kathleen to accompany him to another performance. "A dish of blood was substituted for the head which seems even more disgusting but it was far less barbaric than I expected," she wrote.[75] Then Frank's excitement took its own erotic direction, spilling over into their physical relationship. During the first week of 1911, Kathleen, who considered her family complete, became pregnant.[76]

Accidents cascaded from Frank's passion and intensity. On Christmas Eve, he sprained his ankle beagling. Nevertheless, he took Christopher to the woods to cut down a holiday fir and ran eight miles across country with his men. At forty-two, he came in 125th out of 300, the fastest runner his age. In January, he fell into the Basingstoke Canal with his bicycle as he rode along in a heavy Burberry coat. He sang in a village entertainment, played bridge, painted, and continued to take Kathleen up to London to see the latest exhibitions and shows.

In *Kathleen and Frank*, Isherwood wrote that in the mornings, he watched his father exercising "in his dressing room, naked except for his undershorts," and he remembered "taking a pleasure which was definitely erotic in the sight of his Father's muscles tensing and bulging... and in the virile smell of his sweat."

The earliest overtly sexual fantasy he recollected was about his mother.

He wrote that while still living at Frimley Lodge—so before he was seven and a half years old—he began to masturbate, and that "He imagined himself lying wounded on a battlefield with his clothes partly torn off him, being tended by a woman; Kathleen, no doubt, in disguise. The mood of this fantasy was exhibitionistic; Christopher's own nakedness was what excited him. His 'wounds' were painless." As a wounded, partly naked soldier, Christopher was appropriating his father's identity, but, unlike his father, he was passive.

The man to whom Christopher looked up as a purveyor of knowledge, self-discipline, technical know-how could not be separated from the powerful physical creature who was intensely focused on his own goals. Thus, pedagogy and eros were linked from Isherwood's earliest years, and this link was to play out tellingly in his romantic relationships and his fiction. Sometimes father and son clashed, and Frank would lose his temper and shake Christopher: "Christopher may have been frightened a little, but this too is a sensual memory for him: his surrender to the exciting strength of the big angry man."[77]

When Christopher was six and a half, Frank entered his name for Wellington, the public school founded by the Duke of Wellington for the sons of army officers and regarded as the feeder school for Sandhurst. Frank and Kathleen must have been considering that Christopher might follow his father into the army. Rumors that the York and Lancaster Regiment would be posted abroad had likely prompted them to focus on boarding school, and it was confirmed on the day of their visit to Wellington that the posting would be to Limerick in Ireland.

All through the beginning of 1911, Kathleen felt unwell. By mid-February, she knew she was pregnant, and she lost her self-confidence, lost her social momentum, and lost heart. She went to confide in her mother who was staying at Ventnor, on the Isle of Wight. Christopher and Nanny soon joined them. It was his first visit to the island to which he would often return, and he was, according to Kathleen, "enthusiastic over his 'sea voyage'!!" She took him "to the alluring toy shop where a doll's house was purchased," as if in apology to Christopher for disrupting their ideal home life. The next day she returned alone to Frimley, feeling "seedy" then vomiting during the night.[78] Christopher had not yet been told that he would be playing house in altogether changed circumstances.

Nanny and Christopher stayed on the Isle of Wight until the beginning of March, loosely supervised by Emily and then alone. When they returned to Frimley, Christopher's age-mates were invited to join a regular physical fitness lesson at his house on Tuesday and Thursday afternoons. Frank gave over the drilling to a Sergeant Sturgess. According to Kathleen, "C. loved it."[79]

Absent from the drilling was Arthur Forbes, who had disappeared from Christopher's life during the autumn of 1910, when Arthur's father was posted elsewhere. Before he left, Arthur gave Christopher a book for his sixth birthday, Beatrix Potter's *The Roly-Poly Pudding*, a gift Isherwood kept all his life.[80] He explained in *Kathleen and Frank* that *The Roly-Poly Pudding* was "one of his great early myth-books," because Marple Hall looked so much like Potter's illustrations of the "old old house" of Mrs. Tabitha Twitchit, "full of cupboards and passages" with thick walls that had "queer noises inside them, as if there might be a little secret staircase" and "odd little jagged doorways in the wainscot." In the story, the rats Samuel Whiskers and Anna Maria attack the runaway Tom Kitten behind the attic skirting board and try to make him into a pudding.[81] The tale was as frightening and beloved as Arthur himself.

The friendship also launched a memoir. Christopher collaborated with Kathleen on *The History of My Friends*, a tiny book which she wrote from his dictation, starting in the winter of 1910–11. The first chapter is about Arthur and tells that Christopher fought with him "when the Nannies weren't looking." Now, in hindsight, Christopher wished to commemorate Arthur as if he were a fallen hero: "I have got some Laurel Bushes in my garden, and sometimes we had games there too, we each had our own branches. Now that Arthur is gone, I begin to feel very sorry and perhaps I shall put up a monument to him and hang it on his branch where he got."[82] Arthur had burnished his glamour by leaving town, and Christopher did not find any of his other friends quite so captivating nor so challenging.

The History of My Friends established a principle in Christopher's life, that to have a friend is an achievement and worth writing about. The principle shaped many of his later books, both fiction and memoir. Collaborating with Kathleen on *The History of My Friends* taught Christopher, also, that friendship could be a performance, acted out for the entertainment of others. Performance was to inform many of Isherwood's later friendships and his writing, in which he often built his narrative on a portrait of a friend and on the development of the relationship. From a tiny age, he was committed to having a friend rather than losing one, even when he felt overwhelmed, disappointed, or betrayed, and he was also committed to gaining the upper hand by transforming the friend into a story.

Kathleen's women friends doted on Christopher, and some took him on his own for meals and outings. Kathleen hosted a tea party for his favorites and then felt embarrassed when he showed off reciting prayers and hymns. Mrs. Cooke, wife of Frank's commanding officer, preserved until the 1930s a silver pocket book in which Chistopher printed for her, "I love you ... & 'do you love me' with many xxxs."[83]

One day Christopher and Kathleen "dressed up" and "pretended to be at a ball!" Isherwood recalled that he wore Kathleen's clothes and they danced a set dance, the Sir Roger de Coverley, at which Kathleen had been expert since parties in girlhood:

> Dressing-up meant the excitement and safety of disguise, you had to transform yourself as much as possible, so it was natural that you should change your sex. Kathleen didn't discourage this at all; she draped him in a silk petticoat and let him wear her furs and necklaces and even her switch [. . .] a lock cut from her own hair which she sometimes used to give body to the elaborate hairdos of that period.[84]

He was not only playing the part of a woman, he was playing the part of his mother, acting out the dynamic of their relationship in which they moved easily in and out of each other's minds, experiencing each other's emotions, flipping roles. Later, in his writing, Isherwood was to project aspects of himself through various women characters—Sally Bowles, Elizabeth Rydal in *The World in the Evening*, Maria Constantinescu in *Down There on a Visit*, and Charlotte Wildstein in *The Englishwoman*, his abandoned draft for *A Single Man*.

HE STARTED SCHOOL on May 1, 1911, with a neighbor, who taught five boys at his house. He loved it right away and took his class rank so seriously that he turned down a trip to London to see the street decorations for the coronation of George V: "C. is afraid of being bottom of his class if he went!"[85]

Relations among the boys were intense. "C. returned from school rather in disgrace I fear, & afterwards the other little boy's [*sic*] all ran after him . . . the one idea seems to be to fight each other," wrote Kathleen. He was not quick at sums, and he sometimes clowned. Still, by the end of his first term, he was delighted to win the prize for highest marks.[86]

Now that he had found something in which he *could* come first, Christopher became more self-confident with his age-mates, but he still had irrational fears. One schoolmate, Jack Biddulph, terrified him with a paper snake. Kathleen purchased a compressible wire snake for Christopher to get used to on his own, and he shortly came "home in triumph" having "torn in two" Jack's snake over tea, much to Kathleen's satisfaction.[87]

The snake phobia never went away. In *Kathleen and Frank*, Isherwood described a recurring nightmare about a cobra which followed him along streets, through houses, and even through the ranks of Frank's soldiers lined up on parade, but which never caught him. Vipers and cobras were to feature in some of his early writing, including the Mortmere stories, partly inspired by Conan Doyle's "The Speckled Band," by Kipling's "Rikki-Tikki-Tavi," and by the vipers in George Borrow's *Lavengro* and *The Romany Rye*.

Kathleen saw a link between Christopher's phobias and his struggles with his friends, and she observed that he was happiest playing alone, in particular with a theater he made for himself out of a Quaker Oats box, "anything to do with plays [he] is wild about!" That spring, he fell in love with *A Midsummer Night's Dream* after seeing "pictures of the play in the illustrated papers."[88] Herbert Beerbohm Tree's spectacular production of *A Midsummer Night's Dream* opened on April 17, 1911—a revival of his 1900 production—featuring live rabbits scampering on real grass, sparkling electrical lights on Titania's headdress, child extras to swell the fairy numbers, and countless other details of costume, lighting, and staging that made the enchanted wood come to life in Christopher's six-year-old imagination. Only a few months earlier, he had been taken to see the London department store Christmas decorations including "the Pixie's Cave, which he simply loved: it was all illuminated & toy rabbits ran up winding paths in a glen & fetched back presents!"[89] Kathleen read him Charles and Mary Lamb's version of *A Midsummer Night's Dream* aloud, and he drew pictures of the fairies—Puck, Oberon, and Mustard Seed—and Snug the joiner.[90]

The vision stayed with Isherwood for the rest of his life. In 1970, he watched the Royal Ballet perform Frederick Ashton's adaptation at Covent Garden. Isherwood's friend Wayne Sleep danced Puck; Alexander Grant danced Bottom; tears of joy streamed down Isherwood's face. "For me, the magic quality of *The Dream* is that it seems to express pure happiness," he wrote in his diary. "The world of Fairyland is full of tiffs and feuds but they aren't serious, they are high camp, and high camp is happiness. Puck's relations with Oberon are so beautiful and animal, his vanity is beautiful."

Here was a timeless realm in which sexual affinities were changeable and amorphous, misadventure was only play, unhappy love was both caused and righted by the mischief of fairies, and no real harm could befall anyone. The relation between Oberon and his jesting, imperfect servant Puck offered one model of Isherwood's relation with his father in childhood and, with roles changed, his relation with Bachardy in maturity.

At Covent Garden in 1970, the tears came at "the first modest steps which Alexander Grant essays on his hoofs" because Bottom the weaver, transformed by Puck into an ass, acted out Isherwood's own private identity as Dobbin. Bottom is doted on by the fairy queen as if he were perfect; thus, his wobbly innocence offered an ideal of Isherwood's relation with his mother in childhood. Christopher's feelings for his mother and father had naturally seemed to him more important than their feelings for one another. Even in 1970, Isherwood still saw the adult marriage relationship in the play, between Oberon and Titania, as "merely ceremonious and frigid and uninteresting."[91]

IN MARCH 1911, Frank exhibited at the Old Dudley Art Society for the third time, submitting four pictures—scenes in Spain—which were all hung. Notices in *The Times* and the *Evening Standard* both mentioned his work, among more than 250 pieces: "well above an amateur standard," wrote the reviewer for *The Times*.[92] Frank haunted the private view. Then in mid-May, he was promoted to Major, delighting Christopher, as Kathleen recorded: "The Nursery decorated in his honour & the doll & Teddy Bears in their best, with devices—'Welcome to the Major' 'Congratulations to Major & Mrs. Isherwood & their little boy' etc!"[93]

Kathleen was increasingly unwell and unhappy. She feared the labor and was far more anxious than during her first pregnancy. A London doctor prescribed medication to control her nerves. At the end of July, a new development pushed her to the brink of hysteria. The regiment's move to Ireland was to occur just before the expected birth. Frank had applied for leave so he could stay behind with her, but Colonel Cooke gave it to a more senior officer, Major Ashton. It was already too late to get settled in Ireland before the baby arrived. Kathleen grew more upset. Frank went to London to talk things over with Emily, and they decided that he should leave the army. Kathleen tormented herself for the rest of the summer over how she was ruining Frank's life.

Frank genuinely feared for her health, perhaps for her life, and for the baby's. He may have wished for a calmer wife or a more robust one, but there is no evidence that he blamed her. On the contrary, it seems that he blamed himself for the pregnancy and internalized his guilt and dismay with consequences for his health and for his feelings about the new baby when it finally arrived.

He worried greatly about the loss of pay, including a pension due officers who had served twenty years; he had served nineteen and a half. He looked for other jobs and still hoped to become a professional painter. He resigned in mid-August and distracted himself by making up stories for Christopher. One which he had been making up since Wyberslegh days was about Christopher's two Buster Brown rag dolls, Bobbie and Albert. Buster Brown was an American cartoon strip character who spawned his own Broadway show and a line of children's shoes. The cartoon character had a blond pageboy haircut, elaborate, girlish clothes remarkably like Christopher's, and was full of youthful mischief. He was accompanied on his adventures by a faithful talking dog, Tige, a pit bull, whose words only he could hear. Buster was evidently the first of the boy scamps on whom Isherwood later doted in movies, and Tige was a forerunner of the talking dog in the play that Isherwood wrote with Auden, *The Dog Beneath the Skin, or Where Is Francis?*.

Frank hoped to publish a children's book with his illustrations, and he read the story aloud to his close friend, the Irish writer Ethel Colburn Mayne, with Christopher evidently listening, too. According to Kathleen, Mayne thought the story "delightful,"[94] but there is no evidence that she guided Frank toward a publisher. This episode was to be repeated fourteen years later, when Isherwood decided to submit his first novel to the very same judge for her professional opinion. Like Frank's story of Bobbie and Albert, Isherwood's first novel was never published.

Christopher's seventh birthday was celebrated in Frimley with a last voyage by punt along the Basingstoke Canal into the summer woods, his dream realm of freedom and affection, where, according to Kathleen, the charmed foursome—Christopher, Nanny, Kathleen, Frank—had picnic tea "just as we have done for the last three years in just the same spot!—"[95]

Frank took another step along his bohemian road when, on September 9, he found an art school in Reading to attend that autumn. But the enormous tension in the small family continued. There was gossip about Frank leaving the regiment; nobody had expected him to resign over Kathleen's pregnancy. He fell ill, evidently with another relapse of typhoid.

Ambivalence and regret culminated on September 21 when the regiment held a farewell dinner for Frank, "wearing his uniform for the last time," as Kathleen wrote, "a desperately trying evening for him."[96] Major Ashton's leave was canceled because, without Frank, Ashton was required as the only major. When the regiment finally left, Frank attended his first life-drawing class at Reading, and Christopher had tea with Nicky Ashton, a frequent playmate, who was waiting to be called to Limerick with his mother. Mrs. Ashton's bouquets and apologies that her husband's leave had taken precedence over Frank's—triggering Frank's resignation—could not placate an embarrassed, haughty Kathleen.

IN THE ILLUSTRATED papers, Christopher discovered another Shakespeare play, *Macbeth*, starring Herbert Beerbohm Tree,[97] and Kathleen read the story aloud to him from Lamb's *Tales of Shakespeare*. *Macbeth* was to become as important to him as *A Midsummer Night's Dream*, the hell to its heaven, haunted by supernatural malevolence and dark prophecy, teeming with images of rivalry, worldly ambition, and death. Here in the open was the passion for position that bubbled beneath the surface in the Bradshaw Isherwood family. At Marple Hall, Christopher was surrounded by weapons and armor. He was heir to a mythology of regicide. His mother smoldered with hopes for his future even if she lacked the bloody resolve of Lady Macbeth.

Macbeth was to offer a shorthand, too, for emotions that energized Isherwood's literary friendships, in particular with Auden, Stephen Spender, and Edward Upward, right to the end of Isherwood's career. When Spender was knighted in 1983, he was too embarrassed to inform Isherwood, because in their anti-Establishment youth, Spender had made fun of Auden for turning up at Buckingham Palace to accept the 1937 King's Gold Medal for Poetry from George VI. Spender was unabashedly ambitious for worldly acclaim; the other three insistently mocked it. "Edward Upward, in a letter, made us roar with laughter by quoting Banquo's line: 'Thou hast it now . . .'"[98] wrote Isherwood in his diary. (Banquo, guessing that Macbeth has murdered Duncan to gain the crown, rightly fears he may soon be a ghost himself.)

One image in a 1911 *Illustrated London News* showed Macbeth and McDuff in armor with swords and shields, about to fight. This kind of image, two men poised for combat, was to be offered to Christopher again and again—on the stage, in movies, in works of literature. It figured throughout Isherwood's imaginative and erotic life. Christopher made his own drawings of warriors, too. "The Duel," dated 1911, shows two brightly colored knights ready to close on each other. Other drawings show Christopher's fascination with the chivalric way of life: "In the Fight," "The Hunt," and "Pagaent" (as he spelled it).[99]

On September 22, Kathleen hinted to Christopher that a young rival might soon appear in his own household. He appeared untroubled by talk of the new baby; at seven, he was focused on rivalries with his peers at school. Just a week later, Kathleen's waters broke early: "a son was actually born by 1:15 a.m. Oct 1st rather a disappointment it was not the longed for daughter however F prefers sons," she wrote. In another diary entry, she pretended to talk herself out of wanting a daughter, but in 1934, when Richard was twenty-three, Kathleen told a friend, "Richard is such a good 'daughter' to me!"[100] As a daughter, Richard was as uncomfortably miscast as Christopher in his role of heir to the estate, but unlike Christopher, Richard gradually submitted to his mother's half-conscious fantasy and stayed at home keeping Kathleen company all her life.

Christopher was awakened in the night to see his mother and his new brother. Then, on October 3, he and Nanny were sent to stay with friends. Pushed from the center of family life, Nanny grew resentful. As Kathleen fell under the soothing spell of the maternity nurse, Nanny warned her "how ill the Major looked, which of course upset me <u>dreadfully</u>."[101]

Frank continued to keep silent at this crossroads in his life, but he never formed a strong positive attachment to Richard. After all, Richard was the second son that Frank himself had never been content to be, while Christopher, as heir, promised eventual triumph over the elder brother whom Frank resented and did not respect.[102]

Kathleen, turning forty-three that October, was exhausted by Richard's birth, and Richard had difficulty feeding. At four days old, he refused Kathleen's breast, and the next day, he "even refused his bottle & roared late on into the night."

Then, suddenly, the uncompromising rule of the army again interposed: "A bomb from Ireland came this morning—a letter from the Colonel enclosing communication from War Office—Frank's retirement not accepted unless he goes to the Militia for five years—this means a month's training each August, & might interfere with his taking another job."[103] Frank now had to decide all over again whether or not to leave the army. As a father of two and husband to a woman who required substantial care and comfort, he evidently saw no choice. That autumn, he had five pictures exhibited in a new show at the Dudley, more than ever before, but by mid-October, he was getting estimates for the cost of moving his family to Ireland.

Christopher marked an end to his involvement with the dollhouse that Kathleen had bought him on the Isle of Wight by writing a letter to his mother addressed to the family home from which he and Nanny had been excluded, and adding more than fifty supplicating Xs: "I have packed up the dolls house it is broken."[104] Indeed, it was.

When he returned to Frimley Lodge, Kathleen wrote, "Poor C rather hurt in his mind thinking R was receiving more attention than himself." Nanny was banished on holiday, and Christopher slept in his mother's room in the bed usually occupied by his father. He was bathed and dressed by the maternity nurse. His father walked him back and forth to school, then the cook, then an acquaintance. He focused on regaining his position with Kathleen. On October 29, when she at last dressed to come downstairs for Sunday lunch, he was invited out with friends, but "my first appearance so he refused to go—"[105] Two days later, aiming to impress, he dressed himself for the first time in his life.

In mid-November, the baby was christened Richard Graham Bradshaw Isherwood (partly to honor a bachelor cousin, Sir William Graham Greene, a distinguished civil servant). Then, the maternity nurse departed, and Nanny at last took charge of her new, larger nursery: "with the 2 beds & cot in a row—"[106]

Frank left for Ireland at the end of November. Christopher was looking forward to a day in London and the fulfillment of his most ardent wish—to attend the theater. Off he went with Kathleen on December 6, 1911, to see this year's mechanized Christmas decorations and afterwards to the Coliseum.

He saw "a playlet called *The Slum Angel*," part of a variety show, as he recalled in *Kathleen and Frank*: "a real motor-car and a coach with live horses were driven onto the stage. Christopher can remember his almost frantic delight at this. [. . .] it seemed to destroy the barrier between everyday life and make-believe. If *this* could happen in a theater then anything was possible *anywhere!*"[107]

In *The Slum Angel*, two members of the upper classes venture into east London to take a group of poor children for a day in Epping Forest. Thus, on this early, spectacularly sentimental occasion, crossing the barrier between imagination and reality coincided with crossing another barrier—between classes. This combination of transgressions was to excite Isherwood again and again as his imagination developed in the years to come.

The miracle of theater was closely associated for Christopher with the miracle of Christmas. For several years, he had been dressing up as St. Nicholas to give out gifts at his annual Christmas tree party. In 1910 for Christmas, he had received toy theaters from two of his playmates who already recognized his obsession. In 1911, on Christmas morning, he received a large and splendid toy theater which surpassed all his earlier ones, and within a few months, he was to establish himself as a boy impresario.

While Kathleen and Frank attended a touring production of *Macbeth*, Christopher, left at home, launched his own Shakespeare season. "He pinned posters on the nursery door and expected Kathleen, Frank and Nanny to attend every performance."[108] He began with *Macbeth*, drastically abridging to include only scenes of violent murder and haunting guilt. He soon abridged *Othello* the same way.

For actors, he cast the china animals from his nursery mantelpiece. He preferred them to the cut-out cardboard kings and queens that came with the theater because, he later explained in *Kathleen and Frank*, he was more interested in the essential mythic qualities of his characters' experience than in the realistic details. The china animals had long been part of Christopher's imaginative life. In Frimley, aged five, he had given them a Christmas tree party, digging up a pine tree with Frank and lighting it with candles bought with his pocket money. The china figures were *animals*—creatures as in Beatrix Potter's books—not people with conventional prescribed identities. They had pleased him in many fantasies, and they were reliably under his control. When he later created fictional characters, he likewise used figures familiar to him—from life and from books—then added realistic surface details both to disguise the identity of his original model and to reveal the essential qualities that interested him.

LIMERICK, IRELAND, 1912

Limerick was the main port on Ireland's west coast, in the estuary of the River Shannon. Irish forces withstood a number of English sieges at Limerick in the seventeenth century, and Irish-Catholic supporters of James II made their last stand behind its medieval fortifications before being expelled to France in 1691. Afterwards, Catholics were banned from public office, from owning land, from voting, from practicing their religion in public, while the Protestant upper class, both Irish and English, prospered through the Atlantic trade. The town was expanded in the Georgian style during the late eighteenth century, with wide streets and crescents lined with terraced houses. During the Great Famine in the 1840s, Irish-grown staples like oats and wheat were shipped out of Limerick to England even though the Irish were starving to death, and shipments were sometimes protected by British troops. Tens of thousands of Irish emigrated via Limerick to North America and elsewhere.

Kathleen left Christopher and Richard at Marple Hall with Nanny and went ahead to meet Frank. It was Frank's third tour in Ireland, and the pressure to ensure Kathleen's happiness there was enormous. Two days after she arrived, he had another of his accidents while running with his men and cut an arm and a knee badly. The knee became infected, and Frank was confined to a wheelchair. It was one way to let his wife know that he could not carry all their burdens alone.

She viewed sixteen Limerick houses, rejecting everything in the grander Georgian streets—too large, too many stairs, not intimate. At last, she found Roden House, "a queer attractive rambling old place," tucked behind a recently built technical school and adjacent to the barracks. A glass veranda ran the length of the downstairs and looked onto a fountain and a "spreading apple tree." Steps led down to a vanished orchard through an iron gate with crumbling pillars topped by urns. Upstairs, there were seven windows across the front, "An old beamed anteroom occupied the centre, with stained floor ... and from this the other rooms wandered away." The layout defied military order and sameness. "There was something very romantic too and un-obvious about it all," as Kathleen later wrote.[109]

Christopher arrived by steamship in Dublin with Nanny and Richard on February 15, 1912. Kathleen met them, and they spent a night in Ross's hotel before continuing to Limerick by train. He began school two days later. In fact, it was Miss Mary Mercer's high school for girls, attended by a few boys. Before the end of his second week, Christopher was having snake nightmares and had stopped eating properly. He was sent home early, where he grew worse and vomited: "I think the change & excitement have been rather much for him," observed Kathleen. He "complained of the children being noisy & rough," which disappointed her.[110]

By late March, he was securely at the top of his class even though he struggled to find friends. He, Nanny, and Richard caught colds that went savagely to their chests, partly because they were breathing in large amounts of coal smoke inside Roden House. The chimneys in the drawing room and nursery did not draw, which had been concealed from Kathleen by the house agent.

All through his first school term, Christopher went on coughing until he was finally put to bed. He was far more anxious than anyone realized, and he must have sensed Kathleen's impatience which she confided often to her diary: "if he moves <u>much</u> he still coughs a good deal & seems also in a nervous state crying almost hysterically over the idea of the asp, which he saw a picture of in the illustrated Shakespeare of Cleopatra & which terrified him . . ."[111]

He was evidently looking at Cassell's *Illustrated Shakespeare*, which shows Cleopatra fondling the asp and one of her women already dead, with the caption, "Come, thou mortal wretch / With thy sharp teeth this knot intrinsicate / Of life at once untie."[112] In *Kathleen and Frank*, Isherwood explained of Cleopatra's suicide with the asp, "when younger, he had believed that she actually swallowed it and that it bit her inside, which seemed to him superlatively loathsome." He jokingly threw in a Freudian interpretation about serpents, "that his fear was nothing but a repressed longing to submit to anal intercourse."[113] It was a suggestive aspect of his snake phobia, perhaps revealing more unconscious sexual fantasies about his father and mother. More plainly, the worm of jealousy had been eating young Christopher since the birth of his brother. "C seems to have grown so much quieter than he used to be & quite retiring & shy," Kathleen wrote in her diary. "Richard's advent has rather put him in the background as far as strangers are concerned."[114] Everyone admired the baby, not the boy.

CHRISTOPHER CONTINUED UNWELL, wakeful and vomiting, and seemed too delicate for boyish life in Limerick. Next was a nosebleed, possibly from dehydration as well as the smoke in the nursery. He was never diagnosed with whooping cough, but Kathleen so feared it that she applied the name to his cough, as she was to do with other illnesses later on.

Limerick thoroughly suited Frank, who threw himself back into military life with vigor. His injured knee healed; he ran eight miles and "came in about 150th out of 600," as Kathleen proudly reported.[115] He was often away on training schemes, night attacks, campouts, even court martials. At home, he worked in the garden, assisted by Christopher, and he painted, often in the glass porch, making a subject of Roden House and the apple tree.

Frank also introduced Kathleen and Christopher to the countryside, taking them for drives on Saturday afternoons at a steady clip-clop southwest toward the Clare Hills and the Galtees, then back through Corbally for a scenic view of Limerick Cathedral with bridge and river in the foreground. He bought a mare who was to become a personality in all their lives, proving to be as high-strung, time-consuming, attractive and enduring as Kathleen herself. They called the mare Kitty, which had been Frank's nickname for Kathleen since the days of their courtship. Frank, Kathleen, and Christopher were pulled along through the Irish landscape by this horse-kitten anima much as Frank was pulled along all his married life by Kathleen. Thus, the slow-paced horse-drawn world that Christopher's father grasped by the reins was charged with the unpredictable drama and excitement of Christopher's beautiful mother. The horse-kitten anima was to reappear in the secret myth world of Isherwood and Bachardy. Isherwood's nickname for Bachardy, too, was Kitty.

Kathleen struggled like Christopher to form a new social circle. She did not know how to mingle outside the social parameters in which she had been raised; she automatically befriended the colonel's wife, and even the wife of another major, but recoiled from the wives of officers ranking beneath Frank, the subalterns. Organized religious services were among the things she enjoyed most easily, and she went often. In church, the order of service was printed in advance and the hierarchy was crystal clear, with God at the top, where everyone could look up to Him.

She worried about Christopher's difficulties interacting with other children without recognizing how much his behavior mirrored her own. He expected his childhood friends to treat him with ceremony and found unsupervised play difficult. He was especially challenged by a pair of Irish twins, Bob and Jack Armstrong, partly because there were always two of them. He pushed himself to the limit in their presence, and Kathleen noted that "he always seems to manage some mishap when he goes there!"[116]

In *The History of My Friends*, Christopher and Kathleen wrote of Bob and Jack Armstrong: "A governess called Miss Smith was with them till last Christmas and she made things very nice when I went ... but after she left there was a great difference and somehow we did not seem to get on so well."[117] He was happiest at school where, as for Kathleen in church, the program was planned in advance and the hierarchy was clear, with the teacher to look up to at the front.

In later years, Isherwood was to undergo an extreme and difficult inward revolution, throwing off his mother's shyness and snobbery in order to embrace the so-called inferiors that she feared and did not understand—the servants, the life of the streets, the boys of the Berlin slums, and the barely clothed beachgoers of Santa Monica who knew each other by first name only without any title or rank or by no name at all. In order to change in this way, Isherwood used instincts that his mother possessed but which she directed only toward her intimate family circle—intuition about the inner life revealed through small gestures of dress, behavior, and speech. What Kathleen could read in Frank or her mother and father, Isherwood learned to read in strangers. He was able to get onto an intimate footing with foreigners, outsiders, and "inferiors," and to charm them.

Auden "couldn't understand my capacity for making friends with my inferiors," Isherwood was to write in the 1970s. The theater critic Kenneth Tynan, by contrast, admired in Isherwood "the classlessness that he shares with almost no other British writer of his generation. (I've seen him in cabmen's pull-ups and grand mansions, with no change in manner or accent.)"[118]

IN THE SUMMER of 1912, Christopher made friends with a bossy, imaginative, and savage little girl called Mirabel Cobbold, daughter of Frank's new commanding officer, freshly settled opposite the Bradshaw Isherwoods. As with Arthur Forbes, Christopher was transfixed by a strong personality that threatened to overwhelm him. Mirabel was another only child—like Arthur and his mother, like Kathleen, like Christopher before the arrival of Richard.

Kathleen encouraged the friendship, even though Mirabel brought out in Christopher the passivity that Kathleen deplored. "She hits him & teases him & gives him things & takes them away but he seems to have no sense of retaliation, & never <u>attempts</u> to hit back, & does just as she tells him." Mirabel was three and a half months older, "a head taller," and far more confident. She stole the show from Christopher's other playmates: "it is quite extraordinary the influence Mirabel has on him, how he believes all she says & how he follows her like a dog."[119]

They shared a tempestuous imaginative life. "Mirabel & Christopher played Swiss Family Robinson (which he is now reading!) in the yard of the Technical, fighting wild beasts & sailing on imaginary rafts," wrote Kathleen in her diary at the end of August 1912. Behind Roden House, there was an empty piece of ground that belonged to the technical school. Abandoned materials from design and building projects—"planks, barrels, packing cases, detached doors, broken laboratory apparatus, wire, rope, plumbing fixtures, sheets of glass," as Isherwood recalled in *Kathleen and Frank*—were ideal for making ships, rafts, and huts for desert island adventures.[120]

Mirabel grew up to be a writer like Isherwood and unleashed her personality in her books. There were two fantasy adventure novels leavened with sex, violence, and criminality, *Deborah Lee* (1930) and *Sea-Tangle* (1931), which she wrote soon after being widowed in her first of three marriages. She worked as a journalist in China, Japan, and Macedonia, and published two nonfiction books about her real-life adventures as a member of South Africa's white women's voting and education rights movement, and as a participant in the first trans-African waterways expedition, up the Zambesi, across the interior, and down the Congo.[121]

There is no evidence that Isherwood read Mirabel Cobbold's books;[122] still, he was familiar with the intensity and self-belief with which she delivered them. Themes that appealed to her appealed to him, too, including orphans from privileged backgrounds who travel the world and prevail over fear and cruelty. Theirs was the authorized fantasy world offered to children in classics of English literature in the early twentieth century, acted out in make-believe, repeated to friends at school, imagined again and again.

At ages seven and eight, the frenzy and unpredictableness of Mirabel Cobbold's playing thrilled Isherwood. All his life, he was to seek similar challenges in friendship. In artistic collaboration he was to become a master at directing such imaginative energies, but he did not collaborate with women later on, and sometimes his friendships with women foundered because he allowed himself to be loved, bossed, and managed up to a point and then dismissed any woman who invaded his emotional life too closely or who failed to understand his sexuality. The friendship with Mirabel Cobbold foreshadowed other "big sisters" that Isherwood was to adopt in adulthood, and Mirabel was a forerunner of the fictional character Sally Bowles, yet she was not described in *The History of My Friends*. That original collaboration with Kathleen admitted only boys of a certain class and education.

ON HIS EIGHTH birthday, Christopher received an extraordinary new device from his father: a magic lantern—precursor to slide projectors—that projected images from glass plates: "never had he imagined anything quite so delightful! & he could hardly leave it for a moment."[123] He remained obsessed for months, commanding others to his magic lantern shows just as he did to his toy theater performances.

His world was about to become even brighter, for during September 1912, a cinema opened at 69 George Street. "C. has been excited for weeks past," noted Kathleen.[124] It was called the Gaiety, and it was to give Christopher as much pleasure as anything in his life so far.

Isherwood recalled in *Kathleen and Frank* that "Christopher's lifelong devotion to the movies began as an indiscriminate appetite for any two-dimensional happening on a lighted screen in a dark theater." The content mattered so little that he later found it "hard to remember individual film actors or films from the Limerick days."[125] It was the play of light in darkness that captivated him—like the night light in the nursery where he was safe with Nanny, candles on Christmas trees, a Penny Bazaar lantern carried by his mother through a darkened house in a game of make-believe about a forest,[126] the light on the stage curtain at Frimley when he had been too young to see his father in *In Chancery, or Browne with an E.*, the beams from his magic lantern.

The cinema screen was itself a threshold between reality and make-believe, and his sense of excitement on that threshold never abated. The movie projection was not threatening because it was delivered by a machine, and the darkness offered Christopher anonymity and physical repose. Self-consciousness fell away; he need not perform or attract attention.

Companions to watch with also made him feel safe. First, there was Nanny, then Kathleen and Frank, and later there was a Limerick friend, Eddie Townshend, met at the Wednesday-afternoon drill classes launched by the regiment in mid-October. Isherwood later recalled that Eddie Townshend "needed someone smaller and weaker than himself to boast to and protect . . ."[127]

CHRISTOPHER WAS AT last getting comfortable with moving around. At Christmas 1912, the Bradshaw Isherwoods decamped to Marple Hall, the only time they made the Irish journey as a family. Christopher reveled in the trip and sent postcards to his Limerick playmates from on board ship. For Christmas that year, Frank gave him a globe, and Christopher's other gifts also fed his growing appetite for faraway places: "an atlas, & books about Australia & Canada 'Near Home & Far Off' all of which he liked much as he loves geography."[128] When he shortly had the run of a Penny Bazaar, he added a series called *Peeps at Many Lands*.

Kathleen continued to be the main figure in his religious education, dividing his worship between home services she devised, the garrison church, and, later, Limerick Cathedral, a twenty-five-minute walk from Roden House. One rainy Sunday, "for a sermon," she began to read Christopher *Pilgrim's Progress*. "What shall I do to be saved?" asks Christian, "Whither must I fly?" Down the years, Isherwood was to ask himself the same questions, time and again, as he hurried and over-hurried along his own pilgrim route. They also began the catechism, to which Christopher was to give his responses out loud hundreds of times until he was confirmed at Repton six and a half years later in November 1919. These teachings, too, he took earnestly to heart, promising to renounce the devil and his works and "all the sinful lusts of the flesh," to believe in the Christian faith, and to live by God's will and the ten commandments.[129]

At eight and a half, his life was a constant effort at self-improvement, both physical and spiritual. In addition to drill, which he found difficult now, there were dancing classes at a local hotel and piano lessons with one of his schoolteachers. Even in the holidays, he practiced his multiplication tables and his catechism. Shortly, Kathleen began reading him *A History of England*, a collaboration between Rudyard Kipling and the imperialist historian C.R.L. Fletcher in which the forging of the empire, "the great cause of freedom and Protestantism," was a project just like Christopher. "England's being hammered, hammered, hammered into one!" ran one of Kipling's incantatory poems about England's destiny to subdue other peoples.[130]

Christopher was remorselessly assessed by Kathleen and, increasingly, by himself. In some ways, he was painfully backward, just learning to cut up his own food, use a knife and fork, tie his shoes. Kathleen's wish for him to be tougher and more masculine contradicted the Christian teachings and feminine sensibility in which she schooled him. He tried to please her in all things, and already he was able to present an untroubled surface concealing inner turmoil. His teacher at Miss Mercer's, taken in by this smooth surface, wrote to Kathleen: "Your boy is a most satisfactory pupil in every way, decidedly clever and original, as well as being attentive. He is so straightforward and reliable that I often think he would make an ideal clergyman."[131]

But fear was never far off, especially in Christopher's inner world. One day, Kathleen recorded that Mrs. Cobbold "disturbed me a good deal about Christopher, he so easily gets over excited & frightens himself over the stories he tells himself ... & he is always telling himself stories . . ."[132]

The Easter holidays 1913 saw Christopher's second Shakespeare season—*Hamlet*, *As You Like It*, *Macbeth*—for an audience of dolls and teddy bears. Probably around this time, he also acted out a play he wrote himself, *La Lettre*, in French and evidently influenced by Sarah Bernhardt who had become his idol as well as Granny Emily's. Isherwood described the play in *Memoirs of Pine House*, a fictionalized memoir that he began in 1931 and soon abandoned: "a lady received a letter to say that her son is dead. Whereupon she exclaims, 'O! Il est mort' and falls to the earth."[133]

The play, of course, dramatized Christopher's fantasy that he was the chief object of his mother's affection and that his death would undo her. This fantasy was to be shredded by his father's death two years later, a reality that Isherwood did not mention in *Kathleen and Frank*. According to *Memoirs of Pine House*, the play was banned by Frank: "One day, during a party, I appeared wearing a skirt made out of the nursery table-cloth and performed this play in public. The guests were amused. But my father forbade me ever to do such a thing again." Much later, the adult Isherwood insisted Frank was annoyed because the child Christopher invaded the party "without previous announcement or permission," yet Isherwood knew that his craving for attention had been the real problem: "The indulgent applause of his captive audiences went to his head. He wanted more and more of it."[134]

IN APRIL 1913, Kathleen moved Christopher from Miss Mercer's to the school attended by the Armstrong twins. She and Frank wanted Christopher to go to school with boys. He was soon top, but the pressure of the other boys was nearly overwhelming. He "cut out the little Armstrongs" now that he was in class with them.[135]

Eddie Townshend, who didn't attend the new school, was the only boy Christopher felt like playing with. *The History of My Friends* makes clear, with a tone of melodrama, that Christopher's friendship with Eddie was calculated to make an impression on Jack Armstrong:

> I began to cast off Jack who had long been cool—presently I told him I had entirely cast him off, that his chances were gone and I was now best friends with Eddie—I think this annoyed him. Eddie is twice the size of Jack & me but that doesn't make any difference.[136]

Of course it made a difference. Years later, writing *Kathleen and Frank*, Isherwood still remembered the reassuring size and strength even though he could not remember what Eddie looked like. On the other hand, he did remember what the Armstrongs looked like: "The wrinkled monkey-face of Jack Armstrong and the hot red button-nosed face of Bob, both of them tow-headed, are still dimly printed on Christopher's memory."[137] He was to commemorate the Armstrong twins in the sexually hot character Jane Armstrong, his gender-bending portrait of his 1940s boyfriend Bill Caskey in *The World in the Evening*.

By 1966, when he first began looking at his parents' letters and diaries in preparation for writing *Kathleen and Frank*, Isherwood recognized how completely his childhood playmates had been absorbed into his personal mythology. "As a character or a fact goes into the making of a myth-character (or a mythological circumstance), so its original moves toward oblivion by me." Individual details were forgotten not because the friends were unimportant but because he had assimilated them:

> Arthur Forbes, Brian Wynne, Jack and Bob Armstrong, Russell Roberts, what do I remember about them now? Almost nothing. I see Bob

1: Son of the British Army, Heir to the Estate (1904–1915) / 53

Armstrong's hot defiant red face and bristle of blond hair; the face of Russell Roberts (which now seems much more charming than silly)[.] I see nothing of the faces of the others; not even of Eddie . . .[138]

These brief, intense friendships offered archetypes he reused and elaborated on again and again in his writing. Because he was taken away to England for months at a time, Christopher's Limerick friendships were not entirely real. The same was true of his friendships in England, with children living near Marple, whom he saw only intermittently, and among whom he was often placed on a pedestal as grandson and heir of the squire. His best friend at Marple Hall was his age-mate Alan Coyne, eldest of the gardener's six children. They grew up together in the unbalanced intimacy of above and below stairs, Isherwood possessing a social status that gave him a certain kind of mastery in the relationship; Alan possessing a talent and toughness for outdoor life. With Alan, Christopher played the same games as he played with Eddie and Mirabel, building huts and citadels and fighting imaginary enemies. Outdoors, the Coynes were friends, but indoors, they were servants, allowed to share only kitchen meals and one special party at Christmas.

The moral discipline of continuous interaction and equal status did not exist for a camp follower, a family heir, nor later for a boarding-school boy. Conflicts could be abandoned rather than resolved, a poor preparation for later bonds. On the other hand, the discontinuous unreality of Christopher's friendships was a motive for telling stories about them, to make them real and permanent. But like Mirabel Cobbold, Alan Coyne did not make it into *The History of My Friends*. Nor did Isherwood ever mention Alan in his later work, even though he was to repeat aspects of the friendship in some of his mature relationships.

CHRISTOPHER SAW HIS first moving pictures before Limerick. In London in 1910, there were "Animated Photographs" at the London Hippodrome on Charing Cross Road, likely *A Day at the Seaside*, an eight-minute Kinematograph filmed in Brighton. In 1911, he saw the Pathé newsreel of the coronation of George V after Frank and his men had helped to safeguard the route of the procession.[139] In *Kathleen and Frank*, Isherwood listed what he could recall of films and actors seen at the Gaiety, including Lillian and Dorothy Gish, the Keystone Cops, the Italian version of *Quo Vadis?* and episodes from serials like *The Perils of Pauline*.[140] Later, he saw Forbes-Robertson's *Hamlet* and at least one "exciting detective drama!!"[141] *Quo Vadis?*, based on the 1896 historical novel by Polish Nobel Laureate Henryk Sienkiewicz, was an epic multi-reeler about the dawn of Christianity. Before that, Christopher's first multi-reel film was evidently *From the Manger to the Cross*, which portrayed the life of Christ and was shot on location in the Holy Land with silent titles from the Gospels. He went to the Gaiety at least once a week. His taste for movies, like his taste for people, ranged from the culturally highbrow to the commercial and pedestrian, from the sacred to the profane, though by the time he was a teenager, he was to develop sophisticated critical views.

For his ninth birthday, Christopher received a Kodak Brownie from his Isherwood grandparents. This put the power of the camera into his own small hands. The Brownie was a lightweight cardboard box, about five inches high, covered in imitation leather. It was the culmination of American inventor George Eastman's work from 1878 onward to bring photography to the mass market. With Eastman's pocket Kodak, any amateur could "snap" shots of ordinary life. (The iPhone of the early twentieth century.)

The Brownie was aimed at children, and its brand name was taken from the folklore sprites popularized in North American magazines by the cartoon strips of Palmer Cox and by his illustrated verse volumes, starting with *The Brownies, Their Book* (1887). "Brownies" decorated the cameras and advertisements, adding a toylike whiff of mischief and magic. There was no need to focus or to adjust the aperture or speed. The photographer stood five to eight feet from the subject, held the camera still—against the body at waist height—looked down through the viewfinder and depressed the metal shutter with the thumb. The advice in manuals of the period was to hold your breath and listen for the click. Steadying the camera against the body made an intimate physical connection, the photographer becoming one with the camera. "I am a camera"[142] was to be the most quoted line in all Isherwood's adult fiction, and he was already preparing to write it.

Frank learned how to develop the films in the developing box that came with the camera, and he and Christopher shared this hobby for many months. Probably also for his ninth birthday, Christopher obtained a blue, cloth-bound album with "Camera Studies" embossed in gold on the front, and Kathleen began to paste in and caption his work, mixing in earlier photos by others. There is an action shot of soldiers parading to church in Limerick while little boys in plus-four suits and caps watch from the edge of the road; arguably one of the boys is Christopher. A photograph labeled "Three Generations" shows John Isherwood, Frank with Christopher sitting on his shoulders, and Kathleen at the park gates at Marple on Christopher's third birthday. Frank and his father wear light-colored wool three-piece suits, Frank with a bow tie. Kathleen is wearing an embroidered white summer blouse, a white skirt reaching to the ground, and a wide-brimmed straw hat decked with flowers.

A later shot shows Christopher, Richard, and Nanny, in swimming costumes, grinning and squinting into the sun as they kneel in the wavelets of the Irish Sea at Penmaenmawr; Kathleen took this on September 15, 1919. Immediately underneath is a picture of her in widow's weeds and black hat in front of Beach Hut 29, where her diary records she sat that day. In Isherwood's handwriting, the picture is captioned "Lady into Fox," added after he read David Garnett's 1922 novel of that title, about a shy young woman of twenty-four, tiny and beautiful, with brilliant hazel eyes and reddish hair, who is turned into a fox while out walking in the woods with her husband. The husband continues to sleep with her and to care for her and her cubs, though she grows increasingly wild. Eventually, fox and cubs are mauled by hounds, and he cannot save her. Such was the transformation in the way Isherwood was to see his mother after he passed his sixteenth birthday.

There are photos of Christopher's cousins Joan and Timothy Toogood and of Alan Coyne. The collection unspools into his preparatory boarding school at St. Edmund's, where shots include a favorite teacher, Mr. Sant, and the entrance to the walled swimming pool, scene of excited, semi-nude horseplay. From his public boarding school, Repton, Isherwood stuck in photos of boys playing tennis and of his Officer Training Corps campout at Strensall, where he sits in his khaki uniform outside a tent with fellow "officers" just like his father. Later there are shots of his rooms at Corpus Christi College, Cambridge, and of Edward Upward's rooms.[143]

Isherwood was to make further albums of his friends and his travels abroad. In Berlin, this included boys and boyfriends. Photos or the negatives from which to print them were passed around and traded. Isherwood referred to one German collection as "the Famous Boys Series." He recognized the link between his photos and his emotional life. In 1938, he was to write in his diary: "I am ambitious in my friendships, too. I am proud of them, like a collection—and the affection of my friends is like a large sum of money invested in the Bank."[144] His inclination to collect shaped his life. There were to be many other collections—books, people, places, experiences—all in some way raw material for his art.

THE BRADSHAW ISHERWOODS had arrived in Ireland a few months before the introduction of the Third Home Rule Bill in the British Parliament, April 11, 1912. This third of the four bills it took to achieve Irish independence from Britain triggered rising tension throughout Ireland between those Irish, mostly Roman Catholic, who wanted freedom from British imperial control and those, mostly Protestant, who feared the rule of the suppressed Roman Catholic majority. To Kathleen, as to Isherwood when he was writing *Kathleen and Frank*, animosities in Limerick seemed to be religious, between Catholics and Protestants, rather than between Irish and English. This view permitted British occupiers to see themselves as peacemakers rather than oppressors and perhaps overlook the poverty surrounding them.

Riots broke out in Limerick in October 1912 following a Unionist meeting to oppose the Home Rule Bill. Kathleen blamed Roman Catholics for damage she saw to Protestant shops, churches, and church properties. There is no evidence that Christopher was afraid or even aware of the riots, although he later observed in *Kathleen and Frank* that Nanny "always" exaggerated any threat of danger. "Because of the sensational stories she later told him about their life in Ireland, Christopher grew up believing that the Regiment had been sniped at on its way to service at the Cathedral on several occasions. He only recently discovered this wasn't true."[145]

Other challenges were on the way, for Frank and Kathleen were looking at English boarding schools. As with houses and friends, they were choosy; they knew that their son might not easily conform to institutional life. They were inclining to St. Edmund's, in Hindhead, Surrey, not far from Frimley and Aldershot. It was small, accommodating about fifty boys age eight to thirteen in a large red-brick country house which had been converted to a school in 1900. A chapel, a dining room, a library, classrooms, dormitories, and playing fields had been added in the grounds, thirty acres of woodland, mostly pines. It was run by cousins of Frank, the Morgan Browns.

Frank wrote out a family tree for Kathleen, describing the seven children of his Aunt Fanny Bellairs, who had married the Reverend Morgan Brown, founder of the school. The seven were all either teachers or clergymen, married—if married—to teachers and clergymen, except Cyril Morgan Brown, headmaster since his father's retirement, whose wife had been institutionalized after a breakdown. Beside Cyril's name on the Morgan Brown family tree, Frank wrote: "?Mrs. insane." Cyril Morgan Brown ran the school with his three sisters and his daughter, Rosamira (Rosa), once a pupil herself.[146]

At Marple Hall over Christmas, Frank launched a new craze with this year's gift, "a box of conjuring tricks." Christopher gave his first magic show to the Coyne children and Richard when they gathered for the lighting of the tree; magic was to inform the development of his imagination from then on. Christopher told his mother that Christmas 1913 "was the best he could remember."[147] It was their last as a family.

NINE-YEAR-OLD CHRISTOPHER WAS gravitating increasingly toward his father. During Nanny's New Year holiday, he asked to sleep in Frank's dressing room, "so with electric torch by his side, a supply of books & a clock, he went off very grandly to bed. The <u>first time he has ever slept alone</u>." He repeated the exercise three nights in a row, rising early each morning and dressing himself. He knew by now that he was going to boarding school.[148]

There were extra lessons with his father for two and a half hours every morning, including Latin, probably for the first time. After tea, he practiced piano, and Kathleen then read aloud to him Walter Scott's historical romance *The Talisman* from *Tales of the Crusaders*.

The Talisman opens with a lavishly detailed scene of mortal combat, heavily eroticized and with the participants in disguise. As Sir Kenneth in armor rides slowly across the desert in Palestine, he is set upon by a Saracen at full gallop in turban and green caftan. They close in battle. Each repeatedly throws the other from his horse; both lose weapons and clothing in the fray. Having tested one another's physical strength to the limit, they ride to an oasis where they debate their beliefs, eat, pray, disrobe one another, and sleep beside their abandoned weapons. The Saracen's "sheeny and crescent-formed sabre, with its narrow and light, but bright and keen, Damascus blade, contrasted with the long and ponderous Gothic war-sword, which was flung unbuckled on the same sod."[149] The long encounter, with its ludicrously sexual imagery—swords like spent phalluses—models the kind of fighting-then-bonding relationship that Isherwood, in the 1970s, was to describe as Whitmanesque:

> Whitmanesque homosexuality is concerned with the mating of two completely masculine males. ... A Whitmanesque male must have acknowledged another male to be a real man before he can accept him as a lover. First, they must test each other's virility. Therefore they have to fight. A sex duel is the necessary prelude to sex play...[150]

Fighting-then-bonding offered nine-year-old Christopher an appealing model for his rivalrous friendships with his age-mates, though he was not yet much of a fighter and preferred the idea of others fighting on his behalf. Part of Eddie Townshend's attraction was his talk of boxing. Sometimes Frank went to boxing matches in Limerick.

The Talisman also portrayed the tortured sublimation of courtly love which Christopher assimilated through his mother's voice as she read aloud to him. Whether his lady was kind or cruel, a knight lived only to serve her, "to fulfil her commands, and, by the splendour of his own achievements, to exalt her fame."[151] Wittingly or not, Kathleen cast a spell over her son, a part of whom, for the time being, lived only to serve her.

Christopher was captivated, too, by the male-male bond between

Richard the Lionheart and the minstrel Blondel, for among his childhood drawings of dueling knights, maidens in distress and other scenes from chivalric life, is one of Blondel at the base of the tower where Richard is held hostage, and from where, according to legend, Richard sang out a song Blondel recognized, leading to Richard's rescue.[152] This kind of coded understanding between the master of men and the master of words was also to figure in Isherwood's mature writing.

THEATER TOOK OVER Roden House at the start of 1914. Frank began rehearsals for *The New Boy*, a three-act farce written by Arthur Law and first performed in 1894 in London, and Christopher undertook his third Shakespeare season. Then he accompanied his father to the theater and went backstage during a rehearsal. Isherwood later recalled in *Kathleen and Frank* that during the Limerick years, "He wanted to be an actor, like Frank."[153]

The "new boy" is in fact a mature, married man dressed as a schoolboy. In his puerile, fetching disguise, he is coddled, flirted with, abused, tossed in blankets, and pressured into stealing apples for which he is thrashed by a farmer and sentenced by a magistrate to ten further strokes with a birch. Frank—so recently Christopher's Latin master—was taking the part of the schoolmaster, Dr. Candy, who, in the original production, gave off "a perceptibly chilling atmosphere of impositions and canes."[154] Evidently, Frank was eager to make fun out of the kinds of things that might befall Christopher at boarding school.

Christopher and Kathleen went together to watch the dress rehearsal of *The New Boy*. Two days later, they spent an afternoon getting Christopher photographed in his new school clothes—his own new boy costume—and that night, he went again with his mother to the first performance of *The New Boy*.[155] He took Nanny to the Saturday matinee. He could not get enough of these larking adults who were playing for laughs the initiation looming in his own schoolboy life and who were presided over by his father in a shaggy white wig. Remarkably, by the time he wrote *Kathleen and Frank*, Isherwood had no recollection of seeing *The New Boy*.[156] Considering that he was nine and a half at the time, it is an extreme case of amnesia, evidently protecting him from a truth too painful to recall—that his father had sent him away to boarding school knowing full well the suffering that lay in store there.

Christopher's last few days in Limerick were idyllic. The weather grew hot, and the apple tree that Frank liked to paint blossomed. Christopher, Frank, and Kathleen, with rugs and chairs, sat underneath it. Christopher read *A Midsummer Night's Dream*. It was not unlike the quiet weeks during which Frank, Kathleen, and Emily had awaited his birth at Wyberslegh Hall nearly ten years before. By adulthood, Isherwood was to forget it all.

The night before Christopher left for school, he attended one last show, a charity evening at the barracks. "[C]omic songs & recitation & Mirabel in white-duck trousers & all complete like a boy! Danced the horn pipe to the band she ought to have been a boy without a doubt!" exclaimed Kathleen.[157] Thus, Mirabel previewed the tomboy Sally Bowles, the gamine cabaret entertainer who boldly infiltrated Herr Issyvoo's group of male friends in Berlin. Isherwood later possessed a photograph of Jean Ross, his Berlin friend and announced model for Sally Bowles, dressed like a sailor boy in bell-bottom trousers, her feet spread wide in a defiant stance, hands shoved in her pockets, and on her head, a dark beret, slipped rakishly to one side. This was the androgynous renegade with whom he was to identify once his loving father expelled him from Eden.

BOARDING SCHOOL, HINDHEAD, 1914

Christopher left home in tears, chaperoned by Kathleen, for "a little London Season"—a surfeit of treats pretending that boarding school was something to celebrate. They stayed at Granny Emily's flat at 14 Buckingham Street overlooking the River Thames behind Charing Cross Station, "the center of the city, for the Strand was at the top of the street, and Trafalgar Square only five minutes' walk away."[158]

Dressed in his Eton suit and a straw boater, Christopher went with Kathleen to bookshops, the zoo, Madame Tussaud's, the Natural History Museum, Harrods, Westminster Abbey, and by bus to the airfield at Hendon outside London where, according to Kathleen, they saw biplanes "dropping off bombs & also once looping the loop! C very pleased & excited—" He had loved airplanes ever since living near Aldershot—an early center for aviation in England—where he and his grandfather, out walking, had been the first in the family to see an airplane in flight.[159]

They also saw Harley Granville-Barker's *Midsummer Night's Dream*. As he drafted *Kathleen and Frank*, Isherwood still recalled that the fairies were all in gold, and that he had been enchanted: "The supreme excitement of this magic lay in one's exposure to it; it was right there in the same room, and yet it was utterly other. In this sense it was almost like having a vision."[160]

It was a vision Christopher much preferred to reality. By May 1, he had a bad cold and cough and had to spend the morning in bed before Kathleen took him, dazed and sniffling, to Waterloo Station to meet Cyril Morgan Brown and the group of boys traveling to St. Edmund's. She went aboard the train to say goodbye: "till we actually were sitting in the train I do not think he realized," she wrote, "but he just managed to keep back the tears . . ."[161] Christopher had never even seen the school.

His first letter was a masterpiece of equivocation. "—he said he 'liked school fairly,' & thought 'the Masters looked nice,' & 'rather liked the boys but none specially' and he 'was fairly happy sometimes' but did not think he should ever like games'—" A few days later, he wrote again: "I have liked it much more since lessons started." The timetable included Latin and Greek, mathematics, French, divinity, music, geography, and history. English was not a subject, but spelling, derivations, and synonyms came up as part of geography and history.[162] Divinity included stories and was also literary.

At the end of Christopher's first week, Kathleen spent Saturday night at the school, and she saw him in bed in his dormitory with "eight other little boys." She was to visit at least once a term. But Frank was far better equipped than Kathleen to imagine what was taking place inside Christopher as he tried to adjust to institutional life. In a letter to welcome Christopher at school, Frank adopted a playful tone, expressing his hope that there would be no bullies like Bullock Major in *The New Boy* and challenging Christopher to show off his academic preparation. "I was very pleased to hear that you showed so much pluck," Frank wrote in another letter, after learning that Christopher had held back his tears on the school train, "It will be the greatest help to you in your school life."[163]

However, in *Memoirs of Pine House*, Isherwood depicted how tears held back at Waterloo Station flowed freely at school:

> At intervals, during lessons, or in the dining-hall or at prayers, one of us would begin suddenly to weep—drip, drip, drip, on to the book or the plate, the tears falling faster and faster until they broke into regular sobs; and then the sobbing changing gears into a blurred continuous sound of blubbering. Almost anything would set us off.

Isherwood's favorite master Ivor Sant, fictionalized as "Mr. Samson," comforted the Christopher figure with the words of Shakespeare's Henry V: "He was the only one of the staff who talked my language, the language of the theater: 'Courage, Isherwood, courage. Once more into the breach, Isherwood. Once more into the breach.'"

Memoirs of Pine House disguised identities and dramatically heightened certain essential truths about St. Edmund's. "Orme," a "notable weeper," becomes a target for other boys needing to make a show of strength. The Seniors warn Orme, then bully him in front of the other "New Bugs":

We watched, delighted, when Orme was made to run the gauntlet of knotted handkerchiefs, to lick people's shoes, to stand bare backed and be flicked with a wetted towel. Sometimes we were ourselves allowed to help with the torturing. Orme howled, yelled, cursed, called us sneaks, and cads and beastly rotters and then, when left alone, shed floods of tears. He wept passionately, helplessly, as though a spring inside him had broken and he could never stop. And yet, within half an hour, there he was being as sidey again as ever.[164]

"Sidey" was slang for uppity. Isherwood modeled Orme on Edmund Godfrey Russell-Roberts, who arrived at St. Edmund's the same term as he did and is described in *The History of My Friends*: "he is always rather an ass & violently passionate but I quite like him. He is very cheeky to the bigger boys, but last term he took me out twice."[165] The name Orme hints that Isherwood identified completely with the weeping, high-strung, bullied yet irrepressible boy. The boy could have been Russell-Roberts—Or me.

Memoirs of Pine House also tells about a senior boy scapegoated by his peers. An attractive, successful member of the cricket eleven shines too brightly and is dealt with on what the boys called Pay Day by "gorsebushing." He is hunted through the school grounds then heaved into the gorse bushes. Scratched, bleeding, crying, he limps alone back to the house. "No one spoke to him or touched him. He was an outcast."[166]

Bullying at his preparatory school was to inform Isherwood's understanding of the brutality he witnessed in later years at Cambridge and, enlarged to horrific proportions, in Nazi rampages in Berlin. He considered his role as a victim or a participant to be interchangeable, flippable, like his role in the hauntings at Marple Hall. Anyone might be a victim. Anyone might be a perpetrator. Orme might be Russell-Roberts—*or* he might be *me*. Isherwood was to make this a theme again and again in his writing.

CHRISTOPHER WAS TO repress all memory of Frank playing Dr. Candy in *The New Boy*, reserving the bogie of the stern schoolmaster entirely for his real-life headmaster Cyril Morgan Brown. Unlike Frank, Cyril Morgan Brown was not prepared to let Christopher have his own way. Mr. Cyril, as the boys were told to call him, was older than Frank, nearly sixty, tall and handsome like all the Morgan Browns, powerfully built, with abundant gray hair, shaggy eyebrows, a flowing white moustache, and piercing blue eyes. Behind his back the boys called him "Ciddy." In the memoir following on from *Memoirs of Pine House*, Isherwood named him "Pa,"[167] making light of the frightening father role Morgan Brown adopted among boys and staff. Isherwood's later accounts of his first days at school made much of the clash between his boyhood self and this academically gifted, angry man whom Kathleen described in her diary as "very incapable & dazed."[168]

"I had just spread a slice of bread with butter and was in all innocence, proceeding to cover the butter with a layer of marmalade," says the Christopher character in *Memoirs of Pine House*, when he looked up to find all the boys watching him and the headmaster shouting: "I didn't think you'd be that kind of pig." The marmalade was scraped off the bread back into the marmalade dish. "'Don't let me see you doing that again,' he said. 'You're not in the pig-sty any more now.'" Christopher "blushing furiously, trying to keep back the tears of homesickness, misery and rage," had wanted to tell the headmaster, named Price-Jones in the memoir, that "at Home, I had <u>always</u>, all my life, been allowed to eat marmalade with butter. Nobody had even so much as suggested that this was wrong. [...] Mr. Price-Jones had insulted my home. He'd called it a pig-sty."[169]

Christopher's father loved pigs and had joyfully promoted piggyness to Christopher in at least one Beatrix Potter-like story about Mrs. Porkington Pigiwig, "an old Lady Pig in a blue bonnet," who, with her six piglets, ate up all the gooseberries and carrots in Master Christopher's garden and then forced their way into the nursery "and gave him a great smacking kiss with their great mouths and then began to dance around him in a ring." By contrast, "Price-Jones" expected the boys at his school to rise above their animal instincts. As in the dining hall, so on the sports field:

> If you try to catch a cricket ball on the boundary it hurts your hands very much. Your instinct is [...] to avoid the ball, or let it drop immediately. But instinct must be controlled. Control of instinct is called "character-building." Mr. Price-Jones was very good on this. "There's a pretty large bit of each of you," he remarked, "that's just a pig or a cow. Well, you've got to master it. Unless you want to turn into cows and pigs."[170]

The stand-off between Christopher and Morgan Brown reached a crisis at the school sports day in May. As depicted in *Memoirs of Pine House*, Christopher had been humiliated in the hurdles, obstacle race, and three-legged race, and the headmaster gave him the maximum allowed handicap in the premiere event, deliberately setting him apart as the smallest and least athletic boy in the school. The nearest boy started five or ten yards behind him, and the fastest runners 100 yards behind. "I suppose my smallness of size and my incompetence at cricket had convinced Mr. Price-Jones that I could not run. Actually he was mistaken. Actually, for my age I could run as well as or better than most boys."¹⁷¹ Christopher had often watched his father win running races. *Memoirs of Pine House*, never completed, breaks off as Christopher nears the finish line in first place with cheering spectators running beside him.

But Isherwood was left with a lingering uncertainty as to whether he or Morgan Brown was the victor in this encounter. Because of the long head start, he never allowed himself to believe the win was anything more than a perverse trick Morgan Brown played on them both. In *Kathleen and Frank* he wrote: "Christopher's victory must have disgusted Ciddy—it was a victory of the wrong kind, unearned, flukey, farcical, a sort of send-up of the Morgan Brown way of life, and all the more stinging for being unintentional."¹⁷²

Christopher's uncertainty about the victory was exacerbated by the absence of the audience for which he longed. Kathleen and Frank were both in Limerick, so one of Frank's favorite cousins attended the sports day, Marjorie (Madgie) Reid, née Luce. Then on Prize Day in July, no family or friends at all were present to see Christopher receive the silver cup and the form divinity prize which he also won that term. Kathleen came from London but left before the ceremony. Should Christopher believe these were worthy achievements if his family did not honor them? The theme of undeserved acclaim was to surface repeatedly in Isherwood's work, and it was to become far more complicated once his writing made him famous during the 1930s.

In *Kathleen and Frank*, recalling that Ciddy "preached a gospel of thoroughness, exactitude, levelheadedness and perseverance," Isherwood declared that he had duly acquired all these qualities. Yet he remained in touch with another self, forever tempted to be slapdash, vague, excitable, an opter-out. Boarding school required him to behave strategically and hide such weaknesses. "In retrospect, it seems to have been the most valuable single experience of his life," he averred in his draft for *Kathleen and Frank*. Yet he evoked depression descending, a gray, nondescript nothingness drowning him out:

> The images in his memory aren't painful or ugly, merely rather drab: battered boot-lockers, ink-stained wooden desks, narrow dormitory beds, lists of names on notice-boards, name-tags on clothes, names read out at rollcall—names which make you less, not more of an individual, which remind you hourly that you are now the household darling no longer, just one among many: Bradshaw-Isherwood, C.W. This feeling of lost importance is at the bottom of so-called homesickness; it isn't home you cry for but your home-self.¹⁷³

The conflict between home, where it was possible to be uniquely valued, and the institutional world, which taught him it was wrong to expect any kind of special treatment, grew more nuanced as he matured. At St. Edmund's, C.W. Bradshaw Isherwood began to calibrate just how much and on whose terms he would reveal his private emotions. If his name was the only unique thing his new world acknowledged, he would find a way to make his name stand out.

THE BRADSHAW ISHERWOODS, like most people, did not foresee the conflagration that was about to hollow out their world. Ireland was bristling with fight, and expectation was growing that civil war might break out over Home Rule. However, by the time Christopher returned to Ireland for his summer holiday at the end of July 1914, Austria–Hungary had been at war with Serbia for three days; Germany was poised to join Austria–Hungary, Russia to join Serbia, with Britain and France obliged to support Russia according to treaty. Christopher and Kathleen endured a rough crossing on a ship filled with three trainloads of people, over eight hundred, many seasick, including Christopher, and some fainting. It was only when Frank met their train in Limerick that Kathleen began to understand the European war would affect them all. "They had been expecting news all day to mobilize," she wrote, "it seems so appalling one can't take it in—. I never thought of Irish troops being called upon."[174] In the face of the international crisis, the Irish were to agree to shelve the question of Home Rule.

Isherwood's attention in his later writing to unsuspecting minor characters drowned by world events was rooted in the blindside of his own experience at nine. He had set out alone for the first time to attend boarding school, and he was met by a perfect storm of unexpected change. Nothing could have prepared him for the Great War. Nothing would ever be the same.

In this strange time of readiness and waiting, some things continued as normal. Frank drove Christopher and Kathleen out in the trap to tea with a friend, and Christopher went to play the piano for his old headmistress. On August 4, neutral Belgium asked Britain to intervene against Germany's proposal for free passage through Belgium to France, and Britain declared war on Germany that night. Kathleen made a late addition to her diary: "At 6-pm came a message from barracks that the troops are to mobilize at once[,] on the fifth day they will be ready to go."[175]

Christopher was with his mother when Frank came to share the message. "This is the moment which Christopher's memory has chosen to retain, not only as a picture but as a playback of Frank's voice," he wrote in *Kathleen and Frank*. "Frank looks in, only for a moment; he must hurry back to barracks. He says, 'The order to mobilize has come.' His tone is quiet, gentle, almost reassuring. Then he is gone."[176]

Preparations were rapid. Over the following days, Kathleen and Frank were back and forth to the shops, buying equipment—an air cushion, a sewing kit, a sleeping bag on which they painted his name in white. Christopher went on with his playdates as the carpets were taken up from underneath his feet, beaten, and rolled away. Kathleen gave a month's notice on Roden House and to the cook and maids. Two facing pages of her diary, August 5 and 6, are splotched with water and the ink blurred. Tears might have fallen on those days or on rereadings in subsequent years. On Sunday, August 9, the sun came out, and there was a cathedral service for the soldiers. "They marched down a thousand strong," wrote Kathleen patriotically. "In afternoon the troops were reviewed by the Colonel in the barrack square in their marching order & all their kit inspected."[177]

But the men did not leave. Days passed. The weather grew warm, then hot. Richard was "very irritable and fretful . . ." There was no news. Christopher spent an evening tucked away in front of the flickering screen at the Gaiety. In his draft for *Kathleen and Frank*, Isherwood was to recall that his father used this time "to make Christopher aware of some sort of message." As they waited, resolve suspended, Frank showed Christopher his weapons and expressed his reluctance to use them. In *Kathleen and Frank*, Isherwood was to shift into the present tense, lifting the moment out of time into an endless present: "He tells Christopher that his sword is useless except for toasting bread and that he never fires his revolver because he can't hit anything with it and hates the bang."[178]

Isherwood shaped the memory to resemble the beginning of the Bhagavad Gita, when the warrior Arjuna, facing the enemy armies he is destined to fight, tells Lord Krishna that he does not want to fight and throws down his weapons. In that moment of suspense, with the battle about to begin, Lord Krishna delivers his long, sacred message, the Song of God, explaining to Arjuna that death is not real, that Arjuna must fight because he is a warrior, and revealing himself, Krishna, as God. Thus, in his mature memoir about his father, Isherwood, without naming it, invoked the religious framework which permitted him to recognize his father's ambivalence toward the warrior role and at the same time permitted him to accept his father's devotion to his duty, his dharma. But this was not until the late 1960s, and Isherwood was to quest long and hard for this response to the sorrow of losing his father and to the feelings of confusion and helplessness which accompanied the sorrow. In the meantime, his father was to send more explicit messages, asking Christopher to take his place at home. These messages were to place a great burden on Christopher, a burden which he tried hard to bear and, later, tried hard to forget.

At last on August 13, another order came; the regiment would leave today or tomorrow. A further order came; the regiment would depart at noon on the 14th. But Nanny woke Frank and Kathleen before dawn: "it seems a wire had arrived at midnight, to tell them to be ready to go at 9 & 10 am." Kathleen and Nanny took Christopher and Richard to the barracks and then to see Frank off on the train: "there were a good many people to see them go . . . & it was just heart breaking . . ." wrote Kathleen.[179]

The day after Frank left, "C had a head ache all day & appeared limp." The air continued heavy and close with intervals of rain, and Christopher, like someone fighting to breathe, asked to have his tea on the roof of Roden House, "so we had it there and got a slight breeze."[180]

From Queenstown, Frank sent a postcard, "they have found us an awful old boat on which we are crowding [. . .] The mare will not go on board." A sling was made, but the sling broke and dropped Kitty between the boat and the quay. She "lay on the ledge and gradually slipped into the water. She then swam right round the ship and was headed off by a boat." Kitty had to be left behind. "She is so associated in my mind with you and it is dreadful to think of all the fright and indignities she has had to put up with," Frank wrote in another letter. A few days later, Kitty caught up with him in England, "She is rather bruised and cut about, but nothing at all serious. She walked on board the ship she came over in quite cooly."[181]

Frank was billeted in their honeymoon town of Cambridge. One of Nanny's sisters was married to the porter of Emmanuel College, a Mr. Shaw, and the Shaws "had been out to the camp & actually seen Frank's tent where he was sleeping!"[182] Frank wired Kathleen to come. While Nanny hastily emptied drawers, Kathleen took a moment to measure both her sons. Christopher was four feet three and a half inches. He was three days shy of his tenth birthday. He left Limerick with his mother, Nanny, and Richard, on August 24; from Crewe, he, Nanny, and Richard made their way to Marple Hall.

Kathleen went on to Cambridge. There, on Christopher's tenth birthday, she visited Emmanuel College, where Mr. Shaw "took me to see a picture of Bradshaw as a young man in the Common Room. Decided it would be very nice for William to be a Don."[183] It was a decision made in a time of great uncertainty and distress, and which Kathleen was to hold on to through thick and thin until Christopher was asked to withdraw from Cambridge a decade later. She was trying to see beyond the nightmare unfolding around them.

Frank sent Christopher some toy airplanes and asked him to share responsibility for Kathleen's happiness: "You must try & do all you can for her while I am away. It is a dreadful time for her, & you can do more to make it bearable than anyone else . . ." Later, Frank was to write Kathleen that he hoped "that William will come to 'the scratch' and show 'reciprocity' as Henry calls it. I'm afraid you won't get much out of Richard—"[184]

After Frank left for France, Kathleen joined the children at Marple Hall. She and Christopher sat and talked—initiating the intimate exchange, the reciprocity, that Frank knew Kathleen craved.[185] Christopher raised money from the household for a fund to supply the men in the regiment with socks and shirts, and he accompanied Kathleen and his Aunt Moey to Brabyns Hall to see arrangements for nursing convalescent soldiers. Then he returned to boarding school, where, since she had missed his birthday, Kathleen visited for ten days, bringing Emily and staying in a lodging house.[186]

Frank was reluctant to write to Christopher since the Censor forbade him to say much, but Christopher had been writing to his father ever since Frank left Limerick. In late September, Frank finally communicated from northern France, making it sound as if he were a hobo wandering for pleasure: "one night in a great farm with all the men in the barns & the next night in a church & so on." He mocked the Germans as drunks and thieves: "One night we slept in the bar of the village inn the Germans had been there before us & the whole place was littered with empty bottles & all the contents of the drawers, which had been emptied looking for money."[187]

John Isherwood wrote to Kathleen "saying I was to be sure & make Marple my headquarters & leave the children there whenever I wish to go away." She returned there only on October 26, having missed Richard's third birthday by nearly a month, and was punished for her long absence by the news that "he has begun to see the old woman who haunted Christopher at his age."[188]

Kathleen was stretched thin. The members of her family—including Emily—were scattered in four different places. She spent her second Marple Hall evening looking with Richard "at pictures of trains." Trains connected them. Richard was most at ease when his mind could run along a neat continuous track, where the movement of the cars was controlled and visible in advance. Interruptions and surprises were difficult for Richard. He played with trains to the exclusion of other toys; he watched real trains as if hypnotized. Kathleen herself was obsessed by trains, recording departure times to the minute, whether she caught a "good" train with through service or had to change, also class of travel, where she sat, food, luggage, and every cost.

When Kathleen returned to London, she arranged for Richard and Nanny to join her. She and Frank had decided that Richard was being spoiled at Marple Hall just as Christopher had been. In London, Richard continued fretful and often woke in the night. Kathleen soon realized that Emily's top-floor flat above Charing Cross Station was ideal for trainspotting: "we walked up & down on Hungerford Bridge to watch the trains & signals which are simply an endless delight & he sits for half an hour together at the dining room window quite absorbed!"[189]

Frank wrote to Christopher that two men they knew from Limerick were feared dead; one was Private Bell, who had often helped at Roden House. Frank candidly described a shell destroying the farmhouse where he was having lunch behind his trench, and his flight to the cellar. He was not allowed to say that the shelling was near Touquet, just inside Belgium: "I am living in an erection made of beer barrels and an old door at top, not at all bad but rather cold at night—However I wear 2 top coats & 2 woollen jackets & two waistcoats & a scarf & a woollen helmet & gloves & mittens & two pairs of socks & look just like Tweedle Dum & Tweedle Dee—."[190]

He sent home photographs of himself swathed in the motley layers that made him look like Lewis Carroll's combative twins as they are portrayed in John Tenniel's illustrations for *Through the Looking-Glass, and What Alice Found There*. In Frank's photographs, the men around him wear neat-looking uniforms and regulation hats, but Frank displays his enthusiasm for dressing up even at the Front, where he evidently met the savage cold with humor and his own style of camp.

Kathleen scoured London for wool gloves, trying to order forty pairs for the company; they were sold out in military suppliers and countless civilian stores. She sent weekly parcels of canned food, rum, tobacco, a new air cushion, writing paper, a cheap wristwatch because Frank's got damaged, an electric torch as a gift from his mother, knitting needles after he left his on a train.

For three weeks, Frank camped in a sandpit on the River Aisne, near Vailly, moving forward to trenches facing the German position on the north bank of the Aisne. Then, on October 12, he and his men rushed to help prevent a German advance on Calais. They traveled to the coast by train, then marched east through Flanders, camping in villages each night, pressured to hurry. While they advanced on Radinghem-en-Weppes in the third week of October, they met the enemy in the open for the first time. "I lost 60 killed & wounded in my company, & I think if we had taken it a bit slower it might have been avoided," Frank wrote to Kathleen.[191] He was already close to the place in Belgium where he was to die six months later; after the "Race for the Sea," the war became static, and the regiment would not move far. They were billeted in Bois Grenier, Touquet, Fleurbaix, Le Gris Pot through the end of 1914. From January through May, 1915, the 2nd Battalion York and Lancasters was to camp at Armentières and Chapel Armentières, moving forward from billets into the trenches for up to two weeks at a time.

Once they were no longer on the move, Frank got home leave. He suggested a visit to Christopher: "he might like to exhibit a Father who comes hot from the Front." First was a whirl of pleasures and errands in London and a visit to Marple Hall: "when we got to the house we found quite a party assembled on the lawn to cheer him, & a large 'Welcome home' over the front door & flags flying," recorded Kathleen. Henry and Muriel came from The Oakes; during dinner, Kathleen felt faint and had to leave the table: "I collapsed in the hall & knew no more till I found myself on my bed . . . after which I was very sick!"

The anxiety she had suffered through the autumn, the constant pressure of travel, decisions, correspondence, errands, the sensation of relief at Frank's brief return, the knowledge that he must go back, overwhelmed her. Obviously, Frank was the one in physical danger and unceasing discomfort; still, Kathleen had every member of her family depending on her in a way she was not used to, even Frank for his supplies, and she was determined not to let any of them down.

They spent Saturday and Sunday in Hindhead, where Christopher was "very excited & pleased to see Frank."[192] Afterwards, he sent his father a sprig of white heather, which, according to Scots lore, brings good luck, especially in battle.

During this leave, Kathleen and Frank agreed that she would make a "memory" book about his war. Frank began to send things for it as soon as he was back at the Front, and Kathleen pasted in photographs, newspaper clippings, maps, narratives based on her diaries, postcards, Frank's letters to her and to Christopher. Eventually, she made two books, 1914 and 1915, a literary collaboration with her husband.

The first Memory Book opens with an article from the *North Cheshire Herald*, "A Marple Hero," headed by a photograph of Frank in uniform, hands behind his back, his face still and dignified, blank of expression. The piece ran on Christmas Eve, 1914, when Christopher was staying at Marple Hall and would have seen it:

> Major Isherwood has been in the fighting from the commencement. He returned to Marple a fortnight ago, and spent the weekend with his wife at Wybersley and his father at Marple Hall. He is now back in the trenches in France, fighting with his men, and enduring their hardships and vicissitudes.[193]

The newspaper account placed Frank on a stage, in the public eye, and at a new distance. There were obvious mistakes which Christopher might have noticed—Frank didn't visit Kathleen at Wyberslegh. Christopher might also have noticed that neither of Major Isherwood's two sons were mentioned. The article was unaware of Frank's fond intimacy with Christopher, of his solicitous questions in virtually every letter from the Front about Christopher's well-being and progress, unaware of Frank's wish to enhance Christopher's prestige at school by visiting him there "hot from the Front," unaware of Frank's instructions to Kathleen to give Christopher another London season during these Christmas holidays of 1914: "draw a nice fat cheque from Cox & go to London with Christopher for a nice long burst."[194]

Kathleen clipped other items about Frank from the *North Cheshire Herald*: "the men of the regiment speak in the highest terms of his remarkable pluck & bravery," and—quoting the wounded at what was now called Brabyns Military Hospital—"He was a fine man and a brave one and a soldier who inspired confidence in his men—"[195] The epithet Marple Hero was to be repeated again and again, crowding out the subtleties of Frank's personality, his astringence, his eccentricity, his wit, his slyness, his energy and creativity in varied avenues of art, culture, technology, and agriculture, his all-in willingness to participate, win or lose, success or embarrassment, in countless activities before any audience. Already, public rhetoric was beginning to encapsulate and entomb Frank with false solemnity and blind reverence.

As he began working on *Kathleen and Frank* in the 1960s, Isherwood was to write in his diary that he was digging into his parents' letters and diaries for the first time. Yet more than once he acknowledged that he must have read some of the material before. It seems unlikely that his mother could have worked on the Memory Books without Christopher being aware, indeed, he was sometimes in the same room with her as she did; moreover, when he was at Repton, aged seventeen, Kathleen sent him Frank's letters to St. Edmund's from the Front. While Kathleen focused on the Memory Books and her project of remembering, Christopher tried to forget; he was to turn away from the past with extraordinary determination, gradually repressing much of what he knew about his father.[196]

The Hero of Marple spent Christmas in the trenches, which were now proliferating in all directions, "a labyrinth" as he told Kathleen; "I have already lost myself repeatedly." When it rained, the trenches filled and flowed like streams and sometimes collapsed. The mud became so deep that walking from one place to another was exhausting: "poor old Clemson had to be dug out the other day!" Yet the men were getting fat, "No exercise & lots of food I suppose—" Frank had smashed his new wristwatch and was asking for another: "it is so awkward not knowing the time."[197]

He was horribly bored. Most of the time he was second in command, listening to his superior, Clemson, and doing paperwork. He sent Christopher a wry account of Christmas celebrations at the Front and the widely reported season of mutual understanding when soldiers from both sides left their trenches and fraternized. "They bore us no ill will but they had to fight because they were told to, and they wished the war was over," he wrote. Christopher, anxiously aware that his father was cold, had sent a pair of mittens as a gift. "I will throw away my other mittens, and wear yours when they come."[198]

IN THE ABSENCE of Frank's crackling energy, life at Marple Hall bogged down. "I feel sure the whole thing will collapse if they don't look out, but Father will never start anything on his own account as you know," Frank wrote to Kathleen. Henry was seldom there. In the spring of 1915, the nineteenth-century conservatory that opened off the library was demolished. It had become one of the most leaky parts of the house. "The Library will never be so attractive without it but of course it had got to the state that it was inevitable—" wrote Frank when he heard.[199]

Meanwhile, all through the Christmas holidays at Marple Hall, Christopher listened to Kathleen read aloud Walter Scott's *Ivanhoe*, as he had listened to her read *The Talisman* the year before. The heroes of these overlapping novels, Richard the Lionheart and his Saxon vassal Wilfred of Ivanhoe, are away at the wars in Palestine, and Richard is taken prisoner on the journey home. In their absence, Richard's false and capricious brother Prince John and the greedy Norman nobles oppress the native Saxons, neglecting the land and the people's welfare. Kathleen's voice brought *Ivanhoe* to life during teatime twilights and long dark evenings in the massive, decaying house. The parallels with Frank and Henry were obvious, with the birth order of the brothers reversed. There was even a historical link, since the family believed their Isherwood name derived from Sherwood Forest, fifty-five miles away, home to Robin of Locksley, or Robin Hood, loyal to King Richard.

Ivanhoe, gravely wounded when he competes in disguise as the Disinherited One in the tournament at Ashby de la Zouch, is nursed in secret by Rebecca, just as Richard the Lionheart is nursed by Saladin disguised as El Hakim in *The Talisman*. These manly invalids—Richard the Lionheart and Ivanhoe, kept horizontal by slender oriental healers and forced to postpone their heroic destinies—conform to the fantasy that Isherwood described in *Kathleen and Frank* as his first masturbation fantasy, before he was seven and a half years old, in which he imagined himself wounded on a battlefield and being tended by a woman. During 1915, illness and death were to affect Christopher so extremely as to make such fantasies attractive strategies for real-life behavior. The subliminal pull toward the sickbed and a feminine carer was to have power over him right into his middle age in Hollywood.

On the first day of the new year, 1915, Kathleen and Nanny spent the morning tying up scarves and socks and mittens to send to Frank for fifty new men. Christopher had caught a bad cold. According to Kathleen: "C's leg started acting again The best cure seems, <u>bed & to wrap it tightly</u> in a <u>woollen</u> scarf ... Whether it is a sort of rheumatism subject to change of weather, or cramp, or growing pain I cannot <u>think</u>—he has it everywhere, & used to have it at Frimley too, as well as Limerick—"

Christopher's "acting" leg was revealing distress which he did not—could not—express in words. He was comforted when his "wound" was bound in woolens intended for his father's men at the Front, as if he wished to share his father's misery in the trenches and felt guilty that he could not.

The doctor told Kathleen that the "dull aching pain below the knee in the calf" of Christopher's leg was "a form of muscular rheumatism commonly called growing pain."[200] It appears to have been muscular rheumatism or fibromyalgia. The cause remains unknown. The condition is associated with a heightened sensitivity to pain, and it is measurable by increased amounts of relevant chemicals in the blood. It runs in families.

While his body silently confessed unarticulated feelings, Christopher confidently found words for a poem about the war. His subject was Louvain, the Belgian town sacked by the Germans in August 1914. They had looted and burned the ancient library, the university, the churches, and shot men, women, and children, attracting worldwide condemnation and offering dramatic justification for Frank's absence. He sent the poem to Frank, who, starved of sleep and swamped with paperwork, didn't rise to a reply, though he read it with care. "I really think his poetry is good," Frank wrote to Kathleen, "of course he uses rather stereotyped words, but he got quite an effect of horror and gloom in Louvain."[201]

In January 1915, Christopher joined Kathleen who was already in London for another pre-school season of treats. The centerpiece, hosted by Uncle Henry, was dinner followed by Louis Parker's stage adaptation of *David Copperfield*, in which Herbert Beerbohm Tree doubled the roles of Micawber and Dan Peggoty and the dashing twenty-seven-year-old Owen Nares played David.

The stage adaptation was evidently a first encounter with the Dickens novel that Bachardy later recalled was Isherwood's all-time favorite piece of fiction. Kathleen began reading *David Copperfield* to Christopher the following August. Jack Isherwood, who happened to be in the gallery at the same performance, reported "that Tree's 'Micawber' was vulgar beyond words & that he overdid the whole thing," and Kathleen also dismissed the production as "not convincing."[202] But Dickens broadly played, even camped up, might have been all the more captivating to a ten-year-old. Isherwood was to reimagine the bankrupt Micawber with notably theatrical flair in his celebrated Berlin novel *Mr. Norris Changes Trains*, and he forever associated Mr. Micawber with Uncle Henry, struggling to avoid bankruptcy.

Christopher and Kathleen also saw *Maskelyne and Devant's Mysteries*, the latest version of a magic show he had already attended the previous April and which he now requested whenever he was in London. It was the best magic show of its time, running with various stars since 1873. John Maskelyne specialized in revealing to audiences the ways in which they were being fooled, and he wrote books unmasking everything from con routines and card-marking systems to Madame Blavatsky, the medium who co-founded Theosophy.

Our Magic (1911), written with David Devant, encouraged audiences to appreciate a magic trick as a work of art: "a conjuror is in reality 'an actor playing the part of a magician.'"[203] This is exactly how Christopher liked to see himself, and he was learning both how the tricks were done and how they could be done with dramatic persuasiveness. He later wrote: "He didn't see himself acting in Shakespeare but he did certainly see himself conjuring and very soon after this he began studying card-tricks, reading Hoffmann's books on *Modern Magic, More Magic* and actually buying conjuring apparatus from a shop called Goldston's just off Leicester Square."[204]

Professor Hoffmann's *Modern Magic* (1876) had begun as a series of articles in *Every Boy's Magazine*. Diagrams showed how to do tricks with coins, playing cards, dominoes, dice, rings, handkerchiefs, cups and balls, hats, gloves, strings, and countless other everyday objects. Practical tips included "*Never tell your audience beforehand what you are going to do*" and "*never perform the same trick twice on the same evening.*" Patter was essential; the would-be magician should "cultivate from the outset the art of 'talking,' and especially the power of using his eyes and his tongue independently of the movement of his hands."[205]

These principles became part of Isherwood's arsenal in front of any kind of audience. As a child magician, as an adult speaker, as a writer, he adopted Hoffmann's mantra, repeated by Hoffmann to describe any number of tricks, "a very good effect, especially if introduced in a casual and apparently *extempore* manner."[206] To appear casual required much preparation.

Magic tricks obsessed Christopher throughout his adolescence, and the idea of magic sums up the invisible, potent artistry which Isherwood tried for in all his books. For Isherwood, magic was a style, a subject, and even a code. He later recalled that as a young, unpublished author: "I imagined a novel as a contraption—like a motor bicycle, whose action depends upon the exactly co-ordinated working of all its inter-related parts; or like a conjuror's table, fitted with mirrors, concealed pockets and trapdoors."[207] Moreover, in several of his novels, he was to use magic to reveal and at the same time to conceal the forbidden theme of same-sex love; magic carried a potent innuendo.

With Frank away at the Front, Uncle Jack also treated Christopher to an evening of dinner and theater, and then Christopher spent four days with Aunt Moey in Colchester. Back in London, he and his mother stayed with a friend next door to Kathleen's girlhood flat in Cranley Mansions. In the four and a half weeks since leaving St. Edmund's on December 21, he had slept in at least six different beds in five different places. He had eaten meals with more than thirty people. He had been to nine shows of one kind or another, and to restaurants, galleries, and shops in London, Manchester, and smaller towns. He negotiated this stop–start excitement under intense family scrutiny. Kathleen recorded his adventures and deportment every day that she was with him and some days when she only heard about him from others; Frank tried to manage and assess from the Front: "what a lucky boy," he wrote when Christopher was invited by Moey, "I never went to stay with anyone alone till I went to the Varsity!"[208]

Christopher was expected to take pleasure on the whole family's behalf; then, suddenly, he was on his own again at school; none of the family circle that he worked to charm and to please was available to reflect back to him. Kathleen left him at Waterloo on January 28, and for a month, she didn't mention him once in her diary. Frank sent no letters.

Frank's bleak, claustrophobic winter was brightened when he was mentioned in dispatches "for gallant and distinguished service in the field" and promoted from Major to Brevet Lieutenant-Colonel. These achievements, published in the British newspapers on February 18, meant a great deal to him and to Kathleen, including higher pay. Kathleen savored the public recognition, and Frank admitted to being drunk with congratulatory toasts while writing her. To top it off, he got leave to come home again for a week.

The British blockade of German ports and the German U-boat campaign made crossing dangerous; the leave was promised, canceled, then suddenly allowed. He arrived in London on Monday morning, February 22. At Marple, he made the ritual drive through the village with his father, and he and Kathleen had a glimpse of three-and-a-half-year-old Richard, "very lively & very goodlooking in scarlet coat & black beaver hat." It was to be Frank's final look.

On Sunday, they went to St. Edmund's. Christopher had ceased to thrive. They took him to lunch, and Kathleen noted, "his legs seem to have been bad, & his ankle bound up & he walked quite lame & seemed much less bright than usual—"[209]

The acting leg had now developed into a chronic symptom. It supplied Christopher with an identity as a boy who needed special care, massage from attentive human hands, binding of the "wound," and reprieve from sport. It told a story of loneliness and fear that Christopher did not share out loud or by letter. How could his circumstances compare with those of his father, a hero, mentioned in dispatches for "brave and gallant service," promoted to Brevet Lieutentant-Colonel, heading back to the Front? Anxious and depressed, Christopher was prey to the body chemistry that made him susceptible to pain. Also, he was probably sickening with measles. There were already four or five cases at the school.

He was put to bed on March 1. He was extremely ill for the entire month of March and convalescing throughout April. Kathleen was told it was black measles, a severe form, named for the dark eruptions caused by capillaries bleeding just underneath the skin. Before antibiotics, it was often fatal. Christopher's black measles came on suddenly with the headache characteristic of the virus, followed by extraordinarily high temperatures. The first night he was ill, he had 103.4° Fahrenheit, then overnight March 2, it soared to 105°. It took three long, dessicated days to fall back to normal. He was far too ill to eat.

He was quarantined in the school infirmary with about nine other boys, some with temperatures equally high. Frank begged Kathleen not to try to visit during the quarantine—three weeks—and told her repeatedly that Christopher was probably fine, enjoying himself, and better off getting measles out of the way. But when he heard how high the temperatures had been, Frank consulted the regiment's doctor at the Front. "Purden says that a temperature of 104° or 105° for measles is very high & as all the Brown patients have been like that, he thinks their thermometer is probably wrong—"[210]

On March 7, Christopher was able to eat an egg, and his temperature was normal; on March 9, he tried some chicken. But on March 10, his temperature began to rise again, and it climbed for the next four days till it reached 103 again. He had already been in bed for two weeks, forbidden to read or use his eyes.

Kathleen took her mother to Ventnor on the Isle of Wight. There on March 17, she heard from Rosa Morgan Brown that a specialist and bacteriologist had been called to the school. "Very worrying disturbing news," she wrote in her diary, "darling C. has a touch of pneumonia just developing, & she fears it will be long business."

At last on March 20, Kathleen reached Christopher's bedside and found him "with head bandaged for ear ache & shade over his eyes which have been bad ... & in rather a tearful state—" His temperature went up again to 102 and then began to fall as she sat beside him in the big airy room he was now sharing with two other boys, "all on liquid food & all thin & weak."[211]

Then Kathleen received another blow: "Wire from Nurse her Father very ill could she go . . ." They arranged for Mrs. Dobson, the coachman's wife, to care for Richard at Marple Hall. Christopher, with his arms "like sticks," was still "rather quiet & depressed having a go of ear-ache."[212]

Once the pneumonia patch was gone, the doctor said, Christopher could leave in a week, but Kathleen did not wait. She returned to her mother on the Isle of Wight. Cousin Madgie Reid offered to look in until Christopher was strong enough to travel.

Frank was far more concerned by Christopher's pneumonia than he had been by the measles. "I do hope that this won't leave his lungs affected," he wrote with Moey's health problems in mind.[213] The school pronounced it septic pneumonia, and Christopher evidently had some kind of blood poisoning that caused a rash. Before antibiotics, about a third of those with sepsis died; survivors were left with a range of health issues including chronic fatigue, chronic pain, and post-traumatic stress disorder, all of which arguably played a role in Christopher's subsequent life.

Kathleen dressed down the Morgan Browns about their nursing care, and the Morgan Browns blamed the forty soldiers who were billeted with three officers at the school, but the source of infection was never confirmed. Purden at the Front told Frank the boys probably incubated the pneumonia because they were cared for together.

Frank's moods swung about. He was able to get out riding sometimes on Kitty, and he enjoyed seeing Madgie Reid's son, who had joined the regiment in Limerick and was now thriving as a junior officer. He wrote that Jack Reid was "looking very rosy & cheerful—He has improved in the most extraordinary way & is now quite good looking[.] I have just written to Christopher & hope that he is better—"[214] It was Frank's first letter to Christopher since before the measles.

Despite his illness, Christopher still received a school report. Kathleen and Frank had no patience for criticism during this perilous episode. Having resigned him to the care of the Morgan Browns, Frank now feared for Christopher's unique personality: "I don't think it matters so very much what Christopher learns as long as he remains himself & keeps his individuality & develops on his own lines—though of course I am afraid you ought to sit on him for being lazy—" In April, Frank returned to the theme: "The whole point of sending him to school was to flatten him out, so to speak, and to make him like other boys and, when all is said and done, I don't know that it is at all desirable or necessary, and I for one would much rather have him as he is."[215]

In his draft for *Kathleen and Frank*, Isherwood pondered this. "I shall never know, now, just exactly what Frank meant by having Christopher 'as he is.' What did he think Christopher was? How much did he foresee or guess, as he looked at his mouse-faced, enigmatic, demure little son, with his bright uneasy eyes?"[216] Isherwood decided to accept these two letters as evidence that Frank had not rejected him: "far from disowning his Son, he gave him his blessing."[217] Thus, in the 1960s, Isherwood reversed the amnesia brought on by the cruel exile Frank had imposed on him; he felt certain not only that Frank had recognized and understood him, but that Frank had been glad of his difference and uniqueness, and had wished him to pursue his own path. In 1915, however, Christopher was not able to take in his father's affectionate view of him as a boy unlike other boys—a boy whose gifts lay in his inability to conform.

FRANK VOLUNTEERED FOR whatever duties came along, even if it meant leaving the York and Lancasters: "The Brigade called for the names of people who could speak German & I sent mine in—as I thought it might lead to something." He was determined to challenge himself. "It is raining hard this morning but I went for a gallop in spite of it—I am not feeling so very well & have just taken a dose of castor oil & opium! . . . bhrumm—"[218]

Four days after Kathleen left St. Edmund's, Christopher at last sat up and, briefly, left his bed to have tea beside the fire. On March 31, Madgie Reid collected him for the drive to Portsmouth. There Kathleen, like a general moving troops, had timed the simultaneous arrival of Richard and Nurse from Marple Hall and herself from the Isle of Wight: "he all wrapped up with blankets etc. but very bright & pleased the chauffeur carried him to the boat, & there Nurse & Richard joined us [. . .] We arrived safely Ventnor! C to bed & the Dr to see him, he thought he had stood the journey well—so thankful to have got the children safely here."[219] Nanny had left her father's deathbed to collect Richard.

Kathleen hired a Bath chair pulled by a donkey to take Christopher from the lodging house to the beach and the spring sunshine. On the second day, he walked. The doctor examined his lungs and his legs and pronounced them sound, but Christopher was still very much the invalid, with a special regime—his throat painted daily with antisceptic, a tonic before meals, malt or emulsion after, his legs to be rubbed when they ached, a constant supply of meat teas and fruit jellies. After a week of convalescence, Kathleen recorded, "he rather limps along."[220]

Richard found his new circumstances infuriating. Snatched from the center of attention at Marple Hall back to the edge of the circle in which Christopher so convincingly starred, he immediately threw a terrible tantrum: "it seems sometimes as if a fiend got inside him," wrote Kathleen. "I am afraid he wants a father's attention," Frank advised. "Tell Christopher he must take my place—!"[221] But Christopher was Richard's arch-rival. Kathleen and Emily were reading aloud *The Brothers Karamazov* with its themes of fraternal rivalry and parricide. In later years, Isherwood was to identify with the saintly brother, Alyosha.

For April 8 and 9, Christopher's handwriting appears in Kathleen's diary, taking her dictation: "C. discovered a rash on my face when we woke!" The doctor pronounced measles. Invalid and nurse swapped roles. "C. enveloped in a white petticoat comes & visits me."[222] He read aloud to her—on Sunday the Bible, on Monday the *Daily Mail*.

Kathleen's case was mild; still, she was quarantined until April 18. Then, as she lay in the sun on the veranda, Nanny collapsed with a temperature of 101 and tonsillitis, not to speak of the news received April 6 that her father had finally died. The boys were now looked after by Emily's maid and by a cousin of Kathleen. Illness and convalescence had become a full-time occupation for the group. On April 20, the doctor said that Christopher must not go back to school "till he has lost the wheeziness in his cough."[223]

Christopher had renewed his correspondence with his father, evidently reporting on difficulties sailing his toy boat and Richard's temper. In reply, he received Frank's personal admonition that he must be a strict father to Richard, "I am sorry that your boat & brother are both so ill-behaved you will have to come the heavy father over the latter."[224] This proved to be Frank's last letter to Christopher, written in the expectant lull before the spring campaign. Try as he might "to come the heavy father" with Richard, it was to exceed Christopher's young capabilities. The impulse never left him, though, to try to take care of a boy younger and more needy than himself.

On April 27, the doctor postponed Christopher's return to school for another ten days. Christopher moved into his mother's room because his own had been given up in expectation of leaving Ventnor; Richard moved back in with Nanny.

Nanny now made clear that she did not want to stay at Marple Hall alone with Richard because she was "worried there."[225] From the start of the war, Frank had assured Kathleen that there was enough money to afford her own small home, and he had urged her to use his pay. Perhaps Kathleen feared there really was not enough money, or perhaps she feared to live alone or thought it indecorous. Possibly she did not want to admit to herself that the war or Frank's absence would last long enough to make her own home necessary.

Adrenaline was flowing at Armentières. Frank had told her of a big battle to the north of him, a burst of activity and noise that contrasted sharply with the slow, blossomy carriage drives, tea parties, long walks and longer rests taking place on the Isle of Wight: "we can hear the guns going—The last wires are encouraging & we seem to be pushing the foe back—"[226]

Twenty miles north of Frank's position at Armentières, the Allied front line bulged eastward like a capital D curving around Ypres. This bulge into enemy territory was called the Ypres Salient. The Germans were attempting—for the second of five times during the war—to take Ypres and flatten out the salient. On April 22, they launched their first successful chlorine gas attack against French colonial troops holding the north end of the salient. There were 6,000 casualties, and a four-and-a-half-mile gap opened in the Allied line, permitting a significant German infantry advance. Canadian troops defending the easternmost part of the salient along with two British divisions began the first dangerous counterattacks.

Among the British divisions were the 1st Battalion York and Lancasters, who suffered heavy casualties, including all their senior officers. Frank, having put his name forward repeatedly, was told to leave the 2nd Battalion and hurry north to command the decimated 1st. He announced this guardedly to Kathleen on April 27: "you mustn't be anxious as the fighting up there seems virtually over." Kitty, the mare, remained behind at Armentières. Frank's senior officer, Colonel Clemson, bid him an emotional farewell. "I am very glad to have a show of my own," Frank wrote to Kathleen.[227] She knew him well enough to be distressed, and British newspapers had carried horrifying reports of the poison gas attacks.

Things were not right with Christopher, either. "Poor C. very elderly all day with lumbago in his back & did not go out—a sea fog all the morning & fog signal going."[228] He was still coughing. The doctor was mystified by the lack of "organic" explanation, and he had run out of energizing tonics. He had spoken out against boarding school ever since Christopher arrived in Ventnor, and of course, Kathleen's bedroom was a much nicer place to sleep than the dormitory at St. Edmund's.

Also, Kathleen was using Christopher as a confidant. He had been writing her diary during her measles, and perhaps he had been reading it. He must have been aware on some level of Kathleen's growing dismay about Frank as well as their recent ambivalence about his boarding school.

In her diary, Kathleen fretted about father and son in one barely punctuated breath, and as she grew more anxious about Frank, Christopher's health worsened and his joints swelled. He was channeling his father's destiny. The doctor sent him back to bed, prescribing medicine every four hours and warning Kathleen to watch for rheumatic fever which would require urgent treatment. "He lay there *so* good & uncomplaining reading & drawing & the tears coming when the pain was very bad," she wrote.[229]

Nanny took Richard back to Marple Hall, and Emily returned to London, leaving Kathleen and Christopher alone in Ventnor. The doctor came every day. Rheumatic fever struck fear in them all, and this vigil perhaps gave rise to the idea that Christopher actually did have rheumatic fever, as with the whooping cough in Limerick. But the vigil silently encompassed Kathleen's other fear, potent with controlled hysteria, as she waited for news from Belgium.

ON THE 7TH, 8th, and 9th of May, Kathleen did not hear from Frank. The Ventnor doctor at long last dismissed Christopher, providing letters for the doctors at Marple and St. Edmund's, and Kathleen and Christopher went for one last carriage ride. "—so pretty now," she wrote on the 9th, "with the lilacs out, the mass of fresh green & the apple blossom—one chestnut tree all in flower & laburnums budding [. . .] Nothing from Frank again[,] feel so anxious to know how he is getting on."[230] As it proved, Frank had probably been killed during the previous night.

Isherwood was never able to establish exactly what happened to Frank, though in the 1960s he studied various accounts of what came to be known as the Battle of Frezenberg Ridge. Frezenberg Ridge was at the easternmost curve of the Ypres Salient, and the 83rd Brigade, of which the 1st Battalion York and Lancasters were part, occupied vulnerable trenches on the forward slope. They were relieved from these trenches late at night on May 7 and went to rest in huts to the west of Ypres. Nearly five hundred newly trained men joined them, swelling their greatly reduced numbers back toward full battalion strength, around a thousand. They were called back to the battle Saturday morning, May 8, following a massive German bombardment initiating a series of attacks that overran the forward trenches.

Frank and his men were among those ordered to retake these trenches. Thus, from around 2:30 p.m., they counterattacked under shellfire in the general direction of Zonnebeke, which lies east and slightly north of Ypres and was then behind the German line, about a mile and a half beyond the village of Frezenberg. Beside them, on the other side of a railway line, the 3rd Battalion of the Middlesex Regiment counterattacked in the same direction. They were supported by remnants of seven other regiments. All along the salient, the Allies fought to close the gap the Germans had first opened with chlorine gas and into which more gas was being released.

By about 4:30 or 5 in the afternoon on May 8, Frank and his men occupied support trenches near the village of Frezenberg, between the railway and a hamlet, Verlorenhoek. The York and Lancasters alone among the regiments of the 83rd Brigade advanced beyond these trenches, but they were forced by enemy fire to retire like the others. They were heavily shelled in these trenches and casualties began to mount.

From these support trenches near Frezenberg, the York and Lancasters again attacked under orders, about an hour before sunset. According to the account of the battle quoted by Isherwood in *Kathleen and Frank*, they made the assault at 8 p.m. without preliminary bombardment or covering fire. Only a few of them reached the German trenches, where they were bayoneted. "In this attack," runs the account, "practically every officer present was put out of action . . ." Frank, possibly already wounded when he led the attack, was among four officers who went missing at this point. Two sergeants assembled the surviving men in the support trenches, and the battalion was ordered to attack again at midnight. But the order was countermanded when the brigadier "learnt that there were only eighty-three men" remaining of the whole battalion.[231]

As yet, Kathleen and Christopher knew none of this. They were focused on leaving the Isle of Wight with Christopher still a semi-invalid. Devotion to timetables—of trains, of medication, of meals—protected them from considering the unimaginable: the smoke and noise of howitzers, the blackened, bombed-out countryside, corpses in the leafless woods and unplowed fields, missing limbs, exploded faces, torn uniforms, smashed wristwatches, rotted boots, unraveled knitting.

They left Ventnor on a beautiful spring morning and arrived at Marple Hall in wet gloom. "[I]t was raining which his leg gave warning of before we got there . . . he went to bed almost at once." The next morning came a telegram from the War Office: "Lt Col F.E.B. Isherwood reported wounded 9th of May, nature and degree not stated." It was, Kathleen wrote, "a sad long day of no news, & horrible anxiety."[232]

Within twenty-four hours, she left for London to find out what had happened to her husband, the Hero of Marple. Christopher, so sensitive that his leg could predict the weather, did not see her again for nearly seven weeks. She mentioned him in her diary only three times while she was gone.

Kathleen visited the War Office nearly every day, sometimes twice a day, and she went to the Horse Guards repeatedly to consult the list kept there of wounded officers in London hospitals. She asked at the bank, Cox & Co., again and again, and at two different Red Cross enquiry bureaus. She wrote eight or nine letters a day—to officers still in the field who might know something, to the casualty clearing stations in France, to wounded officers and men who might have seen Frank in the fighting, to anyone powerful enough to advance her questions in new quarters. Jack Isherwood wired all Frank's senior officers.

Evidently, Kathleen prepared to cross to France to look for Frank, for she noted that her passport arrived from Cox & Co. She traveled all over London and suburbs by bus, by tram, and on foot to the bedsides of men wounded fighting near Frank and listened to their stories. One convalescent soldier was only able to repeat what so many repeated: "It was 'orrible 'orrible."[233]

Reports varied: Frank was wounded, killed, not wounded, taken prisoner. Every day, there were rumors and follow-ups. Every day people stopped by Emily's Buckingham Street flat to ask questions and offer advice.

Frank was not at Boulogne, not at Armentières, not among the wounded officers arriving back in London from Ypres. Wires came from the Red Cross in various locales. Kathleen's search for the Hero of Marple presaged the quest for the lost heir in Auden and Isherwood's play, *The Dog Beneath the Skin, or Where is Francis?*, and her tenacity was to be rivaled in Isherwood's efforts to be reunited in the 1930s with his German boyfriend, Heinz Neddermeyer.

As May became June, Kathleen began to receive letters extolling the "fearful & glorious fight" from which so few were left, and a cruel account of the battle was forwarded by Henry. She placed ads in *The Times* and the *Morning Post* requesting information about prisoners. "That is ones last hope now. [I]t is simply heartbreaking—" she wrote on June 5.[234]

On June 19, she received via Henry a letter from a wounded soldier in the Irvine Hospital, Ayrshire, "stating that Frank met his death when leading them in an attack at Ypres on German trenches[,] that he was by his side when he fell, he did not move[,] blood was coming from his head & chest..." She found this letter "most terribly upsetting." She laid hands on what she could of Frank: "Turned out the shelves in wardrobe & refolded F's things—also the moth in his wedding trousers." Then she began to resign herself: "got a black coat & skirt for every day."[235]

Finally, on June 24, nearly seven weeks after she had last heard from Frank, a letter came from the British Red Cross and Order of St. John which she copied into her diary:

> a disc was found on a dead soldier close to Frezenberg early in May with the following inscription / Isherwood F.E.B. / Y&L Regiment / Siehe 5. C of E. / We greatly fear that this disc may have belonged to Col Isherwood...

Kathleen added, "& so passes hope & life."[236]

IDENTITY DISKS ARE called dog tags because they were first used on dogs. They originated in Berlin. *Hundemarken* were put on dogs in the Prussian capital sometime before 1870. The Prussian army copied the innovation to identify soldiers in the Franco-Prussian war which began that year. The British army followed.

A dog tag alone established the fate of Francis Bradshaw Isherwood. Was this the beginning of the connection in Isherwood's imagination between the lost hero Francis disguised as a dog in the play he wrote with Auden, *The Dog Beneath the Skin, or Where Is Francis*? Did it begin earlier, in the nursery, when Frank told him stories about Buster Brown and Tige the faithful talking pit bull?

What did Christopher know about his father's disappearance, as he completed his convalescence from his own near-death experience? Each had approached the abyss that spring; then their destinies diverged. Letters and telegrams were circulating among the family. Each family member expressed opinions about Frank's fate, and the servants around Christopher at Marple Hall, especially Nanny, Anne Pott, and Robert Dobson, surely did the same.

Accounts of the battle of Ypres filled the newspapers, and Christopher was likely to have seen them. Kathleen later pasted into the Memory Book a piece from the *Sunday Observer*, May 16, the day after Frank was listed among the wounded. It included the following passage:

> On Saturday morning, May 8, after a couple of days lull, the attack fell with staggering and appalling violence on our own positions in front of Ypres. [...] The Germans had brought up even the heavy weapons which had been previously used for coast defences. Their accumulated supply of ammunition was such that they poured upon our men not a rain, but a continuous deluge of high explosive. The ground we held at the most threatened points was pounded, riven, churned in all directions. Trenches were blown into shapelessness, scores of their defenders being destroyed at a blast. [237]

It was at Marple Hall that Jack received a letter from Kathleen saying Frank's identity disk had been found. Probably it was Uncle Jack who told Christopher.

Did Christopher know what a dog tag was? Had he seen Frank wearing his? Frank's body had been found, then the dog tag cut off and submitted for recording as was the practice, the body lost again in the mud. Such a loss of identity was to become Isherwood's greatest fear, shaping his behavior through the years. Yet as he approached his own death in old age, Isherwood was to choose to have no grave, like Frank. By the end of his life, he was to have channeled his identity into his work; his memorial was his name as a professional writer. His physical body no longer mattered, as he was to learn from the Bhagavad Gita:

> Worn-out garments
> Are shed by the body:
> Worn-out bodies
> Are shed by the dweller
> Within the body.[238]

AT THE END of June 1915, Christopher, Richard, and Nanny went to stay with Christopher's godmother, Agatha Greene Trevor, her husband, and their seven-year-old son at Maesmor Hall near the village of Corwen in Wales. Kathleen came from London the next day.

"[D]arling C. very sweet & dear it seems so dreadful that such a loss shall have fallen on him so young," she wrote in her diary. In *Kathleen and Frank*, Isherwood was to recall that "He hadn't grieved much for Frank in 1915, but that was because he had then regarded Frank's death chiefly as an injury done to Kathleen."[239] From the outset, Christopher pushed the experience away.

Kathleen poured out her desolation, her fear of the future, her intense longing for a different outcome, to her diary, where she also recorded Christopher's responsiveness, his watchfulness, his anxious, dutiful efforts to be for her whatever she needed.

They spent a whole month at Maesmor, joined by Emily. There was fishing for trout and for eels and motor tours through "pretty country lanes full of honey-suckle and dog roses, & high woods thick with foliage." Here again were the warm, everlasting days that had ushered in Christopher's birth and preceded his departure for boarding school and which he associated with *A Midsummer Night's Dream*. But now Frank was dead, and the idyll was haunted by his memory. Kathleen brooded on what Frank might have enjoyed or chosen to sketch. She paid little attention to the outside world. On Frank's birthday, July 1, she received "Heaps of dreadful letters," which she ignored. Henry Isherwood proposed putting notices of Frank's death in the newspapers, "but I am against doing so at present." She also recorded that "They want me to go to Marple but I don't feel I could face it just yet . . ."[240]

There was a memorial service for Frank in Marple on July 7. Staff from Marple Hall went, including Frank's old nanny.[241] It was the nearest thing Frank had to a funeral. Kathleen did not go, nor any family members. When she received a letter from the War Office repeating that Frank's identity disk had been found on a dead soldier and asking formally "whether I am prepared to accept this information,"[242] she made no record of any reply. She could not bear to formalize Frank's death.

Christopher had a new bicycle which he was learning to ride, and

Kathleen borrowed another so she could accompany him. "I still rather shaky," she noted in her diary. Indeed, despite painful spills, Christopher was far more confident, and he began leading the way. He bought a carrier to take her stream of letters to the post office, safely returning again and again. Such small things could be controlled. Underneath the surface lay their deeply intertwined emotional life.

Around this time, Christopher started collecting cigarette cards. They came inside the packets, serving as stiffeners so the cigarettes wouldn't break. The manufacturers printed pictures on them which could be collected as a series—cricketers, famous inventions, portraits of European royalty, geographical locales. The cards offered pocket-sized access to popular culture of the day in lurid, cheerful colors. At first, Christopher picked up cards that had been thrown away. According to Kathleen, he press-ganged her into hunting with him along the road to Corwen: "on our bicycles searching for cigarette cards." He assembled these bits of detritus into orderly, numbered series, becoming obsessed the summer he lost his father. Isherwood was later to explain that "you could write to the cigarette manufacturers and be sent complete sets of these cards for a shilling or two; but this was considered unsporting."[243] Instead, he got cigarette cards from friends and servants who smoked, creating a new if slender connection with many different—and different kinds of—people.

THE CHILDREN RETURNED to Marple Hall, and Kathleen and Emily went to their annual extension lectures in Oxford. But first, in London, they ordered formal mourning clothes. "M & I each a dull black silk & she a serge too ... hats, etc." Kathleen shopped for "ribbon muslin veils," and she was also fitted for a black silk coat and skirt. By the time Christopher saw her again in mid-August at Marple Hall, Kathleen was shrouded in her official uniform of woe.[244]

In Isherwood's second novel, *The Memorial*, about the effect of the war on his generation, he was to portray the first encounter between the heir to the estate and the newly widowed mother as a dramatic and intense emotional crisis, a single scene so painful for the son that he turns away from her. The heir is called Eric Vernon—playing on his position in both sound (Er/Heir) and sense (sole ruler)—and the mother is called Lily. Eric first encounters her grief on his fictionalized return from school to the Hall:

For a moment he hardly recognized Lily. She was hideous with grief. Her eyes swollen into slits, her mouth heavy and pouting, her face blotched and sallow. He hung back, scared. The smile shrank from his lips. She gave a kind of hoarse cry. He rushed into her arms. That was agony. He knew then that everything he'd imagined he'd suffered at school was nothing, mere selfishness, triviality. She reopened the wound and tore it ten times wider. And now it would have made no difference to Eric if ten fathers had been killed. It was only for her he felt. Father was dead. But she was alive and suffering like this right before his very eyes. He could do absolutely nothing.

Eric "guiltily" takes trouble to avoid repeating the emotional encounter: "It would have been more than he could bear."[245] *The Memorial*, written 1928–30, offers Isherwood's youthful, angry, icily controlled and sometimes vengeful take on the family story he was to address more empathetically in *Kathleen and Frank* when his feelings of rage and betrayal had subsided. In the interim, he also rendered the scene in his fourth novel, *The World in the Evening* (1953), with maximum emphasis on the boy's pain.[246]

Kathleen's grief forced Christopher to feel how much she had loved Frank and that Frank, not he, was her favorite. From this personal hurt, he was gradually to turn away to other entertainments and other affections. Frank had admonished "you can do more to make it bearable than anyone else," and, via Kathleen, "Tell Christopher he must take my place—!" During the first five or six years after Frank's death, until he was about sixteen, Christopher tried to meet his mother's needs—in his emotions, his deportment, and even his choice of career. This was to lead to a false self and a feeling, inevitably, of failure. Of course the role was impossible; he could never take his father's place.

FOR CHRISTOPHER'S ELEVENTH birthday, Kathleen arrived from London bringing him something to collect that was more substantial than cigarette cards—the first volumes of an edition of Dickens.[247] On August 7, in her widow's black, she began to read *Oliver Twist* to him. Within days came the official announcement that Frank was dead. Thus, as their hopes were finally crushed, their imaginations took refuge together in Dickens's story about the lost heir, born in the workhouse, orphaned, snatched by thieves into the underworld slums of London, and yet restored, in the end, to his rightful place in the realm of goodness, daylight, privilege. It had much in common with Christopher's favorite nursery tale, *The Roly-Poly Pudding*, in which that other boy hero, Tom Kitten, is snatched into a den of thieves from which he, too, safely returns.

After his misery at boarding school, Christopher naturally identified with the orphaned heir pushed out of the domestic circle that should have nurtured and protected him. When he fictionalized his boarding-school initiation and his face-off with the headmaster over the marmalade and butter in *Memoirs of Pine House* he obviously had in mind Dickens's "small rebel," Oliver Twist, who draws the fateful lot and approaches the workhouse master, basin and spoon in hand, saying, "Please, sir, I want some more."

Christopher wished to escape his gloomy new world of mourning just as Oliver Twist escapes his apprenticeship at the undertakers, where Oliver mourns professionally at the black-draped funerals of children dead from measles and sleeps among coffins in an under-counter recess that "looked like a grave." On the road to London, Oliver meets "as dirty a juvenile as one would wish to see," Jack Dawkins, the Artful Dodger, short for his age, wearing "a man's coat, which reached nearly to his heels" and exhibiting "all the airs and manners of a man." This "roystering and swaggering" man-child introduces Oliver to another underworld in London, Fagin and his gang of prematurely aged pickpockets smoking and drinking "with the air of middle-aged men"—just the sort of street boys that were to fascinate Christopher for the rest of his life.

At ten, Christopher was about the same age as Oliver Twist and just as "green," listening to Kathleen read aloud about the "game" that Oliver watches the boys play, in which Fagin pretends to be a rich old gentleman and the boys practice picking from his pockets "with the most extraordinary rapidity, snuff-box, note-case, watch-guard, chain, shirt-pin, pocket-handkerchief, even the spectacle case."[248] The "game" was strikingly like the magic tricks that Christopher was then learning to perform. Here was the sleight of hand described by John Maskelyne and Professor Hoffmann; indeed Professor Hoffmann's *Modern Magic* devotes a whole lively, playful chapter to "Tricks with Handkerchiefs."

Oliver Twist's outstanding quality is his purity, plainly visible in his face. He shrinks from crime no matter how cruelly he is pressed by Fagin and by Bill Sikes to become a thief. When wrongly accused, he faints away, and when forced to assist at housebreaking, he tries to warn the victims, is shot, and undergoes a long convalescence. Even the invisible influence of his depraved half-brother Edward Monks Leeford, desperate to ruin Oliver's character and make him ineligible to inherit, cannot corrupt Oliver. Part of Christopher also identified with Oliver's incorruptible purity; he longed to be such a boy.

Henry and Muriel invited Christopher, Kathleen, Richard, and Nanny to The Oakes for a week, and from there, Henry drove Christopher and Kathleen sixty miles through Sherwood Forest to visit Kathleen's Uncle Charles Fry and Aunt Julia Greene Fry in Lincoln. Aunt Julia was Granny Emily's only sister, and Uncle Charlie, Dean of Lincoln Cathedral and formerly headmaster of the public school Berkhamsted, was the male relative Emily had brought in to speak to Kathleen about her future and the future of her sons. Henry now enlisted Uncle Charlie's aid in pressing Kathleen to make Frank's death official. She finally gave in, and Uncle Charlie immediately wrote to the War Office and the bank.

Christopher, on display in front of the two uncles representing both sides of the family, could do nothing to restore his mother's happiness. The next day, "Poor Christopher scalded his foot with his early morning tea upsetting the tea pot over it—caused him agonizing pain." It was a bad burn, and Muriel's doctor was called. "Blister about the size of hen's egg on C's foot," wrote Kathleen.[249] In fact, it was the second time he had burned himself that summer, the start of a pattern of unconscious self-punishment for his failures toward Kathleen.

Frank's father offered Kathleen Wyberslegh as a home; the tenant had just died. But she was afraid to return: "I cannot imagine it without him . . ."[250] For the time being, Kathleen was to lose herself in moving from one temporary accommodation to another and in the commercial entertainments of London. She taught Christopher to do the same.

2

Sacred Orphan (1915–1923)

Christopher returned to St. Edmund's in September 1915 after more than five months' absence to find himself cast in a new role, that of Sacred Orphan. He wore a black crape armband about four inches wide, sewn around the left sleeve of his gray wool uniform jacket just above the elbow. In a 1915 school photograph, he is the only boy wearing such a band. This token of mourning set him apart from his schoolmates and announced his solemn public identity as the son of a dead hero, a father who had made the ultimate sacrifice for them all. "He had now acquired a social status which was respected by everybody in wartime England, including the Crown, the Church, and the Press; he was an Orphan of a Dead Hero," Isherwood explained in *Kathleen and Frank*, "and at first he was vain of it."

Among his schoolmates, though, it was the armband that was sacred, not the boy. "The band mustn't on any account be torn or even rumpled." But like Nanny's pinafore, like a costume for a play, it could be removed. "If [. . .] he felt like ragging, all he needed to do was strip off his jacket and join in the fun."

In the school photograph, eleven-year-old Christopher, hair slicked to his head and painstakingly parted, stands behind handsome, coy Miss Rosa, who nearly blocks him from view; but Christopher leans to his left, and looks around for the camera lens with his characteristically worried, questioning expression. If he is puzzling over what a Sacred Orphan should feel, he is nevertheless determined to be seen. Having been given a role in the national drama, he appears determined to play it and to validate his father's sacrifice, "to be worthy of Frank."

Once again, Christopher was miscast and destined to fail. He was sensitive, intuitive, mercurial, susceptible to anxiety and panic; the role of Sacred Orphan called for steadiness, self-discipline, physical courage, and a certain amount of plodding commitment. In *Kathleen and Frank*, Isherwood wrote of his duty to be worthy:

> Cyril and Rosa were the first to make him aware of this obligation. Later there were many more who tried to do so: people he actually met, and disembodied voices from pulpits, newspapers, books. He began to think of them collectively as The Others. It was easy for these impressive adults to make a suggestible little boy feel guilty.[1]

Over time, Isherwood was to react against this guilt and to direct his passionate outrage not just toward Miss Rosa and Mr. Cyril for criticisms of his behavior and personality, but toward the cultural institutions to which they subscribed and which they represented. He viewed such criticisms as resulting from the values of the British Empire, its caste system, and its racism as articulated by Rudyard Kipling, Cyril Morgan Brown's favorite author—values Isherwood grew to abhor. He came to look upon his St. Edmund's experience as "a lesson," as he wrote in his draft for *Kathleen and Frank*, "that he must never, indeed could never conform. He must recognize once and for all, that he was other than Cyril, other than Rosa, other than Kipling—or cease altogether to exist."[2]

Around the time Christopher returned to St. Edmund's, he wrote a poem called "A Lay of Modern Germany"[3] which was a parody of Macaulay's "Horatius" in *Lays of Ancient Rome*. Macaulay's thumping verse narrative tells how the Roman hero Horatius volunteered to die defending the Tiber Bridge across which the enemy threatened to overrun Rome. While Horatius fought, he gave his compatriots time to dismantle the bridge and close off entry to Rome. Once the bridge was down, Horatius dove into the Tiber, badly wounded and wearing heavy armor. Yet he survived the currents and his own apparent death wish and was greeted in Rome as a hero. The choice of subject for his poem suggests that the self-sacrifice defining his father's heroic death pressed upon Christopher heavily. He longed for a hero who survived.

If Christopher's anger with Mr. Cyril and Miss Rosa was somehow out of proportion, even hysterical, it was because Christopher had unconsciously understood that it was a matter of life and death to oppose them and the beliefs they promulgated. Fulfilling his duty according to their principles was like volunteering to die as his father had done.

In *The Memorial*, Isherwood was to portray this another way. Eric Vernon, the newly fatherless heir to the estate, says, "It seemed that his father's death was in some way connected with the school. That the school was responsible for it [...] the soaked playing-fields and dusty class-rooms and icy-cold chapel—all seemed the atmosphere and scene of Death."[4]

IN LONDON IN the spring of 1916, Christopher was thrilled at last to see Sarah Bernhardt, now in her seventies, in real life. She performed Eugène Morand's dramatic poem, *Les Cathédrales*, in which she and five others, dressed as nuns, represented six great cathedrals damaged or captured by the Germans. The unspoken suggestion of nuns being raped along with what one reviewer called "Belgium's ravished cathedrals" was wildly inflammatory. Decades later, Isherwood still recalled Bernhardt's dessicated rage, camping the performance for Bachardy and telling him how Bernhardt's age and fading powers had increased the pathos.[5]

Christopher also accompanied Kathleen to a Red Cross fundraising exhibition of "relics from the field of battle from Ypres Cathedral." There were "trenches of the most realistic description, with their high mud sides, sandbags dug-outs, & quarters" and a lecture on the bombardment of Ypres "most realistically represented the guns & cannons booming & the burning buildings falling ... it was simply horrible to realize that this is what went on for hours ..."[6] At Marple, Christopher walked to the village and bought twenty-five pounds' worth of Exchequer War Bonds, a big investment for a lad of eleven.

The war was everywhere and inescapable. On August 4, with the family, who were a center of attention, he attended a special intercession church service followed by a rally in the village to mark the second anniversary of the war. A few days later, Christopher went with Kathleen to view Fanny Hudson's expanding hospital arrangements at Brabyns Hall, "her two new tents, each to hold 8. Which will bring her number up to 40 of wounded."[7]

In mid-August 1916 came the news that Madgie Reid's younger son, Bob, was missing in action at the Battle of the Somme. Bob Reid was a lieutenant in the Royal Berkshires, already in command of a company at age nineteen, praised for his bravery and daring. An obituary in his prep-school magazine was to recall that "though not strong in bookwork, [he] showed great aptitude for games, especially Rugby football [...] to play with Bobbie Reid, though only 14, was like playing with another man, so good was his passing and combination."[8] Bob Reid's body, like Frank's, was never found.

Jack and Bob Reid, born just fifteen months apart in September 1895 and December 1896, had offered, as elder cousins, an example for Christopher's education and advancement. Frank had advised Kathleen that Madgie would always be a good source of advice. The Reids also offered an example for grief. Madgie had married a much older man and had been widowed in 1908 after fifteen years of marriage; Jack and Bob were only thirteen and twelve when their father died. They attended public school at Marlborough and then trained at Sandhurst for the army. Jack was the one who had joined Frank's regiment. In Limerick, Kathleen once returned home to find Christopher, aged nine, hosting Jack for tea with gifts Jack had brought from Madgie. Jack Reid had been wounded in the spring of 1916 and his leg amputated above the knee. At the time of his brother's death, he was preparing to return to duty on crutches in the War Office, aged twenty. Later, he became a barrister and a judge.[9]

In 1924, when he was Bob Reid's age, nineteen, Isherwood was to write a story, "Two Brothers," about the death of a twin in a motor accident. Billy dies when the motorcycle he is driving hits a truck; his twin brother, Bob, riding along in the sidecar, survives. The story never mentions the war nor the Reids. It focuses on the sensation of grief and on the question of consolation.

The story is narrated by a schoolmate. At their public school, Billy and Bob were popular athletes and prefects, fitting "perfectly together, like pieces of wood dovetailed." Billy is the leader and the intellectual, Bob "the follower."[10] (Thus the story reverses the fates of his Reid cousins; in real life, Jack was the brain in the pair.) "Two Brothers" evokes Isherwood's buried feeling of twinship with and dependence on his father, who understood him so well, foresaw his enthusiasms and needs, assisted him with his projects, and led him toward a better understanding of himself. Frank had been the "driver" in Isherwood's childhood world as Billy had been the driver of the motorcycle and sidecar in the story.

Isherwood's draft fair copy suggests obliquely how Frank's death had left his creaturely, inexperienced, prepubescent son puzzling over the absence. "For a long time, Bob will go on puzzling and puzzling, asking questions without expecting an answer. [...] Billy's gone, and Bob doesn't want consolation, he wants Billy."[11] It was an insight that was to last a lifetime; Isherwood was to use it again forty years later in *A Single Man*, where he also reused the story's opening line. "Two Brothers" begins with a statement of fact: "Billy is dead."[12] In *A Single Man*, in the narrow kitchen doorway where George used to collide with his lover Jim every morning as they prepared breakfast, George "stops short and knows, with a sick newness, almost as though it were for the first time: Jim is dead."[13]

"Two Brothers" and *A Single Man* both reflect the stoical view that there is no consolation for death, only suffering and the passage of time, and both insist that even memory of the dead will fade. In his draft for "Two Brothers," Isherwood wrote: "Time will pass, and gradually, Bob will forget. He can't be fed on memories, and Billy, I think, wouldn't ask for that kind of immortality. They lived together in the Present. Bob will go on living in the Present—but alone."[14] By 1964, though, Isherwood was to find a more hopeful sequel for bereavement, asserting in *A Single Man* that George will find someone else to love.

AT NEARLY TWELVE years old, Christopher was longing for fun. He began to have neuralgia whenever it was time to go to church, and he was thrilled to attend a summer house party hosted by cousins of Kathleen whose teenaged daughters played charades and taught him roulette "with sham coins." The daughters, Barbara and Angela Pell, returned the visit, so Christopher practiced for a new role, tour guide, by going around Marple Hall "to freshen up his knowledge" with a guidebook prepared by Uncle Henry.[15] He was immersed in the relevant Roundhead and Cavalier history because Kathleen was reading him Walter Scott's *Peveril of the Peak*—a Derbyshire romance featuring the Popish Plot, an imaginary conspiracy to assassinate Charles II—and he was proud to show off Marple Hall. He was to give the tour often in the following years, especially to groups of wounded soldiers convalescing at Brabyns.

Uncle Henry appeared with a friend on the day of the Pells' tour, and Kathleen expressed surprise at their behavior: "Henry & Mr Ross Brown arrived about lunch time & went on in the same juvenile fashion most of the afternoon teasing & tickling each other!!" The ever-observant Christopher may have understood this boyish ragging. In 1979, Isherwood was to write, "Uncle Henry became my first known adult homosexual," and he described a scene that resonates with Kathleen's diary entry:

> I unexpectedly came upon him and a younger friend in the vegetable-garden at Marple Hall. This friend had won the highest decorations for courage in battle during World War One, and he was as handsome as you could wish a hero to be. I had never heard any adults, heroic or cowardly, scream as these two were screaming while they playfully chased each other back and forth around the gooseberry bushes.[16]

Christopher must have noticed that his uncle's commitment to pleasure was unaffected by the war. Family and staff took it for granted that Uncle Henry, as the heir to Marple, was entitled to entertain himself. What a tempting example Uncle Henry offered to Christopher, in the museum of their ancestral home, as Christopher's moods vacillated between enthusiasm and ennui.

That summer, 1916, Christopher renewed his neighborhood acquaintance with Paddy Monkhouse, eldest son of novelist and playwright Allan Monkhouse who worked as a journalist on the *Manchester Guardian* and lived with his family at Meadowbank Farm in Disley. Paddy's mother, Dorothy Monkhouse, was a painter and musician. Frank had been friendly with Allan's sister, the painter Florence Monkhouse, who was a founder of the Manchester Society of Women Painters and regularly showed at the Manchester Academy of Fine Arts. Christopher and Paddy had met as toddlers and were destined to become close friends as teenagers.

A second new friend was Ian Michael Scott, known as Micky. Micky Scott was a year ahead of Christopher at St. Edmund's and lived in suburban Stockport in a mansion next to his father's rope factory. Micky's father, a widower, invited the Isherwoods to tour his factory and meet the rest of his family, a daughter and two more sons. Kathleen described the visit in her diary, noting that "Mr Scott gave me a ball of pink string & some coarser, to take away . . ." This was the first of his attentions to Kathleen.

The Scotts were a kind of opposite to the intellectual, aesthetically inclined Monkhouses, a dichotomy on which Isherwood was to build in *The Memorial*. They showed all the energy and push that Kathleen associated with local industrial fortunes; she wanted nothing to do with them. Two days after the rope factory tour, one of Micky's elder brothers, Gerald, a naval cadet, roared into Marple Park on a motorcycle to ask Christopher to the theater in Manchester and to stay the night. Christopher was shy, and Micky returned later by bicycle with a handwritten invitation from Mr. Scott, extending the theater invitation to Kathleen as well. "I of course declined," sniffed Kathleen.[17] The Scotts bided their time.

ON JANUARY 1, 1917, Christopher began keeping a diary in a small, black leather, page-a-day volume with the words "Collins' Lady's Diary No. 144" embossed in gold on the front. Possibly it was cast off by Kathleen, who typically used the slightly larger Collins' Handy Diaries, No. 166. The fact that Christopher began writing in a lady's diary perfectly suggests how he found his voice partly through his mother. But this was a private diary, written without any collaborator. In the memoranda pages at the front, he wrote out the Morse code alphabet as if he had in mind a secret diary. He used the code only once, though, and the diary is written in exceptionally legible handwriting and clear prose, as would be his habit with his diaries all his life.

From the outset, he was thorough and literal; he left no blank pages in the book. Sometimes he wrote "Nothing much." His picture of family life at Marple Hall that January resembled his mother's, but peppered with reckless energy. His Aunt Esther Toogood came to stay bringing Joan and Timmy, the rivalrous sisters-in-law no longer kept apart in the wake of

Anne Pott's sudden death in September after her twenty-seven years as housekeeper. The cousins played in the barns, had schoolroom teas, walked to church, and tobogganed through mud in the grotto garden because there was no snow. It was evidently now, when he had companions his own age and Anne Pott's ordering hand was gone, that Christopher felt able to see off the Marple ghosts. "Frightened the servants with Timmie in evening," he wrote. They repeated this haunting two days later and "made Edith cry!!!"[18] (One of the maids.)

On a memoranda page, he made a list of books he read that year, another habit pursued through adult life, and he graded them: "V.G." was his highest accolade, awarded to Henry Newbolt's *Tales of the Great War*, Rider Haggard's mystical romance *Ayesha*, John Buchan's spy thriller *Greenmantle*, Harrison Ainsworth's *The Tower of London*, and Marjorie Bowen's occult fantasy about two highly strung medieval scholars who sell their souls to the devil, *Black Magic: A Tale of the Rise and Fall of the Antichrist*.

Newbolt's *Tales of the Great War* (1916) was a fact-based account for schoolboys. On the very first page, Newbolt ran out his view that school games were the best training for warriors: "the useful new subalterns in this war have mostly come from the Public Schools and Universities, and many of the best [. . .] were accustomed to leading in games."

Tales of the Great War delivered plenty of the horror of battle, while manipulating the schoolboy heart to focus on the opportunity for heroic action. "[T]he object of war is not glory but victory, and victory is won not so much by sudden acts of bravery as by carrying on or by holding out," wrote Newbolt. "You will envy and long to imitate [. . .] those who, as my stories will show you, could take punishment without breaking, and hold on after they were beaten, keeping command of themselves and others till defeat turned to victory." Here was propaganda aimed expressly at idealistic boys like Christopher. "I have not invented one word of the book," Newbolt attested in his introduction. Yet he borrowed imagery from favorite stories—*Sherlock Holmes*, *Treasure Island*, *Peter Pan*—to suggest the war was a romantic adventure.[19]

For Christopher, the book was startlingly close to home. The first group of tales, "The Adventures of a Subaltern," was set in the fighting around Ypres just before Frank arrived there; the second group, "The Tales of Two Admirals," featured Elizabeth Isherwood's nephew, Madgie Reid's brother, Captain John Luce. Christopher and Kathleen decided to share it with Elizabeth as she lay in bed recovering from bronchitis: "Mummie read to me in Granny's room afterwards."[20] As Newbolt tells it, the Battle of the Falklands on December 8, 1914, had been Britain's triumphant revenge against the German Admiral Graf Maximilian von Spee for the disastrous Battle of the

Coronel off the coast of Chile on November 1, 1914. John Luce, commanding his light cruiser *Glasgow*, played a dashing, heroic role in both battles, and his heroism was to carry his name into Auden and Isherwood's *The Dog Beneath the Skin*.

Newbolt's tales of the ground war were darker. In "The Adventures of a Subaltern," the hero is an unnamed public-school-educated Oxford undergraduate, captain of the cup-winning college football team and a second lieutenant in the Officers' Training Corps. He is mobilized as soon as war breaks out and reaches the Front, his heart's desire, on April 2, 1915, at Ypres—three weeks before Frank. He fights right next to the 1st York and Lancasters, the battalion Frank was shortly to take over, and the story vividly, cruelly details the decimation of the battalion until a shell blast knocks the subaltern unconscious. On April 27, he is coming around from his concussion in a London hospital. That was the very day Frank had left his 2nd Battalion and gone to take command of the decimated 1st.

At school, Christopher's diary entries were often resigned, even passive. Schoolwork, sport, chapel, choir practice, concerts, lectures by visitors—all happened *to* him. A handful of physical thrills come to life more vividly, for instance, tobogganing off the school grounds after a heavy snowfall: "Run nearly 200 yds long. Went about 20 mls per hr some of the way!!!!!"[21]

There were other things he did not write about until years later—interactions operating underneath the announced rules and schedules of the school, which moved him without his conscious understanding and over which he did not attempt to exert much control. In his diary, he sometimes mentioned ragging in the playroom.

Although he disliked competitive games, which called upon him to suppress his natural instincts, ragging led to laughter and letting go. In *Kathleen and Frank*, Isherwood made plain that the excitement of ragging had been sexual: "He loved tearing around with the other boys, screaming, laughing, scuffling. Wrestling soon became a conscious sex-pleasure. He found boxing sexy too, even though he usually got knocked about."[22] Indeed, according to his diary, he lost all his boxing matches.

In a diary he reconstructed in the 1970s and which was published as *Lost Years*, Isherwood asserted that these early sexual experiences stayed with him all his life:

> Christopher then was and has since remained very much under the spell of his prepub[escent] sexual experiences at St. Edmund's School. If he wasn't quite infantile he was definitely inclined to be small-boyish. At St. Edmund's, all of his orgasms with other boys had been while wrestling.[23]

As a schoolboy, he was afraid of his sexual feelings. In *Christopher and His Kind*, Isherwood explained that he was able to enjoy such feelings only after he arrived in Berlin, where he tried to recover what he had felt at school:

> At school, the boys Christopher had desired had been as scared as himself of admitting to their desires. But now the innocent lust which had fired all that ass grabbing, arm twisting, sparring and wrestling half naked in the changing room could come out stark naked into the open without shame and be gratified in full. What excited Christopher most, a struggle which turned gradually into a sex act, seemed perfectly natural to these German boys; indeed, it excited them, too.[24]

Boxing was more formal, sponsored by the school. Christopher attended a boxing exhibition by Canadian soldiers, and on another occasion, St. Edmund's fought the townees, "the [G]rayshott boys . . ." The boys were encouraged to watch each other fight, so Christopher did. In his 1970s reconstructed diary, Isherwood explained: "Boxing also could be a form of the sex duel, though the pleasure Christopher got from it was of a different quality, tinged with sadomasochism. [. . .] Christopher found a sexual thrill in the very idea of being *matched* with another boy—even if it was with a boy who didn't attract him physically." He had, after all, long been fascinated by individual combat. He objected to rules in boxing, as in games. "[T]he fight itself was spoilt by the formalities of competition," he later wrote. "There were rules and scoring—at the end of the bout, you had lost or won on points."[25] The rules made it acceptable for young boys to hit each other publicly, even though it was not acceptable for them to express physical love for one another.

In his 1917 diary, Christopher recorded the names of boys he boxed and also the names of boys with whom he partnered on his daily, sometimes twice-daily, walks. In general, he didn't walk with the same boy twice in a row; perhaps this was not allowed. For the school Sunday walk, February 25, 1917, Christopher recorded walking with Auden ii—Wystan Auden. (Wystan's elder brother John was Auden i or Auden Major; his eldest brother was not at the school.) The walk was four days after Wystan's tenth birthday; Christopher was twelve and a half. Perhaps it was this walk that Auden still recalled in a 1972 interview: "I was walking with Mr. Isherwood on a Sunday walk—this was in Surrey—and Christopher said, 'I think God must have been tired when He made this country.' That's the first time I heard a remark I thought was witty." Christopher was to record similar walks the following year, 1918, including one during which they became so absorbed in their conversation that "We missed the others and got back late!"[26]

The 1915 school photo captures Wystan sitting in the front row with his knees pulled up to his chest; his big ears, the corners of his mouth, his eyes, and the tips of his large white Eton collar all point solemnly downward. He is two rows in front of Christopher, with Miss Rosa between them. Wystan was then a new boy, aged eight. They got to know each other well only during Christopher's last two years at St. Edmund's. In the autumn of 1917, Wystan, academically advanced for his age, was promoted to the top form while Christopher was still in it. In the summer term, 1918, when Christopher was nearly fourteen and Wystan eleven, they slept in the Blue Dormitory together with three other boys.

In the myth-making memoir *Lions and Shadows: An Education in the Twenties*, which Isherwood wrote in the mid-1930s and in which he launched the comic legend of his literary generation, he sketched an extravagant, mesmerizing portrait of the schoolboy Auden by mixing remembered impressions with things he learned in later years. He mischievously cautioned readers in a prefatory note that the book was "not, in the ordinary journalistic sense of the word, an autobiography; it contains no 'revelations'; it is never 'indiscreet'; it is not even entirely 'true.'" Of course, *Lions and Shadows* does contain revelations, is often indiscreet, and is in many essentials true, but it is written "with a novelist's licence"[27] and artfully, playfully disguises the real events on which it is based.

Lions and Shadows highlighted Auden's boyhood obsession with mining—"his playbox was full of thick scientific books on geology and metals and machines"—his precocious and titillating knowledge of sex gleaned from his father's medical library, and his wildly opinionated personality, always spoiling for an intellectual fight:

> In our dormitory religious arguments, which were frequent, I hear him heatedly exclaiming against churches in which the cross was merely painted on the wall behind the altar: they ought, he said, to be burnt down and their vicars put into prison. His people, we gathered, were high Anglican. As a descendant of a Roundhead judge, I felt bound in honour to disagree with him, and sometimes said so . . .[28]

They argued a lot over the years, as adult friends and literary collaborators, sparring, showing off, pushing one another to the limits of their knowledge and creative powers. Constant intellectual wrestling, suffused with mockery and laughter, defined their artistic relationship; physical wrestling was the foundation of their sexual relationship when it began in 1926. In the early 1970s, Isherwood wrote about the Whitmanesque male–male bond: "in the utter nakedness of the sex duel there is no room for a lie; this is basic physical contact. So it can be claimed that you reveal more of yourself and find out more about your partner while you are wrestling with him than while you are making sex." He recalled that "Auden and Christopher must have wrestled during their sex acts."[29]

The bond between them was to be more intimate, more candid, and more productive than between any other members of their talented literary generation. In 1936, after Auden visited Isherwood in Sintra to work on their third play, *The Ascent of F6*, Isherwood wrote in his diary: "although I was often very much annoyed by his fussing and by the mess he made—still I never for one moment was more than annoyed. I never felt opposed to him in my deepest being—as I sometimes feel opposed to almost everyone I know. We are, after all, of the same sort."[30]

At St. Edmund's, Wystan, like Christopher, had left behind a close family life disrupted by the war. Wystan's father, George Auden, a doctor, was stationed in Gallipoli, Egypt, and France with the Royal Army Medical Corps. Wystan did not see him from age seven to twelve. He later commented, "I lost him psychologically."[31] Wystan's mother, Constance, gave up the family home, just like Kathleen, and stayed with relatives or took furnished rooms in holiday places like Wales, Cumbria, and the Isle of Wight whenever her three sons were out of school.

Like Christopher, Wystan was very close to his mother in childhood. Constance was more educated and more emotionally disciplined than Kathleen. She got a university degree in French, with a gold medal, when few women attended university, and she trained as a nurse with the intention of going abroad as a medical missionary.

Christopher's grandparents were landowners, vintners, socialites; Wystan's were clergy—professional Christians. Constance, the daughter of a rector, was very High Church Anglo-Catholic. Wystan's family prayed together before breakfast and attended Sunday Mass "with music, candles and incense,"[32] and Constance emphasized self-sacrifice, self-discipline, and self-restraint. Kathleen enjoyed attending different kinds of church services depending on who was giving the sermon, and she generally dressed up for them. As often as Kathleen took Christopher to church or conducted services with him at home, she took him shopping, out to eat, to the theater or movies. The Auden house was crammed with books and music, but the Audens were not landed gentry like the Bradshaw Isherwoods. Work rather than leisure shaped their days. Achievement mattered more than pleasure, commitment to the well-being of others more than fashion.

George Auden had a first-class degree in Natural Sciences from Cambridge and went on to be the school medical officer for Birmingham and professor of public health at the university there. He was among the first serious students of psychology in England, and he published articles about juvenile character formation, delinquency, learning disabilities, mental handicap.

The Audens certainly were not conventional. Constance taught Wystan, when he was eight years old, the love-potion scene from Wagner's *Tristan and Isolde*, which they sang together, Wystan taking the demanding part of Isolde.[33] This musical enactment of unrequitable longing evidently took place just before Constance parted with her youngest and favorite son, as he started boarding school. There he continued with his piano playing, progressed to leading the chapel choir, and never found in institutional life any emotional engagement so intense, so challenging, as he had had with her.

Wystan was given Filson Young's *Tales from Wagner* for coming top of his maths set at the end of 1917. As it happened, Christopher had scoured London for the very same book at the beginning of the year after becoming addicted to the "The Grand March" from *Tannhäuser* on Uncle Walter Greene's player piano and hearing it in a concert at Queen's Hall, in London.[34] He perhaps knew how much Frank had loved Wagner.

Wystan was not as unhappy as Christopher at St. Edmund's, partly because he had a brother there. He, like Christopher, lamented the scarcity and nastiness of the food and the bullying—the "fists of big boys," as he wrote in his 1936 autobiographical poem "Letter to Lord Byron."[35] Food was even scarcer from the beginning of 1917 when Germany resumed U-boat warfare on commercial shipping in British waters, causing shortages. Bread was made with bulking additives that gave some boys stomachaches, and Christopher in particular suffered from the war diet. He recorded in his diary when any boy in his dormitory received a food hamper; these were shared—no one at St. Edmund's was allowed to consume treats privately. When Christopher was invited out to tea, he rated the meal, as with his reading.

Wystan was better suited than Christopher to the emotional austerity that Isherwood located in the heart of the junior dorm. In *Memoirs of Pine House*, Isherwood described the bed-sitting room of the Miss Rosa character as "the most ascetic room in the house." He included a motto above the door that he had actually seen on a calendar at Marple Hall: "When God sorts out the weather and sends rain / Why, rain's my choice."[36] In the memoir, the lines—by American poet James Whitcomb Riley—again admonished against the comfort Christopher was used to at home. On the other hand, they articulated a sensibility Wystan shared with Miss Rosa, to whom he grew very close at school. Auden's love of bleak northern landscapes and rainy weather was the source of many jokes in later years and also a theme in Auden's work.

Like Christopher, Wystan had difficulties with Cyril Morgan Brown, whom he considered a good teacher, but whose outbursts of rage seemed to him unpredictable and frightening. Also like Christopher, Wystan experienced these confrontations extremely personally. He felt wounded at the start of his final year when Cyril Morgan Brown passed him over for head of school, although he kept his feelings to himself and got to be head in his next term. Wystan, too, came away from St. Edmund's conscious, for the first time in his life, that he did not want to conform, even if it meant breaking rules in order to preserve his individual identity. In "Letter to Lord Byron" he wrote: "I hate the modern trick, to tell the truth, / Of straightening out the kinks in the young mind."[37]

"GOT A LETTER from Angela & one more 'Polar,'" Christopher had written in his diary at the beginning of 1917 at St. Edmund's. His teenaged cousin Angela Pell had sent a card from the Player's Cigarettes 1915 Polar Exploration series. A week later, "Got the set of 'Historic Events' all but one." And a week after that, "Got a lot of 'Dickens' cards. New set of Players, saw it."

For about a year and a half, Christopher's obsession with collecting cigarette cards had been private, but that spring, he began to collaborate. "Started a firm with Tod," he recorded in May.[38] The cards became a currency, for circulating and making deals, and they drew him into a new kind of power relationship at school, of gangs and groups.

He was to write a story about this in 1927, "Gems of Belgian Architecture," based on his perception that everything the boys did at school had its own set of unspoken rules perpetuating a primitive hierarchy of strong over weak that existed separately from form prizes or silver cups awarded by adults. In a 1965 introduction to the story, Isherwood compared the boys' behavior to the behavior of the heroes in the Icelandic sagas, and he used the vocabulary of anthropology to underline similarities with clan-type etiquette from time immemorial: the "cult of the dead"; the "taboo" against unkind ragging of boys in mourning; the punishment and expulsion of two boys who sinned, one pretending his father had died in the war, another showing undue "side," which was considered far worse.

In "Gems of Belgian Architecture," cigarette-card-trading shapes the power structure among the boys. Some are organized into a gang, "the firm," headed by a bullying older boy and striving to rule the free agents. "It was a question of who'd be the first to get a complete set of Gems." A cowardly boy promises a friend the single card everyone lacks, Number 9, then swaps it, instead, to a spy of "the firm." Afterwards, ashamed, he steals the whole set from "the firm," hides it behind a loose brick in the changing room, and allows another boy to be blamed.

The story was based on a real crime committed against Christopher, who had collected a complete set of Gems of Belgian Architecture. "I seem to remember," Isherwood wrote in 1965, "that some of the rarer cards in it were once stolen."[39] The thief arguably knew he was stealing from a set which had particular meaning since Christopher's father had died fighting in Belgium. Fifty Belgian cultural treasures destroyed or occupied by the Germans are depicted on the cards and described in words on the backs, some with explicit reference to the war. Isherwood's story, though, did not refer to personal feelings, and as with "Two Brothers," the war is not mentioned.

Five years later, some of the boys, now young men, visit their old school. The coward tries to correct his old mistake by producing the complete set from behind the loose brick, but the hiding place is empty. All fifty Gems of Belgian Architecture are lost forever because of the rare Number 9 card. Kathleen thought Frank had died on May 9, and the family marked it as a solemn anniversary. Frank's father died nine years later, on May 9, 1924. Thereafter, the family marked it as a double anniversary.[40] Yet none of them ever knew exactly what had happened that day. The Number 9 card symbolizes this mystery—grief wrapped in layers of code, the longing for completeness in a collection of cards.[41]

Isherwood did not publish "Gems of Belgian Architecture" until 1966, nearly forty years after he wrote it. As he prepared to begin work on *Kathleen and Frank*, he included the early story in *Exhumations: Stories, Articles, Verse*, a collection of abandoned items, like the first cigarette cards he found along the road to Corwen in Wales. "This book [. . .] is just a lot of bits and pieces, fragments of an autobiography [. . .] dug up for display in a museum," he explained in a foreword.[42]

He had not been able to bury his father's body; instead, he had buried his feelings. In the 1960s, when he began to dig them up, they proved to be remarkably physical. He recalled his intense fear of the practice trenches which were dug by soldiers training near St. Edmund's and which the masters encouraged the boys to jump over on their Sunday walks and where he once got lost playing hide-and-seek: "Many of the trenches were seven or eight feet deep; it made me dizzy to look down into them." Christopher had paralyzing vertigo; his father had had it, too. And here, facing Christopher, was the endless maze described in his father's letters home, the cold mud walls that threatened to swallow Christopher like the grave.

In *Exhumations*, Isherwood explained that the army camp near St. Edmund's "was occupied chiefly by Canadians" and that the school staff at first told the boys that the Canadian soldiers were "heroes who had crossed half the world to come to our defence" then later described them as "wild, drunken, dangerous brutes" and banned the boys from walking near their camp. The boys, though, continued to approach the Canadians to ask them for cigarette cards.[43]

There was, in fact, a series called Canadians which Christopher completed in 1916. They depicted the natural resources, new industries, and wilderness beauty spots of what was then still a dominion of the British Empire. The Number 42 card, one of the last two Christopher obtained for his set showed "A Typical Farmhouse," a two-story wooden clapboard structure with a large front porch and a man standing in front holding a rifle. On the reverse was a description of "the pioneer farmer out West" and the information that the settler could "purchase a 'Ready-made Farm,' provided with dwelling-house, barns, and stabling, and with the land ready fenced and the first crops sown!"

This was one of Christopher's childhood fantasies, like Swiss Family Robinson. In 1913, Kathleen had taken him to a slide lecture by a man from Canada who was recruiting missionaries and settlers to pioneer there. After the lecture, Christopher had "played at living in a shack, like the men do out in Canada, pictures of which we saw at the Missionary Meeting last Monday."[44] It was a cultural opposite to Gems of Belgian Architecture and the angry lamentations of Sarah Bernhardt dressed as a ravished cathedral. Cigarette cards linked Christopher to a future of Western frontiers yet to unfold.

IN SUMMER TERM 1917, the weather was unusually hot, and Christopher refreshed himself with a dip in the school swimming pool almost every morning and sometimes again in the afternoon. Even more than swimming, though, he liked military exercises. He filled his diary with "fatigue"—chores and games organized in military groupings.

At the end of May, there were war games in the Devil's Punch Bowl, a dramatic natural hollow near the school. Auden later wrote, "we drilled with wooden rifles and had 'field days' when we took cover behind bushes and twirled noisemakers to represent machine-gun fire."[45] Wystan and John Auden played big roles in that particular field day, recounted in the *St. Edmund's School Chronicle*. Kathleen visited Christopher the following Saturday; he was sunburned and took her to see the Punch Bowl, telling her all about it. "The school is very military now," she recorded, "& the new master Mr Bagnal a very keen soldier—he has been through the new army, but is somehow now unfit for service . . ."[46]

Auden explained in "Letter to Lord Byron" that the war took "the best" men, so that the ones left to teach were increasingly eccentric. He identified Captain Reginald Oscar Gartside-Bagnall as "the oddest" teacher at the school, whose keen soldiering was attested to only by himself—"Your tales revealing you a first-class shot." Bagnall gave beer and biscuits to the boys he liked best, perhaps grooming them for closer friendship. "Went & sat in Mr. Bagnall's room after footer," Christopher wrote in his diary on October 20, 1917. Then in late November, he gave Mr. Bagnall a long set of ellipses—indicating something too significant to record: "Up to Mr. Bagnall's room after prep . . . . . ."[47] He did not specify on these occasions whether he was alone with Bagnall, but he did not mention other names.

In maturity, Auden recalled that Bagnall "had written a play, *The Waves*—a barefaced crib, I later discovered, from *The Bells*—which he used to read aloud in a Henry Irving voice to his awed and astonished favorites."[48] Henry Irving had become a star in 1871 in Leopold Lewis's *The Bells*, playing the burgomaster Mathias who is slowly destroyed by remorse after robbing and murdering a wealthy Jewish merchant. Irving often revived his performance, in particular the scene in which he is haunted by the ghost of his victim.

Isherwood described Bagnall's play a little differently than Auden. In *Lions and Shadows* he told how, in 1925 when he and Auden re-met six years after Isherwood had left St. Edmund's, they tried to "reconstruct the big scene [. . .] in which the villain is confronted by the ghost of the murdered boy." He wrote boy, not man as in *The Bells*, because the dialogue Isherwood attributed to *The Waves* in fact drew on Crabbe's "Peter Grimes," in which the fisherman is haunted by his three dead apprentices. The last and most vulnerable of Grimes's boys dies at sea, after supposedly falling from the mast. Perhaps Bagnall's play was a crib from "Peter Grimes" as well as from *The Bells*, but more likely Isherwood, writing in 1937, made the substitution so the reader would imagine a boy victim. "The waves . . . the waves . . . can't you hear them calling? Get down, *caarse* you, get down! [. . .] Don't stare at me, *carrse* you, with those great eyes of yours . . ."[49] Murdered boys is a dark theme to attribute to a prep schoolmaster, and Isherwood was evidently making a sexual innuendo. Thus, in *Lions and Shadows*, he shouted down Bagnall's inappropriate behavior with laughter.

Auden used an incriminating watery pun in "Letter to Lord Byron," saying that Bagnall's "moral character was all at sea." Yet he expressed gratitude to this apparently drunk and unscrupulous man for teaching him that "the great wide world" outside the school walls was "more like Dickens than Jane Austen."[50] Boys, Auden implied, should know they will be preyed upon by the likes of Bumble, Fagin, Monks, Murdstone, Squeers, Gashford, and so forth.

For both Isherwood and Auden, boyish vulnerability was to be an irresistibly attractive theme, supercharged with emotion. A boy alone is forever on the brink of danger, forever about to become a hero or a victim. The figure of such a boy, resolute, hopeful, tough, leaves footsteps all through their work. He is themselves, and he is many boys they came to know. Such a boy is threatened by many things, but sex was by no means the threat that most worried them.

WHEN RICHARD WAS about four and a half, briefly alone with Kathleen in London, a series of thunderstorms terrified him so badly that the doctor prescribed a bromide sedative to stop the hysterics, and Kathleen decided Richard could no longer stay with her there. The doctor, she wrote in her diary, "thinks R must have been <u>thoroughly frightened </u>at some time by someone about thunder—" Nanny was the likely and indeed the only suspect; yet Kathleen soon packed them off together to Marple Hall, where Richard was haunted by the ghost and continued to suffer terrible "attacks of fear." In the summer of 1916, Christopher and Kathleen found him at Marple "in a nervous highly strung state & the least thing his heart begins to beat so fast, just now his mania is a sort of terror of Nurse going out of his sight." He was also terrified by his grandmother Elizabeth, who, as she grew older, wandered through the house in the dark and was sometimes found sitting on remote staircases having forgotten her mission or lost her way. Kathleen described Richard at bedtime, "begging his Granny <u>not</u> to come & say 'Tummer tum tum' outside his door [. . .] knocking on the door all the while, there is something so uncanny about it . . ."[51]

When Christopher and Kathleen arrived in the summer of 1917, Richard was jealous of the attention Kathleen paid Christopher and rejected her for Nanny. Kathleen blamed Nanny's manipulativeness, but according to her diary, Richard had cause. "C & I sat in the punt in the afternoon paddled round the Duck pond by Ernest Coyne, while I finished reading <u>Nicholas Nickleby</u> out loud."[52] Christopher arranged a bicycle for Kathleen, and the next day, they rode off together. Combined with the punting, it was almost like a romance.

They cycled to Wyberslegh: "the once happiest spot on earth[.] We called on Mrs Cooper & C was interested to see his birthplace again—"[53] They also cycled back and forth to a village called Beamsmoor, where they arranged a cottage for Emily and a cousin, Raymond Smythies. Major Raymond Henry Raymond Smythies, eight years older than Kathleen, was the first gentleman interloper in Christopher's freshly reestablished romance with Kathleen, and he was to make Christopher jealous.

He had retired from the army in 1902 after being decorated in the Boer War, had written a history of his regiment published in 1894,[54] and had spent thirty years assembling a family history, *Records of the Smythies Family* (1912). It was a grander, drier version of Kathleen's own book, "History of Marple and Wyberslegh Halls and the Bradshaw Isherwoods," for which she made watercolors and sketches of interiors, heirlooms, coats of arms, family trees, wrote out mottoes and stories, and cut and pasted historical documents and pictures.

Smythies and later Kathleen joined a London archaeological group, the Peat Society, which toured notable buildings, and he was to accompany her on many trips, sometimes abroad with small groups. He was sufficiently engaged in the art world to have sat for a bust from Henri Gaudier-Brzeska in 1912, although they clashed over style. Smythies wanted a naturalistic "official image" and was uncomfortable with Gaudier-Brzeska's inclination toward abstraction; relations between them were comically prickly.[55]

During August 1917, Christopher and Kathleen made an architectural excursion to Haddon Hall, a medieval manor house passed down through the Vernon and Manners families—the Vernons had built Marple Hall. They bumped into Smythies, already on his way to Beamsmoor, so Smythies toured the house and village church with them. Once Emily arrived, Smythies was ubiquitous. He was included in Sunday lunch at Marple Hall on Christopher's thirteenth birthday. Christopher camped out, pioneer-style, with the Coynes, building a fire and cooking in a tin. "Sat in hut in morning," he wrote in his diary. Perhaps this was a protest. The lunch party was repeated on his grandfather's birthday the next day; then Kathleen spent a day away at Beamsmoor. "Went to meet her but missed," wrote Christopher in his diary.[56] The day after that, he managed to join her, but had to share her with Smythies.

Isherwood eventually punished Smythies by portraying him in *The Memorial* as Major Ronald Charlesworth,[57] the epitome of the retired military man, a veteran of the Boer War, too old for the Great War, tall, thin, lonely, of modest means, devoted to his small flat and three nights a week at his club. At the climactic moment of their slow-growing relationship, Charlesworth cannot bring himself to propose to the widowed Lily Vernon and settles for a paltry intimacy: that they will call one another by first names. He walks away with his meaningless sleepwalker's freedom, like John Marcher from May Bartram in Henry James's "The Beast in the Jungle." Ruthlessly, Isherwood marked Charlesworth's departure with an image suggesting the sex he will never have with Lily: "The lift slid down its shaft. He had passed out of the flat, it seemed, like a somnambulist [...] Now, at last, he could value, as never before, the beauty of his treasure—their friendship. [...] We shall have tea together. We shall talk." Along the street Charlesworth goes, "erect like a hero, swinging his umbrella"—a hero emasculated and trivialized, without a real sword.[58]

IN JUNE 1917, German airplanes reached London for the first time, killing 162 civilians in broad daylight and injuring 432. Nighttime bombing raids began September 3, mostly Gothas, each with six 200-pound bombs aboard. On September 12, before the St. Edmund's train, Christopher and Kathleen inspected the bomb damage near Emily's flat and heard a local report from a girl working in a bookshop.

After Christopher was safely out of London, the raids grew worse, aided by the light of a full harvest moon and clear skies, so Kathleen moved with Emily to Hindhead. Kathleen had already renewed her visits to St. Edmund's, lodging at the school or nearby and spending time with Christopher; during one visit, as she recorded, "we lay in my bed & pulled on wraps & read aloud & ate sweets."[59] Another time, she volunteered her bookbinding skills to mend school hymnals and spent four nights in Miss Rosa's room, Christopher joining her often at Miss Rosa's fire. Once, Richard and Nanny, en route from Marple Hall to a holiday in Lyme Regis, stayed in local lodgings with Kathleen and used the school as a playground. Thus, Kathleen half consciously gravitated to the happier days of Frank's camp and barracks life at Frimley and Aldershot. The school was surrounded by soldiers, and while the "sound of the bugles" made her feel "sad & lonely,"[60] she evidently felt safe.

One Sunday, walking near school, Kathleen and Christopher ran into a London acquaintance also fleeing the air raids, as hundreds of thousands did, and they heard a sensational rumor that Waterloo Station was "a sea of blood" after "70 aeroplanes came—I should think this was exaggeration—" Kathleen wrote. She began tracking the raids, recording the number of Gothas reaching London and the numbers of civilians killed and wounded. Every day, she found Christopher at his break time and often took him out to tea. He was plainly aware of her fears, writing a few months later: "A big air raid on London. It is a very good thing that Mummie has gone to Sidmouth."[61]

These details contrast markedly with a memory Isherwood offered in a 1947 essay, "Coming to London," of Emily's majestic calm in her Buckingham Street flat: "Reclining in a deck-chair on the roof of this flat, during the first Great War, my grandmother liked to watch the daylight raids through her lorgnette." In the autumn of 1917, when the air raids were at their height, Emily was too ill to climb the stairs to her flat; as there was no lift, she had been staying in a hotel before Kathleen moved her to Hindhead. Naturally, Kathleen was frightened; even after the raids had abated and she and Emily had returned to London, she wrote: "it is all very upsetting & keeps me very much on edge at strange noises."[62]

In his diary, Christopher presented himself as all the more manly and military: "Made Lt-cpl . . . ." he wrote on October 13, the copious ellipses indicating another indescribably significant event. He was thrilled by the chance to command junior cadets: "Parade. Took squad drill!!" At the end of the month, there was an outing to Bramshott Camp to observe real soldiers: "Saw Bayoneting Sectional Rushes & entanglement-making. We also shot. Very nice." On November 24, he was again promoted: "Made Cpl!!"[63]

AT THE END of 1917, Christopher was showered with prizes and came third overall in his year. His three days in London included afternoon tea for two at a South Kensington hotel with his old Limerick playmate Mirabel Cobbold, and with Kathleen he attended a solemn imperial service of remembrance for the war dead: "the Choral Commemoration for the 1st 7 Divisions which went out in 1914," as he carefully wrote. All Saturday afternoon, December 15, he and Kathleen sat side by side in a velvet-draped box looking down from the second tier over the vast, jam-packed Albert Hall: "The King & Queen were there. Also Lord French Lord Derby & Mr. Balfour."[64] (Arthur Balfour was Foreign Minister; Edward Stanley, Lord Derby, was War Minister; Viscount French, later 1st Earl of Ypres, had commanded the British Expeditionary Force at the start of the war.) The first seven divisions were represented by the presence of seven hundred survivors.

The choral program, entirely by British composers, told the story of military death as a glorious route to immortality, and Lord Balfour read from Ecclesiastes, closing with "their name liveth for evermore." Lord Derby called out the names of every regiment in the first seven divisions, and a long cheer went up from each, followed by three cheers called for by the King. There was a hymn, then Reveillé, the bugle call to wake, followed by "God Save the King."[65]

"The Banners of each regiment were hung all round the hall," wrote Kathleen, "The Y & L sixth on the left from the orchestra on cream ground."[66] Women from all over the country had contributed stitches to these richly colored memorial tapestries made by the Royal College of Needlework. Hung up among the tapestries were enormous laurel wreaths, symbolizing the immortality of dead heroes. The level of ceremony and the sheer number of people in the rotunda, which could then hold upwards of 8,000, fully displayed the might and the sorrow of the empire. To all of this, Christopher, aged thirteen and a half, was a witness in his role as son of a dead hero. The ceremony was heavily reported in the papers, including the *Illustrated News*, which ran a drawing of the scene showing individual people as if they were specks in a sea.

At Marple Hall that Christmas, Christopher received his own gun from Uncle Jack and practiced at targets with Alan Coyne. "Shot a chaffinch!!!" he exulted in his diary.[67] He carried the gun out walking with Kathleen. At school, he impressed Captain Bagnall with two bull's eyes and was put in the second team for competitions. While he was home, he helped Richard with his music, taught him arithmetic and drilled him, taking their soldier father's place just as Frank had asked him to.

All the while, Frank's parents were running out of money. Kathleen had known for some time that the estate was no longer generating enough to support the family's spending, and she had met with Jack to discuss economies. She was dragged into another discussion with her father-in-law on New Year's Eve 1917. Every day she read aloud to Christopher from *Great Expectations*; all around them, expectations were diminishing.

Kathleen managed her own finances far better than John or Henry Isherwood managed theirs. She had followed up education funds offered by the army, invested in war bonds, and put £100 on deposit at Cox & Co. for Christopher's next school. Whenever she received an allowance cheque from John Isherwood, she put that into a separate account. On January 5, 1918, she painstakingly made a complete domestic accounting for her in-laws. She did this work in her nightclothes: "Sat up in bed till 1. Going through 1917 bills."[68] Her estimate of their expenditures was circulated to Jack and Henry, leading to sandwiches on trays for some meals, fires lit on a rota only once a week in each room, and other economies.

Meanwhile, Micky Scott turned up with a note, again inviting Christopher to stay with his family overnight and go out on the town. This time the invitation was accepted, and the boys went into Manchester to see the Christmas pantomime, *Babes in the Wood*. Christopher was delighted, not least by the late hour of their return, and he was inspired to make a theater out of an old box (his own evidently stored since Limerick) and revive "the 'Witches Cavern' scene out of Macbeth." He also attempted "a fairy play called 'The Dragon'" lit with "a green flash light," after seeing something similar at St. Martin's School in Marple.[69]

He was increasingly fascinated by the supernatural. In London, he took great trouble to find and buy a reprint of Harrison Ainsworth's novel *Windsor Castle* with George Cruikshank's illustrations depicting Herne the Hunter, snatcher of souls, a blue-phosphorescent demon dressed in deerskins. (This was Ainsworth's version of the legendary specter described in Shakespeare's *The Merry Wives of Windsor*.) Kathleen treated him to the theater, and they chose a play by Bayard Veiller, *The Thirteenth Chair*, "about the murder of Edward Wales during a séance [. . .] which he held to find out who killed his friend."[70]

The deaths of so many in the war had increased the attraction of communicating beyond the grave. In 1915, Christopher's old love, Mrs. Cooke, wife of Frank's Aldershot colonel, had written to Kathleen saying Frank had spoken to her through a Ouija board: "Tell her not to sorrow. I am waiting and watching for her--" Kathleen shared excerpts from Mrs. Cooke's letter with her sister-in-law Moey, commenting, "I <u>can't</u> dismiss it without feeling there is <u>something</u>."[71] Kathleen was also captivated by *Raymond*, an account by Oliver Lodge of after-death communications with his son, killed in September 1915. Christopher came to know of these communications and Kathleen's longing to believe in them, and he was to make fun of this longing in *The Memorial* in a scene in which the widow, Lily Vernon, prays to see the ghost of her dead husband then rejects the possibility of the ghost when it appears. It was a private rebuke for Kathleen's lack of objectivity, remorselessly observing that when it came to ghost stories, Kathleen believed according to her emotional needs.

CHRISTOPHER'S 1918 DIARY was far more detailed than 1917, including carefully researched notes and diagrams. His accounts of familiar school events suggest he was finally at ease with institutional life. Indeed, he had become completely assimilated, like a fragment of iron moving in response to a magnet, his own thoughts suspended. His 1917 diary had evinced passivity; in 1918, he began to channel and announce the experiences of the group around him with positive and newly impersonal energy. "All made home-made drawing-to-scale outfits as Mr. Roberts showed us how to. [...] Carpentering which was very nice ... Mr Winchester was not there & had not been for several lessons. Nobody knew why ..."

Christopher was now adopting the role of chronicler for the school community, speaking in a generalized voice and offering everyone's news. "Millais received wire announcing arrival of baby brother."[72] Although he mentioned some personal likes and dislikes and a few private activities, he strived for detachment, listing names of boys and staff, reporting on their lives and achievements without much reference to his own opinion.

School staff knew about Christopher's diary and supported him in keeping it. When he fell and cut his hands during the morning race to the school gates, he dictated his entries to a teacher. He thus made the diary into an authorized collaboration, a semi-official school project. The double-self that was to be a hallmark of his fiction, Christopher as subject experiencing life and Christopher observing and reporting, was increasingly evident in the 1918 diary. This double-self was a natural development of the character, Christopher William, who had appeared as an infant in his mother's diaries and then collaborated with her from age five on autobiographical stories.

At Easter, he joined Kathleen and Emily in Wells, Somerset, and made a journal about the holiday, illustrated with postcards. Then he wrote a poem weighing the vagabond life against the uniqueness of his birthplace, which he knew Kathleen still idealized as the perfect home. Eight rhyming stanzas referenced nearly everywhere he had traveled so far—Cheddar, Wells, Surrey, Suffolk, Hampshire, Wales, Ireland, the Isle of Wight, Cheshire, the Peak District, London—and alluded to places he might still wander; he called the poem "Ode to Wyberslegh."

> But if I travel from Pole to Pole,
> From Greenland to Cape Horn,
> I shan't find a house like Wyberslegh Hall,
> The house where I was born.[73]

WHEN CHRISTOPHER ENTERED the Upper Fourth, the top form at St. Edmund's, in the summer of 1918, he and all concerned believed it was his last term at the school. The next step in his education was unclear and was to expose Kathleen's ignorance of the chauvinistic public-school world as well as her extraordinary tenacity. Despite Christopher's love of cadet corps, she evidently recognized like Frank that he was not cut out to be a soldier, so she ruled out Wellington and set her heart on Charterhouse, less than ten miles from St. Edmund's.

Christopher was to try for a scholarship. He made a colored sketch of the arms of Charterhouse and prepared with excitement for the eight exam papers. He was not told that the school was oversubscribed and would admit him only as a scholar. He did well enough for admission, but not for a scholarship, and was bewildered. Kathleen was so disappointed that she developed a crippling pain in her right arm which "felt as if no strength in it"[74] and puzzled her doctor. Like Christopher's acting leg, her body announced what she would not confide even to her diary, that as a woman without a husband, she was overwhelmed trying to find a way forward for her son.

She arranged for Christopher to remain at St. Edmund's for another term. "I am very glad, as I shall be sorry to leave," he wrote of the school he had once hated.[75] His diary reveals a new relish for breaking rules, defying staff, and lording it over exasperating younger boys. He was banned from swimming for his misdeanors, swam anyway, "& was luckily, not discovered!" One day, playing cricket, "I was comic umpire. Mr Bagnall evidently decided I was mad after the way I behaved." Showing off led to thoughtless cruelty toward younger boys in his charge. "Auden & I had some people to drill, we made them run races, & when Mr Bagnall found out, he was very cross."

Spectating at a first XI cricket match at the end of May, he and Auden demonstrated their signature relationship—playfully apart from the rest of their group: "I scored part of the time," Christopher wrote in his diary, "& sat up in a tree with Auden, till Mr Cyril came & ordered us down."[76] Already, Isherwood and Auden were a combustible combination.

In July 1918, watching cricket, Christopher began to collaborate with Harold Llewellyn Smith on a historical romance, "a story in the time of Henry VIII which is most complicated!!!!" That summer, he cycled to a reference library near Marple Hall, found quotations to use as "headlines for the chapters" and posted them to his collaborator.[77] Their models were Harrison Ainsworth and Walter Scott. Llewellyn Smith much later recalled that Auden had also been involved in planning the novel and that "its 'Gothic' scenario was shamelessly derived from Marple Hall, the ancestral seat of the Bradshaw-Isherwoods," but he was almost certainly crediting to Auden's mature genius and fame more than Auden contributed at the time.[78] Neither Christopher nor Kathleen in their contemporary diaries mentioned Auden being involved. Still, it is easy to picture Christopher talking—boasting—about Marple Hall to entertain and impress, and Auden joining in. The Bradshaw Isherwoods, Marple Hall, its village and community were to become a lasting source of raw material for them both.

Isherwood was a natural collaborator. Auden, by his own account, preferred to play alone. From ages six to thirteen he was absorbed by an imaginary limestone landscape filled with lead mines and based on the Pennine moors in northern England. Until he was twelve, Auden knew this landscape only from photographs and maps, and since he had never been there, he imagined his world as he wanted it to be. There were no lead miners in his imaginary landscape, just as there were no playmates in his game; he once told a lecture audience, "I was the only human inhabitant."[79] What a contrast to Isherwood, with his trips to countless destinations, methodical sightseeing, collections of real objects, and his impulses to record exact appearances and to share everything with a companion.

In middle age, Auden recalled that he had found the constant presence of other children hard to bear: "boarding school ... was a very intense group life in which it was very difficult to be alone." He took it for granted that others did not share his private obsessions: "I knew that the things of greatest interest to me were of no interest to people I met, whether grownups or contemporaries." He was never accepted into any group of age-mates the way Isherwood was. Auden later wrote of the introvert schoolboy: "he sees the extrovert successful, happy, and good and himself unpopular or neglected, and what is hardest to bear is not unpopularity, but the consciousness that it is deserved, that he is grubby and inferior and frightened and dull."[80]

Isherwood managed to break into Auden's solitude and to initiate the kind of shared play that was to fructify richly over the course of their creative lives. When he offered his family lore and other personal material, he did not seem to mind it being taken over and used in Auden's work. Between Isherwood and Auden, ideas and experiences ricocheted back and forth easily and continuously. One being a poet, the other a novelist perhaps made this easier. It was Auden who introduced Isherwood to the Icelandic sagas in the 1920s; Isherwood saw in them the boys from prep school, and they each created something completely different—a short story, "Gems of Belgian Architecture," and a verse play, Auden's *Paid on Both Sides*. Later, they took separate jobs when writing their plays, trusting in the other's ability. They wrestled over what they *believed*, not over what they *owned*. This was different from some of Isherwood's other friendships, notably with Stephen Spender, with whom he was to quarrel over who owned his experiences in Berlin while he was developing them into stories.

Already at St. Edmund's, the connection between Isherwood and Auden was little affected by events and opinions around them. At the end of summer term 1918, they were still talking avidly together, off to one side. "The Choir went up to the Golf-Links for tea, which was very nice indeed. I talked to Auden about the holidays, while the others played rounders," Christopher recorded. The next day, "Mr Cyril read out our marks in the Half-Term Exams. I passed with about 448 marks. In the Upper 4th Clarke, Fletcher i & Auden failed to pass." Wystan was much younger than his classmates and hardly expected to pass yet, but he must have felt dashed by the public announcement he had failed. Christopher's opinion of him seemed unchanged. On the final Sunday walk that summer, he noted, "I walked with Auden."[81]

MICKY SCOTT HAD left St. Edmund's the year before Christopher. He went to Repton, and he encouraged Christopher to join him there. Repton is about fifty-five miles from Marple, in the neighboring county, Derbyshire. It was Uncle Jack's school, which enhanced Christopher's chance of admission.

Repton was founded in the second half of the sixteenth century and greatly expanded in the second half of the nineteenth. It was built on the ruins of a twelfth-century Augustinian monastery destroyed during the Reformation. Kathleen and Christopher visited during the August holidays and saw the outsides of the boarding houses, in particular the Hall and the Old Priory, which form part of an ancient quadrangle with the wall of the village church. The church, "St. Wysten," as Christopher spelled it,[82] was named after the Hamlet-like heir to the Kingdom of Mercia who was murdered in A.D. 840 by a kinsman courting the widowed queen mother. St. Wystan's remains had once been buried in the eighth-century Saxon crypt which Christopher and Kathleen also explored. Wystan Auden's father had attended Repton, and he named his youngest son after the local saint.

Kathleen was not having Christopher turned down again. She took him in person to pin down the headmaster of Repton vacationing in the Peak District. They hiked more than seven miles from the train station at Hayfield through "beautiful wild scenery, the road steadily ascending to 1,700 ft to Edale Cross." On the way down into Edale, Christopher recorded, "The Grouse were as thick as sparrows." They bathed their feet in a stream, picnicked on sandwiches, and arrived by 2:30 at the Church Hotel, where, as if he were a cook, "Mummie interviewed Repton headmaster, Mr Fisher who said he had a vacancy."

Geoffrey Fisher was probably the youngest ever head of a major public school when he took over Repton at twenty-seven. "[H]e & his wife perfect children! but I presume he must be clever to have got such a post—" wrote Kathleen.[83] He was clever indeed, and he later became known for his political conservatism. He was an Anglican priest, common then among schoolmasters, went on to be Archbishop of Canterbury and performed the marriage and coronation of Queen Elizabeth II. Kathleen got what she wanted—a guaranteed place in Uncle Jack's old house, the Hall, where Fisher himself was housemaster.

But as with homes, so with schools: Kathleen could not easily settle. Discussion began afresh back at Marple Hall. Again, Kathleen consulted her male relatives. Christopher tried to defuse the tension with a funny poem, "Choosing a School." Then his legs began to perform: "the rheumatic pains in the calves of his leg returned into the left thigh & then changed over to the other leg." He couldn't get warm, even in winter underwear beside the fire. Kathleen went on fussing to her diary about Charterhouse until September 10, when she finally "posted the momentous letter to Repton,"[84] and Christopher's future was settled.

―――

HE HAD A new collection—crests. Crests are part of a coat of arms, originally mounted on the helmet and used only by those who had fought in tournaments or battles. By the early twentieth century, there were crests for families, clans, schools, colleges, professional groups; they could be cut from documents and from embossed stationery. The boys also copied them, painted or colored them, and circulated them. Christopher bought an album into which he pasted his collection, including "one of the Isherwood bookplates with the complete coat of arms on it" sent by Kathleen.[85]

His research for his historical novel overlapped with his research in heraldry. At Marple, he had been surrounded all his life by the language of heraldry. The entry hall—as shown in a 1902 photo—boasted the coat of arms in gilt above the fireplace, a second simpler coat of arms or perhaps a crest underneath the mantel, and four escutcheons (shields with heraldic markings) flanking above and below the mantel. In *Kathleen and Frank*, Isherwood recalled that in the library at Marple Hall, "The arms of the Bradshaws, the Isherwoods and all their kin by marriage had been painted on the oak-panelled walls and embroidered on the seats of the chairs." These extended from the reign of Henry VIII to the reign of George III. The arms were also carved on the coach house and stables at Marple Hall and on the family coach house next to the church, where the horses and brougham—with the arms painted on its door—waited while the family attended services. Inside the old All Saints church, the coats of arms were painted on the family's box pews. Kathleen had first taken Christopher to see these, along with the Bradshaw monuments there, when he was six, and she included examples of the two family coats of arms with technical descriptions in her "History of Marple and Wyberslegh Halls and the Bradshaw Isherwoods."[86]

Crests and coats of arms were badges rooted in history and reflecting long lineage. They linked Christopher personally to the age of chivalry depicted in Walter Scott and Harrison Ainsworth—an idealized world with codes for loving and fighting. They reached back past the obliterating death that had cut him off from his father, past the badge of his black crape armband, establishing Christopher's identity and position in another network, among earlier generations.

Just before Easter 1918, Frank's sword was finally returned after Kathleen threatened legal action against Frank's last soldier-servant, Private Cope, who professed to have lost it. "It has been hung up in the Hall," recorded Christopher. Thus, nearly three years after his death, Frank joined the generations of military ancestors represented by the weaponry displayed at Marple. Christopher was so pleased that he wrote a personal thank you to the officer in Frank's regiment who helped recover the sword. This was the very sword later recalled as "quite useless for any purpose except for toasting bread."[87] In the end, the sword symbolized outmoded forms of combat, on foot or on horseback, man to man, futile against German gas and artillery.

While Christopher dawdled over his crests and his coats of arms, real historical links were being severed. The Bradshaw Isherwoods decided to sell land to raise cash, and that August Kathleen accompanied her father-in-law to the lawyer's office in Stockport to decide which farms would go. According to a list in her "History of Marple and Wyberslegh Halls and the Bradshaw Isherwoods," in 1831 Christopher's great-great-grandfather, John Bradshaw, owned twenty-five farms and small properties totaling 820 acres; John Bradshaw's elder brother had owned more than twice as much, and had sold 1,000 acres. The nearest factory to Marple was built on the 1,000 acres and could be seen—to the family's distaste—from the drawing-room window. Christopher's grandfather appears to have inherited the remaining 820 acres intact.

Jack Isherwood worked on the details for the sale of five farms, advertised for October 11. The implications were not merely financial. John Isherwood was landlord not only to farmers but also to a publican, a miller, and the Peak Forest Canal Company, which had a major flight of locks at Marple and, just north of there, a ninety-seven-foot aqueduct across the River Goyt. Lime was transported from quarries in the Peak District to lime kilns near the top of the locks; coal, cotton, grain, and manufactured goods also traveled along the canal. Tenants must get along with a landlord, who can, theoretically, throw them out. Selling land diminished the family stature.

Growing hardship was already producing local conflict. One afternoon, Christopher and Alan Coyne came upon "ten Labour Farm boys who were stealing wood." Three hundred trees had been felled for cash urgently needed at Marple. Christopher and Alan told the boys "to clear out," as Christopher recorded with excitement. "Allan pointed his gun at one of them & there was a fight!! Coyne came down & there was a row! Uncle Jack came."[88] The following summer, boys were found stealing apples from the kitchen garden, and Christopher helped Dobson, Coyne, and Alan to catch them. The apple thieves had come from relatively far off, armed with large bags, and after a second episode, the police pressured John Isherwood to prosecute them.

Christopher at thirteen possessed a strong sense of property rights and class privilege, and he supported the empire and the war unquestioningly. He was intrigued by his grandfather's local influence, for instance in the mysterious process of choosing a new vicar for All Saints: "Canon Symonds came over in a cab to discuss about who he should give the living of Marple to. He & Grandad & the two church-wardens had a sort of 'Secret Session' in the Library."[89]

ON THE DAY the war ended, November 11, 1918, Christopher was again on an invalid regime at St. Edmund's, recovering from, probably, Spanish flu. Kathleen was visiting Repton to find out about required clothes and bed-linen. She had arrived all alone in the middle of the Armistice celebrations:

"the JOY Bells were ringing—" she wrote in her diary. "Mr Fisher out, at the Thanksgiving Service, at which I could hear them singing loudly Oh God our help in ages past . . . It is good the fighting is over . . . & it will be a happy day for those whose men will now be coming home . . ."

By the time she returned to London, Kathleen was tired of pealing bells: "the sorrow has been so overwhelming & the joy bells give one a lonely . . . out of it all feeling . . ."[90] Toward the end of November, she was distressed by reports of returning prisoners of war released by the Germans in rags, ill, and starving. Yet she hoped Frank might be among them.

Christopher, by contrast, bounced back quickly from his flu and had triumphed in his Repton entrance exams, coming third out of eighteen. Rosa reported him "looking very rosy & growing enormously." During his last term at St. Edmund's, with the end of the war in sight, he stopped keeping a diary. He was to do the same thing at the end of World War II. Excitement buoyed him, and there was no further need to mark time.

Five and a half weeks after the Armistice, Christopher left St. Edmund's for the last time, on December 19, 1918. In London, he and Kathleen went to see the victorious generals returning home. Christopher's train from school arrived at Waterloo; the generals' train from France arrived at Charing Cross. The generals were cheered by crowds as they traveled in horse-drawn carriages from Trafalgar Square to Buckingham Palace: "immense enthusiasm along the route—we got inside the rails round the portico of S. Martin's Church—" wrote Kathleen about watching the procession.[91]

It had all ended at once, prep school and the war; Christopher had every reason to feel at one with the celebrations. For him, but not for his mother, the end of the war was the beginning, at last, of a new life.

PUBLIC SCHOOL, REPTON, 1919

By comparison to St. Edmund's, Repton was immediately a success. Christopher was put in the top form of the lower school, "to his great satisfaction," as he wrote to Kathleen, and he was "considered to have a good enough voice to be in the Musical class a huge singing society" after never making it out of the second choir at St. Edmund's. In his house, the Hall, he was put in a study with four other boys.[92]

Daytime studies were generally for four boys—a study holder, his "second," and two junior boys, called fags, who had to wait on the study holder. The "second" had no fagging to do but was not allowed to have a fag, as Christopher was to explain in one of the narratives about a fictional public school, "Rugtonstead," that he started writing in 1922 and never published.

At night, the boys slept in dorms of seven or eight: "The beds were reminiscent of a hospital ward—uniform in length—[...] and all covered with the same brown blankets. Big windows, difficult to shut, suggested hygiene and discomfort."[93]

He wrote to Kathleen that the schoolwork seemed "fairly easy," but school life was more mysterious, with "many unwritten laws." He was told off for talking to Micky Scott, who was senior to him at the school: "it appears this is bad form!!" Richard Isherwood later recalled "Micky's vivid charm" and admitted to an intense boyhood crush on him; it seems likely that Christopher also had a crush.[94] At Repton, friendships between older and younger boys implied a sexual or at least a romantic motive and could lead to expulsion.

Rigid hierarchy lies at the heart of Christopher's school narratives. New boys were not spoken to by boys already at the school; fags were not spoken to by older boys except when giving orders; boys from other houses were off limits in the younger forms; boys from the city looked down on boys from the country; banter, never without an edge, aimed at taking a boy down in front of peers. Systematic, almost feudal gradation was reflected in the large, bare dining hall at "Rugtonstead": four tables, two for fags, one for younger study holders and their "seconds," and one on a raised dais for the housemaster, prefects, and senior study holders. All this created intense feelings of loneliness.

The impulse to communicate struggles in the narratives with the need to conform to the hierarchy. Christopher's schoolboy characters are constantly biting their tongues: "It was bad policy to encourage new men—any fags, in fact."[95] In one scene, a study holder and his new-boy fag sit alone together in their study in mounting and comical discomfort as they suppress an almost overwhelming inclination to begin a conversation. For an enthusiastic and nonstop talker like Christopher, such restraint was excruciating.

The only approved way of moving up through the hierarchy was being good at games, the widely accepted path to popularity. It was not necessarily a path to friendship, as some characters observe in Christopher's narratives; anyway, it was not a path open to Christopher.

Naturally, he disliked being at the bottom of the heap, in particular, the humiliation of being a fag. During their first two years, fags had to unpack their seniors' things, decorate the study according to the study holder's requirements, drag their seniors from bed in the cold mornings, fetch water for their baths, run errands. Fags could be cruelly exploited, physically and emotionally. To one friend, Christopher called the fagging system the "white slave traffic."[96]

Fags were not allowed to travel back and forth to school in their own clothes; they had to wear school uniform—an Eton suit for juniors. Christopher despised this extra-muros display of his servitude. He bought a trench coat at a London department store at the end of April 1920 just before returning for his fifth term at Repton; Kathleen thought it "hideous" and presumably associated it with the war that had made it ubiquitous, but she had no idea what he was trying to conceal. In what he later called "Almost the first attempt at fiction I ever made," Isherwood described how, on a train platform crowded with boys returning from the holidays, fags could be seen "hiding away their etons, the hall-mark of a fag, according to tradition, under trench-coats."[97] This was a weird foreshadowing of the far more dangerous degradation of pink triangles and yellow stars under the Nazis.

A further sign of defiance was smoking. During the train journey, safe in a carriage commandeered by posting a "Reserved" notice stolen from the prefects' carriage, Isherwood's fictional fags get out their food, newspapers, and cigarettes, and even the newest boy "'lit up' boldly."[98] Christopher himself started smoking by the time he was in the sixth form. This act of defiance became a habit he struggled till middle age to break. The habit of hierarchical thinking was harder to break, so indoctrinated was he both at school and in his wider, class-ridden world. In Berlin, Isherwood was to reenact the fagging bond with some of his young German boyfriends, and it was to haunt later relationships until he scoured it out with self-scrutiny and self-improvement.

During his first week at Repton, Christopher was reading Edgar Allan Poe, *Tales of Mystery*, for entertainment, just the sort of book he liked to scare himself with; by contrast, he bought himself "a little Anthology of the Hundred best prose writers," probably Adam Gowan's *Characteristic Passages from the Hundred Best English Prose Writers* (1905)—a book for study. Already his ambition eyed the crown Gore Vidal was to settle on his brow sixty years later, when Vidal called Isherwood "the best prose writer in English."[99] Other new projects included an author's calendar (probably the perpetual calendar to which Isherwood added all his life the birth and death dates of favorite authors), and a commonplace book, the first of at least two. In this first, he copied mostly poetry; in his later commonplace book, he copied mostly prose. Like his mother, he also kept a newspaper book, for pasting in cuttings. These literary and journalistic archives replaced his collections of cigarette cards and crests.

By the end of February 1919, Fisher reported to Kathleen the opinion of Christopher's form master, "Writes very good essays," and at Easter, Christopher returned to Marple Hall with "a distinction card for English, which means he is top of his form for Divinity, Essays & literature—"[100] As always, the triumph cost him—the effort to adjust, to make the right impression, to compete with his classmates. He fell ill as soon as the holidays started—a cold, swollen glands, a backache which called for rubbing with liniments and wrapping in flannel.

CHRISTOPHER WAS NOT the only one in the family beginning a new life. Uncle Jack married a rector's daughter, Frida Hill, nineteen years younger than he. He asked for Christopher "to attend him during his last moments of 'spinsterhood,'"[101] but on the wedding day in September, Christopher, Kathleen, and Richard, in a now familiar posture toward family and public events, stayed away on holiday at Penmaenmawr and sent a telegram. Nevertheless, in his adult life, Christopher was to emulate the avuncular pattern of a December–May partnership.

Kathleen had a chance for love in January 1919, but she rejected it. Micky Scott's father renewed his suit, fulfilling Kathleen's worst fears about their sons mixing at school. Kathleen was spending an afternoon with Emily in Buckingham Street when "to our astonishment, in walked Mr Scott! . . . he had got my address from Micky through Christopher at Repton . . . he stayed for tea & had a long talk about the boys & different items of Stockport news, but had come chiefly to say would I come & dine with him at the Carlton! he might as well have asked me to go to the moon!"

Mr. Scott was powerfully attracted. He returned the next day, "wanting me to help him choose a carpet at Hampden's & lunch with him after—" Kathleen helped with the carpet but refused the lunch. Richard recalled years later that she restrained herself because Emily was repelled by Mr. Scott.[102]

Christopher's friendship with Micky Scott opened a crack between mother and son that was soon to widen. Christopher loved entertainment, drama, boys, and nights out. He was eager—desperate—to have fun. In *The Memorial*, Isherwood was to transform the Scott family into the Ramsbothams—Tommy, Gerald, a sister, and their father, known as "our Ram" and "Ram's B."[103]—to hilarious effect. Lily Vernon grudgingly allows Mr. Ramsbotham to carry her dead husband's wreath on the day the village war memorial is dedicated, but she prefers the watery companionship of Ronald Charlesworth. Nevertheless, the brash, effective, unacceptable Ramsbothams, including an ambitious second wife the reader never meets, take possession of the ancestral home, the Hall, and marry into the Vernon family through a cousin of lesser pedigree, Anne Scriven. Thus, Isherwood fictionally fulfilled one of Kathleen's greatest fears, that others might take precedence over Christopher and usurp his inheritance—the Roman Catholic offspring of Henry and Muriel that never arrived, or, worse, the socially unacceptable Toogood children. This was a comic masterstroke and another, crueller rebuke to Kathleen which Isherwood carefully disguised by drawing for Anne Scriven's fictional family on at least three different real-life families, the Toogoods, the Monkhouses, and the Mangeots, whom he befriended in London in the 1920s. His portrait cannot be easily decoded.

He was inspired by the work of E.M. Forster, discovered in the mid-1920s. Isherwood was later to form a close friendship with and to identify Forster as "his master," explaining that "In Forster, he found a key to the whole art of writing. [...] the mental attitude with which he must pick up his pen."[104] Forster's *Howards End* is a spiritual ur-text for *The Memorial*. In it, the postwar generation marry across the divide between culture and industry and settle into the inheritance—a house and the nation it symbolizes—which they must find a way to share. Forster named his cultured characters Schlegel and his brash industrialists Wilcox. Isherwood named them Scriven and Ramsbotham, and he has Anne Scriven, daughter of bohemia, marry Tommy Ramsbotham, son of a manufacturer and sole heir to both his father's houses after his brother dies in a car crash.[105]

Lily Vernon's only reward is the war memorial. There is a real monument to the war dead outside All Saints in Marple, and it bears Frank Bradshaw Isherwood's name, but there is no evidence that Kathleen attended a dedication ceremony like the one portrayed in the novel; it would have been unlike Kathleen to expose herself publicly in this way.[106] Isherwood knew that the memorial Kathleen cared about was the official one, the Menin Gate at Ypres, unveiled in July 1927 by Field Marshal Lord Plumer with a speech by King Albert of Belgium. She listened to the ceremony on a friend's wireless, then read over Frank's letters from the Front and began making a scrapbook about the Menin Gate (the newspapers were full of it).

A year after the unveiling, Kathleen discovered that Frank's name was not on the Menin Gate, "a great piece of carelessness on someone's part," she wrote indignantly in her diary.[107] She contacted the War Graves Commission and learned that because Frank had taken command of the 1st Battalion only a week before he died, his name was included with the 2nd Battalion for the Ploegsteert Memorial, to be unveiled in 1931. She secured an official promise that the mistake would be corrected, but she had to wait several years.

Isherwood intended his heavily satirical family portrait in *The Memorial* to serve as a more meaningful commemoration of Frank than a name inscribed on a piece of stone.

ALL THAT WAS yet to come. As a fourteen-year-old Repton boy, Christopher did exactly what was expected of him. He came top of the Upper Fourth, earned distinctions in English and languages, and won a glowing report from Uncle Henry following a lunch at Marple Hall—"he is a charming boy with perfect manners."[108] He topped his efforts to please by agreeing to be circumcised for the Officers' Training Corps (OTC), which he joined when he matriculated at Repton. At the OTC medical inspection, circumcision was advised because it was thought to reduce the chances of venereal disease, and the Marple doctor, Dr. Burton, concurred.[109]

The matron at Brabyns Hall war hospital, Miss Nettie May Purdie, no longer had wounded soldiers to care for, so she oversaw the circumcision, performed by Dr. Burton with an assistant in Richard and Nanny's bedroom at Marple Hall on a rainy Saturday in August. It proved, in one sense, to be a painful rededication to the culture of war for which Christopher's father had died. On the other hand, Kathleen's diary account, with its anxious euphemisms about "the Event," weirdly recalled her own lying in for Christopher's birth at Wyberslegh in August 1904. She sat with Christopher till he came around, whereupon he threw up. He threw up again when the dressing was changed a few hours later, "a very painful business indeed."[110]

The incision had been stitched, and the dressings were changed constantly, which was excruciating. Nowadays, following adult or adolescent circumcision—which leaves the whole penis bruised and swollen—the bandage would be bound tightly around the wound to control the bleeding, and it would typically remain untouched for four to five days then soaked off in warm water.

Everyone got involved in Christopher's convalescence. Fanny Hudson sent a table to use in bed and came to tea. Kathleen read *Martin Chuzzlewit* aloud, and they played poker patience. Christopher "began a catalogue of his books," another collection that he could arrange, list, annotate—occupying his thoughts and making himself master of something he valued while others had mastery of his physical self. This could not disguise his infantilized state. He was allowed out of bed only with assistance and "had his playbox in." Kathleen evoked an atmosphere of nursery treats to mask the sleepless nights and constant, invasive attention to his private parts: "We had a tea party between 4 & 5 a.m. as C. was uncomfortable & required re-dressing, after that we both slept till 8."[111]

Six days after the operation, Christopher was "partially dressed" by Miss Purdie and "armed" downstairs to the garden, as Kathleen wrote, "where he lay on my long chair outside the Library window" and had his lunch and tea. He spent the next four long summer days horizontal on his mother's garden chair, intimately tended by Miss Purdie. Alan Coyne paid court on August 10. On August 11, "Dr Burton came, & said the stitches could come out when Matron thought best."[112] Even Emily managed to participate, sending calendula ointment which was applied to the wound.

It was Christopher's own doing, joining the OTC, accepting the advice of the Repton school doctor, placing his adolescent penis in the care of Dr. Burton, not to speak of the team of nursing women in his little brother's nursery. It was as near as he could get to being a wounded soldier, and it was, in a sense, a rite visited on himself to assuage his unconscious guilt over the fact that his father had died a hero and that he himself was still alive.

He adored Miss Purdie. A photo in his first album shows a very pretty young woman in a crisp nurse's uniform including a white apron reaching her ankles and a starched white cap crowning her neatly put-up brown hair. So competent was her nursing that she helped care for King George V when he had surgery for lung disease a decade later. For this she was awarded an MBE; she also received the Royal Red Cross for her services as a military nurse. She embodied the ministering feminine presence that Isherwood was to fictionalize again and again—Joan Lindsay looking after her invalid brother Philip in *All the Conspirators*, Margaret Lanwin looking after the troubled veteran Edward Blake in *The Memorial*, Gerda Mannheim looking after the injured Stephen Monk in *The World in the Evening*, Nanny remembered by lonesome George in *A Single Man*. All these women characters combined aspects of Miss Purdie with aspects of Kathleen and Nanny.

As soon as Christopher recovered, he took up tennis. Frank had played. He also went about his grandfather's business maintaining the estate. The solicitor, Charles Symonds, came "to look around, & see how the workpeople were getting on," and Christopher accompanied him, riding "in his new Motor bike sidecar."[113] Christopher was walking further and further into the trap that life had sprung on his father, self-abnegating service to family, tradition, community, and empire. He was determined to charm and to cheer up the woman his father had loved and left to his charge.

Kathleen now suddenly decided that he should become a librarian. She was inspired partly by Christopher's catalogue of books and another hunt he made through the bookshops of London, this time for an edition of Tennyson's *Idylls of the King* illustrated by Eleanor Fortescue-Brickdale with sumptuous watercolors. He went to six different bookshops to find an unblemished copy. Then, at tea with Madgie Reid and her son Jack, who had just passed the Civil Service exam, Christopher's future was discussed, evidently in his presence and perhaps with his participation, and afterwards Kathleen wrote to the Civil Service Commission about posts for librarians. She was advised "to get a nomination as assistant at the British Museum—" Off she went to the British Museum to see the Director and Principal Librarian. She listed requirements for the post in her diary: public school, honors at university, French, German, a competitive exam. She also wrote out the salary, bonuses, and pay increases to retirement. This narrow, quantifiable path might see Christopher through his youth and manhood to a pension "at 65 of half salary per year"—and then the grave.[114]

CHRISTOPHER PREPARED TO be confirmed in the Anglican Church with the same innocent dedication that had led to his circumcision. Years later, describing his conversion to Vedanta in his wartime diary, he wrote: "I can't remember any time in my life when I seriously believed in God. At Repton, when I got confirmed—before I met Edward [Upward]—I was a cautious, diplomatic hypocrite."[115]

Reverend Fisher himself taught the boys what it meant to be a Christian. It was already familiar to Christopher, yet he wrote copious notes in Fisher's lessons. The notes reveal no critical thinking. He shared them with Kathleen when she attended the ceremony, underlining that his confirmation was at least as much for her benefit as his. He took equally thorough notes when he began to study Vedanta with Swami Prabhavananda many years later, but by then his critical faculties were wide awake, and his intention was to spring himself from a trap rather than to lock himself in.

Nowhere in his teenage notes did the newly circumcised Christopher mention sexuality or sexual behavior. He did not yet realize that he needed a religion which would accept him as a homosexual, but he was soon to learn that he didn't need a religion which would not do so.

His school notes reflect the same painstaking application—to Shakespeare, the sonnet, Browning, Milton, English history, modern history, the Holy Roman Empire, chemistry, botany, physics, zoology. He absorbed it all without question, stocking his mind with vast resources of factual information recorded with extraordinary clarity. His program also included Latin, Greek, French, and mathematics. There is not much evidence that he enjoyed it. The schoolboy character Dick Tresham in Christopher's first Rugtonstead novel feels "depressed" as he prepares to return to school after a holiday: "there it was, waiting for him, next day, as if in ambush."[116]

CHRISTOPHER WAS SIXTEEN when he passed his general education certificate exams toward the end of 1920. He then entered the Lower Sixth and was allowed to focus on history, as he told Kathleen in an excited letter at the beginning of 1921: "the cream of my half-week's news. [. . .] I start work as a History Specialist tomorrow!"[117] His history teacher was to change Christopher's style of thought forever, freeing him from plodding literal-mindedness, pushing him to think analytically and synthetically.

Geoffrey Burrell Smith was forty-one when he began teaching Christopher, and he was a relative newcomer to Repton. He had a bristling intellect and a sense of humor both playful and poised. He had studied history and theology at King's College, Cambridge. He married in 1906, but his wife died just three years later. He had worked in intelligence during the war and had already published several of his ten or so books about British and European history. These books show him to have been an astute psychologist, an orderly thinker, a crystalline stylist.

Smith's best-known books were for schools, and he prided himself on making them entertaining. He played constantly with the metaphor of history as theater. His slim and stylish *Scenes from European History*, first published in 1911 and repeatedly reissued, is constructed as a sequence of dramatic episodes shaped by star historical personalities. His announced purpose was "lending a greater reality to some of the more important actors on the stage of Europe."[118] Smith's scenic method had an immeasurable influence on Isherwood, who was to write his own kind of history the same way in book after book. When Isherwood began his 1938 memoir *Lions and Shadows*, he gave it a preliminary working title that alluded to Smith, *Scenes from an Education*. In 1983, starting his final memoir, never completed, about his move to California, Isherwood called it *Scenes from an Emigration*, again paying homage to Smith.

As a historian of the self, Isherwood brought onto his stage the star personalities who had most influenced him. In place of Smith's actors from European history—sainted monks, prophets, emperors, princes—*Lions and Shadows* introduced disguised versions of Upward, Auden, Spender, the princes of his literary world. Smith's influence is also perceptible in Isherwood's interweaving of individual personalities with historical period in the Berlin of the 1930s. In his portrayals of Arthur Norris, Baron von Pregnitz, Ludwig Bayer, Fräulein Schroeder, Sally Bowles, Bernhard Landauer, Otto Nowak, and others, he reveals psychological forces at play below the surface of events. The scenic method is at work again in *Prater Violet*, where Isherwood describes Friedrich Bergmann's face as "the face of a political situation, an epoch. The face of Central Europe,"[119] and again in *Down There on a Visit*. Smith taught Isherwood to use his narrative skills to transform documented facts and gave him permission to put a unique subjective mark on his material.

In *Lions and Shadows*, the first character introduced, the presiding genius of the hero's education, is "a short, stout, middle-aged man with reddish hair [...] His glance was cold, friendly, and shrewd." Isherwood disguised this schoolmaster character with the name "Mr. Holmes," after his favorite brainy detective, Sherlock Holmes.

"'Who was Sherlock Holmes, Daddy?' 'Sherlock Holmes was a detective.' 'What's a detective, Daddy?' 'If you'll listen, you'll hear.'" This simple, repetitive question-and-answer is the last conversation between Eric Vernon and his father Richard in *The Memorial*. The words suddenly stop, and the reader, like Eric, is left waiting and listening for an explanation that never comes: "Eric could remember just how the weather vane on the church tower above the trees had looked as Richard had begun to tell him about Sherlock Holmes." The next paragraph begins: "Eric was very, very sorry to hear that his father had been killed."[120]

In a 1957 essay, Isherwood recalled that the adventures of Sherlock Holmes had been "my favorite escape-reading" since age ten, the age at which he lost his father: "again and again I have turned to them in times of sadness, boredom and ill-health, and never found myself disappointed."[121] In *Lions and Shadows*, Mr. Holmes is the father figure, the mentor, the teacher, who can help Isherwood's generation solve the baffling crime of the war. History holds the clues to their predicament. They must study history together. Solving the puzzle is their only possible consolation.

Isherwood portrayed Mr. Holmes as a showman: "Almost everything Mr. Holmes did or said contributed to a deliberate effect: he had the technique of a first-class clergyman or actor." Holmes took the boys into his confidence and told them what was really going on in their education. His object was "to startle, shock, flatter, lure or scare us for a few moments out of our schoolboy conservatism and prejudice." Like Christopher's favorite magicians Maskelyne and Devant, Holmes "would explain to us gleefully just how this particular trap, bait, or bomb had been prepared."

Forty years later, Isherwood commemorated G.B. Smith again in the theatrical and deliberately disconcerting teaching style of the magicianlike George in *A Single Man*. George is modeled partly on Isherwood, and inside the mature Isherwood was his old teacher, G.B. Smith, fully assimilated. Smith himself thought their bond sprang from a kind of mutual recognition. In a teasing letter sent after Christopher had left Repton, Smith told his former pupil: "Yes you are rather like me and that's a fact and if I could think of anything ruder I would say it."[122]

It was in Mr. Smith's History Sixth that Christopher got to know Edward Upward, from Romford, Essex, the son of a doctor educated at Cambridge with Auden's father. Christopher and Edward only jostled against one another at first, before being thrown together repeatedly. In *Lions and Shadows*, Isherwood called Upward "Chalmers" (a name borrowed from a younger Repton friend).[123] Chalmers was "a pale, small, silent boy, a year older than myself, strikingly handsome, with dark hair and dark blue eyes." He was painfully self-conscious: "On the rare occasions when he got excited and began to talk, his face became flushed; he spoke so quickly and indistinctly, with nervous fumblings of his fingers against his lips, that it was very difficult to understand what he was saying."

As with Holmes, so with Chalmers, Isherwood heightened aspects of the fictionalized character to conform with certain literary themes. "Never in my life have I been so strongly and immediately attracted to any personality, before or since. Everything about him appealed to me. He was a natural anarchist, a born romantic revolutionary," he wrote in *Lions and Shadows*. "Above all things, Chalmers loathed the school to which he invariably referred as 'Hell.' His natural hatred of all established authority impressed me greatly." Isherwood was gesturing to the schoolboy hero in Alec Waugh's 1917 novel *The Loom of Youth*, modeled on Byron, the role in which he cast Upward. Upward won the school verse prize in 1921, and Christopher described him romantically to Kathleen as "the School Poet." *The Loom of Youth* had caused a sensation during the war for attacking the public-school ethos that was producing England's junior officers and for openly referring to boys trysting in their studies. Christopher dismissed it in a letter to Kathleen as "most awful trash."[124] He intended to write a better school novel himself, and he methodically read every book he could lay hands on about schools, boys, and teachers.

The Repton school photo for June 1921 shows hundreds of boys in identical gray suits, white shirts, dark ties, neatly washed and combed, attentive and alert in orderly rows. Because of his short height, Christopher is partly obscured by another boy in front, and is visible only because the other boy is tilting his head. In contrast to his schoolmates, Christopher has filthy, matted hair splayed over his forehead, a shapeless, dirty collar, a dark scowl. His jacket is worn and baggy. His look is homeless, angry, famished, even ghostly, and strikingly different from the scrubbed, polite vanity in so many other photos of him. In this crowd of nearly five hundred boys, he was barely holding his place. Evidently, he didn't groom himself at school, perhaps a sign of defiance, or possibly of depression. In Christopher's first Rugtonstead novel, his character Dick Tresham is teased, "As for you, Tresham—you look as if you'd slept in your clothes for the last week."[125]

In a house photo from around the same time, Upward's posture is even more startling. He sits turned away from the camera, arms and legs crossed, with one trouser leg rucked up around his calf and a piece of paper clutched in his right hand. His hair is greasy and unwashed, and he scowls morosely and determinedly. Upward's rebelliousness was rooted partly in his defiance of his socially ambitious mother. She wished him to rise; therefore, he determined to descend. At Repton, Upward refused to be confirmed; his grandfather had been a Congregationalist with radical Calvinist sympathies, and his father was an atheist. There was suffering in his family of which little is known. One of his three brothers was schizophrenic and lived permanently in an institution; another died in infancy. A cousin, the writer and nonconformist leftist politician Allen Upward, with whom Upward evidently identified, was to commit suicide. In Upward's fictionalized autobiography *The Spiral Ascent*, the protagonist Alan Sebrill is the last boy in his year to be released from fagging, later refuses to use his own fags, and calls for the abolition of the fagging system. In *Lions and Shadows*, Isherwood wrote that Chalmers's refusal to conform was precisely what Mr. Holmes wished to nurture: "nobody could better appreciate than he the market value of the Odd."[126]

Mr. Smith piled on the reading, and Isherwood did it all. He was incredibly diligent, endlessly listing and once reading aloud to Kathleen specialist books on English and European history. He also read for himself, both highbrow literature and books of more pedestrian allure, expressing in his letters confident and acute opinions about Austen, the Brontës, Drinkwater, Goldsmith, Meredith, Borrow, Hardy, Conrad, Wells, Shaw, Ibsen, Hugo, Dumas, Anatole France, Twain, and many others. His timetable now included "library"—free periods up to three hours long "devoted to special reading or to preparing a fortnightly essay."[127]

In *Lions and Shadows*, Isherwood exuberantly portrayed "library" as a privilege the boys abused by writing their own stories, taking naps, or ragging. But in a serious sense, this room of their own, filled with books and comfortable armchairs, was the hub and the fount of their personal intellectual lives, allowing them to discover and pursue their own interests. Hector Wintle, who was specializing in modern languages, managed to write a substantial portion of a public-school novel. Isherwood called him "Philip Linsley" in *Lions and Shadows*: "Plump, smiling, always affable, never in the least upset by criticism however adverse, Linsley was at all times perfectly willing to answer any questions, show us the manuscript and outline the forthcoming phases of the plot."[128] Isherwood made comedy of the boys critiquing Linsley's novel, pouncing on the embarrassing influence of E.F. Benson's idealistic schoolboy romance *David Blaize*. In real life, Isherwood was impressed by Wintle's work ethic and self-confidence; Wintle was already behaving like a professional writer.

In addition to changing his style of thought, G.B. Smith began dragging Christopher politically to the left and turning him against war and the state. Two of Smith's predecessors at Repton had been too open politically and had been sacked. During the war, they had begun a current affairs class, civics, in order that boys could understand the conflict in which they might be asked to die. In June 1917, when Christopher was still at St. Edmund's, the Repton civics class had begun publishing its anti-Establishment views in a magazine, *A Public School Looks at the World*. Incensed conservative masters had responded with angry letters to the existing school magazine, *The Reptonian*, and arguments had raged in the debating society. Reverend Fisher had addressed the school, calling a halt to divisive discussion.

The next issue of *A Public School Looks at the World*, March 1918, had been put on sale at a radical London bookshop, attracting the attention of the War Office, which wrote threateningly to Fisher. Fisher fired the lead master, the second resigned, and a student left the school. The lead master was Victor Gollancz, who had joined Repton as a commissioned officer both to teach and to help with the OTC; Gollancz subsequently pursued his educational mission by publishing pacifist and socialist books under his own imprint and founding the Left Book Club.[129]

Civics survived, inherited by Smith, who walked softly, perhaps because of the scandal and perhaps because it was his nature. Christopher joined civics at the beginning of his third year at Repton, and he attended school debates. In February 1921, the boys argued the extreme leftist motion "that 'the abolition of private property is the only solution of the present Labour troubles.'" In March, members of the Derby Branch of the Workers' Educational Association joined Reptonians to debate the motion that "Environment & not Human Character has been the prime factor in determining the rate & direction of human progress." The teams mixed workmen with schoolboys. Christopher, still an arch-conservative, was taken aback: "The workmen spoke with a frantic accent, but were fearfully well-informed—" he told Kathleen. He made his maiden speech for a politically backward motion "*this house deplores the advent of women in public offices*" and told his mother—who agreed—he voted in favour of the motion "of course."[130]

Christopher also attended a debate on the subject that had banished Gollancz, "the necessity of war," and it was in his attitude to war that he first began to evolve politically. During Christopher's final term, Mr. Smith gave a series of talks, "The Causes of the Great War." In *Lions and Shadows*, Isherwood recalled that "Mr. Holmes [...] had considerably startled most of us by pointing out that the Central Powers were not the only ones to blame." The school also debated the motion that "Patriotism is an obstacle to Civilization," and Christopher opened the debate "by attacking the spirit of revenge and war produced by Patriotism, which fosters ill-feeling between nations and prevents helpful co-operation between them." He was supported by Upward's younger brother, Mervyn, who argued that patriotism always leads to war, and by Mr. Smith, who spoke last. In a speech "which carried the House," Smith argued that "patriotism always leads to the most irrational prejudices, such as prevent intellectual intercourse between nations and so bar progress. Competition has done its work. Now is the time for co-operation." It was Smith's strategy of "agreeing with both sides" before leading the House "gently round" that Isherwood recalled in *Lions and Shadows*,[131] and which he was to adopt for his own literary purposes in the longer run.

He hated war, but patriotism still aroused in him a vague but intense emotion associated with duty, with self-sacrifice, and with his father—"a hard life, an unknown grave," as he copied out for Kathleen from the epilogue to John Masefield's *Sea Life in Nelson's Time*.[132] It was to be many years before he consciously understood the hold such emotion had over him and was able to turn to pacifism.

KATHLEEN AND REVEREND Fisher intended Christopher to go to Oxford, tackling entrance exams at the end of 1922. Mr. Smith initiated a different, accelerated plan. In September 1921, he made the flattering suggestion that Christopher should try to get into Cambridge that very term; so, in just ten gruelling months, Christopher prepared to take the scholarship exams at Cambridge with a cohort of Repton history specialists. The papers went on for a week during early December 1921: general history, Latin and French translation, English history, modern history, medieval history, general questions on art and politics, an English essay. In *Lions and Shadows*, Isherwood recalled Mr. Holmes's advice that it was more a matter of style than content: "Historical knowledge was absolutely unnecessary: all you had to do was to sparkle and startle."

In a break during the exams, Nanny's brother-in-law, Mr. Shaw, took Christopher into Emmanuel College to see the picture of John Bradshaw that Kathleen had seen on Christopher's tenth birthday at the beginning of the war, when she decided he should be a don. The failure of Charterhouse was not to be repeated. "It seems to me that I knew we should succeed," Isherwood was to write in *Lions and Shadows*. "This was Mr Holmes' doing."

On December 15, back at Repton, Christopher received a wire awarding him an exhibition, "a small scholarship ... worth £40 a year." Edward Upward, who had sat the exams with him, also received an award and accepted it for October 1922. Christopher, though, was too young to leave school, and Mr. Smith had already arranged for him to sit the exams all over again in December 1922 "and try and increase my scholarship to £60 or £80, with the CERTAINTY of getting AT LEAST the original £40 a year, HOWEVER BADLY I do," as Christopher told Kathleen.[133] His fate was sealed. He had surpassed himself in pleasing his teacher and his mother.

CHRISTOPHER'S LETTERS TO Kathleen at this time were gallant, intimate, gossipy, and sometimes loverlike. He narrated the ups and downs of his friendships to intrigue and to entertain her, as when they had collaborated on *The History of My Friends*. One boy in his house, George Clifford Hardwick, lived in a semi-detached brick villa in Heaton Norris, a suburb of Stockport, and visited Marple Hall. He was a year younger than Christopher, who pursued him despite the school convention against friendship between older and younger boys. "I am getting rather tired of convention; & people soon give up talking!" Christopher told Kathleen. He tried to get Hardwick all to himself by proposing a cycle tour during the Easter holidays 1921, but Hardwick let him down at the last minute, and Christopher made the tour alone, staying overnight with various cousins en route.

Kathleen turned against Hardwick, and Christopher began to feel he had confided—and complained—too much. He assured Kathleen that he had not given Hardwick a photograph of himself, a customary token of friendship among the boys. Christopher had studio portraits taken—first in Manchester, which he disliked, then again in London—and he was overwhelmed by his popularity, requesting that Kathleen "send half a dozen more, as they seem somewhat in demand?"[134]

He wrote Kathleen almost nothing about his more significant friendship with Ronald (Ronny) Kelsall, another boy a year younger in his house. Years later, in his diary for 1937, Isherwood was to recall being in love with Kelsall at Repton. He preserved a photo in his first album, an informal shot of a slim, fairish boy with glamorous cheekbones and deepset, slanted eyes, in tweed shorts and jacket stirring a pot on a campfire with a stick—the Robinson Crusoe life. Kelsall came from a military family, made his career in the Indian army, and died in his twenties after a riding accident. In the diary, Isherwood grouped him with other lovers who made him inexplicably happy, his German boyfriend Heinz Neddermeyer, an English dancer called John Andrews, and a young Frenchman and teacher of French, Jean Bühler. "Love has its own continuity," he was to observe when he fell in love with Bühler. "This time is part of all the other times. Travelling out in the slow train to Mohrin, wondering if H[einz] would be there to meet me on the platform; hanging about the changing-room at Repton, on the look-out for Ronny; waking up at night in the Hotel Voltaire with John in the neighbouring bed and wondering: 'What on earth is the matter with me? Have I caught a chill? Am I going to be sick? Am I hungry? Am I dying? I feel so strange—' and then realizing: 'No. It's only that I'm happy.'"[135]

Kelsall and Hardwick belonged to a series of younger, physically smaller boys for whom Christopher fell at Repton. In his last term, Christopher was captivated by one of his fags, four years younger, who bore the suggestive surname Darling. To Kathleen, Christopher intimated he was attracted to a quality of celestial purity: "The other morning I heard a kind of far-away chanting going on somewhere overhead. It sounded like angels. I looked up and saw Darling standing over me singing to himself through his teeth!" In Christopher's second Rugtonstead novel, a similar halo protects a fag from a beating. The fag looks "like a seraph" and departs with "a heavenly smile" when his prefect sends him away without punishment for an unspecified crime.

Christopher was probably never beaten himself. In *Lions and Shadows*, he wrote that he escaped it due to the "lazy absent-minded benevolence" of his study holder. However, in a 1923 letter to a friend, he wrote wistfully (perhaps to show off), "Oh for Repton and its rows! I shall never be beaten again [...]." He did beat Darling, evidently for losing his football boots. In *Lions and Shadows*, Isherwood expressed uneasiness at soiling such innocence: "we shared a sense of humiliation like an indecent secret; our relations could never be quite the same again."[136]

AS WITH WRESTLING and boxing at St. Edmund's, violence toward other boys was expected at Repton, even though any friendly or sexual physical relationship was grounds for expulsion. Masturbation, too, was looked on as corrupt. This was the norm in British public schools, where boys were kept active with games and OTC and constantly policed and punished physically or mentally to prevent them from engaging in sexual activity. The amount of sexual activity and the severity of the regime against it varied from school to school. At Berkhamsted, where Uncle Charlie Fry had passed the headship to another cousin, Charles Greene, boys recalled that Greene and his masters roamed the dormitories at night with sticks. Auden's public school, Gresham's, relied on an honor system, and the headmaster expected the boys to turn one another in and even to speak out against themselves. Alec Waugh's *The Loom of Youth* was based on Sherborne, where the boys seemed to run their own world. Upward, in *The Spiral Ascent*, recalled that "immorality" in his Repton house, Latham, reached up to the housemaster, whom he called "Morphew," "interfering sexually with several of these fags, 'tossing them off' as the saying in the House went."[137] The school put out the story that "Morphew" left to join the army.

Sexual disgrace was of intense interest to Christopher. In his first Rugtonstead novel, the mysterious and sudden departure of a talented boy is described but never explained. "[H]e was the sort of man who could do anything. Both teams and a very good scholarship at the Varsity. Nice man, too—But <u>he</u> never had any real friends," says Dick Tresham's prefect. Tresham asks what happened to him. "He had to leave, in the middle of his last term. Wretched business, but they couldn't keep him, of course . . ."[138]

Early in 1924, Isherwood was to write a story called "The Old Game" about a romance between a tutor and a schoolboy a few years apart in age. Both have been banished from their respective public schools before they meet at church and then at a village tennis party. The younger boy, Jack Foster, shares tearful confidences, using euphemisms such as being "horrible" or "amusing" oneself: "Everyone did it. Nobody cared or said anything. It was an open joke. People went about boasting of it. And the ones that had been horrible the night before, laughed and smiled at you in the passage next morning as though nothing had ever happened."

Jack reveals that the first time he was caught, he was thrashed by the headmaster; the second time, "We were caught, by a man in the house, who said he wouldn't tell if he could amuse himself too ... My God!" The third time, Jack was expelled to the hands of his angry father who still isolates him at home: "he went off the rails himself once, so he's extra touchy about me."

The tutor, Charles Bryant, is stirred by the damage to Jack's self-esteem: "It was strange how this old story, with which he had been familiar for so many years, could still move him. The horror, the indignation were still fresh in his mind [...] And thinking of Jack's fate, he remembered, with a curious sense of recognition, the events of his own school life."

Charles takes Jack's confidence as an invitation: "I'm going to be beastly, Jack. Are you sure you aren't afraid?" They never use the word sex. To evade discovery, they go out in a boat. "'Oh, all right,' he said at last; and added with a bitter, tired little laugh: 'Only don't go and upset the boat.'"[139]

Apart from "The Old Game," Isherwood did not write about the sexual policing of boys. Contemporaries who were writers displayed greater outrage at interference in their private physical lives. Christopher, at fifteen, sixteen, seventeen, policed himself more strictly than anyone else could have. He experienced desperate infatuations which he discussed with a small number of confidants. Also, he flirted publicly and successfully with girls.

Christopher found girls exciting, and perhaps he felt safe, knowing that sexually nothing would happen. Kathleen recorded his obvious enthusiasm for his Pell cousins, especially Angela; on the other side of the family, Mary Luce attended his speech day in 1920 and often invited him to the Luces' Georgian terrace house in Derby. Neighborhood friends, the Barlows, fell for Christopher's "charming ways" in January 1921 after hosting him at lunch.[140] Christopher and the teenaged Betty Barlow went to dances, and he played tennis with her, with Paddy Monkhouse's sister Rachel, and with the daughters of local clergy and regimental friends.

His first Rugtonstead novel suggests that around sixteen, Christopher was publicly acting the part of a heterosexual; girls were simply another prize for which to vie in his rivalries with boys. His hero, Dick Tresham, flirts with a fictional Betty simply to take her from another boy. "It was amusing to think of Harold and his defeat. It was nice to think of Betty."[141]

As part of the mask representing his pretend heterosexual self, Christopher wrote poems. The main audience for these poems was Kathleen, his real love, but he teased her: "If ever I take up with a young woman, I shall tell her that all these poems were written to her!" In October 1921, he asked Kathleen to return a "little black book" of poems made expressly for her; he aimed to loot it for a wider audience at school. In exchange, he sent her a sonnet, "The Faithful," already slated as his first publication in *The Reptonian*, paired with "The Dream-Garden." These were pastiches about courtly love and mythical realms and risked nothing personal; they showed that Christopher could play the rhyme-and-meter game. The poems he copied into his commonplace book—Kipling, Yeats, Keats, Tennyson, Browning, as well as Masefield and many others—reveal his taste for romantic, incantatory verses about remote or imaginary locales, solitary adventures, hopeless loves.[142]

But he was open to any unfamiliar poetry. He told Granny Emily that he was studying old ballads: a friend, possibly Upward, "first put me on to them as being most delightful, especially in regard to extreme simplicity." He tried to talk Emily into liking modern verse, praising Robert Nichols, Siegfried Sassoon and Charles Sorley.[143]

Christopher distanced himself as author of his verse by using what he grandly called a "nom-de-plume"—"Cacoëthes," from a phrase in Juvenal's seventh Satire, "cacoëthes Scribendi," which can be translated as "the itch to write." The verses, Christopher's pseudonym implied, were automatic and necessary, like scratching an itch; he was claiming that they involved no conscious, sweaty effort, could not be helped, and should, by implication, be forgiven. What armor he put on to venture into the poetic fray! Evidently, he was wise to do so. His first published poems were attacked as "mawkish sentimentality" in a letter to *The Reptonian* that was signed only "A Connoisseur."[144]

Like so much in Christopher's life at this time, poetry was a contest, a competitive sport; at school, there were prizes to be won. Poetry was intertwined with the chivalric world that had been an obsession since St. Edmund's and in which he was evidently sublimating his yearnings for physical intimacy. Like a medieval knight, he channeled such passions into alternative adventures. At St. Edmund's, ragging, wrestling, and boxing had offered natural opportunities for sexualized contact; at Repton, he played tennis and fives, but physical fighting was now transformed into verbal and literary sparring.

In his last Repton term, Christopher presented a paper to the school literary society; it was titled "Chivalry in English Literature" after a 1912 book about Chaucer, Malory, Spenser, and Shakespeare by William Schofield. Christopher added the Victorian revivalists, Walter Scott and William Morris.

The Christian ideals of French chivalry—renunciation of material gain, pursuit of nobleness for its own sake, generosity, courtesy, just anger, keeping one's word, protecting the helpless, serving women—survived into the twentieth century as the standard of conduct for an English gentleman who subordinates himself in deference to others. Christopher had learned these ideals at home, and they were urged on him again at St. Edmund's and at Repton. He also found them in the masterworks of his literary heroes. "In England, later, chivalry, like Orpheus' lute, was 'strung with the poets' sinews.' There, from the fourteenth century to our own, it has been effectively advanced by men of of letters with moral design," Schofield had written, quoting Shakespeare.[145]

Christopher earnestly held the ideals of chivalry very high, and he strived throughout his life to serve them even when they conflicted with his human nature or his sexual nature, but he was not above making fun of them. One poem he published in *The Reptonian* was witty at the expense of a dance partner, unchivalrously boasting that the poet would not waste his literary skills to immortalize the name of his lady—"Miss—(I forget your name.)"—as "Petrach [sic], Dante, Philip Sidney / And heaps of others" had done. Here was another side to the perfect boy and perfect English gentleman: "fickle," as the poem stated; honest, as the poem demonstrated; and, as the poem also demonstrated, playful and reckless.

Christopher's last appearance in *The Reptonian* in the summer of 1922 was about a failure of chivalry during a wartime air raid. It was called "Gallinamania," *gallina* being Latin for hen. Colonel Cato, retired to suburban life, feuds with his spinster neighbors whose hens eat the colonel's carefully tended tulips. When German bombs set the henhouse on fire, the colonel decides not to save the hens. Afterwards, he goes mad with remorse, like Lady Macbeth or Peter Grimes. He sees hens everywhere and is taken to an asylum.[146]

Barely hidden in the story is Christopher's developing resentment toward women for certain feelings of guilt and inadequacy. His efforts to please were being slowly undermined by a realistic impatience, expressed, for the time being, only humorously. Over the longer term, he was to discipline himself against pretending to be something he was not in order to please. He wanted to be accepted for his real self, and some of his friendships with women foundered when he could not show or they could not fully accept his homosexuality. Those who accepted him for himself were drawn closer, including

Olive Mangeot, Jean Ross, Iris Tree, Dodie Smith, Julie Harris, Jennifer Selznick.

DURING THE CHRISTMAS holidays 1920, Paddy Monkhouse had invited Christopher to spend an evening at Meadow Bank Farm reading a part in Shakespeare's *As You Like It*, in which two pairs of lovers—star-crossed and cross-dressed—pursue one another through the Forest of Arden. The whole family participated, Paddy's mother and father, Paddy himself, his younger siblings Rachel, Johnny, and Elizabeth (Mitty). During 1921 and 1922, the friendship with the Monkhouse family developed through holiday afternoons in the punt, bicycle expeditions, tennis, lunches, teas, and dinners. As in Shakespeare's Forest of Arden, the real-life characters fell in love all wrong, Paddy and Rachel with Christopher, Christopher with Johnny, whom Isherwood later recalled as "a long-legged hockey-playing teenager with an adorable heart-breaking grin." Kathleen labeled him "'Mr. Honeypot' because of his thick yellow hair." Johnny, according to Paddy, "never loved man or woman." Overlooking the tangle of unrequited longing was the father Allan Monkhouse "leaning against the sitting-room fireplace" with "a Shakespearian quotation to fit every occasion."[147]

Whatever he felt for Johnny, Christopher flirted with Rachel, and Allan stirred the pot by writing a novel, *My Daughter Helen* (1922), which portrayed how marriage to someone like Christopher would be far more painful than failing to snare him. It featured a trickster character based on Christopher and contained significant insights into his personality at the time: "He struck me at first as rather a neat little fellow," wrote Monkhouse about his character Marmaduke Abney. "There was something unexpected about him." Monkhouse borrowed the surname from Christopher's Abney cousins whose patriarch, Uncle William Abney—astronomer, chemist, Fellow of the Royal Society, and a Repton governor—died in 1920 and whose womenfolk had received Kathleen's fortune when she was disinherited.[148]

Marmaduke Abney's family line is dying out like Christopher's, and his finances have collapsed, but "He managed wonderfully to evade the dismal and lugubrious by burlesquing them." Marmaduke is witty, entertaining, and dangerous, combining sophistication and recklessness with a boyish innocence. Underneath, Monkhouse described reserve and uncertainty; Marmaduke "was a boy who had done a good deal of quiet shrinking, I think, and now he sometimes adopted a bravura attitude. [...] He would shrink from emotion, secretly fearing and desiring it." Marmaduke talks excitedly about criminals: "Let us be grateful to the criminal for making an interesting world. Some of them are bold thinkers; anyhow, they break across the conventions."

Marmaduke proves to be an *homme fatale*, a kind of amateur Sarah Bernhardt: "He was an actor of extraordinary skill and of a kind of sincerity. He was always putting his case, or part of it, in some subtle way."[149] He wins Helen's heart, but he fails in his career, commits a crime to repay his debts, and ends up in prison. Helen's jealous, protective father—the narrator—is slowly pulled into the catastrophe. The whole family tries and fails to save Marmaduke.

The crime in the novel is forgery, suggesting that Monkhouse observed in Christopher a kind of forged self. Here again is a fictional code at work. The novel warned that Christopher's enthusiasm for Rachel concealed the homosexuality that made him unsuitable as a husband. In 1924, Monkhouse published a sequel, *Marmaduke*, in which Marmaduke returns from prison, goes on the stage, again fails as a family man, and finally agrees to disappear for good after cheating his father-in-law out of some money.

It was 1927 before Isherwood asked Allan Monkhouse outright whether Marmaduke was based on himself. Monkhouse was cagey: "If you like I'll allow you a line & a half but I never suspected you of being a criminal." Years later, remembering the two novels as one, Isherwood reported to a friend: "poor old Allan Monkhouse made me go to prison for forgery in a novel called 'Marmaduke'—a remarkable prophecy [...] in the book I also married his daughter, and how wrong he was ..." Monkhouse's view was corroborated, though, by a letter to another friend in which Christopher had joked, "I shall end by marrying Paddy's sister—the only girl I have ever been sincerely friends with, and who o'ertops me by about a foot!"[150] But, in the end, this is one kind of forgery—marriage to a woman—that Isherwood never committed. Moreover, he boldly commandeered the role of Marmaduke in *Lions and Shadows* by having a fisherman on the Isle of Wight address the Isherwood character as Marmaduke.

Allan Monkhouse taught Isherwood how it felt to be used as a character in a book, and he perhaps made Isherwood feel entitled to use the Monkhouses when creating his own characters. For Isherwood drew on the Monkhouse family again and again—in *All the Conspirators*, *The Memorial*, *The World in the Evening*, and *A Meeting by the River*. As the years passed, it was to become increasingly clear that his fictions talked back hotly to the Monkhouse view of him and aimed to correct it.[151]

Paddy Monkhouse teased Christopher more directly about his sexual and romantic tastes. He sent Christopher a poem, "Found Wanting," that suggests his feelings for Christopher were disappointed when Christopher asked for help with another relationship. The poem contains the lines "you /

Came to me, long ago in trouble, / To ask my help. And then I knew / That all my hope was only bubble / [. . .] / I couldn't help, I grieved you double." Below the poem Paddy wrote, "It isn't quite fair."[152] Failing to break through romantically, he settled for the role of elder brother, advising Christopher on his love life and education. He was five months older than Christopher and a year ahead at school, at Rugby, where he was extremely successful, both in sport and academics. Kathleen idolized Paddy and held him up to Christopher as an example.

At the height of their intimacy, Paddy wrote a funny and cruel poem playing with the conventional idea that men should outgrow boy-love, "Wed a women, and respect her / (Nature has decreed it so)." He wrote from Christopher's imagined point of view, portraying Christopher as loving boys who grow younger with each love affair. The love object is seventeen, then fourteen, then ten, then five, then an infant, until at last the lover turns to the female womb—but only to pursue "the spectre / Of a little embryo"—his own son.[153]

In 1925, Paddy told Christopher that he was becoming sexually interested in girls, and in 1929, he married. Isherwood later conjectured that the friendship with Paddy faded because boy-love became a threat,[154] and in his mature fiction, Isherwood drew on Paddy to create the character type of the lover of boys who fears this aspect of himself and buries it. He never accepted Paddy's admonition that he himself should grow up and turn to women, and he strongly objected to the clichéd suggestion that it was more mature to marry a woman and lie about boy-love than to love boys openly.

IN OCTOBER 1919, as he turned eight, Richard Isherwood finally started school. Kathleen decided on Berkhamsted, where cousin Charles Greene was headmaster. It was twenty-six miles from London; she arranged for Richard to attend as a day boy and live with Nanny in a lodging house.

Richard found school terrifying. He told Kathleen about a master "bellowing at them," and said the same master "took threatening shapes!" When she visited after a month, Richard was nervous, afraid, and unable to play, then blew up completely, "flying into uncontrolled tempers simply stamping & shaking & screaming."[155] By Easter, back at Marple Hall, he looked terrible, had a cough, and could take no pleasure in anything.

Christopher accompanied Kathleen on her next visit to Berkhamsted, where they dined at the School House with Charles Greene, his wife, and three of their six children, including the future novelist Graham Greene, who boarded at his father's school. Thus it was that Christopher's cousin, named after the same bachelor cousin as Richard Graham Bradshaw Isherwood and destined for writing fame like Christopher, showed Christopher over Berkhamsted school where Graham himself was bullied, became depressed, attempted suicide, and finally ran away. The novelist cousins were to maintain a casual friendship as adults, and Isherwood was to read Graham Greene's novels as they appeared.

Charles Greene, having failed to recognize his son's misery before it reached crisis point, was alert and compassionate toward Richard's. He told Kathleen that Richard should be living at home with her. He also recommended psychoanalysis and sent them to the Jungian analyst Kenneth Richmond, who had helped Graham out of his suicidal depression.[156]

Uncle Charlie Fry intervened, asserting he knew better about psychoanalysis and about young boys than his liberal-minded successor at Berkhamsted, and he vigorously warned Kathleen that psychoanalysis was "a most dangerous thing" emerging from the court of the German Kaiser and "developed along sex lines"; that books on the subject were "positively indecent"; that she "would be most unwise to tamper with the mind of a child." He pronounced that he, Uncle Charlie Fry, "could do more for him in a week than any treatment of that sort."[157] Having frightened Kathleen into abandoning the treatment, Uncle Charlie went abroad on holiday with Aunt Julia and offered no further help.

Richard had strong intellectual ability, a need for sameness, extreme fears, recurring bad thoughts, difficulty forming reciprocal friendships, and appears to have suffered from a pervasive developmental disorder, possibly Asperger's syndrome. He was even more highly strung than Christopher, detail-oriented, literal-minded, prone to irascibility, impulsivity, occasional violence. He seems also to have been dyspraxic, with a verbal ability greatly exceeding his mathematical ability, echoing Christopher's normal and productive lopsidedness.

Richard's greatest pleasures—trains and, later, the queens of England—were positive interests, more characteristic of Asperger's than of obsessive compulsive disorder. Trains and queens were certainly coping strategies, but Richard had remarkable knowledge about them. Christopher's collecting activities reflect a similar predisposition that was channeled into his life achievements.

Charles Greene's observation that Richard needed to live in a real home made Kathleen feel guilty. She had been house-hunting in Berkhamsted since Richard arrived there, but she was as choosy as ever and probably didn't really want to live there. Uncle Jack suggested Kathleen and her mother should "join house together" in London, sensible since Emily could no longer manage the stairs at Buckingham Street at all. Emily was far more decisive than Kathleen, and they quickly chose a property just north of Kensington High Street, 36 St. Mary Abbot's Terrace, with "a quite nice garden & airy rooms & in good condition."[158]

Christopher learned about 36 St. Mary Abbot's Terrace by letter at Repton and tried to contain himself: "As you say, I must try not to be excited about the promised house—it seems such a far away dream, like excelsior or heaven or the never never land!" Already, he and Kathleen shared an understanding that he would eventually contribute to household expenses with the mooted librarian job at the British Museum.[159]

By the third week in October 1921, the contracts for the house were signed, and Christopher admitted for the first time how he had missed their belongings, stored since Limerick—seven years. He hinted that he would like to avoid Marple Hall at Christmas.

St. Mary Abbot's Terrace (later demolished) was a big townhouse on five floors, with a bedroom each for Emily, Kathleen, and Christopher, and at least three servants' rooms. Richard shared with Kathleen. The move took place in December, but Christopher did not see the house until January 1922 because he was sitting his first set of exams at Cambridge. He did indeed have to spend Christmas at Marple Hall, and it was far from merry.

When the family had gathered for the previous Christmas and New Year, 1920–21, Elizabeth Isherwood had been preparing to die, and she had spread a restless, ghostly feeling through the household, "asking continually for a cab to take her to her other home," as Kathleen wrote.[160] The doctor had administered a last morphine injection on January 17, but Elizabeth had rallied, lingered for two more months, then died peacefully in March.

Kathleen avoided the funeral, as she avoided most public gatherings with the Bradshaw Isherwoods, but Christopher traveled from Repton and described it in a letter. After the service, they gathered on the steps of the family vault. Christopher was moved by his grandfather's gesture of farewell: "The really touching moment was when poor Grandad, on going away, made a little bow to the vault, as if saying goodbye."[161] This was the family ceremony on which Isherwood evidently drew for the wreath laying in *The Memorial*.

Within a month, Henry proposed that he and Muriel should stay at Marple Hall during the summer, "partly as paying guests."[162] They hoped to save money by not opening The Oakes. John Isherwood resisted.

Everyone in the family was short of money. Kathleen strategically positioned herself partly in and partly out of the Bradshaw Isherwood finances. In April 1920, Jack had proposed selling Wyberslegh, which needed expensive repairs. Kathleen had rehearsed to her diary her lifelong right to live there or to receive rent. Then she discovered that the Isherwoods for seventeen years had annually neglected to pay an extra £100 allowance covenanted to her and Frank at the time of their marriage. Jack discouraged her from claiming it, and suggested that Kathleen should become a trustee of the Marple Hall Estate, replacing a ninety-year-old Luce cousin. Jack himself was the other trustee. It was an obvious way to make Kathleen feel responsible. She agreed and right away she and Jack began discussing how Christopher would manage financially when he inherited.

Just before Christopher's sixteenth birthday, Henry had proposed to liquidate his position and settle his claim on Christopher to save death duties. In exchange, he wanted £10,000 as well as the income he was already receiving followed by an annuity of £700 a year after his father's death. "I do not fancy the scheme," wrote Kathleen drily.[163] Henry's appetite for cash was ludicrous in the circumstances and would have called for selling significant assets of land or furnishings. It underlines his flair for directing resources toward himself and shows he saw clearly where the estate was headed.

Despite John Isherwood's wish to be left alone, Henry turned up at Marple Hall that summer and began to improve his future property by stripping the 100-year-old ivy off the house and felling small ornamental trees. During August, a grumbling Christopher helped prune ivy and trees and clear bushes from the cliff side between the terrace and grotto pond. It was heavy going, especially hauling the debris up the steep slope: "C having a rope passed round his waist to prevent slipping," according to Kathleen. Richard, Kathleen, and Muriel dragged the bushes to a bonfire. Cutting and burning continued for several weeks.

Henry presented Christopher with "a very nice watch which had accompanied him all round the world," distributed bequests in Elizabeth's will and involved Christopher in "re-hanging and re-arranging" artwork inside the house.[164] Later, Henry renewed the gold paint on the picture frames and the black oak wainscoting, to expensive, gaudy effect.

The following August, Henry was to tell Kathleen that his marriage had collapsed and that Muriel was refusing to give him any more money. Kathleen did not believe in Henry's "poverty"; indeed, it emerged that Henry had extracted an allowance from Muriel "on condition that she be allowed to go her own way."

"How horrible the Uncle Henry regime must be getting now," Christopher wrote to Kathleen from school.[165] Uncle Henry's behavior, though, again invited Christopher to adopt a new attitude toward Marple Hall over the longer term. For Uncle Henry continued to offer an example of how to get what you want, and it was a tempting alternative to the insuperable challenge of the hero father.

CHRISTOPHER WAS PRESENTED with the English Essay Prize, the English Literature Prize, and the History Prize at his final speech day in June 1922, but, once again, the ceremony was somehow irrelevant since he was not yet leaving Repton. He had autumn term before him and his second set of scholarship exams for Cambridge in December.

Meanwhile, Mr. Smith invited Christopher to join a group of his students on a walking tour in France during August. Christopher gestured at feeling guilty for abandoning Kathleen during their usual summer holidays—"I realise, Darling, that this is a rather selfish scheme. It would take a large chunk out of our time together"[166]—but he could not conceal his impatience to travel.

Once away from England he reported little. "It is absolutely no good my trying to describe all that has happened or the scenery—in writing," he explained on a postcard from Chamonix.[167] The experience was too big and too new for him to get his pen around it, and he did not relish sharing it with his mother. It was fifteen years later, in *Lions and Shadows*, that Isherwood formulated an account worthy of all the trip meant to him.

They collected Upward in Rouen, where he had been studying French since leaving Repton, and went sightseeing in Paris before taking a crowded overnight train up into the Alps in southeastern France. Upward had been transformed by France, and Isherwood recast him as a French literary rebel: "He had grown a small moustache and looked exactly my idea of a young Montmartre poet." Upward had discovered Baudelaire's *Les Fleurs du Mal*, and Isherwood recalled that "His suppressed excitement set me, as always, instantly on fire." Isherwood claimed that he had run through the cobbled medieval streets of Annecy "to buy my first copy of Baudelaire before the bookshops closed."[168]

According to *Lions and Shadows*, Isherwood and Upward had vowed to each other not to be impressed by the mountain scenery. As they hiked up the pass—the Col des Aravis, leading from Haute-Savoie into Savoie—they couldn't see anything because the mist was so heavy. Thus, they were taken by surprise when they woke to a clear morning and looked out the window at the highest mountain in Europe. "Mont Blanc confronted us, dazzling, immense, cut sharp out of the blue sky; more preposterous than the most baroque wedding cake, more convincing than the best photograph. It fairly took my breath away. It made me want to laugh." This was a comic answer to the famous descriptions by the English Romantic poets—Wordsworth in the sixth book of *The Prelude*, about his 1790 walking tour; Coleridge, who never went but imagined visiting Mont Blanc in "Hymn Before Sunrise in the Vale of Chamouni"; Shelley, who was inspired to write "Mont Blanc" after walking in the Alps with Byron; and Byron in "Manfred." Wordsworth had "grieved / To have a soulless image on the eye / That had usurped upon a living thought."[169] Isherwood, far from grieving, wanted to laugh. The real

Mont Blanc did not usurp upon what Isherwood had imagined; it was better. In a characteristic flourish of understatement, he was careful not to mention the English Romantic poets explicitly.

Still, like Wordsworth, Isherwood was moved because he was so well prepared in advance for the sight of Mont Blanc. The image of the preposterous wedding cake symbolized—as it would in 1939 when he arrived in New York aboard the snow-decked ship resembling a wedding cake—the union of the imagined with the actual, an experience that was to be repeated for Isherwood many other times, moving him sometimes to laughter and sometimes to tears. In Venice with Don Bachardy in 1956, he was to weep at his first sight of the lagoon and Santa Maria della Salute partly because he had seen the view so often in paintings of eighteenth-century Venice.

As the party of Repton historians walked on toward Chamonix, Val d'Isère, and Grenoble, other realities interacted with the literary fantasies shared by Isherwood and Upward, and everything was intensified through the prism of French literature—novels and stories by Flaubert, de Maupassant, Victor Hugo, and the new vocabulary of Baudelaire in which "Sexual love was the torture-chamber, the loathsome charnel-house, the bottomless abyss."

The climax of the trip came, in Isherwood's telling, when Upward read to him on a cliff side safely screened by trees and bushes a poem he had been writing since Rouen, "Stranger in Spring." Isherwood included nine stanzas in *Lions and Shadows*, shifting into present tense to convey the extreme emotion he felt during the private performance, and at the same time, shellacking it with a hard comic shell to protect their adolescent idealism: "I tell him that this is his best poem and that now I am certain, absolutely convinced, that he is going to be a really great poet, the greatest of our generation. My voice trembles with excitement; I keep my eyes fixed on the roofs of the distant village because they are filled with tears."[170]

BACK AT REPTON for his last term, Christopher sat "at the top table in the Dining Hall" and was head of his study and bedder (sleeping quarters).[171] He became co-editor of *The Reptonian* with Eric Falk, a Londoner in his house, one year younger, who was to become another friend. He was learning to manipulate academic, literary, and social masks to protect his feelings. In his second Rugtonstead novel, one of the older boys, a prefect, admires the new boy, Tresham, for his detachment in football. Tresham "was really taking the thing as a game, not a competitive, life and death struggle with everybody else on the field." In fact, the Tresham character is not much of an athlete; like Christopher in real life, he was unlikely to win in sport; Christopher came up with the idea of an "Athletic Mind" for Tresham. The Athletic Mind "makes you look at Life as a Game."[172] This attitude, looking at life as a game, was to be developed over the years, transforming the suffering of failure into a celebration of detachment and difference, but as a teenager, Christopher was still suffering and not yet celebrating. To Paddy Monkhouse, he admitted that none of the social or intellectual games he played, none of the personae he wielded, had any real meaning for him. In the autumn of 1922, he was deeply unhappy. He felt no real interest in anything, and he told Paddy that he didn't want to go to Cambridge. Already he had heard that Upward wasn't happy there.

Paddy, in his role as elder brother, acknowledged Christopher's misery despite discerning a certain teenage self-pity. He advised plenty of activity to burn off sexual tension—"an inconvenient desire"—and a change of plan for university, "why go to Cambridge if you don't want to? If you can get a scholarship there, you can at Oxford . . . If you would condescend to be more explicit, I would be a more able counsellor."[173]

Christopher confided more, and Paddy next advised him to study psychology, listing some books, and to write something every week about his and his friends' states of mind, "a kind of diary." Paddy admitted he had not read Freud; he had learned about psychoanalysis through a Rugby school friend who had tried it. Nevertheless, he was offering himself as a psychotherapist by post, inviting a weekly letter from Christopher, "recording anything which has made an impression on you." He probably hoped to learn Christopher's secrets, but his advice was astute. "From being thus obliged to reconsider your impressions, you will probably pick up something of permanent value. This record—not criticism—of yourself will probably come easiest to you; really preferable would be a little scouting into the minds of your friends—"[174]

Of course, Christopher had already kept diaries at St. Edmund's and (according to *Lions and Shadows*) again at Repton, so Paddy was only reinforcing an existing inclination with a new emphasis on introspection. Isherwood eventually read all the books on psychology and psychoanalysis that Paddy suggested, and more besides. He was to obtain Freud's *Introductory Lectures on Psychoanalysis* on his twenty-first birthday in 1925. The fiction Christopher had begun writing in the summer of 1922, short stories and chapters for his Rugtonstead novel, shows him confidently recording and analysing his personality and the personalities of his schoolmates.

Christopher showed increasing swagger during his last term at Repton, just as he had done at St. Edmund's. For the end-of-term house supper, he and another boy, Sykes, adapted A.A. Milne's *The Red House Mystery*, a Sherlock Holmes spoof. The newly formed House Reading Society tackled Shelley's verse drama *The Cenci*, so depraved that it was never performed in public until that year, in London where Christopher may have seen it. Count

Cenci has his sons murdered and rapes his daughter before she persuades his servants to kill him and then goes to her own death. "I took the part of the wicked Count," Christopher boasted to Kathleen.[175] The role chimed with an identity he increasingly relished—of himself as a bad boy, a seducer, a devil worshiper, who might encourage others to worship the devil with him, like Dirk Renswoude in Marjorie Bowen's *Black Magic*. This was all a pose, generating mental excitement like the confidences he exchanged with Paddy Monkhouse; neither of them had acted sexually on the crushes about which they feverishly corresponded and wrote poems.

CHRISTOPHER WAS TURNING against his subject, history. As he prepared to take the Cambridge scholarship exams for the second time, he announced to Kathleen that "History can only give one nasty clear-headed emptiness (as Mr. G.B.S. himself practically admits), while Literature gives you—well, everything." He felt it useless to explain to Mr. Smith: "the more I read these violent books he gives me, the more I feel how unpractical and prejudiced they are—and how much better Shelley or Browning or Rupert Brooke expressed the same ideas."[176]

Nevertheless, he proceeded like a champion, entering the lists at Cambridge in December 1922 and emerging from the week of grueling exams with double his previous award—the highest possible. He sent Kathleen a nonchalant postcard: "In case you haven't seen—I got £80 schol. Corpus." She recorded an outpouring of pride at home; Granny Emily "even wept she was so delighted." Christopher's name was published in *The Times*, "first name on the list!" Geoffrey Fisher sent congratulations, claiming "I am very attached to him." Fisher also noted that "Mr GBS says of his work he has an intense feeling for style . . . & that his most serious shortcoming is his passion for plowing a lonely furrow."[177]

The scholarship meant something entirely different to his family than it did to Christopher. In *Lions and Shadows*, he created a comic scene in which he announced his true vocation to Mr. Holmes while lying on Holmes's sofa mildly drunk after a celebratory lunch: "I told Mr. Holmes that I wanted to be a writer. [. . .] I'm not really an historian at all." Mr. Holmes has known all along and delivers a lecture, "half-mocking, half-serious, on the value of drudgery, the need for breadth, the necessity of getting inside the mind of people differently constituted from myself 'you butterfly, you cobweb, you s-skimmer of other people's cookery!'" Mr. Holmes advises taking Part One of the History Tripos at Cambridge, then changing to English: "'you'll wriggle and shed several s-skins and be quite a respectable animal at the end of it;

whereas, from the English people, you'll get nothing but a-adulation and d-damnation.'" Isherwood copied this advice from a real letter Smith sent him in February 1923, after Christopher had left Repton.

In the *Lions and Shadows* version, Christopher and Mr. Holmes, having hatched their private scheme for Cambridge, appear before the school in a scene of public triumph which reveals the meaning of all Holmes's teaching. Christopher is warmly applauded even by those who have disapproved of him at school. "And Mr. Holmes, who was sitting beside me, bent over and hissed in my ear. 'You see? N-nothing succeeds like s-success!'"[178] This scene of public triumph, a scene of self-conscious inauthenticity, encapsulates a cynicism and anxiety about public acclaim that Isherwood felt all his life, starting when he won the quarter-mile handicap in his first term at St. Edmund's and recalibrated when he returned to St. Edmund's after his father's death, wearing the armband that marked him as a sacred orphan.

He addressed this theme in a 1924 short story set at Rugtonstead, "The Hero," which charts his continuing response to his father's heroic sacrifice. Two fags, close friends, go out for a walk and nearly drown in a river near the school. One boy, Thompson, falls into the river while reaching for a bird's nest, and the other boy, Wayne, leaps in to save him. The label "hero" is attached to Wayne, but he believes that he does not deserve it, for although he leapt into the river after his friend, he panicked and struck for shore with an "overpowering desire to live, to live!" Both boys are rescued by others.

Wayne allows himself to be publicly acclaimed by the headmaster at speech day in a scene like the one describing the applause for Christopher's scholarship in *Lions and Shadows*: "He saw the timbers of the hall sway before his eyes in a shudder of intoxicating pride, voices sounded triumphantly in his ears, and, as the school surged out under the cold night and the stars, Gerald Wayne knew himself to be a hero." Both boys believe that Thompson is a real hero, who once dragged an injured boy into a bomb shelter during an air raid and who scored two goals for the House in a noble football defeat. Uncomfortable with his supposed debt to Wayne, Thompson ends the friendship.[179]

Like "Two Brothers," "The Hero" draws closely on Henry Newbolt's definition of heroism, from *Tales of the Great War*: a hero has "trained himself to go on when all hell tells him to go back," possesses "the steadiness that comes of long self-discipline," recognizes that "victory is won not so much by sudden acts of bravery as by carrying on or by holding out."[180] This principle was also enshrined in the motto of St. Edmund's School, Per Manendo Vincimus, Through Perserverance We Conquer.

In "The Hero," Thompson possesses the steadiness that comes of long self-discipline; he trains hard for football.[181] Wayne cannot carry on or hold out. Once he leaps into the river, he loses command of himself. Thus, the story reverses the one about Horatius that Christopher had parodied in "A Lay of Modern Germany"; Wayne is pitifully unable to emulate the hero who jumped into the Tiber having saved Rome. Many years later, in *A Single Man*, Isherwood was to reverse these elements of the scenario again, when his characters George and Kenny take a drunken late-night swim, and Kenny, much younger, pulls George from the surf.

An epigraph to Isherwood's draft of "The Hero" pointed to a hidden theme: "Before, a joy propos'd—behind, a dream." It is from Shakespeare's Sonnet 129, about lust: "... till action, lust / Is perjured, murd'rous, bloody, full of blame, / Savage, extreme, rude, cruel, not to trust."

The epigraph hinted that duplicitousness and hypocrisy in the story are linked with sexual appetite. The sonnet suggests that if only Wayne could have acted on his lust, he would have been a better person, and certainly not a liar. Wayne's fault was not the perfectly natural fear that made him strike for shore; his fault was the fear that made him hide the truth, both about his actions in the river and about his feelings for Thompson—feelings in which he longed to immerse himself but feared to drown.

Three days before Isherwood finished "The Hero," in March 1924, he went with Paddy Monkhouse to the London production of Allan Monkhouse's antiwar play, *The Conquering Hero* (1923), about the role of the artist in wartime. The play culminates with a scene of public welcome for another falsely acclaimed hero, drawing again on the Bradshaw Isherwood milieu in ways that must have startled him.

Allan Monkhouse called his artist Christopher. He gave the name Frank—Captain Francis Iredale—to his soldier-hero, who is captured and dies of his wounds. There is also a Henry, not an admirable character, a Sir John, and other familiar details. When war breaks out, the soldier, Frank, leaves immediately for the Front; the artist, Christopher, continues writing stories and telling the truth, which he sees as his vocation and duty. Along with his brother, a parson, he convincingly presents pacifist arguments that the real Christopher Isherwood was to adopt during World War II—that it takes a particular kind of courage to go on stating the truth in all circumstances and that the civilization for which they fight means nothing if the truth is lost.

But when the family butler enlists, the Christopher character feels his position is exposed as a form of class privilege, so he decides to enlist, too. He is unable to cope at the Front, deserts and returns to England, shambling, bent, an invalid, unable to write. He is even too weak to avoid the local public welcome, false acclaim complete with triumphal arch and brass band playing Handel's "See the Conquering Hero." A lesson of the play for Isherwood was that he should have the courage to stick to his artistic vocation and to go on telling the truth.

"All a poet can do today is warn," Wilfred Owen had written in the brief unfinished preface to his war poems. "That is why the true Poets must be truthful." Owen was to become a literary hero for Isherwood, for in Owen's acid candor, Isherwood recognized his own feeling that he had been lied to about heroism. "This book is not about heroes," Owen had written. "English poetry is not yet fit to speak of them." The book was a direct riposte to the likes of Henry Newbolt. "My subject is War, and the pity of War. The poetry is in the pity." Owen's poems stripped away manipulative clichés. "These elegies are to this generation in no sense consolatory."[182] As Isherwood portrayed in his short story "Two Brothers" and much later in his novel *A Single Man*, there is no consolation for death; there is only getting used to it.

Isherwood's mature idea of a hero would have nothing to do with exploits. Eventually, he was to see a hero as someone who could help others to overcome their fear. His father had been able to do this with his aura of calm; his guru, Swami Prabhavananda, was able to do this with his faith. Isherwood told an interviewer after the publication of *Kathleen and Frank* that "real courage [...] consists in giving reassurance to people under terrible circumstances. It's not what you do, sort of roaring and carrying on and killing people. It's the way you make the people who are with you feel, that they're not scared." By then, Isherwood had accepted a report that his father had died unarmed, leading a charge. "When he was killed . . . he just had a swagger stick to make signals to the men to advance. More on the left, or more on the right." Without signals from his father, without Frank's guidance and the reassurance of his physical presence, Christopher felt untethered and afraid for much of his life.

In 1960, in a series of lectures at the University of California at Santa Barbara, Isherwood made another observation about courage: "I think that courage is enormously admirable and that cowardice is to be deplored. But I also think all that really matters about cowardice is not to conceal it. [...] all you really need is the courage to say, when necessary, 'I am afraid' . . ."[183] He had held this view ever since writing "The Hero," in which Wayne's candor fails him.

Paddy Monkhouse, as an undergraduate, solicited "Two Brothers" and "The Hero" for the *Oxford Outlook*, when he was sub-editor under Isherwood's cousin, Graham Greene. "We all liked your tale, 'Two Brothers' immensely," Paddy wrote; and a few months later, "'The Hero' was marvellous well received at Oxford."[184] Upward preferred "The Old Game," about the tutor and the boy having sex in the boat,[185] but Paddy expressly advised Christopher not to submit it, warning that "'Don't upset the boat' might upset ours."[186] When "The Hero" was published, the epigraph from Sonnet 129, alluding to lust, was dropped. So much for candor.

Paddy's mentorship was vital, despite these compromises. He saw Christopher into an undergraduate mainstream. It was Paddy, too, who suggested jettisoning the initials "C.W.B." and using just first and last name in the *Oxford Outlook*. So, with these two stories, "Two Brothers" and "The Hero," published in 1925, Christopher Isherwood was to announce his literary identity.

NOT LONG BEFORE writing "The Hero," Christopher had created a different kind of schoolboy character, who shrinks from public attention and guards his anonymity in order to observe his schoolmates. This was Tuke-Adams, an orphan who lives with a maiden aunt in a cathedral town. Tuke-Adams featured in Christopher's second Rugtonstead narrative, begun in January 1923 just after he left Repton. The name alludes to Henry Scott Tuke, celebrated for his impressionist paintings of nude boys.

Tuke-Adams spends his time "in harmless little stratagems for personal comfort," and his life runs "as smoothly as his new bicycle." He is "unobtrusive" at school, where his personal habits are so fussy and precise that his schoolmates refer to him as Mother Hubbard, a dried-up old lady carefully guarding an empty cupboard. Tuke-Adams reflected the old maid in Christopher, a persona later relished by Auden and joked about by Isherwood.

Tuke-Adams is no mere voyeur. He is intrigued by the enigmatic reserve of the most talented prefect: "Tuke-Adams had always taken an interest, never openly admitted, in this secret side of Traynor." Like Christopher himself, Tuke-Adams is also attracted to the eccentricities of locals and shopowners, "the village characters." He revels in their color, for he himself has none: "he was absolutely without positive qualities of any kind. Caution was written all over him." In Tuke-Adams, Christopher first embodied his observing literary self as a character in its own right. "This strange individuality, which consisted in banishing individualism" was to be a key to his writing throughout his career.[187] It had begun with his diary at St. Edmund's, in which he served as the mediumistic recorder of school life. It was to develop into the detached, camera eye of the Christopher Isherwood narrator in Berlin. In 1938, Isherwood was to write in his diary, "as a person, I really don't exist." But he could call himself into existence by writing.[188]

CHRISTOPHER PLANNED TO matriculate at Corpus Christi College in October 1923—ten months after finishing Repton. For the time being, he settled at St. Mary Abbot's Terrace with his mother, his brother, his grandmother, his nanny, a cook, a maid, and a lodger. The lodger was a post office worker called Herbert Brook Browning who lived over the garage, where he stored his motorbikes.

Christopher was eighteen and a half. He threw himself at London. He cycled, he swam at the public baths, he roller-skated, went constantly to the theater and the cinema, frequented bookshops, heard lectures and concerts, visited galleries and architectural sights with his mother, with visitors, with friends. He attended countless parties, lunches, teas, clubs. He kept up with an extraordinary number of people, from St. Edmund's, Repton, his father's regiment, and his large extended family. He had only to go out his mother's front door to bump into someone he knew. He was alone only when he was sleeping or working. Often, he worked with a friend on hand, occasionally Upward visiting for a day from Romford, sometimes Eric Falk who lived in Hampstead, and, most regularly by the end of February 1923, Hector Wintle, who lived just two miles away in Oxford Gardens, North Kensington, and, like Christopher, was writing a novel. Weekends he visited the Morgan Browns at St. Edmund's, Paddy Monkhouse at Trinity College, Oxford, Uncle Jack and Aunt Frida at their cottage in Shere, near Guildford, Surrey. He came home exhausted from these outings, which included late nights, rich food, and increasing quantities of alcohol.

Kathleen found money to dress him fashionably. They went to a Mayfair tailor to order his first bespoke suit, blue serge, and they hunted in numerous shops before settling on an overcoat, "blue nap" with a plain back, "as those with bands have now been in some time." Isherwood was proud to tell Kathleen that the first time he wore it, he "met several people he knew . . . !" His dinner jacket was updated by Jewish tailors in Shepherd's Bush: "new silk reverses in the right shape." Five months later, he ordered a brand-new dinner jacket, custom-made. He also bought patent leather shoes. There was "a stiff shirt & a Zephyr" from Austin Reed in Regent Street—the first for formal wear, the latter like a T-shirt, with short sleeves and a button opening at the neck. With a view to going abroad again, he purchased "a new soft hat."[189]

Richard had spent his first London year at a nearby pre-preparatory school, Norland Place, where he was happy and successful after a difficult start. He moved up in January 1923 to an all-boys preparatory day school run by two Mr. Wilkinsons, father and son. There, he struggled. In February, he passed an "insulting note" to a classmate and blamed it on a younger boy. Christopher went to the school to conciliate.

In particular, Richard feared disgracing himself in football and gym, so he began skipping both and lying about it. According to Kathleen, Christopher "beat him after long threatening to do so." This must have been distressing for both. After all, Christopher hated football himself. He was suffering from indigestion, and after the beating he went to the doctor, who pronounced, "Nothing organically wrong." Stress was to upset his stomach increasingly for the rest of his life.

Soon, Richard skipped football again. He sneaked away from school before lunch and wandered the streets "afraid to return home" until school let out, when he arrived in a state of collapse and had to be put to bed. The doctor forbade football for the rest of the term. The following Monday, Richard said he "couldn't face" school since "everyone would know of his running off." So Christopher walked him there.

As they reached the school door, Richard bolted, Christopher chasing: "—a few minutes later R disappeared into the mist . . ." Kathleen recorded. "C. could not overtake him & rang me up." Nanny set off to help, and she and Christopher finally found Richard in a nearby churchyard. He was again put to bed. The last thing Kathleen recorded in her diary for that miserable, terrifying day was "Thick fog coming back."[190] It was like the neurosis enveloping the household.[191] Christopher was trapped by illness, physical and psychological. So was Richard. It kept the family together.

Richard's flight was one of many, each more dramatic and frightening. The day he returned to the Wilkinsons, after six weeks off, even Nanny could not control him. As they approached Holland Park Avenue, with the school on the far side, "he dashed across saying he wasn't going back to school & shouldn't return any more & disappeared." He walked all the way to Harrow, about nine miles away, where he bought a train ticket to Berkhamsted and threw himself on the mercy of his old landlady. It was agreed that Richard would live with the Wilkinsons to avoid the daily distress of leaving home. By 9 p.m. on his first night there, he had run away again.

Kathleen was exhausted, afraid, sleepless; Uncle Jack advised "an ultimatum." Richard must choose between the Wilkinsons or boarding school. Despite storms of tears, he was bundled off to Northwood House, at Herne Bay on the Kentish coast, which was "used to dealing with 'nervous cases,'" as Paddy Monkhouse put it. From there, he wrote imploring to come home.

Meanwhile, Christopher himself had made a getaway. In April, he went to improve his French at the same *pension* in Rouen where Upward had studied, Le Vert Logis. He was kept up to date on Richard's ordeal, and he reassured Kathleen by letter that "the third day was generally the crisis of misery, & feeling that we had done the only thing possible in trying this—"[192] Thus, for the time being, he aligned himself with adult authority against his little brother, helping to coerce eleven-year-old Richard who was far more miserable and afraid than Christopher himself had been at the same age at St. Edmund's.

But Christopher only pretended to know what he was doing when he wrote with such breezy certainty to Kathleen. In fact, he had been sharing his worries with Paddy Monkhouse, who thought that boarding school for Richard was a good idea, but reminded Isherwood of the psychotherapy plan abandoned in the summer of 1921. "Richard does not want a schoolmaster: he wants a psychologist," wrote Paddy.[193] Richard's developmental backwardness, paranoia, and emotional instability were to prove insoluble—just like Kathleen's grief.

Christopher turned away to moldable boys like Kelsall, Hardwick, Darling, and Worth, another Repton fag. He would meet the Repton train whenever school broke up and treat his protégés to the movies or theater and tea in London. These friendships were charged with sexual innuendo, but they were also animated by the dynamic of teaching and learning within the hierarchy of older boy to younger characteristic of public-school friendships at the time. Darling showed Christopher a play he had written. Paddy Monkhouse, relishing another chance to teach Christopher strategy in his relationships, advised, "Don't try to be polite, if you think there's anything in him at all: a critical attitude will show him that you are really interested." In turn, Christopher archly berated his younger friend Eric Falk because Falk had failed to extract a letter from one of his protégés: "It would improve his powers of self-expression. In the New Age, in which we live, everybody is out to improve his tarts. I am convinced that Paiderastia is the greatest educational force of Modern Times. (Subject for Essay)."[194] Christopher was attracted to difficulty, but he wanted—needed—someone he could help. Later, he would be attracted to boys who had mental issues like Richard partly because he was always tempted by the possibility of performing a miracle.

It was not just real boys, it was also boys in movies. On February 10, 1923, Christopher and Kathleen saw Jackie Coogan in *Oliver Twist*. They had seen Coogan before, as the orphan adopted by Charlie Chaplin in *The Kid*,[195] and now Christopher became obsessed. He took Nanny to *Oliver Twist* on February 16, saw it alone on March 1, then went again with Hector Wintle on March 5; toward the end of March, he joked to Upward that he was thinking of seeing it for the eighth time. He framed his obsession sardonically as lust: "I think paiderastia is the lowest state of the human soul and the Film Industry the nadir of Commercial Prostitution. My trance, as you call it, is becoming expensive. But they are all shadows."[196] With a film shadow, even more so than with a girl, Christopher was safe from sexual involvement. He could watch the story he loved, *Oliver Twist*, unfold again and again, always with the happy ending that he could not bring about in his own life.

That spring, he began making a movie scrapbook. In the front, he pasted a cutting of Coogan as Oliver, dressed in rags, learning to pick the pocket of Lon Chaney as Fagin in scraggly beard, tattered frock coat and top hat. Edouard Trebaol, as the Artful Dodger, coaches. On the same page, below, Isherwood pasted a photo of Coogan, washed and combed in a velvet suit, restored from vice to grace in Mr. Brownlow's book-filled study, smiled upon by plump, well-dressed members of the upper-middle class.

As with earlier albums and collections, Christopher kept this movie scrapbook meticulously. He made incisive one-line critiques of sixty-seven films in his clear, tiny handwriting, alphabetized by title. "Jackie Coogan mis-cast but unforgettable as Oliver," he wrote. "Edouard Trebaol almost faultless." Coogan was too tough for the part, convincing as a waif but lacking inner purity. Christopher thought him better suited to the ragamuffin ice-cream vendor he played in *Circus Days*: "Perhaps Jackie Coogan's best picture. At any rate, the one in which he seems most at home. The love scene belongs to Great Comedy."

In Rouen, Christopher pasted in cuttings in French about the film adaptation of Anatole France's novel *The Crainquebille Affair*, in which Crainquebille is diverted from suicide by "The Mouse," played by the Cooganesque Jean Forest. Of this film, Christopher—a devoted reader of Anatole France—wrote: "Almost perfect of its kind. Jean Forest justified his introduction into the story."[197] The milieu of poverty and the boy savior were right up Christopher's alley.

ROUEN WAS BORING, and Christopher entertained himself by corresponding "on an enormous scale" with friends and family and by observing three boys in the town, one working in a bike shop, one mending roads, one in the cinema. Eventually he found "some new zests" among his fellow students at Professor Morel's; one was from Scotland, one from Sweden, one from Siam—Niti Guptarakse. Niti Guptarakse was good-looking and—something that always drew Isherwood—tiny in stature. He stands out as evidently Isherwood's first friend with brown skin. They were photographed together in their dinner jackets and Guptarakse later visited London, where Kathleen pronounced him "attractive." As often happened at this time in his life, Christopher had invited more affection than he could handle. He told Falk that Guptarakse "was almost too friendly."[198]

While he was in France, a poem by Christopher appeared in *Public School Verse 1921–1922*. He had competed for selection with public-school boys all over the country and, characteristically, had submitted his poem in secret. It evokes a moment of Glory—anticipated, achieved, then lost—which is vaguely associated with a locale toward which, the poem implies but does not say, young men are marching: Mapperley Plains. The feeling of the poem is feet in motion, three stanzas of six four-beat lines, intriguingly varied and skillfully rhymed.

Isherwood later explained that he had written it while still in uniform and sweaty from an OTC field day during which he had been making up the verses in his head. He was inspired by a contest at Repton in which boys released balloons with postcards attached that requested any finder to write the landing location on the card and mail it back to Repton. In the contest, the balloon which flew furthest was the winner, but Christopher cared only for the sound of the unfamiliar place, Mapperley Plains. "The name thrilled me the instant I heard it, and I repeated it to myself again and again." In *Exhumations*, he was to identify this as the "magic" of place names—the very word used by a reviewer of *Public School Verse*, the Irish poet and novelist Katharine Tynan: "Not often does one find the Natural magic, but it is in C.W.B. Isherwood's 'Mapperley Plains.' [. . .] There is the authentic touch."[199] Natural "magic," a love of incantation, was to shape Isherwood's prose after he gave up poetry, and his love of incantation was to be channeled into his spiritual life when he learned to meditate by repeating a mantra.

In 1923, he was writing other things not intended for publication. Two that he destroyed—plays titled "In the Passage" and "One Man's God"—were evidently sex fantasies. In France, he wrote a story about moviegoing, "The Wrong God," to amuse Wintle, Paddy Monkhouse, and Falk. The protagonist, "Fryne—a real 'character,' like Sherlock Holmes; the complete hunter of Boys," realizes once parted that he cares for his moviegoing companion more than he cares for the flickering image of "Billy Brighteyes, the Wonder Kid" he has idolized on the screen. "Fryne's friend leaves for India; and Fryne, too late, discovers that he was keen on him all the time and only enjoyed the films because of his presence." (The storyline seems to have been triggered by a visit from long-lost Limerick movie-going companion Eddie Townshend the day after Christopher first saw Coogan in *Oliver Twist*.) Christopher told Falk not to "run away with the idea" that either he or Wintle was the Fryne in his story.[200] In fact, by comparing him with Sherlock Holmes, Christopher linked the Fryne character to G.B. Smith.

He and Smith had kept up a teasing, intimate correspondence. They exchanged startling gossip about Repton boys (Darling was among those labeled "hot stuff" for being precociously clever) and squabbled over Cambridge. Christopher had written to the College Tutor at Corpus Christi, William Spens, asking to change subjects from history to English. Spens said no. Christopher blamed Smith, who insisted Spens had made up his own mind. Smith, by way of an inappropriate suggestion, had loaned Christopher Norman Douglas's *South Wind*, about the imaginary Mediterranean island of

Nepenthe and its sexually freewheeling inhabitants, and suggested a trip to Italy together, just the two of them. Christopher resisted but sent provocative letters. Smith was bemused or pretended to be. "Your message from Isherwood left me rather foggy. Am I dull or do I expect too much from him? I think neither. As a matter of fact there <u>are</u> 'two of him, thank God.'"[201]

Isherwood was a chameleon, as Smith recognized. There were *more* than two of him. His mood and desires were constantly changing, and also his mode of self-presentation. In their surviving correspondence, Smith never addressed him twice by the same name:

> Dear Benjie (or shall I say Denis) [or do you prefer Marten]
> My dear Binj
> Dear Binge
> Dear Sir
> Liar & Slave
> Sweet lad
> My dear Bishy
> Dear heart
> My dear Tishy
> My dear Allen[202]

Don Bachardy was to show similar resourcefulness in salutations to Isherwood in the 1960s and 70s, for he was responding to the same quicksilver personality. Over fifteen years of letter writing, Bachardy used more than ninety names for Isherwood.

Smith's next proposal was that Christopher return to Repton in August, after Rouen, to help inaugurate Smith's new post as school librarian: "I am going to weigh in at once and rearrange the whole show by subjects & make a new complete card index cross-reference catalogue in the summer holidays." Smith was inviting assistants to stay with him and work six or seven hours a day. "I won't tell anyone you are coming or have been [...] To me the prospect of turning the whole place upside down is rather alluring."[203] Christopher agreed, arriving at Repton on July 28, while school was still in session, and staying in his old house, the Hall. He evidently felt most comfortable continuing the friendship through books—rearranging, recording, and systematizing.

RICHARD RETURNED TO St. Mary Abbot's Terrace from his first term at Northwood House thin and nervous with "a shrinking look," as Kathleen put it, and a tick: "the jerking up of the right shoulder as if in self defense &

the furtive look accompanying it seem to come on in fits." Possibly, Richard had Tourette's syndrome; later, he grunted and sometimes shouted obscenities, evidently involuntarily. Kathleen took him to a specialist who prescribed Swedish exercises, a mostly vegetarian diet, and "the country rather than London."[204]

Agatha Greene Trevor's son Raymond was in the care of the same specialist, so Kathleen took rooms in the village where the Trevors were spending the summer, Torrington in north Devon. Richard shared Raymond's nurse, who taught the exercises and performed the massage. Christopher joined the convalescent holiday on August 23.

In September, he caught up with his London life. He saw Hector Wintle every day, at the cinema, at the roller-skating rink, and roaming the streets. Wintle was now studying chemistry and physics at a crammer in order to pass an exam for medical school.

Christopher had abandoned his second Rugtonstead novel while in Rouen. He turned instead to a third novel that he was calling *Lions and Shadows*, and into which he put the best of his abandoned material. In his 1938 memoir *Lions and Shadows*, for which he was to recycle the title, Isherwood described the early novel as "a very typical specimen of the 'cradle-to-coming-of-age' narrative which young men like myself were producing in thousands of variations." In style, it was pastiche like "Philip Linsley's" novel, borrowing from the school-based novels of Hugh Walpole, Compton Mackenzie, and E.F. Benson, and "astonishingly slick." Such narratives, as he explained, were indelibly marked by the war: "we young writers of the middle 'twenties were all suffering, more or less subconsciously, from a feeling of shame that we hadn't been old enough to take part in the European war. The shame, I have said, was subconscious: in my case, at any rate, it was suppressed by the strictest possible censorship."

He was trying to write about something he was unwilling to face. In his fiction, he substituted the challenges of public-school life for the war, framing them as "A Test" that could make one a man. After all, the war culture—the military, the literature, the schools—had identified public school as preparation for war and promoted a commingled mythology of public-school games and fighting. He had been taken in by this trick as an adolescent, and he blamed himself. He told Upward after completing his first draft at the beginning of 1925 that he considered heroism "to be the curse of his novel."[205]

His title, *Lions and Shadows*, gestured vaguely toward his powerful, censored emotions. He had found the phrase in the preface to a 1923 collection of stories by an Irish journalist, C.E. Montague, who had worked with Allan Monkhouse at the *Manchester Guardian*. In a notably unclear preface, Montague implied that heroes—"mighty hunters of lions or shadows"—are men who are easily remembered rather than men who are necessarily good and that, in any case, writing is too slow to capture men who are truly vivid and exciting. Yet Montague tried to capture them, for he titled his book *Fiery Particles*, describing it as a collection of yarns about "wild bodies that want to be up and doing something."[206]

In *Lions and Shadows*, Isherwood was to explain that the title "was simply an emotional, romantic phrase which pleased me, without my consciously knowing why, because of its private reference to something buried deep within myself, something which made me feel excited and obscurely ashamed."[207] He chose it, like the title "Mapperley Plains," for its impenetrable incantatory magic. He did not want clarity on his father or the war. Clarity would have been unbearable.

3

Failed History Scholar, Published Novelist (1923–1929)

At Cambridge, Isherwood was to experiment with imaginative games, with alcohol, with sexual flirtations. The experiments were to end when he failed his second-year exams on purpose, rejecting the academic career planned with his mother. Afterwards, he was to focus on his writing and getting into films. To earn money, he tutored and became a secretary. *All the Conspirators*, his novel about the artistic young man struggling to break free of his mother's expectations, was accepted for publication in 1928. The neurosis that afflicted him, his brother, and the protagonist of this first novel was to lead Isherwood, that same year, to enroll in medical school, hoping to become a healer. He was to move out of his mother's house and live on his own, then move back in, all the while taking long breaks away from London, including his first trip to Germany.

CORPUS CHRISTI COLLEGE, CAMBRIDGE, 1923

Isherwood arrived at Corpus Christi College in the late afternoon of October 10 in pouring rain. He had a bad head cold. He was accompanied by his mother. By evening, she had curtains up and a fire lit in his rooms, F-3—a large sitting room and a bedroom one flight up, overlooking the New Quad. It was "New" in that it had been completed in 1827, reviving the Gothic style of the fourteenth century when the college was founded. After Kathleen returned home, she sent Isherwood the old nursery carpet from Wyberslegh "to lay down over the very shabby one now in his room."[1] Cambridge was, for Isherwood, a different kind of nursery, in which he was to be born anew and to try to take control of his life for the first time.

From the outset, he preferred Upward's rooms, below his on the staircase, "low-ceilinged and snug," with Upward's books, his three Dürer engravings, *Melencolia*, *St. Jerome*, and *The Knight, Death and the Devil*, and on the mantel "a pair of long-stemmed clay pipes and a little china skull." In this den, surrounded by memento mori, they began to develop an underground life. They hated the history course at Cambridge. They shut out their academic obligations and focused on their literary destinies, reading authors they selected themselves, writing stories, poems, and diaries for one another in assumed identities, notably as Edward Hynd and Christopher Starn, pornographers, and beginning to create the alternative world they eventually named Mortmere.[2] Isherwood made much of its genesis in *Lions and Shadows*: "Our conversation would have been hardly intelligible to anyone who happened to overhear it; it was a rigmarole of private slang, deliberate misquotations, bad puns, bits of parody and preparatory school smut." It was always very funny. "The mere tones of Chalmers' voice would start me giggling in anticipation, and I had only to pronounce some quite ordinary word with special emphasis in order to send him into fits."[3]

The Gothic menace of Cambridge colored their shared fantasies—medieval architecture combined with foggy weather. Their collaborative world often developed at night, with the youthful energy unleashed by darkness. "One evening, as we were strolling along Silver Street, we happened to turn into an unfamiliar alley, where there was a strange-looking, rusty-hinged little door in a high blank wall. Chalmers said, 'It's the doorway into The Other Town.'" In their imaginations, they squeezed through the doorway together, never admitting that "we were merely playing a sophisticated kind of nursery game."[4]

In the game, Isherwood and Upward's first name for their secret world was "Rats," for which in *Lions and Shadows* Isherwood credited the Chalmers character: "One evening, I happened to read aloud the name under a fluttering gas-lamp: 'Garret Hostel Bridge.' 'The Rats' Hostel!' Chalmers suddenly exclaimed." These "key-words [. . .] expressed the inmost nature of the Other Town."[5] Isherwood did not mention that the door on Garret Hostel Bridge recalled the jagged little doorway into the spaces behind the wainscoting at Marple Hall and at Tabitha Twitchit's house, where the rats ruled in his own favorite Beatrix Potter story, *The Roly-Poly Pudding*.

According to *Lions and Shadows*, Chalmers's "Rats' Hostel" phrase summed up "the special brand of medieval surrealism which we had made our own." They knew nothing yet of the surrealist movement in Europe. Their cult of the weird and foreboding drew on Dürer's animals and his scholastic and alchemical emblems. "Graveyards were 'rats' and very old gnarled trees, and cave mouths overhung with ivy."[6] They also drew on *Alice in Wonderland*, Grimm, Sir Thomas Browne, Poe, and the ballads.

The inhabitants of the Rats' Hostel were their "natural allies" against Cambridge and the history dons. On their side were their favorite writers, in particular Wilfred Owen, Katherine Mansfield, and Emily Brontë: "'Wilfred, Kathy and Emmy,' as we called them."[7] All three of these literary heroes were rebels who tried to expose in their writing the false pieties of the adult world and who died young, Owen on the battlefield and both women of tuberculosis. In fact, Mansfield, the New Zealand-born short-story writer, had died earlier that year, January 1923, aged thirty-four, attracting their attention.

In Upward's final undergraduate year, they were to move the Other Town away from Cambridge to "the edge of the Atlantic ocean," changing it into a village and deciding upon the name Mortmere. They developed Mortmere as a comic satire of English village life with many characters drawn from Isherwood's ancestral home, his family, and the villages and farms around Marple Hall. They also played with the stereotypes and conventions at work in the ghost stories and occult writing of Upward's cousin, Allen Upward, whose poetry was included in Ezra Pound's collection *Des Imagistes* (1914) and who was a prolific novelist and the author of a weirdly grandiose memoir in which he positioned himself among the greatest thinkers and writers as well as crowned heads, prophets, and seers.[8]

Isherwood and Upward turned Church, army, and industrial values upside down, indulging their tastes for pornography, satanism, coprophilia and necrophilia. They invented a pedophile Anglican rector, Reverend Welkin, abuser of choirboys; his drunken, lying fisherman friend, Gunball; the keeper of the Skull and Trumpet Inn, Sergeant Claptree; the engineer, Wherry, whose tunnel collapses on the first train through, killing all on board; the landowner, Henry Belmare, named after Isherwood relatives; Belmare's too-beautiful son and his mannish, artistic sister, Miss Belmare. Gaspard Farfox was a detective from outside the village, once described as a conjuror, once portrayed as a spy disguised in a false red beard.

According to *Lions and Shadows*, they struggled to find a plot in which all their characters could play a role; nevertheless they made "utterly fantastic plans" for a deluxe volume illustrated with real artworks, punctuated by firework explosions, accompanied by music from a gramophone sewn into the cover: "Our friends would find, attached to the last page, a pocket containing bank notes and jewels; our enemies, on reaching the end of the book, would be shot dead by a revolver concealed in the binding." Playing the game was more important than completing the book: "As long as *Mortmere* remained unwritten, its alternative possibilities were infinite; we could continue, every evening, to improvise fresh situations, different climaxes."[9]

Still, they generated plenty of written material, and some survives—stories and fragments, epigraphs from Villon, Blake, Whitman, Bacon, Baudelaire, and Shakespeare, lists of characters, 150 titles for proposed stories, a collation of the books of Mortmere with the books of the Bible, a map, and an "Introductory Dialogue" created in 1925 or 1926 after they had left Cambridge. Only two stories got finished—detective parodies that were not strictly about Mortmere, "The Little Hotel" (Upward) and "The Horror in the Tower" (Isherwood)— because the authors typically stopped writing once the direction of the story was sufficiently indicated to the other. Isherwood's lucid narrative control is already apparent as he parodies Conan Doyle and Edgar Allan Poe in, probably, 1924. Upward is persistently more experimental, even self-consciously modernist, using scientific words and tortured, difficult sentences.[10]

In May 1927, Isherwood wrote "The World War," satirizing his wartime experiences and fantasies. War breaks out during a drunken game of bowls on a summer Sunday morning at the Mortmere Rectory; the narrator occupies the café of a liberated town before engaging in inch-by-inch warfare at the edge of the Belmare Estate, including stupendenous mechanized fighting and gas attacks; countless men, disabled by the same mysterious wound, muffled in bandages, lie helpless in Miss Belmare's war hospital; from one of them, the narrator learns of the foreign monument commemorating the naked choirboy, Boy Radnor, who died "Exhausted by his heroic venery"[11] underneath the corpse of the enemy commander-in-chief; a gigantic air vessel twice circles the Mortmere Rectory, now the Headquarters of the General Staff, and then blows it up. "The World War" was energized by Isherwood's renewed friendship with Auden, who took an excited interest in Mortmere when he heard about it. The Mortmere vision of the sinister in the familiar and the gleeful Mortmere appetite for destruction and anarchy were to be carried into Auden's 1932 work *The Orators: An English Study* and into the theatrical collaborations between Auden and Isherwood, not least in the figure of Destructive Desmond the cabaret artist who destroys a Rembrandt to cheers from the audience and who was cut, to Isherwood's regret, from performances of *The Dog Beneath the Skin*.[12]

Upward produced his most significant Mortmere story, "The Railway Accident," in 1928, but afterwards he grew increasingly uncomfortable about the violence and pornography and refused an opportunity to publish it in the 1930s.[13] In 1952, he destroyed his Hynd and Starn stories and most of his Mortmere writings. Isherwood went away from creating Mortmere freer than he had ever been before; Upward went away more constrained. This foreshadowed their public literary destinies—Isherwood's repeated popular success and Upward's painful struggles to write and get published.

In *Lions and Shadows*, Isherwood recalled his first two terms at Cambridge as "amongst the most enjoyable parts of my whole life," and his and Upward's writing about this period is shot through with erotic energy. Upward was heterosexual, but the infatuation was intense on both sides. "[A]s long as I could be together with Chalmers, which was all day and most of the night, the word boredom didn't exist. I was in a continuous state of extreme mental excitement," wrote Isherwood. "They walked in a rapture of imagery," wrote Upward in *The Spiral Ascent* about his characters Richard Marple and Alan Sebrill. "Alan thought that no other activity on earth—not even making love—could compare with this savouring of words."[14]

But the bond between Isherwood and Upward was ruptured again and again. "If we used my sitting-room at all," Isherwood recalled in *Lions and Shadows*, "it was chiefly to escape from intrusions." There was an Isherwood who relished intrusions, and this triggered Upward's jealousy, particularly of Isherwood's friends among the Poshocracy, as Upward christened the titled, upper-class, wealthy, and good-looking undergraduates who were socially or athletically successful. Isherwood and Upward invented an imaginary third companion, the Watcher in Spanish Cloak, "a macabre but semi-comic figure, not unlike Guy Fawkes, or a human personification of Poe's watching raven." According to Upward's diary, "the Spanish Watcher is a symbol for the theory that everything (almost) that we do is self-conscious; we feel that we are acting before and addressing ourselves to an invisible personage who will appreciate our irony and general inimitability." In *Lions and Shadows*, Isherwood wrote that the Watcher in Spanish Cloak appeared to them "at moments when our behaviour was particularly insincere." It might also be said to embody Upward's jealousy and to make fun of it.[15]

Isherwood always found or invented someone or something to scrutinize and question his authenticity. "It was the Watcher, we said, who disapproved of my presence at Black's poker parties and vetoed all Ashmeade's invitations to bring Chalmers with me to coffee after Hall . . ." Isherwood could not resist the socializing, the college drinking club called the Young Visiters (after the 1919 novel with title misspelt by nine-year-old author Daisy Ashford and which Upward himself had joined), the play-reading society called the Grave Diggers, the Cambridge University Kinema Club. He was unsure of his identity, anxious and even guilty about his enthusiasms and pleasures, searching for a singular self. In a letter of November 1923, a few weeks before the end of Isherwood's first term, Paddy Monkhouse tried to reassure him: "nothing is more delightful than to keep changing one's pose, and ultimately to confront, say, over the luncheon table two acquaintances with totally different impressions of your character."[16]

It may have been during his first term that Isherwood, along with Upward, contributed some poems to a college magazine called the *Benedict*. When the poems were shown to him in the 1960s, Isherwood had trouble owning them. Two sonnets by him appeared in another ephemeral Corpus publication, *Fanfreluche*. One sonnet bid farewell to the poet's toy soldiers and a playmate grown cold; the other was addressed to a crucifix hanging in his room and—characteristically—questioned the purpose of sacrificial death: "You died, you died—but did you die for me?"[17]

Also in his first term, Isherwood heard the film producer George Pearson address the Cambridge University Kinema Club, and he joined the film club trip to the Gaumont Lime Grove Studios in London. The Kinema Club had just been founded by undergraduates Peter Le Neve Foster, Roger Burford, who became a close Isherwood friend, and Cedric Belfrage, who was in Isherwood's year at Corpus. In *Lions and Shadows*, Chalmers teases Isherwood that "as soon as I was inside a cinema I seemed to lose all critical sense." The Isherwood character objects that "I was and still am, endlessly interested in the outward appearances of people—their facial expressions, their gestures, their nervous ticks, their infinitely various ways of eating a sausage, opening a parcel, lighting a cigarette."[18] This was the voyeur in him and also the watcher for poses assumed by others. But in *Lions and Shadows* Isherwood hid the fully alert and critical film sensibility which he had already possessed as an undergraduate; as so often with what he cared for most, he mocked his obsession with the movies.

During his second term at Cambridge, he began to contribute reviews to a new (and short-lived) undergraduate magazine called the *Cambridge Mercury*, edited by Cedric Belfrage. Belfrage went on to become a theater and film critic and, for a time, Samuel Goldwyn's public relations man in London. Isherwood was later friendly with him in Hollywood until Belfrage, briefly a communist and even a Soviet spy, was forced out by McCarthyites.

Belfrage and Isherwood were hired as extras in George Pearson's *Reveille* in the Easter holidays 1924. The film was about the disillusion felt by some during the riotous celebrations at the end of World War I. Isherwood's scene was set in the Savoy Hotel ballroom in London on Armistice Day 1918. In *Lions and Shadows*, he described making himself up with laughable incompetence as a midshipman and dancing all day with a crowd in military uniform and evening dress. "Needless to say," he wrote, the shot in which he might have been recognizable, "was cut out of the finished picture." He didn't tell his mother much about the film, perhaps because it so precisely portrayed the standoff between them, she sorrowful at the war's close, he ready to celebrate. She noted, though, that he was paid twenty-four shillings, the first money he ever earned.[19]

The Cambridge University authorities frowned upon movies as a lowbrow distraction from academic work. The mainstream university weekly the *Cambridge Gownsman* boldly ran an unsigned editorial in May 1924, "In Defence of Cinema," observing that the older generation regarded the cinema "if not as an invention of the Devil, at least as one of his instruments." The editorial made the case for film as "a new form of amusement and a new form of art which already exercises very great influence throughout the world" and pointed out the issue of class as well as age: "those born and bred in humble and squalid circumstances" might receive "vast stores of amusement, content, and knowledge" from cinema. The *Cambridge Gownsman* championed the Kinema Club's first-ever debate about film on May 14, 1924, preceded by a special screening of *Hollywood*, James Cruze's 1923 film about the unreliable allure of stardom; possibly Isherwood attended.[20]

Being a member of the Kinema Club and a film reviewer made Isherwood officially anti-Establishment, even avant-garde. Some of his published reviews were about films he also critiqued in his film scrapbook, where he headed his one-liners "My private opinion . . ." (The Cambridge reviews were of reruns at local theaters; of course, all the films were still silents.) Differences between his two sets of reviews show how carefully he managed his role as a film reviewer. For instance, in his private scrapbook, he economically rubbished *Adam's Rib*: "The nadir of the Society-Extravaganza type of picture. Boring beyond words." Then, for the *Cambridge Mercury*, he produced over a hundred words and softened his blow: "Mr. de Mille sets out to prove that flappers are not so bad as they are painted. [. . .] The setting is florid and the story worked out at unnecessary length." He even managed to praise the actors for "capable performances within the limited scope of their parts."[21]

About a week after Isherwood's first review, the theater where *Adam's Rib* had been screened, the Rendezvous, was put out of bounds to members of the university by the ultra-conservative vice chancellor who happened to be Master of Corpus Christi. The Rendezvous was a dance hall as well as a movie theater. Two undergraduate dance clubs regularly met there, and tea dances were held on Saturday afternoons. These gatherings were frowned on by the university even more than moviegoing since female undergraduates were off limits to male undergraduates and mixing with non-university women at unsupervised parties was prohibited. The proctors, complete with bulldogs, were sometimes seen to snatch offenders from the dance floor. Undeterred, Isherwood reviewed one or two more films showing at the Rendezvous in the winter of 1924.[22]

The following autumn, during his fourth term, Isherwood contributed two full-page roundups of local cinemas to the *Cambridge Gownsman*. Rex Ingram's French Revolution movie, *Scaramouche*, he described as "a very good film, dealing with a hackneyed but arresting subject in an original way." He was weary of European history, and he had studied the French Revolution endlessly at Repton. He preferred *The Covered Wagon*. "It has atmosphere, it has glamour," he enthused: "In the opening sequence—a small, very ugly boy, playing a beautiful old song on a banjo and bawling it, one imagines, at the top of his ugly voice—the director, James Cruze, has managed to strike the keynote of the picture, and, what is more, he contrives never to get out of tune."[23]

The song was "Oh, Susanna," and the boy, kid brother of the heroine, was played by Johnny Fox, an American actor five years younger than Isherwood. Fox was not ugly; he was freckled and tough in a Cooganesque style, and his character, "Jed Wingate," enacts Isherwood's fantasy of the Wanderer, the American Boy. He gets away to summon help when the Indians attack the wagon train, and he makes it all the way to Oregon with his pioneer family to build a home in the wilderness. Here on a screen in Cambridge was the dream of North America that Isherwood had relished in talks by missionaries in Limerick, in childhood games, on cigarette cards collected from Canadian soldiers near St. Edmund's, and in earlier Westerns seen at the Gaiety.

During the Christmas vacation, 1923–4, Kathleen observed that Isherwood was depressed over the size of his college bills, but more important, "he feels the whole thing is so unclear & not helping him on to anything." In *Lions and Shadows*, Isherwood reported that his academic career went wrong at the start, when he read his first essay aloud to his tutor. "'Look here, Isherwood,' he appealed to me abruptly, 'don't you agree yourself that it's all tripe?'" Isherwood liked his tutor, but he couldn't concentrate in lectures, couldn't take notes, couldn't venture to ask a question, because he found the material so dry and the setting so grand. In *Lions and Shadows*, he described "as remarkable, almost miraculous" his 2:1 result in his first-year history examinations in May 1924.[24]

He later told an interviewer that because he had won the best history scholarship in the college, much was expected, not least that he would become an academic,[25] but he was looking for some other path forward. In early January 1924, he went to see a publisher in Covent Garden. Kathleen took this seriously enough that she, too, made enquiries about publishing. Isherwood also spent time on his writing and twice went to see his father's writer friend Ethel Mayne, casting her as his professional mentor. Mayne's novels and short stories won comparisons with Henry James and Katherine Mansfield, though her reputation came to rest on her biographies of Byron and of Lady Byron, published in 1912 and 1929 respectively, on her numerous other fact-based books, and on her translations from French and German. Perhaps Isherwood chose a woman mentor because he happened to know a woman who was a published writer, but Mayne is one of several women to whom he looked for private, almost secret, counsel, free of the bantering rivalry and flirtation characterizing his more public literary friendships with men. Allan Monkhouse, for instance, was a threat and the father of threats.

Kathleen had been suspicious of Frank's relationship with Mayne—sophisticated, bohemian, single, and nicknamed Venus suggesting her expertise in love—but Frank had assured Kathleen that the relationship was platonic.

Mayne affirmed this to Isherwood, who recalled in *Kathleen and Frank* that she "would always insist that they had never been more than friends." On the other hand, Mayne told Isherwood that he was "their spiritual son."

Like Allan Monkhouse, Mayne used the Bradshaw Isherwoods in her fiction. "India-rubber" is a story about a woman resembling herself who disappears from literary-artistic circles when her lover, a painter resembling Frank, marries a young, pliant bride. The painter's two loves meet and both silently conform like India-rubber to his preferred narrative about the friendship: *"There's no past . . ."* In "Still Life," Mayne reimagined Emily, Frank, and Kathleen—the trio of friends—as mother, son, and an interloping daughter-in-law, fictionally intensifying the connection between Emily and Frank and making Kathleen their victim. Isherwood relished the portrait of his grandmother lying serpentlike on "heaped cushions" in a still, shaded room, eying her daughter in-law, called Clare: "To look from Clare's ingenuous face to that upon the cushions was like looking from a bird to a snake."[26]

EARLY IN 1924, advised by the motorbike-riding lodger Mr. Browning, Isherwood bought a motorbike. In *Lions and Shadows*, he presented the motorbike as a response to "My 'war' complex": "'The Test' had now transformed itself into a visible metal contraption of wheels, valves, cogs, chain and tubes, smartly painted black." He felt the Poshocracy watching. "Isherwood becomes a hearty—here was a quaint new pose."

In *Lions and Shadows*, he humorously emphasized his fear of the motorbike, recalling that he had forced himself to "open her flat out" on the straight, country road and then "clung on, horribly scared, with the wind screaming in my ears."[27] In real life, he seems to have handled it competently enough. When his grandfather died on May 9, he rode the motorbike to Marple for the funeral. In June, he rode to Repton; in July, to St. Edmund's; and then a camping trip to the New Forest. In the autumn, though, he asked Browning to sell it.

In its place, "I had decided to keep a journal." Writing was a new version of the Test. This, too, Isherwood mocked: "It was to be modelled upon Barbellion's *Diary of a Disappointed Man*. My chief difficulty was that, unlike Barbellion, I wasn't dying of an obscure kind of paralysis—" Upward visited him in London around this time and also began a diary, titling his "Imaginary Diary of a Poet." In this diary, Upward reported that "Christopher has [illegible] changes of personality, and yet [illegible] he is one person." Isherwood had overlaid his new pose of "Isherwood the Artist" with an image of himself as "a kind of invalid," inspired by his current literary heroes: "Hadn't Kathy and Emmy been invalids? Didn't Baudelaire die of a frightful disease?"[28]

Many years later, in 1979, he was to explain, "I cherished a romantic notion that the artist *has* to suffer in order to create. I saw Mansfield as dying for her art, not just dying. I even called her 'a saint,' by which I meant a person whose chief characteristic is suffering." By 1979, he was to have a different notion of sainthood. "Prabhavananda taught me that a saint is a person who has attained enlightenment and whose chief characteristic is therefore happiness. Happiness doesn't, of course, protect a saint from being persecuted and martyred."[29]

When Isherwood was writing *Lions and Shadows* during 1937, he mocked his artist-invalid pose of the 1920s, because by 1937 melodrama and posing had become embarrassing and unacceptable to him. Yet, as a child and adolescent, he *had* been seriously ill, and he was genuinely encumbered by neuroses. At Cambridge, he was sometimes so vividly theatrical that Upward began to copy him without realizing it. A friend pointed this out to Upward, who reported in his diary toward the end of 1924: "my tone has become dramatic. This is just. My conversation is infused with the Christopheresque."[30]

In the autumn of 1924, Upward was allowed to change courses from history to English. He was extremely excited by his English lectures, in particular the ones given by I.A. Richards, exponent of the close reading of literary texts that was to become known by the title of his 1929 book, *Practical Criticism*. In his diary, Upward called Richards "an amazing genius." Isherwood, too, began attending Richards's lectures. In *Lions and Shadows*, he extolled Richards as "the prophet we had been waiting for." Richards was "our guide, our evangelist," who made them engage with modern literature, with T.S. Eliot, with the newspapers, with Freud: "Now, in a moment, all was changed. Poets, ordered Mr. Richards, were to reflect aspects of the World-Picture."[31]

This meant, according to *Lions and Shadows*, that "everything we had valued would have to be scrapped," in particular the Rats' Hostel and Mortmere: "we were banished from that world forever." In reality, nothing was that clear nor that sudden. On the contrary, after the first Richards lecture, Upward recorded: "In the evening, Christopher and I discussed Mortmere to some purpose; this was-to-be-shit comedy is now becoming allegorical tragedy." The day after that, they walked to Grantchester, talking all the way there and back, and "In the evening we went to our favourite post on Garret Hostel Bridge." After all, Eliot offered his own "rats' alley / Where the dead men lost their bones" in *The Waste Land*.[32]

Upward summoned the courage to approach Richards with a question after a lecture. Richards had been laying out his view that poetry was concerned with states of feeling while science was concerned with objective reality. Upward could not accept that poetry was only about feelings. In *The Spiral Ascent*, he was to portray Richards answering the post-lecture question impatiently, and he sensed that his question had hit a nerve. "His view that a poetic statement could not have any external 'referent' was, as I came to realise before long, central to his whole poetic theory. No wonder my doubts had irritated him a little." Upward blamed this philosophical difference for impeding his progress as a writer, saying that it was not until he found in Marx and Lenin a satisfactory philosophical account of what his poetry could be about, that he was able to write as he wanted.[33] But Upward's own personality and his fragile mental health were to offer an equal if not greater obstacle.

Isherwood's reaction to Richards was far less philosophical. Richards mostly guided him toward new reading material and an updated sensibility. Indeed, the lesson Isherwood took from Richards, that poets "were to reflect aspects of the World-Picture," contradicts the lesson Upward took, that poems couldn't refer to the external world. That autumn, in any case, Isherwood was far more affected by the travails of his inner life than he was by public lectures. He was fractious, unpredictable, temperamental. One night, Isherwood and Upward fought bitterly about Shakespeare, Isherwood asserting that Shakespeare could not draw character, and Upward wrote in his diary, "I could shoot Christopher in his bed."[34]

The pair were involved in founding a new college literary society for presenting original work. At the second meeting, Isherwood brought Christopher Jacobs (son of the writer W.W. Jacobs, remembered for his supernatural tale, *The Monkey's Paw*). Upward described Jacobs as "very pretty and apparently sincere. Christopher believes himself to be partly in love," and "I can sympathize." At the society, "All the buggers of the college took notice of the boy."[35] This kind of attention to one another's companions was constant and problematic, and Isherwood's relationships were consuming more and more of his emotional energy.

With Upward, he plotted against another Old Reptonian history scholar, Smyth, whom they had identified as their archrival and enemy. They nicknamed Smyth the Laily Worm after the Loathly Worm of the English ballad tradition, in which loathly means ugly. "He was the typical swotter, the bookworm, the academic pot-hunter," Isherwood wrote in *Lions and Shadows*.[36] The worm imagery reaches back to Isherwood's childhood snake phobia and to the jealous hysterical tears he had shed over the illustrated *Antony and Cleopatra*, where Shakespeare calls the deadly suckling asp a worm.

Smyth, or "Laily," denied being a boy-lover, yet he propositioned another Old Reptonian, Christopher Orpen, first plying him with sherry. Isherwood was friendly with Orpen and may have been keen on him at the time. He planned, like Hamlet, to expose Laily at a meeting of the Young Visiters club "by acting Laily's crime before his own eyes" during a game of charades.[37]

Christopher Orpen, like Christopher Jacobs, had attracted widespread admiration, and even Upward was obsessed with him, using the code "O-n" in his diary. Orpen was loaned a car by another undergraduate, which he passed off as his own. "He drives it very fast through the worst roads," Upward recorded. "Oh my gay robin beware of death's grin. The world would be blacker if you were killed." Upward was impressed when Orpen escaped with only a large fine after a crash and by Orpen's love affair with a chorus girl: "I feel I could fall at his feet and worship. The variety, life and eloquence." After an Old Reptonians dinner in March 1925, drunk, Upward himself propositioned Orpen.

Isherwood was to use some of Orpen's escapades in *The Memorial*, where the character Maurice Scriven embodies the carefree high spirits that he had admired in both Orpen and Micky Scott. Upward and Orpen invented and performed a card trick that persuaded their undergraduate audience they communicated by telepathy.[38] In *The Memorial*, Eric Vernon watches his father's friend, Edward Blake, the shattered war hero home from his liberating homosexual experiences in Berlin, use a magic trick to captivate the childlike risktaker Maurice, Eric's cousin, with whom the sexually repressed Eric is in love. Only Edward Blake and Eric Vernon recognize the sexual innuendo in the performance which triggers intense jealousy in Eric.

SUCH SEXUAL FLIRTATIONS were not on show at all in *Lions and Shadows*, where Isherwood also left out the death of Granny Emily from bronchitis and pneumonia, a blow that coincided tellingly for him with reading the life story of Oscar Wilde. Arguably, these experiences changed his life as much as anything he did include in the memoir.

"Christopher's grandmother taken ill & expected to die in the night," wrote Upward in his diary on November 10. "Christopher a little irritable. His home, to which he has been called, is a world of tears apparently."[39] Isherwood found Kathleen inconsolable. He went with her to register the death, then Raymond Smythies arrived, closely followed by men from the funeral parlor, wreathes, flowers, and visitors. He bought mourning clothes, wrote letters for Kathleen, answered the telephone. Then he accompanied Kathleen to find her father's grave, neglected since Frederick's death in 1905.

On November 15, Emily was cremated and her ashes scattered over the flower beds at Golders Green Cemetery. The next day, Isherwood and Kathleen laid wreathes on Frederick's grave in Brompton Cemetery. He returned in the evening to Cambridge, where Upward was hosting the new literary society in his rooms. "I read the first act of my play and some poems," Upward wrote in his diary. "Christopher stole in towards the end. He said that it was not the funeral that made him sad but his stomach. This is always out of order." Indeed, Kathleen's emotional needs were overwhelming her son. Two days later, according to Upward, "Christopher ill in hall and afterwards. I am to burn or hide his journal if he dies in the night."

Isherwood immersed himself in the biography of Oscar Wilde written by Wilde's friend, the journalist and critic Frank Harris. Upward was blind at first to the private struggle going on inside Isherwood over his sexuality, though he recorded key details: "Christopher reading a life of the fool Oscar Wilde. Why was the bugger's Christ so bad an artist? Francis entered later in the evening and infuriated Christopher. I did not notice this." David Francis was another undergraduate, pursuing Isherwood for sex.

On November 23, it was Isherwood's turn to present to the literary society, and he read his story "The Hero." "Christopher thinks it the best he has done," wrote Upward in his diary. That night, Isherwood showed signs of continuing inner crisis which he blamed partly on home duties and partly on Upward who saw beneath his poses and stripped them away:

> In the evening Christopher had a fit of misery. The old business of obligations and the social hell. He accuses me of having spoiled his life, destroyed his deliberately assumed illusions, his blagues. He says that he sees nothing but a wilderness before him; the interest has passed from everything; he believes in nothing. These fits are common with him. This one soon passed.[40]

The next day, Isherwood was again absorbed in reading Harris's biography. He had "ordered tea to be sent up for him alone" to Upward's rooms, where Upward found him finishing off the second volume describing Wilde's two years of hard labor, solitary confinement, and special punishments like having his books taken away, as Harris learned when he visited Wilde in prison—"an English prison with its insufficient bad food and soul-degrading routine for that amiable, joyous, eloquent, pampered Sybarite. Here was a test indeed; an ordeal by fire." From this brutal test, Wilde had salvaged his masterpiece, *De Profundis*, but his health was ruined, his dazzling career as a playwright over. Isherwood found Harris's account "Stirring, apparently," as Upward noted condescendingly.[41]

Wilde's was not a test Isherwood wanted to face. His reckless defiance of British middle-class values had obvious appeal to any young rebel; however, his fate was a warning to Isherwood—himself "amiable, joyous, eloquent, pampered"—to follow a less self-destructive path. Through most of his life, Isherwood was to preserve himself strategically from scandal or prosecution. In his encounters with institutional power and the law—from the Gestapo and police to the FBI and the Hollywood studios—he was to employ the circumspection about his sexuality that Wilde had abandoned.

One of the most striking and suspenseful themes in Harris's account is Wilde's persistent refusal to save himself. Harris described the conversation in which he warned Wilde not to bring his libel against Queensbury: "all British prejudices will be against you," since Queensbury would be perceived as a father trying to protect his son. "Don't commit suicide." At this early stage, Harris had urged Wilde to go abroad. Later, when the judgment went against Wilde, and his solicitor offered to delay the arrest long enough for Wilde to escape to Calais, Wilde still refused, as he did even when his friends Robbie Ross and Reggie Turner pleaded with him and when Ross returned a second time with a further plea from Wilde's wife Constance. When Wilde was released on bail, Harris arranged a brougham and a steam yacht on the Thames to take him to France. Wilde again refused the chance to escape, saying, "I'm caught, Frank, in a trap, I can only wait for the end."[42] The brougham and the boat continued available for three days. Still Wilde would not leave.

Hard on the heels of his grandmother's death, with the newly suffocating burden of his mother's need for emotional intimacy unrolling into the future along with her expectations for his narrow professional life, Isherwood's encounter with Wilde's downfall and Wilde's refusal to save himself, began a slow interior upheaval. Isherwood realized that he must not continue resigned; he must act; he must free himself from the trap; he must escape.

He insisted that Upward read Wilde for himself, and Upward conceded that *De Profundis* "has points." Isherwood remained what Upward called "touchy" to the end of term, and they were fiercely quarrelsome even though they shared some fantastic and terrifying insights walking around at night, often drunk. Sometimes Upward empathized, sometimes he kept his distance. "This triviality and meanness in his nature is becoming very noticeable," he wrote. Upward wasn't at ease with Isherwood's friends and especially with Isherwood's boys. They went to a concert at St Bene't's Church: "Christopher's little chastity pimp and mental bumboy was lying in his bosom during the playing. Christopher wore patent leather shoes—as he nearly always does on Sunday. However they seemed more remarkable to-day." After the concert there was an unpleasant exchange. "I left him with the determination to avoid him for several days."

When Isherwood next appeared at Upward's rooms, Upward deliberately insulted him and then shared aloud his unflattering description of Isherwood in his diary. Yet the night after that, having evidently cleared the air, they worked on committing Mortmere to paper, "Christopher dictating."[43]

In *Christopher and His Kind*, Isherwood recalled that "At college, he had at last managed to get into bed" with another boy, and he attributed this "to the initiative of his partner, who, when Christopher became scared and started to raise objections, locked the door, and sat down firmly on Christopher's lap." Possibly he was referring to Christopher Jacobs, for Upward recorded that "Christopher has discovered that Jacobs is not so innocent as he supposed," and then two weeks later, that Isherwood's "passion" for Jacobs "has lapsed lately; in fact, he has renounced homo-sexualism. (Although he intends to possess O-n to-morrow night after the college banquet.)"

Things did not go according to plan on the night of the college banquet, the last night of term. It was formal dress with academic gowns, and wine was poured generously, all in commemoration of the college founders. Afterwards, Isherwood and Upward went back to Upward's rooms, where they were joined by members of the Poshocracy, including many Old Reptonians. All were drunk, and they began to amuse themselves by going through Upward's possessions and then by flicking slices of butter at the ceiling. Upward sensed a plot. "They had obviously come up with the fixed though drunken intent of spoiling my rooms. I therefore went methodically about spoiling their clothes; I did it with a buttered broom," Upward wrote in his diary. He applied butter to the backs of everyone's dinner jackets, then turned off the lights for an instant and threw a lump of butter into the crowd. It landed on the silk lapel of a rugby player who came for Upward and buttered his hair. Upward, infuriated, "attempted to kill him," but someone intervened. "I then proceeded to insult the poshocracy."

What most upset Upward about having his rooms spoiled was that Isherwood made no move to help him. "Christopher was quite incompetent. He was perfectly unaware of all the trouble," Upward recorded, and was then "led away to bed" by two of the party. "I sat down and wrote a letter to Christopher in which I broke with him forever." Decades later, when Upward fictionalized the episode in his trilogy, he pronounced himself still mystified: "He can't have been so drunk as to have been totally unaware of what the poshocrats had been up to. Why hadn't he made at least some gesture against them, however ineffectual, given some sign that he was on my side, not on theirs?"[44]

Upward never delivered the friendship-ending letter, partly because he persuaded himself that drink probably *had* incapacitated Isherwood. Evidently, it did not occur to him that Isherwood *wanted* to be incapacitated. Isherwood simply could not face the pressure to begin a full-fledged physical sex life combined with—and conflicting with—the new pressures from home.

In *Lions and Shadows*, Isherwood left open, provocatively, the question of why Upward's rooms had been wrecked: "As for the alleged 'conspiracy,' I have never quite made up my mind whether to believe in it or not. That the Poshocracy should all have assembled, without invitation, in the rooms of such socially insignificant people as ourselves, was certainly rather queer."[45] He constructed his sentence to close on the word "queer" with its double meaning, raising a teasing question as to what the invading Poshocrats saw in the friendship between Upward and Isherwood, two of the most beautiful boys in the college.

On their return to Upward's rooms from the banquet, before the arrival of the marauding Poshocracy, they had in fact been accompanied by David Francis, the undergraduate who had been pursuing Isherwood for sex and who felt he was in love with him. Francis had taken Isherwood, a few days earlier, to dine at the Pitt Club, looked on by Upward as "the supreme poshocracy club," and Isherwood came away "enraged."[46] He may never have been sexually attracted to Francis, but he permitted his advances up to a point and was apparently flirtatious.

After the end of term, Francis wrote accepting Isherwood's final rejection: "Thank you for saying the worst; of course one knew it all the time." He had evidently accused Isherwood of being scared to commit to a physical relationship. "As to my accusation of being afraid. There is this much of truth in it. When you feel a friendly impulse I don't think you give way to it for fear of the consequences."[47]

During the holidays, Upward's anger turned to depression. He did not blame Isherwood; he blamed his own failure to write a poem good enough to survive his death. He longed for the courage to drown himself; he couldn't write and abandoned his diary. Nevertheless, when the new Cambridge term began, in mid-January 1925, Upward found Isherwood waiting in his rooms and recorded—with a self-conscious deletion—"Very gradually he brought me to life again. He has been happy, he has written. The novel is finished. I felt a real love for him intense as only chaste love of friends can be."[48]

THOUGH ISHERWOOD HAD remained passive during the fight in Upward's rooms, he poured energy into the novel, which he completed during the Christmas vacation, working constantly and hiding from his mother. He had avoided confrontation and sex and reserved himself for this work of the imagination. It was a near-final draft of his first *Lions and Shadows*, about a romantic friendship between two boys, Charles Franklyn and Leonard Merrows.

The boys meet at a roller-skating rink like the rink where Isherwood himself often roller-skated in Kensington. They skate, have tea and cakes, and flirt chastely. One of the boys is older, already working as a journalist. The younger boy's parents are dead, and he is being raised by an aunt and uncle who mostly ignore him. He has not been allowed to attend boarding school like others of his upper-middle-class background because he once had rheumatic fever, and the doctor warns he may have a weak heart. He studies with tutors, longing to have friends, to play sports and games. One day, the two boys bump into each other away from the rink, and the older boy, Charles Franklyn, invites the younger one, Leonard Merrows, home to his nearby lodging house.

In his room at the lodging house, all Charles's life and interests are on display, including photographs of his friends, "people I was at school with" at the imaginary boarding school, Rugtonstead, that Leonard has longed to attend. "'I—I say!' he almost shouted at Franklyn. 'Were you at Rugtonstead?'"

What intrigues Leonard most, though, is Charles's writing:

> He moved over towards the window and the typewriter:
> "Did you write all this?" he asked in tones of awe, gazing at the tumbled sheets covered with small handwriting and scored with corrections.
> "I did. Every bit of it."

"Tumbled sheets" might equally appear on the bed of lovers, and the phrase highlights the erotic thrill of exposing something so private, so intense, as writing.

When Leonard finds notes about the skating rink, Charles acknowledges he is setting a novel there and that Leonard will be in it. Leonard finally approaches the typewriter. "'How do you work this?' he asked. 'I'll show you,' said Charles rising."[49] A typewriter was even more important and personal to Isherwood than a camera. It was far more expensive than a camera, and for capturing his world, it was the camera's secret, demonic double, capable in his hands of far greater depth and complexity.

Charles tells Leonard that the novel will be called *Lions and Shadows*. This was also Isherwood's real title for the novel in which Charles's proposed novel is mentioned. The device, novel within novel, is called *mise en abyme*. The technical name derives from heraldry, that old obsession of Isherwood's, where it refers to the practice of putting a miniature shield bearing the coat of arms at the center of the main shield bearing the exact same coat of arms. As a precocious beginner author, Isherwood was terrifically excited by the interrelation between life and art epitomized in the mise en abyme. He was devoted to a 1923 novel by Hope Mirrlees, *The Counterplot*, about a young woman who writes a play that is acted by friends and family in the garden of her family's country house. The play within the novel is an auto sacramental, a dramatic presentation of the mystery of the Eucharist, set in a convent in late-medieval Spain. *The Counterplot* explores the ways in which art can transpose life into something else, just as the Catholic Eucharist transposes the bread and wine into the body and blood of Christ. This was to be a favorite theme for Isherwood, the similarities between imaginative transformation

3: *Failed History Scholar, Published Novelist (1923–1929)* / 175

and religious ritual. "I find I know whole passages of it nearly by heart," Isherwood was to write of *The Counterplot* in 1955. "It must have been one of the truly 'formative' books in my life."⁵⁰

In the 1938 memoir that he also called *Lions and Shadows*, he described coming across the mise en abyme effect in André Gide's 1925 novel *Les Faux-Monnayeurs* (*The Counterfeiters*). In *Les Faux-Monnayeurs*, an imaginary novelist and diarist, Edouard, is writing a book called *Les Faux-Monnayeurs*, about a gang making false coins. Edouard has never seen a counterfeit coin, but when he tells the title of his book to his friends, one of them, Bernhard, his so-called secretary, pulls a counterfeit coin from a pocket and says: "But why begin with an idea? [. . .] Why not begin with a fact?"

Isherwood recalled that he had first learned about Gide's novel in Forster's *Aspects of the Novel* (1927); what remained in his mind long-term was "my conception of Forster's conception of Gide's original idea."⁵¹ This phrasing conjured a mise en abyme of literary influence; Isherwood introduced Forster as a counterfeit Gide, telling the truth by admitting a fake. So powerful was the impression made by Forster's idea of Gide that Isherwood forgot about Hope Mirrlees, until 1955.

Isherwood read his novel to Upward on January 18; they stayed up all night together. "As a whole, I think it fails, but there are many parts which show that his next will be a great work," wrote Upward in his diary. "Christopher has not slept for two days, yet he does not seem to be tired."⁵² Upward often recalled the all-night session, which seemed to make up to him for the night of the banquet.

In evident revolt against Kathleen's needs, Isherwood now became preoccupied with emotional restraint, leaping up and announcing to his circle of undergraduate friends as they listened to Beethoven's emotion-laden *Eroica* Symphony that "Sentimentality only exists when there is no restraint in relationships between persons."⁵³ His objection to sentimentality was to increase for some years. He was all in on his writing, at the expense of everything else, and he asked Ethel Mayne to read his novel *Lions and Shadows*.

Mayne told him over tea on March 31 that the novel "was complete tripe." Isherwood was morally and physically crushed. Kathleen noted in her diary that "he came back depressed, I know how much it meant to him." In the memoir *Lions and Shadows*, Isherwood did not reveal much more, even though he bravely hyped the scene. He concealed Mayne's identity, expressing only her view that he had yet to find a worthy subject.⁵⁴

He survived the blow partly because he was already three weeks into writing a new novel titled *Christopher Garland*, "a study of a Cambridge young man's life." By mid-April, he was reading *Christopher Garland* aloud to Kathleen, as if to warn her that he no longer planned to be a librarian. For the hero is "gradually committed to art—to the art which he had, at first, not taken very seriously."[55]

ALL THE WHILE, the second-year Cambridge exams, the Tripos, were looming. Isherwood resolved not to try to please his mother or fulfill the expectations of anyone else. "I knew I could never get a First; a Second I scorned," he later wrote. "Rather than that, I would fail altogether." He did not want to return to Cambridge the following autumn after Upward was gone. "I wanted to learn to direct films."[56]

At the time, he confided only in Upward, who, as Upward wrote in his diary, "failed to discourage him." In *Lions and Shadows*, Isherwood claimed that after briefly attempting to cram, he burned his history notes and sold his books to prevent himself from backing out. He went to his exams without any exact plan: "The paper was before me on the desk, the ink was in its bottle, and there lay the printed question-sheet. And now, at length, I had to ask myself: what exactly was I going to do?"

He dismissed any suggestion that he had acted heroically or to achieve a public effect: "Wasn't this the opportunity of a lifetime—for a communist manifesto, a scalding satire, a magnificent passage of obscene libel, a frank reasonable open letter to the authorities on education and the inalienable rights of youth? Of course it was. And I missed it. Alas, I was no Shelley."

Nor was he Oscar Wilde on public trial at the Old Bailey. He had wanted to reframe his destiny with a minimum impact on the university, "this act of mine was a strictly private affair: it had nothing to do with them, personally."[57] It was a quiet act of resistance. And yet the whole episode sets him and his memoir apart among the many written by his generation. In order not to attract attention to himself by leaving the examination hall early, he filled the time in play—writing one answer as concealed verse, another in the style of the humor magazine *Punch*, a third facetiously questioning the question, a fourth as a sonnet, a fifth complaining about the decoration of the room.

He took some pride in his answers, recalling that he copied them out so he could show them to Chalmers. The "private affair" was nevertheless an exhibition for Chalmers's benefit—and for Kathleen. On the day of the exams, Isherwood revealed all in a letter to her, and she "felt quite stunned," as she wrote in her diary.[58] She, like Upward, believed the outcome would have been different if Spens had allowed Isherwood to read English.

It was not until June 18 that Spens telegrammed to London instructing Isherwood to return for an audience. In *Lions and Shadows*, Isherwood wrote: "What was there to say? My act now seemed more than ever unreal to me:

failing the Tripos had merely been a kind of extension of dream-action on to the plane of reality. How was I to tell the tutor that we had often plotted to blow him sky-high with a bomb?" It was, in a sense, the fulfillment of all that Mortmere meant to him and Upward.

Spens invited Isherwood to withdraw voluntarily rather than be sent down, and Isherwood agreed. "I wasn't to be disgraced. I thanked him. He wished me luck. We shook hands."

In *Lions and Shadows*, he finished off his Cambridge chapter with a revealing and entertaining fiction—that he later heard that "Mr. Holmes had got possession, by intrigue or theft, of my Tripos papers; and kept them, ever since, in a locked drawer. I hope this is true. It would be just like him."[59] There is no evidence Smith ever saw the papers, but he invited Isherwood for a weekend to review his situation. Having escaped the fortress of academe that Smith had opened to him, Isherwood avoided Smith's further advice.

He had officially and publicly joined the bad boys. He was now "Outcast, subject to disapproving glances," as he wrote in a farewell poem, "The Recessional from Cambridge," which rejoiced in Mortmere and in the romantic sensibility he shared with Upward: "Yes, tutor, two young men must go alone / Into the night, because Beauty ailed them at the bone."[60] All his years of carefully planned and expensive education, Kathleen's resolve at the outbreak of war that he would become a don, her hope that he would help support the family as a librarian, were exploded. The conventional upper-middle-class future to which Isherwood had agreed in order to please her was rejected. No clear path lay before him.

LONDON, 1925

The week before withdrawing from Cambridge, Isherwood had already made a serious effort to get work as a screenwriter with Stoll Pictures. Sir Oswald Stoll was then the biggest filmmaker in Britain. Isherwood had a preliminary interview at the Stoll offices on the edge of Soho and secured a further interview for himself and his Cambridge University Kinema Club friend Roger Burford, also a writer of fiction and poetry and, eventually, a screenwriter.

While waiting for the further interview, he got to work on his novel. He left London for the Isle of Wight, where he lodged at Marine Villa in Freshwater Bay for just over three weeks. He pressed Upward to join him: "this is Heaven," he wrote, highlighting the possibilities for serious writing. "One can walk down to the beach and back in two minutes while debating the next paragraph."[61] Upward arrived to find that Isherwood had fallen in love with a teenager called George Peck, a cockney on holiday with his parents.

By now, Upward better understood Isherwood's sexual inclination. "I like young girls and women of thirty. The purity and seriousness of young girls," he had written in his diary in April. Isherwood liked the purity and seriousness of young boys, so Upward tried to view them through Isherwood's eyes: "In afternoon saw Joseph Cox the newsagent's boy and interest of Christopher. Surprised to find him not ugly."[62] He was excited by Isherwood's attempt to jump class romantically, and he grew accustomed to drinking with George Peck's father in the bar of the Albion Hotel every night, telling himself he was happy for any opportunity to associate with a cockney and learn about the working class. "Towards ten Christopher and George would come into the bar and sit looking at one another."

Upward cherished Isherwood's confidences, recording in detail what Isherwood said about the love affair: "I have never been allowed to live before this. This is the first time I have been really glad that I am alive." George preferred girls. "Christopher depressed because George had kissed him. 'Thought nothing of it. Simply a joke. He told me that when a girl looks at him in a certain way his spine goes cold. I see now what hopeless odds I have against me.'"

Isherwood soon stopped trying to persuade Upward that he was glad of his presence: "You and George. The two worlds won't fuse." After four days, he asked Upward to leave. Upward felt "Much hurt" and suggested to Isherwood that they "must part forever."[63]

Neither Upward nor Isherwood mentioned George Peck in published accounts of their friendship. Isherwood, though, made an album of the holiday with a glamorous studio portrait of Upward and a shot of Peck in white trousers and dark blazer gazing at the sea from the rail of a ship, his dark hair ruffled by the wind, his round-cheeked face alert, petal lips half open. Isherwood managed to continue the romance during August at lodgings in Reading.

In *Lions and Shadows*, he was to recall that on the Isle of Wight, "I had half-consciously assumed a slight Cockney twang," in hopes of befriending two local fishermen. He called cockney his "disguise-language."[64] Chapter 6 commemorated the Isle of Wight as the locale where Isherwood's fictional self watched the members of his own caste on holiday and recognized that he did not fit in. He made clear that he was attracted to the working class because he was in flight from his own and, without using explicit vocabulary, he made clear he was in flight because he was homosexual: "People like my friends and myself, I thought, are to be found in little groups in all the larger towns; we form a proudly self-sufficient, consciously declassed minority." Isherwood's narrator in *Lions and Shadows* is lonely, melancholy, tired of never belonging: "Does anybody ever feel sincerely pleased at the prospect of remaining in permanent opposition, a social misfit, the rest of his life?" He is adamant that until he finds a place "in the scheme of society," his writing "will never be any good"; he can write only for his homosexual minority, "the connoisseur and the clique," the handful who already understand him.[65] By the time he wrote this passage, German had replaced cockney as the language of disguise and then as the language of access—to sex, in Berlin.

Without an institution like school or university in which to hide, Isherwood began generating impressions to make Kathleen feel comfortable. After Freshwater, he told her he had been invited to stay in Reading, where he could continue with his novel. "[T]he Morgans have a beautiful house standing in a large garden sheltered from road & Mrs Morgan & George Peck fill up the time with different forms of entertainment," as Kathleen understood. When he postponed his return to London, she persuaded herself to sympathize: "On Monday they were out in a boat for 12 hours—so it seems a pity to come back except for the day on Friday to interview the Stoll people."[66] Kathleen almost certainly had not read Isherwood's short story, "The Old Game," with its sexual consummation in a boat, but Isherwood may have been trying to fulfill this fantasy.

He made the day trip to London for the Stoll interview on August 7. He and Burford met with Stoll himself and a colleague at the Cricklewood Studios, in north London, where they were ignominiously rebuffed, which partly explains why in *Lions and Shadows* Isherwood underplayed his knowledge of the movies and his ambition to write them. His hoped-for screenwriting career did not launch. Burford later blamed Isherwood, recalling that Stoll pointed to some shelves loaded with popular fiction and told them, "You will have to read all these books." Isherwood, liberated from Cambridge for not doing the work set him and always discriminating about what he read, reportedly asked, "Why?" It must have seemed obnoxious. Isherwood and Burford next wrote to George Pearson, for whom Isherwood had worked on *Reveille*, and Pearson told them to wait a year and try again.[67]

In the meantime, they maintained their film connections by joining the Film Society founded in London that May to show films overlooked by commercial theaters. Ivor Montagu, who had been director of the Cambridge University Kinema Club in 1924 and who had reviewed films in the same Cambridge publications as Isherwood, also lived in Kensington and was among the founders, mostly established filmmakers and critics.

ISHERWOOD WAS TURNING twenty-one, and he decided to use birthday money from Kathleen to buy a car. Mr. Browning again advised. They chose a secondhand Renault, olive green and "enormous," according to *Lions and Shadows*, "a five-seater which could hold seven—with great brass headlamps, a gate-change gear and black leather upholstery like a cab."⁶⁸ Mr. Browning gave him two lessons, and by the time his birthday came, on August 26, Isherwood was able to drive Kathleen, Richard, and Nanny to Richmond Park solo.

Uncle Henry marked Isherwood's coming of age by inviting him to lunch and proposing that they sell Marple Hall. Isherwood agreed. "Frightfully upset," Kathleen lamented to her diary, "the Christopher of old is dead."⁶⁹ Henry was beleaguered by taxes, caretakers, repairs, and non-payment of rent by at least one tenant farmer; however, he decided to postpone the sale and try to let the property instead.

Meanwhile, Eric Falk had introduced Isherwood to the Mangeot family: André, a Belgian violinist, Olive his wife, and their adolescent sons Fowke and Sylvain. In *Lions and Shadows*, where he disguised the Mangeots as the Cheurets, Isherwood claimed the Renault was his entrée. The younger son, Sylvain, whom Isherwood called "Edouard" (his second name in real life) was laid up with a badly cut knee; "wouldn't I, perhaps, offer to take Edouard out in the car to Richmond Park?"⁷⁰ Kathleen understood that Isherwood's French played a role, since André Mangeot, whose first language was French, needed an English-speaking assistant to help run his chamber group, the International String Quartet.

In addition to the car, Isherwood purchased his own typewriter, a Corona, which he took to the Mangeots' in the mornings and which he used at home for his own writing. The Mangeots lived in a mews house in Cresswell Place, South Kensington. In *Lions and Shadows*, Isherwood described their household and the professional arrangements of the string quartet as a warm enveloping chaos taking place in a mixture of English and French, "nothing was planned, forced, formal, consciously quaint."

There were mountains of letters to answer, concert tours to plan, recordings to schedule. "M. Cheuret," as Isherwood labeled André Mangeot in *Lions and Shadows*, had business stationery printed listing Isherwood with the quartet members. "'Secretary: Christopher Isherwood'—with what furtive pride I read and re-read those three words! They were my passport to the great outer world, the world beyond the schoolroom windows, which I had waited so long and so impatiently to enter."⁷¹ The new life he depicted was not unlike Nicholas Nickleby's career as "Mr. Johnson," launched into theatrical bohemia by Vincent Crummles with the script of a French play: "Just turn that into English, and put your name on the title-page."⁷²

In October, Isherwood drove the quartet in his Renault on a mini-tour through Sussex and Kent, including two performances at boarding schools. There were other excursions, to Sylvain's prep school and performances in Cambridge. Isherwood attended a broadcast at Savoy Hill, concerts at the

Chenil Gallery on the King's Road, and took tickets at a subscription series in Westminster and at Queen's Hall. By the end of October, he began to receive a salary of £1 a week and 10 percent of the quartet's takings. The musical standard was not high. The composer Benjamin Britten rated them "intelligent players," but observed they "aren't really first class intrumentalists." Mangeot was even weaker as a soloist; Britten once described him performing Vivaldi and Haydn concerti "v. badly" and labeled a broadcast of sonatas by English composers "pretty bad."[73]

It wasn't the music that attracted Isherwood, but the family. He stayed for supper and sometimes arrived in time for breakfast at 7 a.m. He went to the theater or to the Film Society with Olive. The Mangeots were gifted at sports like the Monkhouses and claimed among them numerous trophies in tennis and squash. Britten enjoyed playing tennis with them more than playing music.[74] "I had long since fallen in love with the entire family," wrote Isherwood of the Cheurets in *Lions and Shadows*. This was just how he described the fictional relation between Eric Vernon and the Scriven family in *The Memorial*: "For he was in love with them, it was nothing less." And just what he had read in Forster's *Howards End* of Helen Schlegel falling in love with the Wilcoxes and in Virginia Woolf's *To the Lighthouse* of Lily Briscoe falling in love with the Ramsays.[75] And so it would be for Isherwood with other families he was yet to meet in America—the Viertels, the Kiskaddens, the Stravinskys, Iris Tree and her sons, Dodie Smith and Alec Beesley, and even the unconventional family of monastics assembled at the Hollywood Vedanta Society in the 1940s. He was to make a habit of infiltrating, adopting, becoming intimate, seeking "to be acknowledged by them as elder brother and son," as he put it in *Lions and Shadows*.[76]

In *Christopher and His Kind*, Isherwood explained that "Olive was, in a sense, a mother figure in Christopher's life and, as such, a rival to Kathleen. But she was totally undemanding and unpossessive and she never tried to influence him in any direction." Kathleen's diary jealously records plenty of occasions when Olive did influence Isherwood, including asking for his attention when he was trying to write or study. But he did not seem to mind; after all, Olive was a mother figure he chose for himself. He was attracted by her informality and by what he described in *Lions and Shadows* as Madame Cheuret's "genius for making herself comfortable." Kathleen made him anxious; Olive did the opposite: "she was always uncoiling, gently relaxing—and we all, to some extent, relaxed with her."[77]

Relations with the Mangeots grew complicated, as with the Monkhouses. Olive fell in love with Christopher, and Christopher fell in love with Sylvain. Auden made a note in a diary: "O's children are growing up, and she is estranged from her husband. She too wants both son and lover and falls in love with him. C wanting a wife too, falls in love with S, O's youngest son. S has a transference on C, and wants him to be an elder brother, not a husband."[78]

Isherwood explored this new set of star-crossed passions in a novel he began at the start of 1926, *The Summer at the House*. It featured a doomed love triangle—a tutor in love with a boy pupil and the mother in love with the tutor. The novel "was inspired, vaguely, by my vision of the life of the Cheuret family," he said in *Lions and Shadows*.[79] As yet, Isherwood had no opportunity for an open, fully-fledged romantic and sexual life of his own, and so like Puck making sport of Oberon and Titania in *A Midsummer Night's Dream*, he twisted and disrupted conventional bonds among others—undermining father figures, redirecting the love of mother figures toward himself, and loving young boys who embodied his own self-image.

Nevertheless, he imagined a world in which he might be able to live differently, and he continued to explore this in his fiction. *The Summer at the House* borrowed its utopia from Romer Wilson's *The Death of Society: A Novel of the Future* (1921), about a young English war veteran who is bewitched by the wife of his elderly host, a philosopher and critic, in a remote house in Norway. Wilson presents the affair as a mystical love, above sexual passion, a love that might be possible "after the death of society." Her Englishman says, "I am so happy that I love everybody. I love the whole house"[80]—again as Isherwood had Eric Vernon say of the Scrivens in *The Memorial* and Isherwood had himself say of the Cheurets in *Lions and Shadows*.

Olive Mangeot was English, but Madame Cheuret "dark and elegant, a cigarette between her sharply-coloured lips, was rather my idea of a Russian woman out of a Tchekhov story," wrote Isherwood, acknowledging how he saw in his real-life models character types from his reading. In *The Memorial*, he fictionalized Olive Mangeot more thoroughly, imagining her in youth and age as two entirely different characters, as he later explained in *Christopher and His Kind*: "He had put her doubly into *The Memorial*—in the characters of Margaret Lanwin (Olive as she then was) and of Mary Scriven (Olive as she might be in later life)."[81] To both characters he attributed the acceptance, the virtually unconditional motherlike love, that permitted his friendship with Olive to flourish even after he emigrated to the U.S. Of course, neither was based exclusively on Olive; Mary Scriven with two children, poorer cousins of the heir to the estate, inhabits the position of Aunt Esther Toogood, Kathleen's earlier rival, and bears the name of Isherwood's other aunt, Mary (Moey) Bradshaw Isherwood.

André Mangeot later blamed Isherwood for causing emotional turmoil in his household, telling a mutual friend: "Oh, yes, I knew him—to my great sorrow. He broke up my life!"[82] In fact, trouble between husband and wife had begun before Isherwood's arrival on the scene. André was accustomed to having affairs, and until she met Isherwood, Olive accepted them. In 1931 she divorced André, citing a young woman violinist. By then, André evidently knew that Isherwood had introduced Olive to sexual partners, for instance arranging a London hotel assignation between Edward Upward and Olive in the summer of 1929.[83] One of André's affairs was with Rachel Monkhouse who sometimes sang with the quartet; this relationship, too, was facilitated by Isherwood who took them out together in his Renault.

In *Lions and Shadows*, Isherwood transformed André Mangeot into a humble working artist and claimed he had been attracted to Cheuret's contentedness in philistine England, where his talent was hardly recognized: "In London, he wasn't *'le maître'*—except to a small clique of society snobs." Isherwood's Cheuret performed "not according to some showy personal interpretation, but as the composer himself would have liked to hear it played. This was his whole aim as a musician: a faithful anonymous performance." He insisted on equality in his quartet, running it as "a musical democracy of four persons," no instrument leading; "he refused absolutely to call his quartette 'The Cheuret,' even when its three other members wished him to do so." This was all satire.

In reality, André Mangeot kept a firm grip as leader and enjoyed the limelight just as he enjoyed having things his own way at home. With subversive tact, Isherwood in *Lions and Shadows* shouldered the blame for any misunderstanding with his employer, pointing to his own youthful inadequacies, exaggerating his own self-absorption and absolving Cheuret of failings that Mangeot almost certainly possessed: "He never asked for or expected any kind of preferential treatment—either from strangers or members of his own family—"[84] In reality, Isherwood saw Mangeot's expectation of preferential treatment as the root of discord in the household. When he became friends with Stravinsky in Hollywood, Isherwood did not address him as *Maestro* like others around the composer; to him it sounded inauthentic. The Stravinsky household was to offer harmony that Isherwood only imagined with the Mangeots and the Cheurets, and Isherwood was to nestle among the family without explosive outcome despite an echo of old patterns when Stravinsky's assistant-cum-adopted son, Robert Craft, reportedly fell in love with him.[85]

AT ST. MARY ABBOT'S Terrace, Isherwood moved his bed down a flight into his grandmother's old room, creating a top-floor sitting room where he could entertain. In December 1925, he had a craze for a Repton friend, George Fisher, who was about to finish at Christ Church, Oxford. They met for lunch, tea, and dinner, and went to the theater. Fisher's younger brother

Stanley, also at Christ Church, came for tea on December 16, bringing another undergraduate, Wystan Auden, who lived on Stanley's staircase in Christ Church and was staying with the Fishers in Southwark during the holiday because he wasn't getting along with his mother. Auden was now eighteen.

In *Lions and Shadows*, Isherwood transformed this reunion into a star set-piece. "Weston," as he called Auden, had changed very little apart from having grown. "He was expensively but untidily dressed in a chocolate-brown suit which needed pressing," his fingers were stained with nicotine and ink, the nails bitten, and he sat silently smoking a pipe, pulling books off the shelves, paging through them, then dropping them, open, face down, on the floor—until Stanley Fisher left. Once they were alone, Isherwood and Auden began to reminisce about St. Edmund's, culminating in Weston's imitation of a Cyril Morgan Brown St. Edmund's Day sermon. "We laughed so much that I had to lend Weston a handkerchief to dry his eyes."[86]

Before leaving, Weston announced that he now wrote poetry. "I was very much surprised, even rather disconcerted," wrote Isherwood. "Deeper than all I.A. Richards' newly implanted theories lay the inveterate prejudices of the classical- against the modern-sider. People who understood machinery, I still secretly felt, were doomed illiterates." Upward had been crippled by what he learned from I.A. Richards about modern poetry. By contrast, Auden was ready to give voice to all that modern poetry should be, and Isherwood was well prepared to recognize this. He recalled that a big envelope soon arrived by post. "They were neither startlingly good nor startlingly bad: they were something much odder—efficient, imitative and extremely competent."[87] The same might be said of Isherwood's prose fiction at the time.

Like Isherwood, Auden had once sent all his poems to his mother; then he sent them to a Gresham's school friend, Robert Medley, destined to become a painter, and to a journalist friend, Michael Davidson. He now began to send them to Isherwood, who was always on the lookout for a protégé to teach and mold. Isherwood was, after all, two and a half years older, and according to *Lions and Shadows*, "Weston" looked up to him "as a sort of literary elder brother."[88] In this role, conforming to the Paddy Monkhouse strategy, Isherwood was stinting with his praise. "[A] critical attitude will show him that you are really interested," Monkhouse had advised about Darling's play.

Isherwood later claimed that Weston accepted all his suggestions.

> If I wanted an adjective altered, it was altered then and there. But if I suggested that a passage should be rewritten, Weston would say: "Much better scrap the whole thing," and throw the poem, without a murmur, into the

waste-paper basket. If, on the other hand, I had praised a line in a poem otherwise condemned, then that line would reappear in a new poem. And if I didn't like this poem, either, but admired a second line, then both the lines would appear in a third poem, and so on—until a poem had been evolved which was a little anthology of my favourites lines . . .[89]

What survives of their correspondence shows that, in reality, they argued back and forth, playfully and tenaciously, wrestling not only over Auden's poems, but also over writing by others, rating and recommending favorites and new discoveries.

Auden soon fell for Isherwood. Years later, he made a list of people he had been in love with; "Christopher" with the date 1926 came chronologically second after his Gresham's schoolmate Robert Medley.[90] Isherwood, the born collector, librarian, and archivist saved Auden's poems and letters, organized the poems by date, wrote about them in a special double number of *New Verse* in 1937,[91] wrote about them again in *Lions and Shadows*, and made them available to scholars. When Isherwood died, he left behind the largest single gathering of Auden's unpublished work, including more than a hundred items of juvenilia and many later poems. This was Isherwood's own display of love, sublimated in one of his collections.

In the summer of 1926, Isherwood returned to the Isle of Wight, where Auden joined him. Isherwood wrote a jokey, hyper-allusive poem, "Souvenir des Vacances," parodying Auden's current work and his fad for T.S. Eliot. A few lines nestled in the center suggest this holiday launched their sexual relationship, like the holiday in Forster's *A Room with a View*:

> At Marine Villa
>   The lamp gulps mucous blackness: fumbling begins
>   In the room with the view.[92]

Many more lines leading up to and away from these address their unashamedly adventurous reading and writing. In *Lions and Shadows*, Isherwood described Auden's arrival, "striding towards me, along Yarmouth Pier" in "a very broad-brimmed black felt hat" which seemed to represent "something that Oxford had superimposed on Weston's personality" and which Isherwood immediately disliked:

> I will never, as long as I live, accept any of Weston's hats. Since that day, he has tried me with several. There was an opera hat—belonging to the period when he decided that poets ought to dress like bank directors, in morning cut-aways and striped trousers or evening swallow-tails.

There was a workman's cap, with a shiny black peak, which he bought while he was living in Berlin, and which had, in the end, to be burnt, because he was sick into it one evening in a cinema. There was, and occasionally still is, a panama with a black ribbon—representing, I think, Weston's conception of himself as a lunatic clergyman; always a favourite role. Also, most insidious of all, there exists, somewhere in the background, a schoolmaster's mortar-board. He has never actually dared to show me this: but I have seen him wearing it in several photographs.

If there was anything Isherwood understood, it was trying on different hats in the search for an authentic literary identity—the self-consciously ambitious Oxford undergraduate; the T.S. Eliot disciple; the leftist poet; the Anglican clergyman abroad; the rule-obsessed schoolmaster. Isherwood himself tried on many literary costumes, many masks. This made him, at the time, Auden's ideal friend and mentor. He recognized the necessity of such roles as well as their unreality. They were part of the game of poetry and fiction, a part even Upward did not fully understand. Weston "was merely experimenting aloud; saying over the latest things he had read in books, to hear how they sounded."[93]

The Freshwater visit was a watershed for Auden. He talked over all his poems with Isherwood and discarded many. Like Isherwood, Auden learned his craft by imitation; both were masters of pastiche; both read insatiably, mimicked easily. Their appetites and inclinations perfectly illustrated Eliot's idea that the individual talent should immerse itself in tradition in order to learn what has already been written and what still needs to be written.[94] They drew on the writing of the past in order to refashion it, and both were to move on from Eliot's allusive modernism to a more cohesive manner that fearlessly mixed genres and styles, highbrow and lowbrow, without showing, as Eliot showed, the stitching that held together the variety. A shared impulse toward the classical, the austere, meant assimilating rather than revealing their models.

When Auden's first book of poems was handprinted by Stephen Spender in the summer of 1928, Auden dedicated the tiny volume to Isherwood and inscribed Isherwood's copy, "For Christopher. Dura Virum Nutrix." "Harsh nurse of men" was the motto of Sedbergh School where G.B. Smith became headmaster in 1926; Sedburgh had a reputation for a spartan regime.[95] The inscription teased Isherwood for how harshly he had criticised Auden's poems and also acknowledged that this harshness had nourished the austerity of Auden's first collection. The inscription also obliquely complained that Isherwood had never reciprocated in the matter of romantic love. He was mentioned in an early version of the opening poem as "that severe Christopher," his name arising in a conversation about love.[96]

DURING THAT SUMMER holiday at Freshwater, according to *Lions and Shadows*, Isherwood trusted Auden to read a draft of his new novel, *Seascape with Figures*. This was the first version of *All the Conspirators*, transforming Isherwood's escape from Cambridge and an academic career into Philip Lindsay's decision, encouraged by his friend Allen Chalmers, to quit his job in insurance—the safe, guaranteed life—in order to write and paint. "It's got to pay. It will pay, sooner or later," Philip tells his sister Joan. "All I ask is that Mother shall keep me for six months."[97] By the end of the novel, Mother's martyred dismay and his own creative struggle leave Philip an invalid while Joan decides to marry against her sexual inclination a successful Cambridge graduate and clubman named Victor—to whom, as ever, go the spoils.

In the climactic episode, Isherwood deployed the fog that had descended the day Richard ran away from him at the school door. The eviscerating loss of control over Richard proved Isherwood had failed Frank, failed Kathleen, failed his brother; it made him doubt whether he could succeed at anything else since he, too, had run from the school door at Cambridge and was still somersaulting in free fall. He painted his doubts as large as he could in the novel, as if to exorcise them. The day of Philip's planned departure for a dreaded job on an African coffee plantation, he wakes from a nightmare about his prep school and runs out into "thick 'pea-soup' fog, which writhed in strong spirals against the house-fronts, building itself up, layer upon layer, like coil upon coil of inch-thick cable, until it reached the tiles; then sinking upon itself, then rising again, voluminously, an enormous stack of vapour, like cotton-wool which had been soaked in oil."[98]

This fog is thickened by T.S. Eliot's fog that "rubs its back upon the window-panes" in "The Love Song of J. Alfred Prufrock," and Isherwood also imported Eliot's atmosphere of terrified, solitary ennui and "restless nights in one-night cheap hotels" to increase the tension.[99] Philip Lindsay loses his way in a slum, far from the privileges of his class and the mirror of his known acquaintances. From a Jew in a pawnshop—the marginal, magical, healing Jew from Isherwood's reading of Dickens and Walter Scott—Philip buys a thick overcoat, "it was on the large side. The sleeves had to be turned back;" in a parody of the visits to men's shops and tailors recorded by Kathleen, the Jew tells him, "It suits you very well, I think." The overcoat is a forerunner of the hide that will cover Francis in *The Dog Beneath the Skin*; it offers animal comfort and a smell that harks back to Isherwood's horse-drawn childhood in Ireland with Frank and the two Kittys: "The overcoat was his last moral support. As it grew wetter, it stank richly of what Philip vaguely identified as horse medicine. It was like an unfamiliar but reassuring companion."

The coat suggests the masculinity, size, and protective embrace of the lost father, but it cannot protect or liberate Philip Lindsay. He spends the night alone with the coat in a cheap hotel, where his attic room "filled his mind with curious and obscene associations." Dizzy with plans for escape—to the countryside, to the Continent—Philip has a complete mental and physical breakdown, associated with a recurrence of rheumatic fever. Rheumatic fever struck fear in the Bradshaw Isherwoods. It had changed the lives of Henry and Moey, and it had become the name of the hysterical anxiety gripping Kathleen and through her Christopher during their 1915 vigil on the Isle of Wight when he was convalescent and they waited for news of Frank from Belgium. Isherwood's friend Hector Wintle had rheumatic fever twice in the early 1920s and Isherwood spent hours at his bedside; even Kathleen and Emily visited Wintle. It is, in a sense, this fear that fictionally disqualifies Philip Lindsay from public school and from a conventional manly career. His temperature rises and falls, pains shoot through his joints, he is overwhelmed by terror during the night, self-control broken, until he begins to sob and, finally, to pray. The next morning, again wearing the coat, he collapses on the Embankment and vomits before being returned home in a cab by a clergyman. "The astrakhan collar was quite ruined."[100]

BACK AT ST. MARY Abbot's Terrace, Isherwood showed Upward the same draft he had shown Auden. It was the work of only three months, begun at Easter, and it marked a change in approach which Isherwood credited to Upward's influence—a new theory about novel writing divulged during an earlier holiday. They had taken a steamer to the Scilly Isles and stayed a week at a hotel in Hugh Town. Isherwood had brought his existing project, *The Summer at the House*, written in a mixture of styles that went beyond pastiche into medley, like Auden's poems. He had signed the draft "Sir E.J. Fyodor Benson Turgenev Newboltovich"; on the front he wrote, "Scrapped at Scilly."

In *Lions and Shadows*, Isherwood explained that "Chalmers" had picked up his new theory about novel writing from Forster's *Howards End*: "We ought to aim at being essentially comic writers ... The whole of Forster's technique is based on the tea-table: instead of trying to screw all his scenes up to the highest possible pitch, he tones them down until they sound like mothers'-meeting gossip."¹⁰¹ Isherwood was a born comic writer, and nothing excited him more than turning accepted values upside down. Understatement was now the way forward.

He succeeded intermittently with this new theory in *All the Conspirators*, for instance punctuating Philip's hysterical breakdown with the trivial detail of the ruined astrakhan collar. *All the Conspirators* opens on the Scilly Isles, where two young men, the aspiring artist Philip Lindsay and the medical student Allen Chalmers, are staying at a hotel. They talk constantly—arguing, discriminating, challenging each other. "'All the time the wind was south-west you were deadly keen on seals.' / 'Was I?'"¹⁰² Despite rejecting Cambridge, Isherwood was haunted by two Cambridge novels, Forster's *The Longest Journey* and Virginia Woolf's *Jacob's Room*, which celebrate the vitality and joy of tireless arguing among highly educated young men. The arguments in both novels are intensely philosophical and convincingly prosaic, and the young men in them accept no established beliefs and take nothing for granted; they are searching for a new consensus. They argue about whether an object is there if nobody is looking at it; they argue about how to open a tin of beef; they argue about color and form in painting. They argue about writers, historians, philosophers. They knock a volume of Shakespeare overboard into the water while sailing to the Scilly Isles. Like Isherwood and Upward, they do not agree on whether Shakespeare is the greatest writer.

In his diary, Upward said, "We did not quarrel," but rather that Isherwood had "spoilt" the holiday with nonstop talk. "He didn't give me time to think. Endless chatter about literature. I am outgrowing him; he bores me." But then in September, Upward changed his mind. "I was expressing an opinion. It was false to the complete experience. One cannot explain a week in seven words."¹⁰³

In fact, there had been another uneasy holiday later that summer of 1926, in August, when they returned to the Haute Savoie and Mont Blanc together. On the outward journey, they stopped in Paris, where they bought copies of *Ulysses*, banned in England. *Ulysses*, too, opens with an argument between two college men, one a medical student, one a writer, which also influenced *All the Conspirators*. However, Isherwood later decried his use of what he called "Joycean thought stream technique": "Its self-consciously grim, sardonically detached tone doesn't suit any of these characters; even coming from Allen Chalmers it rings false," he was to write in 1957.¹⁰⁴ Joyce's stream of consciousness tends to reveal the isolation of single characters; Isherwood was preoccupied with interaction, with conversation. The style of relationship he shared with his closest friends was playful—testing knowledge and conviction on a foundation of collaboration and shared curiosity, seeking greater intimacy and understanding, seeking the reciprocity it had become unbearable to share with his mother.

According to *Lions and Shadows*, when he finished *Seascape with Figures*, Isherwood again fearlessly submitted it to Ethel Mayne. She advised some changes, and then he sent it to two publishers. It was rejected, so he put it away for six months.

He began something new, "nothing less ambitious than a survey of the post-war generation." He would turn the Test upside down, and write not about the hero, whom he termed the Truly Strong Man, but about "the neurotic hero, The Truly Weak Man." His new metaphor for the Test was crossing the continent of North America. The Truly Weak Man fears experience, so he circumnavigates via the ice and snow of the Northwest Passage and is lost forever. Isherwood planned to call the new book *The North-West Passage*.[105]

He never wrote *The North-West Passage*, but its core ideas about heroism, strength, cowardice, and weakness contributed to *The Memorial*, and much later to *The World in the Evening* and *A Single Man*. *The North-West Passage* was also a working title for *Lions and Shadows*, affirming that Isherwood considered the arcane metaphor to apply to himself, a traveler by the Northwest Passage, unable to take a direct route and missing out on life. Years later, from California, he wrote to his mother, "When I was young, I despaired much more than I do now, because I was afraid I would never get to experience anything."[106]

Isherwood alleged in *Lions and Shadows* that he found the term "the truly strong man" in the work of Swiss psychiatrist Eugen Bleuler, concealing another debt to Gide, for "The Brotherhood of Strong Men" and "The Test" are found together in *The Counterfeiters*. Schoolboys form a gang expressly to exclude a weak and neurotic younger boy, Boris. They devise a test for entry: Boris must stand before the class and pull the trigger of an empty revolver aimed at his head. One boy knows the revolver is loaded. Boris dies. The boy responsible is virtually unmoved, "the truly strong man."[107] Isherwood was stunned by Gide, but ultimately repelled by his lack of compassion and remorse.

"WESTON LEFT NOTHING alone and respected nothing: he intruded everywhere; upon my old-maidish tidiness, my intimate little fads, my private ailments, my most secret sexual fears."[108] In *Lions and Shadows*, Isherwood portrayed himself as unsettled for months after Weston's 1926 seaside visit—not wanting to see anyone, running away to Wales, and even contemplating shooting himself. He decided that he must move out of his mother's house.

He looked at rooms in Vincent Square but did not take them, perhaps for lack of money. Then he went away to see Auden again, telling his mother that the Mangeots could no longer afford a secretary and glossing over conflicts with André. While he was away, Kathleen went to look at the Vincent Square rooms herself. There is no evidence that Isherwood asked her to do this, and she did not record whether he knew. As he began to pull away from home, Kathleen, consciously or not, pursued him. She stalked his movements and copied his behavior, raising the temperature between them. In September, he formally told her he planned to move out, and she took Richard abroad to Annecy, Chamonix, Col des Aravis, Mont Blanc—following in the footsteps of Isherwood's tours there.

She returned from France to find him still at home, unemployed, though he had signed on at a tutoring agency, Gabbitas & Thring. She felt miserable about their relationship: "Everything seems such a tangle & I seem to have grievously failed & to be so utterly alone now." She took a copy of a guidebook for walkers that she had helped her mother to write, *Our Rambles in Old London*, to a publisher friend, hoping to get it republished. In this book, she was at least a character, "K.," a valued companion on each walk and a party to her mother's interest. She had even contributed two sketches. She continued to look for a publisher for several years, like her son.

The struggle between Isherwood and his mother, still mostly unvoiced, was fueled by their distress over Richard. "C's one ambition seems to be to get away from home & me & R's fits & irritability make me very anxious." She had removed Richard from Northwood House at the end of 1925 and sent him to tutors in London. He was made to box twice a week because one of his testicles still had not descended. He turned fifteen in the autumn of 1926 but refused to have his birthday celebrated.

The tutoring was not a success. In October, Kathleen consulted the doctor and psychiatrist Hugh Crichton-Miller, founder of the Tavistock Clinic for Nervous Diseases and a friend of Jung. She found Crichton-Miller "so attractive & convincing" that she brought Richard for a solo interview. Crichton-Miller suggested "an idea that was both astonishing & kind" but which Kathleen was unable to write in her diary—evidently a long separation.[109]

She and Richard chose a tutor, a Mr. Nichol, in Wye, Kent, where she sent Richard by train. Richard aborted, left the train at London Bridge and walked home. So Kathleen took him by car, Madgie Reid driving, and spent one night. After that, she did not see Richard for eighteen weeks. By the time she visited him in February 1927, his clothes were too small. By April, when he came home to London, his voice had begun to break.

Richard remained with Mr. Nichol for most of the next two years, passed his general education certificate and decided on university. It was just his luck that Mr. Nichol suddenly dropped dead in November 1928 as Richard began to study for the Oxford entrance exams.

Isherwood showed Kathleen some kindness by going to meet Hugh Crichton-Miller in October 1926. Afterwards, he invited Kathleen into his room to share his fire and talk over her plan. But during the next two years, he paid less and less attention to Richard. He expressed horror at Richard's lack of interest in his own future, and became, as Kathleen put it, "politely aloof"[110] when decisions had to be made.

On October 20, 1926, Isherwood finished a draft of *Seascape with Figures*. "I don't like the tone as well as 'Lions & Shadows'," Kathleen noted, "much more sexual & vindictive but it is very interesting & a clever study of a family we know!"[111] The greatest vindictiveness lay in Isherwood's requirement that she read it, but she required this of herself, too.

In late November, Isherwood at last got a tutoring job, and this led to another, in January 1927, in Hampstead—Ian Scott-Kilvert, nearly ten. The lessons laid the foundation for a romance that was to blossom a decade later, for Scott-Kilvert was to reenter Isherwood's life in the autumn of 1937 just as Isherwood, coincidentally, had finished portraying him as eight-year-old "Graham" in *Lions and Shadows*, "an exceptionally nervous little boy, with a pale, lively charming face, fair hair standing up in a tuft, and big steel spectacles which were perpetually getting lost."[112] In real life, Scott-Kilvert did not wear glasses, but he had a stammer.

Isherwood's friend Roger Burford was getting married, and Isherwood decided to take over Burford's room in Redcliffe Road, Chelsea. He moved out of St. Mary Abbot's Terrace on January 9, 1927, while Kathleen was away. He may not have known that she had already scouted out his new street for herself. He settled into his Chelsea digs with his books and the armchairs from his Cambridge rooms, but unlike Cambridge, it was Olive Mangeot, not Kathleen, who put up his curtains.

In *Lions and Shadows*, he portrayed himself as having no sex life. The bachelor room at "Romilly Road," as he called it, exhibited "the rigid tidiness of the celibate: that pathetically neat room, as I now picture it, seems to cry out for the disorderly human traces of cohabitation." He dined alone in the evenings on his landlady's cooking, and "the room as long as I occupied it, remained virgin, unravished."[113]

Kathleen visited as soon as she returned to London. He was in bed with a cough. She approved of the room, "which is on the top & very bright & light." She checked on him again the next day, satisfied with his breakfast, "porridge & omelet," but anxious about his state of mind: "he seemed rather depressed poor dear."[114] Shortly, he began going home twice a week, to lunch and dinner and sometimes even tea—incapable of breaking free. Kathleen, still shadowing him unconsciously, moved into his old bedroom at St. Mary Abbot's Terrace, repapered it, and created a new connecting bedroom for Richard.

In mid-May, Isherwood returned to Marine Villa on the Isle of Wight to write for six weeks. In *Lions and Shadows* he portrayed this as a solitary time and offered only a few impressions of locals. He did not mention that Kathleen visited him for five days, staying in the hotel opposite. They talked about his novel and went sightseeing. One trip was to Ventnor, where Kathleen had visited with Frank on December 29, 1900, and Frank had made his second marriage proposal, a "breakthrough," aboard the return train at twilight. "[G]oing down into the town near Alto House, so familiar & sad & dead & all ago," she wrote in her 1927 diary. She had often stayed at Alto House, including during the life-altering spring of 1915, when Christopher was recovering from measles and pneumonia and Frank was fighting his last battles at the Front. The 1927 seaside visit was on sufferance for Isherwood. "I couldn't help feeling rather sad that Christopher didn't really want me."[115]

Isherwood did include in *Lions and Shadows* his encounter that summer with a man he called "Lester," five years older than he, who had served in World War I. "Lester" lived in a tent in a field near the village. He was the perennial homeless veteran, a man so affected by his experience in war that he could not reintegrate into civilian life in peacetime. "He had no business to be here, alive, in post-war England," Isherwood observed. "His place was elsewhere, with the dead."

According to *Lions and Shadows*, Lester had been medically certified disabled; he suffered from headaches, insomnia, constipation. He talked about his war experiences, including being blown up in a tank from which he was the sole survivor. "I tried to picture myself in his place," Isherwood wrote. "But here, as ever, the censorship, in blind panic, intervened, blacking out the image. No, no, I told myself, terrified; this could never happen to me. It could never happen to any of my friends."

In the memoir, he deployed Lester as "the ghost of the War," a ghost that continued to sap Isherwood's strength, like the ghosts at Marple Hall: "Lester had shaken my faith in the invulnerability of my generation."[116] Even though they were safe from the fighting, his generation had been egregiously damaged.

Lester was based on John (Jack) Maunder, who, after years out of touch, was to write to Isherwood from Freshwater Bay in the spring of 1937, asking for guidance finding professional psychological help. Isherwood advised him to contact John Layard, a friend about fifteen years older than he, who was a Cambridge-trained anthropologist and amateur psychotherapist. He also promised to research an institution where Maunder could go.[117]

Layard was abroad and did not respond, so Maunder left the Isle of Wight and checked into a hospital. "I did not then know that it was a mental hospital where they lock you in," Maunder later explained. "But it is." Without realizing it, Maunder had committed himself at Bedlam, relocated from central London to Kent in 1930, and he could not get out. Six weeks later, Isherwood visited Maunder and drove him to see Layard, but he was required to return the patient to Bedlam by 6 p.m.[118] Though he could not help Maunder, Isherwood decided to put him in *Lions and Shadows*; he had been stuck for weeks on the book, but moved forward once this new character reached out to him from his past life.

According to *Lions and Shadows*, "Lester" told Isherwood "you'd make a very good doctor," and Isherwood "felt obscurely flattered and pleased."[119] Perhaps he could be the one to heal the damage epitomized in Lester. He began to think about attending medical school like his friend Hector Wintle and mentioned it to Kathleen. Meanwhile, he went away again, this time with his bicycle, to a boarding house, in Criccieth, North Wales, scene of another childhood holiday. On his return, he gave Kathleen the most recent draft of his novel. It had a new title, *An Artist to His Circle*. The Artist's Circle did not include the Artist's mother. She was only in the audience, though in a sense she was still the most important member of the audience. She found the new draft "very well written the setting depressing & none of the characters in any way loveable!"[120]

Some of the dialogue in the novel carries echoes of Frank's long-buried artistic aspirations. For instance, it mimics language Kathleen had used in her diary in 1910 and 1911, when Frank had his brief moment as a full-time art student intending a professional career, language Kathleen may customarily have used in real life to describe Frank's achievements. Isherwood had of course overheard many conversations between his parents and among his mother's friends, and he perhaps concluded that Kathleen looked on Frank's talent as an exotic accessory to his humdrum identity as a soldier, something she could show off. Isherwood undercut the dialogue with deflating irony. Mrs. Lindsay, boasting of "Philip's artistic successes," manages only to trivialize them, for instance when she reports the sale of three watercolors from "a stall at a bazaar in the Town Hall. It was a very grand affair. Opened by Lady—I forget her name."

The Philip Lindsay character writes *and* paints, combining the artistic talents of Christopher and his father. Philip's writing, like his painting, is referred to by his mother as a glorified hobby that might win a prize or a token sum of money or even serve as therapy but not as a profession. Mrs. Lindsay's companion—Currants, modeled on Nanny—secretly submits one of Philip's poems to a competition for the Best Modern Poem, and

Philip wins second prize, five pounds. "The doctor said it had saved him a week of his convalescence."[121]

The women of his household thus make themselves the custodians of Philip's artistic ambition even though they are unable to recognize in art any intrinsic value. Philip manages to avoid the dreaded career abroad—on the coffee plantation in East Africa—only through being ill; art is permitted to him because he is an invalid and not a real man. His mother, his sister, Currants, all praise and control him like a child. He sits in his overheated room in his invalid's chair, wearing mittens knitted by Currants. The mittens muffle any artistic touch, and they link Philip's helplessness with Frank's, to whom ten-year-old Christopher had sent mittens at the Front. They also recall the woolens wrapped around Christopher's acting leg in childhood, and they recall the bandage, like a single mitten, wrapped painfully again and again around Christopher's circumcised penis as he submitted his sexual self to the care of his female nursing entourage at Marple Hall when he was about to turn fifteen.

After less than a year at Redcliffe Road, Kathleen helped Isherwood pack and carry his things back to St. Mary Abbot's Terrace. He had between five hundred and six hundred books which had to be crated and moved professionally. "The New Life had ignominiously failed," he wrote in *Lions and Shadows*. On the other hand, he had again sent his novel to the publishers.

The title he settled on, *All the Conspirators*, is a phrase from Shakespeare's *Julius Caesar*—distinguishing Brutus as the only one of Caesar's murderers who did not kill from envy.[122] It announced the novel's theme as the toppling of tyrants, children struggling to overturn the matriarchy. But the children in Isherwood's novel are struggling to overturn sexual oppression, not political, and in this regard his title also alluded to one of his favorite Katherine Mansfield stories, "At the Bay," in which Beryl Fairfield alone at night longs for a lover and experiences the "queer sensation that you're a conspirator" and that the night and the garden "were conspirators, too." As Mansfield wrote, and as Isherwood had discovered, "It is lonely living by oneself."[123] In another Isherwood short story, "An Evening at the Bay, 1928," written around the same time and titled after Mansfield's,[124] two young men coach a third, all middle-class summer visitors, to pick up a local girl at Freshwater Bay. Isherwood replaced Mansfield's delicate longing with boisterous, marauding humor; sex is the object of the conspiracy.

IN JANUARY 1928, Jonathan Cape accepted *All the Conspirators*. "I ran all the way to the tube station," wrote Isherwood in *Lions and Shadows*, "and the massed bands were playing their loudest, and the streets were full of waving flags." The Artist shared his excitement with his Circle but not with his mother. Kathleen found out only when Roger Burford dropped by: "he told me in an interval when C had gone upstairs." Isherwood was to receive £30 on publication and royalties after 3,000 copies.[125]

With the novel accepted, he had a burst of professional energy. He left London in mid-February, renting a bedroom and sitting room at Disley Hall Farm in Cheshire. Rachel Monkhouse arranged it. She still had feelings for him, and even years later, the farmer at Wyberslegh Hall Farm, Mr. Cooper, was to recall to Kathleen, "what a set Rachel made at Christopher that time he was up here." She pursued him all that spring. Isherwood recorded in his diary that he "was aware of Rachel's reproachful pathos," and a partly destroyed diary entry seems to refer to an uncomfortably intimate encounter; the surviving text reads only: ". . . me with wistful half-reproachful sex. I must never see her alone again."[126]

While he was away, Kathleen made an offer on a new house at 19 Pembroke Gardens, a property he had viewed with her. St. Mary Abbot's Terrace was threatened by new buildings, and the lease was getting short. Kathleen planned to move in June.

In *Lions and Shadows*, Isherwood did not mention his five weeks of steady, secluded work in Cheshire. He depicted only drunken revels ensuing on the failure of the New Life he had tried to establish at "Romilly Road." At the Mangeots', he met a painter, Bill de Lichtenberg, whom he called "Bill Scott" in the memoir: "a dark sunburnt little man agile and quick as a lizard with naughty prominent blue eyes" who would "take infinite pains over anything which might please or amuse his friends"—dinner, fireworks, charades, a party.[127] As told in *Lions and Shadows*, "Bill Scott" exercised a hypnotic power over the Isherwood character, fueled by the strong cocktails he mixed. His fictional surname commemorated Isherwood's first adolescent nights out in Manchester with Micky Scott, killed in a flying accident in 1925. De Lichtenberg, too, would be dead by 1935, leaving Isherwood free to fictionalize both friendships however he liked.

De Lichtenberg bought a new "French saloon car," and they decided to make a road trip. Isherwood wrote to Kathleen from Inverness in the north of Scotland, then wired from Wick, even further north, asking for his mail to be forwarded and clean clothes. "[I]t sounds wild romantic windswept country with old Norse tradition rather than Scotch," wrote Kathleen in her diary,[128] picking up on the very theme from Isherwood's letter that he was to develop in *Lions and Shadows*. Three weeks later, she made her own trip to Scotland, again shadowing him.

Isherwood and de Lichtenberg drove west along the northernmost coast to Cape Wrath and returned to London on April 25, after nearly two and a half weeks on the road. In *Lions and Shadows*, Isherwood portrayed this alcohol-soaked spree as another futile attempt to run away from the obligations that infantilised him and made him ill: "that dreary governess, that gloomy male nurse will catch you up; will arrive, on the slow train, to fetch you back to your nursery prison of minor obligations, duties, habits, ties."[129]

As Kathleen prepared to move house, he absented himself in Freshwater Bay, then returned to London to celebrate the publication of *All the Conspirators*. He recalled no jubilation when reviews appeared. They were impatient with the teenage angst and Freudian psychology, although the *Times Literary Supplement* noticed the influence of Forster, showing "what can be done without underlining and over-emphasis."

In *Lions and Shadows*, Isherwood pretended to agree with his reviewers and to dismiss his own debut. This was to avoid self-congratulation. He could not help acknowledging that his hometown paper, the *Manchester Guardian*, was "kind and generous." The reviewer was an admirer of Virginia Woolf, Hugh L'Anson Fausset, who appreciated the very subtleties to which others objected and recognized the intensity of the family struggle, which he described as "domestic guerrilla warfare." According to Isherwood, fewer than three hundred copies sold. Five years later, in the *Sunday Times*, Hugh Walpole, from whom Isherwood had freely borrowed in his Rugtonstead novels, was to list *All the Conspirators* among novels "unjustly neglected" since the war.[130]

The day after publication, Isherwood sailed for Germany to stay with his second cousin, Basil Fry, son of Uncle Charlie and Aunt Julia Fry. Basil Fry was British Consul in Bremen, where Isherwood arrived to find the newly widowed Uncle Charlie also in residence. "I hate his benevolently authoritative white beard and his clergyman's grief at the loss of his wife," Isherwood wrote in his diary. "His vitality is loathsome. So was Basil's filial heartiness. 'My dear old father.' They all disregarded me utterly."

But he fell in love with the German boys: "My vision of Germany is utterly the boys' country. In their absurd ingle's coloured lace-up shirts, socks and braided yachting-forage caps. All on bicycles." To the generation of his widowed mother, Germany remained the enemy of the Great War, the enemy who had slain his father, but Isherwood kicked against the moral hierarchy that pronounced the victors righteous and the vanquished evil; in a letter to Upward, he caricatured the British captain's arrogance aboard his tramp steamer *Hero* as they docked: "His barely credible insults to important German officials on the quay. 'Now then, Tirpity—show a leg.' They merely smiled. I know now which side started the War."[131] Grand Admiral Alfred von Tirpitz was the creator of the modern German navy that had threatened British control of the seas during the war.

Soon after his twelve-day visit, Isherwood began turning his Bremen diary into another narrative about the struggle between young and old, but the story was to languish unfinished until he reached middle age and revived it as a sardonic comedy, "Mr. Lancaster," which he was to position as the first part of his seventh novel, *Down There on a Visit*.

IN JUNE 1928, Isherwood stayed a few days in Oxford with Auden and was introduced to Stephen Spender, also an undergraduate. Auden had whetted Isherwood's appetite by showing him in advance a story Spender was writing. "He burst in upon us, blushing, sniggering loudly, contriving to trip over the edge of the carpet—an immensely tall, shambling boy of nineteen, with a great scarlet poppy-face, wild frizzy hair, and eyes the violent colour of bluebells." As with other portraits in *Lions and Shadows*, Isherwood was drawing partly on later knowledge. His phrase "contriving to trip" highlights the contradiction he saw over the years in Spender, who, despite his intelligence, wished to be perceived as not in control and rather that life was an accident befalling him.

Spender's clumsiness, whether an act or an accident, freed his companions to lively, unselfconscious and competitive interaction: "in his company you naturally began to shout, if only in order to make yourself heard at all. [...] His beautiful resonant voice [...] would carry to the farthest corners of the largest restaurant the most intimate details of his private life."[132] As it would prove, Spender could not keep a secret, his own or anyone else's.

Isherwood named his Spender character "Stephen Savage," half fact, half fiction. The fictional half, "Savage," points to striking parallels between Spender and Walter Savage Landor, the nineteenth-century "poet's poet" and political activist whose impulsive anti-authoritarianism seemed to invite misfortune. Landor threw himself into the Spanish Republican cause (against Napoleon), was suspected of spying (for the Prince Regent), and is perhaps best remembered for his prose—a suggestive fit with Spender's career since Spender was to become embroiled in the Spanish Republican cause against Franco, was to be suspected of spying for the CIA, and is perhaps best remembered for his literary-critical prose rather than for his poems.

Spender, being younger, attached himself as a protégé to both Auden and Isherwood. He sought and received advice about his poems, plays and fiction, and did countless literary errands for both—from sending them books they wished to read to introducing them to potential agents and publishers. In Isherwood's account, "He was the slave of his friends."[133] Spender printed Auden's first book of poems by hand in 1928 and later included work by

Auden and Isherwood in the magazines he edited in the 1940s and 50s, *Horizon* and *Encounter*. During the 1930s, Isherwood, Auden, and Spender were often mentioned together by reviewers and critics; in Britain, their fame became permanently intertwined.

———

ISHERWOOD ENTERED HIS name for medical school at the end of May 1928, then went to Freshwater Bay for the summer. Term, at King's College and Westminster Hospital, began in October. He paid no attention to Hector Wintle's advice that he would not enjoy it.

His plan to become a doctor was a fresh expression of his longing to gain control of his life. He yearned for the power to heal—Jack Maunder, Richard, and above all himself. In *Lions and Shadows*, he related how the Isherwood character got a sore throat every time he saw "Weston": "the mere sight of a postcard announcing his arrival would be sufficient to send up my temperature and inflame my tonsils." The Weston character asserts, "It means you've been telling lies!" and labels the tonsillitis "liar's quinsey."[134] The coded implication is that Weston was pressuring the Isherwood character to be more forthright about his sexuality, and, more generally, that Isherwood's whole life was a fragile facade of falsehoods.

Doctors had controlled Isherwood's household since before he could remember. Doctors, like detectives, had methods for identifying a problem and solving it. Sherlock Holmes first meets his right-hand man Dr. Watson in a hospital where Holmes is pursuing his eccentric and exacting studies in the medical lab. Chekhov, whom Isherwood was studying closely in 1928, was a doctor, and so were the heroes in many of Chekhov's stories. Somerset Maugham, another favorite writer, was also a doctor. In his autobiographical novel *Of Human Bondage*, Maugham's fictionalized self, Philip Carey, makes "his third start in life" as a medical student after deciding against university, failing at accountancy and giving up painting. "The medical profession is the only one which a man may enter at any age with some chance of making a living," Maugham wrote. In later years, Isherwood told an interviewer that he wanted to be a ship's doctor (Wintle's first job, about which Wintle wrote a novel, *The Final Victory*) or a police doctor so he could attend the scene of a crime, pronounce the time of death, help solve the mystery. Gore Vidal was to recall that even in the 1950s, Isherwood "often saw himself as a detective or doctor in a mystery movie."[135] Doctors, like magicians, have black bags filled with magic remedies. Isherwood wanted his own black bag; he wanted to acquire the special knowledge that would empower him to cure his unhappiness.

As Auden settled in Berlin to learn German, Isherwood started his medical studies in London. He was five or six years older than his fellow students. He had never studied chemistry; his mathematics had always been weak; physics and botany eluded him; zoology he disliked least. "This was Cambridge again, but worse," he recalled in *Lions and Shadows*. "Worse, because this time, I was honestly trying."[136]

He made one friend at King's, a talented scholarship boy, George Davis, son of a fish and fruit merchant. Davis is remembered as "Platt" in *Lions and Shadows*, "efficient, energetic, patient with me, good at mathematics," chosen to get Isherwood through. "I wasn't keen to meet any more rebels, however interesting. I wanted to stop playing the rebel myself."[137]

It wasn't long before Isherwood reverted from being a doctor to being a patient; again, it was his leg. Setting off Guy Fawkes fireworks in fog on Wimbledon Common, possibly drunk, he fell into a ditch and twisted his knee. Bill de Lichtenberg brought him home to bed after the knee was bound up by a doctor. "I hadn't seen him before," wrote Kathleen of de Lichtenberg, "he has only lately married & is rather a little pet—they have bought an old farm in the S of France with a wonderful view of the sea from the terrace." Kathleen was now invading the imaginative space of her son's next book; in *The Memorial*, Edward Blake, the suicidal homosexual war veteran, lies on just such a terrace in "the deck chair under the tattered eucalyptus tree" above the blue gulf, cared for by Margaret Lanwin.[138] Isherwood was increasingly crippled not only by Kathleen's love but also by her interest in his friends.

He had already started writing *The Memorial*. In *Lions and Shadows*, he reported that it came on him with ferocity: "During those autumn months I wrote like mad. As I had never written before, without hesitation, without pausing to correct, forgetting all my inhibitions, my neurotic etcher's neatness, intent only upon discharging my load of ideas." He described his subject as "the effect of the idea of the War on my generation," indicating with the word "idea" his anxiety that he had been too young to fight and had not faced the reality. His complexes would all be included, triggered by his reaction to "Lester" and by reading *War and Peace*. "Like Tolstoy, I would tell the story of a family; its births and deaths, ups and downs, marriages, feuds and love affairs—all 'The Eternals,' as Chalmers used, rather acidly, to call them."[139]

In his preparatory notes, he also invoked Dostoevsky's *The Brothers Karamazov*, proposing that "There must be a big Dostoyevsky smash-up," but as he worked through three drafts over the following years, the Dostoevsky smash-up was to lose out to the tea-tabling of Forster. In the published novel, tragedy is downplayed; the car wreck and the plane crash kill minor characters, and Edward Blake survives his suicide attempt. Isherwood later described the novel as "a potted epic," which begins *in medias res* and returns to the hero's—Eric Vernon's—childhood only when the reader "is more interested in the characters."

Rather than a continuous narrative, Isherwood presented four books, not in chronological order, a series of "self-contained scenes, like a play; an epic in an album of snapshots."[140] The first part, "1928," portrays the despair of Eric Vernon and Edward Blake, school friend of Eric's father, sending readers back in time to find out why. In "1920," the memorial service at the Hall generates recollections of the prewar years in the thoughts of friends and family attending, carrying the reader even further back in time through linked interior monologues and broadening the context. The next section, "1925," is about Eric Vernon's sexual anxiety at Cambridge and the nurse–invalid relationship between Edward Blake and Margaret Lanwin. Arguably, Eric Vernon represents Isherwood's sexually uptight, frustrated younger self, and Edward Blake represents an older, sexually liberated self who is openly homosexual. In "1929," the Hall changes hands, Eric Vernon becomes a Catholic and Edward Blake escapes to the boys in Berlin.

Isherwood finished the first draft in mid-December 1928, before the events he was to fictionalise in the concluding section called "1929." Despite the ferocious inspiration described in *Lions and Shadows*, he told Kathleen he was "very dissatisfied" with the draft as a result of "only writing in evening after going to King's College."[141] Then he hurt his leg again, knocking it in a taxi and making himself lame.

The day after Christmas, he typed up Auden's play, *Paid on Both Sides*, which Auden had revised and expanded that autumn in Berlin. In the play, conflict is fueled by the mother and her appetite for revenge. *Paid on Both Sides* concludes with a marriage ceremony, conventionally a symbol of transformation and the renewal of social harmony. But Auden's marriage ceremony ends with the death of the bridegroom: "His mother and her mother won," announces the chorus.[142] This was a reminder to Isherwood not to be passive. When he finished typing, he announced more overtly to Kathleen that medical school was interfering with his writing.

In *Lions and Shadows*, Isherwood wrote that "Weston" had returned from Berlin "full of stories"—about the night life, the movies, the cigars, and the liberating theories of an American psychologist, Homer Lane, theories heard from an Englishman met in Berlin, "Mr. Barnard." "Mr. Barnard" was in fact the anthropologist John Layard, who had been Lane's patient. Isherwood could not explicitly mention Auden's stories about the sex, but clearly there were plenty. Auden had written to another friend in England, "Berlin is the bugger's daydream. There are 170 male brothels under police control."[143]

Homer Lane had established a reputation for reforming adolescent lawbreakers by giving them control over their own lives at his residential institutions, in the U.S. the Ford Republic outside Detroit and in England the Little Commonwealth in Dorset. He believed that every impulse is appropriate to some phase of human development and should be allowed to run its course naturally; in his view, repressed impulses caused bad behavior and illness. His social and therapeutic practices were based on love and acceptance.

Lane died young, shadowed by allegations of inappropriate behavior toward women in his care. Layard was still his patient at the time, but already Lane had miraculously restored him from a near-comatose state after the death of Layard's brother in the war had triggered a breakdown and a suicide attempt. Treatment with many other prominent therapists of the day had achieved nothing. Layard spread Lane's teachings as gospel and later wrote a memoir, never published, in which he stated that Lane "had a unique gift for the release of unconscious guilt, and for the turning of anti-social impulses into social ones by perceiving good underlying them." He had exceptional powers of empathy, "a faculty for 'feeling with' used consciously to adapt to any situation . . ."[144]

In *Lions and Shadows*, Isherwood summarized the Lane teachings he had first learned from "Weston": "There is only one sin: disobedience to the inner law of our own nature. The results of this disobedience show themselves in crime or in disease. [. . .] The Devil is conscious control."[145]

The medicine Isherwood was studying offered nothing compared to Lane. "Every disease," Lane had taught, "is in itself a cure—if we know how to take it." In *Lions and Shadows*, Isherwood recalled the voices of Lane and "Barnard" taunting and tempting him: "You're afraid—afraid to trust in your deepest instincts, afraid to take the plunge!" Isherwood returned to medical school in January 1929, but according to *Lions and Shadows*, he had already made up his mind to join Weston in Berlin: "I must leave England altogether—the break with the old life must be complete."[146]

He resolved to visit during his Easter holidays. Acting on his resolve required a tremendous mental effort, and it made him ill. He was in bed with a temperature of 102 the week before he left. He was depressed, his head ached, he couldn't sleep, and he told his mother that the family doctor "was no good & did not understand him." He was still "not feeling too well" when he boarded his train on March 14.[147]

4

Berlin, Sex, Politics, and Fame
(1929–1939)

Leaving Cambridge was Isherwood's first act of self-realization; the second was moving to Berlin, that post-imperial capital bursting with the culturally new, riven by economic inequality, lurching from one fragile government to another. In Berlin he was to have the sex he had feared and longed for, lots of it, and to establish and accept his sexual nature. In Berlin, he was also to find love. He gave himself up to sensual intoxication, but he also wrote constantly. He learned German, taught English, and met the people who were to inspire his most famous characters.

There was nineteen-year-old Jean Ross on whom he modeled Sally Bowles, the nightclub singer and sexual adventurer, embodiment of defiant joy in the face of political tyranny, later played on stage and screen by Julie Harris, Judi Dench, Liza Minnelli, and countless others. There was Gerald Hamilton on whom he modeled Arthur Norris, money-hungry dealer in luxury goods and political intelligence who finds his greatest pleasure with a booted dominatrix. There was Fräulein Thurau who became Fräulein Schroeder, the easygoing landlady wistful over the refined lodgers of bygone years and settling realistically for the prostitute Fräulein Kost, for the washed-up music-hall yodeler Fräulein Mayr, for Bobby, the bartender from a nearby club, for Isherwood himself, transformed into "Herr Issyvoo," honored as a gentleman despite his poverty. There was Wilfrid Israel who became Bernhard Landauer, doomed scion of a Jewish department store family, and there was Gisa Soloweitschik, a Russian émigré banker's daughter, who became Natalia Landauer, cultivated and shockable princess with an instinct for survival. There was Isherwood's lover Walt Wolff fictionalised as Otto Nowak, Herr Issyvoo's host in the family's slum tenement.

When he first arrived in Berlin, Isherwood was absorbed in writing his novel about the impact of World War I on England, *The Memorial* (1932). As he completed this, he was to take an increasing interest in the city around him and begin to explore the darker bruise the war had made on Germany—the poverty and unemployment, the plight of the Jews, the standoff between communists and fascists as Prussian democracy collapsed. He was to work briefly for a communist front organization, believing at the time that the communists would prevail in Berlin and that the Nazis could not possibly control the future.

His writing about Berlin was to include the black-comedy spy thriller *Mr. Norris Changes Trains* (1935) and the collection of interrelated diaries and stories *Goodbye to Berlin* (1939), which took a strikingly different, modernist form. These two books cast the penetrating, disciplined eye of the psychologist and the historian over a cross section of life in Berlin at the end of Weimar, capturing for all time and in telling detail the rise of autocracy from poverty and social dispossession, the insignificant intersecting with the overwhelmingly consequential, freedom partying with its nemesis.

The two novels were conceived from 1932 onwards as part of a single work, *The Lost*. Isherwood separated *Mr. Norris Changes Trains* in the spring of 1934 and published it the following year. Five of the pieces in *Goodbye to Berlin* were published individually through the decade, mostly in the magazine *New Writing*. The first was "The Nowaks" in the spring of 1936. "A Berlin Diary (Autumn 1930)" appeared in the spring of 1937, and *Sally Bowles* came out the same year as a novella. "The Landauers" and "A Berlin Diary (Winter 1932–3)" were finished at the end of 1937 and published in 1938. "On Ruegen Island (Summer 1931)" was completed last, in January 1938, and appeared only in the book. During those same years, Isherwood was to abandon nearly as many stories and drafts as he completed. Some he was to use in later novels—*Prater Violet* (1945) and *Down There on a Visit* (1962).

In 1976, Isherwood was to publish a new account of his life in the 1930s, *Christopher and His Kind*. In it, he was to write candidly as a homosexual for a readership that was coming out of the closet in the 1970s. While it offered new truths, *Christopher and His Kind* also offered new fictions about the past that reflected Isherwood's increasing gay militancy during the 1970s. The earlier works are no less true for having disguised his sexual activity and many other things besides. *Christopher and His Kind* extended his life story to the end of the 1930s, recounting Isherwood's flight from Berlin with his German boyfriend Heinz Neddermeyer in 1933, their search for a country where they could safely settle together, Neddermeyer's arrest and imprisonment by the Gestapo in 1937, and Isherwood's subsequent travels with Auden in 1938—to

China to report on the war there with Japan and circling home via Manhattan, prelude to emigrating to the U.S. for good in 1939.

BERLIN, 1929

Isherwood's first visit to Berlin was short, like his visit to Bremen. Auden described it in a journal he kept in 1929, and his virtually contemporary record offers revealing differences from what Isherwood was to write nearly half a century later in *Christopher and His Kind*. "It begins with the Hirschfeld Museum," wrote Auden. In Isherwood's later telling, it begins with a bar, the Cosy Corner, more formally known as Noster's Restaurant zur Hütte, in the working-class district of Hallesches Tor, because Isherwood wanted to plunge his reader into the action, the sex. "I can still make myself faintly feel the delicious nausea of initiation terror which Christopher felt as Wystan pushed back the heavy leather door curtain of a boy bar called the Cosy Corner and led the way inside."[1] Here again is the curtain that hid from Isherwood the stage on which fantasies became real—his father's theatricals, the miracle of *A Midsummer Night's Dream*, the silver movie screen, and now the sexual and romantic life he had longed for.

Once the curtain was drawn back, according to *Christopher and His Kind*, Isherwood took the stage and began a romance with a young German-speaking Czech, Berthold Szczesny, nicknamed "Bubi"—Baby or Boy—for his adorable looks. Szczesny was the first German-speaking boy who mattered to Isherwood, and Isherwood cast him as the mysterious foreigner, the blond German conqueror, the Wanderer, the Lost Boy. But it was not so simple.

By Auden's account, it was only after the visit to the Hirschfeld Museum and after supper with John Layard, to whom Isherwood was now introduced for the first time, that the three of them continued together to the Cosy Corner, where Isherwood "had" a boy called Paul, evidently his first German boy, who is not mentioned in *Christopher and His Kind*.[2]

The museum was housed in the Institut für Sexualwissenschaft (Institute for Sexual Science) founded in 1919 by Dr. Magnus Hirschfeld, a student of human sexuality and a campaigner for the decriminalization of consensual acts between grown men. The institute offered psychiatric counseling for sexual dysfunctions, treatment for venereal diseases, and legal assistance in sex crime cases.

In *Christopher and His Kind*, Isherwood described his first visit to Hirschfeld's institute as if it had taken place six months later than it did, on his third visit to Berlin, when he was to move in next door. Auden was left out so that Isherwood could focus on the singular experience of recognizing his sexuality:

> He was embarrassed because, at last, he was being brought face to face with his tribe. Up to now, he had behaved as though the tribe didn't exist and homosexuality were a private way of life discovered by himself and a few friends. He had always known, of course, that this wasn't true. But now he was forced to admit kinship with these freakish fellow tribesmen and their distasteful customs. And he didn't like it.[3]

What Isherwood found embarrassing and distasteful were the museum displays suggesting the wide range of human sexual practices—whips and chains for sadomasochists, boots for fetishists, female lingerie worn by Prussian officers, drawings of orgies and erotic fantasies, photographs of celebrated homosexual couples such as Wilde and Bosie, Whitman and Peter Doyle, Edward Carpenter and George Merrill.

If he was embarrassed to recognize his sexual identity in front of Auden, Isherwood was not embarrassed to engage in acts of lust. Auden was watching closely and recorded in his diary that "Pimping for someone on whom one has a transference creates the most [?contrary] feelings." He felt both excitement and sorrow. "[T]he general sexy atmosphere made me feel like a participator in a fertility rite," Auden reflected after watching Christopher and Bubi—showing "bare flesh"—play ping-pong. His sense of exclusion and sexual failure carried him back to schoolboy feelings of loneliness and bewilderment. "I felt the third baboon and a public-school one. Sunday walks to be back in time for chapel." "The third baboon" masturbated alone while watching two others copulate; Isherwood had coined the phrase after reading about baboons with Upward in the library at Marple Hall, where during a summer visit in 1923, they had discovered Uncle Henry's collection of Havelock Ellis, *Studies in the Psychology of Sex*.[4]

"One cannot have a transference on a person unless they love one too. It is not Idol-worship," Auden wrote elsewhere in his diary, but at this time in their friendship, love was too sentimental for Isherwood, as Auden knew. "John in the evening talked about Lane as love. I was ashamed in front of Christopher." Even in 1936 and 1937 when he was writing *Lions and Shadows*, Isherwood never mentioned love. He focused on morality, freedom, and avoiding the hypocrisy of self-sacrifice.

Whether consciously or not, Auden wanted to control Isherwood's sex life. "C and I had an argument about taste in boys. It is very difficult not to treat sexual taste like literary, as something that can approximate to an absolute. I feel that I am disappointed with his choice of Bubi." Possibly Auden had a hand in Szczesny finding out about his rival Paul, because Isherwood, his German still rudimentary, relied on notes from Auden: "the disclosure of Christopher's affair with Paul. I felt beastly. Christopher seemed so babyish in his struggle with his notebook and his sulks." A poem Auden later wrote about Szczesny referred bitterly to a string of lovers, "Before this loved one / Was that one and that one . . ."[5]

According to Auden's journal, Isherwood tried to persuade Szczesny that he respected him as a friend not just a "doll boy": "'Du bist kein puppenjunge. Du bist mein freund.' Unhappy." Auden was not only unhappy but—when Christopher told Bubi he was jealous of another "Beard"—also disdainful: "Christopher appears to have trotted this out alright but cannot understand the answer. We shook hands meaningly as we parted. The writers have condescended." Sensing the disdain, Isherwood left Berlin after eight days, though he had planned to stay ten.[6]

Once Isherwood left, Auden tried to redirect his sexual feelings. "The affect of Christopher's visit was to generate in me a state of libido so that I went walking about trying to get rid of it."[7] He had begun a sexual affair with Layard which he regretted because Layard wanted more from the relationship. In his journal, Auden described two disappointing trysts. Then a sailor, Gerhart Meyer, came on to him in a bar, and they began an affair that was sexually exciting and complicated, and which led Layard to attempt suicide again. The drama provided material for Auden's poem, "1929," and Isherwood, who heard the story secondhand, used it for Edward Blake's attempted suicide in *The Memorial*.

Such episodes contrast with Isherwood's fictional portrait of "Weston" in *Lions and Shadows*: "Weston's own attitude to sex, in its simplicity and utter lack of inhibition, fairly took my breath away."[8] As with "Chalmers," Isherwood made "Weston" more confident and more consistent than his real-life original; this offered a better foil to the fictional uncertainty of his Isherwood character. In fact, Auden's attitude to sex was self-conscious and changeable. He told his brother John that he was celibate during 1927 and 1928 and that he would never marry because the financial pressure would ruin his art. He tried psychoanalysis with the aim of acquiring heterosexual traits and got engaged to a young woman, a nurse, then broke the engagement ten months later. He may not have confided his sexual uncertainty to Isherwood at first, but outward bravado was to give way later in the friendship.

AUDEN DECIDED TO focus on the artistic dimension of the bond with Isherwood and sublimate the problematic sexual one. He invited Isherwood to collaborate on a play, *The Enemies of a Bishop or Die When I Say When, A Morality in Four Acts*, partly set in a boys' reformatory. It was not performed or published in their lifetimes. Auden had already begun a version of it, *The Reformatory*, mentioned several times in his journal: "The Prep School atmosphere. That is what I want."[9] He proposed to explore his boyhood institutional experiences through the kind of rebellious energies presented in Peter Martin Lampel's sensation-causing leftist play *Revolte im Erziehungshaus* (*Revolt in the Reformatory*) about the brutal treatment in a care home of three boys who are driven to incite a riot and try to burn down the building. Lampel, a homosexual journalist and social worker, based the play on his work as an educator in Prussian reformatories and also on his own experience in a Berlin care home. Auden saw the play performed in Berlin in December 1928; Isherwood probably saw the silent film in Berlin later. The film was banned four times and only released in January 1930 after being recut with a soothing idyllic prequel and a conciliatory ending; teenagers were denied entry.

Solitude, fear, continual overstimulation by the presence of other boys feeling the same, sexual appetites forced underground—both Auden and Isherwood were drawn to these traumatic prep-school experiences as an artistic theme, and Isherwood was to continue exploring their effects in his work as late as the 1970s. They rediscovered this atmosphere among the boys they met in Berlin, many of whom had spent time in reform schools, and they relished the parallels between reformatory and prep school. A collaborative imaginative project offered the opportunity for a changed emotional outcome; they could master the material and reform themselves.

According to Isherwood, the Bishop in their play was an idealized portrait of Homer Lane and reflected Lane's role as head of the reform school he ran in Dorset, the Little Commonwealth. The play was dedicated to Szczesny and to Otto Küsel, one of Auden's steady companions who had escaped from a reformatory and, like Szczesny, was trying to elude the police. The character of the Bishop rewrites the unacceptable patriarch Cyril Morgan Brown as a loving, empowering father figure and turns conventional notions of self-discipline and self-control upside down.

Auden may have known that Isherwood had already begun writing a pornographic country house play, *Herds of Lions: An Extravagant Play in One Act*, about unconventional sexual couplings at a house party, where "offstage" is a series of bedrooms, like a brothel, and the characters proposition each other before disappearing there. Isherwood's setting is Tallboy Manor, and the play parodies George Bernard Shaw's country-house play, *Misalliance* (his title rhymes with Shaw's). St. Edmund's School in fact occupied the former Blencathra House, Shaw's country home.[10]

Isherwood and Auden discussed a theory of drama, drafting a "Preliminary

Statement"—in fact a series of statements—about drama, art, psychology, and disease. The manuscript in Auden's handwriting with deletions in Isherwood's handwriting suggests a dynamic in which Auden would proclaim something and Isherwood would object. Of course, they may have agreed on the statements and the deletions, experimenting and then changing their minds, but it was precisely because they did not always agree that their work was so lively. Mutual respect allowed many differences to remain in their finished work.

"Dramatic action is ritual,"[11] Auden began, keynoting his inclination toward the religious or mystical on stage, later reflected in his love of opera. Isherwood deleted this opening, in favor of precise definitions of classical tragedy, Elizabethan tragedy, modern tragedy. Auden's verse was to feature in all their collaborations, coinciding with Auden's wish to move away from realistic theater and individualized characters toward parable, allegory, abstraction. Isherwood was to write most of the prose dialogue and to guard against the grandiloquence and obscurity that tempted Auden. By the time they got to their third play, *The Ascent of F6*, their roles were to be well established. "We interfered very little with each other's work," Isherwood recalled, describing their work process on *F6*, "It was understood, throughout, that Wystan's specialty was to be the 'woozy' and mine the 'straight' bits." But even Isherwood's 'straight' bits were not realistic, as he later explained; they were "full of surreal parody, satire, and pastiche: the characters are like figures in cartoons."[12]

AFTER HIS FIRST visit to Berlin, Isherwood was back in London for only five days, then left with Olive and Sylvain Mangeot for St. Tropez on March 27. He had a slight temperature, but his willpower was stronger than his constitution. He was laid up with flu en route in Marseilles, and Sylvain came down with rheumatic fever; Olive nursed them both. When Isherwood returned to London in mid-April, relations with Kathleen were prickly. According to Kathleen's diary, he lectured her along the lines of the Lane–Layard teachings, "deploring my lack of broadness of view on sexual subjects the charity & kindness with which it should be regarded—also my incapacity of seeing beauty in the ugly things of life . . ."[13]

Uncle Henry had taken a flat at 39 Eaton Terrace, Belgravia, where Isherwood visited after dinner on May 7, his first opportunity to relate his Berlin adventures. Sexual affinities afforded new grounds for intimacy. Isherwood was later to recall: "When they dined together at Henry's flat, they giggled like age-mates over Henry's adventures with guardsmen and Christopher's encounters in the boy-bars of Berlin. 'I find it so extwardinawily soothin', don't you know,' Henry would say, referring to his acts of lust." By the end of the evening, when they were both drunk, "Christopher would get a goodnight kiss which was too warm and searching for any nephew, even one's favorite."[14]

In *Christopher and His Kind,* Isherwood stated that "Christopher couldn't have afforded to live in Berlin without Henry's allowance."[15] It was paid every three months. In exchange, he was to correspond regularly and to dine with Henry when in London. Isherwood was vague as to when they made the arrangement, and it seems likely that he extracted the allowance in exchange for agreeing as heir apparent to support Henry's schemes for raising cash. Perhaps this was a memory so uncomfortable that he censored it.

It was evidently on the night of May 7 that Uncle Henry and Isherwood agreed to sell the Marple Hall furniture. In contrast to their 1925 plan to sell Marple Hall itself, the new plan was at first kept secret—and it was quickly enacted. Within a week, they met with the family lawyer, and Isherwood revealed the plan to Kathleen as a *fait accompli*. She sensed a cruel enthusiasm when he told her, and she could hardly find words to express her shock and hurt. She used nearly thirty ellipses in her diary: "C announced at dinner that he had lunched with Mr. Symonds & Henry & it had been arranged to sell the furniture at Marple Hall which evidently pleases him . . . . It seems like losing an old friend who one perhaps seldom sees but whose existence is a pleasant support."

This supercharged moment between Isherwood and his mother coincided with another announcement that he was moving out. She suggested a repeat holiday together in Freshwater Bay "while he found rooms." He turned her down.[16] In fact, he did not move out, but he began to spend even more time away, mostly abroad.

As trustee, Kathleen had to give permission for the Marple furniture sale, and she attended the law courts to do so on a rainy July 4. The sale was set for July 30 and 31. The illustrated catalogue made her very sad, thirty-one pages, 378 lots. Antique silver and china, arms and armor, paintings, rare and valuable books, cupboards, chests, tables, chairs, four tapestries, including the two Gobelins ones. The family portraits were withdrawn at the last minute, but paintings sold included the one of Queen Elizabeth I and the double portrait of John Donne and Anne More.[17] By chance, Agatha Christie attended and bought two of the fifteen Jacobean oak dining chairs Kathleen loved. She also chose for free the name of the spinster detective she was then creating, Miss Marple.[18]

Symonds the lawyer deemed the sale a success, but Kathleen felt crushed: "only £7,000 for the silver & old tapestries & old oak—" She posted a newspaper account to Isherwood, who showed no sign of caring. He spent twelve days at Freshwater Bay in June, then in July returned to Germany to meet Auden in the Harz Mountains at a village called Rothehütte. Berthold

Szczesny was expected but did not appear, so Isherwood went to Berlin to look for him, to no avail. Szczesny finally wrote from Amsterdam, on the run from the police, and explained that he was shipping out as a deckhand to South America. Isherwood rushed to Amsterdam to say goodbye, accompanied by Auden. He raised funds for travel and for entertaining Szczesny by selling his watch and chain, probably the one given him by Uncle Henry.[19]

In fact, Isherwood was well aware of Kathleen's feelings about the furniture. Furniture turned up in telling fashion in his writing over the following decade, fictionally displaced to Berlin. In *Mr. Norris Changes Trains*, the comic spy thriller that was to win his first large audience with its portrayal of the Berlin demimonde, furniture is at the heart of an astringent dismissal of material possessions, a hidden attack on Kathleen's values and sentiments. Isherwood's narrator, William Bradshaw, overhears whispered conspiratorial telephone conversations brushed off by Mr. Norris as being about "nothing more desperate than the sale of some old furniture in which I happen to be—er—financially interested." After an indulgent dinner at Norris's Berlin flat, Bradshaw reports, "I must have been rather unsteady on my feet, because, when I stood up at the end of the meal, I knocked over my chair. On the underside of the seat was pasted a ticket with the printed number 69." (Isherwood could not resist using the slang term for mutual oral sex.) Norris pretends the ticket is "merely the catalogue number from the sale where I originally bought it." Then, under pressure from Bradshaw, Norris admits that every piece of furniture in the room has been marked by the bailiff, although he cannot bear to name the bailiff in plain English: "I prefer the word *Gerichtsvollzieher*. It sounds so much nicer."[20]

Norris's circumstances are based on those of Isherwood's Berlin friend Gerald Hamilton, whose struggles with the bailiff were real. According to *Christopher and His Kind*, creditors tried to repossess his furniture after Hamilton lost his job selling advertising for the London *Times*.[21] Hamilton's spendthrift ways twinned him naturally with Uncle Henry. They had many other things in common, affording Isherwood the opportunity to reimagine his family's feuds writ large in the political history of Europe with a narrator based on himself who is the unwitting plaything of forces beyond his control just like Christopher had been as the infant heir to Marple Hall. Whether the inheritance is a crumbling house in the north of England, or Europe itself, a Mr. Norris type aligns with whomever holds the purse strings—a John Isherwood, a Muriel Bagshawe, or, as in the novel, a secret agent who is buying and selling political information that means life or death to others and whose power is cloaked with the curiously feminine alias "Margot." *Mr. Norris Changes Trains* is set in Germany, but it smokes with the fires of home.

ISHERWOOD PROBABLY MET Gerald Hamilton in the winter of 1930–31, possibly at the flat of the occultist and writer Aleister Crowley with whom Hamilton lodged for a time, or possibly at Fräulein Thurau's where Isherwood lodged. Hamilton was a large, loose, flapping man with fleshy lips and dainty habits, easily moved to criminal behavior to feed his unquenchable appetite for pleasure. He wore a wig to cover his baldness, and he was full of fibs about his personal history and social position, but it is fairly well established that he was born in Shanghai in 1890 to a Scottish china merchant; his real surname was Souter which he dropped for Hamilton, a given name. His mother died before he was one, and he was sent to her parents in England, educated at a Berkshire prep school and then public school at Rugby. He converted to Roman Catholicism, spent time in Rome, and traveled widely on an allowance from his father, then on a legacy from his mother, and then on another legacy from an aunt. During World War I, he was imprisoned at Brixton, first for suspected homosexual offenses then for treason for his involvement with Irish nationalism. After the war, he spent time in French and Italian prisons for helping to steal a pearl necklace.[22]

Having grown up with Henry, Isherwood was quick to recognize in Hamilton a character type he could explore without the close family connection, an avuncular friend he in fact soon called "Uncle Gerald." Uncle Gerald was, in some ways, a walking parody of Uncle Henry, equally greedy and spoiled, addicted to expensive lunch parties, custom suits, silk underwear, and with a camp personal style that seemed to belong to a past era. Isherwood wrote of Uncle Henry: "He spoke another language, which has long since become obsolete. He thought in terms of 'places' and family relationships, entails and mortgages. He would say contemptuously that a man wasn't 'worth a penny piece,' meaning that he had no unearned income." Hamilton, likewise, was obsessed with social position, describing his paternal ancestry as "faintly ducal"[23] and making much of his connections with minor royalty and aristocrats at the courts of Europe.

From the point of view of the law, Hamilton's crimes were more egregious than Henry's; Uncle Henry appropriated only treasures belonging to his family. He was inclined like Hamilton to sympathize with the "wrong" side; Isherwood later wrote of Uncle Henry that "Italy was his spiritual home: he spent every winter in Rome and always approved of Mussolini, who had made the trains run on time." Uncle Henry's "hardboiled bedroom-eyed Italian valet," as Isherwood once described him (Giuseppe), greeted visitors to Henry's flat with a Fascist salute and was to be interned at the start of World War II as an enemy alien.[24]

Religion, too, was a matter of style and personal comfort, and a way of seeking absolution for "sins" they never tried to stop committing. Hamilton identified as Irish and liked to compare himself with Oscar Wilde, that deathbed convert. About Uncle Henry, Isherwood wrote: "He belonged to a ninetiesish world of smart Catholicism—in which scandal was sniggered over at the end of dinner, and one's confessor was like a rich man's lawyer—paid to get you out of awkward spiritual jams."

Uncle Henry "was a great expert on Dickens, whom he called 'delicious,'"[25] and Isherwood counted on this to make Uncle Henry look favorably on *Mr. Norris Changes Trains*. For while he took pains to obtain Hamilton's written permission to publish, he made no such approach to Uncle Henry. Conveniently, Hamilton proudly and entirely claimed the character, even though, as Isherwood told a correspondent who also knew Hamilton, Norris "is very far from being an actual portrait of our mutual friend." The book unsettled Uncle Henry, and Isherwood expressed surprise, writing to Kathleen, "I'd felt certain that it was just the Dickens aspect of Mr Norris which *would* have appealed to him."[26]

Isherwood's family would have recognized in Norris, helplessly in debt, a Henry-like reprise of Mr. Micawber with whom ten-year-old David Copperfield lodges when he becomes a bottle washer at the London warehouse of Murdstone and Grinby: "The only visitors I ever saw or heard of," says Copperfield, "were creditors. THEY used to come at all hours, and some of them were quite ferocious."[27] Isherwood added plenty of sexual innuendo. In place of Mrs. Micawber's Boarding Establishment for Young Ladies, he introduced Olga's, where the young ladies, equipped with whips and boots, attend to teach rather than to learn.

Norris's wig, his two front doors and many other details gesture to a double life, a private man and a public show, harking back to the over-the-top stage performance by Herbert Beerbohm Tree in *David Copperfield* when Isherwood himself was ten and Uncle Henry's guest. The name Norris also invoked Dickens's New York Norrises in *Martin Chuzzlewit*, the genteel snobs claiming intimacy with the British peerage, grotesquely casual racists, from whose family circle young Martin extracts himself once they learn he has traveled steerage from London and they, "deceived by his gentlemanly manners and appearances," have "received a dollarless and unknown man."[28] Arthur of course also commemorated Isherwood's childhood playmate, Arthur Forbes, who charmed and challenged him, gave him an inscribed copy of *The Roly-Poly Pudding* about a hidden criminal underworld, and then disappeared—just as Arthur Norris does in *Mr. Norris Changes Trains*.

Uncle Henry also objected to Isherwood's narrator being called William Bradshaw, "Why does Henry object to my nom-de-plume?" Isherwood asked Kathleen. "Disgrace to the family or what? I hope the next cash-payment isn't in danger?"[29]

For his William Bradshaw character, Isherwood adopted the naive, curious, and completely unjudgmental persona of Copperfield "so young and childish, and so little qualified" that he didn't even know how best to spend his limited food money. Undoubtedly he also had in mind Proust, who had adopted for his narrator the tone of an ingenu easily fooled by the Baron de Charlus, connoisseur of pedigrees, ruthless pursuer of young men, who at first makes "the impression of a hotel crook" and barely conceals his homosexuality.[30] Behind Proust was the feckless Lucien de Rubempré in the clutches of the master criminal and master of disguise, Vautrin, in Balzac's *Splendeurs et misères des courtisanes* (*A Harlot High and Low*).

Again and again, *Mr. Norris Changes Trains* reveals Bradshaw's helpless and willing entanglement in Norris's greedy deceptions. Bradshaw ignores the warnings of his friends about his fatal tendency to "make up romances about people instead of seeing them as they are."[31] He is slow to discover that Norris once spent eighteen months in Wormwood Scrubs and is £5,000 in debt. He can hardly bring himself to believe that Norris would betray his political ideals for money, and he willingly serves as boy-bait in Norris's scheme to sell information about German Communist Party activities to French intelligence.

But Isherwood thoroughly and knowingly tipped off his readers as to the nature of the web in which Bradshaw is caught. The hook Bradshaw baits is for Baron Kuno von Pregnitz, whose name alludes to Germany's biggest ever homosexual scandal. The real-life relationship between General Kuno, Graf von Moltke, an underachieving Prussian officer, and the powerful, widely resented Prince Philipp zu Eulenburg-Hertefeld was exposed in the press in 1907 and triggered libel actions, blackmail, resignations, and suicides that destroyed many more people than the Oscar Wilde trial in England. Also, the scandal publicized Germany as a natural habitat for homosexuals.[32]

Isherwood told his mother, and she wrote in her diary, that the novel, "like all of my work has a severe underlying moral tone ... in fact it is a tract written in the form of a detective story." His remark insists that he put comedy, sex, spies, and scandal into *Mr. Norris Changes Trains* to beguile his readers while he cautioned them against fascism; otherwise, the novel might have seemed a boring "tract." He also told his mother he was "shocked" when reviewers found the book so funny that they overlooked its message, "they all completely ignore the tragedy at the end. They seem to find German politics just one long laugh."[33]

In a few lines near the end of the novel, Isherwood deftly twisted its parts like a kaleidoscope to reveal his darker theme—that Hitler fooled the whole German nation just as Norris fooled Bradshaw. He put the words in Norris's mouth; Norris, the survivor, the betrayer, the fugitive, the hypocrite, writes to Bradshaw from the New World about the crushing of the Left and the Nazi takeover: "It makes me positively *tremble* with indignation to think of the workers delivered over to these men, who, whatever you may say, are nothing more or less than *criminals*. [...] It is indeed tragic to see how, even in these days, a *clever* and *unscrupulous liar* can deceive millions."[34]

Mr. Norris Changes Trains was widely reviewed when it was published in 1935, as Uncle Henry probably knew. Everyone indeed found it funny; many treasured its psychological subtletly; some enjoyed the reinvention of Mr. Micawber; some were impressed by the portrait of Berlin as Bruening's power dwindled and the Nazis and Communists vied to take over;[35] a few found it repellent. "The great orgy of wickedness and perversion," the reviewer for the *Nottingham Journal* called it, and the reviewer for the *Listener* feared being corrupted.[36] Cyril Connolly, charmed by Isherwood's humorous presentation of Norris's sex life and political intrigues, saw in the novel a hidden autobiography of the William Bradshaw character: "by the end of the book he has grown up."[37] Connolly little knew how closely the plot resembled the particular family romance in which Isherwood indeed had grown up and how daringly it shone a light toward Uncle Henry.

ISHERWOOD WORKED ON the material in *Goodbye to Berlin* intermittently from late 1930 onward. When he assembled the material into a book, he arranged the six pieces to move from the private experience of the lonely foreigner outward into the urban scene that is the focus of national change before the chaotic diaspora of 1933. The opening pieces foreground English characters, the later pieces foreground German characters, developing the links between the former enemy nations. Furniture and property figure again, although Isherwood was more solemn and more oblique about it than in *Mr. Norris Changes Trains*.

The first and last pieces in *Goodbye to Berlin* announce themselves as diaries, including dates. Thus, the opening is titled "A Berlin Diary (Autumn 1930)"; however, the description of the street outside the narrator's window is carefully written to symbolize the intertwined material and moral destiny of Germany.

> Cellar-shops where the lamps burn all day, under the shadow of topheavy balconied façades, dirty plaster frontages embossed with scroll-work and heraldic devices. The whole district is like this: street leading into street of houses like shabby monumental safes crammed with the tarnished valuables and second-hand furniture of a bankrupt middle class.[38]

This fictionalized German locale, complete with heraldic devices, is haunted by Isherwood's English past and the impoverishment of his English family.

His mother's struggle to hold on to physical possessions is doubled in the struggle of his Berlin landlady to do the same.[39]

The objects Isherwood describes in Fräulein Schroeder's flat are imitation German antiquities. They parody Marple Hall with its gilded coats of arms, its hooded porters' chairs before the enormous fireplace, its seventeenth-century Dutch-glass windows depicting Christ, English kings, poets (including Milton's mother who was thought by the family to be a relation),[40] its shrine to Charles I. Here is what Isherwood wrote as he, purportedly, looked around the room he rented in late 1930 at Nollendorfstrasse 17:

> The tall tiled stove, gorgeously colored, like an altar. The washstand like a Gothic shrine. The cupboard also is Gothic, with carved cathedral windows: Bismarck faces the King of Prussia in stained glass. My best chair would do for a bishop's throne. In the corner, three sham medieval halberds (from a theatrical touring company?) together form a hatstand.[41]

In the Marple Hall sale, one lot included two pikes with fine heads and poles covered in velvet, similar to those in the Tower of London Armoury and dated 1480; another lot included a two-handed sword, probably of the reign of Henry VII, and also like one at the Tower of London.[42] Isherwood had once loved such things as he loved the Tower of London, but he refused to be possessed by possessions.

Hidden in these "diary" pages was his evolving argument with his mother. He presented Fräulein Schroeder's things as sham, yet they are cared for with the same passion as Kathleen cared. Things, he suggested, become invested with the ideals and beliefs of their owners; things appear to make an argument about how we should live and what we should believe:

> Here, at the writing-table, I am confronted with a phalanx of metal objects—a pair of candlesticks shaped like entwined serpents, an ashtray from which emerges the head of a crocodile, a paper-knife copied from a Florentine dagger, a brass dolphin holding on the end of its tail a small broken clock. What becomes of such things? How could they ever be destroyed? They will probably remain intact for thousands of years: people will treasure them in museums. Or perhaps they will be melted down for munitions in a war. Every morning Frl. Schroeder arranges them very carefully in certain unvarying positions: there they stand, like an uncompromising statement of her views on Capital and Society, Religion and Sex.[43]

Neither Fräulein Schroeder nor her real-life original Fräulein Meta Thurau was possessed of uncompromising views on Capital, Society, Religion, or Sex. Isherwood portrayed his landlady as the adapter and survivor she appears to have been. It was his mother who seemed to him uncompromising. The more so as he himself began to change. In her diary, Kathleen proudly recorded how she arranged her beloved possessions—furniture, mirrors, china, pictures—in unchanging patterns. "[T]he Japanese screen against the piano," she noted on moving into St. Mary Abbot's Terrace, where she also replicated parts of her mother's flat, "arranged the hall with the same things as at Buckingham St."[44]

Underneath a photo of Kathleen outside St. Mary Abbot's Terrace, Isherwood wrote in his album "The Proprietress." He might have written "The Landlady," for he paid Kathleen room and board when he was in town.[45] Fräulein Schroeder's declining fortunes are a more extreme version of Kathleen's: "Long ago, before the War and the Inflation, she used to be comparatively well off. She went to the Baltic for her summer holidays and kept a maid to do the housework. For the last thirty years she has lived here and taken in lodgers. She started doing it because she liked to have company."

Fräulein Schroeder clings to a genteel self-image, telling "Herr Issyvoo," as she calls him, "'*My* lodgers aren't lodgers,' I used to say. 'They're my guests.'" The downward economic spiral after World War I and the hyperinflation of 1923 took away her choice of guests, then it took away her maid, then her bedroom. A year after the October 1929 Wall Street Crash and the onset of the worldwide Depression, Frläulein Schroeder sleeps on a sofa behind a screen in her living room and does all the housework herself, including clearing up human waste: "'Why I remember the time when I'd sooner cut off my right hand than empty this chamber . . . And now,' says Frl. Schroeder, suiting the action to the word, 'my goodness! It's no more than pouring a cup of tea!'"[46]

AFTER HIS SECOND trip to Germany, Isherwood took another tutoring job during August 1929 with a boy called Wallace Lanigan at a seaside hotel in Bettyhill, Scotland, which he had visited on his road trip with Bill de Lichtenberg. There he had what he described in *Christopher and His Kind* as "his first—and last—complete sex experience with a woman." The woman was Mrs. Lanigan, his pupil's mother. Drunk, after dark, he applied all he had learned in Berlin, felt "genuinely aroused," and recalled a mutually satisfactory outcome. But he was not converted.[47]

He described the experience—like so many key experiences in his life—as if it had come about by chance and was not important. However, the timing and the well-chosen remote location far from friends or family suggest that he may have been looking for an opportunity to double-check whether some kind of heterosexual life was possible for him. His diary reveals that Bill de Lichtenberg had begun a sexual relationship with Mrs. Lanigan on the 1928 trip to Bettyhill and continued it afterwards,[48] so Isherwood knew when he took the job that Mrs. Lanigan liked sex.

Half a century later, Isherwood was to describe his sexual orientation as a personal choice rooted in his need to rebel against conventional values and against his overly intimate relationship with his mother, yet his diction recognizes that he was choosing to embrace the nature he was born with:

> Girls are what the state and the church and the law and the press and the medical profession endorse, and command me to desire. My mother endorses them, too. She is silently brutishly willing me to get married and breed grandchildren for her. Her will is the will of Nearly Everybody, and in their will is my death. *My* will is to live according to my nature, and to find a place where I can be what I am ...

As with the whimsical titles he chose for his books, the incantatory poems he loved, the place names that hypnotized him, there was something about boys which Isherwood could not explain: "their shape and their voices and their smell and the way they move" made them "romantic" in a way girls could never be. "I can put them into my myth and fall in love with them."[49]

At the end of November 1929, he returned to Berlin to stay. After a few days in overpriced lodgings at Tauentzienstrasse 4, he moved into the annex adjoining Hirschfeld's institute on In den Zelten, where Hirschfeld's sister took lodgers and where a friend was already living. He reassured Kathleen about the neighborhood by saying the Tiergarten was the Hyde Park of Berlin and asked her to forward the manuscript he was working on, *The Memorial*. Thus, his novel about the effect of the war on his English generation was to be written in the German capital, where he rested from his work in the arms of German boys. Already, he was initiating the strange imaginative alchemy which would permit him to imbue his impressions of Berlin with the ghosts of his English past when he came to write *Mr. Norris Changes Trains* and *Goodbye to Berlin*. Already, he was experiencing personally the doppelgänger fate of the two warlike empires.

The friend lodging in the Hirschfeld annex was Francis Turville-Petre, a British archaeologist who was being treated for syphilis and who participated in Hirschfeld's work for sexual law reform in Germany and internationally as a member of the Scientific-Humanitarian Committee. Turville-Petre was three and a half years older than Isherwood, "slim and erect," as Isherwood later described him, though his black hair, which "fell picturesquely about his face," was already streaked with gray and his face "shockingly lined."[50] He came from a large Catholic family with ancestral land in Leicestershire, at Bosworth Hall. He had studied anthropology at Oxford and distinguished himself at only twenty-four when he dug up in Palestine, in a cave near the Sea of Galilee, the fossilized remains of the earliest humanoid skull that had yet been found in Western Asia—"Galilee Man." After that, his appetite for alcohol and for boys gradually ruined his professional reputation.

They had first met in July when Turville-Petre had helped look for Berthold Szczesny. Auden had suggested it because, at the time, Turville-Petre's German was much better than Isherwood's, and Turville-Petre was well known in the bars, where he was a regular. The boys called him *der Franni*.

Isherwood and Turville-Petre saw each other nearly every day. Isherwood would write in a café in the morning, then visit Turville-Petre "reading and smoking" in bed with a boy still asleep beside him and perhaps another boy on the couch. The syphilis treatment sometimes required Turville-Petre to rest all day. Isherwood later recalled in him "an aggression" toward anyone who had never had syphilis. "He appeared to feel it was their self-righteousness and cowardice that had prevented them from having it, and that they therefore *ought* to have it for the good of their souls." Despite recognizing that Turville-Petre's attitude harmonized with the teachings of Homer Lane and John Layard, "Christopher begged to be excused."[51]

At night, they would go out together, mostly to boy bars like the Cosy Corner. "Christopher was eager to know everything that Francis could tell him about Berlin, including the weird idioms of Berlinerisch slang," Isherwood later wrote.[52] He also wanted to know how to behave with the boys. Like any tourist, he didn't want to pay too much, and he was shy about it. Turville-Petre enjoyed bargaining. Usually, claimed Isherwood, he himself would go home around 10 p.m., sober, often alone, so he could write the next morning.

According to *Christopher and His Kind*, Turville-Petre didn't much care which boy he ended up with because he "wasn't much interested in making love." What fascinated him "and what began, more and more, to fascinate Christopher, looking at it through Francis's eyes—was the boys' world, their slang, their quarrels, their jokes, their outrageous unserious demands, their girls, their thefts, their encounters with the police."[53] This was the kind of anthropological or taxonomic interest Isherwood had shared with Auden about boarding-school boys, and which Isherwood had aired in his story "Gems of Belgian Architecure."

Before Christmas, 1929, Isherwood accompanied Turville-Petre to an all-male costume ball at a dance hall on In den Zelten. Many of the men were dressed as women. Conrad Veidt, star of countless films, including the 1919 homosexual love story *Anders als die Andern* (which Hirschfeld co-wrote and in which he appeared), "sat apart at his own table, impeccable in evening tails." Isherwood was impersonating his fantasy ideal, a boy of the streets, "in some clothes lent him by a boy from the Cosy Corner—a big sweater with a collar and a pair of sailor's bell-bottomed trousers. It gave him an erotic thrill to masquerade thus as his own sex partner." There was also the thrill of introducing some grit into the evening. In *Christopher and His Kind*, Isherwood recalled with satisfaction that Turville-Petre was criticized for "bringing a common street hustler into this respectable social gathering."[54]

Isherwood and Turville-Petre then went skiing at Riesengebirge, about two hundred miles away in Poland. This gave Isherwood some familiarity with mountain sporting life for the episode in *Mr. Norris Changes Trains* when Bradshaw is used to lure Baron Kuno to the Alps. They returned to Berlin for New Year's Eve 1929–30, a celebration even wilder than the hilariously drunken New Year 1930–31 that Isherwood was to portray in *Mr. Norris Changes Trains*. He wrote to John Layard that it "was like a Pabst film. Francis never went to bed at all. I only for sex purposes. The boy appeared to have delirium tremens and bit half through my lip."[55] The Pabst film Isherwood had in mind was *Die Büchse der Pandora* (*Pandora's Box*), adapted from Frank Wedekind's play and starring the boyish, sexy Louise Brooks. It was released in 1929, and Isherwood had seen it in the spring with Berthold Szczesny.

Louise Brooks became a star as the dancer and prostitute Lulu, and the character remained lodged in Isherwood's mind when he created Sally Bowles. His letter to Layard suggests that he saw in Lulu his boy lovers. The bite "half through my lip" parallels the scene at the end of Act 3 in *Pandora's Box*, in which Lulu bites the finger of her admirer Dr. Schön, triggering his lust. Brooks's marvelously appealing purity of heart also shines through in the androgynous reformatory and brothel scenes in Pabst's *Tagebuch einer Verlorenen* (*Diary of a Lost Girl*). Isherwood was to make a pilgrimage to meet Brooks and watch two of her films in Rochester, New York, in 1977 with Bachardy.

In his New Year letter to Layard, Isherwood offered hot gossip about Berlin boys—"Heine, who was nice but looked very seedy and down at heel," "Pieps, who is prosperous," "Francis' ex-wife, the blonde Gerhardt," forced to retire "to the claphouse," "Gunther (of the Harz), who was very overblown and wanted to start cadging"—just as he had once offered gossip to G.B. Smith about Repton boys. But now his friendships were explicitly sexual, and he reported that he was learning how to handle himself in the boy world: "Have also been seeing Franz, who is much improved—but we had a row the other day because I refused to give tisch-geld to his girl, whom

I'd very goodnaturedly given about ten drinks to at Franz's suggestion." (*Tischgeld* is money placed on the table for extra food, in this case for a tagalong girlfriend.) "I'm still known as a millionaire, but considered extremely stingy, because I simply cannot afford to give boys more than ten marks, a meal and drinks." He boasted he was "not unknown on the Passage," a shopping arcade off the great central boulevard Unter den Linden that was popular for pickups, and he asked, "Do you know the brothers Nowak? I think the older one may have been more or less of a permanent chum while I'm here. He's been away with an aunt in the Harz, and that's why I got bitten by his younger brother."[56]

Isherwood did not pursue either brother for long, but he was to borrow their surname for his story "The Nowaks."[57] He generally disguised boys' identities in his published work, where he blended them into types, but this letter to Layard highlights his interest in their individual personalities.

BACK IN ENGLAND during December, Richard failed his exams for Oxford and was overwhelmed by depression. He took refuge in his favorite book, "the Queens of England & marking in pencil selected paragraphs – I could scream!" wrote Kathleen in her diary, where she labeled this activity "compulsionism." The book was a twelve-volume work by Agnes Strickland; Richard had fallen in love with it at fifteen and bought all twelve volumes secondhand.[58]

He continued fragile in the new year. Kathleen filled the memoranda pages in her diary with proposed next steps—a new hospital for nervous disorders in Kent, a suburban gentleman offering "training to be a parson," the Pitman School of Shorthand, and the tutor Reverend Rabin, who had prepared Richard for the Oxford exam and proposed to try again in his vicarage near Winchester.

Richard volunteered in parish work in Shadwell, east of the City of London, and resisted Kathleen's suggestions. In February, she was pleased and surprised when he found a job on his own initiative. He went off each morning with a sandwich, spent the day writing letters for a Mr. Pollard, and received his first wages. At the end of Richard's third week, Kathleen recorded that he went out to lunch with Mr. Pollard and met Mr. Pollard's wife. After four weeks, she wrote, the lunch was repeated including "another boy too."[59]

Meanwhile, on February 19, 1930, Isherwood returned from Berlin for the first time since November. Relations with Kathleen had deteriorated badly after his first trip to Berlin the previous March, but now they were slowly restored.

The rapprochement between Isherwood and his mother ended abruptly on Saturday, March 22, when Kathleen received a call from a solicitor informing her that Richard had been arrested. She was too inhibited to record in her diary exactly what had happened, but evidently he had exposed himself to a young woman. Isherwood went with her to post bail, £10, and Richard left directly to tell his employer, Mr. Pollard, that he couldn't work that day.

The following Monday, there was a terrible scene, for Richard had confessed to his brother that his job with Mr. Pollard, and indeed Mr. Pollard himself, had never existed. He had made it all up to avoid returning to the country vicarage to study for Oxford.

Isherwood blamed Kathleen, and she poured out her heart to her diary over "the bitter hatred" she had inspired in her sons. "[O]nes death was the only reparation," she wrote melodramatically for having "ruined two lives." Yet on the same day, she frogmarched Richard to a possible typing school.[60]

Isherwood recalled her rage toward Richard many years later in *Christopher and His Kind*: "'If your father was alive,' she told him, 'you wouldn't dare behave like this!'" Looking back, Isherwood recognized that he had failed to support her: "it was his duty to play the affectionate peacemaker and help them work out a new way of living together." But at the time, he had sided with Richard. For him, the conflict wasn't really about Richard; it was about himself: "She had tried to turn Christopher into a Cambridge don, he said, to gratify her selfish daydream of the kind of son she wanted him to be. And since he had foiled her, by getting himself thrown out of college, she was trying to turn Richard into an Oxford don, against his will."[61]

On March 28, the family doctor—Kathleen's only confidant—attended the trial at West London Police Court with Isherwood and Richard, and the case was dismissed. "[T]he young woman looked hardly more than 14 C. said & got rather confused," Kathleen recorded. The solicitor "told R what to say & he said it." None of them recognized any possible injustice to the young woman.[62]

Isherwood wanted, above all, for his mother to understand that both he and Richard were homosexual, so he made clear to her, in explicit physical terms, what that meant. On April 1, according to Kathleen's diary, "Christopher in to lunch & tea & we talked most of the afternoon – largely on Sex." He later recalled that he had "told her coldly and aggressively about his life in Berlin. He made his acts of homosexual love sound like acts of defiance, directed against Kathleen." He felt she understood only "the hate in his voice."[63] He had wanted to speak to his mother like this for a long time, to come out to her and to be recognized without euphemism. The years of frustration made him savage. She wept.

After another long talk with his mother, Isherwood invited John Layard to tea upstairs in his room at Pembroke Gardens and asked Richard to join them but not Kathleen. Afterwards, Layard spoke to Kathleen "with his usual bluntness" and "she agreed meekly that she had made many mistakes." Richard became closer to his brother, sometimes having tea in Isherwood's room, and Isherwood continued his open hostility to Kathleen. He took Richard off to meet Layard a second time, at Layard's lodgings, then on May 8, he returned to Berlin, saying—though he later changed his mind—that he would never live in Kathleen's house again, "he begged that I would refuse to have him again, even if he suggested coming."[64]

Within his family, Isherwood had succeeded in smashing the sexual taboo. Richard tried to find his way into homosexual circles in London, partly through Layard. Layard, whose counseling was not all about sex, also introduced Richard to Christian social welfare activities.

Richard, unlike his brother, never really knew what he wanted to do. When Isherwood was home, life at Pembroke Gardens was like a carnival, with friends in and out and the phone constantly ringing. Richard was included in some of it, but then Isherwood would leave and Richard would feel depressed. Upward took him out every couple of months and once Auden gave him lunch. During 1931, Richard wrote often to Isherwood and even produced some weird, intense Mortmerish fiction.[65]

IN BERLIN THAT May, Isherwood met Walter Wolff, about sixteen or seventeen years old, with whom he began a passionate and tortured relationship that lasted off and on for more than a year. Wolff was much taller than Isherwood, with a lean, smoothly muscled torso and thick hair that went blond in the sun and which he allowed to grow long and flop over one side of his face. He used his glamorous physical presence to keep Isherwood off balance and often got the upper hand in the relationship by openly caring more about Isherwood's money than he did about Isherwood. It was a battle, an obsessive wrestling match, not a sentimental journey, and it brought out Isherwood's masochism along with his determination to triumph in a long game.

Isherwood fictionalized Walter Wolff as Otto Nowak in *Goodbye to Berlin*, making him the center of two stories, "On Ruegen Island (Summer 1931)" and "The Nowaks." Ruegen Island is a holiday destination about 150 miles north of Berlin in the Baltic Sea. It has wide sandy beaches and forests of pine and beech. Isherwood stayed there in the early summer of 1931 with Spender, Wolff, and Auden in a resort village called Sellin. He stayed there again the following summer, with his new boyfriend Heinz Neddermeyer,

Stephen Spender, Spender's brother Humphrey—who was to become a professional photographer—and several other Berlin friends.

"On Ruegen Island (Summer 1931)" drew on both these holidays, and also on a trip with Wolff to Hamburg, where they visited Stephen Spender in the summer of 1930. Despite the specific date, it is not a diary record; on the contrary, it is intensively fictionalized. "On Ruegen Island," like Isherwood's narratives set on the Isle of Wight and later on other islands in Greece and the Canaries, portrayed the oblivious, sensual life at the seaside that Isherwood had loved since childhood. Physical and psychological interactions take center stage while historical forces are trivialized or pushed to the background. Germany's battling factions are represented at the beach by sand forts flying the flags of hometowns or political parties and decorated with clan names and allegiances spelled out in pine cones. "I saw a child of about five years old, stark naked, marching along all by himself with a swastika flag over his shoulder and singing 'Deutschland über alles,'" says the narrator.[66]

The story contrasts the privileged neurotic Englishman of Isherwood's post-World War I generation with the natural, physical, working-class German. Isherwood named the Englishman Peter Wilkinson and made Otto Nowak his lover. Peter adores Otto and is dominated by him physically, as Isherwood shows by describing the kind of subtle and intense chemistry at play in D.H. Lawrence's narratives, for instance between Rupert Birkin and Gerald Crich in *Women in Love*: "Otto moves fluidly, effortlessly; his gestures have the savage, unconscious grace of a cruel, elegant animal. Peter drives himself about, lashing his stiff ungraceful body with the whip of his merciless will."[67]

Otto prefers women. He goes out dancing with the girls at the *Kurhaus* (the spa) and befriends a young woman teacher in charge of a band of orphans on holiday. Otto's malicious triumph and Peter's passivity are reported in ruthless detail by the Isherwood character narrating the story: Otto wrestles Peter to the floor to humiliate him in front of Isherwood; Otto "takes the better chair as if by right"; he challenges Peter: "Why must you always look in the same direction as I do?"[68] Finally, he robs Peter and runs off back to Berlin.

Isherwood based Peter partly on himself and partly on a friend, William Robson-Scott, a linguist and lecturer in English at the university in Berlin and, later, a translator of Freud, who joined him on Ruegen Island in 1932. In *Christopher and His Kind*, he explained: "In real life, William and Otto never even met."[69] The fictional relationship afforded Isherwood imaginative space to explore his own relationship with Wolff, the real-life sexual power struggle that he attempted to win with money and sheer force of will.

In *Christopher and His Kind*, Isherwood quoted passages from the story, replacing the name "Peter Wilkinson" with "Christopher." Thus, he revealed that the triangle in the story—Peter Wilkinson, Otto Nowak, and the narrator—was inspired by a real triangle between himself, Wolff, and Stephen Spender. But this simple substitution made in the 1970s was misleading not only because the Peter Wilkinson character was partly based on Robson-Scott—neurotic as a result of gruesome family tragedies distinct from Isherwood's—but also because the character drew on a literary persona Isherwood enjoyed assuming in front of Spender, Philip Carey in Maugham's *Of Human Bondage* "who becomes the slave of Mildred, the faithless, rapacious teashop waitress"[70] just as Peter Wilkinson becomes the slave of Otto. The substitution was the more misleading because the third-party observer in the story was not so much Spender as Isherwood seeing himself through Spender's eyes.

Already in the early 1930s, Isherwood knew that the struggle of wills portrayed in "On Ruegen Island" was a key to his writing, even if it was embarrassing and attracted painful mockery. "He was well aware of his masochism and his domineering will; they were part of his survival technique as a writer. He needed to be made to suffer; otherwise he would have lapsed into indifference," he explained in *Christopher and His Kind*.[71] The passivity Kathleen had deplored in him in childhood and which had been such a disappointment to Upward was always lurking, and Isherwood was alert to its dangers.

TOWARD THE END of August 1930, Upward made the first of three visits to Berlin, where his growing inclination to communism pricked Isherwood to a greater awareness of their material surroundings. "Here was the seething brew of history in the making—a brew which would test the truth of all the political theories," wrote Isherwood looking back in *Christopher and His Kind*. "The Berlin brew seethed with unemployment, malnutrition, stock-market panic, hatred of the Versailles Treaty, and other potent ingredients." In the September 1930 Reichstag elections, "the Nazis won 107 seats as against their previous 12, and became for the first time a major political party."[72]

Isherwood decided to immerse himself more deeply in working-class life, and in October, he left Hirschfeld's Institute and moved in with Walter Wolff and his family in their slum tenement at Simeonstrasse 4, Hallesches Tor. Later, he played down the enormity of the change: "such slumming seemed a thrilling adventure," he wrote, pointing out he had gone for only a month and claiming that he'd always had enough money to afford something better if he'd wanted.[73] But according to Kathleen's diary, his London bank account was overdrawn from August 1930, still overdrawn in November 1930, and

Uncle Henry was unreliable, holding back the first quarter allowance in 1930 then sending £15 won gambling in Monte Carlo.

When he was writing *Christopher and His Kind*, Isherwood emphasized his sexual motivations for the move; when he was writing "The Nowaks" in the 1930s, he emphasized his financial ones. To this end, he changed the time of the sojourn in the Nowak household from autumn 1930, when he actually lived with the Wolffs, to autumn 1931, after the British decision in September 1931 to abandon the gold standard, a decision which made the value of the pound fall so that all Englishmen in Berlin were poorer. Isherwood had long been exploring friendships outside his social class—with Alan Coyne, with Alfie the newsagent's boy, with George Peck—and it was not just the opportunity for nightly sex that drew him to the Wolffs' tenement. He wanted the complete domestic experience. It was, in its own way, a Test: could he handle real poverty? Naturally, he intended to write about it.

He was influenced a little by Baudelaire. He had translated *The Intimate Journals of Charles Baudelaire* during the autumn of 1929, Auden securing him the job from T.S. Eliot, and the translation was published in the autumn of 1930 with Eliot's introduction. The *Intimate Journals* are diary jottings and notes assembled after Baudelaire's death from syphilis, as Isherwood explained in his Translator's Preface to the 1947 American edition, where he also highlighted themes with which he identified at the time he moved into the Wolff tenement—Baudelaire's preference for poverty and bohemian digs over "the sheltered respectability of the family home," his quarrelsome, sometimes immature-seeming defiance of "bourgeois ethics" and all its representatives, including his mother for whom "he experienced mingled feelings of love, exasperation, pity, rebellion and hatred."[74]

The Wolffs' apartment was in the attic, so it had plenty of light, but the roof leaked. It had a kitchen, a living room, and one bedroom. Isherwood and Wolff slept in the bedroom, where there were two single beds. Wolff's older brother, a twenty-year-old Nazi, moved into a double bed in the living room with their twelve-year-old sister, and the parents slept in the other double bed, also in the living room. The toilet, one flight down, was shared with four other apartments, "unless they preferred to use the bucket in the kitchen." The Wolffs, like others in the tenement, had been told by the housing authority that the apartment wasn't fit for habitation, but they had nowhere else to go. A lodger brought in much needed extra money. In "The Nowaks," the "special treat" for dinner the night the Isherwood character arrives is lung hash, a cheap meal of ingredients some might discard.[75]

Isherwood found it difficult to write at the Wolffs'. He was still at work on *The Memorial*, a third draft. He introduced the project to satirical effect in "The Nowaks" as a novel "about a family who lived in a large country house on unearned incomes and were very unhappy."[76]

In "The Nowaks," "Christoph" takes refuge in the evenings at the nearby Alexander Casino, a fictional cellar *lokal* which resembles the Cosy Corner, and which is frequented by many of the boys Isherwood knew in real life—Pieps, Kurt, Gerhardt. He included their stories of pickups, pickpocketing, shoplifting, brawling, hair-raising escapes from the police, and days on the road; these stories were a true-to-life advance on what he had read in Dickens. Privileged foreigners, from the world Christoph had left behind, appear on weekends at the Alexander Casino, discussing "communism and Van Gogh and the best restaurants. Some of them seemed a little scared: perhaps they expected to be knifed in this den of thieves." In his role as observer and recorder, Christoph identifies with both the privileged foreigners and the thieves; he "could sympathize" as he eavesdropped on one of the sex tourists, even though "it was saddening to know that, two weeks hence," the tourist "would boast about his exploits here, to a select party of clubmen or dons—warmed discreet smilers around a table furnished with historic silver and legendary port."[77] This was just how Isherwood boasted in Uncle Henry's Belgravia dining room.

Herr Nowak is portrayed as a World War I veteran who had been reluctant to shoot the enemy and who had spoken French during the war, doubling Frank Isherwood, who didn't like to fire his revolver and who had written to Christopher from his bivouacks among French civilians that "I am getting a great French scholar & can talk away sometimes like anything." Herr Nowak's work is moving furniture, a comic link with Bradshaw Isherwood preoccupations. The relationship between Otto Nowak and his mother dominates life in the tiny flat, and it is as fraught as the real-life relationship between Isherwood and Kathleen, for many of the same reasons. Mother and son quarrel over Otto's irresponsible pleasure-seeking and his failure to get steady work after the sacrifices Frau Nowak has made for him. When Otto and his mother are both enraged, wrote Isherwood as if in self-recognition, "the resemblance between them was quite startling." And they act out their illnesses competitively like Isherwood, Richard, and Granny Emily: Frau Nowak's tuberculosis, her exhausting cough, her hunger for a better life, vie with Otto's nerves and his failed attempt to slit his wrists: "I wanted to show her," Otto tells Christoph about the suicide attempt.[78] Of course, their economic circumstances tend to justify behavior less defensible among the financially more secure Bradshaw Isherwoods.

Christoph supplies a handkerchief to bandage Otto's wound, and Otto notices that the handkerchief is his own, suggesting the intimacy between them and also the insulation, for the handkerchief marks the moment at which Christoph decides to move on. Otto must nurse his own wounds. Auden once told Isherwood, after reading some of his diaries, "You've always known when to clear out." Isherwood elaborated: "Some sort of instinct in me, a back seat driver that runs one's life without one's knowing."[79]

In "The Nowaks," Christoph moves out of the tenement to a comfortable room in the west end. In real life, Isherwood left the Wolffs for a neighboring slum, Kottbusser Tor, at Admiralstrasse 38. From there, he continued observing the poor. In *Christopher and His Kind*, he was to mock his younger self for imagining that he had gone native—"one of those mysterious wanderers who penetrate the depths of a foreign land, disguise themselves in the dress and customs of its natives, and die in unknown graves"[80]—and to recall that when he went to register his new address with the police, he was flattered to hear he was the only Englishman in the neighborhood. But for a tenderly raised boy who had been unable to cope with the discomfort of boarding school, it was a genuine engagement with living down and out.

Around this time, Frau Wolff was admitted to a sanatorium for her tuberculosis, the first of at least two stays. In "The Nowaks," Isherwood portrayed Otto and Christoph's visit there as a trip to a kind of Hades, populated only by dangerously enticing women—like sirens or the phantom Willis in *Giselle*—from whom Christoph flees. An early version of the episode was titled "Death." Frau Nowak is delighted to receive visitors; they share coffee and cakes with her roommates—young, old, emaciated, incurable, defiant, victims of domestic abuse, a mystery to the doctors. Illness is their respite from the hardships of life.

The women are unnaturally excited "To see a real live man!" and they hungrily watch a married patient emerge with her husband from an implied coupling in a summer house, "the only place in the whole grounds where two people can be alone together." One patient, Erna, only eighteen, decides on Christoph: "her big dark eyes fastened on to mine like hooks: I could imagine I felt them pulling me down." With all the Gothic menace of a vampire, she assures him, "I'm not really a consumptive you know, Christoph." When they dance to a gramophone, she shivers in his arms, and her kiss offers "no particular sensation of contact." The consumptives gather like ghosts around the departing bus: "I had an absurd pang of fear that they were going to attack us—a gang of terrifying soft muffled shapes—clawing us from our seats, dragging us hungrily down, in dead silence."[81]

The story was Upward's favorite: "When you write a whole book as good as The Nowaks then we shall not have lived in vain," he told Isherwood in, probably, 1935. It was to clinch Isherwood's reputation as a cutting-edge leftist writer when it was published in *New Writing* in the spring of 1936. The poet and journalist Geoffrey Grigson, champion of avant-garde writing, singled it out as "remarkable," and the communist poet Cecil Day Lewis said it demonstrated "talent of the first order."[82]

Kathleen was to copy some of the reviews into her diary, tracking Isherwood's interest in the poor alongside her own experiences in London, where she was an almoner for the Charities Organisation Society (C.O.S.) and also made weekly visits to pensioners to deliver grant money for rent and groceries and to check on their well-being. She was moved to write a detailed account—unique in her diary keeping—of "an official visit" to a young couple in Hackney, formerly schoolteachers, who needed money for a uniform so the husband could take a job as a multilingual ship's steward. Emulating "The Nowaks," she described the accommodation in detail, above a tobacconist's—"very dear & no conveniences—for washing up just a gas ring"—their meager income, and their hunger. The wife "seemed to be living on next to nothing in way of food. Half a caulifower & a few potatoes & never had any breakfast."

A few months later, Kathleen wrote a long diary account about attending her first-ever parish funeral for one of her pensioners, a charlady. The other mourners at the funeral worked as maids.[83] Kathleen's miniature narratives about poverty show that she read Isherwood's work closely and was influenced to think about her own experiences in a new way. She was growing and changing. On the other hand, her shadowing had something in common with the terrifying phantoms at the sanatorium gathering around Christoph and Otto's departing bus.

IN DECEMBER 1930, Isherwood left Kottbusser Tor for the shabby but distinctly middle-class neighborhood of Nollendorfstrasse, where he took a room in Fräulein Meta Thurau's large second-floor flat. This was the flat he was to fictionalize as Fräulein Schroeder's in "A Berlin Diary (Autumn 1930)," the flat where Fräulein Kost entertains her gentlemen callers, where Bobby the bartender from the Troika, "a great expert in sexual questions,"[84] walks around in a hairnet, slaps Fräulein Schroeder on the bottom and receives a blow with a frying pan in return, where Fräulein Mayr, the unemployed Bavarian music-hall *Jodlerin*, lies on the floor with Fräulein Schroeder to hear the fight she has engineered in the flat below, and where Sally Bowles was to move in.

Isherwood's keynote in "A Berlin Diary" was urban dusk, a moment of transition from public to private life which excludes the lonely foreigner. "At eight o'clock in the evening the house-doors will be locked. The children are having supper. The shops are shut. The electric-sign is switched on over the night-bell of the little hotel on the corner, where you can hire a room by the hour."[85]

The imagery and rhythms of the prose recall T.S. Eliot's "Preludes": "The winter evening settles down / With smell of steaks in passageways. / Six o'clock." And Isherwood's "street leading into street" recalls the "half-deserted streets, / The muttering retreats / Of restless nights in one-night cheap hotels" in "The Love Song of J. Alfred Prufrock."[86] Looking and writing "from my window" at "the man shaving opposite and the woman in the kimono washing her hair," Isherwood was poised at the same thin partition between inner and outer world that Eliot deployed to portray the isolated, voyeuristic situation of the modern soul: "lonely men in shirt sleeves, leaning out of windows" or, come morning, "the hands / That are raising dingy shades / In a thousand furnished rooms."[87]

Eliot's furtive melancholy, his regretful handling of sexual desire, his use of words like "sordid" and "soiled" in connection with fantasy and the human body were changed by Isherwood to something playful and coy, despite Isherwood's mask of Prufrockian sexual solitude:

> And soon the whistling will begin. Young men are calling their girls. [...] They want to be let in. Their signals echo down the deep hollow street, lascivious and private and sad. [...] It reminds me that I am in a foreign city, alone, far from home. [...] at last I have to get up and peep through the slats of the venetian blind to make quite sure that it is not—as I know very well it could not possibly be—for me.[88]

Not long before Isherwood moved to Nollendorfstrasse, Sinclair Lewis—author of *Main Street* (1920), *Babbitt* (1922), *Elmer Gantry* (1925), *Dodsworth* (1929)—became the first American writer to win the Nobel Prize in Literature. "[F]or his vigorous and graphic art of description and his ability to create, with wit and humour, new types of characters," the Nobel committee announced on November 5, 1930. In the late 1920s, Lewis had lived in Berlin, where he met his second wife, Dorothy Thompson, Berlin correspondent for the Philadelphia *Public Ledger* and the New York *Evening Post*. According to the *New York Times*, Lewis's books were bestsellers in Germany, and his Nobel "brought joy to Berlin's literati."[89]

Following his controversial acceptance speech in Stockholm, the Lewises returned to Berlin, where they were fêted by American journalist friends, and where Dorothy had an emergency appendectomy that delayed their New Year's Day departure well into the winter. The winter of 1930–31 was Lewis's season in Isherwood's Berlin.

Forster had published a review of Sinclair Lewis's work eighteen months earlier in the London monthly *Life and Letters*. Isherwood evidently turned to it when he learned about the Nobel. The review was titled "A Camera

Man." Forster proposed that Lewis's "method" in *Main Street* was to offer "snapshots" of the imaginary mid-Western American town called Gopher Prairie. "And let us at once dismiss the notion that any fool can use a camera," Forster had written. "Photography is a great gift, whether or no we rank it as an art." Isherwood, with his boyhood love of the Brownie, certainly grasped the metaphor. Upward had brought him a new Kodak by request that August.

In his essay, Forster included five passages from *Main Street* exemplifying Lewis's instinctive, casual approach: "Click, and the picture's ours. A less spontaneous or more fastidious writer would have tinkered at all the above extracts, and ruined everything." He admired the way that Lewis positioned himself on a level with his subjects and was, at the same time, detached from them: "Always in the same house or street with his characters, eating their foodstuffs, breathing their air, Mr. Lewis claims no special advantages."[90] Here was an attitude with which the ambitious young Isherwood might pick up his pen or sit at his typewriter. He, too, had been living in the same house and street with his characters, eating their foodstuffs, breathing their air. For this, one might win a Nobel Prize.

In boyhood, Isherwood had learned to steady his camera against his own body while he pressed the shutter. "I am a camera," he now wrote, in what was to become the most famous paragraph of *Goodbye to Berlin*, "with its shutter open, quite passive, recording, not thinking." He was metaphorically describing his activity as a diarist. But he went on: "Some day, all this will have to be developed, carefully printed, fixed."[91] The work of the novelist was to come after the work of the diarist, and it could not be passive. The work of the novelist "developed" the material, transforming it into something considered and literary, with a depth of meaning that would repay rereading.

Lewis's Nobel, applauded by the press, was deplored by literary writers in England and America, and in a sense, it finished Lewis's career. His work dated, just as Forster prophesied in his 1929 essay, where he pointed out that Lewis's knack for spontaneity limited deeper development: "Only occasionally has he thought of the past, the future, international relationships, science, labour, the salvation or damnation of the globe."[92]

Isherwood, though he often deprecated his own seriousness, *was* concerned with the past, the future, international relationships, science, labor, the salvation or damnation of the globe. Throughout *Goodbye to Berlin*, he pressed for connections between the material world that he could see and describe—that a camera might capture—and the underlying, changing direction of history which he understood through his preparation at Repton and even at Cambridge. He was to spend more than half a decade "developing" his material, highlighting patterns and connections among his Berlin stories in order to achieve a fictional whole more penetrating and revealing than individual snapshots, even while he permitted the pieces to be published individually in *New Writing*. He never acknowledged any debt to Lewis because his real debt was to Forster. Don Bachardy later remarked that Isherwood had "little regard for Lewis's work" and didn't possess copies.[93]

Isherwood was introduced to Forster in London in September 1932 by a mutual friend, the South African writer William Plomer. He recalled in *Christopher and His Kind* that Forster praised *The Memorial*, published earlier that year. Isherwood told friends that he cared more for this personal praise from his master than for public acclaim; he even dismissed the Nobel Prize: "My literary career is over—I don't give a damn for the Nobel Prize or the Order of Merit—*I've been praised by Forster!*"[94] But it had not been at all easy getting *The Memorial* published.

IN MARCH 1931, *The Memorial* was rejected by Isherwood's publisher, Jonathan Cape. Friends had called it a masterpiece, and Isherwood had optimistically traveled from Berlin to be on hand for Cape's decision, reconciling with Kathleen and staying at Pembroke Gardens. "The rejection of your second novel—quite a common experience—is more painful than any number of rejections of your first; at least, Christopher found it so," he later wrote. "Christopher's self-confidence was shaken."[95]

Having established himself as a professional, Isherwood was now a failed novelist. He returned to Berlin in a vulnerable state. On Spender's advice, he had passed *The Memorial* to the agent Curtis Brown and received three more rejections. The holiday on Ruegen Island with Auden and Spender and Wolff was filled with career tensions that are not aired in "On Ruegen Island (Summer 1931)." "All in all, this Ruegen visit wasn't a success," Isherwood was to recall. Auden, who had "rather unwillingly" joined the Ruegen holiday, shut himself away from the sun all day writing, "I suppose he was working on *The Orators*."[96] In *Christopher and His Kind*, Isherwood acknowledged that he had felt uneasy because Spender had a camera and was constantly taking pictures. The invading camera also represented the unspoken threat of Spender's pen, which Isherwood did not mention. Spender was at work on a novel about his sexual emancipation in Germany, *The Temple. I* am a camera, Isherwood wrote—not we. Isherwood wanted and needed to be master of the pen or typewriter transcribing his own sexual emancipation. He did not want to be scooped by Spender.

Wading in the Baltic, Isherwood trod on a sharp piece of tin, cutting his toe badly. "The cut festered," he reported in *Christopher and His Kind*, "and he was a semi-cripple for several weeks after his return to Berlin." It was the acting leg all over again. In addition to the infected toe, he came down with a sore throat which confined him to his current digs in Kleiststrasse. From there he wrote to Spender, who was proposing to join him, "I think I could find you something cheaper two doors away. I think it's better if we don't all live right on top of each other, don't you?" As a failed novelist, Isherwood needed space. Auden, too, sometimes felt crowded by Spender, writing to Isherwood before one of his return visits to Berlin, "Don't die, don't leave Berlin before January, and keep Stephen out of it."[97]

Spender carried on as ambassador for Isherwood in London. He gave the manuscript of *The Memorial* with lavish praise to John Lehmann, whom Isherwood had not yet met. Lehmann worked for Leonard and Virginia Woolf at their Hogarth Press. "I am praying to God to soften the heart of Virginia Woolf," wrote Isherwood on August 12. In another letter, he told Spender how grateful he was: "If the Hogarth do take it, it will be entirely because of you."[98] He remained on tenterhooks because the Woolfs decided they wanted to read *All the Conspirators* before making up their minds.

Throughout this period of anxious uncertainty, Isherwood encouraged Spender with *The Temple*, prodded him to send what he was working on, and praised what he received. Spender planned to dedicate his first volume of poems to Isherwood, but he was to change his mind because they quarreled. On a visit to London, Isherwood was introduced to Spender's friends, only to find, as Spender freely admitted later, that "I had already told them most of his stories, and that I had been indiscreet." Isherwood wrote a letter saying that he would not return to Berlin if Spender did because, as Spender paraphrased, "my life was poison to him, that I lived on publicity, that I was intolerably indiscreet, etc." So Spender, "tremendously and tearfully hurt," destroyed Isherwood's letter and gave up Berlin. His *Poems* appeared in 1933 without any dedication. When the volume was reprinted in 1934, Spender restored his intention with the line "Inscribed to Christopher Isherwood."[99] The rivalry between them was to rumble on.

At the beginning of September 1931, the Hogarth Press accepted *The Memorial*. It was the natural home for a book that owed so much to Woolf's writing and to the writing of her friend (and rival), Forster. Isherwood was again a professional novelist. On publication in February 1932, the reviewer for the *Daily Herald* was to write that it "shines out, a brilliant story of postwar England. It scintillates with quick, impressionistic scenes of almost everybody." The reviewer for the the *Times Literary Supplement*, mistakenly identifying it as Isherwood's first novel, was ambivalent about the "original technique," which relied on character and atmosphere rather than plot, and found it "disconcertingly, perhaps unnecessarily, frank" in its portrayal of the relationship between Margaret Lanwin and Edward Blake and Blake's "various *liaisons*" with "his young male friends."[100] Isherwood's controversial career had begun in earnest.

As soon as *The Memorial* was accepted, he began another book about his English past, *Memoirs of Pine House*, the prequel, later abandoned, to *Lions and Shadows*. All the while, Berlin sometimes threatened to overwhelm him. He reported to Spender the old boarding-school sensation of being slowly obliterated, now by the volatile politics of the city: "This Revolution-Next-Week-atmosphere has stopped being quite such a joke and somehow the feeling that nothing catastrophic really will happen only makes it worse. I think everybody everywhere is being ground slowly down by an enormous tool. I feel myself getting smaller and smaller."

As he had done at St. Edmund's, Isherwood fought off his feeling of personal annihilation by making a detailed record. To Spender, he called it "a sort of extra-elaborate diary"; to Upward, he emphasized its documentary plainness: "It has no technique, no gambits, no orchestration and no approaches, but is good hot stuff."[101] This was some of his raw material for *Mr. Norris Changes Trains* and *Goodbye to Berlin*.

Money continued short, and he moved into a cheaper room at Fräulein Thurau's. He was teaching English that autumn, 1931, "going for morning walks with a German-American boy." Spender later recalled that in Berlin at this time, "you not only had to work very hard to earn very little, you also had to be a financial genius to get paid."[102]

Isherwood sent stories to Curtis Brown hoping the agency could place them, and he badgered Harold Nicolson, the writer and diplomat, to commission a regular "Berlin Letter" or book reviews for his magazine *Action*. The British Fascist Oswald Mosley was also a contributor and later commandeered the magazine for the British Fascist Union. Upward, who occasionally gave or loaned Isherwood money during this period, recognized that Isherwood, as a pen for hire, was careless of the political affinities of his employers. "Stephen says you're going to write for Action. They're the dirtiest lot of scum in England," he warned. Upward was by now attending the communist committee rooms at Bethnal Green every day.[103]

The piece Isherwood wrote for *Action* was about the Wandervögel movement, young Germans hiking all summer and sleeping in one of Germany's more than 2,000 hostels, "boys and girls belonging to every conceivable political and religious group, bare-armed, bare-legged, twanging their mandolins and singing as they march." They included both communists and fascists, as he explained, and "a sprinkling of boy tramps, often from good families, sick of town life and eager for adventure."[104]

The Wandervögel headed to the lakes and forests without their uncomfortable Sunday clothes because they wanted "to get away, to be free," like Isherwood himself, from "the pompous bewhiskered fathers of families, the ample, stuffy mothers, the awkward crop-headed sons in their thick black suits and suffocating stiff collars, the heel-clicking, the parade-ground patriotism, the interminable public festivals, the Sunday promenades, the ceremonial drinkings of beer," and the "nasty, half-scared, half-smirking attitude towards sex" hidden by these conventional pursuits. They wore open-necked shirts with "Schiller" collars turned back flat, without buttons, studs or ties. Isherwood had first experienced the excitement of open-necked shirts on his trip to Bremen in 1928, noting laces on some boys' shirts, and he had probably read about the Wandervögel movement, possibly in Lawrence's *Lady Chatterley's Lover*, before coming across it in real life. He optimistically described this counterculture movement as "a mystical ideal" which "stood outside politics." But he soon recognized that however much he needed money, *Action* was not a suitable employer. "It seems to be the rankest John Bull stuff," he wrote to Spender the first time he actually saw a copy.[105]

"SHE WAS DRESSED in black silk, with a small cape over her shoulders and a little cap like a page-boy's stuck jauntily on one side of her head," Isherwood wrote in *Sally Bowles*.

> I noticed that her finger-nails were painted emerald green, a colour unfortunately chosen for it called attention to her hands, which were much stained by cigarette-smoking and as dirty as a little girl's. [...] Her face was long and thin, powdered dead white. She had very large brown eyes which should have been darker, to match her hair and the pencil she used for her eyebrows.

The eccentric clothing, the unsteady hat, the childish dirtiness, the homely, appealing visage might once again have been refashioned from Dickens, offering Sally, the child-woman, as a new kind of Artful Dodger to Isherwood's Oliver Twist. The narrator and his friend Fritz Wendell watch Sally coo down the telephone in German as if she were playing "a performance at the theatre." Then:

> She hung up the telephone and turned to us triumphantly.
> "That's the man I slept with last night," she announced. "He makes love marvellously. He's an absolute genius at business and he's terribly rich—"[106]

Sally is depicted as a more lively actress in her personal life than on stage in her nightclub act, all the better to defy expectation and shock observers in both audiences: "She sang badly, without any expression, her hands hanging down at her sides—yet her performance was, in its own way, effective because of her startling appearance and her air of not caring a curse what people thought of her."[107]

Her boyish, devil-may-care determination to get on with the show hides any inward uncertainty, but Sally is only an amateur, barely getting by. Her nightclub job will last another week; the hoped-for movie offer never comes through. She is immersed in the underworld of a dangerous city, vulnerable, resilient, an instinctive performer; her trade is not picking pockets but picking up men. She is easy prey to the stereotyped, Dickensian, money-fingered Jew, telling the narrator: "there's an awful old Jew who takes me out sometimes. He's always offering to get me a contract; but he only wants to sleep with me, the old swine."[108]

Isherwood endows her with an unstainable purity linked to her childish inability to gauge exactly what impression she makes with her performances. One costume, her black silk dress with the addition of white collar and cuffs, "produced a kind of theatrically chaste effect, like a nun in grand opera. 'What are you laughing at, Chris?'" she demands.[109] Neither of them knows.

As with Isherwood's childhood friend Mirabel Cobbold, the pair in the story fall out over the narrator's wounded vanity. Sally asks Chris to ghostwrite a magazine article for her about the English Girl, then rejects it. In revenge, he plays a nasty trick, bringing the police down on her. But nothing dampens her spirits for long. "The whole idea of the study is to show that even the greatest disasters leave a person like Sally essentially unchanged," Isherwood was to tell Lehmann.[110]

Jean Ross, the real-life original of Sally Bowles, was seven years younger than Isherwood, born in Alexandria, where her father worked for the Bank of Egypt classifying cotton. She was sent to boarding school in England, was thrown out for pretending to be pregnant, was sent to a Swiss finishing school, and then studied acting at RADA for a year on a trust fund allowance.[111] She worked as a model, actress, and singer, and aspired to film. Later she became a journalist.

Ross was nineteen when Isherwood met her, probably in October 1930, at the apartment of a Hungarian baron, Franz von Ullman, portrayed in *Goodbye to Berlin* as Fritz Wendel. According to Spender, von Ullman was Jewish, worked in publishing and perhaps only pretended to be a baron.[112] Ross was then singing at a nightclub intermittently. She was an extra in Max Reinhardt's spectacular production of Offenbach's opera *Tales of Hoffmann* in

Berlin in November 1931, and Kathleen and Richard later saw her in a small experimental production of Ibsen's *Peer Gynt* in London.

With Isherwood's encouragement, Ross moved into Fräulein Thurau's flat early in 1931 and lived there for five or six months until her love life became too exciting even for Fräulein Thurau: "Jean and Kantorowicz made such a mess of their bedclothes that Thurau has forbidden him the house," Isherwood told Spender, evidently referring to the German-Jewish communist journalist Alfred Kantorowicz, who was later a contributor to *New Writing*.[113] So Ross moved elsewhere with a friend, Erika Glück, rumored to be a heroin addict. Meanwhile, she had become pregnant by Götz von Eick, a German-Jewish musician, and Isherwood helped her get an abortion in the early summer of 1931. This was illegal at the time; it was done sloppily and nearly killed her.[114]

The abortion was the chief reason that Isherwood took great care to get Ross's permission before publishing *Sally Bowles*, in which he incorporated it. She said yes when he showed her the story in the autumn of 1936, and Lehmann planned to run it in *New Writing*. Then she changed her mind, so Isherwood gave Lehmann "A Berlin Diary (Autumn 1930)" instead. In February 1937, Ross agreed after all, and *Sally Bowles* appeared as an individual novella from the Hogarth Press.

Isherwood portrayed von Eick as Sally's piano accompanist Klaus Linke, who abandons her by letter from London. In real life, von Eick indeed moved on to London and then New York, earning his living as a pianist and assistant stage director until he resurfaced in Hollywood as the actor Peter Van Eyck, specializing in Nazi villain roles. Tennessee Williams found Van Eyck "*excruciatingly* beautiful" and told a friend that the atmosphere between Van Eyck and his then wife, the actress Ruth Ford, "was charged with an almost hysterical sexuality and torment of jealousy and suspicion although there was much exchange of darlings and kisses all around."[115] The marriage with Ford did not last much longer than the affair with Ross.

In August 1932, Isherwood dictated the first version of the story to his brother Richard, who wrote it out longhand; it included material later separated into "The Nowaks." Isherwood was freshly returned to London from Germany and so was Ross. He visited her four times in six days. They had dinner, lunch, and tea at her digs in Pembridge Square, Notting Hill, dined with her family and with the actor and director Nigel Playfair. Then Isherwood went home to Pembroke Gardens and shared the friendship aloud with Richard as he had once shared *The History of My Friends* with his mother.

The dictation was the culmination of Isherwood's renewed effort to bring Richard into his life. They worked together for three weeks, from August 13 until September 8, then Isherwood typed up the draft himself. Thus, *Sally*

Bowles began as a performance acted out far from Berlin. Isherwood later described the dictation as "a supreme act of intimacy. It is immeasurably more embarrassing for a writer to invent crudely in someone else's presence than to confide to him the most shameful personal revelations." Energy spread through Pembroke Gardens, as with Christopher's childhood Shakespeare seasons, now intensified by secrecy. "Their collaboration brought a feeling of subdued excitement into the household. Something—no matter exactly what—was going on upstairs, behind Christopher's closed door."[116]

In *Christopher and His Kind,* Isherwood said that he borrowed the American composer and writer Paul Bowles's surname for his character, Sally Bowles. Paul Bowles, aged twenty, was in Berlin studying composing with Aaron Copland, and Isherwood sometimes had lunch with him at the Café des Westens.[117] But Bowles was also a family name. Kathleen recorded in her "History of Marple and Wyberslegh Halls and the Bradshaw Isherwoods" that the current owner of Bradshaw Hall in Derbyshire was a Mr. C.E. Bradshaw Bowles, a direct descendant of the original Bradshaw owners. She had taken Isherwood to Bradshaw Hall in 1916, and they had toured the property with a servant. C.E. Bradshaw Bowles was also the author of a history of North Derbyshire which Kathleen had cut out and pasted into her history. Thus, Isherwood was tagging Sally as a runaway heir, like himself, and a kind of distant cousin. Sally's fictional full name, like his real name, is an embarrassing double-barrelled one, Jackson-Bowles, which she has jettisoned for her stage career.

Her first name, Sally, was perhaps borrowed from another friend, Sally Coole, an Oxford graduate teaching English at Berlin University and working as a correspondent for the London *Morning Post*, who appears in *Mr. Norris Changes Trains* as Helen Pratt.[118] More likely, Sally was named for the eponymous heroine of Jerome Kern and Guy Bolton's musical comedy *Sally,* which Isherwood saw in London in 1921.[119] The orphan dishwasher and would-be singer meets her prince in disguise and fulfills her dream of stardom as a Ziegfeld Follies dancer. In a characteristic twisting of the storyline, Isherwood's Sally never gets to marry her prince, but she lives by the spirit of two of the show's most popular tunes, "Look for the Silver Lining" and "You Can't Keep a Good Girl Down."

His Sally Bowles character has lasting vitality because Isherwood conjured her as an ideal type from many different forerunners—from stage, film, books, real life, and personal fantasies. Though she is depicted with the surface particulars of a real woman in the Berlin of the early 1930s, she is not a straightforward portrait of Jean Ross, nor of any single person. There was the tomboy Mirabel Cobbold, with whom Isherwood played and quarreled in Limerick and whom he saw acting the part of a sailor boy on the eve of his departure for boarding school. There was Katherine Mansfield, his literary idol, with her bob and her bohemian lovelife, on the run from her middle-class background in New Zealand. There was the American actress Louise Brooks as Lulu and the Lost Girl in Pabst's films. There was, as Isherwood mentioned in a letter to Lehmann, the faux-naif London society flirt Miss Dolly Foster of *The Dolly Dialogues*, Anthony Hope's comic satire that ran in the *Westminster Gazette* in the 1890s before being collected as a book. There were the various scheming courtesans and grisettes in Balzac's *La comédie humaine*. In the same letter to Lehmann, Isherwood described *Sally Bowles* as "an attempt to satirize the romance-of-prostitution racket" and announced in a further paragraph, "I am reading Balzac."[120] Balzac's interconnected stories about nineteenth-century Paris certainly offered a more general inspiration for *The Lost*.

Then there was Isherwood himself. For Sally Bowles was Isherwood's own boy-girl alter ego, his female double, enthusiastically sleeping her way to nowhere. Casting his alter ego as a girl had the advantage of neutralizing his own sexual transgressions since any bad girl was, in the 1930s, far more shocking than any bad boy. As a woman, Sally is far more "lost" than the Isherwood character, and the Isherwood character can even masquerade as her protector.

Isherwood's childhood fantasy of sailing away to the ends of the earth, first acted out with his Limerick playmates, became in *Sally Bowles* part of a more sophisticated narrative in which Herr Issyvoo and Sally Bowles will be whisked away by Sally's rich, alcoholic, American lover, Clive: "The Orient Express would take us to Athens. Thence, we should fly to Egypt. From Egypt to Marseille. From Marseille, by boat to South America. Then Tahiti. Singapore. Japan." Clive was based on the rich and generous John Blomshield, who passed through their lives with lavish speed.[121]

In the story, Isherwood tellingly juxtaposed this fantasy of escape with the funeral cortège of Hermann Müller, the former chancellor of Germany, whose Social Democrats were trounced by Hitler in the elections of September 1930. The cortège—"Ranks of pale steadfast clerks, government officials, trade union secretaries"—trudges past Clive's window, symbolizing the death of Prussian social democracy; Clive, Sally, and Herr Issyvoo ignore it. "We had nothing to do with those Germans down there," the narrator persuades himself, thus making a pact with the devil as in Marlowe's *Doctor Faustus* or Marjorie Bowen's *Black Magic*:

> In a few days, I thought, we shall have forfeited all kinship with ninety-nine per cent of the population of the world, with the men and women who earn their living, who insure their lives, who are anxious about the future of their children. Perhaps in the Middle Ages people felt like this, when they believed themselves to have sold their souls to the

Devil. It was a curious, exhilarating, not unpleasant sensation: but, at the same time, I felt slightly scared. Yes, I said to myself, I've done it, now. I am lost.[122]

The coming blindside of Hitler was to repeat and amplify the disaster of World War I that Isherwood had experienced in the destruction of his happy childhood life. It was the unprepared, the gullible, the dreamers, the fantasists, the young who moved him. For all her knowing talk of sex, Sally Bowles is one of them, easily tricked. "'You know, Sally,' I said, 'what I really like about you is that you're awfully easy to take in. People who never get taken in are awfully dreary.'"[123] But Isherwood himself was on the alert, bearing witness to the unfolding disaster. He was not taken in, nor did he run away as the realities began to mount up. Instead, in his work, he focused more and more on the power of illusion in all arenas of Berlin life and on the hard line between real and imagined—in love as well as in politics. He was to last in Berlin until May 1933.

AMONG THE ATTRACTIONS holding him in Berlin was his lovable new boyfriend Heinz Neddermeyer. In the spring of 1932, Francis Turville-Petre rented a lakeside house in a village called Mohrin, fifty-five miles northeast of Berlin near the Polish border. To run the house, he hired from Berlin a cook-housekeeper and a boy helper. The cook-housekeeper was a young communist called Erwin Hansen who had served as a fitness instructor in the German army and then as odd-job man at Hirschfeld's institute. The boy was seventeen-year-old Neddermeyer. Turville-Petre invited Isherwood to live with him at Mohrin, and Isherwood later said in *Christopher and His Kind*, "Meeting Heinz was what finally decided Christopher to go with them."[124] In Mohrin, Isherwood and Neddermeyer started having sex and soon fell in love.

Turville-Petre grew bored in Mohrin and began returning to Berlin for the night life with Hansen. "Thus Christopher found himself keeping house with Heinz. This was a kind of happiness which he had never experienced before; he now realized he had always desired it." It depended simply enough on being able to write in a settled domestic arrangement, tucked away from the world. Isherwood told Spender that Neddermeyer "takes it as a matter of course that he shall do all the housework and cooking while I write my novel."[125]

The idyll was short-lived. The all-male household was denounced to the police, partly because Turville-Petre brought back more boys from Berlin.

Also, antagonism developed between Turville-Petre and Neddermeyer because Isherwood introduced Neddermeyer increasingly as a social equal.

Back in Berlin, Isherwood was to be drawn more fully into political developments. Upward's third visit was in April 1932, on his way home from a three-week tour of Soviet Russia "with a gang of Educationalists." "This place is utterly terrific," Upward had written from Leningrad. "No daydream could give an inkling of it."[126] He had also visited Ukraine and Moscow. He was shown a model Russia, not the famine, not the repression. When he returned to England, Upward joined the Communist Party.

Isherwood's own notion of revolutionary communism in Russia had been shaped by books and films. He had watched Pudovkin's film about the revolution, *The End of St. Petersburg* (1927), screened by the Film Society in London in 1929 and told his mother that it was "the finest he had ever seen. [B]ut propaganda & not for general release." According to Spender, he and Isherwood saw many Russian films in Berlin, including *October: Ten Days That Shook the World* (1927), *Battleship Potemkin* (1925), and *Earth* (1930), as well as others less well known. They "conveyed a message of hope like an answer to *The Waste Land*. They extolled a heroic attitude which had not yet become officialized."[127]

In 1928, Isherwood had acquired D.S. Mirsky's two-volume literary-critical history of Russian authors, and in the back of Mirsky's *Contemporary Russian Literature*, he had transcribed an English translation of "The Sons of Our Sons," the Bolshevik poet Ilya Ehrenburg's 1919 address to the generations coming after the horrific violence of the revolution.[128]

He questioned Upward about Lenin's position on homosexuality, but Upward was not well informed on this, and offered only vague assurances. Explaining their hopes in *Christopher and His Kind*, Isherwood was to say that the Russian revolutionary government "had declared that all forms of sexual intercourse between consenting individuals are a private matter, outside the law." But like so many ideals of the revolution, this was subject to the subsequent course of history and did not prove a reliable safeguard for homosexuals in the longer term. Already by 1934, the Soviet government had made homosexual acts punishable by imprisonment. Even in the shorter term, in late 1931, Isherwood told Spender that homosexuals must look out for themselves: "I'm through with the Communists. All politicians are equally nasty. We must work for our own sort of revolution all by ourselves."[129]

Nevertheless, in the autumn of 1932, Isherwood took a job translating for a communist relief organization, the Internationale Arbeiter-Hilfe (International Workers' Aid or IAH), founded by the communist propaganda genius Willi Münzenberg. He was hired by Louis Gibarti, a Hungarian revolutionary known as Münzenberg's right-hand man and "alter ego."[130]

Münzenberg was editor of *Die Welt am Abend*, a newspaper whose title alluded not only to the evening news but also to the twilight hours of capitalism about to undergo the great revolution prophesied by Marx. He had increased circulation from 3,000 in 1926 when he took over to 175,000 by the time Isherwood arrived in Berlin in 1929.[131] Gibarti was on the editorial staff of *Die Welt am Abend* and also on the staff of *Berlin am Morgen*. Münzenberg published many other leftist newspapers, magazines, and books around the world as well as organizing clubs and other initiatives to draw workers, students, and middle-class liberals to the communist cause through welfare activities that concealed links to Bolshevism. Although he had no personal fortune, he lived large on his media empire, acquiring the moniker the Red Millionaire. He was a founding member of the German Communist Party (Kommunistische Partei Deutschlands or KPD) and an elected Communist representative in the Reichstag. Leftist newspaperman Claud Cockburn later wrote that he "was popularly believed to be the real brains and driving force of the German Communist Party."[132]

Isherwood possibly knew Münzenburg personally. Münzenburg was friendly with Hirschfeld and from the mid-1920s rented a flat in the annex to the Institute for Sexual Science where Isherwood lived in 1929. According to Münzenburg's partner and biographer, Babette Gross, "the rooms were also suitable for meeting illegal visitors from abroad," like emissaries from Moscow and the Balkans; "visitors to the institute wandered through our corridors also." Isherwood may have been introduced by Gerald Hamilton, as is suggested by his fictional account in *Mr. Norris Changes Trains*. In *Christopher and His Kind*, he made clear that Hamilton was also involved with the IAH, and he noted, too, that Hirschfeld increasingly aligned with the KPD since the KPD adopted the same stance as the Russian revolutionary party, that sex between consenting individuals was outside the law.[133]

His work with the IAH marked Isherwood's closest approach to German and Soviet communism. In November 1932, he told Spender that he was busy with "a translation of a report on the work of the I.A.H. which Gibarti, Munzenberg's secretary, gave me. I think I shall become a member of the I.A.H. It's the next nearest thing to being a Communist."[134] He cannot have been fully aware of the complexity and risk of the ongoing struggle between the leaders of the autonomous German communist movement and the developing power center in Russia; perhaps nobody was. Gibarti was later exposed as a Comintern operative and double agent for the Soviets.

Gibarti and Münzenberg together were the real-life originals for the red-headed, anti-fascist, anti-imperialist communist activist, orator, and spy-handler, Ludwig Bayer, in *Mr. Norris Changes Trains*. Arthur Koestler, the communist writer, recalled Münzenberg as "a short stocky man of proletarian origin; a magnetic personality of immense driving power and a hard, seductive charm." Isherwood gave such qualities to his fictional Bayer: "His glance was direct, challenging, brilliant as if with laughter, but his lips did not even smile. [...] His mere repose suggested a force of concentration which was hypnotic in its intensity."[135]

As was his habit, Isherwood blurred resemblances to real-life models. "I had seen his photograph two or three times in the newspaper," says the narrator, William Bradshaw, "but I couldn't remember who he was." Similarly, Mr. Norris tells Bradshaw, "I've heard that he began life as a research chemist. I don't think his parents are working people. He doesn't give that impression, does he? In any case, Bayer isn't his real name."[136] Münzenberg used his own name and was proud to be a member of the working class; Gibarti came from a family of doctors, was highly educated, multilingual and used a pen name. There was one detail that Isherwood, writing in 1934, couldn't resist: Gibarti had red hair, as his intelligence files record. Isherwood made his Ludwig Bayer character a Red with red hair.

In *Mr. Norris Changes Trains*, William Bradshaw is attracted to the Communist Party and works as a translator for the IAH like Isherwood in real life. At the fictionalized communist meeting, Norris mounts the platform and gives a rousing speech against British imperialism in China. Protected by his sense of the ridiculous, Bradshaw dismisses Norris in this role. "It seemed so absurd to me to see him standing there that I could hardly keep a straight face." Yet "the audience evidently didn't find Arthur in the least funny."[137] It is one of the novel's distinctive achievements, portraying absurdity and conviction side by side, as in real life.

The scene evokes its antecedent in Dickens's *Hard Times*, when the orator Slackbridge enjoins the workers of Coketown to support the United Aggregate Tribunal in its fight for freedom against the capitalist masters, and the weaver Stephen Blackpool refuses and is ostracized, the first step on his road to martyrdom. Isherwood updates the scene and makes it more revolutionary. His orator Ludwig Bayer exhorts the Berlin workers to "protest against the outrages of the Japanese murderers," to assist "the hundreds of thousands of Chinese peasants now rendered homeless," and "to fight Japanese imperialism and European exploitation." Bradshaw is moved by the "curious restrained passion" of the Berlin workers and depicts them not as rough or uneducated, but as high-minded and refined by privation. Their faces were "pale and prematurely lined, often haggard and ascetic, like the heads of scholars." His portrait asserts that "They were attentive, but not passive. They were not spectators." On the contrary, they "participated" in the red-headed orator's speech. "He spoke for them, he made their thoughts articulate. They were listening to their own collective voice."[138]

For this passage, in which the speaker articulates the thoughts of the audience, Isherwood borrowed from D.S. Mirsky's biography *Lenin* (1931). Mirsky wrote that Lenin "made the plainest listener recognize, in what was expressed by the orator, what he had always felt. [. . .] Lenin, while he brought out the revolutionary passion of his audiences, made them think, transforming their feelings into ideas."[139] The narrator, though, cannot sign up to the movement, or any movement, wary as he is of group emotional experiences like the academic competition, religious training, and patriotism which had deformed Isherwood's adolescence. His political and class feelings, says the narrator, were "muddled" by Cambridge, by his confirmation, and "by the tunes the band played when my father's regiment marched to the railway station, seventeen years ago."[140]

Isherwood was certainly doing his political homework, and he mocked his narrator's political naiveté. William Bradshaw hands over the first report translated for Bayer in September or October 1932. Bayer urges Bradshaw to read the *Communist Manifesto* and gives him some pamphlets by Lenin with more translating work. In November, there is a third translating assignment. Bayer's integrity is highlighted when he saves Bradshaw from being caught inadvertently committing treason by calling him back to Berlin from the mountains where Norris has lured him as unwitting bait in his sale of information. After the Nazis win the March 5 elections in 1933, Bradshaw learns from a journalist friend that Bayer's dead body has been seen in the Spandau barracks with the left ear torn off. "When the first news of the house-searchings began to come in," Bradshaw and his landlady, in a moment of blackest madcap, hide "the papers which Bayer had given me" and "my copy of the *Communist Manifesto* under the wood-pile in the kitchen."

If Isherwood hid his communist reading material in real life, he retrieved it before leaving Berlin. A copy of the *Communist Manifesto*, in German, printed by the Internationaler Arbeiter-Verlag in Berlin in 1929 and with pencil underlinings (possibly Isherwood's) was in his library when he died.[141]

WHEN ARRANGING HIS material for *Goodbye to Berlin*, Isherwood placed "The Landauers" after "The Nowaks," implying a direct contrast between these two very different Berlin families, poor working-class Germans and wealthy, cultivated German Jews. For "The Landauers," Isherwood tried to infiltrate the German-Jewish milieu just as he had infiltrated the German-slum milieu, and he fictionalized a great deal in "The Landauers" to achieve certain aims.

The Nowaks are a struggling, unhappy family; the Landauers are a successful, happy one. They are so clever, rich, and kind that their perfection hangs on the edge of parody. When the Isherwood character tells Natalia Landauer about his novel, *All the Conspirators*, she is mystified: "I do not understand what this modern books mean when they say: the mother and father always must quarrel with the children. You know, it would be impossible that I can have quarrel with my parents." When her mother suffers a migraine, Natalia keeps her company at home, voluntarily and without resentment. When Natalia suffers a fainting fit, she recovers immediately, without neurosis or self-pity, "Oh, it's not so important."[142]

In contrast to Otto Nowak, Natalia seeks intellectual contact and forbids physical contact. She will not chat on her doorstep; she requires a table between herself and the Isherwood character when seated; she will not be helped into her coat; she will not stir her chocolate with the spoon he has used to stir his. She wants and needs nothing from the Isherwood character that he does not offer.

Natalia's father, Herr Landauer, is the author of a doctoral thesis on "the condition of Jewish workers in the East End of London" for which he made himself familiar "with dock-hands and prostituted women and the keepers of your so-called Public Houses."[143] Thus, Herr Landauer long ago descended below the poverty line so alluring to Isherwood, then uncomplainingly turned from his leftist intellectual pursuits to make his fortune in the department store that provides such a comfortable life for the family he adores. Even so, Herr Landauer still reads enough to reduce Mr. Isherwood, as he calls him, to blushing silence with pointed questions as to whether Byron committed incest or Wilde's punishment was justified.

The story hints that Herr Landauer cannot be real. Like so many in Berlin, he is an actor, and he is deliberately making fun in his role as paterfamilias: "He had shiny brown boot-button eyes and low-comedian's eyebrows—so thick and black that they looked as if they had been touched up with burnt cork." Yet the Isherwood character is forced to admit to Natalia: "I think he's the nicest father I've ever met."[144]

Natalia Landauer was partly based on Gisa Soloweitschik, the Russian banker's daughter, Jewish, born in Moscow. Soloweitschik was only seventeen, an art history student, when Spender met her skiing in Switzerland. In his memoir, *World Within World*, Spender recalled that her parents invited him and Isherwood to Sunday lunches at their flat in Wilmersdorf.

Spender scolded Isherwood for his portrait of Soloweitschik in "The Landauers," and Isherwood quoted Spender's letter in *Christopher and His Kind*, where he conceded that his Natalia Landauer character was "a mere caricature." He had portrayed her as "a bossy bluestocking, desperately enthusiastic about culture, sexually frigid and prudish." But he was needlessly siding with Spender against his younger satirical aims, for Soloweitschik herself said that many details were taken from her school friend Annie Joël, whose father was a director at Wertheim's, Berlin's premier department store.[145]

Isherwood invented a meeting between his two characters Natalia Landauer and Sally Bowles "to test Natalia." True to their fictional personalities, Sally boasts about her lovers, and "Natalia is prudishly shocked. She has failed Christopher's test." In real life, Gisa Soloweitschik and Jean Ross never met. Isherwood devised the encounter to create conflict in his story between the conventions of family and the sexual renegades with whom his narrator is secretly aligned and about whom he could not be explicit and still be published.

"I've been making love to a dirty old Jew producer. I'm hoping he'll give me a contract—but no go, so far . . ." says Sally in "The Landauers." This remark—which is similar to dialogue in *Sally Bowles*—causes Christopher to kick Sally under the table as Natalia freezes before their eyes. "I found myself getting increasingly annoyed with both of them—with Sally for her endless silly pornographic talk; with Natalia for being such a prude." He appears to overlook the anti-Semitic slur which might as easily have triggered Natalia's anger. In 1986, Jean Ross's daughter, Sarah Caudwell, published a piece in the *New Statesman* detailing her mother's objections to being the model for Sally Bowles and in particular rejecting this language as alien to her mother's beliefs and style of speech.[146]

But Isherwood did not overlook anti-Semitism in his story. Natalia Landauer's cousin, Bernhard Landauer, is the character he based partly on Wilfrid Israel, also Jewish, who worked for the family department store, N. Israel, opposite the Berlin City Hall. In real life, Wilfrid Israel was not related to Gisa Soloweitschik; Isherwood made Natalia and Bernhard cousins to draw attention to the differences in their stories, two possible trajectories for successful assimilated Jews in the last years of Weimar. Natalia escapes to Paris, where she falls in love with a doctor; she marries happily; she is a survivor. Her trajectory resembles the Soloweitschiks'; they relocated to Paris in late 1931. Bernhard, equally accomplished, equally altruistic, equally self-disciplined, is engulfed by the Holocaust.

Isherwood's portrait of Bernhard explores the link between character and destiny. Why didn't Bernhard leave Germany? This was part of a larger question about character and destiny that had long interested Isherwood, notably in the case of his father and in the case of Oscar Wilde. Why do some people submit to their fate and others kick against it? Why do some follow the code and others break it?

Bernhard Landauer is involved with Jewish communities in Palestine and revolutionary movements around the world, yet he shows off that no toy soldiers or guns are sold at Landauer's department store, and he makes clear he is not a practicing Jew when he mistakenly calls the holy Jewish day of the Feast of the Tabernacles a picnic. Christopher finds him impenetrable: "He will never tell me anything about himself or about the things which are most important to him." When pressed, Bernhard says he believes only in discipline, for himself though not necessarily for others. "He is like Natalia," Christopher observes,[147] but at Bernhard's English cottage on the shore of the Wannsee just outside Berlin, Bernhard reveals the tragedy in his background which mirrors Isherwood's own tragedy in some key details.

The Wannsee villa was built in 1904, the year of Isherwood's birth, for Bernhard's mother who was English. Bernhard's elder brother died fighting in World War I; nevertheless, the family was ostracized, suspected of spying, because of his English mother. In reaction to loss and pain, his mother turned away from both Germanness and Englishness toward the past, like Kathleen, and also toward her own heritage, studying ancient Hebrew texts. Then she was diagnosed with cancer and killed herself.

Bernhard's dark confidence creates uneasiness as well as identification between Bernhard and the Isherwood narrator: "Yes, there is some quality in you which attracts me and which I very much envy, and yet this very quality of yours also arouses my antagonism . . . Perhaps that is merely because I also am partly English, and you represent to me an aspect of my own character . . ." The process of identification and differentiation, present in so many of Isherwood's character studies, was based on real ambivalence in Isherwood's friendship with Wilfrid Israel. In a letter to Spender, in November 1932, Isherwood reported, "He is kind. But he condemns me in his heart."[148]

As with Frau Nowak and the consumptives at the sanatorium, Bernhard is already a sort of phantom, acting without effect in a scenario of death-in-life. A party scene at the Wannsee villa shows his lack of agency, and the same for his guests, as the Nazi nightmare approaches. Isherwood framed the party as a turning point, one of many endless turning points: "However often the decision may be delayed, all these people are ultimately doomed. This evening is the dress rehearsal of a disaster. It is like the last night of an epoch." The night can be identified as August 9, 1931, because there are two real-life events mentioned, the referendum on dissolving the Prussian parliament and the shooting of two police officers trying to shut down a communist rally in the Bülowplatz in Berlin.

The following April, 1932, Bernhard shows Christopher an anonymous letter: "Bernhard Landauer, beware. We are going to settle the score with you and your uncle and all other filthy Jews. We give you twenty-four hours to leave Germany. If not, you are dead men."[149] When Christopher urges him to escape, Bernhard agrees on condition that they leave together that very night. Christopher makes excuses, refusing to recognize the veiled offer of love and making himself complicit in Bernhard's fate.

By autumn, according to the story, Christopher is unable to contact Bernhard. In the spring of 1933, with Hitler in power, he tries harder, visiting the flat, to be told Bernhard has gone away. On the day of the Jewish boycott, Christopher makes a symbolic purchase, a nutmeg grater, in Bernhard's family department store, gesturing in parody to Isherwood's sense that everyone was being ground down to nothing, as he had told Spender, by an enormous tool.

Only when Christopher is himself in flight from Berlin does he learn by chance in a restaurant in Prague, the first stop on his fictional journey, what has happened to Bernhard. He overhears two businessmen discussing in German a newspaper item reporting that Bernhard Landauer has died of heart failure and that the family business will probably be confiscated. The indirection of this report uses a technique favored by Joseph Conrad, offering fragments of a story overheard from strangers while passing through an unfamiliar town, repeated fourth hand by a narrator, leaving the reader to draw his or her own conclusion:

> "Concentration camps," said the fat man, lighting a cigar. "They get them in there, make them sign things ... Then their hearts fail."
> "I don't like it," said the Austrian. "It's bad for trade."[150]

Again Spender criticized Isherwood's portrait, suggesting that the real Wilfrid Israel was more dynamic than Bernhard Landauer. In *World Within World*, Spender recalled that Israel had outlined "a plan of action for the Jews when Hitler seized Germany." The Jews must strike, closing their businesses and taking to the streets in protest "even if the Storm Troopers fired on them." Such a protest "would arouse the conscience of the world." But in *Christopher and His Kind*, Isherwood insisted that the weariness and the apathy he detected in Wilfrid Israel had been real. "I am quite sure that these aspects of Bernhard's character weren't invented."[151]

Isherwood did not mention in *Christopher and His Kind*—arguably he had forgotten—another model for his character, a Berlin refugee met in Amsterdam in September 1935, Walter Landauer, a publisher and a boyhood schoolmate of Wilfrid Israel at Mommsen Gymnasium in Berlin. In his 1935 diary, Isherwood recorded how "Landauer moved about the room like a soft, deprecatory insect—making quiet intelligent remarks," an observation he seemed to be reworking when he described his fictional Landauer as "beaky," "soft, negative" with "the air of a bird." In Amsterdam, Isherwood spent an evening with Walter Landauer and the actress Pamela Wedekind talking about the war and the best place to spend it. Landauer did not have "the least notion what to do." Isherwood observed a kind of death wish in him, noting down his dialogue: "Landauer is particularly fatalistic: 'My generation can't be expected to survive 2 wars.' He is thirty-three."[152] Isherwood gave this death wish to his fictional Landauer, describing him as "overcivilized" in his kimono, "face masked with exhaustion," "perhaps suffering from a fatal disease," the collector of art objects reflecting Chinese or Khmer Buddhistic detachment, all qualities that might illuminate his fictional Landauer's terrible fate.[153] At the time of writing, he did not know that Walter Landauer's publishing career, reestablished in Amsterdam after his flight from Berlin, was to be destroyed a second time when Germany occupied the Netherlands in 1940, nor that in 1943, Landauer was to be arrested and deported to Bergen-Belsen where he died at the end of 1944.

Isherwood's argument with Spender was very personal, as usual. Spender, as he wrote in *World Within World*, was "at least a quarter Jewish"[154] and half German. His maternal grandparents were both German, and his maternal grandfather was Jewish. Isherwood could not share in this minority aspect of Spender's identity. Isherwood's wish to identify with Spender's Jewishness and with Spender's Germanness, his wish to enter in imagination into the Jewish experience, is played out through the fictional relationship between the characters he invented, Christopher Isherwood and Bernhard Landauer. He did not include a Spender character in "The Landauers."

———

IN THE FINAL diary section of *Goodbye to Berlin*, Isherwood again drew attention to those who are easily tricked, and he foreshadowed the coming disaster with any number of sham performances and illusions. The cathedral "betrays, in its architecture, a flash of that hysteria which flickers always behind every grave, grey Prussian façade." The glow of the city, "a mirage of the winter desert," pulls peasant boys from the countryside looking for food and work, only to find "It has nothing to give" and drives them into the Tiergarten "to starve and freeze." The rigged boxing matches at the fairgrounds show that "these people could be made to believe in anybody or anything." The night life, increasingly threatened by a police clean-up, still attracts tourists from as far away as America, who are amazed to see "men dressed as *women*. As *women*, hey?" Rudi, the communist Boy Scout and "Joan of Arc," takes the Isherwood character to his clubhouse, the office of the Pathfinders' magazine, and shows him "dozens of photographs of boys, all taken with the camera tilted upwards, from beneath, so that they look like epic giants." But the sole reality will prove to be a drunken Nazi in a café with his song about smashing the Jewish state: he "thumps the table with his fist, 'Blood must flow!'"[155]

Isherwood had been in training to write this part of his book since his days as a diarist at St. Edmund's, where he first learned to channel the shared experience of the whole community. Now he collected material in the park, from his English-language students, at the communist café, the Nazi café, the Russian tea shop, the artists' café, the Italian restaurant where the foreign correspondents dined, and from his landlady. "[I]t's absolutely necessary for me to stay on here at present. The last part of my novel requires a lot more research to document it," he told Spender toward the end of 1932. His letters included details of the growing violence, for instance a young man stabbed in the eye with the poles of Nazi banners after a rally at the Sportpalast, "The youth was such a clot of blood that we couldn't see how badly he was hurt, but I think one of the spikes had gone into his eye. Some men who were passing put him into a taxi. Six policemen were standing about twenty yards away, but they carefully didn't see anything." In *Goodbye to Berlin*, he would make this description shorter and more graphic: "I got a sickening glimpse of his face—his left eye was poked half out, and blood poured from the wound. He wasn't dead."[156]

He told Spender, too, about a boy they both knew, Willi Müller, trying to get work with the IAH and about to serve three weeks in prison for fighting with a policeman. This he fictionalized as an anecdote about the art student "Werner," based not only on Willi Müller but also on a young Austrian friend, Baron Werner von Alvensleben, later a sculptor and writer, who was a leader of Vortrupp, the Boy Scout-style youth group of the anti-Nazi Reichsbanner movement. Werner is transformed into a hero by the Communist newspaper the *Rote Fahne* (Red Flag). According to "A Berlin Diary (Winter 1932–3)," Werner's photograph appeared in the paper, "captioned 'Another victim of the Police blood-bath,'" after the police shot him in the leg and beat him with their truncheons till he fainted. Christopher visits Werner in the hospital, and Isherwood shaped the scene to convey his longstanding suspicion of public glory, showing how the wish for glory preyed upon the unsuspecting, unemployed youth of Berlin just as it had preyed upon him from the time he was a schoolboy: "Around him, on the blanket, lay his press-cuttings. Somebody had carefully underlined each mention of Werner's name with red pencil."[157]

Isherwood distinguished his Berlin narrative from newspaper reporting by placing his narrator beside an actual journalist at a Nazi demonstration on January 22, 1933, on the Bülowplatz: "I went along to watch it with Frank, the newspaper correspondent." In the scene, Isherwood made Frank the witness. The name "Frank" indicates candor and also alludes to Isherwood's father, bringing his physically reassuring presence to the front line of a new kind of battle:

> As Frank himself said afterwards, this was not really a Nazi demonstration at all, but a Police demonstration—there were at least two policemen to every Nazi present. Perhaps General Schleicher only allowed the march to take place in order to show who are the real masters of Berlin. Everybody says he's going to proclaim a military dictatorship.[158]

"Everybody" was, in fact, another of Isherwood's sources, Rolf Katz, a German-Jewish economist he met in Berlin in 1931. "Katz says there'll be a military dictatorship under Schleicher soon," Isherwood had reported to Spender in November. "They'll try to forbid the K.P.D.—which is now the biggest party in Berlin." Katz had studied natural sciences, philosophy, and economics at the universities of Frankfurt, Munich, and Freiberg, before taking his doctorate in Berlin. He had joined the Communist Party in 1921, and Isherwood later wrote that he was "one of the very few people I have ever met who has really read, studied and digested Marx." He worked as a journalist for publications in several languages. He was about five years older than Isherwood, sometimes hosted him overnight in his Charlottenburg flat, shared at least one boyfriend, and bullied Isherwood like a schoolmaster. "Katz gave me another terrific ticking-off the other day for not being a properly educated revolutionary writer," Isherwood told Spender.[159]

Isherwood took trouble in the demonstration scene to show that the Nazis were not the chosen or even the natural representatives of ordinary working Berliners: "Comparatively few of the hundreds of people round the Bülowplatz can have been organized communists, yet you had the feeling that every single one of them was united against this march. Somebody began to sing the 'International,' and, in a moment, everyone had joined in—" For that brief moment, in Isherwood's telling, "the real masters of Berlin are not the Police, or the Army, and certainly not the Nazis. The masters of Berlin are the workers—" The spirit of the workers shames the Nazis, who "slunk past" with eyes on the ground, offering entertainment worthy of circus clowns: "When the procession had passed, an elderly fat little S.A. man, who had somehow got left behind, came panting along at the double, desperately scared at finding himself alone, and trying vainly to catch up with the rest. The whole crowd roared with laughter."

Isherwood portrayed this laughter, this inability to take the Nazis seriously, as the prelude to a final, irreversible change. Even the journalist Frank does not recognize a threat in something so perceptibly ridiculous. "It was too much like a naughty schoolboy's game to be seriously alarming," the narrative continued,[160] as if the material was suitable for *The Toy-Drawer Times*, the newspaper Frank had made during Christopher's childhood.

It was a week later, January 28, 1933, that Schleicher resigned as chancellor and Hitler formed a cabinet with Hugenberg. "Nobody thinks it can last till the spring," Isherwood wrote in the next section, using the present tense even though he was writing after he had left Berlin and knew that it *had* lasted. "The newspapers are becoming more and more like copies of a school magazine. There is nothing in them but new rules, new punishments, and lists of people who have been 'kept in.' This morning Göring has invented three fresh varieties of high treason."[161] The dull petty-mindedness that Isherwood associated with the hell of his schooldays had taken power in the real world, in the city that had offered him freedom and love. He accelerated the pace of his narrative, like a film running faster and then too fast, delivering events with no discernible meaning, and underneath the speed, a cadence of resignation, as he described the arrests of Jews, intellectuals, communists, the confiscation of books, widespread plans for emigration, and the Nazi police state rapidly taking over.

AT THE BEGINNING of April 1933, Isherwood moved his possessions to London to his mother's house. He dined with Uncle Henry, saw his friends, checked on his publishing prospects, and returned to Berlin for the last time, on April 30, already warned in a letter from Fräulein Thurau that the police had been asking for him at Nollendorfstrasse 17. He would soon be part of the diaspora.

On May 10, he witnessed the enormous bonfire lit to destroy just the sort of leftist novels he was writing. The public burning of "undesirable" books took place in the Opernplatz, the big central square between the opera house, the university, and the Roman Catholic cathedral on the south side of Unter den Linden. It was a fire of symbolic purification—cleansing German culture of writing by Jewish intellectuals, liberals, communists, homosexuals, pacifists, foreigners. A crowd of 40,000 gathered to watch Joseph Goebbels commit the first of thousands of volumes to the flames; similar book burnings took place simultaneously in many German towns that night.

As he watched the bonfire in the Opernplatz, Isherwood knew he was at risk as a writer, a leftist who had done paid work for a communist workers' group, and as a homosexual. The Institute for Sexual Science had been ransacked a few days earlier; its library was now thrown into the flames before Isherwood's eyes along with a bronze bust of Hirschfeld himself, paraded terrifyingly to the Opernplatz on a pike. The names and addresses of the supporters of the World League for Sexual Reform, stored at the institute, were retained by the Nazis with a view to future surveillance and arrest.[162]

This scene was to haunt Isherwood for the rest of his life. He did not write about it in *Goodbye to Berlin*, and in *Christopher and His Kind* he belittled his fear, recalling that he had cried "Shame!" at the bonfire, "but not loudly." The terrifying episode was to surface in his work in other ways as well as in his nightmares, nightmares which could still wake him decades later when he was lying in bed next to Don Bachardy.[163]

GREECE, 1933

Three days after the fire in the Opernplatz, Isherwood took Neddermeyer by train to Prague, then Vienna and Budapest whence via Danube steamer to Belgrade and a train to Athens. He had received an invitation from Francis Turville-Petre to join another men-only kingdom, this time on a Greek island called St. Nicholas (now Ktiponisi). Turville-Petre was hoping to excavate some prehistoric villages on the facing mainland, which was within shouting distance. Erwin Hansen traveled with them, summoned to cook.

St. Nicholas is in central Greece, about eighty miles north of Athens in the Euripus Strait. The island is about two-thirds of a mile long and has the rugged terrain characteristic of so much of Greece—steep hills, rocky ground, heavy pine and scrub woods. It has no fresh water supply, likely explaining why it is uninhabited. In 1933, earthenware pitcherfuls of well water were carried from the mainland by boat. There is one white stucco church, Agios Nikolaos—Saint Nicholas—where services were then performed quarterly.

When Isherwood and Neddermeyer arrived, Turville-Petre had leased the island for ten years from the villagers who lived on the mainland nearby at Chalia (now Drosia), and he was having a house built from the stones of a ruined Turkish watch tower. Masons and carpenters from the mainland were sleeping on the island most nights. Cooking staff and supplemental labor were hired in the bars of Athens—energetic and unruly boys of diverse nationalities and education. Everyone was camping out. Isherwood and Neddermeyer were given the only bed, in a hut built of branches.

Isherwood's diary from the summer still survives, preserved because he intended to turn it into something he could sell. He told Spender before starting for Greece, "I shall write a book as much like Hindoo Holiday as possible."[164] The 1933 diary duly recalls the fictionalized diary by his and Forster's friend J.R. Ackerley, describing the parade of boys at the intensely hierarchical court of the maharajah of "Chhokrapor," who liked to watch his favorite teenagers perform religious plays. As with his story about Bremen, "Mr. Lancaster,"

Isherwood didn't focus on the material until nearly thirty years later when he used it in "Ambrose," the second story in *Down There on a Visit*, where he was to deploy theater as a metaphor for his metaphysical beliefs.

The 1933 diary is alive with observations about the boys. Tasso "wears a beret, a black shirt and mechanic's overalls with a flower by his ear. Nikko is dressed almost in rags. It is noteworthy that, despite the extremely hot weather, both Tasso and the chauffeur wear underclothes." Here again was Isherwood's obsession with collecting and taxonimizing, caricatured in Baron Kuno von Pregnitz's fantasy cult about boys living on a South Sea island in *Mr. Norris Changes Trains*. Kuno has an imaginary collection of English boys' adventure stories; his favorite is *The Seven Who Got Lost*: "cribbed largely from the *Swiss Family Robinson*, of how they hunted, fished, built a hut, and finally got themselves rescued." Like Turville-Petre and like Isherwood, Kuno enjoys discussing the different attributes of each imaginary companion—"good at fishing," "a marvellous climber," "the champion swimmer"[165]—comparing them to boys he knows in real life.

Turville-Petre was paying for Nikko, "very beautiful dark-eyed," to be cured of syphilis. His own syphilis had returned, and he was drinking heavily. The night Isherwood arrived, Turville-Petre got drunk on retsina with Hansen. "I couldn't help admiring F's amazing vitality. He was the last in bed and the first to get up in the morning, as fresh as paint." Isherwood spent his first morning digging a latrine with Neddermeyer. In the evening, they went fishing and after dark joined an expedition to spear an octopus. Such was the boys' paradise, far from Hitler and Berlin. On the second day, he got sick from drinking the water carried over from the mainland. "I am a little alarmed by the stomach ache I now have from the water. I even begin to feel that I may not stay here long."[166]

He was to last about three and a half months, until early September, struggling to work on his novel in the heat, rain, wind, and the cacophony of voices plus music from a "piercing gramophone" that the boys played constantly. His stomach was upset most of the time, with bloody stools, a temperature and in July a diagnosis of enteritis. He reminded himself that "these Boy Scout hardships" were nothing compared to the struggle against fascism, and that writing was his only justification for having retired to a place of safety. "I ran away from the Front Line when I left Berlin. Now I am taking part in an O.T.C. sham fight which no possible mishap can dignify. My only excuse to the Court Martial is that I finish my novel."[167]

Turville-Petre seemed impervious to hardship, whether it affected him or others. Isherwood brooded in his diary on the idea of Turville-Petre as a sacred figure, noting that "one of our visitors remarked that F. very much resembles St. Nicholas." On blank pages facing his diary entries, he developed several descriptions of the island that he imbued with a religious atmosphere drawn from Christian paintings. These were part of his evolving idea that Turville-Petre's self-destructive abandon was a kind of holy masochism, "Francis is a religious maniac. He has just come back from one of his ascetic drinking bouts in Athens—periods of intense mystical absorption, during which he neither eats nor sleeps. His body scarred like that of a martyr."[168]

During the summer, the living arrangements improved. They bought and moved into tents, a roof was put on the ruined cottage that was used as a kitchen, and a kitchen garden was planted. Ducks, hens, and cocks were brought over and penned in a wire enclosure. Turville-Petre bought an old gun for shooting rabbits, a goat for milking, a donkey. The masons began building cisterns to collect rainwater. Isherwood swam early in the mornings, and he and Neddermeyer climbed some of the mountains. Boys came and went. There were illnesses, thieving, cruel practical jokes, drunkenness.

There were several trips to Athens. On the first, Isherwood and Neddermeyer formalized their relationship by exchanging rings. One night on the island, with sunburnt backs, "H and I lay in our tent and talked about Walter and the Cosy Corner and the Berlin Days."[169] Isherwood was reading a volume of pornography, *Günther's Erlebnisse (Aus dem Tagebuch eines Flagellanten)* or *Günther's Experience (From the Diary of a Flagellant)*. On a blank page in his diary, he copied a passage in German, reflecting his preoccupation with masochism and spirituality. In English, it begins: "At Ellen's however, every excess, every indulgence, was taken to a height at which one would no longer feel anything animalistic or crude. Everything was exquisite and was lifted into the realm of the mind, thus becoming a precious experience."

Such reading offered seriocomic inspiration for Olga's, the brothel, in *Mr. Norris Changes Trains* and for Kuno's statement, after being painfully tossed in a blanket by the handsome young men at his country villa, that "the most beautiful things in life belong to the Spirit. The Flesh alone cannot give us happiness."[170]

In the diary, Isherwood longingly conjured the sexy, witty atmosphere of Weimar, listing the nightclubs and dives, the booted prostitutes, the all-male costume balls, and the openly gay life offered in bookshops, newspaper kiosks, and theaters: "Reading the Diary of a Flagellant, I am homesick for the old Berlin. The Berlin of the old Passage, the Eldorado, the massage salons. Red plush. Upholstered vice. Stiefel mädchen, transvestites, the bookshops in the Friedrichstrasse. The Cozy Corner. The Zelten Balls. Revolte im Erziehungshaus. Freud. Schableth and die Freundin."

"Stiefel mädchen" were the booted dominatrixes who wore different colored boots and laces to signify their specialties. Black boots were for buttock cropping, black laces were for punishment with a short whip, scarlet boots—like the ones made especially for Anni in *Mr. Norris Changes Trains*—were for forced feminization and transvestite humiliation. Isherwood's Anni agrees to wear scarlet boots only in private; in public, she wears black boots "with a curious design in gold running around the tops" hinting at an exotic unknown predilection.

Revolte im Erziehungshaus was the Lampel play and film that had attracted both Auden and Isherwood. *Die Freundin* was a lesbian weekly magazine popular with gay men and usually including a section especially for transvestites; the Nazis shut it down.[171]

Neddermeyer was friendly with the group, chatting with the masons, rabbit-hunting with Mitso the chauffeur, and Isherwood began to fret: "I am potentially jealous of everybody on the island—" he wrote in his diary. He battled to keep the upper hand in the relationship, carefully hiding his feelings: "The discovery of my jealousy would put a weapon into his hands." He resolved on "A vital proud core of utter utter indifference."[172]

In a letter to Forster, Isherwood jested that Greece was turning him savage: "Living here has made me fiendishly cruel. We are always murdering some insect or animal. I feel like Macbeth." To Spender, too, he mentioned Macbeth. "Every year I see myself more and more clearly as a sort of comic Macbeth." Like Macbeth, Isherwood needed to rule. He told Spender that "Some of the Mohrin difficulties are beginning to reappear between Fronny and myself."[173] Turville-Petre continued to be irritated by Neddermeyer's status, often insisting on speaking English while Isherwood insisted on German so Neddermeyer could join the conversation.

Isherwood's usual strategy was to step back from confrontation and engage with something else, but on St. Nicholas, this was impossible. In his diary, he admitted his wish to escape: "I imagine / pretend myself to be the demon of the island. [. . .] But I am not really a demon, and so I'd better clear out." Now he was alluding to Shakespeare's Caliban, "monster of the isle," in *The Tempest*.[174] In fact, Turville-Petre argued with nearly everyone.

AFTER COMPLETING WHAT he called Part Two of his novel on July 30, Isherwood stopped writing. The weather grew hotter, and the sea filled with jellyfish. There was an infestation of rats. His battle of wills with Neddermeyer reached crisis point. Neddermeyer agreed to stay with him on condition that they leave for Paris. Evidently, he withheld sex, and Isherwood reminded himself that he had managed to control the outcome of his previous relationship with Walter Wolff: "I must leave him, as I left W., in my own time. It seems as if my sex-life might be over, now, for good."

Neddermeyer gave way when Isherwood treated him to another weekend in Athens: "I spent my birthday very pleasantly, chiefly in bed," Isherwood recorded.[175]

In September, they left St. Nicholas, intending to part in Athens. In Athens, Neddermeyer said, "If you give me 6,000 drachmas, I'll stay with you. I said: Certainly not. I'm not going to buy you." Yet their bond was underpinned by Isherwood's money. In *Christopher and His Kind*, Isherwood stated that, as a young man, "he couldn't relax sexually with a member of his own class or nation. He needed a working-class foreigner."[176] His use of the word "needed" highlights the weakness of his position vis-à-vis his lovers; it does not suggest an exciting transgression of barriers between class and nation. On the other hand, his lovers *needed* money. Isherwood clung to his economic advantage. By keeping hold of the purse strings, he could control Neddermeyer, up to a point.

In his published writing, Isherwood presented the relationship as a love affair, but like all his relationships with boys in Berlin, it depended on his paying for treats and paying for sex. From Mohrin, he had written to Spender, "All boys are sharks—except Heinz—it is only a question how well or gracefully they cadge." In America, soon after the war, Isherwood averred in his diary that the poverty of his Berlin lovers had contributed to his adopting leftist political views: "The people, when I got to Berlin, belonged to a certain class—poorer than mine. I had to spend money on them, and therefore doubted the love. So I became political. Marxism said, I'll remove the barriers."[177]

He had paid for Neddermeyer's journey to Greece as well as for his own, and even, partly, for Erwin Hansen's. He mentioned to Spender that he hoped "to have worked off most if not all my travelling expenses" by autumn, implying he had borrowed from Turville-Petre.[178] Certainly he was in debt to Turville-Petre for room and board on the island. Several times during the summer, he wrote to Forster and Spender that he couldn't leave Greece because he had spent all he had to get there. He felt indentured—like all the boys on St. Nicholas. Calculations in his diary suggest that Isherwood owed Turville-Petre nearly 10,000 drachmas for the sixteen weeks he spent in Greece—perhaps $1,300 or £1,000 in today's money.

In *Christopher and His Kind*, Isherwood said that "Christopher had just inherited a small legacy from his godmother, Aggie Trevor" which meant he could "spend a summer anywhere in Europe or take a short trip farther still." The legacy was £300 (about £25,000 today), but evidently he did not know the amount or have access to the money until after he had left Greece. In his diary, he mentioned it only on July 12.[179] On September 7, when Kathleen heard he was on his way to Paris, she concluded he had not received her subsequent letter giving the amount or he would have traveled further afield.

In Athens, Isherwood was able to scrape together enough money only for Neddermeyer's train ticket, but the Berlin train was crowded: "All sleeping berths were booked. It's a portent, I said."[180] Neddermeyer decided to stay with him.

They took a steamship to Marseilles, then a train to Paris, where they stayed for two weeks in Meudon, in a hotel near Rolf Katz. Katz had fled Berlin in his Chevrolet on March 22 with his eighteen-year-old "nephew" Willi Noeske, as British intelligence files put it.[181] Willi Noeske was actually a paid lover, to whom Isherwood had been giving English lessons at Katz's Berlin flat. Noeske had returned to Berlin in May, and Katz had settled in Meudon, haven also to Arthur Koestler, another Berlin refugee, who was sleeping in a nearby hayloft.

"France was a success," wrote Isherwood, "and [we] were happy."[182] When he could no longer afford the hotel, they traveled on to London and stayed at Kathleen's house in Pembroke Gardens until mid-October. Then Neddermeyer returned to Berlin, and Isherwood stayed in London. Until this moment, the difficulties in their relationship were generated by themselves; after this moment, they would be at the mercy of external forces. This was to tighten their bond.

LONDON, 1933

Jean Ross, fictionalized as a girl who dreams of getting into the movies, in fact got Isherwood into the movies when she introduced him to the Viennese director Berthold Viertel in London in the autumn of 1933. According to *Christopher and His Kind*, Ross gave Viertel a copy of *The Memorial*, and Viertel "leafed casually through" until he came to Edward Blake's attempted suicide. For his next film, *Little Friend*, Viertel needed someone who could write an attempted suicide scene. "'This I find clearly genial,' he had said, pronouncing the word as English but meaning it as the German *genial* 'gifted with genius.' And that was that. Viertel read no further."[183] They met on November 18 at Ross's flat.

Little Friend was based on the Austrian novelist Ernst Lothar's *Kleine Freundin*, in which the main character, a girl nearly twelve years old, tries to kill herself in order to stop her parents from divorcing. She is a child of privilege, cosseted and controlled by her indulgent parents and strict nanny, slowly overwhelmed by the world of unruly sexual passion revealed through her beloved mother's adultery and disgusted by the moniker Little Friend awarded by her mother's lover. Her only real friend is a working-class boy who saves her from being hit by a car during her reckless flight from home.

Viertel saw a more general tragedy in hers: "She expresses the deep bewilderment of the human soul confronted with the futility of illusion," he said in a publicity item for the New York premiere. Isherwood duly made the suicide attempt so convincing that it was banned by the British Board of Film Censors, who reported: "A very pathetic story, well told. Incident and dialogue throughout are free from objection, except p. 137—the shot of Felicity turning on the gas must not be shown."[184]

Viertel's producers, Michael Balcon and his brother S.C. Balcon of Gaumont-British, had originally hired the bestselling novelist Margaret Kennedy to adapt *Kleine Freundin* for the screen. She had adapted her 1924 novel *The Constant Nymph* for the stage, and it was made into a film in 1928, in 1933, and again in 1943, but Viertel wasn't satisfied with her screenplay for *Little Friend*. She was already collaborating on her next play, so Isherwood was hired.

Viertel worked him hard, and Isherwood, true to character, rose to the challenge and was forever changed by it. He completed a draft of the script on December 21, working till half past two in the morning, but Viertel again wasn't satisfied. Together Viertel and Isherwood consulted with Michael Balcon's assistant, Robert Stevenson, already known to Isherwood as a one-time Cambridge poshocrat, then rewrote the script.[185] All the while, the collaboration with Viertel was transforming Isherwood's approach to the novel he was then calling *The Lost*. During November, he had worked on a new draft of the Berlin material, and even Kathleen knew he then scrapped the "new novel nearly finished" in order to "reconstruct it quite differently." Upward stayed overnight Saturday, December 16—an opportunity to discuss it all and start fresh, and the next day, under the heading "Reconsideration of The Lost," Isherwood had written: "From this point, Arthur journeys to Berlin, meeting various people connected with the story. We follow him with the camera eye, objectively. We have none of his thoughts—only see what he sees, hear what he hears."[186]

The discipline of the camera eye telling the story from the outside was to lend *Mr. Norris Changes Trains* objective dramatic strength. But it was to be another six or eight months and several further redraftings before Isherwood decided to separate Arthur Norris from the rest of his Berlin characters and make Norris the center of his own book.

As he brooded on the material in late December 1933, planning to fuse two communist boys into one, wobbling in his conception of the sexuality of another character, he seemed certain only of his main theme, the universal longing for love and the shared moral despair of his characters:

> It is vital to the success of the whole presentation that "Love" is clearly shown for what it is—one of the chief preoccupations of The Lost. Otherwise the book becomes a mere shocker.

> The link which binds all the chief characters is that, in some way or other, each one of them is conscious of the mental, economic and ideological bankruptcy of the world in which they live.

Once an inadmissible word, "love" now tormented Isherwood. His cozy relationship with Neddermeyer was constantly in his mind. He persuaded a boy, Alfy, he met working in a shop, to join him for a meal. "We dined at a restaurant in Charlotte St named Antoine, which was nice and reminded me of the hotel in Meudon." He got home to find a letter from Neddermeyer saying that a visa for England might take four more weeks.[187] Unrealistically, Isherwood also hoped to return to Berlin.

In *Christopher and His Kind*, Isherwood revealed that Viertel did not know while they were working on *Little Friend* about the heartache Isherwood was experiencing over Neddermeyer. Moreover, Isherwood felt that Viertel, at the time of their collaboration in 1933 and 1934, was not capable of understanding his romantic life. He recalled Viertel telling a bawdy anecdote implying that "all homosexual men are hot to go to bed with any male whomsoever" and that any suggestion "that one sex partner might be preferable to another" was mere sham emulation of heterosexuals. He also recalled Viertel's words of disdain for Hitler's homosexual chief of staff, Ernst Roehm, words which "implied that Roehm's swinishness consisted just as much in being a homosexual as in being a Nazi."[188] Writing *Christopher and His Kind*, Isherwood expressed shame that he had been too cowardly to object to such talk along with disappointment that Viertel, a member of a persecuted minority, Jews, had not been more sensitive to the feelings of a member of another persecuted minority, homosexuals.

For, as he also recalled in *Christopher and His Kind*, he had been confident at the time that Viertel *knew* he was a homosexual, and that he "must be deliberately provoking Christopher to make him confess what he was. This, Christopher vowed to himself with cold fury, he would never do." Viertel described the sensual depths of one of his own early love affairs as if he could persuade Isherwood to try women: "You are a typical mother's son, I think. You are very repressed sexually. But you must not be. The right woman will change all that."[189] Isherwood recorded it all in his 1933 diary and later incorporated Viertel's advice verbatim in *Prater Violet*. This sort of talk was insulting to a young man who had fought through his inhibitions and fears to find sexual liberation in Berlin. Even though Viertel and Isherwood were in league together as artistic collaborators against the two commercially minded Balcons and their ambitious assistants, and even though they communicated privately, intimately in German, Isherwood did not try to describe to Viertel his romantic feelings toward boys.

The new year began with more thick fogs and long days of mind-numbing work on the script. Thirteen hours on January 1, twelve hours on January 4. But sooner than predicted, Neddermeyer had his visa, along with a written invitation from Kathleen and money from Isherwood. On January 5, 1934, Isherwood left home "about 10 in a gt hurry as he wanted to put in a long morning at Viertels," according to Kathleen, "before going to Harwich this afternoon to meet Heinz." He had made excited preparations, like a bridegroom, to settle with Neddermeyer in Chelsea, where he had "taken 2 rooms at Mad Mangeot's for himself & H at 30/- a week each for bed & breakfast—"[190] Jean Ross was already a lodger at Olive Mangeot's new house in Gunter Grove. Richard helped move his brother's luggage. Kathleen labored over the bedlinen, marking sheets and pillowcases which she purchased specially. Auden, still on Christmas holiday from his schoolteaching job at the Downs School in the Malvern Hills, accompanied Isherwood to Harwich. Isherwood never moved to Chelsea, because Neddermeyer was denied entry.

He was allowed to come ashore and greet Isherwood before entering the passport office, then, after a nerve-racking wait, Isherwood and Auden were called into the passport office, too, where, as Isherwood later recalled in *Christopher and His Kind*, they saw Neddermeyer "looking humiliated and resentful" and on the table "Kathleen's letter of invitation side by side with Heinz's passport containing that damning word *Hausdiener*." Isherwood had advised Neddermeyer to describe himself as a house servant when they left Berlin for Greece. Now, U.K. immigration officials suspected that Neddermeyer intended to work illegally for Isherwood's family. More problematic, they also suspected that Neddermeyer was in an illegal relationship with Isherwood, for he was carrying a second letter, from Isherwood, revealingly fond, that advised him to say that the money enclosed was a gift from Neddermeyer's grandmother. "I'd say it was the sort of letter, that, well, a man might write to his sweetheart," one of the examiners reportedly teased.

Neddermeyer was told to leave by the next boat. Isherwood and Auden went aboard and had supper with him, and Isherwood paid Neddermeyer's return fare—half price for a deportee. According to Isherwood's later account, Auden declared they had been betrayed by one of their own: "As soon as I saw that bright-eyed little rat, I knew we were done for. He understood the whole situation at a glance—because he's *one of us*."[191]

Isherwood never recovered from this painful, shocking, and humiliating separation. He was to become obsessed by the trip-wires hidden in petty officialdom, paranoid about red tape, and to feel forever bruised and outraged by the invasion of English rectitude into his private emotional life. He tried to fictionalize it during the 1930s in stories he never published, and he was to return to it at the start of the 1960s in "Waldemar," the third part of

Down There on a Visit, as well as telling the tale forthrightly in *Christopher and His Kind*. The separation at Harwich was the beginning of a long, ill-fated odyssey to find a new homeland where he and Neddermeyer could safely settle, an odyssey which more generally shaped Isherwood's life and informed his work.

WHEN ISHERWOOD RETURNED to London the next day, he went straight to work at Viertel's flat. In *Christopher and His Kind*, he recalled his acute embarrassment while he explained "what had become of the German friend whose arrival he had unwisely announced beforehand." His embarrassment was made more acute by the presence of "Frau G," a former theatrical colleague of Viertel's, a Viennese Jew. This was evidently the playwright Anna Gmeyner, with whom Viertel was having an affair. Isherwood sensed that she, like Viertel, looked on his love life as childish, something to be outgrown. When he fled to another room and "shed tears of rage, shame, and self-pity," she followed him and tried to comfort him. "To her, he had become a child, with childish, touching, but funny sorrow."[192]

Isherwood later said that Viertel eventually changed his attitude and treated Isherwood's sex life with respect, but he never forgot his embarrassment, his passionate anger and disappointment, and how hard it was to continue with the grueling sessions on the script.

He confided to Kathleen that he was "longing now to go abroad as soon as possible." One night, she waited up for him, and they talked things over until after midnight. Viertel wanted him to work as dialogue director while *Little Friend* was being shot but made no definite offer; Isherwood wanted to join Neddermeyer.

Rolf Katz and Gerald Hamilton both warned it wasn't safe for Isherwood to go to Berlin. Isherwood wrote to William Robson-Scott, who was there, asking him to help Neddermeyer get a visa and ticket for Paris with a view to continuing to French Morocco or Tahiti. "[I]f I seem terribly tiresome, please remember that my state of health is far from normal," he told Robson-Scott. "This film and the Harwich incident have been a little much for me. I am having a sort of nervous breakdown, it seems, without the relief of breaking."[193] Later, he showed his gratitude by dedicating *Lions and Shadows* to Robson-Scott.

Isherwood met Neddermeyer in Amsterdam on January 20, and they went to Paris. Viertel agreed to keep open the job as dialogue director on *Little Friend* if Isherwood would return by the end of the month, but the French authorities refused permission for Neddermeyer to stay in France, so

Isherwood was forced to beg for more time through a network of helpers and attentive busybodies. He would call Kathleen from Paris; she would call "Feartell" as she once wrote it; Viertel would call the studio. Replies were wired care of Katz's Meudon address. Isherwood took Neddermeyer back to Amsterdam, settled him "with a family to learn English," and managed to return to London on the evening of January 30 after all. He rushed back to work at Viertel's the next morning, only to learn that nothing was going to happen "for at least another week, very annoying," as Kathleen recorded.[194]

The cast was yet to be finalized. Isherwood tried to get the part of Felicity's mother for his actress friend Beatrix Lehmann, John Lehmann's youngest sister. He recalled in *Christopher and His Kind* that "he took Viertel to see her play the young Elizabeth on stage in *The Tudor Wench*" and then introduced them: "Beatrix arrived dressed—or so my memory assures me—in an incredible femme-fatal outfit consisting largely of green feathers." She did not get the part, but she and Viertel began a love affair with an ease of access not possible for Isherwood and Neddermeyer, and Viertel cast her in his next film for Gaumont, *The Passing of the Third Floor Back*.[195]

WANDERING, 1934

The ardor and friction of his collaboration with Viertel was to produce rich fruit, later, in *Prater Violet*, and also in the near term, in *Mr. Norris Changes Trains*. At the end of March, Isherwood rejoined Neddermeyer in Amsterdam, and they shipped out together from Rotterdam, voyaged south via Lisbon and Madeira all the way to Las Palmas, Gran Canaria, in the Canary Islands. In Las Palmas, they found a room on the roof of a hotel by the beach. There, with a view of the surrounding rooftops occupied by goats, drying laundry, and flowers, Isherwood managed to write the first chapter of *The Lost*, "a novel about Norris alone," as he recorded in his diary on May 23. He abandoned all the rest of his material. For the time being, Arthur Norris seemed to him "to be the only workable character."[196]

Writing *Little Friend*, Isherwood had been forced by Viertel to throw away, again and again, anything that didn't work. They had cut much of Lothar's novel and focused on the central character, the young girl called Felicity. Now, he found the energy and discipline to repeat this with his own book. He acknowledged his debt to Viertel repeatedly in their correspondence, calling him "dear Master" and thanking him for "those horrible but fascinating months" which he said "have been worth more to me than my whole education." After the novel about Norris was accepted, he acknowledged the debt again: "My experiences during the making of Little Friend have completely changed me. If my new book is good at all it is largely because of what I learnt then."[197] It wasn't just the writing sessions with Viertel; it was also the anguish and anxiety he experienced trying to sustain his bond with Neddermeyer; the travel and communication challenges forced him to simplify his life in order to focus on Neddermeyer's destiny. He edited away his other friendships for this single workable, real-life individual.

In the Canary Islands, far from Viertel, so bossy and controlling, Isherwood resolved to tell his own story in his own way, and he hit on a narrative strategy that could not be invaded by any other point of view; it was a strategy that he would stick to and that he would use again. In his 1934 diary, he wrote "I think it must be in the first person. The narrator being myself." He later explained in *Christopher and His Kind* that "Christopher wanted to make the reader experience Arthur Norris just as he had experienced Gerald Hamilton." In the novel, he did not reveal that his narrator William Bradshaw was a homosexual because "he feared to create a scandal." He hesitated to embarrass Kathleen and even Uncle Henry to that extent. Also, he later said, he wanted the reader to focus on Mr. Norris; "the Narrator had to be as unobtrusive as possible." A homosexual narrator "would have become so odd, perhaps so interesting, that his presence would have thrown the novel out of perspective." But Isherwood "scorned" to make his narrator heterosexual, and so gave him no "explicit sex experiences in the story."[198]

There is a further reason, never touched on by Isherwood. In his publicity piece for the New York premiere, Viertel explained that he selected the novel *Little Friend* because he wanted to make a film with a new kind of hero: "I decided to have a child, a 12-year-old girl, as a heroine. It was my own choice." Quoting the epigraph from *The Idiot* used by Ernst Lothar at the front of the novel, Viertel went on:

> But, as the great Dostoevsky says, "Children do understand everything." They don't know our real reasons and the mechanism of our grown-up passions, but they understand everything with their hearts. And so little Felicity, left alone with her fairy tales, her dolls and her mother-fixation, has to find out everything else by herself.[199]

She is just the sort of innocent observer figure that Isherwood created in William Bradshaw, sensitive, inexperienced, well meaning, willing, easily tricked, like Maisie in Henry James's *What Maisie Knew* or like Isherwood's favorite, David Copperfield.

The narrator in *Mr. Norris Changes Trains* is and is not Christopher Isherwood. Isherwood expressed his ambivalence toward the character by giving him the two middle names that he himself did not want, William Bradshaw.

According to *Christopher and His Kind*: "They had always embarrassed him," and they made his name too long to fit on travel documents. But it was not until 1946, when he became a U.S. citizen, that he took as his full legal name Christopher Isherwood.[200] Meanwhile, putting William Bradshaw into a novel, as Isherwood put so many of his real-life friends and acquaintances, signaled that Isherwood was done with this aspect of his personality. Afterwards, in *Goodbye to Berlin*, *Prater Violet*, and *Down There on a Visit*, the narrator was to appear as Christopher Isherwood.

From Gran Canaria, Isherwood and Neddermeyer went to the island of Tenerife, where in the garden of a *pension*, Pavillon Troika, Isherwood set up his Corona underneath "the spotted leaves of a rubber tree, with banana plants and hibiscus around him," and got back to work on *The Lost*.[201] Sometimes he gave Neddermeyer lessons in geography, history, and English. A friend had taken Neddermeyer with his passport to the German consul in Las Palmas to change the professional description *Hausdiener* to *Sprachstudent*, so Neddermeyer was no longer a domestic servant but a student of languages. At night, Isherwood and Neddermeyer drank and danced on the patio. They also went climbing—El Nublo on Gran Canaria in June, and in July the Pico de Teide volcano on Tenerife with a guide and two mules to carry their bedding and food. Eventually they toured the westernmost Canaries.

In *Christopher and His Kind*, Isherwood dismissed the film of *Little Friend* because it had a happy ending and an "old-fashioned sentimental theme."[202] In Lothar's novel, the divorcing parents come from different social backgrounds; class and ethnic differences destabilize the marriage, and the novel presents this as symptomatic of the wider social situation in which increasing friction between the bourgeoisie and the proletariat in Vienna is intertwined with growing suspicion of the Jews. The half-Jewish, half-Catholic heroine is surprised to discover her Jewish patrimony and feels torn by class and ethnic hatred within her family circle. These social and political themes were cut from the film.

Adapted for British audiences, the story was moved to London; the marriage is between a man and woman of similar social background, and it is broken by adultery rather than societal animosity. The friendship between the privileged heroine and the working-class boy offers, as it might in Dickens, the opportunity for the boy to better himself rather than for him to attack the social structure. Thus, the Viertel–Isherwood film addressed not the war between social classes and ethnic groups but the middle-class war between generations which Isherwood had portrayed in *All the Conspirators* and in *The Memorial*.

On the other hand, the film had a notably modern aesthetic. Inspired by the dream sequence at the beginning of Lothar's novel, it used Freudian symbolism as a storytelling device. The rigid schedules and prohibitions visited on Felicity addle her dreams and contrast tellingly with the destructive rule-breaking of the adults in her waking world. The same sort of dream sequence was to be used in MGM's *The Wizard of Oz* half a decade later.[203]

In *Christopher and His Kind*, Isherwood recalled that his friends were "indulgent" about the film. Some told him it was "really quite good"; others "took it for granted that he couldn't be held responsible for the film in its final form, since, obviously, the Gaumont-British vulgarians must have altered every word of the screenplay." A third group considered him "an amusingly cynical whore." He knew of himself, however, that he needed to work on a commercial movie story, both for the money and for the dose of reality: "He, the arrogant dainty-minded private artist, needed to plunge his hands into a vulgar public bucket of dye, to get them dripping with it, to subdue his nature temporarily to it and do the best he was capable of under the circumstances."[204]

By chance, the film opened in London on Isherwood's thirtieth birthday, August 26, 1934. He was far away in the Canaries. His mother and brother were intoxicated by the coincidence of dates, attending *Little Friend* the day after it opened, on the birthday of grandfather John Bradshaw Isherwood which Kathleen had always liked to celebrate as Isherwood's birthday. Kathleen was "fearfully thrilled" when she saw Christopher Isherwood's and Margaret Kennedy's names together in the credits and sat through the film a second time to see this again.[205]

Little Friend received good reviews and did well at the box office. Felicity was played by Nova Pilbeam, exquisitely slender, unblemished and brainy, who soon afterwards starred for Alfred Hitchcock in *The Man Who Knew Too Much* and *Young and Innocent*. The *New York Times* praised the film as "very close to being a masterpiece of its kind." Far from finding it sentimental, the reviewer thought the film austere, noting "it is unfortunately possible that the quality of understatement which gives it its distinction may also damage it in the film public's esteem."[206]

Forster, the master of understatement, couldn't get enough of it. He knew Lothar's novel, which treated the same kinds of social friction and hypocrisy he fictionalized himself. Isherwood had taken Forster on the set, and Forster wrote a few years later that he "should have told you how much I liked Little Friend. It was wonderfully little spoilt. I went three times."[207]

Meanwhile, Isherwood's sojourn in the Canaries provided material for two short stories set there and published in 1935. "The Turn Round the World" was about two traveling con men destined to be rivals as they wander in constellation from country to country, island to island, begging funds. "A

Day in Paradise" was a leftist, antiwar satire about holidaymakers disappointed when the imaginary island paradise purchased in advance from travel brochures abuts poverty and a military base on the real island they visit.[208]

Isherwood preserved photographs and requests for financial support from the real-life traveling con men along with brochures and maps of his own travels from that summer and autumn. These highlight the fact that he and Neddermeyer were strangers everywhere they went, relying on public information rather than on the hospitality or local knowledge of friends. They finally left the Canaries from Las Palmas at midnight on September 6, exactly one year after leaving Turville-Petre's island in Greece, voyaging to Spain, and then to the North African coast, where they disembarked at Ceuta in what was then Spanish Morocco. They toured Tetouan and the blue village of Xauen (Chefchaouen) before starting north again, via Granada and Madrid, toward their next temporary home, Copenhagen, where they spent the winter.

IN 1930, AUDEN wrote a play about a wandering Englishman, *The Fronny*—his English version of *der Franni*, as the boys in Berlin called Turville-Petre. *The Fronny* included a short poem that begins with the haunting alliterative line, "Doom is dark and deeper than any sea-dingle . . ." The poem is about a quest of unknown purpose and about the longing to return home. Eventually Auden titled the poem "The Wanderer" after the Anglo-Saxon poem that inspired it.[209] The poem became famous; the play, except fragments, was lost.

The fragments show that Auden associated his Fronny character with the fool in traditional English mummers' plays, who undergoes a ritual death and rebirth to empower the next generation to marry and procreate. The mummers' plays are rooted in earlier fertility rites. In *The Revesby Play*, which Auden included in his anthology *The Poet's Tongue*, the fool lists out loud what he wills to each of his five sons before they kill him for his "estate."[210] Auden's Fronny makes a will, leaving his letters and manuscripts to Isherwood and Upward and leaving other possessions to reward friends for their virtues or to address their sexual and psychological problems.

Auden returned to the theme of death and rebirth over the next few years, subverting the connection between inheritance and procreation which did not align with his interests as a homosexual. In 1933, he wrote a socialist play called *The Dance of Death*, in which the dancer, adopting many roles, represented the English middle classes; in his last will and testament, the dancer leaves his property to the workers and cedes the stage to Karl Marx. Isherwood later revealed that the unnamed character mimed by the dancer at the end of the play was the Fronny: "As the paralyzed patron of a boy bar, he is wheeled onto the stage, makes his will, orders drinks all round, and dies." The leftist Group Theatre performed *The Dance of Death* to sensational effect in London in 1934 and again in 1935.[211]

In 1934, Auden wrote another play, *The Chase*, incorporating parts of *The Fronny* which he had by then abandoned. He sent *The Chase* to Isherwood for comment, as he sent most of his work at the time. Isherwood was settled in Copenhagen with Neddermeyer. On November 18, in his diary, he sketched some "Possible scenes for play" using Mortmereish ghastliness to satirize current political and economic struggles in European capitals and introducing the rival nations Ostnia and Westnia. He worked these up into a scenario which he sent Auden a few days later, and they began collaborating by post, each writing different new scenes and revising existing scenes. In January 1935, Auden flew to Copenhagen, where, Isherwood later recalled, "they worked through the play, making minor alterations." They called the new play *Where Is Francis?*; later, *The Dog Beneath the Skin* was added in front of this.[212]

It was a madcap satirical pantomime again foretelling political and social revolution. It drew on Brecht and on Gilbert and Sullivan as well as the mummers' plays, taking the audience on an absurdist quest from an English village in the grip of Church and army through the nightmare unfolding in Europe at the start of the 1930s—collapsing monarchies, burgeoning dictatorships, vibrant red-light districts, overpopulated lunatic asylums, all peopled by self-deluding dreamers, proprietors on the make and on the take, prostitutes, drug addicts, runaways, crooked financiers, bogus entertainers, sold-out journalists, ignorant destroyers of art and culture promoting themselves as entertainment. With the new material introduced by Isherwood, Mortmere seemed to have engulfed Europe.

The motive for the quest is the search for a lost heir, absent for a decade from the village. Instead of undergoing a ritual death and rebirth, the lost heir, Francis Crewe, disappears and returns in disguise. This was a favorite plot device of Isherwood, who probably first encountered it at age ten when his mother read him Walter Scott's *Ivanhoe* during the Christmas holidays in 1914 while his father was away at the Front. Scott's knight, Desdichado, the "Disinherited," returns home from the Crusades to claim his patrimony disguised in a suit of armor. In Auden and Isherwood's play, the disguise is a skin, a standard theatrical resource of the time, and Francis, as he announces at the end of the play, does not wish to reclaim his patrimony: "you can keep Honeypot Hall and do what you like with it."[213]

Auden had used a dog skin in *The Chase* as a disguise for a minor character. Isherwood put it on the central figure, as meaningfully as he put the astrakhan coat on Philip Lindsay in *All the Conspirators*. In the play, the dog skin suggests the unconscious loyalty that pulls the lost heir home to his village, and it also makes him into a comic figure, like the fool.

Auden had already used names from his own and Isherwood's families in *The Chase*. These proliferated in *The Dog Beneath the Skin* alongside material from Bradshaw Isherwood family life at Marple Hall, characters from nearby villages, and local lore. Throughout Isherwood's childhood, his grandmother Elizabeth was accompanied by her faithful dogs when she walked in Marple Park. One was called Dash; another with black fur had the now unacceptable name Nigger. After Frank Isherwood's death, one of Elizabeth's dogs often walked with Kathleen to the various small churches she attended in the neighborhood. "After lunch, Mummie & I walked to Chadkirk ... Nigger came with us, & waited for us the whole time we were in church," wrote Isherwood one Sunday in 1918. The faithful, mirroring companion was a cliché of great resonance, central also in his beloved childhood cartoon of Buster Brown and the faithful talking dog Tige. In addition, the dog skin alludes to Nana, nanny to the Darling children in J.M. Barrie's *Peter Pan* and played by an actor in a dog skin in the popular stage adaptation which Isherwood saw in 1917.[214] Peter Pan spirits the children away to Neverland while Nana is chained in the garden.

In *The Dog Beneath the Skin*, the dog-hero keeps a diary like Isherwood, illustrated with photographs. Viewing the world from "a dog's eye view" changes the hero's opinion of the people in his village, as he makes clear in his third-act speech: "As a dog, I learnt for the first time with what a mixture of fear, bullying, and condescending kindness you treat those whom you consider your inferiors, but on whom you depend for your pleasures." Isherwood told Spender that in this speech (written by him, not by Auden) Francis is "condemning his 'dog's-eye view' as superficial, condemning his diary"; the underdog perspective, the diary, was only a way of hiding from larger truths and obligations, for instance the obligation to take action for change. "In fact, the whole allegory of the dog-skin disguise is: 'Proust is not enough.' "[215]

The title *The Dog Beneath the Skin, or Where Is Francis?* referred not just to one lost heir, but to a representative type forever changed by World War I, sacrificed and reborn in the next generation as an educated bourgeois hero with an evolving leftist consciousness.[216] Isherwood, like Francis Turville-Petre, was heir to his family's estate, and like Turville-Petre, he spent his share of family money to fund his wandering, down-and-out life abroad. Like Turville-Petre, Isherwood was not interested in the house and lands, nor in continuing the family line—inheritance and procreation as in the fool's age-old fertility rite. His father had been the last member of the family who knew how to husband the family properties. Isherwood's father's real name was not Frank but Francis—like Francis Turville-Petre. When Francis Bradshaw Isherwood went off to war, all that came home was his dog tag.

In 1936, the play was performed by the Group Theatre in London, directed by the dancer Rupert Doone. In Doone's hands, the theme of class warfare was more prominent than any personal mythology. Isherwood was abroad, and Auden rewrote the ending even though the play had been published in 1935; in Auden's new version, the hero, Francis, when he reveals himself, is assassinated by a woman from the village.[217] This small significant change illuminated the difference between Auden's world view and Isherwood's. Auden had a death wish articulated tellingly throughout his work; Isherwood identified in his imagination as a survivor.

IN MAY 1935, Isherwood had begun to outline a new novel, *Paul*, about a young man wandering through Europe. "Greek Island—the Ostriches," he noted in his diary, indicating that he was thinking of St. Nicholas as a place to put heads in the sand and ignore what was happening politically. The main character, Paul, was to be a kleptomaniac, an idea inspired by a real kleptomaniac, an Englishman, met in Berlin. According to Spender, Isherwood had cured the kleptomaniac by making him keep a ledger of his thefts, thereby accepting them and rendering them mundane.[218]

Auden had featured kleptomania in *The Orators*. In the section called "Journal of an Airman," his mysterious hero, the Airman, is a kleptomaniac. Wilhelm Stekel, briefly John Layard's analyst, had studied kleptomania and published his view that kleptomania was rooted in repressed or disguised homosexuality. But Auden did not accept the narrow link to sexuality; he grouped kleptomania with all criminal acts as a form of rebellion. In his 1929 journal, he had written that "Every criminal act is a revolt against death. [. . .] Stealing is an attempt to perform a miracle." In "Journal of an Airman," the Airman observes of his hands, "They stole to force a hearing."[219]

For Isherwood, kleptomania was more about stealing an identity, a possible life to lead. "The figure of the young man, Paul," he mused in his diary, "constantly being submerged and reappearing amidst varying groups of people." His will-o'-the-wisp character easily disappears and becomes anonymous or camouflaged; he "is always having heroes or heroines, with whom he falls violently in love. And he is always violently reacting from these enthusiasms—so that one affair blows him headfirst into the next."[220] Paul cannot stop himself from stealing the genius of others.

He masquerades as the person he imagines he must be to succeed in the milieu where he finds himself. "Paul lies about himself," Isherwood noted as he planned the novel, sometimes "posing as a Baron (no, a 'von')"—i.e., a hereditary member of the German nobility. Auden's kleptomaniac Airman undertakes a heroic mission against a mysterious, generalized enemy; Isherwood's Paul was to redeem himself "with some great hysterical venture: Paul's attempted return to Germany to murder the Leaders."[221]

Isherwood sketched detailed relationships between Paul and his other characters, but Paul was slipping from his fictional grasp, so he decided to jettison the other characters and focus on Paul, changing the title to *Paul Is Alone*.

The new title reflected Isherwood's growing sense of isolation as he moved from one city to another with Neddermeyer and returned to London intermittently to work. Wherever he was, he missed something—either Neddermeyer, or the companionship of his writer friends, especially Upward, Forster, Spender, and Auden. Without his friends, he felt he was "without a looking-glass," as he wrote in Holland on September 1, "in a kind of trance; only half alive."

Spender had just visited for a few days: "When I am with him, I seem the same as ever, I suppose." Spender was industriously translating Hölderlin's poems from German; his energy and confidence impressed Isherwood: "as he says himself, he isn't more than half English and half German. 'You see, I'm really a German poet.'"[222]

So strong was the impression Spender made as a half-English, half-German poet, that the impression went right through Isherwood into his novel. Paul was to be half English and half German, also reflecting Isherwood's status, half in, half out, but at home nowhere. In Paul, he planned to express the empathy with Germany and Germanness that he had experienced both in the abstract and through his relationships with Neddermeyer and other German boys. "If I could only write the book partly in German—so as to make the very important symbolic point: that Paul speaks better, more educated German than English."[223]

During May 1936, Isherwood roughed out two chapters presenting Paul's escape from his past and from a disembodied, threatening "Them," as a masochistic adventure in the Greek landscape, where Paul, his "naked flesh [...] bleeding from a dozen places, like the body of a martyr," is hungry, thirsty, lost, tired, blistered, bruised, cut, and nearly drowns, vowing he will never give in, never go back.[224] The chapters were influenced by Frederick Rolfe's *The Desire and Pursuit of the Whole* (1934), given to him by Auden for Christmas, and by Ernest Hemingway's *A Farewell to Arms* (1929). In the former, the gondolier's daughter, a "boy by intention but a girl by defect," is pulled from the water, stripped of her erotically clinging garments and wrapped in a blanket like a foundling as she presses her service on Nicholas Crabbe, insisting she would rather die than leave him. In the latter, Lieutenant Frederic Henry, rather than be shot, deserts from the Italian army by leaping into a river where he nearly drowns before crawling out downstream.[225] Paul encounters the happy-go-lucky German wanderer of his dreams, a communist youth on the run from the Nazis, offering fictional opportunities for Isherwood to explore political and sexual liberation and a train of vaguely erotic fantasies flowing from the hedonistic outdoor life of the Wandervögel.

But the character of Paul was not strong enough. "He isn't in the least demoniac—he is only a little cissy who steals," Isherwood confided to his diary. "He must be capable of sexual vice, debauch, drug-taking, anything. Such people attempt to redeem whole lifetimes through one tonic act of violence." The other characters, so interesting in themselves, "eclipse Paul."[226] Like Paul Dombey, the old-fashioned child so sensitive that he gathers impressions from patterns in wallpaper and lives vicariously through his sister Florence in Dickens's *Dombey and Son*, Paul lacks the force to fulfill his own destiny. Suddenly, on May 29, Isherwood decided to abandon the novel, "all I'd planned was a daydream." He was to resurrect and transform the material many years later in "Paul," the final story in *Down There on a Visit*.

For now, he proceeded instead with a "book of autobiographical fragments,"[227] which in fact became his next three books. He made a list of individual stories that would eventually comprise *Lions and Shadows*, *Goodbye to Berlin*, and *Prater Violet*. He had already written rough drafts of most of the material. The long period of fantasizing and frustration presaged a whirlwind of achievement. He began reworking the material about Sally Bowles and finished the story in less than a month.

HITLER HAD INTRODUCED conscription on March 16, 1935, as part of rearming Germany, and this made Neddermeyer's exile dangerous. "As soon as he's been formally called up and has formally refused to return to that mad-house, he becomes, of course, from the Nazi point of view, a criminal," Isherwood explained to his mother. Neddermeyer's German passport was due to expire in 1938; as a draft evader, he would be unable to renew it. "[H]e must get another nationality," Isherwood declared.[228] This preoccupied Isherwood night and day from 1935 to 1937 as he and Neddermeyer scurried from one rented lodging to another all over Europe.

In December 1935, they left the Low Countries for Portugal, where they rented a villa in São Pedro, a village above Sintra, with Spender and his Welsh boyfriend, Tony Hyndman, formerly of the Coldstream Guards. After Spender and Hyndman moved on, others joined the household, including the Irish writer James Stern and his German wife, Tania Kurella, a physical therapist who later collaborated with Stern as a literary translator. On June 25, 1936, a letter caught up with Neddermeyer from the German consulate in Lisbon requiring him to report for military service. "At present, my only reaction is a fierce warm sick feeling," wrote Isherwood in his diary. "My thoughts scamper round inside my head like scared hens."[229]

By chance, Kathleen, approaching her sixty-eighth birthday, arrived for a visit four days later. The bucolic setting of the stuccoed villa surrounded by gardens and farmland reminded her of Isherwood's birthplace: "the bees buzzing over the flowers & perfect stillness. [. . .] that marvellous open view, one used to get at Wyberslegh . . ." She delighted in the sunshine, the chattering local maids and Isherwood's productive contentment, and she shared his distress: "it is really the most settled & domestic life they have had & now it is all threatened . . ."[230]

Isherwood was frantically seeking help from a Lisbon lawyer and from a local friend who was a civil servant. From a neighbor's villa, he would telephone Brussels where Gerald Hamilton was negotiating on Neddermeyer's behalf with an English lawyer, Cecil Salinger, who sometimes worked with the British Embassy there. From noon to one each day, he waited for the mail to arrive with any news. Sometimes he walked to the post office in the town square to telegram Hamilton. Kathleen recorded that they "get quite jumpy each time the doorbell rings which it does very often!!"[231]

"I am told they are quite capable of extraditing H. on to a German boat," Isherwood reported to Forster. He moved Neddermeyer out of the villa to stay with friends because the address was known to the German consulate. A second letter in August was to create "further panic"; it was also ignored.[232] Isherwood told his mother that money was the answer and asked her for £1,000, an extraordinary amount, roughly £70,000 in today's money.

Her son's four-year-old relationship with Neddermeyer mystified Kathleen. She considered Neddermeyer a social inferior, "he does not speak unless spoken to." However, she recognized a domestic bond in financial intimacy—"they share everything & every evening H. makes up 'our accounts' & asks C just what he has spent during the day!" —and she was committed to her son's happiness. So on her return to London, she went to her bank to arrange funds for Salinger. On the same day, civil war broke out in Spain, which delayed letters between England and Portugal and made it difficult for her to communicate with Isherwood. Moreover, it was ten days before she heard from Salinger, "pretty cool," she wrote in her diary.[233] He wanted payment in advance and would not explain or guarantee his plans.

Kathleen returned to her bank supported by her bachelor cousin, Sir William Graham Greene, now retired from the Admiralty and about to turn eighty. Her diary suggests that she did not find it easy to reveal Isherwood's situation to her elderly cousin and that she blurted it out to him at the bank. Once he knew, Cousin Graham began contacting well-placed friends for advice. Nobody favored Isherwood's plan to obtain a new nationality for Neddermeyer in Belgium. A friend at the Foreign Office warned that it might "involve C in trouble."[234] One of Isherwood's own friends, with whom he had been at medical school in 1928, Robert Moody, visited consulates in London and reported to Kathleen what countries might be open to applications for new citizens.

All the while, Isherwood was cabling Kathleen to send the money right away to a bank in Brussels. Neither Isherwood nor Kathleen really trusted Salinger, nor for that matter Gerald Hamilton who had introduced him. Paranoia crept in. "It is difficult to know how much it is safe to write to C in letters," Kathleen fretted.[235] In mid-August, she asked him to return to England so they could discuss the matter in person.

Isherwood was afraid to leave Neddermeyer alone in Portugal, so he brought him as far as Ostend, in Belgium, and continued alone. Cousin Graham joined them at Pembroke Gardens, "to talk over the Brussels—Equator—Brazil possibilities with C." as Kathleen put it in her diary.[236] Edward Greene, a younger brother of Cousin Graham, had lived in Brazil, where he built a fortune in the coffee trade, and also offered help. They knew less about Ecuador, as Kathleen's spelling makes clear.

Isherwood found this intimate family counseling uncomfortable to say the least. He was turning thirty-two that week; he had been living largely abroad for seven years and, as a homosexual, he had been living outside the law. He had tacitly assumed that Salinger might have to bribe someone, hence the need for such a large sum. As he later explained in *Christopher and His Kind*, "he felt out of place siding with [Kathleen] against Gerald and the lawyer. If they were lawbreakers, well, so was he."

As they all knew, and as Isherwood explained in *Christopher and His Kind*, "Under the new Nazi laws, the penalty for attempting to change your nationality was a long term of imprisonment: it could even be death." Belgium now seemed too close to Germany to be safe. It could be invaded. Therefore, Isherwood "was now making up his mind to emigrate with Heinz to some country in Latin America."[237]

On August 26, Isherwood returned to Ostend, accompanied by Forster, and celebrated his birthday there with Neddermeyer, Forster, Gerald Hamilton, Robert Moody and William Plomer. Kathleen again returned to the bank, embarrassed that the bank official "obviously thought I was being <u>very foolish</u> as I expect I am . . ."

Her diary around this time reveals another flow of thought about duty and military service. "Nurse & I looked through Frank's uniform in tin boxes—" The twenty-year-old uniform and the duties and sacrifices which it so powerfully symbolized were outmoded, yet she could not bring herself to discard them. She ran into one of Isherwood's expatriate English neighbors, home from São Pedro, who had hosted Neddermeyer to hide him from the German consul, and she wrote, "I fancy the general opinion had been it was a pity that H did not go & serve his time—"[238] Kathleen feared and hated war, but she revered her husband. She had been an army wife at the height of the British Empire, when "the general opinion" was that military service was an honor and a glory. She was extremely sensitive to the opinions of others—the Greenes, the bank manager, the neighbors—yet what she fancied must be the general opinion of the expatriate British in Portugal was in fact a suppressed opinion of her own.

Salinger shortly reported to Isherwood that he was applying for Mexican citizenship for Neddermeyer at a cost of £700. Two and a half months elapsed, then three, then six. Neddermeyer moved from Ostend to Brussels, to Spa, back to Brussels, to Paris—stalked by the expiry dates of short-term permissions to stay and with no job or even chickens to occupy him. He had left a beloved puppy dog behind in Portugal. Isherwood had left his books and manuscripts, which he and his mother and a relay of friends and neighbors spent months retrieving. He perched with Neddermeyer in each European locale, tenaciously continuing with *Lions and Shadows*. "Like most of my generation," he wrote:

> I was obsessed by a complex of terrors and longings connected with the idea of "War." "War," in this purely neurotic sense, meant The Test. The Test of your courage, of your maturity, of your sexual prowess: "Are you really a Man?" Subconsciously, I believe, I longed to be subjected to this test; but I also dreaded failure. I dreaded failure so much—indeed, I was so certain that I *should* fail—that, consciously, I denied my longing to be tested, altogether.

He dreaded the same for Neddermeyer, and was determined to protect him from any such Test. Humphrey Spender had joined the Sintra ménage for a time and observed in his diary that Isherwood was wary of anything that could take Neddermeyer away from him: "The fact that Heinz is not allowed to stay in first one and then another country is the deciding factor in Christopher's life," he wrote. "Christopher shields Heinz to the point of depriving him of all independence."[239] Neddermeyer's own feelings are unrecorded, although his family was evidently glad he was safely outside Germany.

DURING LATE 1936 and 1937, Isherwood crossed and recrossed the English Channel, roosting with Neddermeyer in Europe then attending rehearsals and doing rewrites with Auden in England for *The Ascent of F6*, about the inner demons of a mountaineer attempting to scale the world's most challenging peak, the fictional F6. Here was another variation on the Test, the Truly Strong Man and the Truly Weak Man—themes that obsessed Auden as well as Isherwood and to which they now gave tragicomic shape.

The hero, Michael Ransom, was based partly on T.E. Lawrence, Lawrence of Arabia, though Ransom's real challenge is essentially a religious one—a crisis of conscience like Thomas Becket's in T.S. Eliot's *Murder in the Cathedral*. In a 1935 review, Isherwood had called the spiritual conflict in Eliot's play "extremely interesting" but Eliot's approach "uncertain" and showing "confusion."[240] A better play on the subject was called for. Michael Ransom undertakes his mission for the glory of the empire but suspects his motives are impure and that he secretly wants the glory for himself and is ready to sacrifice even his friends and colleagues to achieve it. The expedition sets off in a frenzy of public attention. When Ransom meets his nemesis on the mountaintop, it proves to be his mother. He dies there, again fulfilling the message of Auden's charade, *Paid on Both Sides*, "His mother and her mother won." For Auden and Isherwood at this time, the psychology of the family romance seemed to rule not only bodily health but also the forces of nature. The avalanche thundered within. And as with their mountaineer hero, fame itself was starting to become a problem—a temptation and a distraction that confused them both, though in different ways.

The Ascent of F6 was staged by the Group Theatre at the Mercury Theatre, Notting Hill, opening on February 26 while Auden was away observing the Spanish Civil War. It was Isherwood's turn to rewrite the ending which had already been published in book form; he tried out a different version every night. There was music by Benjamin Britten, whom Auden had befriended while working with him at the GPO Film Unit. Isherwood took Britten under his wing, encouraging him to explore his homosexual inclinations, spending a night with him at the Jermyn Street Baths, and sometimes putting him up at Pembroke Gardens. Britten liked Isherwood to read aloud to him and described Isherwood in his diary as "a grand person; unaffected, extremely amusing & devastatingly intelligent."[241]

The Ascent of F6 was Auden and Isherwood's biggest critical and commercial success. It transferred to the West End after fifty performances, ran four nights in Cambridge, and was revived two years later at Birmingham Rep and a year after that at the Old Vic. "This time Auden and Isherwood have brought it off," wrote the reviewer for the *New Statesman*, recognizing the central theme that had at last emerged clearly, "the exploitation by imperialists of all that is best in the youth of the Empire." "[N]o show in London better worth seeing at the moment," said the *New English Weekly*, launching Isherwood's reputation as a dialogue specialist with additional praise, "probably nobody to-day writes better contemporary dialogue than Mr. Isherwood." In the U.S., the published play was reviewed by the *New York Times* and workshopped by Yale drama students.[242] So Isherwood and Auden began a fourth play, *On the Frontier*.

In the spring of 1937, Isherwood fell ill from a botched wisdom tooth extraction. A fragment of tooth festered in the gum, and by April 10, he developed a fever and inflamed tonsils. For nearly two weeks, he was seriously ill at Kathleen's house, living "on slops" by doctor's orders and having the infection syringed every few hours. Kathleen moved him into her own bed and slept elsewhere. His temperature rose to 103. Nevertheless, a parade of visitors talked and smoked around his bed all day long; Auden played the piano and sang hymns. William Coldstream painted Isherwood's portrait in oils.[243] On April 13, Isherwood woke with a mouthful of new ulcers discharging pus and his jaw so stiff that he couldn't talk and had to write down his needs.

Meanwhile, leaving no stone unturned, Neddermeyer had applied again for permission to enter the U.K. Forster wrote a letter of support. The application was denied. The Home Office confirmed to Salinger that Neddermeyer's 1934 exclusion had been on moral grounds and could not be reversed. Security was especially tight leading up to George VI's coronation on May 12, 1937. This was to prove an unlucky day for Isherwood and Neddermeyer.

While Isherwood was incapacitated by his infected tooth, Neddermeyer was expelled from France as an undesirable alien. He had been questioned by the Paris police about a jewelry theft, and although he was not charged, he was put down as belligerent; also, the police discovered he had lost his identity card, and when they visited his lodgings, they were told he was a male prostitute.

Isherwood was far too ill to help. An American friend, Tony Bower, "then somewhat in love with Christopher," volunteered to go to Paris and take Neddermeyer to Luxembourg.[244] By April 25, Isherwood was well enough to join Neddermeyer in Luxembourg, but in the meantime, the French police were sharing Neddermeyer's undesirable status internationally. Soon there would be nowhere for him to hide in Europe.

On coronation day, while Isherwood and Neddermeyer were sleeping in their bed at the Hotel Gaisser in Luxembourg, Kathleen rose at 4:30 a.m. in London and walked to Marble Arch to watch the celebrations from a club overlooking the route of the royal procession. In Luxembourg, two police officers woke Isherwood and Neddermeyer and told Neddermeyer he "was expelled from Luxembourg and must leave immediately."[245] Isherwood and Neddermeyer did not yet realize that they had just spent their last night together.

Salinger proposed an emergency short-term visa for Belgium, but in order to obtain it, Neddermeyer would have to reenter Germany. So Neddermeyer crossed the border by train from Luxembourg to the German city of Trier. Salinger discouraged Isherwood from accompanying Neddermeyer, in order to avoid attracting attention or questions. Reluctantly, Isherwood took a train to Brussels to wait.

Kathleen was still watching the coronation procession: "besides the coaches there was a most <u>wonderful procession of soldiers sailors airmen</u> etc from all parts of the Empire—India Australia New Zealand South Africa the Gold Coast etc etc," she wrote in her diary. "It <u>filled one with pride</u> to belong to such an Empire! & to be <u>English!</u>" As she listened to the service relayed from Westminster Abbey, Kathleen thought about King Edward VIII, who, in December, had given up the throne to his younger brother and sought refuge in France rather than try to rule without the support of the woman he loved, the twice-divorced American Wallis Simpson. Kathleen had commented in her diary at the time of the abdication that the king "shirked his responsibilities . . ." Now, during the pomp of his brother's coronation, she wondered how the Duke of Windsor felt listening to the service, "an exile by his own doing in a foreign land—"[246] Her son's unacceptable love affair had secretly shadowed the zeitgeist. Isherwood, too, had chosen, and would choose again, to be an exile from the empire his mother loved.

In Trier, Neddermeyer spent the night of May 12 alone in a hotel. The next morning, Salinger met him by car and took him to the Belgian consulate to collect the visa. After they left the consulate to drive back to Brussels, Gestapo agents appeared and asked Neddermeyer for his papers; then they arrested him for draft evasion. Additional charges were added later.

Stephen Spender and Olive Mangeot told Kathleen that they suspected Gerald Hamilton may have shopped Neddermeyer. Kathleen had been suspicious of Hamilton all along. In *Christopher and His Kind*, Isherwood fully aired his own suspicion that Neddermeyer's fate had been determined by Hamilton's constant need for money: "Gerald was *capable* of this crime."

Something in Isherwood liked to rely on people he knew would betray him. Was he repeating the betrayal that he had experienced in childhood when his utterly reliable father let him down by being killed in the war? Or was this another test, to discover whether he himself was tough enough to handle betrayal and go on with the game?

As a writer, Isherwood prided himself on being able to plumb any character, to tell authenticity from sham. He could not quite get to the bottom of Hamilton. In *Christopher and His Kind*, he wrote: "If Christopher was able to be present at Gerald's deathbed, he would kneel beside it and ask, 'Gerald, did you do it?' If Gerald answered 'Yes,' Christopher would forgive him; if 'No,' Christopher would believe him but would feel subtly disappointed." He found the idea of Gerald's crookedness exciting, and as a homosexual he felt he belonged among crooks. In any case, Isherwood was attracted to the emotional satisfaction of forgiving Hamilton—because being in a position to forgive meant that he, Isherwood, had the upper hand in the end, whether or not he had been tricked. He had already portrayed this in *Mr. Norris Changes Trains*. When Bradshaw learns that Norris used him as bait in his moneymaking plot, he is disappointed of any reconciling confidence, let alone an apology: "Arthur's orientally sensitive spirit shrank from the rough, healthy, modern catch-as-catch-can of home-truths and confession; he offered me a compliment instead." Bradshaw himself supplies the pity, the sentimental emolument: "I felt a sudden anxiety to protect him from a realization of what he had done."[247]

On July 7, 1937, Neddermeyer was convicted of draft evasion and reciprocal onanism. Isherwood told Robson-Scott that Neddermeyer had "admitted everything, not merely about deliberately disregarding the consul's summons at Lisbon, but also moral charges."[248] There was an appeal, with no change in the outcome. Neddermeyer served six months in prison at Trier, including the time awaiting trial, followed by a year of labor for the state and two years in Hitler's army.

Isherwood was named at the trial as the man with whom Neddermeyer had committed reciprocal onanism—in fourteen foreign countries and in the German Reich. Certainly Isherwood could not return to Germany. The earliest he and Neddermeyer could hope to see one another again was 1941. But Neddermeyer had avoided the worse fate of being "sentenced to an indefinite term in a concentration camp, as many homosexuals were." Isherwood later explained in *Christopher and His Kind*: "In camp, Heinz would have been treated as an outcast of the Reich who differed from a Jew only in having to wear a pink triangle on his clothes instead of a yellow star. Like the Jews, homosexuals were often put into 'liquidation' units, in which they were given less food and more work than other prisoners. Thus, thousands of them died."[249]

LONDON, 1937

Back in London, Isherwood got a small film job, translating a script from German for Alexander Korda, a project later abandoned. It was late July, stifling hot, and his mother and brother were away. "I think all day of Heinz over there in prison," he wrote in his diary.

Throughout his five years with Neddermeyer, Isherwood had other sexual affairs and even fell in love outside the relationship. For instance, during rehearsals for *The Ascent of F6* at the Mercury Theatre, he had begun an affair with the ballet dancer John Andrews, whose troupe, Ballet Rambert, rehearsed in the same theater. He introduced Andrews at home, took him to stay with Auden at Threlkeld in the Lake District where he and Auden were doing rewrites for *The Ascent of F6* and starting *On the Frontier*, and to his favorite Paris hotel. But his feelings for Neddermeyer more deeply tapped his long-standing need to look after someone else and to serve something pure and innocent. The July diary entry continued, "I suppose it isn't so much H. himself that I miss—but that part of myself which only existed in his company. That aching, melting tenderness: 'Mein kleiner Bruder.' I want to watch over him, protect him, serve him—anyhow, anywhere, on any terms."[250]

In mid-November, Isherwood heard that Neddermeyer had been released from prison and was home in Berlin living with an aunt and beginning his term of hard labor. This alleviated his guilt over taking Neddermeyer away from Germany and being unable to keep him safe. He began another affair, with the French-language teacher, Jean Bühler.

He savored the sensation of being in love, but he still felt lonely: "I want, above all, to be strong—to give protection, like a tree. This isn't mere conceit. It is part of my deepest nature," he wrote in his diary. "I can be strong for others—not for myself."[251]

Then he fell in love with someone else. This time, it was his former pupil, now an undergraduate at Cambridge, Ian Scott-Kilvert. In a grand hall in St. James's in the center of London, Isherwood and Auden appeared together at the Fifth National Book Fair, introduced on stage by their friend the poet Cecil Day Lewis. They read from *On the Frontier*, "first one at the microphone then the other but necessarily standing close together—"[252] wrote Kathleen, who was proud to attend.

In *On the Frontier*, two imaginary European countries glide slowly, terrifyingly, toward war. On opposite sides, like Romeo and Juliet, like Isherwood and Neddermeyer, are the lovers Eric and Anna, "Looking for a place where I could really be myself, / For a person who would see me as I really am." Eric and Anna meet only in a spotlight on the stage; when the spotlight is off, their love affair does not seem to exist. That day in the hall in St James's, Isherwood reveled in the exposure—"the applause, the autographing of our books"—but afterwards, he felt "mildly ashamed": "It was like Satan's view of the Kingdoms of the World—and didn't I play up to it: grinning, handshaking, theatrically putting my arm on Wystan's shoulder? This kind of thing really constitutes the greatest possible danger to my integrity. I am a born actor."[253]

Into the spotlight, that moment of excitement, walked Ian Scott-Kilvert, "A strikingly handsome young man, whom I'd noticed almost as soon as we entered the hall," and whom, a decade before, Isherwood had begun to school in his own style of thinking. Scott-Kilvert introduced himself and they arranged to have a drink. It felt like a momentous reunion: "that ridiculous meeting, in a corner of the Langham lounge, was something quite unique in my life. It was like discovering a long-lost brother." He found Scott-Kilvert "so vivid and gay—just as I remember him: with the same awful stammer." The spotlight was on again.

They planned to meet in Cambridge, and Isherwood was further bowled over by an "astounding letter" from Scott-Kilvert, filled with promises of which he tried to be wary: "is it the kind of thing Henry James writes about in 'The Pupil'—or is it just a kind of sublimated undergraduate literary snobbery?"[254]

James's story about a university graduate and a boy of eleven, then twelve, thirteen, fourteen, who form an intimate bond over their private lessons conformed to Isherwood's deeply held fantasy about an ideal intellectual romance. James had presented the bond between the tutor and the boy as a form of marriage. At the tutor's interview, the boy "looked straight and hard at the candidate for the honor of taking his education in hand," and they are pulled around Europe in the wake of the boy's siblings, "a band of adventurers," who are trying and failing to achieve advantageous marriages in the conventional sense before the family runs out of money.[255] Isherwood's sexual promiscuity never weakened his longing for a marriage-like bond.

In Cambridge, waiting alone in Scott-Kilvert's rooms, he looked over the books, the music, the photographs, even the letters, with possessive intimacy. At thirty-three, sexually experienced, beginning to be professionally famous, he was back at his old university, where he had been miserable, sexually uptight, and an academic failure. He relished the comparison with his younger self implied in Scott-Kilvert: "He is all angles and prickles and sharp corners—so young still, and so angular that it makes one want to shed tears. Underneath this, I think, he is soft and feline—yes, a bit catty: awfully like myself at the same age."

With helpless vainglory, Isherwood recorded the seduction on the sofa:

"'What am I s-supposed to do now? Fall into your arms?' My answers seemed to amuse him. He said, in the morning: 'I'm still in a mist of admiration for the way you handled things last night.'"

Meanwhile, Isherwood continued his affair with Jean Bühler, spending a night with him in Brighton. "I told him, before we started, all about Ian. He was sad, of course. But things went off quite well, nevertheless." On December 9, Isherwood and Scott-Kilvert flew to Paris, stayed at the favorite Hotel Quai Voltaire, "in the same room I've had four times already," and "wandered about the streets in a kind of daze" with Isherwood hanging nervously on Scott-Kilvert's reactions.[256]

However, the spotlight was about to dim, and the lights to come up on the broader stage. On the evening of December 15, as he sat in his room at Pembroke Gardens writing up the Paris trip in his diary, Isherwood's arm was already stiff with his first round of typhoid and cholera injections for China.

He had gone to Primrose Hill for lunch with the writer Charlotte Haldane, a Communist Party member organizing and fundraising for the Spanish Republicans. She was preparing to take the singer and actor Paul Robeson and his wife to Spain in January, and she invited Isherwood and Auden along. Auden had already been to the Spanish Civil War, from January to March, and subsequently he and Isherwood had been invited to the Second International Writers' Conference for the Defense of Culture, a gathering of anti-fascist intellectuals in Valencia in July, but they had been unable to get travel permits. (Spender had traveled out with the communist writer Sylvia Townsend Warner, and it was he who communicated the shortage of permits to Isherwood, raising the possibility that Spender, having lost out to Isherwood over Berlin, did not do all he could to help Isherwood get to Spain.) Auden and Isherwood agreed to join Charlotte Haldane's trip provided it could take place before the trip to China that they had already begun to plan. She directed Isherwood to the Lister Institute on his way home from lunch to start his China inoculations.[257]

"Ian will just have to take his place in my life—I can't alter it to suit him," wrote Isherwood.[258] Travel permits for Haldane's group were delayed, and the trip postponed, so Isherwood and Auden decided to leave for China without going to Spain. They were to be away for six months.

CHINA, 1938

They had been commissioned by Auden's publisher Faber and Faber to write a travel book. They produced *Journey to a War*, a hybrid volume of poetry, prose, map, and photographs about the war between China and Japan that broke out in 1937 after years of rising tension following the Japanese invasion of Manchuria in 1931. They collaborated on a diary, taking turns recording the material that Isherwood, after they got home in July 1938, revised as the main text for publication. Auden contributed sonnet sequences to open and close the volume—"London to Hong Kong" and "In Time of War," the latter with a verse "Commentary," and a dedicatory sonnet to Forster.

Auden's curt, oracular poems gave the book a unique grandeur. They theorized about the material realities reported in the diary, hallmarking the Sino-Japanese war as another theater of a worldwide struggle. "This is one sector and one movement of the general war / Between the dead and the unborn," Auden wrote,[259] gesturing toward socialist revolution, a war between past and future. Individual tragedies and private comedies were scattered throughout. Port by port, country by country, provincial town by provincial town, the book described a colonial order about to be swallowed up in a universal conflict. By century's end, the map was to be so altered as to make Auden and Isherwood's journey difficult to trace.

In January 1938, Isherwood and especially Auden were experiencing a new level of prominence as politically engaged writers. On top of the excitement generated by their plays, Auden's poem "Spain" had appeared as a pamphlet in May 1937. It charted in a time scheme familiar from Ilya Ehrenburg's "Sons of Our Sons" the prehistory of the civil war, the centrifugal pull attracting fighters on the right and on the left from outside the country, and a possible Marxist future. In June, Auden had also stated his support for the Republican government in Valencia in Nancy Cunard's pamphlet, "Authors Take Sides on the Spanish Civil War," published by the *Left Review*. It was in November 1937 that George VI awarded Auden the King's Gold Medal for Poetry, the first of the reign, for a talent already displayed in three brilliant volumes—*Poems* (1930), *The Orators* (1932), and *Look, Stranger!* (1936; *On This Island* in the U.S.). It was also in November 1937 that *New Verse* devoted the double number to Auden's work. Auden had opened season on himself with his funny and revealing autobiographical poem "Letter to Lord Byron," included in his 1936 travel book *Letters from Iceland*, a collaboration with the Irish poet Louis MacNeice. Isherwood's *Lions and Shadows*, mythologizing the formation of their literary clique, was to appear in March 1938 while they were away. All the while, the little stream of Isherwood's Berlin material continued to appear in Lehmann's magazine, *New Writing*, and the novella *Sally Bowles* had appeared in October 1937.

They were given a wild party the night before they left London, headlined by the nightclub singer Hedli Anderson performing Auden poems set to music by Britten. By the end of the evening the guests were so drunk that they began fighting and knocking each other down. Britten wrote in his diary, "Beastly crowd & unpleasant people. [...] Christopher leaves in temper." Britten was staying with Isherwood at Pembroke Gardens but found himself locked out until breakfast the next morning. "I do not think C & W enjoyed it very much," Kathleen reported.[260]

The press followed Isherwood and Auden to Victoria Station, where they boarded a boat train for Paris, heading eventually to Marseilles and embarkation on the *Aramis* for Port Said. They were swarmed by lenses like a movie star couple. Photographs show them wearing white shirts with ties, dark wool pullovers, and overcoats unbuttoned with the collars turned up as they smoke and laugh at the door to their train compartment. Auden's spotted bow tie is awkwardly twisted, and his camera, in a leather case, is slung over one shoulder on a strap. Isherwood wears a plaid wool scarf layered casually around his neck.

In Egypt, they visited Cairo with Francis Turville-Petre, who took them drinking in a café surrounded by street boys and introduced them to a professor at the university. They also saw the Pyramids and the Sphinx while their ship threaded the Suez Canal without them. They reembarked at Port Tewfik (now Suez Port) and traveled down the Red Sea to Djibouti, crossed the Indian Ocean to Colombo in Ceylon (now Sri Lanka), and from there sailed on to Saigon. This part of their trip generated a magazine piece for their future American public, "Escales," published in *Harper's Bazaar* in October. They reached Hong Kong after nearly a month traveling, on February 16, 1938. Telegrams home were signed Wystopher.[261]

According to *Journey to a War*, Hong Kong in 1938 was "all about dinner-parties at very long tables, and meetings with grotesquely famous newspaper-characters—the British Ambassador, the Governor, Sir Victor Sassoon." They departed from Hong Kong by boat, up the Pearl River for Canton, safer than traveling by the Kowloon–Canton railway which "was being bombed, almost daily, by Japanese planes operating from an air-craft carrier anchored somewhere off Macao." From Canton, they continued north by train to Hankow, at the mouth of the Han River where it meets the Yangtze, "the real capital of war-time China," they wrote.[262] Peking, Shanghai, and Nanking had fallen to the Japanese. From Hankow they planned to continue by stages to the Yellow River Front.

China had been overrun not only by the Japanese but also by English diplomats, German military experts, American and Canadian missionaries, Swiss and Scottish doctors, White Russian refugees, Australians, Norwegians, Italians, who were serving as sea captains, journalists, relief workers. Auden and Isherwood met Chinese generals, officers, and soldiers of all ranks, toured hospitals spilling and stinking with wounded and dying. "The train coming up to Hankow took 3 nights and 2 days," Isherwood wrote to Olive Mangeot. "It went at a walking pace nearly all the way—with all the passengers hanging out of the windows, spitting inexhaustibly, eating rice, making jokes." They read Scott's *Guy Mannering* and Trollope's *Framley Parsonage* aloud to one another, "the two stodgiest books we could find."

It was early March when they reached Hankow, blizzarding. "Chang himself is here—we hope to see him shortly," Isherwood reported further to Olive Mangeot. "He has an English advisor named Donald, who has never spoken to him—for Chang knows no English and Donald no Chinese."[263] By Chang, Isherwood meant Chiang Kai-shek, the Nationalist Generalissimo, whose Australian advisor, the former journalist Henry Donald, had known Madame Chiang since childhood. Isherwood and Auden interviewed Donald and Madame Chiang, fluent in English, and met the Generalissimo.

They also met the Communist statesman Chou En-lai and interviewed the pro-communist American journalist Agnes Smedley. They photographed the Hungarian-born war photographer Robert Capa, befriended on the boat from Marseilles, and specimen Chinese—a politician, an intellectual, a railway engineer, a sailor—honoring like social scientists their assignment to observe. They pondered who would win the struggle within China between the Nationalists and the Communists once the Japanese were gone. "Hidden here are all the clues which would enable an expert, if he could only find them, to predict the events of the next fifty years," they wrote in *Journey to a War*. "History [. . .] has fixed her capricious interest upon Hankow."[264] Capricious indeed. Hankow is now part of the megacity Wuhan, which hid the clues to the much later birth of Covid-19.

While Isherwood and Auden were in Hankow, Hitler annexed Austria on March 12, 1938. Suddenly they were at the wrong bit of history in the making. "And here we are, eight thousand miles away. Shall we change our plans? Shall we go back? What does China matter to us in comparison with this?"[265] It was only human nature to think one war mattered more than another, though it was perhaps out of the ordinary to admit this so candidly in their book. It was all the same war in the end, as Auden was to say in the poems he was working on.

Throughout their time in China, both Auden and Isherwood had been uncomfortably aware of their inexperience as war correspondents: "we were not real journalists, but mere trippers, who had come to China to write a book." Isherwood had been fighting off his intense fear of guns and bombs. His diary account of one air raid, seen from the roof of an American bank to which he determinedly climbed in darkness, one of the tallest buildings in Hankow, was to inform the conclusion of *Prater Violet*: "far off, the hollow, approaching roar of the bombers, boring their way invisibly through the dark. The dull, punching thud of bombs falling, near the airfield, out in the suburbs. The searchlights criss-crossed, plotting points, like dividers: and suddenly there they were, six of them, flying close together and high up."[266] Afterwards, he and Auden heard that six Chinese planes had been destroyed on the ground.

Only one sentence in *Journey to a War* acknowledged that for Isherwood China was a journey toward his father's destiny in World War I. Describing their arrival in Cheng-chow (Zhangzhou), closer to the northern front than Hankow and far more heavily bombed and strafed, he observed: "moonlight heightened the drama of the shattered buildings; this might have been Ypres in 1915."

Isherwood had visited Ypres two and a half years earlier, on November 11, 1935, Armistice Day, with Neddermeyer, guided by a Belgian acquaintance. He had found the bloody battles veneered over by new life, affirming his belief that the dead are forgotten. "Almost all the houses are new and bright pink—here and there, the darker bricks mark the outlines of a former ruin. There are no trenches to be seen," he had written in his diary. He thought the Menin Gate memorial was ugly and absurdly too big for the little street of which it formed the end: "We searched for Daddy's name and finally found it, high up in a corner, heading a list of Addenda."[267]

In *Journey to a War*, self-mockery and literary fantasy neutralized the real-life anxiety Isherwood had clearly felt as they set off by rickshaw from Sü-chow (Suzhou), accompanied by their Chinese attendant, Chiang, to progress yet nearer the front: "Auden, in his immense, shapeless overcoat and woollen Jaeger cap, seems dressed for the Arctic regions. Chiang, neat as ever, might be about to wait at a Hankow consular dinner-party. My own beret, sweater, and martial boots would not be out of place in Valencia or Madrid."

The description of Isherwood's clothes alluded to the Spanish Civil War, which he never ceased to feel uneasy he had missed. His narrator in *Down There on a Visit* was to say: "In China I was scared several times during air raids or when we were at the front, but I was never panic-stricken; and—however ridiculous this may sound—I know it was largely because we were wearing our own civilian clothes!" Jittery with war fears in Copenhagen in 1934, Isherwood had written in his diary: "I dread the Army itself—like going back to school again—"[268] It was as a boarding-school boy in uniform that he had lost for the first, original time, his sense of personal identity, what he later called his "home-self." In losing that, he had lost all sense of personal value and self-esteem.

Choice of costume was like his name or like the choice of words in a narrative; it was an aspect of Isherwood's imaginative agency, his inner readiness to meet what was coming. Having the right clothes meant being prepared, rather than being taken by surprise. When he was eight, Kathleen had read him an improving Sunday allegory for children by the Anglican Bishop Samuel Wilberforce, "Agathos, or the Whole Armour of God," about spiritual readiness. Agathos patiently wears his full suit of armor even while he sleeps, ready to fight the dragon. The other soldiers grow bored waiting, cast off their armor and are eaten when the dragon finally comes, but Agathos is ready and vanquishes the dragon.

In China, Isherwood and Auden risked two journeys on the Lunghai railway past Japanese guns mounted on the north bank of the Yellow River. Isherwood reported that onboard their train he "slept uneasily" with his clothes on, like Agathos, "not wishing to have to leave the train and bolt for cover in my pyjamas. Auden, with his monumental calm, had completely undressed."[269] They rode ponies to the second-line trenches and then proceeded on foot to the frontline trenches, ignoring military advice for their safety. They came upon many corpses, some headless, a severed arm being eaten by a dog, the horrifically maimed, the hungry, the ill.

Isherwood later said in *Christopher and His Kind* that the trip to China alleviated "his neurotic fear of 'War' as a concept." This was the first step toward becoming a pacifist. In his diaries written during the 1940s, he explained, "Before China, my pacifism was so entangled with cowardice that I could never examine it at all. After China, it was only a matter of time before I should stop repeating slogans and borrowed opinions and start to think for myself."[270]

The diary accounts in *Journey to a War* grow funnier and more moving the longer the authors are in China, illustrating the way other emotions gradually percolated up through the fear. As they set off for a village called Meiki at the southeast front in mid-May, they were overtaken by the hotshot British correspondent and adventure writer Peter Fleming, educated at Eton and Oxford, elder brother of Ian Fleming, the creator of James Bond, reportedly inspired by Peter. "In his khaki shirt and shorts, complete with golf-stockings, strong suède shoes, waterproof wrist-watch and Leica camera, he might have stepped straight from a London tailor's window, advertising Gent's Tropical Exploration Kit."

As his clothing indicated, Fleming was a professional; moreover, he was disciplined, naturally brave, and easily able to outwalk everyone on the expedition. He took "exhaustive notes" and typed his dispatches at night as Auden and Isherwood collapsed into their camp beds. He understood a little Chinese and was "a born leader," who flattered others into raising their game so he could get to the fighting over mountain passes and through torrential rain. Against expectations on both sides, they became friendly, but Auden and Isherwood couldn't keep up with Fleming. Auden was overwhelmed by stomach cramps, and Isherwood's feet became a mass of crippling blisters; both had to depart from the front at Meiki in sedan chairs borne by coolies: "We gazed at their bulging calves and straining thighs, and rehearsed every dishonest excuse for allowing ourselves to be carried by human beings."[271] Admitting this in print was to tarnish their leftist credentials, as was the raillery in *Journey to a War* that drew on the vocabulary of public-school valor and competitiveness. Their diction cast Fleming as the hero-prefect type and Isherwood and Auden as his juniors, thereby showing them all to be members of the same privileged middle class.

Shanghai was under Japanese control, no impediment to their visit since Britain was neutral in the war. Yet they saw Japan, the imperialist aggressor, as the enemy, as they explained in a newspaper article written after they arrived in Tokyo: "If you have just spent four months in the interior of wartime China, visited two fronts, a dozen military hospitals, and the site of many air-raids, it becomes difficult to remember that you are supposed to be an impartial neutral, whose country maintains 'friendly diplomatic relations' with each of the two belligerent governments." In Tokyo Station, Auden and Isherwood watched a troop train pull out for China, "amidst cheering and waving banners."[272] For Isherwood, the aggression in China was to bleed into World War II.

MANHATTAN, 1938

Auden and Isherwood returned to England via North America, making a full circle of the globe. On the long summer voyage from Yokohama to Vancouver, they revised *On the Frontier*. They crossed Canada by train, and spent nine days in Manhattan, guided by the literary editor for *Harper's Bazaar*, George Davis, whom they had met in England the year before and who was publishing some of their journalism. Davis "had a genius for melodramatic showmanship," Isherwood later wrote in his diary, and Davis promised them more magazine work in a new kind of future unrolling before their eager imaginations. "We shot up and down skyscrapers, in and out of parties and brothels, saw a fight in a Bowery dive, heard Maxine Sullivan sing in Harlem, went to Coney Island on July the Fourth." They met intellectual celebrities like Maxwell Anderson and Orson Welles, "drank all day long and took Seconal every night to make us sleep." Isherwood fell for his first American boy, Harvey Young, met in a New York establishment called Matty's Cell House. This taste of Manhattan made both Isherwood and Auden hungry for more. "America was obviously the next place on the list," Isherwood wrote.[273]

Nothing would ever be the same for them after China and New York. Their friendship was changing, too. It would easily survive the petty frictions of prolonged close quarters during their trip, "the longest continuous confrontation" they had in their lives, as Isherwood later wrote. Auden had sometimes accused Isherwood of willfulness and of sulking when he didn't get his way, and worse, of being cruel and unscrupulous. They both knew that Auden was fascinated rather than repelled by these qualities. Isherwood considered that Auden "was incapable of cruelty but that he had a streak of masochism in him which could invite it from others."[274]

In these frictions, larger themes were revealed. Auden was now taking the dominant intellectual position. Isherwood, with unpitying self-observation, laid out his jealousy of his former protégé in his diary: "In China, I sometimes found myself really hating [Wystan]—hating his pedantic insistence on 'objectivity,' which was merely a reaction from my own woollymindedness. I was meanly jealous of him, too. Jealous of his share of the limelight; jealous because he'll no longer play the role of dependent, admiring younger brother." Equally gimlet-eyed, Isherwood also recorded his own asendancy in the sexual sphere and Auden's anguished confidences about sexual failure: "Then, in New York, and on the Atlantic crossing, we had those extraordinary scenes—Wystan in tears, telling me that no one wd ever love him, that he wd never have my sexual success."

When they reached London, he did not let Auden stay at Pembroke Gardens because he "wanted to stage the Returning Hero act all by myself." Isherwood reported this freely in *Christopher and His Kind*, quoting his diary without any self-protective excisions. According to another recollection, 1938 marked the end of their occasional sexual encounters. Nevertheless, he described Auden in his diary as "my 'best friend,'" and affirmed that "My essential feeling for Wystan is untouched by all this, and will remain so."[275]

The bond between them was strong enough to allow each to grow and change, which set their friendship apart. Both were domineering personalities capable of driving away lesser spirits, an important example being Britten who was to end his friendship with Auden in the early 1940s, when Auden swamped him with opinions, advice, expectations, and far too many words to set to music.

LONDON, 1938

As Isherwood approached his thirty-fourth birthday, he made "a portrait of myself" in a long diary entry, starting with his physical appearance and personal habits and progressing to the state of his soul. "Ever since Heinz's arrest, I have been a heavy smoker. I now have the nicotine addiction, and can't give it up without becoming nervous and irritable." Sex was not much different: "I also masturbate enormously—at least every night, and often twice a day as well."[276]

The self-portrait makes clear how deeply he cared for and worked to improve Auden's opinion, for much of what Isherwood wrote about himself in August 1938 responds to observations made by Auden, some dating back to, roughly, Isherwood's thirty-third birthday a year before, well in advance of the China trip, when they were together in Dover and Auden had written a poem for Isherwood inside a volume of D.H. Lawrence verse, *Birds, Beasts and Flowers*. Auden's poem described Isherwood as "A cross between a cavalry major and a rather prim landlady," deftly conjuring the blend of Frank and Kathleen. And it teased him about his willfulness: "Don't you love to boss just everybody, everybody / [...] / Turning on your wonderful diplomacy like a fire-hose." But Auden also exhorted Isherwood against his fatal passivity: "Use your will. We need it."

Most intriguingly, the poem described Isherwood as pretending to be "Anonymous" until "there's an opening in the conversation, or a chance to show off / And you strike like a lobster at a prawn." This went to the heart of a real division in Isherwood: his feeling of being anonymous, "nobody in particular," as Auden put it,[277] was no pretense. This feeling had come and gone ever since St. Edmund's, where he had first experienced the obliteration of his identity, later at Repton where he had invented his literary persona Tuke-Adams, later still in Berlin and on his wanderings. It was in his 1938 self-portrait that Isherwood wrote: "I once read the title of a German novel (I forget [what] the author's named) Der Mann ohne Eigenshaft. That, I've come to feel more and more, just describes me. For the more I think about myself, the more I'm persuaded that, as a <u>person</u>, I really don't exist."

Der Mann ohne Eigenschaften (*The Man without Qualities*) was the title of Robert Musil's gigantic, unfinished Viennese novel in which the hero permits himself to be formed by the world around him. Maybe this, maybe that, the hero thinks, as he wavers between science and mysticism. The first two volumes were published in Berlin in 1930 and 1933. Isherwood usurped Musil's hero's lack of identity for himself, like his kleptomaniac character, Paul, who faded away in the mid-1930s while frantically trying out one identity after another. "My 'character' is simply a repertoire of acquired tricks, my conversation a repertoire of adaptations and echoes, my 'feelings' are dictated by purely physical, external stimuli."[278] He considered his personality to be an outward show, like clothing.

In his self-portrait, Isherwood recorded arguing with Auden "over the 'personality' question" on the way out to China. "I maintained that Christopher in Saigon and Christopher in Kensington were two different people. This sounds self-evident, but Wystan disputed it. This feeling of being quite different in different places and with different people is very strong in me."[279]

Being "different in different places and with different people" enabled Isherwood to adapt to any social milieu in any locale, to mirror the emotions and psyches of any number of acquaintances, to befriend strangers. In his writing, it enabled him to enter his characters, to identify with and become the object of his imagining. But he was far less sure of who he was than Auden, and crisis was bearing down on them. He was to discover again and again through painful experience that he needed to be in a good place and with good people in order to be the person he wanted to be.

By the time Isherwood returned to England in July 1938, he felt cut off from himself as never before. The lovers who looked up to him, for whom he could be someone, had become geographically or emotionally remote. Without an intimate companion to mirror and reciprocate his behavior—as Nanny or Kathleen had done throughout his childhood—he could not access his emotions. He could not *feel*. Visiting the Isle of Wight, he wrote: "Feeling has dwindled to mere nostalgia—nostalgia for the island of Tennyson and of the 'twenties, for George Peck and his family—for Harvey with the gold Catholic amulet round his neck, in New York—for Heinz building Hitler's Berlin on a scaffold on the Potsdamerplatz."

Between him and Scott-Kilvert there was a complete barrier. On his travels, Isherwood had imagined that the friendship "was to be a challenge, an assertion of the right to live and be happy—a challenge to this whole deathstruck era." But on his return, they were tongue-tied: "There is no electric current between us, at the moment: nothing but embarrassment."[280] He tried other liaisons, a sojourn in Dover with Spender's boyfriend Tony Hyndman, in Richmond with a wealthy young American studying at Cambridge, Hugh Chisholm, an affair with an Oxford graduate, Richard Buzzard.

Love affairs had become part of Isherwood's repertoire of nervous tics, like smoking and masturbating. One night he stayed up with his straight friend Robert Moody drinking and comparing sex adventures: "Robert, like myself, has just discovered that he can have absolutely anybody he wants to. We boasted, and were very hearty and jolly."[281]

Lehmann visited Berlin and returned in early September 1938 with a report on Neddermeyer which "impressed me tremendously"—perhaps because it came from afar and was filtered through the viewpoint of someone else. "H, it seems, has been actually hardened and strengthened by his time at Trier. He now lives only for the day when he can get out of Germany and meet me again. Also, he is fully politically conscious: he knows we may be in for a war." Thus, as the Munich Crisis began to unfold and war between their respective homelands seemed increasingly likely, Isherwood's sense of commitment to Neddermeyer was reignited: "I must remain free. I must be ready for H. if he needs me."[282]

During August and September 1938, Hitler was demanding self-determination for Germans living in the Sudetenland. One by one, the European powers agreed to let Hitler annex these territories just across his eastern border in Czechoslovakia rather than risk war with him. Until the pact was signed at the end of September, war was increasingly expected, and fear was widespread. Czechoslovakia busily strengthened its fortifications against Germany, and in London, trenches to serve as air-raid shelters were dug in Hyde Park; gas masks were issued through the mail.

Isherwood was transfixed by the Munich Crisis. The months of uncertainty—when war was constantly threatened, constantly postponed—were a Test for even the strongest people he knew. "Morgan says he's afraid of going mad—he might suddenly turn and run away from people in the street. But he isn't weak. He's immensely, superhumanly strong," Isherwood wrote in his diary after lunching with Forster on September 24. "This crisis is really like a newly discovered area of life. Hitherto, scientists have supposed that the zone between peace and war was narrow, and quickly crossed. Now we find that this neutral zone is enormous: we might conceivably live in it for the rest of our lives."[283]

Indeed, part of Isherwood did live there ever afterwards, because he had already lived there before, in Limerick, in August 1914, when his father was preparing to leave for the Front, when there was no news about where Frank was headed or what to expect, and when Christopher, only ten, battered by his first term at St. Edmund's, had had no idea of the gigantic slow-motion disaster about to befall his family and the whole world. This had been the period during which Isherwood later felt his father had tried to give him a message whose meaning was to become clear only in the fullness of time. The message that came through—to take Frank's place at home, to look after Kathleen and be a father to Richard—was not a message Isherwood wanted to remember or reflect on by 1938; he had tried and failed. He was waiting to hear something else, and he was still desperately auditioning younger brother types in hopes of finding someone for whom he could be a hero.

During late August and early September 1938, he managed to write two articles about China for *Cosmopolitan*, the New York magazine. They were never published. On September 19, he began work on *Journey to a War*, but the China diary project now lagged behind the movement of history and behind his personal political evolution.

By September 26, he was no longer in command of himself: "The crisis is getting me down. I have stopped sleeping properly, or wanting to eat. Nothing seems any use." Love receded before the growing threat of war: "I hardly even think of H. now. I daren't. And Harvey is just a dream." On September 27, he got his gas mask: "You can hardly breathe through them at all." On the 28th, the German army mobilized and conscription was introduced in the U.K. "Everybody is enlisting, or running away," he recorded. "I have written to the Foreign Office, to offer my services in propaganda work."[284]

Newspapers were appearing with fresh headlines every twenty minutes. He recorded that he bought them compulsively as if by paying close enough attention, he could control what was happening. His diary is littered with thumbnail news bulletins and summaries of current expert opinion. It was his own emotions that Isherwood was really trying to control. As tension mounted, he craved a steady newsfeed like an intravenous drip, just as his brother Richard craved the certainty of trains running to schedule on a continuous, clearly laid track.

Then, suddenly, the crisis was over. Chamberlain and Daladier met with Hitler and Mussolini in Munich on September 29, and they agreed that Britain and France would allow Germany to occupy the Sudetenland without resistance. Czechoslovakia was not even invited to the conference.

Isherwood observed in his diary that for him, emotionally, the two worst moments during the crisis occurred when he received alarming news bulletins while he was in the company of lovers "whom I couldn't help, and who were therefore millstones round the neck." When he was alone, he had felt "quite cold and calm—with, underneath it all, just a flicker of excitement," which reminded him of China, "that night on the Lunghai railway, when we got up steam for our dash past the Japanese guns." Attracted and moved as he was by the young, the needy, the stammerer, the idea of the little brother whom he wanted to protect like a tree, he had been forced to learn during the crisis that he had only enough strength for himself or for a distant lover, like Neddermeyer, whom he could hold as a constant in the mind's eye. After his lunch with Forster, on September 24, Isherwood had written in his diary, "I don't feel I want to see any weaklings nowadays: they are like sufferers from a dangerously infectious disease."[285] Or like the weepers he described in *Memoirs of Pine House*. He did not, after all, possess courage like his father's that "consists of giving reassurance to people in terrible circumstances."

Meanwhile, he was steadily in the public eye. He attended countless private parties, frequented the Café Royal, lectured on China, on drama, appeared on stage, spoke on BBC radio, contributed numerous book reviews to the *Listener* commissioned by J.R. Ackerley. Glimpses of him at this time, in his last intermittent months in London, surface in the diaries of others.

A younger writer, Alan Pryce-Jones, met him at a dinner party and clearly saw the hollow man, the calculating romantic, cut off from his emotions by tension and dread: "Isherwood . . . dangerously pointed, both in revolver and bodkin sense. Bodkin, I think, rather than dagger. Very quick bright eyes, with a look of fear in them. [. . .] Seduced more boys than any other individual in Berlin, one is told with aghast admiration."[286]

Virginia Woolf, on the other hand, older, was enchanted by him, just as Mrs. Cooke and Kathleen's women friends had once been. After their first meeting in February 1937, she wrote: "I[sherwoo]d rather a find: very small red cheeked nimble & vivacious. [. . .] a most appreciative merry little bird. A real novelist, I suspect; not a poet; full of acute observations on character & scenes . . . I[sherwoo]d & I were such chatterboxes."

The older generation were interested in his destiny as parents are interested in the destinies of their children. A year and a half later, Woolf bumped into him on Sibyl Colefax's doorstep. Isherwood had turned up at the society decorator's party despite a terrible cold. He exuded energy, and seemed to Woolf ready to run, as if in a horse race, and to win all the literary prizes: "He is a slip of a wild boy: with quicksilver eyes. Nipped. Jockey like. That young man, said W. Maugham 'holds the future of the English novel in his hands.' Very enthusiastic."[287] Maugham had fallen for Isherwood over lunch with Forster in 1937, and he chose "The Nowaks" for an international short-story anthology he was assembling around that time.[288]

That same year, Cyril Connolly, sophisticated and untrickable in his literary insights, placed Isherwood with George Orwell above all their generation as "the ablest exponents of the colloquial style [. . .] superlatively readable," and Connolly placed Isherwood alone with his elders, Forster and Maugham, in his "mastery of form."[289]

In mid-November 1938 Isherwood and Auden attended rehearsals and opening of *On the Frontier* at the Arts Theatre in Cambridge, staged by Rupert Doone's Group Theatre with music by Britten and designed by Robert Medley. It never transferred to the West End.[290] The standoff they had imagined between fascist Westland and the decrepit monarchy of Ostnia was nothing like as gripping as the real standoff between Hitler and his appeasers. History had overtaken their plot. John Maynard Keynes, underwriter of the Arts Theatre, asked them if they would like to revise the play, but Isherwood and Auden had lost interest. Their thoughts were on America.

They went to Brussels in mid-December to finish *Journey to a War*. Isherwood brought yet another new lover, Jack Hewit, an English would-be dancer who was the longterm companion of a mutual friend, Guy Burgess, the former Cambridge history student later exposed as a Soviet spy. Hewit temporarily abandoned Burgess for Isherwood in hopes of accompanying him to America. Brussels offered an interlude of promising domesticity, with Hewit cooking meals and Isherwood working. To one friend, Isherwood wrote, "My married life is being a great success, and we have a dear little flat."[291]

They stayed for Christmas and New Year with Auden. Britten arrived to perform his piano concerto with the Belgian Radio Symphony Orchestra, and his friend Lennox Berkeley, unrequitedly in love with him, admonished him to "try and behave nicely there in spite of being in the possession of mysterious addresses."[292] Isherwood and Auden were now notorious not just for same-sex love, but for their involvement with professional sex workers at such addresses—all the more reason to emigrate.

They hoped to pay for their trip with another travel book, *Address Unknown*, but this fell through, making money tight. Isherwood used this as a reason to tell Hewit he must remain behind, though he promised to send a ticket from the U.S. Back in London, Hewit saw Isherwood and Auden off at the train for the boat to New York on January 19, 1939, and Isherwood later recalled in his wartime diary, "Jacky cried in the taxi to the station and gave me a keepsake, his first champagne cork."[293] The cork was from the New Year's Eve party given by Auden in Brussels, at which he had read aloud a reckless and funny poem, "Ode to the New Year (1939)," with a stanza each for Hewit, Isherwood, Gerald Hamilton and two other friends present that night as well as lines to many friends who were not. Hewit's stanza included a tactful reprimand to Isherwood, couched as a wish for Hewit to find a less fickle lover: "You will find One worth your devotion . . ." Years later, Isherwood observed, "I think Auden identified with Jack, a little."[294]

Another reprimand was to come from Forster, in June 1939 by letter in the U.S., after Isherwood broke his promise to send Hewit the ticket to join him. Hewit's friends, Burgess and Anthony Blunt, tried to involve Forster on Hewit's behalf, but Forster refused. "I guess the situation and feel very sorry for the boy. This much I will say, that now you know you can miscalculate you will be more careful another time," Forster told Isherwood.

Isherwood admitted to Forster that he felt "ashamed."[295] He did supply Hewit with money, repeatedly authorizing Lehmann to lend and then simply to give Hewit, out of earnings from *Goodbye to Berlin*, "as much as was necessary, without limit."[296] This was the generosity of guilt. His careless treatment of his many boyfriends, not just Jack Hewit, contradicted everything Isherwood believed in and wished to be, yet, after his experience with Neddermeyer, it is hardly surprising he decided not to take another boyfriend into exile.

Over Christmas and New Year in Brussels, Auden had read the proofs for *Goodbye to Berlin*. He took special note of the concluding section, "A Berlin

Diary (Winter 1932–3)," with its descriptions of peasant boys lured to Berlin by hopes of food and work, and the hunger and cold that drove them into the Tiergarten, that cruising ground, or into the arms of the communists, the Nazis, the Pathfinders and any organization offering a role.

Auden responded to the proofs with several poems. "The Capital" tells about the same kind of starving boys; "Brussels in Winter" describes their likely source of income: "And fifty francs will earn the stranger right / To warm the heartless city in his arms." The most famous poem from this group, "Musée des Beaux Arts," elaborates on Isherwood's point that the world takes little notice of such boys, and little notice of suffering in general. "About suffering they were never wrong," Auden observed of the Old Master painters, "how it takes place / While someone else is eating or opening a window or just walking dully along."[297]

Isherwood's narrator remains preoccupied with the innocent, the gullible, the illusionists, the unprepared, the vulnerable, the ones who were taken by surprise: "I am thinking of poor Rudi, in his absurd Russian blouse. Rudi's make-believe, story-book game has become earnest; the Nazis will play it with him. The Nazis won't laugh at him; they'll take him on trust for what he pretended to be. Perhaps at this very moment Rudi is being tortured to death."[298] Rudi recalls Barnaby Rudge, the fictional teenager in Dickens's eponymous novel, who leads the anti-Catholic rioters in London in 1780 through the dangerous accident of being "simple."

Just as he had done in his account of bullies and weepers in *Memoirs of Pine House*, in which the roles of victim and perpetrator at prep school might be reversed—you *or me*—Isherwood implicated himself among passersby in Berlin, behaving cheerfully, according to his nature, even though he noticed and recorded what was taking place: "The sun shines and Hitler is master of this city [. . .] I catch sight of my face in the mirror of a shop, and am horrified to see that I am smiling. You can't help smiling, in such beautiful weather. The trams are going up and down the Kleiststrasse, just as usual."

Auden noticed this truth again when he looked at Breughel's painting of Icarus in the picture gallery in Brussels, in which the sun also shines, regardless of large or small disasters, and in which the world continues with its business:

> ... the sun shone
> As it had to on the white legs disappearing into the green
> Water; and the expensive delicate ship that must have seen
> Something amazing, a boy falling out of the sky,
> Had somewhere to get to and sailed calmly on.[299]

In the figure of Icarus flying too close to the sun as he flees the Labyrinth, Auden also gestured to the voyage he was about to make with Isherwood across the Atlantic. They, too, were attempting to flee a labyrinth. What was to become of them?

Aboard the *Champlain*, the political wings on which they had soared to new heights of fame melted. According to Isherwood's later account, he said to Auden on deck one morning that he no longer believed any of it, "the united front, the party line, the antifascist struggle," and Auden surprised him by agreeing. They wanted to disappear into the sea that was America and rediscover their artistic intentions: "We had forgotten our real vocation. We would be artists again, with our own values, our own integrity, and not amateur socialist agitators, parlor reds."

Isherwood realized "that I had always been a pacifist." It was not just his feelings about his father, it was also the German boys he loved who were now "a part of the Nazi machine": "Suppose I have in my power an army of six million men. I can destroy it by pressing an electric button. The six millionth man is Heinz. Will I press the button? Of course not—"[300]

5

Hollywood Screenwriter and Hindu Monk (1939–1945)

MANHATTAN, 1939

Auden and Isherwood settled at the George Washington Hotel, run by a hospitable Englishman, and Harvey Young soon joined them. After a few months, they moved to an apartment in Yorkville, home to Manhattan's German community and alive with pro-Nazi activity. For Auden, their new life was better than he had expected; for Isherwood, it was worse. He told Spender: "Everybody invites us out, and says nice things, but there's very little money to be earned. This is a cruel hard town. Very expensive to live in." He later reported in his wartime diary that his first months in New York were "a bad, sterile period for me."[1]

He didn't know what kind of job he wanted, and he wrote little. There were book reviews (mostly for the *New Republic*, where George Davis managed to place extracts from the China diary), a piece about up-and-coming British writers jointly with Auden (for *Vogue*),[2] and an account of his friendship with the leftwing playwright Ernst Toller, met in Portugal. Toller, a Jew, was exiled by Hitler and hanged himself in a Manhattan hotel room in May 1939, overwhelmed by the triumph of fascism and by the news that his brother and sister were in concentration camps. Isherwood intended his Toller piece for Lehmann's *New Writing* but decided it sounded "patronising and rather offensive" and withdrew it.[3] Later, in 1953, he allowed it to appear in *Encounter*.

During March and early April 1939, he fell into a torpor in New York. Meanwhile, back in London, *Goodbye to Berlin* was a big commercial and critical success.[4] "[T]he mark of imaginative greatness, is to be able to impose a personal vision," wrote the Bloomsbury novelist David Garnett in the

New Statesman and Nation, "Christopher Isherwood has this power." Garnett's review of *Goodbye to Berlin* recognized that Isherwood had broken free of conventional attitudes and class values—"he finds the people whom we all conspire to overlook, really fascinating"—and observed how much skill and hard work this required. "Isherwood's style of writing appears simple and colloquial, for which reasons many readers are likely to overlook its most remarkable quality: its exactness. He never uses a cliché."[5]

The British papers praised again and again Isherwood's keen power of observation, relishing his humor, his irony, even accepting his apolitical stance,[6] but some reviewers lamented the epic he had not written.[7] They had fallen into a trap set by Isherwood in a self-deprecating preface explaining that the six pieces in *Goodbye to Berlin* were "the only existing fragments of what was originally planned as a huge episodic novel of pre-Hitler Berlin. I had intended to call it *The Lost*."[8] For the generation raised on *The Waste Land*, there was hardly a more glamorizing word than "fragments"—an aesthetic keynote of modernism. Isherwood surely had in mind the often-repeated line from Eliot's fifth and final section: "These fragments I have shored against my ruins." Isherwood's six fragments were as carefully composed and sequenced as a poem.

In America, Isherwood as yet had almost no audience, and though he eschewed political notoriety, he was not comfortable with complete anonymity. "'Goodbye to Berlin' is being pre-regarded as a flop, over here, and not pushed at all," he vented to Lehmann about his new publisher Bennett Cerf at Random House. "[T]hough various people who read it were full of praise," he wrote to Kathleen.[9] By the time Edmund Wilson's reputation-making review appeared in the *New Republic*—the review that called Isherwood a master of social observation and compared the transparency of his prose to Pushkin's[10]—Isherwood was to have left New York.

Cerf had given him an advance on a new novel but wasn't interested in *Lions and Shadows*, and Isherwood feared his career as a novelist might be over. "Maybe I have come to the limit of my talent, and shall just go on being 'promising' until people are tired of me," he wrote to Kathleen. "I could describe anybody, anything, in the world; but I can't make it all into a pattern. Perhaps that is the penalty you pay for not believing in anything positive."

On the other hand, he reported, Auden "flourishes exceedingly. Never has he written so much. And he seems to be formulating his ideas, and making the most impressive speeches." This success was part of the problem for Isherwood. He needed space, as he admitted to his mother: "My real instinct is to go away by myself for a while."[11]

He confided to Forster, as he had confided to Kathleen, that he was unable to write. He told Lehmann the same thing, but Lehmann kept badgering him anyway for something to publish in his magazine. Isherwood was longing for a mentor to guide him as Layard, Katz, and Forster had done in the past: "But where is Vergil?" he asked Forster in a letter. "The only one I can espy on this continent is Gerald Heard, so I must go out west to talk to him."[12]

He was corresponding with Heard, an Irish-born Cambridge academic specializing in the history of religion, who had relocated to California in 1937 in tandem with his fellow spiritual trailblazer Aldous Huxley, the Oxford-educated intellectual who had achieved world fame with his dystopian novel *Brave New World* (1932). Heard had been a London friend of Auden, who had introduced Isherwood in, probably, 1932. Heard and Huxley were both pacifists, and they had both become disciples of Swami Prabhavananda, founder of the Vedanta Society of Southern California in Hollywood. Prabhavananda was teaching them about Ramakrishna, the nineteenth-century Bengali holy man who was widely accepted as an incarnation of God and who began the revival of Vedanta, the Hindu philosophy founded on the ancient Sanskrit texts, the Vedas. Prabhavananda was also training Heard and Huxley in the ancient techniques of mind control—prayer and meditation—that are among the methods, called yogas, for achieving union with the divine. The teachings of Homer Lane had once helped draw Isherwood to Berlin; now the teachings of Ramakrishna helped draw him to Hollywood and toward another, equally profound change of life.

An idea of America also lured Isherwood. "The real America, for me, was the Far West," he was to write in his diaries. "All my daydreams were based on D.H. Lawrence's *St. Mawr*." The daydreams were also based on the movie Westerns he had loved for years. He felt that he could experience the real America only "through the eyes of an American."[13] As with his cockney boyfriend George Peck, and his German boyfriends Szczesny, Wolff and Neddermeyer, Isherwood looked on his American boyfriend Harvey Young as the means to infiltrate his new surroundings. Young was to be "Whitman's American Boy" and also "the hardboiled twentieth-century city youth." Young, Isherwood wrote in his diary, "had run away from home at the age of fourteen and hitchhiked to Texas; this made him seem a specially suitable traveling companion." To his mother, Isherwood described Young as a promising art student and a new edition of Neddermeyer, "rather German in appearance and mentality (his ancestry is English and South German) not unlike Heinz." To Spender, similarly, he wrote that Young "often reminds me of Heinz in his solemn bespectacled moods."[14]

Young was never to conform to Isherwood's fantasy of the ideal American Boy. Bachardy later observed that Young was bisexual: "it was just as easy for him to have sex with one as with the other."[15] He later married—twice—and with his first wife, he had a son whom he named Christopher after Isherwood.

(Neddermeyer, too, was to marry and to give his son the middle name Christian after Isherwood.)

LOS ANGELES, 1939

Isherwood and Young set off across the U.S. by Greyhound bus on May 6, 1939. The trip took three weeks. They arrived in downtown Los Angeles on a Saturday night, May 27: "the streets were swarming with drunks. We saw three sailors carrying a girl into a house, as though they were going to eat her alive. From the hotel, we telephoned Chris Wood. 'How wonderful,' he said, 'to hear an effeminate British voice!'"[16]

California marked a new beginning. "How I love the sun," wrote Isherwood to his mother. "I feel as if we'd arisen from the tomb—full of energy and gaiety."[17] Chris Wood was Gerald Heard's former lover and longtime companion who had relocated with Heard from London to Los Angeles, "handsome, shy but friendly, rich," as Isherwood later wrote. The family business made jams and canned goods. In London, Heard had been Auden's friend, and Isherwood had gravitated to Wood, with whom he had perhaps had a sexual liaison. Wood took them out to eat at "all the best restaurants," and made a loan of $2,000 while Isherwood looked for work.[18]

Isherwood and Auden both had already applied for quota visas back in New York. In mid-June, Isherwood crossed the border into Mexico, collected his visa at the American consulate in Ensenada and reentered the U.S. fully employable. After six weeks at the Rose Gardens Apartments in Hollywood, he and Young established themselves in "a very beautiful little house, up in the hills above Hollywood," 7136 Sycamore Trail,[19] and bought an old Model T Ford which they soon traded for a new Ford convertible.

During July, Berthold Viertel—last seen in the Café Royal the night before Isherwood left London—arrived in Santa Monica, returning home to his wife and three sons who lived there. Viertel had signed with Fox in 1928 after directing silents in Europe. In Hollywood, he had directed four films for Fox, moving to sound for the second two, then one for Warner Brothers and four for Paramount, but he had feared for his artistic integrity and fled from success back to Europe, directing one more film in Berlin before moving to London and Gaumont-British. As Isherwood later recalled, Viertel had worked with "several famous actors and actresses, including Paul Muni, Claudette Colbert, Charles Boyer, Tallulah Bankhead."[20]

Isherwood had tried and failed to get movie writing work through an agency, and now Viertel, his screenwriting guru, invited him to collaborate again. The project was an anti-Nazi story about Hitler, *The Mad Dog of*

Europe, which Viertel planned to thoroughly rewrite. They worked for three or four months developing a treatment which they titled *The Nazi*, about a German officer, a veteran of World War I, who is slowly won over to the Nazi Party. But once the war began, Hollywood had no interest in an empathetic study of the psychological evolution of the enemy.

Isherwood managed to get a studio job with Samuel Goldwyn by selling him the rights to *Mr. Norris Changes Trains*, and he arranged for Viertel to work with him on the script. Goldwyn was not satisfied with anything Viertel and Isherwood wrote. He made a series of "contradictory suggestions and objections" about the plot, until Isherwood, growing frustrated, complained with "a mock-polite letter to the story department." The letter sparked an embarrassing scene with Goldwyn, who tried to ingratiate himself with Isherwood, claiming "he thought of me as a friend." The head of Goldwyn's story department, Eddie Knopf (who happened to be the brother of New York publisher Alfred Knopf), had seen it all before. "Tell him he hasn't acted like a gentleman, and he'll crawl," said Knopf. Isherwood later realized that Goldwyn's strategy all along, with himself and countless other writers, was to "make him produce the maximum number of story ideas in a very short period" and then fire him.[21]

As with Ethel Mayne and Jean Ross, it was again a woman who advanced Isherwood's career, launching him professionally at the Hollywood studios. Viertel's wife Salka, a Viennese actress turned MGM screenwriter—often for Greta Garbo, her close friend[22]—introduced Isherwood to her lover, Gottfried Reinhardt, film-producer son of Viennese impresario Max Reinhardt. Gottfried Reinhardt hired Isherwood to write dialogue for an Ingrid Bergman film, *Rage in Heaven*. This got Isherwood an MGM studio contract, leading to a second job, on dialogue for *A Woman's Face*.

Isherwood was back writing for the movies, the career of which he had long dreamed. Over the years, he was to take studio jobs whenever he needed money. Screenwriting was to have a significant impact on his literary writing, both good and bad, as with *Mr. Norris Changes Trains*. It took time and focus from his fiction, but it disciplined him to reach a broad audience, an American audience. The great number of creative refugees in Hollywood meant that this American audience was about to develop and change as it digested the contributions of the European diaspora. It was the audience of the future.

IN THE SUMMER of 1939, Isherwood squeezed out a short story called "I Am Waiting." It was a first-person narrative about time travel, set on July 25, 1939, as the world waits for the outbreak of war. The joke is that the narrator, a failed writer, "self-effacing, anonymous," travels into three perfectly unimportant moments in his nondescript future and learns nothing about the crisis. "I Am Waiting" is a comic homage to H.G. Wells's *The Time Machine*, and it plays on the news addiction that had controlled Isherwood during the Munich Crisis. It also responded to the accident of Auden and Isherwood being misplaced in China for the Anschluss and to Isherwood's unspoken fear that, by going to America, he might find himself in the wrong place again.[23]

What Isherwood was really waiting for during the summer of 1939 was a new way to think about time and about the future; the mechanistic, pseudo-scientific time travel of H.G. Wells led him nowhere. He needed a new kind of vision.

Gerald Heard came through for him, putting before Isherwood "the most exciting proposition I had ever heard. He told me what Life is for," Isherwood wrote in his wartime diary. "Life, said Gerald, is for awareness. Awareness of our real nature and our actual situation." Heard was referring to the eternal, all-pervading reality, called *Brahman* in Vedanta, which can be known when the ego personality is shed. The ultimate goal, *samadhi*, is analogous to the Buddhist nirvana or the Christian mystic union.

Heard had studied the the Tibetan Book of the Dead and the Christian mystics and, like Huxley at this period, saw common ground among them. He focused with confidence on the parts of Vedanta he found most useful to his spiritual quest and was unconcerned that some beliefs might seem outlandish to a European Christian, like reincarnation and the notion that karma—an act and the consequences of an act—carries over from past lives. For Isherwood, disillusioned with all he knew, the more outlandish the better: "If Gerald hadn't been so interested in yoga and opposed to Christianity, he would never have been able to influence me the way he did," Isherwood later recalled. "I could only approach the subject of mystical religion with the aid of a brand-new vocabulary. Sanskrit supplied it." Vedanta "was suddenly revealed as a precise, practical, clearly stated philosophical system, the only one I had ever been able to understand."

Heard, with his glowing eyes and goatee beard, was developing his awareness of reality by meditating six hours a day. He taught Isherwood that day-to-day reality is an illusion—called *maya*, another Sanskrit word. Meditation excludes consciousness of the illusory world and turns the mind inward. It is one of the four yogas, one of of the four ways to seek union with the divine.

Here was a different kind of response to the world crisis and to Isherwood's personal crisis. "And why was I never told this before?" Isherwood kept asking himself, until he decided he had been told many times, "Only—I hadn't been ready to listen." Now he recognized something he had in fact already undertaken in his writing: "Religion is the struggle for greater awareness of reality, deeper understanding of the nature of life. Art, also, struggles for awareness and understanding. The goal is identical."[24]

Isherwood was ready, in the summer of 1939, to be converted. Heard introduced him to Swami Prabhavananda at the end of July or the beginning of August. This was to be, next to Kathleen and to Don Bachardy, one of the most important relationships in his life and the subject many years later of his final book, *My Guru and His Disciple*, in which he described the friendship with his usual unsparing candor, illuminating his need for unconditional love from a father figure and his need to devote himself to an ideal outside of and greater than himself.

"I have absolutely no memories of my first visit," Isherwood wrote with deflating wit in *My Guru and His Disciple*. Thus, his very first description of Prabhavananda, written on August 4, is of someone whom he already knows, hitting on a theme in Prabhavananda's own life story of being already known to his own guru on first meeting and also accounting for the power of the contact between them: "His smile is extraordinary. It is somehow so touching, so open, so brilliant with joy that it makes me want to cry." Prabhavananda's small stature appealed intimately to Isherwood: "He was considerably shorter than I was. This made me able to love him in a special, protective way, as I loved little Annie Avis, my childhood nanny, and as I should love Stravinsky."[25]

Their meeting was so personal as to be, for Isherwood, embarrassing, as it had once been embarrassing to confront his homosexual tribe in Hirschfeld's museum in Berlin. "I felt terribly awkward—like a rich, overdressed woman, in the plumes and bracelets of my vanity." He tried to push Prabhavananda away, but was disarmed with laughter. "I explained how I had always thought of yoga as silly, superstitious nonsense. The Swami laughed: 'And now you have fallen into the trap?'" Indeed, triggered by years of longing and anxiety kept at bay by sex, smoking, drinking, restless travel, on the verge of despair about writing more fiction, Isherwood had fallen into the trap. Or perhaps he had fallen out of one.

He had already begun meditation under Heard's supervision. Prabhavananda instructed him again, suggesting four steps, written down for Isherwood, who copied them into his diary. Ever the self-improver, Isherwood right away began meditating afresh, cross-legged on the floor, spine straight. He found Prabhavananda's first two steps fairly easy. First, try to feel the presence of an all-pervading Existence; second, send thoughts of peace and goodwill toward all beings. The fourth step was to meditate on the real self. As part of this instruction, Prabhavananda had written, "The Self in you is the Self in all beings." As Isherwood had already recognized in his meditation with Heard, this was like his writing, in which he constantly exercised his power of imaginative empathy.

But Prabhavananda's third step, Think of the body as a temple housing the Reality, Isherwood found difficult. "Much involved with thoughts of sex," he wrote in his diary. "I am always trying to reassure myself that there is nothing and nobody in the universe I really want. Hence, my sexual adventures. To be able to say, 'Oh, I've *had* X.' So X. is taped, X. is eliminated. Then jealousy—because X. won't stay taped."[26]

This struggle with lust and possessiveness was to pursue him for decades. In *My Guru and His Disciple*, Isherwood recalled that he had asked Prabhavananda right away whether he could lead a spiritual life if he was having a sexual relationship with a young man. Prabhavananda had told him, "You must try to see him as the young Lord Krishna." Isherwood had understood this as a metaphor, comparing the physical attraction of Harvey Young with the spiritual attraction of Krishna, a challenge to "try to see and love what was Krishna-like" in Young. "[I]t was far more permissive than I had expected," he later said. "What reassured me—what convinced me that I could become his pupil—was that he hadn't shown the least shadow of distaste on hearing me admit to my homosexuality."[27]

Nevertheless, the goal was chastity, in order to preserve energy for the higher aim of enlightenment. About fifteen months after beginning his instruction, Swami told Isherwood that "all sex—no matter what the relationship—is a form of attachment, and must ultimately be given up. This will happen naturally as you make progress in the spiritual life."[28]

Isherwood's progress was dogged not only by lust but also by laziness, by prejudices of which he had been previously unaware, and also by something deeper and more stubborn—inarticulate defiance toward the whole spiritual undertaking. In January 1940, Isherwood wrote in his diary: "The opposition is enormously strong. Incredible as it seems, part of me actually *wants* to wallow in black, lazy misery, like a pig in filth."[29] Ever since St. Edmund's, part of him had wanted to remain a pig.

He was by now working hard at MGM on *Rage in Heaven*, and he began to fall ill. He wrote to Lehmann that he was under the care of a doctor for "a kind of nervous breakdown, I think: sleeplessness, exhaustion and headaches." The doctor, Josef Kolisch, was another Viennese émigré, "very brilliant and amusing,"[30] who was also a follower of Prabhavananda. Kolisch attended the monks and nuns at the Vedanta Center, prescribing vegetarian diets for them as well as for Aldous Huxley and his wife, Maria, and Greta Garbo.

In March 1940, Isherwood recorded that the Swami urged him to "think about the word Om which is God." But Isherwood didn't like the word: "Om says nothing. [...] I'm afraid the Swami is altogether too Indian for me, with his mantras and his parables." Isherwood was homesick—overwhelmed and lonely amid the unrelentingly strange and new. He had an attack of despair, telling Young that he hated America and Americans and would have to go back to Europe. Then, in his diary, he tried to recover his balance, observing, "I meant: I hate myself." He went on to write, "I love this country. I love it just because I don't belong. Because I'm not involved in its traditions, not born under the curse of its history. I feel free here. I'm on my own. My life will be what I make of it."[31]

PRABHAVANANDA NEXT INSTRUCTED Isherwood to do something more exotic: "Imagine there is a cavity within you. In the middle of this cavity there is a throne, in the form of a red lotus. In the middle of the lotus, a golden light is burning. Approach this light and say, 'O Self, reveal yourself to me.'"

Isherwood was repelled: "My imagination revolts from this: it sounds like a stage scene at the Radio City Music Hall." Nevertheless, he was determined: "But I shall try to do it. [...] perhaps the lotus is better, just because I *don't* like it. A very subtle aversion is mixed up with this question. Maybe, even, a certain racial snobbery, against anything Indian."[32] In adolescence, he had adored some of the most lurid and fantastic romances, from Walter Scott to Rider Haggard, Marjorie Bowen, and Sax Rohmer. He had relished films portraying oriental magic, Arabian nights, and religious sentimentality. His imagination was nimble and resourceful; moreover, he was skilled at directing it.

There were other forces at work, too, not least the disapproval of his friends. Friendly antagonism fired his resolve. The year before, at the beginning of August 1939, Auden had arrived in California, completing his own cross-country trip with eighteen-year-old Chester Kallman, a student at Brooklyn College and a future poet, with whom he had fallen in love in April. Auden had what Isherwood described as "a long but rather unsatisfactory talk" with Heard, who commented on Auden's "jittery behavior and chain-smoking, and predicted that he would end up a Catholic." Auden accused Heard of being "a life hater."[33] Isherwood tried, in his diary, to explain away these strident disagreements, because they implied disagreement between Auden and himself.

It was immediately after this disruptive summer reunion that Isherwood had decided to make his second visit to Prabhavananda, the key August 4 visit that he was later to remember and write about, when Prabhavananda instructed and relaunched him in meditation. Contact with his old life, in the form of Auden, had reminded Isherwood why he wanted a new one.

Then, on August 6, Isherwood wrote a long letter to Upward explaining his new way of life. Feeling out of harmony with Auden, he wanted to square himself with at least one other close friend. "Only hold your hat on, because there's a bit of a shock coming," he warned. He described to Upward the New York life shared with Auden and his feeling that he had never committed himself properly to the Left as Upward had done:

> [T]his stupid little phase of notoriety as a writer pitchforked me into the limelight as Wystan's second fiddle. We went to China, and I produced this travel-diary which so annoyed the Left, because it was messy, personal, sentimental and confused, like myself. That is the way I will always be: personal. So I don't belong in any movement; and I cannot really take sides in any struggle.

He was apologizing to Upward because *Journey to a War* had been attacked in the *Daily Worker* by Randall Swingler, a mediocre poet and composer but a serious communist. Swingler had scolded Auden and Isherwood for being "too preoccupied with their own psychological plight to be anything but helplessly lost in the struggle of modern China." They were "playing at being war correspondents, at being Englishmen, at being poets."[34]

Play was not something Swingler could value as Auden or especially Isherwood valued it. In the days of their adolescent conspiracy, Isherwood and Upward had rebelled against the institutions that raised them by playing the Mortmere game, but their increasingly political radicalism during the 1930s had failed to change anything. "So what remains for me but pacifism, of some kind?" Isherwood asked Upward rhetorically. "And what revolution can I promote but a revolution inside myself?"

Isherwood went on in his letter to explain, "Heard believes that mankind can only escape from its present revolutionary-counterrevolutionary cycle (excuse this jargon) by attempting a new phase of evolution: psychic evolution." Socialism will only "bog down in materialism, unless men themselves are really and radically changed." To that end, Heard wanted to train a new group of leaders in the principles of yoga, "not pure eastern Yoga, but Yoga adapted to the needs of the west. (Are you still reading, or have you fallen under the table in a dead faint?)"[35]

Acknowledging how arduous and unlikely his path was, Isherwood used the image of a narrow, rocky goat track. He was recasting the travail of his hero in *Paul Is Alone* who had struggled along just such a "rough zig-zag goat-track." "Yes, believe it or not, your unlucky Starn has set his foot on the bottom of this crazy goat-track which is to lead over the peaks of the never-never mountains." This precarious zigzag to utopia was to replace in Isherwood's world view the spiraling Marxist dialectic to which Upward was still devoted. "No. I am not going back. I can't help what people will think of me. I can't worry about my writing. This is more important. It is also the only way in which I can even remotely hope to be of use to anybody, now."[36]

HEARD WAS A prolific author. His bestselling detective stories are witty page-turners, but his numerous books on the history of religion are so learned as to be intermittently incomprehensible. They are rooted in the theory of evolution. He expected, or at least hoped, that the next phase of evolution would involve an expansion of human consciousness.

Isherwood was to portray Heard as Augustus Parr in "Paul," the last story in *Down There on a Visit*. The story describes a perceptible metamorphosis in Augustus Parr from the "fastidiously clean-shaven, barbered and tailored" lecturer and BBC science broadcaster who had frequented Bloomsbury parties, dined in the Oxford and Cambridge colleges, studied in the British Museum, to the bearded, blue-jeaned ascetic eating scraps from the fridge in someone else's house in California only when his host was out.[37] Isherwood was struck by these very changes in Heard in real life, as he recorded in his diary.

Auden did not believe people could change. He once wrote a letter to Isherwood in which he said:

No doubt in Purgatory we shall still be having the same argument.

Christopher "But I know I'm not the same person I was on earth."

Wystan "But I know I am."[38]

It was the old argument "over the 'personality' question" they had had on the way to China, when Isherwood had "maintained that Christopher in Saigon and Christopher in Kensington were two different people." Now Isherwood began to see such changes as part of progress toward a goal, the extinction of the ego, oneness with the infinite. Auden never accepted Isherwood's Hindu beliefs, although out of friendship he sometimes gestured at them positively.

Arguments between Auden and Isherwood were nothing compared with arguments with outsiders. In Britain, the press turned against them. Isherwood thought this was touched off by a letter he sent Gerald Hamilton. To amuse Hamilton, he had described some German refugees in Hollywood as "very militant and already squabbling over the future German government" while "Others are interested, apparently, in reconquering the Romanisches Café, and would gladly sacrifice the whole British army to make Berlin safe for nightlife ..." Hamilton, without Isherwood's permission, passed the letter to Tom Driberg, then gossip columnist for the *Daily Express*, where it was quoted on November 27, 1939, three months after the war started.[39]

In February 1940, Cyril Connolly and Stephen Spender printed an editorial "Comment" by Connolly in their new magazine *Horizon*. It described Auden and Isherwood's departure as "the most important literary event since the outbreak of the Spanish War." Connolly called them "ambitious young men, with a strong instinct of self-preservation, and an eye on the main chance, who have abandoned what they consider to be the sinking ship of European democracy."[40] In April 1940, Harold Nicolson, by now a Labour MP and parliamentary secretary, accused Auden, Isherwood, Huxley, and Heard in the *Spectator* of undermining the possibility of American support for the war effort; Americans were unlikely to commit against Hitler if "four of our most liberated intellectuals refuse to identify themselves [...] with those who fight." Nicolson's views were echoed in the *Daily Mail*. By June, questions were being asked in the House of Commons: would Auden and Isherwood, men of military age, "be summoned back for registration and calling up, in view of the fact that they are seeking refuge abroad?" Shouldn't their British citizenship be revoked if they did not at least register as conscientious objectors?[41]

Isherwood was determined not to apologize or make any public statement about his position on the war. Privately, though, he objected to Spender vociferously. He was helping Spender to promote *Horizon* in California, buying subscriptions for friends and local bookstores. Little did he know what he was promoting. "I must say, I was a little staggered when I read the 'Comment'—" He told Spender he had no intention of answering the wider attacks, "But when you, or Cyril, writes something, it is different." It was a public betrayal by close friends. In his letter, Isherwood countered the *Horizon* "Comment" point by point, defending Auden even more fiercely than he defended himself because he considered Auden lacked the kind of worldly ambition the piece attributed to them.

The *Horizon* "Comment" reflected disappointed fantasies, hurt feelings, and envy on the part of both Connolly and Spender. Isherwood accepted that his circumstances, "living in safety, in a beautiful climate, earning money," were enraging, "And I often feel guilty about this." He reminded Spender, "This emigration wasn't a last-moment flight. It was a deliberate act, planned a long time ago." He pointed out that "even the British authorities agree that those who are in the U.S. should stay," and he insisted upon his longterm plans to remain in the U.S., quite apart from the war: "Why have I decided to become an American citizen? Because I believe that the future of English culture is in America, and that the building of this future will be assisted by the largest possible cultural emigration." He was bitterly disappointed that Spender doubted his new religious beliefs and his pacifism: "You cannot seriously think that my interest in Yoga (not 'Yogi'!) is a pose, or that my change of feeling about violence is not sincere." He had believed the friendship between them was unconditional: "I accept you completely—and woe betide the skunk who calls you any nasty names!"[42]

Friendships were failing all around, and the war was engendering hard new attitudes. Spender had fallen out with Lehmann by soliciting contributions for *Horizon* even though he was already on the board of Lehmann's *New Writing*. Lehmann had been trying to get financial support from their mutual friend Peter Watson, heir to a dairy fortune and patron of the arts, but Watson gave his money to *Horizon*. Lehmann had fallen out with another mutual friend, the writer and critic Cuthbert Worsley. Isherwood wrote to Lehmann: "It makes me very sad to think that The Gang is splitting up."[43]

On Auden's advice, and as Auden had already done, Isherwood wrote to the British Embassy in Washington "asking if these attacks represented the official British attitude and offering, if necessary, to return to England and serve in a noncombatant capacity." He received a reply on July 12, 1940, affirming what he had told Spender, that "your position in the United States, like Mr. Auden's, is understood and that the offer of your services is much appreciated." He copied the letter into his wartime diaries, where he also explained that the British consulate later asked all British residents to return to England, "but only on condition that you signed a paper agreeing to accept *any* kind of service you were assigned to. This ruled out conscientious objectors."[44]

Being made fun of hurt most. Anthony Powell wrote a verse that ran in part, "The dog beneath the skin has had the brains / To save it, Norris-like, by changing trains." When Isherwood heard it, he wrote, "Why does this sting me so? Simply because it is really clever. It succeeds in making me look ridiculous—in a way that mere abuse can't." It prompted him to further self-questioning, but only in the privacy of his diary: "If I were told that somebody else had 'run away from England' I should ask, 'What did "England" mean to him?' 'England' to me meant a place that I stayed away from as much as possible during the past ten years."[45]

Auden's and Isherwood's reasons for leaving England were so personal and so complex that even their closest friends couldn't understand them. Upward, Forster, Spender, Connolly, E.R. Dodds (Auden's Oxford don friend) were among the few to whom they took trouble to explain themselves. On the day the war broke out, September 1, 1939, Forster, who *did* understand, wrote to Isherwood that he must not return: "*Whatever one does is wrong*, so do not come back here, that is the wrongest." Six weeks later, Forster exhorted Isherwood further, that he and Auden must make a point of surviving because "you both must and can carry on civilization."[46]

Auden and Isherwood themselves were changing as quickly as the circumstances around them. By the time the war broke out, Isherwood had already begun to feel he had found the home for which he had been searching. "I know I certainly wouldn't leave Los Angeles if the Japanese were to attack it tomorrow."

He feared "the atmosphere of the war, the power which it gives to all the things I hate—the newspapers, the politicians, the puritans, the scoutmasters, the middle-aged merciless spinsters."[47] This was the atmosphere—encroaching conservatism, rigid institutional attitudes, ritualized and unnuanced public conversation—that he had feared and resisted since he was a schoolboy. As a homosexual, he had long been conducting his sexual and romantic life outside the law and outside popular morality, but neither he nor Auden could say publicly that they emigrated because they were gay. Both sought the anonymity and freedom which seemed possible in the sprawling social setting of America where they had no relatives and no school friends.

Isherwood was to begin circulating his wartime diaries among near friends in the late 1940s. By then, he had added bridging narrative to fill gaps, and he had revised and expanded many of the entries. The diaries are not a work of fiction, but he shaped them to explain and to justify his choices, and in this run of diaries he made a thorough case for his emigration and conversion.

The wartime diaries were not published until 1997, long after Isherwood's death, but in the meantime, they began to present the Americanization of Isherwood to a new insider audience with whom he had some experience of America in common: in California, the English writer Dodie Smith and her husband Alec Beesley, the Stravinskys to whom Robert Craft read them aloud, and possibly the Huxleys and Gerald Heard. He showed them in New York, too, and arranged through Lincoln Kirstein to have them deposited for safekeeping with the head of manuscripts at Yale while he traveled abroad after the war. Yale kept a microfilm copy.[48] His New York writer friend Glenway Wescott traveled to Los Angeles especially to read the diaires in 1949. Don Bachardy read them in the summer of 1956 and again in the autumn of 1966. Isherwood read passages aloud to Auden in the autumn of 1951.[49] Later Gavin Lambert and John Rechy read them.

NOT LONG AFTER the German Blitzkrieg started over England during July 1940, Auden visited California a second time, and Isherwood again resorted to the word "unsatisfactory" in his diary: "It has been an unsatisfactory visit: we had hardly any time for a proper talk. In any case, we are both too much disturbed to be able to talk properly."[50] They were greatly troubled by events, and they were looking for different kinds of answers.

On the day Auden was to arrive, Isherwood awoke "in a muddled state" with his head full of news of Nazi air raids on Dover and "A feeling of complete bewilderment, as though I had lost the thread of life. I could no longer remember even the intellectual reasons why one should believe God exists, or try to be good. Meditation seemed longer than ever before." He collected Auden from the airport and, right away, questioning began, first about Isherwood's diet. "He would rather see me take to dope than become a vegetarian,"[51] Isherwood wrote in his diary. Two days later, they made an excursion to Palos Verdes for tea, and Auden delivered a stream of unequivocal assertions about Heard's teachings. "'No one can be a pacifist,' he said, 'who isn't trying to live Gerald's life. The truth is, I *want* to kill people.'"

Auden told Isherwood that he would allow himself to be drafted if the U.S. entered the war; like Isherwood, he had already applied for U.S. citizenship. "Wystan is suspicious of Gerald's ideas," Isherwood observed in his diary, "because Gerald thinks Time is evil. Wystan likes Time, and the material world." Moreover, Auden was preparing to return to the Anglo-Catholic beliefs of his childhood. He had been reading widely in theology, and that autumn, he was to begin attending Episcopalian communion. "He has a whole new lingo of Christian theology, very abstruse. He said how much he disliked Sanskrit words. I told him I feel just the opposite."[52] In fact, until then, Isherwood had not liked Sanskrit words at all. In March, he had rebelled against Om; at the end of July, only a few days before Auden arrived, he had revolted against Prabhavananda's red lotus throne. Auden's friendly hectoring tightened Isherwood's focus.

Two days after Auden left from this second West Coast visit, Isherwood was back in the temple, and Prabhavananda gave him "new and much more elaborate instructions" for meditation.[53] Isherwood felt the meditation was helping him cope with depression brought on by news of the bombing and the increasing expectation that the Germans were about to invade Britain. Soon he recorded a week in which he managed to meditate every single day.

That autumn, he had two minor mystical experiences which he evidently did not record until six years later when he revised his wartime diaries. The first occurred at an aquarium in San Francisco. "I was looking at a small tank of damselfish—tiny, vivid specks of brilliant blue. All at once, I saw them, as it were, within a universe of their own: embraced, sustained by an intensely living 'presence.' And I said to myself: 'He cares for *them*, too.'" The perception had greatly moved him, and it remained intensely vivid. Did he notice the pun—damn selfish—guaranteeing God's love to all creatures whether or not they were absorbed in their own universe as he himself so often was?

The second experience was driving home in evening traffic on Sunset Boulevard. He had a spasm of cramp in his leg and swore involuntarily, "Oh God." "The word, which I have misused ten million times, produced a kind of echo in my consciousness. Like the vibration after a bell has been struck. It seemed to vibrate down, down into the depths of me. It was so strange, so awe-inspiring, that I longed for the cramp to return. I thought, 'I have called upon God.'"[54]

The more Isherwood thought about Sanskrit words, the more they meant to him. As with his cockney accent in the 1920s and German in the 1930s, he was entering a new world through its language, now with Prabhavananda as his guide. Within a few years, he and Prabhavananda were to translate the Bhagavad Gita together, the first of many collaborative projects in translation that were to be a constant activity in Isherwood's life and to bind him ever more closely to Prabhavananda. Isherwood never learned Sanskrit, apart from individual words, and so relied on Prabhavananda all the more.

Early in the morning on November 8, 1940, Prabhavananda formally initiated Isherwood as his disciple.[55] Isherwood described the process minutely in his diary. Following Prabhavananda's instructions, he meditated in the shrine and offered flowers to Ramakrishna; to Sarada Devi, Ramakrishna's wife, also known as Holy Mother; to Christ; and to Prabhavananda as his guru. Prabhavananda instructed him to meditate again, on Ramakrishna. "Then he taught me my Sanskrit mantram (which I must never repeat to anybody) and gave me a rosary, showing me how to use it, repeating the mantram and meditating on Ramakrishna's body—"

They had toast and coffee then celebrated Holy Mother with more offerings including a special meal for her. Last was the fire ceremony, in Prabhavananda's study, which had a fireplace. "All our actions, good and bad, were symbolically offered up and purified in the fire. The Swami made a sign on our foreheads with the ash, to symbolize the opening of the third eye, the eye of the spirit."[56]

A few months later, at the beginning of 1941, Heard formally split from Prabhavananda. He was becoming increasingly ascetic and disapproved of Prabhavananda's comfortable and relaxed domestic arrangements which depended on a number of women disciples: "'the holy women' were too much for him, and the little tea parties, the automobile and the other minor luxuries which the Swami permitted himself—especially his cigarette smoking," Isherwood explained in his diary. So Heard stopped lecturing at the temple and contributing to the Vedanta Society magazine.[57]

Isherwood remained closely involved with both Heard and Prabhavananda. "Gerald offered me discipline, method, intellectual conviction. But the Swami offered me love." He decided to give up smoking, a trivial austerity in the pandemonium of World War II, but smoking was the habit for which Heard most looked down on Prabhavananda, and Isherwood was determined "to take some definite step toward 'purgation,' however small." He called it "the final test," as he might have done in the 1920s.[58] For two weeks, he found it a torment, but he didn't smoke again for two years.

All the while, from England and the East Coast, he sensed the questioning of friends like Upward and that other chain-smoker, Auden. He and Auden had agreed during their summer visit in 1940 "to do nothing about going to England without consulting each other first." They both knew that if Isherwood decided to get in deeper with Prabhavananda, he would certainly not return to England, regardless of what Auden decided. By letter, Auden pressed Isherwood urgently to be certain of his vocation, and barely concealed his doubt that it was real:

> As you know, I regard the contemplative life as the highest and most difficult of all vocations, and therefore the one to which very few people are called—fewer even than are called to be creative artists, among whom, rightly or wrongly, I believe my place to be: for the other I am not good enough. If you are <u>certain</u> you are called, then of course you must obey, but you <u>must</u> be certain, otherwise it is just presumption.[59]

NEARLY A YEAR after the start of the war, Isherwood hosted lunch at the Beverly Hills Brown Derby for three American friends who had fled Europe for Los Angeles, Cyril Connolly's estranged wife Jean, née Bakewell, Tony Bower, educated at Marlborough and Oxford, who had escorted Neddermeyer from Paris to Luxembourg in April 1937 when Isherwood was too ill to go, and a young man from Florida, Denham Fouts, the paid lover of princes and millionaires. Luckily, the chaperone role suited Bower, for Jean Connolly and Fouts needed looking after. According to Isherwood, they were hungover at lunch and "steadily tanking up for the next blind."[60]

Fouts was being kept by Peter Watson, the arts patron and collector, who remained in England during the war. If Isherwood had met Fouts before, he took note of him for the first time in August 1940 when Fouts was twenty-six and Isherwood was thirty-six.[61] He recalled his impressions in his diary, translating Fouts to the realm of the imagination by describing him as a figure in a painting:

> I think of the lean hungry, tanned face; the eyes which seemed to be set on different levels, slightly overlapping, as in a late Picasso painting;

the bitter little rosebud mouth; the strangely erect walk, almost paralytic with tension. He had rather sinister clothes—wash-leather jerkins, bell-bottomed sailor's trousers, boxer's sweaters. They were sinister because they were intended for laughing, harmless boys, not as a disguise for this tormented addict, this wolflike inverted monk, this martyr to pleasure.

Similarities between Fouts and Francis Turville-Petre are evident; so are differences. For Turville-Petre, Isherwood had referenced Christian religious paintings. For Fouts, he chose Picasso, in part because Peter Watson had given Fouts a Picasso, *Girl Reading* (1934), which Fouts was to hang in his Santa Monica apartment and then bequeath to Isherwood, "in consideration of debts I owe to him & because he is my best friend," as Fouts poignantly wrote in 1945.[62]

In October 1940, Fouts told Isherwood that he wanted to become a disciple of Swami Prabhavananda, so Isherwood took him to the Vedanta temple, and they sat together in the shrine; a few days later, he introduced Fouts to Prabhavananda. But Prabhavananda turned Fouts away, telling him that "what he needed was not meditation but hard work." Fouts, in private with Isherwood afterwards, "burst into tears, sobbing that he was rotten, everybody despised him, and he'd better kill himself with heroin as soon as possible." This made a big impact on Isherwood, who "said far more than I meant. I told him that *I* didn't despise him, that I admired him and liked him and wanted to be his friend."

He next introduced Fouts to Gerald Heard. Heard, "flattered and pleased at being able to demonstrate his superior charity, immediately accepted Denny as his protégé and disciple." The situation naturally put pressure on Isherwood's relationship with Prabhavananda. Moreover, Prabhavananda's rejection "made Denny oppose the Swami's influence over me on every possible occasion."[63]

During the autumn of 1940, Fouts lived with Heard as his disciple until Heard sent him to a Pennsylvania farm where he could learn skills for the contemplative community Heard was planning and which he called Focus. While Fouts was away, Isherwood and Harvey Young split up, and Isherwood moved into an apartment on Green Valley Road in Laurel Canyon, next door to Heard and Chris Wood. "Gerald and I had supper together practically every day," Isherwood later recalled.[64] After five months, Fouts returned, and Isherwood invited him to share his apartment. Fouts was now waiting to be drafted into war work as a conscientious objector in Roosevelt's peacetime draft.

So began the unlikely period, fictionalized in "Paul" in *Down There on a Visit*, when Isherwood and Fouts established a daily routine of meditating for an hour at 6 a.m., noon, and 6 p.m., reading aloud from books of philosophy and religion, in particular William James's *Varieties of Religious Experience*, "a badly written book which we both criticized violently,"[65] and attending classes to learn hatha yoga breathing and physical exercises. On behalf of the local Quaker relief organization, they distributed bundles of clothes to the "Okies," refugees from the agricultural disaster of the Oklahoma Dust Bowl, and they also assisted European refugees in Hollywood.

Fouts began writing a novel about a trio of international pleasure-seekers resembling himself, Jean Connolly, and Tony Bower, who reunite at the Glendale airport six months or more after their European playground is closed by the war. "Sefton" is the character that Fouts based on himself, and Isherwood, rereading Fouts's manuscript as he worked on "Paul" in 1960, toyed with using the name "Sefton" for his character Paul.

Fouts was evidently aiming to get control of his life not only through studying Vedanta but also through writing. "Notebooks like Chris," he jotted in a list of errands in the notebook in which he started his novel. Isherwood was again playing a chaste but intimate game, fueled by erotic excitement that was not acted on. He wrote in his diary:

> Everything we did seemed interesting and amusing. The apartment acquired a kind of nursery atmosphere of innocence.
>
> We had agreed, of course, to give up sex. [...] We didn't give up thinking about sex, talking about sex, even boasting of our glamorous love lives.[66]

ISHERWOOD'S EXPERIMENTAL LIFE with Fouts in the spring of 1941 was successful while they remained cut off in their private spiritual cocoon. Then, from July 7 to August 7, they attended a religious retreat, the La Verne Seminar, organized by a Quaker group, the American Friends Service Committee. Heard with some colleagues and followers joined the Quakers in an empty college dorm in the town of La Verne, east of Los Angeles in orange-growing country. They planned to meditate, pray, study religious texts, and to talk about the relative merits of the contemplative life and the life of service.

Isherwood later explained that Heard "wanted to see how far he could go along with the Society of Friends." The La Verne group included Christian ministers with wives and children, schoolteachers, a healer, a folk festival organizer, Heard's publisher, a magazine editor, a journalist, a few college students, and, by chance, a cousin of Isherwood's, Felix Greene, who had been working for the BBC in North America and was one of the organizers.

"For the first time, I understood the basic appeal of a monastery," Isherwood commented in his diary. "The group meditation periods were what I most looked forward to, throughout the day." They gave him a feeling "of safety, even of comfort." He learned "what continuous vigilance ought to mean," and how to guard against compulsive behavior like constantly checking for news in a period of crisis. "Nazi armies were pushing deeper and deeper into Russia, and one longed to sneak out to the drugstore and peep at the latest headlines," he later wrote. The discipline was "To try to annihilate your ego, to let the Real Self walk about in you."[67]

The La Verne Seminar was the subject of the first American writing that Isherwood finally released to the importunate Lehmann, let down several times. He had been avoiding Lehmann's coterie audience back in England: "Every time I sit down to the typewriter, I think of Cyril waiting for me to take up an 'attitude' or make a 'statement,'" he told Lehmann in 1941, "and that freezes me." But when he was about to set off for La Verne, he suddenly offered "a short plain account of the doings and findings there."[68]

He cast himself in the familiar role of visiting observer and wrote the piece impersonally, like a laboratory report: "We had gathered, as researchworkers in any field may gather, to compare notes, to discuss techniques, and to get the inspiration which a feeling of companionship in effort can give." In the driest of tones, he described the daily schedule and presented the topics of discussion, formulating the latter as generalized rhetorical questions without any immediate connection to his personal dilemma: "Is the life of prayer a form of escapism, or is it perhaps the most direct sign of action?" The piece was both humble and strangely showy, dissolving individual concerns into the group monastic experiment, extolling Heard's skill as chairman, sharing an imposing list of religious and philosophical books. In wartime London, "The Day at La Verne,"[69] as it was titled, must have seemed boring, eccentric, high-minded and irrelevant. Far from inciting further attack, the piece successfully drowned opponents in worthiness and sobriety. Like so much that Isherwood wrote about his conversion, it concealed as much as it revealed about what really happened at La Verne.

As Isherwood recalled in his diary, Heard's "orations were as spellbinding as ever; but Denny and I knew them practically by heart, and so we were hypercritical." They were a terrible influence on one another at the seminar. "I think the breakdown of our chastity resolutions had a lot to do with this," Isherwood reflected. "As soon as we were alone together, we would begin picking everybody to pieces, from Gerald downwards: Gerald, of course, was our special victim."

He didn't specify how their chastity resolutions broke down. He later told Bachardy he never had sex with Fouts, but they were together at the La Verne seminar for a whole month. Much went unrecorded in the diary: "the bad days aren't mentioned, because then I didn't feel like writing at all."[70] Once, Heard asked Isherwood to speak with younger members of the seminar "on the subject of confidences." Isherwood couldn't face it. "They were having a discussion of their sex problems. Gerald wanted me to take part in it, and be frank. I refused. I'm bored sick of confessions."[71]

When the La Verne Seminar ended, Fouts received his conscientious objector's draft call-up to a forestry camp at San Dimas. "We spent a melancholy two weeks buying his ugly trousseau, the stiff blue denim work clothes and the clumsy boots," wrote Isherwood.[72] He drove Fouts the forty miles to Glendora, where Fouts was collected to go up into the mountains. Then Isherwood flew to New York to visit Auden and to be interviewed in Haverford, Pennsylvania, by the director of a refugee hostel where he hoped to work. He had decided against Heard and Prabhavananda: "the contemplative life was not for me—at any rate, not yet. I must do some social work."[73]

DESPITE HIS PROFESSIONAL success and his outward bravado, Auden was no happier than Isherwood. His love affair with Chester Kallman, which Auden had come to regard as a marriage, nearly ended that July after just two years, when Kallman revealed he had another lover and wanted his freedom. Auden was so distressed that he tried to strangle Kallman in his sleep.[74] Sexual relations between them were over for good, though for the rest of his life Auden supported Kallman financially; later, they collaborated on opera librettos.

When Isherwood arrived, Auden and Kallman were vacationing in Jamestown, Rhode Island, with a wealthy friend and patroness, Caroline Newton. "She was in love with Auden," Isherwood later wrote. Isherwood thought Newton "silly, snobbish, well-read [. . .] with very little taste, often pathetic and always kind hearted." The situation was itself like a comic opera, including both suffering and farce. "The atmosphere was in the highest degree embarrassing," Isherwood recalled. "I had to keep going on walks, alternately with the three others, to discuss the latest developments. Wystan was in a difficult, strained, provocative mood, and kept attacking Gerald and talking theology." On top of everything else, Auden's mother died on August 21. Isherwood reported to his own mother that Auden "was a good deal up-set—"[75]

Isherwood was relieved when they left Rhode Island for Brooklyn, where

Auden was sharing a house rented by their friend George Davis, the one who had introduced them to Manhattan in 1938. Number 7 Middagh Street was the echt-bohemian establishment which Davis and Auden famously shared with the writer Carson McCullers, the stripper Gypsy Rose Lee, Paul Bowles and his writer wife Jane Bowles, and Benjamin Britten and his new companion, the tenor Peter Pears, who were testing the idea of settling in America: "an attractive, insanely untidy place," wrote Isherwood.

From Brooklyn, he went to meet another Caroline, Caroline Norment, a former college dean, who ran the Quaker refugee hostel (the convener of the La Verne Seminar had supplied an introduction). Isherwood committed to move to Haverford later that autumn. Even so, "poor Wystan cried when I left for Los Angeles, toward the end of September."[76]

HAVERFORD, 1941

Isherwood returned to Haverford on October 11. He persuaded himself that he was continuing the spiritual journey he had begun at the Hollywood temple, even though he was putting 3,000 miles between himself and his guru: "I had come to Haverford, I told myself, as a sort of invisible monk: my spiritual life was to be neither seen nor heard. As I had a room to myself, I should be able to meditate without difficulty, at any rate night and morning."[77]

The refugee hostel was in a rented mansion next to the Haverford College campus. Isherwood and a few refugees slept at another house around the corner, hosted by a Mr. and Mrs. William Yarnall. The project was called the Cooperative College Workshop, and it drew on the elite intellectual resources of Haverford College, Bryn Mawr College, and Swarthmore College (where, by coincidence, Auden had taught). Many of the refugees had been teachers, and even the non-teachers were planning to take teaching jobs as soon as they could speak English well enough. They also had to learn what Caroline Norment called the American Way of Life, promoted through social events, lectures on municipal government and civil liberties, and tours of nearby schools and colleges.

Isherwood taught five or six individual English lessons a day. "I and my pupils ploughed through grammar, correcting exercises, reading aloud from the *Reader's Digest*, or drilling with verbs and consonants ('You're a Yank yourself, yelled Yetta)." But these were not the kind of students he had had in Berlin when he gave English lessons in the early 1930s. Everyone at the hostel was uprooted and engaged in a forced transition to become American. "The lessons were not really lessons, they were psychiatric sessions," he later wrote, for "badly rattled, middle-aged people whose lifeline to the homeland had been brutally cut, and whose will to make a new start in the new country was very weak."

Into his busy schedule at the hostel, Isherwood fitted sessions of meditation; his nerves frayed when he could not meditate. "Sometimes, I had really bad breaks, when I flew right off the handle and barked at the refugees like a drill sergeant, or said something really inexcusable."[78] Meditation and prayer had become a centerpiece of his mental health as well as the engine of his spiritual quest.

There were numerous interpersonal dramas, especially as the session approached year end. On Christmas Eve, a refugee, Gretl Ebeling, a German communist concentration camp survivor, married and with a child, told Isherwood that she was in love with him. In the new year, she left with her family, but she kept returning melodramatically to Haverford. Isherwood was to transform her into the character Gerda Mannheim in *The World in the Evening*, another of his nurse-sisters, who cares for the protagonist, Stephen Monk, when he is hit by a truck. In fact, Gretl Ebeling's feelings toward Isherwood were an obstacle between them, not a bond as in the novel: "We could have been real friends if it hadn't been for this business," Isherwood wrote in his diary.[79]

He also described many of the other refugees in the diary. None appeared to him to be in control of his or her destiny. For the time being, they were victims, exhausted by the horror of war, by flight and resettlement. He was to try and fail to write a novel about them, but even his proposed title, *The School of Tragedy*, seemed to recognize they had little to offer him—no scope for the comedy, romantic illusion, or spirited defiance at which he had shown himself adept.[80] Nevertheless, it was to take him many years to move on from *The School of Tragedy* to the novel he did write about this period, *The World in the Evening*.

As an invisible monk among the Quakers, Isherwood reentered the spiritual landscape of his Christian childhood. On Sundays, he did an hour of Bible study and attended Quaker Meeting; on Mondays, he went to a class in which he was taught to read the gospel closely, as if "for the first time," and try to imagine Jesus as a living individual: "It was like a weekly visit to the theater or the movies," he wrote. "And, for the first time, very dimly, I caught glimpses of an extraordinary figure moving behind the inaccuracies, contradictions and propaganda of the gospel story."[81]

In Pennsylvania much more than in California, he felt the shadow of his old English life, partly because America entered the war when Pearl Harbor was bombed on December 7, 1941, bringing Europe closer. Also, the Philadelphia area reminded him of northern England. Less than five miles from Haverford was a small town called Marple, founded by English Quakers;

many local place names—Bryn Mawr, for example—were Welsh, like the villages of his childhood holidays.[82]

In the new year, after three months in Haverford, he went downtown for a concert of Benjamin Britten's music and was again reminded of home. "Philadelphia in mid-January and wartime is a kind of nightmare Manchester, drearier than the grave, and full of naval and military drunks," he wrote. After the concert, he and Britten and Peter Pears got drunk themselves at a seafood restaurant. They were sad because Britten and Pears had decided to return to the U.K. and register as conscientious objectors. Britten asked Isherwood to write the libretto for his proposed opera *Peter Grimes*, based on George Crabbe's poem, but Isherwood decided he could not make time in "a life like the one I lead at present," and anyway, they would be "so far apart."[83]

Also in January, he was summoned for a meal with the Bloomsbury philosopher and activist Bertrand Russell, at Little Datchet Farm in Malvern, "tucked away in one of the lonely valleys out beyond Paoli, which so resemble the Derbyshire Peak District, especially in winter." Russell's pacifism during World War I had cost him his job at Cambridge University, but he renounced pacifism during World War II because he thought fascism a greater evil than war. He was lecturing at the Barnes Foundation for the Philadelphia pharmaceutical millionaire Alfred Barnes. Staying with Russell was Aldous Huxley's brother Julian, an Oxford zoologist who worked on evolution and genetics, "over here for a few weeks on some British propaganda mission," explained Isherwood in his diary.

Isherwood had met them both in Hollywood in 1939; now they cross-examined him about Aldous Huxley's new way of life: "'Did he—I mean—er, that is—do you mean to say he actually, er, really—*prays*?' 'And why,' asked Bertie, 'does Aldous talk about Ultimate Reality? Surely one kind of reality isn't any more or less real than another?'"

These sceptical, agnostic British intellectuals decided that Aldous was seeking "a psychological adjustment," a phrase allowing them to avoid the question of belief in God and the challenging possibility of real change in Aldous. Yet, later the same evening, Julian Huxley took Isherwood aside and asked furtively, "'And you—you do this thing too?' 'Yes,' I said, 'I do.' 'And you believe in it? It really helps you?' 'I believe it's all that really matters.'" This won a concession from Huxley. "'You know,' he told me, 'you look quite different from when I saw you last. It's an extraordinary change.'"[84] Isherwood shaped the whole passage reporting on three star brains of the time—including Aldous Huxley in absentia—to persuade eventual readers of his wartime diaries that change was possible.

At the time, he was corresponding with Forster about the difference between the British and the Americans when it came to sex and religion. He and Forster agreed the British were squeamish about both. In late 1941, Forster had received a letter from Heard "partly about praying," and Forster wrote to Isherwood: "I believe it is much more like going to bed with someone than is generally supposed. Hence the shyness. Hence the great advantages *or* disadvantages which may ensue."

From Haverford, Isherwood had replied: "I agree with you about prayer. It *is* like going to bed: just as 'getting religion' (that horrible expression) is like falling in love. And prayer, in its turn, has various consequences, like consummation." As for the benefits of prayer and meditation for himself, Isherwood echoed Forster's own phrase about the inner life from *Howards End*: "'it pays,' in better balance, better integration, greater contentment, and, much more important, in an increasing appetite for it and commitment to it." He found it "a lot more satisfactory than physical marriage ever was," but asserted he was still open to physical marriage of the sort he had had, for instance, with Neddermeyer. "If the right person came along, that could be more wonderful than ever."[85]

ISHERWOOD NEEDED TO connect with others. He could not last long without some kind of live current, some kind of reciprocity, whether physical or spiritual. The longer he was in Haverford, the more involved he got with East Coast friends outside the workshop. Chief among these was Lincoln Kirstein, whom he had met in March 1939 not long after arriving in New York: "I had taken one of Wystan's Benzedrine tablets, and the afternoon passed with an effect of terrific, smooth, effortless speed. Neither Lincoln nor I stopped talking for a single moment. We were intimates at once."

Right away, Isherwood had seen Kirstein as a character from a book, though he couldn't decide which book or which character. Kirstein's blue pea jacket made him look like "a mad clipper captain out of Melville," but "his hair cropped like a convict's" made him look like Victor Hugo's Jean Valjean. His height gave him "the air of protecting everybody, of holding up the world. He is like Gulliver among the Lilliputians."[86] Kirstein was indeed a giant of a man, poet, painter, critic, connoisseur of literature, art, and ballet. He was heir to a retailing fortune, co-founded the New York City Ballet with George Balanchine, and helped found the Museum of Modern Art. In 1941, he married Fidelma Cadmus, sister of the painter Paul Cadmus, but he was bisexual and nearly always had a boyfriend living in his house or nearby. He was bipolar and prone to occasional complete breakdowns.

Isherwood made visits to New York, where he saw Kirstein, the photographer George Platt Lynes, the British playwright John Van Druten, Britten and Pears and their Long Island hostess Elizabeth Meyer, Berthold Viertel, James and Tania Stern. In February, he posed for a portrait by Paul Cadmus. He visited his agency Curtis Brown. His life became less and less like the life of an invisible monk.

More friends were being drafted. With Jean Connolly, Isherwood visited Tony Bower at army training camp on Long Island. One of Kirstein's lovers, a ballet dancer, Jesús José Martínez Berlanga, known as Pete Martinez, had volunteered for the navy and was turned down despite being an American citizen, because he was Mexican by background. Kirstein suggested that Martinez go to work at the Haverford refugee hostel, which he dubbed "Humble Hall."[87]

Isherwood saw in Martinez both gaiety and "a strange Mexican mournfulness" that captivated him, "Partly Spanish, partly Indian." This was combined with the physical discipline and wit of the trained dancer. "All his gestures are graceful and comic. He is a walking parody of the ballet."[88] Martinez joined him in Haverford in mid-February. "He charms everybody," Isherwood wrote. After introductions and supper on Martinez's first night, "we ran most of the way to Ardmore—to see Garbo in *Two-Faced Woman*—screaming hysterically with laughter and release from tension."

The friendship quickly warmed with the playful erotic energy characteristic of so many of Isherwood's friendships, with a notable element of camp: "Life at the workshop, since he arrived, has turned into a kind of private game between us. It is like a parody of itself. Everything that happens seems startlingly funny." Martinez patiently gave English lessons "to the two weakest members" of the group, and he made a striking impression outside of class. "I happened to meet him in the hall and asked him what kind of a day he'd had. 'Darling,' he exclaimed, for the benefit of several people who were listening, 'if you don't kiss me I shall *scream*!' "[89]

Isherwood felt that the Quakers might be shocked "by my novels, by the conversation of my friends, by my literary and artistic tastes," and the presence of Martinez highlighted his sense that "a lot of their 'plainness' is just provincialism, middle-class prejudice." Once again, he was living in a conspiracy of two. "Instinctively we spend our time trying to shock the Quakes, just because they are so shockable."[90] It delighted him.

A month after Martinez arrived, they started sharing a bedroom to make way for a new arrival. In *My Guru and His Disciple*, Isherwood referred to Martinez, without naming him, as "a sexual playmate,"[91] and letters to Kirstein and Cadmus make clear the romance was sexual. "I had no conscience pangs. I had never felt that Quakerdom demanded celibacy of me; they all approved of sex, even if it was only of the lawful kind." By April, though, he was growing uncomfortable; the Puritan in him disapproved of their drinking bouts, and when Martinez left toward the end of the month, Isherwood felt "curiously relieved."[92]

He made other local friends. René Blanc-Roos, French by background, was an assistant professor of French and Spanish at Haverford College and coached the wrestling team, which Isherwood enjoyed watching. "Like Denny, he is sour," noted Isherwood in his diary. "It is a relief to suck his sourness like a lemon, after too much sweetness and light."[93] Blanc-Roos had damaged his spine wrestling and drank to relieve the pain. He was separated from his wife but continued a sexy, quarrelsome relationship with her. He and Isherwood discussed French literature, and Blanc-Roos pushed Isherwood to start writing again. So Isherwood eked out a short story, "Take It or Leave It," which appeared in the *New Yorker* that October, earning him nearly $500.

"All writers get ideas which don't really belong to them," Isherwood wrote in the opening paragraphs of "Take It or Leave It." Accordingly, the narrator charts his transformation into someone else: "You notice, I'm even beginning to talk with a different accent? It's not my voice any longer. That's the influence of this story, which isn't mine." The story was about a heterosexual marriage going wrong, like Blanc-Roos's, but the real-life author, Isherwood, was a homosexual. Also, the real-life author was an Englishman writing about two Americans; he was a writer no longer confident of his talent; he was a spiritual convert falling away from his newfound path.

In the story, wife and husband spill out their misery on paper. The wife writes a diary; the husband fills a notebook. Secretly, they read each other's accounts of woe, enabling a rapprochement not possible face-to-face: "It is a game, but they have to play it seriously and very carefully [...] The diary grows warmer. The notebook responds."[94] For Isherwood, writing enabled self-understanding. His double was another self pursued on paper, a self reflected in a piece of writing, a self who wrote to be understood and read to understand.

In "Take It or Leave It," the narrator introduces three precursors for his tale of self-transformation: *A Tale of Two Cities*, *Dr. Jekyll and Mr. Hyde*, and *The Picture of Dorian Gray*." All three stories are about doubles—repressed, monstrous, and ready to overturn the status quo. "Take It or Leave It" was not only about the process of identification and transformation the author must undergo to write the story, but also about the difficulty of becoming an American, the difficulty of becoming a Hindu, and about the hidden self which threatened to overturn the public, published narrative about Christopher Isherwood.

In a later essay about *Dr. Jekyll and Mr. Hyde*, Isherwood identified "a tension" between Robert Louis Stevenson's "inherited Puritanism and his natural inclinations"; he often identified the same tension in himself: "Dr. Jekyll is the average sensual man whose sensuality is inhibited by his sense of duty and his regard for the proprieties."[95] Jekyll's daydream is "the separation of these elements."[96] In Isherwood's view, "Stevenson's Puritanism" dulled his insight just as Isherwood's inner censor had often done in the past. "The real tragedy of Jekyll—as Stevenson would have seen if he had permitted himself to face it—is that he disowns Hyde, his libido, and calls him evil."[97]

Isherwood shared the daydream of splitting himself into two separate identities, but he also wished to unite them, to embrace his libido as he had embraced Denny Fouts and Pete Martinez. In 1942, the Puritan in him was beginning to frown on this embrace, and in "Take It or Leave It," the rapprochement fails. The wife startles the husband in the act of reading her diary; the explosion leads to divorce. The reconciliation that seemed possible for husband and wife when mediated and controlled through writing is not possible in the flow of real life; it, too, is only a daydream.

Blanc-Roos remarried soon after Isherwood left Haverford. His second wife was a twenty-three-year-old Bryn Mawr graduate. Within a year, she shot herself. "She was very young. She was going to have a baby, and René thinks she thought he didn't want her to have it," Isherwood reported in his diary. Blanc-Roos, "on the verge of complete collapse," evidently told Isherwood that "it'll help if I write to him a lot"; so Isherwood wrote to him every day for a month. Many years later he told Dodie Smith that "at the end of that time I stopped and I have never seen him since."[98]

However, the epistolary gesture was not all, because Isherwood dedicated his first novel written in America, *Prater Violet*, to Blanc-Roos, who had pushed him to write, first the short story and then the letters. Blanc-Roos "was, to some extent, the model for one of its characters, Lawrence Dwight."[99] Dwight is the angry-looking head film cutter who has lost a leg and killed his new wife in a car wreck and who honors technicians above all others. He rants against the sentimentality of artists, even though he admires the work of the Friedrich Bergmann and Christopher Isherwood characters.

ALL DURING THE spring and summer of 1942 in Haverford, Isherwood was waiting to be drafted. He had volunteered for non-military service at a government forestry camp the summer before, when he was thirty-seven, two years above draft age, and was not wanted. After Pearl Harbor, the draft age was extended down to twenty and up to forty-four; he told Forster that his age group was required to register on February 16, 1942. Years later, he recalled an offer to serve in Washington, "promoted, I'm nearly certain, by Lincoln Kirstein. I think it was an intelligence job—was in an office—not amidst cloaks and daggers, but dignified by a military rank (major?). This I refused, on pacifist grounds."[100]

The call from the draft board did not come; they wanted men willing to serve in combat. In mid-May, Isherwood volunteered for an American Friends' ambulance unit in China, but he was told that only trained doctors and trained mechanics were eligible. In June 1942, he mailed his Form 47 to the draft board applying for conscientious objector status, 4-E, and had a medical exam.

The hostel was closing down, the refugees had been dispersed, and by early July, Isherwood was ready to leave Haverford for good. Auden was staying with Caroline Newton at her main residence in Berwyn, about eight miles from Haverford, so Auden and Isherwood saw each other three or four times before saying goodbye on July 6. They did not meet again until after the war, in January 1947, four and a half years later. On board his departing train, Isherwood wrote, "In spite of leaving behind so many people I'm fond of, I must admit that I'm wildly, indecently happy. My only thought is, I'm going back to the West. Hurrah. Hurrah..."[101]

LOS ANGELES; LAGUNA BEACH; TRABUCO, 1942

Because of the draft, Isherwood's future remained uncertain, so when he arrived in Los Angeles, he did not get a place of his own but stayed alternately with a friend in Beverly Hills, Peggy Rodakiewicz, and with Chris Wood, who had bought a new house about sixty miles south of Los Angeles in Laguna Beach. Gerald Heard had moved to Laguna with Wood.

Peggy Rodakiewicz was a beautiful socialite, coincidentally from Ardmore, Pennsylvania, next to Haverford. She was born Margaret Plummer, and her first husband had been Curtis Bok, a Quaker lawyer and judge from one of Philadelphia's most prominent families, publishers of *Ladies' Home Journal* and the *Saturday Evening Post*, philanthropists and pacifists. With Bok, Peggy had traveled to England, where she met Aldous and Maria Huxley and Gerald Heard, friendships which led to her becoming a devotee of Swami Prabhavananda. She had three children with Bok—the youngest, Derek, became a lawyer and a president of Harvard University. She divorced Bok in 1933, and married a Polish documentary filmmaker, Henwar Rodakiewicz, with whom she settled in Beverly Hills. This second marriage was breaking up in 1942. In July 1943, she was to marry a Los Angeles plastic surgeon, William Kiskadden, with whom she had a fourth child.

Isherwood had met Peggy Rodakiewicz through Heard when he first arrived in Los Angeles in 1939. "I think of her with the kind of love-hate I'd feel for a sister," he wrote in his diary. "In some ways, we are deeply alike. I think the most dominant of her characteristics is her bad conscience." In Isherwood's view, she was trying to repay the wealth and privilege of her first marriage by solving everyone's problems, but she expected those she helped to make good according to her standards. She had kept Isherwood's books and baggage at her house and forwarded his mail while he was in Haverford, encouraging him to "regard her place as my permanent home."[102]

"Being back in Los Angeles dazed me with joy," Isherwood wrote in his diary. "Had California always been like this? It seemed ten times more beautiful than ever."[103] He collected his car from storage in a garage on Sunset Boulevard, and he was soon seeing the Huxleys, Tony Bower, now stationed at an army camp in San Diego, and Denny Fouts, on leave from firefighting camp.

From Chris Wood's new house, 1 Rockledge Road, Laguna Beach, he visited Heard's nearby contemplative community, Trabuco, named after the wild canyon where it had been conjured from a dream while Isherwood was away in the East: "the buildings were there and inhabitable—a miracle in itself, considering that this was wartime." Heard's plan had been realized by Isherwood's cousin, Felix Greene, who had helped organize the La Verne Seminar. Greene, five years younger than Isherwood, had resigned from the BBC when the war started, to run a Quaker camp for conscientious objectors and to read Heard and the Bible and meditate.[104]

Trabuco was "a series of cloisters which mounted, in flights of steps, the slope of a little hill." Heard compared it to "a small Franciscan monastery in the Apennines." There was a bell tower, big wooden gates and red tile roofs, and a big circular meditation room with no windows. The outer courtyard was planted with fruit trees. From the cloisters, the ocean was visible, twenty miles away.

Isherwood was just as susceptible to the physical suggestion of architectural surroundings as he was to the human company he kept. This traditional monastic setting stole into his imagination almost unnoticed. The buildings offered sanctuary and calm where he was to retreat again and again for crucial intervals in the coming years.

He felt, though, that Felix Greene had built more than Heard had envisioned. Greene had "worked all winter, with his superhuman energy, collecting materials, bullying contractors, grabbing the last available supplies of wood and metal fixtures before the government froze them." Evidently, he possessed some of the qualities of the Victorian empire-builder that ran in the Greene and Fry clans. "The snug little anonymous retreat for four or five people, 'Focus,' had been swallowed up by 'Trabuco College,' which was capable of holding fifty. Already, Felix was talking of a printing press to issue pamphlets, and was planning next year's seminars."[105]

The requirements of leadership embarrassed Heard partly because he was, in Isherwood's phrase, "commuting regularly between Trabuco and Rockledge Road," where Chris Wood was hosting a "Very thin, very blond" young man called Paul Sorel, a painter and versifier, unstable and prone to "bursts of utterly irresponsible rage" which alternated with days of fasting, praying, and Mass-going. Heard "was jealous of his influence" over Wood. More problematic, "several members of the college knew and disapproved of Paul."[106]

Wood's house had been designed by the same architect as Trabuco, Garrett Van Pelt, but it offered a different kind of calm—luxurious, male, familial. Whereas Trabuco climbed up the landscape, the Laguna house plunged down a cliff, as if symbolically. "At first you see only the tiled roof of the house, below you, on the very edge of the cliff. It comes gradually into view as you descend the steps, terrace by terrace, past the oleander bushes and the pomegranates and the orange and scarlet zinnias." Balconies led to bedrooms where Wood and Heard slept, and a corkscrew staircase cut into rock led to Isherwood's bedroom. "The ocean is right at your feet, bubbling and creaming over huge lava reefs."

Isherwood would breakfast with Heard discussing "Vedanta, Trabuco, the difficulties of purgation, the failings of the Quakers and the Catholic doctrine of sin." At ten, Wood and Sorel would join them in bathrobes. At 11:15, they would swim; lunch was at one. "Gerald and myself inside the dining room, eating vegetables, served by Josephine, the ancient, skinny, talkative Irish cook; Chris and Paul outside on the terrace, taking their beer and sandwiches on two trays." There would be a walk or cycling in the afternoon. Tea at four. Tomato juice on the terrace at seven in the dark because they were banned by the wartime blackout from showing lights seaward.

On one walk, they "talked about the Bloomsbury group, and intellectuals in general." As émigrés from Bloomsbury, they continued to enjoy its characteristic privileges and freedom. In the living room at night, they might read aloud their manuscripts: Heard's crime stories; Wood's ghost stories; Isherwood's one-minute dramatic monologues which he wrote and tape-recorded in advance to entertain the others: "a man in a telephone booth, desperately calling the police, as gangsters close in to murder him; a homicidal madman in an asylum, talking to a visitor; a husband raging at an unfaithful and sulky wife."[107] Sometimes Wood played the piano, which he did to a professional standard.

From this ambivalent heaven, divided between metaphysical aspiration and sensual indulgence, even Wood was waiting to be exiled. He, too, was registered for the draft as a conscientious objector; he, too, expected to be sent to Civilian Public Service camp. This was the period when Isherwood made his first revision of the wartime diaries, "working at breakneck speed, like a dying man, because I expected the draft board's call to camp at any moment."[108] He was working on the entries written 1939 through summer 1942. The second revision, in 1946 when the war was over, was to include new material written after Haverford, up to the end of 1944.

This review of his life since arriving in the U.S. perhaps contributed to Isherwood's decision to apply to the draft board in late September "asking for 4-D reclassification" as a theological student instead of 4-E, conscientious objector, which he had already received. "Actually, if I were working with the Swami," he mused in his diary, "I should be a theological student within the meaning of the act."[109] His phrasing makes clear that he was looking for an authentic position, not a semantic loophole. He proposed to turn his spiritual quest into something like a job, with tasks that could begin and end: studying and discussing texts, learning rituals, assisting at ceremonies, editing, translating.

That September 1942, Isherwood attended another seminar, this time at Trabuco. He was taking up his spiritual quest where he had left off in the summer of 1941, when he had decided at La Verne that he had to do some social work before he could attempt the contemplative life. At the Trabuco seminar, there were nearly thirty people, many repeats from La Verne. Aldous Huxley also participated, commuting from Laguna with Heard and Isherwood. Isherwood recorded Heard's thoughts on prayer, and he used them years later nearly verbatim for Augustus Parr in "Paul."

After Huxley returned to L.A., Tony Bower and three other friends descended on Chris Wood's house: "over the light blue hills there came a noise of revellers, and it was Bacchus and his crew," wrote Isherwood. How well he knew from Heard's teaching that alcoholic intoxication was not a constructive way to alter the consciousness. "If only one could keep commuting! But that way lies destruction."

The very next day, Prabhavananda proposed by telephone to write a letter to the draft board supporting the application Isherwood had made for reclassification as a theological student, 4-D. "But first, he wanted me to assure him that I really intend to become a monk." Taken by surprise on the telephone, Isherwood agreed. However, he had questions, so he drove to Hollywood the next morning to talk to Prabhavananda. He wanted the tests of chastity and poverty, but not the lecturing and lunching with other devotees. "Swami waved my doubts aside. Of course—he said—I wouldn't be asked to do things I wasn't fitted for or wasn't inclined to do. 'Why,' he added, 'I would accept even an atheist if he would take the vow of chastity.' *If!*"[110]

Back Isherwood drove to Laguna, then back again on October 5, to stay with Peggy Rodakiewicz in Beverly Hills. He was still commuting; he still had not committed.

AS HE WAITED to hear from the draft board about his new classification, Isherwood started the first and most important of the many Vedanta literary projects he was to undertake at Prabhavananda's request over the next thirty years. The project, which Prabhavananda had already begun, was an English translation of the Bhagavad Gita, the Gospel of Hinduism, its most widely read sacred text, in which "incarnate God speaks to man," as they eventually put it in their Translators' Preface.[111] Bhagavad Gita means Song of God. It was probably composed between the fifth and second centuries B.C., and, early on, it became part of the epic poem called the Mahabharata, begun before the fifth century B.C.

Prabhavananda could not have chosen better war work for his pacifist disciple. The Mahabharata is about war—the protracted dynastic wars between the descendants of King Bharata in ancient India. The Bhagavad Gita is a long conversation that takes place on the decisive battlefield, Kurukshetra, just before the eighteen-day battle that made the virtuous Pandavas undisputed rulers of India and vanquished their evil cousins.

The warrior hero Arjuna asks his divine companion and charioteer, Lord Krishna, to drive him out onto the battlefield, into the space between the two armies. There, Arjuna sees the faces of his relatives in the enemy ranks and realizes that he cannot fight. He cannot kill his relatives any more than Isherwood could kill Germans who might include Heinz Neddermeyer. Arjuna asks Krishna to halt the chariot; he throws down his weapons and is overcome with sorrow and tears. In despair, he says (as Prabhavananda and Isherwood rendered it in their translation):

> Evil they may be,
> Worst of the Wicked,
> Yet if we kill them
> Our sin is greater.
> How could we dare spill
> The Blood that unites us?[112]

As Isherwood explained in a much reprinted essay "The Gita and War," "Krishna's reply to Arjuna occupies the rest of the book."[113] There on the battlefield, while the armies wait, Krishna reassures Arjuna that death is only an illusion; he teaches Arjuna to meditate so that Arjuna can "become indifferent to the results of all action, present or future";[114] and he reveals himself as God in all his terrible glory in order to prove his power and to show his love for Arjuna. The Bhagavad Gita, as Isherwood further explained, "deals not only with Arjuna's immediate personal problem, but with the whole nature of action, the meaning of life, and the aims for which man must struggle, here on earth." Like a forerunner of Hamlet—who, lacking a Krishna, converses with himself in soliloquies—Arjuna questions and learns until he understands himself and his universe. Only then can he act. "At the end of their conversation Arjuna has changed his mind. He is ready to fight. And the battle begins."[115]

Krishna persuaded Arjuna to fight, but he did not persuade Isherwood. In "The Gita and War," Isherwood argued against the view "that the Gita 'sanctions' War." This was a matter "of the greatest importance" to him as a pacifist. "The Gita neither sanctions war nor condemns it. Regarding no action as of absolute value, either for good or for evil, it cannot possibly do either."

Nevertheless, Isherwood demanded of the Gita that it be relevant to the unfolding world crisis. He worked on the translation from the autumn of 1942 until the winter of 1944, and it was probably February 1944, during tremendous fighting in Europe and the South Pacific, when he imagined "a similar dialogue taking place today," and asserted that "If the Gita has any validity, its reference is equally to this war and this very year."[116]

By inheritance, Isherwood was a member of the warrior caste, but he did not look on Krishna's advice to Arjuna as applying in any explicit sense to himself. Arjuna is more easily compared to Isherwood's father. "He corresponds to the medieval knight of Christendom," Isherwood wrote, the knight who passed down the code of the English gentleman by which Frank had lived and died. Krishna reminds Arjuna that he is from the warrior caste, and that it is his caste duty to fight, "to a warrior, there is nothing nobler than a righteous war. [. . .] if you refuse to fight this righteous war, you will be turning aside from your duty."[117]

Isherwood, who had once hoped that communism could improve the social order on earth, now argued that "spiritual growth" would result from accepting the caste system which "is presented as a kind of natural order" in the Gita. Each of the four castes, he explained, "has its peculiar duties, ethics, and responsibilities; and these must be accepted." Revolution was not possible, only incremental progress. "A man must go forward from where he stands. He cannot jump to the Absolute; he must evolve towards it."[118]

For himself, Isherwood sought to deviate from the pattern of his caste, to break the rigid code in which he was raised and to act according to his own nature. He was confident that his duty—his dharma—lay elsewhere.[119] He wrote about duty as something to be discovered only with difficulty, and not as something inescapably assigned by birth. "For the majority, much self-analysis, much trial and error, would seem to be the only way." And he used the word acceptance, not resignation: we must "accept the consequences of being ourselves. Only through this acceptance may we begin to evolve further." Still, he considered that there was always a choice between two ways of making an action: "The Christians call it 'holy indifference' and the Hindus 'non-attachment,'" he wrote. "Freed from fear and desire, he offers everything he does as a sacrament of devotion to his duty. All work becomes equally and vitally important. It is only towards the results of work that he remains indifferent."[120]

Since Isherwood never learned Sanskrit, he worked with Prabhavananda's existing, evidently crude, English version and discussed every nuance with Prabhavananda. In mid-October 1942, he wrote in his diary: "Some of the Sanskrit words have meanings that sound very bizarre in English, and the Swami, who has long since learnt to paraphrase them, has practically to be psychoanalyzed before he'll admit to the literal translation."[121] Thus, the would-be divinity student, who in March 1940 had disliked even the Sanskrit word "Om" for God, reached behind the language, seeking to make his new beliefs comprehensible and attractive to other Westerners.

It took Isherwood a year to finish a rough draft of the Gita translation. Then Peggy Rodakiewicz began offering criticisms which were both helpful and irritating, especially to Prabhavananda. In November 1943, there was "a really historic showdown," when she told them both, "It's dull and it's clumsy and it reeks of Sanskrit." She had already shown some of it to Huxley, who agreed with her. "It was an awful moment."[122]

Yet Isherwood wrestled new inspiration from this heavy blow. He took the manuscript to his room and struck out in a new direction, reimagining the whole rendered in a variety of verse forms and prose styles that could reflect its great range of voices and moods. When he showed the new opening to Prabhavananda and Rodakiewicz, all three of them became immensely excited by what he had done so far. Isherwood copied it into his diary:

> Krishna the changeless,
> Halt my chariot
> There where the warriors,
> Bold for the battle,
> Face their foemen.
> Between their armies
> There let me see them,
> The men I must fight with . . .[123]

Years later, he explained, "I had turned a passage of creaky antiquated prose into some lines of verse which were alliterated and heavily stressed in imitation of an Old English epic."[124] In fact, the lines recall the haunting drive of the poems that Auden had begun to write in the summer of 1927, aged twenty, just as he was discovering his poetic voice:

> I chose this lean country
> For seven day content,
> To satisfy the want
> Of eye and ear, to see
> The slow fastidious line
> That disciplines the fells . . .[125]

Auden had synthesized this voice from a wide array of models. That summer of 1927, he had moved on from the fragmenting influence of T.S. Eliot to the lyrical austerity of later Yeats, epitomised in the third part of Yeats's "The Tower."[126] Also, Auden had been studying the alliterative verse of Middle and Old English, and he had continued to be obsessed by the Icelandic sagas, about blood feuds between kinsmen in medieval Iceland.

These were the sagas he had persuaded Isherwood to read in 1926—*Burnt Njal*, *Gisli the Outlaw*, *Grettir's Saga*—and which had suggested how to write, in "Gems of Belgian Architecture" and *Paid on Both Sides*, about the feuding and fighting that surrounded them in wartime at prep school. Isherwood called the language "hybrid" because it combined "saga phraseology and schoolboy slang"; it was enigmatic and heroic and had the effect of intensifying emotion and distancing it at the same time.[127] This language of their school-saga world—their equivalent of Mortmere—had been irradiated with erotic energy, for it had been invented during the period when Auden fell in love with Isherwood and they had first gone to bed together.

In 1943, in the midst of another war, Isherwood rediscovered the linguistic excitement he had experienced with Auden and their school-saga world, and he drew on it for a new purpose. Their remembered boyish exuberance helped him bring to life with remarkable intimacy and informality the incarnation of his new God, Krishna, and the warrior hero Arjuna. While he was at it, he had in mind to best Yeats, student of Theosophy, author of poems about Krishna and Arjuna, and translator of the Upanishads. He dismissed Yeats's Upanishads in a letter to Kirstein: "Alas, like most readable translations, it is wildly inaccurate."[128] Prabhavananda and Isherwood's Bhagavad Gita was to be both readable and accurate.

The translation progressed "as if by magic." Isherwood felt he had "never worked so hard," but he felt, too, as if the work was part of a military exercise, such as he and Auden had trained for during their wartime schooling: "The whole thing seems to be already in my head: it's as though I'd been secretly assembling it there, like an invading army, all these months."[129]

"The result is a distinguished literary work," pronounced *Time* magazine after the Prabhavananda–Isherwood translation of the Gita was published at the end of 1944. It was "[s]impler and freer than other English translations." Long preliminary passages of epic poetry were compressed into a lucid narrative preamble, "Gita and Mahabharata," which invitingly set the scene for the dialogue between Krishna and Arjuna, and the esoteric details of Hindu cosmology were tucked into an orderly, brief Appendix.

Huxley contributed an introduction that shared themes with *The Perennial Philosophy*, the anthology-like volume he assembled to demonstrate his view that all religions share the same four fundamental doctrines and that these doctrines seem different only because they have been articulated at different moments in history in different languages and different cultural settings.

Observing that Heard, Van Druten, and Maugham as well as Huxley and Isherwood were gathered around Prabhavananda, the *Time* reviewer identified a school of expatriate English writers creating "a minor but noteworthy literary movement."[130] By 1945, Isherwood had begun co-editing the Vedanta Society magazine, *Vedanta and the West*, to which they all, apart from Maugham, contributed for free. Each had a unique literary identity, and each was traveling an individual spiritual path, but they were all pacifists, and as a group, their project was nothing less than to articulate and promote a universal religion that might help bring an end to world conflict.

AROUND THE TIME he began translating the Bhagavad Gita in the autumn of 1942, Isherwood took a job at Paramount adapting Maugham's novel *The Hour Before Dawn*, conceived as a propaganda piece for the Ministry of Information in Britain and published earlier that year. The story is set in the darkest hour of the war, after the British evacuation from Dunkirk, during the Blitzkrieg. It focuses on an upper-middle-class British military family not unlike Isherwood's, with a conscientious objector son. Isherwood was hired to articulate the conscientious objector's position, working with the screenwriter Lesser Samuels. But now that the U.S. was in the war, Paramount grew nervous about portraying a conscientious objector and ignored Isherwood's suggestions, instead presenting the conscientious objector as "a pathological 'case'" formed by earlier trauma. "We're not allowed, of course, to suggest that conscientious objection is 'right,'" Isherwood noted acidly. The script was rewritten by someone else.

Isherwood never heard anything more from the draft board. He decided to move into the Hollywood monastery as Prabhavananda's student anyway, even after the draft age was lowered again to thirty-seven and he, at thirty-eight, was no longer eligible to be drafted. The ideal of the monastery drew him, and he wanted to live according to his beliefs: "my life has been a mess and a lie, a messy lie," he wrote in his diary. He wanted to simplify and unify it.[131]

On the last day of 1942, he wrote a story, "The Wishing Tree," about the Kalpataru tree, mentioned in the earliest Sanskrit literature, a divine tree which grants all wishes. Most wish for money and power, according to "the rules of the world's wishing-game." The more their wishes are granted, the less they are satisfied. Only one boy recognizes that the tree is divine, the tree of life. This boy, viewed by his siblings as "'a bit of a saint,' by which they meant that he was a trifle crazy," never wishes for anything at all. "Nobody ever heard him say, 'I wish' or 'I want'—" The boy might be recognized as Ramakrishna or as any of his followers on the path to enlightenment.

Isherwood read his new story aloud to Heard, Wood, and Sorel in Laguna. "Paul, with his usual flair for malice, commented that it was 'very delicate.' It sure is," Isherwood cynically agreed. "You could blow it over with a Bronx cheer."[132] But he had not written it for them; it was for the Vedanta Society magazine, whose readers were more likely to appreciate the story's secret—not to wish, not to desire.

The day after Isherwood wrote "The Wishing Tree" was January 1, New Year's Day and also Kalpataru Day, the anniversary of the day in 1886 when Ramakrishna revealed himself to some of his non-monastic followers as a divine incarnation. He had been living in a suburb of Calcutta, at a place called Cossipore Garden House, where he was dying of throat cancer. While walking in the garden, he went into an ecstatic state, touching his followers and sending them, too, into altered states, giving some visions. By revealing himself in this way, Ramakrishna was preparing his followers for his death. One follower said that Ramakrishna had himself become the Kalpataru tree, hence the name Kalpataru Day. The time was approaching for Isherwood to give up desire.

BRAHMANANDA COTTAGE, HOLLYWOOD, 1943

Since 1929, Prabhavananda had lived in the Hollywood house of an American devotee, Carrie Mead Wyckoff, known as Sister Lalita or just Sister. She was nearly thirty-five years older than he and had begun to follow Ramakrishna in 1900 when her family in Pasadena had hosted Ramakrishna's disciple and missionary to the West, Vivekananda. Sister heard Prabhavananda lecture in San Francisco, asked to assist with his work and then offered her home at 1946 Ivar Avenue for a new Vedanta Center. Thus, they founded the Vedanta Society of Southern California. (When freeway construction turned the end of Ivar Avenue into a cul-de-sac in 1952, the street address was changed to Vedanta Place.)

Sister Lalita supported Prabhavananda with a monthly annuity and eventually deeded her house to the Vedanta Society. She was a widow and had lost her only child, a grown son, in an accident. Prabhavananda in a sense replaced him. By the time Isherwood arrived in California, Sister had donated more funds to build the Hollywood temple in her garden—a white stone onion-domed building resembling the Taj Mahal.[133]

In 1942, the Vedanta Society of Southern California bought a neighboring house, 1942 Ivar Avenue, and refurbished it to accommodate young men who wished to become monks. Isherwood described it as "a small, Spanish-style, stucco-walled house with a tiled roof." There were four bedrooms, a living room, two bathrooms, and a washroom. Prabhavananda named it Brahmananda Cottage, after his guru, widely acknowledged as Ramakrishna's spiritual son. He opened it on Brahmananda's birthday, February 6, 1943. It was usually referred to as "the monastery."

In *My Guru and His Disciple*, Isherwood remarked of Sister's house, the temple, and Brahmananda Cottage: "These three buildings could hardly have been less alike." The exterior of the temple, as Isherwood wrote to one friend, was "by far the most exotic thing about it. Inside, it is a very plainly decorated lecture hall, with a small inner room at one end which is used for meditation, and contains a shrine." Sister's house was American Craftsman style. The buildings "formed a kind of unit simply by being so close together."[134] It was not a conventional monastic setting like Trabuco.

The residents were also not conventional. Four men besides Isherwood moved into the Brahmananda Cottage monastery when it opened. Asit Ghosh, Prabhavananda's twenty-five-year-old nephew, was planning to be a film director, not a monk. He had been trapped in the U.S. by the war while studying cinematography at the University of Southern California. Isherwood described him as full of happy vitality, "lazy and wildly untidy," but also "charming."

George Fitts, a New Englander about the same age as Isherwood, was devoted to Prabhavananda and obsessively recorded everything he said, either in a notebook or with a tape recorder. He transcribed the tapes by typewriter, sometimes chanting loudly as he typed. He paid to have his room "walled off from the rest of the house" with a separate outside entrance. There he collected photographs of Ramakrishna, Holy Mother, Vivekananda, Brahmananda and Prabhavananda, also busts, statuettes, altar lights, incense, and withered flower offerings from the shrine. "George, in his own eccentric way, was very nearly a saint," observed Isherwood in his diary.

There were two teenagers, close friends, who were students at Hollywood High, "not the ideal place for would-be monks."[135] By mid-April, 1943, one had left.

Sister Lalita lived in the main house with a number of other women. Two became important friends to Isherwood. Helen Kennedy, a probationer nun given the Sanskrit name Sudhira, had first come to Ivar Avenue in her professional capacity as a nurse, and she often nursed Isherwood when he was ill. Isherwood considered Helen Kennedy to be "one of the most beautiful women I have ever met—in the same class as Garbo and Virginia Woolf. Her beauty wasn't so much in her features or her figure as in her manner, her voice, the way she carried herself: she was physically aristocratic." Tragedy hung over her; she had been widowed on the third day of her marriage to a flier killed in an accident. "I suppose that, within the limitations of our respective neuroses, we were in love with each other," Isherwood wrote in his diary in February 1943.[136] Helen Kennedy was the meaningful original of the Gerda Mannheim character in *The World in the Evening*, though her identity is partly disguised by that of the Haverford refugee Gretl Ebeling. As with so many fictional characters, Isherwood layered surface detail from one model over essential qualities in another he knew or cared about more deeply.

Ella Corbin was an Englishwoman, who came to Hollywood after the failure of her first marriage and was hired as a housekeeper by Sister Lalita and Swami Prabhavananda in the early 1930s. Prabhavananda gave her the Sanskrit name Amiya. "A marvellous cook and a born manager, she was jealous and bossy," wrote Isherwood, "she wanted to be undisputed mistress of the household." She, too, "must have been very pretty, but was now running to fat." Isherwood told his brother Richard in a letter that Amiya "startlingly resembles Mummy at moments!" In 1952, Amiya was to remarry, to George Montagu, the 9th Earl of Sandwich, twenty-eight years older than she, and to move back to England as the Countess of Sandwich.[137] She became friendly there with Kathleen and Richard.

"It seemed absurd to think of 1946 [Ivar] as a convent and of 1942 [Ivar] as a monastery in the ordinary sense of the words," Isherwood wrote in his wartime diary, "for how could nuns and monks be isolated from each other when they were living at such close quarters? In fact, the inmates of the Center were now like members of a family."[138] In some ways, the Swamitage, as the Bok children dubbed it, offered Isherwood a setting reminiscent of his itinerant childhood on army bases, at his grandfather's estate at Marple, and at his first boarding school, St. Edmund's—a variety of mismatched dwellings and communal spaces and a large number of women tending to the needs of a few men. Everything was operated on behalf of one all-important man at the top—Isherwood's father or grandfather, a commanding officer, a headmaster, and now Prabhavananda.

As he prepared during January and February 1943 to enter the monastery, Isherwood wrote several times in his diary about his hopes for one "last fling," "some wild, last-minute adventure,"[139] sexual, alcoholic—the adult version of the indulgences his mother had offered him in the theaters, sweet shops and toy shops of London before his boarding-school terms. He finished advising on *The Hour Before Dawn* on January 29. He was staying with Peggy Rodakiewicz in Beverly Hills, and he grew anxious that she would interfere in his new life by communicating privately with Prabhavananda, just as his mother had done with his headmasters and teachers when he was a schoolboy, "passing hints to the Swami on the telephone, or getting him up here to lunch for a 'good talk' about my case. I've already had a violent row with her on this subject."

Returning to institutional life, the life he had feared and hated in childhood, was a dreadful test. "I'm scared that I may behave badly and possessively about my books," he wrote in his diary, "the last belongings I cling to." And he feared his fellow monastics would disturb his writing. For he was ready to get back to writing in earnest: "Above all, I'd like to get started on the first of the stories I've planned—the one about Berthold Viertel and Gaumont-British."[140]

In the end, the last fling was a double scoop. He had lunch at the Brown Derby with Viertel, who disapproved "with all the jealousy of his fatherly affection and his liberalistic Marxism" of Isherwood's move to the monastery: "what am I doing with this old, unfashionable Indian stuff? What relation can it possibly have to America and 1943?" Then he spent an evening at a gay nightclub, Café Gala on Sunset Strip, with Chris Wood and another friend. "My farewell visit to the End of the Night," Isherwood called it as he wallowed in the tawdry luxe of the evening while describing it in detail in his diary. It reminded him of "all the other times." He was equally nostalgic about the beach in Santa Monica, itemizing the beloved sights and smell of the honky-tonk scene. "Goodbye. Goodbye. I shall see you often—but differently, I suppose."[141]

In *My Guru and His Disciple*, he was to recall a Gothic fantasy—partly inspired by *The Garden of Allah*, Robert Hichens's 1904 Sahara Desert romance about a renegade Trappist monk—of being snatched from the world "Against my will" by the monks: "They are all inside, in the shadows, cowled and black-robed, waiting for me. Within a moment, they have stripped me of my clothes and forcibly robed me. I stammer the irrevocable vow."[142]

The move to Ivar Avenue proved to be an anticlimax. The world did not end. There was a puja (a ceremony of worship) to dedicate the newly refurbished cottage. Prabhavananda wore his orange robes, the monks their Sunday suits, and "Peggy came, in her smartest clothes, like a mother to a prizegiving at her son's school." Prabhavananda marked the occasion by jettisoning "Mr. Isherwood" for "Chris"—"he pronounced it 'Krees,'" Isherwood later recalled; he himself began to refer to Prabhavananda as

"Swami" instead of "the Swami." After the reluctance, the fear, the self-pity, and the excitement came . . . "Nothing. As a matter of fact, my subconscious hasn't even cocked an eyebrow or twitched an ear, yet," Isherwood pronounced two whole days after moving in.[143]

Neither he nor any of the other monks had taken any vows yet. In Vedanta, there is a five-year probationary period before the first ones, brahmacharya. Still, "there is a very real discipline and routine here, though it is all self-imposed," as he reported to his brother Richard. "Everything is built around the hours of worship in the shrine room of the temple—seven to eight, twelve to one, six to seven. The food we eat is taken there and offered to the Lord first." Knowing Richard to be obsessively literal-minded and anxious about rules and religion, Isherwood emphasized the relaxed decorum of his new life: "people talk about God without the least embarrassment from morning till night, and often jokingly."[144]

FOR ISHERWOOD THE shrine was very important. "Sure, God is everywhere," he wrote to Richard, "but nearly all of us [. . .] need the concentration, the essence of God's presence, in a shrine."[145] Long before arriving at the monastery, Isherwood had begun to develop a relationship with the Hollywood shrine that might be compared to the relationships he developed with his closest friends or with characters as he prepared to write about them: "there is such a sense of contact. Like sitting face to face with someone you know very well, and not having to speak." He had long feared spending the night alone. In the monastery, he slept alone in his cell, but he took the shrine for his companion: "The fact of its being there, always, right in the midst of our household. It's particularly wonderful at night. You feel so safe there."[146]

In the monastery, love and acceptance combined with absorbing new tasks and intelligent companionship alleviated Isherwood's guilt, panic attacks, and mood swings. "So let's, at worst, agree that it's a reasonably efficient mental clinic," he told Kirstein.[147] To Kirstein, he described the midday ceremony that he was learning to perform, tagging connections to Christian rituals familiar from his Anglican childhood and to a broader cultural context:

> One sees where the Mass comes from, and the Corn King and the Spring Queen, and every sort of magic the South Seas are full of. You project God out of yourself into pictures and images and symbols, then call on him to transform you, finger by finger, leg by leg, into himself; and then you have lunch together. It takes nearly two hours, offering flowers, pouring water into bowls, ringing bells and waving incense-sticks.

The Corn King and the Spring Queen is a historical novel by Naomi Mitchison, a Scottish writer friend of Auden and Heard. Mitchison borrowed mythology about pre-Christian fertility rites from *The Golden Bough*, James Frazer's massive comparative study of early religions. These ancient rites in which the king or god must die and be reborn (often digested or planted for fertility) were the kind that Auden had had in mind when he wrote *The Fronny* and *The Dance of Death*. With the phrase "every sort of magic the South Seas are full of," Isherwood alluded to shamanic practices symbolizing death and rebirth among the Stone Age tribes that had been the subject of John Layard's South Sea studies before World War I and which Layard had written up in a book, *Stone Men of Malekula* (1942).[148]

Performing the worship bound Isherwood into the present moment even as it carried him out of himself—like acting and like writing. As he repeated the ceremony again and again, he brooded on the many mythologies that shared common ground with Vedanta, and he made physical the deep processes of the imagination which, throughout his career, had produced some of his best writing. In creating his characters—for instance, Sally Bowles, Mr. Norris, Bernhard Landauer—Isherwood projected his own "gods," his characters, out of himself "into pictures and images and symbols," just as he told Kirstein he did in the temple ritual. He identified with his "gods" over the course of his narratives, transforming himself into them, "finger by finger, leg by leg." Then he differentiated himself again by the end of his stories and broke away. In *Prater Violet*, Isherwood was to project his character Friedrich Bergmann in exactly this way. Five weeks after moving into Brahmananda Cottage, Isherwood told Kirstein that he had, at last, begun the story about writing *Little Friend* with Berthold Viertel. This was his first attempt since emigrating to pick up the threads of his earlier imaginative life, and Viertel was right there in California, giving new life to the notes Isherwood had made a decade earlier. He and Viertel—the real-life Bergmann—often met for lunch or supper.

Isherwood was now trying to frame a relationship between his identity as a writer and his identity as a monk, but before long, he would discover a fundamental conflict between the uniqueness of his writing personality and the aim, in Vedanta, to give up the ego. This conflict would push him gradually to forge a path partly inside and partly outside Vedanta, with certain writing tasks discharging his commitment to Vedanta, others discharging a commitment to his art. For the time being, he continued to argue vehemently and resourcefully that the two vocations were one and the same. In letters to friends and strangers, he placed the active life on one side, the contemplative life on another, and asserted that his vocation as a writer was part of the contemplative life he was now pursuing. As a pacifist in wartime, he felt a constant, unrelenting pressure to defend his position; he never stopped thinking about how best to formulate it, often simplifying, sometimes exaggerating, to give clarity and weight for those who could not understand him or agree with him.

Even Forster, unique among Isherwood's English friends in expressing no extreme surprise or disagreement with Isherwood's new life, empathized less as the war worsened and their circumstances became increasingly different. Forster's long-term lover, the policeman Bob Buckingham, had volunteered that spring, 1943, as engineer on a bomber, greatly distressing Forster and Buckingham's wife and son; then at the last minute, he was rejected because of his eyesight and had to satisfy himself with pulling victims from bombed-out buildings and fiery, collapsing rubble in London, still alarmingly dangerous. Isherwood lamely tried to cheer Forster up from his safe distance: "those who are always volunteering and plunging ahead tend to survive," he wrote.

He described his new religious activities to Forster with a self-conscious wish to ingratiate them, relying on the fact that Forster had lived in India and written about it. "I understand your ritual and drag easily," Forster assured him, but he stubbornly demurred from Isherwood's trust in God. "I do not understand your feeling that God will help you—i.e. I don't ever feel that I shall ever be thus helped myself. When I was so upset about Bob's being taken from me, I seemed to go through it all alone."

Isherwood tried again. He remembered that Forster had confided some years earlier about "one curious episode: the sacrificial burning of a number of short stories in 1922 in order that a Passage to India might get finished." Isherwood saw this ritual propitiation as evidence that Forster *did* believe in some kind of help from God. "You half sarcastically acknowledged its existence when you burnt those stories in order to get on with The Passage to India," he pointed out.[149] The argument about God was to continue between them in subsequent letters.

AFTER THREE MONTHS in the monastery, Isherwood wondered, "Have I made progress?" He had performed the ritual about eighteen times. "Nearly always, I at least manage to get a great sense of *responsibility*. Here am I, with all my karma upon me, presenting myself before the unthinkable majesty of God's throne. 'I'm sorry, Sir. I was the only one they could find to send.'"

Ten days later, he was managing without notes, though he forgot a symbolic hand gesture over the food and "a whole chunk of the purification ceremony slipped right out of my mind" along with "the prayer for the liberation of earthbound spirits and all the precautions against psychic obstacles."[150]

It was spring in California, and he was thinking more and more about sex; his concentration was lapsing. "I'm going through an ebb-tide phase," he wrote on May 22. "I must watch myself, or I shall be apt to grab some excuse for leaving Ivar Avenue altogether—such as an order from the draft board." Any excuse might permit him to return to sex, which he was picturing "in entirely promiscuous terms: I've no desire whatever for any kind of relationship."

As he explained to Caroline Norment, he didn't have to break off friendships while living at Ivar Avenue. "I go out and visit people when I have time—though that isn't so often!—and all kinds of visitors are with us continually." At Rockledge Road, he found the atmosphere "bad and squalid" and felt "shaken and insecure" away from the monastery. He stayed with the Huxleys at their ranch in Llano on the edge of the Mojave Desert and with John Van Druten and his boyfriend Carter Lodge at their ranch near Indio in the Coachella Valley; he went to parties at the Viertels'; walked with Greta Garbo; lunched with Peggy Rodakiewicz and with Dodie Smith and Alec Beesley. But, as he also reported to Norment, "About celibacy, yes, there is a vow—a conditional one, which can be terminated after three years; and a lifelong one, which is made after ten, when one becomes a full-fledged monk and presumably takes up some kind of ministry."[151]

For a man who craved intimacy, both intellectual and physical, celibacy was a gigantic challenge. Isherwood's daily life focused more and more on managing his sexual energy, changeable as quicksilver, no sooner extinguished than raging like a wildfire. His dynamic investment in the shrine, his acting out and memorizing of the ritual, his platonic love affairs with Sudhira, Amiya, Peggy Rodakiewicz, the distance he adopted from the Wood–Sorel–Heard ménage, all evidenced the struggle with his libido. Even books became a battleground. "I am reading and thinking often of Yeats, just now: he represents a most elegant kind of sexual sublimation," he wrote in March. The Yeats was the "Chorus from *Oedipus at Colonus*" in *The Tower*. During a bout of flu, he read Arthur Waley's translation of the Chinese novel *Monkey*, Edwin Arnold's *The Light of Asia*, about Buddha, and Buddhist writings from an anthology by Lin Yutang which made him feel "very strongly, we must not rave against the body. It is *not* a lump of corrupt filth, it is *not* evil. It is our faithful, loyal servant, in sickness and in health."[152]

His reading was mostly translations, consulted while he worked on the Bhagavad Gita with Prabhavananda. As his cerebral self worked to translate Sanskrit into English, Isherwood's physical self struggled to translate sexual energy into spiritual energy. He was trying to reverse the powerful urge toward sexual liberation that had carried him to Berlin in 1929. In the Berlin days, he had come to believe that repressing his sexuality had made him ill.

In the monastery, he repressed his sexuality in hopes of a higher kind of liberation, and it was to make him ill all over again in due course.

In the midst of his struggle, Tennessee Williams arrived in L.A. with an introduction from New York friends, and Isherwood rebuffed him. Like two heroes in Walter Scott, they only traded blows and took the measure of one another at first, but they were destined to draw close.

Williams had a script job at MGM, a lingering cough, and no friends; he was longing for companionship. He had just read *Goodbye to Berlin*. Isherwood "interests me profoundly," he had written in his notebook before they met. "Sally Bowles a brilliant study. A new something in it." Williams imagined he had found a twin, a better self: "Isherwood seems strangely like me—his mind, his attitude. Only clearer, quieter, firmer. A better integrated man."[153]

Williams took Isherwood to lunch at the Brown Derby, and his intense identification continued. To the mutual friend who had suggested they meet, Williams reported: "I recognized him at once, just by instinct, and he does look just the way I imagine myself to look—it was funny." It had not occurred to Isherwood that he and Williams, seven years younger, made any kind of pair: "He's a strange boy," he wrote after their meeting, "small, plump and muscular, with a slight cast in one eye; full of amused malice."[154]

To his notebook Williams confided, "he has ignored me since the one meeting, in spite of a letter I sent him. It was foolishly done, the letter. But I wanted someone to be with and talk to So badly."[155] Next, Williams dropped by what he called the "seraglio" at Ivar Avenue, interrupting an evening lesson from Swami on karma yoga. Isherwood suggested a walk, and Williams told a friend that "he was nearly as relieved as I was to escape the overpowering atmosphere of outraged sanctity which my entrance had evoked," but he also remarked that "Herr Issyvoo is not one to speak very frankly all that he is thinking or feeling." Still, he found him "charming."[156]

Isherwood reported the scene slightly differently to Kirstein, mentioning that Williams had a New York friend in tow. He had wished to scare Williams away or to disappear himself—"It was one of those times when one wishes one had two heads, or none."[157]

Isherwood persisted in protecting his monastic discipline, but Williams would not accept a brush-off and wrote again: "Ordinarily I only like people who like me (vanity, you know) but the attachment and sympathy I felt for Herr Issyvoo in Berlin has even withstood the intensely Anglican cold-shoulder which he has given me in Hollywood." Isherwood replied: "I don't quite know how to convince you that I 'like' you. Ordinarily, I should have solved the problem by asking you out to dinner and getting very drunk. I haven't been a monk long enough to know how to convey the same impression on CocaCola. Forgive me." He resented being expected to impersonate a fictional self left behind in a book; he was trying to become someone else: "I suspect that the truth is that you don't really want to see me: you want to see Mr. Issyvoo, and I can't produce him."

Then Isherwood challenged Williams, as if to a duel: "I'll meet you whenever you like, if you're sure you want to. But what are we going to talk about? I'm not really interested in anything except this place and this kind of life and what they imply; shouldn't I bore you to death?"[158]

Just as Isherwood seemed about to career off his spiritual path, Prabhavananda, alert to Isherwood's state, was called away to another Vedanta Center, so he invited Isherwood to move into his bedroom. "I am very conscious of his presence here—[...] It will help me a great deal," Isherwood wrote. The too-close quarters in Brahmananda Cottage had begun to rattle him, especially because a new arrival, a lapsing Roman Catholic priest, was openly conducting a romance with a young woman. "Hardly any trouble since I've been in Swami's room."[159]

When Prabhavananda returned, the extraordinary connection with Isherwood was immediately reestablished: "'Love' is too possessive a word to describe it. It is really absence of demand, lack of strain, entire reassurance," wrote Isherwood. The dynamic between them was both loving and teasing, affectionate and coldly realistic: "He touched my cheek with his finger and giggled, because *The New Republic* had referred to me as a prominent young writer. I told him how free I'd been from sexual thoughts and fantasies during the past weeks, and he said, 'Yes, I saw that in your face yesterday. But don't get too confident. They will come back.'"

Within only a few days, during a special all-night puja in the temple, Isherwood was swept by storms of lust that made him long to give up Vedanta and pacifism and "get into a uniform and be the same as everybody else," as he recorded in his diary. "I really wouldn't care what happened to me, I thought, provided I could spend a few more rousing Saturday nights."[160]

He was hanging on by a thread—almost literally. During meditation, he was relying on the mechanical task of telling the beads on his rosary. As he explained in *My Guru and His Disciple*, the Vedanta rosary has 108 beads, plus a separated bead with a tassel which represents the guru. "Repeating your mantram is called making *japam*. When making japam with your rosary, you repeat your mantram once for each bead. On reaching the tassel bead, you reverse the rosary and start it the other way around."[161] The devotee makes one hundred repetitions for his or her own spiritual progress, and eight for mankind. It was like the knitting his father had done in wartime, a stitch-by-stitch shaping of time, when circumstances seemed unbearable. To his diary,

Isherwood confided, "If you ask me what I want, I reply: Sex, followed by a long long sleep. If offered a painless drug which would kill me in my sleep, I would seriously consider taking it."

In August, he made it to a watershed: "six months at Ivar Avenue, six months of technical celibacy. Last year, that achievement would have seemed positively supernatural. Now I see it as the very first step."[162] He was determined to stretch himself much further.

BUT FIRST, IN mid-August 1943, Isherwood took a ten-day break. He moved into a rented room at 206 Mabery Road, across the street from the Viertels in Santa Monica Canyon and just below the house on Adelaide Drive where he was later to live with Bachardy. From there, he tracked down Tennessee Williams at 1600 Ocean Avenue, opposite Santa Monica Pier, "a very squalid rooming house called The Palisades," as Isherwood recounted in his diary. "We had supper together on the pier and I drank quite a lot of beer and talked sex the entire evening."[163]

Williams told his friend and publisher James Laughlin that they discussed writing a play together: "Isherwood has temporarily withdrawn from his monastery and become a fellow beach-comber. I am trying to agree with him upon a subject for dramatic collaboration—"[164]

Since being rebuffed, Williams had tapped his sense of twinship with Isherwood and his admiration for *Sally Bowles* in a story about a writer and his fantasist, feminine alter ego. He wrote it in June when he was supposed to be busy with his studio job—adapting someone else's bad novel as a star vehicle for Lana Turner. On his MGM stationery, Williams had reported to Isherwood that he was secretly working on "'Portrait of a Girl in Glass' about my sister" while Turner was "galloping madly up and down the corridor beyond my locked office door." From "Portrait of a Girl in Glass" Williams was to develop his play *The Glass Menagerie* which made him famous two years later, in March 1945, when it opened on Broadway.[165]

Isherwood decided to end his spiritual vacation and return to the monastery at once, "two days earlier than I'd intended," following a sex adventure. He said little more in his wartime diary, but according to an account he wrote in the 1970s, he was swimming with his trunks around his neck when a man came along the beach, took off his own trunks, swam out and groped him; they laughed together, and Isherwood became aroused but resisted having an orgasm until he was alone at home.[166] This proved to be a critical incident in eventually breaking down his commitment to celibacy. He hurried back to the monastery on what happened to be his thirty-ninth birthday, performed the worship and slept near the shrine rather than expose himself to the temptation of any other kind of birthday celebration.

In the wartime diary, he mentioned that the swimmer in his sex adventure was a deaf mute—unable to kiss and tell.[167] This makes a meaningful contrast to Williams, with whom Isherwood also went swimming. Williams was articulate and outspoken, and he had been pressing during the summer to be allowed to write a piece about Isherwood's new life as a monk. Isherwood knew he couldn't handle the scrutiny. "You are welcome to write down your impressions of this place, of course," he had told Williams by letter. "But I can't collaborate. However 'fair' and 'respectful' the account might be, it would still have the fatal distortion of self-advertisement: ISHERWOOD and Vedanta—instead of VEDANTA and isherwood."[168]

Williams had intended the piece for James Laughlin. Eventually, in November 1943, Isherwood met with Williams and Laughlin for lunch, but the piece was never written. Isherwood had managed to silence Williams and to prevent his story being hijacked by another professional storyteller; thus, Williams proved as safe as the deaf-mute swimmer. Conceivably, the deaf-mute swimmer was Isherwood's disguise for Williams in his carefully censored wartime diaries. For the encounter with Williams was the real challenge to Isherwood's celibacy and, more important, to his life in the monastery.

In a 1985 interview, Armistead Maupin asked Isherwood if he and Williams had gone to bed together. "Yes, but that was actually neither here nor there. [...] It was not a big deal; we just found each other very sympathetic, and went to bed together two or three times, I imagine." After Isherwood's death, Edmund White reported that Isherwood told him of a love affair with Williams in the 1940s "when we were both still rather presentable." However, in Key West in November 1954, Bachardy heard Williams tell how Isherwood rebuffed a pass, most likely on the August night that Isherwood had tracked down Williams in his rooming house on Ocean Avenue: "When they were sitting side by side on a small cot, Tennessee had managed to pull Chris down in a kissing embrace. 'This won't do,' quoted Tennessee as he imitated Chris quickly pulling himself up."[169]

Sometime after 1946, Isherwood gave Williams a glamorous photograph of himself with an inscription recalling their wartime intimacy: "For Tennessee, to remind him of those black out nights on Sta Monica Pier." In Key West in 1954, Williams made a return presentation, to both Isherwood and Bachardy, of a self-portrait painted during their visit.[170] Later still, Williams gave Isherwood his copy of Robert Louis Stevenson's *A Child's Garden of Verses*, "the one his mother used to read to him from, when he was a child." The gift reflected the purity of the sentiment Williams came to feel toward

Isherwood, and which he described in his *Memoirs*: "There was an almost sentimental attachment between us but it didn't come to romance: instead, it turned into a great friendship, one of the continuing friendships in my life, and one of the most important ones."[171]

ONE EVENING DURING Isherwood's vacation from the monastery, Berthold Viertel took him to meet Bertolt Brecht and Brecht's actress wife Helene Weigel. Hanns Eisler "the Red composer" was also there. "I liked Brecht immediately," wrote Isherwood in his diary, but they did not become friends.

Isherwood had translated the poems in Brecht's Dickensian novel *Dreigroschenroman* when it appeared in English as *A Penny for the Poor* (1937) with the main prose text translated by Desmond Vesey. Brecht looked on Isherwood with greedy ambition as a possible English translator for upcoming work. They met three more times over the next few days, including at a big party at the Viertels', where a heavy political-philosophical discussion began in front of a large gathering: "Eisler attacked what he calls 'religion' (he means clerical politics) and I had to defend 'pacifism,'" Isherwood recorded. "It was silly and futile. I felt like a fake."[172]

In September, after Isherwood had returned to the monastery, he and Viertel again went to dinner at the Brechts', where Viertel raised the subject of Vedanta, and, as Isherwood recorded: "Brecht fairly blew his top. To him, it's all fascism and superstitious nonsense. Frau Brecht joined in—like a Salvation Army lass—calling on me to repent and remember my duty as a revolutionary writer." Viertel "tried to suggest that it was only temporary; that, in fact, I might be regarded as a sort of spy in the enemy's camp. If only—after two or three years—I'd write a book 'showing up' mysticism once and for all, then my retirement would have been well worth while." Isherwood, with his endless social resourcefulness, took the attack as funny until it focused on Huxley, who wasn't there. "Brecht said he was 'verkauft'—had sold out. I was so angry that I nearly got up and left the house at once. I *did* leave very shortly afterwards."

Summing up in his diary, Isherwood revealed his great admiration for Huxley's integrity, attested by Huxley's lack of a personal agenda. By contrast, Brecht wished to forward only himself and his own projects. "He's just as arrant an individualist as I am, and pretty much of an opportunist, too."[173]

The episode gave rise to agonizingly apologetic letters between Viertel and Isherwood, Viertel claiming that affection had motivated Brecht's "bitter fight for your soul [. . .] even if he should lose an ideal translator." For his own part, Viertel did not want to lose one of the last friends "who connects me with these ominous years since 1933," despite the fact that he objected to

Isherwood's decision to enter the monastery. Viertel pronounced the argument about political revolution and the inner life as "the great struggle of our time being fought between *friends* in this room—and, as I felt, the battleground was your heart, your sensibility (and mine too)." Thus, Viertel, with his gift for seeing the universal in the particular, introduced in his 1943 letter the agon that Isherwood was to place at the heart of *Prater Violet*, the novel ostensibly about events that had occurred ten years earlier. Viertel went on, in the letter, to offer the unconditional love which Isherwood was to portray in his conclusion to the novel and which had grown up between them during the elapsed decade: "Would I stop you if I could? I have to answer with 'yes.' You see, love does answer without hesitation, so does conviction. But I cannot stop you. I can only wish you the very best, fullheartedly. [. . .] My feeling for you is unchanged."[174] This was the kind of friendship Isherwood had looked for elsewhere, from Spender, for instance, and felt disappointed.

Brecht had indeed lost a translator. Accusing Huxley of selling out was, in Isherwood's view, "denunciation" not discussion, as he told Viertel and also wrote in his diary.[175] The following spring, Brecht visited Isherwood at the monastery and spent a whole hour asking him to translate *The Caucasian Chalk Circle*, Brecht's version of Klabund's 1925 play, *The Circle of Chalk*, adapted from the Chinese. "He is an expert wheedler, and I nearly gave way," wrote Isherwood.[176]

ALL THROUGH AUGUST and September 1943, Isherwood battled with sexual urges and a growing feeling of being trapped. He wrote to the draft board to see if he could join the Army Medical Corps, "My only visible means of escape from this place," but he no longer expected his age group to be drafted, and nothing came of the query.

He turned increasingly to his friendship with Denny Fouts who had been discharged from CPS camp after being accused of bringing in liquor and marijuana and who was sharing a nonstop party house in Silver Lake while studying for his high school diploma. "Being with Denny unsettles me," wrote Isherwood in his diary, "and yet I need him more than ever before, because he's the only person who can view my life as a whole, and therefore the only one who can give me any valuable advice."[177]

On September 20, Isherwood had another sexual encounter with a swimmer on the beach in Santa Monica, and the next day Pete Martinez came to town on leave from the army. Isherwood surrendered to the flesh and spent the night with Martinez in a cubicle at the Pershing Square Turkish bath. Two days later, Martinez invited Isherwood to Long Beach to spend another night together and to meet his family, recently relocated there. They ate tacos, drank tequila and smoked. Martinez's sisters sang Mexican songs, Isherwood read poetry aloud. "I felt like quite a different version of myself—Pete's Christopher," Isherwood wrote, knowing he was substituting worship of Martinez for the worship he might otherwise have been doing at Ivar Avenue. "The whole legend, the whole cult of Pete which Lincoln has established, made the room into a sort of shrine, with Pete himself cross-legged in the middle of the floor, a minor but authentic deity."[178]

Isherwood was referring to a particular legend created by Kirstein in a romantic memoir co-authored by Martinez and based on stories about Martinez's family. The memoir was titled *For My Brother*, alluding to Martinez's renegade elder brother, who died after an accident on a construction site near Mexico City. Isherwood adored the book and helped persuade Lehmann to publish it in England at the Hogarth Press. According to Kirstein's biographer, Martin Duberman, Isherwood even worked on the manuscript, cutting it drastically and transforming it from a memoir into a novel. He also tried to find a U.S. publisher, praising the book to Tennessee Williams and James Laughlin among others. The memoir proved to him that Kirstein was a far better prose writer than poet, a theme to which Isherwood gingerly returned in letters to Kirstein.[179]

On the last night of Martinez's leave, Isherwood returned to Long Beach with Fouts and two other friends, and they drank and stayed up all night at a bathhouse. Prabhavananda decided it was time to send Isherwood traveling on Vedanta business: "I'm glad to be getting away from Ivar Avenue, which is verging on an eruption," Isherwood wrote in his diary at the end of September. He was headed to the Vedanta centers in San Francisco, Portland, and Seattle. In Portland, he was to assist at a three-day Durga Puja and to attend the laying of a foundation stone for a temple at the Vedanta retreat outside the city in Scappoose. "Amidst my baggage is one unusual article," he told a friend, "a copper tray for use in the Hindu fire ceremony which has to be performed when a new shrine or house is opened."[180]

Isherwood's pathway was itself on fire. At Ivar Avenue, his fellow monastics were having problems with sex, drugs, insomnia, fainting fits, tears. He had written in his diary in late August:

> ... mustn't there be something radically wrong with this place, if everybody is so hysterical? But that objection arises from the fallacy that the aim of religion is to make you happy in a worldly sense. It isn't. The death of the Ego was never supposed to be pleasant; and this misery may really mean that we are getting ahead with it. So let the squeezing process go on, as long as we can take it.[181]

At the other centers, he was impressed by the Indian swamis, describing them variously in his diary as intelligent, ambitious, charming, tyrannical, joyful, joking, hardworking. He was less impressed by the American probationer monastics, including a man called Al Clifton, "the only real monk in the whole of American Vedanta," who had "actually taken the first vow, of brahmacharya." Clifton seemed to Isherwood "nice, but somehow *crushed*." The three-day puja simply overwhelmed Isherwood: "An avalanche of flowers, fruit, sandal paste and six-armed sacred pictures has been pouring down between me and Ramakrishna. No—it's better not dwelt on."[182]

He recorded in his diary that the train ride from San Francisco to Portland was "the nicest part of the trip, so far" because he fell in love with Charlotte Brontë's heroine Jane Eyre. Huxley had written dialogue for a screen adaptation at 20th Century–Fox, and Isherwood wanted to read the novel before he saw the film. He had evidently forgotten reading *Jane Eyre* in 1921, when he told his mother that it did not have "half the power of Emily's *Wuthering Heights*." It made a stronger impression now: "she's one of my favorite characters in fiction. I *so* understand her when she says, 'I never in my life have known any medium in my dealings with positive, hard characters, antagonistic to my own, between absolute submission and determined revolt.'"[183]

Jane slaves reluctantly to learn Hindustani so she can help her cousin St. John Rivers prepare to go to India as a Christian missionary, and she even agrees to accompany him, but she revolts against his insistence that they marry. "I am ready to go to India," Jane tells him, "if I may go free." She clings to her identity and her inner life: "I cannot marry you and become part of you." She cannot become Mrs. St. John Rivers; she must remain Jane Eyre.

Prabhavananda had proven he did *not* have a positive, hard character, yet suddenly Isherwood, traveling alone on his mission to the other centers, dreaded something inescapable might be delivered to him through this most flexible of men. "A sudden gust of aversion and fear that Swami will give me a Sanskrit name," he wrote.[184] A Sanskrit name would absorb his identity into the culture in which he still felt so uncomfortable and obliterate him as an individual.

He was to fictionalize his anxiety in the concluding interior monologue of *Prater Violet*. Walking home after a late party beside Friedrich Bergmann, at "that hour of the night at which man's ego almost sleeps," the Christopher Isherwood character feels "The sense of identity, of possession, of name and address and telephone number" grow "very faint." Without mention of Vedanta or a monastery, his character envisions the escape Vedanta seemed to offer from the fears that had pursued him since childhood, from loneliness and from the failure of love: "how infinitely faint, how distant, like the high far glimpse of a goat track through the mountains between the clouds, I see something else: the way that leads to safety. To where there is no fear, no loneliness, no need of J, K, L, or M. For a second I glimpse it."[185]

Here again was the "rough zig-zag goat track" along which Isherwood's 1930s Paul character struggles in Greece, and the "crazy goat-track which is to lead over the peaks of the never-never mountains" which Isherwood had used to explain his new beliefs to Upward in his 1939 letter. The image of the distant, ascending path also evokes the concluding chapters of a novel he had recently reread, Rudyard Kipling's *Kim*, in which Kim, the Dickensian orphan of Lahore, torn between his Indian upbringing and his white Irish patrimony, a gifted speaker in both Hindustani and English, a British secret agent in the Great Game with Russia, climbs up into the Himalayas with the Tibetan lama who is his guru and adopted father figure on their long, shared walk to enlightenment.[186]

But when the Isherwood character glimpses the high goat track in *Prater Violet*, "the clouds shut down, and a breath off the glacier, icy with the inhuman coldness of the peaks, touches my cheek." The escape route, for him, is impossible: "'No,' I think, 'I could never do it. Rather the fear I know, the loneliness I know . . . For to take that other way would mean that I should lose myself. I should no longer be a person. I should no longer be Christopher Isherwood.'"[187]

His personal identity, embodied in his name, stood between Isherwood and enlightenment. So did his need for an intimate sexual relationship.

"THERE'S BEEN A lot more trouble with sex," Isherwood wrote in his diary toward the end of 1943. As the discipline of celibacy crumbled, he focused on telling the truth. "The other day, Swami said to me, 'Do you know what purity is, Chris? Purity is telling the truth.'"[188] This was the essence of Isherwood's life as a writer, and it was to become the chief way in which he could honor his commitment to Ramakrishna.

In his wartime diary, he reported that in March 1944, he started to fall in love "with someone whom I'll call X." It was the same convention he used in *Prater Violet*, identifying his lovers by letters of the alphabet. "There is a reason for this, other than mere discretion; because, as far as I was concerned, X. wasn't a human being at all but simply a state of mind." The love was unrequited: "even if X. had returned my feelings, I would never have left Ivar Avenue on that account." However, as he openly revealed, "I indulged it, and even gratified it, as they say, physically."[189]

X. was a beautiful young man called Bill Harris, who seemed to fulfill

Isherwood's ideal of the American Blond. Fouts had introduced Harris in August 1943, when Isherwood was taking his fateful vacation from the monastery. Nothing happened for seven months, until the spring of 1944, when Isherwood began slipping away from Ivar Avenue to spend time with Harris, often at Fouts's new apartment on Entrada Drive near the beach in Santa Monica Canyon. Even then, he continued to struggle against sexual temptation and to fulfill his duties at the Vedanta Center.

"I had to talk about it to someone," Isherwood noted in his diary in mid-April. He decided on Helen Kennedy, and she responded by confiding something worse—that she might have colon cancer. She planned to kill herself with an overdose; being a nurse, she knew how, and had already stocked up on morphine. Isherwood was overwhelmed. He found himself "bursting into tears, uncontrollably, at odd moments." He tried to pray, "'Master, let me have it instead of her'—but I couldn't. I was scared. I could only say, 'Your will be done, and help us to accept it.'"

Kennedy's diagnosis proved uncertain; X-ray treatment was planned. During June, she was nursed at the home of some devotees, tried to escape, and was admitted to the hospital after fainting and hurting her head. She confessed to Isherwood that she had taken "three cc's of typhoid vaccine—thirty times the maximum dose—she can't understand why she didn't die."[190]

Isherwood, too, was increasingly unwell. First of all, there were his teeth, rotten and troublesome since childhood. He had two pulled in February, two more pulled in May, a fifth in the autumn. The rotten teeth were accompanied by swollen glands, scalding sore throats and raging temperatures which repeatedly confined him to bed—as in the spring of 1937 at Pembroke Gardens. On April 22, while he was at the movies with Kennedy, he discovered a hemorrhoid, and he asked Bill Kiskadden, Peggy's new husband, to cut it out. This perhaps unnecessary masochistic gesture was to be unexpectedly painful and to require a long recuperation.

"It hurt like hell. I yelled clear around the block, and immediately knew I'd gotten a black mark for doing it. Bill is a Spartan," Isherwood wrote in the wartime diary. Yet he claimed the pain was "a great relief, because, for the moment, it takes the sting out of the X. situation. You can't be in love when you have a sore behind."[191] He was in bed for nearly two weeks. In his struggle with celibacy, he was psychosomatically reenacting the dramatic episode of his circumcision just before his fifteenth birthday, a punishment for which he had volunteered just as he volunteered his hemorrhoid. He had long since recognized his addiction to being ill and to luxuriating passively, dangerously, on the threshold of mortality.

The movie at which he discovered the hemorrhoid was *For Whom the Bell Tolls*, adapted from the 1940 Hemingway novel. Isherwood had reviewed the novel two years earlier in a long, eccentric essay, "Hemingway, Death, and the Devil," in which he projected onto Hemingway his own predicament as a spiritual aspirant and a would-be American novelist and claimed Hemingway "was a philosopher, even a mystic."[192] As he sat watching the film beside Kennedy, the story of the wounded hero and the Spanish Civil War had evidently triggered Isherwood's overlapping fantasies about being maimed and being nursed. The ministering power of his beloved nurse Miss Purdie and all the related women, real and fictional—Nanny, Kathleen, Olive Mangeot, Mrs. Lindsay, Joan Lindsay, Currants, Margaret Lanwin—had come to life again in Helen Kennedy, "Sudhira": "To me, she was the universal, cosmic Nanny; the beautiful, mysterious figure whom we meet twice in our lives, at the entrance and the exit, the midwife and the hospital nurse, the life giver and the bringer of death. [. . .] In a way, she *was* death, and our relationship could only really exist as long as I was sick."[193]

Nearly two years after the hemerrhoid, Isherwood was to require another operation, in January 1946, to remove a blockage from the top of his urethra, inside his bladder. This, too, he faced with a mixture of relief and masochistic satisfaction—relief that the blockage was not malignant and satisfaction "because he felt that he *deserved* some ritual penalty for his failure to remain a monk," as he later recalled. The constriction had been intermittently painful, and he visited at least four different doctors during the autumn of 1945 before being operated on by a Dr. A.D. Gorfain in the Santa Monica Hospital.

As with his teenage circumcision, hygiene was prioritized for the patient's supposed benefit, this time with an unexpected outcome. "[I]t was Gorfain's practice to guard against infection during this operation by tying the patient's sperm tubes, thus making him sterile," Isherwood wrote in *Lost Years*. When Gorfain came to explain this to Isherwood before he operated and to ask permission, Isherwood had already been given tranquilizing drugs, and the conversation went ludicrously wrong: "Christopher misunderstood Gorfain to say, 'You aren't planning on becoming a *parrot*, are you?' The question seemed to him, in his condition, to be funny but not at all strange. He replied, smiling, 'Well, Doctor, whether I planned it or not, I couldn't very well become one, could I?'" Isherwood had previously revealed to Gorfain that he was homosexual, so "Gorfain found Christopher's answer perfectly sensible—" He did his best to recreate the party atmosphere Kathleen had introduced when he was recovering from his circumcision in 1919 and which had also marked the crisis of his infected tooth in the spring of 1937: "He 'invited' Sudhira to come to the hospital during the two or three days he would have to be there, and act as his private nurse. Sudhira, of course, was delighted to do this." He recovered quickly, with only one after-effect, according to *Lost Years*: "he could no longer ejaculate sperm—at least, not until several years later, when a few drops would, very occasionally, work their way through the tied tubes as the result of an exceptionally violent orgasm. Otherwise, his sensations were the same as usual." He did not mention that he suffered intermittently from impotence which may have been linked to the median bar operation or to the much earlier circumcision. There is a statistical correlation between adult circumcision and impotence.[194]

DURING THE SPRING of 1944, Isherwood was working with Huxley on a screenplay, *Jacob's Hands*, about a faith healer from the Mojave Desert who is overwhelmed when he is promoted in the churches, theaters, and medical facilities of the Big City, Los Angeles.[195] Huxley and Isherwood also met with Wolfgang Reinhardt, brother of Gottfried, to discuss another screenplay project, *The Miracle*. They planned to adapt the stage spectacular that the Reinhardts' father, Max, had first mounted in Germany in 1911 and brought to London and later Broadway. Huxley and Isherwood's friend, the English actress and poet Iris Tree—a daughter of Herbert Beerbohm Tree, giant of Isherwood's childhood theater world—had played the two leading roles on alternate nights, sharing with her friend Diana Cooper, the British aristocrat and society beauty, during the U.S. tour in 1925–26.[196]

The Miracle was based on a twelfth-century Spanish legend about a nun who runs away with a knight. A statue of the Virgin Mary comes to life and takes the nun's place, protecting her reputation. Huxley and Isherwood intended to transform the love story into "a parable of sanctification and salvation." They wanted to show the elopement as a pathway toward God, making a profane love lead to a sacred one. In their proposal, the nun knows that she is hurling her soul into eternal damnation. "Her sacrifice for the man is thus of a supernatural order . . . the love capable of producing such a sacrifice must be of an almost frantically obsessive quality."[197]

"Frantically obsessive" also described Isherwood's feelings for Bill Harris. The notion that giving in to temptation was the way to transcend it articulated again the teachings of Homer Lane so essential to Isherwood's liberation in Berlin. The screenplay never progressed beyond the proposal, but it suggested that Isherwood was longing for a miracle in his own life.

That May, with the Huxleys, he drove to Ojai to hear Krishnamurti speak and to have lunch with Iris Tree and Alan Harkness, the Englishman with whom Tree was running the High Valley Theater Company in Ojai. Isherwood had met Krishnamurti once before, in November 1939, at what he called in his wartime diary "an all-star picnic organized by the Huxleys at

Tujunga Canyon." The guests had included Krishnamurti, Desikacharya and Rosalind Rajagopal, Berthold and Salka Viertel, Bertrand Russell and his family, Anita Loos, and Greta Garbo. At both meetings, Isherwood found Krishnamurti attractive and convincing. "Certainly, he didn't impress me as Prabhavananda did; but he had a kind of simple dignity which was very touching. And—there was no getting away from it—he had done what no other man alive today has done: he had refused to become a god."[198]

Krishnamurti and his younger brother had been adopted in India by the leaders of the Theosophical movement, Charles Leadbeater and Annie Besant, taken to England, and trained there as the vehicle and an alternate in which the Theosophists believed their Lord Maitreya, the World Teacher, was to be reincarnated. The boys' health suffered from the English climate, so in 1919 they were sent to an orange ranch in Ojai. There, Krishnamurti's brother died of tuberculosis and Krishnamurti first experienced "the process," a set of physical symptoms that seemed to express both ecstasy and suffering and which were evidently triggered by his longing for feminine love. It was later revealed that his life of supposed celibacy revolved around sexual affairs with the women who nursed him through these periods of illness.[199] It was like the psychosomatic illnesses Isherwood suffered as he struggled to sublimate his sexual appetite.

In 1929, Krishnamurti had marked his religious maturity by renouncing leadership of the Theosophical movement and rejecting the guru–disciple relationship and the devotional aspects of Hinduism. He broke with the movement completely when his adoptive mother Annie Besant died in 1933, though he went on speaking to devotees for the rest of his life, often to huge crowds.

Isherwood's childhood friend Leonard Tristram, the son of Kathleen's admirer Mamie Tristram, had lived with Krishnamurti at Eerde Castle in Holland in 1927 and traveled to California in his entourage in 1928. At the start of the trip, Krishnamurti had spoken in London at the central meeting house of the British Quakers. Kathleen, after reading some of Krishnamurti's writings, had attended with Leonard, Mamie, cousin Madgie Reid and Madgie's son Jack, and she had described it vividly: "the whole place was packed--every gangway. On the roof were people listening in through the open skylight—he only spoke for three quarters of an hour—harmony & truth which brings liberation & happiness no outward forms or ceremonies or churches to be founded—happiness is within ourselves." Isherwood had been home in bed at Pembroke Gardens recovering from a cold.

So impressed was Kathleen that she accompanied Mamie to Waterloo Station where Leonard and the man Kathleen now called "the prophet Krishnamurti" were catching the boat train for America. By June 1928,

Leonard had bought a ranch in Ventura, and he married without telling his mother, writing that he wanted "to live his own life & make his home, 'free from interference & inquisitiveness.'" Mamie reported everything to Kathleen who noted in her diary, "How familiar this all sounds . . ."[200]

Through the spring and summer of 1944, Isherwood forced himself to carry on with his devotions at the Vedanta temple, including, once each month, the immensely taxing day of silence which symbolically abraded his need to have a writerly voice. In April, he overheard Prabhavananda asking another devotee, "Why do you read novels? All books that do not give the word of God are just trash." The next day, Isherwood resigned as president of the Vedanta Society. He explained to Prabhavananda, "I dislike taking any official position here because I want to feel free to walk out at a moment's notice." Years later, he wrote in *My Guru and His Disciple*: "Swami didn't tell me *not* to write any more novels. He simply took it for granted that I would devote all my available time and my literary abilities to our Gita translation, articles for our magazine, and similar tasks. The fiction writer was forced to go underground."[201]

Isherwood continued with the editing and translating work, writing and gathering pieces for the Vedanta Society magazine, getting the magazine printed and helping to mail it out. He corrected the page proofs for the Bhagavad Gita and found a local publisher and distributor, another Englishman, Marcel Rodd, who ran the London Bookshop on Hollywood Boulevard and sold pornography under the counter. When Isherwood assembled and introduced an anthology selected from the magazine, *Vedanta for the Western World* (1945), Rodd published that, too.

In June 1944, Isherwood fell ill again. He was attended by Dr. Kolisch, and they had a long talk. "He believes that everybody who tries to lead the religious life is sure to get sick; it's part of the process of renunciation, 'dying to the world.' If you persist, you snap out of it again and your health improves." Then Fouts went out of town, leaving his new apartment available; Isherwood spent four days there with Bill Harris, June 25 to 29, when he and Harris evidently had sex for the first time.

On June 30, back home at the monastery, Isherwood confessed everything about the relationship to Prabhavananda: "Swami rose to the occasion, as he always does. 'Once you have come to Ramakrishna, you will be taken care of,' he said: 'I promise you that. Even if you eat mud, you will be all right.'"[202]

Along with his confession, Isherwood presented a plan for keeping himself on the straight and narrow. He told Prabhavananda that he would leave the monastery and settle nearby with his ex-lover Harvey Young, observing all the rules of the monastery in his own way as he had once done with Fouts.

Back in 1941, after splitting with Isherwood, Young—according to Isherwood—had lived alone in Hollywood, "painting a little, drinking a great deal, and having promiscuous sex off the boulevard." One night he "swallowed half a bottleful of Seconal tablets," but Isherwood and a friend found him unconscious and managed to bring him around.[203]

Young had gravitated home to New York and visited Isherwood in Haverford with a view to living with him again. Isherwood had resisted. Then Young had been accepted at a Benedictine monastery, Holy Cross, on the Hudson River north of New York City. Instead of entering the monastery, he had gone on a retreat in the nearby Catskill Mountains with another boy who had also applied to the monastery but had been rejected. Whether he knew it or not, Young was copying Isherwood, who had set up his monastic life with Fouts after Fouts was rejected by Prabhavananda.

A social worker, Alfred Gross, gay himself and an acquaintance of Auden, corresponded with Auden and with the Assistant Superior at the Holy Cross monastery about settling Young more securely. Gross wrote to Isherwood in September 1942, suggesting Isherwood should take Young under his wing again in California, urging that Young was unlikely to survive the winter in a leaky shack in the Catksills and that he was unsuited to the Benedictine monastery. Isherwood, still expecting to be drafted to CPS camp, had again resisted. Young and his friend lasted only a few weeks in the Catskills. Then Young "drifted unhappily about New York"[204] until, in the spring of 1944, he himself wrote to Isherwood proposing his return to Los Angeles.

Prabhavananda agreed to Isherwood's plan to share his religious life with Young, but he wanted them both to live in the monastery. In the chess game Prabhavananda and Isherwood were now playing, Prabhavananda made a brilliant next move. According to Isherwood's diary account, he raised the spiritual stakes: "I don't want you to leave here, Chris. I want you to stay with me as long I'm alive. [. . .] I think you have the makings of a saint." Isherwood was "really staggered" and laughed off the idea that he could ever become a saint. "No," said Swami, "I mean it. You have devotion. You have the driving power. And you are sincere. What else is there?" Within a few days of this new spiritual challenge—to become a saint—Isherwood was in bed with a fever, "my usual reaction to being fussed."[205]

Nonetheless, he completed his rough first draft of *Prater Violet* on July 24, egged on by Dodie Smith. "Every time we meet, she asks firmly, 'How many pages?'" he wrote in his diary.[206] Smith and her husband Alec Beesley were living in America because Alec was a pacifist. She had left behind her many London stage successes and was writing scripts for Paramount. She started her first novel, *I Capture the Castle*, but stalled, so she and Isherwood encouraged each other, she as a beginner novelist, he trying to begin again.

Young arrived by train on August 12 and stayed in Brahmananda Cottage before moving into an apartment Isherwood rented for them at 2050 Ivar Avenue, but Isherwood never joined him there. For some time, Prabhavananda had been shopping for land on which to build a new center so he could move the Vedanta Society out of the city. Suddenly, "a house and several acres of land, up above Montecito, near Santa Barbara" was given to him by a wealthy devotee, Spencer Kellogg, a linseed oil heir and trained painter from upstate New York.

George Fitts gave Prabhavananda money to purchase an adjacent seventeen acres, making, eventually, forty-five acres. "It's still quite wild country," Isherwood observed, "with lots of deer and mountain lions and coyotes." The house was called Ananda Bhavan—Sanskrit for Home of Eternal Bliss. From its windows, as Isherwood recorded, "You look over the bay, with its islands: a much finer view than any around Santa Monica." Prabhavananda intended to put Amiya in charge at Ananda Bhavan full-time and send others from Hollywood by turns. He himself would commute back and forth until after the war, when he planned to move everyone. In the end, he was to move only the women. Ananda Bhavan eventually became the Sarada Convent, and a temple was built in the grounds by 1956.

Prabhavananda invited Young to live at Montecito. Spencer Kellogg had an art studio on the grounds, and Young would be able to work on his painting. "I'll probably spend most of my time at Montecito, myself," Isherwood decided. He felt calmed by Young's presence, and "the X. situation has practically ceased to exist," he wrote in his diary. In *My Guru and His Disciple*, he acknowledged that he had used Young "to neutralize my sex drive."[207]

He moved to Montecito in late September, ten days after Young. Young wasn't happy for long, and he began to avoid Isherwood and then to be hostile because he felt trapped. On November 11, Isherwood admitted in his diary, "The [Harvey] experiment has failed." Painfully, Isherwood was learning that he could not make his lovers or his friends conform to his private needs. He once apologized to Kathleen for his youthful cruelties to her, writing, "My punishment has been that I have always, in one way or another, made the people I loved behave to me as I behaved to you."[208] He was deeply discouraged by all his personal relationships. In his diary, he ran through his California friends—Young, Helen Kennedy, Peggy Rodakiewicz, Denny Fouts (now busy studying medicine at UCLA), Chris Wood, the Huxleys, the Beesleys—recognizing that he could not live with any of them. Without a domestic companion, he felt homeless.

"The X. situation is beginning again," he wrote in his diary on November 30 after moving back to the Hollywood Vedanta Center. He now grew possessive of Harris and made a scene over one of Harris's other lovers. Harris, barefoot and wearing only his bathrobe, ran out of his apartment into La Cienega Boulevard: "All this *love*—" he exclaimed, "I can't stand it!" A few days later, Harris left for New York, ending the affair for good, though, luckily for Isherwood, not ending the friendship.

Isherwood continued to live at the Hollywood center even though he was not celibate. "An awful lot of my guilt about this is simply fear of appearances. Suppose somebody found out?" he wrote in his wartime diary. In fact, friends already knew about his affair. "Denny, Bill Harris, the Beesleys, John Van Druten, Carter Lodge, etc." he later wrote, "their tolerance was humiliating."[209]

It was Prabhavananda, again and again, who offered Isherwood the only feelings of calm and safety he experienced as 1944 drew to a close. One night, unsettled after visiting Fouts in Santa Monica, Isherwood returned to the Hollywood center to find Prabhavananda waiting by the fire: "'You will live long,' he told me—and explained that he had been thinking about me just as I came in. Suddenly, I felt such peace."[210]

Looking back years later, Isherwood felt certain that staying at the Vedanta Center had been the right choice. "What mattered was that he was getting exposure to Swami, that his relations with Swami continued to be (fairly) frank, and that he never ceased to be aware of Swami's love." Losing face with outside friends for living in a monastery when he was not celibate "was a hundred times better than if he had fooled everyone into thinking him a saint."

He feared the spendthrift solitude of his rich and selfish Uncle Henry. "Can I grow old messily, like poor Uncle Henry?" he asked in his diary.[211] So he remained with Prabhavananda.

DESPITE EVERYTHING, ISHERWOOD had completed his revision of *Prater Violet*, first conceived in 1935. It is one of his most perfect creations, spare in execution yet assimilating, through its narrative construction, diction, and imagery, multiple layers of personal and public history.

In a service flat in London, the Christopher Isherwood character collaborates with the refugee Viennese-Jewish director Friedrich Bergmann, writing a film called *Prater Violet* that is set in pre–World War I Vienna, before the great woes of the twentieth century began. The film is a schmaltzy love story about a prince and a flower girl. The Isherwood and Bergmann characters battle with one another, with their script, with their studio bosses to produce this piece of commercial entertainment while Hitler consolidates his power in Germany, and the Left in Austria makes its last doomed uprising, prelude, eventually, to the Anschluss. Isherwood used the title *Prater Violet* both for the novel itself and for the imaginary film on which his Isherwood character collaborates with Bergmann. The mise en abyme of the film *Prater Violet* within the novel *Prater Violet* brings the imaginary and the real into dizzying proximity. Historical events flash past the windows of the characters' private experience as Isherwood obliquely retells the story of the 1930s, the disillusioning decade that turned him toward mysticism. His narrative focus was sharpened by his argument with Brecht about the duty of the artist in a time of revolution, and the story movingly insists that true friendship, of the kind he shared in real life with Viertel and which Viertel affirmed in his letters following the argument, could overcome differences of politics and religious belief.

Isherwood brings Hitler's rise into the center of *Prater Violet* by having his director character, Friedrich Bergmann, act out the Reichstag Fire Trial while he is supposed to be working on the film script. The Reichstag Fire—the arson attack on the lower house of the German parliament—was the crucial turning point that allowed Hitler to end democracy in Germany and make himself dictator. For his audience of two—the Christopher Isherwood character and a secretary—"Bergmann enacted the entire drama and represented all the characters."[212] This narrative strategy allowed Isherwood, in the novel he was writing in the 1940s, to recall in detail the real-life radio broadcasts and press reports that went out from the trial in Leipzig and Berlin from September to December 1933 and to add his own sensational, satirical, and entertaining edge.

Hitler, Goering and Goebbels had declared that the arson attack on the Reichstag on the night of February 27, 1933 was the start of a communist putsch to take over the country. It was the very next day that the ailing eighty-six-year-old president of Germany, the once-powerful World War I Field Marshal Paul von Hindenburg, gave in to Hitler's request for emergency powers and signed the Reichstag Fire Decree for the Protection of People and State. The decree suspended a wide range of civil liberties, allowing Hitler to jail communists and others without trial, ban unfriendly publications, ban public gatherings, and search houses without warrants; it also enlarged the definition of treason to include many forms of dissent, among these any statement that the Nazis themselves had started the fire.

The theory that the Nazis had started the fire with the intention of blaming the communists took hold immediately on the Left and was never proved or disproved.[213] They arrested over a thousand people on the night of the fire, including left-wing intellectuals and trade union leaders who were beaten and tortured, and arrests continued for weeks. The next national elections, on March 5, 1933, were the last to take place in Germany before the war. It was two weeks later that Hindenburg signed the Enabling Act, permitting Hitler to rule by decree and thus cementing his dictatorial powers, as Isherwood had described in *Goodbye to Berlin*.

The Reichstag Fire Trial was a political showpiece, expected to illustrate and affirm the need for Hitler's unlimited emergency powers and allowing him to further scapegoat and isolate his communist opposition. The indictment alleged that as many as twenty-three separate fires were started in less then fifteen minutes in different locations inside the Reichstag with heavy and cumbersome materials, implying many arsonists. But the trial produced only one convicted perpetrator—Marinus van der Lubbe—who had no significant links to the leadership of the Communist Party and who was widely thought to be a tool of the Nazis. This outcome infuriated Hitler.

In *Prater Violet*, Isherwood's Bergmann character impersonates the president of the court and the five accused communists—van der Lubbe from Holland, Popov, Tanev, and Dimitrov from Bulgaria, and Torgler, the only German and the leader of the elected Communist Party members of the Reichstag. Bergmann also acts out "Goering, the straddling military bully, and Goebbals, lizardlike, crooked and adroit."[214] For Bergmann, as for many on the Left, the hero of the trial and Bergmann's own favorite role, is the Bulgarian Georgi Dimitrov, a high-ranking Communist Party member (and after World War II, a prime minister of Bulgaria), who ably conducted his own defense.

Bergmann's van der Lubbe reacts to the courtroom commands of the Nazi police chief like someone brainwashed, tortured, and drugged, as many believed he had been: "The head jerks up at once, automatically, as if in obedience to some deeply hidden memory. The clouded eyes wander around the courtroom." Then he laughs like a madman, "laughs and laughs, silently, blindly, his mouth open and dribbling, like an idiot's." Here was another hapless, unsuspecting piece of human collateral damage, unemployed, partially blind from a work accident, rumored to be a lover of SA commander Ernst Roehm; on December 23, 1933, when hard at work on *Little Friend* with Viertel, Isherwood had written in his diary: "Despair. Van der Lubbe sentenced to death."[215] Van der Lubbe was twenty-four when he was executed by guillotine on January 10, 1934, and buried in an unmarked grave.

Bergmann's secretary exclaims in horror at his performance of van der Lubbe's mad laughter: "Those Nazis aren't human." Bergmann admonishes: "But they are human, very human, in their weakness. We must not fear them. We must understand them. It is absolutely necessary to understand them, or we are all lost." This was the kind of understanding that Viertel and Isherwood had offered in *The Nazi*, the film treatment they had been unable to sell in Hollywood in 1939. Isherwood was offering it again in a different way in *Prater Violet*, to show how the fascists had seized control.

From playacting the Reichstag Fire Trial, Isherwood's Bergmann turns directly to the fictional film script, *Prater Violet*, in which the hero, Prince Rudolf, "loses his future kingdom of Borodania through a palace revolution. A wicked Uncle seizes the throne. Rudolf returns to Vienna, a penniless exile."[216] Life and art are juxtaposed, pushing the reader to consider the ways in which they are the same and not the same: Hitler, the wicked uncle, as in an old fairy tale or a familiar stage piece like *Hamlet*, takes over Europe through a palace revolution, creating countless penniless exiles. Rudolf, disguised as a student, wanders in the Prater, where he begins a romance with a poor flower girl, Toni, selling violets.[217]

Bergmann tells the Isherwood character that their hero, Rudolf, stands for themselves as leftists and as artists. "The dilemma of Rudolf is the dilemma of the would-be revolutionary writer or artist, all over Europe." This was the ground opened in Isherwood's argument with Brecht. The imaginary love affair at the center of the fictional movie, *Prater Violet*, brings the "artist prince" to a turning point: "He now has to make a choice. He is declassed, and he must find a new class. Does he really love Toni?"[218]

The androgynous name "Toni" belonged in real life to Tony Hyndman, to a Viennese lover of John Lehmann, and also to Toni Altmann, the German lover of Isherwood's wealthy Old Etonian writer friend Brian Howard. Like Neddermeyer, Toni Altmann had left Germany and wandered with Howard in search of a new homeland. Howard and Altmann had overlapped with Isherwood and Neddermeyer's exile in Amsterdam, and Howard had proposed settling as a foursome in Portugal where they would "buy a ruined palace," as Isherwood recorded in his diary[219]—two princes with their penniless lovers. Isherwood and Neddermeyer had instead settled with Spender and Hyndman in Portugal.

Privately for Isherwood, the story within the story also portrayed the drama that still obsessed him of his love affair with Neddermeyer. In *Prater Violet*, he was carrying several themes at once, exploring the intersection of the personal and the political while continuing to veil his sexuality. The narrator alludes to the secret of his romantic life with only two short sentences: "I was glad I had never told Bergmann about J. He would have taken possession of that, as he did of everything else."[220] This aside seals the narrator's bond with the reader, creating a special intimacy, a trick Isherwood also used in other stories.

Bergmann's political idealism is tested by the further unfolding of real-life events—the failed February Uprising of the Left in Austria in 1934 (sometimes called the Austrian Civil War). From February 12 to 16, there were armed clashes between the Left and the Right in a number of Austrian cities, and they became most violent in Vienna. Workers barricaded themselves in their apartment houses, the Karl Marx Hof, the Engels Hof, the Goethe Hof, where they were rumored to have secret stores of weapons. The conservative chancellor of Austria, Engelbert Dolfuss, along with his deputy, the founder of the Fatherland Front, Prince Ernst Starhemberg, crushed the uprising, bringing out the army as well as the police, declaring martial law, and ordering the Karl Marx Hof to be shelled.

As Isherwood told it in *Prater Violet*, "Without definite orders, without leadership, cut off and isolated into small groups, the workers went on fighting." Hundreds of workers were killed, thousands wounded. Their leaders went into hiding or fled; those caught were executed. The uprising, like the Reichstag Fire Trial in Germany, proved to be the last public death throe of the Left in Austria. It was a boon for Hitler. "Berlin looked on, smugly satisfied," wrote Isherwood. "Another of its enemies was being destroyed and Hitler's hands were clean."[221]

In writing about the February Uprising, Isherwood was revisiting the same intertwined political, sexual, and artistic themes that Spender had addressed in his long poem *Vienna* (1934). Spender had been present in Vienna just a few months after the uprising while his Tony, Tony Hyndman, had his appendix removed. Isherwood followed the gestation of Spender's poem encouragingly, counseling in several letters that the poem was too obscure. It was rushed to publication and harshly reviewed. Spender tried, unsuccessfully, to have it withdrawn following publication.[222] Now Isherwood, after a decade for consideration, served up the same material with dramatic clarity.

His character Bergmann is reduced to tears by news of the February Uprising; Bergmann's wife and daughter are still in Vienna. "How can I leave them alone at such a time?" he asks the Isherwood character. "You cannot know what it is like to be an exile, a perpetual stranger ... I am bitterly ashamed that I am here in safety." Of course, Isherwood himself did know what it was to be an exile, a perpetual stranger, and to feel ashamed of safety. Bergmann's lament evoked Isherwood's own complicated feelings about abandoning Neddermeyer in Germany and his more general sense of guilt about friends and family at risk in World War II while he sat writing the novel in the monastery between stints of work at the Hollywood studios.

Bergmann's guilt turns him against his own film: "It lies and declares the Danube is blue, when the water is red with blood ... I am punished for assisting at this lie. We shall all be punished." Pressed by the studio, Bergmann continues to work, but in a state of savage despair, bullying his actors and his crew. Then, in its own show of power, the studio—pointedly named Imperial Bulldog Pictures—threatens to bring in another director. Bergmann's rushes are shared without his permission, the press is alerted, a candidate for Bergmann's job is publicly paraded. Bergmann, fearing that the new director will "carefully annihilate every fragment Isherwood and I have built up, so lovingly," vows to "re-shoot everything. I work night and day." With this promise, Bergmann's personal uprising against the studio collapses, and he delivers himself body and soul, a helpless worker, back into the hands of his boss, Chatsworth, who behaves like Samuel Goldwyn even while resembling the British producers, the Balcons: "'Of course you will!' Chatsworth put his arm around Bergmann's neck. 'But you'll have to sell me your new ideas first ... Look here, let's have dinner together this evening, the three of us. Then we'll get down to brass tacks.'"[223]

Isherwood introduced into his novel yet a further analogy—with ancient Rome: the decadence of the sprawling empire, the rebellious spirit of the Jews and other enslaved peoples, the spread of Christianity in a period of epochal change when politics were useless and individuals helpless except in their private spiritual inclinations. He had told his brother Richard as he was roughing out *Prater Violet* in the spring of 1943: "I have been rereading Shaw, 'Androcles and the Lion,' how very good he is."[224] Shaw's play is based on Aesop's fable in which the runaway slave, Androcles, befriends a hungry lion by removing a thorn from its paw; Shaw's Androcles is a Christian. Captured with Androcles are other Christians, all struggling to hold on to their faith as they prepare to be devoured by the lions in the Colosseum in Rome.

Cecil B. DeMille's 1932 Hollywood spectacle about the spread of Christianity in ancient Rome, *The Sign of the Cross*, had opened in Germany in February 1933. It starred Charles Laughton as the Emperor Nero playing his lyre on a balcony while he watches Rome burn. Right after the Reichstag Fire, when the communist press was newly outlawed, Willi Münzenberg's publicity machine made a pamphlet disguised as a review of the film and distributed it in movie theaters in German cities. On the cover of the pamphlet, the movie title, *Im Zeichen / Des Kreuzes*, was split top and bottom with a cross between. Underneath ran "Ein C. d. Mille-Film der Paramount." Inside, the text had a coded meaning; leftists were to read "communist" where the pamphlet said "Christian."

"I too went to the Sign of the Cross," Isherwood had written to his friend William Plomer in February 1933. "The arena scenes are revolting without being funny." He knew of Münzenberg's pamphlet, and he preserved with his diaries another pamphlet, published in England a few months later, *The Communist Party of Germany Lives and Fights [The banned literature distributed under the Hitler Terror]*.[225] The pamphlet Isherwood saved described the continuing work of the banned Communist Party in Germany and the diligence of the illegal press—hundreds of communists still secretly printing and distributing material at the risk of imprisonment, torture, deportation to the camps, and death. The pamphlet included a facsimile of the cover of the DeMille "review" with its first paragraph translated into English, including the coded polemic about the Reichstag Fire and aftermath in which Nero stands for Hitler and the Christians stand for communists: "The bloody tyrant Nero ordered his slaves to set fire to the city of Rome and accused the Christians of being the incendiaries. This served as an excuse for the most ruthless *persecution of Christians*."[226] From this kind of propaganda, Isherwood learned techniques for concealing alternative meanings and risky polemics in his own work, just as he learned them from the work of George Bernard Shaw.

He found in Shaw's play *Androcles and the Lion* a view of the relationship between the individual and society that harmonized with his own view as it had continued to develop since 1933. Shaw's Androcles is persecuted not for his faith but because he does not fit in, as Shaw explained in his "Preface on the Prospects of Christianity" which he published with the play: "a Christian martyr was thrown to the lions not because he was a Christian, but because he was a crank; that is, an unusual sort of person." For Shaw, as for Isherwood, the particular always implied the universal: "Therefore my martyrs are the martyrs of all time, and my persecutors the persecutors of all time."[227]

In Shaw's dramatization of the relationship between individual Christians and the persecuting Roman Empire, Isherwood saw the relationship he had observed between the cultivated Jew and Hitler's Reich and also the parody of this which he sketched in *Prater Violet* between the creative artist and the film studio bosses. Moreover, he recognized his embattled self, a homosexual, a pacifist, a Hindu—a crank—misunderstood and attacked by friends and strangers alike. In his letter to Viertel about being attacked by Brecht for giving up the ideals of communist revolution, Isherwood had written: "I am well aware that I will never be able to fit into the new world he desires. I will be killed quite soon, for being an individualist, and I will be glad to die. I could never breathe that air." He assured Viertel that he liked Brecht just fine, but he opposed violence just as Huxley opposed it: "I even find Brecht's violence sympathetic. But I will never submit to it—that's the difference between being a pacifist and being a slave."[228]

Throughout *Prater Violet*, the reader is led to consider, Who triumphs? The tyrant who appears to have financial and political power, or the storyteller who understands what is taking place, and, if he is clever, controls the narrative? At lunch with Chatsworth and Bergmann, the Isherwood character attributes power to the artist, the Aesop figure, the Greek slave who wrote the fables. In the theater of the imagination, the artist can play both roles, emperor and slave. Isherwood gives Bergmann "The head of a Roman emperor," and also "the dark, mocking eyes of his slave." The slave is an enigma on whom the master depends "utterly—for his amusement, for his instruction, for the sanction of his power; the slave who wrote the fables of beasts and men."[229]

FROM ALAN WATTS'S *The Spirit of Zen*, Isherwood learned about jujitsu, "a method of self-defense without weapons, founded on the principle of defeating one's opponent by yielding to him and using his own strength."[230] Jujitsu suited Isherwood's personality and inclinations. As a teenager, he had seen off the ghosts at Marple Hall by pretending with his cousin Timmy to be one and scaring the maids. In *Christopher and His Kind*, he was to analyse the real-life power struggle that played out between him and Viertel, revealing not only how he himself had liked to play both roles, master and slave, but also how his ability to flip from one role to its opposite was a strategy for preserving his imaginative freedom. He had been Viertel's ideal collaborator when they met in 1933 because Viertel "needed an amateur, an innocent, a disciple, a victim. He needed someone he could teach—" Isherwood had been "eager to learn the craft of film writing and prepared to begin at the beginning. Why shouldn't he play the humble novice?"

In fact, while Isherwood was playing the novice scriptwriter, he had been secretly playing another role, observing Viertel: "trying to memorize his vocabulary and mannerisms. This was part of Christopher's instinctive functioning as a writer. He often caught himself studying someone without having been conscious that he or she was a model for a prospective fiction character." Isherwood didn't accept Viertel into his closest circle because Viertel was "never silly, never frivolous," as Isherwood pronounced in *Christopher and His Kind*. "Comparing him with Forster and Auden and Upward and seeing the vast difference between Viertel and them, Christopher said to himself that only those who are capable of silliness can be called truly intelligent."[231] The collaboration with Viertel remained, for Isherwood, a game which had only a provisional outcome and which forever had the potential to be played in a different way.

In *Prater Violet*, Isherwood had the "game" end with the participants in the roles of spiritual father and son:

> We had written each other's parts, Christopher's Friedrich, Friedrich's Christopher, and we had to go on playing them, as long as we were together. [...] Mother's boy, the comic Foreigner with the funny accent. [...] Beneath outer consciousness, two other beings, anonymous,

impersonal, without labels, had met and recognized each other, and clasped hands. He was my father. I was his son. And I loved him very much.[232]

Isherwood's musings elsewhere on his real father and on his ancestor John Bradshaw show a similar interest in the way that actions publicly recorded by history oversimplify the personality and conscious intention of the actor. In the imagination, in the theater, in a story, in a process of thought, in a dialogue, flipping to the opposite position, playing the opposite role is always possible. A hero is also an antihero; an antihero is also a hero.

Like Isherwood's own father, Bergmann is sworn to a particular duty, and he will carry it out, write the script and make the film for which he is paid. But however many stories he can imagine and act out, Bergmann can complete only one version of his film. In it, the provisional world of the imagination must finally take shape in an unchangeable outcome. The reality of movie-making is dictated by money. The film is not in any case the creation of one individual or even two intimate collaborators; it is the creation of a group, as the Isherwood character shows when he takes the reader by the hand on his own virgin trip into the film studio, introducing the reader to what were—in the 1930s and 40s—mysterious and glamorous new technologies and to the many workers in the studio, each with his or her own individual role and individual name. In the midst of this corporate undertaking, Bergmann and Isherwood have to fight to keep control of their story.

ISHERWOOD SHOWED VIERTEL a draft of *Prater Violet* in October 1944, assuring him in advance that "it is obviously 'about' you, and yet it is not; because certain aspects of your character are exaggerated and others quite ignored, and the incidents are mostly imaginary." Another model for Isherwood's "Jewish Socrates"[233] was Rolf Katz, as evidenced by the episode in which the Isherwood character travels to Brighton with Bergmann, a trip Isherwood made in real life not with Viertel but with Katz. Also, it was with Katz in Berlin that Isherwood had witnessed and discussed the Nazi violence represented in the nightmare the Isherwood character has while dozing in the train on the way home from Brighton. (The nightmare in *Prater Violet*—about the trial and about violent persecution of communists and Jews by Nazis—was based on a real nightmare Isherwood had in April 1944 when he fell asleep on the sofa underneath Denny Fouts's Picasso, and to present it in the novel, Isherwood used again the Freudian dream sequence technique used in the film *Little Friend*.)

Viertel relished the novel's magic. "It moves, as light as air, and as fast as a sunbeam. It is utterly unsubstantial and very substantial at the same time, imaginary and real," he wrote. He professed himself touched and honored to be accepted as Isherwood's imaginary father and moved by the poetry of their shared nighttime walk, but he also felt marginalized and even vanquished. "The hero of the novel is Chatsworth," he declared, "the mastermind." Unconvinced by the identification between himself and Isherwood as outsiders, Viertel suspected Isherwood of preferring the Englishmen, even though Isherwood had satirized them sharply, and Viertel objected above all to the suggestion that he would have placed such a film, "a Viennese film with Valse music, the thing I contempted most and refused to do always," above the safety of his family. In a second letter, he suggested revisions, but then urged Isherwood not to mar the work: "Your technic [sic], as of the younger generation (and of English understatement) is, to use a slight touch where I would elaborate it and endanger, by that, the chastity."[234]

Meanwhile, Isherwood made some revisions of his own and shared the draft more widely. In January 1945, Auden wrote saying he had read it three times, then read the final soliloquy aloud to his literature students at Swarthmore and "had them fainting in the aisles." He hoped for more of "the directly serious note" of the final soliloquy which he compared to the sanatorium episode at the end of "The Nowaks": "Not that I don't love the comedy, but you can do that standing on your head."

Like Viertel, Auden had advice for changes, and as with Viertel, Isherwood largely ignored them. Auden called one "A doctrinal point," illuminating again the divergence in their religious beliefs and artistic identities, rooted in the same soil and producing different fruits. "Surely it's incorrect to say that the True Way means that you will no longer be Christopher Isherwood, but that you shall be Christopher Isherwood as God wished him to be, ie the real person instead of the faux monnayeur," Auden wrote, using shorthand that referred to Gide's novel *The Counterfeiters*.[235]

Auden could not accept the annihilation of the ego as a religious objective; nevertheless, he had hit on a live element in *Prater Violet*, the continuing unresolved question of Isherwood's vocation. In November 1943, Isherwood had written in his diary: "To be a monk and to be a writer are the same, there's no clash of purposes." But he was discovering that they are not the same. In the spring of 1944, while he was at work on his first draft of *Prater Violet*, he had performed a day of silence as a devotional austerity. His identity and his need to speak out in his own voice had again welled up defiantly: "Storms of resentment—against Asit [Ghosh], against India, against being given a Sanskrit name (extraordinary how violently I react against this)." Years later in *My Guru and His Disciple*, Isherwood was to quote this passage and again address the numinous importance to him of his name: "To me, 'Christopher Isherwood' was much more than just my name; it was the code word for my identity as a writer, the formula for the essence of my artistic power."[236]

In 1944, his identity as a writer was hanging on the success of *Prater Violet*. Huxley told Isherwood it was "first-rate," and Heard thought it showed Isherwood was a "genius."[237] Among the reviews from strangers, Diana Trilling in the *Nation* had the clearest insight: "the most charming novel I have read in a long time," she wrote: "It is a book written in the author's own person, yet utterly without ego; it is a novel about movie writers which is yet a novel about the life of every serious artist; it is a book without a political moral, but a profound moral-political statement; it is gay, witty, sophisticated, but wholly responsible."[238] She rightly feared *Prater Violet* would not win the readers it deserved partly because it was short.

Edward Upward agreed. Ten years after it was published, he told Isherwood that brevity was the only reason it was not given its due in England. Rereading left him "filled with admiration and despair." He praised it above Hemingway, "how much better it is than for instance *The Old Man & the Sea*, good though this too is in many ways."[239]

Timing may have been the real problem. *Prater Violet* was published in *Harper's Bazaar* in America in July 1945, two months after Germany surrendered on May 7 and only weeks before the atomic bombs were dropped on Hiroshima and Nagasaki, leading to Japan's surrender on August 14. It came out as a book in the U.S. that November. In England it appeared only the following May, because, until then, there was not enough paper to print it.[240] The war was finally over, and the world wanted to celebrate the success of the heroes rather than remember the failures of the 1930s.

6

American Apostate (1945–1953)

Isherwood abandoned his diary at the beginning of 1945. He was, for the time being, done with examining his behavior and measuring his spiritual progress on paper. He continued to jot down his activities in day-to-day diaries, the pocket-sized appointment books he kept through much of his adult life. In these, he recorded the names of people he saw, meals shared, books read, movies or plays seen, work accomplished. For 1946, even his day-to-day diary is lost. He began his diary again in September 1947 to fulfill a commission from Random House for a travel book, *The Condor and the Cows*, about Latin America, but when this was completed, he continued his diary only erratically until after he settled down with Don Bachardy in 1953.

The hole in his life story was to become of interest to Isherwood a quarter of a century later. On his sixty-seventh birthday, August 26, 1971, he was to begin assembling the memoir that he called a "reconstructed diary" and which was published posthumously as *Lost Years*. He consulted his scattered diary entries from the late 1940s and early 1950s, his day-to-day diaries and his letters, asking friends to return certain ones. Otherwise, he drew on his memory, which he questioned freely and constantly. He referred to this work of reconstruction as "knitting," an activity which "might keep me amused."[1] As it proved, this "knitting" also subdued the years of anxiety, conflict, and disruption into a recognizeable shape—like a sock made by his father, a toy train track assembled by his little brother, japam made by himself as he repeated his mantra and counted the repetitions on his rosary.

Lost Years is his main account of his life from 1945 to 1951. Like the published memoirs he wrote just before and just after it—*Kathleen and Frank* and

Christopher and His Kind—*Lost Years* was conceived under the influence of Jung's autobiography, *Memories, Dreams, Reflections*, which Isherwood read in the summer of 1971, evidently for the second time. He recognized a familiar truth in Jung's statement in his Prologue, "My life is a story of the self-realization of the unconscious," and Jung inspired him to pursue more consciously and more analytically the project in which he had already been long engaged, and for which he adopted Jung's phrase, "to tell my personal myth."

Jung, the inventor of the collective unconscious, also valued the singular consciousness, writing: "Whether or not the stories are 'true' is not the problem. The only question is whether what I tell is *my* fable, *my* truth."[2] This emphasis on the personal partly explains why memory was to become just as important to Isherwood's writing in the last third of his career as anything he could document in the external, material world. The reconstructed diary was a draft; Isherwood never corrected it. Although it is sometimes factually unreliable, it is subjectively true. In it, Isherwood can be observed trying to recover and to understand who he was and what he wanted during a period of his life when he could not live according to his announced intentions. For, after six years of climbing a difficult pathway toward God, he seemed in 1945 to throw himself in the opposite direction. Only in the early 1970s did he want to know why.

His tone in the reconstructed diary is more cynical than in his other work, and he appears more selfish. He is a self-admittedly fallible narrator, but in contrast to the Herr Issyvoo of his Berlin novels, he is a narrator with a very busy sex life and an even busier fantasy life. Unlike his wartime diaries, 1939–1944, the reconstructed diary is not an apologia. It is not trying to defend decisions or justify a choice of life. It opens the way to understanding psychological forces, powers greater than the self which the self cannot control. These powers erupted into Isherwood's life in the postwar years, energizing, destabilizing, mysterious, irresistible. They made it difficult for him to write fiction, and his next novel, *The World in the Evening*, was to take him seven years.

SANTA MONICA CANYON, 1945

On February 21, 1945, Isherwood began work at Warner Brothers on an adaptation of *The Woman in White* by Wilkie Collins. He read the novel at the monastery, in bed with one of his inflamed throats, before signing on at $600 a week. He produced a story outline and two treatments and started the screenplay before he was moved to another project, for Wolfgang Reinhardt, an adaptation of Maugham's *Up at the Villa*.

He found the writers' department at Warner Brothers congenial, recalling gleefully in *Lost Years*: "It was said that Jack Warner and the other front office executives were afraid to venture into the building." Parties were thrown during daytime office hours by writers finishing their assignments "complete with liquor (which was officially forbidden) and dancing."[3] As the war drew to a close, spirits rose, and the atmosphere became so playful that Isherwood's colleague, the British fantasy writer John Collier, whom Isherwood had befriended at Salka Viertel's (and who was later to write the disappointing screenplay for *I Am a Camera*), was forced to do his studio writing at night.

Collier's favorite author was Proust. He was straight, but Isherwood took trouble to interest him in homosexual life: "as a Proustian voyeur, he was curious to get a glimpse of Christopher in actual pursuit of sex; and Christopher was delighted to oblige him." They treated the studio as if it were Proust's Grand Hotel at Balbec. The entertainment value came not so much from sex as from secrecy, the fact that there was something hidden to reveal, to decode, to expose, to show off.

According to *Lost Years*, the mail room at Warner Brothers "was just then the center of a lot of gay activity, and had several attractive messenger boys." Participating was risky, especially for well-known actors. Nevertheless, Isherwood became involved with a messenger boy who hoped to become an actor and had adopted the name Steve Conway:

> Collier found it thrillingly Proustian to look out of his office window and watch the discreet flirtations of the messenger boys—the glances and conspiratorial exchanges of dialogue—which Christopher had now taught him to observe and interpret. For [Christopher], it was like the discovery of a secret society; he was now prepared to believe that nearly the entire studio was queer.[4]

During 1945, Isherwood finally read all seven volumes of Proust. He also caught gonorrhea from Steve Conway. He visited a Dr. Zeiler on June 5, 1945, and was quickly cured by a series of penicillin shots. Penicillin had only become widely available after 1940, making "a happy contrast" to the first time he had caught gonorrhea, "those burning douches of potassium permanganate which the Brussels doctor squirted up his smarting urethra, day after day, in December 1938."

In Brussels in the winter of 1938–9, there had been "fucking à gauche et à droite," as Auden made outrageously clear in his "Ode to the New Year." In the Ode, Auden had blessed the "trade of old Brussels" and teased Isherwood with a New Year wish, "May even your oncers be healthy." After his 1945 cure, Isherwood felt uncomfortable with his retrograde motion into hypocrisy. "Here was yet another situation in which he felt ashamed of himself and, at the same time, contemptuous of his shame. It was shaming to return from a V.D. clinic to a monastery, but only shaming when he imagined Swami somehow finding out."[5]

He was receiving attention from *Time* magazine that made him even more uncomfortable—the Gita translation and Maugham's new novel *The Razor's Edge* (1944) brought a *Time* photographer to the monastery on January 15, and *Time* printed its glowing review of the Gita on February 12. The review identified Isherwood as Maugham's model for his main character Larry Darrell and publicly fanfared the way of life Isherwood had already secretly abandoned. Isherwood squirmed and eventually dismissed the rumor in a letter to the editor. "I am not, as you have twice stated in your columns, the original, or part-original, of Larry in Maugham's *The Razor's Edge*. I can stand a good deal of kidding from my friends, but this rumor has poisoned my life for the past six months, and I wish it would die as quickly as possible."[6]

Yet Maugham certainly had taken advantage of insights gained from observing Isherwood's progress with Vedanta, and he had drawn on Isherwood's friendship with Denny Fouts to create Larry Darrell's fictional friendship with the once shy and bookish Chicago girl, Sophie Macdonald, whom Larry meets again in Paris and tries to marry in order to save her "lovely soul, fervid, aspiring, and generous" from addiction to sex, alcohol, and opium.[7]

The suggestion that he might be Larry Darrell was deeply slighting to the grit and ardor of Isherwood's religious struggle, and it was embarrassing since, by implication, it made claims of saintliness that he would never have made about himself. He told Kirstein: "I think The Razor's Edge fails because its hero lacks any kind of inner conflict."[8] In "The Problem of the Religious Novel," Isherwood observed that "Maugham is rather vague" about "that decisive moment" at which the religious hero "becomes aware of his vocation and decides to do something about it." He professed to admire Maugham for attempting the subject, but "Unfortunately [...] one gets the impression that becoming a saint is just no trouble at all."[9] The problem was epitomized for Isherwood in the novel's title, *The Razor's Edge*, which Maugham had borrowed from the Katha Upanishad and mistranslated in his epigraph. He and Prabhavananda had tried to explain to Maugham, "one should *not* say, 'It is difficult to cross,' as some translators do, but rather, 'It is difficult to tread.'"[10] Maugham settled on "The sharp edge of a razor is difficult to pass over," repeating the error. Isherwood had learned that enlightenment was not a one-time event, like crossing a razor blade at a right angle; rather, it was an endless, narrow path, both difficult and also *painful* to travel, like walking along the edge of the blade in bare feet.

As in 1938, fame was becoming a problem for Isherwood. He was torn between exhibitionist tendencies and the desire to control his own narrative.

He resented having to hide his homosexuality, and he wished to entertain. The spotlight was about to shine on another love affair, but his new love object, William (Bill) Caskey, unlike earlier lovers, was not a teachable protégé type. Caskey was outspoken, sexy, and socially confident. He was cool, sophisticated, a born party-giver with a will nearly as strong as Isherwood's. Isherwood had begun to change, and the relationship with Caskey was to develop into the most serious and balanced romantic attachment in Isherwood's life so far, but ultimately into a stalemate without reciprocal empathy and yielding and without the possibility for longterm imaginative growth.

In *Lost Years*, he recalled that the affair with Caskey began as "a theatrical performance" for Fouts,[11] who dared Isherwood to lure Caskey away from another lover. The seduction duly took place on the night of Caskey's twenty-fourth birthday party, June 2, 1945, but friction soon arose between Fouts and Caskey, because Isherwood excluded Fouts as he became more seriously involved.

Isherwood was still living at the monastery, so he and Caskey met at Fouts's apartment, and at the apartment of Caskey's ousted lover, Jay Laval, a big blond chef who ran Café Jay, a restaurant at the bottom of Santa Monica Canyon that was a trysting place for celebrities.

Caskey sometimes washed dishes at Café Jay, so he and Isherwood also met in the kitchen there and at the Friendship, across from Café Jay, "the chief neighborhood bar and one of the very few gay bars in West Los Angeles." The Friendship was busy throughout the war, "crammed every weekend with servicemen and their pursuers, female and male," Isherwood was to recall in *Lost Years*. "This was the scene of Christopher's courtship of Caskey; they seem to have felt more at ease with each other in such a state of public isolation than when they were actually alone together."[12]

But this recollection may have been colored by the fictional portrait he had by then already written in *A Single Man*, in which the Friendship became the Starboard Side, a place of symbolic romance, where any courtship might be conducted, where passion quickly boiled over in fighting, and where high spirits recklessly defied law and order:

> You pushed aside the blackout curtain and elbowed your way through a jam-packed bar-crowd, scarcely able to breathe or see for smoke. Here, in the complete privacy of the din and the crowd, you and your pick-up yelled the preliminary sex-advances at each other. You could flirt but you couldn't fight; there wasn't even room to smack someone's face. For that, you had to step outside. Oh, the bloody battles and the sidewalk vomitings! [...] The siren-wailing arrival of the police; the sudden swoopings of the shore patrol.[13]

The blackout curtain marks the threshold between restraint and intoxication, between monkish solitude and the intimate, untrammeled warmth of the party crowd promising sex edged with violence. This is the curtain hanging across other key thresholds in Isherwood's work, the curtain which opens to reveal fantasies acted out, secrets revealed, a stage where the spotlight is on.

When Japan surrendered on August 14, 1945, gas rationing in the U.S. ended immediately. Isherwood recalled "a great outburst of automobile driving—just driving for driving's sake." On August 15, he drove up the coast with Caskey to Riviera Beach on Point Dume near Malibu, a secluded spot "then bare-ass."[14] They returned often, alone and with friends, in the ensuing weeks as Isherwood gave way to physical joy and sensual pleasure along with everyone around him.

This, too, he commemorated vividly in *A Single Man*—the "mad spree of driving," the celebratory bonfires now that the blackout was over, and the unselfconscious sex-making: "The magic squalor of those hot nights, when the whole shore was alive with tongues of flame, the watchfires of a vast naked barbarian tribe—each group or pair to itself and bothering no one, yet all a part of the life of the tribal encampment—swimming in the darkness, cooking fish, dancing to the radio, coupling without shame on the sand." George's happy life with his younger lover, Jim, is launched in this moment of permitted intoxication at war's end. "George and Jim (who had just met) were out there among them evening after evening."[15]

These were the energies that finally propelled Isherwood out of the monastery. At the end of August 1945, he moved into the tiny chauffeur's apartment at the Beesleys' current rental house on the Pacific Coast Highway between Santa Monica and Malibu. Two days after he moved in, Bill Caskey came to spend the night. About a month later, on September 29, they sublet Fouts's apartment at 137 Entrada Drive; Fouts had left by plane for Manhattan.

The apartment was upstairs in a low brick building, overlooking the street, so close to State Beach that there was sand on the sidewalk and in the gutters. In *A Single Man*, George reminisces about the seedy neighborhood Isherwood loved, with nearby West Channel Road disguised as "Las Ondas" (The Waves), shabby but sexy: "The motels are new but cheaply stuck together and already slum-sordid; they cater to one-night stands. [. . .] seashells are still less easy to find here than discarded rubbers."[16]

ISHERWOOD AND CASKEY lived and traveled together for most of the next six years. At first, Isherwood turned his back on Vedanta, and he later said this was partly because he wasn't confident Vedanta would stand up to

Caskey. Caskey was part-Cherokee, part Irish-Catholic; two of his great-uncles were priests. According to Isherwood's account in *My Guru and His Disciple*, written thirty years after he and Caskey parted, Caskey had stopped going to confession aged sixteen because he did not want to tell the priest about his sexual relations with men and he was as passionate as Isherwood to tell the truth.

Isherwood was confident that Caskey believed in God, and Caskey appeared to be so entangled with the Catholic conception of sin that Isherwood feared the Vedanta conception of sin would seem to him "hopelessly unserious." In *My Guru and His Disciple*, Isherwood declared: "I never discussed Vedanta with him," though Prabhavananda and Caskey occasionally met.

Prabhavananda did not reproach Isherwood for leaving the monastery, and Isherwood agreed to polish Prabhavananda's translation of Shankara's *Vivekachudamani*, or *Crest Jewel of Discrimination*, "to prove my continuing loyalty to him." The *Crest Jewel of Discrimination* is an austere work of Vedanta philosophy written in verse by the eighth-century Indian monk Shankara. The translation took until the end of 1946 and was published in 1947. In *My Guru and His Disciple*, Isherwood wrote: "I was simply glad to be living out in the open at last, with no appearances to be kept up and no need for pretences."[17]

According to *Lost Years*, Caskey was a little shorter than Isherwood, "very sturdily built, with square shoulders and the slightly bowed legs of a horseman." His father bred horses, and he had ridden since childhood. He had gray-blue eyes and curly brown hair which he cropped short because he did not want the curls to show; curly fuzz covered his whole body. He had bad teeth and only one testicle. He was the opposite of shy, and despite his youth "he had an impressive air of having 'been around'—as indeed he had." He was attractive to Isherwood partly because he was "a social amphibian," comfortable anywhere: "Red-eyed, drunk and unshaven, he looked every inch a Eugene O'Neill Irish lowlife character; washed and shaved and sober, dressed in a Brooks Brothers shirt and suit, he was fit for the nicest homes." He was "able to project a southern upper-class charm to go with his Kentucky accent," and "nearly everybody liked him."[18]

During the war, Caskey had served in the navy in New Orleans and in Florida, doing mostly office work, alleviating the boredom with parties and sex, and "then came one of those big homosexual witch-hunts; a few boys were caught and they named names." Caskey received a blue discharge "neither honorable nor dishonorable," and traveled to California with a friend, Hayden Lewis, fired in the same scandal; "they were what used to be called 'sisters,' not lovers."[19] Isherwood and Hayden Lewis never liked each other. Lewis warned "that Caskey was 'a bad boy,' implying that he didn't think Christopher would be able to handle him." Isherwood was excited by the challenge. "Caskey's temperament, with all its unpredictability, offered Christopher a new way of life."

After his effort at self-control in the monastery, Isherwood was determined on recklessness. In 1929, when he had first launched himself into the world of the street boys in Berlin, he had relished wrestling and rough play, and he described a dark echo of this physical violence with Caskey, with whom he sometimes became so angry that he lost control of himself: "During these scenes he would yell at Caskey and occasionally hit him. Caskey, who was stronger than Christopher, very seldom hit him back. To have provoked the blow was, for Caskey, a kind of triumph."

Right from the start, the relationship was a power struggle. "Christopher spent their first few months together trying to get Caskey to make a real unequivocal declaration of love." At bottom, Caskey was an *opponent*, with whom Isherwood engaged most directly through fighting, not lovemaking. "From Christopher's point of view, at any rate, drinking was a built-in dimension of their relationship; while sober, he felt, they never achieved intimacy."[20] So they drank more and more.

Isherwood explained in language adapted from Jung that Caskey stood apart from all his other lovers in one respect: "Christopher didn't have a myth about Caskey. [. . .] The nearest he got to a Caskey myth was in regarding him sometimes as a nanny figure. But a nanny isn't romantic . . ." Annie Avis's job and identity depended on Isherwood being a helpless child who could not dress or bathe himself or sleep alone at night. When Richard was born, Nanny infantilized Richard instead. Isherwood wrote in *Lost Years* that "He used to think of the relationship between himself and Caskey as being more down to earth and therefore more mature than any other he had previously experienced."[21] Yet his inclination to see Caskey as a nanny figure promoted in Isherwood childlike passivity.

His imaginative life withered. They camped and played very little. Isherwood was on his guard against Caskey, and therefore on guard against himself. Caskey triggered the same anxiety as Paddy Monkhouse, Spender, Connolly—that Isherwood was childish. But the child in Isherwood was the wellspring of joy, silliness, creativity.

Caskey derided some of Isherwood's sexual preoccupations, perhaps to gain the upper hand rather than because he disapproved. During the winter of 1946, Isherwood frequented the Pits, hollows in the dunes at the back of State Beach along the wall bordering the actress Marion Davies's beach house: "he enjoyed the exhibitionism more than the sex he got there." He told Caskey about these visits, and Caskey "made jokes" implying that "The Pits belonged in the category of Christopher's immature sexual tastes." When Isherwood suggested to Caskey that they wrestle, Caskey called it "'prep school stuff' and Christopher was so embarrassed that he never mentioned it again."[22] Caskey meant American prep school, aged thirteen or fourteen to eighteen. For Isherwood, though, erotic interest in wrestling went back to St. Edmund's and before that to Limerick, in particular to his friendship with Jack and Bob Armstrong, the rambunctious Irish twins with whom he had had a physically passionate and testing friendship: "My personal opinion of Jack is that he is rather boasting and is very fond of saying 'I'll wrestle you' to other boys without carrying it out," Christopher and Kathleen had written in *The History of My Friends*.[23] The Armstrong twins had been among Isherwood's original opponents. They had Irishness in common with Caskey, and it was their energetic chemistry Isherwood was to conjure when he gave their surname to the character based on Caskey, Jane Armstrong, the hard-drinking, sex-loving second wife of the protagonist in *The World in the Evening*.

Isherwood recorded in *Lost Years* that Magnus Hirschfeld had categorized his sexuality as "infantile."[24] If he remained under the spell of his prep-school sexual experiences in the 1940s, he nevertheless engaged in a wide range of sexual activities. According to *Lost Years*, he and Caskey "did everything in bed which normal homosexuals do—cocksucking, rimming and fucking." He recalled that he had believed at the time in "a balanced active-passive relationship" and therefore began to allow Caskey to be the active partner even though Caskey "was smaller than himself and anyhow, from Christopher's point of view, unalterably female." He let Caskey take the active role more and more often, "until the time came when he stopped fucking Caskey altogether."[25] This was another kind of flipping.

The sexual dynamic between them was further shaped by the fact that Caskey's "greatest sexual pleasure was in going to bed with basically heterosexual men."[26] Isherwood later asserted that their promiscuity in itself hadn't "as a rule, upset the balance of their relationship," even though he was "much more prone to jealousy than Caskey was."[27] However, "Caskey's preferences for heterosexual men," wrote Isherwood in *Lost Years*, "irritated and frustrated Christopher throughout their relationship."[28]

Isherwood made a point of recording in *Lost Years* a number of Caskey compliments about his sexual prowess, for instance a claim he overheard a drunken Caskey make to a sceptical young houseguest: "He's the best lay on the Pacific Coast!" But Caskey exhibited none of the boyish vulnerability so attractive to Isherwood in many younger lovers. Instead, they shared an image of themselves as bad: "Caskey felt guilty not only as a lapsed Catholic but also as a dishonored navy man." Isherwood felt guilty as "a failed monk."[29]

Guilt had stopped Isherwood writing during his first years in America, and now it stopped him again. After *Prater Violet*, he made plans but no progress. He told the reviewer for *Time* magazine that he was working "on a novel about physically and spiritually 'displaced persons.'" He told a subsequent interviewer that *Prater Violet* was the first of a trilogy about refugees. This idea of a trilogy of novels—novelettes, as he sometimes said—had been in Isherwood's mind since the early 1940s though the components repeatedly changed. On New Year's Day 1945, he began what was probably a second story for the trilogy. Then, sometime during 1946 in Santa Monica, he worked out a draft for the longer novel, *The School of Tragedy*. All through the late 1940s, he continued to think about both projects and made many attempts to start fresh or move forward. None was sustained.[30]

Nevertheless, his public career was busy. In December 1945, James Laughlin of New Directions published *Mr. Norris Changes Trains* and *Goodbye to Berlin* "in one big volume" titled *The Berlin Stories*.[31] For American readers, this omnibus edition obscured the artistic differences between the two works. *Mr. Norris Changes Trains* was constructed like an old-fashioned novel, "a sort of glorified shocker; not unlike the productions of my cousin Graham Greene," as Isherwood had told Lehmann.[32] But *Goodbye to Berlin* had dispensed with page-turning plot for the fictionalized diary form that permitted more detailed observation of material and psychological reality, and helped launch a whole new way of writing about real events, admired and developed by writers of non-fiction and New Journalism, including Isherwood's friend Truman Capote with *In Cold Blood*.

In 1946, *The Memorial* appeared for the first time in the U.S. Then, to feed his American audience, Isherwood resurrected another project of his youth, his 1930 translation of Baudelaire's *Intimate Journals*.[33] He continued to attract interest from journalists. The romance of the accomplished, worldly young writer withdrawing to a monastery stoked his fame. *Life* magazine sent photographers for a story which never ran about him and Prabhavananda, and there were numerous smaller features and interviews. During 1946, admiring reviews of *The Memorial* and *The Berlin Stories* appeared in the *New York Times*, the *Washington Post*, and the *Saturday Review of Books*.[34]

Haloed by past achievements, Isherwood did virtually no new work while living with Caskey at Fouts's apartment. "One memory of any living place (no matter how temporary) which I nearly always retain is the memory of the spot where I worked. At Entrada Drive I simply cannot picture it." He remembered drinking, hangovers, and the songs on the record player, in particular Frank Sinatra, which gave him "a sweet but sickening sense of being bewitched, entrapped, unable to escape."[35]

In April 1946, Fouts returned to Entrada Drive, and he and Caskey began quarreling. "Caskey saw his advantage and pushed their quarrel to the point at which Christopher had to choose between them," Isherwood recalled.

Isherwood and Caskey escaped to Salka Viertel's garage apartment at 165 Mabery Road. For his mother, Isherwood detoxified the feud, comparing himself and Caskey to the underworld characters in his favorite Beatrix Potter story: "we were to be seen, like the rats in the Roly-Poly-Pudding, scurrying through the dusk with enormous packages in our arms—and settled in a very charming room over the Viertels' garage."[36]

Fouts soon drifted east again, and then back to Europe. He and Isherwood were to meet over a few days in Paris in April 1948, their last meetings. In *Lost Years*, Isherwood recalled: "Though he had sided with Caskey, his sympathies remained with Denny. Looking back on the two relationships, it seems to me that Christopher and Denny came closer to each other than Christopher and Caskey ever did."

Nevertheless, he described the period in Salka Viertel's garage apartment as "the happiest in Christopher's whole relationship with Caskey—I mean, the happiest for Christopher." Salka's house was two streets up the hill from the beach and from the Friendship and faced away from the ocean, "on a respectable street," affording privacy and calm. "[B]each acquaintances and other near strangers were scared of wandering in there uninvited." Company was available by choice in the main house, "Salka was always glad to see you and she usually had visitors."[37]

In the spring of 1946, Salka's household included her mother, her younger two sons, Tommy and Peter, and Peter's wife and stepdaughter. Peter Viertel, the star son, a novelist and screenwriter, had written his first book *The Canyon* (1940) when he was only seventeen and got it published by the time he was twenty. He had attended Dartmouth and UCLA, served in the marines and was decorated four times during World War II. Greta Garbo—who had already made her last film and had time on her hands—was often there, and Isherwood later recalled that Garbo "hadn't the least hesitation in shouting up to the garage apartment and even climbing the stairs, to find out if they were home or not."[38] Once Isherwood and Caskey hid under the bed to avoid going for a walk with her.

The garage was a white wooden building at the rear of the garden looking out toward the ocean. Upstairs, the long, narrow bed-sitting room had big windows and was filled with light; there was even a balcony for sunbathing. As Isherwood knew, it had been Berthold Viertel's room before Viertel returned east to New York and then Europe, and it still contained some of his books and papers. A writer for British *Vogue* interviewed Isherwood there. "Christopher Isherwood sits at a desk covered with proofs and manuscripts," she wrote. "He looks very boyish in a clean white sweater and faded blue jeans."[39] The same issue had profiles of Maugham and Huxley. Now that the war was over, expatriates were back in fashion.

The desk was covered with proofs and manuscripts because in the security of his new home, Isherwood was back at work on Prabhavananda's Shankara translation and on his own wartime diaries, typing out his handwritten entries, filling the gaps with explanatory narrative passages, and producing "a typescript of at least 130,000 words." It was a reckoning. Meanwhile, he mixed happily at Salka's "salon." In contrast to the impromptu gatherings and the record-player music at Entrada Drive, "He found many of her guests really interesting and he enjoyed introducing them to Caskey."[40] Caskey made photographic portraits of some. He took a two-month photography course and began launching a professional career.

Isherwood was planning to travel to England for the first time since 1939 as soon as he could earn enough money and resolve his immigration status. There were no royalties yet from *Prater Violet*, so he began work for Wolfgang Reinhardt, adapting Ibsen's *Rosmersholm*. He moved the action from Norway to New England and reduced the three suicides to one, Rosmer's wife. His Rosmer died defending a child in the revolution, and his Rebecca West departed alive.[41]

The job lasted only four weeks. "[T]he head of Enterprise Studio was horrified when he found out what Rosmersholm is about," Isherwood reported to his mother. He was to reimagine the explosive relationship between the tradition-bound clergyman and the free-thinking beauty young enough to be his daughter in a later film treatment called *Judgement Day in Pittsburgh*, devised on spec at the end of 1946 with his old studio colleague Lesser Samuels.

According to *Lost Years*, *Judgement Day in Pittsburgh* "was originally Samuels's idea." But Isherwood, as he did often in collaborations, surreptitiously, irresistibly, pulled the story toward what interested him. *Judgement Day in Pittsburgh* "was about a young iceman who invents one of the first automatic refrigerators and a girl art student who falls for him and does a painting of his head attached to a nearly nude body she has copied from a Michelangelo print, thus causing a scandal."[42] By the time the movie was made (by RKO) the inventor had disappeared; what survived was the artist struggling for freedom in a provincial community.

The girl became a clergyman's rebellious daughter, expelled from art school for asking to paint nudes from life. She wins a competition with an anonymous entry, creating a scandal that threatens her father's career. The idea for the film drew not only on Ibsen but also on the New Woman—the "unwomanly woman"—who appeared in the plays of Ibsen's disciple and another Isherwood idol, Shaw.[43] But the studio supplied a meaningless new title, *Adventure in Baltimore*, and cast Shirley Temple. *Rosmersholm's* Scandinavian isolation and suicidal despair were replaced by American family, friends, and community, all won over by the adorable, smiling Shirley Temple character who marries the boy next door; the father ends up a bishop. It was to earn Isherwood and Samuels lots of money.

AS A CONSCIENTIOUS objector, Isherwood could not become a U.S. citizen during World War II because, as he explained in *Lost Years*, "no exceptions or reservations were allowed in taking the loyalty oath; you had to swear to defend the country, no matter what your age or sex were." In July 1945, with the war nearly over, his immigration counselor advised him to apply in hopes that the regulations would soon change, "and because, if he didn't apply, his application might be refused later."[44] He took the advice and told his mother that he would soon be able to visit her.

His concern for Kathleen surfaced increasingly in his letters to her. He knew that food and fuel shortages were continuing in England after the war and that Kathleen, like everyone, was afraid of the atomic bomb. He was returning to England chiefly for her sake. He told Forster: "When I think of England, it all really adds up to my mother and you."[45] Indeed, he dreaded seeing the rest of his circle: "Oh, my heart is like lead at the prospect," he confided to Kirstein. "They will all think I'm creeping back, repentant."[46]

At his citizenship interview, Isherwood could not swear, as was still required, to fight for America. He was offered a second interview, and "he was asked if he would be prepared to load ships in wartime. 'Yes,' he said, 'if they were carrying food.' 'But not if they were carrying arms?' 'No—not if they were carrying arms.'" However, it turned out that he had demonstrated satisfactory willingness to serve when, in September 1943 while living at the monastery, he had volunteered for noncombatant service in the Army Medical Corps despite being over military age. So his application for American citizenship was granted.

He took the oath of allegiance on November 8, 1946, the sixth anniversary of the day on which he had been initiated by Prabhavananda. He got an American passport and took a preliminary jaunt with Caskey to Mexico City for Christmas and New Year, beginning an article about their trip for *Harper's Bazaar*. Then, on January 17, 1947, he went to the British consulate: "He found it strange and slightly disagreeable that he now needed a visa before he could set foot in England."[47]

ENGLAND, 1947

Isherwood had returned to England countless times between 1929 and 1939. "But, of all these returns, I think that only one will remain with me vividly for the rest of my life. It is my return from the United States at the beginning of 1947." So he said in "Coming to London," written during the three months his visa permitted him to spend in postwar England, from mid-January to mid-April. The piece described his reunion with friends at John Lehmann's London flat, "one of the most moving experiences of my life," and his happy discovery that "my friends and our friendship seemed to be essentially what they had always been, despite the long separation." Yet when Isherwood reprinted "Coming to London" in *Exhumations* in 1966, he introduced it, contradictory fashion, by emphasizing change more than continuity: "Now, suddenly, we have to accept each other as live people, separate people who have been alive and changing, all this long while. Can we ever catch up with each other again?"[48]

By the time he wrote *Lost Years*, Isherwood was no longer sure that the vivid reunion had been a single real event, and his day-to-day diary suggests it was at least two. What in 1966 he called "the 'inwardness' of the scene" had in fact been developed in his imagination; it was the experience he *wished* to have—of finding his friends and friendships "essentially what they had always been." He was in town for only three days in January before leaving for Wyberslegh and returned for two more weeks in March.[49] He socialized constantly, trying to fit in everyone and to please them.

He was cautious about his friendship with Lehmann, who had helped make his reputation in the 1930s by publishing his work in the magazine *New Writing* and at the Hogarth Press where Lehmann had worked for the Woolfs; Lehmann had now established his own firm. Advance letters were formal and punctilious. Lehmann sensed that Isherwood was nervous about how he would be received, but in *Lost Years* Isherwood wrote that Lehmann overestimated this: "Lehmann, in his heart, felt that Christopher *ought* to be nervous *and* penitent, because he hadn't stayed in wartime England—and, incidentally, been available to help Lehmann with his publishing projects."[50]

Isherwood was also cautious about Spender to whom he had been so close in the 1930s and by whom he felt so betrayed by the "Comment" on his emigration with Auden that had appeared in Spender and Connolly's *Horizon* in 1940. Spender had been in the National Fire Service during the war, and with a photographer, John Hinde, had assembled a book about the Blitz and about the Civil Defence response to it, *Citizens in War—and After*, which Isherwood had received for Christmas 1945 from his mother. Text and large color pictures depicted the suffering, the exhaustion, the sacrifices, and solemnly considered how the heightened sense of social responsibility on the Home Front could be carried over into peacetime. It wasn't until March 2 that Isherwood toured the bombed areas of London. He was driven around by Britten and Pears, but recorded nothing about the devastation, honoring Spender's eyewitness account. He recalled only that he had been comfortable seeing the wreckage with Britten and Pears, with whom he still felt "a special kind of rapport" over their sojourn in America at the beginning of the war.[51]

He was mostly well received, and he liked postwar England more than the England he had left. "It seems much more alive and much less snooty," he wrote to Kirstein. "But I could never live here." He was teased about his "alleged American accent," and Lehmann later reported the accent and mannerisms seemed to come and go as if "he was, in spirit, being pulled to and fro across the Atlantic all the time." Isherwood demurred: "he hadn't succeeded in doing much beyond altering his vowels; his speech rhythms remained British." In England, though, he felt challenged to display a change: "He had to prove to the English that his emigration had been a serious action, that he had put down roots and become, at least partially, American."[52]

The fact that he was socially in demand ignited old jealousies. "Toward the end of his visit, Stephen told him, with typical malicious hyperbole, 'You're the most popular man in England.'"[53]

He reunited with two old lovers, Jack Hewit, with whom he had spent his last European Christmas so contentedly in Brussels, and his former private pupil Ian Scott-Kilvert. He spent at least one night with Hewit, in part to make up to Hewit for having reneged on the promised ticket to America, and he had supper at the Reform Club with Hewit's on-and-off lover Guy Burgess who, with Anthony Blunt, had fruitlessly pressured Forster to intercede with Isherwood on Hewit's behalf. Ian Scott-Kilvert, that youthful stammerer with whom Isherwood had begun the 1937–8 affair that briefly promised to change both their lives, was now married with a son and starting a career at the British Council. Isherwood was sharply aware that Scott-Kilvert had been a hero in the war, "As a conscientious objector, he had gone to Africa with the Friends' Ambulance Unit, where he had narrowly missed being killed." Then a Cambridge friend in Scott-Kilvert's unit, once a romantic rival of Isherwood's, had died in a bomb blast, so Scott-Kilvert had given up pacifism, joined the army, and served with Greek guerrillas behind the German lines in Greece.[54] Isherwood had their love story in mind as he worked on *The World in the Evening*.

Isherwood had a lot of money to spend in England because earnings and interest had accrued to his bank account during the war. Some of it was royalties, mostly for *Goodbye to Berlin*.[55] The paperwork for a foreign citizen to declare the money was arduous, so he spent as much as he could, entertaining lavishly, buying gifts, and, with Brian Howard's help, choosing a Keith Vaughan painting to take back to California where Vaughan's work was then unknown.

He made a special visit to his Repton and Cambridge friend Edward Upward, now settled in Dulwich, south London, with a wife and two children, met his new publisher, Alan White at Methuen, saw his Berlin friends Gerald Hamilton and William Robson-Scott. The latter, "to everybody's amazement," had also married.[56] He traveled to Cheltenham to stay with his beloved mother figure from the 1920s, Olive Mangeot, and to visit Jean Ross who lodged near Olive and now had a daughter with the leftist journalist Claud Cockburn. Isherwood had passionately admired Cockburn "for telling the truth" in the 1930s, and he had been a devoted reader of Cockburn's *The Week*, receiving it regularly while he lived abroad.[57]

NOBODY IN ENGLAND had been more eager to see Isherwood than his real mother. She looked on his visit as a homecoming and had yet to understand how complete was his new life in America, despite the many indications he had given her. He carried his family inside him, as he himself was to understand fully only when he wrote *Kathleen and Frank* two decades later, but survival—emotionally, psychologically, spiritually—had depended on escaping them. Any visit home carried the renewed threat of suffocation, yet Isherwood knew Kathleen craved his company and affection, and he risked this for her.

"We have been expecting him for so long . . ." she wrote in her diary, where she always referred to one bedroom at Wyberslegh as his, set aside for him since she moved there in 1941. "It was a most happy moment to see him again, looking so well & kind & not a bit changed in appearance, perhaps a shade older, but hardly perceptibly so—. & there was so much to hear—" Repeatedly, she applied the adjective "kind," and once she described him as "very serene."[58]

Isherwood later recalled in *Lost Years* that Kathleen, too, seemed little changed. But he was shocked by Richard: "Richard's face looked mad and somehow psychologically *skinned*, all its protective coverings stripped away down to the raw, the quick of defenseless misery." The years had told hardest on Anne Avis. "Little old Nanny sat by the kitchen fire, bright-eyed but infirm, chuckling at Kathleen's novice attempts at cookery. Kathleen and Richard waited on her."[59]

Kathleen and Nanny had stood by one another through many hardships of which Isherwood was unaware. Of her twelve siblings, Nanny had stayed in touch only with a few near her in age, and they had died during the war. She had become ill with a shaking palsy leading to falls, stiffness in her left arm and left leg, mysterious enlargement of her left hip, and reduced vision in her left eye—probably Parkinson's disease[60] and perhaps a mild stroke. The family doctor attended regularly, and Kathleen fetched the prescriptions from the chemist, bound up Nanny's bloody head when she cut it against the washstand, took her to the optician, and collected her pension from the post office. A stroke was to kill Nanny in November 1948.

What else had happened to his family that Isherwood did not know? Kathleen and Richard had fled Pembroke Gardens on August 31, 1939, the day before Germany invaded Poland, traveling in a packed train to Manchester with what belongings they could carry; Forster, by telephone, "strongly urged us to do so 'while the going was good,'" Kathleen had written in her diary. They took refuge at Brabyns Hall with their friend Fanny Hudson. But the first chaotic adrenaline had subsided, and the cinemas had reopened, "everyone taking their gas masks."[61]

Three weeks into the war, Kathleen and Richard had left Cheshire for North Wales, where Maud Brunton, daughter of Kathleen's godmother, offered them two bedrooms and a sitting room in her house at Penmaenmawr. Nanny had joined them, and then Elizabeth Besley, the cook, put up in servants' rooms. For nearly two years, Richard traveled the ninety miles back and forth from Wales to Cheshire about once a week so he could work at Wyberslegh Farm, where he rented a room from the Coopers. Farmworkers were protected from conscription early in the war.

With joy, Kathleen had received cables and letters from Isherwood. She went to the movies often in Penmaenmawr, and she went to church every day, sometimes twice a day, saying her prayers as methodically as her son— though she prayed for victory while he prayed for peace.

It was not until she read the issue of *Horizon* containing Cyril Connolly's item on Auden and Isherwood leaving for America that she discovered Isherwood had applied for naturalization. "I <u>had</u> so hoped he wouldn't . . . it seems so to <u>cut</u> us off . . ." Nevertheless, she took his side instinctively when he was publicly criticized for emigrating: "it <u>infuriates</u> me that insinuations should be made that it was to escape from the European trouble—" She felt the attacks personally, recording them all in her diary—the questions in Parliament, Harold Nicolson in the *Spectator* ("that flabby <u>worm</u>" she called him), the verses by Anthony Powell. Isherwood hardly knew what an ally he had in her: "I hadn't referred to the Question in the House of Commons," he told her in one letter, "because I hoped you mightn't have heard about it & I knew it would upset you."[62] But she followed the press avidly, and she was in touch with his friends.

Forster, on whom she looked as an unassailable moral eminence, had reassured her by letter, and Forster had alerted Kathleen when he wrote to the *Spectator* calling for "a close time for snarling at absent intellectuals." In his *Spectator* letter, Forster pointed out that the attacks seemed to be motivated by "unconscious envy" and would be better directed at wealthy and aristocratic Nazi sympathizers in Britain who were an actual danger to the country.[63] Kathleen had copied this gallant intervention into her diary along with other snippets of public support for her son.

IN THE SPRING of 1940, Uncle Henry had begun to have life-threatening bladder trouble. Surgery was required to drain an infection, and afterwards the Bradshaw Isherwood family gathered around his bed in the nursing home—Jack, Esther Toogood, her daughter Joan Toogood Duke, Joan's five-year-old daughter Shirley, Kathleen and Richard. Henry's estranged wife, Muriel Bagshawe, raced to his bedside by bicycle and train from one of her country estates, still in her muddy work boots, after years without meeting. It was May 9, the anniversary of Frank's death at Ypres in 1915 and of John Isherwood's death in 1924. Henry received the last sacrament.

But Henry did not die until July 10, back home in his flat. Kathleen found herself unexpectedly sad. In California, Isherwood wrote that he and Uncle Henry had been genuinely fond of each other. He had given up the allowance from Uncle Henry only a few months earlier, explaining via Kathleen that he was earning nearly £100 a week at Metro Goldwyn and didn't need it. Kathleen, too, had stopped her allowance to Isherwood from the end of March 1940 "by his wish."[64]

In June 1940, during Henry's last illness, Isherwood had written to Kathleen that he wanted the Marple Hall Estate to go to Richard. When he heard that Henry was dead, he repeated by cable: "I want Richard to have Marple and money as I told you in previous letter—" In his wartime diary, he elaborated: "the absurd boyhood dream of riches is over forever. It is too late to invite my friends to a banquet, to burn the Flemish tapestry and the Elizabethan beds, to turn the house into a brothel. I no longer want to be revenged on the past." Richard, on the other hand, "loves the place and is prepared to live there."[65]

Kathleen found Isherwood's wishes both touching and upsetting: "from his babyhood I always thought of C living there some day . . . & it makes me sad to think of him an exile & no settled home—"[66]

Although he rejected his material inheritance, Isherwood had already taken a different kind of legacy from Uncle Henry, since *Mr. Norris Changes Trains*, the novel that made his reputation and which gave him his first foothold in Hollywood when he sold it to Samuel Goldwyn, was inspired just as much by Uncle Henry as it was by Gerald Hamilton.

In June 1940, Henry had made a new will, designating his brother Jack his sole executor, a role previously shared with Isherwood, and leaving all his personal effects to Jack instead of Isherwood.[67] The estate itself, of course, was not Henry's to leave.

Kathleen cared about the Bradshaw Isherwood ancestral property at least as much as any of the family into which she had married, and she fought to preserve it. Near the front of her 1940 diary, she recorded the gross value of Henry's estate as £75,787-0-9. Personal property accounted for £31,787-0-9 and the Marple Hall Estate £44,000. In addition to the houses, farms, and parkland, the estate drew income from rents and financial instruments including about £32,000 in mortgage securities and government bonds. A small amount of furniture was settled in the estate. She listed the properties and other sources of income, but recording gross values was wishful thinking. When probate was granted, the figure for personal property was much smaller—£3,122-4-8 gross and £2,402-11-9 net. Out of this came legacies and tax, leaving well under £200 personal worth.[68]

Death duty on the Marple Hall Estate was £20,000. The family lawyer, Charles Symonds, managed to raise £11,000 in ground rents from houses along the park. One tract of land was already slated for sale at £1,100; other parcels were sold perforce during the following three years. Marple Hall with its outbuildings needed urgent repairs, as did other buildings belonging to the estate, but during the war, the government had limited expenditure on such work, so all but the most urgent had been postponed.

A Manchester businessman expressed interest in purchasing the estate, but Richard did not want to sell. Neighboring properties were changing hands. When Fanny Hudson died in 1941, unmarried and childless, Brabyns was acquired by the town council; then it was demolished in 1952 for lack of funds to maintain it. Thomas Legh, 2nd Baron Newton, also died during the war; his heir donated Lyme Hall, family seat of the Leghs since 1398, to the National Trust because no buyer could be found.

By holding on to the Marple Hall Estate, twenty-nine-year-old Richard became "one of the very few remaining Cheshire squires," as Uncle Jack flattered him in a 1940 letter. "No words can describe how deeply & sincerely grateful I feel to Christopher . . ." Richard wrote to his mother from Wyberslegh Farm.[69] But Richard was irrationally obsessed by the question of who would inherit after him: Christopher's children or his own children? What if the children were daughters? This obsession—pointless, indeed absurd—underlined Richard's inability to feel that the property was really his.

Charles Symonds traveled to Penmaenmawr first class at the expense of the Marple Hall Estate, and Kathleen nearly dozed off with boredom while he read aloud the draft of the new settlement. When Richard read the draft, he was told "it would be less complicated to leave the property to C. & then to his children failing these to Jack & his descendants & then Esther & hers..." He was fobbed off with an allowance while his newly inherited estate paid the huge stamp duty and lawyer's fees for the resettlement document which did not reflect his wish to leave the estate to his own children.[70]

THE LONDON HOUSE in Pembroke Gardens was damaged by bombs in October 1940. Windows and shutters were blown in, including in Isherwood's old room, and the conservatory was shattered. At Penmaenmawr, Kathleen slept through air raids on nearby Manchester and Merseyside, but woke repeatedly at 4 a.m. worrying about her furniture in London. Early in 1941, she managed to move it north by van and store it at Marple Hall despite gas rationing and labor shortages. She sold the lease on Pembroke Gardens and began to think about moving back to Wyberslegh.

At the end of 1940, Richard had announced that he could not go on living and working at Wyberslegh Farm, where an able young French refugee had made him feel unneeded, so Kathleen arranged work at another farm belonging to the estate, Dan Bank, about three miles from Wyberslegh near the village of Marple. She rented Richard a room in the village and also arranged a bedroom at Marple Hall, "to take up his position there," which was advised by the lawyer.[71]

The following summer, Richard was targeted by an anonymous "Poison Pen." Then he brought home to tea an eight-year-old boy who lived along the edge of Marple Hall Park: "very much all there, & not at all shy but not particularly attractive," wrote Kathleen in her diary. The day after the tea party another poison pen letter came. Richard was "very fussed over the wretched woman at M.H. who doesn't seem able to leave him alone," she recorded. The "wretched woman"—and probably the poison pen—was the caretaker's wife, Mrs. Cotton, paid to provide meals, fires, and hot water for Richard, which she never did, although she constantly tried to wheedle more money from him. There was no Forster to stand up for Richard; "it makes one feel so lonely that such things should happen—" wrote Kathleen.[72]

Wyberslegh Hall had been rented to a well-liked Greek family called Natzio. Rachel Monkhouse married the son, Eustace Natzio, and the two of them settled in the house. During the war, Eustace Natzio joined the RAF, so Rachel moved to a smaller place, subletting Wyberslegh for the income. She maintained through a lawyer that she was entitled to extend the lease every six months till the war ended, and Kathleen finally hired her own specialist lawyer to get Rachel out. Ill feeling lasted years.

Kathleen moved back in during the summer of 1941. She traveled between Penmaenmawr, Wyberslegh, and London, packing, unpacking, arranging furniture and china, hanging pictures, mirrors, curtains saved for more than thirty years, laying rugs, staining floors. At the train station in Penmaenmawr, there were no longer porters or taxis; she carried her own suitcase through the village. She was nearly seventy-three. Soon she was growing a wide variety of vegetables with hired help, making gooseberry tarts from her own bushes and jam and bottled fruit to stretch the sugar ration. She felt close to Frank and to the rhythm of rural life: "The men busy with the hay cutting & heaping into mounds..."[73]

Richard helped with the harvest—heavy work. After the hay came barley and wheat. The last night of the harvest, at the end of September 1941, he knocked over a lamp in Kathleen's bedroom and cut himself on the bulb. He couldn't work for a month. Every day, he went to the pub. On Sundays, he began to skip lunch, preferring to drink during the hours the pub was open. "[E]very young man is or should be doing war-work," wrote Kathleen in her diary, well aware of local opinion.[74]

It was the beginning of a pattern for Richard, stints of work broken off by injuries, misunderstandings, transportation difficulties, and bouts of heavy drinking, depression, and exhaustion. He was kicked by a horse, which broke a bone in his right hand. He sprained an ankle. He got ringworm from one of the calves. He slammed a train door on his thumb. Eventually, he adopted the habit of rising before dawn on Sunday mornings to milk the cows so other laborers could have a morning off. Then he would sleep in the Oak Parlour at Marple Hall and have lunch there before doing the afternoon milking and carrying the pails.

One night in March 1942, something unspeakable happened at Marple Hall, which Kathleen recorded but did not describe in her diary. She was more passionate and more oblique than ever, reporting that Richard was "very upset over the scandalous & disgraceful behaviour at M.H." and that he "felt he would never forget the horror of it..."[75] She sent him to stay with friends in Hull. There, he had a nervous collapse. The Marple doctor, Dr. Hastings, prescribed nerve pills, which Kathleen took with her to Hull when she collected Richard. These became a staple, possibly the cause of painful hemorrhoids and other symptoms.

Richard and Kathleen decided that the Cottons had to leave Marple Hall.

It took the lawyer, Symonds, and a younger colleague, Herbert Sidebotham, two months to get them out. They were replaced by a couple from Hull, the Essex-Crosbys, who moved in at the end of June 1942 exposing a horror of trash and filth and many unreported leaks.

War news, when at last it favored the Allies, featured destruction on a scale never known before: "it tells even on the people who are not in it, like ourselves ..." wrote Kathleen in November 1943 after Berlin was bombed every night for a week. "Felt frightened, & depressed all day."[76] Richard began to shake all over, and his gut was in constant turmoil.

As 1943 turned to 1944, Richard was waking in the night, terrified by howling wind, violent indigestion, and sharp pains in his chest. Dr. Hastings proposed a new medication, Elixir Bromo-Valerianate, a powerful and addictive patent sedative.[77] It combined the tranquilizing effects of bromine and valerian root, and probably calmed Richard's sex drive; it could cause intoxication, hallucination, confusion. Dr. Hastings supplied Bromo-Valerianate steadily to Richard, and he counseled each month—February, March, April—that Richard might be ready to go back to work in another two weeks after getting through a few more bottles. But Richard tired easily and was often too nervous to go out alone. He read and typed out letters and stories. He never returned to farmwork.

BEFORE HE MOVED into the monastery for the first time in 1943, Isherwood had arranged a report card about himself which he knew would reassure his mother: "Found such a nice letter from Peggy Rodakiewicz about Christopher," wrote Kathleen in her diary in February 1943, "they all seem *so* fond of him ..."[78] She worked hard to understand exactly what kind of monk Isherwood was trying to become, copying into her diary an explanation of yoga received from a friend and comparing it to the drill of Isherwood's childhood and the Pelman memory training course that both she and Isherwood had undertaken by post when he was preparing for public school.

From America, Isherwood sent food parcels, his new publications, and in May 1943, he sent Felix Greene to visit. Kathleen professed herself "delighted" with the Isherwood–Prabhavananda translation of the Bhagavad Gita, which reached her in November 1944, followed by Isherwood's article "The Gita and War" in the Vedanta Society magazine. She helped deliver her own parish magazine around Disley every month, and she liked to identify with her son's activities, but pacifism challenged her. She and Richard went to see the *The Hour Before Dawn*, and she noted in her diary that Isherwood had developed the pacifist point of view for the script, "certainly one has every sympathy with him,"[79] a lukewarm pronouncement implying she did not.

She also went to see a film to which Isherwood—along with hundreds of others in Hollywood—contributed for the British War Relief Fund, *Forever and a Day*, "simply bristling with stars! & the script by well known authors," she enthused, proud to see her son's name on the screen alongside Alfred Hitchcock, James Hilton, C.S. Forester, and Donald Ogden Stewart.[80] The story was calculated to promote British-American friendship—an American sheltering from the Blitz in the cellar of an old London house learns the history of the house and of Britain overnight. She went twice.

In October 1944, the cook, Elizabeth Besley, fractured an arm and a leg putting up blackout curtains and retired after a long hospital recuperation.[81] So Kathleen learned to cook in earnest. She washed her own laundry and hung it outdoors to dry, and she scrubbed the floors rather than having Nanny, who could no longer get down on her hands and knees, complain they looked dirty.

"Very excited," Kathleen wrote when the typescript of *Prater Violet* arrived at the end of January 1945.[82] She and Richard read it aloud in the evenings before she forwarded it to Isherwood's London agent as Isherwood requested.

On May 2, when Hitler's death was announced, she wrote, "Somehow the news falls flat."[83] Nanny and Richard collapsed with sore throats and ear infections. Kathleen carried trays up and down stairs. The garden was full of weeds. Ration books were reduced from twenty-four points a week to twenty, and there were no potatoes for sale at all.

As the war ended in Japan and Isherwood took to the road with Caskey in California, Alan Coyne's youngest brother, Edwin, turned up on his motorbike to see Richard, "quite <u>unself</u> or class conscious," according to Kathleen.[84] Edwin brought his wife to tea, arriving in a new blue car. Outings to the cinema were soon followed by impromptu suppers with the young Coynes. "What <u>would</u> the Reeves have said[,] the married couple we had, when we lived here before, to see us entertaining in the kitchen!—a room I never went into except to give daily orders at 10 am! . . . . . . My Trifle & Jelly quite a success!" wrote Kathleen in January 1946. She daydreamed of her mother Emily, with her aristocratic bearing: "I can still see her there in my mind's eye." In June, she grieved to her diary that the Private Drive at Marple Hall was no longer known as the Private Drive (indeed, it was no longer private since it had houses built along it): "as I write," she continued, "I have just observed a mouse running into my velvet shoe—"[85]

Kathleen, like Richard, found repose in visits to Marple Hall, where the new caretaker reliably laid a warm fire and his wife brought tea. She would shut herself into the Oak Parlour, "the only really cosy room in the house" according to Isherwood,[86] and write letters. She spent hours altering an old pair of curtains to hang in the windows and putting fresh red velvet around the needlework chairs with their coats of arms.

"Alas," she wrote in May 1946, "the pond practically dried up, & the Grotto in ruins . . ." This was the fantasy hermit's cottage in the Mere Pool behind Marple Hall. The new caretaker had caught some local boys "deliberately knocking the little house on the island to pieces, just for the sake of destruction."[87]

Only a few weeks before Isherwood arrived at Wyberslegh in 1947, Kathleen had gone to the lawyers' office in Stockport to sign away the cricket field. It had been used as farmland during the war; now, just as in post-war California, there was a housing shortage. A builder paid £1,787.10, and she and Jack Bradshaw Isherwood were resisting pressure to sell Marple Hall Park.

IN DECEMBER 1944, Kathleen had purchased a wireless radio for Wyberslegh. Snobbery about proper social intercourse had kept her from the pleasure until then. It was installed in the drawing room, but she learned how to move it into the kitchen so she could listen to a church service while cooking Sunday lunch. At 9 p.m., she and Nanny and sometimes Richard listened to the news. Otherwise it was concerts, radio plays and broadcasts of books read aloud.

One night, Isherwood was the subject of a program called *Living Authors*. Kathleen managed to dash down some comments by the presenter, poet and critic W.J. Turner: "Humour & tolerance & his broad sympathy are the characteristics of Mr. Isherwood's work [. . .] the best comic writer living today [. . .] it is his rare courage & charity which make him so charming—"[88]

When "the best comic writer living today" finally arrived at Wyberslegh, the weather was savage and the gas supply so weak that temperatures inside the house fell below freezing even with the gas fires burning. "Towards evening the water froze in my washbasin (in the big bedroom,) & C who had a bath before supper found the water would not run away after—!"[89] On January 31, the electricity was switched off because of the national coal shortage. Isherwood kept warm by shoveling snow. At night, they huddled around the radio listening to adaptations of Shaw, Melville, Henry James, Rattigan. It was the coldest January in fifty-two years. The Thames froze, and so did parts of the sea.

Many evenings, they talked. Almost as soon as he arrived, Isherwood told his mother about the operation on his bladder. Despite all his revelations over the years, it was this operation that signaled to Kathleen the end of the family line. She confided her disappointment to her diary: "sad that it should have been necessary . . . I wish I might have had grandchildren . . ."[90]

Even though Isherwood had never wanted to marry or have children and was now sterile, Kathleen and Richard insisted on revisiting the question of the succession. They were so absorbed in the decaying Marple Hall Estate that they could not believe Isherwood would never want it back. Their anxiety persisted, until, at the end of March, he accompanied them to the lawyer in Stockport, carrying Richard's typewriter to prepare what Kathleen called a "supplement" to the "Marple Deed of Gift."[91]

Kathleen became indignant in front of the lawyer about Isherwood's operation: "the violence of Kathleen's reaction took [Christopher] by surprise. She seemed to regard Christopher's sterilization as a crime quite equal to that of abortion, and she cast all the blame for it on poor Dr. Gorfain. 'He ought to be put in prison!' she exclaimed." Only years after her death did Isherwood articulate his own anger: "How dared they assume that he should *want* to have a child, anyway?"[92]

The possessions that mattered to Isherwood were the papers and diaries and books which he had left behind at Pembroke Gardens when he emigrated. In the anxious days in London before the war broke out in 1939, Kathleen had folded her dresses on the bed in the spare room, sorted through her underwear, taken the silver to the bank, and "packed C's papers & diaries in a suitcase." She took the suitcase with her to Penmaenmawr; later, she took a second suitcase containing more papers, photo albums, and first editions.[93] Both suitcases were eventually carried from Penmaenmawr to Wyberslegh. Isherwood's books were moved later, in stages, sorted by John Lehmann, before Kathleen left Pembroke Gardens for good.

Isherwood now went through the suitcases alone in his room at Wyberslegh, where he shivered in his overcoat. He had not seen the material in at least eight years. One evening, in a gesture of openness or gratitude, he read part of a diary aloud to Kathleen, "the beginning of the arrival at the Greek Island, & of Francis T-Petre. Very descriptive & full of possibilities . . ." she commented.[94] Isherwood was later to use it in *Down There on a Visit*.

By mid-February, he had begun to burn things in the gas-fired Cosy Stove in the Stone Parlour. He salvaged only what he wished to carry forward from his old life. According to *Christopher and His Kind*, this did not include the Berlin diary on which he based *Mr. Norris Changes Trains* and *Goodbye to Berlin*, for he had already burned it in the 1930s when he finished writing the books because "it was full of details about his sex life and he feared that it might somehow fall into the hands of the police."[95]

From his beloved collection of books, he chose many to ship to America. The rest he sold to a bookdealer in Stockport. He visited every bookshop in

Manchester, including the secondhand ones, looking for more books to buy. He also shopped for books in London, once with Forster, with whom he stayed on his second visit there when he also stayed with Spender and again with Lehmann. Eventually, he shipped two tea crates containing about three hundred books. "[H]is many books," Richard told Lehmann, "I always think express his personality."

With this sifting, sorting, and reassembling of books and papers Isherwood was reweaving a ragged tear in the fabric of his life, collecting again some of what he had abandoned during his wanderings. Kathleen was to feel his spirit leave home for good in April with the tea crates, "all his books have gone [...] they seemed part of him!"[96]

Meanwhile, the extreme weather continued, made into a greater hardship by continuing strikes, shortages, electricity failures. On some days, roads were blocked by new or drifting snow, trains couldn't get into the station in Manchester, milk from Wybersleigh Farm had to go out in sledges, but Kathleen was utterly content shut in with her sons.

Isherwood worked on his pieces for *Harper's Bazaar* about Mexico and London and then began writing about Los Angeles for Cyril Connolly and *Horizon*.[97] He corrected the proofs for the English edition of the Bhagavad Gita. According to *Lost Years*, "He also wrote a hard-core sex story about a sailor whose nickname was 'Dynamite.'"[98] For the first time ever in his mother's house, he helped with housework, making his bed, washing dishes, buying food, cooking. He even learned to light the kitchen fire in the mornings, which Kathleen had found the hardest of all her tasks at Wybersleigh.

On February 27, a thrilling cable about *Judgement Day in Pittsburgh* arrived from Beverly Hills, read by staff at the village post office at High Lane and by Kathleen and Richard as well as Isherwood: "Meta sold story to RKO for Fifty Thousand. Yes I said Fifty Both send love Lesser—"[99] Meta Reis, later Rosenberg, was Lesser Samuels's agent. All the writing on spec had finally paid off. The squire's grandson was a success in Hollywood.

DUTIFULLY, ISHERWOOD MADE the rounds of friends and acquaintances in Cheshire just as in London. The Monkhouses interested him most. His old friend Paddy now had "a high-up post on the *Manchester Guardian*" and was, in Isherwood's view, one of the "most distinguished-looking men in England." Paddy was at his mother's, Meadowbank Farm, the day Isherwood called with Kathleen, but Isherwood "was aware of a gulf" between them because Monkhouse had become "solidly a family man." Isherwood went on walking expeditions with Paddy's youngest sister, Mitty, who now lectured and did social work,[100] and Mitty confided about her love affair with a married man. This reencounter with the Monkhouses, their passions and tangles, proved to be a crucial spark for the Quaker novel. A few days later, Isherwood opened a diary he had begun in Holland in 1935 and abandoned in London after the Munich Crisis. On blank pages at the back, he made another attempt to start the novel set in Haverford.[101] He got nowhere at the time, but eventually, he was to express in it his long-repressed anger and confusion at the way Paddy and his father Allan Monkhouse—in friendship and in fiction—had looked down on him for being a lover of boys.

Kathleen prepared to let go of Isherwood, using her diary to talk herself through it again and again during April. "I quite see he will never be happy to settle again in England," she concluded on April 12. He sailed on April 19. Two weeks later, she received the April edition of British *Vogue* from a friend; the profiles of Maugham, Huxley, and Isherwood were already a year old.

MANHATTAN, 1947

Reunited with Caskey after three months, Isherwood "felt himself falling in love, all over again." Caskey had driven their car east from California. He met Isherwood on the dock in New York and whirled him away for a night at the Park Central Hotel. Then they moved into an apartment on East 52nd Street sublet from James and Tania Stern, who had left to spend some time in Europe.

Isherwood placed himself in Caskey's hands, never attempting to learn his way around Manhattan by car and instead conceding the driver's seat literally and figuratively. "Christopher wanted to relax and surrender his will (in all matters that weren't important to him) to a nanny figure who would wait on him and relieve him from the tension of making decisions."[102] He had not been happy living in New York in 1939; now it was up to Caskey to make it work for them both.

Caskey was ready to cook and entertain, and they had a wildly social spring and summer. Auden, Kallman, and Kirstein remained the core of Isherwood's Manhattan circle, and this reconnected him with Fidelma Kirstein, Pete Martinez, Paul Cadmus, and George Tooker. There were drinks and meals with Monroe Wheeler and Glenway Wescott, Irving Drutman and Mike de Lisio. Forster was visiting from England, accompanied sometimes by Bill Roerick, an American actor who had served in England during the war. The world was on the move again, passing through or pausing in Manhattan—Tony Bower, the Charlie Chaplins, John Goodwin, who was a wealthy writer friend of Denny Fouts, John Van Druten with his new boyfriend Walter Starcke, Amiya, Klaus Mann, Berthold Viertel with his lover the Viennese actress Elisabeth (Liesl) Neumann. Peggy Kiskadden turned up, as did Chris Wood and Paul Sorel, and Wood introduced Isherwood to John Gielgud. Isherwood's day-to-day diaries tag countless other names in New York's interconnected circles of painters, writers, photographers, architects, and their wealthy, party-giving hosts.

He made no record of religious observances during this period. He joined a gym, though, on the West Side, frequented by dancers from Balanchine's New York City Ballet. The German émigré running it, Joseph Pilates, told him, "'If you'll just touch your toes one single time, every day of your life, you'll be alright'—which made Christopher think of a saint begging some hopelessly worldly householder to please try to remember God for at least one moment during each day." With his instinct for cultural trends, Isherwood was now a disciple of the founder of the Pilates method known worldwide in the next century.[103]

In mid-May, his books arrived. He had to store them in the basement because the bookshelves in the apartment were full of the Sterns' books; this hindered settling down to work. Some years later, he explained to an interviewer that he preferred to work with his books around him. "I like to get up very often and open some book—nothing relevant necessarily to the material—and just kind of take a swig at it. [. . .] I find this very stimulating."[104]

At the Sterns', Isherwood managed to produce only a few pages of his novel. Studying the pages years later, he noticed they were "written very neatly" and recalled that in Manhattan, "he had to keep wiping the side of his sweaty hand (the weather was hot and humid) to stop it from smearing dirt over the page." He hated working with dirty hands. "The filthy city with its noises and its horrible climate soon began to get on his nerves." He wrote best in a garden, at an open window, on a balcony, even on a rooftop; "he couldn't, wouldn't settle in New York."[105]

For the next five months until he left for South America with Caskey—who was to collaborate with him as photographer on *The Condor and the Cows*—Isherwood floated and idled, coasting on his reputation. He met with Mary Louise Aswell, editor of *Harper's Bazaar*, for whom he had been writing. He was interviewed for *Mademoiselle*, which his old friend George Davis was now editing, and he was approached by writers from *Town & Country* and *House & Garden* as likely magazine fodder. He was also interviewed on NBC radio by the seminal talk-show team Jinx Falkenburg and her husband Tex McCrary.

On May 1, he went to Random House to see Bennett Cerf about the proposed South America book. There, he was introduced to Truman Capote, "the marvellously gracious little baby personage," aged twenty-two, about to publish *Other Voices, Other Rooms*, his extravagantly poetic Southern Gothic romance about a hyper-imaginative twelve-year-old boy who flees his paralyzed father with a tomboy alter ego reminiscent of Mirabel Cobbold only to be captured by a gay uncle—catnip to Isherwood. Forewarned that Capote "could only be compared to Proust," Isherwood preferred a more eccentric literary analogy: "To hell with Proust; here was something infinitely rarer and more amusing, a live Ronald Firbank character!"[106]

A few months later, Isherwood and Caskey stayed on Nantucket with Capote and his much older boyfriend, Newton Arvin, a Smith College professor who was writing a biography of Melville that was to win the 1951 National Book Award. "As a host, Truman was like a masterful child leading a gang of children; he knew what *he* wanted, he was determined to enjoy himself, and he took it for granted that the rest of them would follow him," wrote Isherwood. They swam and cycled and attended some frolicsome all-male parties at Hagedorn House, a converted coastguard station near Quidnet rented by Leo Lerman, the magazine editor and *Vogue* gossip columnist who ran a Sunday-evening salon in Manhattan.

Capote flirted with Isherwood, two decades his senior: "You're going to be *awfully* attractive when you're a bit older—another five years, *and you watch out!*" Bachardy believed that "had Truman ever thought he had a chance, he would have gone after Chris when they first met in 1947."[107]

The puckish pair—Isherwood and Capote—evidently caught glimpses of themselves in one another. Such was Capote's admiration for Isherwood's work that he later reinvented Sally Bowles as Holly Golightly in *Breakfast at Tiffany's* (1958). After that, Capote sought to ballast his work with the gravitas of evil—as the Nazis had ballasted *Goodbye to Berlin*—scouring the newspapers until he found news that was bad enough, the multiple murder he was to report in his masterpiece *In Cold Blood* (1966). His claim to have invented the nonfiction novel rested on Isherwood's earlier achievements.[108]

As the summer wore on, Isherwood and Caskey left Manhattan more frequently for nearby beaches—Jones Beach, Point Look Out, Long Beach and the Lido Beach at Town Park—for lunches out across Long Island and house parties up the Hudson. From Nantucket, they continued to Provincetown to join Cadmus, Tooker, Jared and Margaret French, and Donald Windham and Sandy Campbell, all transplanted from New York during the hot weather. Isherwood later recalled the beauty and seclusion of the beach near Provincetown where they swam and sunbathed without clothes. Jared French photographed Isherwood and Caskey nude.[109]

Auden had rented a shack in Cherry Grove on Fire Island that summer, and Isherwood visited him numerous times, sometimes overnight. On one July visit, Isherwood and Kirstein had to share a bed. Isherwood later wrote:

"Lincoln, for the first and only time, made a pass at Christopher—a half-joking, tentative pass, which Christopher jokingly declined." His reason was not that he found Kirstein unattractive but that "he hated mixing sex with giggles."[110]

He spent his birthday at Cherry Grove. In *Lost Years*, he recalled that he had passed out drunk the night before in Manhattan and woke up in the car on the way to the Fire Island ferry. "'The last thing you said last night was, "Take me to Wystan,"' Caskey told him. 'So I'm taking you.' Christopher was delighted. This was Caskey in his aspect as the perfect nanny."[111]

They went back to Fire Island in mid-September when Kirstein, Spender, Chris Wood, and Berthold Szczesny (Isherwood's Berlin boyfriend "Bubi"), gathered with Isherwood, Caskey, Auden, and Kallman. Spender was teaching at Sarah Lawrence College in Bronxville. Szczesny was visiting from Buenos Aires with his wealthy older lover, the Countess Tota Cuevas de Vera Atucha, wife of a Spanish nobleman, and Tota's grown-up daughter.

Thus, the hedonism of pre-Hitler German summers on Ruegen Island was reanimated on Fire Island. It was the first time Auden, Isherwood, and Spender had been together since 1939, and Caskey photographed the trio posed with Isherwood in the center just as they had been posed for Spender's automatic shutter release on Ruegen Island in 1931. Much later, in the 1970s, as he worked on *Lost Years*, Isherwood looked at the Fire Island photographs and saw in them the person he had fictionally explored in his story "On Ruegen Island (Summer 1931)"—the person he had been before he emigrated, before he met Prabhavananda, before he had learned to meditate and tried to become a monk. He also saw how his rivalrous friendship with Spender had limited his development but at the same time prevented him from being carried away by a sense of his own self-importance. In one Fire Island photo (taken by Spender, he thought), "His legs are apart, his fists are clenched, his plump little figure is rigid with self-assertion. He looks at the others as if he were demanding their submission to his will, but in fact no one is paying him the smallest attention."[112]

In the summer of 1947, Isherwood was not exercising his celebrated will at all. He was passive, moved by currents around him like seaweed in water, living in an alcoholic haze, and letting Caskey nanny him.

ONE OF THE strongest currents was created by Kirstein. One day, Kirstein initiated Isherwood and Caskey into his obsession with the Polish-born sculptor Elie Nadelman, driving them to the Bronx to see Nadelman's work stored in the house where Nadelman killed himself. Another day, he took them to Washington, D.C., where they saw in secret under military police guard some of the 6,500 European masterworks stolen by the Nazis and hidden during the war in a salt mine at Altaussee near Salzburg in Austria. As a private in the U.S. Army, Kirstein had been assigned to the Arts and Monuments Commission, and he had been one of the first two Americans to enter the salt mine. He described this amazing discovery in several magazine articles published during the summer and autumn of 1945 and in his poems.[113]

Kirstein had intelligence connections in Washington predating his military service, and these were to influence Isherwood's plans for the South American trip and provide many contacts. Nelson Rockefeller, an old friend of Kirstein, had been appointed Roosevelt's "Coordinator of Inter-American Affairs" in 1940, with three and a half million dollars to spend on trade, finance, and culture. Securing friendships in the Western hemisphere had become urgent for the U.S. as Hitler overran Europe and pro-Nazi sympathy resounded in Latin America. Rockefeller had invited Kirstein to plan a ballet tour, and Kirstein signed up George Balanchine as artistic director of a traveling company, American Ballet Caravan. Kirstein and Fidelma with Pete Martinez, who was one of the thirty-five dancers, had toured Latin America for five months in 1941. Throughout the tour, according to Martin Duberman, Kirstein was also "doing informal intelligence work that centered on reporting the effectiveness of the United States' ambassadorial and consular representatives."[114]

In 1942, Kirstein was sent on a second tour, to buy paintings for the Museum of Modern Art. Money was supplied by Rockefeller, who wanted Kirstein to continue reporting privately on local politics because the State Department had failed to line up Argentina, Chile, and Brazil against the Axis.

SOUTH AMERICA, 1947–8

Even before the days of looking for a country where he could settle with Neddermeyer, Isherwood had dreamed of traveling to South America. "I know I shall never be happy till I've visited the places one sees on cigarette cards," he had written to Forster long ago from Berlin. In *Christopher and His Kind*, Isherwood observed that he was attracted to certain destinations "chiefly because of their remoteness." Two names in particular "had haunted him since boyhood—Quito and Tahiti," the middle of the earth and the middle of the ocean. The names pulled his poetical ear like mantras—keys to a world that existed inside the mind. "The magic of Quito had almost nothing to do with Quito the place," he wrote: "What excited him was the concept of a city poised at ten thousand feet above the equator, with days and nights of eternally equal duration and the round of seasons repeated every twenty-four hours. [. . .] An earthly model of paradise—or of limbo, according to the way you thought of it."[115]

Part of Berthold Szczesny's allure had been his escape by ship to South America. Rolf Katz had found refuge there in the way Isherwood had imagined he and Neddermeyer might. Isherwood had been further moved to fall in love with Latin culture through his relationship with Pete Martinez. As with so many things that he imagined, he was determined to slip into the scene and make it real.

In mid-September, Caskey's mother Catherine arrived in New York; "she was pretty, flirtatious, campy and quite unshockable," wrote Isherwood in *Lost Years*. Moreover, she was just as devoted to her son as Kathleen was to Isherwood. She was among the party seeing Isherwood and Caskey off on the *Santa Paula* on September 19 for Curaçao, La Guaira and Puerto Cabello in Venezuela, en route to Cartagena, Colombia.

Isherwood dedicated the American edition of *The Condor and the Cows* to Caskey's mother and the English edition to his own mother, making them, as he later explained "an unsanctified pair of mothers-in-law."[116] In this regard and in most others, *The Condor and the Cows* was a dutiful book; it fulfilled its obligation to publishers, readers, and the countries traveled. Isherwood observed closely, and he reported methodically and thoughtfully. Even though he was fulfilling a boyhood wish to see Quito, the book described a trip he made for others, not for himself. He wrote it as a diary but with almost no introspection, commenting on local industry, religion, culture, and politics with clarity and occasionally with passion. His intended readers were not a circle of close friends, as with his wartime diaries, but the general public. Perhaps he half consciously wished to protect himself from the criticisms of *Journey to a War*, that he and Auden had been "too preoccupied with their own psychological plight to be anything but helplessly lost in the struggle of modern China," and that they had been "playing."[117] In the South America book, he was resolutely earnest, adult, and objective.

And yet, like all his books, *The Condor and the Cows* is revealing about Isherwood himself. "I now see *The Condor and the Cows* is one of my best books," he later told an interviewer. "I managed to put an enormous amount of things into it that I wanted to say," and "I think a travel book is a marvellous medium for political and philosophical remarks."[118]

He explained the title in a preface: "the Condor is the emblem of the Andes and their mountain republics, while the Cows represent the great cattle-bearing plains, and, more specifically, Argentina—no offense intended." In Lima, the U.S. Ambassador to Peru, Prentice Cooper, who kept a jaguar, an ocelot, a vicuña, a deer, and a heron as pets, told Isherwood: "Condors will peck the eyes out of cows and then drive them with their wings off the edge of a cliff; the cows get killed and the condors eat them."[119]

Isherwood and Caskey traveled south down the west side of the continent, along its mountainous spine and the adjacent low-lying coast. They spent five months in Colombia, Ecuador, Peru, Bolivia, and Argentina; they saw almost nothing of Venezuela, Brazil, Chile, or the other smaller Latin American countries. "My deepest impression is that we have been travelling through an empire in the final stage of its dissolution," wrote Isherwood in a grand, prophetic conclusion to *The Condor and the Cows*, "the new republics aren't yet really free, really integrated. They haven't yet become nations."

With uncanny accuracy, he foresaw "Decades of upheaval. Military rule. Mob rule. Endless violence, relieved only by periods of sheer exhaustion." What remained of his belief in the dialectical development of history was overwhelmed by the extreme contrasts and the violence he observed in both nature and mankind:

> Thunder and avalanches in the mountains, huge floods and storms on the plains. Volcanoes exploding. The earth shaking and splitting. The woods full of savage beasts and poisonous insects and deadly snakes. Knives are whipped out at a word. Whole families are murdered without any reason. Riots are sudden and bloody and often meaningless.

His rhetoric reflected his fear that the monumental agony through which the world had just passed during World War II was only part of a larger, unimaginable, undescribable process, "whatever it may be, it *is* cooking. And it will go on doing so, mysteriously, noisily, furiously, through all the bad times that are coming."[120]

He titled the opening section of *The Condor and the Cows* "The Voyage Out," after Virginia Woolf's debut novel about a party of English people who travel to South America and there lose to a mysterious fever a young girl on the brink of life, newly in love. In Woolf's novel, Richard and Clarissa Dalloway, stars of her masterwork *Mrs. Dalloway*, make a preliminary appearance as messengers from the milieu of sophistication and power at the heart of the British Empire, a life that beckons and then closes to the ill-fated heroine. Isherwood cast himself and Caskey as a similarly unexpected pair, harbingers of expanding curiosity and associated risk, called upon to transform a geographical voyage into a metaphysical one.

He assumed this role for himself with the sense of duty that permeates the whole book. Like the Dalloways, he was a minor celebrity; his public surrounded him among the passengers aboard ship. Fixing his imagination on the married couple with whom he and Caskey shared their table, he wrote, "I must tell stories about China, England, Germany, Hollywood; about Nazis, missionaries and movie stars. I must appear bohemian, lively, happy-go-lucky. But I must also drop reassuring hints of wander-weariness. [...] And I must make it clear, especially to him, that I really earn and respect money."

Indeed, using this persona, updated from Conrad and Maugham, Isherwood established treasure as a central, troubling theme of his South America diary. For the conquistadores, it had been gold; for Conrad in *Nostromo* it had been silver; for Isherwood, it was oil: "The single brutal word, SHELL, painted black on silver storage tanks in the harbor, should be enough to recall the tourist from his daydreams."[121]

Isherwood obliquely announced that *this* travel book would not be about the best hotels, restaurants, museums, and beaches; it would take you below the surface, into the future, on an adventure, like the Jules Verne fantasy journeys he had loved in adolescence. Tourists appear in *The Condor and the Cows* for the sake of contrast, offering an occasional comic sideshow with their predictable reactions to the new and the challenging. On arriving in Cartagena, "the average guest" catches an airplane for Bogotá, less than three hours' flight. "However, we have other plans," confided Isherwood, in a signature gesture of intimacy with readers, "to travel inland up the Magdalena River to a point from which we can take a train to Bogotá. That way we will see more of the country."[122]

The road to Barranquilla, where Isherwood and Caskey could board a river steamer for the nine-day voyage up the Magdalena, was arduous, twisting, pitted, and worsened by rain. Their driver—without consulting them—bribed the customs official not to search their luggage. The bribe was a bottle of rum, to be paid for by Isherwood and Caskey. Isherwood was outraged, but he hardly knew why. "Isn't it simply a specimen of that delightful picturesque South American dishonesty? Isn't it part of the national charm? Isn't it a huge joke?"

Throughout their five months in South America, he never became comfortable with the small-scale rule-breaking that infected officialdom and which he sensed was part of more dangerous corruption. The shady, the dirty, the crooked had been a subject for comedy in his 1930s writings, but to the Isherwood of 1947 it was unacceptable. He longed for purity and cleanliness. Waiting for the riverboat at Barranquilla, Isherwood and Caskey toured a soap factory and a waterworks for filtering and chlorinating the riverwater. To Isherwood, "It was almost as good as visiting a monastery."[123]

In Bogotá, Isherwood was introduced to Colombian intellectuals, and he was struck by the high number of bookstores but disappointed to learn this was because there were no lending libraries. Two ethnologists guided him and Caskey to an All Souls' Day festival at a resort town, Silvia, that was heavily attended by the Guambia Indians who farmed in the surrounding high mountains. Dr. Gregorio Hernández de Alba and Dr. John Rowe from the Smithsonian Institution in Washington, D.C., with local nuns and clergy pointed out ways in which the festival blended Indian and Christian beliefs. (Throughout *The Condor and the Cows*, Isherwood referred to the native Latin Americans as Indians, then the norm in English.) Rowe gave Isherwood his monographs about Inca culture at the time of the Spanish Conquest and about the survival of the Indians and their languages in Peru.[124]

On November 6, Isherwood and Caskey set off by bus and mail car to a frontier post at Ipiales on the Guáitara River. "Behind it, Ecuador towers into the sky, a tumultuous and forbidding wilderness of mountains." They continued south through desolate, rainswept moorland, crossed the Laguna de San Pablo in a rowboat with all their luggage, "romantic, though a bit complicated," and caught the rail bus to Quito, where Isherwood's boyhood fantasy of crossing the equator dissolved into familiar reality: "The Equator is just another valley; you aren't sure which and you don't much care. Quito is just another railroad station, with fuss about baggage and taxis and tips."[125]

He and Caskey lodged in a now shabby grand villa with a Jewish refugee landlady from Prague, inviting comparison with his arrangements at Fräulein Thurau's at Nollendorfstrasse in Berlin. He bumped into a friend from pre-Hitler Berlin, who described her hair-raising escape with her brother from the Gestapo; she now ran a leather goods shop.

Quito, then, was an anticlimax. "The old central section of Quito is very much as I had imagined it," Isherwood wrote in the South American diary.

> The best view is from the top of the Panecillo Hill with the snow peaks of the eastern range for a background—Cayambe, Antisana, Cotopaxi, all more than 18,000 feet high. This kind of beauty is so authentic, so immediately convincing, that you "recognize" it at once, like a famous masterpiece of which you have already seen countless reproductions...

To Upward, he reported in a letter dated the same day as the published diary entry that, actually, just as Mont Blanc had been shrouded in fog when they climbed the Col des Aravis in 1922, he had not seen the mountains from Quito yet because they were "hidden in the clouds, so far." He also told Upward that despite being reminded of their beloved Mortmere, he found the poverty, the suffering, and the social stratification overwhelming: "Quaint, rats, grotesque, picturesque as all these Andean places are, one seldom shakes off a sense of depression. Oh yes, there are jeeps and drugstores, and a new hospital here and there, but the psychology is still so largely colonial."[126]

As in Berlin and in China, he was eager to gauge the condition and mood of the citizenry and the workings of local power structures. He visited social, political, and cultural institutions and talked to the professionals who staffed them. At the old city madhouse, the Manicomio, four hundred patients were in the care of two doctors who reported some success with psychoanalysis, Metrazol injections, and electric shock treatment. Isherwood remarked as a "frustrated doctor" that he would never "miss a chance to see anything medical." He and Caskey returned to watch the shock treatments being administered. He described the machine, called an Offner, as "not much larger than a typewriter," as if the psychiatrists were trying to rewrite their patients' life stories.[127]

At the prison, he admired the atmosphere of freedom inside the locked gates—no guards, no uniforms, private weekly visits for the men with their wives or with prostitutes, plenty of music, games, shoemaking.

He was struck by the challenge facing Quito's poets, painters, and sculptors of creating a national tradition drawing on European achievements, as well as on the complex racial and cultural tapestry of contemporary Ecuadorean life. Writers, he learned, could hope for publication only in a newspaper or magazine. "There are no publishers except the government offices. If you want to bring out a book, you must buy your own paper."[128]

He was pained by the lack of resources which he attributed partly to fickle American self-interest. In a draft essay about Quito, he wrote:

> During the last war, the United States did a great deal in Latin America. Hospitals and schools were built, roads were made, all kinds of public assistance was forthcoming. This assistance, as all but the most brazen hypocrite would admit, had a political motive: Nazi influence had to be countered, and raw materials were wanted for the war effort.[129]

He picked up the theme in the published diary, pointing out that Ecuadoreans clearly saw "Now you don't need us, so you don't bother."[130] He lamented that the British Cultural Institute was closing and the American Cultural Institute was underfunded, despite their role as propaganda centers, which in any case fooled nobody.

The oil companies were the ones spending money. The manager of the Shell Oil Company of Ecuador drove Isherwood and Caskey to Shell-Mera, an oil camp in the Amazon jungle in the east of Ecuador. "The Camp is a big, well-lighted, solidly built town of huts, workshops, and hangars, with a military atmosphere of order and tidiness," Isherwood wrote. "Only a few years ago, the site was swampy virgin jungle." There was a school for the children and a night school for the illiterate adults. Funds were being raised for a hospital. The library had been purchased from the soon-to-be defunct British Cultural Institute.

They toured the area by plane, and Isherwood was filled with admiration for the men who cleared the forest and kept it cleared. The jungle, "left to itself for a few months," he wrote, "would begin to throttle the road, to close in upon the huts, to coil up the derrick, to creep among the engines."[131]

IN EARLY DECEMBER, Isherwood and Caskey headed to Peru. They were introduced to pisco sours, and one night Caskey, drunk, slapped Isherwood's face over dinner. Isherwood included this in *The Condor and the Cows* but nothing else about their relationship. Below the surface, the dynamic between them was shifting; it was Isherwood's trip, and Caskey was growing passive. Isherwood wrote to Kirstein in early January: "I couldn't bear to make this trip with anybody who was energetic or enthusiastic or adaptable. Porky just sits in the midst of it all, an irreducible Anglo-Celtic lump."[132]

Lima, with its colonial center reaching back to Pizarro's time and the surroundings reminiscent of nineteenth-century Paris, impressed Isherwood as "the most imposing city we have seen in South America so far." But his diary entries about Peru again articulated the uncomfortable reality, clearer as the Latin American journey progressed, that he admired the British and American presences, even though they were associated with the empire-building he abhorred, because he respected the energy for social progress and cultural enrichment. At Christmas in Lima there was a food shortage, and the poor stood in line for bread. Alongside this suffering, Isherwood observed thievery and corruption: "I suppose one must ultimately blame the Conquistadores; their original crime haunts this land like a curse."[133]

But "The Incas were imperialists, too," he recorded. "At the height of their power, they had subdued all the other tribes of Peru, and conquered the Bolivian highlands, most of Ecuador, northwestern Argentina, and northern Chile." The treasure which might have paid for social progress seemed to Isherwood to have corrupted the whole continent, just as Conrad had shown in *Nostromo*, published, he noted, the year he was born and "still, after forty-five years, a wonderfully life-like picture of a backward South American state—never mind which."[134]

The gay scene is not mentioned in the published diary, but Isherwood wrote to Kirstein from Quito deploring the self-deception of the homosexuals he met: "The Homintern as such I find gruesomely dreary and corrupt.

They spend three quarters of their time and all of their money pretending not to be, and are mean and vile in their personal relationships."¹³⁵

On January 9, Isherwood and Caskey flew to Arequipa, then continued by train to Cusco, the one-time capital of the Inca Empire. The altitude made Isherwood feel sick, as it had in Bogotá, but he managed the vertigo-inducing pathway to Machu Picchu, "one of the principal stations of this great *via dolorosa*," on a skittering mule. Inca culture did not appeal to him: "I find them, as we used to say during the Evelyn Waugh Period, madly ungay." After rereading one of the monographs given him by John Rowe, *Inca Culture at the Time of the Spanish Conquest*, he concluded that "It was a culture of mass, of authority, of order. [. . .] Much ritual, little spirituality. Much gold, little elegance. Much feasting, little fun."¹³⁶

Isherwood could not fathom, nor could he find out from local intellectuals, what was to become of the Indians nor what they themselves wanted. Assimilation and advancement seemed closed to them. Their language, Quechua, was not taught in schools or used in government business.

With Caskey, he attended a Roman Catholic Mass conducted in Quechua. The religious activity he observed in South America reminded him how highly he valued the spiritual life. In imperfect Catholic efforts in South America, he saw the shining truth learned earlier in California, that human progress must be built on transformation from within. "[I]t can't be denied that the Church in South America is a disgrace to Catholicism," he wrote; yet he felt Catholicism might be the only hope for the Indians, a better hope than the leftism that had attracted him in youth.

He admired the missionary zeal of the Protestants, which produced hospitals, schools, and hygiene, but "I can't help feeling," he wrote, "that Protestantism isn't really suited to the Indian temperament. I believe that the Indians are very devotional; their psychology demands sacraments, shrines and images." He might have been writing about himself and Vedanta. He objected to what he called "Protestant ethical standards," too; the Protestants had too many sins on their list for the Indians to understand which ones mattered. "Where is the difference between telling a lie and smoking a cigarette?" Drinking and chewing coca were part of the Indian way of life. Calling once more upon John Rowe's scholarship, Isherwood remarked "intoxication was a ritual act among the Incas—they only got drunk during religious ceremonies, on prescribed occasions" and "ritual intoxication is still practised among the highland Indians."¹³⁷ For him, drinking was not a sin. As when he had written about Berlin in the 1930s, he was also writing about himself when he wrote about South America and the Indians, obliquely revealing changes in his attitude to religion since leaving the monastery, changes which would shape his fiction in the coming decades.

In late January, they crossed Lake Titicaca to Bolivia and attended another festival at Copacabana at the southern end of the lake. It was attended by hundreds of Indians from towns all over the plateau. Isherwood was attracted, as in Vedanta, to the intimate continuity between spiritual life and ordinary life: "There was a perpetual coming and going between the church and the square. Dancers still sweating from their exertions kept entering the shrine, kneeling for a few moments before the image of the Virgin, then coming out again to dance and drink some more."

He was also attracted to the masked figures, who "operated independently, like harlequins. One of them was a demure and sinister cat; another a bright yellow lion." The masked figures teased and pinched the children; even the adults seemed afraid of them. "It was as if they embodied some sort of totemistic magic."[138]

To learn more about the Latin American Church, he spent a day and a half with a priest of the Catholic Maryknoll fathers, who guided him around a poor Indian area outside La Paz, Villa Victoria. He learned that there were not enough priests—just as there were not enough doctors, schoolteachers, or technicians.

FROM LA PAZ, it took four whole days to reach Buenos Aires by train across the "boundless grasslands" of Argentina. Berthold Szczesny met them at the station and drove them to his house in the suburb called Beccar. Tota Cuevas de Vera and another lover, a man, had set Szczesny up as part-owner of a stone mill. Isherwood was moved by the life Szczesny had created—paintings and books, a phonograph and records, a swimming pool seen through sliding glass doors, a Jeep, a Great Dane. Szczesny was about to marry a young Argentine woman of privileged background. It was an unexpected outcome to "the Szczesny Saga"—he had been a stoker, a boxer, a bartender, a cowboy, helped smuggle German refugees into England and been imprisoned by the Gestapo. Now that he was comparatively rich, his hospitality knew no bounds.[139]

Isherwood dined several times with Rolf Katz, who reported to him on the prosperity that made Buenos Aires so attractive and which made Argentinians "politically apathetic."[140] He saw the abundance in person at Tota's 86,000-acre *estancia*, El Pelado, which sent a weekly trainload of produce to Buenos Aires from its own railway station.

By the end of February, he and Caskey were 250 miles south of Buenos Aires at a seaside resort, Mar del Plata, where they were hosted by a Kirstein friend, Victoria Ocampo, publisher of the Argentine literary magazine *Sur* (*South*). She let Isherwood read her copy of *The Mint*, T.E. Lawrence's then unpublished novel about his experience in the Royal Air Force after World War I, when he had tried to shake off his public identity as Lawrence of Arabia and enlisted under an assumed name. Ocampo had never met Lawrence, but she knew his family, and she had written a book about him, later published with a foreword by one of Lawrence's brothers.[141] Isherwood had never met him either, but in the hero of *The Ascent of F6*, Michael Ransom, he and Auden had taken possession of Lawrence.

"I am much closer to him, in a sense, than she could ever be," wrote Isherwood in *The Condor and the Cows*: "He is part of the mess I am in. What binds me to him are his faults—his instability, his masochism, his insane, inverted pride. Like Shelley and Baudelaire before him, he suffered in his own person the neurotic ills of an entire epoch. And I belonged to that epoch. I can never escape him now."[142]

Isherwood persistently tried to escape these faults, yet at the same time, he needed them as part of his identity as a novelist, in particular his mediumistic gift for suffering the neurotic ills of his epoch. Auden had recognized and commemorated this just before they emigrated in his December 1938 sonnet for Isherwood, "The Novelist," who "in his own weak person, if he can, / Must suffer dully all the wrongs of Man."[143]

Isherwood twice visited the Ramakrishna Ashrama, the only Ramakrishna mission in South America. It was an hour's train ride from Buenos Aires, in Bella Vista. "To me, it was like coming home," he pronounced. "Sitting cross-legged on the floor, before the shrine with its familiar photographs, and listening to the familiar Sanskrit words, I felt myself back in our temple on Ivar Avenue in Hollywood." He was longing for the relief that he had felt in the presence of Prabhavananda's unconditional love, a love that he associated with laughter. In *The Condor and the Cows*, he articulated this more clearly than he had ever done before:

> Ramakrishna's own spiritual genius was frequently expressed in humor—not the sly clever kind, but real rampageous clowning, childlike silliness, extravagance worthy of the Marx Brothers. [...] It is utterly subversive, outrageous, unselfconscious, improper, infectious. Indeed, it is one of the purest and most beautiful aspects of Love.[144]

PARIS, 1948

On March 27, 1948, Isherwood and Caskey left Buenos Aires aboard a French ship, the *Groix*, bound for Le Havre. At sea, Isherwood worked on *The Condor and the Cows* and reread *Nostromo*. He had already written magazine pieces about the trip for an impressive array of publications, and these, with very little revision, were to become chapters in *The Condor and the Cows*.[145] He continued making diary entries, though they were no longer for the travel book.

He sent Kirstein a postcard from Paris on April 29. He was in high spirits: "Paris . . . youth . . . springtime . . . the chestnuts on the Bois . . . the Eiffel Tower . . . the Mona Lisa . . . Gore Vidal—but I can't go on."[146] Vidal, with unabashed and methodical ambition, had introduced himself to Isherwood, twenty-one years his senior, in Les Deux Magots. He had already sent Isherwood his third novel, *The City and the Pillar*, about a love affair between "two 'normal' all-American boys."[147]

Isherwood had not been impressed by the novel, describing it to Kirstein as "better than many, but the usual defeatist trash about poor little me, I'm so queer and horrid and should be put away somewhere quietly, or maybe have a bit of my brain cut out, so I won't know a marine from a monkey."[148] Nonetheless, he admired Vidal for tackling the homosexual theme and for publishing against the advice of his publisher, and he had written from Lima, laying out his own longterm intention to change cultural ideas about homosexuality. He admonished Vidal that it was not enough just to write about homosexuals; they must be portrayed in a positive light with self-conscious political intent:

> There are certain subjects—including the Jewish, Negro and homosexual questions—which involve social and political issues. There are laws which could be changed. There are public prejudices which could be removed. Anything an author writes on these subjects is bound, therefore, to have a certain propaganda value, whether he likes it or not.

He advised Vidal that the "tragic ending: Jim's murder of Bob" in *The City and the Pillar* would encourage the reader to conclude that homosexuality leads to "tragedy, defeat and death." To this, Isherwood objected:

> [M]any homosexuals are unhappy [. . .] But there is another side to the picture, which you (and Proust) don't show. Homosexual relationships can be, and frequently are happy. Men live together for years and make homes and share their lives and their work, just as heterosexuals do. [. . .] Certainly, under the present social setup, a homosexual relationship is more difficult to maintain than a heterosexual one (by the same token, a free-love relationship is more difficult to maintain than a marriage), but doesn't that merely make it more of a challenge and therefore, in a sense, more humanly worthwhile? The success of such a relationship is revolutionary in the best sense of the word. And, because

it demonstrates the power of human affection over fear and prejudice and taboo, it is actually beneficial to society as a whole—as all demonstrations of faith and courage must be: they raise our collective morale.

This was fighting talk in 1947, well ahead of contemporary attitudes, and remains inspiring in the twenty-first century when artistic representations of queer happiness continue to offer necessary defiance to repressive norms. Though it was to prove that Isherwood had not yet achieved this happy longterm relationship in his own life, he wished to write a book that would persuade the Others, the mainstream world, that it was possible. "Forgive me," he begged of Vidal. "I'm really lecturing myself, because I, too, have been guilty of subscribing to the Tragic Homosexual myth in the past, and I am ashamed of it."[149]

He decided that Vidal was "a pretty shrewd operator." In Paris, Vidal asked for career advice, and Isherwood observed: "He is very jealous of Truman, but determined not to quarrel with him because he feels that when a group of writers sticks together it's better business for all of them. (He drew this moral from the Auden–Spender–Day Lewis–MacNeice–Isherwood gang, he says.)"

Vidal certainly was shrewd, flattering Isherwood with this mixture of praise and emulation. By announcing to Isherwood his position vis-à-vis Capote, Vidal was inventing the group to which he wanted to belong. Isherwood later observed: "I believe he really thinks about 'posterity' and its 'verdict'—just like a nineteenth-century writer!"[150]

Isherwood liked Capote's *Other Voices, Other Rooms* better than Vidal's *The City and the Pillar*. He insisted to Kirstein, who didn't much appreciate Capote's work, that "Truman's style, not his content, is remarkable." He wrote careful puffs for both books. Years later, he noted that he "much preferred *Williwaw*," Vidal's first novel, an intensely masculine psychological thriller set on board a storm-tossed ship in wartime. Also, he conceded that Capote's books were "mere skillful embroidery, unrelated to himself and therefore lacking in essential interest."[151] Capote as a character interested Isherwood more than Capote as a writer.

As for characters, Vidal and Capote were both eager to meet Denny Fouts, about whom all three of them were to write in due course. Vidal accompanied Isherwood and Caskey on one of the evenings they spent with Fouts in his apartment on the Rue du Bac. Auden and Kallman were also in Paris and shared a separate visit with Isherwood, Caskey and Fouts. "[T]he thundering herd of Fire Island queens [. . .] have invaded Europe. We met all of them in Paris," Isherwood told Kirstein.[152]

One night, Isherwood and Fouts quarreled—a familiar power struggle over Caskey. Fouts asked Caskey to connect with his opium dealer waiting outside the restaurant where they were eating; Isherwood made Fouts buy the opium himself, fearing Caskey might be arrested. Nevertheless, Isherwood later tried the opium himself. "It tasted like incense and had no apparent effect whatsoever," he wrote in his diary.

He began to imagine Fouts, in his nocturnal opium addict's life, as a creature from beyond the grave, a lost dandy as portrayed by Oscar Wilde. "Denny joined us for cocktails at the Ritz—like Dorian Gray emerging from the tomb—death-pale and very slim in his dark elegant suit, with black hat and umbrella. He looks like the Necropolitan ambassador."[153] These were their last encounters.[154]

ENGLAND, 1948

When at last he was at Wyberslegh in mid-May, Isherwood got back to work on the travel book. Caskey joined him and was "quite a success with the Mater." Caskey was also a success with Isherwood's London friends, including at a party at the *Horizon* office and with Forster at High Table in King's College.[155] They went to see Britten's 1945 opera *Peter Grimes*, for which the English poet Montagu Slater had written the libretto instead of Isherwood, and they also went to Britten's new opera *Albert Herring* at the first-ever Aldeburgh Festival in Suffolk.

In London, they intersected with Capote on his way to Paris to meet Fouts for the first time, and Vidal soon caught up with them, ambitious to enter Isherwood's British circle. Tennessee Williams also appeared. Forster invited Vidal and Williams to Cambridge toward the end of June and reported to Isherwood that "Tennessee Williams got up too late to reach Cambridge. Vidal arrived, and I wish he hadn't, as I disliked him a lot."[156]

Williams sensed that Isherwood was miserable in England, and that misery made him cruel. He described a scene of covert savagery in a letter to their friend Carson McCullers: "he felt called upon to tell Gore, very obliquely and through the mouth of his intimate companion, that he did not think Gore's work of paramount importance. Gore is not able to take this kind of criticism. A real crise developed. Gore spent three sleepless nights, and then left England."

Vidal took revenge on Isherwood—and Forster—years later. In his memoir *Palimpsest*, published a decade after Isherwood was dead and could not reply, Vidal falsely claimed that Forster had publicly humiliated Isherwood by dismissing *Prater Violet* in front of all their literary friends at what Vidal incorrectly declared was their first reunion since the war. He described this supposed humiliation as "a ritual English social blooding," saying it took place at a party for himself and Tennessee Williams given by Lehmann, U.K. publisher of *The City and the Pillar*.[157] In fact it was Vidal who had been publicly humiliated, not Isherwood, as Williams described in his letter. In both accounts Caskey is dismissed as a mere creature channeling Isherwood's opinions, but Caskey generally had his own opinions and was not shy of expressing them.

Vidal announced in *Palimpsest* that although he liked Forster's novels, he had instantly disliked Forster and that neither he nor Williams had wanted to go to Cambridge for lunch with him. The account reveals how badly Isherwood had hurt Vidal.

The botched meeting with Williams and Vidal was only of passing concern to Forster: "What I am really writing about though is *Maurice*," Forster told Isherwood, referring to his unpublished homosexual novel: "I should very much like a talk alone with you during the next week or so. I am ashamed at shirking publication but the objections are formidable."[158]

Their conversation about *Maurice* was to continue for years. Isherwood reread *Maurice* late in 1951, and encouraged Forster to publish it.[159] Early in 1952, when Isherwood was again in England, they spent an evening over supper at the Reform Club discussing how to rewrite it. At his death, Forster entrusted the U.S. publication to Isherwood, and Isherwood assigned the proceeds to the National Institute of Arts and Letters to fund a U.S. travel grant for British writers.

333 EAST RUSTIC ROAD, SANTA MONICA, 1948

Around the beginning of July 1948, Isherwood got movie work at MGM, adapting Dostoevsky's funny and terrifying novella *The Gambler* for Gottfried Reinhardt. He was to revise a script written by Ladislas Fodor, the émigré Hungarian playwright. Isherwood and Caskey took the *Queen Elizabeth* to New York, arriving July 14; Isherwood stayed one night and then boarded a train for Los Angeles, leaving Caskey in Manhattan.

He put up in a Santa Monica hotel, the El Kanan, on Ocean Avenue opposite Muscle Beach. He told Kirstein that he worked long days at the studio and returned to the hotel "only very late at night, drunk."[160] On August 14, he had supper with twenty-nine-year-old Jim Charlton, a Frank Lloyd Wright-trained architect and former air force pilot, and Charlton began spending occasional nights at the El Kanan.

During September, Isherwood and Charlton went away together to Laguna and up into the mountains and to Warner Hot Springs. Isherwood later regretted that he didn't write in his diary about "the wonderful drive around Mount Palomar, which was one of the happiest days of my life."[161] So happy, in fact, that he and Charlton went away again the next weekend, this time to Ensenada in Baja California.

Caskey rejoined Isherwood on September 20, and they settled at 333 East Rustic Road. This was the house and the street Isherwood was to fictionalize as Camphor Tree Lane in *A Single Man*. They rented it from Paula Strasberg, the actress famous as Marilyn Monroe's acting coach. It was two stories, heavily overhung by a huge sycamore tree at the left and a steep cliff behind. In front was a creek running parallel to the road. The creek had been widened and lined with a permanent cement channel to prevent flooding; this gave it a municipal touch. The property was reached by a wooden bridge just wide enough for a car.

Number 333 East Rustic Road was both intimate and isolated, shaded by woods and dappled by shafts of brilliant light. The ground floor had a small galley kitchen and a living room. The ceilings were low, the rooms dim. Up the narrow stairs were two bedrooms, a bathroom, and a glassed-in porch, where Isherwood worked on the South American book. He told Kirstein that once they had found the house, "Pig sprouted wings and has been cooking, painting, carpentering and sewing ever since. [. . .] We now lead a life of the stodgiest domesticity." Within a few days of returning, Caskey met Charlton over supper with Isherwood. Charlton had the temperament to make a third in any relationship, sexual, romantic, or just friendly. He easily became part of their ménage, forming his own friendship with Caskey.

The Dostoevsky movie started shooting on October 6. It was called *The Great Sinner*, and Isherwood's revised script included material from *Crime and Punishment* and from Dostoevsky's own life story. Also, it had a happy ending. "I know he'll <u>never</u> speak to me in heaven," Isherwood told Kirstein.[162]

Gambling was transformed into a metaphor describing the writer's relationship with his material. Down on his luck, the writer—played by Gregory Peck—pledges his work notes at the casino, and gambles away his literary future. He is about to rob the poor box in a church when he has a vision of Christ and undergoes a religious conversion. In his final scene, miraculously cured, he tells the casino owner he has found something more exciting than gambling—"Writing about it."[163]

The casino owner was given the name de Glasse, and mirrors reflected the spiritual condition of the characters. The script itself reflected Isherwood's attitude toward writing for Hollywood. Having won big with a share of $50,000 for *Judgement Day in Pittsburgh*, he was now playing roulette. Should he place his bet on this movie story, that movie story? This producer?

That director? Which project would solve his money problems? Which would make him rich enough to turn back to his novel? Was he gambling away his literary future by writing scripts? "Every time I do one," he admitted to Lehmann, "the dyer's hand is a little harder to wash clean."[164]

ISHERWOOD HAD RETRIEVED his wartime diaries from Kirstein when he passed through New York in the summer of 1948. He was anxious, though, about his books, which were still waiting to be shipped west. The Sterns' basement had flooded, and he wrote to Kirstein that the books "are being eaten by cockroaches, rats, bats, etc. If you are down that way, would you go and look at them?" At last they arrived in early January. "When he saw several of his especially beloved volumes stained and crinkled and cracked, he shed tears."[165]

He saw a private screening of *The Great Sinner* on March 16, and there was a preview for the public a week later. "Peck was awful. He did his best but he was hopelessly miscast," wrote Isherwood in *Lost Years*. His co-star, Ava Gardner, was no better. "[T]he total effect was mediocre, Hollywoodish, saccharine."[166]

Isherwood finished *The Condor and the Cows* on April 2 and sent it off to his publisher with Caskey's photographs.[167] He then turned to his novel and eked out a chapter, about eighteen pages long, which he later abandoned.

With Forster, he was elected to the ultra-highbrow National Institute of Arts and Letters, but he didn't record this in his diaries or date books or mention it to friends, apart from square old John Lehmann, who he knew would be impressed: "I am now respectable [...] and may wear a rosette," he boasted.[168] Meanwhile, without studio work, he had begun collecting $25 a week government unemployment insurance; he went to the office in person.

During the summer of 1949, he developed a new script idea with Lesser Samuels, *The Easiest Thing in the World*, about the tragic effects of slander in small-town America. It featured a beautiful, fanatical young woman evangelist, and it breathed the atmosphere of the coming McCarthy era. "It's the easiest thing in the world," the hero proclaims, "to make us believe evil—of anything—a play, a book, a person, a faith." Isherwood had recently reread *The Bostonians* by Henry James, "my favorite long novel by James," in which the voice of the feminist movement speaks through the charismatic young orator, Verena Tarrant.[169] Once again, he tried to sneak a rebellious literary heroine into a Hollywood movie. This one carried some of the real-life attributes of Aimee Semple McPherson, the Pentecostal evangelist who denounced theater and films as the work of Satan while using all the tricks of show business to turn herself into the first-ever religious media star. The studios showed no interest.

THERE WERE DINNERS at Salka Viertel's with Garbo, Montgomery Clift, Charlie Chaplin and his fourth wife Oona O'Neill. At Peggy Kiskadden's, it was the American producer Sam Zimbalist with his wife and the Viennese director Fred Zinnemann with his wife, Renée. New York publisher and Hollywood producer Frank Taylor and his wife Nan entertained for Robert Penn Warren, for Chaplin, for Edgar Snow. In December 1948 and again in March 1949, Isherwood went to parties given by Thomas and Katja Mann. He had been friendly with their son, the novelist and magazine editor Klaus Mann, since 1931 in Berlin.

Klaus was the second of six children. In 1935, his elder sister, Erika, had been declared an Enemy of the Reich for writing and performing in a satirical anti-Nazi cabaret, so Klaus asked Isherwood to marry her and provide her with a British passport. Isherwood, in Amsterdam at the time, passed the marriage request to Auden who met Erika, sight unseen, off a train in Ledbury, Herefordshire, and married her at the local registrar's office on June 15, 1935.[170] Klaus also lost his German citizenship—for publishing an anti-Nazi literary magazine, *Die Sammlung* (*The Collection*).

Klaus and Erika emigrated to America, where they continued to oppose the Nazis by lecturing and writing, and they were the first to greet Auden and Isherwood on the *Champlain* in January 1939: "They had come out to the ship on the quarantine launch, posing as journalists who wanted our interview," wrote Isherwood in his diary. Thomas Mann was then a guest lecturer at Princeton, where Auden and Isherwood visited and were photographed with the family for *Time* magazine. Isherwood described the scene in *Christopher and His Kind*: "'I know Mr. Auden's your son-in-law,' said the photographer, 'but Mr. Isherwood—what's his relation to your family?' Thomas's prompt reply made everybody laugh but the photographer, who didn't understand German: 'Family pimp.'"[171]

In 1941, Thomas and Katja Mann had moved to Pacific Palisades, where the family reassembled gradually. All had been deprived of German citizenship after Thomas made a statement in 1936 opposing the Nazi regime, and his books were banned. Katja was Jewish. During the war, Isherwood had found Erika strident and even vengeful in her attitude to Germany, and he had felt more comfortable with Klaus's equivocation. Klaus told Isherwood that he was a pacifist even though he favored war against Hitler: "he couldn't possibly kill anyone personally."[172] Klaus became a U.S. citizen and served in the army, despite being homosexual and a longtime heroin user.

In the autumn of 1948, Isherwood and Klaus worked on a film script about the Dutch painter Han van Meegeren, who forged Vermeers and de Hoochs that were so convincing they were hung in the Rijksmuseum in Amsterdam. According to Isherwood's later account, "This project was entirely Klaus's idea; he had studied Van Meegeren's career while he was in Holland." They gave an outline to Frank Taylor, then producing at MGM, but the project stalled, and Thomas Mann wrote witheringly to Klaus about involving himself with the "starry-eyed" Isherwood and Hollywood: "The starry-eyed one seems to have failed—anyone who counts on the movies is throwing himself on Satan's mercies."[173]

The following year, Klaus killed himself in Cannes. It was not his first attempt. Suicide ran in the family; two aunts and later his youngest brother also killed themselves. It fell to Isherwood to tell Klaus's current boyfriend, Harold Fairbanks, who was in the merchant marine and friendly with Caskey. Isherwood wrote a memorial portraying Klaus's reserve, his European manners, his sympathetic ambivalence, and vulnerable sophistication: "Birdlike, he seems to be balancing upon the truth, as if upon a slender, unsteady twig. He is so anxious to say precisely what he means."[174] Writing the memorial was made more poignant by the fact that when Virginia Woolf had committed suicide in 1941, Klaus had persuaded Isherwood to write a memorial about *her* for his wartime magazine, *Decision*, ending one of Isherwood's worst-ever dry spells.

OCCASIONALLY, ISHERWOOD WENT to the Vedanta Society for tea, for supper, and for ceremonies on holy days. After the Ramakrishna Birthday Puja on March 1, 1949, he wrote in his diary "Swami still keeps a room in the other house—the one behind 1946—which he says is for me. It rather scares me—the way he waits. Shall I ever find myself back there? It seems impossible—and yet—"[175]

That year, Heard gave up on Trabuco College and donated the site to the Vedanta Society. Prabhavananda was to consecrate it as a monastery in September 1949, and it was to become another refuge for Isherwood.

For now, he made japam only "when he remembered to,"[176] and when he prayed, he seldom prayed for Caskey. He managed to produce a foreword for a biography of Swami Shivananda, the second president of the Ramakrishna Order and a direct disciple of Ramakrishna. With Prabhavananda, he began translating the yoga aphorisms of Patanjali.

Living with Caskey was getting difficult, and Isherwood turned to his neglected diary in torment, warning himself, "It is absolutely useless and self-destructive to get mad at Caskey about his all-night record playing." As he later explained in *Lost Years*, the struggle over the record player was simply one expression of "the clash of their wills." Isherwood wanted a comfortable, predictable, quiet daily life so he could work. Caskey wanted "surprises, unexpected guests, parties which snowballed into roaring crowds, out-of-town trips taken on the spur of the moment."[177]

The conflict affected Isherwood's health, and by the end of May 1949, he feared he was "really verging on some kind of a nervous breakdown." He bubbled with the same kind of resentment he had felt toward Harvey Young in 1940. "He is lazy. He won't earn money. He won't even try to draw his pension. He stays out late. He is cold, bitchy, selfish, etc. etc. I rehearse bits of this great accusation as I lie in bed in the morning, until it seems as if my thoughts would wake him up, they are so loud."

He was unable to imagine living alone, and wrote in his diary: "Leaving Caskey—quite aside from being terribly painful—wouldn't really solve anything. Unless there were someone else to go to—which there isn't. Or unless I were prepared to return to Ivar Avenue—which I'm not. Therefore we have to stay together."

He advised himself to accept Caskey "*exactly as he is*," and he used his diary—as his mother used hers—to instruct himself. "I *must* stop trying to subdue Caskey, to shame him, to make him feel guilty," he wrote. "It *is* possible if you build up your inner life of prayer, meditation, artistic creation, physical exercise and routine, and simply let Caskey do as he pleases—"[178] His good intentions achieved little, but he was rehearsing for his relationship with Bachardy.

ON AUGUST 6, 1949, Isherwood went to an all-night party given by Sam and Eddie From, twin brothers from the Midwest. Isadore (Eddie) From worked for Technicolor and later became a psychotherapist. He was once picked up by the police for a homosexual offense, and Isherwood helped him in some unspecified way; that's how they met.[179] The brothers shared a house on Benton Way in Silver Lake with their friend who owned the house, Ruby Bell, a librarian, and Charles Aufderheide, who also worked at Technicolor as a camera technician and was an amateur poet. They were the nucleus of what become known as the Benton Way Group, intellectuals and professionals living together in an unconventional ménage and communally examining their lives and sexual relationships.

Evelyn Caldwell, a psychology professor at UCLA who was studying the homosexual community in Los Angeles and offering counseling to homosexual clients, attended the August 6 party; she was to become well known by her married name, Evelyn Hooker. Also attending were the writer Paul Goodman, the philosopher David Sachs, Sachs's friend George Bill, and Alvin Novak, a pianist studying philosophy at UCLA. In the 1970s, Isherwood recalled about the party: "That night, Goodman, David Sachs and Christopher probably did most of the talking. I think that the nature of homosexual love was discussed at enormous length, and that they quizzed Evelyn on her knowledge of gay slang and kidded her, saying that they were going to smuggle her into a gay male bathhouse."

At dawn on August 7, Isherwood drove from Silver Lake back to Santa Monica with Sam From and Alvin Novak. They went to the beach and swam and then to 333 East Rustic Road, where Sam From fell asleep and Isherwood and Novak had sex. "[H]ighly romantic," Isherwood observed, looking back. "It was unique, at any rate. Christopher never went to a party that was quite like it."

The all-night discussion followed by a sensual dousing in the ocean was a real-life forerunner of the fictional night that George spends with Kenny Potter in *A Single Man*, and Isherwood's remarks in letters and diary about the figure of Socrates show that he was reimagining the *Symposium* in the novel. By the time he wrote *Lost Years*, he had come to look back on the all-night party as a Platonic Love Feast. In *Lost Years*, he designated Paul Goodman as "the Socrates of the group" and Alvin Novak as "the Alcibiades of the evening's *Symposium*."[180] In the intervening years, he had reread the *Symposium* at least twice, and he had also read Angus Wilson's story collection about Socrates, *Hemlock and After* (1952). He told Kirstein that he felt "terribly disappointed" by Wilson's book:

> It was meant to be heroic (according to Wilson himself, whom I met while last in London) but it fails to make you feel that, I think, utterly. Sands was supposed to have been a modern Socrates, but Wilson fails to show a single scene in which he is even corrupting, much less instructing, the Youth. I never felt he had any relation to those boys, or slept with them, or liked them at all.[181]

Sands is Wilson's protagonist. Isherwood's disappointment highlights not only how central love and sex were to his conception of the pedagogic friendships between Socrates and the Youth of Athens, but also that Isherwood felt such friendships should be—or anyway *could* be—shown in a heroic light. He was to find his own way to do this, portraying George in *A Single Man* as a modern Socrates, corrupting, instructing, trying to sleep with and certainly liking the Youth of southern California. Meanwhile, Isherwood's homosexual tribe, its tradition and sensibility, threatened and driven underground by

Hitler and the war, was preparing to reemerge; the Benton Way Group was an early ripple in the gay liberation movement in Los Angeles.

There was no end to Isherwood's sexual itch, nor to his pedagogic impulse. During 1949, the names of sexmates frequently appear in his diary. In addition to Jim Charlton, he mentioned Russ Zeininger, Paul Porter, Don Coombs, who was an English professor, and many others. He had supper with the Benton Way Group again a few weeks after the party. He was reflecting all the time on the sexual behavior of his tribe, trying to codify it, and sharing his code with younger men.

In a letter to a young acquaintance serving in the coastguard—written at the end of 1943 when Isherwood had first begun to lose his grip on celibacy in the monastery—he offered the sort of advice he must have offered to many young men, advice reflecting his ideal of sexual deportment as kind, generous, truthful, and without rivalry, guilt, or gossip: "If you are promiscuous, then don't tell each one he's Mr. Big; and never steal boy friends just to get the sense of power; and never have sex with anybody unless you yourself want to, or—when you like someone and want to do him the pleasure—if you are quite sure you can avoid the whole thing going sour on you afterwards."[182]

In *Lost Years*, Isherwood pondered his state during the last months of the 1940s: "Did Christopher ever relax? Yes—in the ocean, plunging his hangover headaches into the waves—drinking, especially if Caskey wasn't around—naked in bed with Jim Charlton or some other sexmate—but such respites were short. Most of the time Christopher was under tremendous strain."[183] Sex and drinking, frowned upon by even some of his most liberal friends, were part of an earnest, everlasting exploration.

Heard, Huxley, and Prabhavananda admonished Isherwood about his way of life. The drinking was not all due to Caskey. In *Lost Years*, Isherwood described occasions during which he was so drunk that he couldn't participate in what was happening. In June 1949, there was a dinner at the home of an accomplished French chef who cooked only by appointment. Isherwood never got to taste the food: "He was drunk already when they arrived, and went to sleep in a hammock on the front lawn." Another memory, during an evening at the Stravinskys' with the Huxleys, was "Christopher lying on the floor, dozy with drink. Christopher looks up and sees Aldous towering skyscraper-tall above him—ignoring Christopher with English tact, as he talks aesthetics to Igor in French." Charlie Chaplin ended their friendship after Isherwood reportedly peed on a sofa in Chaplin's house after passing out there. Caskey, who was with Isherwood at the house, said the story was untrue, but Iris Tree and her screenwriter son Ivan Moffat believed it. Isherwood never discovered any other reason why Chaplin stopped inviting him to parties, nor was he able to effect a reconciliation.[184]

In November 1949, Isherwood and Caskey agreed on a temporary split. "One symptom of their weariness," Isherwood later wrote, "was that they had stopped quarrelling." Caskey hitchhiked to Florida to see his sister. Isherwood expressed his distress with a sore throat, "very bad, sometimes I can hardly swallow."[185] His first night alone, Jim Charlton showed up. Isherwood's anxiety to fulfill his romantic destiny was compulsive but led nowhere. The next morning, he took off for Trabuco with Russ Zeininger. Four days after Caskey's departure, he wrote in his diary: "I'm already tired of wasting money in restaurants, making infinitely cautious overtures to prospective affairs, etc." He gave up smoking, a symbolic austerity. He felt safe with Charlton and slept long, sound hours at Charlton's apartment, but these were "domestic, not [. . .] romantic" episodes. He found Charlton "too restful, too easy to be with, too predictable to be all absorbing." Also, he knew Charlton was not likely to commit himself to a single relationship. "There would be other people in his life, and scenes about them."[186]

Britten and Pears were giving some concerts in Los Angeles, and Isherwood and Charlton heard one on the night of Thanksgiving. They took Britten and Pears away to Palm Springs and Laguna Beach, then Isherwood threw a party to introduce Britten and Pears to cute boys. Britten confided that he had sex only with Pears: "I still feel the old charm."[187]

The cute boys were really for Isherwood. He felt "jittery" before the party because he hadn't smoked for six days and because he was worried "that he wouldn't be able to remember all their names. He kept repeating them, to reassure himself." He felt jittery, too, about his debut, temporarily single, in front of the crowd of young men. "Waldo Angelo, Hank Burczinzky, Hanns Hagenbuehler, Nicky Nadeau, Victor Rueda, Leif Argo, Russ Zeininger, Ted Baccardi [sic], Amos Shepherd. American names."[188] He wrote them in his diary, as if trialing them for use in a future story set in America, or auditioning the boys for a future role in his life. He had been desperately trying to replace Caskey since long before Caskey had left town. Ted Bachardy was a key to his future, but as with the Nowak brothers in Berlin in 1929–30, Isherwood was to dally for a time with the wrong brother.

THE HOUSE AT East Rustic Road began to frighten Isherwood as Marple Hall had once frightened him. His landlady Paula Strasberg had told him, "It's a very lonely house," and laughed when he asked whether she meant haunted. On three separate occasions, a figure was seen moving upstairs, and during a Ouija board session, Caskey and some companions thought they contacted a woman who had killed herself in the house. Isherwood was impressed by "the intensity of the unpleasant psychic atmosphere,"[189] more potent than anything he had sensed before.

At night, lit up, the house looked snug from the outside, "But it never seemed snug to Christopher. It seemed secret, unhomely, *unheimlich*." The sycamore trees dropped limbs without warning, and one tree fell over during the night, narrowly missing the house. Isherwood later recalled that he "woke abruptly, about a half a minute before this happened." Working at his desk upstairs in the glassed-in porch, he would sense someone nearby but could never turn quickly enough to see them, and when he slept alone in the house, "he would sometimes wake thrilling with fear." He came to understand it as a dark harmony between his inner and outer worlds: "The longer he lived there, the more he felt that its psychic atmosphere was *both* something which had belonged to the place before he came there *and* something which was a projection of his own disturbed, miserable, hate-filled state of mind."[190]

In his diary, Isherwood described killing ants in the kitchen in the dead of night then making eggs and recalling one of Nanny's comforting nursery jingles. He was to use the diary passage in *A Single Man* to portray his character, George, facing middle age alone after the death of his lover, Jim. It captured the spectral quality of past time inhabiting present time, and it also evoked the mind's efforts to defend itself from large fears by substituting smaller ones—to make a campfire circle that might hold at bay a wider, more threatening darkness, like the Shell-Mera Camp that had impressed Isherwood in the encroaching Ecuadorean jungle. Nanny's jingle made Isherwood feel sad: "You hear a cheery little voice saying it—a voice which takes no account of the atom bomb, the Sermon on the Mount or Beethoven's C-sharp minor Quartet. The false snugness of the tiny nursery pleasures; and all around, the howling wilderness of life."[191]

Only two nights before he made this diary entry, Isherwood and Charlton, with whom Isherwood felt so safe, had been arrested in a raid on the Variety, a bar on the Pacific Coast Highway. They were questioned at the Santa Monica police station. Both denied being homosexual and were released, but Isherwood was enraged at the police and disappointed with himself for not having "called their bluff, insisted on being locked up, hired a lawyer, taken the case to the Supreme Court, started a nationwide stink."[192]

Later, in *Lost Years*, he described the humiliating treatment he and Charlton received from the police sergeant, who "declared that he recognized Christopher from the 'faggot bars' downtown." After checking to see whether they had criminal records, the police sergeant asked "Are you two having a romance?" Ever ready to forgive his tormentors and blame himself, Isherwood wrote: "This actually not very dreadful ordeal has haunted Christopher ever since. Even as I write these words, I feel bitterly ashamed of him for not having said he was queer. And yet I'm well aware of the counterargument: why in hell should you give yourself away to the Enemy, knowing that he can make use of everything you tell him?"[193] He was still a survivor, not an Oscar Wilde.

He learned that a neighbor across East Rustic Road had reported him to the police as a homosexual. The police watched his house one night from a parked car. It transpired that the neighbor was psychotic and had made outlandish accusations against others in the street, so Isherwood signed a neighborhood petition asking the district attorney to ignore her testimony.

Literally haunted by his shortcomings, determined to guard his privacy and his freedom, constantly aware of risks all around him, Isherwood needed a tribe and also a companion. He was utterly stuck with his novel about the refugees and the Quakers that he had begun and abandoned repeatedly since finishing *Prater Violet* in 1945 and with which he would not really get traction until 1951. Before the end of 1949, he began yet another romance, this time with a young would-be writer called Michael Leopold, from Texas, who stayed over Christmas and New Year. According to *Lost Years*, Leopold was "intelligent, ardently literary, a tireless talker and sex partner." More than that, he was "eager to become Christopher's literary disciple," asked questions about books and writing, and worked on a story of his own when Isherwood worked.[194]

In no time, Isherwood was jotting down new story ideas. One was about an established middle-aged writer going through a period of "complete impotence" and a younger writer, "still unpublished," invited to stay, who finds himself writing as he has never been able to write before. The established writer pretends to work, reconfiguring Henry James's tales of erotic inspiration between mentor and disciple. "Does the young man unconsciously 'cure' him?" Isherwood wondered in his diary. "Perhaps."[195]

Revisiting the diary passage in *Lost Years*, Isherwood commented: "Barely ten days after their first meeting, Michael has been 'assimilated' and transformed into a fiction character."[196] Of course, Isherwood had assimilated many other young men in the same way.

After recording his new story ideas, Isherwood made a long diary entry about his novel, why he was stuck and how to proceed. All of his thoughts were about the material itself; none was about his way of life. He felt inspired by Leopold, yet he was incapable of sustained creative effort. Every few months he would have another burst of energy, write in his diary or a big planning workbook, then nothing for weeks.

At the start of 1950, Bill Harris, "Mr. X.," stayed at East Rustic Road, keeping Isherwood company through most of January, and Isherwood wrote two more film scripts, on spec. One, *Below the Equator*, with Huxley, their third collaboration, was about a failed leftist revolution in an imaginary

Latin American country and drew on Isherwood's recent trip. The other, with Lesser Samuels, also their third collaboration, was called the *The Vacant Room*. This was a ghost story updating and Americanizing the doppelgänger thrillers Isherwood loved, *Dr. Jekyll and Mr. Hyde* and *The Picture of Dorian Gray* among others, and Isherwood worked on the screenplay again in later years.[197]

CASKEY RETURNED IN April after five months away. His father had died, so, after Florida, he had gone home to Kentucky to settle family affairs. By June, trouble was brewing. Isherwood was trying to land an assignment with a monthly literary magazine, *Tomorrow*, for a series of long book reviews that might release him financially from film-script roulette. The editor of *Tomorrow*, Bill Kennedy, was visiting Los Angeles. Over dinner with Kennedy and Isherwood, Caskey "denounced Kennedy for belonging to the entrepreneur class, staying at the Miramar, etc." The next day, Isherwood found he could make no progress with a review promised elsewhere, about *A Field of Broken Stones* by the painter Lowell Naeve, a conscientious objector during World War II.[198] He felt sick and had to spend the afternoon trying to mend the situation with Kennedy.

Despite Caskey's abrasive behavior, Isherwood got the reviewing he wanted. He began with Ray Bradbury's *The Martian Chronicles*, which he praised as the outstanding fictional response to the threat of nuclear annihilation, "the story of a purely American immigration," fantasy not science fiction, and worthy, in Isherwood's view, of comparison to Edgar Allan Poe, "the greatest master of his particular genre." According to Bradbury, Isherwood's piece "turned my career around, that year."[199]

That summer, Caskey planned a trip to Baja California with Jay Laval and Lennie Newman, who had been assistant chef at Café Jay and one of Laval's lovers. Isherwood occupied himself with his own excursions. The longest, in August, was a two-week road trip with Peggy Kiskadden and her three-year-old son to visit Georgia O'Keeffe in Abiquiú, New Mexico.

During the trip, Isherwood worked on a review of Ford Madox Ford's tetralogy *Parade's End* for *Tomorrow*. "The character of Sylvia Tietjens made him think of Caskey and the quarrels at Rustic Road."[200] Christopher Tietjens, guided by his English gentleman's code of conduct, never blames his promiscuous wife for the failure of their marriage. Isherwood likewise had no intention of blaming or curbing Caskey's promiscuity or his own, nor did he consider their infidelities as sins. Yet they were quarreling, and although he buried it, Isherwood felt hurt and betrayed.

O'Keeffe drove Isherwood, Kiskadden, and the three-year-old to Taos to see the Lawrence Ranch and Frieda Lawrence and her lover, Angelo Ravagli. Isherwood had met them a decade earlier when Frieda asked him to help dramatize Lawrence's novel *The Plumed Serpent*. "It is exactly as Lawrence described it in *St. Mawr*," wrote Isherwood with satisfaction in Taos. The house in which Lawrence had lived intermittently from 1922 to 1925 and where he had written much of *St. Mawr* and *The Plumed Serpent* in the summer of 1924 seemed to Isherwood "strangely joyful." He cast a pilgrim's eye over Lawrence's possessions and expressed surprise that Lawrence's paintings had been allowed to get dirty (even though he didn't like them). Frieda and Ravagli had moved into a new house built by Ravagli, "blocking out the view from the old Lawrence house behind it, from jealousy, probably."

Isherwood found the atmosphere of the new house "squalid," and he described Lawrence's tomb as "very amateur-dauby," but nothing could dim his admiration. "Peggy was shocked because I signed the guest book. Didn't tell her that I also took two red flowers from the hillside in front of it and pressed them in my billfold for relics."[201]

On his own, Isherwood drove to Sante Fe to visit the photographer Carl Van Vechten and the poet and translator Witter Bynner. Bynner had traveled to Mexico with the Lawrences in 1923 and was portrayed by Lawrence as Owen Rhys in *The Plumed Serpent*. He had written his own book about this, *Journey with Genius*, which Isherwood pronounced "an extremely interesting but rather bitchy, envious book."[202] Leaving Santa Fe to return to Abiquiú, Isherwood was stopped by the police for drunk driving. They offered him a fine on the spot instead of a trial—thirty dollars.

The New Mexico trip tested Isherwood's friendship with Peggy Kiskadden. He sensed that she couldn't accept his boyfriends, and there were many she didn't even know about. When they got back to Santa Monica, they found a "wild mess" in the house at East Rustic Road. Isherwood surmised that Caskey had given a party before leaving for Baja with Laval and Newman, and that he had planned to be home and clean up before Isherwood got back. "There were spider's webs in some of the glasses and drowned insects in others. The food, in that damp atmosphere, was already furred with mold. And there was an odor of decay in the air." Kiskadden was horrified. "'Let's get away from here, darling,' she said urgently and in a hushed voice, 'you can come and stay with us—for as long as you like.'" He persuaded her to go and let him clean up, and he decided that they could no longer "be intimate" if he was living in a homosexual relationship. "She would always try to undermine it and make Christopher feel guilty."

The next day, he found out that Caskey had never reached Baja. He was in jail. Like Isherwood, Caskey had been arrested for drunk driving. The judge had offered him a fine, just as the police outside Santa Fe had offered Isherwood, but Caskey had refused to pay and was given three months in the Santa Ana jail. Isherwood visited and proposed hiring a lawyer, but this, too, Caskey refused. "His Catholic conscience imposed this penance, to some extent; he felt that it was time for him to be punished for his drunkenness," Isherwood explained in *Lost Years*. "Also, he wanted to keep away from Christopher for a while, knowing that Christopher's martyred forbearance would make him feel more guilty, as well as hostile."[203]

For the rest of the summer and into the autumn of 1950, Isherwood visited Caskey in jail every Saturday. Caskey got time off for good behavior and was released at the end of October. The jail sentence had again postponed solving the problem of their relationship, but when Isherwood brought Caskey back to East Rustic Road, he himself took to his bed and stayed there for a week. He came to see his collapse as psychosomatic, recalling in *Lost Years* that one of his symptoms was "numbness in the legs," and that perhaps he was trying to punish Caskey or appeal to Caskey to nanny him.

Dr. Kolisch attended and then Prabhavananda. On November 7, Isherwood got up to look for a new place to live with Caskey because their lease was expiring. Then he went back to bed, and Kolisch attended again, delivering "the most memorable piece of medical advice he has ever received," as Isherwood later thought: "You have the kind of constitution which is capable of simulating every species of pathological condition. So I would urge you, never consult a doctor again, as long as you live. It will only be necessary once—and then it will be too late."

Writing about the episode in *Lost Years*, Isherwood noted that John Van Druten had recently suffered numbness in his legs, diagnosed as "senile polio," and that his own body seemed to be emulating Van Druten.[204] He did not mention something equally likely: his involvement with a group of paraplegic World War II veterans.

As a form of social service, Isherwood had been visiting the paraplegic veterans at the Birmingham Hospital in Van Nuys several times a month since June 1949, and he gave parties for them at East Rustic Road, where they visited in their wheelchairs with girlfriends and wives. When Norman Mailer came to Hollywood to make a movie of his World War II novel *The Naked and the Dead*, Isherwood arranged for Mailer to attend one of the parties and tell war stories.

In June 1950, the paraplegics had been relocated to Long Beach Veterans Hospital, where Isherwood continued to visit them and also to visit tuberculosis cases. In *Lost Years*, he recalled with cynicism that he was "posing as a fearless Francis of Assisi."[205] The visits were another iteration of his mission—like Oliver Twist or Lawrence of Arabia—to venture among the poor, the oppressed, the afflicted, confident that he would safely return to tell his tale. Though he later scorned his exhibitionism, his acts of charity were real.

Fred Zinnemann had directed a film, *The Men*, in which some of the veterans appeared as extras alongside Marlon Brando playing a paraplegic veteran, Brando's first film role. Brando had lived at the Birmingham hospital for a month preparing. Isherwood saw *The Men* with Frank and Nan Taylor in mid-January 1950 and again at the Birmingham Hospital the week following with the paraplegics, and he met and became friendly with Brando later in the year, when Tennessee Williams came to town to polish the script for the movie version of *A Streetcar Named Desire*.

While Isherwood was visiting Caskey in jail regularly, he stopped visiting the paraplegics. The drive was too far, especially after they were relocated to Long Beach. He was to restart his visits a few years later, but meantime, guilt about the failure of his relationship with Caskey evidently combined with repressed feelings about the war veterans—reminiscent of the veterans he had visited at Brabyns War Hospital during World War I—reduced him to the passive role of cripple that he had played in childhood whenever he felt overwhelmed. His recurring sense of helplessness and paralysis were to be symbolised in his next novel *The World in the Evening* in the broken leg Stephen Monk suffers when he is hit by a truck—the novel Isherwood was still unable to write.

LAGUNA, 1950

By November 10, Isherwood was out looking at houses again with Caskey, and after Thanksgiving, they extended the search to Laguna where they signed a lease for 31152 Monterey Street.

The street "wound around the hillside above the Coast Highway, looking down on Camel Point and the beach below it," Isherwood recalled in *Lost Years*. The house was built in "country-cottage style" with a long garden sloping down toward the road and a view over the tops of the houses on the other side of Monterey Street toward the islands of Catalina and San Clemente and, to the north, the Palos Verdes headland.[206] When they moved in, in mid-December 1950, he wrote in his diary that he liked the house for its "atmosphere of 'Old Laguna'—the original colony of third-rate watercolorists, mild eccentrics, British expatriate ladies who ran 'Scottish' tea shops, astrologers, breeders of poodles, all kinds of refugees from American city life." It was a backwater, outside the mainstream, and it reminded him of the seaside locales he had loved in childhood:

this whole area of small houses, gardens of flowering shrubs and sheltered winter sunshine, sandy lanes winding up and down the steep hillside, takes me back to early memories of Penmaenmawr and Ventnor. I have an agreeable feeling of having come to the very last western edge of America, looking out over the pale bright Pacific—much cleaner than at Santa Monica—with nothing between me and Catalina but mist and a huge telephone pole.[207]

He was experiencing more than nostalgia. The edge-of-the-world feeling in Laguna recalled the narrow last ledge of childhood happiness on which he and his mother had sheltered together in Ventnor in April and early May 1915 when he was recovering the use of his legs after measles and pneumonia and just before the news came that his father was missing in action. It had been their last hopeful time together.

On the other hand, Caskey was attracted by the fact that the new house had been a bordello during the war: "several whores had lived at 31152 and had entertained service men there. Caskey felt that this had given the place a 'party atmosphere.'"[208]

Nest-making seemed to promise a happy new life. Caskey started building bookshelves, and they drove Isherwood's books down from Santa Monica in their station wagon, then rented a truck and brought furniture in time for Christmas.

Isherwood recognized that he was circling back into a beloved and familiar trap. As they were moving in, he made an outline for a film, *The Day's Journey*, conceived as an allegory like Bunyan's *Pilgrim's Progress* about the journey of the soul toward God. The journey was to take place in a Vedanta framework rather than a Christian one. Isherwood imagined a young man in a bar—drunk, recently in a fight—trying to make a telephone call. The telephone call symbolizes the choice the young man has to contact God; he is repeatedly delayed by the pleasures and temptations of the world. "He seems hopelessly astray," Isherwood wrote, as he outlined the film with some help from Jim Charlton:

> This is, of course, a symbolic story. "The Day's Journey" is the span of a human life. The Boy is Everyman. The bar in which we first see him represents a sort of limbo between the end of one life and the beginning of another. The Barman and the Proprietress are personifications of the power of Maya, seeking to bind him to the Karmic wheel of birth-death-rebirth. The Boy, through all his rough experiences of ignorance and illusion in a previous birth, has been dimly aware that it is always possible to "telephone"—i.e. to make contact with the power of Reality and thus free himself from the Karmic wheel.[209]

The young man is so engaged with the struggle of his life that he never makes the telephone call, and so he is doomed to be reborn. Isherwood planned to symbolize this through California car culture—the boy would leave the bar, jump into an unfamiliar vehicle, and go for another ride. Affirming the pattern, that January, he and Caskey got a new car, turning in their station wagon for a Ford Anglia and renewing their dissipated, conflict-riven life together.

But in Laguna, Isherwood did write. It was mostly the small projects to which he had been clinging for his professional literary credentials and as a follower of Ramakrishna. For *Tomorrow*, he had already finished his third essay review, about a biography of H.G. Wells, and the first one he wrote in Laguna was about Robert Louis Stevenson. During March, he finished his introduction to *Vedanta for Modern Man*, a second big anthology from the Vedanta Society magazine, and he inched through a few more of the Patanjali aphorisms. Caskey earned some money working as a gardener. Finally, Isherwood even began to devote strings of continuous days to his novel.

In April, he worked on a roundup for the *Observer* called "Young American Writers." This was the start of a series introducing readers of the British Sunday paper to American writers being published in England; it mentioned more than thirty writers whose work he knew well and admired. All, Isherwood argued, were writing about loneliness:

> American loneliness is of three kinds. First, there is the brute physical loneliness of the individual in a land of huge spaces and cities. Secondly, there is the loneliness of the social or psychological misfit within a society which recognises only the claims of the norm. Thirdly, there is the loneliness of being an American in a world which envies, mistrusts and often misunderstands America.

Each kind of loneliness had its own hero. The first, Isherwood explained, was "a wanderer, temperamentally footloose but chronically homesick for his birthplace as he knew it in childhood." The most numerous was the misfit, "a rebel or a victim," a criminal, an outcast or "the prejudged member of a minority—Jew, Negro, homosexual or other." The third "is the man with a national conscience, confronted by people of other nations and trying to be just and wise in his dealings with them."

Continuing by threes, Isherwood proposed: "There are three ways of dealing with loneliness. You can defy it stoically. You can try to resolve it into a relationship with another person. You can sublimate it by means of religious faith or a sense of social brotherhood."[210] He knew, because he had tried all three ways. He did not mention another way of dealing with loneliness—writing. These young American writers were his colleagues, his fellows, his brothers and sisters. He was personally acquainted with about half of them, and a quarter were among his closest friends. In their books, in their imaginations, he knew them all, and he shared their loneliness.

From the beginning, Isherwood took breaks away from the new home in Laguna—with other romantic interests, with friends in L.A., at Trabuco, and at the Huntington Hartford Foundation, a writers' colony funded by A&P grocery heir Huntington Hartford in Rustic Canyon next to Santa Monica. There he could work in a cabin and swim in the pool. He was shepherded onto the foundation's advisory board by publisher and producer Frank Taylor and, as he told Upward, read "manuscripts by young writers who get scholarships."[211]

He spent time there with several young writers, including Speed Lamkin, whom he met in 1950, when Lamkin, from Monroe, Louisiana, and educated at Harvard, turned up in Hollywood aged twenty-two, about to publish his first novel. Before that, Lamkin had made some short-lived conquests in New York, including Auden and Kirstein. Isherwood disliked Lamkin's name-dropping and feared his gossiping tongue, yet he expressed guarded admiration in his diary: "With his vulgarity, snobbery and naive appetite for display, he might well become a minor Balzac of Hollywood."

Lamkin, as Isherwood put it, "made Christopher one of his projects" in March 1951: "Christopher *had* to leave Billy—with whom, however, Speed was on the best of terms—and come to live at the foundation and put his future in Speed's hands." They began "clowning an affair" and went to bed together several times. Lamkin's sway arose from what Isherwood called his "absurdity." At certain turning points in his life, Isherwood was able to move forward only on the level of play, for example when, seeking release from academic suffocation, he wrote joke answers on his exams at Cambridge. "Speed could influence Christopher because Christopher didn't take him, or his concern for Christopher's future, seriously."[212]

Lamkin persuaded Isherwood to let him and another friend, Gus Field, adapt *Sally Bowles* for the stage. Isherwood was impressed by a draft they completed in late January 1951, but Dodie Smith and Alec Beesley thought the Lamkin–Field script didn't work and intervened by challenging John Van Druten to try.

Meanwhile, guests frequented the house in Laguna, and the ones who visited from Los Angeles tended to stay overnight. As Isherwood built up a head of steam with his writing, a clash with Caskey became inevitable. The partying reached a pitch on Saturday, May 19, when an all-night romp ended abruptly. "Everybody left," Isherwood wrote in his day-to-day diary for the Sunday, and on Monday, he left too, this time with the intention of settling at the Huntington Hartford Foundation: "life with Billy had become unbearable," he wrote in his diary. He never recorded exactly what happened at the party, and by the time he wrote *Lost Years*, he could not recall.

Caskey went to San Francisco to take a course for prospective merchant seamen. "I am very unhappy," wrote Isherwood after a week living at the foundation; he was also "worried and scared."[213]

The very day that he wrote about his unhappiness, May 28, 1951, Van Druten read aloud to him the draft for the stage play which was then still called *Sally Bowles*. "I think [Christopher] disliked the character of Christopher Isherwood from the beginning and never changed his opinion," wrote Isherwood of his younger self in *Lost Years*. Nevertheless, he went to Van Druten's ranch and spent five days there working with him on the script. By the time it was finished at the end of June, the play was called *I Am a Camera* and included additional material from *Goodbye to Berlin*.

Ambivalent though he was, Isherwood allowed himself to rely more and more on the promise of the play, on Van Druten's connections and his history of successes on Broadway. The play offered not only money but also "the glitter of footlights."[214]

DESPITE TAKING BACK the play from Lamkin, Isherwood had trusted him to read the current draft of his novel. Lamkin, like others, had already read the first chapter—in which the protagonist Stephen Monk discovers his second wife Jane Armstrong in flagrante with another man at a Hollywood party—because the chapter was due to be published in *New World Writing* in 1952. Lamkin took only a day to read the rest—it was the same day that Isherwood heard Van Druten read *Sally Bowles*. "Next day, May 29, Speed delivered his verdict: 'The refugees are a bore.'"

Isherwood accepted this as ruthless and life-giving. "The sentence was like an axe stroke, cutting the novel in half."[215] Isherwood had been forcing himself to include the refugees, making lists of their proposed names, assigning them bedrooms in the fictionalized house, diagramming their places in the dining room. Again and again, he had commented in his notes that he didn't know enough about them to make them interesting. He had already reduced them in number. "I seriously believe that this is the cause of my block," he now wrote in his work journal. "I don't want to write about the refugees."[216]

The refugees embodied some of Isherwood's most troubled and complicated feelings about the war. His work with them was in effect a contribution to the war effort, and certainly it reflected his commitment to the German people among whom he had lived for four years, freely and happily according to his true nature as a homosexual. In his novel, the refugees were a link back to the milieu he had portrayed in his Berlin stories and by which he had made his literary reputation. He had explained to Upward in 1947: "'The School of Tragedy' is the refugee hostel itself, and, more generally, the whole experience of persecution, imprisonment, flight and emigration under the Hitler terror. And it should suggest the idea that life's most pathetic figures are those weak unheroic people who are called upon to play tragic parts entirely beyond their powers."[217]

The fate of his shattered Berlin milieu was a dark subject, and nearly all of his refugee characters were Jews. The threat that had hung over 1930s Berlin had proved far worse in fulfillment than in imagination, and he had been unable to find in his refugee material any spark of defiance, heroism, or even suspense.

Isherwood quickly sketched the unburdened novel he eventually went on to write, leaving the problem of his feelings about the war and about his relationship with Germany for his next book, *Down There on a Visit*. He was influenced by working with Van Druten on the stage play just as much as he was influenced by Lamkin. His sudden clarity of vision, his impulse to simplify, was like the clarity he had found after working with Viertel on the script for *Little Friend*, when the economy required for film writing had galvanized him in 1934 to jettison all his characters except Mr. Norris. Collaboration had pushed him then, as now, to find his own voice. But he had written *Mr. Norris Changes Trains* hidden away in the Canary Islands; in his complicated Los Angeles life, he had no place to hide.

"What in the world are you doing at the Huntington Hartford Foundation?" Lincoln Kirstein wrote from New York. Kirstein scoffed at Hartford's support of the arts, pointing out that Hartford hadn't been able to sustain focus on *The Rake's Progress*. "For 15 mins. as Bob Craft will tell you, he was interested in Strawinsky's [sic] and Auden's opera. Maybe it was 14 mins." As for Lamkin, he was now entirely off Kirstein's list: "I won't see him, even, angel, for you."[218]

By early July, Isherwood drifted back into his Laguna life with Caskey. They hosted Caskey's mother for a long, tense visit during August, and by the time she left, Isherwood had another sore throat. On August 22, over lunch at Trabuco, Prabhavananda urged him, "more strongly than ever before," as Isherwood recorded in his diary, to come to the monastery to live. "He said, 'It *must* happen. I've wanted it and prayed for it so much.'"

Isherwood was evasive. He consulted Heard, who said "without hesitation that I should obey Swami and go to live there." On August 23, "on a sudden impulse," Isherwood drove to Trabuco and talked to Prabhavananda about living there or at Ivar Avenue. Prabhavananda revealed that both Heard and Huxley "had come to him and told him things about the way I was living and asked him to remonstrate with me." Isherwood didn't commit. Instead, he rushed off to Los Angeles for the weekend, testing another possibility and rejecting that, too: "Jim definitely offered to live with me. I said no—and I'm glad I did; and he later said I was right."[219] Nevertheless, for a week in October, he stayed with Charlton in Iris Tree's apartment on Santa Monica Pier.

He managed to keep one shoulder to the wheel, producing a review of Santayana and an essay for the Vedanta Society magazine, "What Vedanta Means to Me." For the *Observer*, he reprised his review of *The Martian Chronicles* when a new version of Bradbury's collection was published in England as *The Silver Locusts*,[220] and the day after he mailed in the Bradbury review, he completed a draft of the Patanjali yoga aphorisms. All the while, Sally Bowles beckoned from Broadway.

NEW YORK, 1951

Isherwood finally left for New York on October 19, 1951, and Caskey stayed behind. Caskey wanted his independence. "I feel I must try something completely on my own with no influence of any kind and it would have been much harder if I felt I was hurting you in carrying out such a plan," he wrote to Isherwood.[221]

Determinedly, Caskey dismantled the nest, then went to San Francisco to ship out with Harold Fairbanks in the merchant marine. He arrived after an all-night drive through disorienting fog to find that Fairbanks had gotten into a fight and shipped out the day before: "What a character he is," said Caskey without rancor. Every day, Caskey attended the seamen's hiring hall with hundreds of ordinary seamen, hoping to get hired without any experience or insider's leverage. In his boredom and loneliness, he kept an eye on the progress of *I Am a Camera* in the papers. "I'm delighted with your success," he told Isherwood.[222] He also understood Isherwood's mixed feelings: "I just hope the stage Chris isn't too embarrassing."[223]

As soon as Isherwood had arrived in New York, he was photographed by Richard Avedon with Julie Harris in her costume as Sally Bowles. "I decided to treat her as Sally," he later recalled, "to conceal a certain dismay, a disconcerting sense of strangeness." For the character was no longer his. "Oh, yes, it was *like* Sally Bowles, but it wasn't my creation. It wasn't Julie's. It wasn't John's. It had a life of its own."[224]

He was far more dismayed when he encountered an apparition of *himself* at the rehearsals which he attended over the following month, as he wrote in the *New York Herald Tribune*:

> For here am I, a middle-aged man, sitting watching the rehearsal; and there, before me on the stage, is the young man who answers to my name. It is true that William Prince, who plays him, doesn't look like me physically, any more than Miss Harris looks like the original of Sally Bowles; but who am I to claim that I am more essentially the Christopher Isherwood of the play than Mr. Prince is?[225]

The man without qualities, the man who doubted that he had a personality, the man who had clung to his name fearing that his beloved Swami might make him anonymous with a different, Sanskrit one, was face-to-face with the fact that he had, after all, given away his identity—to a nondescript young actor who didn't even look like him. One reviewer was to observe that "Mr. Prince does not, in all honesty, play the part very well."[226]

Again in 1954, and again in 1975, Isherwood was to describe the unsettling experience of having his fictional past taken over and transformed by others,[227] but only this first time, for the *Herald Tribune* that November 1951, did he so clearly reveal his feelings about the imposter on stage. In Vedanta, Isherwood had feared the extinction of his identity; now he had achieved it in the theater. He had obliterated himself. "I have nothing left that I can call entirely mine; nothing, either real or invented, that is strictly personal to me."[228]

At least he was surrounded by friends—Auden, Kirstein, Vidal, Wescott, Tota Cuevas de Vera, Capote, Lerman, and, shortly, Tennessee Williams and his lover Frank Merlo. After two nights at Auden's apartment, Isherwood moved in with Andrew Lyndon, a would-be writer friend of Capote from Macon, Georgia, with whom he had begun a flirtation on Nantucket in the summer of 1947. During the first week of November, he found another sleeping partner, the socialite art dealer, John Hohnsbeen. For a time, Kirstein's friend Jenson Yow rented Isherwood a room of his own on Bethune Street in the West Village. Later, after leaving New York, Isherwood told Kirstein that he slept ten hours recovering from "those white New York lovenights."[229]

The play opened in Hartford, Connecticut, on Thursday, November 8. Coincidentally, this was the anniversary of Isherwood's initiation by Swami Prabhavananda in 1940 and his U.S. citizenship in 1946. On the 7th, before the evening dress rehearsal, he found time to donate at the local blood bank. Isherwood donated blood regularly until he caught hepatitis in 1956; still, it was extraordinary to fit this in. Was he marking November 8 with a small ritual act to benefit mankind? Was he taking the opportunity to place himself briefly, passively, in medical care?

The next day, before the performance, he wrote in his diary for the first time since September: "This isn't my own child. But it certainly is a milestone. Here I am, in this gloomy New England town; and there are Billy and Jim out there on the Coast."[230]

He left Hartford after the Saturday matinee, delighted to return to New York and spend another night with Auden. Many years later, he recalled in *My Guru and His Disciple* that these were the first visits in years when he and Auden had been alone together, "able to have long, intimate talks, as in the old days." They managed to talk about religion "without getting into any arguments," and he showed Auden passages from his diary about living at the Vedanta Center. Auden dismissed Vedanta as "heathen mumbo jumbo," but he did not dismiss Prabhavananda: "Your Swami's quite obviously a saint, of course."[231]

Isherwood went to Philadelphia for the second out-of-town opening on November 12 and spent a day working with Van Druten on changes. He was yearning for his lost center of gravity: "The place in the United States I think of as home—and I feel very homesick for it as I write these words—is the stretch of ocean front running five or six miles south from Santa Monica Canyon to Venice." In his Philadelphia hotel room, he was writing an essay about his beloved shoreline that was originally conceived for a book of photos by Caskey. They never finished the book, so Isherwood published the essay as "California Story" in *Harper's Bazaar* in February 1952.[232]

With Tennessee Williams and Frank Merlo, he watched part of Williams's play *The Rose Tattoo* which had just closed in New York, and he saw Anita Loos's stage adaptation of Colette's *Gigi* which was to open on Broadway on November 24, just four days before *I Am a Camera*. It was a season for gamines, Julie Harris as Sally Bowles in pre-Hitler Berlin and Audrey Hepburn as Gigi in belle époque Paris. Hepburn went on to become the bigger star in films, but Harris outdid her on the stage, starting with *I Am a Camera* which was to run two months longer than *Gigi*.

I Am a Camera opened at the Empire Theater, Broadway, on November 28.[233] Isherwood was interviewed relentlessly and even did a radio broadcast with William Prince, the actor playing him. But after Hartford, he made no more diary entries. Evidently, there was nothing more he wished to say. On January 10, 1952, he was to record in his day-to-day diary "50th performance of 'I am a Camera.' Julie Harris became a star." Already on Christmas Eve, she had appeared in a *Life* magazine photo spread; Isherwood labeled the photos "divine."[234] She won a Tony award. He adored her and grudged her nothing.

While William Prince impersonated him under Van Druten's direction on the New York stage, the real Christopher Isherwood sailed for England on the *Queen Elizabeth* on December 14, his third trip since the war. From there, he was to return, at last, to Berlin and come face-to-face with survivors from his former life—some who were portrayed in Van Druten's play and others who were not.

BERLIN, 1952

At the *Observer* offices in London, Isherwood was a center of attention. He was newly established as a commentator on recent American fiction, and the play adapted from his celebrated book about Berlin was a hit in Manhattan. On January 9, he met with the editor, the literary editor, and the Berlin-born Cold War correspondent to plan his return to Berlin.[235] There was another planning meeting on January 23, and on the 30th, he was given lunch at the Waldorf, where Harold Nicolson joined them.

Meanwhile, Isherwood had fallen ill. He was to explain in his *Observer* piece: "I dreaded meeting the people I had known. I dreaded seeing familiar places in ruins. I had quite made up my mind to go, but my unconscious still protested; so I developed symptoms of duodenal ulcer and nearly broke my leg on a staircase."[236]

The fall on the stairs, yet again incapacitating his legs, occurred the day after the *Observer* luncheon. There were X-rays and appointments with specialists. He was put on a "strict diet" for his ulcer symptoms.[237] His final checkup was on February 4.

With his medical all-clear, he flew from Northolt on February 10 to spend six days in Berlin. The city was occupied by the Russians in the east and by the Allies in the west and marooned inside Russian territory one hundred miles from West Germany. "I had arrived prepared—over-prepared—for a shock," he wrote. He landed after dark, so his first shock was the brightly lit prosperity of the Kurfürstendamm with its shops and bars and the modern Hotel am Zoo, populated by "thick-necked cigar-smoking tycoons and elegant women who might have stepped right out of the cartoons in which Georg Grosz satirises the plutocracy of the inflation period." Such figures had not changed, as far as he could tell, but he himself had changed, and he could now afford to stay with them in the same hotel.

In the morning light, the true state of Berlin, seven years after the end of the war, was revealed to him. At the end of the Kurfürstendamm, he saw the heavily bombed nineteenth-century Kaiser Wilhelm Memorial Church, "now more Gothic than ever in its jaggedy pinnacled ruins, and, one must admit, far more beautiful." Beyond the church, the Tauentzienstrasse looked to him like "an avenue of broken monuments." There were mounds of rubble everywhere, and the Tiergarten was a "treeless plain." Berliners had stripped it for firewood during the last year of the war and in the aftermath. Replanting had only just begun.[238]

Isherwood was driven around the city by Melvin Lasky, the American editor of the liberal anti-communist magazine, *Der Monat* (*The Month*), a highbrow German-language publication aimed at German intellectuals. Later, Lasky was an editor with Stephen Spender of the British cultural magazine *Encounter*. He had remained in Berlin after serving in the military during World War II, and his magazines were funded by the Marshall Plan, the Ford Foundation, and the CIA. He was a founder of the Congress for Cultural Freedom, and he was long-rumored to be a CIA agent, although his support for cultural and psychological warfare against the Soviet Union was never a secret. Richard Lowenthal, a German-Jewish political science professor who worked as a journalist for Reuters and for the *Observer*, accompanied them. Toward the end of his visit, Isherwood attended a meeting of the small Committee for Cultural Freedom, which supervised the Congress.

He visited reconstruction projects, was interviewed by the German press, talked on the radio, and lunched at the British Press Club. With the German film producer and screenwriter Wenzel Lüdecke, he went out on February 14 to the bars: "Kleist Casino, Bart, etc."[239]

The American poet Edouard Roditi, who was a member of the Benton Way Group, and an editor friend took Isherwood to Hallesches Tor, where Isherwood had lived at Simeonstrasse 4 in the attic tenement with Walter Wolff and his family in the autumn of 1930 and where he had set "The Nowaks." Bombs had destroyed the whole street in February 1945.

The flat at Nollendorfstrasse 17, where he had lived with Jean Ross, had also been hit by a bomb, but living a few doors away, he found his beloved landlady, Fräulein Meta Thurau,[240] portrayed as Fräulein Schroeder in *Goodbye to Berlin* and now being played by Olga Fabian as Fräulein Schneider on the New York stage. In his *Observer* piece, Isherwood wrote that she uttered a "Wagnerian scream" when she recognized him.

Fräulein Thurau was in her seventies now, slimmer than she had been in her fifties, and full of stories. She had suffered illness, increasing poverty, and months of bombing that drove her into the cellar. After that came the Russians and the fear of being shot or raped. Through it all, Isherwood observed, Fräulein Thurau—Schroeder as he again disguised her in the *Observer* piece—had managed to hold on to her "only asset," her furniture: "she has clung, throughout the years, to its reassuring bourgeois solidity. Now, in this smaller flat, it makes the place seem like an overcrowded museum. Here was the massive bed I used to sleep in. Here was the immense washstand carved like a Gothic shrine. Here was my ponderous writing-table."[241]

As a memento of their reunion, Fräulein Thurau gave Isherwood the brass dolphin clock that had stood on the writing table and which he had described in *Goodbye to Berlin*. "During the war, the dolphin was hurled from the table by a bomb-blast and its green marble base slightly chipped; the tiny scratches are its only record of the passage of those violent years." He proposed to treasure it "for the rest of my life, as a souvenir of my dear friend and a symbol of that indestructible something in a place and an environment that resists all outward change."[242] The dolphin clock still sits on the table in his workroom in Santa Monica.

For the *Observer*, Isherwood wrote that he was "awestruck" by the damage the war had done to Berlin; he was awestruck, too, by what had survived—his friends, their homes, their possessions, but above all, their style of speech and their stories: "The indestructible something—that was what I had really come back to Berlin to look for. And I seemed to sense it almost at once in the very air of the city and in the sound of its inhabitants' voices." It was the German language. "I only wanted to speak and hear German."

Vagabond that he was—not precisely from Manchester, an outsider in Berlin, only a naturalized Californian—Isherwood felt at home again in the language he had loved and the storytelling he had relished in Berlin: "Berliners love to talk, and most of all, they enjoy telling tragi-comic tales of disaster and horror."[243]

Back in London, Isherwood worked on his piece for six days; he was still revising when he left for New York on the *Queen Elizabeth* on February 28, and he continued in New York before he finally submitted it on March 8. Evidently, his editors didn't want political comment because he cut away paragraphs about the 1948–9 Allied Airlift that supplied West Berlin with food during the Soviet blockade; paragraphs about the triumph of the Communist Party in East Berlin, the imposition of communist ideology, and the power of the Soviet propaganda machine; paragraphs about growing divisions in the intellectual and cultural life of the city. Later, Isherwood told a friend he was "ashamed" of the resulting piece, "So superficial."[244]

What his editors wanted was personal and literary reminiscence. He added material about three further survivors from the days of *Goodbye to Berlin*, presenting them as fictional characters. Bobby the bartender had served on the Russian Front, and Otto Nowak, "that eternal spiv," had shown up recently at Nollendorfstrasse in expensive clothes and offered to buy Fräulein Thurau's carpets. (Isherwood had tried and failed in Berlin to contact Nowak's real-life original, Walter Wolff.)[245]

The third survivor was a character never mentioned before in Isherwood's published work, "Luis." Isherwood obligingly made this character's story funny. "Luis" had reportedly been taken prisoner by the Americans, who had "more or less allowed him, and a number of others, to escape and had later forwarded his mail, marked 'escaped,' to his home address."[246] Luis was Heinz Neddermeyer, with whom Isherwood in reality spent more time during his 1952 Berlin visit than with anyone else.

After the war, Isherwood had first heard from Neddermeyer in March 1946, a postcard that took seven months to reach him from Neddermeyer's POW camp in France via the Hogarth Press and the Vedanta Center: "You'll be astonished to hear from somebody whom you think will be already dead." Kathleen also heard from him. "[H]e is acting as an Interpreter," she wrote in her diary, and "he has learnt to typewrite." He had made it home to Berlin by the beginning of October 1946.[247]

Before the war started, Kathleen had sent a monthly allowance to Neddermeyer on Isherwood's behalf until this became impossible in September 1939. Since hearing from him after the war, Isherwood had been sending packages of food, and he had tried through Lehmann to help Neddermeyer find work as a chauffeur or a dishwasher in the British sector.[248]

Isherwood and Neddermeyer had dinner together in Berlin four times in February 1952, twice with Neddermeyer's family—his wife, Gerda Scholz, and his son, Peter Christian, already twelve years old. One day, Isherwood visited Neddermeyer's flat in Weissensee, a leafy area around a small lake in the Russian sector, and boldly traveled with the whole family on public transport from Weissensee back to Fräulein Thurau's flat in the west.

These reunions with Neddermeyer were not mentioned in the *Observer*. On top of longstanding reasons for keeping the friendship private, Neddermeyer now had a family, and he lived on the wrong side of Berlin. The meetings would have to wait for Isherwood to fictionalize them as his final reunions with the character called Waldemar in *Down There on a Visit*. In real life, this was not the last time Isherwood saw Neddermeyer; they were to meet again in London in 1961.

DURING HIS TIME in England, Isherwood was immersed in a widening circle of friends, attended to his career with his publisher and agent, was interviewed on the evening news, spoke on the radio, read from his novel at the new, radically inclined Institute of Contemporary Arts, and gave time to several lesser known writers.[249] At Christmas, his mother and brother came down from Wyberslegh and stayed with him at a hotel in South Kensington;

they remained until February, and Isherwood included Kathleen in lunch and dinner parties and took her to films and theater. However, it was to be another fifteen years before he could write empathetically—in *Kathleen and Frank*—about Kathleen's shrinking material world, her homes and her furniture, in the way that he wrote about Fräulein Thurau's in *Goodbye to Berlin* and for the *Observer*.

A favorite London haunt for Isherwood was Muriel Belcher's Colony Room Club in Soho, where he drank with the painter Francis Bacon. Bacon had visited Berlin in the late 1920s, but Isherwood evidently met him for the first time over supper on December 20, 1951 with his old friends from the Group Theatre, Rupert Doone and Robert Medley. Bacon impressed Isherwood strongly, both the man and his paintings. "I remember Francis saying to me that he always tries to 'get down to the nerve.' He certainly has genius of a sort," Isherwood once wrote after seeing a Bacon exhibition. In 1956, he was to use Bacon's phrase to describe the authenticity he was trying for in his writing. He wanted to get under the skin and bring, as Bacon did in his painting, perception directly onto the nervous system, reinventing his technique as he worked.[250] He was to use the phrase again in a lecture title in 1960, "What Is the Nerve of Interest in the Novel," part of a revealing series of lectures delivered in Santa Barbara.

When he was again on board the *Queen Elizabeth* returning to New York at the beginning of March, Isherwood made his first diary entry since the Hartford opening of *I Am a Camera*: "But now, listen to me. We have come back here to work, and to learn self-discipline, and to regain what we lost in those messy years of unhappiness since 1948." Comparing himself implicitly to Forster, he remarked that he had chosen a different kind of life, and that he must advance in ways for which Forster could offer no example: "This place is a jungle, a wilderness—it isn't venerable and traditional and mentally cozy, like King's College. One can only live here by being strong and standing alone. And how does one get to be strong and stand alone? By opening the heart to the source of all strength and all love and not-aloneness."[251] He planned to spend most of the summer with Prabhavananda working on their translation of the Patanjali yoga aphorisms and on his novel.

In New York, he reconnected with his nearest friends, and then despite his intentions, suddenly flew to Bermuda on March 19 for a romantic holiday with a young man he met just a few days after his ship docked, Sam Costidy.* For a week, they swam, cycled, went sightseeing and attended local parties. On March 20, he recorded "this has certainly been the happiest day of my life since 1948, when I went to Ensenada with Jim." But he warned

---

* Not his real name.

himself: "This island—including the cove where we swam, with its blighted cedar woods and dried Portuguese man-of-war—is only a token, or symbol of experience."[252]

THE GARDEN HOUSE, BRENTWOOD, 1952

Always his path spiraled, obsessively circling through old patterns of behavior even as he resolved on a new course. Isherwood returned to the West Coast via San Francisco and a road trip with Caskey, a reunion disrupted by a fight over a pickup of Caskey's. In Los Angeles, he again stayed with Jim Charlton on Santa Monica Pier, then moved to the Huntington Hartford Foundation, where he began flirting with another attractive young writer, Tom Wright, from Louisiana, a friend of Speed Lamkin.[253] Then Caskey caught up from San Francisco, and four days later, Sam Costidy flew in from New York, a perfect storm of romantic complications recalling the fame-addled period of 1938.

Isherwood now played Virgil to Costidy, guiding him around his own Californian life and pointing out possible paths forward as a homosexual. He introduced Costidy to Evelyn Hooker (married in 1951) and the Benton Way Group and to Prabhavananda and the Vedanta Society, and they made romantic getaways. Isherwood wrote to Kirstein: "I think I can help him—not to be a writer; that's his own struggle. But to find out what he wants. Is this sheer megalomania?"[254]

Isherwood lasted only three weeks at the Huntington Hartford Foundation, where there were insoluble management problems. Next, he moved to Trabuco, where he stayed another three weeks doing his share of physical labor with the monastics. He was rereading Dante's *Inferno* in a dual-language edition, a book that was to shape his outlook powerfully for the rest of the decade. On days not devoted to the Patanjali aphorisms, he pressed steadily on with the novel.

At Trabuco, he had no sex, and at first he felt no craving for it: "I certainly needed the rest." He told his beads but could not meditate successfully; his thoughts raced—over his novel, Sam Costidy, Tom Wright, and his financial situation: "the 'take' on *Camera* is down again," he recorded.[255]

Costidy began "bothering" Isherwood to live with him, and then he started a relationship with Tom Wright, left town with him, and never returned. "I was glad to see them go, I'm afraid," Isherwood wrote in his diary.[256] He resigned from the Huntington Hartford Foundation, moved his things to a temporary apartment in Santa Monica and arranged with Evelyn Hooker to rent the garden house at the home she shared with her husband Edward on Saltair Avenue, in Brentwood. It was about three and a half miles from the beach, promising privacy and quiet. Jim Charlton agreed to remodel it.

Isherwood looked back longingly to the domestic security his mother had provided in London, Nanny helping with housework, Elizabeth Besley cooking, and Kathleen doing errands, managing his finances and dealing with his agent and publishers: "I must confess, I want to be looked after. I want the background of a home. I see now how well the arrangement at Pembroke Gardens suited me, during the last year or so in England (much as I complained about it). [. . .] What I really want is solitude in the midst of snugness." He resolved to live alone and look after himself for the first time in his life. The garden house was ideal for one person, "a perfect dream study bedroom," as he wrote to a friend.[257]

Charlton made the most of every inch, designing and building in cupboards, counters, drawers, bookshelves, and a big L-shaped desk running under the main window. Even in bed, Isherwood was to be surrounded by his reading and his writing. Alongside his books were framed photographs of family and friends, souvenirs from his travels, his record collection and record player. The sleek, professional orderliness was almost nautical, with Isherwood proud and content at the helm of his life. He announced to another correspondent that his new address, 400 Saltair Avenue, was "more or less permanent."[258]

Caskey's current ship was in port nearby, so he and Charlton got Isherwood settled in the garden house in mid-August. The first night, Caskey stayed over. The second night, a young designer, Phil Burns, stayed. The night after that, it was Charlton. These were partners for the night, not for life. Isherwood was genuinely resigned to solitude. One night, he dreamed about his father:

> My father, in uniform, at a table. I'm sitting beside him.
> "Are you lonely here, Daddy?" I ask.
> "Yes."
> "So am I. But never mind. You get used to it."
> I pat him on the shoulder, rather deliberately, never having done this before but feeling that it's right. A very strong feeling of rapport, between us
> Woke happy. This was a good dream.[259]

In the dream, he was sharing his father's destiny, solitude, and he was the one to reassure his father—rather than his father reassuring him, as in childhood.

Caskey shipped out for Japan in September, then returned for another road trip and to attend the Los Angeles opening of *I Am a Camera* at the Biltmore on November 24. Caskey was "weepy" in the car and told Isherwood that "moving into the garden house was 'ruthless.'" Isherwood did not cope well with the confrontation and the guilt. Progress on the novel came to a halt, again.

He didn't give up. "Got started, today, on chapter four," he wrote on December 1. "I'm making another effort to bust this 'writer's block' by just going ahead." In January, Caskey shipped out again: "Pray for me sometimes," he requested. Isherwood struggled with a breaking heart: "He has never been gentler or sweeter."[260]

He returned to Trabuco, where Prabhavananda was temporarily in residence. He didn't hear from Caskey all month. He worried, smokeless since Christmas, sleepless, and nervy. He spent many hours in the shrine, went without alcohol and sex, and managed to work every day on the novel. He felt he was wrestling the devil for his soul, and he even called on Ramakrishna to assist him. "I actually said to Ramakrishna in the shrine: 'If it's your will that I finish this thing, then help me.' And so we began to move."

He completed a rough draft at the end of January. "I feel as if my whole future as a writer—and my sanity, almost—had been at stake."[261] It was by no means a book, but it now seemed that a book might be possible if he could sustain his discipline and concentration away from the monastery. He left Trabuco for the garden house, where he read through the draft on February 4, 1953. The very next night, the Hookers' garage burned down.

Isherwood felt on the night of the fire that he might lose everything he owned because his house was attached to the garage, separated by only a thin plaster wall. In his diary, he wrote: "I woke, around 2:30 a.m., from a nightmare that I was being chased by Nazis who'd seen me watching them bury the corpses of murdered children. There was a strange unpleasant smell which I didn't immediately identify as burning, but I went to the door—hearing roaring, crackling sounds in the high wind—the garage was full of fire."

The disaster somehow lightened and purified his life. He compared it to the sacrificial *homa* fire in Hindu ritual: "thinking that for sure everything I owned was burned, I felt a very curious exhilaration. It was almost as if I understood, for the first time, the meaning of the homa fire. 'Okay—a real fresh start, then, if that's your will. What do you want now? Tell me. I'm ready.'"[262]

The garage fire brought to the surface grim, longstanding horrors thinly covered by Isherwood's Californian equanimity. It occurred almost exactly a year after his return visit to Berlin, and his nightmare about the Nazis, one of the many he had all his adult life, suggests he was continuing to repress powerful anxieties about his role as a witness to their atrocities, some written up in his published work, others still kept private, for instance the fire in the Opernplatz onto which Goebbels and other Nazis had thrown thousands of "undesirable" books—many pillaged from the library of the Institute for Sexual Science along with the bust of Magnus Hirschfeld. His new California landlady, Evelyn Hooker, strikingly reprised Hirschfeld, a liberal-minded academic studying the local homosexual community. Once again Isherwood was living in an annex linked physically to the scientific study of his tribe, just as he had when he lived next door to the Institute for Sexual Science.

It was three days after the Burning of the Books that he had fled Berlin in May 1933. Now, twenty years later, he had drafted exactly the sort of novel—candidly portraying homosexual love and companionship—that would have been thrown onto the Nazi bonfire. Isherwood's car and bicycle and the Hookers' car were destroyed in the fire, but nothing in the garden house or the main house was damaged. The draft of the novel survived, but the risks of being homosexual and writing about it persisted, and Isherwood knew that the novel courted such risks more openly than his earlier work.

Christopher William Bradshaw Isherwood, 11½ months, with his distinctive slanting eyes

Kathleen holding Christopher William, Wyberslegh, Christmas 1905

Major Francis Bradshaw Isherwood, the Hero of Marple, on his way to the Front, 1914

Kathleen Machell-Smith, later Bradshaw Isherwood, in her twenties

Marple Hall, before 1915

Henry Bradshaw Isherwood, around 1907

Christopher and nanny Anne Avis, Ventnor, Isle of Wight, March 1911

Marple Hall, dining room, 1902, with double portrait of John Donne and his wife

Mirabel Cobbold, forerunner of Sally Bowles, with her father, Colonel Ernest Cobbold, Frank's commanding officer, Limerick, August 1914

Christopher and his brother, Richard, to whom he tried and failed to be a father, June 1913

Christopher (center right) watching the York and Lancasters march to church, Limerick, April 1914

Wystan Auden (front row, center), Rosamira Morgan Brown behind him and Christopher behind her, St. Edmund's School photo, 1915

Cyril Morgan Brown, headmaster, St. Edmund's

Edward Upward, around the time he finished Cambridge, 1925

Geoffrey Burrell Smith, the history master who changed Christopher's way of thinking, Repton School, 1921

Ethel Colburne Mayne, nicknamed Venus, "whom I took as my literary judge," Isherwood wrote in 1929

Olive Mangeot, Isherwood's chosen mother figure, after she divorced and moved to Chelsea

E.M. Forster, in whose work Isherwood discovered "the mental attitude with which he must pick up his pen," Dover, August 1937

Auden, Stephen Spender and Isherwood, Sellin, Ruegen Island, Baltic Sea, Germany, summer 1931

Francis Turville-Petre, the Fronny and the model for the homosexual philosopher king Ambrose, about 1930

Isherwood and Walter Wolff, model for Otto Nowak, on Ruegen Island, summer 1931

Gerald Hamilton, criminal, spy, bon vivant and model for Mr. Norris

Jean Ross, model for Sally Bowles, in boyish sailor-style bell bottoms and beret, Berlin, about 1931

Oliver (Jackie Coogan), coached by the Artful Dodger (Edouard Trebaol, left), learns to pick the pocket of Fagin (Lon Chaney). Christopher pasted this cutting into his film book.

Boys in Berlin: Heinz Neddermeyer (second from left), about 1932

Isherwood and Neddermeyer, touring the Canary Islands, 1934

Berthold Viertel, Isherwood's screenwriting master and model for Friedrich Bergmann, 1930s

Isherwood and Auden on their return voyage to England from New York and China, summer 1938

Gerald Heard, the spiritual pioneer who introduced Isherwood to Vedanta

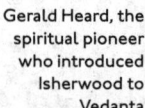

Isherwood with his Vedanta guru and literary collaborator Swami Prabhavananda, outside the temple at the Hollywood Vedanta Center, 1943

Isherwood, Prabhavananda, and the English intellectual and visionary Aldous Huxley, Hollywood Vedanta Center, early 1940s; Ramakrishna's image hangs behind.

Lincoln Kirstein in uniform during World War II

With Dodie Smith, author of *The One Hundred and One Dalmatians*, and one of her Dalmatians

Denny Fouts, legendary courtesan, in his Entrada Drive apartment, Santa Monica, 1945–6

Bill Caskey in Salka Viertel's garage apartment, Santa Monica, where he lived with Isherwood in 1946

On Crystal Beach, Ocean Park, before the 1950s clean-up that demolished the gay-friendly Crystal Baths and Rendezvous Ballroom

The smoking yogi, about 1946

Iris Tree, model for Charley in
A Single Man, late 1940s

With Tennessee Williams on the set of *The Rose Tattoo*,
Key West, November 1954

With Truman Capote, 'Sconset, Nantucket,
July 1947

Gore Vidal, around the time he introduced
himself to Isherwood in the late 1940s

John Van Druten, who turned Isherwood's Berlin material into the 1951 hit Broadway play *I Am a Camera*

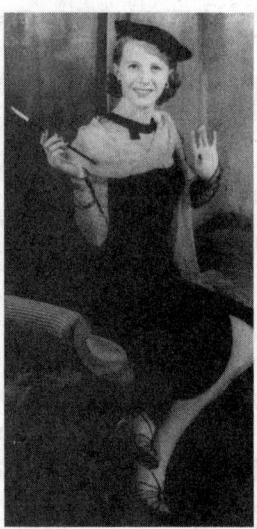
Julie Harris as Sally Bowles in *I Am a Camera*, for which she won her first Best Actress Tony Award

Isherwood at work in his garden house, Saltair Avenue, Brentwood, June 1953

With architect Jim Charlton in a photo booth

Ted (left) and Don Bachardy, State Beach, Santa Monica, about 1953

Marilyn Monroe signing an autograph for Don Bachardy outside the Bergen and McCarthy radio show, Los Angeles, October 1952

Isherwood and Bachardy on Muscle Beach with their writer friend Gavin Lambert (center), September 1963

English film director Tony Richardson on the set of *The Loved One*, 1965

Anthony Page, English stage director, 1968

With David Hockney at film director John Schlesinger's birthday party, February 1976

Isherwood and Bachardy in front of Hockney's portrait of them, hanging in the Chester Square dining room of Marguerite Littman (née Lamkin), London, February 1970

Christopher Isherwood by Don Bachardy, June 1961, pen and ink on paper

Marguerite Lamkin during her second marriage, to actor Rory Harrity, by Don Bachardy, December 16, 1961, pencil and ink with brush on paper

Life imitating art imitating life: Isherwood mugging in front of a Bachardy portrait, 1983

At 145 Adelaide Drive, January 1980

7

The Ideal Companion: Don Bachardy (1953–1961)

Most weekends in the late 1940s, the teenage Bachardy boys, Don and his elder brother Ted, rode the streetcar from Atwater out to Santa Monica, transferring in downtown L.A., and walking the last mile and a half to Will Rogers State Beach. It took nearly two hours, until the summer of 1951 or 1952 when Ted had saved enough money to buy a used Pontiac Coupe, a 1939 two-seater with a rumble seat, which he painted sea-foam green.

The brothers were good-looking, with glossy dark brown hair, slim, lightly muscled physiques and porcelain skin that turned olive in the sun. They had lustrous, incendiary eyes. Don's were hazel—clear green with brown flecks—changing in the light to reveal in quicksilver succession soulfulness, excitement, intrigue, defiance, hurt, laughter. Don had a dimple on his chin, and, at eighteen, his face was still plump and babylike. He was five foot eight; Ted, four years older, was five nine and a half. The brothers wore Levi jeans with the bottoms rolled up, loafers or flip-flops and white T-shirts from Sears. They carried towels and changed at the beach into bathing trunks. Ted had a low-fitting blue pair which he bunched down even lower on his lean hips; Don's were pure white and rose to the waist.

"It was a way of looking for sex for Ted," Don later recalled. "I was uncertain I wanted it and uncertain how to do it. And leery of getting in above my head. Ted was a responsible older brother. He could defend me."

Don was reserved and had no friends of his own age. "I knew I was queer. I already wasn't interested in what people my age had to offer." And yet, he was a risk-taker. "Whenever Ted was away at work, I would take the car and drive through the Atwater neighborhood to a big field where I practiced shifting gears."[1] He didn't have a driving license or Ted's permission. At fifteen or sixteen, Don had even frightened himself when he climbed over the wall and dived into Marion Davies's swimming pool on the beach at Santa Monica, "looking under the water to the dark, deep end of the pool completely terrified me. So I leapt out and *ran* and climbed out over the wall as fast as I could. I was trespassing on private property."[2]

Ted taught him to shoplift—a cashmere coat right off a mannequin in Bullock's department store for their mother's birthday, groceries so that he could pocket the money he was given to buy them. During one brief, intense friendship at Washington Irving Junior High School, Don and another boy were caught by a plain-clothes detective stealing "lipticks, rouges and cheap perfumes." They were released to their angry fathers with no charge, then two months later, on Halloween, "we took a red streetcar to Grauman's Chinese Theater in Hollywood to see *Forever Amber*, both of us in heavy make-up and dressed to the teeth in female clothes, and hats, false hair and high-heeled shoes!"[3] They were thirteen years old; it was 1947.

Equally bold was Ted and Don's habit of slipping into movie premieres uninvited, to mingle with the stars. They dressed in their best suits and carried a camera, easily persuading their favorite actors and actresses to be photographed with them—for instance, sixteen-year-old Don with Marilyn Monroe at the 1951 Academy Awards.

Glade Bachardy, their mother, had begun taking the boys to the movies when Don was three or four years old. They spent countless daytime hours in the dark, looking up at the gigantic actors on the screen, the gods and goddesses of their heaven. In the Bachardy household, there was no churchgoing.

When Don started school, he found it uninteresting compared to the movies. He was given almost no books in childhood, apart from one with photographs of "dressed-up kittens and their mother cat" and another containing illustrations from the 1937 movie *Snow White and the Seven Dwarfs*.[4] But there were plenty of movie-fan magazines at home. The brothers cut out faces to trace and sketch. This was the beginning of the obsession with faces that was to motivate Don's development as a portrait artist. The scissor blades permitted only one accurate cut, requiring already the precise, economical line that was to be a hallmark of his work, from his early delicate pencil portraits to his later freely painted portraits in jewel- and marine-colored acrylics. In childhood, the brothers always sketched women, for it was women with whom they identified.

Their father ferociously disapproved of the moviegoing, the fan magazines and the drawing. Jess Bachardy worked shifts on an airplane assembly line at Lockheed. He was a first-generation American of Hungarian

7: The Ideal Companion: Don Bachardy (1953–1961) / 447

parentage with a flair for mechanics and no high school diploma; he grudged the money and the lack of practical results. The boys and their mother conspired against him. Glade exaggerated the cost of groceries to get money for movie tickets and taught the boys to lie to their father. They disliked him for being grumpy, uncommunicative, and critical. Don made a point of getting straight A's in school to avoid being scolded for wasting time. Both brothers wanted to be movie stars. Don had an instinct for the limelight that would gradually propel him to the center of a world as yet entirely unknown to him.

One Saturday night, when Don was an eighteen-year-old freshman at UCLA, Ted took him for after-dinner drinks at the apartment of some friends in Hollywood. Isherwood was there, finishing supper. Don knew Isherwood slightly from the beach, where Isherwood often appeared in his close-fitting dark blue trunks, barrel-chested and narrow-hipped with shapely legs and the alert, super-erect posture of a soldier. Isherwood at five six and a half was shorter than both the Bachardys. His nose was beaky and sunburnt, and by now his eyebrows grew right over his downward-slanting, gray-blue eyes. His tan was heavy, with white crow's feet at the corners of his eyes, pale creases around his mouth, and a flashing white grin.

That night, November 1, 1952, Bachardy learned that Isherwood was a writer. He had never met a writer before. Bachardy later recalled that he liked Isherwood's "vitality, sparkling eyes, British accent and charmingly attentive manner." But Isherwood was forty-eight, "too old for me to consider him in the running as a sex-partner."[5]

Everyone got a little drunk, and the party began to swing. One of the hosts began kissing Ted and, standing up in the dining room, Isherwood began kissing Don. "I was not repelled nor eager to disengage myself," Don later wrote. But alcohol was new to him, and he had had too much. They fell against a window and cracked a pane, and Don suddenly felt alarmed. "I was drunk and in strange circumstances. I was determined to leave the apartment." Ted drove him home. "I was inexperienced when I met Chris. Although that would certainly have changed within six months or a year." In fact, Don's first sexual experiences with older men were not with Isherwood. In response to questions in later years about the age difference, Don liked to joke, "Well, I mean, the idea of this middle-aged man deflowering this young boy, it was exactly what the boy wanted, and he flourished."[6]

It was just a few weeks later that *I Am a Camera* opened in Los Angeles. "Camera is going great guns here," Isherwood reported to the Beesleys, "last week broke our record, including Broadway, I believe."[7] The Bachardy boys, adept at getting into any show that interested them, managed to see it, though Don later recalled that it took him a long time to connect the man who kissed him on November 1 with the character Herr Issyvoo in the play.[8]

Christopher Isherwood wasn't an actor and he wasn't a director, yet he was the star of his own show, a stage character as well as its creator.

———

IT WAS TED Bachardy who first attracted Isherwood's attention. They had met on the beach by November 1949, perhaps earlier, and there had been sexual encounters. During February 1953, they had what Isherwood called a "reunion."[9] He cooked for Ted, took him out to restaurants and movies, and spent time with him on the beach. On February 8, Ted brought Don along to breakfast at Isherwood's garden house, and afterwards the three set off in Ted's car since Isherwood's car had burned.

They went to an actor friend's beach house on the Pacific Coast Highway where a group of young men were gathered to swim, eat, drink, and talk. Later, they drove up the coast to Trancas to drop in on a painter and his boyfriend and then up into the mountains overlooking Malibu, where Caskey's friend Hayden Lewis and Lewis's companion Rod Owens were hosting a cookout. Jim Charlton was there and took an interest right away in Don Bachardy. This led to an assignation at Charlton's apartment, where, according to Bachardy's later account, the sex was a failure.

The partying continued the next weekend—at the same beach house; over dinner at a fish restaurant in Malibu; at the house of Jerry Lawrence, the playwright who co-authored *Auntie Mame* and *Inherit the Wind* and who often entertained for attractive young men hoping to be actors. On the way home from Lawrence's, Ted stopped at the garden house to drop off Isherwood. There, to everyone's surprise, Don got out and stayed the night. It was Valentine's Day.[10]

The next night, Isherwood took Don to see a disturbing and highbrow double feature, *The Strange Ones* and *Los Olvidados*. The first was in French, the second in Spanish, both with subtitles. *The Strange Ones* (1950) is Jean Cocteau's film adaptation of his own 1929 novel about sibling rivalry, *Les Enfants terribles*. *Los Olvidados* (*The Forgotten*, 1950; released in the U.S. as *The Young and the Damned*) is Luis Buñuel's dreamlike documentary portrayal of slum children in Mexico City. Isherwood had been interested since adolescence in the subjects of both films—the inner world of psychological and sexual manipulation and the underworld of childhood poverty—and *Los Olvidados* was to obsess him increasingly over the next decade as he developed his own south-of-the-border inferno in his novel *Down There on a Visit*.

Just a few nights later, Isherwood took Ted Bachardy out for a completely different kind of evening: dinner at Bublitchki on Sunset Strip, followed by a musical at the Players Ring, and then a couple of nightclubs, Ciro's and

Mocambo. It was a glitzy and expensive marathon. After this ritual courting display, Ted spent the night.

If Isherwood was excited by Ted's unquenchable appetite for fun, he was about to be reminded that it was part of a serious illness. Ted Bachardy was a manic-depressive schizophrenic. His first breakdown had occurred in 1945, when he was fifteen. He had gotten in trouble at his high school, been sent home, and, as Don later recalled "couldn't remember where he had been or what was happening to him." He had lain about on the sofa with his clothes suggestively unbuttoned, dopey but also defiant and provocative. A train of doctors and psychiatrists put him in a mental hospital where he received electric shock treatments.

"When I realized there really was something wrong with Ted," wrote Don later, "I felt betrayed and abandoned. I saw before me the immense task of remaking my life without any reliance on him." It had taken two years for Don to overcome his reserve and make friends with the junior high classmate with whom he was arrested for shoplifting and went to the movies in drag. Ted had his second breakdown that year, 1947, and Don ended the junior high friendship abruptly, betraying the boy as he felt he had been betrayed—by going alone to a film they had agreed to see together. He never spoke to the boy again, and he took trouble to prove to himself that he didn't need to rely on anyone at all—not his school friend, not Glade, not Ted.

Ted had a third breakdown around the time he first met Isherwood in 1949 and evidently a fourth about two years after that. He beat up his father, probably because he was jealous of Don. "Jess had a cruel streak that he indulged by making it clear to Ted that I was his favorite," Bachardy recalled of their childhood. "After dinner each night, Jess sat in his upholstered chair in a corner of the living room next to our sleek console radio with three standard props: a lit cigarette, the evening newspaper and me on his lap."[11]

In February 1953, Ted was accelerating toward another breakdown. He became self-destructive and confrontational. He was unemployed, unable to sleep, ricocheting back and forth to the beach, frantically trying to amuse himself. A few days after their big date, Isherwood saw Ted again; then later the same day, he collected Don at home and drove him to Griffith Park to talk about Ted's problems. Insurance money had allowed Isherwood to replace his car—a blue convertible Sunbeam-Talbot—with the brand-new 1953 model, a car unlike any Bachardy had ever seen.

Isherwood felt enormous sympathy for Don. His own teenage years had been lit with the adrenaline induced in his mother and himself by Richard's mental health crises. He felt guilty that he hadn't been able to solve Richard's problems, and he was attracted to little brothers he *could* help partly because they salved the tragedy of his biological one.

Now that Don had begun to have his own sexual adventures, he stopped confiding in Ted, but Ted was curious and possessive. After all, they still shared a bedroom. Ted discovered that Don was having dates and sex with a TV camera operator introduced by himself, and he went to the man's apartment and gave him a black eye. Isherwood drove into town to talk to Ted about the fight, and he brought Ted back to meet with Evelyn Hooker for counseling.

That evening, he introduced Don to the ballet. They dressed in jackets and ties and went out to supper before the performance, a mixed program of Russian and French classics including excerpts from *Swan Lake*. Don was enchanted. It was the start of another great new theme in his life.

Twice that week, in his day-to-day diary, Isherwood wrote "Don" then crossed it out and corrected it to "Ted," as if the cerebral side of him, the writing side, was already focused on Don even though the sexual side of him continued to shift the brothers around like coins in his pocket. But his friendship with Ted was no longer a romance; it was a helpline. He wrote to friends that Ted had become "a daily problem; usually committing some act of violence and then coming around to tell me about it."[12]

Meanwhile something was blossoming with Don. One morning, they picnicked in a cove up the coast at Point Mugu State Beach. The weather was dazzling. The beach was deserted. They climbed over reddish slopes of rock at the southern end onto a hidden ledge and a patch of sand, where they stripped off their clothes and lay in the sun making love. Then they plunged into the water, yelling at the cold.

"I suspect that the cove Chris introduced me to that morning had been used before by him for the same purpose," Bachardy later wrote.[13] Indeed, it was a ritual. In Isherwood's final novel, *A Meeting by the River*, the lovers, Patrick and Tom, frolic at a hidden spot, "Tunnel Cove," and afterwards, the younger lover, Tom, gives the elder lover, Patrick, a copy of a cheap romance containing the love scene they have just acted out together. The world-weary, boy-chasing, scriptwriting Christopher Isherwood knew that no love scene is ever the first or the only love scene; yet certain actors can make the script come to life. In Bermuda, with Sam Costidy, the love affair, the cove, had been "only a token, or symbol of experience";[14] now the symbol became real again. For Bachardy, everything was new: the open blue car flying along like a speck of sky, the coarse whole-wheat hunza bread they ate, the avocados and tomatoes and sharp, unfamiliar cheeses. He later recalled that their lovemaking was restrained—necking and rubbing, orgasms but no penetration. They were shy, not abandoned.

Isherwood's knowingness, his having-done-it-all-before nonchalance, concealed and protected a quality of innocence, even purity, in his sensibility and his sexuality. Caskey taunted Isherwood that he had been "sexually naive" in 1945 despite "all those German boys": "You sure hadn't done much when I met you at the age of 41. [...]—you just bellyrubbed!—"¹⁵ Isherwood's reputation as a bad boy of Berlin arose just as much from the circles in which he moved as from any acts which he may or may not have performed. Bachardy once said: "Chris was a Virgo, you know. [...] Virgo is the sign of the Virgin. There was something in Chris that stayed virginal all his life. Sometimes he seemed to me to be younger than I was. He was innocent. Susceptible. What he lacked in sexual experience he made up for in intelligence."

Isherwood knew this about himself. According to Bachardy: "Chris was very careful about what would have an impact, an effect on him. He was careful about his vulnerability. It was what made him so wonderful to be with, how this survived in him all his life, this innocence."¹⁶ When they first met, Isherwood observed the same natural, unstainable purity in Bachardy that Bachardy saw in him.

TED BACHARDY DIDN'T like Evelyn Hooker, and his mental state was deteriorating rapidly. After the picnic, Isherwood went to see Prabhavananda at the Hollywood Vedanta Center and then visited Don again; Ted had been taken away in the meantime. "The Ted Bachardy case was very ugly and horribly tragic," Isherwood wrote years later. "The parents sent for the police, and Ted was dragged away, screaming and fighting, in handcuffs. And his little brother Don cried in my car afterwards: 'Chris, he's really *insane*.' "¹⁷

Ted was committed to the state mental hospital at Camarillo for nearly six weeks. Meanwhile, Don lived alone with their mother because Jess and Glade had decided to divorce three years before, in 1950, and Glade had moved with the boys from Atwater to an apartment on Harold Way in Hollywood. In fact, the divorce was never legalized, and Jess often came around, whether or not he was wanted.

Glade was helplessly unworldly. Childhood polio had left her with a withered leg and a limp, and she was pretty but painfully self-conscious and shy. She had been born in Port Huron, Michigan, and grown up in Cleveland, Ohio, on the edge of Lake Erie. Her father, Waldo DeLand, likely of French-Canadian descent, was captain of a steam-powered cargo boat that worked the Great Lakes. He was "authoritarian and possessive" and "humorless," Don recalled.¹⁸ Her mother, Isabelle O'Connor, remembered by Don for her very pale blue eyes, was Irish by background. The family—including Glade's two younger sisters—spent summer holidays on board the steamer. In the summer of 1928, Jess had also been aboard, employed as crew. Don later wrote: "Glade, from under her parasol as she stood on the captain's bridge, first espied him, stripped to the waist, loading cargo onto the boat. Imbued with the ideals of movie romance, she was immediately smitten and made her interests unmistakeable to Jess, who was flattered to win the attentions of the captain's daughter."

Jess was shorter than his sons and less self-confident, but he was just as handsome. At twenty-three, when Glade "espied" him, he had just returned from California, the land of Glade's movie-obsessed dreams, where he had been working as a chauffeur in Pasadena. Captain DeLand objected to the match between his daughter and "an uneducated and penniless common laborer,"[19] but Glade fought to marry quickly before Jess could lose interest. The wedding was in Cleveland in December 1928. Glade was twenty-two. Jess drove her to Hollywood for their honeymoon.

By 1930, when Ted was born, Jess and Glade were settled in Glendale, and Jess was working in the developing aviation industry as a mechanic, at Kinnear. Eventually he rose to be a tool planner.

Glade had a powerful inner life, and Don felt she never fully emerged into the real, adult world. She collected dolls secretly, and she bought clothes for herself in a size she wished to be. She wanted her second child to be a girl, and when a boy arrived, she named him Don after her sister Donnabell, known as Donna. This, too, was magical thinking, because Glade's father had made the able-bodied Donna his favorite daughter after Glade was disabled by polio. Jess sanctioned a family movie outing on Sunday nights to affordable second- or third-run theaters in their neighborhood, but every week, Glade found a way to sneak downtown to first-run films, sometimes with the boys, and she drew them further and further into her fantasy world.

She did not know what homosexuality was until Ted had his first breakdown and it became evident that he was having sex with older men, probably in their twenties.[20] Glade certainly did not understand the difficulties their sexuality presented for her sons in the late 1940s and 50s when, in the state of California, oral sex and sodomy were criminal acts even between consenting adults regardless of gender or marital status. Sodomy could be punished by life in prison for repeat offenders. California became one of the first states (in 1947) to require sex offenders to register, and also one of the first to legislate against psychopathic offenders. Vice prosecution was on the rise mid-century, in keeping with the conformist trends of the McCarthy era. Loitering with intent to solicit sex could get you arrested and so could vagrancy, an ill-defined crime which gave the police discretion to pick up anyone who was in the wrong place at the wrong time or with the wrong people.[21]

At eighteen, Don was outgrowing the need for Ted's protection from sexual predators, but he had not outgrown the need for companionship and sexual understanding, and as the youngest member of his family, he was accustomed to being looked after. "Ted had been for many years the pivotal person in my life," Don later recalled, "my moviegoing partner and the only link I had to the homosexual society I more and more craved."[22] Once launched into an active sex life, Don couldn't do without it, but he wanted more than sex. It was "homosexual society" he craved—that vast, amorphous network that lay partly hidden in the culture all around him and to which Isherwood could provide not just the link once provided by Ted, but also some understanding of what homosexual society might be.

Don Bachardy was the first person in his family to attend college. When his German-Hungarian paternal grandmother, Laura Elenore Lednisky Bachardy, emigrated from the Austro-Hungarian Empire in 1892, aged twenty-six, she could not speak English. She never learned. She settled in Passaic, New Jersey, where she worked as a dressmaker and where Jess was born in 1905, soon after the death by accidental drowning of his father Stephan Bachardy. Family lore said that Laura had thirteen children; she evidently raised six in Passaic, three boys and three girls.

Jess was ashamed of his Hungarian background and hid it, starting with his name, Jas, which he Americanized to Jess. Don recalled meeting his Hungarian grandmother only once. "Jess was tense and embarrassed in front of his sons."[23] They grew up knowing only their uncles Ted and Joe Bachardy. Once they met an Aunt Julia. Jess never spoke Hungarian to his sons and didn't want them to hear it or learn it. Perhaps that unconsciously influenced Don to major in modern languages at UCLA.

After graduating from John Marshall High School, he had started at UCLA in the autumn of 1952, but he felt lost in the big lecture courses with two hundred students taking notes, so he transferred to Los Angeles City College in Hollywood, smaller and much closer to home. In February 1953, when he began seeing Isherwood, he was between schools, but formal education never really engaged him. He was later to say that his real education came from Isherwood, who nurtured his curiosity and his intensely discriminating sensibility by exposing him to books, movies, plays, music, and artworks, and to the people who made such things. Isherwood had never had a younger friend as receptive as Bachardy.

ON THE LAST two Saturdays in March, Isherwood drove Bachardy to Camarillo to visit Ted, and they met with Ted's psychiatrist. Ted was released on April 7. Bachardy now felt uncomfortable around his older brother and increasingly unhappy at home.

Isherwood had taken him to Mexico, that favorite spot, Ensenada in Baja, where, according to Bachardy's recollection, their sex progressed to anal penetration. Bachardy confided to Isherwood that he had been wanting but fearing to allow the TV camera operator he was seeing to penetrate him, so they agreed that Isherwood would teach him how and be the first. Isherwood had also begun introducing Bachardy to his friends, including John Van Druten at his desert ranch.

Meanwhile, Caskey returned to Los Angeles on March 14, and Isherwood saw him nearly every day for two and a half weeks and spent several nights with him. Caskey found it difficult to accept that Isherwood had established a new life without him. He pronounced the garden house "piss elegant," and one night, drunk and angry, he smashed some spotlights mounted on the bookshelves around Isherwood's bed.[24]

What a contrast to Bachardy, who brought his homework to the garden house, shared a supper of shrimp jambalaya, then sat working quietly while Isherwood got on with his novel. This was the kind of companionship Isherwood longed for—quiet absorption side by side, solitude in the midst of snugness.

In mid-April, Bachardy suggested that he move in with Isherwood. They were on their way to see the 1952 film of Oscar Wilde's play *The Importance of Being Earnest*. "Chris was visibly surprised by my suggestion," Bachardy later wrote. He "became grave" and "questioned me delicately to test whether I was serious and whether I was fully conscious of what it seemed to him I was proposing."[25] Isherwood knew his Oscar Wilde. He was well aware that Wilde, in *De Profundis*, had blamed his downfall on his own weakness of character in failing to drive away Lord Alfred Douglas and get on with his writing. Isherwood was in love, but having struggled so hard to free himself from Caskey, he was cautious and said no.

What happened next shows Bachardy's uncanny intuition. Two days later, at the garden house, Bachardy offered to help Isherwood with his novel by typing to his dictation. He had learned to type in junior high school. Far from taking Isherwood away from his work, Bachardy made himself indispensable to it. As with Richard at Pembroke Gardens in 1932, the dictation was a supreme act of intimacy for Isherwood. It was not just that Bachardy was typing; he was also providing an audience. His young, American ear was an ear that Isherwood, as a writer, had not yet reached.

The scene in the garden house brought to life the fantasy Isherwood had entertained ever since he had decided to become a writer, about meeting a boy who would take an interest in his work, just as Leonard Merrows takes an interest in Charles Franklyn's work in Isherwood's first, discarded novel, *Lions and Shadows*. Isherwood had given this fantasy a variety of literary forms, casting it different ways in different stories, sometimes changing the sexes of the characters, and playing with the narrative point of view. The scenario was intoxicating for him, and he never tired of trying it again in new ways.

THE SUCCESS OF *I Am a Camera* and the loss of his personal past to the public domain had increased the pressure for Isherwood to reinvent himself as an American novelist. How had he become a novelist the first time? For *The World in the Evening*, he delved backward into his early attempts at fiction and the literary models that had obsessed him in the 1920s, when he had launched his career.

He reread *Les Faux-Monnayeurs*, evidently prompted by Gide's death in 1951, and he managed to obtain a copy of the far more obscure Hope Mirrlees's *The Counterplot* to reread as well. He again decided to use the mise en abyme. In *The World in the Evening* an English writer Elizabeth Rydal is the author of a book called *The World in the Evening*. A young man twelve years younger than she, Stephen Monk, takes an interest in her writing, as Leonard Merrows takes an interest in Charles Franklyn's in Isherwood's early novel, abandoned when it was savaged by Ethel Mayne. Elizabeth Rydal and Stephen Monk marry, and he offers to type her current manuscript and soon becomes her secretary. Their love story takes place in Europe in the 1920s and 30s and is told through flashbacks during a present set from April 1941 to late January 1942, in the buildup to Pearl Harbor when World War II is raging and the U.S. prepares to enter the fighting. Elizabeth Rydal dies and Stephen Monk marries again, to the character based on Caskey, Jane Armstrong, whom Stephen is divorcing throughout the novel.

Stephen is a wealthy American raised partly in England, a lapsed Quaker, a pacifist. He shelters from the wreck of his second marriage with his adoptive aunt in Haverford, Pennsylvania. There he is hit by a truck. Recuperating in bed, he rereads Elizabeth Rydal's letters, reflects on both of his marriages, and also on his failed love affair with a man. He falls in love with his nurse, a woman, and he also falls for his doctor and his doctor's partner, both men. The healing in the book is not only to his broken leg but also to his broken psyche.

Stephen Monk's first marriage fulfilled another fantasy of Isherwood's youth, the consummation of his one-sided love affair with Katherine Mansfield. In April 1951, Isherwood reviewed a literary-critical biography of Mansfield for *Tomorrow* and reminisced that "For several years I was violently in love with 'Kathy,' as my friends and I (who never knew her personally) used to call her." In his 1951 review, he stated plainly that back in the 1920s, "I identified myself romantically with her sufferings and her struggle."[26]

Mansfield's adored younger brother was killed in World War I, making her memories of their New Zealand childhood, Isherwood explained in the book review, "more precious, more sacred than ever." It was in a "mood of spiritual collaboration" with her dead brother that she had written "the New Zealand stories which contain so much of her finest work." But, argued Isherwood, her writing was marred by an "acute internal conflict" between her childhood self and her adult personality. "Had she lived to achieve her own psychological integration she would naturally have merged the two writers into one."[27]

When he wrote this in 1951, Isherwood was working to achieve his own psychological integration and to merge his English and American selves into one, "feeling my way toward an Anglo-American style," as he told Upward.[28] He had once endowed his Christopher Isherwood narrators with a childlike innocence partly inspired by *David Copperfield* and by Felicity in *Little Friend*; like the Mansfield he described, he was riven with internal conflict and obsessed by the idea that he must find a way to express himself as a fully grown-up writer. He tried to do this by turning Mansfield into a fictional character, Elizabeth Rydal, and developing his narrative through her personality.

The Mansfield review was one of Isherwood's pieces for *Tomorrow*, founded by the Irish-born literary saloneuse Eileen Garrett, known as a psychic. In March 1953, Isherwood attended a dinner with Garrett, hosted by Aldous and Maria Huxley and also attended by Heard who, like Huxley, was keenly interested in extrasensory perception and parapsychology. Huxley and Heard were following experiments to test Garrett's powers of ESP, and Isherwood was fascinated. He once told an aspiring novelist: "More important than the art of writing is the trance state you must first get into,—in communion with your subject."[29] The metaphor of the writer as medium recurs throughout his work, and so does the language of the occult.

In *The World in the Evening*, Isherwood raised Katherine Mansfield from the dead and reimagined her as Elizabeth Rydal so that his Stephen Monk character could commune with her as if at a séance. Stephen Monk first "contacts" his dead wife during a Quaker meeting; then, after his accident, Stephen communes with her while lying in bed reading her letters. His reverie technique is borrowed from Mansfield. In her journal, Mansfield had recorded that when she became really ill with the tuberculosis that finally killed her, she received a "consolation prize" of being able to relive the past "at will" in complete detail: "lying here in bed, I begin to *live* over either scenes from real life or imaginary scenes. [. . .] I am *there*."[30]

In June 1951, Isherwood wrote in his work journal: "the private title of this novel is 'Ghosts.'"[31] He had in mind Henrik Ibsen's play *Ghosts*—another text he had idolized in the 1920s and which had influenced *All the*

Conspirators—in which the young artist Osvald Alving is forced to abandon his painting career in Paris and return home to his mother in provincial Norway because he is ill and going mad with an unnamed disease (presumably syphilis) inherited from his father. The theme of *Ghosts* gripped Isherwood again as he struggled with his first truly American novel. In *The World in the Evening*, the past is another world mysteriously nearby and within, like the presences that haunted Isherwood at 333 East Rustic Road and, long before that, at Marple Hall. "It is becoming much more like Freudian analysis," Isherwood told Upward. "I'm far more interested to see what I will discover about myself than to see how it will develop as an artwork."[32]

ISHERWOOD MODELED THE Rydal–Monk marriage partly on the real-life marriage of Dodie Smith and Alec Beesley. Alec, tall, handsome, physically fit, was seven years younger than Dodie and devoted to managing her career—from typing her manuscripts and doing her accounts to choosing her wardrobe and packing her expensive luggage.

Planning, in 1951, how he would write the first meeting between Elizabeth Rydal and Stephen Monk, Isherwood had decided that Stephen should come to life from Elizabeth's imagination: "She has imagined this character. In he walks."[33] This is what Isherwood had always wished for himself, and in 1953, in walked Bachardy like a blank page. It was the mise en abyme in reverse. Down sat Bachardy at Isherwood's typewriter, performing the role of Stephen Monk in the novel that he was typing to Isherwood's dictation.

The text Isherwood and Bachardy produced bears the mark of private interaction not necessarily intended to be understood by readers outside the garden house. For instance, the fictional Rydal–Monk marriage offered instructions to Bachardy on how to succeed in his relationship with Isherwood: "I must never let myself get jealous of Elizabeth's work," Stephen tells himself. This was a mistake Caskey and other Isherwood boyfriends had made. Stephen shares in Elizabeth's work in order to overcome his resentment of her fame and his uneasiness around her literary acquaintances, who treat him "as an attractive boy, Elizabeth's pickup." Stephen recalls how the beginning of his marriage with Elizabeth seemed like "a kind of game" or "'a camp' . . . to prevent anyone from suspecting that we two had discovered a new, unnamed kind of relationship."[34]

In the imaginative game Isherwood and Bachardy were now playing, identity was not fixed, characters and roles could be slid in and out of, just like sexual identity. Bachardy played Stephen Monk, who was based partly on Isherwood, partly on Alec Beesley, partly on bisexual friends of Isherwood's boyhood and youth, Stephen Spender and Patrick Monkhouse, as well as on Frank Taylor. Isherwood played Elizabeth, partly based on himself, partly based on Dodie Smith, Katherine Mansfield, Virginia Woolf, E.M. Forster, and Ethel Mayne. Even in 1953, Isherwood was still trying to please Mayne who had died in 1941.

Bachardy instinctively joined Isherwood's game even though he cannot fully have understood it. Isherwood had imagined a whole career for Elizabeth Rydal, listing the titles of her publications in a timeline in his work journal so that he could offer convincing glimpses. These imaginary publications resonated with Isherwood's real past. The title of the third one, *A Garden with Animals*, "the most autobiographical of her novels,"[35] was a pair for *Seascape with Figures*, the preliminary title for Isherwood's own first novel, *All the Conspirators*. Garden and shore had been the happy realms of Isherwood's first ten years.

A Garden with Animals was also a coded caption for the scene unfolding between Isherwood and Bachardy in the garden house. Almost right away, they adopted the pet identities Dobbin, the plodding reliable horse, and Kitty, skittish, unpredictable, and needing protection. For Bachardy, who as yet knew nothing of Beatrix Potter or of Kathleen, the latter referenced the kitten figures in one of his only two childhood picture books. Soon Isherwood and Bachardy began to refer to themselves as the Animals, launching just the kind of private game or camp that Stephen Monk describes in *The World in the Evening*, "a new, unnamed kind of relationship."

Their game was rooted in the world of childhood imagining, where Isherwood had played with Beatrix Potter, Buster Brown and Tige, and his father's stories about Bobby and Albert and Mrs. Porkington Pigiwig and her piglets. At twenty-one, working for André Mangeot and besotted with eleven-year-old Sylvain, Isherwood had composed poems to accompany Sylvain's sketches of animals, some dressed in human clothes. The poems and sketches were assembled in a homemade book, *People One Ought to Know*, gesturing to Edward Lear, whose *Complete Book of Nonsense* includes the poem "How Pleasant to Know Mr. Lear."[36] With Auden, there had been *The Dog Beneath the Skin*. With Kirstein, camping and clowning revolved around cats, which Kirstein adored. Bill Caskey's pet identity was "Pig." With Vidal, Isherwood played Mole to Vidal's Toad from *The Wind in the Willows*.[37]

Through the identities of Dobbin and Kitty, Isherwood and Bachardy formed the secret unbreakable bond which, over the years, they were to imbue with sentiments—and sentimentality—they could not articulate directly. One of the most important characteristics of the Animals was their innocence of ulterior motive. They embodied the instinctive life—the submission to creaturely needs and to a humble, unforeseeable destiny. The camp drew not only on Beatrix Potter, but also on Walt Whitman who described these animal qualities in "Song of Myself":

> They do not sweat and whine about their condition,
> They do not lie awake in the dark and weep for their sins,
> They do not make me sick discussing their duty to God,
> Not one is dissatisfied, not one is demented with the mania of owning things,
> Not one kneels to another, nor to his kind that lived thousands of years ago,
> Not one is respectable or unhappy over the whole earth.[38]

At St. Edmund's, Cyril Morgan Brown had humiliated Isherwood for piggily putting marmalade and butter on his bread and admonished him to control his instincts unless he wanted to be a pig or a cow. The Animals opposed such school values, and lived according to the intimate freedoms of home, where they slept together in what Isherwood and Bachardy called "the basket." Isherwood once described his father's story of Mrs. Porkington Pigiwig as "downright revolutionary"[39] for its overturning of nursery rules and of conventional relations between humans and animals. The Animals secretly possessed the appetites and sexual energy that could overturn or transform the fabric of society. In Isherwood and Bachardy's game, the Animals were homosexuals. The Others were in general straight people, but they were also any outsiders.

In Bachardy, Isherwood had encountered a fact that he could not counterfeit. He later wrote: "I did feel awed by the emotional intensity of our relationship, right from its beginning; the strange sense of a fated, mutual discovery."[40] So intense were his developing feelings that the fictions he had made since boyhood—the stories he had told himself and his friends, written down, made into plays, film scripts—temporarily ceased to excite him, overwhelmed as they were by real life. In his diary that April, he described a feeling of creative "impotence," a "lack of inclination to cope with a constructed, invented plot—the feeling, why not write what one experiences, from day to day? And then, as I slid my door back, this sinking-sick feeling of love for Don—[...] Why invent—when Life is so prodigious?" It made him dissatisfied with *The World in the Evening*: "it's so lifeless."

IN ADAPTING *Goodbye to Berlin*, John Van Druten had commandeered not only Isherwood's identity but also his artistic approach. In a preface to his script, Van Druten asserted that plot was no longer necessary in the theater: "The mood of the play—the establishment for the audience of what it felt like to be living in Berlin in 1930, and the kind of life and people that one met there, then—is its most important quality." In the 1930s, Isherwood had been a disciple of Chekhov; he had excelled at characterization and mood, but with Van Druten laying public claim to this trend in theater, Isherwood, seeking artistic elbow room, lurched back to plot. He told the Beesleys that *The World in the Evening* had "turned into a novel of situations and character-collisions, instead of that kind of atmosphere-embroidery I've always specialized in before."[41]

Isherwood and Van Druten were close friends for nearly twenty years, and they had much in common, being born and educated in England, transplanted to New York, where they had first met in 1939, and then California. They were both pacifists and both followers of Vedanta. But Van Druten was rich from his stage work in New York and London. His strength was light comedy, and from Isherwood's point of view, there was something altogether lightweight about him. Isherwood once told Kirstein: "He writes as one wrote when one was seven. Without pain. And the telephone hums with calls from New York, offering him the gold of the Andes if he'll do this, that or the other."[42] And yet this innocent success was something Isherwood could not help but envy.

In *The World in the Evening*, he fictionally consigned Van Druten to a diminishing minor role as Cecilia de Limbour, younger sister of Elizabeth Rydal, whom Stephen Monk suspects "of nursing a permanent grudge against Elizabeth's talent"[43] and to whom Elizabeth writes unguarded letters, confident that Cecilia won't notice any revelations and will write back only about herself. Dodie Smith exchanged letters with Van Druten as often as four times a day; "they were the closest and deadliest of rivals," wrote Smith's biographer, and Van Druten was "a leech," who stole embryonic ideas Smith shared with him: "It's wonderful having John to argue with – I enjoy it more than I can say," wrote Smith. "But John doesn't extend my mind as Christopher does."[44]

Elizabeth Rydal puts a rhetorical question to Cecilia de Limbour, about "the Original Sin of novelists." Isn't it "that they've tried to persuade their readers, and themselves, to see human beings as 'characters'; beautifully complete three-dimensional wholes?" And she answers the question herself: "This lie of the novelists is a sin because it encourages the belief that you can treat human beings as characters; that you can know them fully, and possess them—in the same way that one can know and possess Emma Bovary or Alyosha Karamazov." Elizabeth is building upon Forster's view, stated in *Aspects of the Novel*, that "what we call intimacy is only a makeshift; perfect knowledge is an illusion. But in the novel we can know people perfectly..."[45] By way of Van Druten's adaptation of *Sally Bowles* Isherwood had become a victim of his own original sin. He was being treated as a character who could be fully known. But he was still alive and changing.

A crucial scene in the last part of *The World in the Evening* suggests that real intimacy might be knowledge *with* another person rather than knowledge *about* them, and this kind of knowledge is available to the spiritually prepared. The refugee Gerda Mannheim describes how Sarah Pennington, the devout Quaker who raised Stephen Monk after his parents died, sat silently with her, experiencing "all that I am feeling, everything," as Gerda weeps for her husband Peter, lost in a Nazi concentration camp: "The room gets very still. [. . .] It is all right—even if Peter is *not* safe—even if the worst happens, to him and to me. Suddenly I knew that. Sarah made me know it..."[46] Isherwood portrayed Sarah Pennington as a saint. Her initials, S.P., also stand for Swami Prabhavananda. Outwardly she resembles Caroline Norment who ran the refugee project, but her inner qualities, her empathy and faith, derive from Prabhavananda.[47] Thus, Isherwood offered Gerda's quasi-mystical experience in a Christian formulation which he considered his readers would more easily understand and accept than a Hindu one; Vedanta is never mentioned.[48]

THE OPENING SCENE of *The World in the Evening* announces sexual betrayal as a central theme, and in writing the book Isherwood seems to have been trying to alleviate the wound of Caskey's infidelities and also to arrive at a better understanding of jealousy, promiscuity, and polyamory. There was little sex in the marriage between Dodie Smith and Alec Beesley,[49] so he based the Rydal–Monk marriage on other marriages, too, both fictional and real. His Caskey character, Jane Armstrong, is part of an orgy-bent, pleasure-seeking tribe, undiscriminating in physical partners: "They were like a pack of young animals, playing together and sometimes squabbling, but without any strong individual relationships." The tone of sour sophistication mixed with innocent, unquenchable desire is borrowed from Cyril Connolly's novel *The Rock Pool* (1936).[50]

Isherwood borrowed far more from Gide, staking out a hidden critique of his marriage to Madeleine Rondeaux as he saw it portrayed in Gide's novels *L'Immoraliste* (*The Immoralist*) and *La Porte étroite* (*Strait is the Gate*), and in *Madeleine, ou Et nunc manet in te* (*Madeleine, or And Now He Is in You*), his 1947 memoir about his late wife.[51] The three books together suggest how Gide manipulated his wife to serve his private sexual and artistic purposes. In revenge for her husband's love affairs Rondeaux burned his letters to her, knowing he had planned to base future work on them. By contrast, Isherwood's Elizabeth Rydal preserves her letters and leaves them behind so Stephen Monk can learn from them.[52]

The World in the Evening dismissed conventional Christian attitudes toward sex. Isherwood's hero is a sinner only if he sees himself as one. In Vedanta, sex is an attachment to overcome, not a sin. Isherwood had observed in his work journal: "If Stephen's 'conversion' means anything, it means that he can accept an apparent paradox—i.e. he still believes in God—or more than ever believes in God—while doing something the God-mongers condemn—that is, loving another man. [. . .] This is what makes the story really significant."[53]

Isherwood had met Gide in Berlin in 1929, when Gide toured Hirschfeld's institute, presenting himself, as Isherwood later recalled, "in full costume as the Great French Novelist complete with cape." He labeled Gide a "sneering, culture-conceited Frog."[54] Yet he mocked himself in the same way, time and again, for playing a role, dressing up as a writer: "Isherwood the Artist," "Curaçao Chris," "Isherwood-in-Hawaii."[55] He came to honor Gide "as one of the heroic leaders of our tribe."[56] But he could not honor Gide's unyielding heart. As late as the 1960s, Isherwood was still rewriting Gide. In *A Single Man*, he was to offer a lifelike, erotically charged Platonic dialogue to replace the stiff, cold ones in Gide's *Corydon* (1911), and thereby to make Gide's argument that pederasty is "natural" and "normal" far more compelling.[57]

Isherwood overloaded drafts of *The World in the Evening* with sex partly because he expected his publishers to make him cut some of it, and he wanted to begin with a position from which he could be seen to negotiate. He told Kirstein: "The novel is very strange, rather like Moravia, a chain-reaction of fucks, both kinds."[58] In the same way that he was trying to squeeze Vedanta into Christendom through the door of the Quaker Inner Light, he was trying to squeeze homosexuality into a mainstream novel through the door of promiscuous heterosexuality.

AS THE GERMAN communist refugee character Gerda Mannheim points out to Stephen Monk, the title of Elizabeth Rydal's novel, *The World in the Evening*, "was also the name of a Communist newspaper in Berlin. Before Hitler came."[59] This was Willi Münzenberg's *Welt am Abend*, mentioned in *Mr. Norris Changes Trains*.[60] Gerda Mannheim, with her communist convictions, hates Elizabeth Rydal's novel because it focuses on the emotions of privileged characters safe in a beautiful house in England while "People are taken in concentration-camps and beaten and tortured and burned like garbage in ovens."[61] But Gerda, too, learns, through her relationship with Sarah Pennington, the solace of mysticism when politics have failed, and Isherwood's leftist political inclination reemerged in the book exclusively aligned for the first time with the drive for sexual freedoms that had been only a tag-along leftist cause in the days of Magnus Hirschfeld and Willi Münzenberg in Berlin.

When the *The World in the Evening* was still a seven-page embryo focused on German-Jewish refugees, Isherwood had told Upward: "I'm aiming of course, at a parallel, as in Proust, between the Jewish and the homosexual minority."[62] But that was back in 1947. Once he cut the Jewish refugees from the book, Isherwood was able to focus on the homosexual minority directly. Charles Kennedy, who is Stephen Monk's highly competent doctor, and his partner Bob Wood are Isherwood's first middle-class, American homosexual characters—educated, adult, solvent. They are neither artists, aesthetes, con men, nor the hungry unemployed of England and Europe. They are not weaklings or victims. Bob Wood goes off in uniform to fight in World War II saying: "I can't be a C[onscientious] O[bjector], because if they declared war on queers—tried to round us up and liquidate us, or something—I'd fight. I'd fight till I dropped."[63] Thus, Isherwood made good on the advice he had offered Gore Vidal, creating, as few authors dared in the 1950s, an attractive and happy homosexual couple: they are not psychologically twisted; they are not doomed to tragedy,

The pair was inspired by Dallas Pratt, an American doctor, and his English companion, John Judkyn, a converted Quaker, who hosted Isherwood at Brandywine Farm outside Paoli, Pennsylvania, in the spring of 1942. "The Quakes are puzzled by him, no doubt," Isherwood wrote of Judkyn in his diary, "and by Pratt, but they accept them because Pratt is a doctor and Judkyn is very efficient at organizing relief work. Nevertheless they don't fit in at all. They are really outsiders."[64] As so often in Isherwood's novels, these two outsiders were surface models only. Deeper models supplied the psychological and emotional chemistry—Wood was based on Jim Charlton, who had flown twenty-six missions over Germany during the war, including a daylight raid on Hamburg in July 1943, and Kennedy was based on Lincoln Kirstein.

In one draft, Wood crashes and dies in the war, and Isherwood roughed out a scene in which Kennedy and Monk visit his body at the mortuary, find it horribly disfigured, and have the casket lid screwed down to spare the family. In his work journal, Isherwood wrote of Kennedy: "He himself doesn't go to the funeral. I want to show his exclusion from the ritual, because his relationship is unrecognized by Society." For the time being, he dropped the idea as "too daring";[65] instead he integrated the gay lovers, showing how they fit in, rather than emphasizing their position as outsiders. But he used it in *A Single Man*, fifteen years later.

In the characters of Charles Kennedy and Bob Wood, *The World in the Evening* portrayed for a mainstream audience what might be called a homosexual sensibility. The novel made clear that homosexuality was not only about sex. This was groundbreaking. For instance, Charles Kennedy tells Stephen Monk all about camp, explaining the difference between Low Camp, "a swishy little boy with peroxided hair, dressed in a picture hat and a feather boa, pretending to be Marlene Dietrich" and High Camp, which "has an underlying seriousness. [. . .] You're expressing what's basically serious to you in terms of fun and artifice and elegance. Baroque art is largely camp about religion. The Ballet is camp about love . . ."[66]

A decade after *The World in the Evening* was published, Susan Sontag, the American philosopher and critic, pointed to this scene as the first description of camp in literature. Sontag called for more on the subject and berated Isherwood for providing only a "lazy two-page sketch." This was to give herself a platform. Isherwood, far from being lazy, disciplined himself to deliver the scene with the light touch appropriate to camp: "You have to meditate on it and feel it intuitively," says Charles Kennedy.[67]

Camp was the language Isherwood and Kirstein spoke together. During World War II, Isherwood confided to Kirstein the alienation he felt from his English friends due to his pacifism and his absence from England. "Somehow, I don't in the least feel that your experience, or mine, will 'come between' us. Why do I say this? I suppose because we have something in common on an entirely different plane: the camp that passeth all understanding."[68] Camp was a private game of the theatrical, exaggerated sort that Isherwood had been playing since childhood. For him, such games came to life in the playing, in new material, and with new collaborators.

ISHERWOOD CONTINUED TO resist letting Bachardy move in with him because it was too great a responsibility. Bachardy grew so distressed that he began vomiting his mother's cooking, "even those very special dishes of hers which I had loved in my childhood." So Isherwood helped Bachardy move into a room on Spalding Avenue in Hollywood, "cheap and clean but rundown-looking and with a small, lumpy bed."[69] Most nights Bachardy stayed at the garden house anyway, and Isherwood drove him back and forth to school. Bachardy had a week off starting May 4, so they made a six-day road trip which they came to look upon as their honeymoon.

Isherwood dropped their itinerary into his diary on a loose sheet, commemorating its significance without trying to describe it in detail: Blythe on the Arizona border, then Gallup, New Mexico, then back into Arizona to explore Canyon de Chelly, an ancestral home of the Pueblo and Navajo people. They drove the two-lane highways with the top down on the Sunbeam-Talbot, then traveled into southern Utah on a dangerously sand-swept dirt road to Monument Valley, sacred to the Navajo. The towering red-rock formations had been made famous by John Ford, winner of four Academy Awards, who directed seven Westerns there, including *Stagecoach* (1939). "Isn't it magnificent?" Isherwood had written to his mother after they had each seen the film separately during his first few months in the U.S.[70]

Isherwood and Bachardy checked into Harry Goulding's Lodge—single-story, ranch-style buildings huddled under a mesa—and went into the mess hall to eat. There, completely by chance, they bumped into Ford himself, "eye-patch and all," as Bachardy later recalled. "The scene deserved musical accompaniment."

Ford was probably hiding out from negative publicity surrounding the release in May 1953 of his controversial comedy about race relations in a Southern town, *The Sun Shines Bright*. With him were "eight or so scruffy-looking, gruff-sounding men," including the Irish film director Brian Desmond Hurst. Ford and Hurst were both about ten years older than Isherwood. Bachardy felt too uncomfortable to talk in such a macho setting, but he recalled that Isherwood remained at ease, though it was a "stilted, wary conversation between Chris and Ford."[71] Everyone was hiding something. Hurst had become friendly with Gerald Hamilton in Tangier after the war, and in later years became known for his candor about his homosexuality, referring to himself as the Empress of Ireland.[72] Bachardy did not guess that Hurst was gay.

That night, Isherwood and Bachardy slept "in separate bunks in a one-room bunkhouse [...] shared with several of the men." The next day, they toured the valley by Jeep with a majestically tall Navajo guide dressed all in black and photographed each other, diminutive in stature, freshly shaved and combed, their shirts neatly tucked into their trousers, grinning happily or staring romantically at the rugged rock formations as they acted out their private script on what was, in a sense, the largest film set in the world.[73]

On the homeward journey, they stopped in Las Vegas. Bachardy was on the edge of his seat as they drove along the Strip, go-go lights beckoning through the palm fronds, and he relished the floor show at the Flamingo by the musical stars Marge and Gower Champion, but back at the garden house, he was overwhelmed by sorrow: "I felt I'd consumed some crucial bit of my youth, and despite my full enjoyment of the feast, it was gone."[74] Isherwood was only beginning to feed Bachardy's passionate, insatiable appetite.

IN MID-MAY, BACHARDY moved again, into a spare room in the apartment of Isherwood's friends Harry and Marguerite Brown, acceptable chaperones to Bachardy's parents and to conservative Hollywood society because they were married. He continued to spend most nights with Isherwood. Harry Brown, educated at Harvard, had won an Academy Award as co-writer on *A Place in the Sun* (1951) and was writing scripts for 20th Century–Fox and MGM. Marguerite was Speed Lamkin's sister and had followed Speed to Hollywood. She was a Louisiana belle, descended from cotton-growing aristocracy and living off Delta Airlines stock. She was open-minded, though she liked appearances to soothe expectations. She also liked to have fun. She once described people who were able to function on both sides of convention as "zigzag."[75] Her party-girl aura is evoked in the character Angelica O'Brien, heroine of her brother's second novel, *The Easter Egg Hunt* (1954), which was dedicated to Isherwood and in which Isherwood appears as Sebastian Saunders.[76]

Bachardy fell for Marguerite's looks, "gangly in a delicate, distinctly feminine way," and her dress style. Above all, he was enchanted by her "[s]oftly insinuating" Louisiana accent. "She quickly became my best, most adored friend," he later wrote.[77] And she made herself a foundation stone in the establishment of Isherwood and Bachardy's life together by offering sanctuary to their unconventional relationship.

The second draft of *The World in the Evening* was done by June 8, just before Stephen Spender arrived on a lecture tour that included an engagement at the UCLA English department arranged by Edward Hooker, who was a professor there. In the 1930s, when Isherwood had sometimes felt pushed and crowded by Spender, the pressure had helped him to get work finished. Now, in June 1953, he seemed to be responding to a work deadline imposed by the reentrance of one of his band of literary brothers. Spender, as it happened, had a big role in *The World in the Evening* as a model for the bisexual character, Stephen Monk.[78]

Like Stephen Spender in real life, Stephen Monk is orphaned with an income; like Spender, whose grandmother joined the Quakers during World War I, Monk is raised by an overly affectionate female "relative," a Quaker; like Spender, Monk is tall; like Spender with his lover Tony Hyndman, Monk falls in love with a man whose destiny is tied up in the Spanish Civil War.[79] Isherwood evidently found many reminders of Spender's past in Spender's memoir *World Within World*, which he read in proof in 1950 and reviewed for *Tomorrow*.

In his review, Isherwood pronounced *World Within World* "a very important book" because it showed that Spender had never taken sides politically or sexually in an era which had seemed to demand this. Spender was briefly but not genuinely a communist,[80] he was bisexual, had affairs with men and women, and had two marriages: "he has teetered back and forth, and even now his balance is uncertain," wrote Isherwood. In the memoir, Spender presented his involvements with communism and homosexuality as being over, but in fact he continued to fall in love with young men and hid this from his second wife.

Building on the insights of his 1938 portrait in *Lions and Shadows*, Isherwood in his review described Spender as "an essentially comic character" with "an instinctive flair, amounting to genius, for revealing truth through farce." He cunningly disguised this judgment as admiration, saying that Spender "seems to preserve an ultimate integrity simply by virtue of laying himself so ridiculously open to criticism."[81]

Isherwood was not the only friend to say such things. Auden wrote to Spender about *World Within World*, "while confessing your sins of weakness, you pass over in silence your sins of strength; ie of calculation and coldness of heart."[82] The "inspired simpleton" was also "shrewd and ambitious, aggressive and ruthless, a publicity-seeking intellectual full of administrative energy and rentier asperity," said Connolly in a review for the *Sunday Times*.[83] Spender epitomized a style of duplicity at the heart of the 1950s, nurtured by Cold War fears, dependent on the widespread and complacent acceptance of convention, on open but unarticulated secrets. In 1953, Spender became co-editor of the magazine *Encounter*, secretly funded by the CIA. Friends thought he knew about the CIA funding, and some warned him. When the CIA funding was exposed in the newspapers in May 1967, Spender resigned. All the while, he was attacked in the press by friends and adversaries alike.

Isherwood, as ever, had a peculiarly intimate motivation for what he wrote about Spender and how he used him in his fiction. When he had seen Spender in January 1947, for the first time in eight years, Spender was established as a married man with a son; a daughter was born in 1950. For Isherwood, who had supervised Spender's early steps toward homosexual liberation in Berlin and kept house with Spender and their respective boyfriends, the new closeted Spender was a curiosity and an emotional challenge. Isherwood had observed Spender's first unsuccessful marriage to the novelist Inez Pearn which lasted from 1936 to 1939, and before that, he had been privy to Spender's growing interest in erotic relationships with women. In 1934, during an affair with the American psychoanalyst and resistance agent Muriel Gardiner, Spender had written to Isherwood that he had been having "quite a lot of normal sex lately," as he called it, and that he preferred it. "I find boys much more attractive, in fact I am rather more than usually susceptible, but actually I find the actual sexual act with women more satisfactory, more terrible, more disgusting, and, in fact, more everything." He rejected the bar life and the cruising they had shared, "the whole life of the lokals and of the people I see pursuing boys, is too much for me now, when I feel, like you[,] that we are in the last whirlpool."[84]

In his reply, Isherwood had jokily dismissed the idea of "normal" sex and evinced some cautious nostalgia for their German adventures: "I should be sorry if we either of us ever came to despise the old jokes and haunts; we had some fun there, didn't we, in our day?"[85] Some of this developing disharmony about sexual preferences may have been rooted in the fact that Isherwood had never found Spender sexually attractive. Spender told Auden's biographer in 1980: "I should think that Auden (and Isherwood for that matter) regarded me as sexually inhibited and inhibiting."[86]

As he reconsidered his and Spender's shared life in the 1930s and their respective sexual destinies, Isherwood found he couldn't admire or even fully empathize with the bisexual character he was creating in his novel. He understood the character to be a homosexual hiding from straights and gays alike and also hiding from himself, afraid to commit, teetering. He teased Spender about his political and sexual ambivalence by referring to Spender's memoir as WhirledWithinWhirled.[87]

Stephen Monk tries to hide his homosexual inclinations and activities from himself and from his wives, besmirching his integrity and authenticity, endlessly repenting and apologizing. The wandering, risk-taking, disillusioned Michael Drummond character, who is in love with Monk, appears at key moments to challenge Stephen to be true to himself. But the sexual encounters between Monk and Drummond seem immature, partly because Monk refuses to fully acknowledge them, partly because Isherwood's publishers pressured him to remove any suggestion of physical arousal. Elizabeth Rydal, like the mother figure Margaret Lanwin in *The Memorial*, indulges Monk's homosexual side, which infantilizes him further. Their marriage is a sexual failure, as Isherwood made explicit in his work journal and as he represented in the novel by the miscarriage of their only child. He contrasted all this sexual floundering with the adult honesty of the relationship between Bob Wood and Charles Kennedy.

The World in the Evening carries an oblique polemic against the notion that a homosexual who marries and has children is somehow more grown up and responsible than a homosexual who never undertakes heterosexual family life. Isherwood was pushing back, and not just against Spender. In *Enemies of Promise* (1938), Cyril Connolly had stated that the experiences of his and Isherwood's generation of middle-class English boys at their boarding schools were "so intense as to dominate their lives and arrest their development." These were the boys educated to run the declining British

Empire. "[T]he greater part of the ruling class remains adolescent, school-minded, self-conscious, cowardly, sentimental, and in the last analysis homosexual," wrote Connolly. He labeled this "The Theory of Permanent Adolescence," a phrase vivid and succinct enough to enhance the currency of the idea.[88] Isherwood later described a prickly personal exchange on the matter which had occurred in 1937 in Paris. Connolly had asked,

> in a tone which Christopher found patronizing, how he felt about Heinz—the implication seeming to be that Cyril couldn't believe that an intelligent adult like Christopher could take such a relationship altogether seriously. To this, Christopher replied casually but nastily: "Oh, very much as you feel about Jean, I suppose." Cyril obviously found this insulting, to Jean and to himself. But he couldn't very well say so.[89]

Notably, when Isherwood first read Connolly's novel *The Rock Pool* in 1936, he had disliked it on the grounds that "it wasn't socially conscious." He did not mention but cannot have liked the fact that Connolly's English girl barkeepers in the South of France ban "fairies"—conforming to Connolly's ban on his own homosexuality when he became interested in women after leaving Oxford.[90] In 1936, Isherwood had been, after all, writing rival stories set in Berlin, and they were mostly about "fairies."

And then there was Patrick Monkhouse, "practically my oldest friend" as Isherwood described him in 1955.[91] Monkhouse visited Los Angeles to lecture on behalf of the Foreign Office in February 1951, another mature married man who had once fallen in love with boys rather than girls and who no longer acknowledged this as Isherwood had uneasily sensed when they met in Disley in 1947.

In a 1949 draft of *The World in the Evening*, Stephen Monk was called Stephen Monkhouse.[92] Isherwood later explained to a would-be biographer that he returned to Stephen Monk "to rewrite his character in some respects" in his last novel, *A Meeting by the River*.[93] He pointedly named this later version Patrick and made him into the type of the closeted bisexual who marries and hides his boyfriends from his wife. To behavior he observed in Stephen Spender and Patrick Monkhouse, Isherwood was to add observations about other bisexual friends: Lincoln Kirstein, Frank Taylor, and the film director Tony Richardson. Gay liberation and marriage equality later made this bisexual type an anachronism in many social milieux, but to Isherwood at the time, it embodied unacceptable mendacity. In *A Meeting by the River*, the "good" brother is Oliver, the name Isherwood had associated with purity ever since reading *Oliver Twist* in 1915. The "bad" brother is Patrick because Patrick lies, in particular to those closest to him. Oliver enters the monastery: a Monk House. He is worthy of his vocation because he is honest, and he does not allow his elder brother to talk him off the pathway he has chosen. In these codes, Isherwood spoke to his adolescent past of embarrassment and shame, insisting that goodness was telling the truth.

———

FOR A WHOLE week in June 1953, Isherwood devoted himself to Spender, unlocking all the compartments of his life and introducing his friends. There were cocktail parties, barbecues, and breakfasts with members of the UCLA English department, lunches at MGM and at the Vedanta Society, a day on the beach, an evening when Isherwood left Spender alone with one of his own young sex partners.

Afterwards, Isherwood got back to work on the third draft of *The World in the Evening*, and Bachardy, done with classes, began retyping it. Isherwood took Bachardy to meet Gerald Heard, who was, as Bachardy recalled, living "in simplicity and seclusion," celibate, emaciated, in a garden house in Pacific Palisades, where he gave spiritual guidance to his wealthy hostess and her friends instead of paying rent. Bachardy sensed that Isherwood was "skittish" about the introduction, fearing Heard would disapprove of a boyfriend so young, but Heard seemed to accept Bachardy and took trouble to focus his high-flying talk directly at him.[94]

As for Prabhavananda, Bachardy had already been introduced to him over tea at Isherwood's own garden house. In *My Guru and His Disciple*, Isherwood reported: "All I now remember is that Swami made some approving remark about the look in Don's face. [. . .] From that moment, I felt that Don, and thus our relationship, was accepted by him."[95] This glossed over the extraordinary turbulence introduced into Isherwood's religious life when he fell in love with Bachardy, turbulence which he mostly repressed.

Isherwood finished the draft of *The World in the Evening* on August 5 and mailed a copy to Dodie and Alec Beesley. Dodie "is bothered by the sex," he wrote in his work journal ten days later.[96] He altered a bedroom scene between Gerda and Stephen, substituting a kiss, and sent the typescript to his publishers.

Then he had a revealing dream. Sex, both real and literary, was very much on his mind: "I dreamt that I was sharing a bed with Swami in a hotel which I knew to be a male whorehouse. Except that we were sharing a bed, our relations were as they always are. I was full of respect and consideration for him." In *My Guru and His Disciple*, where he later included this dream, Isherwood pointed out that "Sharing a bed with Swami represents a situation of absolute chastity," and that the dream might have been inspired by his memory of sleeping in Prabhavananda's bedroom at the Hollywood Vedanta Center when Prabhavananda was away in 1943.[97] The dream fulfilled Isherwood's wish to believe that no matter what his sexual activities, they could not besmirch his relationship with Prabhavananda.

Breaking with Caskey had offered Isherwood the opportunity to draw closer to God, and he had even, briefly, returned to the monastery at Trabuco. But he had accepted only what he wanted at Trabuco—the safety and quiet in which to hammer out a draft of his novel—before leaving to meet a new, and newly problematic, partner. He needed, wished for, and would continue to receive unconditional love from Prabhavananda. In his dream, Isherwood's unconscious reassured him with a new permissive mantram, as if he were being initiated all over again. "Swami said, 'I've got a new mantram for you, Chris. It is: Always dance.'"

The new mantram "seems to me to refer to Ramakrishna dancing in ecstasy," Isherwood was to explain in *My Guru and His Disciple*.[98] Ramakrishna is often described dancing in ecstasy in *The Gospel of Sri Ramakrishna*. But also, in July 1953 Bachardy had begun taking dancing lessons at Arthur Murray Dance Studios; moreover, Isherwood himself had enjoyed dancing lessons in his Limerick childhood. Now that he was free of Caskey and had finally completed *The World in the Evening*, Isherwood longed to turn away from guilt and suffering toward pleasure and playfulness, toward the innocence and freshness of youth embodied in Bachardy. He believed that Ramakrishna and Prabhavananda countenanced such joy, such dancing of the spirit.

HE TOOK BACHARDY off to San Francisco for ten days of wild pleasure. They saw everything from Cliff House and the gigantic Sutro Baths to the Presidio and the Bay Bridge. They took the ferry to Oakland, climbed the Twin Peaks and the Coit Tower atop Telegraph Hill, went to Stinson Beach. They ate German-Swiss food at the Shadows, Chinese food at Cathay House and Hang Far Low, French food at the Poodle Dog, Italian food at Dante's in the Castro and at the more glamorous Ernie's. They had cocktails on top of the Mark Hopkins Hotel and at the Fairmont. They heard Odetta sing at the Tin Angel, took in the female impersonators performing at Finocchio's, Rae Bourbon in drag at the Chi-Chi, Mexican musicians at Cantina Sinaloa. They even spent two evenings with Caskey, including one in Sausalito hitting the Valhalla and the exotic Four Winds.

The trip harked back to Isherwood's pleasure-seeking years in Berlin, the clubs and cabarets and cellar lokals where he had partied and which he had fictionalized in *Mr. Norris Changes Trains* and in *Goodbye to Berlin*. It harked back further to London trips with his mother throughout his childhood and adolescence, when Kathleen had piled treat upon treat until, sometimes, he was literally made ill. He and Bachardy even repeated the airfield trips, during which, as a child, Isherwood had watched stunts from the ground. On September 1, he and Bachardy flew over San Francisco, seeing from the air the length and breadth of the feast devoured that week.

But Isherwood and his beloved boy were about to be cast out of Eden. Three days after their return to Los Angeles, Evelyn Hooker visited the garden house for a private conversation while Bachardy was out. "When she had originally made the offer of the house to Chris, Evelyn explained, she and Edward had not foreseen that there would be anybody other than Chris living in it," Bachardy later recalled, noting how embarrassing this conversation must have been for Evelyn, since she was championing gays in her professional life as a psychologist. "Chris guessed that her mission had been precipitated by an ultimatum from Edward."[99]

Isherwood reported to Spender that the conversation was indeed tortured. The Hookers feared Don's presence "might lead to scandal which would compromise Edward with the UCLA faculty." They were not comfortable harboring a love affair between two men thirty years apart in age. "But I don't think that was the real reason. I think they just didn't want too much life in their garden." Bachardy later said that he felt Edward had an "aversion to the very people she's fighting for."[100] During the summer, Edward Hooker had spotted Bachardy picking blackberries at the back of the garden; Isherwood had advised Bachardy to share what he had picked; Hooker had refused the offering.

Whatever Isherwood felt at the time, he kept it from Evelyn, writing to Spender: "I really believe Evelyn still doesn't realize how I feel about it. My friends were much angrier than I was." According to Bachardy, years later, after Edward Hooker's death, Evelyn asked Isherwood whether he felt she had behaved badly, and Isherwood told her frankly that he felt she had, and she wept.[101]

Thus, Isherwood left the home which meant so much to him. His books and papers remained, and he used the garden house as a study until 1955, when Evelyn made it her consulting room.

Isherwood did not expect heterosexual friends to take risks on behalf of his homosexuality. Nor would he admit to them that this attitude cost him any effort; on the contrary, he managed to give the appearance, socially, of being at peace with the conventional heterosexual world. After nearly half a century as a homosexual, he knew how to conduct himself without seeming strange or difficult, without causing others awkwardness. He submitted to being evicted with no show of emotion, revealing even to Bachardy only a "grave manner" when he shared the news.[102]

Homelessness had been a full-time occupation for Isherwood during the 1930s, when he had wandered through Europe with Neddermeyer. Before that, during his childhood, he and his mother had followed his father from one army camp to another until World War I broke up the family home, and it had been seven years before his mother set up house again. He had learned not to struggle against their vagrant life, not to permit himself to long for a home. This continued to be a strategy for preserving his emotional equilibrium.

HOMELESS, 1953

Isherwood stayed with Bachardy at the Browns' until they found an apartment in West Hollywood, at 1326 Olive Drive, where they moved in together on September 19 before Bachardy started back at L.A. City College. There followed a period of constructive domesticity, cooking meals and spending evenings on Bachardy's homework.

But Isherwood was worried. On September 22, alone at his old desk in the forbidden garden house, he wrote in his diary: "I'm very happy in my father relationship with Don, except that he makes me feel so terribly responsible. It's nearly as bad as Heinz all over again. Nearly, but not quite, because Don is a lot brighter, and really much more able to look out for himself."[103] Isherwood had about $6,000 in the bank and friends owed him about $3,000 more. He didn't expect to make much money from his novel, partly because he had borrowed in advance from Random House.

His editor there, Bob Linscott, wanted changes: "I love the writing and everything about Elizabeth, but I'm troubled by the character of Stephen," Linscott wrote. What troubled him was Monk's "lack of empathy. (How could Elizabeth have loved him?)" Linscott also thought that two episodes of male sex was heavy-handed and asked Isherwood to tone down the physical intimacy. Worse, he found some of the characterization unconvincing, in particular: "the false (to me) heartiness of Bob Wood." Finally, he rejected the ending for its "patness."[104] Reviewers were to raise nearly all these issues when the novel eventually appeared. The bits of hokey American dialogue and the happy ending reflected Isherwood's exposure to Hollywood movie talk.

Alan White at Methuen had not written at all because he had panicked and was consulting three colleagues: "Sexual abnormalities are almost stock ingredients of Christopher's books," he wrote to one, "but always in the past the aberations [*sic*] have been on the part of <u>other</u> characters [. . .] This time it is the 'I' who is queer and it seems to make a difference."[105]

The colleague, Leonard Strong, a published novelist and critic as well as a director of Methuen, praised the novel, calling it technically "astonishing" and spiritually advanced.[106] However, he feared the homosexual scenes would be "painful and alarming" to *women* readers who "have to fear the competition, not only of other women, but of certain men as well." This could affect chain-store sales, as White told Isherwood's London agent: "It is a cracking good novel, but it does contain a few things likely to put us on the wrong foot with Boots and perhaps others."[107] Strong, like Linscott, had suggested toning down both sex scenes, but White bravely asked Isherwood to change only the first.

Isherwood promised the revisions by the end of October and promptly began to have stomach pains. "It is horribly hard to rebuild at this point," he told Kirstein. "But I will try. Also, I'm feeling quite sick, which is probably due to tension about the novel and having now set myself a deadline."[108] He went to the doctor, then finally settled down to work on the 29th, neutralizing the all-male sex scenes and removing altogether the love scene between Gerda and Stephen. The American part of the novel still didn't satisfy him. He sketched changes for the American characters, then cut the last part of the book ruthlessly. Caskey, Kirstein, and Gus Field had all now read the novel and offered advice.

Isherwood's stomach continued to articulate his anxiety. In mid-November, he had X-rays to look for an ulcer. The eventual diagnosis was pyloric spasm—painful tightening of the sphincter muscles in the upper part of the digestive track which can result from stress, alcohol, poor diet. He finished the revisions just in time for Thanksgiving dinner with Bachardy and the Browns. He had spent more than seven years on the book.[109]

He was already planning another treat for Bachardy—two weeks in New York City during Bachardy's Christmas vacation from college. He took Bachardy to a tailor and had him measured for a custom-made suit in charcoal-black serge, recalling that he himself in his youth had always gone out in a black suit, white shirt, and black tie. Once again, he was reenacting his relationship with his mother, who had shepherded him to the tailor as often as she could afford and lovingly recorded every detail, including the effect he achieved.

On the day he and Bachardy left for New York, Isherwood again spent some time alone at his desk in the garden house: "This place is really all the home I have anywhere—despite the behavior of the Hookers, and I always leave it with regret. There is a good smell of work here, despite much lazing and mooning about." As before the San Francisco trip in August, his unconscious had produced a reassuring dream about Prabhavananda. They were getting ready for bed and Isherwood was helping Prabhavananda into his dressing gown. "[W]e found that it was entangled in mine—the sleeves of my gown were pulled down into his. Swami said, 'Oh, so you have a dressing gown? I was going to give you mine.' And I said, 'But I can throw mine away.'"

The dream fulfilled Isherwood's wish to see himself eagerly receiving whatever Prabhavananda had to give—blessings, love, a dressing gown—and it also expressed his deep, hidden wish to act on his identification with his own father and play the role of father as well as son. At Christmas 1914, when Isherwood had sent his father an item of clothing as a gift, Frank had promised what Isherwood dreamed, "I will throw away my other mittens, & wear yours when they come."[110]

"The practice of non-attachment gives value and significance to even the most ordinary incidents of the dullest day," Isherwood and Prabhavananda had written in their commentary on the yoga aphorisms of Patanjali, published that very year, 1953: "we are renouncing nothing that we really need or want, we are only freeing ourselves from imaginary needs and desires."[111] But in his waking life, Isherwood was increasingly attached to Bachardy.

Bachardy wore his new suit for the overnight flight to New York and carried an overcoat belonging to Harry Brown. They arrived on December 18 and checked into the George Washington Hotel, where Isherwood had stayed with Auden for two and half months in 1939. Within twenty-four hours, Isherwood and Bachardy had been to the Statue of Liberty and the top of the Empire State Building and dined with Kirstein, Auden, and Kallman. Such was Bachardy's appetite and enthusiasm that he wrote the entries in Isherwood's day-to-day diary for the first nine days of their visit.

They saw a Broadway show practically every day, took the train to Philadelphia to see Julie Harris in *Mademoiselle Colombe*, accompanied Kirstein to a rehearsal of the New York City Ballet's *Nutcracker*, were photographed by Carl Van Vechten, and attended countless Christmas and New Year parties. Bachardy was thrilled to be able to order his own drinks in the bars rather than sneak sips from Isherwood's as he had to do in California where the drinking age was twenty-one.[112] He later recalled that a rumor went around New York that Isherwood had brought a twelve-year-old with him.[113]

"Lincoln immediately took a great shine to me, and enveloped me with his overpoweringly forceful personality," Bachardy later wrote. "I was treated to bearhugs and playful animal-maulings." He found Auden more daunting, partly because he knew that this was Isherwood's closest friendship. With

Kallman, Bachardy was immediately at home: "Chester's New York Jewish humor and funny, eye-rolling mannerisms made him more accessible to me than shy, British, intricately sensitive Wystan."

By and large, Isherwood's friends were besotted with Bachardy. George Platt Lynes, the photographer, contrived to spend time alone with him by taking his photograph, with Isherwood's permission, while Isherwood was meeting with his publisher. Lynes later sent prints to Bachardy in California, including nudes shot from the back, which Bachardy showed to Isherwood. "I hadn't told Chris about any of the nude shots [...] when he saw them he teasingly said: Oh, the naughty thing!" Lynes circulated the photos in New York, to Kirstein (who admired them) and to others. He kept for himself some frontal nudes with an erection.[114]

Isherwood evidently never knew about the frontal nudes nor did he know that Lynes seduced Bachardy with a blow job on New Year's Day 1954 while Isherwood was having lunch with Auden and visiting the New York Vedanta Society. "[I]t seemed an inevitable culmination not only of my first trip to the big city but of the most eventful year of my life," Bachardy later recalled. Still, he found it a challenge to go straight from Lynes's arms to meet Isherwood for drinks at the Plaza Hotel with that "preeminent sniffer-out" Speed Lamkin: "Yes, I felt I'd betrayed Chris, but what happened with George happened so easily and naturally, without conscious premeditation (at least on my part) that it seemed more our business than anyone else's. I knew that telling Chris would upset and hurt him, and perhaps destroy his confidence in me."[115]

Bachardy and Lynes began a secret correspondence using Glade's address. They discussed Bachardy's education and his future, including the possibility that he might like to study in New York instead of California. "It's evident at this point that I did fall in love with you. [...] I can't in good conscience try to seduce you away from Chris," wrote Lynes. "Any asking- or offering-in-marriage can only come from you." Lynes followed this with anxious descriptions of his limited finances: "Room and board and carfare, certainly, but a paid-for education and the things that go with it I can't manage now."[116] Bachardy eventually wrote back: "it's too big a chance to take – for either of us." He had no job in New York and no prospects of one: "I love Chris, I know he loves me, and he's been wonderful to me. I feel guilty and ashamed for any invitations and dares I've made to you, because you see, I can't make them good myself."

Bachardy and Lynes met again in New York in January 1955, when, at a party at Lynes's apartment, they "managed a few minutes alone and an intimate embrace."[117] The last time Lynes wrote to Bachardy was May 1955, to congratulate him on his twenty-first birthday. Lynes was in the hospital being investigated for a chest infection. It turned out that he had lung cancer, and he was dead before the end of the year.

ISHERWOOD WAS INDEED better equipped than Lynes to care for Bachardy and to make his dreams come true. Just a few weeks after returning to Los Angeles, he abandoned his literary plans for 1954 and took a high-earning job at MGM writing the script for *Diane*. He reported to Kirstein: "am writing a nistorical [sic] opus about Catherine de Medici, Henri Doo of France, and Diane de Poitiers, who kept beautiful by taking an ice-cold bath every morning. There is poison in it and a tournament-accident and a delayed execution and a party where there are boats sailing all over the ballroom."

The script—in which Diane de Poitiers and Catherine de Medici vie for the love of Catherine's husband Henri II—allowed Isherwood to indulge his boyhood love of chivalry and to draw on his training as a historian. "I have to do lots of research," he told Spender excitedly.[118]

His boss was Eddie Knopf, who, back in 1939 on Isherwood's very first Hollywood job at Samuel Goldwyn Studios, had told Isherwood he had "touched Sam on his sore spot" by implying Goldwyn was not a gentleman. Hollywood had not become any gentler. "I talked to Marvin Schenck about the CP," wrote Isherwood in his day-to-day book on January 21. Schenck was a nephew of two of the most powerful men in Hollywood, Nicholas Schenck, a head of MGM and Loew's, and Joseph Schenck, a head of Loew's, United Artists, and 20th Century–Fox. The CP was the Communist Party. In response to Senator Joseph McCarthy's anti-communist crusade, the studios had adopted the uniform position that they would not knowingly employ a communist or a member of any group proposing to overthrow the U.S. government.

Marvin Schenck presented Isherwood with a list of evidence linking him to the Communist Party and questioned him about his loyalty to the U.S. The evidence included items gathered from the communist and socialist press that mostly showed only that the leftist press sometimes followed Isherwood's career. There were many errors and omissions.

One item reported that Isherwood had signed a petition demanding a review of the case against the Hollywood Ten—the writers, directors, and producers including Dalton Trumbo and Ring Lardner who were jailed for refusing to cooperate with the House Un-American Activities Committee and who were blacklisted by the major studios.[119]

More concerning was a section of the document headed "Lists reference as *Mrs. Viertel*." It was reported that Salka had signed a petition to the U.S.

Supreme Court on behalf of two of the Hollywood Ten, and that she had signed a Lawyers Defense Committee appeal on behalf of Communist Party leaders. Salka's living room had of course been the center of the German and Austrian émigré community in Hollywood during the 1940s, where the likes of Thomas Mann, Heinrich Mann, Arnold Schoenberg, and Bertolt Brecht felt entirely at home. Many were leftists, some were communists. She was friendly, too, with the Soviet filmmaker Sergei Eisenstein and the communist composer Hanns Eisler whom Isherwood had met with Berthold Viertel and Brecht. Salka had been on a U.S. government watch list since 1942, and in 1951, she was added to another list called the Communist Index.

Worst was a report from the House Un-American Activities Committee identifying Mrs. Peter Viertel as a Communist Party member.[120] This was Salka's daughter-in-law Virginia, known as Jigee, a former Paramount dancer, who had recently separated from Peter. Jigee's first marriage had been to the writer Budd Schulberg, with whom she had been active in the Communist Party. Schulberg had renounced the party and named names to the House Un-American Activities Committee.

The interview with Schenck was just the kind of situation to give Isherwood—or anyone—nightmares. Fifteen years later, in 1969, Isherwood told Jim Charlton that it was one of the chief things in his life of which he felt ashamed, and he made clear in his diary in 1969 that he wished he, like the Hollywood Ten, had refused to cooperate. By 1969, refusing to cooperate was standard behavior; many Americans were engaged in mass protest movements against the Vietnam War, and the feeling of risk had faded: "my prospective job was at stake, *maybe*, plus the possibility of being put on an 'uncooperative' list," he wrote disparagingly of his earlier reaction.[121] In 1954, however, the questions were threatening, in particular because Isherwood feared to be exposed as a homosexual.

Direct confrontation was not Isherwood's style, but he wrote a follow-up letter to the studio at Salka's request, trying to defuse the situation with methodical understatement and by ingenuously presuming upon mutual understanding. "Gentlemen," he began—thereby invoking the code of behavior that had challenged Samuel Goldwyn, the code by which Frank had lived, in which he himself had been raised, and which had developed from the ideals of chivalry portrayed in the very film he was being asked to write, *Diane*—"As I explained to Mr. Schenck, the chief political emotion of the thirties was anti-fascism, and none of us are to be blamed if we welcomed as allies any political party which promised cooperation against Hitler. That we were deceived by the communist party in this connection is a matter of history."

He explained that he had signed the petition for the Hollywood Ten "with entirely non-political motives—simply as a civil liberties issue," and disavowed his decision: "I don't think I would do the same thing now—" He affirmed he had never been a member of the Communist Party and pointed out that he had been thoroughly investigated by the FBI in order to obtain his citizenship. He concluded by inviting his prospective employers to see themselves as members of his own thoughtful, courteous elite—gentlemen—rather than as hysterical arch-conservative anti-communists, and he claimed them as friends in the way Sam Goldwyn had once claimed him:

> ... the communist party has no more determined enemies than liberals such as myself. The tendency to confuse liberals and communists is not only completely unfair; it is actually playing into the hands of the communists themselves. I am sure that you, gentlemen, are well aware of this; and I make this personal explanation to you with confidence that you will receive it as friends, not judges.

Of Salka, he wrote: "She is one of my closest and dearest friends. [. . .] I know nothing about her alleged political activities, but I must say that I do not believe for a moment that she has ever been a member of the communist party."[122]

Hollywood was not run by gentlemen. Salka was blacklisted; her income dried up; she had already been forced to sell the house in Mabery Road. Even though she was an American citizen, she was denied a passport to visit Berthold on his deathbed in Vienna; later she managed to escape to Switzerland on a temporary passport. Jigee Viertel developed a drinking problem and burned herself to death in 1960 after falling asleep with a lit cigarette in her hand.

When he recorded his shame and regret in his diary in 1969, Isherwood made no reference to other fears guiding his behavior in the 1954 interview with Schenck. Not only was he concealing his homosexuality, but also he was concealing that he had shared his boyfriend Jack Hewit with Guy Burgess, the British intelligence officer and Foreign Office official who *was* a communist, a spy for the Soviet Union, and had defected in 1951 with Donald Maclean, also a Foreign Office official.

Burgess and Maclean were part of the five-man spy ring that was eventually revealed to include Anthony Blunt, Kim Philby, and John Cairncross; all had studied at Cambridge University and were recruited by the Soviets in the 1930s. Burgess and Maclean disappeared by ferry from Southampton to France on May 25, 1951; their disappearance was announced June 7, 1951, and by 1952 it was assumed they were in Russia, although this was confirmed only in 1956. Meanwhile, intelligence agencies had launched a massive international hunt for them.

Maclean had had access to U.S. atomic secrets. The press had ignited with the spy story, including the suggestive detail that the night before the diplomats had disappeared, Burgess had tried to contact Auden in London. Burgess had telephoned the Spenders' house, where Auden was staying en route to Italy for the summer. He had spoken to Natasha Spender, and she had supplied another number for Spender's study nearby, where Burgess reached Spender.

Whether or not Burgess's request to speak was passed on to Auden is a matter of dispute, but Spender, with his love of publicity, passed it to the press.[123] The *Daily Express* interviewed Auden, and sensationalized the story despite Auden's insistence he had had no contact with Burgess since March in New York. Then Spender shared with the *Express* a letter from John Lehmann affirming—based on private information—that Burgess must be a spy. Lehmann was furious with Spender; the private information had come from his sister, Rosamond Lehmann, who had realized that Burgess had recruited one of her lovers for the KGB: "now all the pieces fitted together. She was absolutely sure," Lehmann had told Spender in the leaked letter.[124]

On June 15, 1951, two men from the FBI had visited the Huntington Hartford Foundation to interview Isherwood about his friendship with Burgess. Isherwood told them he had read about the disappearance of Burgess in *Time* magazine. He acknowledged that in the late 1930s in London, he had often seen Burgess at the Café Royal, at private parties, and even at Burgess's apartment, and that he had worked with Burgess on a 1938 BBC radio show about his China trip. According to the FBI memorandum, Isherwood described Burgess as "a highly emotional person and a heavy drinker" who was "trying very desperately to be 'one of the group.'" He also said that Burgess was "known to be a homosexual," asserting that this "would not be considered unusual in the London of that period" and wasn't "a weakness which could be used to advantage by the Soviets." This was a strategic argument that, by implication, would defend any homosexual in their milieu—for example, Isherwood himself. He averred that "he actually did not really know BURGESS as well as some people thought;" for example, they didn't write letters to one another.

On being asked to name others who knew Burgess, Isherwood had listed Forster, Auden, Spender, J.R. Ackerley, Rudolf Katz, Lord Inverchapel—Britain's ambassador to the U.S. during the war—Jack Hewit, and someone called Tony whose surname he said he could not recall, but which he later

7: The Ideal Companion: Don Bachardy (1953–1961) / 481

supplied. Tony was Anthony Blunt, once Burgess's flatmate, eventually also exposed as a member of the spy ring. Isherwood described Jack Hewit as "an advertising man in London." The FBI memorandum continues: "ISHERWOOD said he did not know HEWITT very well but did know that probably HEWITT knew BURGESS better than anyone else."[125] But Isherwood did know Hewit—very well.

Hewit had also been Anthony Blunt's lover, and was living with Burgess at the time of Burgess's defection in 1951. It was Burgess who had introduced Hewit to Isherwood. Isherwood's lie to the FBI, that he didn't know Hewit well, was designed to conceal his homosexual private life.

The FBI had returned for a second interview on July 17, 1951. In this second interview, Isherwood talked mostly about Rudolf Katz, whom he referred to as Rolf Katz, safely living in Buenos Aires. In the first interview, Isherwood had told the agents that Burgess had briefly worked for Katz in London on one of Katz's magazines about economics and politics.[126] The FBI knew that Isherwood had visited Katz in Buenos Aires because Gerald Hamilton had shown the relevant passage in *The Condor and the Cows* to agents from MI5 and Special Branch in London.

Isherwood was made to elaborate on this, and reportedly said he believed he had been introduced to Burgess by Katz. In essence, he repeated what he had already said about Katz in *The Condor and the Cows*, that Katz was a leftist who "at one time had probably adhered to the Communist Party," but that he was too much of an "independent thinker" to be "a true follower of Communism." (British intelligence already knew that Katz had joined the Communist Party in 1921.)[127]

In fact, Isherwood had been wrongly identified by U.K. intelligence as an acquaintance of a completely different person, Otto Katz,[128] a known Soviet agent, and this excited attention on both sides of the Atlantic. Otto Katz had worked closely with Willi Münzenberg, spied on Münzenberg for the Soviet secret police, and probably played a role in Münzenberg's death by "suicide."[129] Isherwood just missed Otto Katz in Berlin, where from 1927 to 1929 he had managed a theater in the Nollendorfplatz. He just missed him again in Hollywood, where Katz "charmed German émigré actors, directors and writers," according to Babette Gross.[130] Otto Katz had been a Comintern fundraiser and helped to found the Hollywood Anti-Nazi League in 1936. Salka Viertel had joined, and she had remained a loyal member through the 1930s, even after her film director friend Ernst Lubitsch had warned her it was controlled by communists. She and Berthold had been friendly with Otto Katz since the 1920s, when they had first met him in Berlin.[131] Katz was expelled from the U.S. in November 1940 and hanged by Stalin in 1952.[132] Isherwood made clear to the FBI that he had never met Otto Katz and assured them that "he recognizes the evil of Soviet Communism and would do anything in his power to combat it."[133]

He had been contacted again by the FBI, September 26, 1951, evidently by telephone. He recorded nothing about these FBI interviews in his diary and noted them only in his day-to-day book. The secrets about which he cared most remained undiscovered. His affair with Jack Hewit was not exposed.

Still, espionage and conspiracy haunted him. In notes written between 1955 and 1957 for his next novel, *Down There on a Visit*, there are scattered references to arrests and interrogations, to spies roving mysteriously between the realms of politics and art, to an artists' colony like the Huntington Hartford Foundation, and to a millionaire patron with a network of spies who was more like Münzenberg than like the profligate Huntington Hartford. The Isherwood character, called William in the notes, is suspected of being a spy by all parties:

> "Señor N. has been detained for questioning. You had better go back to the Hotel."
>
> a character who has been "investigated"
>
> An "uncooperative witness"—
>
> Who is the "spy" from L[os] O[lvidados], who comes to the town & joins in the gambling—
>
> He might be a spy of the millionaire's [...] He might know something about the C.P.—
>
> Group A suspects William as a reactionary bourgeois writer & a spy of the FBI. Group B. suspects William as a writer who has sold out, and a spy of the millionaire.[134]

It would take Isherwood some years to shed these adrenaline-induced ideas clogging the development of his next novel.

Meanwhile, he and Bachardy agreed not to introduce Bachardy into his professional friendships with Eddie Knopf or others at the studio. For the time being, it was safer that way. Isherwood's new commitment to the studio funded their life together, but it began subtly to deform their relationship.

MESA ROAD, SANTA MONICA, 1954

Four days after discussing the Communist Party with Schenck, Isherwood signed his contract with MGM; he was to be paid $1,000 a week. His American advance for *The World in the Evening* and *The Condor and the Cows* together had been only $2,500 in 1947. For the next six months, he drove the nearly ten miles to Culver City every day and dictated to a series of female secretaries while Bachardy attended L.A. City College.

In 1954, MGM was still the preeminent Hollywood studio. It was a world of its own, and a busy one. Isherwood ate lunch at the Writers' Table, cultivating numerous old and new friendships, and he tore into his new project. By mid-May, he and Knopf were sharing his treatment with the head of production at MGM, Dore Schary, and Isherwood began writing the screenplay. It had a new title, *The Cage of Gold*. The title didn't last, but it spoke to the circumstances.

As the paychecks rolled in, Isherwood and Bachardy house-hunted. They signed a lease for a small, two-story house, 364 Mesa Road in Rustic Canyon, a few blocks from State Beach, and moved in on February 15, 1954. Bachardy later described it as "our modest pre-fab"; there were seventy-five stairs to climb from the street.[135] In April, they remodeled, adding a room over the garage as Bachardy's lair, and Isherwood bought Bachardy a longed-for car of his own.

They now had a spare room. Auden stayed for a week in March to lecture at Occidental College and UCLA, and they gave parties for him and took him to the beach. In the spring and summer, Julie Harris filmed Elia Kazan's adaptation of John Steinbeck's novel *East of Eden*, and on weekends she came out to stay from her motel near the Warner's lot in Burbank. Isherwood and Bachardy went on the set and attended the end-of-filming party. When Kazan ran the rough cut for Harris's co-star, James Dean, Isherwood and Bachardy sat in. Kazan invited them to see the film again the next day and discuss it over lunch, and, according to Bachardy, "made several cuts, particularly in the ending, based on his discussions with Chris."[136]

Bachardy's appetite for movie stars was obsessive. One night Isherwood and Bachardy gave a dinner party for Greta Garbo, and there were countless studio visits, premieres, and industry parties which Isherwood might have otherwise skipped. "Chris [...] never made the slightest fun of my awe of stars," wrote Bachardy years later. The people Bachardy wanted to meet were drawn to Isherwood, and Isherwood was a brilliant conversationalist: "I could observe his interlocutor without strain," Bachardy recalled.[137] It was to become Bachardy's lifelong habit to attend social events with a companion who could do the talking.

Finished copies of *The World in the Evening* arrived on Bachardy's birthday, May 18. Reviews, starting in June, were ruthless. The American reviewers didn't like Elizabeth Rydal, didn't like Sarah Pennington, hated Stephen Monk. The English loved Elizabeth but hated everyone else. Some reviewers found the structure too complicated. Most sensed that Isherwood was not sure of himself emotionally; the tone was sentimental, "soggy," hearty, off.[138]

Few were convinced by the spiritual dimension. They longed for the comic genius, the crooks and the gold diggers of Isherwood's earlier work and found his new interest in goodness too earnest. Why had he turned his camera eye inward, "away from the contemporary picture to a contemplation of his own problems?" asked the reviewer from Isherwood's hometown paper, the *Manchester Guardian*. "Clamped in the mind of Stephen Monk, he is reduced to feeling what Stephen feels and seeing what Stephen sees," said Edwin Muir in the *Observer*. *Time* magazine called it "second-rate" and complained that Isherwood "has splashed all the water out of his stagnant, neurotic pool," a euphemistic reference to the homosexuality. In the *New York Times Book Review*, Mark Schorer tied himself up in knots trying not to offend Isherwood: "a brilliant enigma," he pronounced.[139]

And so it went, the *Washington Post*, the *Saturday Review*, the *Irish Times*. In the *New Statesman*, V.S. Pritchett called it "a calamity." Isherwood's friend Angus Wilson wrote an intimately well-informed and condescending piece in Spender's new magazine, *Encounter*, saying Isherwood "has tried to stick out his spiritual neck a great deal further than it will stretch."[140]

There was plenty of praise for the writing. Horace Gregory, in the *New York Herald Tribune*, called Isherwood "the real thing, the unforced, unfaked writer of genius," and there was a general recognition that Isherwood was attempting, as Thom Gunn put it in the *London Magazine*, "something far more serious, far more complex, than before" and also something calling for compassion. John Wain wrote admiringly in the *Spectator* that "we get for the first time, an Isherwood book in which the 'I' is a real, suffering, developing human being."[141]

An anonymous profile in the *Observer*, where Isherwood had so recently been a contributor, asked sympathetically: "Will this charming, clever and serious man have the strength to survive the comparative failure of his attempt to re-emerge in new colours? Or may it be that the private diary which Isherwood has been keeping for the last quarter of a century will prove to be his subterranean life-work and his most enduring monument?"[142]

And really, that was the question. For he was famous and widely admired;

otherwise, he would not have commanded so many column inches. Indeed, the language of some of the reviewers was strangely possessive, and not just from reviewers who had met him. Isherwood had been so personal with readers—putting himself into his books as a character, sharing his life—that they felt he was their own. He had taken his readers to exciting places, the edgiest edges of their world. Expectations were high; they felt that they had been waiting since 1939, discounting *Prater Violet* which was overlooked because it coincided with the end of the war and because it was short.

Isherwood tracked down and read his reviews. Bachardy later recalled that he was grave but showed "no hint of emotion": "His belief in himself was strong enough to withstand any attack by critics." On the other hand, Bachardy's own belief in Isherwood was tested, in particular by *Time*, then widely accepted as a national news channel: "This rejection of Chris in print, the first for me and so official-sounding, shook me." In July, Isherwood summed up: *The World in the Evening* "is sort of a flop, both here and in England, but with some good notices, much discussion and fair sales."[143]

But there was more to come. He had pressed Methuen to release the U.K. edition of *The World in the Evening* during the the London run of *I Am a Camera* which opened in March 1954, and the timing led to an attack in the magazine *Punch*. "I Am a Chimera," a playlet by Julian MacLaren-Ross, presents Herr Issyvoo and his typewriter in a "camp bed," where he is visited by Elizabeth Rydal, Charles Kennedy, Aunt Sarah Pennington, Baron von Pregnitz, Mr. Norris, and Sally Bowles, while struggling to write his next book. The playlet captured the speech of Isherwood's characters to cruel and hilarious effect, and the revealing dichotomy between the Truly Strong Man and the Truly Weak Man which Isherwood had developed in *Lions and Shadows* was also mocked.[144]

As ever, Isherwood was able to empathize, even with his critics: "I suppose I do seem a completely bogus figure to people who dislike me—a preacher of sloppy uplift, a self-obsessed, weak-kneed, whining bore." But he did not agree with them. "I know, quite solidly and finally, that the uplift is neither bogus nor sloppy—however unconvincingly I may preach it."[145]

Near the end of his life, Isherwood pronounced *The World in the Evening* "my worst novel."[146] Yet it is the hinge joining the English Isherwood and the American Isherwood. In the sprawl of this subtle, multilayered, hyperallusive novel, with its cracked voice still developing, is a trove of clues about Isherwood mid-century as he tried to make a single narrative out of all that had shaped and changed him so far. It is deformed by his reluctance to show some of his themes openly—audiences were not ready for his Hinduism—and his former leftism is cloaked by vagueness in the increasingly dangerous McCarthy period. But the novel's clearly messaged homosexual subject matter did not offend reviewers or readers in the way that his publishers feared. On the contrary, the book was to find its way to a new kind of audience in Isherwood's adopted country, an audience for whom it was a different kind of hinge—a hinge on the closet door that was to open gradually in the second half of the twentieth century. "I have lots and lots of fan-mail of the type you can guess," he wrote to Spender. "I believe if I gave the word, right now, I could start a queer revolution."[147]

To many, Isherwood's homey, Hollywood-American slang felt familiar and even inviting. One fan stayed up all night reading the novel a second time and "crying like a baby." Then he wrote a passionate letter to Isherwood in language not unlike some of the maligned dialogue in the novel:

> But dammitall, I can't sleep for talking to you. So here it is! [. . .] I have felt your love as though it were directed personally to me. [. . .] Part of me is fighting you and your book. But I think you really understand. [. . .] To say that I am Stephen would, I suppose, be absurd and presumptuous. At best, I'm Stephen in the first day of the cast ... or perhaps your book is the truck just running me down in the street.[148]

Isherwood had wanted to break free from a coterie, and at last he was succeeding. It released a gush of sentiment in him as well as in his fans, which he also confided to Spender: "Actually, it's heart breaking, the sense you get of all these island existences, dotted about like stars and nebulae, all over the great black middle west."[149]

AS HE TURNED fifty, he asked himself what he should make of his next twenty years. The answer seemed to be personal and emotional, as he observed in his diary a few weeks later: "The one real responsibility I have is Don. Everything revolves around him, at the moment."[150]

His feelings about Bachardy were very intense, and that summer they led him into a violent display of jealousy at a farewell party given by Iris Tree, who was leaving California for Italy. The party was Saturday night, July 3, at her apartment on Santa Monica Pier, and Isherwood and Bachardy both got drunk. A filmmaker called Curtis Harrington brought a dark, handsome young man to the party, a writer called Robert Phippenny, who made advances to Bachardy. For nearly an hour, they sat talking and "the young man covertly pressed his knees against mine under the table," Bachardy later wrote. "I was unaware of being observed by Chris." As Isherwood and Bachardy said goodbye to Tree, Harrington joined them. "I have a distinct impression of an amused smirk on Curtis's face the instant before Chris hit it," Bachardy recalled. Isherwood was shorter than Harrington, but he "dispatched several quick, short-range jabs."

Everyone was taken by surprise. Harrington made no effort to defend himself. Bachardy felt guilty and filled with regret. On the drive home, Isherwood "made no recriminations of any kind against me."[151] Isherwood woke up the next morning with a bad hangover, disgusted by what he had done, and called Harrington to apologize, but Harrington was unforgiving. He sued for $600. A doctor attested that both Harrington's eyes were blackened and that swelling and headaches persisted for weeks, although Harrington returned to work within two days. They settled for $350.[152]

Harrington told his story in a memoir published long after the event, misleadingly claiming that Isherwood's friends persuaded him not to sue but that nevertheless he was "forever ousted from the charmed Isherwood circle." In fact, a year after the punch, Harrington wrote to Isherwood asking forgiveness for involving a lawyer, so Isherwood forgave him. The year after that, in 1956, they found themselves employed on the same film, and Isherwood described his relief once they finally bumped into each other in a corridor. "Said hello. So the spell is broken."[153]

Isherwood and Harrington had liked each other at first—quite a lot. Tree had introduced them in 1949; there were supper and film dates, they spent several nights together, had a rendezvous in London in January 1952, and even talked about a film collaboration.[154] Harrington continued to visit Isherwood at the garden house after Bachardy appeared there, but he had been disappointed by Isherwood's waning interest; "my coolness toward you," Isherwood explained in one letter, "was due to my feeling that you were becoming an habitual gate-crasher."[155] In other words, Harrington had worn out his welcome in "the charmed Isherwood circle" long before Isherwood punched him, and Isherwood was reacting to what he perceived as Harrington's attempt to take revenge through Bachardy by permitting—perhaps encouraging—his date to pursue Bachardy and prove him publicly disloyal.

Bachardy was not all troublemaking. "Don has taken up painting quite seriously and is going to classes during the vacation. He also lifts weights, so as to have a chest with breasts," Isherwood told Spender. Bachardy had started going to Isherwood's gym, emulating his discipline. The art classes were taught by the painter Howard Warshaw, but Bachardy found them too theoretical. He wanted to draw from life, not to discuss perspective, and he left halfway through the third class. Nevertheless, although he did not realize it yet, he had found his vocation. That summer, he continued to draw, including "some quick sketches of me," as Isherwood recorded.[156]

"It is a happy time," Isherwood told Spender, "in spite of worrying about

Indo-china and how Don might be involved. I often think of the Heinz days."[157] In 1954, American men had to register for the draft at eighteen and could be called up from eighteen and a half to twenty-five; the military had kept the draft alive after the Korean War and already foresaw needs in Vietnam. This was another threat to Isherwood and Bachardy's domestic life, just as Hitler's draft had been a threat to Isherwood's life with Neddermeyer.

Bachardy decided to tell the draft board that he was gay. He also decided to get professional support from Evelyn Hooker, despite badly bruised relations over the garden house. He attended his physical on October 5, armed with a letter from Hooker, who had administered a Rorschach test and gave her professional opinion about his sexual orientation. On his questionnaire, he indicated he was homosexual. He was then interviewed by a psychiatrist who, as Bachardy later recalled, glanced at Hooker's letter and said: "You mean to tell me you couldn't control yourself if you were in a shower with another naked man? I suppose I could, I had the nerve to say, if I were sure he didn't like me."[158]

Bachardy's abiding impression was of the psychiatrist's sneering disgust. He was called for a second physical exam a month later and classified 4-F, not acceptable for service. Isherwood summarized this painful, undignified process as "a horrible experience."[159] It was weirdly analogous to his Communist Party interview with Marvin Schenck.

Free-floating, lifelong anxieties about war and annihilation continued to haunt Isherwood, metamorphosing now into fear of East–West nuclear apocalypse. In September 1954, he wrote in his diary: "my pylorus is busy manufacturing anxiety in case it's needed suddenly in gigantic quantities. I wake, most nights, around 3 a.m. fairly shaking with terror. I convince myself that spies or thugs are coming up the stairs from the street."[160] The crisis of his flight from Berlin and his years on the run with Neddermeyer had never left him, and his fears were reawakened by his feelings for Bachardy and the opportunity for a different outcome. He was also exhausted by the pace he had been setting.

He had pushed through ill health, starting with measles during March then debilitating back pain in August, to finish the script of *Diane* in time for his birthday, a deadline he often worked to; then without a pause, he was back in the studio with Knopf, revising and cutting. The mixed reception for *The World in the Evening* made it all the more important to succeed with *Diane*. Dore Schary pronounced the script "brilliant" and requested only minor further revisions. "Felt awful," Isherwood recorded. "Pains in the penis, bladder and rectum."[161] He had two days of medical tests, including a barium enema, X-rays, and electrocardiogram, with a new doctor, an endocrinologist, Jessie Marmorston, who was the wife of MGM executive Larry

Weingarten. She started giving him vitamin and hormone shots once or twice a week, and they seemed to have a remarkable effect, although Bill Kiskadden warned the hormone shots could cause prostate cancer. Perhaps they did; it was prostate cancer that was to kill Isherwood at eighty-one.

Isherwood went back to work at MGM for four days in October and again felt sick. When he was done, he had another shot and took Bachardy on the overnight train to San Francisco. They spent five days with Auden who was lecturing there.

By chance, Salka Viertel was also in San Francisco, and so was the Chinese-American cinematographer James Wong Howe. Isherwood and Bachardy had a new Bell and Howell movie camera with them. "At the top of Telegraph Hill, Jimmy demonstrated with our camera a firm-handed, unhurried panning shot over San Francisco Bay, Alcatraz, Coit Tower, and the Bay Bridge, with Salka, Chris and me in the foreground," Bachardy recalled.[162] The next morning, Bachardy filmed Isherwood and Auden dancing in the garden of Auden's hostess—evidently, the Sir Roger de Coverley that Isherwood had danced with his mother in childhood. Kathleen had taught the dance to Auden and some of his friends at a New Year's party in 1936 for the GPO Film Unit documentary *Calendar of the Year*.[163]

BACHARDY CARRIED THE Bell and Howell again a few weeks later, to Key West, Florida, where Isherwood took him to visit Tennessee Williams and Frank Merlo and to watch the filming on location of *The Rose Tattoo*, adapted from Williams's play. They spent two weeks on this southernmost U.S. island with its toy-size conch houses and nineteenth-century mansions festooned with porches, verandas, wrought-iron balconies, picket fences, and bougainvillea.

Bachardy wasn't allowed to film on set, but, by coincidence, James Wong Howe was the cinematographer and filmed a rehearsal scene for him with the Bell and Howell, the only color footage since the film was black and white. Bachardy also worked as an extra, playing a passenger in the backseat of a car. He was on set at 8 a.m., wasn't called until after lunch, and was invisible in the movie.[164] This killed his ambition to be an actor, but making home movies thrilled him, and he began to wonder whether he might become a director. Isherwood was sympathetic since he had experienced the same obsession in his own youth.

One night in Williams's little clapboard bungalow on the corner of Pearl and Duncan Streets, Williams read them his new play, *Cat on a Hot Tin Roof*. The next night, Williams read the first act of another version he had revised for Elia Kazan, his proposed director, and Isherwood briefly fell asleep. Williams was battling Kazan, who wouldn't commit without revisions to the character of Brick. Kazan had leverage because he had achieved a hit with *A Streetcar Named Desire*, for which Williams won a Pulitzer Prize, and Williams wanted Isherwood's advice about *Cat on a Hot Tin Roof*.

Williams told his agent Audrey Wood that Isherwood "loved it, said he thought it in many ways my best play." Isherwood, too, advised revisions but more in keeping with Williams's own conception: "He felt only that the story of Maggie-Brick-Skipper needed to be developed more fully to make it more clearly understood, what had actually happened, as that was the heart of the story."[165] By the time he wrote to Wood, Williams had already started on the changes Isherwood suggested.

Williams proposed that he and Isherwood meet with Kazan when the *Rose Tattoo* filming moved back into the studio in Hollywood. So, on November 30, Isherwood joined Williams and Kazan over drinks in Williams's room at the Beverly Hills Hotel to talk about *Cat on a Hot Tin Roof*. In the small hours following their discussion, Williams wrote to Kazan about the play, using the terminology of clinical psychology: "I now believe that in the deeper sense, not the literal sense, Brick *is* homosexual with a heterosexual adjustment."[166] Kazan was asking for a heterosexual ending in Maggie's bed, an ending to illustrate that Brick could recover from the death of his football buddy Skipper. Isherwood was familiar with this kind of accommodation to heterosexual tastes and with the suggestion that love between men was a form of immaturity: "Maggie declares that Skipper and I went into pro-football after we left 'Ole Miss' because we were scared to grow up," says Brick.[167] This was the battle Isherwood had fought with *The World in the Evening*. Moreover, the friendship between Isherwood and Williams had a quality of innocent boyish affection—the "sentimental attachment" Williams mentioned in his *Memoirs*—not unlike the affection between Brick and Skipper.

Kazan teased from Williams the changes he wanted. *Cat on a Hot Tin Roof* was a hit when it opened on Broadway in March 1955, and Williams won his second Pulitzer Prize as well as "every theatrical award for best play." But he went on expressing his feeling that Kazan had made him sell out his "harder and purer [...] blacker play" for a commercial success. He published both endings with a note of explanation that, as Kazan fumed in a letter to Williams, "gave people generally the idea that I had forced you to rewrite 'Cat.'" Williams's biographer, John Lahr, observed that "Williams owed Kazan more than he could admit to himself, or to the public."[168]

Yet how could Williams have staged his preferred version of the play without Kazan's enthusiastic belief in it? How could any homosexual writer defy his publisher, director, or producer? Brick's name expresses his immutable stubbornness; the revised ending turns him to malleable clay, and reduces the importance of his love for Skipper. By publishing his preferred version of the play, Williams found one little door through which to squeeze a different message. Arguably, the disillusion audiences felt with Williams later in his career might have been less if they had been afforded more insight into his true nature.

Bachardy recalled in his unpublished memoir that he and Isherwood "were dismayed by the alterations" which "weakened the play."[169] Isherwood's professional pragmatism had no trouble accepting the revised version, but he disliked the casting when he saw a preview in Philadelphia in March 1955, and he thought the expressionistic set was wrong. "This play absolutely demands realistic staging. It is not symbolic. It means exactly what it says."[170] After the preview, he discussed the play one last time with Williams and Kazan and watched a second performance, but he never saw it on Broadway. In 1956, he met with Kazan for a drink and decided, "He isn't a very pleasant character, I think. He talked quite bitchily of Tennessee."[171]

The day after Isherwood and Bachardy got home from Key West, while they were setting up their projector to watch the movies shot there, Caskey dropped in with a friend. So the four men watched together. In front of Isherwood's old boyfriend, Bachardy was mortified by a sequence of himself in the hotel pool at the Casa Marina imitating Esther Williams, and Caskey and his friend rubbed it in. "Now you stop that, Don! scolded Caskey in between his and his friend's derisive laughter, Naughty! Naughty!'"[172] Bachardy stayed cool till the guests departed, then lost his temper with Isherwood, cut the sequence from the film and destroyed it. A year or two later he gave up filming.

While Williams and *The Rose Tattoo* cast were in town, Isherwood and Bachardy entertained them at home, took them out to restaurants, and drank with them at the Beverly Hills Hotel. Bachardy had fallen for Williams. By December 3, he was writing in his diary. "I am so in love with Ten. He is little and insecure and so in need of comfort and reassurance." He recorded his erotic fantasies and a dream about a love affair with Williams. In Key West, Williams had "talked about his crazy sister, Rose, who is two-and-a-half years older" and was given a lobotomy at twenty-eight. "She and Ten were very close," Bachardy wrote. In return, "I told him a little about Ted."[173]

Ted Bachardy was included in some of the nights out in Los Angeles, and he stayed overnight with Williams on December 7. Bachardy recorded no jealousy of Ted, but he did recall feeling jealous when Williams invited Caskey out to dinner with Anna Magnani, who starred in *The Rose Tattoo* opposite Burt Lancaster, and he was relieved when Caskey turned up so drunk that Magnani refused to go.

Bachardy kept his feelings to himself, but he confided to his diary that

Williams praised his intelligence and noticed him more than Isherwood seemed to. "I want to be accepted for myself, not because I'm the friend of Christopher Isherwood," he wrote. At the same time, he recognized that he was inclined to "take refuge in my role as 'wife,'" pretending he had no time for a career with all the housework and cooking when, in fact, the problem, as he unsparingly wrote, was: "A lack of confidence in myself—that's <u>all</u>. And so, must I leave Chris? Throw away the crutch I'm leaning on? And if I do, won't I just find another crutch, another excuse?"[174]

"SLOWLY, SLOWLY. MAKE no plans for writing. Don't say: I *ought* to write. Just wait until inspiration orders." Near the end of his career, Isherwood was to explain: "Psychologically, I need, as it were, to sneak up on a problem rather than attack it frontally by sitting down at my desk and willing myself to start; willing invites frustration." He recalled that "during the Thirties," at his mother's London house, "I would make such rough sketches standing up, with my paper on top of a chest of drawers which happened to be just the right height. Standing was also an informal posture which didn't make me feel committed to work."[175]

Inspiration for *Down There on a Visit* came to him in December 1954 while he was driving to Mexico to celebrate Christmas and New Year. "The idea of The Border. What it means. Two worlds." A week later, he proposed:

> Something quite unlike me—Kafkaesque—about a journey. A journey which is meticulously described and yet unreal: the reality being the relationships between the characters. Maybe they are all dead—as, in a sense, the characters are in Hemingway's *The Sun Also Rises*. Also, I see elements in it of *The Day's Journey*, my projected film.[176]

(*The Day's Journey* was Isherwood's allegorical film about the young man doomed to be reborn because he fails to make the symbolic telephone call to God.)

In these glimmerings, Isherwood already had the ideas for his next two novels, *Down There on a Visit* and *A Single Man*. *Down There on a Visit* was to have a deceptively documentary surface and to be "Kafkaesque" in that the fantasy would "be made not as fantastic but as realistic as possible," as Upward put it in 1955.[177] It was to trace a journey from the narrator's youth into his forties among characters whose life choices he explores and discards along the way. *A Single Man* was to portray a whole life unfolding in one day as in the proposed film, a life closely resembling the life Isherwood settled on in reality. Isherwood was to pull the two novels from his imagination slowly and patiently, untangling one from the other like a fisherman separating two lengths of line. Indeed, the prologue first written for *Down There on a Visit* was to become the opening of *A Single Man*. In draft, it ran: "Whatever it is that wakes up in the morning says *am, now*. It lies looking at the ceiling until it recognizes I, and deduces I am, I am now."[178]

It was on December 9, 1954, that Isherwood disappeared with Bachardy on the four-week road trip south, dropping out of their high-voltage Hollywood life to travel with a relatively anonymous couple from the neighborhood, Jo and Ben Masselink, with whom Isherwood had been close friends since 1949. Jo designed bathing suits and sportswear, some for movie stars. Ben wrote for TV and later published short stories and two novels; he had served in the marines during the war. One night on leave, Ben got drunk in the Friendship, the bar in Santa Monica Canyon, and went home with Jo, who lived a few doors away. After the war, he found her again and stayed with her for twenty years. She took his name, although they never married. Her own name was Jo Lathwood. She had been married and had a son and daughter left behind in North Dakota, but she concealed her age and her past from Ben because she was about twenty years older than he; according to a note Isherwood made in 1958, she even had a "facelift and arm trimming."[179]

Isherwood's diaries and day-to-day books show that he and Bachardy spent as much time with the Masselinks as with anyone else they knew. There were many home-cooked suppers and evenings out together. The Masselinks had a gift for cosiness, and the age gap between them approximated to the age gap between Isherwood and Bachardy. They were quietly present at most of the gatherings Isherwood recorded with more famous friends.

The Masselinks were not subjects of Isherwood's fiction. Apart from one line in *A Single Man* telling the story of how they met during the war, Isherwood wrote about them only in his diaries.[180] Yet their company set him free to think about his fiction. "It's so restful being with Jo and Ben. Jo really bosses everything, decides everything—and that's what I need right now." On the way to Mexico, Jo did all the planning. Ben did all the driving. The car was the Masselinks', too, a yellow 1949 Ford convertible.

After three days on the road, the four travelers reached the coast at Guaymas, and the Masselinks hired a boat to take Isherwood and Bachardy fishing: "Don and I were the first to catch fish—a mackerel and a sea trout respectively. Then we got into a school of mackerel and all caught lots. And then Jo caught a real big fish, a sixty-pound grouper, and made such a fuss that it was exactly like a woman having a baby in the street." It was difficult for Isherwood or Bachardy to take this Hemingwayesque episode seriously. "When we got home, Don somewhat surprised me by saying exactly what I'd been feeling—that he'd enjoyed himself up to a point, but that he found the catching of the mackerel boring and inhumane—it was so ridiculously easy."[181]

Hemingway had just won the Nobel Prize that autumn, prompting Isherwood to read a Hemingway fishing story, *To Have and Have Not*. He had already read *The Old Man and the Sea* (1952), which was published in *Life* magazine, won the Pulitzer and made Hemingway rich. Isherwood had been following Hemingway's career with admiration since the 1920s. In the foreword to his 1957 anthology *Great English Short Stories*, he was to mention a single American writer—Hemingway. "The world of Ernest Hemingway for example is nowadays as crowded as a national park; and I remember nostalgically how I used to visit it before the season opened."[182] Isherwood never liked to be part of a crowd, and he carefully underplayed the inspiration Hemingway had offered him.

Hemingway was only five years older than Isherwood, a World War I hero, wounded and decorated for driving a Red Cross ambulance rather than fighting. *The Sun Also Rises*, published as *Fiesta* in England in 1927, had articulated the state of mind of the generation that grew up in and survived World War I, the generation achieving fame just as Isherwood was starting his career.

In his Berlin novels, Isherwood had reimagined Hemingway's expatriate story from an English, homosexual, comic point of view. Hemingway's promiscuous, gold-digging, upper-middle-class English heroine, Brett Ashley, can be compared to Sally Bowles; his detached narrator figure Jake Barnes, who cannot consummate the romance at the heart of his story, can be compared to the Christopher Isherwood figure; other parallels are evident in the insistent, drunken gaiety in bars and restaurants, the precoccupation with heroism, with culturally enshrined, ritual violence—bull fighting and Nazi bullies—with anxiety about Jews and anti-Semitism.[183]

The Sun Also Rises was the first novel Isherwood advised Bachardy to read, and he gave Bachardy his own British edition. The second book Isherwood gave Bachardy was *The Great Gatsby*, by Hemingway's friend, F. Scott Fitzgerald. During the Mexico trip, Bachardy was reading Fitzgerald's *Tender Is the Night*.[184] Thus, Dick and Nicole Diver and their circle of friends, lovers, and hangers-on—representatives of the "Lost Generation" of the 1920s and early 1930s, burdened like Stephen Monk and Elizabeth Rydal by money, ill health, and fatally attractive sexual glamour—were accompanying them in the Masselinks' yellow convertible for the Christmas and New Year festivities in Mexico City.

The next alchemy, life into fiction, was already beginning. Driving south along the Gulf of California toward Mexico City, Isherwood began to think about how the country around them could be a sort of limbo or purgatory for people living there but not from there—expatriates. At Álamos, "a sort of ghost town—formerly founded on great riches of silver," they put up in a hotel called Casa de Los Tesoros, an eighteenth-century convent, where "you have to 'mingle' with" the owners: "The Gordons are writers, documentary movie-makers, puppeteers, professional bohemians, owners of Mexico's beauties—you've got to see them through their own eyes."

If the Gordons were "professional bohemians," they were amateur at everything else, and ran the hotel on "luxury-amateur lines," in Isherwood's phrase.[185] Meeting them revived impressions of countless other "exiles, expatriates and permanent tourists," as Isherwood later wrote in his work notebook, met during his vagabond years in Europe in the 1930s, in China in 1938, in South America in 1947 and 1948 as well as in the novels of Hemingway and Fitzgerald. Each of these expatriates was a reflection of himself, in flight from the center of the culture, searching for another way to live—except that Isherwood was a writer, a *professional* writer, who had determinedly differentiated himself from the leisured class of his forebears and the class ideal of amateurism.

Isherwood considered that the character and quality of his observations as a writer set him apart from any milieu in which he immersed himself. When he slaved in the Hollywood studios, surrounded by other writers, they were all professionals together. Of the main character in his new novel, he noted: "I see him as a successful writer—corrupt to some extent, but consciously so and not too apologetic about it, either." By contrast, he sometimes referred to his expatriate characters as representing "a cult of failure."[186]

The plan for Mexico City was to make merry with Jay Laval who had fled unpaid debts in the U.S. and opened a grand new restaurant. The fiesta proved to be nothing like Hemingway's; instead, it was like a parody of the psycho-physical traveling in Gide's *The Immoralist* or Paul Bowles's *The Sheltering Sky*. Isherwood, then Bachardy, then Jo Masselink fell ill with fever, chills, and cough. Bachardy confided to his diary that he hated Isherwood for being ill and suspected it was deliberate, "to test my faithfulness."[187]

The ragtag group struggled out in twos and threes to climb the Aztec pyramids and view Popocatépetl. Once the flu symptoms passed, the gripes hit. As they drove away, Isherwood looked out the rear window "for a final view of the august volcanos rising above the city" and "intoned, 'Goodbye, Death Valley.'"[188] This filled the car with laughter. They were ill all the way home, and Isherwood went on suffering from amebic dysentery until spring.

AS HE PREPARED to return to work at MGM, Isherwood felt homesick for the self he had fleetingly contacted while moving through the landscape in the open car with Bachardy and the Masselinks: "What I miss is the contemplative side of my life. I want time alone—time just to stare out the window and take stock. [. . .] The inner life has to be recultivated ruthlessly."[189]

Then, on February 12, 1955, Aldous Huxley's Belgian-born wife Maria died of breast cancer. She had kept the seriousness of her illness a secret, even from her husband, until a week before she died. Maria was elegant and enchanting; she was fluent in French, English, and Italian, telling a correspondent that "one single language becomes very boring."[190] She had devoted herself to looking after her husband. Isherwood attended her small Episcopal funeral with a bad cold. Afterwards, "I cried all the way to the studio, and I was really crying for myself."[191]

This was the pilgrim self which, in 1939, had followed Heard to California to find a new way of life—a contemplative life with a mystical dimension. A life too often drowning in material preoccupations. Maria had understood and shared this life, the only reliable haven against the flight of time and advancing middle age. According to Huxley, Maria had had "a number of genuinely mystical experiences" while living in the Mojave Desert in the early 1940s. "For her, it was not merely a geographical region; it was also a state of mind, a metaphysical reality, and unequivocal manifestation of God."[192]

The Huxleys had renovated an old house in the tiny desert town of Llano and moved there early in 1942. There were fruit trees, almond trees, vines, and water running through irrigation ditches lined with poplars. A few large trees shaded the main house. Isherwood had often visited during World War II, becoming, in Maria's phrase, "a sort of habitué sans habitudes. Part of the family,"[193] as with the Beesleys.

Once, on "the kind of spring day on which you feel that perhaps you will live forever," Isherwood had sat on the Huxleys' hot, sunny terrace describing in his diary their view of desert and distant snow-covered mountains. "Maria is in the kitchen cooking wildly, with everything boiling over. [. . .] There is no sign of the war, except the olive-drab army trucks, moving almost invisibly through the landscape, along the road below the house."[194] With the Huxleys, he had felt safe from the war, from criticism, from self-criticism. Huxley's reputation offered refuge, since Huxley, the renowned public intellectual, product of Oxford and London's literary bohemia, a pacifist and a Hindu, was an international exemplar of the new life which Isherwood had adopted in California. With them, he had felt accepted and understood as an émigré and a pacifist.

Isherwood had been slow to warm to Huxley, who was "so very very donnish," as he had reported to his mother.[195] He had felt the same way about Huxley's novels: "he simply hasn't the gift—which scores of the dreariest little hacks possess—of 'making his characters live.'"[196] But Huxley's benevolence had won Isherwood over, and Huxley had trusted Isherwood, as he had not previously trusted anyone, to give an opinion of one of his novels in draft.[197] Huxley's brain combined with Isherwood's popular touch had seemed to offer a promising collaboration—reminiscent of Auden and Isherwood—though none of their screenplays sold.[198]

Unlike Heard, Huxley did not meditate, but he spent many hours thinking.[199] He had been temporarily blinded by a rare illness at sixteen and never recovered much of his sight. He turned to his inward eye, the mind, and became obsessed with the possibility of mystical vision. In the early 1950s, he had begun experimenting with chemical routes to visionary experience—mescaline, LSD, psilocybin—experiences he revealed in his 1954 book *The Doors of Perception*, ur-text of psychedelic drug culture.

When Maria died, pattern and repetition stirred in Isherwood's memory. With the Huxleys, he had visited the real Death Valley during a motor trip in May 1941, but on the road, he had "felt excluded from their quietly affectionate domesticity," which reminded him of his recent break with Harvey Young. "From Dante's View, we looked out over the gigantic wilderness," he had written in his diary about the overlook point that developers of the Death Valley tourist trade had named after Dante Alighieri. "A desert is a great empty picture frame, and we can't resist using it for a portrait of our private disaster. To me, the scene was beautiful but horrible—like a vast geographical demonstration of Harvey's total absence."[200]

For Isherwood, not to have a partner, not to be able to make a success of a relationship, was indeed a kind of hell, and with Bachardy, he was determined not to repeat earlier mistakes. This called for carrying his past with him at all times in the present, and so at the start of 1955, he made a significant practical change in his life. Ten days after Maria Huxley's funeral, on February 24, Ramakrishna's birthday, he attended vespers at Vedanta Place, and he resolved to write in his diary "*at least* twice every week until the birthday comes round again next year."[201] During the Caskey years, his diary keeping had dwindled away; since meeting Bachardy, entries had swelled to a dozen a year, and then a dozen and a half. He had already made eight entries during the Mexico trip as preparation for his next novel. He pretty well kept the vow, and these acts of recollection and self-examination were to restore him gradually to a sense of living his life on purpose.

DEATH VALLEY, WHETHER playfully evoked out the rear window of the Masselinks' car leaving Mexico City or seen for real from Dante's View with the Huxleys, had a powerful hold on Isherwood's imagination. Starting in

May 1955, he modeled his new novel on Dante's *Divine Comedy*, and for the next four years, he tried to use his vision of this desert, the great empty picture frame, around a portrait of himself descending into hell.

In the literature he had loved as a boy, the hero could risk everything and yet survive and return, alive and pure in heart. No brush with evil could smirch his goodness, no fight with the devil could hold him. This was the narrative offered by Dickens when Isherwood's mother had read *Oliver Twist* aloud to him in August 1915 while they waited and hoped to hear news of his father missing at the Front. It had fallen on his ears at a time of unbearable suspense with its promise that no matter what darkness he passed through, the hero would be restored, like the soot-covered Tom Kitten, hero of Isherwood's nursery, to his clean and rightful place.

Isherwood was the survivor that his father had failed to be. However guilty he felt or had been made to feel about this, about his personality, about his sexuality, he also possessed a lifelong conviction of his inner goodness. His right to survive, his sense that he was worthy, was rooted in his literary imagination and bound up from adolescence with his evolving identity as a writer. He recast the stories of Tom Kitten, Oliver Twist, David Copperfield over and over again in his fiction, charting his descent into the slums of Berlin, reporting on the petty vices and large evils he saw there. In April 1935, he had described to Spender "a big novel (they always start off big, with me)" modeled on Dante, that other visitor to the underworld, about a group of refugees from Germany who "set off on a kind of Dante's Inferno tour of Europe" which was to include a visit to Fronny's island and scenes from the English film studios such as later included in *Prater Violet*.[202]

Isherwood returned to the idea in early drafts of *Down There on a Visit*. At first he set the new novel in Mexico and named his American expatriate colony Los Olvidados, the Forgotten. This became a working title, borrowed from the Buñuel film about the slum children of Mexico City. He quickly realized that Dante's hell was no use to him since the fate of his characters was not final like the fate of Dante's characters: "this Inferno is more a Purgatorio, because nobody in it is permanently damned—only temporarily self-detained." His characters were in the grip of a psychological condition which they could choose to change, like the young man in his film who can choose to make the phone call to God, and his hell was "a place of self-exile, which you can leave at any time if you a) become aware that you are exiled, and (b) want to leave."[203] Isherwood didn't believe in hell in the Christian sense or even in the existentialist sense toward which he was gesturing. In Vedanta, there is no hell, no place where one dwells eternally as a result of committing sins. In Vedanta, there are no sins, only errors. In any case, since childhood, long before he encountered Vedanta, Isherwood had believed in redemption.

Nevertheless, he went on playing with the idea of hell in his notes and drafts. He wouldn't find his way forward until 1959.

AT MGM STUDIOS, early in 1955, Isherwood was given a new job, rewriting a script about Buddha, *The Wayfarer*. The project aligned with his spiritual interests, and he even gave a talk about it at the Vedanta temple. He told Upward (who had written a prizewinning undergraduate poem about Buddha): "It is to be very authentic: made in India with Asian actors and the full approval of the Buddhist church." But right away, he had to invent "characters, motives and situations because the canonical story is so terse and jumpy."[204] Also, as he told an interviewer: "We couldn't have anything about the enlightened Buddha, because that's not allowed on the screen in Buddhist countries." Glenn Ford was proposed as Buddha, and the project was in the gossip columns as late as 1958,[205] but it was never completed.

At the same time, Isherwood was still doing rewrites for *Diane*, which was lurching away from his conception as casting progressed. Lana Turner, leveraging her fifteen years at MGM and her box-office sex appeal, insisted on playing Diane, despite being too old and all wrong for the part. "She's a restaurant hostess," Isherwood told Bachardy. Opposite, as Catherine de Medici, was Marisa Pavan, more than ten years younger. Roger Moore was to play Henri, the dauphin both women wanted. Isherwood was proud of his script and disappointed by the casting and by the director, David Miller. Marisa Pavan had a thick Italian accent, not inappropriate since Catherine de Medici was Italian, but Pedro Armendáriz had a Spanish accent—confusing since he was playing the King of France, Francis I, Henri's father. Isherwood "fantasized retitling the movie 'Revenge Of The Pig People'" while he resolutely cultivated friendships with everyone involved.[206]

Shooting began in May, but not before Joseph Breen, director of the Production Code Administration, attacked the film for condoning adultery. Breen was a conservative Roman Catholic. "If they had their way, adultery would be punished by stoning and homosexuality by being burned alive," Isherwood raged to his diary.[207] Breen made sure the characters were fully clothed in the bedroom scenes and punished for their sins.

Isherwood continued to conceal his own domestic arrangements. When he was invited to dinner by the Knopfs or other studio executives, he went alone. Sometimes there were stars at these evenings, Irene Dunne, Oscar and

Dorothy Hammerstein, Ronald and Nancy Reagan, Florence Vidor, Walter and Ruth Pidgeon, but star-loving Bachardy was not included.[208]

When Bachardy spent time at home with his family, Isherwood, similarly, was not included; in fact, he was "not to be mentioned," Bachardy recalled. Jess let it be known that he was "straining his principles and sense of propriety by deigning to see his fallen son at all." Bachardy felt that his father was jealous: "He knew I'd replaced him with someone much better equipped to play his role."[209] Glade, though, sometimes visited Isherwood and Bachardy for a meal.

Early in 1955, Jess Bachardy moved back in with Glade on condition that he would not interfere with Ted, a condition he ignored. In mid-March, Ted had another breakdown, and was sent back to Camarillo. Isherwood noticed that Don became hypersensitive and unpredictable, bursting into tears over small slights and challenges. He felt that Don was "suffering on a much deeper level the backwash of Ted's breakdown. The terrific undermining shock to his security such a disloyalty—for Ted's breakdowns *are* a kind of disloyalty, or refusal to cooperate—must be."[210]

In his own diary, Bachardy wrote: "I don't seem to fit in anywhere I want. I even dread seeing Mom and Dad or Ted. I'm almost afraid of them—afraid they might get hold of me again." During that winter and spring, Bachardy tried to write a play about Ted's 1953 breakdown, when Ted had been tied up and dragged away by the police. His notes for the play suggest that he did not know who "the other brother" was, or what the other brother character should do, any more than he knew of himself in real life.[211]

Nevertheless, as 1955 began, Bachardy resolved, like Isherwood with his diary-keeping vow, to change course in his life. He transferred from L.A. City College back to UCLA and changed majors from Languages to his new passion, Theater Arts. It wasn't just Tennessee Williams. In January, before the semester started, Truman Capote had visited Los Angeles to try to sell the movie rights to *The House of Flowers*, the musical based on his short story. Capote stayed with David Selznick and Selznick's wife, Jennifer Jones, a favorite star of Bachardy, and even took a thrilled Bachardy off to meet her.

The next day, Capote persuaded Isherwood and Bachardy to fly to New York to see the musical. Off they went that very night. Reckless of expense, Isherwood and Bachardy checked into the St. Regis Hotel and spent five days lunching and dining with New York friends. Such was their lack of preparation for the spree that Isherwood had to buy an overcoat in Manhattan for the cold weather.

But Theater Arts was not the answer. In March, after another trip east, to the Philadelphia opening of *Cat on a Hot Tin Roof*, Isherwood wrote of Bachardy: "He hates school. Doesn't want to be a student." How could school compare to Bachardy's "real" life, powdered with so much stardust? The new course of study proved as disappointing as being an extra in *The Rose Tattoo*, and Bachardy found himself committed to twenty nights of scene shifting for a UCLA campus production, "a compulsory chore for Theater Arts students." Dutifully, he complied.

Speed Lamkin warned Isherwood that he was apt to make young people "despise all kinds of occupations, without giving them any positive interest,"[212] and he suggested Bachardy work for an interior decorator, Tony Duquette, who was designing the sets and costumes for Vincente Minnelli's *Kismet*. Duquette had recently bought a Santa Monica building with a theater, where he hoped to stage new plays. By May, Bachardy was working alongside Duquette's wife, an artist known as Beegle, assisting as she painted a mural for a Duquette client. He pretended to like the job, but he wasn't being paid, and he soon decided he wasn't being taught anything either.

Isherwood knew Bachardy was restless and frustrated. After a party, drunk, Bachardy told Isherwood that he hated all the guests and wished he were dead: "I want them to like me for what I really am, but I don't know what I am."[213]

On May 18, 1955, Bachardy turned twenty-one. Isherwood organized a birthday celebration at Marguerite Brown's to which he and Marguerite invited a crowd of movie stars including the ones in *Diane* and—abandoning caution about his reputation at work—the Eddie Knopfs, the director David Miller, and his new doctor, Jessie Marmorston. One by one the stars begged off. None of them came. "I was so angry that I actually shed tears of rage," Isherwood wrote in his diary.

Nevertheless, there was drinking and dancing, including a kick line to "Glad Rag Doll," a hit recording of a ragtime classic. Spirits were high. Then too high. "[T]here was a big dramatic climax: Marguerite left Harry—walked out of the house." When she returned the next day to pack her clothes, "Harry pulled a gun on her, said he was going to kill her and himself."[214] The Brown divorce provided melodrama for months.

What upset Isherwood and Bachardy most about the birthday party, though, was that Glade made the bus journey to the Browns' apartment and never came inside. Bachardy saw her from the window, standing alone in the street in her best black dress and shoes with her two black braids coiled on her head and topped by a black-and-purple velvet bow. He ran down to meet her, but she was far too shy to come in and be introduced.

He reflected that he had asked too much of Isherwood and too much of his mother. Why should the stars turn out? Why "perform for something of no value to themselves. For their own protection they must be elusive, or else be constantly exploited."[215] Yet his appetite to be around them was nearly uncontrollable. Also, he had an insatiable need to share in and ultimately to *have* anything he observed Isherwood to have.

Despite all this, their domestic life had a magical intimacy. As a private surprise, Isherwood tape-recorded some plays for Bachardy to listen to, and a few days after the birthday, he read aloud to Bachardy in bed from a favorite Hans Christian Andersen fairy tale, "The Snow Queen."

GORE VIDAL GOT a screenwriting job at MGM in July 1955, and he and Isherwood often lunched together that summer. Vidal later wrote: "The common denominator in the rare friendships that I have had with other writers is laughter." Laughter disarms rivalry. With Isherwood, "I laughed a great deal," Vidal recalled. "'I am American literature,' I announced one day. 'I feared as much,' he said."[216]

When they first met, Isherwood had observed that Vidal's "conversation is all about Love, which he doesn't believe in—or rather, he believes it's Tragic." Vidal had the self-discipline and institutional nous to cope with Hollywood, but Isherwood noted in 1955 that Vidal was depressed "because he finds himself unable to care for anyone seriously."[217] His long relationship with Howard Austen, of whom Isherwood grew fond, was not a love affair. Even though Isherwood had enormous affection for Vidal and relished his wit, he was perpetually on guard against Vidal's self-conscious and corrosive mistrust of happiness, and this guard enabled a lasting friendship.

Lunching was another part of his life that Isherwood didn't share with Bachardy. Day in, day out, Isherwood lunched with people who intrigued him, mostly at the studio. In June 1955, the British poet Thom Gunn turned up, "en route for Texas. Liked him so much I asked him to come on with us [. . .] for supper."[218] He also pursued flirtations with younger men, picnicking with one on an empty studio lot. In July, in tears, Bachardy told Isherwood he was "'so terribly unhappy'" because he had "no friends of his own." Bachardy's feelings were more intense than Isherwood realized. To his diary, Bachardy confided: "I resent Chris's having been successfully promiscuous for so many years, and been bold enough to get so many people I would never have the courage to get. [. . .] I want power—I want people to run after me and beg for favors. I want to get even with them and show them."[219]

The lease on the Mesa Road house was due to expire at the end of the summer. *Diane* finished on July 12. Isherwood was feeling "completely insecure" and wondered "What in the world is the point of all this work at Metro, these efforts to get another house—if Don suddenly leaves me?" He got "paralytically drunk" at the closing party on the set. "I'm told that I actually licked someone's face."[220]

Studio pressure and Bachardy's ups and downs continued to cause stress-related symptoms, sharp darting pains in the top of his head that triggered half-hearted fears of a brain tumor. Like an automaton, Isherwood repeated but did not act upon his good intentions—to count his beads on his Vedanta rosary, to work on his new novel. Bachardy's intensity cut through every inclination: "Don is by far the most interesting person I've ever lived with. Why? Because he *minds* the most about things." Isherwood knew that, on his side, the relationship was deeper and more permanent than the storms it caused. Self-understanding began to emerge at night, the only hours of his life that were not frantically overscheduled. Instead of nightmares, he began to experience a new kind of clarity:

> I wake—not with the horrors, but calmly and lucidly. Then I know certain things clearly—it's almost as if they belonged to another order of reality: that I shall die one day—that much of my life has been wasted—that the life of the spirit is the only valid occupation—that I really care for Don and that I have, as it were, adopted him, much as I adopted Heinz, but more completely. In the daytime, these facts are obscured by studio noise and as-if behavior, and insane resentments and mental and physical slumping. Also, I know that all occupations, even Art, are symbolic, and all are valid, so long as they represent right livelihood.

In September, they moved out to Zuma Beach, Malibu, where Isherwood was blissfully happy: "It's a strange place, full of the atmosphere of childhood and the beach."[221] He described it to Upward through two of their favorite writers: "It's so wonderful—partly Kathy's At The Bay, but also rather Conrad—'Marlow began—' "[222]

He swam before breakfast, as he often did in Santa Monica. "He was happy to go alone and always returned invigorated, wet hair askew and wearing over his wet white boxer trunks his wool-lined, heavy-leather aviator jacket, what we both called 'his skin,' " as Bachardy later wrote.[223]

He felt liberated from the movie studio. One day, "I stayed home with Don," he wrote, "and we had one of the best days we've had in this house—walking on the beach in the marvellous afternoon light and watching a dog chase the gulls. Again it was there—*le bonheur*."[224]

Now that Bachardy was twenty-one, they planned to go to Europe, sailing from New York on October 19. But first came warning signs that *Diane* would be a fiasco. Isherwood saw it in the projection room, then went to a Burbank preview. Viewers thought the film was too long and Lana Turner boring. Marisa Pavan looked good, but Isherwood thought her acting amateurish. "Well, I did my best, and they ruined my dialogue and drowned it in Hungarian music—at the cost of $2,300,000."[225]

The movie was to dog him on his travels. In Paris, "lousy notices of *Diane*" arrived from *Variety* and the *Hollywood Reporter*. In London, *Diane* played at a big central theater, the Empire in Leicester Square, and Isherwood was to record his surprise that "I actually mind because it is having bad notices and is a flop." He continued to believe in his script, and he later told an interviewer:

> It should have been done in a High Camp style with a British cast. The lines were not designed to be said by people with south Los Angeles accents. For instance, Diane has to say to the king something like, "Sire, God has lent you the greatness of his power. Show his greatness also in your mercy." It takes a professional to talk like that. It isn't much use if it comes out like, "Aw, Your Majesty, let him go this once."[226]

As with *The World in the Evening*, Isherwood was resilient and already busy with something else. He responded with similar stoical objectivity when he saw the British film of *I Am a Camera*: "a truly shocking and disgraceful mess . . . everything is awful except for Julie who was misdirected."[227]

GRAND TOUR, EUROPE, 1955–56

Just over a decade and a half after his arrival in New York harbor in January 1939, the promise of the snowy wedding cake was fulfilled. Isherwood traveled back to Europe with the American boy he had hoped to find and to whom he was now committed: "I could hardly hold back my tears—it was so beautiful—the Hudson full of fussing tugboats and brimming with silver light—the thought that it was Don's first voyage, never never to be quite duplicated for him—"[228]

They decided to disembark at Gibraltar and make a side trip to Tangier, in Morocco, to visit Paul Bowles. Swarmed by memories of travels with Neddermeyer twenty-one years earlier, Isherwood relished "the Casbah; the veiled women, and the baggy-pant men."[229] He took Bachardy sightseeing with a German friend they bumped into in the post office, the photographer Herbert List, and they spent an evening watching Arab dancing boys.

One night, they went to Bowles's penthouse, where they got high on hashish, an experience that proved overwhelming. They smoked *kif* in a pipe and ate *majoon* from a tiny coffee spoon. It was prepared by Ahmed Yacoubi, the Moroccan painter and storyteller who was Bowles's muse. Isherwood was careful to take very little; nonetheless, he became dizzy, claustrophobic, and so acutely nervous that he disliked even writing about it in his diary two days later.

At first, Bachardy didn't get high, so he smoked and ate much more, leading to a near-psychotic experience that exposed his fear of going mad like his brother. He had paranoid delusions that Bowles and Yacoubi were trying to incapacitate Isherwood so Yacoubi could rape Bachardy while Bowles watched, and he thought Yacoubi was a witch. Isherwood managed to get Bachardy back to their hotel, where they clung to each other through the night. Bachardy feared that he wasn't in Tangier at all, but still in California and insane. The experience brought them closer than ever.

Isherwood was to draw on the harrowing episode for a story called "A Visit to Anselm Oakes," initially conceived as part of the last section of *Down There on a Visit*. He set the story in a suburb of Paris, and Bachardy did not appear in it. Instead, Isherwood combined Bachardy's experiences with his own and portrayed the fears through minor characters. He embellished the atmosphere with satanic and black-magical themes, modeling his Anselm Oakes figure on Aleister Crowley as much as on Paul Bowles. During the European trip, he was reading a life of Crowley, *The Great Beast*, by John Symonds. "The truly awful thing about Crowley," Isherwood observed in his diary, "is that one suspects he didn't really believe in anything. Even his wickedness."[230]

In the story, Isherwood proposed that such a lack of conviction was the essence of evil: "if a Devil *did* exist, the most terrifying thing about him might be simply this: that he wasn't interested in anything, even in damnation."[231] Satanism had fascinated Isherwood since he was a schoolboy reading Marjorie Bowen's *Black Magic*. For Mortmere, he and Upward had written stories about the Christian Church perverted—raped choirboys, excrement, Gothic settings, succubi, incubi, mad bell ringers. Unlike Bowen or Crowley, their Mortmere stories had been funny. Isherwood reread *Black Magic* for at least the third time in 1958, calling it a book "which I've loved for more than thirty years."[232] That same year, he also read or reread Maugham's novel *The Magician* (1908), in which Aleister Crowley is portrayed as Oliver Haddo. What interested Isherwood in the 1950s was the state of mind of the determined sinner. This was a subject of his new project.

Despite his bad experience with hashish, Isherwood continued to experiment with drugs because he wanted to understand their role for both saints and sinners. In California, with Heard, he had already tried inhaling a mixture of 70 percent oxygen and 30 percent carbon dioxide. "I got a most unpleasant feeling—that the oxygen cylinder was breathing *me*, forcing me to inhale and inhale, and preventing exhalation, until I thought I would choke and had to take off the mask." Heard had attributed Isherwood's reaction "to a fear of death—that is, a fear of losing one's sense of identity." Isherwood was irritated by this acute insight. He tried again, and the ceiling seemed to open, revealing the night sky filled with stars. "Other than this, I can't say that the experience was particularly exciting or interesting. There is a terrific sense of 'lift,' that's all."[233]

He was more curious to emulate Huxley's experiments with psychedelics, but his friends interfered: "Salka greatly shocked me by telling me that Maria Huxley said they had decided never to let *me* have mescaline, as it would undoubtedly prove fatally habit forming—since I'm so weak willed!" Heard "more or less admitted" to Isherwood that he had told Humphry Osmond, the doctor who supplied mescaline to Heard and to Huxley, not to supply Isherwood because he "had 'been through so much.'"[234] They misjudged him, probably because of his bond with alcohol.

On his way to Europe with Bachardy, Isherwood had obtained seven tablets of mescaline from a friend in New York. In February 1956, in London, with Bachardy present to look after him, he took one tablet. He experienced the heightened colors Huxley had described in *The Doors of Perception* along with feelings of exhilaration and delight, but there was no mystical breakthrough: "the whole mescaline experience was, for me, quite unspiritual [. . .] I had no drastic adventures, gained no spiritual insights, went neither to heaven nor to hell."[235]

Bachardy persuaded Isherwood to drop the Anselm Oakes episode from *Down There on a Visit*. Perhaps he remained uncomfortable about the Tangier experience. He considered the fictional hashish episode a "cheap thrill," a merely chemical adventure that involved no inward transformation or spiritual or philosophical work on the narrator's part, and unworthy of being presented alongside the narrator's religious journey. Sceptics, he pointed out, might dismiss Isherwood's religious beliefs as if they, too, were only an experiment or a moment of irresponsibility.[236]

Bachardy knew, as Isherwood did, that Swami Prabhavananda opposed drugs of all kinds. "[D]rugs could never change your life or give you the feeling of love and peace that you get from spiritual visions," Prabhavananda admonished. "Drugs only made you marvel—and then later you lost your faith." Prabhavananda believed Huxley had lost his faith in this way.[237]

From Tangier, Isherwood and Bachardy went to Capri and Ischia—where they saw Chester Kallman surrounded by another "tiny colony" of expatriates such as Isherwood was planning to write about[238]—then Naples, Pompeii, the scenic towns along the Amalfi drive, and on to Rome. Isherwood had never visited Italy and later said he was "duly stunned."[239] Iris Tree, with her penchant for living at the picture-postcard heart of things, had an apartment overlooking the Spanish Steps. It was reached by an outdoor spiral staircase, an inconvenience which didn't seem to faze her any more than the constant music from the carousel did when she had lived on Santa Monica Pier.

On November 15, Isherwood and Bachardy visited the grave of Denny Fouts in the Protestant cemetery. Fouts had died of a heart attack in Rome in 1948, addicted to opium and heroin.[240] At his grave, Isherwood cried for Fouts and for himself, just as he had cried when Maria Huxley died: "It all seemed such a wretched tangle—his life, and mine, too."[241] With Fouts alone among all his friends, Isherwood had performed both spiritual austerities and libertine debaucheries. He could not accept the "wretched tangle" as Fouts's epitaph, and he was to offer something far better in the last section of *Down There on a Visit*.

By November 24, he and Bachardy were in Venice, where they had Thanksgiving at Peggy Guggenheim's. Florence, San Gimignano, Lucca, Pisa, Milan—they took in cultural highlights and lowlife, the chapels, the Old Masters, the little-known dives, and the cultish clubs. At the invitation of Mario Soldati, they visited the set of *War and Peace* and watched 3,000 soldiers from the Italian army, dressed in Napoleonic and Russian uniforms of 1812, reenact the battle of Berezina in the ice and fog along the banks of the Po. They made a pilgrimage to the impossibly luxurious Villa Mauresque on Cap Ferrat in the South of France to stay with Somerset Maugham and his companion Alan Searle. In preparation, Bachardy tore into Maugham's novels, and Maugham was charmed by him.

Isherwood never tried to take Bachardy to Berlin, and Germany barely figured in their Grand Tour. They flew to Munich for Christmas, where Bachardy got food poisoning and spent Christmas Day in bed. It was a dark, cold disaster after the splendid embrace of the Villa Mauresque.

In Paris, they checked into the Hotel Quai Voltaire, and Isherwood was again flooded by memories of old love affairs: "(this must be at least my fifth visit—I was here four times in the thirties that I can definitely remember—with Heinz, Johnny Andrews, Ian Scott-Kilvert, and Wystan, on his way to the Spanish war)." He gave way to "black depression" as they drew closer to the suffocating atmosphere of his former homeland: "The truth is, I dread going to England. I dread seeing M. and Richard and reopening the whole dismal tragedy."

Crossing the English Channel on January 7, 1956, Isherwood was "in an absurd state of jitters" because "I can never forget that traumatic experience with Heinz."[242] It was almost exactly twenty-one years earlier, on January 5,

1934, that Neddermeyer had crossed alone and been refused entry. This was to become another subject of *Down There on a Visit*.

"AND MAYBE IT wouldn't have been so *very* unfortunate if we had been turned away from the white cliffs," Isherwood observed in his diary once they had successfully landed at Dover and settled in London. "After two days at John Lehmann's, Don announced that he just couldn't take it any more—he even thought we'd have to stop living together—because my friends all treated him like dirt, or worse." Isherwood was disappointed, too, that Lehmann couldn't see how much he, Isherwood, had changed, "he has no curiosity. He dismisses Vedanta, Gerald Heard, California, the United States. He isn't prepared to listen to anything I tell him about the life I lead in Los Angeles." Isherwood and Bachardy moved out of Lehmann's flat to the Cavendish Hotel.

But it wasn't just Lehmann. It was also Spender and his wife Natasha, Lehmann's flatmate the ballet dancer Alexis Rassine, William Plomer, Peter Watson, Francis Bacon, and so on. Isherwood's London friends didn't take up Bachardy as his New York friends had done. All through January and February, during dinner parties, theater outings, sightseeing excursions, Bachardy felt slighted again and again. His behavior became so sulky and self-pitying that Isherwood felt he was "in need of treatment." Yet Isherwood also saw that the complaints were often justified: "There is no question: many people treat him (and indeed all young people) as if he were a small mess made by the cat."[243]

Dodie Smith and Alec Beesley were among the few to be sympathetic to Bachardy during visits at their thatched cottage in Essex. Bachardy was charming in return. Before the second visit, he went with Isherwood to Samuel French, the drama publisher, where they bought scripts of all Smith's plays, and Bachardy read every single one. "It gave me an insight into who she was," he later recalled. Bachardy sketched portraits of Smith and Beesley, and Isherwood talked with Smith about his novel.[244] Before visiting Forster, Bachardy prepared by reading *The Longest Journey* and *A Passage to India*. This visit was also a success.

In France, Bachardy had devoured *Wuthering Heights*, which introduced him to the northern English landscape of Isherwood's childhood and the romantic torments of Isherwood's adolescence. Wyberslegh and Marple were about forty miles from Haworth Parsonage, the Brontë home in Yorkshire, and Isherwood later said that when he read *Wuthering Heights* and the poems of Emily Brontë in his youth, he had "at once superimposed their myth" on the wild, desolate moorlands and bleak hills around Marple Hall: "It was as Heathcliff that he rode his bicycle uphill and down, through the familiar but transformed landscape, dreaming of death and despair and hopeless love." But Isherwood didn't take Bachardy to Cheshire. "I had to come here alone," he wrote in his diary.[245]

Richard met him at the train station in Stockport, and Isherwood was shocked all over again. It was four years since their last meeting: "His cheeks are rough red and his nose quite purple—[...] Several of his front teeth are missing. His hands are nicotine stained, chapped and usually covered with coal dust." By comparison, Kathleen, now eighty-seven, seemed "pretty and feminine," with eyes, ears, and memory sharp, her energy undiminished: "she still cooks the meals, counts the laundry and attends to all kinds of chores." Wyberslegh Hall was "sponge wet": "The books in the shelves smelled of corpses, the bedclothes were like shrouds, you smelt stale smells everywhere of old fat in unscoured skillets." Then it snowed and turned cold. "Even standing in front of the fire you can see your breath—but the smell of damp and the stink of dirt are less noxious. The countryside is beautiful under the snow."

Isherwood had left Bachardy behind partly to protect him from the filth and discomfort, but also to protect him from his family and from his own complicated feelings about them. Two days after Isherwood arrived, Richard got drunk and overturned the dinner table, yelling, "This is the end! I'm at the end of my tether! I haven't a friend in the world! You're all prigs—all of you!" Then he turned on Isherwood raising an arm as if to strike him: "I hate you! You come up here so smug and tell me my Mother's overworked. I hate you! I hate you!" Isherwood could not take him seriously, and when Richard apologized "and told me he loved me very much," Isherwood felt embarrassed. "Because I don't love *him*—most certainly not as a brother. I have had a hundred brothers already and a thousand sons—and all this talk about blood relationships nauseates me. It's the evil old sentimental lie."

A few days later, Isherwood narrowly restrained himself from continuing forthrightly to his mother on the same themes: "M. had been needling me by talking family—did I remember this or that cousin's cousin? I didn't go so far as to say—as I have often said before—that I hate the whole idea of being 'related' to anyone."[246] Already, he was articulating another theme that was to become widespread among gay and transgender people in later decades, the rejection of biological family in favor of chosen family. He did permit himself to say, "I'm glad that my life is what it is—wandering, insecure, imprudent. I'm glad that I have no idea what I'll be doing ten years from now, glad that I'm still thrilled by Carmen's words about 'la chose enivrante.'" "The intoxicating thing" is freedom; the gypsy heroine of Bizet's opera sings to her lover that she must be able to wander where she pleases.[247]

"There's only one thing I really fear and that's dependence," Isherwood continued in his diary. He had gained the courage to be alone by devoting himself to Vedanta. He wanted nothing to do with the social position his mother clung to, nor with the farmland, parkland, and manor house of his forebears. Experience had shown him that holding on to the past, struggling to preserve an outmoded way of life, was entirely destructive.

The next day, Isherwood drove the three miles with Richard to Marple Hall, now a ruin, with the front staircase unusable and the chimney stack collapsed through the roof. "The only intact thing left in the house is the pink marble fireplace which Uncle Henry brought back from Venice and had fixed up in the drawing room." In vain, he urged Kathleen to have it removed.

Isherwood saw Kathleen's "eyes fill with tears" when he left Wyberslegh, and Bachardy cried on being reunited in London. There was another brief meeting with Kathleen and Richard in London a month later, including Bachardy, before the departure for New York in mid-March.[248] Soon, Isherwood was to bring his biological family and his chosen lover into a fictional relation with one another in "Mr. Lancaster," the first story in *Down There on a Visit*.

SYCAMORE ROAD, SANTA MONICA, 1956

"I've bought the house," Isherwood wrote to Upward from Los Angeles in July. "It's just one in a row, in a street near the beach."[249] It was the first house Isherwood ever owned, 434 Sycamore Road, three minutes' walk up the canyon from the old rental in Mesa Road and five minutes from the East Rustic Road rental shared with Caskey. There was a patio in front full of flowering plants, and a terraced garden climbed the hillside behind. Inside, "I have a most attractive book-lined workroom, and Don has a charming upstairs room of his own, with a sundeck."[250] It used up all his savings.

He had moved in alone on April 30 because Bachardy was in the hospital with hepatitis. It wasn't long before Isherwood, too, came down with it. He was hospitalized for nine days in June, followed by bed rest and quarantine at the new house. So ended the wandering, imprudent life about which he had told his mother he was still glad.

In England, Isherwood had visited Upward's house twice, a modest one in Dulwich, near the private school, Alleyn's, where Upward taught English for nearly thirty years. He lunched with Upward, Upward's wife Hilda, and their two children, including a son named Christopher after him. Hilda was also a teacher and member of the Communist Party of Great Britain.

The Upwards, Isherwood was later to say, "lacked a certain fashionable

7: The Ideal Companion: Don Bachardy (1953–1961) / 511

urban sophistication." This was part of their attraction for Isherwood, "their simplicity" and their safe distance from the London literary scene.[251] They were doctrinaire Marxists, and, to him, exemplary leftists, like Gerda in *The World in the Evening*. Isherwood, who had tried and failed to become a monk, who struggled to live by his religious beliefs, keenly admired how authentically the Upwards lived by their political beliefs.

He had not taken Bachardy to Dulwich because he hesitated to introduce his young male companion in front of the Upward children, and he worried Bachardy might feel bored or even jealous of the friendship with Upward. After lunch on the second visit, Isherwood and Upward sat by the fire and talked about work in progress—work that was to become *Down There on a Visit* and *In the Thirties*, the first volume of Upward's autobiographical trilogy charting his conflicting struggles to become a writer and to participate in the workers' revolution as a member of the Communist Party of Great Britain.

In the same year that Isherwood had published *Lions and Shadows*, 1938, Upward had published a widely admired surrealist narrative, *Journey to the Border*, about his decision to join the party. Then his literary career had stalled. In a 1937 essay that became notorious, "Sketch for a Marxist Interpretation of Literature," he had argued that the writer "must first of all become a socialist in his practical life, must go over to the progressive side of the class conflict" if he wished to do his best work. He had rejected his gift for fantasy because "fantasy implies in practice a retreat from the real world into the world of imagination."[252]

Upward became completely absorbed with Communist Party work and with earning enough to support his family. The party, though, forced him out in 1948, because he believed that, in Britain, it had become a party of reform rather than revolution. His wife believed the same and was forced out with him. He suffered from political disillusionment and isolation; on the other hand, he found time, at last, for writing. Isherwood helped him to get "The Railway Accident," his Mortmere story, published in the U.S., but Upward was so reluctant to own this youthful work that it appeared under the pseudonym "Allen Chalmers" given him by Isherwood in *Lions and Shadows*. Isherwood wrote a foreword calling the author "profoundly and subtly influential."[253]

Upward's mental health was fragile. Once, when he had stayed overnight at Kathleen's house in London, she recorded in her diary: "Dreadful screams in the night – it turned out to be Edward Upward having a nightmare." Isherwood later observed: "I think he *lives* very near to madness and perhaps always has."[254]

Upward struggled to write, doubting every sentence. During the 1940s and 50s, he drafted and redrafted the opening of *In the Thirties*, in which the character based on Isherwood abandons the character based on Upward during a writing holiday on the Isle of Wight. This rupture stood for the many real-life partings between them. The most important had been in May 1928, when Isherwood left Upward on the Isle of Wight and went to London to celebrate the publication of *All the Conspirators*. It had been a professional turning point. They loved one another too well to acknowledge directly any literary rivalry or jealousy—and yet there it lay, under the surface. In *Lions and Shadows*, Isherwood described hiding from his friend "Chalmers" his excitement about the advance copies: "every time he went out of the room, I kept furtively opening them and peeping at my name on the title pages."[255] He made no mention of the fact that Upward had remained behind on publication day "to make a start at last on the novel I had been planning for a very long while," as Upward later revealed.[256]

In the fictional account that Upward eventually produced, "Alan Sebrill" finds he cannot write alone. He is filled with self-hatred, fear, "nervous agony."[257] He falls in love with a girl who rejects him; he decides on suicide, but cannot go through with it. His eventual recovery from this psychological crisis leads to his joining the Communist Party.

Upward wrote and crossed out with such ferocity that he made holes in his paper; his health worsened. In 1949 and again in 1951, he and Isherwood discussed their illnesses by letter, humorously casting their symptoms as neurotic. Isherwood exhorted Upward to remember the way in which they used to play together, invoking D.H. Lawrence and Robert Louis Stevenson to support his view that the creative life should be joyful and even reckless:

> Lawrence was so right about "art for *my* sake." I never cease to be grateful to you for having helped me acquire the play-instinct early, with Mortmere. [...] Dreadful old R.L.S. said that true realism consists in finding "where the joy resides, for to miss the joy is to miss all." He meant—or I want him to have meant—the glee, the insane Mortmere-anarchic element in all experience, however ghastly.[258]

Upward struggled on with his book. Anxiously, Isherwood enquired, "did you see Stephen's recantation of Communism in 'The God That Failed?'" In his essay for this anti-communist collection, Spender pilloried Upward as the type of the English intellectual who had converted to communism with such mystical fervor that he was unable to change his position in response to unfolding events. Using the Isherwood pseudonym, Spender devoted four pages to the political and artistic folly of "Chalmers," born with a bourgeois sensibility that could not be exchanged for a working-class one just so he could write a revolutionary novel. Spender recalled that in 1937, he had asked Chalmers for his thoughts on Stalin's show trials and Chalmers had replied, "There are so many of these trials that I have given up thinking about them long ago." Upward believed that news in the West about the purges was propaganda circulated to discredit the Soviet Union, and he changed his mind only after Stalin's death.[259]

Upward finally had a complete breakdown. Early in 1953, during the months when Isherwood was falling in love with Bachardy and engaging with the problems of Bachardy's schizophrenic brother, Upward was ordered by his doctor to give up his novel. Hilda wrote secretly to tell Isherwood.

Upward recovered and returned to writing the following summer. Thereafter, Isherwood was especially protective of him. When Upward finally finished a draft of *In the Thirties*, Isherwood praised it lavishly, "every inch of every scene is so true. [. . .] this is part of a masterpiece." Across the top of his letter, he added: "You know what's so different about Alan? He's a moralist. We haven't had a moralist in literature since when? Gide <u>called</u> himself a moralist, but his moralising was trivial: all about his marriage which he didn't believe in anyway."[260]

In his next letter, Isherwood pressed Upward to strengthen Alan's moral position further, even if it reflected badly on the Isherwood character, Richard Marple: "(It's quite possible that you may have avoided doing this because of some conscious or subconscious scruple about <u>my</u> feelings? If so, remember what Stephen did to me in World Within World—and I wrote and <u>begged</u> him not to omit anything!)" He urged Upward to heap blame on Richard Marple for the collapse of Alan Sebrill's life, as if he wanted to be held responsible in fiction for Upward's suffering and so to pay a penance for his own happiness, his freedom, and his literary success. "Even in Richard's desertion of Alan, I sense an opportunity missed. Shouldn't Alan resent this much more than he does?"[261]

When *All the Conspirators* first appeared in the U.S. in 1958, Isherwood renewed the book's original dedication to Upward, extending it to Upward's family and claiming Upward as "the judge before whom all my work must stand trial and from whose verdict, much as I sometimes hate to admit it, there is no appeal."[262] For the rest of his life, Isherwood continued to turn to Upward for advice on work in progress, and he continued to help him find publishers. In 1977, in the *New Statesman*, he called Upward's complete autobiographical trilogy, *The Spiral Ascent*, "one of the most truly original books in modern literature."[263] By then, however, Bachardy had not only replaced Upward as Isherwood's first reader but had also become

Isherwood's collaborator. Upward never collaborated with anyone else; Isherwood collaborated promiscuously.

AFTER THEIR MISERABLE conflicts in England, Isherwood and Bachardy entered a more harmonious phase. It was partly the stability and independence of home and partly the hepatitis, which contributed to "A sort of nursery-sickroom atmosphere, which reminds me of the last scene in O'Neill's *All God's Chillun*. Kittycat and old Dobbin."[264] Eugene O'Neill's play pairs a white woman and a black man, at least as taboo when it was staged in 1924 as two men with a thirty-year age gap in the 1950s. The characters, Ella and Jim, are ready to destroy each other rather than let go; in the last scene, they take refuge in the childhood identities that first formed the unbreakable bond between them—Painty Face and Jim Crow. Bachardy and Isherwood, too, rested from fighting with the world and one another in their Animal identities.

Smashing a taboo is not easy. Bachardy accepted that he needed psychological counseling and consulted Evelyn Hooker. "She didn't think it neurotic of him to be upset, under the circumstances," wrote Isherwood. "In other words, she thinks that our life together constitutes a genuinely big problem." At first, this threw him: "I can't, in my weakness, help feeling hurt when I'm treated as a sort of classic monster—a standard monster, almost—out of a textbook like a dragon in a fairy tale." Yet he recognized a pattern: "Go back twenty years. For Don, substitute Richard. For Evelyn, John Layard, for me, my mother." In fact, it was more than twenty-five years since the crisis over Richard's future in 1929 and 1930, when Isherwood had introduced Layard to counsel Richard in the face of their mother's expectation that Richard complete his education and get a job.

With Hooker's support, Bachardy became a little more confident and happier. Isherwood was forced to accept a different image of himself: "Don, on his side, cannot understand that I mind. I ought to accept my monsterhood humbly, he thinks."[265] Of course, Bachardy had none of Richard's longterm problems, and Isherwood himself was determined to change.

Less than two weeks after Isherwood and Bachardy had returned to Los Angeles from Europe, Bachardy had gone to Chouinard Art Institute in Westlake to find out about classes. He got home, Isherwood noted in his diary, "suffering from psychosomatic stomachache—because the Chouinard had depressed him or scared him."[266] He enrolled in a summer course on July 2, 1956, and ended up studying there for the next four years.

Something else happened in the spring of 1956 that made Isherwood feel like a monster. In May, he received a letter from Neddermeyer proposing that Isherwood "sponsor the immigration of Gerda, Christian and himself to the States, and that we shall then all live together in a house that I'm to buy," as Isherwood recorded in his diary, where he commented, "I'd rather die than agree."[267]

Neddermeyer and his family were still living in East Berlin, governed by the Soviet-aligned, communist East German regime. Movement back and forth between East and West Berlin was becoming increasingly difficult. East and West Germany were beginning to rearm. In November 1956, during the anti-Soviet Hungarian Revolution, Isherwood heard again from Neddermeyer, who had fled to Hamburg in West Germany "for fear of arrest after a political argument in his factory."[268] Isherwood sent money, but he felt guilty about Neddermeyer's hope to emigrate and began to turn against his younger self for inspiring such hope.

Just then, Gerald Hamilton was publishing a memoir, *Mr. Norris and I . . .*, and Hamilton asked Isherwood to contribute a prologue. Isherwood found this "very difficult" to write.[269] It was a delicate task to acknowledge Hamilton as the model for Mr. Norris and not accuse him of the extremely bad behavior depicted in the novel.

While writing *Mr. Norris Changes Trains*, Isherwood had focused on the Norris character; now he focused on his younger self, the author, and felt repelled by his own book: "It is a heartless fairy-story about a real city in which human beings were suffering the miseries of political violence and near-starvation. The 'wickedness' of Berlin's night-life was of a most pitiful kind; the kisses and embraces, as always, had price-tags attached to them . . ." Isherwood deplored the role he had played in this. "The only genuine monster was the young foreigner who passed gaily through these scenes of desolation, misinterpreting them to suit his childish fantasy."[270]

As he reflected on his past behavior, he was increasingly aware that Bachardy was doing the same, from another point of view. In May, Bachardy read two letters Isherwood had sent to Caskey from Wyberslegh in 1947, "and it hurt him to find that they were exactly like the letter I wrote Don from Wyberslegh this trip." During June and July, Bachardy read the wartime diaries, 1939–44, and asked about "Mr. X.," with whom Isherwood had fallen in love in 1944 and for whom he had left the monastery: "Don returns again and again to the examination of my character—with the furious impatience, indignation and fascination of one who studies a book which is full of matters vitally interesting to him, but which is very badly and ambiguously written. What *does* the goddam author mean?"[271]

Bachardy wanted to know everything about Isherwood without ambiguity. His judgments were sometimes harshly negative, but on the other hand, he found much to emulate. For instance, he began to take an interest in Vedanta.

Prabhavananda came to tea at Sycamore Road with two other monks: "Don was pleased, because I told him that serving a meal to a Swami would probably save him five hundred rebirths. He also drank the remains of Swami's tea as prasad." (Prasad is food that has been consecrated by being offered to a god or to a saintly person.) Next, Bachardy accompanied Isherwood to Vedanta Place along with Huxley and Huxley's new wife, the Italian violinist Laura Archera. "It was rather a success. Swami seems to have accepted Don's relation to me as a matter of course. He said to Don, as we were leaving, 'Come again—every time Chris comes.'"[272]

The intensity of Bachardy's attention was binding them together more and more tightly. It was a challenge and a responsibility for Isherwood, to measure up to Bachardy's scrutiny. Moreover, in Bachardy's behavior, Isherwood began to see his own youthful behavior from a new angle.

Despite the hepatitis, Isherwood worked hard all through the spring and summer of 1956, even in the hospital. He wrote 102 pages of *Down There on a Visit* by the end of July, and he began a project Prabhavananda had long urged on him, a new biography of Ramakrishna. This biography was to take Isherwood nearly ten years to complete. Portraying an incarnation of God on earth, which Ramakrishna's followers believed him to be, was to challenge Isherwood, a challenge increased by the bureaucracy of Belur Math, the Ramakrishna monastery near Calcutta, and by conservative attitudes that were crystallizing around Ramakrishna's freely expressed spirituality.

At first Isherwood worked on the biography in little bursts every day, reading and taking notes from two existing biographies, *Sri Ramakrishna, The Great Master* by Ramakrishna's direct disciple Swami Saradananda and *The Life of Ramakrishna* by the French writer, mystic and Nobel prizewinner Romain Rolland. He made good progress on his novel, and he was also assembling his anthology, *Great English Short Stories*, commissioned by Frank Taylor for Dell, and for which he expected to be paid about $3,500. He timetabled each day rigidly.

Then in mid-September, he was hired by 20th Century–Fox to write a movie script adapted from *Jean-Christophe*, Rolland's ten-volume novel about a musical genius modeled on Beethoven. Isherwood was now in deep with Rolland, by coincidence, and settled down to read the gigantic book right away. He signed a contract on September 28; he was to be paid $6,000 for the treatment, which he completed October 10.

He and Bachardy agreed with a contractor to remodel their new house, and soon there was a hole in the roof for a skylight, holes in the walls of

Isherwood's workroom for two new windows, painters at work, a tile floor being laid in the living room. Some days, Isherwood felt completely exhausted. He had never really allowed himself to recuperate from the hepatitis. On October 20, he started a new series of hormone shots, and he began taking hormone pills as well. At last he confided to his diary a worry he couldn't bring himself to name: "I'm depressed because of this psychological difficulty with Don—due perhaps, on my side, to aftereffects of the hepatitis. It makes me feel so insecure, although at present he's taking it very well."[273] Isherwood was impotent.

Bachardy indeed took it well. The vulnerability in Isherwood aroused Bachardy's generosity and compassion, but the impotence danced like a will-o'-the-wisp between them, sometimes presenting a terrible obstacle, sometimes vanishing. In mid-January of the new year, Isherwood wrote in his diary: "My physical problem loomed large yesterday because we discussed it, and assumed the air of tragedy. Today, because nothing was said about it, it solved itself absolutely—for the time being."

Then, in February 1957, there was a cancer scare, "a bump on the side of my belly," which his doctor, Jessie Marmorston, wanted cut out immediately. The night before the operation, Isherwood sought reassurance from Prabhavananda about his fear of death, but he couldn't bring himself to ask about his fear of being separated from Bachardy: "What if Don were excluded from the Ramakrishna loka?"[274]

The tumor proved benign. Nevertheless, it made Isherwood sharply conscious of his mortality. Dr. Marmorston blamed the hepatitis for the tumor and urged Isherwood to make a more complete recovery. He was also experiencing shooting pains in his right hand, caused by arthritis in his thumb.

Despite his fears of illness and death, or perhaps because of them, Isherwood observed in his diary that his life with Bachardy was now "truly idyllic." His novel and his movie work both interested him keenly. And there was Vedanta: "most important of all—I feel a new or renewed relationship to Swami. This has been growing for months. It's as if he were exposing me to stronger and stronger vibrations of his love—yet, all the while, making almost no personal demand."

Bachardy had no intention of being excluded from the Ramakrishna loka. He accompanied Isherwood more frequently to the Hollywood temple, just as Prabhavananda had invited him to. In March, Isherwood went alone to Santa Barbara to lecture at the Sarada Convent, where he took note of a ten-year-old boy who was attracting attention for his saintly mien. "Maybe he's a junior saint," Isherwood wrote in his diary. "And already everybody is kidding him about becoming a monk." Bachardy half seriously feared the competition. "I hate child prodigies!" he said when Isherwood told him about the boy.

That very night, Bachardy accompanied Isherwood to the Hollywood temple for vespers, a puja celebrating Ramakrishna's birthday, and he insisted on being "touched by Swami with the tray of relics." The relics, shared out by Belur Math, are tiny bits of bone and hair gathered from the cremation sites of Ramakrishna, his wife Sarada Devi, and his best-known disciples, Vivekananda and Brahmananda; at the Hollywood Center, they are shown only four times a year and touched to devotees' foreheads. Bachardy had refused to participate in this ritual only a month before. "Now I feel he has joined the Ramakrishna family," Isherwood wrote after the puja. He was confident that Bachardy had been made safe from spiritual harm. He had already made Bachardy materially safe, for in January 1957, he had signed a will leaving Bachardy the house and his money.

Isherwood was uncomfortable with the happiness he was experiencing fully for the first time in his life. "It scares me, and so I keep fearing its end, and dwelling on the danger of its ending. I would do much better to try to understand it and learn something from it. *Why* are Don and I so happy right now? *Why* isn't everybody?" His happiness was not the result of chance. He had pursued it with determination, cunning, recklessness for years—a place to live, a way to live, someone to live with. At last he had found his ideal partner and drawn him fully into a family circle. But he could not settle into it. On May 9, he noted in his diary, "The day my father was killed."[275] He had not written anything about this date for some years. As his feelings for Bachardy deepened, buried recollections began to emerge—of his parents' happiness which he had shared as a child and which had been snatched from them.

ISHERWOOD FINISHED WORK on *Jean-Christophe* on June 9, 1957; gossip had Brando starring.[276] On June 13, Bachardy flew alone to New York, where he stayed with Lincoln Kirstein for two weeks. Chouinard was on break, and Bachardy wanted to spread his wings. He spent a weekend on Fire Island with Isherwood's and Fouts's friend John Goodwin, went to the theater, and saw Tennessee Williams and Frank Merlo. Isherwood had long guessed and accepted that Bachardy wanted "some kind of sex adventures"; he looked on this as "only natural."[277]

The sexual dynamic between him and Bachardy was immensely subtle. When Isherwood's impotence abated, Bachardy drew back. On May 3, Isherwood had noted in his diary that his "sex feelings" had "returned to quite an extent." It was just three days later that Bachardy announced he wanted time away, explaining that "he feels incapable of having any relationship to anyone while I'm around." Two days after that, there was "Some tension with Don." According to Isherwood, "He says he is bored by my affectation of strength and would like me to lean on him more. But when I do lean on him, he gets rattled." After another two days, Bachardy evidently burst out: "'I feel I'm stifling here!' He talked a lot about my qualities as a monster—how I force people to leave me, etc." Isherwood was a strong dish. The writer Charlie Locke, who worked next door to him at Warner Brothers, repeated something others had suggested since Isherwood was eight years old, "that I ought to have been a minister of the Gospel because I had so much inner strength."[278]

Alongside his drive for independence, Bachardy had what Isherwood described as "almost pathological feelings of insecurity about our life together [. . .] As I see it, Don feels compelled to test the relationship in all sorts of ways. Is there anything that'll make me break it up?"[279] The struggle to control one another was to escalate as Bachardy matured. It was always laced with sexual tension, and the challenge and risk it offered to both parties was a vital, binding component in the relationship. It kept them interested.

It was not sexual adventures Isherwood feared, but sentimental ones. He worried that Bachardy, on his own in New York, would form "all sorts of new relationships outside my sphere, and maybe one in particular which will keep pulling his thoughts eastward after his return." In his diary, Isherwood insisted he felt glad that Bachardy was having a wonderful time away, but he also admitted that he was miserable without him. "Melancholy. Stomachache. Loneliness—terrible sad unromantic loneliness." He had forgotten how to be alone.

Around this time, he reread Colette's masterpiece, *Chéri*, about the charms and tortures of a great love between two people far apart in age—forty-nine-year-old Léa, "nearing the end of a successful career as a richly kept courtesan,"[280] and her boy-lover, reaching the age when he must marry someone else. Such a love could not preclude other loves, but it could never be replaced by them.

When Bachardy returned in July, Isherwood seemed to find happiness itself unbearable: "underneath I feel only gnawing anxiety, despair, the deadness of everything." Dr. Marmorston took him to a specialist who said Isherwood's vagus nerve was "causing this upset in the pyloric region. So I'm to take belladonna to stop the spasms." His stomach improved, but he continued to feel anxious about earning money. He was planning a long trip to the Far East with Bachardy. On August 15, *Jean-Christophe* was shelved at

Fox. "So that's that. It looks like I shall earn no more money before we leave. [...] I smell a period of unsuccess."[281]

SCROUNGING FOR OTHER remunerative work brought new friends if not income. That summer, Isherwood collaborated on a speculative television series for Hermione Gingold with an English writer, Gavin Lambert, twenty years younger than he. Lambert had come to Los Angeles in March 1956 to assist Nicholas Ray—recently famous for *Rebel Without a Cause* (1955). He was also Ray's lover and shared Ray's bungalow at the Chateau Marmont for a time. Lambert was writing his first book of fiction, *The Slide Area: Scenes of Hollywood Life*, a group of interconnected stories in which he appeared as narrator, like Isherwood in *Goodbye to Berlin*.[282] Dodie Smith found it an uncanny impersonation: "No, I SWEAR on Ramakrishna's beard, I did NOT write the Slide Area!" Isherwood playfully assured her.[283]

Lambert had a long, clear view of the Isherwood–Bachardy relationship: "They not only endured conflicts, tensions, and separations that would have torn most couples apart, but loved each other to the end." He thought Isherwood's drinking was caused by hidden unhappiness, remarking that Isherwood was "not quite as overwhelmed by bliss as he claimed. Otherwise, I wondered, why did he get drunk so often?" Isherwood was certainly chemically hooked; he had had a drinker's sweet tooth from early childhood. But in addition, there were the relentless anxieties that pursued him all his life, his nervous temperament, his inability to relax, his fear of death.

Alcohol offered respite of a different kind than Isherwood found in Vedanta. Krishnamurti told Lambert that Vedanta meditation worked like a tranquilizer: "Fixing the mind on a mantra and excluding every other thought, is just spiritual Valium. True meditation," for Krishnamurti as for Huxley, "means setting the mind free and totally aware, then following it where it takes you." But Isherwood set his mind free in his writing all the time; from his religion, he wanted something to ground and stabilize him. The repetitiveness was not an end in itself; it placed him on a spiritual pathway. It was Isherwood who introduced Lambert to Krishnamurti, and according to Lambert, Isherwood never tried to persuade him to take up Vedanta, "he only talked about it when asked."[284]

Bachardy helped Isherwood and Lambert with the TV series, taking notes and typing the treatment. It was about an impoverished, middle-aged Englishwoman, from a landed family, who is on a secret mission to take over America for the British. She wears Edwardian clothes but is a master of disguise and operates out of a magic shop, where she serves tea and crumpets, promotes cricket and croquet, and tells fortunes—a blend of the real-life psychic Eileen Garrett, who was Irish, with Isherwood's mother and grandmother, Emily. The show was called *Emily Ermengarde*. "No matter what happens—always behave as it if hadn't . . . That's what we do in England," advises Emily over the teacups.[285]

Gingold was filming *Gigi* at MGM and proved difficult to pin down. Financing was offered by the Burns Brothers, the comedians, but she lost interest. Isherwood was relieved to be free of the commitment. Later, in 1958, Elsa Lanchester considered the material, but the show was never made. Lambert continued to come up with ideas, and in 1959, he and Isherwood worked on *The Vacant Room*, the ghost story which Isherwood had written with Lesser Samuels.

Cecil Beaton was in town designing the costumes for *Gigi*. He took Isherwood and Bachardy on the set and brought the young star Leslie Caron to supper at their house. "She is rather a magic person," Isherwood was to write in 1968, "so gay, almost affectionate, but with a welcome dash of lemon in it."[286] Beaton he had known since the late 1940s, when Beaton came to Hollywood with a production of *Lady Windermere's Fan*. Isherwood and Bachardy took Beaton for a beach picnic with Don Murray and his wife Hope Lange, who were making a film of William Inge's play *Bus Stop*, in which they had both appeared in New York. Murray was starring opposite Marilyn Monroe.

Murray was a pacifist. He had served jail time as a conscientious objector and volunteered with the Red Cross in the Korean War. He and Lange used their earnings from *Bus Stop* to build a refugee resettlement community in Sardinia. Isherwood took an excited interest in this project.[287]

In 1958, Murray acquired the production rights to *Jean-Christophe*, hoping to use Isherwood's shelved script. Later, he hired Isherwood to write a treatment for a film about the savage feuds among Sardinian clans, titled after the village where the true story happened, *Bandits of Orgosolo*.[288] According to Murray, Isherwood had a reputation as a serious and sensitive writer who wouldn't "put things into a script just to attract stars." He surrounded himself with "people who had ideas," and what made him so attractive to others was "his interest in *them*."[289] Isherwood adored Hope Lange, "an enchantingly attractive girl," he wrote in his diary.[290]

The most valuable friendships, to Isherwood, had no material motive or lost it along the way. This was epitomised in his friendship with Igor and Vera Stravinsky, with whom he experienced an embracing contentment that recapitulated and perfected his relationship with the Mangeots during the 1920s, including the French elements he had observed and the Russian elements he had invented when he portrayed the Mangeots as the Cheurets in *Lions and Shadows*. The integration in Stravinsky of creaturely innocence with the highest moral qualities aroused Isherwood's intense affection: "His cuddly animal smallness, his spontaneous warmth and unembarrassed kisses, his marvellous multi-lingual conversation, his wit."[291] Isherwood's feelings for Vera, once an actress, later a painter, were similar.

He had been introduced by the Huxleys in 1949, and he later recalled that Stravinsky welcomed him to their first evening together "by saying 'Shall we listen to my mass before we get drunk?'" What Stravinsky recalled was that "On Christopher's first visit to my home, he fell asleep when someone started to play a recording of my music. My affection for him begins with that incident." Drinking was a bond between them, and the acceptance of the unguarded self which drunkenness can reveal. "We have often been drunk together," Stravinsky recorded, "—as often as once a week, in the early 1950s, I should think—"[292] Another bond, unremarked, was religious devotion. To Isherwood, Stravinsky's studio, where he composed, was "doubly a sacred place, since it contained an icon to which he prayed."[293]

In June 1957, Isherwood attended Stravinsky's seventy-fifth birthday concert in Los Angeles. The program included *Canticum Sacrum* and *Agon*. "Of course I didn't enjoy the music," he wrote in his diary, "nervous stabbing sounds, the creakings and squeaks of a door swinging in the wind. Little fizzes of energy from the violins. Short desert twisters of revolving noise, which soon pass."[294] In July, Isherwood and Bachardy went to Santa Fe to hear *The Rake's Progress*, with greater pleasure since the opera offered a story and Auden and Kallman's libretto. As he later admitted, Isherwood "actually did like a lot of classical music, including some of Stravinsky's, but he never told the Stravinskys so—the gross compliments of their courtiers disgusted him."[295] He had been around music all his life and was familiar with the professional music milieu through working with André Mangeot's string quartet, so he recognized that he did not speak Stravinsky's language—music. He had turned down the opportunity to collaborate with Stravinsky on *The Rake's Progress* as he had turned down the opportunity to collaborate with Britten on *Peter Grimes*. Lyrics and librettos were Auden's job, and it was Isherwood who suggested Auden and Kallman to Stravinsky as collaborators on *The Rake's Progress*.

Isherwood saw Stravinsky's achievement as a spiritual one comparable to the mystical achievements of Prabhavananda, for Stravinsky had transcribed a truth offered by the universe when he composed *Le Sacre du printemps*, the work that had made his reputation in 1913. "I am the vessel through which *Le Sacre* passed," Isherwood quoted in a 1968 introduction to Prabhavananda's book *Religion in Practice*. "Stravinsky's use of the word 'vessel' has tremendous significance," he explained, for: "The truly spiritual man knows that he is only a vessel; however great his efforts may have been, they cannot command the coming of experience, for that is always a gift of grace. The most he can do is purify the vessel so that it is ready to receive the gift at any time—"[296]

He had observed similar attempts at purification by his idol Katherine Mansfield and by E.M. Forster (even though Forster did not agree with his analysis), when Forster burned short stories in order to be able to progress with *A Passage to India*.[297] Isherwood still sought this purification, this readiness, for himself.

THE FAR EAST AND INDIA, 1957

Just before midnight on October 8, 1957, Isherwood and Bachardy took off for Honolulu on the first leg of a proposed three-month tour around the Far East and India. In India, they were to be hosted by the monks of Belur Math, the main Ramakrishna monastery near Calcutta, and Isherwood aimed to gather material for his biography. They made a collaborative record of the trip with a view to a travel article. Bachardy sometimes wrote Isherwood's day-to-day diaries, and the journal Isherwood typed when they were back home in 1958 drew freely—"sometimes with acknowledgement, sometimes not"—on another diary Bachardy kept while they were traveling.

In Tokyo, World War II felt close to Isherwood, as it had in Berlin in 1952: "The city was terribly damaged in the great raids at the end of the war, and much of it is still emergency-rebuilding," he wrote. During the single night that he and Auden had spent in Tokyo on the way home from China in 1938, they had experienced a small earthquake while standing in the lobby of the Imperial Hotel. Isherwood returned there with Bachardy, and now, twenty years later, his memory offered a potent image of the world already wobbling before the onslaught of the Axis powers: "I see a Nazi officer in full uniform standing talking to a Japanese officer, right in the middle of the lounge, under a big chandelier. As I watch them, the chandelier begins to sway; and this is my first (and only) Japanese earthquake—a mild one, admittedly." He considered the memory "suspiciously symbolic," as he recorded in the 1958 journal, but he held on to its essential truth and used it in *Christopher and His Kind* with confident embellishment: "the Berlin–Tokyo Axis personified," he wrote. "They exchange Nazi salutes, then bow Japanese-style, then shake hands."[298]

In the 1958 diary, Isherwood wrote that the night life in Tokyo reminded him "of Berlin in the twenties." At one coffee bar, "there were a lot of quiet crafty-looking Japanese juveniles sitting sullenly around." In another, "Only a few exaggeratedly graceful Japanese boys with spit-curls or high fluffy pompadours [...] called 'Sister-boys.' Tokyo's night-life offers every kind of boy-lover, from boy-geishas in full drag[,] rice-powder and black wigs to U.S. style tough guys with leather jackets and motor-cyclist's boots in the manner of James Dean." He also described with critical self-reference the dynamic between rich foreigners and impoverished locals: "Ah, how disgusting this sexual colonialism is! And how guilty [...] I have been of it, myself, when young!"[299]

They visited temples, shrines, and the Imperial Palace in Tokyo as well as the red-light district, working-class bars, upmarket bars, and a striptease musical. They saw kabuki and enjoyed the animal pleasures of the Japanese bathhouses. Isherwood was interviewed on the radio and gave a talk; Yukio Mishima, who had visited in Los Angeles, made the introductions by letter. Mishima also connected Isherwood with Meredith (Tex) Weatherby, who let Isherwood read his draft English translation of Mishima's second novel, *Confessions of a Mask*. Later, Mishima credited Isherwood with supporting the book to U.S. publication and thanked him, touchingly, for his blurb.[300] When Mishima committed seppuku in November 1970, Isherwood observed: "I suppose he had become completely crazy. I just cannot relate this to the Mishima we met."[301]

From Tokyo, Isherwood and Bachardy flew to Hong Kong, privately unspooling Isherwood's journey with Auden in the opposite direction in 1938. They were bound not toward the terrifying reality of war but toward the mythical fantasy of the "East" depicted in the writing of Conrad and Maugham. They left Hong Kong aboard a Dutch East Indies liner for a twenty-day sightseeing cruise through the Indonesian archipelago, but, as Isherwood told the Masselinks, they did not find the romance he had imagined, "thousands of little islands—and on some of them maybe old ruined Dutch plantation houses standing deserted in the midst of pepper-orchards, and the wind bringing delicious whiffs of spices, oregano, snuff, and fine herbes over the water [...] a volcano or two, with fire coming out."

Instead, Djakarta bristled with "a menacing sense of military activity." Anti-Dutch sentiment was graffitied on buildings, and in Semarang, where they arrived on a national festival day, they were discouraged from going ashore because "incidents against foreigners are expected."[302] In Bali, they overdosed on tourism—temples, shrines, caves, tombs, sacred springs, sacred monkeys, the ritual monkey dance.

On board ship, Isherwood read *To the Lighthouse* "(for maybe the 3rd time)," *The Brothers Karamazov* and Conrad's tragic final novel, *Victory*, "all about this part of the world," as he wrote to Van Druten. "I loved it right up to the final scene which seems to me an inartistically total holocaust."[303] His disappointment was a seed for a new approach to Conrad's island theme in *Down There on a Visit*.

"[O]ur great mistake in planning this trip was to include the voyage to Bali," Isherwood later told Prabhavananda, "we wasted a great deal of time en route and became tired out."[304] They continued to Angkor Wat in Cambodia, but they had had enough of being tourists, of being foreigners. They still faced the real purpose and justification of the trip, researching Isherwood's biography of Ramakrishna. Isherwood felt just as uncomfortable in the role of religious biographer as he had felt in the role of war correspondent with Auden twenty years before. He was a renegade from all forms of institutional life, and now he was about to come face-to-face with the institutional base of the religion he had joined in its exotic outpost in California.

In Singapore, Isherwood and Bachardy made a preliminary visit to the Ramakrishna Mission and Boys' Home, and Isherwood's gut was already reacting. He got sick and grew worse on the flight to Calcutta, where he took to his bed in the hotel. He wrote to Prabhavananda that he had "a high fever and bad cough in the bargain," but he also blamed his liver, still sensitive after the hepatitis: "I think I can stave it off if I'm very careful not to eat fats and spiced food."[305]

However, Bachardy was to recall years later: "Of all his psychosomatic adventures, this was the most extraordinary. He almost made me into his accomplice. Swami had laid this task on him, to write the biography, knowing Chris would do anything Swami asked. This kind of obligation filled Chris with apprehension."

Looking back, Bachardy thought that "The problem was we were together. Seeing it through my eyes, as well as his own, was torment."[306] Bachardy was unhappy during the trip, which he recorded in his travel diary, where Isherwood was surprised to come across "a most wounding outburst against the misery of our relationship at that time and his longing to be free of it."[307]

Isherwood had to hold his nerve, arriving at the monastery, a bastion of celibacy, with his young lover in tow. Prabhavananda had accepted Isherwood's way of life, but what about the other monks? Isherwood was now playing the role of Prabhavananda's star disciple, representing his guru to his guru's colleagues and superiors. He had feared this even before he left Los Angeles, and in Honolulu he had recorded that a chance encounter with a fellow mystic had enhanced his dread: "I just cannot dare to picture the embarrassment of our both being there."[308]

As he lay in bed in the Great Eastern Hotel in Calcutta, Isherwood was waited on by two swamis from Belur Math. It was three days before he felt well enough to go out. On December 3, yet another swami, Vitashokananda, drove Isherwood and Bachardy to sites associated with Ramakrishna, starting with Cossipore Garden House, the suburban villa where Ramakrishna, surrounded by his direct disciples, spent the last nine months of his life in 1885–6.

Afterwards, they went to lunch at Belur Math itself, just west across the Ganges (the distributary called the Hooghly) in Howrah District. Belur Math stands on forty acres beside the river. In 1898, Vivekananda had carried Ramakrishna's relics there in an urn and worshipped them, consecrating the location, where he then spent the last four years of his own life. Before Vivekananda died at the young age of thirty-nine, he planned the building of the main temple, which was begun in 1935 and designed by a fellow monk to incorporate motifs from all religions in keeping with the Vedanta ideal of being a universal religion. The multi-domed structure of reddish-brown sandstone, over one hundred feet high, resembles a cathedral, a mosque, a Hindu temple, a Buddhist temple. The floor plan is in the shape of a Christian cross, and the facades and decoration draw on the stylistic and symbolic traditions of many other sects and geographical regions. Scattered over the gardenlike grounds are smaller temples built on sites where Ramakrishna's direct disciples were cremated, including Vivekananda, Brahmananda, and Sarada Devi.

On December 4, Swami Vitashokananda took Isherwood and Bachardy on another tour before moving them into the Belur Math guesthouse. Among the sites was Udbodhan, the house built for Sarada Devi to use when she was in Calcutta. Sarada Devi was married to Ramakrishna when she was five years old and Ramakrishna was twenty-three; she remained with her family until she was eighteen, and even after she joined Ramakrishna, they never consummated their marriage because he was devoted to his spiritual practices and she wished to follow and support him in these. Although she took no vows, she lived as a nun, became a great teacher with many disciples and continued Ramakrishna's ministry after his death. She is worshipped in her own right as Holy Mother.

Next, they drove a little further north up the Ganges to see Dakshineswar, the temple to the goddess Kali where Ramakrishna spent most of his adult life. He became head priest there in 1856, taking over from his elder brother. On another day, they saw the location of Ramakrishna's funeral pyre, the wood-burning "ghat," or steps, leading to the Ganges at Cossipore. Everywhere they went, Bachardy was filming.

"I was still feeling shaky, with waves of fever, and I could hardly eat anything," Isherwood wrote to Prabhavananda about the first lunch at Belur

Math. By December 5, he was planning to cut the India visit short. "I cannot go around from mission to mission demanding special diets, and suddenly getting sick and having to lie down and rest." He resolved to see "everything which is required for the Ramakrishna book" and then go straight to England. His letter explaining this to Prabhavananda is painstaking with guilt: "I fear you will be greatly disappointed to hear all this. It makes me sad to have to tell you."[309]

Throughout his visit, he made *pranams* only once—prostrating and taking the dust of the feet of the president of the order, Shankarananda (i.e. touching the feet with both hands and placing the dust on his own head). "I didn't bow down to any of the other swamis," he later wrote, "because I didn't want to embarrass Don," who "couldn't bow down because, in those days, he wasn't a devotee."[310] This excruciating time laid the emotional foundation for Isherwood's final novel, *A Meeting by the River*, which was to articulate the conflict between his religion and his sexual and domestic life and to conclude with a meaningful bow of the worldly to the spiritual.

At Belur Math, Isherwood met the head of the Ramakrishna Order, Swami Madhavananda, who was to oversee the Ramakrishna biography, reading "chapter by chapter" and supplying "corrections, added information and comments."[311] Never before had Isherwood written a book to be approved by an official authority; Madhavananda reportedly imposed his views lightly, but Isherwood chafed under the mere idea of censorship, later admitting to a friend how adversely this affected the project: "There is that in me which will never write its best to order."[312]

In the 1980s, in *My Guru and His Disciple*, Isherwood explained that he had wanted to write more about Ramakrishna's sexuality. He revealed that Prabhavananda had once "persuaded or intimidated" another author into deleting from her book a passage that suggested Ramakrishna was "a homosexual who had had to struggle hard to overcome his lust for his young disciple later to be known as Vivekananda." Isherwood considered Ramakrishna too frank and childlike to have been able to keep such a thing secret.

He pointed out that Ramakrishna's expressions of love for his young male disciples were "extremely emotional," which could easily be misunderstood. In addition, Ramakrishna sometimes dressed in women's clothes. "As a boy, he did this for a joke," Isherwood wrote, but:

> As an adult, he wished to experience every sort of religious mood, including the mood of a female devotee of Krishna. [...] when he took part in certain pujas, he wore woman's clothes, with ornaments and a wig, to complement his devotional mood. This naturally scandalized

the conventionally pious. Ramakrishna regarded the distinction between the sexes as a part of *maya*, the cosmic illusion; therefore, he can't have thought of himself as being exclusively masculine or feminine.[313]

ON DECEMBER 6, Isherwood and Bachardy "started out on our great pilgrimage" to visit Ramakrishna's birthplace, a tiny village called Kamarpukur in Hooghly, West Bengal. In his letters to Prabhavananda, Isherwood described the journey in minute detail, as if he were trying to stretch his eight days in India into the six weeks originally proposed. He knew how much each crumb of information would mean to Prabhavananda, who lived so far from his monastery and was so anxious that Isherwood be received hospitably. Plain diction and almost halting syntax masked Isherwood's uneasiness about his situation vis-à-vis Bachardy, but they also hinted at his growing emotion and respect for Ramakrishna. He was to adopt a similar understated style in the biography, in which he was almost perversely careful not to try to persuade the reader that Ramakrishna was a divine incarnation nor to convert the reader to Vedanta.

Both Ramakrishna and his wife grew up in small family compounds comprised of mud huts with roofs of straw. Their families were Brahmins, traditionally the priest caste, educated, independent, but poor; Ramakrishna's father farmed rice on half an acre. When Isherwood visited Kamarpukur, a temple to Ramakrishna had already been built, and worshippers were finding their way to it. Isherwood told Prabhavananda that he was more struck by Sarada Devi's birthplace, Jayrambati, "chiefly because the village seems still to be so much as it must have been in Holy Mother's time." Reticent as he had been to make pranams to the swamis at Belur Math, he prostrated before every rural shrine.

Finally, they visited Prabhavananda's own birthplace, an even tinier village called Surmanagar, where Prabhavananda's two elder brothers laid on a meal. "We spoke of you with tears in our eyes," Isherwood reported. They visited the local temple and "reverently stood before the spot where Prabhavananda was born."[314]

In Surmanagar, Prabhavananda had read about Ramakrishna and his disciples Vivekananda and Brahmananda by the time he was fourteen. One day, by chance, he saw Sarada Devi sitting outside a country inn, and he made pranams to her. As Isherwood reported in *My Guru and His Disciple*, Sarada Devi said to Prabhavananda, "Son, haven't I seen you before?" A few years later, when Prabhavananda had become a student at City College of Calcutta, he visited Belur Math and saw the late Vivekananda's room, kept as a shrine. As he left, Prabhavananda bumped into Brahmananda who said, just as Sarada Devi had said, "Haven't I seen you before?" This "spiritual recognition," as Isherwood called it in his 1968 introduction to Prabhavananda's *Religion in Practice*, "was accompanied by an intense emotion of love, such as he had never experienced before in his life."[315] It set off a spiritual ripple which drew Prabhavananda irresistibly to become Brahmananda's disciple.

Isherwood's accounts of Prabhavananda's early life feature a display of anti-British defiance corresponding to Isherwood's own youthful leftism. While he was studying in Calcutta before World War I, Prabhavananda "joined a revolutionary organization and wrote pamphlets for it, which were secretly distributed," wrote Isherwood in *My Guru and His Disciple*. In his 1968 introduction to Prabhavananda's *Religion in Practice*, Isherwood was bolder, calling it "a terrorist organization," the pamphlets "subversive," and declaring that Prabhavananda "resolved never to marry until India won her freedom—thus becoming, as it were, a political monk." When he was not yet twenty, Prabhavananda had taken charge of "some revolvers which had been stolen from a British storehouse: he hid them in his room." A friend "threw a bomb at the Viceroy and had to escape from the country." Another friend was arrested and died in prison, possibly tortured.[316]

Prabhavananda and his friends had no military training, but they had seen it as their duty to overthrow British rule in India, and Isherwood was moved by their vulnerability as well as by their idealism and courage. Abanindra Nath Ghosh, as Prabhavananda had been called before he became a monk, "wasn't even sure how to use his revolver—but they were risking their lives just as much as the veterans of the movement." This was similar to what Isherwood recalled about his father, "that he never fires his revolver because he can't hit anything with it and hates the bang." Such behavior was characteristic of Isherwood's "Anti-Heroic Hero,"[317] described repeatedly in his writing, the figure he devised so that he could group his soldier father among his heroes. It was an imaginative feat to portray inward characteristics shared by his guru and his father, for after all, during the years when Prabhavananda was a student revolutionary in Calcutta, Frank had been an officer of the occupying imperial force in Limerick, where the Irish were trying to achieve Home Rule.

After City College, Prabhavananda had specialized in philosophy at Calcutta University College and visited Belur Math to study Shankara with one of the swamis. When he graduated in 1914 at age twenty-one, he joined the order and abandoned his revolutionary activities. He adopted the view, as Isherwood explained, that "the awakening of India would never come through political action but only through an intensification of the nation's spiritual life."[318] In 1923, the year Isherwood started at Cambridge, Prabhavananda had been sent to America, where he assisted at the Vedanta Center in San Francisco and then founded the center in Portland, Oregon. It was in 1929, the year Isherwood first visited Berlin, that Prabhavananda had moved to Los Angeles at the invitation of Sister Lalita.

———

IN LONDON, ON the last day of 1957, Isherwood experienced something extraordinary. He recorded it in his diary only the following May, observing, "I knew at once that this wasn't merely a dream but a vision—" Prabhavananda thought so, too. It was about Brahmananda, "to whose personality I've never been particularly drawn. I really felt that tremendous love radiating from him, of which Swami so often speaks."

Despite the emotional conflict he had experienced while in India, Isherwood's gift for throwing himself into the mind and mood of someone else allowed him to feel what Prabhavananda felt about Brahmananda. Thus, he was drawn into a chain, directly in contact with his guru's guru: "I dreamed that I had a talk with Brahmananda. He remarked that he didn't know why Ramakrishna moved around at all, since he could see God everywhere. I went away, thought this over, and decided to ask Brahmananda why *he* moved around so much—actually far more than Ramakrishna."[319]

Isherwood's dream, or vision, was about travel and, in a larger sense, about mission. Ramakrishna, Vivekananda, Brahmananda, and Prabhavananda had spent time as wandering beggars after taking their final vows; this was customary. Afterwards, they had continued to move around as teachers. Vivekananda had become the prime missionary for the order and founded Vedanta societies in the U.S. as well as lecturing. Brahmananda "had to travel from one monastery to another in the course of his duties as Head of the Order," as Isherwood was to tell in *My Guru and His Disciple*. Prabhavananda, although he had hoped "to be permitted to lead a contemplative life,"[320] was sent abroad to teach.

Isherwood traveled by choice. When he had a professional commission—to write a book about the war in China, to write a biography of an incarnation of God in India—he was inclined to question and even mock his puffed-up status as a special observer. A journey to a war, a journey to India—were these authentic quests for knowledge and understanding? Or were they merely highbrow sightseeing, a form of escapism, a privilege of the few? Was he making these trips and writing these books for himself or for his readers?

In his New Year's Eve dream, Isherwood was really asking *himself* why he moved around so much if he could see God everywhere.[321] Underneath this question lay another, subtle and insidious: must he write about God in order to testify to his belief? Could he devote himself in silence, or was he devoting himself in order that he could write about it?

In the dream, Brahmananda prostrated to Isherwood, reversing the roles of worshipped and worshipper. At Belur Math, Isherwood had refrained from prostrating, but in the dream, he prostrated in response, "with tears, thinking of my many impurities but feeling at the same time great joy." He "felt Brahmananda's hands touching the back of my head in blessing," which would have been, he noted, "physically impossible" since Brahmananda was sitting six feet above him. He did not ask his question about why Brahmananda moved around, and the purity of his own motives and the sincerity of his quest were silently recognized and blessed. As he walked away, others asked whether Brahmananda had told him "anything you may tell *us*?" In the dream, Isherwood shook his head, weeping; yet already he had begun to feel vain of the experience and "take credit to myself for the great honor of this experience," and he woke up.[322]

The dream admonished Isherwood that, like it or not, he must accept the public responsibility of telling what he had found out about God. He must not allow concern for his reputation as a writer—acclamation or derision—to confuse him. Ramakrishna's biography was a duty and a privilege visited upon him and for which he need not and must not take personal credit. Up until he visited India, his religion had been a private experience shared with a small group of close friends in California. Now it was an institutional matter, public, and out of his hands. Isherwood was never comfortable with the institutional side of Vedanta; the Protestant in him wanted a direct dialogue with the Lord, embodied for him in his guru. His discomfort with Belur Math was like the discomfort of Dostoevsky or Gide with the Church; they all preferred to follow the Gospel with no intermediary.

As to whether Isherwood's dream was a vision or a fulfillment of his wish to make his own choices without guilt, it made no difference provided he wrote the biography of Ramakrishna that the order wanted him to write. This was the mission given him, as the mission of traveling and teaching had been given his guru and his guru's guru. "The Ramakrishna book bores me to death," he was to admit to his diary in 1959, "but that doesn't faze me so much; after all, it's an austerity."[323] And so it was—a spiritual discipline undertaken in order to grow closer to illumination.

WHILE THEY WERE in London, on their journey by stages back to Los Angeles, Isherwood and Bachardy heard that John Van Druten had died. He had been ill for more than a year following a heart attack and a stroke. Van

Druten had made Isherwood an executor of his will, but by February 1958, Van Druten's former boyfriend, Carter Lodge, "blandly informed me that I'm no longer the literary executor. Johnnie made three different wills last year. I wonder who was responsible for that." Isherwood already knew that Van Druten's most recent boyfriend and business partner Walter Starcke had been cut out two weeks before Van Druten's death, and he "was aware of a slight defensiveness on Carter's side."

He felt invested in Van Druten's literary and financial affairs since they shared rights in *I Am a Camera*. Van Druten had the larger portion of their sixty-forty split, and that portion now went to Lodge and Lodge's new partner Dick Foote. To his diary, Isherwood admitted, "I had hoped there would be some money coming to me from Johnnie's will."[324]

Far more than money sparked Isherwood's confusion and regret. Van Druten was only three years older than he, an alter ego, a rival. Isherwood reread some of Van Druten's plays and then Van Druten's diaries. "Piqued because there is very little about me. The salutary truth: he was far less interested in me than I was in him!"[325] He also dreamed about Van Druten, repeatedly, dreams in which Van Druten was dead, and they conversed anyway, Isherwood wanting to ask about God and whether Van Druten still believed in the teachings of his guru, Joel Goldsmith, the Christian Scientist founder of the Infinite Way, but waking too soon for an answer.

Into the midst of his brooding on Van Druten and the possibility of knowledge from beyond the grave came a cable from Richard Bradshaw Isherwood, on April 30: "Deeply regret to tell you Mum seriously ill following stroke writing fondest love." Richard expected Kathleen to die. Isherwood had last seen her en route from India, just after Christmas at Wyberslegh. The news made him feel wretched, but he decided not to tell anyone except Bachardy because he couldn't bear the effort and the distress of grief.

Already the next day, another cable reported his mother was better, but he went on feeling sad and dull. His mother's mortality felt like his own. He revived a phrase from his nursery childhood to express his feeling that he was still in the middle of playing, and that he was not ready to stop simply because Kathleen might be ready to stop: "I think how I might die right now, leaving everything 'out on the floor.' And yet—is there any way to tidy it up—and—far more important—is tidying up really desirable?"

On May 9, he was acutely ill and "spent the night vomiting."[326] Perhaps it was food poisoning. Perhaps it was a symptomatic recollection of the fact that on May 9, 1915, his father, alone and far away, was flattened under a barrage of German artillery fire.

There were a great many strands in Isherwood's life just now; "tidying up" certainly did not feel either desirable or possible. Film writing had captured his attention again—the financially rewarding game that kept him from writing his novels and which would have kept him from his mother's deathbed. The current film job was especially glamorous. "Today I suddenly got the call to see Selznick next Monday—on *Mary Magdalene*," he had written in his diary on March 13.

Isherwood had built a reputation for being able to script religious stories. He was at David Selznick's command until mid-June for $1,250 a week. At first, Selznick wanted Mary Magdalene to be "rather like Brett in *The Sun Also Rises*." Then they agreed on "a Shavian comedy with a background of violence." By the time they were on the eighth draft for the treatment, Isherwood was restless to get back to the Ramakrishna biography and to his novel, and by September, he had turned against Selznick's *Mary Magdalene*: "Loved him, hated her," he quipped to Dodie Smith.[327]

He tried not to mind when Selznick returned to the project in October with a different writer, for he and the Selznicks had become good friends, and Isherwood's extraordinary capacity for intimacy once again sidelined the matter of making movies. Jennifer Jones became a disciple of Prabhavananda, and some years later, in June 1965 when Selznick died after a series of heart attacks, she was to ask Isherwood to be a pallbearer. On the day of the funeral, as he received George Cukor's instructions alongside the likes of Sam Goldwyn and CBS chief executive Bill Paley, Goldwyn—with whom Isherwood had parted ways on such uneasy terms in 1939—was so friendly as to seem positively sentimental. Isherwood recorded in his diary: "He said to me, referring to David, "He was very fond of you," and then added, "We're all very fond of you." So I had to forgive him. If I'm not careful, I soon won't have any mortal enemies left—"[328]

Isherwood's likableness also made him a popular guest on a Hollywood talk show hosted by the composer Oscar Levant during the late 1950s and early 1960s. On a typical evening, as Gavin Lambert recalled about *The Oscar Levant Show*: "Levant cracked a joke or two about his neuroses and medications, played a piece or two by Gershwin or Ravel on the piano, then cued Christopher to recite poetry, tell stories about Auden, Thomas Mann, Virginia Woolf, Berlin, and Hollywood."

Isherwood appeared on the show about a dozen times from 1958 to 1961. Soon he began to be recognized in public, and he had a fight with Levant on the air, for which he blamed his ambivalence: "I didn't want to go on the Levant show any more—so I worked myself into a rage in order to quarrel with him in order not to go on." But Isherwood had cause; the fight was really about his position on World War II.

According to his diary, he had told Levant that he admired Winston Churchill as a man but did not like Churchill's far-right politics. Levant prodded Isherwood to say whether he admired Churchill as a writer, pointing out that Churchill had won a Nobel Prize for his writing and his speeches. Isherwood finally retorted, "Yes, and I think it was disgraceful. They only gave it to him because he's such a celebrity."

On a subsequent show, when Isherwood was not there to defend himself, Levant said, "In 1941, when Churchill was making his great speech, Isherwood was in Hollywood writing *I Am a Camera*." Churchill's famous speech was presumably his "Now we are masters of our fate" address to the Joint Session of the U.S. Congress on December 26, 1941, after the Japanese bombed Pearl Harbor. In fact, Isherwood was then living in Haverford teaching English to German refugees, and of course he didn't write *I Am a Camera*. Levant's public innuendo that Isherwood had shirked his war duty stung painfully, and Isherwood demanded and received an apology from Levant before agreeing to appear again on air.

Levant triggered the show-off that Isherwood disapproved of in himself. After one appearance, Isherwood observed, "I was good, I guess; but I have to stop this ingenue-oldboyish act which is inseparable from appearances with Levant."[329] Nevertheless, he found it hard to resist going on the show, just as he found it hard to resist working with Selznick. According to Bachardy, he didn't want to hurt Levant's feelings, and of course, with Selznick, he wanted the money he could earn. But also, his tortured compulsion toward the limelight tapped his vestigial defiance of his mother. He had his toys out on the floor, and he was determined to play with them.

BACHARDY WAS STILL attending Chouinard, and from February to October 1958, he also took painting lessons from Isherwood's first American boyfriend, Harvey Young. He was often away all day, and once or twice a week he stayed away overnight. In his day-to-day diaries, Isherwood recorded that Bachardy was staying at his parents', but by May 1958, he abandoned this pretense. For himself, he recorded evenings spent with other young male friends, sometimes including sex.

Isherwood thought continually about finding someone who could replace Bachardy, but no single individual ever materialized to fill the role. He imagined romances and sentimental friendships with various boys, imaginings which were to develop and coalesce in the fictional character he named Kenny Potter in *A Single Man*—a boy who attracts, who suggests a possibility, but with whom there is little or no sexual involvement and no disappointment. One of the models for Kenny was Kent Chapman, a student who stopped by with a girlfriend and, as Isherwood wrote, "talked a lot about the

Beat Generation and Venice West."[330] Chapman was a pacifist and an aspiring writer, and Isherwood liked his work.[331] The character Kenny is a "crazy" boy, in the 1950s sense of crazy—curious, a free spirit, a more Whitmanesque type than Bachardy. In the evolving slang of the mid-twentieth century, he might have been called a hobo, later a beatnik, and later still, a hippie.

Occasionally, Isherwood ate alone at home; more often, he ate at Vedanta Place, where on Wednesday evenings he often stayed to perform the reading. He missed Bachardy's company, but he believed in the new modus vivendi. "It really is better, I guess, since his 'freedom' has been officially recognized. Anyhow I know it's the right thing and I'm in favour of it unshakably—in principle." He called it "our design for living" after Noël Coward's 1933 play about a long-lasting three-way love affair.

He found it hard, though, when Bachardy went away for more than one night at a time. In September, Bachardy made a six-day trip with a friend to a party in Yosemite. Isherwood fell into a "[b]lack depression" the day before the departure, and when Bachardy returned, he made a scene. "My possessiveness hates to face the fact that he can have important experiences with other people. Well, I have got to face it. The trick is to stop minding without ceasing to care for him." He especially minded that Bachardy kept him off balance: "He decides at the last minute so I shan't be able to make any plans. Is he aware of this?"[332]

Bachardy had learned in childhood to occupy the central position on his father's lap, where Jess made a nightly favorite of him over Ted. Now, Bachardy was strategic about protecting his claim on Isherwood even as he established his new freedom. Toward the end of September, Bachardy proposed giving up his art studies to "be my secretary and collaborator," as Isherwood recorded. "He said, 'Am I intelligent enough?' 'Do you like me as well as love me?' "[333]

Two weeks later, Bachardy left again with a friend, to spend a long weekend in Ensenada, where he and Isherwood had shared one of their first and most intimate romantic trips in 1953. The friend was Paul Millard, a good-looking actor, who had lived with Speed Lamkin for a few years. Isherwood distracted himself with his sex friend Phil Burns. "We had such a wonderful time together," he wrote in his diary:

> Yet he couldn't make me feel better about Don's going to Ensenada. I *mind* that. It burns deep. I sort of hate him for it.
>
> Yes, and I know one *should* mind. It is inhuman to be reasonable about these things. And yet, in the last resort, one must be fair, must show understanding, must admit that being twenty-four and fifty-four are two worlds.[334]

Bachardy pressed the idea of working together, and they decided to write a play based on *The World in the Evening*, using their recent Far East trip for settings. They called it *The Monsters*, Bachardy's title for his play about his family. A second draft was finished in mid-January 1959, and they mailed it to the Beesleys. Then Bachardy spent a day reading through Isherwood's old reviews, perhaps imagining the reception their play might receive. In February, they gave a copy of *The Monsters* to Cecil Beaton. "Cecil Beaton doesn't like our play *at all*," Isherwood groaned to his diary. "He couldn't find one good word to say about it." Neither could the Beesleys. "Whatever possessed us to write this crap?"[335] Isherwood wondered when he reread *The Monsters*. But while they were working on it, they were as happy as they had been in the early days of their relationship, when Bachardy sat typing Isherwood's novel in the garden house.

Next to Bachardy, "the reallest person" in Isherwood's life, he noted in his diary, was Swami Prabhavananda, and Isherwood realized toward the end of the 1950s that he needed to spend more time with his guru. "I *would* like to be with him often—quietly, without speaking, like a dog." A few months later, he again described himself as a dog, "Tonight I went up to Vedanta Place. Suddenly I was so glad to be sitting on the floor beside Swami—without a word, like his dog." At the beginning of 1959, Prabhavananda urged Isherwood "to come and live in one of the apartments of the new apartment house they are going to build." Isherwood considered it "quite out of the question at present because of Don, and anyhow I do *not* want to become part of the 'congregation.'" He decided not to mention the offer to Bachardy "because I know it would upset him and make him feel insecure."

The offer also upset Isherwood: "I fear it means the start of another come-back-to-Vedanta offensive, such as Swami waged while I was with Caskey."[336] Prabhavananda was just as strategic as Bachardy, and he sensed that the dog beneath Isherwood's skin was longing to devote himself simply and abjectly to a master.

ISHERWOOD NEEDED TO make money. Script jobs were too brief, and schemes to sell material written on spec weren't panning out. "Very low finances," he had written in his diary on March 11, 1959. "And now we have to pay huge assigned-risk insurance as punishment for our accidents."[337] These were car accidents, and some were not their fault, but neither he nor Bachardy were reliable drivers. The worst crash was just before Thanksgiving 1958, when Isherwood fell asleep driving home from dinner and slammed into a parked vehicle, breaking his nose, bruising his eyes, cutting his left knee, and, most painful of all, tearing his pleura. Bachardy had received five traffic tickets, the most recent for running a red light.

Bachardy was just beginning to earn money for his artwork. He completed the semester at Chouinard in triumph, with eleven drawings in the year-end show in the spring of 1959, and he got a part-time job drawing for a department store, the May Company, along with freelance fashion advertising jobs.

Meanwhile, an altogether new source of income presented itself. Isherwood was invited to teach at Los Angeles State College. He described the campus to the Beesleys as "brand new and built, so its faculty members say, in 'late supermarket.' All brick and glass. Wonderfully clean. Perfectly equipped." He signed on in March 1959. "It seems strange, after running away from Cambridge to avoid becoming a don, that now I am a real professor!" he wrote after classes began in the autumn.[338] Even without a university degree, Isherwood was seen as a desirable teacher, and indeed, he had plenty of experience as a private tutor and language teacher.

Another major change was in the offing: Isherwood and Bachardy decided to move away from Sycamore Road. "I do not love the Hine boys," Isherwood wrote in May 1959 about the family across the street. From his window during the last three years, he had often watched the Hine and Stickel children playing in the street and on a vacant lot opposite. The noise shattered his concentration, and he found himself "roaring like a cross old bear."[339] He was to take it all away with him, as with his observations about his neighbors in Berlin, and use it in *A Single Man*. He knew exactly what time the fathers brought the daughters back from swimming; he saw how the mothers dressed to put out their garbage; he watched them mow their lawns; he overheard their conversations. He was to fictionalize himself as a monster in his lair, whom the neighbors feared for his sexual nature.

He and Bachardy looked at a beach house for sale and then 145 Adelaide Drive. What they wanted most of all was privacy and quiet. The Adelaide Drive house was tucked beneath the lip of the canyon at the end of Ocean Avenue. It had nearly a third of an acre, secluded by vegetation. The rear walls were overhung and protected by the cliff behind it. In front, it had panoramic views of the canyon floor, the beach, the ocean to the west and the mountains to the north. They made an offer in early June and sold Sycamore Road by the end of July, planning to move in the autumn.

Meanwhile, Bachardy arranged an entirely separate option for himself, like an escape clause, borrowing a guesthouse in West Hollywood to use as a studio. It belonged to Paul Millard, the actor with whom he had been conducting an affair. Isherwood visited the guesthouse in mid-July and returned to pose for Bachardy in mid-August, but he did not know how involved

Bachardy was with Millard. In any case, Isherwood had renewed his own friendship with Jim Charlton. One night, when Bachardy was staying in town, Isherwood and Charlton got drunk together, "and we more or less got back to our old relationship, which was very nice."[340]

Before the move, Isherwood and Bachardy took a summer vacation to New York and Europe, and Bachardy accompanied Isherwood to Wyberslegh, where they arrived the day before Isherwood's fifty-fifth birthday. Kathleen had "recovered largely from the stroke," though she had lost sight in one eye and movement in one arm. Richard, though, had "a wild look of dismayed despair which I have never seen before," wrote Isherwood. The house was in a worse state than ever, and Richard cooked them a sickening meal. He showed no sign of being able to cope alone.

Isherwood and Bachardy took Kathleen out to supper, and the next day, they went for a drive that Isherwood had made countless times—in his childhood with his grandfather in the horse-drawn coach emblazoned with the Bradshaw Isherwood coat of arms; in the 1920s with family friends who had large open cars; in taxis; on bicycles. The two great loves of his life were in the car with him that day, Kathleen Isherwood and Don Bachardy. One had seen him in and the other would see him out.

He experienced the drive, as he experienced so many of the most satisfying moments of his life, as partly real and partly imaginary, enhanced by the power of a favorite book: "—Glossop, the Snake [Pass], Castleton, Miller's Dale, Buxton; and the weather was perfect. It was like that sinister summer passage in *Wuthering Heights*, when they go up to Penistone Crag and it is so lovely, but the shadow of the oncoming winter and death is over everything."[341] This was the last birthday he spent with Kathleen, who had cared so much to celebrate birthdays with him throughout his childhood.

145 ADELAIDE DRIVE, SANTA MONICA, 1959

"The day before yesterday we moved here—to 145 Adelaide Drive," Isherwood wrote on October 2, 1959. "We can see the hills from our bed. Don is so delighted, it warms my heart. But this is a real house, a long in-and-out place of many rooms and half-rooms, passageways and alcoves." Nearly half a century earlier, Kathleen had described Isherwood's childhood home in Limerick—Roden House—in similar phrases, "all surprises—little passages and endless doors running in and out."[342] The Adelaide Drive house was a kind of burrow for the Animals, hidden below the level of the street above. It was built "in Californiano style, stucco and a heavy tiled roof," as Isherwood told the Beesleys. "The living-room is paved with the most attractive old tiles; the other floors are hardwood. We have a fireplace, but oh how it smokes! This is to be investigated."[343] Of course, the houses were completely different, yet at Roden House, too, the floors had been stained wood, and the chimneys had smoked so badly that some rooms were uninhabitable in winter.

Isherwood was "home." This was the house where he was to live with Bachardy for the rest of his life. He was to inhabit the physical space so completely that it became part of his interior psyche, gradually suffused with the lightness and magic of his devotion to the immaterial.

Bachardy was repainting the rooms as Isherwood sat describing it all to the Beesleys by letter, and Isherwood soon agreed to expensive remodeling. Workmen removed beams from the roof, replastered walls and mended the floor. Shutters were added to the living-room windows, and Bachardy painted them sky blue. Thus, he created the background for David Hockney's double portrait, *Christopher Isherwood and Don Bachardy*, conceived eight years later in the living room at Adelaide Drive.

Isherwood had accepted a second semester of teaching at L.A. State: "So at least we'll have *some* money."[344] On Tuesdays, he taught "Selected British Authors" and "20th Century British Literature." On Thursday mornings, "Selected British Authors" met again, and sometimes, on the way home, Isherwood stopped at Brooks Steam Baths where, as Bachardy later recalled, Thursday was queer day. Then he would go on to the Vedanta Society. He also helped with rehearsals for a student production of *Hamlet* that autumn, harking back to the days of his toy theater.

His classes recapitulated the literary history of his generation. He talked about Auden, the Spanish Civil War, Robert Graves's *Goodbye to All That*, Cyril Connolly's *Enemies of Promise*, Forster's *Howards End* and *Aspects of the Novel*. In his teaching as in his writing, he pushed himself to deliver something that mattered. He labored over Huxley's *After Many a Summer*: "It is *so* dry and prissy. I know how my students' stomachs will be turned by it."[345] Yet he was determined to find a tone of voice, a persona, that could bridge the gap between the high culture of Bloomsbury and the easygoing youth of California.

He was immediately successful and popular. When he began his second semester, in early February, nearly eighty students signed up for his evening class, and the college library created an exhibit: "'Christopher Isherwood— Man of Letters,' with the foreign translations of my books which I gave them, plus newspaper articles, etc. etc. I was really touched and pleased and surprised." He was also honored with a reception: "The president shook my hand and told me, 'You're the kind of person we want here.' How often I have been told the opposite!"[346]

He secured another teaching job for the autumn of 1960, at the University of California at Santa Barbara. From his public identity as a college literature professor, he was to create the fictional character George in *A Single Man*: based on himself and on the persona he developed for teaching, and yet separate.

"TED SEEMS LIKE he is getting ready to have another of his breakdowns after all this time," Isherwood recorded toward the end of January 1960. Bachardy got jumpy, partly in reaction. His car broke down, and he had to share Isherwood's for a week. He began saying he shouldn't be living in Santa Monica at all: "*his* studio, *his* school, *his* gym are all in town."[347] After only five months in the new house, Isherwood found this irritating.

He was conscious that he was adding to the tension by conducting an affair on the nights when Bachardy stayed in town. He had met the young man, Paul Kennedy, at a New Year's Eve party at Jerry Lawrence's house. When Bachardy found out, his distress was increased by the recollection that it was after a party at Jerry Lawrence's that he and Isherwood had spent their first night together in 1953, but, after all, he had taken his Paul—Paul Millard—to Ensenada. The liaisons with Paul Kennedy continued for about a year, and the relationship was to figure in *A Single Man*.

Ted committed himself to a sanatorium, and from there he made collect calls to the new house. Bachardy refused them, but the pressure turned him against the very domestic stability and commitment he craved. He was determined not to depend solely on Isherwood. He needed something else, as Isherwood needed Vedanta, and he told Isherwood that "he'd like to have an apartment near school and spend about four nights there a week." On February 10, Ted ran away from the sanatorium and got through to Isherwood on the telephone, asking if he could stay at Adelaide Drive. "No, I said, very firmly."[348]

So Isherwood and Bachardy reached the end of their first seven years together. It was partly the irrational in Bachardy that held Isherwood's attention, the unpredictable internal struggle between contradictory impulses that Bachardy himself could hardly control, along with his reckless passion for life.

That winter and spring, Isherwood read aloud to Bachardy from Walt Whitman's *Leaves of Grass*. He recorded that Bachardy "shed tears" listening to "As I Lay with My Head in Your Lap, Camerado" and "Vigil Strange," about outlaw love and about the death of a companion. "Why are the animals so happy, nowadays?" asked Bachardy a few weeks later.[349] Neither of them ventured a reason.

THE ISHERWOOD–BACHARDY MÉNAGE was attractive to others who wanted something like it. Charles Laughton became interested in buying the house next door, 147 Adelaide Drive, "so as to have a place to get away from Elsa."[350] He was involved with an English model and would-be actor, Terry Jenkins, and he had invited Jenkins to visit from England. He made an offer on 147 in July 1960.

Isherwood had known Laughton's wife, Elsa Lanchester, since 1958, when she considered taking the lead in *Emily Ermengarde*. He soon became closer to Laughton, whom he had admired on stage and in films since the 1920s. This made Lanchester jealous. Recently, Laughton had been touring the U.S. with dramatic readings from Shakespeare, the Bible, and other classic literature, and he asked Isherwood to help him with a one-man play about Socrates. Isherwood confided to his diary: "I think his chief reason for wanting to work with me is so he can talk freely about his private life. And why not?"[351]

They reviewed Laughton's existing material in April 1960, meeting twice a week at the house he shared with Lanchester on Curson Avenue in Hollywood. Then Laughton was unexpectedly hospitalized with gallbladder trouble, but they began work again during the summer, framing a three-part piece: first, Socrates's political thinking, then his ideas on love, and last his trial and execution by suicide. They read the *Republic*, the *Symposium*, the *Phaedrus*, the *Gorgias*, the *Apology*, the *Crito*, meeting to choose "bits we like," and cutting and pasting them to "see how they all fit together."[352] While they were still at work, Laughton began trying out the material, and Isherwood's excerpts from the *Phaedrus* were recorded live and released on a double album of some of Laughton's favorite readings.[353]

Laughton reminded Isherwood of Van Druten, "his eagerness to be the bright boy in class who puts his hand up, and his underlying inferiority." Sometimes Isherwood felt bored by Laughton "because he's stupid, vain, *and* pretentious [...] *much* stupider than Johnnie." But he also identified with Laughton and tried to understand him both as an actor and a homosexual. He had seen Laughton's Lear at Stratford-on-Avon in the summer of 1959, and recalled: "I cried twice; it was wonderful on the heath, with the Fool clinging to his enormous skirts, and wonderful at the 'Never, never, never, never' end. [...] Charles is a megalomaniac. [...] I am fond of him, though."

I do like monsters. Charles says he is a monster. And that I am one, too." Matching himself with Laughton made Isherwood feel more contented as a middle-aged lover. "Charles and I wallow naked in the pool like a pair of old hippos."[354]

Early in July, Laughton insulted Bachardy, who had asked him to sit for a portrait. In his diary, Isherwood saw Bachardy's side, writing that Bachardy took the insult "perfectly; he left, smiling pleasantly." But Isherwood feared "a tremendous, slowly growing feud."[355] Lanchester had already been rude to Bachardy.

Bachardy began spending nights in town for the first time in over a month. During one absence, he told Isherwood he was apartment sitting for Paul Millard who was in Europe, but when Isherwood phoned Bachardy at Millard's apartment about an appointment, Millard picked up the phone, already home from Europe, and professing not to know where Bachardy was. Isherwood turned to his diary, "sick with worry." Eventually Bachardy phoned and persuaded Isherwood that he had been ill, had stayed at a friend's after discovering Millard was already home, and hadn't told a lie; Isherwood, relieved, accepted this. Bachardy had taken great pains to conceal his long-running affair with Millard, but "Chris must have sensed what was going on," Bachardy reflected years later. "Imagine what I was dealing with at the other end, handling Paul!"

Bachardy was also concealing other affairs. It was understood between Isherwood and Bachardy that they had sex outside their relationship, but neither wanted to report everything he was doing. "I identified so strongly with Chris," Bachardy later said. "I knew he kept so much of his earlier life from me. Was he going to deny me the adventures he had had? Never."[356] In fact, Bachardy's instinct for autonomy helped to preserve the relationship. Isherwood never succeeded in fully understanding everything Bachardy did, nor turning him into material for a story as with so many other friends and lovers.

When Terry Jenkins arrived from England, Laughton expected Bachardy to befriend him, and even though Bachardy ended up liking Jenkins, the implied comparison made him feel trapped. On August 21, Bachardy and Isherwood got drunk, and according to Isherwood, Bachardy "had one of his most violent and apparently unmotivated 'Black Tom' attacks." He played at wrecking the car, then ran away. When he came back, he smashed a memento, "our dear old Mexican money pig that Julie [Harris] gave us." Isherwood feared that "these attacks may become really insane like Ted's." When they discussed it a few days later, Bachardy explained that the attack was not unmotivated. "I forget how difficult it is to live with me—I am so dominating, etc."

The "Black Tom" attack came on as Isherwood and Bachardy got home from watching a rehearsal for *A Taste of Honey*. Tony Richardson, the British director, was bringing his stage production from the Royal Court Theatre in London to the Biltmore. Gavin Lambert had introduced him. "Tony is interesting—quite sly and subterranean, and with a wild manic side to him (after brandy) which promises great talent. Don thinks him very attractive," wrote Isherwood after they entertained Richardson for supper one night at Adelaide Drive. "Yes, there is something really stimulating in Tony—a wildness."

Isherwood did not know, and he evidently never found out, that Richardson and Bachardy had begun an affair during the two nights that Bachardy claimed he was apartment sitting for Paul Millard. It was to go on intermittently for years, and as with George Platt Lynes, Bachardy was to consider leaving Isherwood.

While he was in Los Angeles, Richardson was also directing a film adapted from William Faulkner's novels *Sanctuary* and *Requiem for a Nun*. Isherwood and Bachardy watched him direct at Fox in August: "He told me he loves directing—would like to direct all the time, without even bothering what became of the pictures," wrote Isherwood.[357] Indeed, in his real life, Richardson was generally at the center of a clique animated by talent and complicated sexual energies that he manipulated with the same creative intensity he brought to directing, sometimes with sadistic relish. From the beginning of their friendship, Isherwood was both attracted and wary. In the coming decade, he was to work on a number of adaptations for Richardson, yet he always kept his distance.

Bachardy also worked for Richardson. He was hired to make some "bad" drawings to be used as props in *A Taste of Honey*. Then he did portraits of the cast to be hung in the theater lobby when *A Taste of Honey* opened in New York. This was to afford Richardson and Bachardy time alone in Manhattan.

ISHERWOOD WORKED UNRELENTINGLY that summer to finish a rough draft of the last section of *Down There on a Visit* before his fifty-sixth birthday in August 1960. This was in spite of a crippling slipped disk, resulting from a fall on Tony Richardson's garage steps. Often, he boosted his focus by taking Dexamyl. Bachardy took Dexamyl, too, every day, with his doctor's approval, to ward off "storms of anxiety, resentment and melancholia."[358]

Isherwood was driven partly by his reluctance to think about the death of his mother. Prabhavananda, alerted by Amiya now living in England as the

Countess of Sandwich, telephoned on June 8 to warn him that Kathleen was fading. On June 14 there was a letter from Richard and then on June 16 a cable saying Kathleen was dead. "I am sad, yes," wrote Isherwood, "but I don't really feel M's loss. Perhaps I never shall, perhaps I've been through it already. My feelings aren't important, anyway."[359]

He had, in fact, self-defensively dived into work on June 10, following Swami's call. In addition to the last part of *Down There on a Visit*, he had begun the introduction to a long-planned book of selections from Vivekananda, *What Religion Is: In the Words of Vivekananda*. This was being assembled by John Yale at the Vedanta Society, though Isherwood had intended to do the book himself as early as 1942 and had even aspired to writing a biography of Vivekananda who, as Bachardy later recalled, was his favorite Vedanta author.[360]

Isherwood's feelings about Kathleen assailed him indirectly. Stravinsky's frailty as he prepared for a South American tour warned Isherwood "that I may not see him again if he goes," and this reminded Isherwood how he had hurried back into Kathleen's bedroom at Wyberslegh the summer before "to give her what I guessed might be a goodbye kiss—an extra one after we'd already said goodbye."

Richard reported that Kathleen was cremated and her ashes buried at Wyberslegh Hall, "'Close to the remains of her two dear pussies.' That makes me cry as I write it," Isherwood admitted, "but I know that's because pussies are part of the great sensitive area in my feelings surrounding Don."[361] He was close to recognizing how alike Kathleen and Don were: both nicknamed Kitty, both intense, obstinate, passionate, sometimes irrational, sensitive, energetic, intuitive, beautiful to look at, with a gift for intimacy, controlling, jealous, possessive and yet bound to betray Isherwood with another lover, in Kathleen's case, his father. Isherwood did not seem to be aware how hard he was working to recreate with Bachardy the family circle that had been shattered when his father died.

ISHERWOOD AND LAUGHTON heard from Isherwood's film agent that the impresario Sol Hurok "believes the Socrates project is really box office, and will back it," so they began meeting again at 147 Adelaide Drive. Laughton had been back in the hospital to have two gallstones removed, and he appeared with a chauffeur and a masseur, "Like a punch-drunk old fighter groggily declaring that he'll make a comeback."

Clear-eyed as he was about the drain on his time and energy, Isherwood could not resist Laughton's charisma and dramatic gifts: "He is an old man of [the] sea and would dearly love to spend every moment sitting on my back," wrote Isherwood in his diary, "and yet I can't refuse him and anyhow I'm fond of him."[362]

When Isherwood launched himself at U.C. Santa Barbara on September 29, 1960, he measured his performance against Laughton: "Really, the fuss these old hams make! What a temperament *I* could have thrown over my first lecture at Santa Barbara last Thursday! As a matter of fact, it was a truly smashing success."

Later that year, he performed with enormous confidence at a writers' conference at Berkeley, "nearly cracked the mike during the fishing scene from 'Mr. Lancaster' and made Mark and Ruth Schorer roar with laughter." Schorer, the novelist and biographer, was a professor of English at Berkeley and department chair. Soon there was another job, at UCLA, where Isherwood held out for a large sum of money to give three Sunday-evening lectures for the University Extension—open to mature and continuing education students as well as undergraduates. After his final UCLA lecture, "a couple who were present sent me a box of red roses, as if I were an opera singer!"[363]

Isherwood's lectures were always about writing, and he generally read aloud from the works he discussed. At Santa Barbara, he gave eight lectures that focused for the first time on himself—why he wrote, what influenced him, his idea (referencing Francis Bacon) of the nerve of interest in a novel, and his relation as a writer with theater, films, and religion. The Santa Barbara series, called "A Writer and His World," was broadcast on the radio in 1961, and a contemporary transcript was published after Isherwood's death.[364] His lecture style was congenial and discursive, in contrast to his writing which was always sharpened by economy.

His first Santa Barbara lecture, "Influences," introduced autobiographical material that he was to develop in greater depth in *Kathleen and Frank*—including the history of the Bradshaw Isherwoods and his father's prescribed role as a second son. He suggested how his father's career in the army, where Frank's gifts for music, painting, and acting were not relevant and where Frank's personality offered a mismatch to any obvious warrior ideal, had helped to form his own ideal of the Anti-Heroic Hero.

He told the anecdotes about his father using his sword to toast bread, never firing his revolver because he "hated the bang," and leading his final military charge carrying only "a small cane."[365] He made clear that his idea of Forster as the Anti-Heroic Hero stemmed from feelings about his father, and he introduced the dark forerunner to his Anti-Heroic Hero, Judge John Bradshaw, who sentenced King Charles I to death, telling his Santa Barbara audience that he had often considered writing a historical novel about Bradshaw. He was intrigued in particular that after Charles was executed in 1649,

Bradshaw evinced signs of revulsion over his own role, picking a fight with Oliver Cromwell and denouncing "the use of force, the use of soldiers to create a military dictatorship." In short, Isherwood was suggesting that after the execution, Bradshaw turned toward pacifism. According to Isherwood's lecture, Bradshaw further revealed his inward change by showing mercy to the Quakers. George Fox, founder of the Quaker Society of Friends, recorded in his journal that Bradshaw was one of only two judges to give the Quakers a fair trial when they were "being persecuted by everybody in England."[366]

Bradshaw's uncomfortable fit with his public self resounded in the schism between atoners for and celebrators of the regicide in the Bradshaw Isherwood family, and in Frank, and in Isherwood's own ambivalence.[367] Isherwood was to explain of himself in *Kathleen and Frank* that in his own youth: "He loathed Puritanism and Puritans, which made it impossible for him to side wholeheartedly with the Parliament. He rejoiced in the Restoration because it did away with the Puritans' killjoy ordinances and brought back whores, orgies and sexy plays. But he hated nearly all monarchs—"

Isherwood liked to "boast of being descended from the Regicide,"[368] but he was simplifying for effect and asserting his right to choose his ancestors, for he was not actually descended from Judge Bradshaw, who had no surviving children. Isherwood was in fact descended from John's elder brother, Henry, a colonel in the parliamentary army, who was tried as a regicide and acquitted. Thus, in a sense, he was descended from the original Uncle Henry, and like Uncle Henry, Isherwood vacillated toward Catholicism and experienced the guilt felt by so many in his family.

Through explaining himself to his American students, Isherwood unlocked new self-understanding. In November 1960, Genevieve Watson Haight, who trained English teachers at U.C. Santa Barbara, invited him to her popular children's literature class, where he talked spontaneously about how his literary imagination had begun to form in childhood, focused from the outset on the border between fantasy and reality in Beatrix Potter, H.G. Wells, and Harrison Ainsworth, whose fictional worlds seemed so like, so proximate to, his real world. In Mrs. Haight's class, he also held forth on fairy tales, in particular Hans Christian Andersen, in whose stories "the stark truth is told about suffering and love and death."[369]

He toyed with making Genevieve Haight into a fictional colleague at the imaginary college St. Tomas State in *A Single Man* and drafted a lunch scene with a Dr. Cynthia Leach, once an Oxford don and the author of an academic study of Beatrix Potter. In the end, the character he devised was the more sophisticated but less personally revealing "handsome young New Yorker, Sarah Lawrence-trained, the daughter of a rich family" whose specialty is not described.[370]

After the years of running from his past, Isherwood was getting ready to take it on, to explore his psychological makeup more deeply than ever before and to look for a way to articulate what he was to call, under Jung's influence, his personal mythology.

Teaching brought him faculty friends at U.C. Santa Barbara. Douwe Stuurman, a classicist who taught English, and Howard Warshaw, the painter whose classes Bachardy had fled in 1954, sometimes put him up overnight. Both were straight and married. Alcohol flowed in the evenings with them and other colleagues.

But "the most interesting" acquaintance Isherwood made that autumn was in Los Angeles, with the young Texan writer John Rechy, who was the same age as Bachardy. Rechy had already published his story about the white-wedding fantasy of a downtown Los Angeles queen, "The Fabulous Wedding of Miss Destiny." He showed Isherwood additional material for the collection in which it was to appear, *City of the Night*, and they discussed Rechy's writing. "One of the characteristic things about John is his fear of inventing; he wants to record everything exactly as it happened. So I spent a lot of time trying to convince him that this would be undesirable and anyhow impossible."

Isherwood was keenly interested in Rechy's life as a gay hustler. The Rechy characteristics Isherwood noted in his diary hit points of resemblance with himself—exhibitionism, a fascination with mirrors, compartmentalized friendships: "And, with his 'mental' friends, he is exaggeratedly nonphysical; he hates to be touched, even in the most casual way. (I remember how Edward [Upward] used to laugh at me for this, at Cambridge.) I think he thinks of himself as being always in disguise."

Rechy became friendly with Gavin Lambert as well as with Isherwood and Bachardy, and his portrayal of all three in his 1967 novel *Numbers* caused turmoil. He used the Adelaide Drive ménage to represent middle-class homosexual life peopled by the "creative and sophisticated" among whom Rechy's avatar Johnny Rio—once a hustler, still addicted to cruising—craves but cannot find understanding. Rechy took trouble in the novel to praise the artwork of his Bachardy character, but Bachardy was not susceptible to this kind of flattery, and he insisted that his drawing of Rechy which appeared on the cover of *Numbers* be removed from future editions.

Even without Bachardy's drawing, insiders could not miss the connection. Speed Lamkin had named his Isherwood character in *The Easter Egg Hunt* Sebastian Saunders, and Rechy echoed him by using the name Sebastian Michaels. Both implied an unwelcome comparison with Evelyn Waugh's Sebastian Flyte in *Brideshead Revisited* (1945). "Sebastian" of course conjured the saint riddled with arrows, often read as a masochistic or homosexual figure, and the surname "Flyte" had marked Waugh's expatriate character as escapist. The wounded foot of Sebastian Flyte's German lover had symbolized how the relationship crippled them both. Isherwood was acutely sensitive to any comparisons with Waugh, with just cause, as will be shortly explored.

In *Numbers*, Johnny Rio declines an invitation to stay the night with Sebastian Michaels because he knew he would afterwards feel "the famous writer had listened to him only because of a sexual interest and not—as Johnny wished—because he wanted to be an understanding friend."[371] This concealed Rechy's real-life sexual liaisons with Isherwood, liaisons which Isherwood recorded in his day-to-day diaries.

TO BACHARDY'S DELIGHT, Cecil Beaton and the artist and fashion illustrator R.R. Bouché both praised the cast drawings for *A Taste of Honey*. Julie Harris hosted Bachardy in New York while he was supervising the framing and hired him to do another set of posters for her upcoming play, *Little Moon of Alban*. Then Tennessee Williams requested posters for *Period of Adjustment*. Bachardy made a second trip to New York in mid-October and came home to Santa Monica on November 4, "the longest stretch of time we've ever been separated," Isherwood recorded.[372]

Bachardy's work was now on display in three New York theaters. His secret affair with Tony Richardson was absorbing and difficult, and he was constantly aware of competitors for Richardson's attention. He developed a painful stress-related stomach complaint like Isherwood's, perhaps an ulcer. He had also began a sexual relationship with Tennessee Williams.

Howard Warshaw asked to see Bachardy's work, so Isherwood and Bachardy took some drawings to Santa Barbara. Warshaw "praised the portraits very highly." Nevertheless, Isherwood observed that "Don is going through a deep depression, with all his masochism in full play. After the success in New York—nothing." Warshaw's attention aside, Bachardy was again being ignored by Isherwood's older friends at dinners out. He told Isherwood that he wanted an independent life, "after all he had given me so much of his life, and it was time that counted. [. . .] he never feels the house belongs to him. It isn't his home. Etc., etc. With much hatred of me in his voice."[373] Almost immediately, there were apologies and a rapprochement, a pattern that had been developing for some time.

By the end of the year, Bachardy found a path forward. An acquaintance, Russell McKinnon, offered to pay for art study in London. Isherwood, who felt that his mother had tried to control his own professional future, encouraged Bachardy to go. Stephen Spender arranged for Bachardy to attend the Slade School of Fine Art headed by the painter William Coldstream, his and Isherwood's longtime friend.

In the month remaining to them, Isherwood and Bachardy grew closer than they had ever been. Isherwood wrote in his diary on the last day of 1960, "Yesterday evening—I forgot to record—we did something we haven't done in ages; danced together to records on the record player. A Beatrix Potter scene—the Animals' Ball."[374]

Bachardy left Santa Monica on January 23, 1961. On what Isherwood described as "one of his last minute whirls," he rushed Isherwood to an art nouveau exhibition at the L.A. County Museum, then to Hollywood to see (again) Buñuel's *Los Olvidados*, then for drinks with Paul Millard, then to UCLA to see Pirandello's play *Six Characters in Search of an Author* from which they had to be towed away because Bachardy damaged the car while parking. Back at home, Bachardy tried to draw Isherwood for the next lecture brochure, then he packed and wrote letters. They stayed up all night.

They had agreed to avoid the tension of an airport parting, so Isherwood drove Bachardy to the Miramar Hotel to catch a bus to the airport at 6:55 a.m. "We both cried as the bus went off." Much later Bachardy recalled: "I knew he thought that I wasn't coming back. It was one of the worst moments of my life. There was nothing I could say to him. I knew by how upset I was just how important he was to me. That I could never leave him. We were both sobbing."[375]

8

Existential Isherwood: The Outsider (1961–1964)

During the next three years, Bachardy was to establish himself as an independent adult and a professional artist, and tensions between him and Isherwood were to mount to breaking point. The pair were to split, then come together again in a new, recalibrated relationship, with Bachardy the dominant partner. Isherwood was to let go control by drawing on everything he had learned from Prabhavananda and from his past relationships as well as by exploring his emotional circumstances in his writing. He was to complete the four stories that comprise *Down There on a Visit*, stories that revisited the sequence of crises during the first half of the century which had defined his position at the edge of mainstream culture, and he was to write the masterpiece of his maturity, *A Single Man*, creating another unforgettable character, George, the outsider, uniquely free and joyful with the semi-secret of his homosexuality despite the difficulties of solitude and advancing middle age. George was to become a star in his own right, like Sally Bowles, through stage and film adaptations, such as Tom Ford's 2009 movie.

ISHERWOOD HAD WRITTEN over five hundred pages of *Down There on a Visit*, revised and then scrapped them with increasing frequency until January 1959, when he had finally decided that "all the fantasy and hell-stuff can wait." By mid-March that year, in a characteristic act, he had jettisoned everything: "I think I have got to forget all about what has been written so far."[1]

Instead, it was to be three character studies which "are related, through the character of the narrator, to each other." He listed "Mr. Lancaster. Ambrose. Paul." He went on to finish "Mr. Lancaster" in less than a month and conceived a fourth, "Waldemar," to come third in the sequence. "Mr. Lancaster" is set in 1928 and describes the narrator's visit to a family friend in Bremen, Germany, a visit which coincides with the start of his career as a professional writer. "Ambrose" is set in 1933 and recounts the narrator's sojourn on a Greek island, where he finds that he cannot settle on a utopian life away from the mainstream. "Waldemar" is set in England during the Munich Crisis in 1938, when the narrator's inward crisis aligns with the world political crisis. He encounters a pair of lovers arriving in England, one English, one German, and recognizes that such a destiny was never his. In "Paul," set in Los Angeles in the early 1940s and in Paris and Berlin as late as 1953, the narrator turns to the life of the spirit, testing his new faith through another religious convert far more troubled than he.

Isherwood mined the material he had rediscovered at Wyberslegh in the winter of 1947—diaries from 1933 to 1938 and drafts for stories begun during that period—as well as his diaries written since arriving in the U.S. But twenty years had passed and a world war had intervened, changing everything. So he decided on an unusual time frame—the novel was to be set in both the present and the past. "The Narrator, myself, speaks from the viewpoint of himself today. But he also projects into the character [...] I am therefore able to describe the feelings of both parties."[2]

Down There on a Visit was Isherwood's existentialist novel, his account of himself as a Dostoevskyan Underground Man, a bitter, sour, alienated talent who does not fit in, a crank, a monster, an outsider seeking an authentic life. His narrator revolts, first, against his background and education (in "Mr. Lancaster"), and second, against his fellow rebels (in "Ambrose"). He suffers a full-blown moral crisis and rejects even his own once dearly held fantasies of his romantic future (in "Waldemar") before choosing a new way of life, the path of the mystic, about which he continues to experience agonies of scepticism (in "Paul") but a path by which he believes true freedom can be attained.

Isherwood had known for a long time that the novel could not be about a visit to a fourteenth-century Christian Hell like Dante's, because, as he was to tell an interlocutor plainly in 1967: "I simply do not accept the Dantean conception of damnation or his classified approach to Sin—as you will realize if you have read our comments on the Patanjali Yoga Aphorisms."[3] But it took enormous imaginative effort and discipline to loosen the grip of the Christian mythology in which he had been raised and to keep his newly adopted mythology before him—to replace Dante with Vedanta.

PRABHAVANANDA AND ISHERWOOD intended their Patanjali yoga aphorisms as "a practical aid to the spiritual life; an aid that can be used by the devotees of any religion—Hindu, Christian, or other." Yoga doctrine had been "handed down from prehistoric times," as Isherwood told in a foreword to the yoga aphorisms, and Patanjali restated it "for the man of his own period" sometime between the fourth century B.C. and the fourth century A.D. Prabhavananda and Isherwood restated it again for twentieth-century Westerners. Their Patanjali yoga aphorisms offer a lucid manual to the practices and beliefs which lay behind Isherwood's new novel.

In their commentary to Sutra 19, Prabhavananda and Isherwood explained that a Hindu

> believes in many planes of existence other than this earthly one—some infernally painful, some celestially pleasant. To these planes we may go for a while, after death, impelled by the karmas we have accumulated here on earth. But we shall not remain in any one of them eternally. When the good or the bad karma which earned them is exhausted, we shall be reborn into mortal life—the only condition, according to Hindu belief, in which we are free to make the act of yoga, to unite ourselves with the Atman.

Karma is an act and also the consequences of this act—"what we call our 'fate.'"[4] The fate of those in Dante's Hell cannot be reversed or escaped; karma, though, like a debt or indenture, can be slowly worked off, even if it takes several lifetimes. Isherwood did not believe in Original Sin or the Fall; he believed in many planes of existence and in the repeated, constant opportunity in mortal life to be united with the Atman, the name for Brahman within each person.

In the autumn of 1957, Albert Camus had won the Nobel Prize in Literature, and Isherwood, always alert to this honor, read Camus' 1956 book *The Fall*, which, as it turned out, already occupied the fictional ground he himself was treading. "Have you noticed that the concentric canals of Amsterdam are like the circles of hell?" asks Camus' main character, Jean-Baptiste Clamence, buttonholing the reader, his double and his initiate.[5] Clamence is referring to Dante's nine circles of Hell in the *Inferno*. Camus situates Clamence in a bar called the Mexico City, referencing a high place which symbolically contrasts with Amsterdam's position below sea level, and further introducing the metaphysical geography of Dante's *Divine Comedy*.

This coincidence, including Mexico City, didn't leave Isherwood much imaginative elbow room. He had largely dismissed Camus and also Sartre when he read them in the late 1940s. He called Camus' *The Stranger* "one of the classic bogus masterpieces of this century" and thought Sartre's *No Exit* equally "phoney." On the other hand, he admired Camus' *The Plague* for its "anti-heroic" message "that suffering and death are not romantic and that even a brave and noble doctor would rather not have to fight a plague." In a draft for *Down There on a Visit*, Isherwood tried to square his problem with a joke. Before setting off to visit Hell for a *Life* magazine story, his narrator pitches a TV show to a producer called Timmy Thomas who tells him "that what was wrong with my idea was that I had never read a French writer called Kay-moose." The book to read, says Timmy Thomas, is "La Shoot."[6] (*La Chute* is Camus' title in its original French.) Isherwood abandoned this joke along with the draft, though in the published book he was to reuse the name Timmy—reaching back to his nursery nemesis, cousin Timmy Toogood—for a different, more irritating rival.

The collision with Camus focused Isherwood's intention. In a letter to the Beesleys, he explained without naming authors that he had wrestled the novel away from any crowded general trend back to the unique narrative of his personal experience: "It is about mental hells. And it is also about the attitudes to life which one individual can hold at different times—engagement versus disengagement, to use the French post-war jargon." In the same letter, he wrote, "it's about me, at four different ages, with four different attitudes."[7]

Even this personal space—"me, at four different ages, with four different attitudes"—was bristling with competitors. "[W]e are someone other than the 'me' that we have called ourselves," John Van Druten had written in the foreword to his 1957 memoir, *The Widening Circle*, and he made the point again and again. "Whatever I mean by 'me' today is a semblance, a personality that results from everything that has ever happened to me, but it is more than that."[8]

Isherwood had read Van Druten's memoir before it was published, and he had dismissed it privately as "dreadfully sententious."[9] The book is indeed shallow and dull; after more than two hundred pages, Van Druten still gestures only vaguely toward the non-dualistic teaching of Vedanta and Joel Goldsmith's Infinite Way, "I know only that none of these parts of 'me'[...] is me at all, and that there is another and eternal me outside of them." He simply did not possess the ability to reveal in a prose memoir the self that is part of a larger metaphysical self, nor did he possess the ability to show how the imaginary characters he created in his plays "are a part of me."[10]

Isherwood *did* possess this ability, and he knew that he did. Van Druten's death was another push for him to turn to the long-neglected material that was his alone after the years hidden in suitcases at Penmaenmawr and Wyberslegh. The material offered a fresh opportunity to take back his identity from the man who had hijacked it with such astonishing commercial success in *I Am a Camera*, and it also offered a way to explore the relation between the changing self and the larger reality that Vedantists call Brahman.

Isherwood made rivalry with other storytellers into a propulsive theme in *Down There on a Visit*. Jostling with their voices and imaginations heated his mind and helped him forge his narrative and control the thread. His 1928 Christopher triumphs over Mr. Lancaster by having a vision of his second novel; he refuses to be incorporated into Mr. Lancaster's "epic song of himself"[11] and insists on being the author of his own life story. In "Ambrose," the 1933 Christopher becomes obsessed by the publishing success of a contemporary back in England. "You think you can make me jealous? You think I'm coming back to compete with you [. . .]?" he fumes after chancing on a rave review of a London novel by his school and university friend "Timmy North."[12] The rivalry pulls the 1933 Christopher back into the literary fray, so that he abandons his friend Ambrose and their shared idyll in Greece.

In "Waldemar," the power struggle occurs with one of his characters, who tries to redirect the story and create a different future for himself. The 1938 Christopher learns that Mr. Lancaster's clerk has changed his name to Eugen because Waldemar strikes him as "a name for a working-class boy."[13] Eugen means well-born. The 1938 Christopher continues to use the old name, and Waldemar's new lover copies Christopher, so that Waldemar, despite his own intention, is contained in his original fictional identity—just as Isherwood wished to contain Neddermeyer in Germany rather than helping him reinvent himself in America. In "Paul," Isherwood's minor characters reject the saintly imago of Paul built up by the Christopher narrator of the early 1940s. They attack Christopher for pushing a destiny Paul could not live up to. "Being serious just did not suit him, let's face it. He had a genius for enjoying himself, and perhaps if he'd devoted his life to that, he'd be alive today."[14] But Isherwood suggests in the narrative that there is another way to understand Paul's story.

FOR "MR. LANCASTER," ISHERWOOD took inspiration from his father's favorite Conrad tale *Youth*, in which Marlow recalls for his middle-aged contemporaries the romance of his first death-defying voyage to the East. Conrad had narrated from several points of view, starting in the first person then handing over to his character, Marlow, aged forty-two, who describes his maiden voyage at twenty under a doubting old skipper of sixty. Likewise, Isherwood narrates as himself in middle age and as himself at twenty-three: "a separate being, a stranger almost," a young man not much older than Bachardy, who had more recently taken his first voyage, to Europe.[15]

His twenty-three-year-old Christopher travels aboard the tramp steamer *Coriolanus*, named for the Roman general who, in Shakespeare's tragedy, dies from trying too hard to please his mother, and, at first sight, Germany has all the allure the East had offered Marlow; it is the enigmatic, intoxicating foreign locale of Christopher's sexual destiny. Fear of the former national enemy is transformed into erotic excitement. "You must feel that Chris is horny. *All through* the story," Isherwood had written in his workbook. In *Christopher and His Kind*, he was to make clear that in real life "he had no love adventures" in Bremen.[16] He invented erotic details for the story—including an afternoon of sex with Waldemar, Oskar, and Oskar's girlfriend—in order to position sex at the heart of Christopher's future in Germany. He was reaffirming the power sex had had over him as a young man partly because he was experiencing it in the behavior of the young man he was living with in 1960, a young man who often spent his nights away.

"He must *not* be apologized for," Isherwood noted in September 1960 in his workbook. "The oldsters are as unreal to him as dinosaurs. I must express my belief in him—in his genius."[17] The genius Isherwood had in mind was his own youthful promise as a novelist, and it was also Bachardy's still untested talent. About Bachardy, he wrote in his diary: "I do now firmly believe in the *psychological* possibility of his becoming a really good artist. I mean, he has the right attitude toward the object. He is genuinely, passionately interested." Isherwood was even prepared to invest his own time: "I've told him I'll sit and sit for him, by the hour if necessary."[18]

In the story, Christopher has just published his first novel, called *All the Conspirators*, attesting to his passage into adult professional life, yet Mr. Lancaster with his "patronizing air" treats him "as though I were still a school boy,"[19] enraging and humiliating him just as Isherwood's London friends had enraged and humiliated Bachardy, just as Laughton continued to do, just as Kathleen had enraged and humiliated Isherwood even after his postwar return to Wyberslegh. In an introduction to a U.S. edition of *All the Conspirators* that Isherwood was writing while he worked on "Mr. Lancaster," he explained that "The Angry Young Man of my generation was angry with the Family and its official representatives; he called them hypocrites, he challenged the truth of what they taught. He declared that a Freudian revolution had taken place of which they were trying to remain unaware."[20]

Mr. Lancaster, sprung from the British institutions of Church, army, and Civil Service, rejects Freud in favour of the classical and public-school ideal of "a healthy mind in a healthy body." He is modeled on Isherwood's cousin Basil Fry, whose father Uncle Charlie Fry, clergyman and headmaster, had given Kathleen empty advice about schools and rejected Jungian analysis for Richard. Uncle Charlie had worn the foaming white beard "of the genuine Victorian paterfamilias" that Mr. Lancaster's father wears in the story. The Lancasters, father and son, represent all the values against which Christopher rebels.

In keeping with the fact that Isherwood hated "the whole idea of being 'related' to anyone," he has Christopher say, "Even my mother, who delighted in kinship, had to admit that [Mr. Lancaster] wasn't, strictly speaking, related to us."[21] Using the title "Mr." reinforced this. But Lancaster was a family name on his father's side, represented among the family portraits at Marple Hall;[22] moreover, his father and grandfather's regiment was the York and Lancasters. The 1928 Christopher resists the temptation to be guided by his male relatives, and he fights for his autonomy by making a hate object out of Mr. Lancaster in order to stay strong. His vocation as a writer insulates him: "Wasn't I a novelist?" Here was a life strategy—for the 1928 Christopher and for Bachardy. "You had to study him, like lessons."[23] Study your elders like lessons, and use them in your art.

"Mr. Lancaster" was an offering to Bachardy's youth. It was a gesture of understanding, a lengthy piece of advice, and also a kind of promise, for the story makes clear that the 1928 Christopher will get satisfaction through his art. During a fishing trip aboard Mr. Lancaster's yacht, Mr. Lancaster yells at Christopher to pull hard on the tiller and when Christopher does, the engine falls in the water, leaving the boat helpless, to Christopher's delight. At this "very instant" of conflict with Mr. Lancaster, Christopher has a vision of his next novel. This is his answer to Mr. Lancaster: "I had seen it all—the pieces had moved into place—the composition was instantaneously *there*. Dimly, but with intense excitement, I recognized the outline of a new novel."[24]

Bachardy liked "Mr. Lancaster" the least of the stories in *Down There on a Visit*, and "attacked it brutally at the time."[25] It felt uncomfortably personal. Yet he took Isherwood's advice. He studied his elders, read their books, saw their plays. More to the point, he watched their faces, their expressions, their gestures, their clothes—with exceptional intensity. This was to become his art and his future pathway. His vocation was to serve him in exactly the way Isherwood's story promised.

"Mr. Lancaster" was a very English story, and American magazines turned it down. Isherwood's American publisher, Random House, did not offer for the novel it was to be part of, so Isherwood signed a contract with Simon & Schuster, a move he had been considering since as early as 1956.[26] An early version of "Mr. Lancaster," with less sex, appeared in the *London Magazine*, where John Lehmann positioned it and the forthcoming episodes of the new novel as a continuation of the reputation-making earlier work, "all originally forming part of a never-to-be-executed plan for a huge novel, *The Lost*."[27] His influential but outdated boost hindered understanding of Isherwood's technical achievement; it overlooked the genius work *Prater Violet* and entirely underestimated the ambition of the new novel to address the changed existential concerns of the postwar era.

8: Existential Isherwood: The Outsider (1961–1964) / 557

"AMBROSE," THE SECOND story in *Down There on a Visit*, responds to *The Tempest* and various works reimagining it—Conrad's *Victory*, Maugham's *The Narrow Corner*, and Auden's *The Sea and the Mirror*—each with its own Prospero, Miranda, Antonio, Ariel, Caliban, and so forth. Isherwood had been disappointed with Conrad's *Victory*, and he had not liked Auden's Commentary on *The Tempest*. "I am very dashed that you don't care for The Sea and the Mirror," Auden had written in 1944, "because I think it is one of the few pieces of mine which are 'important', and if you don't like it, no one will."[28] *The Narrow Corner*, on the other hand, Isherwood called "Maugham's one really magic novel [...] I love its setting in the Spice Islands, its dreamy languid equatorial atmosphere, its romantic queerness."[29]

Isherwood commandeered the island theme to serve his own agenda. Though he used his 1933 Greek diary as a basis for the story, he omitted the personal struggles with Neddermeyer so painfully recorded there and focused on transforming his main character Ambrose into a would-be homosexual saint and philosopher king, "one of Shakespeare's exiled kings." He resisted any explicit statement about Prospero, preferring the name Ambrose, after St. Ambrose, patron saint of Milan, where Prospero had been duke. On St. Nicholas in the summer of 1933, Isherwood had read *Ambrose Holt and Family* (1931) by Susan Glaspell, which featured another wanderer, Ambrose Holt, who abandons his family to seek a free and meaningful life as a tramp. As with Katherine Mansfield and Hope Mirrlees, he found a way into his material through a less-known woman writer.

Isherwood resisted, too, any explicit statement that his Ambrose was a saint, instead writing things like "Ambrose has the sort of indifference to discomfort and hardship which you would expect to find in a great hero or saint."[30] His narrator mockingly evokes the miracles of Christ—"I can quite imagine you getting out and walking on the water," he tells Ambrose—and he alludes to Christ's suffering and death—"Behind us, the folded tent was being carried by the boys, like an enormous dead body. [...] I thought it was like a painting of the descent from the cross."[31] These and similar phrases were taken verbatim from the 1933 diary and deployed, now, in silent relation to the teachings of Vedanta.

Returning from India and the South Seas, where Isherwood had daydreamed of Maugham and read *Victory*, he and Bachardy had seen John Gielgud's *The Tempest* in London, experiencing afresh its themes of fraternal rivalry and usurpation. Prospero's final speeches about magic and about theatricality itself, long familiar to Isherwood, harmonized almost uncannily with Isherwood's mature belief as a Vedantist that the material world is an illusion: "The cloud-capped towers, the gorgeous palaces, / The solemn temples, the great globe itself, / Yea, all which it inherit, shall dissolve..."[32]

Indeed, theater offered a rich metaphor to illustrate his beliefs. Explaining in Patanjali's yoga aphorisms that a spiritual aspirant produces no more karmas after achieving liberation but that karmas produced earlier still govern the remainder of his life on earth, Isherwood and Prabhavananda had written: "He is like an actor on the last night of a play. He knows that the play will never be performed again [. . .] Nevertheless, he must play it through to the end until the final curtain falls and he can go home."[33]

Isherwood used the metaphor in the story to introduce his beliefs without naming them. The Christopher character describes life on Ambrose's island as "a play which had to be performed day after day in its original version but with a cast that was no longer big enough." With the departure of various boys, "I had to double the roles of Christopher, Geoffrey, Hans and Waldemar. And thus I almost ceased being myself, or anybody else in particular." He submits because "I needed to reassure myself *that I wasn't alone!*"[34] Like Paul in Isherwood's abandoned novel *Paul Is Alone*, the Isherwood character finds relief in being someone else, in extinguishing his personality. Ambrose is trapped forever repeating old karmas; he will never go home.

Isherwood cast Hans (based on Erwin Hansen) as Caliban, "monster of the isle" and Prospero's slave. Aleko, who makes the 1933 Christopher think of "a sorcerer's familiar," is the Ariel of Isherwood's story (a composite of two real boys, Mitso and Alekko). Aleko goes unpunished for attacking Hans with a broken bottle and paralyzing his hand—a real injury suffered by Erwin Hansen. As restitution, Ambrose makes Hans heir to half his estate as Caliban is heir to Prospero's island (and as the sons of the fool in the Revesby mummers' play that influenced Auden and Isherwood in the early 1930s are heirs to his). Isherwood reversed the destinies of Caliban and Ariel; Aleko blows up Ambrose's house, and Hans flees to safety, leaving Aleko in possession of the island until he tires of it and returns to Athens.

As for Miranda, Prospero's finest creation, Isherwood reinvented her as Maria Constantinescu, root of discord on his island rather than means of reconciliation. Whereas Prospero gives his daughter to Ferdinand, heir to the king of Naples, admonishing him not to "break her virgin-knot" before the holy rites of matrimony are performed, Maria Constantinescu is a sexual marauder, "driven by her nameless lust." She arrives uninvited in pursuit of the outspoken, aggressively heterosexual Englishman, Geoffrey, and Circe-like enchants the boys with her gramophone, her whisky, and her hashish, making herself "absolute ruler of the island." She loudly proclaims her love of "pederasts," has unashamed sex with Waldemar, scandalizes everyone by swimming naked in broad daylight, then departs, carrying off her drunken, sleeping lover Geoffrey.[35]

Tiny, bossy, peroxide-blonde Maria Constantinescu was modeled on Maria Britneva St. Just, a close friend of Tennessee Williams. Isherwood met her at the beginning of 1955. She was born in Russia and educated in England, where in 1956, she married an English banking heir, Peter Grenfell, 2nd Baron St. Just. She failed at acting but succeeded in being selected by Williams as his literary executor. Bachardy later recalled that she was snubbed by most of Williams's friends. "She was very feisty and loved irritating people."[36]

In *Christopher and His Kind*, Isherwood made clear that "the visit of Maria Constantinescu never happened." But he had wished for it. In their worst moments of boredom on St. Nicholas, he and Neddermeyer had agreed that "what we lack on this island are one or two really nice women—"[37] Moreover, the tradition of enchanted island literature in which Isherwood was working in 1959 required a woman.

Conrad, like Maugham and Isherwood after him, had parted ways with Shakespeare by making his female character the root of discord on his enchanted island. Also, he turned Shakespeare's Antonio into the desperado Mr. Jones, the uninvited incarnation of evil that cannot be escaped, "an outcast—almost an outlaw." Conrad hinted that Jones's "tastes" are homosexual—"his thin, waspish, beautifully pencilled eyebrows,"[38] his hatred of women—and he had Jones fire the tragic bullet that precipitates the deaths of everyone else in the final scene that Isherwood called an "inartistically total holocaust" in his letter to Van Druten. Jones is just the sort of homosexual character Isherwood warned Gore Vidal they must not write if they wanted to change public opinion.

In *The Narrow Corner*, Maugham hinted that his character Dr. Saunders is homosexual, with his girlish Chinese boy servant and his memory of a cruising locale in London, the Front at Piccadilly Circus, where at midnight "There was a sense of adventure in the air. Eyes met and then . . ."[39] Still, opium addiction masks the doctor's sexuality, and his reason for living as an outcast is never revealed. Tragedy is delivered by the sexy, straight, boyish murderer Fred Blake.

On Ambrose's island, everyone is homosexual, and the wreckage caused by the woman, Maria Constantinescu, is comic not tragic. Ambrose fails as a king because, like the real-life Francis Turville-Petre, he is an anarchist, bossing his subjects only when he wants to and declining to adjudicate disputes. In his workbook, Isherwood wrote: "The climax should be some horrendous yet basically farcical scene of violence, which somehow arises out of Ambrose's passivity."[40]

Isherwood saw Maria Constantinescu as acting out his own malevolent fantasies about being the demon of the island, making trouble for fun, like

Puck. Before she leaves, Maria recognizes her double in Christopher, telling him, "You are an old, old monster like me," and she asserts that curiosity about other people is the only thing that truly engages them both: "You cannot hold a monster by his emotion, only by puzzling him. As long as the monster is puzzled, he is yours."[41] The monster, Caliban, is the writer, who puzzles over his friends until he has solved them, and then discards them once he has created his story. Maria Constantinescu has the same initials as Isherwood's childhood friend Mirabel Cobbold, with whom he first played the utopian island game of Swiss Family Robinson. Maria also has Mirabel's domineering personality, her playful savagery, and her appetite for adventure; she was an old, old double, indeed.

JUST AS "MR. LANCASTER" was a private offering to Bachardy, "Ambrose" was a private offering to the island-loving Upward and an apology for the bold inconstancy with which Isherwood had pursued the gypsy freedom and literary success he knew Upward had longed for. Upward had been terrifically excited by Isherwood's sojourn in Greece. "Tell me the details and whether it's possible to live on an island for nothing and forever," he had written in the spring of 1933. "If it is I'll come."[42] But already it had been too late for Upward, teaching in the suburbs and committed to Communist Party work.

In the story, the Christopher of 1933 wills himself to believe that life on Ambrose's island is all he has ever wanted. But "it didn't ring true. I wanted to force it to be true, and I couldn't . . ." Suddenly, the romance is over. "I've got to leave," he says. "I have to be getting back to London—quite soon." Isherwood modeled this dialogue on the island parting between Alan Sebrill and Richard Marple in Upward's *In the Thirties*: "I can't wait any longer. I've got to go to London," says Marple on the Isle of Wight.[43] Reading Upward's manuscript, Isherwood had experienced from Upward's point of view how the end of their shared dream of being writers together had felt like betrayal.

He had urged Upward by letter to heap blame on his Richard Marple character for the collapse of Alan Sebrill's life, and he had called Sebrill "a sort of saint"[44] for his commitment to his beliefs. Now Isherwood inscribed Upward's reckless and innocent commitment in Ambrose and heaped blame on the Christopher figure, even evoking the painful episode at university when Upward's rooms were wrecked and he himself had failed to object. Ambrose confides that he decided to leave England after his Cambridge rooms were wrecked by college rugby players and oarsmen during the Michaelmas term of 1923. Not only does this recall what happened to Upward, but it also makes a wider reference, for it is a common tale—the crude bullying of aesthetes by hearties, the hatred of the mob for any fine thing a mob cannot understand. The tale is told, famously and cruelly, in the opening scene of Evelyn Waugh's first novel *Decline and Fall*, a satiric comedy set partly in Oxford. *Decline and Fall* was published in 1928, making it a rival of Isherwood's first novel, *All the Conspirators*. It was far more successful commercially—just like the imaginary novel by "Timmy North" that enrages the 1933 Christopher when he spots it reviewed in an old magazine.

Isherwood drew *Decline and Fall* to the reader's attention by having Maria Constantinescu praise the 1933 Christopher for writing it: "'This young man who is a schoolmaster and becomes imprisoned for the traffic in the white slaves—*quel esprit!*'" cries Maria. "'I'm afraid that's by Evelyn Waugh,' I said, not charmed." The description of "Timmy's" novel—"a carefree, hilarious, altogether uproarious novel of London stage and society life"—plausibly conjures Waugh's second novel, *Vile Bodies*, published in 1930. Again, Isherwood artfully smudged the references. By 1932, when Isherwood himself had published his second novel, Waugh was already on his third, *Black Mischief*. Isherwood had admired Waugh's skill but objected to his cynicism, telling Spender in a letter: "It is very well done, but he's such an utter little unbeliever. He declines to back *any* of the horses."[45]

The violence portrayed in *Decline and Fall* is the drunken brawling of privileged, thoughtless upper-class young men—the Bollinger Club. It falls by chance upon a hapless, orphaned theology student, Paul Pennyfeather, who is so miserably out of the know that he cannot foresee or defend himself against the debagging—stripping off of his trousers—that will ruin his life. Isherwood saw little humor in this kind of satire which touched experiences he had fictionalized from his earliest boarding-school days of new boys being bullied and successful boys being gorse-bushed and which so vividly portrayed everything he hated about England.

In his workbook Isherwood wrote: "The truth is, bogus tho it sounds, I am only interested in compassion." A few years later, he told a lecture audience that he was haunted by a sentence from the *Tao Te Ching*: "Heaven arms with pity those whom it would not see destroyed," and he admonished, "the person you are really harming by cruelty is yourself, and that is the tremendous power of this sentence."[46]

Isherwood presented the Geoffrey character as Ambrose's contemporary at Cambridge, the type of the athlete who had hated Ambrose—evidently for embodying a part of himself which Geoffrey wished to repress. Imagining that both had had homosexual experiences, Isherwood wrote in his workbook: "G is a ruined athlete, just as A is a ruined aesthete." For a time, he planned to establish plainly in the narrative that "G wrecked A's rooms at

Cambridge,"[47] but he pulled back from anything so neat and coincidental, preferring instead to portray Ambrose and Geoffrey as exemplars of two tribes locked in permanent antagonism.

In "Ambrose" the 1933 Christopher remarks, "I don't for a moment believe that he left England simply because his rooms were wrecked; that's just the kind of incident you dramatize and dwell on because it expresses a general attitude of mind." This instructs the reader how to understand Ambrose's tearful narrative—as a dramatization that expresses a general attitude of mind. The room-wrecking can be read as a gay-bashing or, more generally, as group brutality toward an individual of different sensibility: "what astonishes me is how violently I was affected by his story," says the Christopher character. "While he was telling it, all my undergraduate hostilities came back to me." He goes on to explain that "I've been living outside England myself, and in the presence of public enemies, the Nazis, against whom you feel a different sort of hostility—public and proper and respectable."

The story resists mentioning the ransacking of the Institute for Sexual Science and the Burning of the Books in the Opernplatz which Isherwood had witnessed in Berlin just three days before leaving for Greece. The raid on the institute, as Isherwood recalled in *Christopher and His Kind*, was made by "a party of about a hundred students" who "spent the morning pouring ink over carpets and manuscripts and loading their trucks with books from the Institute's library, including many which had nothing to do with sex: historical works, art journals, etc." The pillaging students were from the Hochschule für Leibesübungen—the college for physical education teachers. Thus, the action was a kind of state-sanctioned bashing of aesthetes by the undergraduate hearties of Berlin.

Isherwood wanted the reader to recognize the hidden, more primitive hostility—toward the oddball with a different sensibility, different sexuality, different beliefs—that secretly feeds such public acts of violence. To achieve this, he acknowledged this hostility in the character representing himself: "The other kind of hostility—which isn't respectable or proper, but which sometimes goes much deeper—you can perhaps only feel for your own class and kind."[48]

In March 1960, Isherwood sent "Ambrose" to Spender to publish in *Encounter*. Spender cabled "marvellous" and then rejected it. "He seems chiefly to dislike the reason why A. left England, adding strangely, 'I am not just concerned with the fact that people will say this reflects your own point of view about leaving England.'"

Isherwood felt Spender's rejection as a blow. The story certainly did reflect Isherwood's own point of view about leaving England. Moreover, Spender had confided in the winter of 1956, when Isherwood and Bachardy were in London, that he himself was tired of England and longed to get away: "There's nothing here but personal relationships and maneuvers—and I'm tired of both."⁴⁹ Yet Spender could not bring himself to leave his island. Nor could he bring himself to honor Isherwood's reasons for leaving. Upward, on the other hand, understood, writing that the "Ambrose" story moved me to the core," and that the novel "promises to be the best, the most moving, you have done yet."⁵⁰

HALFWAY THROUGH World War II, when England had already been heavily bombed, Evelyn Waugh had published *Put Out More Flags*, his novel satirizing the behavior of the British ruling classes during the first year of the war. In it, Waugh mocked "two great poets [...] who had recently fled to New York," calling them Parsnip and Pimpernel. Of course, he had in mind Auden and Isherwood, as was widely recognized at the time. Waugh's Parsnip and Pimpernel are the darlings of the artistic left, intimate friends and literary collaborators, and the authors of "Guernica Revisited"—alluding to Auden's 1937 Marxist poem "Spain," later disowned—and "the Christopher Sequence"—alluding to Isherwood's Berlin stories. Followers of Parsnip and Pimpernel are mentally tortured by the question, which they discuss over and over again, "how these two can claim to be *Contemporary* if they run away from the biggest event in contemporary history"—the war. Few knew at the time that Auden and Isherwood had neither "fled" nor "run away" but had planned the move in advance and left long before the war started. Waugh's mockery gave a sharp, literary edge to the wider, equally inaccurate criticism of Auden and Isherwood in the British press, in Parliament and by colleagues, acquaintances, and close friends.

Waugh supplied Parsnip and Pimpernel with a friend and leftist fellow-traveler, Ambrose Silk, a homosexual-aesthete writer. Ambrose Silk stays in England during the war even though he does not fit in. His story offers a fictional counterpart to the flight of Parsnip and Pimpernel. As a "cosmopolitan Jewish pansy," Silk struggles and fails to find the right job in the war effort.

Like Cyril Connolly, Waugh had put behind him the homosexual affairs and romances of his own youth. He saw no possible future for the homosexual-aesthete type in England, and consigned Ambrose Silk to the past, laughably out of fashion in wartime: "A pansy. An old queen. A habit of dress, a tone of voice, an elegant, humorous deportment that had been admired and imitated, a swift, epicene felicity of wit, the art of dazzling and confusing those he despised—these had been his, and now they were the current exchange of

comedians . . ."⁵¹ As Isherwood had observed, Waugh declined to back any of his horses. Parsnip and Pimpernel were mocked for leaving, Ambrose Silk for remaining—because they were homosexual. Waugh's wartime England offered them no place.

Ambrose Silk was mostly based on Brian Howard, the friend who had proposed sharing a Portuguese palace with his lover Toni Altmann and Isherwood and Neddermeyer.⁵² Howard was partly Jewish, born in England to American parents. At Eton, he had started a magazine with Harold Acton—Waugh's lesser model for his homosexual-aesthete character—and founded the Eton Society of Arts. Howard's early celebrity had continued at Christ Church, Oxford, and beyond. He had been a dandy and a legendary partygoer before venturing to Germany for sex. In Ambrose Silk, longing to join Parsnip and Pimpernel in America, Waugh united the myth of the wandering Jew with the predicament of contemporary homosexuals, destined to seek and not to find a safe homeland with their lovers: "the dark, nomadic strain in his blood, the long heritage of wandering and speculation allowed him no rest. Instead of Atlantic breakers, he saw the camels swaying their heads resentfully against the lightening sky, as the caravan woke to another day's stage in the pilgrimage."⁵³

After the war started, Howard had returned to England, where he worked for War Office Intelligence until he was let go. He then volunteered for the RAF and was again let go. All the while he brooded on his absent boyfriend Toni Altmann and drank heavily. He never fulfilled his youthful promise as a writer and died a suicide at fifty-two while Isherwood was writing *Down There on a Visit*. If this was the likely fate of an Ambrose type in England, how wise and how brave it had been for Auden and Isherwood to emigrate. Indeed, how urgent. Lincoln Kirstein, serving in England as a private in the U.S. Army during the spring of 1944, had seen this clearly: "God—how Right you and Wystan were to leave," he told Isherwood in one letter.⁵⁴

As Isherwood returned to his Ambrose material, abandoned since the 1930s, he might easily have chosen a different name for his main character. But the coincidence of Waugh choosing Ambrose for his homosexual-aesthete offered an opportunity to counter Waugh's insults with a rival narrative. Isherwood and Waugh repeatedly developed similar themes and characters in opposite directions. Waugh's Ambrose Silk is useless and out of fashion in wartime because he is homosexual; by contrast, Isherwood's Bob Wood recognizes he is not a pacifist and joins up because he knows he would do the same in a war against homosexuals. In *Brideshead Revisited*, Waugh lovingly conjured the ancient seat of the Marchmains as the locus of mother love and Catholic piety; Isherwood wanted Marple razed to the ground and in *The Memorial* he gleefully delivered its fictional counterpart into the hands of new money. Waugh fell in love with the upper classes, which made him willing to serve them; Isherwood fell in love with the lower classes, which made him long for a classless life.

The 1933 Christopher does not fit in—neither to class nor nation. He abjures a fantasy life on Ambrose's island and returns to England to fight for a place in the mainstream, "the world in which Timmy could sell twenty-thousand copies." But England is only an interim stop on his journey; "I knew that I didn't belong here, either."[55] Like Odysseus, he must wander on until he finds his sexual homeland, where he can live authentically as himself.

IN "WALDEMAR" ISHERWOOD was making his first public—published—attempt to portray his emotional state at the end of the 1930s and his attitude to the war. He had begun to think about writing "Waldemar" only in April 1959, about nine months after being attacked on television by Oscar Levant.

He drew heavily on his 1938 diaries, incorporating with negligible changes the portrait he had made as he turned thirty-four of the man without qualities, the man who was certain that he had no soul and who considers his personality to be an outward show, like clothing, put on or off depending on circumstances. Again, he mined Auden's observations, referring to Auden in the story as if he were a whole group of friends: "To judge from the jokes they make about me, they see a rather complex creature, part despot, part diplomat. I'm told that I hold myself like a drill sergeant or a strict little landlady; I am supposed to have an overpowering will." The friends consider him "sly" because "I pretend to be nobody in particular just one of the gang." The Christopher of 1938 takes trouble to show interest in others, charms the young with his "romantic, slightly world-weary air of having been places and seen things" and charms the old with his "beautiful manners." He is a celebrity, "my writing is fashionable to exactly the right degree—chic, not vulgarly famous." He has made a success of himself at "The Others' game" as he calls it in "Waldemar."

But the 1938 Christopher considers that all his achievements are only in reaction to the society in which he was raised—rivalry, reaction, rebellion, forced through by "this celebrated will of mine—"[56] At this pinnacle of attainment and public recognition, he does not know what he is for, and the mirrors reflecting back at him have gone dark.

No reference to Neddermeyer's arrest, trial, or imprisonment occurs in "Waldemar." Instead, Isherwood invented a romance between Waldemar and a young Englishwoman he called Dorothy. Returning across the

Channel from Paris, the Christopher of 1938 bumps into these two old friends from Berlin traveling together as lovers and preparing to marry. In the relationship between Dorothy and Waldemar, Isherwood fictionalized his real-life relationship with Neddermeyer—the bond across differences of nationality, class, and education, which had been so painfully challenged as Europe moved toward war.

He had first proposed this way of telling the story in a diary entry he made on July 24, 1938: "an English girl, lives in pre-Hitler Berlin. She has revolted from a rich upper-middle class family, refuses to take their money. She teaches English. She has become a member of the K.P.D. and gives lessons at the Marxist Workers' School." The English girl begins an affair with one of her pupils, a carpenter. She is thirty; he is only twenty-one. She has "a kind of masculine quality which makes her relationship [...] sometimes appear almost homosexual." In another set of notes incorporating characters based on Brian Howard and Toni Altmann, he had written: "She's sometimes taken for a lesbian." About the marriage, Isherwood had observed: "It's what she's always wanted—to denaturalize and declass herself." He had also proposed that the boy would reveal he has worked as a prostitute; this would establish the boy's honesty and his poverty as well as the singularity of the affair.

Like Isherwood and Neddermeyer, the pair were to be forced to run from Hitler, and so to begin wandering about Europe, constantly shadowed by fear of the German authorities before being separated for good. Isherwood had got stuck in the summer of 1938: "the story is really the story of a homosexual seduction," he realized. "The truth is I just don't know how to make them go to bed together for the first time."

He had decided to leave out the seduction and begin with the characters arriving at Dover: "The love affair has already started, and is taken for granted."[57] He changed the girl's name repeatedly—from Karin to Helen back to Karin then to Janet—as if her essence was still metamorphosing in his mind.[58] He was trying to represent a changing aspect of himself. The boy, on the other hand, was called Erich in all the drafts.

Reading over the 1938 material in 1960, Isherwood found it "good. Maybe it's the simplest and neatest storyline I have ever contrived." The story still needed telling.

For the arrival at Dover in *Down There on a Visit*, Isherwood used many details from the real-life episode at Harwich in 1934, when Neddermeyer was deported. However, in "Waldemar," Dorothy and Waldemar are both allowed to enter—but only for one month. This synchronized the time frame of their relationship with the time frame of the Munich Crisis, amplifying the atmosphere of oncoming catastrophe. Dorothy and Waldemar, Hitler and Europe have one month. This was how it had felt to him, that anxious time of public and private crisis. In his work journal, he called it "the idea of a limbo [...] which is neither peace nor war." The idea was in fact a sensation reaching back for Isherwood to Limerick at the start of World War I—the sensation of waiting passively, helplessly, for a certain doom. "It is an Agony in the Garden—after which the crucifixion will be positively a relief."[59]

Traveling aboard the same ship as the lovers, the jaded 1938 Christopher is the observer of his own past romance. Dorothy is mocked as a trend-follower "who had caught communism like flu," and uses it as "an instrument of aggression against her family, her own class, and England in general." Her anger toward her mother for treating Waldemar like a member of a lower social class evokes Isherwood's own youthful anger. Waldemar is reduced to an object in an old struggle. Dorothy's mother begs her to send him back to Germany. In his notes, Isherwood proposed: "we see—though she doesn't —that a tiny part of her wants Waldemar to go. But she'll never admit that,"[60] a kind of acknowledgment that in youth he had clung to Neddermeyer in part to defy his mother and all his mother symbolized to him.

Waldemar adopts the same view as Dorothy's mother about his return to Germany, telling the Christopher of 1938, "I'll never be a Nazi. You know that. But I'm German, and home is home." But when Waldemar learns that Christopher is leaving for "Amerika," he proposes to abandon Dorothy and asks "very softly and persuasively, 'Will you take me with you Christoph?'" The 1938 Christopher rejects this as "absolutely impossible."

In real life, it was only in 1956 that Isherwood had fended off Neddermeyer's plan to join him in America. Isherwood offset his guilt about this with the final fictional affirmation that Waldemar's request is purely opportunistic. Already, Waldemar has a taxi waiting; his train for Berlin leaves in twenty minutes. "We shan't meet again. Ever," he announces conclusively.[61] Thus, Waldemar sets Christopher free.

As Isherwood made clear in *Christopher and His Kind*, the Waldemar character is a fictional composite, based partly on Neddermeyer and partly on Isherwood's previous lover, Walter Wolff, who had already been the model for Otto Nowak. The name "Waldemar" neatly fuses the Wal- of Walter with -demar for -dermeyer. Neddermeyer's innocence is suggested in the remembered, younger Waldemar, Wolff's slyer hardness in the mature Waldemar, who wishes to be called Eugen and join a higher social class.

In "Waldemar," Isherwood undermined the leftist credentials his writing had earned him in the 1930s, as if he had been merely showing off. In fact, he had already begun to critique his political posturing in the 1938 drafts by bringing his young woman character, a serious communist, face-to-face with his earlier narrator in several scenes. "She spoilt my act," the narrator concedes.[62]

In the character of Dorothy, Isherwood also exposed his youthful possessiveness, attributing Dorothy's need for sexual fidelity to her privileged background. Waldemar would "go to bed with almost anyone who flattered him enough," she confides. "I hate and despise myself for minding, but I do. It's all part of this ghastly way I was brought up—this awful bourgeois thing they teach you about *owning* people . . ."

Yet Dorothy, as sharp as Maria in "Ambrose," identifies with the monster, Christopher. "You know, Christopher, I envy you! You do travel light, don't you? You don't ever get involved with anyone."[63] She is describing a mask that Isherwood had presented to the world. Behind the mask, another Isherwood had been helplessly involved not only with Neddermeyer but also with numerous other lovers, and he had been helpless during the anxiety of Munich to engage fully with any of them. In "Waldemar," these lovers can't be brought onto the stage because they are men.

"WALDEMAR" SETS THE stage for the great changes in the Christopher character when he finally crosses the Atlantic, and it dramatizes the arguments for his emigration that Isherwood had rehearsed in his diaries. Isherwood gave his 1938 Christopher character two fictional mentors, one English, one German, "E.M." and "Dr. Fisch." E.M. offers an example of how to behave in the crisis, Dr. Fisch holds the key to what might happen. E.M. is easily identifiable as E.M. Forster; Fisch is based on Rolf Katz.

In his workbook, Isherwood proposed Forster as "the great liberal." In "Waldemar," he called E.M. "the anti-heroic hero" who "is as anxious and afraid as any of us, and never for an instant pretends not to be. He and his books and what they stand for are all that is truly worth saving from Hitler."[64] "Dr. Fisch" is "the Cassandra" of the Munich Crisis. The 1938 Christopher rushes to get his opinions on each new development. In reality, it had been Katz who contacted Isherwood, by telephone over and over again, to offer them.

E.M. "lives by love, not by will," whereas Christopher relies only on will, vacillating between his announced beliefs and his determined forgetting through sex and alcohol. But he wants to live by love. "I hereby make a bargain with fate—if, by some miracle, we get through this without war, then I am going to America," he says, "I am going to live with V. and try to unlearn my madness and forget my ancestors and become sane again."[65] V. stands for Vernon, the name that Isherwood gave Harvey Young in *Christopher and His Kind* and *My Guru and His Disciple*. This was a piece of private code, for Vernon was the family name he had given the characters based on his immediate family in *The Memorial*. The Vernon family, builders of Marple Hall, were more ancient and grand than the Bradshaws. In America, Isherwood and Young had visited George Washington's home, Mount Vernon, named after the same family. So the name identified Christopher's American Boy as his intended American family.

The move to America is presented in "Waldemar" as the realist's solution adopted by Dr. Fisch, who predicts fascism in England and prepares to leave for South America: "'Back to the private life.' Europe is lost, he says." The revolution has failed, and history is not unfolding along the lines predicted by the Marxist dialectic. In reality, Rolf Katz's return to the private life was motivated, like Isherwood's, largely by his sexuality. Katz was reported to the British authorities for an affair with a young stoker aboard a British navy vessel. Despite his ferocious anti-Nazism, evident in correspondence intercepted by MI5, he was tagged as a possible Nazi spy and required to leave the country even though MI5 established that his friendship with the stoker was romantic and posed no security risk. He was never allowed to return.[66]

The private life, of course, was to prove the ultimate challenge for the Christopher of 1938, the man without qualities, the man relying on his will, on the right company or on the distraction of a new love affair. In "Waldemar," he blinds himself to the life of the spirit even as it bears down on him. "I haven't got a soul [. . .] When I hear the word 'God' I want to vomit," he insists to the character called Hugh (Auden's middle name). "Hugh would laugh good-humoredly and say, 'Careful! Careful! If you keep going on like that, my dear, you'll have *such* a conversion, one of these days!'"[67]

IN FICTIONALIZING HIS conversion to Vedanta, Isherwood approached obliquely via another character, an interlocutor, a double, who was far less likely than he to find salvation in religion: "Establish Paul's reputation as an international cocotte, drugtaker, golddigger,"[68] he instructed himself for the early part of "Paul." This would make the story sexy, colorful, and shocking. It would also take the reader's scrutiny away from the conversion of the Christopher character, obviating the need for detailed testimony about his inner transformation and new beliefs.

Isherwood planned the relationship in the story as "a love-affair on the metaphysical plane"—physically chaste. Paul has been impotent for three months, making his reputation as "the most expensive male prostitute in the world" meaningless and triggering his crisis. Nevertheless, the bond between Christopher and Paul is intensely erotic. "We see how Paul adapts himself & becomes what C. wants him to become," Isherwood wrote in his workbook—in effect, Christopher's spiritual geisha.

At first, Isherwood planned that Paul was to die from opium addiction: "But his death isn't tragic; and perhaps the insights he obtained will help him. What is a good life, anyway? Take an example of some static 'good' person & some static 'bad' person. Neither of them ventures far enough. Paul ventured."⁶⁹ The ending Isherwood eventually wrote leaves Paul cured of his addiction and completely disintoxicated. But before he dies—of a bad heart—he has a "relapse" which Isherwood depicts as a prelude to a new spiritual metamorphosis.

About the relapse, Paul tells Christopher that he has returned to the life he lived before his conversion, because "I wanted to see if I was *really* changed by any of what happened to me in California—meeting Augustus, and meditating, and all of that." Christopher wants to share in this reckless test. He asks to smoke a pipe of Paul's opium. Paul only laughs: "You know, you really are a tourist, to your bones. I bet you're always sending postcards with 'Down here on a visit' on them. [. . .] It's absolutely no use fooling around with this [. . .] you have to let yourself get hooked."⁷⁰ As a writer, the Christopher character wants to know as much as Paul knows, to enter the underworld, the den of thieves, and yet remain confident that he can be restored to the hearts of friends and tell his story.

DENHAM FOUTS ATTRACTED the legend-making skills of Gore Vidal and Truman Capote as well as Somerset Maugham and Isherwood. Their fictions transformed Fouts into a symbolic American lost to the wickedness of Europe, a boy (in Maugham's *The Razor's Edge* a girl, Sophie Macdonald) who becomes an object of pilgrimage for his uninitiated compatriots fresh off the boat after World War II.

In *The Judgment of Paris* (1953), Vidal had portrayed Fouts as the Virginian opium addict and courtesan Jim, fragile, forlorn, and unreachable. "Looks like a baby, doesn't he? [. . .] But he's taken it every way, one time or another." Then, in his 1956 short story "Pages from an Abandoned Journal," Vidal created a kind of homosexual oracle, Elliott Magren, again an opium addict. In another Vidal short story, "Three Stratagems," set in Florida but referring to "exile in the foreign cities," a college boy type hustler reveals his Fouts-like strategy of remaining silent to attract clients, "waiting for the proper moment to assume the character of the other's dream."⁷¹

Maugham and Vidal created their Fouts-inspired characters before Isherwood wrote "Paul," Capote afterwards. Capote was to introduce Fouts by his real name in "Unspoiled Monsters," the first part (published in *Esquire* in 1975) of his unfinished final work *Answered Prayers*, in which Capote drew on Isherwood's "Paul" and pretended he was revealing a journalistic truth behind Isherwood's story while in fact inventing and exaggerating audaciously.⁷²

Fouts was born in 1914 in Boca Grande, Florida. His father was a Yale graduate with smalltime management jobs, an ice-cream parlor, a bakery, a broom factory, property developments. Sex with older men became Fouts's career path, but his personal taste was for boys aged fourteen to sixteen. He worked in his father's bakery, and, at probably age nineteen, was sent or ran away to Washington, D.C. to work for an uncle in the Safeway grocery store chain. By 1934, he was bagging groceries in Manhattan. Through a roommate who worked in a bookstore, he met Isherwood's friend Glenway Wescott and was introduced to Wescott's long-running ménage à trois with George Platt Lynes and Monroe Wheeler, eventually head of publications at the Museum of Modern Art.

It was Wescott who wrote to Isherwood on Christmas Day 1948 to report Fouts's death. In his letter, Wescott recalled Isherwood's long-ago confidence that Fouts was driven partly by anxiety about having a small penis, a "sense of disendowment in the particular of virility,"[73] as Wescott orotundly put it. In "Paul," Isherwood changed this to impotence, Isherwood's own disendowment.

Peter Watson, the philanthropist and art collector who kept Fouts from the 1930s onward, told a friend that Fouts "never did and never has told me how he first came to Europe."[74] According to Watson's 1948 recollection about Fouts, "We met in 1933, about, in a nightclub."[75] Until World War II, Fouts lived with Watson in London and Paris, and Watson supported him until near the end of Fouts's life.

Fouts was yet another character who seemed to be conjured by Isherwood's imagination; certainly, he was gradually refashioned by it. Isherwood had abandoned his proposed novel *Paul Is Alone* in May 1936 through frustration with his character Paul being "only a little cissy who steals" when Isherwood wanted to create a character "capable of sexual vice, debauch, drug-taking, anything," a demoniac figure who might "attempt to redeem whole lifetimes through one tonic act of violence." In walked Fouts in 1940, giving new potential to Isherwood's young con man, wandering through Europe pretending to spring from the milieu of privilege in which he once worked as a waiter, claiming to be a German baron, an English gentleman, a committed communist activist.

Already in November 1940, Isherwood had begun to describe in his diary elements of romance and drama in Fouts's situation, revealing in advance the sort of spiritual outcome he wished to see in Fouts's story. "He has extraordinary reserves of willpower, backed up against a huge black rock of despair, like a creature at bay. His despair isn't noisy. It's quiet and well mannered: the dynamic despair which makes dangerous criminals and, very occasionally, saints." Isherwood had been excited when Heard reported that he saw Fouts "as a figure 'with something standing behind it'—an embodiment, perhaps, of certain acts, with a being of its own,"[76] his debauched past attached to him like an aura.

Isherwood later clarified: "My original Paul character had nothing to do with Denny—indeed I thought of him long before Denny and I met."[77] As with Ambrose, Isherwood could have changed the character's name, and in fact he considered other names in his workbook, but instead of dropping the name Paul, he ceded it to his new character, affirming an essential link. The new Paul, modeled on Fouts, could more richly articulate themes Isherwood had been brewing since the 1930s.

Of course, the name Paul for a religious convert resonates with the Christian story about Saul of Tarsus, converted on the road to Damascus. Isherwood drew attention to this: "How odd that he should have that name!" observes Augustus Parr after spending his first day with Paul. "Although, at present, perhaps *Saul* would be more appropriate."[78]

With regard to religious conversions, the story was a riposte to Maugham's *The Razor's Edge*, in which, as Isherwood had argued in "The Problem of the Religious Novel," Maugham had made sainthood seem like it was "just no trouble at all" and portrayed no inner conflict in Larry Darrell. At the end of *The Razor's Edge*, all Maugham's characters, as the narrator observes, "got what they wanted [. . .] Sophie death; and Larry happiness."[79] Isherwood saw the destinies of sinner and saint as more perplexing and never complete. In "Paul," he revitalized and recomplicated the narrative of his conversion and his friendship with Fouts—the narrative which Maugham had plundered and oversimplified in the relationship between Larry Darrell and Sophie Macdonald.

Isherwood republished "The Problem of the Religious Novel" twice, emphasizing its importance, and he also discussed the portrayal of saints in his 1960–1 Santa Barbara lectures. The essay and his lectures offer many clues to what he was trying for in "Paul" and in his last novel, *A Meeting by the River*. As he made clear in the sixth Santa Barbara lecture, "A Writer and Religion," he was especially interested in the moment when a monastic discovers his or her vocation, the moment of insight which causes "gradual movement of life away from the pattern." A novelist must show this moment resourcefully, since an ordinary reader identifies with the ordinary. When the saint takes up his or her vocation, Isherwood advised, readers "will find something at once chilling and forbidding about his behavior, and we will say to ourselves, I can't understand that." (He had used such phrases to Tennessee Williams from his real-life monastery when ducking Williams's friendship in 1943, "Maybe the life I am trying very feebly to lead makes you uncomfortable, chilly down the spine?")[80]

This uncomfortable, chilling moment was the one about which Isherwood felt Maugham had been too vague in *The Razor's Edge*. Huxley had left it out altogether in *Time Must Have a Stop*, skipping over the development of his main character with a time lapse. George Moore had done it better in *Evelyn Innes* (1898) and *Sister Teresa* (1901), his pair of novels about an opera singer who becomes a Roman Catholic nun. After she enters the convent, Evelyn, now Sister Teresa, overhears the other nuns chattering impiously about trivialities, and she thinks she will go mad if she stays in the convent. Then she recalls the chatter of her aristocratic former friends and her companions of the stage, and she thinks she will go mad if she returns to her singing career. "And so she finds herself passing through the agony of belonging no place," Isherwood explained to his Santa Barbara audience, "and this, of course, is the beginning of her understanding of why she is really in a convent and what the religious vocation has meant to her."[81]

But the best accounts, in Isherwood's view, were in Dostoevsky's *The Brothers Karamazov* and Tolstoy's *Father Sergius*. Dostoevsky "doesn't quite tell you what triggered the whole mutation" in Zossima from officer to monk, but the night before the duel which Zossima forces upon the husband of the girl he fancies, Zossima wonders for the first time in his arrogant young life, "what am I worth that another man, a fellow creature, made in the likeness and image of God, should serve me?" He rushes to beg forgiveness of his servant whom he had struck, and at the duel he throws away his pistol. "We share the young man's exquisite relief when he finds himself suddenly able, by fearlessly asking his opponent's pardon, to break the bonds of a rigid military code which has hitherto conditioned his behavior, and to perform his first act of pure free will," Isherwood had written in "The Problem of the Religious Novel." "This is the kind of scene I should like to have in my novel—something slightly comic and entirely natural." At the end of his life, "a great saint—a man of extraordinary insight," as Isherwood put it, Zossima realizes "the terrible fate that lies in store for Dmitri Karamazov" and "he bows down before him to the ground, just as, in another context, he bowed down before his servant in his full uniform."[82] Isherwood found such empathy and compassion excruciatingly moving; the holy man bowing down to his spiritual junior had formed the center of his vision of Brahmananda on the last day of 1957.

Tolstoy's Father Sergius also begins as an upper-caste military man. Disillusioned when he discovers his fiancée has been the Tzar's mistress, he enters a monastery, but there he has a new worldly ambition—to be the *best* monk. Each of his spiritual attainments leads to a new temptation until, in despair, he becomes a wandering beggar, is arrested without a passport and transported to Siberia where he works "in the kitchen-garden, teaches children, and attends to the sick." Isherwood identified the story as "the best account that I know of a life progressing in this manner towards sainthood." Yet he said, "even in this remarkable work the kind of fun which I would like to see is absent."[83]

What did Isherwood mean by fun? "Why should the temptation of St. Anthony be a dreary scene?" he asked. "Why is there not a certain joy, a certain glee, in this whole process?" None of his predecessors, even Dostoevsky and Tolstoy, had fully succeeded in showing this in a religious novel.

In nonreligious novels, Isherwood could point to examples of the kind of energy—joy, glee—that he meant. He told his Santa Barbara lecture audience that he took the word "joy" from Robert Louis Stevenson's essay "The Lantern Bearers," and that he had in mind "a kind of higher fun, a kind of mad vitality which exists in the universe." The end of *Moby-Dick*, he said, "illustrates almost more vividly than anything that I know in literature this point about this joy, this underlying, enormous exhilaration, the wildness behind the actual events of the story." Ahab meets his tragic destiny when at last he harpoons the white whale and it turns and sinks the ship. "But my goodness, what a ball they are all having, and how in a strange way you feel that Ahab and the white whale and everybody else all adore each other and are part of an extraordinary kind of cosmic fun going on."[84]

Another example was the end Conan Doyle invented for Sherlock Holmes, wrestling with his nemesis the arch-criminal Dr. Moriarty above Reichenbach Falls and plummeting with him to their deaths. Isherwood once compared them to Ahab and the whale and identified Holmes as "one of the truly great comic characters in our literature."[85] He planned that his Christopher and Paul characters would likewise wrestle with their destinies embodied in one another. The dynamic reached back to Isherwood's childhood enthusiasm for mortal combat, to the knights in Walter Scott and to his first discovery in the *Illustrated London News* of Macbeth armored to fight Macduff. At Santa Barbara, he traced Melville's achievement to "the great roarings and bellowing of Shakespeare."[86]

Isherwood spoke about this joy, this mad vitality, not as something created by an artist but as something found by the artist at its source, whence the artist unleashes it. He considered it a sacred, metaphysical energy. "The saints have almost all been unanimous," he told his lecture audience, "insofar as they've expressed themselves on the subject in saying that in some way which the rest of us can't understand everything is finally all right. It is marvelous." His view looked past death, past the jaws of any whale.

He sourced his word "joy" not only in Robert Louis Stevenson but also in a saying from Hindu scripture: "In joy the universe was created, in joy it is sustained, in joy it dissolves." He recognized that his audience might find the

Hindu saying "unfeeling" because it "expresses a kind of indifference toward human suffering." But he pointed out that "some of these great men of compassion and mercy did in fact, in the midst of terrible suffering which they were working all through their lives to alleviate, nevertheless rejoice." He added an anecdote which Ramakrishna liked to tell, and which Isherwood included in his biography, about a wandering monk who visited the temple at Dakshineswar: "He used to come out of his cell twice a day and sit on the edge of the Ganges as though he were a spectator in the theater, and clap his hands and say, 'Bravo! Excellent!' as though the whole universe were an enormous theatrical performance."[87] For Isherwood, this kind of enagagement with joy was not frivolous; it was religious and profound. It was the performance put on by the universe in the illusion of maya.

In *Down There on a Visit*, Paul's first attempt to meditate is just such a gleeful performance, progressing from sobs to coughing to panting: "Then he actually started to roll about on the mat, jerking his knees up to his chest and relaxing them again; until one realized that this literally was a kind of accouchement. Something was being violently expelled and perhaps brought to birth. And the suffering was desperate."

This melodramatic account is reported by the only witness, Augustus Parr, the Heard character. It is both comical and frightening. "Do you know, Christopher," says Parr, "his face—it was suddenly the face of a pre-adolescent boy? One was in the presence of true innocence." The process reverses Dr. Jekyll's, when he drinks his "transcendental medicine" and is transformed into the monster Mr. Hyde in Robert Louis Stevenson's story;[88] Paul is transformed from evil to good, as if in an exorcism. Parr tells Christopher that Paul's experience "*might* have been the first sign of a true mutation, and not just a temporary emotional reaction," referring to Heard's theory of psychic evolution.

The importance of the physical process is underlined by Isherwood's remarks on D.H. Lawrence in his fourth Santa Barbara lecture. Lawrence created "a real revolution" because he had "a great sense of the physical" and a "fearlessly subjective approach." Isherwood explained that "we have somehow become divorced from what [Lawrence] described as the dark—he was very fond of the word *dark*—instinctive part of our nature, and have become too cerebral, too mental." Isherwood illustrated this with his favorite Lawrence story about the animal passion of the horse, St. Mawr, satanic when subjected to excessive control. And he begged his students to read "The Blind Man," included in his anthology *Great English Short Stories*. The blind man vanquishes his wife's suitor by feeling his rival's head and face and asking to be touched in return. The suitor feels annihilated and revulsed by the interaction. In his anthology preface, Isherwood equated Lawrence with the blind man, saying that he "writes, as it were, by touch rather than by thought; his greatest gift is his understanding of physical contact and its implications."[89]

Isherwood grounded "Paul" in Lawrentian darkness and physicality right from the opening lunch scene by giving his Ruthie character the comatose sensuality of Marilyn Monroe: "She is a big girl altogether; big hips, big bottom, big legs. I've seldom seen anyone look so placid, so wide-open to visitors, so sleepy-slow." At the lunch, Ruthie wears, as Monroe often did, a black silk dress cut so low it might be a nightgown and over the black silk dress a fur coat. She is drunk; indeed, she is always drunk or high, but her drunkenness is not evil: "She is an animal person; she has the cosy quality of a subhuman and therefore guiltless creature." In Ruthie's second scene, she is naked, lying by a swimming pool. "She grinned her slap-happy grin at me, without the smallest embarrassment."[90] She is surrounded by young men, and Paul tries to shock Christopher by fantasizing aloud that Ruthie has had sex with them all.

Ruthie was mostly modeled on Isherwood's friend Jean Connolly, but he met Marilyn Monroe a number of times in 1959 and 1960, and he enjoyed touching her. "I got drunk and hugged Marilyn Monroe a lot," he wrote after one Sunday-afternoon party.[91]

Ruthie and her reveling friends serve as a foil to the spiritual development of Paul, intended to keep readers engaged as the path of the saint grows strange and alienating. In his sixth Santa Barbara lecture, Isherwood explained that in any novel about a saint, "the others, his friends, his neighbors, the other characters in the book, are in fact themselves searching for the same thing that the saint is searching for. Only they're searching for it in the wrong direction and with the wrong means."[92] Fun-loving Ruthie is just one of the characters in "Paul" searching for meaning in drink, drugs, money, sex, or violence.

BACK IN 1941 when Heard took Fouts as his protégé, he had given him $10,000. It was part of the $100,000 that Heard had saved up to start his contemplative community, and Heard told Isherwood that it was perfectly logical to use the money to help future members of his community. Isherwood, however, observed that the money had a corrosive effect, like "a kind of bribe." He later wrote: "As soon as Denny had taken it, he was obligated; as soon as he was obligated, he began to feel guilty." Fouts's guilt grew "into resentment and near hatred."[93]

Isherwood reframed this to create the first attempts at free acts for his spiritual aspirants in "Paul." He had the Christopher character, not the Heard

8: Existential Isherwood: The Outsider (1961–1964) / 577

character, give a large sum of money to Paul: half his savings. "How tremendous—for once in one's life—to do something quite without compulsion, to break the greed-and-fear pattern by an absolutely free act!" But the narrative shows that this gift is not a free act, and the money corrupts Christopher's relationship with Paul just as it had corrupted Heard's relationship with Fouts in real life. The guardians of Plato's Just City are to have education but no material wealth; they are to value the higher good in acting for the happiness of the whole city and not just for their own happiness, as Isherwood was reminded by his reading of the *Republic* with Laughton. As the story unfolds, Christopher is shown to be merely bribing Paul to stay with him. "Already, out of the corner of my eye, I was watching to see how Paul was going to spend *my* ten thousand dollars." Paul buys gifts for his co-workers, repeating Christopher's mistake, "bribing them."

But with his own money, Paul expects nothing in return. Some Mexican-American teenagers, pachucos, swear Paul into their gang, talk him out of his money, crash his car, then abandon him to the police. He sees them as acting true to type and identifies with them: "After all, I'm a hustler, too. [...] Giving the kids that money made me feel wonderful."[94] Toward the end of "Paul," Christopher gives Paul 30,000 francs to buy opium. This dark echo of the original corrupting gift has no premeditated intention, no agenda for redemption, and leaves Paul free to make his own choice. Paul hastens away to start smoking up his new wealth. This freedom is the necessary prelude to his cure.

Paul undergoes other tests—sexual temptation and a trial by fire. At the religious retreat modeled on the La Verne Seminar (in an imaginary town waggishly called Eureka), Isherwood introduced two pubescent sisters, Allana and Dee-Ann Swendson, fourteen and twelve, who attend with their parents and cause sexual mayhem. Allana, feeling jealous, fabricates a story that she has seen Paul having sex with Dee-Ann. Paul, careless of the opinion of others, accepts the guilt for this even though nothing happened. Later, he is exonerated. At his C.O.'s firefighting camp, he rescues two firefighters trapped in a canyon, demonstrating recklessness in bravery equaling his recklessness in debauchery—debauchery for which he is expelled from the camp even though accusations of partying (marijuana, alcohol, gay sex tinged by racism and racial transgression) are unproved.

Throughout "Paul," Isherwood reversed conventional notions of virtue and vice in order to reveal vice as a pathway to virtue. "[I]s 'good' really good—is 'bad' really bad? In other words, isn't enlightenment what matters?" he asked in his workbook.[95]

In November 1961, as if chastened by the effort to write "Paul," Isherwood told an audience of Vedanta devotees in the temple in Santa Barbara:

> The portrayal of saints in fiction is quite beyond the power of most of us, and therefore it's much more satisfactory to try to write about them in terms of biography. I have often thought this since I have been working on a biography of Ramakrishna. [...] the moment you have an imaginary figure, and the moment you have to invent fictional circumstances, then you have a much greater difficulty convincing the reader that all this could possibly have happened.[96]

He had turned from "Paul" back to the Ramakrishna biography a few months earlier, and had to rein in his imagination. Instead of the exciting subjectivity he so admired in Lawrence and emulated in "Paul," he could record only what happened in Ramakrishna's life.

But Ramakrishna was an avatar, not a saint: "a saint is still a human being and an avatar is not," Isherwood explained in the biography. "An avatar has no 'past' in this sense, for he has no karma. He is not driven by his karma to be reborn; he takes human birth as an act of pure grace, for the good of humanity."[97] Thus, Isherwood could not identify with Ramakrishna in the way he customarily identified with his human characters. Moreover, he never had any opportunity to observe Ramakrishna in person and was forced to rely on the reports of others. This placed him in a humble relation to the life writing project.

In "Paul," by contrast, he was inventing and rearranging fearlessly. Comparison with his diaries shows myriad changes for the sake of the narrative. Among these were setting the final meetings between the Paul and Christopher characters in Paris in 1952, leaving out other friends who were present, and having Paul die there in the spring of 1953—the period when the real Isherwood was beginning his life with Bachardy—rather than in 1948 when Fouts died in Rome. Despite his humble statement to the Vedanta devotees in the temple, the novelist in him was boldly transforming Fouts's story into a portrait of a possible saint—a fiction more meaningful and more hopeful than the wretched tangle he had surveyed when he visited Fouts's grave. He was making yet another private offering, this time posthumously, to Fouts. He was also developing his apologia for his own life by winding Paul's story inside the larger fiction in *Down There on a Visit*.

There were other important changes to timing and locale. Isherwood kept his Ruthie character alive two years longer than Jean Connolly (dead of a stroke in 1950), so that the Christopher character could bump into her resurrecting the pre-Hitler bar life in Berlin on the last night of his 1952 visit there. Accompanying Ruthie in the Berlin bar is Ronny, the character based on Tony Bower. Bower "seemed to me to be a perfect specimen of the denier, the person who is roused to fury by any mention of the spiritual life and those who try to practice it," Isherwood later explained.[98]

He made Ronny the mouthpiece for comments about Fouts voiced by various real-life friends, comments synthesized and shaped to imply a spiritual trajectory that Ronny doesn't fully understand. The comments drew on New York gossip reported by Auden—that Fouts had given up Vedanta and returned to his life of sex and drugs and was the better for it. The comments also drew on details of Fouts's last days in Rome shared by John Goodwin, who wrote to Isherwood that not long before his death, Fouts had decided "he wanted to live, which was something he hadn't cared one way or another about for a long time."[99] In addition, Goodwin passed along the report from Tony Watson-Gandy—who found the body—that Fouts had not died by suicide or drugs and that his face showed no pain.

Isherwood seized on these details to devise the positive ending in which Paul has overcome his addiction and dies disintoxicated—a death befitting a potential saint. Ronny reports of his last visit that Paul was surrounded by young intellectuals arguing about the impossibility of life after death. "Paul, who had been listening to them without making any remark, suddenly said, 'You little fools!' My dear, you ought to have heard him! It was positively shattering. And he said it with such an air of authority; it was as if he actually *knew* something."[100] This Parisian scene, with its seriocomic gesture to a reality outside the narrative, again talks back to Gide.

In *Lafcadio's Adventures*, the English translation of Gide's *Les Caves du Vatican* (1914), which Isherwood read or reread in 1945, the free act can be either a crime or an act of virtue, and Lafcadio does not know why he chooses to commit one or the other. He rescues two children from a burning house (the trial by fire that Isherwood also used) and gives his reward to their mother, but he throws his brother-in-law from a moving train to his death. Lafcadio does know, however, that while the self can be improved, an action cannot be changed. "It's the power of revising that makes writing such a colorless affair—" he reflects. Life is more vivid because "erasures aren't allowed."[101] Lafcadio's novelist half-brother, his wan double, reaches the same conclusion, but he reaches it only in his imagination, by thinking not by acting, and he is easily frightened into abandoning his insight and playing safe.

Gide leaves Lafcadio free to make his final decisive act outside the covers of the book—will Lafcadio give himself up for murder? Isherwood lends his double Paul the same authenticity by leaving Paul free to make his last spiritual play outside the story Isherwood is writing. In the first three stories in *Down There on a Visit*, the narrative masters the characters; none of them is truly free. Paul, like Lafcadio, is allowed to break the frame, and the narrator accepts for himself the role of mere witness, a wan double like Lafcadio's half-brother, who lives by imagination not by action, playing it safe.

In the end, the story affirms that for the narrator what's really important is love. The Christopher character has trouble saying "love" aloud to Paul just as, at the beginning of their friendship, he has trouble saying "God." For Paul, knowledge is more important than love; he accepted no euphemism for God, and he wants clarity. "'All I can say is, you'd better start making up your mind before it's too late. Either be a proper monk or a dirty old man!'" he tells Christopher. It is for certain knowledge that Paul risks everything.

Isherwood's own spiritual journey was about love more than about knowledge, but "Paul" does not reveal much about Isherwood's conversion. Only Isherwood's diaries and later *My Guru and His Disciple* which drew on them make clear that it was not a one-time event or even a single episode but a long, spiraling sequence filled with conflict and setbacks as well as joy and laughter.

ISHERWOOD HAD AGREED to join Bachardy in England in the summer of 1961. Meanwhile, at home, he wore Bachardy's sneakers, noting in his diary, "I like to have on something of his." He reminded himself again and again to let Bachardy be genuinely free. "I must get over the most basic part of my possessiveness—wanting him to experience everything through myself as an intermediary."[102] All the time that he was writing "Paul," Isherwood was brooding on how to give Bachardy his independence without losing him altogether. They sometimes argued over his expenses when Bachardy was away from home with another lover; Isherwood grudgingly covered these.[103] Now that Bachardy's studies in London were being paid for by Russell McKinnon, the dynamic between Isherwood and Bachardy was subtly changing. Isherwood balked when faced with genuinely sacrificing his economic advantage over his beloved—a means of control ever since Berlin—and yet he was determined to do it, like the narrator in "Paul."

Bachardy wrote from London that he was desperately homesick, and they spoke on the telephone to mark their anniversary. Then Isherwood decided to join Bachardy earlier than planned, in April, as soon as he had finished giving his UCLA extension lectures, funding the trip with money due him from his mother's will.

Meanwhile, he invited a young man called John Zeigel to stay with him at Adelaide Drive. "[A] very sweet boy," he wrote in his diary, "intelligent, though on the prissy, academic side, and capable of serious love." The serious love in Zeigel's life was another older man, a former Trabuco monk, Ed

Halsey. Eventually, Isherwood put Zeigel on a plane to Mexico to join Halsey and concluded in his diary, "I guess, if there had never been a Don, I would have had a try at living with him; and I think it could have worked out. But then, so it could have with lots of people. That doesn't make him a Don, or even a Don-substitute, by a million miles."[104]

There were plenty of other trysts, with Paul Kennedy, Michael Hall, Jim Charlton, John Rechy, and Ben Underhill.* All the while, according to his diary, Isherwood was "absolutely impotent" but felt "terrific";[105] he was meditating and making japam, going to the gym regularly and losing weight.

When he finished revising "Paul" on March 14, he shared the typescript with Gavin Lambert, who thought it "the best thing I've done and altogether extraordinary." Next, he showed it to Heard, who did not like it. "I suspect that his feelings are somehow hurt." Heard's secretary and companion, Michael Barrie, thought Isherwood had portrayed Heard as a fake. Certainly Isherwood had extracted maximum comic effect from Heard's eccentric housekeeping and raggedy clothes. He mailed a copy to Bachardy, who reassured him that the Heard character was "a triumph," and who rushed to Dulwich to pass the typescript to Upward.

"This whole book is for you," Isherwood wrote to Bachardy. "It will be dedicated to you of course. But it will also be sort of privately dedicated in a way only Kitty and Dobbin will understand, because this is Dobbin's way of laying the best he knows how to do at Kitty's paws."[106] He was reminding Bachardy that although the four stories in the book were from his past life before they had met, each one contained details from their six years together along with coded messages of advice and understanding for Bachardy.

HAMPSTEAD, LONDON, 1961

Isherwood settled in with Bachardy at 11 Squire's Mount, a small brick house on the southwest side of Hampstead Heath. It belonged to Richard Burton and his first wife, the actress Sybil Williams, both away in New York where Burton was appearing on Broadway in *Camelot*. Isherwood and Bachardy had befriended the Burtons at a Hollywood party, and Isherwood had worked on a screenplay for Burton of Robert Louis Stevenson's story "The Beach of Falesá."

Bachardy seemed to Isherwood "desperately tense and full of his usual fears, plus a new one—that he won't ever be able to paint in oils." He found his tutor Keith Vaughan shy and "astringent," as he had told Isherwood in

---

* Not his real name.

one letter, and "frank and tough in his criticisms." Bachardy was determined to prove himself, and he was doing private sittings with writers and theater people met through John Gielgud's doctor and close friend, Patrick Woodcock, and through Isherwood's address book. Isherwood sat for two portraits as soon as he arrived. "Don seems more vulnerable, more nervous but also more alive here," Isherwood typed on a clunky manual typewriter he rented. "He is like a burning fuse, almost; a fuse that is burning eagerly toward the point of explosion."[107]

Upward came to Hampstead to talk about *Down There on a Visit*, and Isherwood developed the frame uniting the four episodes. He also sent the typescript to Auden, who, commenting on "Ambrose," "objected to Christopher's reasons for leaving the island; the urge to go back and compete with Timmy North."[108] The criticism revealed how firmly Auden ruled out rivalry with contemporaries as a motive for action. Isherwood remained determined to portray his nature honestly, whether it showed him to be heroic or merely human. After two months in England, he delivered the typescript to Alan White at Methuen and sent a copy to Curtis Brown in the U.S., then sold the manuscript to a collector for fifty pounds.

In June, Bachardy was offered a show of his drawings at the Redfern Gallery in Cork Street, Mayfair. "Triumph!" Isherwood crowed in his diary. They had been on the edge of their seats while the gallery looked at Bachardy's work, asked to see more, considered further. "He thinks it was largely the fact that he had gotten Stravinsky and Beaton to pose for him that did the trick!" Isherwood wrote. "He will only have one little narrow room—but it's the Redfern, and the Redfern is THE TOP." He considered the show to be "a justification" of Bachardy's whole stay in England. "Don is wild with joy. And I am spinning plans, how best to exploit the victory and turn it into a rejoicing for our friends and a rebuke to our enemies." He believed in Bachardy's talent completely and reveled in his personal qualities. After a dinner party given by his old school friend Eric Falk, Isherwood typed that Bachardy "absolutely sparkled like a diamond. He seemed a creature of another kind, altogether." [109]

AUDEN ARRIVED IN London on June 7. Hans Werner Henze's opera *Elegy for Young Lovers*, for which Auden and Kallman had written the libretto, was to open on July 13 at the Glyndebourne Festival sixty miles south of London. "[O]n the stage it should be marvellous," wrote Isherwood in his diary after reading the libretto, but at the premiere, the music "reminded me of pangs of arthritis, sudden and sharp and unpredictable."[110]

Plans were afoot, also, to work with Auden and Kallman on a musical about Sally Bowles. Carter Lodge and Dick Foote had mooted the project in June 1958, and Isherwood had heard some proposed music on a New York trip in the autumn of 1959. Frank Taylor had introduced a possible financial backer, and Isherwood had fretted when Taylor "went all around town asking people if Wystan can really write poetry." He was anxious that Auden might be "too cerebral," but he was loyal. In any case, Taylor had refused to put up money "till Wystan and I can work and be together." Taylor had proposed casting Marilyn Monroe as Sally Bowles.[111]

In the spring of 1960, Auden had written to Isherwood that he wanted to create a new kind of musical, and he had warned that the result "might be, commercially, the most frightful flop."[112] Giving the material to professional musical comedy writers might be more lucrative. Nevertheless, in this and a subsequent long letter he had flooded Isherwood with ideas for the project. Isherwood had explored a collaboration with Sandy Wilson, creator of the 1953 musical *The Boy Friend*, and Wilson wrote a few songs, but the effort came to nothing.

By the spring of 1961, the musical had attracted the interest of Tony Richardson and the British stage and film producer Oscar Lewenstein, and the three collaborators would at last be able to meet in person. However, Isherwood wasn't optimistic. In one of his letters, Auden had endorsed a suggestion from Kallman that they start from scratch with a new main character: "Herr Issyvoo must go and be replaced by a new hero—possibly a sort of mixture of you, me, and Stephen [...] he ought to be quite overtly queer." As an afterthought, Auden had mentioned, "We shall need Sally, of course, but there will be no misunderstandings about the heart." Between them, Auden and Kallman seemed likely to push Isherwood off the stage, just as Van Druten had done. They outnumbered him artistically and financially. To his diary, Isherwood admitted, "I don't really like Chester," and "they want us to split three ways, while I feel that I should have something extra as the original author."

They worked together half a dozen times during June and July in London, and Curtis Brown negotiated with Richardson and Lewenstein. Isherwood continued to think Auden and Kallman's ideas were unworkable, but above all, he sensed that neither was genuinely interested, and perhaps this was partly why he couldn't get interested himself.

Eventually, Auden and Kallman proposed a new setting for the musical, jettisoning even Berlin. "It can be that our mistake is in fixing our minds on Berlin," wrote Auden later in the summer, and he revealed that, for him, inspiration had to come from his own artistic personality: "the essential donnée at which the imagination catches fire, has not yet been granted to us.

When Chester, I and Henze started discussing Elegy, the same thing happened to begin with. Then the moment we realized that our central figure was a great poet, everything came to life." The great poet Mittenhofer in *Elegy for Young Lovers* is a version of Auden himself.

As Auden and Kallman had written in an Afterword, "The Theme of *Elegy for Young Lovers* is summed up in two lines by Yeats, 'The intellect of man is forced to choose / Perfection of the life or of the work.'"[113] Mittenhofer, the poet, chooses work, and the opera depicts him as a kind of murderer. He sends the lovers on an errand in the mountains, where they freeze to death in a blizzard, yielding a subject for the elegy. Isherwood, in contrast to Auden, had not abandoned hope that something close to perfection was possible in both his life and his work. He was unwilling to choose between them. The days when these two large personalities, Auden and Isherwood, could collaborate, were long over; each had a different kind of story to tell. A third collaborator, Kallman, didn't help. A few more letters were exchanged, and the musical project was dropped.

Berlin itself, however, was in the headlines all summer. On June 3 and 4, 1961, President Kennedy and Soviet leader Khrushchev held talks in Vienna at which they failed to agree about the future of the divided city. Khrushchev intended to transfer Soviet authority over East Berlin to East Germany, ending the agreements made among the four victors at the end of World War II and forcing the Western Allies to negotiate with communist East Germany, a new country they were reluctant to recognize, while they continued sending supplies to West Berlin. Kennedy told Khrushchev that the West had a moral obligation to the two million people in West Berlin and would not give up its right of access. There was military buildup on both sides, and residents of East Berlin fled to West Berlin in increasing numbers. By mid-August, the East Germans closed the border within the city and began to build the Berlin Wall. The crisis lasted until mid-October when the U.S. agreed to accept the reality of two German states and urged West Germany to do the same. The new status quo continued to be extremely dangerous; East German imposition of new passport checks led to another face-off in late October, with tanks on either side of the new wall, a hundred yards apart, and tactical nuclear weapons nearby.

Isherwood was continuously reminded of the 1938 Munich Crisis and shuddered over every headline. His greatest fear was being separated from Bachardy if war broke out. As the crisis built and Bachardy's show neared, Isherwood felt the same powerless indignation that had haunted his final years in Europe before he emigrated.

Despite the crisis, Neddermeyer visited London with his wife and son, borrowing Forster's flat in Chiswick in early July. He had managed to resettle his family in Wanne-Eickel, Herne, West Germany. Isherwood feared being drawn into any plans they might have to emigrate to the U.S., but when they met, he was impressed by Neddermeyer, who, nine years after their last meeting in 1952 in Berlin, had a deep voice and had grown "enormous—not merely fatter, but taller and broader." To please his wife, Neddermeyer had given up smoking, drinking, and gambling; he was focused on saving money and securing his family's comfort and safety after their wartime suffering. Isherwood was surprised to find on this meeting that he liked Gerda, too.

He did not introduce Bachardy. He was protecting Bachardy and Neddermeyer and also Gerda and Christian, who, if they had been brought face-to-face with Isherwood's sparkling young American lover, might have been forced to see husband and father in a new light. Bachardy came to regret this missed opportunity.

One night, Isherwood and the Neddermeyers had dinner with Auden and Kallman: "we got drunk and sang a little," Isherwood recorded, and he was moved to revise *Down There on a Visit* before he handed his final changes to his publishers, making the last fictional reunion with Waldemar in Berlin "warmer."

He continued to circulate the typescript, fearlessly sharing it with bigtime talkers. Capote, who was in London, delighted Isherwood "by calling to say that it is the best thing I have ever written!" Capote wrote to Andrew Lyndon: "Liked it very much. Sort of 'Goodbye to Berlin' brought up to date. It's almost *too* frank."[114]

RELATIONS WITH BACHARDY were changeable. "It's the old story: he can't have any friends of his own as long as I'm around, because, even if he finds them, they take more interest in me as soon as we meet." Bachardy wanted elbow room, but he was ambitious for his work and he also wanted the entrée that Isherwood could provide: "he knows I'll be useful when he has this show."

Each had outside sexual interests, and their affairs intermittently blew up between them. Once when Isherwood didn't return home overnight, Bachardy subjected him to a day of silent fury. "When he is in this mood, he is absolutely *black*," wrote Isherwood, and he continued to feel frustrated when Bachardy made last-minute dates, leaving him with a solitary evening too late to plan.

Bachardy was increasingly absorbed by his work. He told Isherwood that he felt "miserable unless he can draw for three hours at the very least, every day."[115] With the show in his sights, he worked like a fiend, making portraits of Dodie Smith and Alec Beesley, Vivien Leigh, Auden, Kallman, Albert Finney, Joe Ackerley, Margaret Leighton, Lotte Lenya, Forster, and Gielgud. One morning he drew seven portraits of Isherwood. On the side, he continued to earn money doing fashion drawings.

They spent a weekend with Cecil Beaton at Reddish House in Wiltshire, where Bachardy drew with Beaton. Afterwards, Isherwood began reading Beaton's diaries, *The Wandering Years, 1922–1939*, which made him see Beaton in a new light: "He is an extraordinarily heroic figure. In the last resort, he has nothing except his work. No friends. No alleviating vices. No real faith. Nothing. And he knows that." After an evening with Beaton at the theater, Isherwood wrote, "for almost the first time, I felt affection."[116]

Isherwood went to Manchester at the end of June to participate in a TV talk show with Auden, Spender, Connolly, and four younger British writers, but Richard wouldn't permit him to visit Wyberslegh. He was allowed to return a month later for the first time since Kathleen's death. Guilt no longer hung over the wild northern landscape, and he felt more positive at Wyberslegh than he had felt anywhere else in England this visit, describing in his diary sensations he was to give George almost word for word in his next novel, *A Single Man*: "it seemed extraordinarily cheerful, joyful, almost, with a sort of childhood joy when I woke in the morning and heard the wind seething in the beeches, and looked out and saw the line of the moors, which is so different in different lights but has a sense of always-thereness like the sea."

He also described Richard's obsessive and crippling class-consciousness; his affection for Alan Bradley, his "pal and best friend," who tucked him into bed at night when Richard stayed at the Bradley home; his ten-bottles-of-beer-a-day alcohol habit; his appearance of insanity while being, in Isherwood's view, completely sane. Most poignant was Richard's feeling that he had been "left behind."

The mound where Richard had buried Kathleen's ashes was right outside the front door at Wyberslegh. "It's admirably Buddhist in feeling," Isherwood noted. "I went out in the windy morning of my last day there and tried to dedicate the spot with *mantrams* to Ramakrishna."

Just before leaving England, in October, he squeezed in another visit and met Alan Bradley and his family. They sat up drinking illegally after closing time at a local pub, the Ploughboy, before spending the night at the Bradleys' house. Alan and his wife Edna assured Isherwood that "I needn't worry about Richard because they had solemnly promised my mother on her deathbed, etc. etc." until Isherwood grew tired of hearing it. "I do see the snugness and consolation which Richard gets from them."[117]

At the Ploughboy, Isherwood recorded, "a 'character' named Reg appeared," a Mortmere type. "He said, 'The Americans are living in a world of fantasy,'" and quoted poetry, in particular Henry Newbolt's most famous poem "Vitaï Lampada," which Isherwood had known since boyhood. The poem compares a hard-fought cricket match to a disastrous battle in the failed campaign to relieve the siege of Khartoum before General Gordon and his men were massacred there by the Sudanese Mahdists in 1885. It was a poem glorifying empire and bloodshed, and the refrain "Play up! And play the game!" which Isherwood mistakenly recalled as the title, summed up everything he objected to in the game of the Others; indeed it was a likely first source for Isherwood's lifelong theme. The idea that school games prepared Isherwood's generation to fight the wars of the British Empire had helped drive Isherwood from England. He was to incorporate Reg into *A Single Man*.

IN JULY, TONY Richardson's production of John Osborne's *Luther*, starring Albert Finney as the Roman Catholic monk who launched the Protestant Reformation, had opened at the Royal Court followed by "a big showy party on stage."[118] Isherwood and Bachardy attended, and Richardson invited them for a holiday at a farmhouse he and Osborne had rented in the South of France. Isherwood half-heartedly agreed, partly because remaining in England long enough for Bachardy's show would make him liable for British income tax; ten days in France would solve this.

"La Baumette is a tall stone farmhouse with blue shutters, surrounded by vines and olive trees," Isherwood wrote. It was in the hills above Cannes, near a village called Valbonne, with a distant view of the sea from the highest point of the property. It was the setting for heartbreak because Osborne, who had just left his second wife Mary Ure, was conducting two love affairs, one at La Baumette and a new one off site in Venice. Fascinated though he was, the strain distressed Isherwood. "Awful depression, caused by/causing pyloric spasm and stomach sickness. Misery, sulks," he noted of the second day.

They lay by the pool, Richardson reading *A Passage to India*, Isherwood trying to interest him in a movie idea. "Our fearful mistake was to come here and stay with him. When you are at his mercy, he can drive you absolutely nuts. You have to do exactly what he says, every moment of the day." Then, suddenly, Richardson left in the middle of the night with one of the guests, rushing back to London for a press preview of his film adaptation of *A Taste of Honey*. Osborne with his betrayed lover left the next day, and Richardson returned, reporting that the preview had been a success and that Bachardy's portraits of the cast "are framed and exhibited at the theater." There were twelve drawings at the Odeon in Leicester Square, all the actors plus Richardson and the playwright, Shelagh Delaney.

In Richardson's absence, Isherwood and Bachardy shared a sumptuous, drunken lunch with Maugham and Alan Searle at Villa Mauresque, and Isherwood had a climactic professional face-off with Maugham, recorded in his diary. Maugham recalled the success he had once imagined for Isherwood, back in 1938 when he had praised Isherwood to Virginia Woolf as the key novelist of his generation, "and then you threw it all away" for personal happiness and for Vedanta. "'And' said Willie, 'I envy you.'" Isherwood countered "that the game wasn't over yet, and he should wait till he read my new novel."[119] Maugham did not yet know that Isherwood had reimagined *The Narrow Corner*, *The Razor's Edge*, and *The Magician* in *Down There on a Visit*.

METHUEN WAS USING one of Bachardy's pencil portraits of Isherwood as the author picture for the jacket of *Down There on a Visit*, and for the main image on the front had accepted a Bachardy design with a sketch of an Isherwood-like figure looking at his younger self in a mirror. Isherwood was uncomfortable with the visual suggestion that the character in the book was himself rather than a fictional being. "I'm sure the mirror idea is good, but making the faces look like me makes the whole thing somehow indiscreet."[120] He gave in when he saw the proof. In New York, Simon & Schuster decided on the same cover.

Bachardy's opening on October 2 was a knockout. He had persuaded the Redfern to give him a bigger room, and still the crowd stood crammed halfway up the stairs. "Don was interviewed and photographed by the press, while I kept away in a corner, nearly splitting with pride," wrote Isherwood in his diary.

"Willie Maugham created a major sensation by appearing for a short while with Alan Searle. Forster and Joe Ackerley stayed quite a long time." Amiya attracted press attention in her role as Countess of Sandwich, and she was photographed with Bachardy in front of her portrait. Some of the portraits sold, and Bachardy received many commissions. "After it was all over, we took Francis Bacon out to supper at Gale's. He had stayed all through the show and somehow given it his blessing, although obviously he couldn't have thought very highly of this kind of work."[121] Bachardy had persuaded Bacon to sit for him and got the portrait framed just in time to hang it in the show.

ADELAIDE DRIVE, SANTA MONICA, 1961

Back in Los Angeles, the thirty-year-old English novelist and critic Colin Wilson was lecturing at Long Beach. Wilson's book about existentialism and religion, *The Outsider*, analyzed the figure of the Outsider in Dostoevsky, Sartre, Camus, Hemingway, Henry James, William James, Shaw, Thomas Mann, T.E. Lawrence, George Fox, Ramakrishna and others. "It didn't interest me much as a book. But as a theme it is of prime significance," Isherwood had written when he read it in 1956. "I not only take it for granted that I'm an Outsider but I really am only interested in modern books if they are written from an Outsider's point of view. An Outsider but not a No Sider. [...] The Outsider stands outside the modern conformist world, looking in—but with passion, with sincere involvement, with heartfelt hostility."[122]

Wilson wanted to meet Aldous Huxley and Henry Miller, both mentioned in his book,[123] so Isherwood, Wilson, Miller and Miller's thirteen-year-old son drove up to see Huxley in the Hollywood Hills. Huxley's house in Deronda Drive had burned to the ground in a brush fire in May. He and Laura had managed to save only the manuscript of the novel he was writing, *Island* (1962), Laura's Guarneri violin, and a few clothes. They were now living further up the same hillside with Laura's close friend Virginia Pfeiffer.

Wilson, who in *The Outsider* had attacked Huxley's novels for seeming to accept that "absolutely nothing can be done" to make man "stronger," and "less of a slave of circumstances," was "very brash and rather embarrassing," according to Isherwood, asking why Huxley wasn't more like Hemingway. Huxley was reticent. "It simply isn't in him to defend himself," wrote Isherwood.[124] Deep down, this triggered Isherwood's protective impulse, as it had on the savage night with Brecht and Viertel. In *A Single Man*, Isherwood was to take up Huxley's defense, revealing his profound reverence and shy love for him.

He went to countless other lunches, dinners, movie outings, and parties—all just to distract himself. He felt "sick with misery" as he waited for the next word from Bachardy. "Without him my life is pointless. Jaw still bothering me. And I have the shits. I am at the lowest ebb."[125] For weeks, his jaw had ached and felt sticky, but he resisted the temptation to go to the doctor, partly because he recalled Kolisch's advice that it would be necessary only once when it was already too late, and partly because he didn't want to learn that his symptoms were serious.

He forced himself to spend a few days at Trabuco in early November. Prabhavananda was there and took note of Isherwood's deep unhappiness. Isherwood asked, as he had asked before, whether Prabhavananda was certain God exists and whether God helped him bear his misfortunes. Prabhavananda reassured him: "I just know He will take care of me. . . . It's rather hard to explain . . . Whatever happens, it will be all right." Another swami joined them in the cloister where they were sitting, and in front of this witness, Prabhavananda proposed to make Isherwood a swami, skipping the preliminary brahmacharya vows and administering the final ones: "Stay here, Chris, and I'll give you *sannyas*. You shall have a special dispensation from the Pope." Recording this in his diary, Isherwood recalled, "He said this laughingly, but I have a feeling that he really meant it [...] it staggered me."[126]

He signed on for the spring semester at Los Angeles State College and began to plan two literature courses and a writing course. It was not really for the money. He had received over $14,000, about half the money due him from his mother's will, and he had not yet touched the American advance for *Down There on a Visit*. He was working steadily if unenthusiastically on the Ramakrishna biography, and he was brooding on what he should write next. "I keep thinking of a possible father-son novel, about Don and me, more or less."

During November, he returned to work with Charles Laughton on the Socrates project. He was inspired by a new approach which he described to Bachardy as, "Sort of Pirandelloish, but different." He was referring to *Six Characters in Search of an Author*, which he and Bachardy had seen on the emotion-filled night before Bachardy left for London in January. To the existing three-part draft, he added a new opening in which the actors break character to discuss how to bring Socrates to life. Laughton was to say to the audience: "Socrates is in the Dialogues, of course. His arguments are, and his methods of arguing—they give you clues. But that's all. [...] we've got to look for him where he's still alive. [...] Here in the Present Moment. In our world. Today."

The Socrates project was to be abandoned when Laughton died at the end of the following year, but Isherwood was to cast his character George in *A Single Man* as a Socrates for the 1960s. George is a teacher, a philosopher, a pederast, with "bulges of flesh over the belt of the shorts." He may be compared, as Alcibiades compares Socrates in the *Symposium*, to the busts of Silenus with pipes and flutes in their mouths, busts which can be opened to reveal images of the gods inside. He may also be compared to Marsyas the Satyr. George is at home in the "physical democracy" of the gym, where naked men of varying ages work side by side to improve their physiques, as they did in fifth-century B.C. Athens. After his late-night swim with Kenny, George sees the blanket in which Kenny wraps himself as an ancient Greek garment, until Kenny yawns and stretches: "The chlamys slips off his other shoulder. He pulls it back over both shoulders as he rises, turning it into a blanket again and himself into a gawky twentieth-century American boy comically stranded without his clothes."

The ritual of the drunken "Platonic dialogue" takes place at the Starboard Side, and Isherwood distinguishes the quality of the communication between George and Kenny from ordinary conversation: "George can almost feel the electric field of the dialogue surrounding and irradiating them." The parties to the dialogue are symbolic opposites, "in this case, Youth and Age," and the dialogue is impersonal, permitting them to "say absolutely anything"[127] and thereby to open new ground.

Thus, the time spent with Laughton suggested to Isherwood how he could build on the August night spent discussing homosexual love with the Benton Way Group as he developed his ideas for his father-son novel and reanimated the ideals of ancient Athens in Santa Monica Canyon.

BACHARDY WAS OFFERED a debut exhibition in New York for January 1962. He cabled details from London, proposing that he and Isherwood spend Christmas in New York with Julie Harris and her producer husband Manning Gurian.

Bachardy was to arrive first, in early December, but the plans became confusing, and Harris telephoned Isherwood on December 4 to ask why Bachardy had not appeared. On December 9, Isherwood received a letter from Bachardy, dated December 6, saying that Harris had never confirmed the invitation. Bachardy was still in London, would travel soon and would cable his plans. Isherwood bought a plane ticket to fly east on December 14, but on December 11, he received a cable from Bachardy, who was already in New York: "STRAY KITTEN FOUND IN NY MEWING FOR A HORSE IF YOU KNOW THIS CAT COME AT ONCE. =NYSPCA="

Isherwood flew to New York that very night, touching down at dawn on December 12. Bachardy never told Isherwood that he had in fact arrived in New York on December 10 to be with Paul Millard. He had not seen Millard since leaving for the Slade, and he now ended their affair. The trouble he took disguising his activities created a week of anxiety for Isherwood, who wondered repeatedly in his diary "where was Don?" Whether or not Bachardy intended to hold Isherwood's attention by keeping him guessing, he had succeeded.[128]

The New York visit proved to be a cruel test. Bachardy's show was at the Sagittarius Gallery, run by one Count Lanfranco Rasponi, a publicity agent for Italian opera and New York restaurants and a society party fixer who ran his gallery on the side to showcase young artists. After seeing photographs of Bachardy's work, sent from London, Rasponi had challenged, "Haven't you anything else besides portraits? [...] I cannot base a show on the question mark of how many portait commissions we can get." But Cecil Beaton had made the connection for Bachardy and reassured him that Rasponi was "reliable, a gentleman and a good business man."[129]

As soon as he arrived, Isherwood came down with a "toxic" sore throat accompanied by a high fever and was forced to see a doctor, David Protetch, a friend of Auden and the Stravinskys. Protetch was reassuring, and Isherwood felt soothed by a visit from Auden, a born nanny. After a day in bed on pencillin, the throat improved; but Isherwood's jaw felt sticky, and his stomach began to flutter. "[C]an I be of use to Don here?" he wondered to his diary. "Otherwise I'd be far better off in California, getting on with my work."

The Christmas bustle included parties, shopping, a trip to the ballet with Kirstein, a snowy weekend with Gore Vidal and Howard Austen at their country house, the Philadelphia opening of Vidal's new play, *Romulus*, and a preview of Tennessee Williams's new play, *The Night of the Iguana*, preceded by dinner at Sardi's with Williams and his family and Frank Merlo. On his own, Isherwood saw *The Play of Daniel* for which Auden had written the narration: "beautifully done and I guess enjoyable if you like twelfth-century religious drama with quaintness and chanting in Latin. It was in a church." Bachardy drew one society hostess after another and a few celebrities, constantly in a rush.

On the day of the opening, January 2, Isherwood and Bachardy were at the Sagittarius Gallery from 2:30 until 7 p.m. Auden, Kirstein, and Julie Harris with Manning Gurian loyally appeared right at the beginning; the movie star Myrna Loy, whose portrait was in the show, also came, and Marian Winters who had played Natalia Landauer in *I Am a Camera*. Finally, "[a]n hour and a half before closing time, Marguerite appeared, bringing with her socialites and journalists; and cameras flashed," as Isherwood wrote gratefully in his diary of Marguerite Brown who was nearing the end of her second marriage, to actor and would-be writer Rory Harrity. Nearly half of the thirty-five drawings sold.

Once the show was open, the mood between Isherwood and Bachardy soured. Bachardy wanted to stay in New York fulfilling commissions, but he had an airplane ticket to California which would expire on January 19. He asked Isherwood to use his ticket, pretending to be Bachardy; he would later use Isherwood's ticket, pretending to be Isherwood. Isherwood resisted. He didn't want to leave so soon, and he feared the embarrassment of being caught. Bachardy became furious and "said he didn't want to see me any more if I wouldn't do what he said."

In London, Bachardy had experienced a feeling of extreme letdown after his show opened at the Redfern. Isherwood had sympathized, and he recognized that it was made worse because the newspapers, which always commented abundantly on his own work, made almost no comment on Bachardy's. *The Times* had printed a portrait of Auden; another, of Albert Finney, appeared in the *Arts Review*, both with mild praise. In New York, Bachardy was interviewed only by the *New York Herald Tribune*. His behavior got out of hand. On January 12, Isherwood wrote cryptically: "My face is healing up nicely now, from the marks of where Don slammed the taxi door on (in?) it." The cuts required attention from Dr. Protetch and then four visits to a Dr. von Linde, presumably a plastic surgeon.

Isherwood was defiant: "I have every intention of surviving somehow. *I shall return*." He decided to remain in New York after all, for a meeting at the National Institute of Arts and Letters on January 24, and then return to California by train. He received first copies of *Down There on a Visit* from Simon & Schuster and did publicity interviews. "A boy named Andy Warhol," as he described the future phenomenon, drew Isherwood's feet for "a book of foot drawings of well-known people!"[130]

Bachardy worked relentlessly. Among the many portraits he drew during January were Jerome Robbins, Paul Newman and Joanne Woodward, Norman Mailer, Anita Loos, and Isherwood himself, as a thank-you gift for Julie Harris.

Before returning his rented typewriter and boarding his train, Isherwood tapped out a bitter farewell:

> So goodbye to one of the nastiest, most miserable phases of my life. I hate this city anyhow, and I've hated being here this time because of the way Don has acted. Right now, he is nerve-strung almost to the screaming point and it is misery to be with him. I'm sure he hates me and I rather hate him, I mean on the surface. Underneath, things are more or less as they've been for years. Whether we shall go on living together, and whether we ought to if we do, remains to be discovered.

Snow blanketed the country, "right across the Plains and the mountains," until his train descended toward the California border, at Needles, on the Colorado River. Rolling across the desert at sunset, drinking Scotch, he roughed out a letter to Bachardy. He set aside their Kitty and Dobbin personalities as "sentimental" and wrote from his heart: "You are so much the reason for my life—my writing, the house, my teaching. You say, that's just accident. Anyone could have been the reason. No. You know that's not true." Isherwood had searched the world for a partner, and he continued to spend time, curious and open-minded, with any boy who interested him. They both knew that Bachardy was the one. "My selfishness is that I want you to stay with me. Your selfishness is that you ask yourself, couldn't you do better; considering you are young. So my selfishness is really much more sinister than yours."

He never sent the letter; he only copied it into his diary. Bachardy called from New York the day after Isherwood arrived home, saying he would be coming back to Adelaide Drive sooner than he thought, and that, as Isherwood recorded, he was "considering buying six chairs for the dining room at the cost of six hundred dollars. So he certainly seems to mean to stay!"[131]

THEY WERE HEADED into a long period of turbulence. While Bachardy was still away, Isherwood failed to settle down to work. He drank too much, stayed out late, and couldn't function the next day. He found Bachardy's letters "puzzling and disturbing" because "he utterly ignores all the things he said to me in New York. It's just Kitty and Dobbin as it was in the beginning." Bachardy proposed to return in time for their Valentine's Day anniversary, another bit of sentiment. "And then what?" Isherwood wondered in his diary.

Bachardy didn't return until three days after the anniversary. Isherwood asked no questions. "[W]e have been very harmonious," he wrote after a week, but he observed a change. "What I see is a reserve. He doesn't seem so childishly open as before. [. . .] he seems more in control of the situation."

Bachardy had been away for more than a year. He was worried about his work now that he was not in school and had no show for which to prepare, and he resolved to get to grips again with the challenge of painting. But, as Isherwood wrote in his diary, "The temptation, in a way, is to have another show here, of drawings."[132]

Isherwood himself was bound for a new flurry of public attention. *Down There on a Visit* was already available in some bookstores, and friends were reading it. David Selznick phoned from New York asking permission to show the novel "to 'several top-flight dramatists'" because Jennifer Jones wanted to play Maria Constantinescu on stage. Bachardy had written to Isherwood while still in New York that Julie Harris and Manning Gurian, Marian Winters, her husband Jay Smolen, and the playwright Bill Inge "all praise 'The Dub's Story' very much." Bachardy had given his own copy to Tennessee Williams. Anita Loos was also reading it. In L.A., Ivan Moffat, Alan Campbell, Dorothy Parker and Chris Wood were "enthusiastic," and Parker was reviewing it for *Esquire*. Auden read it again and told Isherwood it was his "'finest to date' and that Paul is 'quite magnificent.'" Kirstein chimed, "the structure of PAUL is pyrotechnic." Mark Schorer phoned from San Francisco to express his enthusiasm. The poet Henri Coulette, Isherwood's colleague at L.A. State, wittily and perceptively observed, "Dostoevsky in a beach towel." John Lehmann sent advance galleys of Julian Jebb's review for the *London Magazine*, in which Jebb called "Ambrose" Isherwood's finest work so far.[133]

In America, the book was highly praised by the reviewer for the *New York Times*, Gerald Sykes, who compared Ambrose and Paul as homosexual characters to Proust's Baron de Charlus. William Peden in the *Saturday Review* also noticed Isherwood's debt to French literature, placing the novel beside Rousseau's *Confessions* and Gide's *Journals* and hearing in it "the authentic ring of a small, offbeat classic." Isherwood conjectured that the long, showoff piece of mixed praise and barbs by the *Time* interviewer "will sell copies."[134]

But Herbert Mitgang reviewing for the *New York Times Book Review* was uncomfortable with the homosexual themes and resorted to euphemism, labeling it "an apologia for abnormality." The reviewer for the *New York Herald Tribune*, Gouverneur Paulding, was overwhelmed by disgust, and described the book as "loathsome," "sordid," "unhappy," "sad and disquieting." Isherwood took pity on him, recognizing "a conditioned reflex puritan attack on the subject matter."[135]

The reaction in England was more personal. "I doubt if Mr Isherwood has written a single line that has not given me pleasure," wrote Cyril Connolly in the *Sunday Times*. Connolly was enthralled by *Down There on a Visit* partly because, as he acknowledged, he had known "one or two" of the characters in real life. In fact, he had known far more than two, and he had been married to the original of Ruthie: "at any moment one hopes to come on a flattering description of oneself," he joked. Still, he recognized the skill with which Isherwood had transformed his raw material: "The technical mastery of the time factor, of the integration of novel and diary is so complete that one takes it for granted like a smooth running engine."[136]

The good reviews in England were not all by friends. "[C]ompulsively readable," Norman Shrapnel pronounced in the *Manchester Guardian Weekly*, "and as funny as hell." Richard Mayne in the *New Statesman*, like Connolly, saw it as "the perfect vehicle for [Isherwood's] formidable and dangerous charm" which was "offset by a new gravity and immense moral fastidiousness."[137]

In fact, as reviewers, Isherwood's friends again proved to be his deadliest enemies. Angus Wilson in the *Observer* berated Isherwood for returning to the manner of earlier stories rather than progressing with the "constructed novel" he had attempted in *The World in the Evening* and suggested that "his cult of the private emotion and the personal relationship" was "trivial." Spender in the *New Republic* appeared miffed to be shut out from favored-friend insights. He simply could not read the book as fiction: "One assumes that some things are real, others invented. But which?" He complained that "this book only visits the edge of horrors"—Berlin and the Nazis. "Possibly this book is a preliminary for a novel which will really visit Hell."[138]

Isherwood had of course jettisoned the Dantesque version of *Down There on a Visit* in which the narrator really visits Hell, because he knew such a visit was, for him, a sham on several levels. Spender continued to attack his friend for being absent from the Hell of England during the war, and he continued to envy the life Isherwood had chosen elsewhere.

Forster told Isherwood privately that he didn't like the book. "I didn't want Christopher or his variant to guide me through a book by you any more." He admitted that he had reacted the same way to Conrad's Marlow, and with regard to the Christopher character went on: "I don't always find him a help towards the matter in hand. And your matter is important and enormous." Isherwood's reply to Forster was loving and robustly confident. He had long since decided that he must break out of the artistic world of his mentor. There were readers who *did* need a guide into his world; he was not writing just for Bloomsbury or his old London literary clique. Conrad used Marlow to heighten the mystery, beauty, or horror at the heart of his tales; Isherwood used Christopher to reduce these qualities, to tame his socially unacceptable characters so that he could bring them into mainstream drawing rooms. "There is a part of me, of my literary and personal character," he told Forster, "which is very far from what you are and stand for, which is perhaps one of the reasons why I love and admire you so much!"[139]

The reviews went on and on. Kingsley Amis in the *Spectator* asserted that Isherwood's "talent took a nosedive as soon as he left England" and that Auden, too, had been unable "to write a line of verse worth reading" once their boat had passed the Isles of Scilly. Amis baited Isherwood about sex, criticizing *Prater Violet* for lack of explicit sexual detail and then asserting that "Ambrose" shows how "that tolerance which is the condition of a homosexual mode of life [...] slides into condonation of any and every kind of nauseous behaviour and thus into total moral and emotional chaos."[140]

Naturally, Isherwood minded. "The bad unfair ones depress me far more than they should," he wrote in his diary. "I realize that I was counting on a resounding success and vindication." In the face of homophobia, he wished friends would support him, at least in public. "I am shocked to find out how vindictive I feel towards Stephen, Angus, Kingsley Amis, etc."[141]

Reviewers did not see what he was trying for, and there was nothing he could learn from them. In early April, the weather turned hot, and he felt "lousy—a big pyloric flap. I'm exhausted, want to lie down all the time. Sick to my stomach and yet can't throw up."

It did not help that Ted Bachardy was being sent to the L.A. County Honor Farm, a minimum security correctional facility, to serve a three-week sentence for shoplifting. Ted's breakdowns were coming closer together, about once a year, which darkened his prognosis. He had had a bad one in February 1961 when Don was in England, but he had been hospitalized for only a few weeks, without being "properly cured yet" as Glade told Isherwood.[142] Now, things again looked precarious for him.

On April 6, Isherwood and Bachardy went to the movies with Ted and a boyfriend, Vince David. Vince David knew a student taking one of Isherwood's classes at L.A. State and reported that "most of the students are puzzled and bored." This hit Isherwood just as hard as the book reviews: "I find myself far more sensitive to criticism, lately, than I'd supposed I was." The next day he was forced to admit, "I'm sick. This morning I woke up to find I have a discharge."

He had been avoiding his L.A. doctor for a long time, and he feared being subjected to a full checkup, so he found a new doctor through Gavin Lambert, a Dr. Alan Allen, who diagnosed a prostate infection, "much more tiresome than the clap; harder to get rid of."[143] Dr. Allen required Isherwood to stop drinking and gave him some pills. Five days later, the infection had not yet cleared up. Allen gave him more pills.

On the same day, Bachardy "made another of his declarations of independence," as Isherwood put it in his diary. "He has got to have a studio of his own, here at the house, and his own telephone, and his own money and his own friends. I am making him sound tiresome, but actually this outburst wasn't hostile; was even full of love." Isherwood suggested Bachardy would be more independent if the studio was away from the house, but Bachardy joked that "he wants to keep an eye on me." Isherwood thought, "this isn't entirely a joke. He is afraid of leaving me *too* much alone. He doesn't want *my* independence."[144]

Bachardy slept out for the next two nights. He had committed to two more exhibitions, one in September at the Rex Evans Gallery in L.A.—owned and run by the British music-hall comedian and Hollywood character actor—the other in New York. Soon he was invited to show in Santa Barbara and at Stanford, and he was asked to New York to do pen-and-ink drawings of Oleg Cassini, the Paris-born designer who dressed Jackie Kennedy as First Lady. The assignment, for full-page ads in *Vogue* and *Harper's Bazaar*, included drawing Jackie Kennedy's sister, Princess Lee Radziwill, and the movie star Merle Oberon in Cassini gowns.

Isherwood's prostate infection was gone by April 21, but his jaw and neck still ached, so Allen sent him for X-rays which revealed arthritis. After the months of secret worry about his jaw, Isherwood was relieved by the diagnosis. He did some writing—another page of the Ramakrishna biography, some notes for an upcoming lecture at L.A. City College, and two pages of a brand-new novel. "*Felicidad*," he wrote in the diary.[145] Happiness was an absence of anything being wrong. It was also starting the brand-new novel.

SUFFERING OVER BACHARDY and over the mixed reception of *Down There on a Visit* was stirring a vast creative reservoir. Isherwood had gotten the idea five or six weeks earlier. "I shall call this new novel project provisionally *The Englishwoman*," he had decided in his diary.

It was to be "a Study in Exile," set in Santa Monica Canyon, "Time about nowadays," with a character based on himself living alone in the house he had shared with Caskey more than a decade before, 333 East Rustic Road. "One of my neighbors," he proposed, "is an Englishwoman." He imagined that she had married an American GI in England during the war and returned with him to America; they had a son. "What interests me in this novel is to show America through British eyes."[146]

He pictured his Englishwoman alone and brooding on the past, as in the inexorable unfolding of Maupassant's first novel *Une Vie*, which he had long admired, about the slow crushing of the life dreams of the daughter of a country baron in Normandy. *Une Vie* portrays the decline of the family circle and the gradual stripping away of hereditary house and lands, the process that had, in real life, been so painful to Isherwood's mother.[147] Deep in his imagination lay Kathleen's tragedy, and *The Englishwoman* began as a fantasy about someone like Kathleen transplanted to California. It was a tragedy that required exploring before he could move on to his real subject. Like the refugees who had hampered progress on *The World in the Evening*, the Englishwoman reflected Isherwood's guilt about the past he had left behind, and she was to become an important character for the novel he eventually did write, *A Single Man*. As in childhood collaborations, he began with a shared narrative, projecting himself through an imaginary Kathleen before he pushed her character into a minor role. Already, she had a name: "The Englishwoman's name is Charlotte. Some people call her Charley."[148] Isherwood, that lover of unexplainable sounds, of incantation, was exceptionally confident about this name, and he never changed it. It has two syllables and a double letter, like Kathleen, called Kitty by some, yet it is cross-dressed with a soft Ch, like a feminine Christopher, called Chris by some.

Charley was modeled on Iris Tree, the haute-bohemian English actress and writer, twice divorced mother of two American sons, who had been Isherwood's best woman friend until she moved back to Europe in 1954.[149] The masculine nickname Charley signaled the possibility of androgyny and linked through Charles Kennedy in *The World in the Evening* all the way back to Isherwood's original elder brother character, Charles Franklin, in the first *Lions and Shadows*, and before that to the tutor Charles Bryant in his short story "The Old Game." The longer, feminine form, Charlotte, also linked back to Madame Cheuret in *Lions and Shadows*, modeled on Olive Mangeot, the bohemian mother of two half-Belgian sons. Like Iris Tree, Olive Mangeot ended up divorced and alone though she had numerous lovers.

The Kenny Potter character in *A Single Man*—modeled on so many young men and embodying American youth, freedom, the hunger to learn—first appeared in *The Englishwoman* as Charley's son, Colin Wildstein. "Colin" alluded to Colin Wilson, whose 1956 book *The Outsider* addressed a theme calling out to Isherwood for richer development. "Wildstein" departs from "Wilson" just enough to suggest something wild in the character Isherwood was inventing (possibly Isherwood knew through their mutual friend Angus

Wilson that Colin Wilson had slept rough on Hampstead Heath while writing his first novel).

In *The Englishwoman*, the triangle familiar from Isherwood's life and writing in the 1920s—mother, son, interloping elder brother figure—recurs, and there is a dead soldier father. Isherwood was to move past this pattern in *A Single Man*, in which none of the characters is biologically related. Although he had long ago articulated his wish to have no family relationships, it was as difficult for Isherwood to clear his family romance from his imagination as it had been for him to clear Dante from his religious mythology when writing *Down There on a Visit*.

IN FEBRUARY 1962, around the time he first conceived *The Englishwoman*, Isherwood made notes for a story about a middle-aged writer and professor who receives part of a student novel about a frustrated homosexual love affair set on campus. The professor is uncertain whether the student author is homosexual, so he is cautious. Months later, the completed novel arrives. The professor finds it "clumsily written and dull,"[150] but he takes the boy out to supper, and the boy talks openly of the unrequited love portrayed in his book and of his real-life homosexual experiences with a hustler. The boy begins a second novel and announces that he wants to go to bed with the professor. To the professor, the sex seems successful, moreover, the boy's new novel is better than the first. But now that the professor is really interested in the boy and believes himself to be the first important love interest in the boy's life, the boy is noncommittal and leaves for Europe.

The story notes were inspired by Isherwood's friendship with a student called Frank Wiley,* who had been in his class at U.C. Santa Barbara. In October 1960, Isherwood had read Wiley's novel in progress and they met and talked. In January 1961, after Bachardy had left for London, Wiley dropped a manuscript at Isherwood's house, and Isherwood took him to supper to discuss it. A year later, in early February 1962, while Bachardy was still away, Isherwood took Wiley to supper again, and Wiley spent the night. Then Isherwood read Wiley's current manuscript. He also met Wiley's stepmother, in whom he was disappointed, finding her rich, spoiled and nondescript. Eventually, Wiley joined the Naval Reserve and went to serve abroad. In 1963, Isherwood recommended his novel to a New York publisher.[151]

Isherwood's creative response to Wiley echoes his response to Michael

---

* Not his real name.

Leopold in late 1949, when he was living at Rustic Road. The donnée of the older writer who is intrigued and inspired by the younger writer interested Isherwood obsessively, as it had Henry James. This was Isherwood's own marriage plot, a plot for which he could generate countless stories. In the Michael Leopold variation, the older writer was experiencing a period of impotence, and the younger writer, working near him, was able to write as never before.

When he started drafting *The Englishwoman*, Isherwood introduced a third variation. Instead of the impotent older writer being "cured" by the younger writer, or the younger writer being inspired by the older writer, the younger writer is prevented from writing at all.

In *The Englishwoman*, the professor instructs his visiting student, Colin Wildstein, to cut out and paste into a scrapbook a series of magazine articles written by the professor; thus the professor imprisons the younger man in the disciple role. This reimagines Hans Christian Andersen's "The Snow Queen," in which the Snow Queen kidnaps the boy, Kay, and forces him to puzzle out the word "Eternity" from ice fragments on her frozen lake.[152] It is just what Charles Laughton had done to Isherwood with the Socrates project, asking Isherwood to cut and paste from Plato's work in order to make a star vehicle for Laughton, while shutting down Isherwood's other creative work. Isherwood identified with both roles, and easily flipped from master to disciple, basking in Laughton's stardom, asking flattering questions, falling in with Laughton's personal needs as well as his professional ones. But he knew that an ideal master–disciple relationship should set the disciple free, as he wished Bachardy to be free, as Prabhavananda continued to teach Isherwood how to free himself. In *The Englishwoman* the professor goes upstairs to write, finds that he can't and falls asleep—only to be discovered in his middle-aged helplessness by Colin who, in a characteristic fulfillment of an Isherwood wish, is portrayed as a natural nanny.

In his workbook notes, Isherwood planned that when Colin finally leaves home, his mother, the Englishwoman, decides to return to England. "The epilogue, so to speak, is when I ask myself: why don't I go?" In real life, Isherwood had no intention of moving back to England, but putting his character in this situation would allow him to explore what America meant to him. "I know already that this study in alienation, in foreignness, appeals to my deepest artistic appetite."

The material prosperity of Southern California, to be represented in the new novel by what Isherwood called the Good Life of the Canyon, could not bring happiness. He wanted to show that any next step had to be an existential step—a spiritual leap: "achieving The Good Life merely means that you have reached the edge of a tremendous precipice," he wrote in his workbook.

In 1950, he had observed this precipice as a physical coastline in Laguna, "the very last Western edge of America," and his Laguna experience reached all the way back to the emotional ledge on which he and his mother had sheltered in Ventnor on the Isle of Wight in 1915, their last happiness before everything was smashed. As a ten-year-old boy, he had had no choice but to jump with Kathleen back toward the remains of an earlier life. He had been trying to jump in the opposite direction ever since.

Charley, by returning to England, would be returning to the old, familiar striving. She would be like the boy in the bar in Isherwood's proposed film, *The Day's Journey*, who instead of making his phone call to God jumps in a car to go for another ride. The character based on Isherwood would remain in California, at the margin, an outsider looking in at "The Lost (i.e. the nice normal Americans)," and he would make the leap into the future. Everything Isherwood had learned from Heard and Prabhavananda about spiritual growth was to be reflected in his new project.

Already, his unconscious was delivering spontaneous gifts. In May, "a Japanese girl character whom I'd introduced for no reason apparent to myself [. . .] suddenly acquired symbolic status as another Foreigner."[153] She was to become Lois Yamaguchi, Kenny Potter's girlfriend in *A Single Man*, shipped to an internment camp with her family as an enemy alien during World War II, despised by all Americans except blacks and pacifists.

The first draft rushed along; by his birthday in August he had written fifty-six pages. But there he stuck.

ON HIS READING list for 1962, Isherwood had put *Mrs. Dalloway*. Spender had asked him to write an essay about Virginia Woolf for *Encounter*, but after scratching out a draft, Isherwood decided: "I simply do not have enough to say about her."[154] He broke the commitment to Spender, and he started reading *Mrs. Dalloway* while he was at work on *The Englishwoman*.

He was floored. In his diary, he described it as "one of the most truly beautiful novels or prose poems or whatever that I have ever read. It is prose written with absolute pitch, a perfect ear. [. . .] Could I write a book like that and keep within the nature of my own style? I'd love to try."

On his fifty-eighth birthday, August 26, 1962, fog shrouded the beach, and Isherwood stayed at home finishing *Mrs. Dalloway*. He declared it better, more authentic, than Joyce: "Woolf's use of the reverie is quite different from Joyce's stream of consciousness. Beside her, Joyce seems tricky and vulgar and cheap, as she herself thought. Woolf's kind of reverie is less 'realistic' but far more convincing and moving. Joyce's emotional range is very small."[155]

A few weeks later, Isherwood reread his draft for *The Englishwoman* and then, sitting on the beach one morning, discussed it with Bachardy. "Don, after hearing all my difficulties with it, made a really brilliant simple suggestion, namely that it ought to be *The Englishman*—that is, me." All his themes—America through British eyes, Loneliness, the Lost, Middle Age in relation to Youth, his public image as a college professor, and Death as seen from Middle Age—"are much better approached from my viewpoint." He decided to make himself the central character and to write about himself in the third person. For now, he used his own abandoned name William: "this book is a study of William as a public image, a physical creature, an exiled spirit."[156]

He planned to show William teaching, fighting off age at the gym, discovering a tumor that he fears might kill him. Also, "I have to show William's spiritual life—what makes him bear all this. This is difficult without dragging in the Vedanta Society, but I must do it." He had faced the same challenge when writing *Prater Violet*. "What makes you go on living? Why don't you kill yourself? Why is all this bearable?" wonders the Christopher character as he walks home beside Friedrich Bergmann; he considers it "the only question worth asking our fellow-travellers."[157] Isherwood didn't explicitly mention Vedanta in either novel. Already, he began to see ways to handle the spiritual aspect and to present his beliefs though he would not name them: "the house he lives in ought to be haunted. And the haunting should show the awful power of resentments, samskaras, etc." (Samskaras are recollections of past intentional actions.)

Finally, there was William's personal chemistry, his sex life: "Above all else, William is an observer. [. . .] His real sex life should be in his masturbation fantasies. This is very important." George in *A Single Man* falls asleep and misses out on the possibility of sex; when he wakes up, he masturbates to fantasies he scripts like a film, expunging figures he knows in favor of figures he has observed at a distance, two boys on a tennis court, entirely under his imaginative control.

But George is not without deep human connections. Isherwood proposed in his notes that his central character "should have had a long-standing homosexual affair before the book opens," with a character who "has died recently." This longstanding relationship kept William in California. "Also, the death of the friend opens the theme of The Past. Was it really so marvellous? Does it really matter? And the answer seems to be: it doesn't matter very much to William."[158] The past is past, but it offered the opportunity to portray for a general audience a committed love relationship between two adult men.

IN THE EARLY summer of 1959, while he was still working on "Ambrose," Isherwood had already written a story about a committed love relationship between two men, but it was not for a general audience. He described it as "a queer story" which was "absolutely frank," and he had used the phrase picked up from Francis Bacon, "I just want to see how near I could get to the nerve." As so often when something was important to him, he had begun without premeditation, "on a sudden impulse." The title was "Afterwards."[159]

"Afterwards" gave vent to his jealousy over Bachardy's sexual infidelities, to his fear of losing Bachardy, and to his rage and anger at heterosexuals who could not or would not understand what sexual love felt like to him. He used the diary form with a first-person narrator, a writer, whose lover, Tom, has been killed in a light-plane crash. Thus, the story previewed George losing Jim in a car crash in *A Single Man*—the kind of loss Isherwood had decided against for *The World in the Evening* when he dropped the idea of having Bob Wood die fighting in World War II and Charles Kennedy excluded from the funeral. Now he made this homosexual grief a central donnée which could not be brushed aside as the fate of minor characters in a world war.

"Afterwards" was an imaginative letting go, a story Isherwood had not yet allowed himself to write. The narrator opens with a bitter attack on the literature of heterosexual love and on his "best friends," a cozy heterosexual couple, reminiscent of the Masselinks, who cannot fully empathize with the depth and authenticity of his grief over Tom's death. "I loathe all heterosexuals of all ages everywhere. I loathe the poignant restrained heartbreaking books that are written about their nasty amours. [...] I find their love as disgusting as they find mine."[160]

These eruptions of rage were to be reimagined in *A Single Man*, where George broods on his hatred for the procreating heterosexual community represented by the families in his neighborhood—the Stickels, the Garfeins, the Strunks, modeled on Isherwood's former neighbors in Sycamore Road. George never tells his neighbors Jim is dead because he knows they cannot understand what this loss feels like to George: "The fiend that won't fit into their statistics, the Gorgon that refuses their plastic surgery, the vampire drinking blood with tactless uncultured slurps, the bad-smelling beast that doesn't use their deodorants, the unspeakable that insists, despite all their shushing, on speaking its name."[161]

"Afterwards" includes vivid and explicit accounts of sex between the narrator and other men. There is a one-night stand of ferocious, cynical appetite quickly forgotten and a carefully developed love triangle between the narrator and two younger men, an established couple. In the triangle, the narrator is attracted by the couple's youth and good looks, but even more so by the unguarded helplessness with which they love one another. He begins a secret affair with one of them, the affair is exposed, and the betrayed lover confronts the narrator. They fight viciously, and the fight turns into sex. The narrator ends up with the betrayed lover.

Toward the end of "Afterwards," the narrator makes clear that he, too, is a betrayed lover. Tom betrayed him often, but the narrator cannot admit his hurt to his heterosexual friends because he cannot trust them to understand it any better than they understand his grief over Tom's death: "as far as they, and the rest of the outside world, are concerned I still present my life with Tom as a little showcase of homosexual domestic bliss, and perfect faithfulness."[162]

Isherwood felt this pressure to show his heterosexual readers not just a successful homosexual relationship, but a perfect one—and a perfectly faithful one. Therefore in *A Single Man* he had Jim betray George with a woman, Doris. George's jealousy of Doris is powerfully and bitterly expressed, but readers could continue to enjoy the sentimental ideal that the relationship between the two men was, in a sense, still faithful.

Isherwood's workbook shows that he initially imagined the Doris character as a man, "a youngish man dying of cancer who has, maybe, had an affair with William's friend."[163] This youngish man was based on Isherwood's real-life sex friend, Paul Kennedy, with whom he had begun an affair in January 1960. Isherwood learned in 1962 that Paul Kennedy was dying of cancer and visited him in the hospital during the spring and summer, each time making a diary entry on which he later drew in precise detail for the hospital scenes in *A Single Man*.

Thematically, he saw the dying young man as "a kind of duty to William, an ex-object of jealousy and a memento mori." In real life, Kennedy was an ex-object of jealousy to Bachardy, not Isherwood, but the fictional character served for them both, a knot tying up all the angry strands running through Isherwood's and Bachardy's emotional lives—Isherwood's jealousy of Paul Millard, Bachardy's jealousy of Paul Kennedy and of Jim Charlton, and so on. All these toxic emotions were projected onto the mortally ill character, Doris, so that they would die with her.

In "Afterwards," the narrator blames possessiveness for his young lover's death. "Although I approved on general principles of our being mutually free, I still couldn't be generous about it." He recalls making "a spiteful scene of jealousy" on Tom's last morning alive as Tom set off to go flying (a symbol for having sex, hence betrayal). This scene, he believes, is what killed Tom: "Didn't I somehow will it?" And he undertakes "that if ever there is anybody else, and we start a life together and these problems arise—I will try to be more understanding and more generous."[164]

"Don is delighted with 'Afterwards,'" Isherwood had written in his diary on August 7, 1959. But the story was unpublishable and dangerous to both author and readers. Isherwood left it on Kirstein's desk in person on his way through New York. He managed to get copies to other friends, including Lehmann and Laughton. Forster read it in secret at Lehmann's flat, writing afterwards to Isherwood: "Double envelope cannot move from John's fireside, and I read it there last week in comfort and with great interest."[165]

Forster was about to be the key witness for the defense in the obscenity trial of D.H. Lawrence's last novel, *Lady Chatterley's Lover*, which was published in an unexpurgated version in 1960 for the first time in England and exonerated by the trial. In the U.S., Isherwood agreed to testify for Henry Miller's *Tropic of Cancer*, also being prosecuted for obscenity. He was not called, but the case went all the way to the Supreme Court where the book was ruled not obscene in December 1963. Lawrence's and Miller's novels featured explicit straight sex; a story about sex between men was far more likely to be viewed as pornography. Nevertheless, Isherwood was to find a way to put sex at the heart of *A Single Man*. Times were changing and he was part of the change.

THERE WAS, OF course, the much earlier antecedent to George's loss and his grief in the 1924 short story "Two Brothers," inspired by Isherwood's cousins Jack and Bob Reid and evoking Isherwood's hidden feelings about the death of his father. Already at nineteen, Isherwood had been an expert on grief, and a cynic. "Billy is dead," he had written in 1924; "Jim is dead," he wrote in 1964. The narrator of "Two Brothers" knows his letter of condolence cannot change anything for Bob, the creaturely half of the perfect whole once made by the twins: "Bob is up against a blank wall," as Isherwood had put it in his fair copy.[166] In *A Single Man*, George, too, is up against a blank wall, experiencing the dumb animal suffering for which there is no consolation. "He stands quite still, silent, or at most uttering a brief animal grunt, as he waits for the spasm to pass."[167]

In both narratives, Isherwood used a random motor accident in order to focus on the grief itself rather than on any cause. And in both narratives, he stoically affirmed the continuation of life. "Bob will forget," he had written in 1924. "They lived together in the Present. Bob will go on living in the Present—but alone." Now the lost partner is a chosen partner, not a biological one, and Isherwood suggests George will not be alone for long: "He believes he will find another Jim here. He doesn't know it, but he has started looking already. [. . .] It is Now that he must find another Jim."[168]

George possesses the desire "to live, to live" that Isherwood had given to the schoolboy Gerald Wayne in "The Hero," the 1924 partner story to "Two Brothers"—Wayne who jumps into the river after his friend Thompson, then panics and strikes for shore. Wayne awakes in the infirmary, where Thompson, not drowned, wrapped in a rug and a dressing gown, comforts him with praise during their last moment of intimacy. In *A Single Man*, Isherwood cast himself as the elder figure, rescued after going underneath "an apocalyptically great wave" by the younger Kenny, who is wrapped only in a blanket when he undresses George and puts him to bed. The new sequence exonerated the desire "to live, to live" and fictionally redressed Isherwood's guilt over the fact that in 1915 he had surfaced after measles and pneumonia while his father went under at the Front.[169]

Fear of losing his ideal partner had haunted Isherwood since childhood—long before he met Bachardy. When he grieved at the prospect of losing Bachardy, he was grieving as well for losing his father. Being a father to Bachardy allowed Isherwood to fulfill the role Frank had abandoned too soon. If he could not be a father to Bachardy, he would be a father to someone else.

IN FACT, BACHARDY had begun a determined campaign to make Isherwood move out. This had broken into the open one night in June following an evening at Gavin Lambert's. "After the party, drunk, Don told me he wants me to go away to San Francisco and leave him alone all summer."[170]

Isherwood had finished teaching at L.A. State at the end of May, and he wanted to work on his book. He had turned down an invitation to lecture at U.C. Berkeley, but Berkeley increased the fee, so he decided to go for a few days at the end of the summer partly to please Bachardy.

Bachardy was wrestling with conflicting feelings about independence and security. He pushed Isherwood away, looked for other sources of strength, and spent nights out; yet, at the same time, he found ways to institutionalize their involvement. For one thing, he took an ever-increasing interest in Vedanta, the source for Isherwood of so much patience and resolve. He read Vivekananda's lecture "The Real Nature of Man," and in June, at the very time that he asked Isherwood to go away, he announced that he wanted to become Swami Prabhavananda's disciple. "Swami seems to have been pleased and surprised—as well he might be, after nearly ten years! He told Don how to meditate and said he'd initiate him next December."

Isherwood felt confused by Bachardy's contrary impulses and by the possibility of being pulled uncomfortably close to the Vedanta Society. Bachardy was as intense in his pursuit of Vedanta as he was in all things. He told Isherwood that "he is afraid that this whole thing may take over, and that he may find himself getting in too deep and thinking about nothing but finding God."[171]

When Bachardy flew to New York in July to fulfill the Oleg Cassini commission, Isherwood saw him off at the airport, and they got so engrossed talking that Bachardy missed his flight. "[H]e said he was very happy with the life we are leading now, and asked if I was, too," Isherwood wrote in his diary. "And at the same time, he said he wished we could speak frankly about *everything* that we did. I said this wasn't desirable. He said, 'But I get to know almost everything you do, anyway.'"[172] Bachardy was watching Isherwood as closely as ever. He was also hinting that he wanted to tell Isherwood more about his own sexual and romantic life.

One thing making Bachardy happy was a long-considered plan to convert the garage into a studio. Work started on June 14, and within ten days a startling transformation was underway, with a new deck extending along the dining room and front bedroom. "Don and I lay on the deck, which still has no railing and seems as insecure as a flying carpet, with the wind blowing up between the floorboards and the whole Canyon floating in the air around you."

The studio was to have running water and a toilet, creating a second domestic space. Isherwood felt "an almost superstitious dread of spending all this money for such a purpose," and blamed his puritanical nature. "I can only do it by firmly reminding myself that it is entirely for Don's pleasure, reassurance and morale. He has got to feel that this is his home, created by himself."[173] At least they had plenty of money. Kathleen's personal legacy was arriving in chunks, converted to American currency and totalling nearly $20,000. In addition, the Agatha Greene Trevor trust fund invested in London promised a further $10,000–15,000. He still had not touched his advance from Simon & Schuster.

For the main house, they bought a new dining-room table, chairs, a chandelier. A full-height mirror was installed along the dining-room wall, carpets went down, and draperies were hung in the front bedroom and in the studio. They gave their first dinner party in the newly decorated house on August 22. Entertaining the famous and the fascinating was an ever-growing theme in their relationship; any number of guests were to see themselves reflected in the mirror over the years and to catch the glances of hosts and companions observing one another. Once the house was completed, in September, they each bought a new car to put in the new carport. Bachardy got a Corvair, wine red with black upholstery and silver buttons, Isherwood a black Volkswagen.

Fresh talk of a Berlin musical promised even more money. Carter Lodge was handling negotiations. He recommended a lawyer-accountant who counseled Isherwood and Bachardy that a business merger would save on income taxes, so they combined their finances in Bee-Eye Enterprises, for Bachardy-Isherwood, further formalizing their bond.

Bachardy was receiving many portrait commissions and earning money and praise for his work, but he was plunged in "deep deep gloom." The night before Isherwood's birthday, alone in his brand-new studio, Bachardy had what Isherwood described as "a drunken fit of crying [. . .] so loud that I could hear him from the house." Isherwood walked over to the studio, "and he said to leave him alone, he liked to cry. I really felt he was on the edge of a breakdown."[174] The next morning, as if nothing had happened, Bachardy presented birthday gifts, "inscribed in the Dub and Kitty idiom," shirts, socks, "and a beautiful Japanese model horse, white with trappings of orange, green and gold." Then he left to draw David Selznick.

Isherwood was a year older than Bachardy's father. He had given Bachardy everything Bachardy wanted. But he could not change the fact that his fifty-eighth birthday offered a stark longterm prospect for his twenty-eight-year-old lover.

BACHARDY'S WEST COAST debut show opened at the Rex Evans Gallery in September. He felt the opening party was "a great disappointment," but his spirits were boosted when the show was praised in the *Los Angeles Times*: "an impressive appearance by a highly skilled and perceptive draughtsman who captures the personality as well as the appearance of his sitters with elegant lines." The reviewer, Henry Seldis, observed, too, that Bachardy was working against the fashion of his time: "The art of portrait drawing is so far removed from the Contemporary abstract emphasis that it is surprising to find a very young artist among its most expressive practitioners."[175] A number of portraits sold.

Over lunch at Ted's Grill on Entrada Drive, Bachardy discussed his future with Isherwood. Russell McKinnon had offered more money to study abroad, but London, Paris, Rome, and even New York did not appeal. Isherwood felt obliged to give Bachardy space, so he wrote to Mark Schorer and applied for a Regents' Lectureship at Berkeley for the spring of 1963.

Meanwhile, he returned to his novel, focusing more on the relationship between the two men, one recently dead. Even though they were so deeply at odds, he showed Bachardy the first twenty-eight pages of the second draft, and Bachardy was impressed. "He made me feel that I have found a new approach altogether; that, as he put it, the writing itself is so interesting from page to page that you don't even care what is going to happen."[176]

Isherwood had already decided that the action of the novel "covers one day"—as in *Mrs Dalloway* and *Ulysses*. He was writing in the present tense and he was still calling his main character William. He wished to show William as "paradoxical" and changeful, like Clarissa Dalloway, bringing out "His eccentricity, his senility, his lingering youthfulness, his dullness, his brilliance, his sympathy for others and his indifference." He described the project as "a sort of Virginia Woolf poem about life, specifically about male middleage," and he wished "to avoid plottiness" in favor of emotional continuity: "one thing which should be strongly stressed is the <u>ebb and flow of vitality</u> throughout the day."

His aims had certainly changed. In 1937, he had told Virginia Woolf that he admired her novels, but that he admired Forster's more. She had recorded Isherwood's reason in her diary: "I'll come out with it then Mrs Woolf—you see, I feel youre a poetess: he does the thing I want to do ... a perfect contraption."[177]

Now, like Woolf, he was going for something deeper than literary character, deeper even than stream of consciousness. He was excited by "the sense of William's being 'put together,' 'assembled,' every morning out of raw consciousness, and dressed up and made into a recognizable person and going out into the world and playing his role, or roles." This was like, and not like, Woolf's handling of what she called "the soul," for instance when Peter Walsh approaches Clarissa Dalloway's house for her party: "The brain must wake now. The body must contract now, entering the house, the lighted house, where the door stood open, where the motor cars were standing, and bright women descending: the soul must brave itself to endure." Isherwood knew he needed to get exactly the right balance between the "two strands of styles interwoven in this sort of writing—"

> the lyric, sub specie aeternitatis thing which observes William like a wild creature, an antelope, with his daily habits and his whole symbolic meaning as a type, and then there is the mere plot approach, which ties this particular individual William up with this particular individual Charlotte and Colin. Too much of the second is death to the first.[178]

He stepped outside of any narrative voice he had used before. "This novelette is, as it were, written by his Id, or by God. <u>It knows things about him which he does not know</u>." In addition to reading Woolf, he was reading *The Book of the It* by the German doctor and psychotherapist Georg Groddeck, who had studied and corresponded with Freud and had influenced Freud's conception of the Id. "Wystan used to rave about it in the twenties," Isherwood exclaimed in his diary.[179] Indeed, he was rediscovering a conception of the self that he had already assimiliated through Auden in the twenties, for Isherwood had been on the trail of the Id most of his adult life.

"I hold the view that man is animated by the Unknown, that there is within him an 'Es,' an 'It,' some wondrous force which directs both what he himself does and what happens to him," wrote Groddeck, who framed his book as a series of letters written by one Patrik Troll. "Of this It, we know only so much as lies within our consciousness," Patrik Troll explained, "by search and effort we can extend the limits of our consciousness and press far into the realm of the unconscious."

In his work as a medical doctor, Groddeck found that all his patients' illnesses, even broken bones, had a psychological basis: the It acting out conflicts as symptoms. He used psychoanalysis to coax the It into the open, the conscious mind, and to persuade the It to act out in ways less damaging to the body. He looked upon mental life as "one continuous symbolization" in which disease served as "a vital expression of the human organism."[180]

Groddeck implicitly compared the It to the Atman, quoting the Sanskrit phrase *tat tvam asi* (you are it), and he described human experience with the theatrical metaphors familiar in Vedanta, but referring to a psychological rather than a cosmic performance. "If we like," he wrote, "we can think of life as a masquerade at which we don a disguise, perhaps many different disguises, at which nevertheless we retain our own proper characters, remaining ourselves amidst the other revelers in spite of our disguise, and from which we depart exactly as we were when we came." Isherwood might have written this himself.

In his draft called *The Englishman* and later in *A Single Man*, Isherwood offered another metaphor, "a lot of rock pools," to represent the relation between individual identity and a larger consciousness. This metaphor, tested in a simpler form on Forster years earlier in their correspondence about whether God exists and will help us, was one way he could illustrate his religious beliefs without mentioning Vedanta. At ebb tide, the rock pools are "individual entities" which can be named and which may be filled with personal appetites and fears; when the ocean rises, the rock pools are flooded and become one, "that consciousness which is no one in particular but which contains everyone and everything, past, present and future, and extends unbroken to the uttermost stars."[181] Rock pools had been used by Cyril Connolly in *The Rock Pool*, by Virginia Woolf in *Jacob's Room* and *To the Lighthouse*, and by Katherine Mansfield in "At the Bay," to suggest discrete worlds of complex beauty and mysterious threat. Isherwood's rock pools gesture to his literary forebears as well as to his religious beliefs; the imagery distinguishes him as a unique literary identity in a larger literary ocean and shows again the continuity between his adopted religion and his literary being.

Groddeck's Patrik Troll hoped to rid himself of his "I," his ego, as he aged: "I am still at the beginning of the process generally called 'growing old,' which seems to me to be like 'growing childlike.'" In this vein, Isherwood's main character looks in the mirror and sees his former selves, "the face of the child, the boy, the young man, the not-so-young—all present still." Toward the end of the novel, he is returned to his childlike former self—"crazy, he thinks. That is my secret; my strength."[182]

In his effort to get deeper than stream of consciousness, deeper than Woolf's reverie, Isherwood also drew on another account of the mind–body connection, in the work of the endocrinologist and bestselling diet doctor, A.T.W. Simeons. He lifted George's coronary occlusion from Simeons's 1960 book *Man's Presumptuous Brain* as he mentioned in a 1975 interview.[183] But he lifted more. Simeons had described how the conscious part of the human brain had evolved by censoring stimuli that could divert its development, and how the conscious part, the cerebral cortex, no longer had access to the primitive animal part of the brain, the diencephalon, buried deep in the brain stem. The diencephalon still regulated the animal life of the body—heartbeat, digestion, urination, sleep, sex, nerves, glands—as if regulating primitive humankind in the wild, but animal reactions to fear, rage, hunger, sex were no longer useful or comprehensible to the conscious part of the brain in modern, sedentary humankind.

In his first complete draft for *The Englishman*, Isherwood made plentiful use of Simeons to describe the functioning of his main character's body, nailing his character's inner world to science rather than to Woolf's elusive "soul." Simeons's vocabulary survived in the opening and closing chapters of *A Single Man*, where the cortex, "that grim disciplinarian," takes conscious control on waking, ignoring the involuntary spasm of the pylorus which it cannot distinguish from a spasm of grief. "These morning spasms are too painful to be treated sentimentally. After them, he feels relief merely. It is like getting over a bad attack of cramp." At the book's close, neither the cortex nor the diencephalon can prevent the "almost indecently melodramatic situation [. . .] the formation of the atheromatous plaque" which might kill "with the speed of an Indian strangler."[184] The suggestion that George is being lived—operated—both from within his conscious mind and from somewhere else permeates *A Single Man*.

What struck Isherwood above all in *The Book of the It* was Groddeck's teaching about ambivalence in love, "that there can never be great love on the human level without great hate." Ambivalence had defeated Isherwood in past relationships with family, friends, and lovers, and he was struggling to handle it in his relationship with Bachardy:

> Don instinctively understands Groddeck's proposition about love-hate much better than I do. I mean, I think he would be prepared to accept and live with it, if I would, too. But I am sentimental—in the worst possible way—the way my mother was ... I have a great deal of that attitude which makes women say, "not before the servants," "not before the neighbors." Only the "neighbors" in my case are some kind of an internal audience.[185]

In the novel he was able to show both love and hate in front of George's neighbors, and he grew increasingly determined to topple his inner censor.

As he worked on his drafts for *A Single Man*, Isherwood discovered other underlying continuities between his past and present selves, fragments that assembled into patterns. In Colin, comprised of many boys, Isherwood even imagined the wild English boys of the 1920s—himself, Upward, and Auden, in the exuberant, playful days when they had first begun to break bounds, chancing it in their life and in their art. He introduced Colin wearing, of all things in the Californian heat, "an Icelandic sweater with one of those very dramatic patterns." Colin's sweater "gives him an air of somehow taking part in a game."[186] The Icelandic sweater alluded to the saga world to which Isherwood had been introduced by Auden and in which Isherwood had recognized the boys at their prep school, launching their imaginative game in which saga and school worlds became one.

Isherwood delved deeper and deeper, trawling his diary for events from the 1940s and 50s in the canyon and on the beach in the aftermath of World War II—during his life with and without Caskey at the haunted house in East Rustic Road, during his life with Bachardy and the neighbors in Sycamore Road, in his teaching life—and remembering childhood experiences with Nanny and in his native Cheshire landscape.

Increasingly, as work progressed, he associated negative emotions with illness, reflecting Groddeck's idea of the It acting out conflict. In real life, he was surrounded by cancer; it was not just Paul Kennedy. Isherwood had known since 1960 that Huxley had found a malignant tumor on the back of his tongue and refused surgery because it which would have affected his ability to speak. The tumor had been burned away with a radium needle, and friends were told he was cured, but a second tumor had appeared in Huxley's neck and then a third. Harvey Easton, who ran Isherwood's gym, had cancer in his liver. Charles Laughton had cancer in his kidney.

Laughton was scheduled to have the kidney removed in New York, but he returned to Los Angeles without surgery. Isherwood went to see him and afterwards wrote: "we talked quite frankly about death, God, etc. [...] He said he was appalled how unprepared he was to die."

The cancer spread to Laughton's spine, causing uncontrollable pain; a disk was operated on at Cedars of Lebanon. The cancer that kills Doris in *A Single Man* carries all the melodrama of Laughton's long decline, and it embodies Isherwood's own fears: "all my fears are centered on cancer," he wrote in his diary in June 1962. He feared illness more than death: "I am terrified of going over the edge, knowing the illness is terminal, knowing the doctors and nurses have got me in their cruel kingdom of insufficient pain-killing. But I have faith, too. I believe that I shall be somehow sustained."

Isherwood went on visiting Laughton at Cedars of Lebanon and recording the visits unflinchingly. Laughton's brother "smuggled in a Catholic priest who gave Charles the last rites," outraging Elsa Lanchester who was not a believer and feared Laughton would leave money to the Church. Laughton confided to Isherwood that he wanted another priest, and Isherwood reassured him that seeing the priest didn't matter: "He should speak to God, ask for help. Because God is there. 'I know,' Charles said." Then Isherwood sat holding Laughton's hands "and praying to Ramakrishna to help Charles through his suffering and dying." He described in his diary the presence of silly and self-important human nature even in these gravest of circumstances: "All mixed up with the praying—which moved me and caused me to shed tears—were the caperings of the ego, whispering, 'Look, look, look at me, I'm praying for Charles Laughton!' "[187]

On December 14, Isherwood went to visit Laughton back at home, but Laughton was unconscious and died the next day.

BACHARDY WAS INITIATED by Prabhavananda on December 18, 1962. The following day was Laughton's funeral. Isherwood was a pallbearer, along with Raymond Massey, the actor; Taft Schreiber, the MCA executive who was Laughton's agent; Frank Lloyd Wright Jr., son of the architect; Jean Renoir, film director son of the impressionist painter; and Bill Phipps, another actor friend. Isherwood spoke about Laughton and read from Prospero's parting speeches in *The Tempest*. He was horrified by the fake piety of Forest Lawn and by the invasive news coverage, "when I got a little weepy over the 'I am the Resurrection and the Life' speech, there was a movie camera whirring away at me instantly, like a rattlesnake."[188]

Laughton's death coincided with a preliminary climax in Isherwood's power struggle with Bachardy. Isherwood had agreed to spend Christmas in

Mexico with Bachardy and Gavin Lambert, but as Laughton declined, he had turned against the idea. Bachardy accepted this with difficulty. On December 21, Bachardy brought home a lover, Bill Bopp, to spend the night at Adelaide Drive—while Isherwood was there.

To add to the drama, Bachardy's new car was stolen the same night, December 21, when he left it outside a Hollywood restaurant with the key inside. It was recovered smashed up and requiring expensive repairs. Isherwood and Bachardy quarreled. "When I suffer, I suffer as stupidly as an animal. It altogether stops me working. I am ashamed of such weakness," Isherwood wrote in his diary the day after Christmas.[189]

Again as Bachardy pushed Isherwood away, he offered something to pull Isherwood back. This time, he confided that he had long thought the bond between them was a mystical one. He told Isherwood that during their hashish night in Tangier, his near-psychotic paranoia had alternated with spiritual ecstasy, a blissful recognition of his love for Isherwood and of Isherwood's unconditional commitment to him. He had been too overwhelmed to explain this at the time. Since then, he had read about the kundalini, the spiritual energy that rises from the base of the spine through the seven chakras to illuminate the brain, and recognized that he must have had a mystical experience. In his diary, Isherwood commented that the "sudden revelation" was "a bit mystifying to me,"[190] although he saw the Tangier experience as a possible reason for Bachardy's decision to be initiated by Swami.

Bachardy continued to bring Bopp home for the night, and often he stayed out. Bopp was two years older than Bachardy; he had an administrative job at the Burroughs Corporation, a data-processing company, and lived in an apartment in Hollywood. Isherwood kicked back, chasing pleasures of his own. While Bachardy was away in January drawing portraits on commission, Isherwood had "a sort of Indian summer of fun," drinking and partying at Jerry Lawrence's and spending nights out with Charlton and others. There was a "midnight swimming escapade on State Beach," which he labeled "curious because it paralleled the scene in my new novel."[191]

Toward the end of 1962, through the Masselinks, Isherwood and Bachardy had met the painters Paul Wonner and Bill Brown. "They have studios on the vast empty top floor of an old building in Ocean Park, and their work is influenced by Francis Bacon and (a little bit) Keith Vaughan," Isherwood wrote. The four went on the beach and had dinner together, and Isherwood spent the night with Bill Brown. "Don was quite displeased," he confided to his diary, but he also noted that "much as I often don't like it, the Bill [Bopp] situation certainly does seem to make Don behave better around the house."

He dreamed that Bachardy had read his diary. "I hope he won't, because it would upset him." Then he dreamed repeatedly about Bachardy and

Bopp, who were out together nearly every night. "What I am miserable about is the feeling that Don is gradually slipping away from me," he wrote.[192] Bachardy assured Isherwood he would never want to live with Bopp, but he did not tell Isherwood—yet—that he was beginning a new affair. On Christmas Day, 1962, Isherwood and Bachardy were photographed by the Russian-born photographer George Hoyningen-Huene. Huene was assisted by a young man called George Kramer. On January 20, 1963, the two Georges both took pictures of Bachardy. Isherwood watched the session, but he evidently did not see, or at least he did not record in his diary, the excitement plainly evident on Bachardy's face when he was photographed by George Kramer.

IN EARLY FEBRUARY 1963, Isherwood finished his first complete draft of *The Englishman*. At last, he had settled on the names George and Jim. These ordinary-sounding American names had special significance, like all Isherwood's names. Jim was the name of that constant, symbolic rival to Bachardy, Jim Charlton; and George was the name of Isherwood's most recent rival for Bachardy's affection, George Kramer. By naming the younger character for Bachardy's real-life rival, and the older character for his own real life rival, Isherwood was addressing the challenge of Groddeck's love–hate relationship—flipping the identities, as if they were, in some sense, the same. Repeating the names as he typed them, concentrating on them intently, Isherwood was using them like mantras to make spiritual progress, to advance beyond rivalry to equanimity and even love. Over and over again, typing Jim, typing George, Isherwood neutralized jealousy, overcame possessiveness. The novel itself was a meditation, a pathway to detachment and to love.

There were other Georges, of course. George Cukor, George Hoyningen-Huene, and George Dangerfield, the British historian with whom Isherwood was friendly at UCSB and whom he and Bachardy visited in December 1962 when laying groundwork for Bachardy's Santa Barbara show. Dangerfield was known to his friends as "Geo," the nickname used in the novel. Behind all the Georges was Georg Groddeck, who had revealed to Isherwood the "It" that Isherwood decided to call George.

In his workbook, Isherwood listed George's choices for a life without Jim: to live alone, to return to England, to live in a brother-sister relation with Charlotte, to find "some substitute for Jim, in a father-son relationship with Colin." He decided that George was past caring—but then, not quite: "indifference seems to win out. But, right toward the end, George exclaims 'I want love!'" Isherwood intended to leave the end of the novel ambiguous.

"Everything is left undecided, including the coronary occlusion. It is only 'let us suppose that—' "¹⁹³

Over the five months that followed, he revised steadily, despite challenging interruptions, and finished the third complete draft on July 25, 1963. As his writing approached perfection, his personal life fell apart completely.

ON THEIR TENTH anniversary, February 14, 1963, Isherwood had presented Bachardy with a copy of *Down There on a Visit* to replace the one Bachardy had given Tennessee Williams. He inscribed the new copy: "Let's put our faith in the Animals. They have survived the humans and will survive." In his life, as in his work, Isherwood was relying on deep, unconscious forces. Bachardy slept away the night before the anniversary, and he slept away the night after. The night after that, Bill Bopp came to stay with him at Adelaide Drive.

At the end of the month, Bachardy left for Santa Barbara and Stanford for shows of his drawings. While he was gone, Isherwood invited Paul Wonner to Adelaide Drive, where they slept in Isherwood and Bachardy's bed. He and Wonner walked on the beach together and had lunch at the house. Isherwood did not conceal these romantic doings when Bachardy returned. Bachardy later recalled that he and Isherwood both knew Wonner possessed qualities uniquely threatening—in particular, an animal sensuality that Isherwood adored in Bachardy. A battle was raging. Bachardy revealed to Isherwood that he had experienced "feelings of sheer hatred" while he was in Stanford, and Isherwood now learned of the relationship with George Kramer.

They continued with surface courtesies as they searched for a modus vivendi that would permit both honesty and freedom, goals that were in some ways incompatible as Isherwood recognized. Bachardy sensed he was gaining the upper hand. On March 6, 1963, Isherwood reported to his diary: "He said yesterday, 'Dub used to be my jailer, now he's Kitty's convict.' The George Kramer situation, into which I never probe, seems to make him permanently happy and at the same time much fonder of me—in all ways."¹⁹⁴

Bachardy fended off questions about Bopp, who had suddenly stopped coming to the house, and he left again on March 11 to drive to Phoenix, Arizona, where he had commissions and was planning another show. Isherwood wrote him a long letter, trying to untangle what was happening. "[Y]ou feel that I am trying to own the relationship or sponsor it, or whatever you say, just by talking about it," he posited. "I really do accept it as part of our life together. But even if I say *that* much, it sounds sort of possessive, as though I were trying to make it into a mere colony of the Kitty-Dobbin empire." He admitted that he had slept with Wonner out of rivalry but also because he hated being alone at night: "It has always been a weakness of mine, and one which I should get over. It's childishness, really. Something to do with the dark." All through childhood, there had been Nanny, then Richard; at boarding school, he always shared with other boys. Even then, during school holidays, he sometimes shared with his mother until he was at least seventeen. He was programmed to have a bedfellow or a roommate.

As Bachardy bore east toward Phoenix on Highway 10, six hours, mostly through desert, Isherwood sat at his typewriter, sketching a scene that repeatedly played out between them, when they were face-to-face and failed to communicate successfully:

> Oh—I am so saddened and depressed when I get a glimpse, as I do so clearly this morning, of the poker game we play so much of the time, watching each other's faces and listening to each other's voices for clues. And then you say, for example, Dobbin's in a strange mood, and then things start to get tense. And, because I know this, I start playacting to get them untense again, and that makes everything worse.[195]

Physical distance released them, and so did triangulating through their Animal personae. Accustomed though he was to having the upper hand in his relationships, Isherwood prepared to give way, as he had never given way before. He implied it might be easier if Bachardy forced him, but he recognized Bachardy wanted him to volunteer:

> I was so happy the other day when you said that about Dobbin having been a jailer and now being a convict. I sort of wish that were true all of the time. Masochism? Oh, Mary—what do I care what it's called? I only know that it isn't a *wrong* thing for me to feel. Our relationship is really so very strange. No wonder it gives us trouble. I mean, I often feel that the Animals are far more than just a nursery joke or a cuteness. They *exist*. They are like Jung's myths. They express a kind of freedom and truth which we otherwise wouldn't have . . .

It was two weeks before Isherwood made another diary entry. "This is a strange period, and I feel I don't want to make any statement about it until it is over. Seriously, it is possible we might have parted by the summer."[196] He remained upbeat and socialized as always. Cecil Beaton was back in Hollywood working on costume and production designs for George Cukor's film of the musical *My Fair Lady*, and Auden stayed at Adelaide Drive during a western lecture tour in March. Once, Isherwood stayed overnight with Charlton.

JONES STREET, SAN FRANCISCO, 1963

On April 12, Isherwood made a jail break, driving his black Volkswagen to San Francisco to lecture at Berkeley. It was a series of three called "The Autobiography of My Books," a chronological account of his novels and of the plays and travel book he had written with Auden. In the lectures, he mapped some of the territory he was to cover in *Christopher and His Kind*, initiating a retrospective self-understanding that was to develop and preoccupy him increasingly in the coming years.

He borrowed a house, 2424 Jones Street, from a painter friend of the Masselinks. He liked the view from the roof—San Francisco Bay, the ships passing and Alcatraz, that real jail, in the background. "[A]t present I am concerned with my psychological convalescence," he wrote in his diary.[197] He established a strict routine, rising early, making japam on the roof, doing exercises from the Royal Canadian Air Force book, grooming, breakfasting, and getting to work.

Beaton came north one weekend to visit a lover, and Isherwood began writing an introduction for a book of photo portraits in which Beaton had laid several negatives on top of each other so that the sitters appeared to be moving or to be haloed by an aura. The book, called *Images*, included portraits of Auden, Garbo, T.S. Eliot, and Anna Magnani. In Beaton's cubist experiment, Isherwood described a psychological exploration like the one he was making in his novel: "Here are records of journeys made from the bright surface-world of things-as-they-normally-appear into the dark hinterland, the exciting, beautiful and sometimes terrifying interior."[198]

Bachardy was riding the roller coaster, as he made clear when he finally wrote: "The screws are on. I can't remember a more difficult time. I can't paint, I can't read, I can't relax—" He was holding out for a personal transformation: "I don't want to need you. I want to be able to rely on myself. I have so many years of bad habits, selfishness and weakness to overcome. I sometimes feel it's almost hopeless to try to change, but then I don't know what else to do. I don't have any other choice which is acceptable to me. It seems I must change."

Isherwood wrote back reassuringly: "I have never in my life gone so *far* in a relationship with anyone before. In a way, I feel as if we *couldn't* be separated any more. I don't mean physically, of course." He offered to stay away a little longer. To his diary, he confided: "I am even losing my confidence that this will end all right."[199]

Jim Charlton came to San Francisco to visit, and there were sex friends—Ben Underhill, Bob Davis—but these romantic boys reminded Isherwood of his failures in love. Walking with one young friend in Golden Gate Park, "I was suddenly blue, overcome by memories of Harvey, of Caskey, of Don. The past came crowding in . . ." He caught a virus which gave him an extreme backache, "the beginning of a truly great Blue Period," he wrote in his diary. He spoke with Bachardy on the telephone on May 6, and Bachardy said, "hesitantly" as Isherwood noted in his diary, "that he *would* like me to stay on up here." This made Isherwood "sad as hell"; he got drunk and had to deliver his final lecture hungover "feeling like death." After the lecture, he got drunk again.[200]

Then there was a real death, an unexpected one, Larry Paxton, recently returned to San Francisco from New York where he had worked in an art gallery, died of diabetic shock on May 7. He had been raised as a Christian Scientist and decided to return to principles and stop using insulin. Isherwood hadn't known Paxton well. He had taken him out to dinner a couple of times since arriving in San Francisco, and Paxton had stayed one night at Jones Street. The family asked Isherwood to speak at the funeral.

"It was ghastly," Isherwood wrote in his diary. There was an open casket, a drunken mother, an innocent, forlorn teenage half-brother who clung to Isherwood. Isherwood read Donne's sonnet "Death, be not proud" and was "trembling all over" by the time he finished. The congregation was swept with grief and fury over the loss of someone so young and vital, and one friend, a Greek who had flown in from New York, perhaps a lover, "suddenly let out a great roar of frustration and despair, and banged against the casket with his fists." In the refrigerator at Jones Street, Isherwood still had some tomato juice that he and Paxton had bought together. He also had a "funny photograph" of himself and Paxton wearing derby hats.[201]

ADELAIDE DRIVE, SANTA MONICA, 1963

Isherwood drove back to Los Angeles to celebrate Bachardy's twenty-ninth birthday on May 18. He went to a fancy jewelry store, Kazanjian Brothers downtown, bought Bachardy a ring set with a dark blue Australian sapphire, and presented the ring with a Hallmark card picturing a smiling beribboned white kitten. Inside the card, he wrote, "I dreamed of Kitty. I dreamed Dobbin died and someone said, 'Was he very beautiful?' and Kitty said 'No.'"

Whether or not Isherwood meant the ring as a proposal, his dream suggested that he already knew the answer. Bachardy turned the ring down. Isherwood recorded: "This morning at breakfast he shed tears, said he couldn't accept it. Our relationship is impossible for him. I am too possessive. He can't face the idea of having me around another ten years or more, using up his life."

Over this painful truth, the veil of courteous business-as-usual was immediately drawn. "I said I absolutely agree with him. If it won't work, it must stop." There was a birthday dinner party and guests to prepare for; Bachardy went out. "I cried a bit. Then drank coffee, felt a lot better, and began figuring. Don should start by getting a studio away from this place, where he can stay whenever he wants to. Also, he should go to a psychiatrist. (This is his idea.) And we must start thinking about selling this house." But even before writing this in his diary, Isherwood, with characteristic self-possession, had already sat down and worked on his novel for the first time in a week. "I must keep hard at it from now on in," he admonished himself. [202]

By June 2, he had completed seventy-seven pages of his new draft. "I do so want to get all this work squared away before I face a complete break with Don—if there has got to be a break." He was again avoiding writing in his diary, observing after a gap of two weeks: "Part of Don wants to run me right off the range and wreck our home beyond repair; part wants to keep on and see how things work out."

He spent a few days at Trabuco with Prabhavananda and returned to find George Kramer at supper with Don and staying for the night. "The scene worked out as well as could be expected, so today all is fine again. Don says he can't make his case against me stick. He asks forgiveness. I forgive (no shit) and so we go on."[203] It was a long, hot summer of ménage à trois. Kramer was often at the house or on the beach with Bachardy and Isherwood, went out to supper with them, and was included in larger supper parties at home. Bachardy and Kramer took two trips away together to Santa Barbara.

Just as agreed, Bachardy rented a studio away from Adelaide Drive. It was in Wonner and Brown's building in Ocean Park. Around the middle of June, he began seeing Gavin Lambert's psychiatrist, a Dr. Oderberg. His mood improved. "No more gloom," Isherwood observed, though he attributed this to the relationship with Kramer and to working alongside Wonner and Brown, "he is at grips with his great problem—*can* he paint and if so does he really *want* to?" Bachardy was also making japam regularly.

Isherwood was impressed by this all-out effort. Bachardy continued to make Isherwood his example and to seek his approval. "Don is very conscious of the existence of this 'old black book,' as he calls it," Isherwood noted in his diary. "He's sure it's full of criticism of him. I tell him, well, when I die, all he has to do is burn it."[204] In fact, when Isherwood died, Bachardy was to read through the whole diary. Then he was to oversee publication, including the accounts of his own floundering struggles to grow and change, to gain power in the relationship with Isherwood, to have as many lovers, and to get Isherwood to accept this emulation, which was both homage and punishment.

That summer, Isherwood spent many evenings with other friends and sometimes stayed the night with Jim Charlton or Phil Burns. He drank far too much and had more car accidents. On June 22, he sideswiped a parked car on the way home from Bruce Zortman's. The police were involved, and Isherwood hired a lawyer to pay for the damage without revealing his identity. Repairs to the two cars cost nearly $400, and the lawyer was $500. "And all I need have done was to sleep on Bruce Zortman's couch, or for that matter take the most expensive hotel room in town—"[205]

He had a second crash, far worse, involving two other cars, on August 10. He broke a rib and did $600 worth of damage. Two men gave him coffee, drove him home, and then asked to meet again before testifying whether Isherwood had been drunk. Isherwood refused the meeting and directed the blackmailers to his lawyer. Despite his guilt and shame, he did not reform. On April 7, 1964, on the way home from a restaurant, he was arrested for drunk driving and jailed until 6 a.m. the next morning. He posted bail, appeared in court and was fined. Two years later, in May 1966, he hit another car.

George Hoyningen-Huene ended his domestic arrangement with George Kramer in August 1963, and Kramer moved in with friends. He was all the more available to spend time at Adelaide Drive. Bachardy chose the day of Kramer's move to show Isherwood some of his recent paintings, again pulling Isherwood close as he pushed him away. The paintings were of dolls. "One or two of them are curiously poignant," Isherwood wrote in his diary. "You feel the tragedy of their not being human—just as one occasionally feels the tragedy of some human beings not being *more* human." Dolls were a revealing subject for Bachardy, objects of devotion, fantasy, manipulation, without any life of their own.

He had been making dolls for himself most of his life. His mother embroidered their faces, and Bachardy added different-colored hair from embroidery thread that could be combed. He mostly kept the dolls secret from Isherwood. Once in 1956, when they were packing to come home from New York, Isherwood found one, a stocking doll with a black silk dress made from a scarf. "Don usually kept it stuffed into an overcoat pocket, during this trip—but he doesn't know I've examined it. When I seemed about to discover it, he got excited and cross. I suppose it is some very private kind of magic."[206]

When Bachardy and Kramer returned from their second trip to Santa Barbara in mid-September, Isherwood told Bachardy that he did not want to see Kramer anymore. In his diary he wrote: "That kind of thing is messy and was messy in the days of Lord Byron, and always will be messy." But the initiative failed.

A month later, he wrote: "Jealousy: Not what they do together sexually.

But the thought of their waking in the morning, little pats and squeezes, jokes, talk through the open doorway of the bathroom. For that one could kill." He had tried to accept the ménage à trois, but domestic intimacy was too important to him. He told Bachardy again: "I have said definitely that I do not want to see George any more, under any circumstances. I also asked Don to please take the photo of George into his studio. He had put it up on the desk in the back bedroom ..."[207] After that, Kramer's name dropped from Isherwood's day-to-day diary. The affair was in fact reaching a natural end and now served mostly to disguise Bachardy's other liaisons.

Tony Richardson was in Los Angeles several times that autumn. He was approaching the apex of his career. His comic film *Tom Jones*, adapted by John Osborne from Fielding's novel and starring Albert Finney, launched at the Venice Film Festival on September 29. Two weeks beforehand, Richardson gave an all-male dinner at Chasen's and included Isherwood and Bachardy. The night Richardson attended the premiere in Italy, Isherwood and Bachardy watched the film with Gavin Lambert at the Screenwriters Film Society in L.A. In Venice, Richardson won the Golden Lion; later, he won Golden Globes, BAFTAs, and the 1964 Academy Awards for Best Picture and Best Director. By November 14, he was back in Los Angeles, and Isherwood noted in his day-to-day diary that Bachardy was away from home for seven nights. Then in mid-December, Bachardy went to New York. He continued to make a serious play to leave Isherwood for Richardson, and Richardson continued to resist.

BACHARDY READ *The Englishman* on July 29, 1963, generating one of the uncanny moments of shared insight which still fired the core of his relationship with Isherwood: "In bed, on Monday night, Don was silent for a long while. I thought he had fallen asleep. Then he suddenly asked, 'How about *A Single Man* for a title?' I knew instantly and have had no doubts since that this is the absolutely ideal title for the novelette ..." Later Bachardy, "that wizard at name finding" as Isherwood called him, picked the character names Kenny and Doris that Isherwood was to use in his final draft.[208] Eventually, Bachardy designed the jacket for the U.K. edition.

Upward sent three letters of praise when he read the current draft. "The book as a whole cuts the reader to the heart, and dazzles him too. And I think your new manner comes off 100%." Upward saw the novel as the start of a new episode in Isherwood's career. "I dream that you are now beginning to tap an immense reservoir of experiences which for one reason or another have had to be dammed back until now."[209]

In September, Isherwood discussed the novel with Gore Vidal, who was in Los Angeles making a film of his play *The Best Man*, and he told Vidal he wanted to dedicate *A Single Man* to him. Vidal was evidently taken by surprise and shyly underreacted. He wrote when he got back to the East Coast, expressing stronger feelings: "After the fact, to say how pleased, touched, honored and all the rest of the by no means bullshit I am to have the novel dedicated to me. I'm not very good at confrontations of any sort (so that is why you became a writer, Mr. Vidal) and I did the occasion less than I meant..."

The dedication was the fruit of the long-running discussion between Isherwood and Vidal about their social and political mission as homosexual writers. Here at last was the book, Isherwood implied, that they had been discussing and attempting to write since 1947, before they had even met—a beautiful work of art that was also a powerful piece of propaganda presenting a well-adjusted homosexual to a mainstream audience.

When Vidal read *Down There on a Visit* in 1962, he had written several paragraphs of praise before getting to the cautious criticism: "Now my one nervousness, a curious thing for me to fret about: I think there is a kind of homosexual chauvinism in the book which puts one off."[210] As Isherwood by then knew well, Vidal had sophisticated political instincts that shaped such a judgment. He sprang from a political family and hungered for public office. In 1960, Vidal had run as the Democratic candidate for Congress in the traditionally Republican 29th Congressional District in New York, upstate from Manhattan. He resented the fact that his sexuality was an obstacle to his political career, and he defiantly published work that made his sexuality evident. Isherwood saw writing as Vidal's real political task. He had been impressed by *The Best Man*, about two politicians vying for their party's presidential nomination, when he saw it staged during Vidal's unsuccessful 1960 congressional campaign, and he had implored, "Don't desert the arts too much—you are needed badly."

In their conversation about *A Single Man* in September 1963, they debated strategy again. Vidal evidently said that this new novel also evinced too much homosexual chauvinism. But after years of caution and courtesy, Isherwood was unwilling to soften George's rage against the procreating heterosexual middle class. "I'm afraid you may be disappointed because I have left in all of the homosexual aggression; it seems necessary for my character," he told Vidal a month later.[211] Isherwood did, however, make the bond between George and Charlotte warmer, on advice from both Vidal and Upward.

It was only in the final draft that Isherwood had George and Charlotte talk about buying a pub together in England. He wanted to show George seriously considering a return to England in order that he could show him rejecting it. He decided on a business that promotes drunkenness, George and Charlotte's usual route to intimacy as it had been Isherwood and Caskey's.

The real-life pub Isherwood had in mind was the Ploughboy near Wyberslegh, where he had sat up drinking with Richard and the Bradleys in September 1961 and where the local character, Reg, had quoted Henry Newbolt, "Play up! And play the game!" comically epitomizing the glorification of war and empire that had first turned Isherwood against England.

Isherwood also decided to introduce into the scene between George and Charley "a tongue-kiss" in order to show that as a homosexual George could not be lured toward bisexuality, even with a woman he loved. Charlotte "suddenly sticks her tongue right in," during their goodnight embrace. "She has done this before, often. It's one of those drunken long shots which just might, at least theoretically, once in ten thousand tries, throw a relationship right out of its orbit and send it whizzing off on another."[212] But the kiss does not change anything for George. His sexuality is fixed; the reader must recognize it as real.

A few years later, reciprocating for *A Single Man*, Vidal was to dedicate his gender-breaking novel *Myra Breckinridge* to Isherwood. This first-ever mainstream fiction about a sex-change operation was to carry the Isherwood–Vidal conspiracy to change cultural attitudes right into the twenty-first century. "HONORED AND DELIGHTED," Isherwood was to telegram on receiving the unpublished manuscript from Rome in August 1967. He read it twice and wrote to Vidal, "it's your very best satirical work. Wildly funny and wildly sensible." He saw in the book "an entirely realistic and very subtle psychological self-portrait."[213]

ISHERWOOD HAD AT last polished off the biography of Ramakrishna in September 1963, "the longest and cruellest of all my Vedanta chores." He had been reading aloud from his draft at the Vedanta Society, and he had permitted it to be published chapter by chapter in the Vedanta Society magazine. He titled it *Ramakrishna and His Disciples*. Now Prabhavananda invited Isherwood to accompany him to India for the closing celebrations of the Vivekananda centenary, revealing a whole new set of obligations that fell to Ramakrishna's official biographer. "The idea fills me with blank horror," Isherwood declared in his diary.

The year-long celebration of Vivekananda was to conclude in January 1964; they were to set off in December. Driving hard, Isherwood completed his final draft of *A Single Man* and sent it to his publishers in late October: "I am almost certain that it is my masterpiece; by which I mean my most effective, coherent statement, artwork, whatever you want to call it."

Predictably, his health was breaking down. A cough and cold produced a sore throat that had lasted all summer and made him hoarse. He decided that it was a psychosomatic symptom brought on by writing about the throat cancer that killed Ramakrishna. A shot of penicillin did nothing. By the end of October, still unwell, he was blaming the approaching India trip: "A *passionate* psychosomatic revolt is brewing."[214]

Around the edges of his consciousness, another big subterranean theme was leaking. The friends who had anchored his Californian life were declining. Stravinsky was eighty-one, frail and intermittently forgetful, and Huxley was dying of throat cancer—which had killed Ramakrishna and which Isherwood's symptoms had been copycatting. Isherwood visited Huxley on November 4 at Cedars of Lebanon: "He looks like a withered old man, grey faced, with dead blank eyes, speaking in a hoarse voice, hard to understand. But his mind seems to be as good as ever—that marvellous instrument, about to be swallowed up in the ruins and shattered."

In April, working on *A Single Man*, Isherwood had written in his diary, "I am off on a digression about Huxley's *After Many a Summer*, but that doesn't matter. I'll just keep writing until I write myself out of it again."[215] *After Many a Summer* was the last novel Huxley published before World War II. Its theme was the passage of time, and it fictionalized the ideals for which Huxley, Heard, and Isherwood had changed their lives at the end of the 1930s. Isherwood's digression was really more of a defense—a defense of Huxley, incapable in Isherwood's view of defending himself against the attacks of Colin Wilson and before that Brecht, a defense of Heard, and of himself. *After Many a Summer* evoked a key turning point in Isherwood's life, and it offered him another way to refract the central themes of his own novel—youth and age, timelessness and time, minorities in a majority culture, or outsiders as he often called them.

Huxley had taken his title from Tennyson's poem "Tithonus," about Ganymede's twin, to whom Zeus gave immortal life but not immortal youth. Tithonus ages but cannot die, a fate Huxley had visited upon his character the Earl of Goniston, as a warning to his other characters who are satirized for their varied obsessions with youth. Only the philosopher Propter, modeled on Gerald Heard, points to the possibility of transcending time in the higher consciousness achieved through nonattachment. In *A Single Man*, George's students are assigned to read *After Many a Summer*. They are mystified by the ideal of nonattachment and give up discussing it without understanding it. They are far more engaged by the Tithonus myth, which brings Isherwood's theme of boy-love obliquely into the open.

Isherwood used magic, as he had once done in *The Memorial*, to suggest a hidden homosexual theme in George's mind. "Slowly, deliberately, like a magician, he takes a single book out of his briefcase and places it on the reading desk."[216] The book allows George to perform in the casual extempore manner once advised by the adolescent Isherwood's favorite magicians a simple and astonishing trick. One student asks about the persecution of the Jews: "Mr. Propter says the stupidest text in the Bible is '*they hated me without a cause.*' Does he mean by that the Nazis were right to hate the Jews? Is Huxley anti-Semitic?" The persecuted group in *After Many a Summer* is the Okies not the Jews, but this goes unremarked. "No Mr Huxley is *not* anti-Semitic," cries George. "The Nazis were *not* right to hate the Jews." Thus with deft sleight of hand, one minority group is substituted for another; the Okies, the Jews, "people with freckles." George has homosexuals in mind, but in a college classroom in the early 1960s, he cannot say so without threatening his job. So Isherwood used George's silent eye contact with a boy who files his nails and plucks his eyebrows. "I am with you little minority-sister," thinks George, as he looks at the boy.

Abracadabra. This was how Münzenberg had used Christians to mean Communists in his propaganda pamphlet pretending to review DeMille's *The Sign of the Cross* after the Reichstag Fire in 1933. Isherwood did not use the word homosexual in the novel, but his sequence of substitutions insisted that homosexuals are a minority like any other minority, an idea not widely established at the time and, to many, thoroughly shocking. He stacked George's classroom with outsiders—a Jew, a Black, a Chinese, a German, a Swede, a Hispanic, a Roman Catholic nun—in order that he could place a homosexual among them and push the reader to recognize the plight of the homosexual as the universal plight of the minority, of the outsider. "So, let's face it," says George,

> minorities are people who probably look and act and think differently from us, and have faults we don't have. We may dislike the way they look and act, and we may hate their faults. And it's *better* if we admit to disliking them and hating them, than if we try to smear our feelings over with pseudo-liberal sentimentality. If we're frank about our feelings, we have a safety-valve; and if we have a safety valve, we're actually less likely to start persecuting [. . .] And, of course, persecution is always wrong.

George also pushes his students to accept that "minorities are people; *people*, not angels."[217] As a homosexual, Isherwood didn't expect to be liked; he expected to be treated justly. He was to say this more directly, in propria persona, as the years went by.

Huxley died on November 22, the day of President Kennedy's assassination. Isherwood labeled it "Black Friday." Huxley had no funeral. Instead, family and close friends gathered for a walk. Afterwards, Isherwood experienced a massive cadence of closure. *A Single Man* had been accepted by both his publishers. He handed over his typescript of *Ramakrishna and His Disciples* to the Vedanta Center. "Well, the books are done now. Maybe I shall die soon [. . .] Life goes on, or stops. If it goes on, it will change for me."[218]

BELUR MATH, NEAR CALCUTTA, 1963

Christmas 1963 was the first one Isherwood and Bachardy spent apart since they had met ten years earlier. The uncertainty surrounding their relationship intensified Isherwood's anxiety about traveling to India with Prabhavananda. He did not want to end up as a monk; he was determined to remain a dirty old man. To still his travel fears, he began taking Librium a few days before the trip: "The idea is that I shall be riding high before the take-off."[219]

At Belur Math, he stayed in the new guesthouse, built since his 1957 visit with Bachardy, just outside the gates of the monastery compound on the Ganges riverbank. He described the monastery as "far more delightful" than he remembered, and the singing at vespers "more thrilling." Whereas in 1957, he had been reluctant to make ritual bows which might embarrass Bachardy, he now relished taking the dust of the feet of the swamis: "This time I am playing it very broad with pranams."

The magic quickly dissipated. He ran out of Librium by December 23, and he had many obligations. There were readings, tours to the order's educational and numerous other projects where he was sometimes asked to speak, a separate Women's Conference to which he was also a delegate, and countless people from India and all over the world to greet, including the press. Meals were eaten in a crowd, sometimes on the floor, with hands and no utensils; Isherwood found this "messy and unsnug."

In addition to preparing and recording his own speeches, he helped John Yale prepare a slide lecture about the Vedanta Society of Southern California. Yale had taken hundreds of photographs to illustrate Isherwood's biography of Ramakrishna. One morning in India, they went through them, and Yale told Isherwood that he didn't think the biography—which he had been reading chapter by chapter—was "really 'great.' " In his pocket diary, Isherwood wrote, "I agree with him, of course." His resentment welled up. Censorship by Belur Math, he made clear to Yale, had turned the project into a lifeless bore. "I added that I could probably draw a much better portrait of

Ramakrishna to a sympathetic stranger one evening when I had had a few drinks."[220]

He decided to take a stand on the photographs. The Math had never permitted publication of the full death picture of Ramakrishna taken August 16, 1886—Ramakrishna's corpse surrounded by more than fifty devotees on the way to the ghat for cremation. In existing published versions, the corpse had always been cropped out so that the devotees looked intently at something beyond the picture frame. Prabhavananda supported Isherwood's argument that showing the corpse was not repulsive or in bad taste and pointed out to the monks making the decision that the dead Christ was depicted openly in churches and even his wounds portrayed.[221] So the full photo appeared in *Ramakrishna and His Disciples* when it was published

On Christmas Eve, at the puja for Jesus in the temple at Belur Math, Isherwood read from the Gospels. He tried to write to Bachardy but found he "could say nothing coherent." He felt dazed. Huge canvas tents on bamboo frames, called pandals, were being set up in the monastery grounds for speeches and mass meals at the centenary closing ceremony. "Also, in the field in front of the guesthouse," Isherwood wrote in the diary, "they have dug latrines and shit holes." On December 28, he wrote: "It *is* an experience, being here. I *am* getting something out of it, I know. And yet I strain like a leashed animal to escape."[222] Already, he had made a plane reservation to fly to Rome in early January. On the 29th, he moved with Prabhavananda and George Fitts (Swami Krishnananda since taking his sannyas vows in 1958) to the Ramakrishna Mission Institute of Culture in Calcutta so they could more easily attend the meetings of the Parliament of Religions.

The first session lasted three hours. "Next to the hashish experience in Tangier, this was the least endurable time stretch I have ever known," wrote Isherwood. The audience was about 8,000 people; the speeches were "droned out" from prepared scripts in English, though Isherwood thought that few in the audience could really understand English. "When it was my turn, I spoke too loudly and too urgently—rather like a communist speaker in the thirties." The next day, at the second session, he gave a speech titled "Vivekananda and the West"—"a tribute to Vivekananda by a descendant of their oppressors," he wrote in *My Guru and His Disciple*.[223]

Throughout his visit, Isherwood noticed power struggles. The swamis "push their disciples around," he wrote. "They push the younger swamis around, even." He insisted on seeing this as a remnant of British imperialism rather than as part of traditionally hierarchical Indian society, even though he felt that he, too, was being pushed around. By December 30, he was ill with stomach pains and diarrhea; he lay awake all night, shivering. His "It" was in revolt. On the last day of 1963, he aired his feelings in his pocket diary, resolving to tell Prabhavananda that his role viv-à-vis the Vedanta Society must change, and his public appearances cease: "As long as I quite unashamedly get drunk, have sex and write books like *A Single Man*, I simply cannot appear before people as a sort of lay minister." But he was given some pills by a doctor, and off he went, achey and sleepy, without saying a word of this aloud, to another Ramakrishna project—schools, clinics, a farm—at Narendrapur, in the countryside south of Calcutta.

Isherwood began in his imagination to negotiate with Prabhavananda, postponing any confrontation and identifying particular tasks he *was* willing to perform: "I still am resolved to tell Swami I won't give any more religious talks; but I'll do so only after my talk at Belur on the 6th; and I'll offer to give two talks about this trip, in Hollywood and at Santa Barbara, and also two readings on other Sundays while he is still away."[224] Once he had written out this strategy, his symptoms improved a little.

Despite being ill, he took his turn presiding as president of an afternoon session of the parliament. He gave another speech, "chiefly about Girish Ghosh and the ways in which I identify myself with him." Girish Ghosh, the celebrated Bengali actor and playwright, had been a devotee of Ramakrishna, and through their close relationship, Ramakrishna had become patron saint of Bengali drama. Ramakrishna's portrait hung backstage in most Calcutta theaters. Indeed, on the first night of the Parliament of Religions, Isherwood, Prabhavananda, and Fitts attended a play at the Star Theatre, where Ramakrishna had watched Ghosh perform and where Ghosh's portrait hung with Ramakrishna's backstage.

Ghosh was known not only for his theatrical and literary genius, but also for his drinking and whoring. He visited Ramakrishna at all hours, even on his way home from the brothels, and they danced together when Ghosh was drunk. In *My Guru and His Disciple*, Isherwood was to relate how the sight of drunkards reeling inspired Ramakrishna to "think of the way a holy man reels in ecstasy." And he was to explain that "Ghosh became a kind of patron saint for me—I felt closer to him than to any other member of Ramakrishna's circle" because "Ghosh dared to reveal himself shamelessly to Ramakrishna, thereby making a sacrifice of his own self-esteem and self-will and submitting totally to Ramakrishna's guidance." But Isherwood was not as bold as Ghosh, any more than he was as reckless as his character Paul. "I am sorry, now, that, throughout my long relationship with Swami, I never once came into his presence drunk. Something wonderful might have happened."

In his diary, Isherwood remarked that his speech about Ghosh was "better than the other, though less well received." When he finished, he was handed a note: "Continue for fifteen minutes." Another speaker had failed to appear.

Isherwood found the situation "enormously insulting, however unintentionally."[225] He did not comply.

The next day, his "It" was again unruly. He accompanied Prabhavananda with a group to visit Brahmananda's birthplace, a tiny village east of Calcutta, Sikra Kulingram, where they were to spend the night. Throughout the three-hour drive, Isherwood felt awful, "Partly upset stomach and headache, but chiefly rage against the Parliament of Religions, the Ramakrishna Math, India, everything." At the birthplace of Prabhavananda's beloved guru, Isherwood decided he would finally tell Prabhavananda about the inner conflicts he had experienced throughout the years of their relationship. His diary account reveals how intensely he longed to be a perfect disciple and how difficult he found it to blemish his perfection in the eyes of his own beloved guru. But the Isherwood–Prabhavananda relationship, like the Isherwood–Bachardy one, required recalibration if it was to last. Isherwood wanted more freedom; like Bachardy, he still had growing to do. In India, as Ramakrishna's biographer, he felt trapped by the kind of institutional structures he had feared all his life; he ugently needed to make another jailbreak.

He had to build up a head of steam emotionally first, lying down in his room: "I realized that I was going to make a scene and I needed time to rehearse it." Then he found Prabhavananda and asked for a car to be ordered so he could travel back alone to Belur Math. Prabhavananda acquiesced, bewildered. Isherwood launched into his reasons. "Swami—it isn't just that I'm sick. I feel awful about everything. I've made up my mind: I can't ever talk about God and religion in public again. It's impossible. I've felt like this for a long time." He did not promise the readings and talks back in Hollywood that he had imagined as his bargaining chips, but instead went for maximum emotional effect. "It's the same thing, really, that I told you years ago when I was living at the center: the Ramakrishna Math is coming between me and God. I can't belong to any kind of institution. Because I'm not respectable--" Prabhavananda laughed, more bewildered, and praised Isherwood's frankness. Isherwood ruthlessly pressed on. "I can't stand up on Sundays in nice clothes and talk about God. I feel like a prostitute."

They were walking up and down a pathway between some bushes, but the rest of the group could see them. "I felt that everybody knew a scene was taking place. I also felt that I was acting hysterically." Prabhavananda hardly seemed to understand what was happening and registered only hurt and dismay. "'I don't want to lose you, Chris,' he said."

Isherwood was echoing Bachardy's behavior, thousands of miles away from him. The relationship with Prabhavananda had long asked more than Isherwood wanted to give, and Isherwood demanded to continue it on his own terms, with Prabhavananda's blessing, and without guilt. "I felt better immediately. [...] Through the eyes of my relief, India suddenly seemed charming."[226]

Now it was Prabhavananda's turn to be ill. The next day, he went to bed with a cough. "The country dust is blamed; but I got a strong impression (later confirmed by Prema) that the sickness has a lot to do with me." (Prema Chaitanya was John Yale's Sanskrit name given when he took his brahmacharya vows; his name was about to change again when he took his next vows.)

Isherwood had known that Prabhavananda, too, found India emotionally challenging. He had written to Forster before leaving Santa Monica: "He dreads all this just as much as I do. And the mere sight of his native land usually throws him into a fever. Last time he went there, he was sick every single day."[227] Indeed, Prabhavananda had already spent a day in bed in Tokyo during the outward journey. Yet Isherwood rebelled.

Now that he had written *A Single Man*, Isherwood had begun to access, as Upward had recognized, an immense reservoir previously dammed back. In future he would still perform some tasks set him by Prabhavananda—regular readings at the temple, occasional lectures to the congregations in Hollywood and in Santa Barbara, even some literary jobs—but he asserted at last that his identity as a writer could not be subsumed in the needs of the order or directed by it. He had carefully avoided mention of Vedanta in his fiction; his next novel was to be all about Vedanta, following the dictates of his own imagination.

JOHN YALE HAD already been present at Belur Math when Isherwood arrived with Prabhavananda from California. Yale was preparing to take his final vows, sannyas, on the last day of Vivekananda's centenary celebrations. Also at Belur Math preparing for sannyas was another American monk from the Hollywood Vedanta Society, Kenny Critchfield, known as Arup Chaitanya.

Yale had first been drawn to Vedanta in the late 1940s, when he read Prabhavananda and Isherwood's translation of the Bhagavad Gita. He had left his job in Chicago, where he was a director of Science Research Associates (SRA), a publisher of educational tools and psychological tests later absorbed by IBM, and moved to Los Angeles to become a disciple of Prabhavananda. He had first met Isherwood at the Vedanta Center in 1949. He was nine years younger. Yale had also taught high school and edited textbooks; later, he got a doctorate in education from USC. He developed the Vedanta Society bookshop, building a mail-order business, and he edited the Vedanta Society magazine, taking over from Isherwood. He had worked with Isherwood on the chapter-by-chapter magazine publication of the Ramakrishna biography, and he had also published in the magazine his own book, *A Yankee and the Swamis*, about his journey to Belur Math and other Indian holy places in 1952–3 before he took his brahmacharya vows.

Isherwood was intrigued by Yale's sex life, which Yale guarded closely. Back in Chicago, Yale had been interviewed by Alfred Kinsey for *Sexual Behavior in the Human Male*. Recounting his sexual history for Kinsey had made Yale ill, so he had decided to give up sex. Isherwood presumed he was homosexual. Isherwood saw in Yale an example of what he himself might have become if he had remained at the monastery, but he also noted a single-mindedness he did not possess.[228] He was to draw on Yale's experiences for his character Oliver in *A Meeting by the River*.

On January 4, Yale and Critchfield had their heads shaved, leaving only a tuft. As brahmacharis, they had worn white robes; now they were issued with *gerua* (ocher) clothes to be put on during the sannyas ceremony on the last day of the Vivekananda centenary. They ate as much as they could for supper on January 4 because they would begin a two-day fast the next morning.

Isherwood's health was improving, but he was in a bitter mood, impatient for his freedom. "A terrific wailing and drumming burst forth at about 4:30 a.m. announcing the Big Day," he wrote on January 6. On January 5 and 6, he masturbated, "as a protest."[229]

Prabhavananda frightened them all by saying he wished to leave his body in India, *mahasamadhi*. The atmosphere between him and Isherwood was awkward, even petulant. Resting adjacent to Vivekananda's old room, kept as Vivekananda left it, Prabhavananda asked Isherwood to massage his hand, a reference to an important moment in the past when Brahmananda had asked Prabhavananda to massage his feet. Isherwood did his best, sensing that Prabhavananda still wished to exert control over him and chafing against his position as a disciple.

On the day of his departure, Isherwood woke with a meaningful sore throat to hear the ceremonial music again blasting through the loudspeakers. It took him three hours to drag himself from bed; finally, he went to find "the new swamis." They had renounced the world, died, undergone a spiritual rebirth, and received new names. Prabhavananda and most of the other swamis had attended the ceremony in the temple in the dead of night; no one else was allowed to see it.

To Isherwood, the two American monks seemed genuinely transformed. First he found Critchfield, looking "absolutely marvellous in his gerua." Together, they found Yale, "in a group of other new-made swamis on their way to beg alms. [. . .] I ran out to him and prostrated and he hugged me warmly; the onlookers were much edified, I felt, to see us Westerners playing the game according to their rules."

Isherwood slipped alone into Vivekananda's room when he saw it was open for cleaning. There he prostrated and prayed: "'Give me devotion to you, give me knowledge of you—even against my will. And be with me in the hour of death.' And I prayed the same for Don. Then I touched my forehead to the bed." He repeated these furtive rituals on a balcony Prabhavananda had shown him, where Prabhavananda had first encountered Brahmananda. Later in the day, Isherwood returned a second time to the balcony: "I brought my beads and touched them to the spot on the floor of the balcony where I guess Maharaj and Swami must have stood."[230]

It was after midnight when he took off from Calcutta airport for Karachi, Damascus, and Rome. He was to stay with Vidal and Austen before joining Bachardy for a few weeks in New York. He had a terrible mucousy cold. Nevertheless, he stayed awake on the airplane, adding notes to his pocket diary before his memories faded. Airborne, he was struck with the inspiration for his final novel, *A Meeting by the River*. "Later, when talking about that night, I used to claim jokingly that it was then I had first become aware that Vivekananda—grateful, no doubt, for my help in celebrating his centenary—had given me a charming thank-you present, an idea for a novel."[231]

ADELAIDE DRIVE, SANTA MONICA, 1964

Isherwood's stomach was upset for a long time after he returned from India, with a prolonged attack of pyloric spasm. Dr. Allen prescribed pills and proposed X-rays, but Isherwood had plans, so he told Dr. Allen that he was fine now. "I don't know if I really am, but I do know that I want to be. I want to work with Tony Richardson on *The Loved One*."

It was Richardson, not Evelyn Waugh's satire of the American funeral industry, that attracted him. He had read the novel when it appeared in 1948, and he was later to write that "He passionately hated *The Loved One* for its condescending attitude toward California" and considered it "a mean-minded, sloppily written production, probably Waugh's worst and utterly unworthy of his talent."[232] He began adapting it toward the end of March 1964.

During the same period, he was rereading his diaries for passages about Huxley so he could contribute to a memorial volume. One night, he dreamed that Igor Stravinsky was dead, "But the corpse could talk. This dream was somehow reassuring."[233] It seemed to promise that he would have time to say all he had in mind to say with his own writing even though he had now taken on another film job. He was thinking about the new novel based on John Yale taking sannyas, and his British publisher, Methuen, had proposed a retrospective book—reviews, essays, poems, stories. Isherwood had considered this idea before, in the summer of 1961, and it was now that he decided to call the collection *Exhumations*. He got started May 27, then put it aside to concentrate on Richardson's script.

He finished his screenplay in late May at MGM. In mid-June, the American novelist Terry Southern was also hired, and they worked together for a month. There were rushes of the film by August 31, then frustration: "They are shooting *The Loved One*, with dialogue about ninety-nine percent Terry Southern's; all that's left of my script is some of the skeleton," Isherwood reported in his diary. In fact, much more than a skeleton remained, but the feel of the script was changed.

Southern's comic sensibility shared something with Isherwood and Upward's Mortmere—dark and grotesque, with deliberately offensive humor that relied on extreme exaggeration—and Isherwood was impressed by Southern's ability to invent dialogue on set, but Isherwood was a master of the well-made plot, with tightly structured causal connections, learned from years of screenwriting. Southern's narrative was shaped by appetite—for sex and food—and by random chance. In his style of satire, depravity triggered disgust, awe, and laughter, but there was no moral intention. Bachardy felt that Richardson wanted to work with Southern because Southern and his sense of humor were "in."[234] Southern was twenty years younger than Isherwood.

Still, Isherwood remained closely involved with the movie; he was often on the set, and he advised on the editing when the movie came out far too long. Southern was asked for alterations, but Richardson had lost confidence and turned back to Isherwood. The first rough cut Isherwood saw was four hours and nineteen minutes. When it was released, the film was two hours. A pink typescript survives, labeled in Isherwood's hand "Dictated by Tony," with the edits they discussed.[235]

He went on ignoring his health; he was determined to work, to keep the pace, to have fun. There were parties all summer with lots of movie stars, on the beach, around swimming pools and at Adelaide Drive when Bachardy was in town. In June, Isherwood had shooting pains in his groin which spread down his leg. In August, it was a bad sore throat kicked off by a tooth abscess. His back had begun to bother him again, too. He saw Dr. Allen six times in one week in mid-September; X-rays showed a disk wearing thin. The pain continued and spread to his ribs, but he felt certain that work kept worse health at bay.

8: *Existential Isherwood: The Outsider (1961–1964)* / 635

Before taking Isherwood off *The Loved One*, Richardson had already given him another job, adapting Carson McCullers's Southern Gothic love-hate story, *Reflections in a Golden Eye*. The story catered to Richardson's fascination with unmanageable passions, here set off by the rigid discipline of an army camp. He told Isherwood in September that he was "delighted" with the script but then could not assemble the cast he wanted. John Huston later adapted the story.[236]

Richardson next proposed that Isherwood work on Marguerite Duras's novel *Le Marin de Gibraltar* or on Colette's *Chéri*. By mid-December, Isherwood had drafted a screenplay from Mervyn Savill's English translation of the first, *The Sailor from Gibraltar*. It was difficult to structure: "The chief technical problem is the fragmentation of the flashback," Isherwood wrote in his diary. Richardson used other writers and then finished the script himself. When Isherwood saw an early cut at Twickenham Studios in London two years later, he was "horrified." Richardson confessed he had been having an affair with his star, Jeanne Moreau, and Moreau had begun an affair with a Greek naval cadet playing a sailor on the yacht at the center of the story: "this had made Tony so insanely jealous that he had 'lost control' of the picture." Richardson's wife, Vanessa Redgrave, whom Isherwood thought "radiantly beautiful in the film" began divorce proceedings. Ever the professional, Isherwood tried to help, advising Richardson "to take out some of the narration, as they easily can." In his memoir, *The Long-Distance Runner*, Richardson was to describe Isherwood as "one of my greatest friends." Decades before the memoir, he told Isherwood on New Year's Eve 1966 "that I am one of his few real friends and that he loves me."[237]

Relations with Prabhavananda had mostly calmed down. Isherwood dedicated *Ramakrishna and His Disciples* to Prabhavananda, and he attended the Vedanta Society regularly for worship and to do readings. Once in a while, Bachardy accompanied him for supper.

Isherwood and Bachardy bought their first television in March, their "new vice in common," and watched old movies together late into the night. Bachardy turned thirty in May and left for Egypt and Greece to travel with a new love interest, Lee Garlington, an acting hopeful who was also conducting a secret affair with Rock Hudson. In his diary, Isherwood wrote: "This is Don's 'birthday present' for his thirtieth birthday. He said he wanted to do it 'with my blessing.' "[238] A friend of Garlington's was also on the trip.

Isherwood missed Bachardy painfully and failed to get much pleasure out of the affairs he conducted at home—a weekend at Big Sur with an aspiring writer he liked, Bill Jones, a night at Adelaide Drive with one-time football star Ronnie Knox who also wanted to become a writer, a series of romantic trysts with Bob Christian. He often took out a protegé of Richardson's, Budd

Cherry, a Creative Assistant on *The Loved One*, and at least once spent the night with him; mostly they talked about Richardson.

Bachardy continued from Greece to Vienna. "The trip has failed," he wrote to Isherwood, "we've all parted and gone our separate ways, and I am in a dazed state, not knowing why on earth I am in Wien." Auden hosted him in Kirchstetten overnight, and Bachardy was able to describe to Isherwood, who never went, the cozy house that made Auden so happy. More important, he saw the Klimts and Schieles at the Leopold Museum and the Österreichische Galerie Belvedere. He had studied them in books because they were little known in the U.S. until 1965 when the Guggenheim held a first major exhibition. In 1963, Bachardy and Isherwood had managed to see some Klimts and Schieles in an exhibition at the Pasadena Art Museum, "Viennese Expressionism 1910–1924."

Bachardy preferred Klimt's watercolors and drawings to the oil paintings which seemed to him disappointing and gray, like Austria: "There are marvellous ones, too—the Judith with the head of Holofernes is as good as I'd hoped." But he was most impressed by Schiele: "The Schiele oils are actually better than any I'd seen—there is one really magic one. I have lots of inspiration now which I hope I can hang onto."[239]

In the autumn, back in California, Bachardy began to break through with his painting. "Paul Wonner and Bill Brown have at last told him that they like it and think he ought to exhibit some of it," wrote Isherwood.[240] Still, in 1964, Bachardy showed only drawings, first in San Francisco, then in New York. The New York show—at the Banfer Gallery in October—included portraits of Auden, James Baldwin, Leslie Caron, Glenn Ford, Forster, Gielgud, Paulette Goddard, Huxley, Isherwood, Vivien Leigh, Simone Signoret, Spender, the Stravinskys, Barbra Streisand, Virgil Thomson, Gore Vidal, and Natalie Wood. Isherwood did not attend, but Spender reported a sizable crowd at the opening.

Following the Banfer Gallery show, Bachardy stayed away in New York for a long time, partly because Lincoln Kirstein commissioned him to draw the twelve principal dancers of the New York City Ballet. In L.A., Isherwood took Truman Capote to watch *The Loved One* being filmed at Greystone Mansion, and he read the first three parts of *In Cold Blood*. "[T]errifically impressive," he observed.[241] A couple of overnight visits from Spender, on a Western lecture tour, were heavier going.

He sensed Spender's guilt toward his wife for "his sex activities," and found him lacking in generosity toward Auden's success. "He hates Wystan, and says Wystan is one of the most famous people in the world." As he assessed his old friend and rival, Isherwood also assessed himself: "Stephen's vice is ambition. Mine is vanity. Stephen would never bother about his personal appearance, I imagine. I bother very little about whether or not I have succeeded; maybe because I feel that I have, according to my rules. What *I* am concerned about is whether or not people recognize the fact of my success. And this concern arises from vanity, not ambition."[242]

Isherwood had indeed succeeded. Early in 1964, Auden had sent him a telegram reiterating earlier praise that *A Single Man* was "BY FAR THE BEST THING YOU HAVE DONE." But Auden voiced three criticisms to Bachardy in New York and repeated two of them in a letter. Isherwood summed them up in his diary: "(1) That George stays far too long in the bathroom. (2) That there is too much made of the homosexuals' right to be regarded as a minority, in the same category as the Negroes and the Jews. (3) That Wystan was shocked when George thinks he will 'make a new Jim.'" Isherwood concluded that Auden thought "my upholding of the homosexuals was indirectly anti-Semitic."[243] Certainly his own feelings about Jews were shaped by his disappointment that, in his era, the persecution of homosexuals was not equally recognized.

Isherwood's and Auden's views on homosexuality had grown further and further apart. In his lifetime, Auden never publicly announced that he was homosexual though he acknowledged it mostly elliptically toward the end of his life. After his return to the Anglican Church, he considered homosexuality a mortal sin for which he hoped to be redeemed by God's grace. "I do wish he wouldn't say homosexuality is sinful," wrote Isherwood a few years later.[244] Isherwood had long been committed to the idea of homosexuals as a minority entitled to the same rights as all other minorities. As for making a new Jim, it is a testament to their individuality that after years observing Isherwood's need for companionship Auden could still be shocked.

Heard told Isherwood that he thought *A Single Man* "by far my best book. 'Now, obviously, you can write anything.'" Capote announced his pride and admitted his envy, calling it "A stylistic tour-de-force of the greatest distinction [...] It is harrowing stuff, and yet very funny, and always, always deeply moving." Spender and Lehmann gradually warmed to it.[245]

Isherwood's former student and sex friend Bill Jones typed out a three-page letter in the middle of the night. "You emerge caring in this one. [...] I doubt you'll ever teach at LASC again. Ha! Well, that'll be alright anyway. [...] P.S. God! I adored it. It absolutely breathes fire." Paul Cadmus sent three pages of praise. Erika Mann also thought it was Isherwood's best, "overwhelmingly convincing and most intriguing in its seeming simplicity." Some years later, John Rechy wrote, "I consider it one of those rare, perfect, gem-like works—"[246]

Incredibly, there weren't many truly positive reviews. As Vidal had warned, the homosexual chauvinism was a problem, though reviewers found many ways to avoid addressing this clearly. Alan Pryce-Jones, writing for the *New York Herald Tribune*, called it "a small masterpiece" even though he averred that Isherwood had deliberately made George unattractive. Elizabeth Hardwick in the *New York Review of Books* was well informed, puritanical, and determined to see a waning of powers: "tired . . . sad . . . biological melancholy running through it." David Daiches in the *New York Times* was cautious: "not the sort of novel that Christopher Isherwood's earlier works have led us to expect of him," he wrote, longing for another Berlin book and blind to the new achievement. *Time* magazine acknowledged George as a homosexual, yet clumsily described Jim as his "roommate" whose death is a "deprivation" that "has no meaning." It was not much different when the book came out in England. Anthony Burgess in the *Listener* was lapidary and impenetrable, alive to the Socratic gravity of the dialogue between George and Kenny and dead to the fun.[247]

For the first time in his career, Isherwood made no mention in his diary or day-to-day books of publication date or individual reviews. He no longer cared. "*[A]ccording to my rules*," he wrote in November, "*A Single Man* is a masterpiece; that is to say, it achieves exactly what I wanted it to achieve. I keep dipping into it and always I feel yes, that is exactly the effect I was trying for."[248] Compared to the novel, the reviews were old-fashioned and uninteresting; he had left the professional critics behind. His friends, and over the years his readers, knew better; they loved the book, and it was to achieve an unassailable position as a classic.

9

The Animals' Golden Age
(1964–1986)

Bachardy visited home over Christmas and New Year, 1964–5. It was idyllic. "I told him that this short time together has been the best I have ever had with him. He said, 'Lately I've been thinking that the Animals haven't seen anything yet; they still haven't had their golden age.' I said, 'They better hurry.'" Indeed, there were wars yet to come between them. Bachardy was, after all, only thirty. Isherwood in his sixties was to find the intrigue and the difficulty of his young lover almost overwhelming, but his appetite for work and his continuing professional success were to keep Bachardy engaged as helpmeet and collaborator as well as domestic partner. Moreover, as Bachardy began to achieve his own professional success, he gained in self-esteem and self-confidence, and Isherwood was flooded with joy and pride in him.

BACHARDY PLANNED AT least two more months in New York working on the ballet portraits, so he rented an apartment. Kirstein loaned furniture, and Rouben Ter-Arutunian, the ballet and opera designer who had worked on *The Loved One*, loaned a bed. Not all their friends understood, as Bachardy reported to Isherwood: "Marguerite's first words (in bated breath) when I told her I had this apartment were: 'Is Chris upset?' I assured her there was absolutely no disaster to celebrate and that Kitty was more devoted to his dear than ever before." Home on the East Coast existed in relation to home on the West Coast. Isherwood headed letters Casa de los Animales or The Casa; Bachardy replied from "The Anti-Casa."[1]

Isherwood lasted just a few weeks alone. He completed his commentary for *Exhumations*, then joined Bachardy for ten days in February, carrying a copy of the new collection for his New York publishers.

He found New York "dirty, cold and brutish as usual," and Bachardy transformed into "an ardent ballet lover." Kirstein had arranged for George Balanchine's New York City Ballet to move into the New York State Theater in 1964, "and he has megalomaniac schemes to make it the most famous theater in the world," Isherwood recorded.

Kirstein had big plans too for Bachardy, whom he had commissioned to draw not only the ballet company but also the actors appearing at the American Shakespeare Festival Theater in Stratford, Connecticut, where the New York City Ballet performed in the summer. Tension arose over who was in charge of Bachardy's career.

> Lincoln says that Don will be the Sargent of our time, and that he shouldn't be bohemian but dress stylishly and live in extreme elegance. That was why he advised Don to take this two hundred dollar apartment, and it must be said in Lincoln's favor that he did offer to pay the rent. But Don refused, and camps out there in squalor and depression.[2]

Kirstein also proposed to work with Isherwood on a staged performance of selections from his verse volume *Rhymes of a PFC*. Isherwood was helping choose poems for a second edition. He had tried in vain to collaborate with Kirstein before—on a Brecht libretto, *Der Jasager*, adapted from Japanese Noh drama, and on a ballet of *Sleeping Beauty* for a film to be choreographed by Balanchine. For *Sleeping Beauty*, Isherwood had submitted detailed suggestions but was never allowed to work directly with Balanchine. Kirstein and Balanchine decided against spoken dialogue, Isherwood's specialty, and Isherwood had been forced to point out there was no room for his input.[3]

Back in California, he took up a Regents' Professorship at UCLA, which he had delayed for *The Loved One*. He was to teach for a full quarter, longer than the lectureship of a few weeks at Berkeley. At his first public lecture, there "was standing room only—in fact, they said they turned two hundred people away!" This was a new level of attention.

He also gave a talk, introduced by Heard, at the homosexual support and advocacy group One, Incorporated. The talk, "A Writer and a Minority," was one of his first public statements, without any fictional mask, about homosexuality. He was attacked by a homosexual police officer in the audience for lacking commitment. In his diary, Isherwood objected: "I do stick my neck out quite far, in my own way." The police officer saw "'the struggle' in terms of group action."[4] Isherwood saw the struggle from the point of view of the individual, the outsider, and he considered private freedoms crucial to self-determination. He supported the American Civil Liberties Union, often attended ACLU events, and at least three times was a speaker. In this, he emulated Forster, the first president of the U.K.'s National Council for Civil Liberties founded in 1934.

During Bachardy's absence in New York, Isherwood had marked their twelfth anniversary by starting the novel he had been planning since his airplane flight from Calcutta. The novel was about "two brothers who meet in India just as one of them is about to become a monk." Isherwood had already decided on a title—*A Meeting by the River*—and he never changed it.

The idea was "a simple confrontation" between the brothers. "[E]ach of them represents a world, a view of life; there is a kind of struggle between them, each wants to win the other over to his way of thinking." Isherwood had described the confrontation idea years earlier in his workbook, when he was planning *Down There on a Visit* in 1958, and it was rooted even further in the past in his original ideas for his Paul character of the 1930s. Over the years, he had repeatedly put this confrontation narrative to one side, until, at Belur Math, "I saw that Paul ought to be a monk."[5] In the published novel, the younger brother is called Oliver, and he indeed becomes a monk, but not before the elder brother, Patrick, travels to India to try to stop him. In their struggle, their personalities and histories are revealed, and the younger brother's bond with his guru is explored. The guru has died before the novel begins, and the climax involves a supernatural intervention.

Isherwood made rapid progress, even though he was teaching at UCLA and reading student manuscripts for his heavily oversubscribed class. He drafted twenty-five pages in about a month. Then he began to reconsider his method. He decided "to tell the story through letters and a diary or diaries." He began again. For the time being, he changed the names to Leonard for the younger brother and Martin for the elder. In Leonard, he was evidently borrowing details from his childhood friend Leonard Tristram, raised in Cheshire and educated at Cambridge, who had become a disciple of Krishnamurti and settled in Ventura. He had first used the name Leonard for the younger boy, Leonard Merrows, in his early novel *Lions and Shadows*.

He was departing sharply from "the observer-viewpoint" he had used in *A Single Man*. "In this book there is to be no objective view of any of the characters. They are all seen through Martin's or Leonard's eyes."[6] He was also departing from the question-and-answer dynamic of the Platonic dialogue, in which one character, like Socrates, possesses all the knowledge gradually drawn out by his interlocutors. This time, he was creating opponents, equals who possess different kinds of knowledge. This made for a new kind of suspense and called for a different kind of resolution.

He was partly inspired by his own 1942 *New Yorker* short story, "Take It or

Leave It," which he was reprinting in *Exhumations*. This was the story written in Haverford about the couple who secretly read each other's diaries and find themselves involved in "a game" that is "deadly important to them; perhaps their last chance of happiness together." Through writing, they approach a confrontation they cannot achieve face-to-face: "Slowly, slowly, they advance toward one another. [. . .] The diary grows warmer. The notebook responds."

"Take It or Leave It" had reworked the Jekyll and Hyde dynamic, and now in *Exhumations*, Isherwood was also reprinting his essay about Robert Louis Stevenson, in which he observed that Stevenson had been pressured by his wife to cut from the *Strange Case of Dr. Jekyll and Mr. Hyde* a character based on his student-days lover, a Scottish country girl met in the Edinburgh streets, Kate Drummond. Isherwood felt that Jekyll's disowning of Hyde, the evil libido, referred to this suppressed mistress. Jekyll and Hyde symbolized to him the conflict within Stevenson between his "inherited Puritanism and his natural inclinations."[7] As for himself, Isherwood had gradually learned to embrace his libido as he had been unable to do when he wrote "Take It or Leave It." In "Take It or Leave It," the marriage fails; in *A Meeting by the River*, written more than two decades later, "marriage" between the two parts of the self is no longer necessary. At last, Jekyll and Hyde go their separate ways and cease to torment each other.

Isherwood was also inspired by Thornton Wilder's epistolary novel *The Ides of March*, about Caesar and Cleopatra's meeting by a different river, the Tiber, in Rome, where he had been headed the night he conceived the novel. Already at Belur Math, the spectacle of the boats on the Ganges had conjured a fantasy of the Nile that Isherwood had recorded in his pocket diary: "All kinds of craft pass along the swiftly flowing river; small steamers, high-prowed barges, boats with huge square sails like junks, galleys rowed by standing oarsmen which look as if they were straight out of Cleopatra's Egypt." Wilder had portrayed the meeting between Caesar and Cleopatra as the prelude to Caesar's assassination and the power grab that transformed the Roman Republic into the Roman Empire. He called his novel "a fantasia" on the last days of the Roman Republic because he freely rearranged historical events. Isherwood thought it "seriously, a masterpiece."[8]

In Wilder's novel, the two stars—both tyrants—meet to fulfill their cosmic love affair, the elder needing to teach, the younger needing to learn. They are led into misunderstanding and reach a personal impasse. Caesar, aware of the conspiracy against him, is illuminated by a new kind of understanding when he secretly visits the deathbed of Catullus, aligned against him. He speaks with Catullus about love and about the power of the imagination embodied in the work of the Greek tragedian Sophocles. Despite her cruelty and depravity, Caesar praises the woman for whom Catullus wrote his love poems, and Catullus dies listening to Caesar recite a chorus from Sophocles's *Oedipus at Colonus*, in which Oedipus, fallen from power, blind and a beggar, accepts his destiny and dies.

Wilder's masterpiece informs the confrontation between Isherwood's two brothers—the elder brother a tyrant over family, lovers, employees, the younger a tyrant over himself. The dead swami, like Catullus, speaks the language of love rather than the language of power. Both novels contrast the epic grandeur of public performance with the intense intimacy of private thought in diaries and letters. Both novels culminate with an important and secret religious ceremony.

As usual, Isherwood's imagination was also fired by the flow of his current life. Richard Burton had continued to ask for a script based on "The Beach of Falesá." On January 24, 1964, not long after returning from India, Isherwood had gone with Gavin Lambert to see Burton and Elizabeth Taylor "at bay in the Beverly-Wilshire," as he told Bachardy. "They were very sweet, when we finally got to them through a cordon of newsmen, photogs and cops."[9] Burton and Taylor had begun their romance on the set of *Cleopatra* in 1962, when Burton had played Cleopatra's next lover, Mark Antony, who led the campaign against Caesar's murderers. Like their onscreen characters, they had become the most scrutinized, scandal-ridden lovers in the world, divorcing their respective spouses to marry in 1964.

"[T]he setting of this narrative shall be, as it were, 'mental,'" wrote Isherwood in his diary, because he wanted to focus the reader's attention on the spiritual drama and to make the reader experience the mystical vocation as the matter of life and death that he believed it to be. To critics of his pacifism and his monastic retreat during World War II, prayer and meditation had seemed irrelevant and unreal amid the massive physical destruction and suffering of the war. He was anxious, too, not to depict a monastery that could be recognized as Belur Math, nor to offer the kind of detailed descriptions of time and place so admired in his earlier work.

In some respects the two brothers reflected opposing impulses in Isherwood himself, but he developed them with individual personalities that were markedly different from his own. "[A]m *very* tempted to make Martin a bisexual counterfeiter—I mean, to make him cheat on his wife with a boy," he proposed in his notes.[10] In the novel, Isherwood brought into opposition as types the closeted bisexual who indulges his sexuality and lies to conceal this indulgence and the monastic who represses his sexuality because he disapproves of it and is unwilling to lie about it. The first he had observed in Patrick Monkhouse, Stephen Spender, Frank Taylor, Lincoln Kirstein, screenwriter and producer Charles Brackett, Charles Laughton, and Tony Richardson; the second in John Yale and others.

Bachardy made another visit home during April and May 1965, then returned to New York because Kirstein was promising to put up "'some' of my drawings at Stratford." He was spending time with the group around the poet Frank O'Hara, including Joe LeSueur, J.J. Mitchell, and Larry Rivers, and he was friendly with the artist Joe Brainard. Virgil Thomson adopted Bachardy, invited him to dinner and introduced him socially. But Bachardy felt unsure what Kirstein expected. "I am hoping to get some kind of coherent statement about Lincoln's plans for me," he told Isherwood in June. "I don't want to leave feeling defeated, dejected and depressed."[11]

In California, Isherwood was receiving manic communiqués, sent special delivery, enclosing the latest drafts of Kirstein's poems and asking which ones should be included in *Rhymes (& More) Rhymes of a PFC*. Kirstein also shared plans for a stage version of the poems on which he still hoped to collaborate with Isherwood.

Much like Isherwood with Tony Richardson, Bachardy responded energetically to the frenzied challenge of Kirstein's super-normal energy and was drawing two sitters a day. But when Kirstein gave a "lukewarm reception" to the most recent portraits, Bachardy confided to Isherwood that he was losing patience: "I don't fit into any of his preconceived ideas about The Artist. He can't explain to himself how I could possibly be any good *really*." Still, Kirstein proceeded with plans to publish Bachardy's ballet drawings in "a portfolio of reproductions, each on single sheets without binding and with perhaps a biography of each dancer on the back, to be sold at the theater but quite independent from the souvenir program."

Bachardy's sense of himself as an artist was undergoing a major evolution. He told Isherwood that he was confident Kitty had done "some first-rate drawings" and that with the completion of the ballet drawings, "a phase of his career" was coming to an end: "The period of the Bachardy Drawing, as we know it, is over, and if he draws again, which is not absolutely certain, his work will be totally different from what has gone before."[12]

Isherwood forged ahead with *A Meeting by the River*. After reading through his first rough draft in June, he changed the professional background of the worldly brother to enhance his power over his younger brother, his lover, and his wife: "He should be more important. A producer, if in the movies at all. Or a director. (Tony Richardson would suspect it was him!)" A few weeks later, Isherwood proposed to himself: "When you read his letters [...] you should rub your eyes in amazement—<u>can he</u> be such a hypocrite?"[13]

Bachardy returned again at the beginning of July, anxious to put Kirstein's drawing assignment behind him and progress with his painting. "He wants to live a more independent life, sleep out in the studio, eat breakfast alone, etc.

He feels overpowered by my being around," wrote Isherwood, unperturbed. "[W]e are really not each other's problems. Don has to come to terms with success-failure. I have to come to terms with death." When Bachardy finally broke "the curse," as Isherwood heard him telling a friend on the phone, and painted a picture he didn't hate, it was a picture of Isherwood.

Bachardy took his time reading the draft of Isherwood's new novel, but when he did, he was as generous as ever. "Don loves *A Meeting by the River*," Isherwood reported in his diary. Lambert also read it and seemed "impressed, though with reservations."[14] Isherwood made a copy for John Yale, and on July 28, he drove up to Montecito to stay with Yale at the Vedanta Retreat and pick his brain about becoming a monk. It was a high point in their monkish friendship; they went swimming, had supper on the Santa Barbara Pier, and saw two movies.

Yale shared aspects of his past for the backstory and many points of religious ritual and cultural practice, including secret parts of the sannyas ceremony which Isherwood had not been allowed to see in India: "two days before, the monk, having been given the gayatri mantra, invests himself with the sacred thread. Then he performs his own funeral rites. [. . .] Then, he strips completely, before all the swamis in the monastery, and the head of the monastery formally accepts him and then he puts on the gerua—the loincloth is most important. He begs for three days."[15]

The Gayatri mantra, for meditation upon the sun as a symbol of the supreme reality, is given at first vows, brahmacharya. The sacred thread, worn across the chest, symbolizes membership in the highest Hindu caste, the Brahmin priest caste, joined so that the initiate can renounce earthly rank from the highest possible position. The thread is typically given to a boy by his father, but Yale would have received it from the head of the Ramakrishna Order. The initiate performs his own funeral rites because a monk has no children to do this for him, and he performs the funeral rites of his parents, grandparents, and so forth, fulfilling his duties to them in advance, because a monk renounces family and social ties and is not eligible to perform such rites. The funeral rites, called Shraddha, symbolize the death of the old life; in a sense, the initiate is a ghost until the ceremony two days later.

During the sannyas ceremony, Yale would have thrown his sacred thread into the purifying homa fire along with his last remaining tuft of hair, cut off by the leader of the order from Yale's otherwise shaven head. Then he would have stripped naked, prostrated to the head monk, and left the temple to bathe in the Ganges. After bathing, he would have put on his new gerua robe, returned to the temple and prostrated again to the head monk. Isherwood discreetly omitted the naked prostration and bathing from the novel.

As he prepared to start his second draft, he came up with his final names. "Patrick" grooved the connection to Patrick Monkhouse and tagged the elder brother character as the "It" of the novel—after Groddeck's letter writer "Patrik Troll." Oliver is the purehearted one who descends to an underworld and returns unbesmirched to the embrace of his true patrimony, in this case, abandoning the middle-class hearth in order to join a spiritual gang whose Fagin teaches love and nonattachment rather than thievery. Isherwood also changed Patrick's wife's name from Jennifer to Penelope. This signaled an imaginative shift from a personality like Jennifer Jones, wife of the late and straight movie mogul David Selznick, to faithful Penelope, Odysseus's wife, who fended off suitors for twenty years while her husband fought at Troy and wandered the seas on his way home.

One night, driving home from supper with friends, Bachardy had a muscle spasm in his chest. It was so painful that Isherwood had to take over shifting the gears in the car. At 2 a.m. they summoned Dr. Allen, who gave Bachardy a shot to relax him and explained that the pain was intense because Bachardy's muscles were strong from exercise at the gym. Dr. Allen did not say what triggered the spasm. In his diary, Isherwood recorded: "While he was drowsy and a little high from the shot, Don told me that he really does love Ramakrishna, but can't feel much for Swami. He has tried to ask Ramakrishna to make his presence felt. And he believes that Ramakrishna has shown him that the signal that he is present is pain—pyschological pain just as much, if not more, than physical."

Isherwood expressed delight at this: "I am so happy that Don is getting this kind of experience. It is better than anything else I could wish for him."[16] Reading Isherwood's draft of *A Meeting by the River* evidently reminded Bachardy how much Vedanta meant to Isherwood. That autumn, Bachardy accompanied Isherwood to supper at Vedanta Place and stayed to listen to him read to the congregation in the temple. Even in New York, Bachardy regularly made japam.

THE ENGLISH PAINTER David Hockney introduced himself to Isherwood one afternoon in early February 1964 during Hockney's first visit to Los Angeles. He admired *Goodbye to Berlin*, and he was eager to meet the man who had ventured into the boy bars back in 1929.[17] He stopped by Adelaide Drive from his room at the Tumble Inn at the bottom of the canyon then returned later the same evening to meet up with Jack Larson and Jim Bridges, close friends of Isherwood and Bachardy, actors who also wrote for stage and screen and directed. A few days later, Hockney came back to be introduced to Bachardy just home from New York, but it wasn't until the following summer that the friendship developed. Hockney reappeared in L.A. in August 1965 with the British painter, Patrick Procktor, who had a commission for a mural in the home cinema of the widow of Harry Cohn, head of Columbia Pictures. Isherwood and Bachardy had known Procktor since London in 1961. Procktor was tall, bony, dandyish, acerbic, exotic, giraffe-like. "The thing I loved about Patrick was his flamboyance," Hockney told Christopher Simon Sykes. "I also liked him because he could mock the art world. He felt he was a bit more outside it than I was, and anybody who mocks pomposity I'm attracted to."[18]

Over the following weeks, the three young painters were often together. Bachardy was thirty-one, Procktor twenty-nine, Hockney twenty-eight. They went on the beach, to an art show, to a party, dined at Adelaide Drive with Isherwood, went out with Isherwood to the movies. One day, Bachardy drew Procktor. Soon after that, Bachardy went to supper with Procktor and Hockney and stayed out for the night.

Bachardy was buoyant about his work. He hung eight of his pictures in the house, framed, and on September 26, he and Isherwood picked out paintings to show Rex Evans, who suggested another exhibition for January 1966. Bachardy checked in with Kirstein in New York, learned that the portfolios of his ballet portraits wouldn't be manufactured until January, and decided to stay in Los Angeles and paint for the new exhibition.

There were more supper parties with Hockney and Procktor, at restaurants and at home, with Larson and Bridges, Paul Wonner and Bill Brown, and with other new friends, including Nicholas Wilder, from Rochester, New York, who was to become a leading Los Angeles dealer and represent both Hockney and Bachardy. Wilder was the same age as Hockney. On the surface, he was an East Coast establishment type. He had graduated from potted-Ivy Amherst College and studied law at Stanford before his love of art burst his buttoned-up preppy veneer. He opened his own gallery in Los Angeles in April 1965. In addition to Hockney and Bachardy, Wilder showed Joe Goode, Robert Graham, Billy Al Bengston, Cy Twombly, Ken Price, Ed Moses, John McCracken, Kenneth Noland, Helen Frankenthaler, Jules Olitski, Agnes Martin, Sam Francis, Bruce Nauman, Hans Hofmann and many others.

Thus, Isherwood found himself at the heart of the new L.A. art scene. For October 15, 1965, he recorded in his day-to-day diary: "To Gemini Studios, to see David Hockney's lithographs being pulled." These were a series called "A Hollywood Collection," featuring stereotyped genre images in elaborate frames; they mocked local collectors who needed to be told what art they should buy. The next night, Isherwood and Bachardy went to a show at Wilder's new gallery on La Cienega, then out to supper and on to a party thrown by Wilder. The energy level was high and culminated when Hockney, Procktor, and Hockney's current Californian boyfriend, Bob Earles—known to many as Princess Bob—piled into a car and drove off to New York.[19]

Isherwood wrote in his diary that the summer and autumn of 1965 with Bachardy was "one of the best periods we have ever spent together."[20] He kept steadily on with *A Meeting by the River*, finished the second draft on October 10, and mailed it off to Edward Upward. Upward advised him to build more tension between the two brothers. Considering this in his diary, Isherwood revealed an inner bias against his character Patrick, for his lack of depth and commitment. "My feeling is that Patrick is really incapable of being serious enough and passionate enough to take any drastic steps to get Oliver out of the monastery—*and that is his tragedy*." The real struggle had to take place inside Oliver. "Yes, I can see Oliver in agony because of the struggle Patrick has started up inside him; and Patrick not really caring—"[21]

Again, he consulted John Yale, who had made notes throughout Isherwood's second draft and typed out for Isherwood an entry from his own diary describing his sannyas: "It ends, 'Chris remained till the day of our glory, and rushed up to prostrate. Bless his heart.' There is really a deep affection between us, I believe."

Isherwood decided to dedicate *A Meeting by the River* to Yale. Yale asked for the dedication to be to Swami Vidyatmananda, the name given to him when he took his sannyas vows, "since John Yale was no longer alive," as Isherwood put it in his diary.[22] Prabhavananda agreed, but Swami Pavitrananda, head of the New York Vedanta Society, objected; Yale turned down the dedication to his former self, and Isherwood dedicated the novel to Gerald Heard who first led him to Vedanta.

IN THE AUTUMN of 1965, Isherwood started a new piece of writing, a book about his parents, which he proposed to call *Hero-Father* and then *Hero-Father, Demon-Mother*. Right away, he had difficulties.

First of all, he tangled with the physical problem of his personal papers. Now that he wanted to focus on them, he felt anxious to safeguard them. Huxley had lost everything in the wildfire that burned down his house in 1961. Isherwood wanted to be able to get them out of the house when he wasn't working on them, so his photographer friend Peter Gowland, who built cameras, built a box made "to fit exactly to the measurements of the rack in the safe-deposit vault of the bank,"[23] and Isherwood sorted letters and manuscripts into it. Thus, the writer famous for his phrase "I am a camera" entrusted his literary remains to a box that might have been a camera. It was the first step in a preservation job carried on by himself and later by Bachardy that ensured the record of Isherwood's life and times was available not only for the three memoirs he was to write over the final creative period of his life but also for readers and scholars who came after.

Isherwood's proposed title *Hero-Father, Demon-Mother* gestured again to the Romantic-Gothic oppositions of Robert Louis Stevenson, the Brontës, and others. He was now recasting the everlasting combat of opposites in the gendered roles of the family romance that he had so long rejected. After the two weeks spent locking down his sources, he tried to start again. "I can't," he wrote in his diary. "Something inhibits me." He was trying to open a door that he had kept firmly closed for years—a door to the past.

He pondered what form to use, how to speak to his audience. Who should he be while he revealed who he *had* been? He considered a lecture form, "but that seems so contrived. Perhaps I should attempt a sort of notebook." He didn't want to write sentences and paragraphs: "it seems too literary, too *urbane*."[24] He wanted informality, intimacy, to be right there with his readers and not have his public persona, his literary reputation, intervene. He was a man in his sixties eager to embrace an audience ever-younger than he, to communicate with the students in his classes, the boys on the beach, the exuberant artists around his dinner table. In what voice should he speak about the past to the generations of the future?

He began to spot in himself inclinations he associated with his mother, "her horror of 'progress,'" and he was determined to rout these out: "Undoubtedly there is a great deal of snobbery mixed up in it—a snobbery which goes back into my heredity. The snobbish horror of my upper-class family at the triumph of the caste of the merchants."[25] He tried not to feel threatened by change as the city of Los Angeles boomed. At the end of his street, excavation had begun for a thirty-two-story apartment building which would be one of the tallest buildings in Santa Monica, deeply unsettling him. He had touched on this in *A Single Man*, where George dislikes a new apartment building between him and the beach. It was to prove a central theme of *Hero-Father, Demon-Mother*, the book which he would eventually retitle *Kathleen and Frank*.

Isherwood had been guided to look more closely at his prejudices by Prabhavananda. Only a few weeks earlier, Prabhavananda had admitted that he was "astonished" to discover prejudice in himself against members of the untouchable caste. He had invited an untouchable to lunch, "but had been 'so relieved' when the invitation was refused!" The prejudice was irrational, "He's an educated man! He is sent by the Indian government!"

Prabhavananda had exclaimed.[26] But the prejudice was nonetheless real and difficult to overcome. Prabhavananda's admission had impressed upon Isherwood how deeply such prejudices are rooted, how energetically they must be scourged.

By the third week in November, Isherwood gave up wrestling with *Hero-Father, Demon-Mother* and started his third draft of *A Meeting by the River*. "There must be definite *moves* (in the sense of chess moves) in this game." Each action brings a response, as the brothers draw closer, feinting and parrying in their lifelong rivalry now elevated onto the spiritual plane. At the beginning of 1966, Isherwood noted:

> the main action of the book is temptation—the temptation of any saint by any satan. [. . .] The key line is when Oliver says that he was inviting Patrick to come and judge the swami. He has to have Patrick's okay. He doesn't ever get it of course. What he does get is a spiritual intervention by the swami himself, proving to him that Patrick "belongs" whether he likes it or not, knows it or not.[27]

For the spiritual intervention, Isherwood turned to Dostoevsky, drawing on Alyosha's vision of Father Zossima in *The Brothers Karamazov*. His character Oliver falls asleep while standing up, slumps down and sees the swami, then wakes on the ground, just as Alyosha falls asleep while kneeling to pray, slumps down and sees Father Zossima, then wakes to hear Father Paissy continuing to read the Gospel over Zossima's stinking corpse. In his vision, Oliver is boiling the kettle to make water into tea for his swami; during Alyosha's vision, Father Paissy is reading about Christ's first miracle, turning water into wine at the Wedding at Cana. Oliver, like Alyosha, is filled with rapture and cries tears of joy.

In another diary entry, Isherwood explained that after his vision Oliver "suddenly no longer sees Patrick's world and his world as hostile opposites. It's like the moment of *satori* in Zen, the *koan* becomes meaningless, Oliver and Patrick are united within Swami's love." He had once explained the puzzle of the koan to Kirstein, borrowing an example from Alan Watts's book on Zen Buddhism: "Suppose you are hanging from a tree by your teeth. A man asks you: 'What is Zen?' If you don't answer, he will remain ignorant. If you do answer, you will fall and be killed." This was during his own attempt to become a monk, in 1943, when he was also reading George Moore's novels *Evelyn Innes* and *Sister Teresa*, containing the scene which became a touchstone for him, in which the opera singer turned nun is repelled by her new life just as much as she is repelled by her old life: "She can't go forward. She can't go back," he had told Kirstein, "he really conveys the sense of sheer vertigo, which I've experienced myself, once or twice." Of Sister Teresa's situation and his own, he had concluded: "It is the Koan, of course. And the only way to solve it is to relax towards it."[28]

Isherwood himself still longed for that moment of insight and resolution imagined for more than twenty years, and he shaped his final scene in *A Meeting by the River* as a piece of theater played by the two brothers for the sake of their Indian audience; what unites the brothers is understanding their effect. Oliver recognizes that Patrick, prostrating before him to take the dust of his feet, "had done the theatrically perfect thing!" He pulls Patrick up and hugs him. "I did this to cover an uncontrollable attack of giggles—I was shaking with it, and as I held him I felt him beginning to laugh, too." Here is the cosmic joy that Isherwood had described in his Santa Barbara lectures in 1960. Oliver continues: "At that moment I seemed to stand outside myself and see the two of us, and Swami, and the onlookers, all involved in this tremendous joke."[29]

Back in 1960, Isherwood had told his Santa Barbara lecture audience that he found this mad vitality, this glee, in Robert Louis Stevenson, in the battle between Ahab and Moby Dick, in *Macbeth* and *Lear*, in Hindu scripture, in Ramakrishna's story of the wandering monk who sits at the edge of the Ganges each day like a spectator in a theater applauding the universe as if it were a theatrical performance. He did not tell them that he had also found it in Forster's *A Passage to India*, a locus he acknowledged in general but never in particular. Perhaps it was too important.

In "The Temple," Forster's Professor Godbole, dressed in white, barefoot, with a pale blue turban, attends the ceremony symbolizing the birth of God, Sri Krishna. In contrast to Isherwood's theatrically astute English brothers, Forster's Indian singers, musicians, and crowd of townfolk "did not one thing which the non-Hindu would feel dramatically correct; this approaching triumph of India was a muddle (as we call it), a frustration of reason and form." Even the message "God si Love" is misspelled. But at the moment of the incarnation, the birth of Krishna, "All sorrow was annihilated, not only for Indians, but for foreigners, birds, caves, railways, and the stars; all became joy, all laughter; there had never been disease nor doubt, misunderstanding, cruelty, fear." Games are played to amuse the newly born God; a nobleman removes his turban, puts butter on his forehead and waits for it to slide down into his mouth; another snatches the butter and eats it. "There is fun in heaven. God can play practical jokes upon Himself, draw chairs away from beneath his own posteriors, set His own turbans on fire, and steal His own petticoats when He bathes. By sacrificing good taste, this worship achieved what Christianity has shirked: the inclusion of merriment."[30]

Isherwood had first read *A Passage to India* in, probably, 1924,[31] again in

1946 and likely other times. He waited many years to write his own religious ceremony, and wrote his differently than Forster, but he hoped to release for readers the same cosmic joy. In the meantime, he had been silly like this, with Forster, with Auden, with Upward, in the most serious way.

BACHARDY'S JANUARY 1966 show at the Rex Evans Gallery was a smash hit like his first show at the Redfern, and his painting was vindicated. Friends and celebrities thronged the opening and bought seven of the portraits painted in acrylics and two portrait drawings. In mid-February, Bachardy again left for New York.

Isherwood had another Regents' Professorship, this time at the University of California, Riverside, and taught on Tuesdays and Wednesdays. He spent many evenings with Lambert, Larson, and Bridges and often went to supper at Jennifer Selznick's. There were countless engagements with his wider circle of friends and sex friends.

He finished the third draft of *A Meeting by the River* at the end of May. "And now I have got to show it to Swami," he wrote in his diary, "which makes me squirm inside. I hate the thought of him reading the parts about Tom—but *why* should I, actually? I'm not ashamed of them, I would never apologize for them artistically or morally, they are absolutely right for the book." Tom was the sexy, young American boyfriend of Patrick, and it was not just Prabhavananda that worried Isherwood. About a year earlier, he had told Bachardy, "I don't know if I could ever publish it without mortally offending the Ramakrishna Order. There isn't one word about them in it, but they are so touchy and they will identify, in one way or another."[32]

Some reviews of his Ramakrishna biography had been harshly negative, and Isherwood believed this undermined his position with Belur Math, not to speak of Prabhavananda's position. Indian reviewers had been impressed that Isherwood had actually visited India and was a Vedanta devotee, though they observed that he neither endorsed nor rejected Ramakrishna's divinity.[33] He stated only that Ramakrishna was "a phenomenon"—echoing Jung on the Virgin Birth. This was generally accepted and widely repeated, but still Western reviewers questioned whether Ramakrishna was an incarnation of God.[34]

"In our culture any claim to be God is the very hallmark of insanity," Alan Watts had written sympathetically in the *San Francisco Examiner*. Other reviewers fell back on reciting Ramakrishna's supernatural achievements— for example, in the *New York Times Book Review*: "clairvoyance, clairaudience, mental telepathy, healing by touch, prolonged periods of holy ecstasy (*samadhi*)"³⁵—and on describing Ramakrishna's skills as a teacher and his unusual innocence and childlike playfulness in personal relations.

The British, with their imperial history in India, were the most sceptical. Malcolm Muggeridge, for the curmudgeonly right, sneered at post-British India, at California, at mysticism. Raymond Mortimer dismissed the two main accounts on which Isherwood had drawn as "naïve hagiographies." Frank Kermode, writing with erudite condescension, had hoped for extravagant camp but found superstition, "uncriticized *Aberglaube*," which he obliquely compared to Jung's eccentric obsession with alchemy: "I admit that I am incapable of a sympathetic appreciation of the phenomenon Mr. Isherwood describes." By contrast, Stevie Smith noticed something entirely different: "The author seems to have caught, or found in himself, all that is best in god-loving, god-hungry India, and to have let the worst go."³⁶

It was difficult to dismiss a story less than a hundred years old reported by so many witnesses in so much detail and offering so many parallels with the story of Christ, and some reviewers remarked on the Western intellectuals who had been impressed by Ramakrishna—including Jung, Huxley, and Ramakrishna's previous biographers Max Müller and Romain Rolland. Moreover, Isherwood's literary skills were recognized by even his most severe critics. The handful who found the book "devoid of any real literary interest" or called the writing "flat and uninspired" nevertheless praised the way in which Isherwood had condensed the prolix narratives about Ramakrishna's life and above all Isherwood's "lucid and sympathetic" account of Hindu beliefs. In the *New York Times Book Review*, Nancy Wilson Ross wrote that Isherwood "unfolds a fantastic story with a calm finesse that should make it possible for even confirmed Western sceptics, living in a culture where Divinity and humanity are not on intimate terms, to suspend judgment at least temporarily."³⁷

Alan Watts took up the question of sex explicitly because he did not believe that celibacy was necessary for spiritual realization: "this passionate exclusion of sex is surely inconsistent with teaching that the whole universe is the playing of God, and the more so in that Ramakrishna did not idealize withdrawal from life."³⁸ Isherwood of course agreed with Watts, but the biography had to satisfy the Ramakrishna Order.

As it proved, the true story of God was far more important to Prabhavananda and to the Ramakrishna Order than whether an imaginary character in a novel had sex with another imaginary character. Only a few days after dropping off the typescript of *A Meeting by the River*, Isherwood received a telephone call from Prabhavananda: "As I finished reading the last scene there were two tears running down my cheeks," Prabhavananda reported. "In fact, he went so far as [to] suggest that it ought to be sold at the Vedanta

Center bookshop!"[39] Moved as he was, Prabhavananda told Isherwood that the monastery was easy to identify as Belur Math since there was no other monastery on that part of the Ganges.

BACHARDY HELD ON in New York until late April. When the engravings of the ballet portraits were finally ready, George Balanchine decided he wanted to be included in the series and also asked for three of the portraits to be redrawn. Then Bachardy discovered that Kirstein had never asked Balanchine's permission to sell the ballet portfolios at Lincoln Center because Kirstein feared it would be assumed Bachardy was a boyfriend being promoted. Bachardy received a copy of the portfolio with Balanchine's red-ink comments (personal remarks about the dancers, some criticizing the likenesses). The project was scrapped, after a year and a half of work. Bachardy was furious and let Kirstein know. They never spoke again.

Kirstein also ended his friendship with Isherwood. At first Isherwood expected a reconciliation, and later he longed for one, but Kirstein was headed for a mental breakdown that would see him committed to a sanitarium outside Boston for seven weeks in the summer of 1967. In 1971, Isherwood wrote what he called a "peace note," and was saddened by Kirstein's "utter rejection of the two of us."[40] He hoped for reconciliation again in the spring of 1975 when Kirstein had a massive heart attack. It was not to be.

Kirstein cut others out of his life, too—Rouben Ter-Arutunian, the architect Philip Johnson, a young boyfriend Freddy Maddox, the British ballet critic Richard Buckle—but Bachardy blamed himself for the end of the friendship. Dealing with a manic depressive was especially unsettling for him, considering his brother's illness. Evidently, Bachardy never revealed to Isherwood that his relationship with Kirstein had been made more volatile by a sexual affair. For Bachardy, Isherwood would accept any loss. It only made him more committed.

Reunited in Santa Monica, Isherwood and Bachardy had a happy summer, destabilized by another cancer scare, a lump on the inside of Isherwood's lip which proved to be a nonmalignant cyst. Isherwood sent *A Meeting by the River* to his publishers in July, and considered various movie offers. The best opportunity was a television job, "my first," he observed in his diary.

The project, for ABC, was "a Christmas Spectacular about how 'Silent Night' was composed, in 1818." The money was good, and he was to work with the director of the film adaptation of *The Rose Tattoo*, Danny Mann, whom he had got to know in Key West in 1954. Isherwood wrote an outline, and he and Mann arranged a September visit to the village church in Austria where the song, with music by the church organist, Franz Gruber, and words by the priest, Joseph Mohr, had first been performed. The church, aptly named St. Nicholas, was in Oberndorf, near Salzburg.

Two years later, Isherwood and Mann would find themselves making "Violent last-minute attempts" to have their names removed before *The Legend of Silent Night* was aired on Christmas Day 1968. The commercial schmaltz of the finished program horrified them both, but it got good notices from the *Hollywood Reporter* and *Variety*,[41] and it was aired all over again on Christmas Eve 1969. Isherwood's residual was $10,000. More important, his symbolic reimmersion in German-speaking culture marked the beginning of the great, final retrospective phase of his career.

ISHERWOOD WAS ENCHANTED by Salzburg, pronouncing it one of his three favorite towns, along with London and San Francisco. It touched a sentimental wellspring: "Salzburg is so snug in the best medieval way, ratlike tunnels and alleys and cellars, and the setting is so beautiful." He was moved in particular by the horses he saw depicted everywhere in varied moods and characters, the sculpture fountains of the central square, the paintings around the pond where the royal horses were once washed and watered, the real horses still at work. "Salzburg is dobbintown."[42] It was not just a fairytale world, it was also his childhood world, a long-ago life conducted at a clip-clop pace without motorcars, to which his mind was returning.

Afterwards, in London, he stayed with Neil Hartley, Tony Richardson's collaborator in Woodfall Productions and associate producer on *The Loved One*, and Hartley's American boyfriend, Bob Regester. He went to the theater, gave a party with Patrick Procktor, and went to hear Auden preach at Westminster Abbey. By late October, he was in Disley, where Richard was now living full-time with the Dan Bradleys, brother and sister-in-law of Alan, in their house on Bentside Road built by the local council. He and Richard visited Wyberslegh to delve into family papers, and he began to read his mother's diaries.

There were nearly seventy small volumes, each about the size of an open palm, filled with Kathleen's handwriting, similar to his own, but looser, less controlled. Her writerly self was also similar to his, less trained, less detached, but no less observant and searching. Kathleen had kept a diary for a year as a girl of fourteen in 1883, then she started again in earnest at age twenty-two. Isherwood now regretted that he had never asked her why.

"I like being able to look up and see what I was doing, on such and such a day," he later conjectured on her behalf, for "After Frank's death, Kathleen lived increasingly in the past; it was her cult." By contrast, Isherwood kept his own diary in order to analyze the present. "I am not trying to bring back the past, for nostalgic reasons. I am trying to find out what life is—and life is always experienced as the present."[43] But now he wanted to find out about the past, and he turned immediately to Kathleen's volume for 1915 to read about his father's death. So arresting were the entries that he began to copy them into his own diary.

Who was the man who had disappeared? Together, Isherwood and his brother began to read Frank's letters to Kathleen, and the letters completely changed their view of their father. Isherwood was at first unable to articulate his own emotion, so he focused on Richard, who said: "If he was really like he sounds here, I might even have got to like him. [...] Everyone kept saying how perfect he was, such a hero, and so good at everything. He was always held up as someone you could never hope to be worthy of, and whenever I did anything wrong I was told I was a disgrace to him."[44]

There can be little doubt that Isherwood shared Richard's anxiety about not measuring up to their hero-father, but as he read, he learned that he was capable, at least, of measuring up emotionally. "God, my mother's and father's letters are fascinating!" he wrote to Bachardy from Disley. "In one of them, my father makes a strange apology to her for 'lack of reciprocity' and he seems to mean some sort of coldness, sexual or emotional. As for my mother, she says, bitter against Uncle Jack, 'None of the Isherwoods feel things much'!"[45] Isherwood himself had felt it all, deeply, in his childhood. He was opening the door, preparing to enter the chamber of the past from which he had been in flight all his life.

He and Richard took a taxi to the grounds where Marple Hall had stood. "[B]ig, airy pleasing buildings" of the Marple Hall Grammar School had been built on the Private Drive, now renamed Marina Drive. "You could barely trace the foundations of the house, they were thickly grassed over. Only the stone over one of the doorways to the terrace lies there in the grass, engraved with the date 1658." This peaceful scene was for him an ending and a beginning. Children were in their classrooms and playing football on the old Barn Meadow. He felt relief and hopefulness still colored by the favorite books that had cast their atmosphere over his adolescence: "The Hall and its curse were forgotten, or remembered only as something romantic and mildly benevolent. And I felt as the narrator feels at the end of *Wuthering Heights*, when he sees that the graves are becoming overgrown by the vegetation of the moor and thinks that you could not imagine unquiet slumbers for the sleepers in that quiet earth."[46]

Now that the house and its inhabitants were gone, Isherwood was free to bring them back to life according to the needs of his own imagination. In telling the story of his parents, he was to share the stage, allowing Kathleen and Frank to speak in their own voices as recorded in their letters and diaries. He was to give the largest role to Kathleen. This was an act of extraordinary generosity for a man who had fought throughout his youth to get his own story away from his mother, his childhood collaborator, and tell it himself. He kept to a discipline of documentary accuracy; his versions of family texts are reliable, though he occasionally corrected or slightly improved them. Even so, memory, intuition, and deep private inclination were to guide his attention, and much was to be omitted or remain hidden even from himself.

WHEN ISHERWOOD RETURNED from England to Santa Monica at the beginning of November 1966, *Cabaret* was about to open on Broadway. He was determined not to go to New York to see it, even though he and Bachardy had been invited to Truman Capote's decade-defining "Black and White Ball" to be held just after Thanksgiving at the Plaza Hotel. He had never liked New York, he did not want to travel away from home again so soon, and all the difficulties and challenges of seeing his early work, indeed his early self, taken over by others—as in *I Am a Camera* back in 1951—could only be worse with a musical. He knew that he must stay away and protect his imagination from this new invasion. "Don and I are engaged in one of our strange psychological wrestling matches," Isherwood wrote in his diary. "He wants to go to New York, attend Truman's ball and see *Cabaret*. I don't."[47] He was convinced Bachardy would have more fun without him, even though Bachardy said he would feel embarrassed to appear at the ball alone. What excited Isherwood that autumn was *Hero-Father, Demon-Mother*. He was thinking about it constantly.

Cabaret opened on November 20 with music by John Kander, lyrics by Fred Ebb, book by Joe Masteroff, directed and produced by Harold Prince. Joel Grey played the Master of Ceremonies and Lotte Lenya was Fräulein Schneider. "It is quite a hit, although the notices haven't all been good," reported Isherwood. The *New York Times* was more enthusiastic than *Variety* or the *Los Angeles Times*. Jill Haworth, as Sally Bowles, "was described as a hole in the production."[48] Nevertheless, it played to sold-out houses for fifteen weeks at the Broadhurst Theater before moving to the larger-capacity Imperial, where it continued to sell out. In March 1967, it was to win eight Tony Awards: Best Musical plus seven more Bests in the Musical category—Director, Featured Actor, Featured Actress, Original Score, Scene Design, Costumes, Choreography. In June it was to win the New York Drama

Critics' Circle Award for Best Musical. It moved again, to the Broadway Theater, eventually playing 1,165 performances. Isherwood's small percentage of the proceeds, with record album sales, tours, later the film and revivals, made him financially secure for the rest of his life.

Bachardy left for New York two days after Thanksgiving. "He went to the ball, which he found tacky but very enjoyable, and he saw *Cabaret*, which he found merely awful," wrote Isherwood. Isherwood had Ronnie Knox to stay one night and Byron Trott another, and he was entirely content at home with the theater of his imagination. "I find my father and mother in me. I find all the figures of the past *inside* me, not outside." His past life welled up into his present life, and he lived in layers of time and memory. On a page of his draft he typed: "I believe that my Father and Mother are not only alive inside me but becoming more alive, more dominant, as I grow older."[49]

In his poem for Isherwood's thirty-third birthday, Auden had described Isherwood as "A cross between a cavalry major and a rather prim landlady," recognizing already the blend of Frank and Kathleen. On the landlady side, characters swarmed in and out of Isherwood's imagination just as guests had swarmed in and out of Kathleen's house and lodgers had swarmed in and out of Fräulein Thurau's flat. Once, talking about his Berlin epic *The Lost*, Isherwood explained to an interviewer that as a young man, he had to turn many of them away: "all these characters, all the people I'd known in Berlin, were all waiting as though I were a refugee officer in some place like Hong Kong where these people are crowding in. You had to find a place for them. And you look in despair, because you cannot imagine how you're going to fit them into the available housing."[50]

His imagination was the stage for countless applicants who craved the limelight for at least one scene. Isherwood had decided which acts to feature, and he had taken the stage alongside them. In his draft *Hero-Father, Demon-Mother*, he wrote of his younger self: "As for becoming an actor, he may have considered it. But he sought and found a larger stage and a more demanding role. Throughout his life, with the utmost energy, enthusiasm, with varying degrees of hamminess, and then with increasing technique, he was to play the part of himself."[51] In New York, the makers of *Cabaret* had introduced what seemed to be a new character, a Master of Ceremonies—a cult role for Joel Grey and, later, Alan Cumming—but in a sense they had only revealed the entertainer hidden all along behind the bland narrator figure, Herr Issyvoo—the baby impresario, the would-be actor, the show-off exhibitionist. In 1959, planning their Berlin musical, Isherwood, Auden, and Kallman had proposed to make Christopher a comedian.

Isherwood was turning inward now to write about his past, but at the same time, in the present, he was more than ever on public show. He was approached for more TV work and also for stage work. In Los Angeles, there was a George Bernard Shaw story to adapt for the Mark Taper Forum, *The Adventures of the Black Girl in Her Search for God*, and he met with the producer, Lamont Johnson, and the director, Gordon Davidson, to discuss the project which would come to fruition in 1969. In England, there was an adaptation of Wedekind's Lulu plays, *Erdgeist* (*Earthsprite*, 1895) and *Die Büchse der Pandora* (*Pandora's Box*, 1904) for Anthony Page to direct at the Royal Court. The Wedekind seemed to offer an opportunity for Isherwood to reengage with material that had inspired him in Berlin, where he had first watched Louise Brooks as Lulu.

Anthony Page was only thirty-one yet had already been Artistic Director at the Royal Court during an illness of George Devine in 1964. He had visited Wedekind's daughter Kadidja in Munich about mounting the play. According to Page, Kadidja Wedekind offered him "scenes that had never been performed before due to the censor."[52] Page had met Isherwood in Los Angeles through Tony Richardson, and they had other friends in common—Patrick Procktor, Bob Regester, Neil Hartley. In London, Page had given Isherwood the new material, and Isherwood promised to read it.

For the time being, Isherwood focused on the book about his parents. He proposed to ground the new project in psychology, invoking Jung:

> The book should be preoccupied with the concept of the autobiography as myth, following Jung's remarks at the beginning of his autobiography, and there should be a lot of examples given of how myth is created out of the materials of experience. Therefore there will be quotations from my books, showing how different aspects of the myth were developed.

In fact, this described the approach he was to take in *Lost Years* and in *Christopher and His Kind*. As had happened before, notably with *Down There on a Visit* and *A Single Man*, he conceived several works at once and slowly untangled them from each other. For *Kathleen and Frank* he was to settle on "a much straighter kind of narrative, a study of their marriage, primarily, without time jumps and other such tricks."[53]

Both *Kathleen and Frank* and *Christopher and His Kind* involved Isherwood in unpicking the fictions he had woven in the first trajectory of his career. Ever since his April 1963 lectures at Berkeley, he had been trying to find a way to write what he had called "An Autobiography of My Books." Once, he had referred to this project as "'The Autobiography of my Characters' (or 'Books')," which, again, points to the narrative he was eventually to unfold in *Christopher and His Kind*, telling how he had developed the characters in his books from real people he met. He saw the autobiography of his books in

Jung's terms as "a story of the self-realization of the unconscious." In his encounters with the subjects of his writing, in the imaginative transformations he had performed on them, he was to trace his own history, the story of his inner, hidden life, the "personal myth."[54] Of course, the story began with his parents and the other characters of his childhood world.

Jung, Groddeck and Simeons are not included in any of Isherwood's lists of "Books Read" in his day-to-day diaries. The psychology books—exploring what can and cannot be known through consciousness—were so fundamental to his struggle to understand how we know what we know that they themselves slipped from consciousness.

———

ONE THING ISHERWOOD irrationally, perhaps unconsciously, and perfectly naturally, held against his father was simply absence. His notion of fatherhood called for presence and for intimate engagement, as he had shown in his relationship with Bachardy and with countless other young men.

While he was working out his ideas for *Kathleen and Frank*, he and Bachardy had supper with Timothy Leary and Alan Watts, hosted by Virginia Pfeiffer. It was the second time they had met Leary. "He really is a fake," wrote Isherwood in his diary. They attended Leary's show, "A Psychedelic Religious Celebration: Illumination of the Buddha" at the Santa Monica Civic Auditorium—slide projections, singing and dancing "by a group which calls itself The Grateful Dead," as Isherwood reported. "Leary, all in white and barefoot, addressed us through a mike." He was no Socrates, in Isherwood's view. "He appealed to all the young to 'drop out, turn on, tune in,'" making free use of pot and acid, Isherwood recorded, but "He wasn't really offering any reliable spiritual help to the young, only inciting them to vaguely rebellious action—and inciting them without really involving himself with them."

Later the same year, Isherwood went with Jo Masselink to hear Maharishi Mahesh Yogi, the Indian holy man who taught Transcendental Meditation to, reportedly, more than five million people including the Beatles and the Beach Boys. "I was quite favorably impressed—I mean, I don't think he's an out-and-out fake," Isherwood wrote afterwards, although he found the Maharishi's talk about the Self "confusing" in relation to the Atman, and the Maharishi's claims of speedy results through mass teaching unconvincing.

After seeing the Maharishi, Isherwood renewed his own efforts at meditation. He decided to chant his mantram aloud, as he had once been taught to do whenever meditating alone, and to pray "for those I love *and for those I hate*." A month later, he "suddenly had the impulse" to meditate "according to the instructions Swami gave me all those years ago. I don't know how long it is since I dropped it, but ages certainly." He found it "incredibly difficult,"[55] but the counterculture, which had caught up with him, now swept him further along his old pathway.

Father figures preoccupied Isherwood. When he next visited Prabhavananda, he learned that the assistant head monk at the Vedanta Society had asked to go back to India, potentially leaving seventy-four-year-old Prabhavananda alone to train someone else. Isherwood told him this meant "you'll have to live another ten years at least!" Prabhavananda humorously protested. "But I got the feeling that he did indeed somehow accept the duty of not dying too soon." Isherwood craved similar responsibility for himself, but not in public at the Vedanta Society. He wrote in the same diary entry: "Which reminds me that Ronnie Knox rang me up in the middle of last night and told *me* not to die, because he needed my fatherly influence—though he didn't put it quite like that. He was very very drunk."[56]

Isherwood pressed on with *Hero-Father, Demon-Mother* until he reached the point at which his father left for the war. He never got any further with this draft. "I realize more and more clearly that I'm going to rely chiefly on my mother's diaries," he wrote on April 7. He needed more time with them. Accordingly, he set off for England again in May 1967. In London, he stayed with Bob Regester but found him bossy in Neil Hartley's absence. "[H]e showed a kind of possessiveness by harping on the theme that I am a hopeless alcoholic." Isherwood moved to Chester Square, to the house where Marguerite Brown Harrity now lived with her third husband, the English barrister Mark Littman. She included Isherwood in meals and parties and enthusiastically accommodated his drinking. One day, the Littmans took him to Cambridge to picnic in a punt, and they got drunk. "The Backs were full of punts. Undergraduates jumped into the water or pretended to fall in, with all their clothes on. The trees were enchantingly green. It was almost like being young, but better; no anxiety." Indeed, it was like a journey into long-ago summers, when he was transported by punt to the picnics of his childhood birthdays in Frimley, near Aldershot, before World War I. He labeled this his "Happiest day in England."[57]

Forster had suffered a stroke, and Isherwood visited him at Bob and May Buckingham's in Coventry. Joe Ackerley was also there, and Ackerley died only a few days after the visit. While he was in Coventry, Isherwood met a man called Harry Heckford, who was planning a book about him and with whom he had been corresponding. He could find nothing to like in Heckford but answered his questions and provided photocopies of lectures and unpublished work. Heckford's book was never published, but his questions stirred Isherwood's thinking about his own book.

At last, he visited Richard, who read the 124-page draft of *Hero-Father*,

Demon-Mother and felt persuaded by it to let Isherwood take away Frank's and Granny Emily's letters and a key stretch of Kathleen's diaries, from 1897 to 1915. In Cheshire, Isherwood drank no alcohol because he feared being overwhelmed by depression, and he did not want to encourage Richard to drink. Bachardy later recalled that Isherwood was able to give up drinking whenever he made up his mind to do so, and there are many sober periods mentioned in Isherwood's diaries.

There was one other project he was keen on. "I have taken a great liking to Anthony Page," he noted in his diary, "and let him know that I will definitely work on the Lulu adaptation." Together he and Page had been to watch Mick Jagger's girlfriend, the singer Marianne Faithfull, make her stage debut in Chekhov's *The Three Sisters* at the Royal Court. Page thought Faithfull "might do for Lulu," as Isherwood reported to Bachardy. Page later recalled that they went to dinner afterwards at the Casserole in the King's Road. There was a Bacon painting of naked wrestlers upstairs and a gay disco in the basement. They drank a lot of wine, and Isherwood talked about Bachardy, confiding "that he sometimes wished that Don could have a lover nearer his own age." They also discussed Colette's *Chéri*, which Isherwood told Page "he would love to adapt because it dealt with this subject." Page revealed his "profound inhibitions about being openly gay and how I couldn't shake them," and he told Isherwood about his affairs abroad, one with "someone I thought I could possibly have loved." Isherwood encouraged Page to go abroad again, find that lover, and act upon his feelings. "You should never be cynical about love. I never have been. . . . Tell him what you feel and see where it leads."

They walked along the King's Road back to the Littmans' house, where, on the doorstep, Isherwood gripped Page in a drunken embrace and invited him inside. Page played it down and went home. "Finally, he accepted that I was unwilling and let me go, bidding me a tipsy, but still friendly goodnight." Like Regester, Page was left with the impression that Isherwood was a hopeless alcoholic, but Page was inspired by him nonetheless. He acted on Isherwood's advice to meet his foreign lover again, "determined to find the courage to enjoy life openly as I should have long ago—and as I was sure Christopher had with all those German boys in Berlin."[58] When he got home to Santa Monica, it took Isherwood nine months to start making a rough translation from Wedekind's German.

British reviews of *A Meeting by the River* began while Isherwood was still in England. "*Times* poor, *Daily Express* fair, *Daily Telegraph* very good," he wrote to Bachardy. Robert Baldick, in the *Telegraph*, called it "a remarkable *tour de force*."[59] In the U.S., Stanley Kauffmann in the *New Republic* noticed a special dynamic: "like one of those optical illusion drawings," he wrote, "it changes as one reads it." This was the chess game, the Zen koan that

Isherwood had planned. The novel presented an apparently insoluble contradiction, reduced the contradiction to its elements, examined it from every point of view, and resolved it in laughter. "[A]n enigma variation," wrote Christopher Wordsworth in the *Guardian*. "Mr Isherwood remains the supreme craftsman, working away with invisible nails at the inscrutable, the sublime, the absurd."[60]

Gerald Sykes for the *New York Times* attacked the novel savagely, then conceded that it was charming, readable, honest, and "far more authentic" than Maugham's *The Razor's Edge*, precisely the religious novel that had so long chafed and challenged Isherwood. As with most of Isherwood's work, opinions varied in the extreme: "it is the evil Patrick who runs away with the book," pronounced the reviewer for *Time* magazine. "Patrick is fully as alive as Sally Bowles," he enthused, "and could support a longer novel."[61]

ONE OF HIS writing students from L.A. State had approached Isherwood to endorse the Vietnam Summer antiwar project started in April 1967 by the Quaker American Friends Service Committee with support from Martin Luther King and Benjamin Spock. Isherwood said no by letter, and recapped in his diary his uneasiness about the peace movement, highlighting differences with Gandhi's movement in India, where the protesters were subject to a foreign imperial power. He reminded himself that as a pacifist he needed to oppose all wars, not just wars to which he had political objections: "I believe Aldous would have agreed with me. And Gerald Heard." He saw no public role for himself in the peace movement and later wrote: "It's far more effective to give a little prod unexpectedly now and then, in the midst of what's officially a course in English literature. When you speak at a peace rally everybody knows in advance what you're going to say." This position at the margin of organized politics reprised his stance toward communism in the early 1930s.

He was carrying his pacifism into a new age of conflict without being able to consult his key pacifist mentors from World War II. Heard was suffering a long series of debilitating strokes. With the first, in 1966, he lost the use of his left arm then gradually recovered it; with the second, he lost the power of speech then gradually recovered it; there were many more. Access was strictly controlled by his companion, Michael Barrie. In August 1967, Isherwood and Bachardy insisted and were allowed to visit Heard in bed: "He seemed hugely amused by us, we were *maya*, absurd and trivial and yet absorbingly interesting to him."[62] The bedside visits would continue until a few months before Heard's death in 1971.

The summer of love was also a summer of hate. In July, a police raid on a black after-hours bar in Detroit triggered five days of violence and looting. Isherwood observed from the press coverage that whites as well as blacks were rioting, establishing for him that the cause was not just race but economics, like the riots that had occurred in Berlin and Vienna in his youth.

Closer to home, the relationship between the Masselinks fell apart. Jo discovered that Ben had a young girlfriend, Dee Hawes, a dancer. There were scenes of sorrow and drunkenness, and every detail was subject to implicit comparison with Isherwood's own domestic relationship. "Don identifies more with Ben and I with Jo." Isherwood was horrified by Jo's anxiety about her age, and even more by her jealousy, "like a terminal disease."

By the end of the summer, both the Masselinks were seeing psychiatrists, and Ben moved out. He married Dee Hawes a year later. All through the breakup, Isherwood recorded that he was as happy as he had ever been with Bachardy, but it set him on edge: "I keep thinking, what a lesson to me, and I needn't preen myself on having cured myself of the disease. The George Kramer days aren't so far behind."[63]

A few days after his sixty-third birthday, Isherwood made one of his summary assessments in his diary. His life with Bachardy was "in a marvellous phase of love, intimacy, mutual trust, tenderness, affection, fun, everything." They had plenty of money and his health was good. "I am of course terribly uneasy about my 'worldly' happiness; fearing to lose it and yet knowing that of course it will be necessary to lose it before I can find *ananda*," he pronounced. But then he admonished that one was a pathway to the other. "How *can* love be profane if it really is love? In my own case, hasn't my relation with Don now become my true means of enlightenment?" A few months later, he wrote: "the real point of a householder's life is not simply that he is not a monk but that he loves a human being rather than God. So he must learn to love God through that human being."[64] His biggest test in this regard was yet to come.

IN FEBRUARY 1968, Isherwood and Bachardy celebrated their fifteenth anniversary in Palm Springs with Truman Capote, and *Cabaret* opened in London to strong reviews; Judi Dench played Sally Bowles. Isherwood finally turned to the Wedekind plays for Anthony Page. He had made a synopsis of *Earthsprite* within a week, and in March he began working on *Pandora's Box*.

David Hockney moved into an apartment in Santa Monica, on 3rd Street, with his Californian boyfriend Peter Schlesinger, met in Hockney's UCLA drawing class in the summer of 1966. Isherwood and Bachardy saw them whenever Hockney and Schlesinger were in Los Angeles, often joined by Larson, Bridges, Lambert and others. Hockney was fresh from the success of his fourth one-man show at the Kasmin Gallery in London. Schlesinger had just been accepted to study at the Slade, like Bachardy in 1961. The Slade term didn't begin until September, and for the time being, Hockney didn't need his flat in Notting Hill, so he offered it to Isherwood and Bachardy.

Isherwood was immersed in his mother's diaries, and he was up to his eyebrows in other work—rewrites on *The Adventures of the Black Girl in Her Search for God*, rewrites on a TV adaptation of Dickens's *A Christmas Carol* for Hunt Stromberg Jr. at Screen Gems with Rex Harrison as Scrooge, a speech on Auden's behalf for the American Academy and Institute of Arts and Letters which was presenting Auden with its Gold Medal, a recording of selections from the Prabhavananda–Isherwood translation of the Gita.[65]

Bachardy, on the other hand, was at a loose end, so he took up Hockney's offer and left on April 1 for a proposed ten-day break. "After I'd seen him off I noticed that time seemed to slow down, to an uncanny extent," Isherwood wrote in his diary. The weather was terrible. "[R]aining hard in heavy gusty showers. The sea grey, the trees drinking, the slides sliding. Just the right weather for the situation in this house . . ."[66]

On April 4, Hockney sent Bachardy a note in London: "I'm thinking of doing another giant portrait of Chris & you like this." He drew an arrow pointing to a sketch: two figures seated side by side with a space between them, like monarchs on their thrones or actors on a stage, with the flat plane of a coffee table in front of them and a big window, like a void, behind them. He enclosed a bundle of twenty photos of Isherwood and Bachardy taken in their living room on March 30, two days before Bachardy left town, some showing the same pose, others showing close-ups of their faces.[67] He had made watercolor sketches and drawings of the scene, and he got started on the portrait while Bachardy was away. It was in a sense the mise en abyme again, since Hockney was painting a double portrait in which one of the sitters was at work on another double portrait—of his parents, Kathleen and Frank. The painting and the book were to prove a kind of shared meditation on the marriage relationship, harking back for Isherwood all the way to childhood meals beneath the Marple Hall portrait of John Donne and Anne More.

Hockney later said that Isherwood often sat for him, and he published an ink drawing of Isherwood posing in the rented room Hockney was using as a studio across from his and Schlesinger's 3rd Street apartment. But Hockney worked on the portrait mostly alone, painting from his sketches, his photos, and his memory. According to Schlesinger, Hockney "painted mostly from photos at that time. Paintings of me were mostly from photos even though I was there." It was not until April 20 that Isherwood saw the painting,[68] and he made no comment on it in his diary, nor did he mention any sittings.

He talked to Bachardy regularly on the telephone and learned that Bachardy had stayed with the Littmans for a few days then moved to Hockney's flat "which fills him with horror, it is so dirty and messy and cold and far away." Bachardy reported that nobody in London was glad to see him; he felt "inclined to come right back home." But on April 17, after more than two weeks there, he postponed his return, planned for the next day. Instead of the reunion, Isherwood visited Dr. Allen for a stomach pain. Allen prescribed pills which seemed to help, but the pain persisted, and it was to grow worse over the coming weeks.

On April 22, Bachardy again postponed his return. "I feel very sad," Isherwood wrote in his diary. "But it's good, actually, because he's done this job for the Royal Court and now the whole trip is justified." The job at the Royal Court was for Anthony Page, portraits of the cast of John Osborne's new play *Time Present*, which Page was directing. The portraits were to be used as posters in the theater and to be printed in the program. Isherwood was having a bad time alone, feeling "depressed and sick" with stomach pain and diarrhea. "I long for Don to come back—so I can love and think and feel and be a human being again. At present I'm just a dull old dying creature."[69]

Bachardy wrote after three weeks in London that he had not yet booked a flight home "in case some unforeseen emergency arises concerning the posters." He had moved from Hockney's flat to Bob Regester's. He forgot to tell Isherwood that Iris Tree had died on April 13, and he skipped her memorial service. He was clearly preoccupied.

On April 27, on the telephone, Bachardy postponed his return again. On April 30, he wrote saying he was too busy drawing the cast to see any of their London friends. He was constantly at the Royal Court, and he planned to get a plane reservation for the following Monday, May 6. "Don't call me here except in an emergency," he warned. "I feel very uncomfortable around Bob & Neil and so spend most of my time away."

Isherwood received this letter on May 2. That day, he was sent by Dr. Allen for the dreaded medical tests, including barium X-rays to check his gallbladder and stomach. "So terribly longing for Don, and also with an upset stomach, vagus nerve or whatnot," he wrote in his diary. But the tests showed that everything was functioning normally. "So I will just have to ignore the whole thing. Probably it will get better as soon as Don gets home." The physical symptoms were caused, as so often in the past, by anxiety that Isherwood was trying to ignore.

On Sunday May 5, Bachardy phoned again and said he was not yet coming home. By now, he had moved to Page's flat, at 68 Ladbroke Grove, back in Notting Hill near Hockney's flat. "I was so ill at ease at Bob and Neil's," he declared casually in another letter, "that I asked him if he would put me up for a few days." He hinted that there might be further calls for him to stay on in London. He was having trouble getting a good likeness of John Osborne. "Kitty is being terribly fussed and rattled and dazed by all these Show Biz people who keep plucking at his fur and spinning him around."[70]

Bachardy and Page had begun an affair. Page, already a prestigious director with an important job at the Royal Court, was eighteen months younger than Bachardy. He was supremely intelligent, well educated, well read, well traveled, a fine musician, acute in his intuitions, witty, playful, glamorous-looking. He was just as highly strung and sensitive as Bachardy, with a similar capacity for intimacy and obsession. According to Page's later recollection, he and Bachardy were introduced in London by Procktor, though in fact, they had met five years earlier at Tony Richardson's all-male dinner party at Chasen's in the run-up to the premiere of *Tom Jones*. "Patrick told me that, when in England, Don looked for figures unlike the stocky Christopher. Tall, gangly people like himself and Tony Richardson. And me." Since Isherwood had confided to Page that Bachardy ought to have a younger lover and had himself made a pass, Page had no scruples: "I saw nothing amiss in inviting Don over."[71] Moreover, Bachardy assured Page that Isherwood would not object. None of them foresaw the power of the connection between Bachardy and Page, and the affair was to prove the most significant threat so far to the bond between Isherwood and Bachardy.

Isherwood reacted as his mother might have. "[W]e both felt very loving after our talk," he reassured himself in his diary after phoning Bachardy at Page's flat, pretending, as Kathleen used to pretend about Isherwood when he was young, that he knew how Bachardy felt. But he also reacted as himself: "I keep reverting to the rather horrible feeling that this is a kind of illness, his not being here, from which I may not recover. Suppose he died, over there. I wouldn't have any reason to go on living. That thought is simply terrifying."[72] In childhood, too, Christopher's father's absence had been a kind of illness—beginning with measles and pneumonia in March and April 1915.

Isherwood had been considering some kind of writing collaboration with Bachardy, and in one letter, Bachardy reported that Page had been offered a film deal to adapt a French thriller and suggested the three of them work together. "If Anthony does ask you to do it, a kitten might lend a paw if asked. That way the Animals could put their heads together out of the basket as well as in." Ever since he had fallen for Tennessee Williams, Bachardy had wanted to write a play and to enter the theater world of Williams, Richardson, and now Page. A film script would be at least as exciting.

Isherwood developed a backache. On their May 12 phone call, Bachardy again delayed his return. The next day, Isherwood again saw the doctor. "I am miserable for Don. And there is absolutely no substitute," he lamented in his diary. He went to the gym to have heat applied to his back and visited the doctor twice more. He phoned in the small hours of May 18 to wish Bachardy a happy birthday. "His voice was so beautiful; it seemed full of tears and yet perfectly happy."[73]

Isherwood was having a breakdown. He could not bring himself to recognize consciously what his diary entries make clear—that he was reacting not only to his anxiety about Bachardy but also to the tragedy which had befallen his parents and his childhood self and which he was reliving as he worked through their diaries and letters. He was grieving for all he had lost long ago and for which he had never grieved before.

In youth, Isherwood had escaped and triumphed over Kathleen's fate; now he was falling prey to it, and he became more conscious of his mother as a rival. "Everything Kathleen does seems compulsive," he observed reading her diaries. "And yet at the same time she was an extremely perceptive person in many ways. Sometimes in later life she used to talk as if she viewed the whole of human activity as a sort of masquerade." He described himself in his diary much as he had described Kathleen, compulsive in all his actions, unless they were acts of love. He brooded on Bachardy as Kathleen had brooded on Frank: "It is all a sort of vague dream, governed by compulsion. I go out to supper, like last night, and immediately know that I would rather be by myself at home. I want to be alone and just think about Don, brood on him, rather. And why do I like doing this? Because brooding on Don is love ..."

He grew sicker and was woken by pain in his gut. He stopped drinking; he tried a massage. Two more letters from Bachardy were full of details about time-consuming difficulties with printing the program, about the Brighton opening of *Time Present*, about Page's film of *Inadmissable Evidence* and about the possibility of portraits for another Osborne play opening in July at the Royal Court, *The Hotel in Amsterdam*, a commitment Bachardy soon confirmed to Isherwood by phone.

"It was a painful disappointment," Isherwood grieved to his diary after the call. "A dreadful mad silly voice says suppose he never comes back ... Actually he keeps reassuring me—and I do believe him—that's he longing to return, loves me, longs to be with me, etc. Well, anyway, shit. I'm not going to be like poor old Jo ..."[74] After that, he made no more mention of Bachardy's absence. He read the two Osborne plays, *Time Present* and *The Hotel in Amsterdam*. He had not sent Bachardy a single letter all the time Bachardy was in London because he wanted to pressure him to return as soon as possible.

Isherwood's private despair was unfolding in a wider atmosphere of uncertainty and fear. President Johnson had announced he would not run for a second term because he could not spare time to campaign when Americans were fighting overseas in Vietnam and the country was so divided. This amounted, as Isherwood described it, to "Johnson's resignation." On April 4, Martin Luther King was assassinated. "Oh fuck them all," Isherwood wrote in his diary. "How blood-horny this'll make the killers on both sides."

Riots broke out in cities all over the country. On June 5, Robert Kennedy was assassinated. In his day-to-day diary, Isherwood jotted: "To see Swami. Felt sick, back and throat bad. Came home and ate alone." Awash as ever in the wider crisis, he could hardly separate his private mood from the sorrow and anger around him. At last, on June 10, Bachardy returned. "My throat is bad, and I am full of anxiety. A kind of dread—but of what? Of new developments? Silly old superstitious horse. Even the smell of happiness makes him tremble and twitch his nostrils."[75]

Hockney and Schlesinger photographed Bachardy for the double portrait, then Hockney left by car for New York and flew on to London, taking the rolled-up canvas. The painting he was making shows a domestic scene: two men at ease in their living room. In a subtle change from the sketch Hockney had sent Bachardy, the double window behind is shuttered—with the blue louvred shutters painted by Bachardy—suggesting privacy. The viewer is inside their world, not a voyeur. The colors are pale and fresh, the light clean, with a quality of purity rather than anything the least bit shady, nocturnal, debauched, or even secretive. The surfaces are spartan, the composition stable, anchored by the piles of books. It's a confident, luminous portrayal of a same-sex relationship—quietly revolutionary. But Hockney was having a great deal of trouble painting Bachardy's face.

JIM BRIDGES LIKED *A Meeting by the River* enough to suggest adapting it with Isherwood for stage or film. Bridges also wanted Isherwood to help with a film adaptation of Tennessee Williams's 1948 story "One Arm," about a boxer who loses an arm in a car wreck, turns to hustling and then murder. Williams favored Isherwood to write the script: "I'm the only one he would trust not to falsify it because I'm the only one who has never lied about homosexuality in my writing or my life, etc.," Isherwood noted in his diary; so he agreed, "*if* it is clearly written into the contract that Jim Bridges is to be the director." But the proposed producer didn't want Bridges as director. Williams visited Los Angeles in September 1968, bringing his own script and inviting Isherwood to help him. "This is of course out of the question," wrote Isherwood, because Bridges had been dropped.

Meanwhile, Isherwood and Bridges finished a draft of the stage adaptation of *A Meeting by the River* in late April. Bridges had accompanied Isherwood to Vedanta Place for a reading and attended a Sunday lecture. He had also read *An Approach to Vedanta* and begun to meditate. But, gradually, Isherwood sensed that "Jim doesn't want to write this play, only direct it."[76]

Isherwood was still unwell, and not long after returning from London Bachardy fell ill, too, with a sore throat. Collaboration was the cure, as it had been for Auden and Isherwood in 1929 when Auden, the unrequited lover, had asked Isherwood to help with his play. By July 5, Bachardy was rereading *A Meeting by the River*. "[W]e shall work on this together if it seems at all possible, without saying anything to Jim Bridges who, luckily, is now busy with a musical of his own."

They started on July 12. "Don is very much on the alert to prevent me from attributing ideas to him which I have actually had myself—this is part of what he calls buttering him up. Nevertheless I do genuinely find it hard most of the time to remember which idea belongs to whom." He enjoyed their sessions enormously. "I love taking things apart and putting them together differently; and Don is always wonderful to work with."[77]

At the same time, Isherwood pressed on with his mother's diaries and the seventeen or more packets of letters. On August 5, close to the date that England had declared war on Germany, he finished working through the year of his father's death, 1915. "I feel that I know Frank now for the first time," he observed in his diary. He had over four hundred single-space typed pages. He made Jerry Lawrence laugh when he said, "I'm afraid this is going to be just another *War and Peace*."[78] The joke illuminated the link back to his second novel, *The Memorial*, also greatly influenced—in different ways—by *War and Peace*.

He and Bachardy finished their draft script of *A Meeting by the River* at the end of August, and Bachardy typed it up and took it to New York to show Bridges, who was there directing a play. Bachardy was candid that he might continue from New York to London to see Page. "[T]his is something I have got to come to terms with, and I will," Isherwood resolved in his diary.[79]

He was determined not to fall apart as he had done during Bachardy's last absence. He swam off the beach every day, went on refining his notes from Kathleen's diary and pondered exactly how to write the book about his parents. At last, he began a letter to Kathleen to use as the opening. He addressed her by her name, which he had never done before. "I know, I can feel it already, that calling you Kathleen makes all the difference; it's going to be a real release for me," he told her in the letter. In his diary, he wrote: "It opens something up. It's a bit like meditation was, when I first tried it in 1939."

Morever, he thought the connection came more easily since Bachardy was away. "Somehow being alone strengthens my sense of the confrontation between the two of us."[80]

Now that he had read through her diaries, Isherwood had a more complete view of Kathleen. He recognized, as if for the first time, how much of his work was written in dialogue with her: "I always talked to you about my work, planning it out loud. This is odd, now I come to think about it, because you didn't really much like anything I wrote." Rehearsing all the old points of friction, he abandoned the typewriter and continued by hand. "But what I objected to in your nostalgia was that it implied such a determined sulky disapproval of the present [. . .] you did admit, again and again, while Frank was still alive, that your marriage was happy . . ." Then, as he wrote his father's name, he had a breakthrough:

> For Christopher, from the age of ten onward, Frank <u>was</u> The Past. Frank was the Ideal, and your marriage to him the Lost Paradise, against which all people and states of existence would henceforward be judged—and found to have fallen short.
>
> Christopher began by accepting your cult of the dead and the past. He tried for a while to respect it. Then it began to anger him. He was passionately jealous of it. And so he turned against The Past.

Through his relationship with Bachardy, Isherwood had begun to learn how to cope with jealousy. In the midst of his anxiety that he might lose Bachardy to Page, he saw at last how jealousy of his father and of his parents' happy marriage had turned him against his mother, against the past, against history, against England. "Why have I waited so long? To make use of your diaries and Frank's letters? I knew they were there at Wyberslegh."[81] Now he was ready to celebrate his parents' life together in *Kathleen and Frank*.

Bachardy returned from New York without going on to London. Bridges liked their play and wanted to direct it in Los Angeles and then in London. So Isherwood and Bachardy revised it, and on October 8, Bachardy left for England after all, taking the play with him, intending to show it to Tony Richardson. A week later, a vivid and distressing dream "that we were actually in the act of parting" woke Isherwood early in the morning: "I felt he was slipping away from me; indeed that he had only partially come back to visit me and that, although he wanted to, he couldn't stay."[82]

Isherwood stuck in harder on the book, and he wrote yet another article about Vedanta for a twenty-four volume encyclopedia of the supernatural to be published in England.[83] He jogged every day on the beach. He and

Bachardy had agreed not to telephone during this separation; after all, it would have been awkward in those days of landlines for Bachardy to talk on the phone while staying at Page's flat.

"I think Anthony rather dreaded my visit," Bachardy confided in his first letter home. Page was incredibly busy. *Time Present* and *The Hotel in Amsterdam* had both transferred to the West End, and Page was now rehearsing a third Osborne play, a revival of the 1956 reputation-making *Look Back in Anger*, to open at the Royal Court on October 29. He asked Bachardy to draw just one actor in the revival, Victor Henry, playing Jimmy Porter, for a poster and for the program. Bachardy soon chased down portrait commissions of his own.

"Have told no one so far of the play and begin to feel that maybe I won't show it to anyone," Bachardy reported to Isherwood about *A Meeting by the River*. He was inhibited by a kind of stage fright about the script. Isherwood, robust with experience, urged him to show it to both Richardson and Page and get their opinions. "I now am *certain* that it is good [. . .] *somebody* will like it and it will be performed somehow. So let us risk a little disapproval." When Bachardy finally told Richardson about the play, Richardson didn't ask to read it, so Isherwood advised dropping the matter. "Anyhow let's see what we can do with it here first."

In California, Isherwood was continuing to discuss the play with Bridges, and when Isherwood and Bachardy's agent, Robin French, read it, French telephoned Isherwood and "really carried on wildly" declaring the play "perfect."[84]

Bachardy had tea with Hockney and Schlesinger in Notting Hill and updated Isherwood on the double portrait: "the figure of me is in grave danger of being *overworked*. Otherwise I very much like the painting." In the painting, Isherwood turns toward Bachardy attentively, and Bachardy looks out at the viewer, half his face veiled by shadow. His expression is charged but unrevealing, as if frozen in a state of sparkling excitement, conscious of being an object of scrutiny. Isherwood at last expressed some interest: "Do they have any idea where it will land up? Hope it'll be in London, at any rate I don't want to have to make a pilgrimage to some obscure provincial gallery."[85]

As Bachardy's second London visit to Page stretched on, his letters to Isherwood opened up about the friendship. He praised Page's intelligence, his versatility, and his directing skills. Isherwood went to see Page's film *Inadmissable Evidence* in Los Angeles and asked Bachardy to pass on his considerable admiration.

On October 25, Page asked Bachardy to do a new portrait for *The Hotel in Amsterdam* because Paul Scofield was leaving the play, and Page wanted a poster with the next star, Kenneth Haigh. "As soon as the bad old phone rang, Dubbin KNEW, and later when Kitty's letter from last Friday came, speaking of Kitty's certain arrival, a few tears fell," Isherwood wrote to Bachardy on October 29.[86]

It was not just the portrait that delayed Bachardy. He and Page had quarreled about *A Meeting by the River*. Page had begun reading the script. Halfway through, he passed it to a colleague, the playwright and director Nicholas Wright, who ran the Theatre Upstairs, a small space at the Royal Court. Bachardy wrote to Isherwood: "I was *furious* and lost my temper in a way I have never done with him before. As you can imagine, he was very surprised. We had quite an argument. This is another reason why I didn't want to leave yesterday, in a cloud of ill feeling."[87]

Page later recalled that he had felt the play was "complicated and clumsy compared to the book," but that he kept this to himself, hoping "that through my lack of enthusiasm Don would realise that I wasn't ever going to direct it." He had given it to his colleague in order to show he was making some effort over it. Bachardy's temper stunned Page, who feared all the neighborhood could hear Bachardy shouting and stamping his foot: "it was only then that I realised how deeply he cared about my reaction." Page considered the matter finished: "He can scarcely have believed that I would seriously consider directing it after this incident."[88] But he did not say this to Bachardy, and he was unaware that Bachardy was detailing Page's criticisms of the play to Isherwood as a blueprint for revisions.

When he got back to California in November, Bachardy wrote Page that Bridges was organizing a reading of the play. This went ahead in mid-November. Bachardy also told Page that Edward Albee and Richard Barr were interested in the project.[89] John Houseman requested copies to show in New York.

Isherwood had bounced back from his breakdown. He had spent some time with Paul Bowles while Bowles was guest teaching at San Fernando Valley State College. He had given a day to filming with the BBC for an *Omnibus* program about his life and career, released as *Christopher Isherwood— Born Foreigner*. His Shaw adaptation was scheduled for spring 1969 at the Mark Taper Forum and casting was already being discussed. He was at work on the second chapter of *Kathleen and Frank*. He began taking some antiaging pills, KH3, procaine hydrochloride, procured in London by Bachardy, and he took Alertonic, a vitamin and mineral compound. He had become a committed jogger, on the beach when the tide permitted or along San Vicente Boulevard, often accompanied by Bridges. Bachardy ran separately on the beach, further and faster than Isherwood.

Meanwhile, in London, the director of the National Portrait Gallery, Roy Strong, had seen Bachardy's drawings for the Osborne plays, got in touch through Richard Buckle, and asked to see more work. Bachardy reported to Page: "I sent him a book of photographs of my drawings, mostly those of writers, painters and composers (in whom he was most interested) and got an enthusiastic letter from him last week saying he wanted 'to place before the trustees' several of the drawings." Phone calls and letters continued between Bachardy and Page. "I do miss you and want very much to see you," wrote Bachardy in January 1969.[90]

All through the winter, heavy rains blew through Santa Monica Canyon, and the land was washing away into the sea. "The waves are brown," wrote Isherwood in late January. "A tremendous torrent is pouring out of the hills down the channels; on Rustic Road the water takes the curves like a racing car, so that the whole stream tilts sideways, spilling out over the road." A chunk of their hillside lot at Adelaide Drive slid down into Ocean Avenue Extension below, including part of their retaining wall, threatening the steps to Bachardy's studio. A month later, just north of Santa Monica, a whole house slid onto the Pacific Coast Highway. Bachardy was getting restless. "Don is unsettled, unhappy, aggressive, then sweet again. This is one of the cloudy periods. There is much we can't discuss. Earthquakes are in the air," wrote Isherwood.[91]

For himself, he was worried about a painful lump developing on his finger. He grew more alarmed when he discovered a second lump, in his palm, and thought he had a malignant tumor which had spread. Visits to his doctor and then a specialist revealed the lumps were the first sign of Dupuytren's contracture, a condition in which the connective tissue in the palm and fingers develops fibrous cords which gradually shorten, contracting the fingers into a bent position.

On February 20, Bachardy received a telephone call from Page. "Don is happy, now he smells England. I say I want nothing but his happiness. Well then, why aren't I rejoicing? Because I'm jealous. So what else is new."

Another, bigger piece of the bank at the bottom edge of the Adelaide lot slid into Ocean Avenue, closing the road. Great chunks of the retaining wall went with it. "They had to break it up with drills before they could truck it away." Through the spring, Isherwood recorded in his diary earthquakes of various magnitudes all over southern California. One night, he and Bachardy ran some of their old home movies, "sweet and nostalgic but saddening," Isherwood observed. "What phantoms such film-figures are; the bright flicker of activity and compulsive fun, gone in an instant and forever. And behind it, the mystery. What *is* Life really about?" Next came a cable from Page asking how soon Bachardy was arriving because he wanted to go with him to Morocco.[92]

Rehearsals for Isherwood's Shaw adaptation, *The Adventures of the Black*

Girl in Her Search for God, had begun on February 12, 1969, at the Center Theater Annex downtown. Douglas Campbell, a Scottish actor, took the role of the Irishman who becomes Bernard Shaw, and the Black Girl was played by Susan Batson, a black actress who had recently appeared in the original off-Broadway production of *Hair*. Isherwood attended rehearsals, and he saw great promise in Batson. There was African singing and dancing "directed by native experts," which Isherwood found very exciting. There was also, as he recorded, "interracial hostility" among the cast.[93]

In Shaw's satirical picaresque, the Candide-like questioning of the Black Girl, converted by a Christian missionary, exposes the contradictions and hypocrisy of the white man's religious doctrines and institutions—Christian, Muslim, scientific. The Black Girl is anti-authoritarian and a lively proto-feminist. Voltaire, appearing as a character, advises her to cultivate a garden to God's glory and to marry the Irishman. The black actors, led by Batson, complained the marriage was a sellout. Isherwood's script stayed close to Shaw's story, a requirement of the Shaw Estate, although he managed to change the ending.

Arguing continued into March. Batson was "splendid" in Isherwood's opinion, reviews were mixed, audiences were enthusiastic, and the show did good business.[94] There were nightly discussions between actors and audiences after the show, some heated about race. Isherwood and Batson appeared together on a TV arts show, *Tempo*, and they spoke at a round table fundraiser for the ACLU. Batson won the 1969 Los Angeles Drama Critics Best Performance Award for her Black Girl. There was even talk of a film.

In the middle of the excitement, John Lehmann arrived from London to lecture at UCLA on "British Poets of the Thirties." He stayed with Isherwood and Bachardy, who threw a dinner party for him, and he attended a preview of the play. At UCLA, Isherwood introduced Lehmann to the audience as "an absolutely unique authority on the thirties; the only person who had known its poets on three levels, as friend, fellow writer and editor-publisher." But Lehmann flunked his Hollywood debut. He read from a prepared script, "so dull and dead that I was quite embarrassed," wrote Isherwood, who was forced to admit to himself that their connection was emotionally finished. "Now he can say we have entertained him and introduced our friends to him. But it is the symbolic aspect of anything which really impresses him—for instance, that Don has had a drawing bought by the National Portrait Gallery and that he is going to draw the Harewoods."

The news from the National Portrait Gallery had come on March 6. The trustees had decided to buy Bachardy's 1967 drawing of Auden. Isherwood was thrilled. "His first sale to a public gallery!"[95] Moreover, Richard Buckle had secured Bachardy a commission to paint a first cousin of Queen

Elizabeth II, the Earl of Harewood and his Australian second wife. Symbolism had great meaning for Isherwood, too, when it gathered around Bachardy. Bachardy bought a ticket to fly to England on March 31.

Four days before Bachardy's planned departure, he and Isherwood spotted a beautiful four-masted schooner at anchor in the bay. "Don said, 'At last—our ship's come in!'" Within the hour, Robin French phoned to tell them a project was afoot to make a movie of *Cabaret*. Isherwood was asked to write the script, and Bachardy was accepted as his collaborator. Bachardy postponed his London trip indefinitely.

The proposed director was yet another British Tony, Anthony Harvey, who was having a big success with his film *The Lion in Winter*, adapted from the Broadway play about Henry II and Eleanor of Aquitaine. *The Lion in Winter* won three Academy Awards, including Best Actress for Katharine Hepburn, and Harvey had a Best Director nomination. "At present the whole thing seems too good to be true, because Tony is charming and our sort of person and he wants to get right away from the stage musical and shoot the picture on location in Germany," Isherwood reported.[96]

It was a complicated deal. Sidney Beckerman, president of Allied Artists, was buying the film rights, and Robin French secured a sale based on Isherwood's rights in John Van Druten's stage play, $6,000 to $7,000 a year for six years. Bachardy left for England after all; he was planning to stay with the Harewoods and draw them at Harewood House in Leeds and otherwise to stay with Page.

It was April 29 before French was able to finalize the second deal, for Isherwood and Bachardy to write the screenplay: $10,000 for a treatment, $90,000 for the screenplay, and a bonus of $25,000 if Isherwood and Bachardy were the sole credited authors. Bachardy rushed home on May 6; they roughed out a treatment in three weeks, revised it in two further drafts, and mailed it to Tony Harvey on June 9.

Harvey rejected it. Isherwood and Bachardy had trouble collecting their $10,000, and Harvey himself was soon off the project. But Isherwood's and Bachardy's lives were too full to spend time lamenting this fiasco.

Bachardy's friendship with Page continued to be volatile. About a week after arriving in London, Bachardy had moved out to Richard Buckle's in Covent Garden. Page was launching a new production of Thomas Middleton's 1657 tragedy *Women Beware Women*, a play he had directed for the Royal Shakespeare Company in 1962. His focus on that, followed by frustration when the production didn't go ahead, contributed to rising tension. But the romance wasn't over. They spent a weekend together in Devon, and when Bachardy returned to Santa Monica, there was a phone call followed by a letter: "I really just wanted to hear your voice," Bachardy wrote. "And it helped some though I still miss you terribly."⁹⁷ Page corresponded separately with Isherwood, asking him to write a screenplay of Evelyn Waugh's novel *A Handful of Dust*. Then he telephoned to discuss the project; Isherwood turned down the job.

In London, Marguerite Littman had told Bachardy that her close friend, reportedly her lover, John Foster, an Australian-born barrister, Conservative MP and professional mentor of her husband, had bought Hockney's portrait of Isherwood and Bachardy as a birthday present for her. The painting was exhibited in Hockney's New York show at the André Emmerich Gallery that spring. Afterwards, Marguerite hung it in her dining room, where it became familiar to her wide social circle. When Foster died in 1982, the painting was claimed by his estate, and she did not try to get it back, perhaps to avoid embarrassing her husband. According to Hockney's British dealer John Kasmin, who had hoped to see the painting go to the National Portrait Gallery, "Hockney was broken-hearted about this. He literally wept. I couldn't believe it had happened."⁹⁸ Since then, the portrait has been shown publicly a handful of times—in Berlin in 1997 for the centenary of the founding in 1897 of Magnus Hirschfeld's Scientific-Humanitarian Committee,⁹⁹ and in Hockney's major retrospectives in London, Paris, and New York in 2017 and 2018.

TAHITI AND AUSTRALIA, 1969

In May 1969, Tony Richardson asked Isherwood to revise a script for a film adaptation of *I, Claudius* by Robert Graves. "I said yes, *we* would; but am still not sure he really understands about my partnership with Don," Isherwood wrote in his diary. He and Bachardy began to discuss ideas. Richardson was then making a film about the Australian outlaw Ned Kelly with Mick Jagger in the title role. Bachardy longed to visit the set, "unimaginably far off in the Australian outback," as Isherwood wrote in his diary, so they decided to go via Tahiti, setting off in July.

It was one of the two place names that had haunted Isherwood since boyhood, Quito and Tahiti, the middle of the earth—on the equator in Ecuador—and the middle of the ocean. "Ben Masselink said in an article that he had thought of Tahiti every day of his life. I probably had too. I had thought of it as utterly alone (disregarding the thousands of other islands) on a vast blue empty map; the most distant point."¹⁰⁰

From Tahiti, they went by boat to Moorea and by plane to Bora Bora. On Western Samoa, Isherwood, ever the literary pilgrim, insisted on visiting the house and tomb of Robert Louis Stevenson. "[I]t was sort of a funeral rite on

Frank's behalf," he explained in his diary, "the very last of his South African letters I copied out before leaving is about the Stevensons and how he wishes he and Kathleen could have visited them." About nine locals pushed and dragged them to the tomb at the top of Mount Vaea. The view was "tremendous" with Stevenson's house, Vailima, below, the rooftops of the village, Apia, the mountains, and the vast ocean. The last two lines of Stevenson's "Requiem" appear on the tomb, and Isherwood recited the rest, "also a ritual act offered to Frank."

He told Bachardy that their first day on Tahiti was one of the happiest days of his life. The day on Western Samoa was another. "You get such a feeling of joy in these islands anyhow. Don was feeling it too and our being here together made it perfect."[101]

They flew on, via New Zealand, to Sydney and Canberra, met Neil Hartley and drove to the ranch, Palerang, where Richardson was shooting in a stony riverbed.

> Ned Kelly and the rest of the gang are trading for horses in the rain; a hose is spraying them. Tony Richardson looking like the Duke of Wellington, in a kind of Inverness mackintosh cape; we embraced in front of the whole crew and the actors, including Mick Jagger. It was such an improbable encounter, after these thousands of miles, like Stanley and Livingstone, rather.

Isherwood was impressed by Jagger, but when he saw *Ned Kelly* the following year, he found it "foggy" and confused and thought Jagger "miscast."[102]

He and Bachardy talked with Richardson about *I, Claudius* and submitted their outline. "[H]e seemed so languid and bored and yet dogmatic during these discussions that we were on the point of telling him to forget all about it. Then suddenly he said it was fine and we should go ahead."[103] On the way home to Los Angeles, Isherwood spent two days in Honolulu with Jim Charlton, who was living there, then caught up with Bachardy for a single week of work on the screenplay before Bachardy went on to London to meet Page.

ADELAIDE DRIVE, SANTA MONICA, 1969

By the time Bachardy returned to Santa Monica on September 8, Isherwood feared there wasn't time to meet Richardson's deadline. They submitted their screenplay on November 3; Richardson wrote saying he liked some of it, and they were paid, and then a month later, Isherwood heard that Richardson had written another script himself.

The surviving Isherwood–Bachardy draft is marked by the tensions between them. First of all, Bachardy didn't like the material: "*I, Claudius* is such a bore," he had written Isherwood from London.[104] Second, Isherwood was mad at Bachardy about the affair with Page. Third, as Isherwood recognized, *I, Claudius* was a sprawling challenge, with many characters and events to fit in, and they had wasted precious time.

They had turned all these issues into private jokes in their draft, which drew heavily on Graves's sequel, *Claudius the God*, about the marriage between Claudius and his third wife, seventeen-year-old Messalina. They saw Claudius—trained as a historian and secretly a diary keeper like Isherwood—as a patient, willfully blind Dobbin playing the fool to survive, and they saw Messalina, with her craving for power and her endless train of lovers, as a frantic kitten. Their Messalina begins by scratching her husband's face, drawing blood and blaming her bad behavior on boredom: "You say I'm an Empress, yet here I am, shut up with the servants! Please, can't I help you somehow—I mean <u>really</u> help?"

Thus they mocked Bachardy's push to control Isherwood by becoming his professional collaborator, and they mocked how Bachardy maximized his freedom to pursue his own ambitions and sexual appetites. Messalina wheedles for her own apartments, just as Bachardy had insisted on having his own studio at Adelaide Drive; she even invokes Plato to end their sexual relations: "After all, sex isn't essential to love if there's some other strong bond between the lovers. I do agree with Plato about that."[105]

Much of their dialogue satirizes the Dobbin–Kitty power struggle, parodying their own conversations and giving black comic insight into their relationship. When Messalina is killed, as in the novel, by a vassal of Claudius, Claudius survives on a potion that makes him feel like a god. KH3? Alertonic? He asks for a mirror and imagines he looks good. The script leaves him in a land of delusion.

Thus, the collaborators tried to package and seal the affair with Page. But the affair was not quite over, and it was tangled with their stage adaptation of *A Meeting by the River*, in which there was continuing interest from the Mark Taper Forum, from John Houseman and from Bridges. In London, Bachardy met with Robin French, Bridges, and Larson, and he reported discussions to Isherwood about possible directors and venues, including a Royal Court production directed either by Page or by Bridges. A British producer with financing had attached himself to the project, Clement Scott Gilbert; he visited Isherwood in Santa Monica and tried hard over many months to put together a London production, to no avail.

Meanwhile, Bachardy had confided in a letter to Isherwood that he wasn't getting on well with Page and that he wasn't certain he could work with him. According to Page, Bachardy had received a harsh insult from Page's circle. About a week before Bachardy arrived in London in August 1969 following the Tahiti trip, Page had told Procktor and the actor Nicol Williamson how much he admired the drawings Bachardy had done for the Osborne programs. Page recalled the following exchange between himself and Procktor:

> "But he's not an artist," said Patrick emphatically.
> "You can't say that."
> "I certainly can. Those are just magazine drawings."

Later, in Bachardy's presence, Williamson drunkenly reminded Page of the conversation, twisting it unkindly: "you both agreed that Don wasn't an artist." Page assured Bachardy that he had not agreed with Procktor. "I felt a terrible pain for him although he maintained a stylish apparently unaffected brightness for the rest of the meal."

That night, according to Page, Bachardy surreptitiously removed the revised script of *A Meeting by the River* which Page had been reading. The next night, he brought up Williamson's comment, telling Page that Williamson deliberately caused trouble because he wanted reassurance that Page cared for him; Page understood that Bachardy wanted the same reassurance: "I felt he was talking about himself," wrote Page. He saw the episode as ending his affair with Bachardy. "Later that night we made love fiercely, and the next morning he moved out."[106]

Page now wrote to Isherwood telling him he considered the novel *A Meeting by the River* better than the play and that he favored staging a dramatic reading. Isherwood replied that a dramatic reading offered him no fresh creative opportunity, described revisions he still had in mind for the play and finished coldly, "As for Lulu, I'm afraid I've rather lost my enthusiasm for it."

On Christmas Eve 1969, Isherwood received a telegram from Page asking for the return of the Lulu materials. Isherwood sent a paperbound book containing a version of the two plays in German, made by Kadidja Wedekind. Page never received it. During Isherwood's next visit to London, Peter Schlesinger tried to intercede. Isherwood still refused to see Page, so Page wrote him a note. Isherwood replied that he didn't want to meet. "[S]o that's that." Even then, intense emotion lingered. One day, Isherwood saw Page in the street near the Royal Court—"I was going into the Underground and had to pass quite close. Probably he saw me." Ten days later they bumped into each other at the opening of Hockney's first retrospective, at the Whitechapel Gallery, where they were surrounded by friends and acquaintances. This brought out the worst in Isherwood, as he unapologetically reported in his diary:

> I made rather a thing of shaking hands with him, which I now regret. Why not have just turned my back on him [...]? (When I got to the flat, yesterday, I found a note from him saying he is "very unhappy and distressed about everything; whatever my failings have been I've always wanted the friendship between you and Don and me to be there." Ha ha. She ends, "I'm simply writing now hoping your feelings will change and that we can make it up.")[107]

The next night, Isherwood had a dream about jealousy; repulsive eels kept turning into lovable kittens and then back into eels. Accidental meetings with Page continued awkwardly, along with Chinese whispers through Schlesinger and also Dodie Smith. Isherwood could not see that he was displacing onto Page the anger and sense of betrayal he felt toward Bachardy.

Page wrote to Bachardy in the new year, 1970, still trying for reconciliation. In his reply, Bachardy insisted nothing had gone wrong. "Your letter makes it seem as though you think there is a quarrel between us to be made up. I don't think that way. And I don't see that there is anything to 'forgive.' I just don't want to see you anymore."[108] Many years later, Page and Bachardy were to renew their acquaintance, and in 2018, Page was to direct Isherwood and Bachardy's adaptation of *A Meeting by the River* in a two-part podcast starring Dominic West as Patrick and Kyle Soller as Oliver.

BACHARDY WAS DETERMINED to prove that he was not merely a magazine artist as Procktor had said, and he refocused on his art career at the beginning of 1970. He had been working toward another show at the Rex Evans Gallery when Evans suddenly died of a heart attack in April 1969. "One of the last things he did was to send a notice to the *Los Angeles Times* about Don's drawing of Wystan being bought by the National Portrait Gallery," Isherwood had noted in his diary. Evans's companion of twenty years, Jim Weatherford, planned to keep the gallery going, so Bachardy continued to paint with the show in mind. Then he was contacted by another gallerist, Irving Blum, and decided to move on.

Blum had visited Bachardy's studio to see Bachardy's work at the end of June 1969, and he wanted to show the drawings. Blum "shows very New Order people like Lichtenstein, Oldenburg and Newman," Bachardy had told Page. "He says he's wanted to ask me for a long time but never dared because he was a friend of Rex Evans."[109] Contemporary California artists like Ed Ruscha and Ed Moses were also exhibited by Blum. Bachardy had been saying for a long time that he didn't want another drawing show, but Blum did not want to show the paintings. By Christmas 1969, they agreed on a show of drawings for early 1970. The subject was to be artists, art dealers, and art-world figures.

Bachardy secured sittings with Roy Lichtenstein, Richard Diebenkorn, Robert Irwin, Larry Bell, the collector Betty Asher, Henry Geldzahler, curator of twentieth-century art at the Metropolitan Museum in New York, and Brooke Hopper, daughter of the Hollywood super-agent Leland Hayward and wife of Dennis Hopper with whom she collected. He had already drawn Hockney and Bacon. In January, he went to New York, where he drew Andy Warhol at the Factory, Jasper Johns, and Salvador Dalí.

Isherwood joined him in New York on January 30, and they continued together to London; then Bachardy returned alone to Los Angeles for his opening with Blum in March. He captured the lead position in the *Los Angeles Times*'s coverage of local exhibitions: "His technique is, itself, glamorous, existing in a tradition stretching from Ingres to *Vogue* magazine illustrations. But he gives us more than the superficial gloss of faces from a public demimonde. They are finally psychological studies." Beside the review, like a prophecy, was a reproduction of Bachardy's portrait of Nicholas Wilder, whose career as a dealer was on the rise.

Bachardy was receiving growing support from fellow artists. Isherwood recorded that the strapping, Kansas-born, motorcycle-riding, surfing, womanizing dynamo Billy Al Bengston, whom Bachardy had first met in 1967 when *Harper's Bazaar* commissioned him to do Bengston's portrait, said "that all the artists he knows who have seen Don's work think very highly of it and that the opinion of artists is all that matters in the long run, Don just has to wait until their opinion is accepted which will probably take at least two years or more."[110] Bengston also said he wanted to show Bachardy's work at his own studio, which doubled as a commercial gallery.

CHELSEA, LONDON, 1970

Isherwood stayed in England for two months trying to push forward a London production of *A Meeting by the River*. He kept a detailed diary and worked on *Kathleen and Frank*, again visiting Richard and collecting more material from Wyberslegh. He lived in a Chelsea flat belonging to his old friend Bill Harris, arranged by Bachardy who paid Harris with forty dollars' worth of amyl nitrite.

Twice Isherwood visited Forster in Cambridge. When he got the news in June that Forster had collapsed in the dining hall at King's and died in Coventry with the Buckinghams, he cried a little but decided not to be sad. "I have been living so long with him in my head that I know he won't fade out until I do." Vidal, who so disliked Forster, remarked, "Well, we've all moved up one rung higher."

Isherwood met with Forster's biographer and friend Nick Furbank, who gave him photocopies of some early Forster stories that Isherwood had not seen before, but Isherwood could not return the gesture, explaining to Furbank that he didn't want Forster's letters to him used in the biography. Furbank asked how "intimate" Auden had been with Forster. "I said not very, and added that Wystan has always found it difficult to be intimate—he's shy in that way. Even this little confidence I somehow regretted as soon as I'd made it."[111] Isherwood was as anxious as ever to keep control of his material, and he was protective of his friends, especially Auden.

He made some new, younger friends, including the American novelist David Plante, met through Spender, and the ballet dancer Wayne Sleep, met in Los Angeles when Sleep was on tour there with the Royal Ballet. One Saturday night, Robert Medley threw Isherwood a party thick with painters, dancers, Cambridge dons, actors both aspiring and successful, and even Christopher Gibbs, antique-dealer friend of the Rolling Stones, who brought greetings from Jagger. In his diary, Isherwood described the alluring, hip bohemianism of this all-male London frolic at the dawn of the 1970s. The next morning, he found Hockney's portrait of himself and Bachardy in the Sunday papers, in an *Observer* spread about Hockney. He was back at the heart of the London scene from which he and Auden had departed in 1938 for China, but the scene had been transformed, and so had he.

On March 23, he flew to Nice with Hockney and Schlesinger, and Hockney drove them to Tony Richardson's new property, Le Nid du Duc, then took them on what Isherwood called a "whiz tour" to Carcassonne, Arles, Aigues-Mortes, Nîmes, Les Baux. Isherwood was terrified by the speed at which Hockney drove, "literally, at 100 mph," he reported to Bachardy, but he found both Schlesinger and Hockney irresistible: "And indeed this trip has made me love them both even more than before."[112]

Back at Le Nid du Duc, he described in his diary the games, repartee, and squabbles among the large cast Richardson had assembled for the Easter holiday, including Hartley and Regester, the playwright Edward Albee, Richardson's two little daughters, a nanny, a secretary, a chauffeur, a housekeeper, five miniature greyhounds and a parrot. "Le Nid de Duc," Isherwood wrote, "is a former village of about eight houses, old stone buildings on the slopes of a steep valley, amidst cork oaks, with a stream tumbling in occasional waterfalls." Peacocks wandered through the grounds, and there was a heated swimming pool.

Richardson had invited Hockney to convert one building into a studio; Hockney never did, but he returned often and made some dazzling paintings of the locale. His 1972 *Portrait of an Artist (Pool with Two Figures)* shows Schlesinger bending to look into the pool at an underwater swimmer—evoking Schlesinger's life partner, Swedish designer Eric Boman, about to surface as the Hockney–Schlesinger love affair foundered. It is one of Hockney's most beautiful paintings. In the background of the painting, "Low wooded hills rise into a gap of light toward the sea," exactly as Isherwood had described in his diary.[113]

Isherwood felt anxious for Hockney. After the retrospective at the Whitechapel, he wrote:

> David's overwhelming success must make anyone who loves him (and I do) afraid. Surely the world will make him pay for it, cruelly. For David is not only a "golden boy," as the press calls him, but a crusader for his way of life, for our minority. (He kissed me on the mouth, without the least affectation, when I came into the gallery.) Many people must be gunning for him.

These were the fears of a past generation. Hockney handled his public situation confidently, without hiding his sexuality. Isherwood was soon to demonstrate again that he was able to learn from the young as well as teach them.

All the while, he was privy to the difficulties arising between Hockney and Schlesinger. Schlesinger, like Bachardy, wanted more freedom and more privacy; in particular he wanted his own apartment. Isherwood's diary attests that he considered warning Hockney about being too possessive but held his tongue. When Isherwood left London on April 29, Schlesinger, who had begun to wear silver paint on his eyelids, told him, "You cheered me up."[114]

ADELAIDE DRIVE, SANTA MONICA, 1970

Back in Santa Monica, Isherwood devoted himself to *Kathleen and Frank* and to further revising the stage adaptation of *A Meeting by the River*. On May 28, Hockney unexpectedly arrived from London. "He seems to have left England quite suddenly. Don feels there is something wrong between him and Peter. David merely said he had to get away and draw." Hockney began working right away, drawing everything in his hotel room at the Miramar.

He joined them for supper, and Isherwood felt he "wasn't entirely present." Later, in a letter to Isherwood and Bachardy, Hockney explained that he had grown bored by sex with Schlesinger and begun making trips to California for the bar scene. But he found the pickup scene lonely, missed Schlesinger, and felt eager to get back to him. Schlesinger told Hockney's biographer that Hockney kept his Los Angeles sex affairs to himself, and that Schlesinger discovered them only when he saw Hockney's drawings of the boys.[115]

Over Memorial Day weekend in L.A., Hockney, Isherwood, and Bachardy went to a Gay-In at Griffith Park. For Isherwood, this proved to be an in-person public debut in the gay liberation movement. One of his former students, Lee Heflin, introduced them to Morris Kight, who had founded the Gay Liberation Front in 1969. Kight was directing the proceedings "wearing a silk dressing gown and a funny hat." He presented Isherwood to the crowd and asked him to speak: "so I said, in my aw-shucks voice, 'I just came here because I'm with you and wanted to show it.'"

Only a few months earlier, Isherwood had appeared in an eight-part NBC television documentary about the lifestyles of homosexuals. His performance was praised by Evelyn Hooker, Gavin Lambert, and George Cukor, and the interview was reused in a one-hour TV special, *Out of the Shadows*, promoted in local TV listings as a look at "a little-known subculture in Los Angeles." *Out of the Shadows* was broadcast in June. It included interviews with a minister of a homosexual church, the transsexual Christine Jorgensen, psychiatrists, and what the newspapers called "members of the homophile community."[116]

On TV, Isherwood was joining a national conversation which had begun in 1967, when Mike Wallace presented on CBS the first-ever network news report on homosexuality, "The Homosexuals." Isherwood and Bachardy watched "The Homosexuals" the night it aired, March 7, 1967. It gave a frightening picture of what the gay liberation movement was up against two years before Stonewall. CBS had commissioned a survey which found that Americans considered homosexuality more harmful to society than adultery, abortion, or prostitution; moreover, Wallace reported:

> The CBS news survey shows that two out of three Americans look upon homosexuals with disgust, discomfort, or fear. One out of ten says "hatred." A vast majority believe that homosexuality is an illness. Only ten percent say it is a crime, and yet, and here's the paradox, the majority of Americans favor legal punishment even for homosexual acts performed in private between consenting adults. The homosexual, bitterly aware of his rejection, responds by going underground.

Shadowy black-and-white footage showed secret clubs, lonely city streets, the men's room arrest of a nineteen-year-old boy. Faces were concealed, apart from one brave, articulate young man speaking directly to camera about the importance of his sexuality to his inmost sense of self. He said that he felt no more guilt about being homosexual than about having blond hair.

Wallace's monologue gripped like a horror movie: "No one knows how many homosexuals there are in the United States. There is no reliable way to find out, for most of them are unwilling to acknowledge it. [...] This much is certain, male homosexuals in America number in the millions and their number is growing."

The program was complete with distinguished expert psychiatrists pronouncing beliefs of the time, that "Homosexuality is in fact a mental illness which has reached epidemiological proportions," that no one is born homosexual, that homosexuality is typically caused in the first three years of childhood by an overanxious mother preventing her son from joining the rough and tumble of masculine play, that prevention and cure were up to the father whom the psychiatrists called upon to stop competing with and belittling the son and instead to engage with him intimately and affectionately. "The father can do a great deal [...] first he recognizes this is *his* son as much as it is his wife's son." The "disease" was threatening family life and traditional values: "The average homosexual, if there be such, is promiscuous. He is not interested in nor capable of a lasting relationship like that of a heterosexual marriage. His sex life, his love life, consists of a series of chance encounters at the clubs and bars he inhabits and even on the streets of the city." According to the experts, the "Happy Homosexual" was "a myth": "The fact that somebody is homosexual, a true obligatory homosexual, automatically rules out the possibility that he will remain happy for long."

Gore Vidal, among the last to be interviewed, scoffed at it all. He invoked Gide, argued that homosexuality was the most natural thing in the world, practiced since the dawn of time, and pronounced American sexual mores the laughing stock of Europe. Marriage, said Vidal, was outmoded; the idea of having sex with only one person for sixty years was nonsense. He roguishly denied any special influence of homosexuals in the arts even though he and Isherwood and others they knew had for years strategized how to acquire and use such influence: "the artist is an artist first and a homosexual or heterosexual second. I've never seen any sign in any of the arts of there being a 'homintern' as alarmed editorialists like to write."[117]

Isherwood was invited to speak at the National Gay Students Liberation Conference in San Francisco in August 1970. He could not help being attracted by the kind of national attention Vidal was receiving, but he refused the invitation because he feared embarrassing Prabhavananda "by making a spectacle of myself which would shock his congregation and the women of Vedanta Place!"

A year went by, and he searched his conscience again, this time about taking part in the Christopher Street West Parade, the second annual Gay Pride parade commemorating the 1969 Stonewall Riot on Christopher Street in New York. He longed to be "one of the Grand Old Men of the movement," but dismissed it as "vanity."

It was 1975 before Isherwood's public engagement with gay liberation caused any distress at the Vedanta Society. He appeared in a question-and-answer session at Cal. State Long Beach as part of the college's Gay Pride Week. William Scobie, a journalist friend, wrote it up for the *Advocate*. Scobie's piece fell into the hands of a nun who was "terribly shocked." But Isherwood decided her reaction was old-fashioned: "she was afraid all the queers would now start coming to the temple! As if they hadn't started thirty years ago!" The next time they met, he was with Bachardy, and the nun "couldn't have been friendlier."[118] Her hypocrisy convinced him to move on from the issue.

His religious life was undergoing a revival in the early 1970s as he became increasingly aware of Prabhavananda's solitude and mortality. He saw Prabhavananda as a hero in the mold of Forster, nourished by an invisible wellspring within himself, a wellspring Isherwood labeled with a touchstone phrase from *Howards End*: "Swami has lived all these years in an alien land, amidst the most alienating people and surroundings, and now he is an old man and all alone—for however much we love him we can none of us really understand him—and behold, 'The inner life has paid,' his faith is its own absolute reward."

In July 1969, before the Australia trip, Isherwood had borrowed the key and let himself into the shrine room in Hollywood, trying to reanimate the spiritual energy of 1943, when he had lived at the monastery and made the shrine his nighttime companion. "It seemed extraordinarily important to do this, though I didn't 'feel' anything much while I was in there." A week later, at the Trabuco shrine, he had "sat in the dark, saying, 'speak to me.' It didn't. In fact I couldn't possibly feel drier than I do now." So he had continued to rely on Swami. "He sits there and shines. He is the beacon which shows the way out through the reef."[119]

After the Australia trip, Isherwood discovered a new method of meditating at home; he imagined that he was sitting alone in front of the shrine, exposing himself to its power. "The shrine is a piece of furniture that is *alive*. I have to be absolutely alone with it to feel this; it's a sense of radiation. You don't do anything, don't even pray, just expose yourself to the radiation." On another occasion, he explained in his diary: "When I am alone I get the sense of confrontation, the 'setting face to face' which is so wonderful and which I try to recapture when I'm meditating here at home."[120] Thus, he conjured the shrine in his imagination, just as he conjured characters in his head when he was writing.

At his request, Prabhavananda gave Isherwood new instructions for meditation in late August 1970.[121] Isherwood found it difficult to imagine God in any abstract way, but the acts of devotion and the personalities—Ramakrishna, his wife Sarada Devi, Vivekananda, and Brahmananda—were real to him. "And when I try to assemble the two Ramakrishnas, Maharaj, and Swamiji in the room I get a feeling, *where are they all going to sit?*"[122]

One day, with Prabhavananda, "I tried to meditate on the fact that I was in the presence of The Guru." Focusing in the presence of the Guru helped Isherwood prepare to meditate in the absence of the Guru: "I find that I can now meditate on the memory of having done this, just as I meditate on the memory of having sat in front of the shrine."[123] In Prabhavananda's room, where they sometimes meditated, Prabhavananda's guru, Brahmananda, was represented by a photograph hanging over the mantelpiece. When Isherwood summoned this photograph to mind, he felt: "Swami is always in his presence." It was the mise en abyme all over again, a saint in the presence of another saint, belief guaranteed by belief. As he had once felt excited and compelled by the borderline between life and art, Isherwood now felt excited and compelled by the borderline between life and the spirit.

Late in 1972, he began meditating on a photograph of Sarada Devi, and he imagined other monastics gathering with him to worship. He directed them like the cast of a play inside his head: "I try to conjure up the shrine with all of them sitting in it, and I say the meditations Swami told me to say as if they were being said by different monks and nuns in turn, or else speaking in chorus."

These mental practices were a bulwark against solitude and death. "I feel that I would not be at all afraid to die, if I might be carried to Swami's room to do it, or even put in front of the shrine." The boy who had feared to pass a night alone had grown into a man who gathered a crowd around him in his meditation while he prepared for his death. The glass animals that had starred in Christopher's toy theater were replaced by Hindu saints and California monastics, conjured before Isherwood's mind's eye. Bachardy, too, was present at the mental shrine: "I can picture him sitting across from me, also at Swami's feet, as he so often does."[124]

In September 1970, Prabhavananda told Isherwood that it had been very difficult for him to run the Hollywood Vedanta Center: "I had no education." Isherwood was surprised, "those English-run Calcutta colleges had very high standards in his day," he wrote in his diary, but "I suddenly saw that he must have felt his lack of education strongly in the presence of Aldous and Gerald—but then, anyone who didn't would have been a fool." Prabhavananda went on to confide "that he wished so much I had stayed with them, so I'd now be able to give lectures." Prabhavananda was still waiting for Belur Math to send him an assistant who could one day take over the center; Isherwood, with his education, would have been the ideal conduit for Prabhavananda's mission—some of which had already been fulfilled in the books they had made together. Isherwood recorded in his diary that he had no regrets:

> haven't I, by doing what I did do, fulfilled at least a part of my *dharma*? How can I regret the books I've written since then? [. . .] My life with Don has been happiness-unhappiness raised to an intensity I'd never dreamed of before, much more and better than that, it's been a discipline in which I've often failed but from which I've learnt a great deal of what I now know.[125]

Isherwood had a special status at the Vedanta Center that was widely recognized. One Indian swami who was briefly groomed as Prabhavananda's successor took trouble to treat Isherwood with special courtesy; at pujas, he called Isherwood first after the monastics to be touched by the relics. Prabhavananda permitted Bachardy to participate alongside Isherwood as his partner; Isherwood and Bachardy made pranams together when they visited him. At home, they meditated at the same time in different rooms. Isherwood wrote in his diary that their bond over Vedanta, "has formed very slowly, imperceptibly almost, and yet it is perhaps the most important feature of our whole relationship."

Bachardy felt differently. On a car journey to Palm Springs to stay with the film director John Schlesinger one Christmas, Isherwood asked how he felt about his meditation: "he said that it is now definitely part of his life but that he doesn't at all share my reliance on Swami as a guru. 'If anybody's my guru, you are.'"[126]

Prabhavananda still bound Isherwood to him with literary tasks. In 1973, Isherwood was revising and writing an introduction to Prabhavananda's translations of *Narada Bhakti Sutras*, rewriting Prabhavananda's Shankara translation, *A Garland of Questions and Answers*, and writing a foreword to Chetanananda's Vivekananda anthology on meditation. Serving his guru and renewing his efforts in meditation built up extraordinary emotion inside Isherwood. One night toward the end of 1973, Prabhavananda asked Isherwood whether "I had had any experiences." This was a trigger: "I found myself instantly in a state of emotion. I told him that if I hadn't met him my life would have been nothing, that I knew this now, and that I like best to meditate on his room because I know that Maharaj is there. My voice was shaking and tears ran down my face." Such scenes of emotion and release were to happen again and to be recorded in Isherwood's diary.[127]

Isherwood also recorded encounters showing that Prabhavananda deliberately challenged his complacency. In April 1973, Isherwood had asked Prabhavananda whether he would have given sannyas to Gerald Heard if Heard had stayed at the monastery. Prabhavananda said yes, "And you, too, Chris—even now—why don't you come back to us?" Prabhavananda joked later the same day that "Chris is going to become a monk!" sowing doubt in Isherwood's mind. "Doesn't Swami accept my present way of life, after all? I had begun to believe that he did." On another occasion Prabhavananda criticized Isherwood harshly for asking impertinent questions about Brahmananda in public. Isherwood was forgiven, and came to the conclusion that "his scolding had really been a true blessing." After all, Prabhavananda had shared stories about scoldings he himself had received from Brahmananda which he had learned to see as blessings. On another occasion, Isherwood overheard Prabhavananda saying to one of the nuns: "I don't scold you for now but for after I'm gone."[128]

Prabhavananda was weakened by heart problems and careful how he used his energy. "I feel that our relations are so much less personal than they used to be," Isherwood wrote in February 1974. "There is no shit here, no sentimentality, absolutely none. And I do feel 'in the presence' when I am with him—the truth is, 'he' has very nearly disappeared."[129]

Accounts of his religious experiences increasingly filled Isherwood's diary. As his spiritual life gained importance, connections between his religion and his homosexuality became more obvious to him in hindsight. He was later to state clearly, "my personal approach to Vedanta was, among other things, the approach of a homosexual looking for a religion which will accept him."[130] Vedanta had been a refuge, but it had also been a way to break out, to find liberation in all senses of the word.

ISHERWOOD'S POSITION IN the gay liberation movement was far from avant-garde. In 1970, he had attended a group called the Society of David and found himself cast as "an old liberal square celebrity" confronting "the young activists of the Gay Liberation Front." He sensed disapproval from the radical leadership: "A big swarthy baldish guy named Don Kilhafter (I think) put me down, without absolutely directly attacking me personally. Old Kight aided him without seeming to." The dynamic felt familiar;

Isherwood noted in his diary that Kilhefner (as it was spelled) "had the more-engaged-than-thou, dogmatical rudeness of a thirties left-winger."[131]

Evelyn Hooker asked him to lend his writing skills to promote her psychological research, much as he had loaned them to Prabhavananda to promote Vedanta: "She wants me to work with her on a 'popular' book on homosexuality," Isherwood noted in December 1970. They had first planned this in the early 1950s, when he was living in her garden house. Since then, she had tried and failed to write an academic book by herself, and the effort had driven her to a mental health breakdown and a spell in Mount Sinai Hospital.

Hooker had first presented her work to her peers at a conference in Chicago in 1956, marshaling Rorschach tests to show that similar percentages of homosexuals and heterosexuals were psychologically normal. This minority view was mentioned by Mike Wallace in his 1967 TV news report, and yet, more than a decade after Hooker's paper, the majority opinion that homosexuality was an illness still prevailed. In the meantime, she had published further academic articles based on her voluminous interviews, counseling notes, and other clinical tests.

The pressure on Hooker was extreme. She had lived alone since her husband died of a heart attack in 1957, and in 1961, she had been indicted by a grand jury, along with four others, for conspiracy to obtain a criminal abortion for a young woman; Hooker's indictment was dropped for lack of evidence, but she believed the police had pursued the charges against her because of her work on homosexuality. They had visited her university office to question her, threatening her job, and she became so anxious that she decided to remove from her files personal information that might identify her subjects. This consumed a whole year.

She leaned heavily on Isherwood, asking him to read sixty case histories and turn them into accessible prose. "She seemed very emotional still; once she actually shed a few tears while describing the goodness of her sister to her during her breakdown. [. . .] She is a very good woman and her intentions are of the noblest and I would like to help her." She gave him two files early in 1971, but Isherwood was dismayed by the impenetrable jargon. "I really can't imagine myself working with Evelyn on this sort of thing; it would be like having to write a book in a foreign language."[132] Translating from Sanskrit with Swami was different. He was forced to tell Hooker that he couldn't collaborate with her.

He was nevertheless influenced and radicalized by her work. Toward the end of 1970, he received a visit from a gay liberation activist, Michael Silverstein, and recorded some of Silverstein's thinking: "He dislikes the idea of presenting 'normal' queers to the world (as Evelyn Hooker wants to do in her book) because he says how can any of us be normal as long as we are subjected to this persecution." A few days later, Isherwood revised a sentence about himself in *Kathleen and Frank* to be "much more aggressive." Instead of "he is now quite certain that heterosexuality wouldn't have suited him. And he has always felt content and well-adjusted, being as he is," he wrote, "Despite the humiliations of living under a heterosexual dictatorship and the fury he has often felt against it, Christopher has never regretted being as he is. He is now quite certain that heterosexuality wouldn't have suited him; it would have fatally cramped his style." Though he attributed this change to Silverstein's visit, Isherwood's line of thought in fact grows out of concepts made familiar to him by Hooker. A decade earlier, after discussing her paper "The Homosexual Community" (presented to a convention of psychologists in Copenhagen), Isherwood had written in his diary, "I must say, she makes it sound madly glamorous and thrilling, a mixture of the Mafia, the Foreign Legion and Alice Through the Looking-Glass. She refers to a heterosexual as 'a representative of the dominant culture'!"[133]

Kathleen and Frank was the first piece of writing in which Isherwood, without a fictional mask of any kind, made clear that he was homosexual. The British press had led the way in August 1970 with a profile of him in the *Daily Telegraph* (by Brendan Lehane) that "says I am homosexual, quite flatly, without further explanation." Soon Isherwood was saying that he didn't know why it took him so long. "I regret that I didn't do it earlier in one way or another and I think perhaps I should have," he told an interviewer in 1972: "But I never felt that I was concealing it, as far as my own life and my own relations with other people were concerned. In the first place, over a great period of my life I lived in a domestic relationship with some other man, and we've always gone around everywhere together."

His life with Bachardy in Hollywood was brave, if not reckless; so was his life with all his earlier boyfriends; but explicitly stating and insisting on his homosexuality was new. Among writers of his stature, he was one of the first to do so. Despite being a leftist, he had never joined the Communist Party, and he had been as cagey about stating political convictions as he had been about stating his sexuality, always relying on the veil of fiction. Now he encouraged others to come out, too, and from the summer of 1971 onward, he promoted his sexuality, making certain "to talk to all interviewers about my queerness."[134]

His age and his fame made him a model for others; the young looked up to him as a father figure offering unique affirmation by his way of life and his relationship with Bachardy. But it was through his books rather than his activism that Isherwood made his contribution to gay liberation. He should be remembered not with politicians like Harvey Milk or Franklin Kameny, but with younger writers like James Baldwin, Allen Ginsberg, Jan Morris, and of course his friends Gore Vidal, Truman Capote, John Rechy, Thom Gunn for changing attitudes with his art. They along with Isherwood's immediate forebears Forster, Woolf, D.H. Lawrence, Gide, even Maugham helped prepare the ground for a gigantic culture shift by changing imagination and perception below the surface, by redefining what was acceptable, even sought after, in any drawing room, by offering new ideals of the beautiful and the lovable. Only a skilled artist can alter taste and sensibility, leading the way for concrete political change. Hockney and Bacon also contributed to this change. As an out writer, Isherwood offered special inspiration to a next generation including Edmund White, Armistead Maupin, Alan Hollinghurst, and, later, Olivia Laing.

Despite his outspoken commitment to the movement, when Isherwood learned that a new foundation to lobby for the rights of gays and lesbians was using his name—the Isherwood–Radclyffe Foundation—he objected: "it will compromise me; I shall have all the disadvantages of being dead without any of the advantages."[135] He insisted his name be dropped, and it became instead the Whitman–Radclyffe Foundation. His name was as personal as ever, and, more important, he was still creating the literary identity attached to it.

ISHERWOOD TARGETED HIS sixty-sixth birthday as the deadline to finish his draft of *Kathleen and Frank*. The project continued to affect him deeply. His mother's diary account of her search for Frank "nearly makes me cry whenever I read it," he wrote in July 1970. Also, the project opened the way for his next book: "I see that I can't write very much about Christopher at the end; it would be beginning another story."[136] He sent copies of *Kathleen and Frank* to his publishers toward the end of November.

Billy Al Bengston, as good as his word, invited Bachardy to exhibit in a group show at his studio with "a very distinguished gathering," as Isherwood noted,[137] the core of the developing Venice art scene—Ed Moses, Larry Bell, Joe Goode, Tony Berlant, Ron Davis, Ed Ruscha, Ken Price, Peter Alexander, and John McCracken. All were to have big careers, rooted in the physicality and outdoor brilliance of Californian life and in the polished glamour of Hollywood. Los Angeles-born Peter Alexander—willowy, curly-headed, educated in architecture as well as sculpture and painting, passionate about all forms of beauty—became with Bengston one of Bachardy's closest artist friends.

Isherwood invested in these nascent bonds. One day he accompanied Bachardy, Bengston, Joe Goode, and two girlfriends, Penny Little and the writer Mary Agnes Donoghue, to watch motorcycle races at Ascot Park in Gardena: "We did it, as Don said, for 'business'—" Isherwood wrote in his diary. It was the kind of Hemingwayesque adventure which impressed him even though he could not take it fully seriously: "they were really just like bullfight fans. And as always with aficionados you wondered, justly or unjustly, can they *possibly* care that much?"

Bengston's flirtatious macho fascinated and challenged Isherwood: "What a masked, playacting character he is!" He grew fond of him, and studied his work until in 1978, looking at some new watercolors, "I had a sudden insight into the quality of Billy's art in general [. . .] it all seemed to relate to itself as one enormously long chain of variations on his themes."[138]

In December 1970, Bachardy had a joint show in San Francisco with Ed Ruscha, and the following March, he exhibited in "Drawings '71" at the San Pedro Municipal Gallery alongside Bengston, Goode, Alexander, Price, Ruscha and others. He was emerging as a visual diarist of his group, depicting the intimate friends of his artistic generation as Isherwood had depicted Auden, Upward, and Spender in *Lions and Shadows*. "Don Bachardy presents suave Ingres-like portraits of artists. He draws very well but his major talent is in evoking character," wrote William Wilson in the *Los Angeles Times*.[139] Bachardy's pencil drawing of Peter Alexander with brooding liquid eyes and hair like wildfire was the only item from "Drawings '71" reproduced in the newspaper.

In January 1971, Isherwood and Bachardy started work on a TV adaptation of *Frankenstein* for Hunt Stromberg Jr. As with *I, Claudius*, they transformed *Frankenstein* into a camp about themselves. This time they lighted on a universal homosexual narrative in which the monster created by Dr. Frankenstein implicitly represents the "monstrous" homosexual so many Americans feared—solitary, loveless, predatory.

Mary Shelley had titled her novel *Frankenstein: or the Modern Prometheus*, but Isherwood and Bachardy drew less on Prometheus and more on Pygmalion—the sculptor who falls in love with his statue—which George Bernard Shaw put on the stage and in which their friends Rex Harrison and Audrey Hepburn appeared in the film version of the Lerner and Loewe musical *My Fair Lady*, directed by yet another friend, George Cukor. Their monster is indeed "fair" until the moral depravity of his makers begins to show in his face. On one level, they were playing with the story of Bachardy, brought to life by Isherwood and gradually corrupted. Thanks to Wilde's *The Picture of Dorian Gray*, in which the portrait hidden in the attic reveals the moral decay of the young man who continues outwardly to look young and innocent, their script offered a tale easily decoded by their tribe.

The struggles of their Frankenstein's creature hilariously exaggerated

Bachardy's predicament, and sly, charming, old-fashioned Dr. Polidori—the mad scientist they named after Byron's real-life physican, John Polidori—parodied Isherwood's. The hands of their Polidori have been eaten away by an accident with his chemicals, symbolizing the moral deformity which results from his craze for power. Because of his hands, Polidori depends on an assistant, just as Isherwood with his arthritis and his Dupuytren's contracture depended on Bachardy to type for him.

Bachardy did far more on the script than type. In his diary, Isherwood muttered: "without him I wouldn't work on the fucking thing at all. And he does very often have good and even brilliant ideas." Isherwood was eager for the income, despite the fact that he and Bachardy had sizable savings and had even made a real estate investment to offset their taxes: "although we have about $74,000 in the savings accounts, plus the Hilldale property half paid for, I always feel we ought to have more, to at least not start living on capital."[140] He had become as financially careful as his mother.

Covertly, Isherwood and Bachardy made their relationship the butt of their script collaborations, but Isherwood found he could not write anything else about their life together. While they were at work on *Frankenstein*, he began what he called "a sort of notebook on Kitty and Dobbin": "I'll try to write it rather like a study in natural history; their behavior, methods of communication, feeding habits, etc. I had a very strong feeling that I ought not to record all this, that it was an invasion of privacy. But where else have I ever found anything of value? The privacy of the unconscious is the only treasure house."

In the past, when he had written about his friends, Isherwood had consumed the friendship in the work, extinguishing the mystery through his exploration. He sensed a risk, and after two months, he decided that his history of the Animals had failed. "I shall never, as long as we are together, be able to fully feel or describe to myself all that our love means; it is much much too close to me."[141]

As collaborators, Isherwood and Bachardy grew closer than ever. Despite repeatedly bolting for freedom, Bachardy identified more and more closely with Isherwood. One morning, after knocking off scriptwriting, they made an interview tape about Bachardy's portrait work, his methods and his attitudes to his sitters. "We were both amazed to find how alike our voices sounded," wrote Isherwood in his diary. "If bits of this tape had been played to me, I couldn't have been certain who was speaking."[142]

As with Caskey, Isherwood was now content to give up the driver's seat in the car whenever he and Bachardy drove together. But Bachardy's fast driving played on his nerves, so Isherwood began to lie down in the back of the Volkswagen. From there, he could see only treetops and tall buildings. In

August 1972, Bachardy bought a white four-door Fiat so that it was easier for Isherwood to get in and out of the back. Eventually, they added a blanket and pillow. "[W]e have long intimate talks, punctuated only occasionally by a terrific jerk as he stands on the brake, having just avoided a smash!"[143] The white Fiat was a new incarnation of the mail cart (also white) in which Kathleen and Nanny had pushed the infant Christopher around the Cheshire countryside.

Isherwood called these years in the early 1970s "my idea of 'the earthly paradise.' " He wrote about Bachardy that he treasured "the wonderful intimacy of sitting with him in the movies and feeling his closeness. And the joy of waking with him in the basket—the painful but joyful tenderness—painful only because I am always so aware that it can't last forever or even for very long, Kitty and Old Drub will have to say goodbye."[144]

In 1973, he asked Bachardy about sex. According to Isherwood's diary, Bachardy replied that "he doesn't mind our not having sex together anymore; he agreed with me that our relationship is still very physical." They slept in the same bed, and Bachardy later recalled that they did once or twice have sex after this time. By 1975, Isherwood was writing that he and Bachardy were "no longer entirely separate people; and I do suspect that we communicate deeply during sleep." His compassion for Bachardy's situation was ever-growing. "Some of the inner rage he feels against me is because of the fact that I am going to leave him. He feels that this is a trick which I shall play on him—have, indeed, already played, by involving us so with each other."[145]

After they finished the *Frankenstein* script in September 1971, Isherwood finally had to go under the knife for his Dupuytren's contracture. He spent two days in the California Hospital in downtown L.A., "the frontier post of death."[146] The operation took about an hour, and he came home with his left hand in a bandage and splint. He used this as an excuse to cancel his publicity tour to England for the publication of *Kathleen and Frank*. The real reason was that Caskey planned to be in London at the same time looking for a publisher and a gallery for his photographs. Isherwood and in particular Bachardy did not want to see him. In fact, Isherwood was in vigorous health and recovered quickly from the hand surgery.

A few days after the operation, he got a telephone call from Hockney "from London in tears," as he wrote in his diary. Hockney had just received a letter from Isherwood commiserating over his split from Schlesinger. Schlesinger had sent Isherwood and Bachardy a postcard saying that he had left Hockney, but on the phone, Hockney seemed surprised. Isherwood wrote to Schlesinger "begging him to be absolutely frank with David." Schlesinger wrote again, making clear that he and Hockney had thoroughly discussed their relationship over many weeks.[147]

Next, Isherwood and Bachardy received a long letter from Hockney saying he was more unhappy than he had ever been before. Schlesinger had told him it was too difficult to live with an artist so famous while trying to do his own work. Hockney objected that he didn't think of himself as a famous artist, and he wanted Isherwood to explain it all to him.[148] He arrived alone at Adelaide Drive and stayed one night on his way to San Francisco and Japan with a friend.

After talking things through, Hockney still did not understand about the independence Schlesinger wanted. "Oh, yes, indeed, David is a monster in the making," wrote Isherwood in his diary. "But I love him and Don loves him and he is lovable, truly lovable and wonderful and kind and generous and full of life."[149]

Hockney had wanted to have sex outside the relationship, as he freely reported to Isherwood and Bachardy by letter, and he had not initially minded about Schlesinger's new relationship with Eric Boman. But he was not prepared for the depth of Schlesinger's feelings for Boman any more than Isherwood had been prepared for the depths of Bachardy's feelings for Page. Moreover, he had been taken aback when Schlesinger no longer wanted sex with him.[150]

Hockney was well aware that Isherwood and Bachardy had found domestic and creative channels for their affection which were separate from their sexual relation; he had observed their relationship closely. But evidently he did not recognize, or did not wish to emulate, how much Isherwood had changed himself in order to continue his domestic life with Bachardy.

JOHN LEHMANN, VISITING Los Angeles that autumn to give another lecture, brought Isherwood a clipping from the *Financial Times*. "[F]ar and away his best work since the early Berlin novels," wrote C.P. Snow about *Kathleen and Frank*, with "the psychological implications of a very good novel." Snow predicted that *Kathleen and Frank* would be as popular as the TV series *The Forsyte Saga* adapted from John Galsworthy's novels (the *Downton Abbey* of the 1960s). *The Economist* titled its review "The Isherwood Saga."

The coverage was extensive. "This is an unexpected and extraordinary book," wrote Roy Fuller in the *Listener*, relishing the surprising new details about a writer he already admired. "The sense of the past—that potent gift handed on from mother to son—fills the thick book with an extraordinary detail and animation," wrote John Bayley in the *Guardian*.[151]

But Isherwood was hurt—again—by Spender in the *Sunday Telegraph*: "one of his half-assedly bitchy lukewarm putdowns," he lamented in his diary. "Why did he have to review the book at all? It is sheer aggression and envy." Another "friend," Angus Wilson, was methodical and stuffy in the *Observer*, managing to suggest that he understood the book far better than its author did.[152]

Isherwood was now an institution—"a legend" as Colin Wilson wrote in the *Spectator*. Wilson observed that Isherwood's central aim was "total honesty, rather in the manner of Gide." This total honesty, combined with eager self-criticism, made Isherwood vulnerable to attack. Moreover, because he was now an institution, reviewers took the opportunity to score their own professional points, showing off their expertise, their writerly skills, or parading their politics.[153]

"The Beesleys obviously think that I have had a triumph," Isherwood wrote in his diary, yet in the U.K., "the cold fact remains that the sales up to the 20th of November were only 1,185!" Things went better in the U.S., where the book came out some months later and, despite smaller expectations, sold 8,848 copies by the end of March 1972.[154]

The anonymous reviewer for the *New Yorker* called the narrative "entrancing"; indeed, from an American perspective, it might as well have been fiction, for the time and place hardly seemed real: "Isherwood's memories of his parents' way of life are so vivid that it is impossible to believe that everything (including Marple, the Isherwood estate and the ghosts that haunted it) has vanished entirely, and equally important to believe that that life—its conventions, its pieties, its private incomes—existed within this century."[155]

Some reviewers observed that Kathleen had been the inspiration for much of what Isherwood wrote and for his determination to reach the polite, conventional drawing-room audience. For instance, Ronald Blythe in the *New York Times Book Review*: "One of the aims of *his* writing, he confesses, 'was to seduce her into liking it in spite of herself.' [. . .] She was a provocation he could count on."[156]

Kathleen and Frank was widely seen as an act of reconciliation with both parents after a lifetime of rebellion, and Isherwood's candor about his homosexuality triggered a slow avalanche of attention. Now more than ever, readers were interested in Isherwood himself. He went to New York for the U.S. publication and appeared on national TV "speaking out about my queerness," as he wrote in his diary. He was a guest on *The Dick Cavett Show*, on *The Today Show* with Barbara Walters, and on Arlene Francis's radio show. He gave print interviews for the *New York Times*, the *Boston Globe*, and *Vogue*, for which he was photographed. He was also interviewed on videotape for the archives of the Gay Activists Alliance by a reporter from the *Village Voice*, Arthur Bell.[157]

He boldly offered a range of views long rehearsed in private. "I have written about homosexuals in my novels," he told another *New York Times* interviewer, "and in taking up the cause of one minority, that of homosexuals against the dictatorship of heterosexuals, I have spoken out for all minorities. And we are all minorities in one way or another."[158] To Bell, he made clear that he wished through public appearances as an out homosexual to "persuade a few timid souls not to be so timid, because, by degrees, they begin to think, well, after all, he hasn't been struck by lightning, why should I be?"

For the first time, he put forward his objections to the hypocrisy of the closet, "the absurd attempts to pass" and the "forced relationships that homosexual men indulge in to try and cover up their real nature. And everybody knows about it, that's the tragedy." He openly avowed opinions voiced by his fictional character George in *A Single Man* nearly a decade earlier: "The truth is, I respect prejudice. [. . .] I can understand that people, because of some weakness or mixup in their makeup, find themselves deeply disturbed by being with homosexuals." He also boosted the kind of open relationship which had brought him both suffering and great happiness: "one of the beauties of the homosexual relationship should be that there's a great deal more freedom between the partners than in conventional marriage." Homosexuals, in his view, had something to teach the paired-off procreating mainstream: "There's no question that the average heterosexual couple would like to be promiscuous from time to time."[159]

ISHERWOOD SAW A preview of *Cabaret* the movie on January 21, 1972. For him, the best thing about it was "beautiful broken-nosed Michael York." He had named York with Jeanne Moreau the "most intriguing celebrities" he had met in 1969, and after seeing York's earlier film, *Something for Everyone*, he had confided to his diary "Two things distract me chiefly at present; lust and my book. Right now, I am thinking of the extreme shortness of Michael York's shorts."[160] His enthusiasm recalled his adolescent obsessions with Jackie Coogan, Mickey Rooney, and Jean Forest. Long ago in Berlin, Isherwood had gotten an erotic thrill by dressing as his own sex partner, a boy from the streets, to accompany Francis Turville-Petre to the all-male In den Zelten Christmas Ball; in *Cabaret*, he was thrilled by seeing his younger self impersonated by a favorite sexy movie star.

But Isherwood fiercely objected to some of the dialogue in *Cabaret*, which in his opinion, suggested that "The queer is just an impotent heterosexual." The character based on himself, called Brian Roberts in the film, is portrayed with vague sexuality, neither bisexual nor homosexual, but certainly not straight, and ambivalent about any physical relationship with Sally

Bowles. They quarrel over her love affair with the character called Baron Maximilian von Heune: "Sally exclaims, 'Oh, fuck the Baron!' (meaning that he's unimportant) and Chris replies coyly, 'I do.' That's the kind of thing which offends *my* dignity as a homosexual," wrote Isherwood in his diary.

In November 1972, he saw the film a second time and reported that he "liked it much better than before." He found York "not only adorable and beautiful but a really sensitive and subtle actor." Liza Minnelli, on the other hand, seemed to him "clumsy and utterly wrong for the part, though touching sometimes, in a boyish good-sport way."[161]

Nevertheless, he could not help being delighted by success at the Academy Awards: "Triumph of *Cabaret* over *The Godfather*. They got only three awards, we got eight," he crowed after watching the television broadcast. Minnelli won Best Actress, Joel Grey reprising his stage role as Master of Ceremonies won Best Supporting Actor, and Bob Fosse won Best Director. The film made Minnelli an international superstar. In the run-up to the Academy Awards, she was the first person ever to appear on the cover of *Time* and *Newsweek* simultaneously. She was pictured in costume as Sally Bowles with captions alluding to movie roles played by her superstar mother, Judy Garland: "The New Miss Show Biz" and "A Star Is Born." In the end, she won over Isherwood personally when they met to be photographed for *TV and Radio Times* in advance of the 1974 TV broadcast: "I rather liked her. She has a complete manner for such encounters; she genuinely enjoys them, so it doesn't seem false."[162]

In 1972, the Mark Taper Forum staged *A Meeting by the River*. It was directed by Jim Bridges as part of a season called "New Theater for Now," opening April 26 for six performances. Isherwood told an interviewer that the play was "a religious comedy" and implied a comparison with Shakespeare: "It's about serious matters, but a comedy nevertheless—an all's-well-that-ends-well situation." He noted in his diary that the theater was "packed every night, because there are so many regular subscribers" and this created "an atmosphere of success."

Isherwood felt invigorated being back at the Mark Taper every day, and there were strong reviews and expectations of a longer run. The *Los Angeles Times* called it "one of the most civilized evenings NTN has given us," and the reviewer for the gay-friendly entertainment magazine *After Dark* enthused: "the Mark Taper Forum's New Theater for Now season struck a beautiful opening chord under Jim Bridges' direction."[163] Another positive review appeared in the July issue of *Coast*.

A New York repertory company chose *A Meeting by the River* for their series "Sideshows," and the Mark Taper cast reprised the main parts. Isherwood and Bachardy flew east and were interviewed on ABC's morning TV program by one of the actors, Larry Luckinbill, who played Patrick. Sam Waterston, who played Oliver, joined them. Reviews were encouraging, and the audience loved it.[164]

Bridges now wanted to direct a film adaptation. Isherwood and Bachardy got straight to work on a screenplay, but by the time it was ready, Bridges was busy with something else. They offered it to Ismail Merchant and James Ivory, but negotiations eventually foundered when Merchant and Ivory's film, *The Wild Party*, turned into a fiasco.

Meanwhile, a different iron was hot. Universal was ecstatic over the Isherwood–Bachardy *Frankenstein* script. Stromberg exclaimed to Isherwood on the telephone: "the dialogue has the distinction of Shaw or Wilde!" Sidney Sheinberg told Robin French: "I've got the best script I've ever had!"[165] Universal planned to make it their biggest production for 1972, a feature, and to film it in England.

Stromberg signed them up for another thriller, *The Mummy, or The Lady from the Land of the Dead*, and they started the screenplay at the end of October, inspired partly by a scholarly book about ancient Egyptian religion given to Isherwood by Gerald Heard, partly by *The Turn of the Screw*, and partly by *Rosemary's Baby*, which they had seen October 8.

Jon Voight, whom Isherwood and Bachardy had met at the 1969 premiere of *Midnight Cowboy* directed by their friend John Schlesinger, wanted to play Dr. Frankenstein, but Universal wobbled between shooting for film or TV. Stromberg "signed Jack Smight, a C director, behind our backs," as Isherwood recorded, and Voight backed out.

Nevertheless, Universal paid for Isherwood and Bachardy to fly to London first class and gave them $600 a week each for expenses. They left Los Angeles on January 22, 1973, in "a honeymoon atmosphere," drinking champagne on the flight. "We held hands and kissed and Don said it was fate that we had met and that he adored me for being so lucky. I felt an intense bliss of togetherness—"[166]

NOTTING HILL, LONDON, 1973

They stayed at Hockney's flat in Powis Terrace and attended a dinner party at Spender's where Isherwood was captivated all over again by Francis Bacon—"that powerful star [...] most affectionate and kissy"—and arranged to visit at Reece Mews, South Kensington. "The studio seems as intensely 'charged' as a shrine, but its atmosphere isn't in the least shrinelike; it doesn't calm you. This *is* the battlefield; the awe-inspiring scene of Francis's desperate victorious struggles to 'get down to the nerve'—I can never forget that phrase of his." Stirred by rivalry, as always, he recorded Bacon on Hockney: "Francis said of David Hockney's work, 'She's no good.'"[167]

He telephoned Auden in Oxford, where Auden was now living at his undergraduate college, Christ Church. Kallman answered the phone, and, according to the account that Isherwood wrote when he got back to California, "there was a feeling of awkwardness between us. Then Wystan got on the line and said quite firmly that he couldn't see us that day. Perhaps he didn't want to, with Chester around. I don't blame him."[168] As Isherwood had realized when they worked on the Berlin musical, he didn't really like Chester; evidently, the feeling was mutual. That was the last time Isherwood and Auden spoke. Auden died suddenly from a heart attack seven months later in September 1973.

In Cheshire, Isherwood found the hillside below Wyberslegh a muddy sea of new houses under construction, "Wybersley Rise." Richard owned a completed one, where Isherwood stayed, but Richard himself always slept at another of the new houses that he rented for the Bradleys. He was drunk throughout the visit. Wyberslegh was shuttered and smelling of damp and rot. Richard "made a great point of giving me—pressing me to take—a watercolor of Wyberslegh Hall painted by the Mr. Standen who had given painting lessons to Frank."[169] Isherwood came to believe the gift was an apology for something Richard did not tell him but which Evelyn Bradley let slip—that Richard had sold all Frank's watercolors to a dealer. A friend found one in a Disley shop and bought it for Isherwood. Isherwood had evidently already acquired a study of the apple tree in bloom at Roden House in Limerick—the tree once forgotten along with the carefree days before boarding school and the war when he had sat reading *A Midsummer Night's Dream* underneath it. He hung both of Frank's watercolors in his workroom in Santa Monica along with Standen's view of Wyberslegh Hall.

From England, Isherwood and Bachardy went to the tiny mountain village of Klosters in the Swiss Alps to visit Salka Viertel, now a very old lady, Peter Viertel, and Peter's second wife, the actress Deborah Kerr. Then he and Bachardy spent "a strangely joyful" twentieth anniversary in Rome with Gore Vidal, Howard Austen, and Gavin Lambert.[170]

Frankenstein began shooting in mid-March in England, with a rather remarkable cast including Leonard Whiting as Frankenstein, Nicola Pagett, David McCallum, James Mason, John Gielgud, Agnes Moorehead, Margaret Leighton, Ralph Richardson, Jane Seymour, and Michael Sarrazin as the Creature. It wasn't until mid-August that Isherwood and Bachardy saw an undubbed print in the projection room at Universal Studios: "worse than anything I'd expected," according to Isherwood in his diary. He wrote two paragraphs attacking the directing, the acting, the casting, the makeup, the butchering of the script by Stromberg and Smight: "This wretched pair have taken months of our work and destroyed it." But then he and Bachardy shrugged it off: "the life we have together now makes all such disasters unimportant, even funny."

NBC, on the other hand, was delighted with the film and broadcast it during two prime evening slots. Critics raved over the script, and Michael Sarrazin made the cover of the *Advocate* as "A Monster we'd like to get stuck on a desert island with!" The film was nominated for a Nebula Award by the Science Fiction and Fantasy Writers of America, won the prize for Best Scenario when it was screened at the 1976 International Festival of Fantastic and Science-Fiction Films, and generated a lasting cult following. The screenplay was published by Avon paperbacks. What's more, Stromberg offered yet another job, adapting *A Tale of Two Cities* for TV. Isherwood, despite feeling friendly, wrote in his diary: "It is really unthinkable that we should work with Hunt again. We can't trust him..."[171]

ADELAIDE DRIVE, SANTA MONICA, 1973

John Lehmann wanted to publish the letters he and Isherwood had exchanged in the late 1930s and during World War II. Face-to-face in London in early 1973, Isherwood had agreed and promised to write some notes. Back home in California, he regretted this: "I fear that the letters must be a thundering bore." Six months later, in August 1973, he received from his agent a contract Lehmann had already signed with Methuen. He told Lehmann he couldn't add his own signature without seeing copies of his letters first; once he reread them, he withdrew his consent. In his diary he explained: "They are dull, mechanical, false."[172]

The misfire with Lehmann ignited Isherwood's long-neglected impulse to tell the story of his emigration. "I quite suddenly decided to make a stab at my autobiographical book about America—" he wrote a few days later. He was determined to omit anything petty or false in the chrysalis he had shed, including the persona that had once corresponded with Lehmann. The self-realization of his unconscious was to be toward the light, toward joy. "My inspiration is Jung's resolve 'to tell my personal myth,'" he declared in his diary. "Therefore, I shall try to dwell only on the numinous, on the magical and the mythical. I shall try to avoid much reference to characters who lack these qualities and arouse negative emotions in me. [...] I want to write about my sex life very frankly and without the least hint of self-defence."

He heard back from Lehmann toward the end of September, a letter of understandable hurt and reproach. He admonished Lehmann not to assume his friendship was false because his letters had been and advised him to reread the letters objectively. In his diary, he addressed the question of *"why my letters to him during the war were so false [...] I knew he didn't believe I was serious about Vedanta or pacifism and I knew he would disapprove, on principle, of any book I wrote while I was living in America. I was false because I didn't want to admit how deeply I resented his fatherly tone of forgiveness for my betrayal of him and England—"*[173]

Then, on September 29, Auden died. Isherwood heard the news when a journalist from Reuters phoned and woke him before dawn. A second journalist phoned, from the BBC, and told him that it was a heart attack in a hotel room in Vienna after speaking to a literary society there. Did Isherwood have any comment? The BBC was recording the call and broadcast it on September 30: "the sense of shock and grief in Isherwood's voice was an unforgettable testimony to a friendship," wrote one listener.[174]

Auden's death certainly took Isherwood by surprise. Isherwood had protected himself carefully from death—distancing himself from the deaths of family and friends, preparing fastidiously for his own. Auden had been part of this protection ever since China, when, as reported lightheartedly in *Journey to a War*, Auden had "popped his head above the parapet" at the front line to photograph the enemy trenches and had undressed and slept easily beside a fretful, fully-clothed Isherwood as their train ran past enemy guns, assuring him the Japanese would not shell the train because "Nothing of that sort ever happens to *me*." Auden was, after all, two and a half years younger. Isherwood had to write out the news in his diary and then read it over in order to process it: "His death seems uncanny to me because he was one of the guarantees that *I* won't die—at least not yet. I think most of us, if we live long enough, have such guarantee figures. On the other hand, the fact that he has gone first makes the prospect of death easier to face. He has shown me the way."

Isherwood wept for the poignancy of an unfulfilled ambition that he knew remained close to Auden's heart, "he didn't get the Nobel Prize, after all. He did so want it—" He felt certain that Auden had sent him a psychosomatic reminder of the journey they had begun together in Berlin from neurosis to self-understanding: "That night he died—or rather, in the afternoon here, which might well have been the exact time of his death in Vienna—I started a sore throat [...] I like to believe that he sent me a message which got through to me."[175] It was, again, "the liar's quinsey" that had afflicted Isherwood in youth. Telling the truth in his art and in his life had gradually become Isherwood's main preoccupation. He had rejected the falseness of his correspondence with Lehmann; he was all the more resolved by Auden's death to continue with the truth.

"[T]he cloud of Wystan's death" hung over him as he continued to search for an entry point into the new book. "My difficulty is that I want to have this book start with our departure for America. But I have now realized that I can only put our departure in perspective if I begin with Germany—why I went there—'to find my sexual homeland.'" He decided to shift back in time and begin with his emigration to Berlin, "taking up more or less where *Lions and Shadows* left off."[176] His provisional title was *Wanderings*.

It was now that he began to reconsider Auden's role in his story. In *Lions and Shadows*, Isherwood had described Weston and the John Layard character, Barnard, as the motivating force behind his journey to Berlin: "I was in their hands, and content to be. [. . .] I was only a traveller, given over, mind and body, to the will of the dominant, eastward-speeding train." In the new autobiography, Isherwood himself was to be the central character, and his own will was to be revealed. His impulse to make himself the central character was partly protectiveness; he would not reveal for publication that Auden had been unrequitedly in love with him and had been, as Auden had testified in his own diary, a wistful voyeur of his first German romances. More important, Isherwood wanted to untangle his personal myth from the myths of friends and collaborators. So often, he had moved on the wind of someone else's willpower; now he would take responsibility for his story. So he decided to begin with his third visit to Berlin, "my real emigration,"[177] in the autumn of 1929, when he settled there. Thus, he began to develop the narrative that departed from Auden's account in his contemporary journal.

The new book excited him as nothing had for a long time. "It seems to contain everything I want to say," he wrote in his diary. At sixty-nine years old, he worried that he was no longer up to the task. "When I reread my earlier work, I feel that perhaps my style may have lost its ease and brightness and become ponderous. Well, so it's ponderous. At least I still have matter, if not manner." He reread Auden's letters and the poems Auden had begun sending him in 1925: "I seem to see the whole of his life, and it is so honest, so full of love and so dedicated, all of a piece." He berated himself for having allowed them to drift apart: "He loved me very much and I behaved rather badly to him, a lot of the time. Again and again, in the later letters, he begs me to come and spend some time alone with him."[178] On the other hand, Auden could be bossy and overwhelming, which cost him his friendship with Benjamin Britten. Isherwood knew—and demonstrated in friendship after friendship—how to be intimate and to keep his distance at the same time.

By Easter Sunday, he had written two hundred pages "up to our arrival in New York in January 1939," and in August he decided this comprised a "first volume: March 1929 to January 1939."[179] It was the eventful 1930s—the friends, the sex, the politics, the fame, and finally the disillusion—told with stunning candor and lashings of self-reproach from the point of view of the 1970s, at the start of the queer revolution.

He found himself quoting extensively from *Goodbye to Berlin*, from Spender's autobiography *World Within World*, and from Kathleen's diaries: "I feel so uninventive," he fretted. But he did not need to invent. He only needed to reveal truths hidden by the fictions he had created in the past. The work was hard; advancing age was against him, and he had to revise each sentence over and over again. Just after his seventieth birthday, he wrote in his diary: "The 'shutter' of my brain is only open for about three-quarters of an hour in the morning—I mean, really open." He began drinking coffee after a long period without it: "it seems to blow the nearly dead embers of my imagination into a faint red glow. Also I occasionally increase the effect with a Dexamyl tablet."[180]

The pressure increased when he learned that Spender was revising and expanding *World Within World*. They spoke on the telephone, and Isherwood got the impression that Spender "was very anxious to see the manuscript of my book"; so he promised to send it before it went to the publishers. "In the midst of this conversation, I got a most uneasy feeling that history was repeating itself; Stephen is attempting to scoop my material, as he did back in the thirties. He doesn't even quite know that he is doing this. It's just that he's so competitive."

Spender also wanted Isherwood's help with a book about Auden that he was planning to write with Auden's literary executor Edward Mendelson. The book was never written, but the project alerted Isherwood to his own concern for Auden's legacy:

> He is well aware that he is going against Wystan's expressed wish, not to have his life written. But then so am I, on a much smaller scale. I am writing little bits about Wystan in my book. And, I must say, I can't help feeling, wishes or no wishes, it is better if those who knew Wystan write now, instead of leaving it to those who didn't know him, a generation or two later.[181]

By late 1975, two biographers, Brian Finney and Jonathan Fryer, were also tracking Isherwood, though they promised to wait for him to publish.

All the while, Isherwood worked on stage productions and film scripts, traveled to New York several times, kept up the usual busy social life, gave TV, radio, and personal interviews, and made numerous public appearances. He had appeared at the Hollywood Authors Club to receive an award for A Lifetime of Distinguished Contribution to Literature. He spoke to John Rechy's writing class at Occidental College. He went to bookshops to promote the paperback publication of *Kathleen and Frank*.

In April 1974, he was invited to speak at the Honors Convocation ceremony at Cal. State Los Angeles, where he had begun his academic teaching career in 1959 when it was still called L.A. State. He observed the transformation in the institution as well as in himself. "I used to regard the place as a rough and ready teach-factory." Now, it had all the trappings of Cambridge-style academia. He was required to wear a gown and a mortarboard, and he walked in a procession with the president led by someone carrying a silver mace. The audience was huge. He delivered a version of his last Santa Barbara lecture, "A Writer and His World": "But this time it included a gay lib statement." A few days later, he was flown to New Orleans to give a reading at Loyola University. He chose passages from *Goodbye to Berlin*, *A Single Man*, *Lions and Shadows*, and *Kathleen and Frank* and, as he noted in his diary, he again "made a gay lib declaration which brought them to their feet, clapping."[182] He also read poems at a Tribute to Auden at USC. In 1975, he was awarded the Brandeis Medal, by Brandeis University, again in recognition of lifetime achievement in literature; Bachardy went to New York and delivered the speech Isherwood wrote.

BACHARDY ONCE TOLD Isherwood that he had "a temperamental horror of making plans" about his work. "He feels that plan making destroys his artistic impulse. If he tries to plan, he loses all desire to paint the picture. So he confronts himself, as it were, with an emergency, a fait accompli, which demands to be dealt with."[183]

Over the years, Bachardy developed many strategies for intensifying the sense of emergency. He painted almost exclusively from life with his subject sitting in front of him. In a long sitting, his subject might struggle with fatigue and muscle spasms, make faces, surreptitiously shift position, or fall asleep. Time was always short for the perfection Bachardy demanded of himself. Often his subjects were famous, some famous for being impatient and difficult.

It may have been partly his innate temperament and sensibility; on the other hand, Bachardy had begun to assimilate ideas about art as soon as he sat down at Isherwood's typewriter in the Hookers' garden house in 1953 to take dictation for *The World in the Evening*. At the time, Isherwood had been rediscovering the lessons of his own artistic youth, for instance Forster's discussion of truth in life versus truth in art, in which Forster had identified something new in Gide, "the attempt to combine the two truths, the proposal that writers should mix themselves up in their material and be rolled over and over by it; they should not try to subdue any longer, they should hope to be subdued." Forster had compared this with an anecdote about an old lady who "agreed with Gide," because she rejected logic in favor of the offerings of the subconscious mind: "'Logic! Good gracious! What rubbish!' she exclaimed. 'How can I tell what I think till I see what I say?'"[184] This had gone right through Isherwood to Bachardy who, equally, might have said, How can I tell what I see till I see what I paint?

In December 1972, Bachardy had been invited to have a summer show at the Los Angeles Municipal Art Gallery in Barnsdall Park. "This will be his biggest—and he will have, for the first time, a proper illustrated catalogue!" Isherwood crowed.[185] Bachardy fretted over the show all spring, bringing on ulcer-like pains. Irving Blum wrote an introduction to the catalogue which seemed to Isherwood patronizing and sloppy; it failed to mention any of Bachardy's many earlier shows apart from the one at Blum's own gallery. Then Barnsdall Park declined to cover the full cost of framing the work, and plans for the opening night party were entrusted to the socialite art collector Brooke Hopper, whom Bachardy did not trust.

Just as Bachardy was being sucked into a vortex of negativity and angst, Billy Al Bengston proposed to give another smaller party "for the inner circle," and, more important, Nick Wilder offered Bachardy a future group show followed by a solo show in his gallery. Wilder told Bachardy that "he now realizes that the portraits of celebrities are only a small part of Don's work." This was a turning point for Bachardy.[186]

The Barnsdall Park show opened on July 12, 1973. Isherwood and Bachardy previewed the pictures in the morning. "They look splendid—" Isherwood reported, "truly an oeuvre, a human comedy ranging from Norton Simon to Gregory Evans, from Mrs. Reagan to Candy Darling." He was prouder than ever.

"The opening was certainly a success. Hundreds came, including a few stars." Isherwood listed many in his diary. "Don was at his best—he blazed with manic brilliance, greeted everyone, knew everybody's name and submitted to much photography by a fumbling amateur."[187] The supper afterwards was hosted by Bengston, Wilder, and Joe Goode in an open-air rooftop restaurant, Ceeje's. They failed to include in the inner circle the *Los Angeles Times* art critic William Wilson, a long-time fan of Bachardy's work, and Blum felt certain this poisoned Wilson's review.

Wilson saw the work before the show opened. His piece, as Isherwood put it, was "the strangest mixture of panning and praise, self-contradictory and double edged." Wilson attacked Bachardy for courting fame with portraits of international cultural stars—Stravinsky, Virgil Thomson, the "luminaries of Venice's art mafia," New York artists Jasper Johns, Lichtenstein, and Warhol, as well as writers and movie actors—and he made a few detailed technical criticisms; then he conceded a triumph: "Yet the Bachardy exhibition remains among the most absorbing socio-psychological documents I have ever seen in an art gallery."

As in his earlier reviews, Wilson recognized that Bachardy was portraying something essential about the personalities of his sitters: "He responds with sympathy, detachment and an unnerving, stainless steel insight. We see a handsome young artist being slowly engulfed by satanic madness, a millionaire collector who has seen too many tragedies, the shrewd stare of a hip dealer, the wistfulness of a faded actress, all presented without a hint of sentimentality or satire."[188]

Isherwood copied the review into his diary, guessing the identity of the individuals mentioned and picking apart Wilson's writing. He did not observe that Wilson might have been reviewing a piece of writing by himself. For Bachardy had achieved in his drawing the economic and lucid portrayal of character that had made Isherwood famous as a writer.

In September Bachardy heard that the National Portrait Gallery in London wanted to buy more of his work. Over the coming decades, the NPG acquired nine Bachardys including the Auden.[189] In early December, Bachardy showed some paintings to Wilder, "mostly the blotty watercolors," as Isherwood described them in his diary, and Wilder offered him "a show in which the whole front room of the gallery is full of the watercolors with a few drawings in the back room."

Bachardy was exuberant. "Now I can begin to live!" he exclaimed. Perhaps Isherwood was even happier: "if I had been told I could have one wish granted to me (within the bounds of possibility) this would have been it." He had no end of admiration for Wilder: "he is quite consciously out to alter Don's image—from that of celebrity-hunting portraiteer who got the chance to draw famous people through his association with Isherwood to that of a serious artist who has to be respected for his talent." They set a date in November 1974 for the exhibition.

The wound inflicted by Patrick Procktor and his circle would never heal, but Bachardy was now certain that he was an artist. He told Isherwood that he "no longer wonders."[190] Since adolescence, Bachardy had fought his fear of going mad like his brother. The affirmation of his identity as an artist allowed him to recognize that his strangeness and his unpredictability were part of his creativity and originality, gifts rather than weaknesses. Others were certain, too. William Wilson told Isherwood that the paintings had altered his view of Bachardy as an artist, and Isherwood recorded that Richard Diebenkorn had seen and praised four of the paintings when they were hanging in Isherwood's workroom. Henry Seldis, who reviewed the Wilder show for the *Los Angeles Times*, compared the "absolutely fascinating watercolor portraits on paper using anonymous friends and acquaintances for sitters" to Egon Schiele, and, more closely, "to Kokoschka's probing of the psychological aspects of the people he painted."

Bachardy had found his style. As Isherwood observed, "They are so absolutely Bachardy and no one else."[191] Another show followed, at the Dootson-Calderhead Gallery in Seattle in December 1975, and there were many commissioned sittings. In 1976, Bachardy enlarged his studio at Adelaide Drive, building a second story. That winter, he sometimes drew with Hockney, including sessions at Gemini, where they made engravings.

ISHERWOOD AND BACHARDY'S penultimate screen collaboration was an NBC TV adaptation of F. Scott Fitzgerald's 1922 novel *The Beautiful and Damned*, about the last members of a gilded American leisure class. Like Isherwood's own family, Fitzgerald's characters are accustomed to living on inherited money and so uncomfortable with work that they sink into poverty and addiction rather than take a job. This kind of American had fascinated Isherwood since he first read Hemingway's *Fiesta* in 1927. They were lost souls even before the Great War, desperate to have a good time.

They had a shooting script by late August, but the film was never made. Bachardy later recalled that interest in Fitzgerald seemed to evaporate in the wake of Jack Clayton's *The Great Gatsby* (1974) scripted by Francis Ford Coppola,[192] which, though it got mixed reviews, occupied (and perhaps muddied) the imaginative space.

For the first four months of 1976, Isherwood devoted himself entirely to the book which he had begun to call *Christopher and His Kind*, a title once again suggested by Bachardy. He sent off the final version on May 6 to a new literary agent in New York, Candida Donadio. She had found him a new publisher, Farrar, Straus & Giroux, where his editor was Michael di Capua. Isherwood and Bachardy flew east to be introduced over a dinner attended by Roger Straus, Robert Giroux, Susan Sontag, and Barbara Epstein, cofounder of the *New York Review of Books*.

LONDON, 1976

They went on to London where the National Portrait Gallery was launching an exhibition, "Young Writers of the Thirties," and Isherwood was again a center of attention.

Hockney drove them on a zigzag tour from London to the Suffolk Coast, west to the Cotwolds, then north to Edinburgh and all the way to Inverness.

At Aldeburgh in Suffolk, Isherwood saw Benjamin Britten for the first time since 1949. He later told an interviewer: "I knew Ben was ill, but I didn't know how ill he was. Any emotion was bad for him. He was so moved [...] that he could hardly trust himself to speak. The others left us, and Ben and I sat in a room together, not speaking, just holding hands."[193] The opera that night at Snape Maltings was the Britten–Auden *Paul Bunyan*, which had failed when it was performed in Manhattan in 1941, hastening the end of the friendship between Auden and Britten.

ADELAIDE DRIVE, SANTA MONICA, 1976

After a month in England, Isherwood and Bachardy joined Gavin Lambert in Tangier, where on July 4, they heard by telephone that Prabhavananda had died. It was the anniversary of Vivekananda's death in 1902. They had been expecting news of this kind, and took ten more days traveling home. Together, they attended three services for Prabhavananda, two in Hollywood and one in Santa Barbara. The head swamis from seven American centers gathered to perform the rituals and to speak. Isherwood spoke, too, at the memorial services at Santa Barbara and at Vedanta Place.

The problem of the succession had not been resolved. Belur Math had told Prabhavananda that they would not send a new assistant until he separated the monks and nuns as in India. In 1971, the Math had sent Swami Chetanananda, but Chetanananda was considered too young to run the center, so after Prabhavananda died, the Math installed Swami Swahananda, possessed of an M.A. in English from the University of Calcutta and head of the Berkeley Vedanta Center. Isherwood had delivered lectures and readings during Prabhavananda's last illnesses, and he filled in as necessary after Prabhavananda's death.

In contrast to Auden's death, Isherwood had long been preparing himself to be parted from Prabhavananda: "I feel that Swami is very much 'there,' in a sense that he never was while he was alive. He knows everything now, I say to myself; there is no concealment."[194] Isherwood mused on what to write about their long relationship and began jotting down thoughts for a new book. Meantime, he could now promote *Christopher and His Kind* without fear of making trouble for his guru.

THE LAUNCH OF *Christopher and His Kind* was a kind of victory tour. The first appearances were planned for San Francisco, San Diego, New York, and

Los Angeles in late November and December 1976. Isherwood was seventy-two years old. As he set off on the first leg, San Diego was canceled because local TV and radio stations felt their sponsors "would veto" mention of his homosexuality or even general discussion of the subject. "Well, so be it," he wrote in his diary. "Let the situation carry me wherever it wants to. This is all *maya*."[195]

Everywhere else, attention proved remorseless. He held his own in the interviews, attributing his quick responses to KH3 tablets, which he had begun taking again in mid-November. "But I couldn't possibly have gotten through the New York trip without Don, who was sustaining me throughout. I have *never* known him to be more marvellous and angelic."

The outpouring of approbation from the huge numbers of gay readers was affirming and fulfilling:

Perhaps the most moving experience was going down to the Oscar Wilde Memorial Bookshop in the village and signing copies of my book, with a line of people, mostly quite young, stretching all the way down Christopher Street and around the corner. I had such a feeling that this is my tribe and I loved them. ("They're beginning to believe that Christopher Street was named after you," Gore said, with his sly grin, half flattering, half mocking, at dinner . . .)[196]

The tour continued in January 1977 to Rochester, Toronto, Chicago, Minneapolis, again generating a deeply affecting combination of disapproval and rapturous support.

It hardly mattered what the reviewers had to say because Isherwood had reached his audience directly. As he set off to make what he called "propaganda for my book," he recorded in his diary opposition which was political, not literary-critical. *Publishers Weekly* was "hostile": "always his ultimate measure of the world seems to be sexual." The *Chicago Tribune Book World* was "vicious": "The big, bold book of fact has become a fairy tale." Isherwood predicted that such viciousness would "sell a lot of copies and inspire loyal indignation in the hearts of Chicago queers."[197]

The *New York Times* cultural critic John Leonard wrote a rambling, uncertain review in which he accepted the boys but made fun of Isherwood's Eastern religion and objected to Isherwood's criticisms of his younger self, asserting that the modernists—Joyce, Eliot, and their generation—were greater geniuses than Auden, Isherwood, and their generation. But Leonard did not hold his modernist geniuses to the ethical standard to which Auden and Isherwood held themselves—that they try to be good people as well as good writers, that they examine and, if necessary, change their beliefs to do so. Peter Stansky, then a professor of history at Stanford University, writing for the Sunday *New York Times*, similarly focused on the "revisionism" of Auden and Isherwood in their later careers and agreed that Isherwood's new book tended to trivialize the Christopher of the 1930s. However, Stansky recognized that for Isherwood, the cultural change around homosexuality not only permitted but called for a new kind of book. He also saw that Isherwood had set out "to do in his legend" in part as "revenge on the 'camera' image."[198]

These issues were raised again in England. C.P. Snow, who had been such a fan of *Kathleen and Frank*, objected that *Christopher and His Kind* was really "a manifesto." Rebecca West reacted with puritanical indignation, asserting that Isherwood's portrait of "insanitary" male prostitutes, dirty, drunken, treacherous children and adolescents afflicted by disease along with their grown-up patrons, would give honorable homosexuals a bad name. The only other woman to review the book, Gabriele Annan, born in Berlin in 1921 and raised there until 1932, was not shocked or even surprised. She was fascinated by Hirschfeld and the Institute for Sexual Science, and she found Isherwood's intoxication with "the defiant, romantic, dangerous aspect of homosexuality" attractive: it is "dashing, reckless, gay (in the old sense of the word), and umpompous, it is a wonderful seedbed for jokes." Looking at Isherwood's work as a whole, she pronounced that "one way or another, first as an act of defiance and then as a fight for equal rights, it has always been a homosexual campaign."[199]

Many straight reviewers couldn't handle the homosexual sex. Philip Toynbee evasively said that he preferred "the sheer *atmosphere*" of the Berlin novels to the outright candor of *Christopher and His Kind*. John Bayley, though, recognized that Isherwood's revelations were not just about sex; they were about emotion, for both Auden and Isherwood: "each was in his way in search of love—this is the moving fact to emerge from the book."[200]

Nearly four years later, in his review of *My Guru and His Disciple*, Spender was to weigh in on Isherwood's reassessment of earlier work and also on the use of fictional techniques to shape both memoirs and novels. "[F]iction and nonfiction add up to a whole which is closer to the truth than the fiction alone," wrote Spender about Isherwood unpacking his earlier work. He averred that Isherwood had been "so successful in intensifying the reality of people that the fictitious character seems more like the person described than that person seems like himself or herself." Neither Isherwood nor Spender could think of Jean Ross or Gerald Hamilton without thinking of Sally Bowles or Mr. Norris. "Consciousness of the real person standing behind the fictitious character makes Isherwood feel guilty," claimed Spender, repeating the example of Bernhard Landauer being depicted as passive in

Goodbye to Berlin when his real-life original, Wilfrid Israel, heroically helped many Jews escape Germany.[201] But it was Spender making Isherwood feel guilty—by demanding historical accuracy from fictional creations.

Isherwood knew what it felt like to be a character in someone else's fiction. He had been made into a character by others again and again, starting early, with his mother, then Allan Monkhouse. But for all its use of fictional skills, *Christopher and His Kind*, unlike the Berlin novels, is not fiction.

In 1978, before *Christopher and His Kind* appeared in Germany, Isherwood wrote to Heinz Neddermeyer for permission. He had been extremely protective of Neddermeyer in all his earlier writing. He sent Neddermeyer the newly completed German translation, assuring him that the publisher did not know his identity, pointing out that no surname had been used, and offering to change the name "Heinz" to something else. He also invited Neddermeyer to veto publication altogether.

Neddermeyer wrote back expressing "horror and dismay." His letter, in German, said that he was appalled by Isherwood's candor, which had brought him to the edge of despair; by luck his wife, Gerda, had not read the book, but he was anxious about who else had read it. He would rather be dead than appear in Isherwood's story—strong words from someone who survived Hitler and the war. Isherwood replied that he was "really really sorry" that Neddermeyer felt "insulted," and he assured him the book would not be published in German. Bachardy later observed of Neddermeyer's reaction: "That would have hurt Chris's feelings."[202] It was, after all, a love story. Isherwood must have worried, too, about how widely read the book already was in English. Neddermeyer returned the manuscript, and *Christopher and His Kind* was not published in German until 1992. There is no evidence that Isherwood ever wrote to Neddermeyer again.

Two friends went to bat for Isherwood in their reviews of *Christopher and His Kind*, Vidal and Upward. Vidal wrote a legacy-shaping essay for the *New York Review of Books*. "As memoirs of the Twenties, Thirties, Forties now accumulate, Isherwood keeps cropping up as a principal figure." Vidal understood Isherwood's position among the friends of his youth, including the rivalries that had fueled the attacks when Isherwood emigrated: "In every generation there are certain figures who are who they are at an early age; stars *in ovo*. People want to know them; imitate them; destroy them. Isherwood was such a creature and Stephen Spender fell under his spell even before they met."

Vidal made the case for Isherwood's 1939 realization that he was a pacifist and could not risk fighting Neddermeyer, and he made the case for Isherwood's commitment to gay liberation. Vidal also excused the aggressive homophilia that he himself had in the past criticized in private: "If his defense of Christopher's kind is sometimes shrill ... well, there is a good deal to be shrill about in a society so deeply and so mindlessly homophobic." As for wasting his talent in Hollywood, Vidal spun Isherwood's decision to become a screenwriter into cast-away praise: "From that time on the best prose writer in English has supported himself by writing movies."[203] Thus, Vidal's greatest tribute was reserved for the writing. His essay was a small masterpiece, hitting every point.

Upward, too, did Isherwood proud with a detailed and unflinching account of the rebellious impulse that became focused for Isherwood in his sexuality. He also made the point that Isherwood's career was not all about sex. "To be a writer was even more essential to him than to be a homosexual," he wrote.[204]

"[T]HE MORE YOU think about a thing the less it frightens you," Isherwood told an interviewer in 1977. "Feeling death near is as though you're in the approach pattern for the airport. You want to land properly and not upside down."[205] Isherwood had been frightened of death ever since he could remember. Alcohol, travel, sex had seemed to offer release from this fear. But now, as he drew nearer, Isherwood was determined to be in clear-headed control.

He was sorting through his domestic life and preparing to take his toys up off the floor. In October 1976, he got a new doctor, a woman called Elsie Giorgi, "someone to ease me onto my deathbed, when the time comes." Dr. Giorgi was a successor to Miss Purdie and to Helen Kennedy—when the time came, he could permit himself to be supine at last under the supervision of a certain kind of woman. "She is a nonstop talker, an egomaniac, a show-biz snob and extremely sympathetic. Don is in favor of her, too."

Dr. Giorgi helped arrange for Isherwood's corpse to be donated to the UCLA Department of Anatomy: "there won't be any kind of 'resting place' to which my darling might feel obligated to come, on anniversaries, with wreaths."[206] He chose for himself the physical oblivion visited on his father, whose body had never been found in Belgium. He did not want anything like the official memorial to his father's sacrifice, that awkward, trivializing addendum on the Menin Gate which his mother had pursued through years of administrative error and bluster. Isherwood's memorial was to be his work.

But he had a decade remaining. Dr. Giorgi found him in perfect health for his age. He had injured his knee falling down the steps of Bachardy's enlarged studio, so she gave him an anti-inflammatory drug called Butazolidin, telling him it was administered to racehorses to make them run faster, and she went on boosting his energy and his spirits with vitamin shots and, at least as important, her attention.

He officially adopted Bachardy in a ceremony performed in a judge's chambers in Santa Monica in June 1977. This was an estate-planning decision that also suited the emotional dynamic of their relationship. Isherwood wrote in his diary that the judge "said 'good luck' to us both when it was over, which made the ceremony seem like a marriage."[207]

He began the memoir of Prabhavananda in February 1977, a long look back over his own spiritual life and a further preparation for death. He progressed steadily with his rough draft until he completed the account of Prabhavananda's death. Then he found he could not write the final chapter, the Afterword, in which he planned to summarize all it meant. "What is holding me up?" he mused in his diary in late October:

> Am I perhaps inhibited by a sense of the mocking agnostics all around me—ranging from asses like Lehmann to intelligent bigots like Edward? Yes, of course I am. [...] I must state my beliefs and be quite intransigent about them. I must also state my doubts, but without exaggerating them. Yes, that's it. I must give the reader a glimpse of myself in a transitional stage, between Swami's death and my own.[208]

As he worked on the book, Isherwood found his meditation had become "a dead telephone line." It was more and more difficult to think about Prabhavananda "unless I'm actually writing about him." Then, early in 1978, he felt that he was at last experiencing some emotion when he meditated, but "What I do not feel is any sense of visitation. I have never once really felt Swami's presence since he died."[209] It was an admission that he had unconsciously expected to have in real life the vision he had created for Oliver in *A Meeting by the River*.

Bachardy opened another successful show at the Nick Wilder Gallery in September 1977. For the first time, he included a male nude and a seminude. Fellow artists were impressed. "There was a feeling that this show is his best to date," Isherwood recorded. William Wilson gave him top billing in the *Los Angeles Times*'s "Art Walk" column on September 30. "He's always been an absorbing, virtually literary talent," he wrote. Wilson was fascinated by the stories and character analyses he saw in the work, yet he didn't mention Isherwood as an influence or a comparison, only other artists, all major talents. "He begins to remind us of Egon Schiele, Francis Bacon, David Hockney or Richard Avedon. His subjects are as decorous as if they were posing for Ingres or Holbein..."[210]

Jess Bachardy died of lung cancer in December; he had reconciled himself enough with Isherwood to share family restaurant meals a few times a year from 1971 onward.[211] Glade had lost her memory. According to Isherwood's diary, she vacillated between contentment all alone in the apartment she had shared with Jess and sudden recollection when "she's scared and thinks she's been deserted by her sons and cast adrift. This is heartrending."[212] Bachardy drove into town often to eat with her, and he persuaded Ted to move in with her.

Isherwood's injured knee continued to be a problem. He had to give up jogging, and an X-ray revealed a badly torn ligament needing surgical repair. The operation was scheduled for January 31, 1979, but Bachardy couldn't handle the thought of the general anesthetic, so they canceled it. A second opinion and a physiotherapist brought no improvement. Isherwood became depressed and neglected the book.

Bachardy, feeling destabilized, began an affair with a movie critic and would-be actor, Bill Franklin. Isherwood was mostly content at home, sipping beer in front of the TV while he waited for a report on what he called Bachardy's "mousing," but when Franklin was included in their private life, Isherwood labeled him "The Downer" and excused himself. One night, he came across Franklin cooking spaghetti in the kitchen: "I had such a vision of his doing this after I'm dead."[213]

He pushed on with the book about Prabhavananda by taking Dexamyl, rationing himself to one every third day. He had a cataract in his left eye, which was getting dimmer. By April, he was blocked on the book and "terror whispers in my ear that that's because there is something wrong with the whole project."[214] In mid-May, he feared for his wits. He heaved himself onward through the summer, running down to the beach despite the torn ligament and the pain, cranking out more pages, waking in the night in a fret.

On his birthday in August 1978, he resolved to make japam three times a day, morning, noon, and night, "*with beads*." The following month, he made another resolve like the ones his mother had introduced in his childhood, to follow a daily self-improvement scheme; this time it was isometric exercises devised by the Olympic wrestler Henry Wittenberg. "I'm living an exceptionally compulsionistic life," he wrote in his diary. "I have to do my various specimen tasks each day—my midday beads, my isometric stretchings, my bit of the Swami book, and this diary. Perhaps it is the only way I can function now."[215] He was relying on his famous willpower.

Toward the end of 1978, Bachardy went to Mexico for ten days with Bill Franklin. "[A]nd why the hell shouldn't he?" Isherwood demanded in his diary, as he tried to come to terms with it. "Am indulging in some interesting physical symptoms; I begin to feel a certain weakness in my right knee, the first twinges in many months. Also, today, I peed blood twice." He was lonely, but now he also admitted to his diary: "I feel old and, oddly enough, a bit nervous by myself—another dream about a fire."

Eventually, he insisted that Franklin be pushed out of the Animals' domestic ménage. Bachardy took other lovers, and Isherwood felt less threatened by numbers, noting with satisfaction that there were "three part-time successors."[216]

In 1979, *A Meeting by the River* finally went to Broadway. A producer called Harry Rigby had contacted Isherwood back in 1975, "wildly enthusiastic" about the play.[217] Rigby introduced a co-producer, Terry Allen Kramer, and a director, Albert Marre. They planned to open at the University of Tennessee at the beginning of March, then two weeks in Boston, and then New York. Isherwood and Bachardy worked on more rewrites, and Isherwood temporarily abandoned the Prabhavananda book. Marre traveled to Belur Math with the designer and with the actor playing Oliver, Simon Ward, to learn about the rituals, music, and dance.

Isherwood and Bachardy attended New York rehearsals in January and February. Press interest in Isherwood was strong, and he again appeared on *The Dick Cavett Show*. Bachardy was also sought after by reporters, and their social life was manic. David Hockney was in town with his new lover Gregory Evans and Nick Wilder; Peter Schlesinger and Eric Boman were also there. One night, Bachardy went out dancing at Studio 54 with Truman Capote and Andy Warhol. In addition to rewrites for the play, and getting music composed, Isherwood started back on the Prabhavananda book on February 1. Bachardy was doing portrait sittings whenever he could. Isherwood broke out in a rash.

Back in Los Angeles, Dr. Giorgi diagnosed psoriasis, prescribed a cream and gave Isherwood another vitamin B12 shot. Bachardy soon learned to administer these, and he also took over cutting Isherwood's hair. Isherwood managed to keep working on the book, now titled *My Guru and His Disciple*. He submitted seventeen chapters, and Michael di Capua called to say he liked them.

On March 1, Isherwood and Bachardy flew to Knoxville for the opening of *A Meeting by the River*. For ten days, they did rewrites after almost every performance, then went on to New York; the two-week try-out in Boston had been scrapped. The *New York Times* reported that it "went so well in Knoxville" they would open three weeks early on Broadway.

In the rush, Patrick's young boyfriend, Tom, was cast only at the last minute, with Keith McDermott. The scene in which Tom first appears, exposing Patrick's duplicity toward his wife, triggered arguments between Marre and the two leads, Simon Ward playing Oliver and Keith Baxter playing Patrick, and they wrote a letter to Isherwood and Bachardy. Ward and

Baxter got angry again on the day before the final preview. Bachardy later recalled that "Baxter wouldn't play the character as written. He didn't want to be too unsympathetic. He was always fighting the interpretation of the part."[218] They opened on March 28, and Isherwood wrote in his day-to-day diary: "Decision to close play immediately because of bad notices."

Richard Eder for the *New York Times* slammed the play as "dated" and cruelly suggested that the key religious action occurred while the audience was out of the room: "Transformation comes suddenly; in the intermission between the second and third acts, to be precise; and we never see how." The acting seemed to him so false that he suggested the actors were "guying their parts" deliberately: "Albert Marre has directed in what seems to be a state of desperation." Others were more admiring. The drama critic for Gannett Newspapers called the play "a thing of delicate beauty and considerable dramatic value" and praised the "elegant, and very effective symmetry of plot."[219] But it didn't matter.

According to Bachardy, the fatal mistake was the theater. The cast was already in Knoxville when Marre went to New York, alone, to negotiate for the venue; he ended up at the Palace, suited to musicals and far too big for *A Meeting by the River*. "Oh, it was just awful, this *huge* hall for this tiny little what do you call it—chamber piece—which should be done in a small intimate theater." Another problem was that Sam Jaffe, who played the Swami, had trouble remembering his lines. He was nearly fifteen years older than Isherwood, "still remembered for his performance as the high lama in the 1937 film *Lost Horizon* and last seen on Broadway 40 years ago," as one journalist put it. Bachardy recalled that "We never knew what would come out of his mouth. Or he would just sit there smiling as if one of the other actors had forgotten his lines. Lots of old actors do it." Even worse, there had been no advance ticket sales; it would have taken weeks to promote the 1,800-plus seats.[220]

If Vedanta could not light up Broadway, how was Isherwood to overcome his block and complete *My Guru and His Disciple*? He believed that "Thoughts are things," a phrase he and Denny Fouts had long ago read together in William James's *The Varieties of Religious Experience*, and which he and Bachardy had put into the mouth of their Swami character.[221] But the wider world did not believe in anything it could not see. Was this side of his life to prove unrevealable? As ever, being attacked brought out the fighter in Isherwood. At home in Los Angeles, he went straight back to work on his book about Prabhavananda.

On May 25, Isherwood learned that Richard had died ten days earlier "in Dan Bradley's arms. It was a heart attack, without warning." Richard had divided his share of the Agatha Greene Trevor Trust between Isherwood and their cousin Thomas Isherwood, the only child of Jack and Frida. Isherwood gave the Bradleys his share of Richard's money from this trust, evidently between £35,000 and £45,000.[222]

He submitted his manuscript of *My Guru and His Disciple* at the end of May, and he gave Harvey Young a copy, fearing Young might object like Neddermeyer. Young "thought it was beautiful," and he wrote "a sweet but embarrassing letter saying that I am one of the few people one meets in a lifetime that one can really trust and signing himself my disciple." Isherwood also shared a copy with the Vedanta Society, through a monk supervising publications and the bookstore, Bob Adjemian. There were no objections, but Adjemian reported that trouble was expected after the book was published: "Swahananda's only fear is that my book should give the impression that Vedanta endorses homosexuality."[223]

Isherwood's notoriety in the gay liberation movement continued to grow. *A Single Man* and *Christopher and His Kind* generated the sort of passionate enthusiasm of which he had been suspicious most of his life. In September 1979, he offered readings and conversation at a fundraiser for Gay Advocates in San Francisco:

> Amidst the cheers and standing ovations, I felt somehow like a conductor conducting a piece of music which isn't his own composition. I don't mean that I was consciously trying to say only things I thought they'd like to hear. But I *was* trying to be one of them, whether in agreement or in disagreement. I felt that I was a member of the tribe...[224]

That fall, Isherwood and Bachardy collaborated on an illustrated diary, *October*. Bachardy drew an ink portrait—sometimes more—each day of the month, and Isherwood made the prose entries. He adopted a semi-public tone with frequent explanatory gestures to his audience, gestures he did not make in his private diary. October 1 was Richard's birthday, so he began by writing about Richard's death. There were new reflections about Kathleen and Emily, who also had October birthdays. Bachardy drew Isherwood for the first illustration in the book, and Isherwood made a sketch of Bachardy in words: "He himself, with a pen gripped in his mouth ready for use when it is needed instead of a brush, reminds me of a pirate carrying a dagger between his teeth while boarding the enemy. He seems to be attacking the sitter."

Isherwood also recorded telling Peter Alexander about how he and Bachardy worked: "I said that our respective art-forms—Don's single-session drawings or paintings which he never retouches; my gradual production, by much trial and error through many months, of longish proseworks—seem closely related to our characters. Don is all impatience, energy, aggression. I'm patient, lazy but persistent."[225] Yet both strived for the effect of casual, instantaneous reality and for insight into personalities obtainable only by the acute glimpse.

October established a shared Isherwood–Bachardy style that was spare, precise, unflinchingly candid and intense, beautiful, intellectually hip. The format was lavish in size (10˝ by 13˝), yet the material was austerely printed in black and white. The drawings included one striking male nude, of Curt Klebaum, who worked at Nick Wilder's gallery. The book helped position the Isherwood–Bachardy partnership and its aesthetic at the center of highbrow gay culture, inviting readers inside the day-to-day routine of the riveting, complicated, haloed couple depicted in Hockney's double portrait. Hockney was later to make another giant painting, *A Visit with Christopher and Don, Santa Monica Canyon* (1984), which portrayed them at work in the shared domestic compound that afforded them both privacy and interconnection, Isherwood at his desk in the house, Bachardy in his studio.

ISHERWOOD WASN'T CONFIDENT that *My Guru and His Disciple* would be popular when it was published in the summer of 1980. "I can imagine really savage attacks on it and yet in a way I think it is the most worthwhile book I have written *and* probably one of the best modern books of its kind."

Again, he made exhausting promotional trips—to San Francisco, London, and Amsterdam. In San Francisco, he was interviewed for two days solid. Bachardy shared some of the interviews with him "like a professional."[226]

William Hogan in the *San Francisco Chronicle* called *My Guru and His Disciple* "a religious adventure story." James Atlas for the *New York Times* found the style "bland," but the narrative "artless in its simplicity." He was moved by Isherwood's humility and pronounced himself "convinced that Swami was enlightened."[227]

In England, Philip Toynbee stole the show among reviewers by proclaiming in the *Observer* his spiritual alignment with Isherwood, writing that Isherwood's earlier biography, *Ramakrishna and His Disciples*, "remains for me one of the outstanding religious revelations of my life; and I believe, with Isherwood, that Ramakrishna was something more than a great teacher and prophet; I believe that he was in a supreme degree what all of us are in varying degrees of littleness—an incarnation of God."

Toynbee recalled that Isherwood's biography of Ramakrishna had met with "facetious and arrogant contempt" among reviewers, and he feared that in *My Guru and His Disciple* Isherwood "lays himself even wider open to this kind of treatment. He describes his love affairs as frankly as he describes his spiritual quest; and he makes no bones about the equal importance to him of both of these complementary elements in his life." Toynbee declared *My Guru and His Disciple* "fascinating," "often very funny," and above all "as much a book about man and God as, say, the Book of Job or the Acts of the Apostles." He thought Isherwood's publishers "unwise" to head their jacket copy with the conversation in which Isherwood asked whether he could lead a spiritual life while he was having a sexual relationship with a young man and Prabhavananda replied, "You must try to see him as the young *Lord Krishna*." Indeed, nearly every reviewer mentioned this passage.[228] Isherwood had long worked to change the relationship between religion and sex and to recalibrate conventional notions of vice and virtue; his publishers were at last prepared to take some risks along with him.

Michael Ratcliffe, in *The Times*, harmonized with Philip Toynbee in pointing out that "Few of his English admirers [...] have ever quite come to terms with the great leap in Isherwood's life around 1940." The Vedanta Center and its shrine, he said, "must be understood as the background to Isherwood's entire life and work in California over the past 40 years. It will not go away." In the *Times Literary Supplement*, the novelist and critic Paul Binding was philosophically at odds with the whole project because he didn't believe in God; he attributed all Isherwood's achievement to his education in the liberal humanist tradition and none to his conversion to Hinduism. The anonymous reviewer for *The Economist* refused to be convinced by anything less than perfection in the religious life, focusing on Isherwood's "reluctance to commit himself wholeheartedly" to the monastery and on Prabhavananda's "lapses into competitiveness and self importance." John Lehmann managed to affirm Isherwood's view that he, Lehmann, was not interested in anything he didn't already know: he pronounced himself "confused" and "put off" by the proliferation in the book of words like "pranam," "puja," "mantram," "japam."[229]

Spender, writing for the *New York Review of Books*, now produced the review addressing the reinventions in *Christopher and His Kind*: "*My Guru and His Disciple* is autobiography in which Isherwood draws upon all the devices of fiction." He saw in this last book the "coming together" of Isherwood as novelist, autobiographer, biographer. "It is probably his best book," he conjectured.[230]

Younger gay writers, fans, wanted more from Isherwood, just as Isherwood had once wanted more from Forster. Edmund White, in the *New York Times Book Review*, was among those disappointed by Isherwood's "plain style": "a seeker after wisdom may free himself of the senses, the writer mustn't." Still, he admired Isherwood's "direct, even jaunty appreciation of how preposterous, certainly precarious, spirituality can be today"; he recognized the comic absurdity, something approximating the glee Isherwood had longed for in religious novels. "No other writer I'm aware of" had reported what it was like "to be a clever, upper-class Englishman, a socialist and a skeptic, a handsome party-boy, a celebrated novelist who sits down and begins to meditate for the very first time."

Alan Hollinghurst found Isherwood's spiritual experiences less interesting than the sexual ones revealed in *Christopher and His Kind* and saw little in Vedanta to illuminate Isherwood's artistic achievement: "the book is almost silent on the subject of his writing and (with an excusable reticence) of his private life since he met Don Bachardy."[231]

That Isherwood was in a vanguard was to become increasingly clear in the fullness of time. The British literary scholar Christopher Ricks evinced doubt that an Englishman could really become a Hindu. He invoked T.S. Eliot's observation that "You can be eclectic in ideas, but you have no such freedom to choose your ancestors."[232] Isherwood had often described the obstacles that India put between him and Vedanta, but his devotion made him part of a much wider process of cultural mixing that was only just beginning and was to prove Ricks wrong.

Armistead Maupin had sent Isherwood *Tales of the City* in September 1978, a few months after they first met, and Isherwood couldn't put it down. "The mood of it, the kind of campy fun, is perfect of its kind. I kept thinking how Wystan would have loved it," Isherwood wrote. He recognized in Maupin powers of insight and empathy similar to his own: "He seems to be absorbing impressions constantly, which means that he is tremendously 'responsive' in Kathleen's use of the word, and kind of mediumistic in the way he has psychic feelers out, testing the atmosphere." Later, Isherwood described *Tales of the City* as "a modern Dickens novel." Maupin's work developed and extended ideas in Isherwood's fictions about substitute mothers, fathers, uncles that showed you could indeed choose your ancestors. Forty years on, Maupin was to identify Isherwood as his logical grandfather, "the obvious tribal elder for our new breed of open queers," and "part of a lineage that reached back through Forster and Maugham to Wilde and Whitman and Carpenter and every unknown soldier and working-class roughneck who had ever rolled in the hay with them."[233]

In the U.S., *My Guru and His Disciple* sold nearly 10,000 copies by the end of July. Isherwood heard from one American monastic that in India the book "has shocked some, pleased others."[234]

Already, Isherwood had begun writing something else. Back in July 1979, he had looked again at his friend John Van Druten's memoir, *The Widening*

Circle, and noted that Van Druten had used his ranch as the setting for his thoughts and memories. Isherwood decided to use Adelaide Drive in a similar way. "The house will be the image of me, the old man, in constant danger of collapse."[235] Over the following weeks, he developed the idea to include all the houses where he had lived during his California life and the relationships that had unfolded in each one; his working title was *California*.

He was, though, slowing down. By May 1981, he had only eleven pages. He was considering the title *Scenes from an Emigration*, harking back to his teacher G.B. Smith's long-ago history textbook *Scenes from European History*.

In mid-July 1980, he had learned that Caskey had been found dead in the apartment in Athens, Greece, where he had settled after moving abroad in the late 1960s. He felt "Relief that we're rid of the tiresome menace of Billy's jealousy of Don," but he was saddened when a mutual acquaintance wrote that Caskey had been dead for a month before the police found his body. This "vision of Billy leading a life so utterly without friends" shocked Isherwood. He still felt grateful to Caskey "for making the break between us when it had to be made and I perhaps wouldn't have made it myself."[236]

FOLLOWING THE BROADWAY fiasco, Bachardy had continued his work as diligently as Isherwood. In the spring of 1979, he showed on the campus of Redlands College, in Houston, and in a portrait exhibition at the Barnsdall Park Municipal Gallery. He was doing portrait sittings nearly every day. Nicholas Wilder had begun to share his gallery with another dealer, Jim Corcoran, and Wilder soon told Bachardy he was giving up altogether. Jim Corcoran kept four of Wilder's artists—Sam Francis, Ron Davis, Hockney, and Bachardy.

Bachardy's first show at the Corcoran Gallery opened on March 1, 1980—portraits of women. The reviewer for the *Los Angeles Times* was a woman, too, Suzanne Muchnic, who announced a new fashion for portraiture after decades of abstraction. Isherwood copied her praise into his diary: "Now that human likenesses are enjoying a revival of interest, his work looks better than ever."

There was a huge crowd at the opening party, sales were good, and there were commissions. Wilder's support had been enormously important to Bachardy, validating his maturity as an artist. Isherwood's suppport was even more important. "You were the only one who encouraged me, I'd never have gone on without you," Bachardy had told Isherwood in July 1972.[237] He repeated this often as the years went by.

In September 1980, Isherwood flew with Bachardy to New York to open another show, at the Robert Miller Gallery. They carried copies of their book, *October*, and arrived in time to attend *The Elephant Man* and be charmed by David Bowie at a party afterwards. Andy Warhol and Bob Colacello had published excerpts from *October* in their magazine *Interview*, and Isherwood and Bachardy went to lunch at the Factory. Nick Wilder supervised the hanging of the show for the gallerists Robert Miller and John Cheim. A Swedish dealer bought thirty Bachardy paintings, "a first European beachhead," as Isherwood proudly wrote in his diary.

Bachardy had also been commissioned by Bruce Voeller, the biologist turned activist who had founded the National Gay Task Force and who later devised the name Acquired Immune Deficiency Syndrome, to do a series of twelve portraits of gay and lesbian leaders for Voeller's Mariposa Foundation.[238] He began the commission during the trip to New York, where he also drew Robert Mapplethorpe.

On the same New York trip, Isherwood and Bachardy met with a producer and agreed to collaborate on a screenplay of "Paul." As soon as they were home, Isherwood began making an outline.

One day, while he was at his desk and Bachardy was out in the studio, intruders broke into the house, one carrying a knife. Isherwood cried for help in hope of scaring them away. They hit him in the face until his lip bled, tied him up with the belt of his bathrobe, took the money in his billfold, his rings and his watch, then forced him down on the floor of his workroom, gagged with a sock and with his bathrobe wrapped around his head, promising not to hurt him if he was quiet while they searched in the next room.

Writing up the episode in his diary, Isherwood insisted that he had never felt frightened. His imagination automatically came to his defense, converting the episode into fiction even while it was happening: "My situation seemed to me corny in the extreme—something which only belongs in a book." After the robbers fled, he managed to free his feet, walked out to the studio with his hands still tied, and banged on the door with an elbow, gleefully maximising the emotional payoff in presenting himself to Bachardy. "Darling cried out in dismay when he saw Dobbin all bloody—all the rest of the day he was so sweetly concerned. Then the police came."

He had a sore rib for ten days, though his lip healed quickly. Bachardy was mortified. "My encounter with the burglars, I know, has given him a much greater shock than it gave me," Isherwood wrote, but he was more upset than he admitted, even to himself, because the burglary highlighted his increasing helplessness. The fears he repressed surfaced, as they always had, in his dreams. There was growing pressure on Bachardy, as they both knew. One day, Isherwood drank too much at a party, spilled wine on himself, and had to be helped from the room. Bachardy reprimanded him on behalf of them both. "'I played the scene very well,' Darling told me, but I know they were all thinking, 'How awful it must be for Don.' So Drub swore to reform."[239] He drank nothing at all for some time. Parties were more and more unwelcome to him anyway.

In April 1980, Dr. Giorgi had discovered that Isherwood had a hernia. He had been experiencing stomachaches and nausea for some time, and she advised him to lose weight and not to wear his belt tight. The pain grew worse over the following year. In April 1981, he wrote in his diary: "I feel I might die quite suddenly—the vital supports are beginning to give way." He was increasingly reluctant to leave the house or see friends; his relationship with Bachardy was "largely a nursery world of sleeping together, cuddled like children." He also had pains in his right leg and in his back. Still, he ran down to the beach, swam, worked at his writing, and determinedly recorded his physical and spiritual condition: "Loss of hair. Loss of taste and consequent loss of weight—down to 147 and ½—no big deal, this."

At last, he dreamed about Prabhavananda. "It was definitely an 'appearance,'" he wrote in his diary. "What I dreamed was just being with him—in his room at Vedanta Place, I suppose—and being moved by the faith and joy with which he spoke about God. You could call it a vision or just a vivid memory, since I experienced the same thing many times in his presence when he was still alive."

Dr. Giorgi sent Isherwood to a surgeon who wanted to operate on the hernia. Bachardy was opposed. Isherwood himself was opposed, but he was suffering "real electric shock pains in the upper legs," which reminded him of his near-death illness in childhood. "Having these pains makes me remember what cruel pain I often had when I was young. Probably the rheumatic fever pains were the worst, when I was ten."[240] (Evidently, he believed he *had* had rheumatic fever, although this had been a fear not a fact.)

To fight off depression, he began a new draft of the "Paul" screenplay, but in May, he and Bachardy agreed to abandon it. Bachardy was busy with four exhibitions that spring, including a show of the Mariposa Portraits at the National Gay Archives.

Isherwood focused on his California memoir. The pain in his gut grew worse, and his weight began to drop precipitously. He started taking Butazolidin again, and he was also taking four aspirin every day and receiving massages and acupuncture for his back. At the end of June, Dr. Giorgi insisted on the hernia operation. As he signed off work on his memoir, Isherwood had a surge of interest. "It's tantalizing, how clearly I seem to see my way ahead on the *California* book just when I have to stop work because of going into hospital."[241] He had four chapters roughed out. He had lost ten pounds.

After the operation, the pain continued, and Isherwood's weight went on falling. He was back at work on his book, walked to the park most days, and shared evening meals with friends. By his birthday, he had lost more than fifteen pounds and weighed only 132. He tried a new doctor. He had ice packs on his back, followed by hot baths. One day, he couldn't get out of the bathtub; Bachardy had to help him. Once again, he started taking Butazolidin. By mid-September, he weighed only 130 pounds. He made two visits to a specialist back pain center, and then he checked back into St. John's Hospital, where they put him on methadone.

In his day-to-day diary for September 23, 1981, Isherwood recorded: "Dr. Brosman told me about tumor in prostate." He had a biopsy, consultations with all his doctors, and started taking pills for his back pain. He left the hospital after three days. It was three weeks before he mentioned the tumor in his diary. "Don is heroic, heartbreaking in his devotion. He keeps me off the pain pills as much as possible, to prove to me that I can do without them." Bachardy also encouraged him to work on his book. They saw friends and watched lots of movies. "I pray and pray to Swami—to show himself to me, no matter how—as we've been promised that he will, before death." Sometimes the pain was bad. "I get fits of being very very scared."

On December 23, Isherwood had another biopsy. It was negative. "Did I ever have cancer at all? Can cancer come and go so casually? Or did Brosman merely mean that he *thought* I had cancer, originally?"[242] By February 14, 1982, the Animals' twenty-ninth anniversary, his weight was back to normal—147. By May, his back was better, his legs were stronger, he felt up to walking and even running. He did have cancer, but, for now, treatments were working.

Although Isherwood struggled with depression and death fears, 1982 was another busy year. Bachardy ensured their life together continued as before. Isherwood read the Katha Upanishad at Vivekananda's breakfast puja in January 1982 at the Hollywood Temple as he had done for many years. Bachardy opened another show at the Corcoran Gallery in March. Hockney marked the day of the opening by making a composite photograph portrait of Isherwood and Bachardy. Isherwood reached page 100 in his California memoir and kept going. He also carried on with guest-teaching and interviews for TV, radio, and print.

In 1983, Isherwood received a PEN award for a Distinguished Body of Work and the *Los Angeles Times*'s Robert Kirsch Award for Lifetime Achievement. The mayor of Los Angeles, Tom Bradley, declared May 21, 1983, to be "Christopher Isherwood Day." The mayor of Santa Monica followed suit. In October 1983, Isherwood and Bachardy flew to New York for a symposium commemorating the tenth anniversary of Auden's death. Isherwood was assisted to a podium at Columbia University and read aloud to a packed room some of his friend's earliest poems. Bachardy hovered near. I sat in the back row, the only time I ever saw Isherwood.

He was writing less and less. The entries in his diary and his day-to-day books show proliferating corrections, then dwindle away. He made his last diary entry on July 4, 1983, the anniversary of Prabhavananda's death. Two and a half years remained to him—without writing. He never wrote about AIDS, first reported in California in 1981 and identified in 1983, though he had friends who died of it after he stopped writing.

AT THE START of 1981, Isherwood had written in his diary: "my death—I sincerely believe—would set Darling free. He wouldn't collapse. He would spread his wings and fly higher." A few weeks later, he had put the question to Bachardy: "'What'll Kitty do when Dobbin has to depart?' Kitty answered, without hesitation, 'Give him a great send-off.' "[243]

And so he did. At the end of Isherwood's life, it was evident to Bachardy that although Isherwood could do almost nothing, he could still sit for his portrait. So Bachardy gave up all his other sitters and painted only Isherwood. They worked together nearly every day, through sickness and pain, for about five months, starting on Isherwood's birthday. Bachardy used a Japanese paintbrush and black acrylic paint suited to the solemnity of this final collaboration. He wrote about their sessions in his diary: "While Chris was sitting for me on Thursday evening, his eyes on me and the view of the ocean, mountains and canyon behind me, he suddenly said:, 'There's so much to describe.' His eyes filled with tears." Was it nostalgia for the writing he had been forced to abandon? Or joy for the beauty that continued to surround him?

At the end of October 1985, Isherwood was admitted to St. John's for chemotherapy and radiation. He and Bachardy began the sittings again in mid-November. During the hiatus, Bachardy had asked himself: "am I so insistent about these sittings with Chris as a means of *extending* the time I have left with him, thereby impressing this time all the more firmly in my mind?" He felt guilty insisting on the sessions, "Yet it is the only way now that I can really be with him intensely, in a way which challenges me as much as him. Perhaps it's my revenge on him for getting old and sick. If so, so be it. I know that he forgives me. I know that he understands."

Isherwood was so ill that he stopped commenting on the pictures, so Bachardy stopped showing them to him. One day, as Bachardy gathered up work spread on the floor to dry, Isherwood unexpectedly said, "I like the ones of him dying."

Dr. Giorgi suggested Isherwood be readmitted to hospital for a morphine drip on January 2. Bachardy put it off. "I felt it would be a capitulation," he wrote in his diary. "Also, I might not get Chris out again. (I want to do the death drawing and might be prevented from doing it in hospital!)" As he lay dying, Isherwood was "coughing, moaning and grimacing, occasionally calling for Nanny and mumbling some unintelligible complaint." Bachardy went on working with his Japanese brush. The last drawings are unquestionably some of his greatest work.

Isherwood died on January 4, 1986, at home in his bed as he had always wished. Bachardy painted his corpse. "I was able to identify with him to such an extent that I felt I was sharing his dying ... It began to seem that dying was something which we were doing together."[244]

Sri Krishna:

There was never a time when I did not exist, nor you, nor any of these kings. Nor is there any future in which we shall cease to be.

Bhagavad Gita II,
"The Yoga of Knowledge"

Acknowledgments

Don Bachardy has opened his life to me without reserve, sharing everything he knows about Christopher Isherwood and insisting on absolute candor about their relationship. His intelligence, his bravery, his charm, his curiosity, his fine powers of discrimination, his sense of humor have made writing this book the adventure of a lifetime.

Sarah Chalfant, my agent, first suggested the project, and she has steadfastly stood by me through the thickest of thick and the thinnest of thin.

My friends the filmmakers Tina Mascara and her late husband Guido Santi made this journey with me, their steps in pictures, often leading the way.

Xenobe Purvis, intellect in angel wings, has worked untold hours as my researcher, finding things out and noticing what's wrong (remaining wrongs are mine, not hers).

My publishers Clara Farmer and Jonathan Galassi fought through thousands of pages now on the cutting-room floor; Isherwood would be grateful for their rigor.

Other generous and tenacious early readers were Michael Carroll, John Fuller, Matthew Greenburgh, Rachel Kelly Grigg, Verlyn Klinkenborg, Edward Mendelson, Anthony Page, Roger Pasquier, Richard Sassin, Erik Tarloff, and above all Pravrajika Vrajaprana, my guru in all things Vedanta.

My heart swells painfully as I reflect on the time and wisdom given me by each of the people listed above and all I have learned from them over the years. It's been a long project, building deep gratitude.

So many other friends, acquaintances, and strangers have answered questions, helped me to materials, given time to conversation. I treasure these exchanges: the late Peter Alexander, Anne Alvarez and the late Al Alvarez, Lisa Appignanesi, the late Billy Al Bengston, Leslie Caron, Sally Carton, Kent Chapman, Mary Agnes Donoghue, Gregory Evans, Robin French,

Susan Bradley Hasledine, Bettina von Hase, David Hockney, Jennie and Steve Hoffman, Val Holley, Michael Holzman, Lisa Janssen, Alan Jenkins, George Lawson, Julian Machin, Stephen Miller, Stephen Morley-Mower, Don Murray, Alvin Novak, the late George Ramsden and his widow Jane Ramsden, Paul Rassam, Joseph Rodota, Peter Schlesinger, Roger Scott, Wayne Sleep, Matthew Spender, the late Sir Stephen Spender, Jeremy Treglown, Swami Tyagananda, the late Edward Upward and his daughter Kathy Allinson, James P. White, Professor Jonathan White.

Isherwood's earlier biographers have a place in my heart—Peter Parker, Brian Finney, Jonathan Fryer—as does Norman Page for his book on Isherwood and W.H. Auden in Berlin. The biggest place belongs to Edward Mendelson (*so* deservedly) for his lifetime achievement editing, writing about, and teaching the work of W.H. Auden. The late Samuel Hynes introduced me to *Goodbye to Berlin* in 1979; I owe a great deal to his teaching as well, and to his books, *The Auden Generation* and *The Edwardian Turn of Mind*.

I had research assistance from Zennor Compton and from Angelica von Hase, who is an English-German and German-English translator of nuance and sophistication.

At the Wylie Agency, I am eager to thank Luke Ingram for his continuously thoughtful support; at Chatto, Rosanna Hildyard, Rowena Skelton-Wallace, Rhiannon Roy, Priya Roy, Katherine Fry, John Garrett, Stephen Parker, Lily Richards and Rosalynne Otoo for their patient and clear-headed editing, copy-editing, proofreading, bold design, picture wizardry and all manner of strategic masterminding. At Farrar, Straus and Giroux, I would like to add Katharine Liptak. Christopher Phipps has assembled the expert index to which I know some may turn first.

The Huntington Library has been a wellspring of seemingly magical resources. It is also a sanctuary. Stephanie Arias, Anne Blecksmith, Sandra Brooke Gordon, Nick Degala, Sarah Francis, Steve Hindle, Sue Hodson, Alan Jutzi, Holly Mendenhall, Karla Nielsen, Jazmin Rew-Pinchem, Bert Rinderle, David Zeidberg are among the remarkable professionals who helped me there. At the Harry Ransom Center, another sanctuary, I had generous and thoughtful assistance from Jean Cannon, Cathy Henderson, and David Ramos. Staff at nearly every library in which I worked were kind and able, and I am especially grateful to librarians and research assistants whose names I failed to record because, together, we were focused on Christopher Isherwood. Please be honored by the anonymity which shows your devoted professionalism. I would also like to acknowledge Mary Ellen Budney, Yale Collection of American Literature, Beinecke Rare Book and Manuscript Library; Todd Gustavson, Curator of Technology, Eastman House, Rochester, NY; Lucy Hughes, Archivist, Corpus Christi College, Cambridge; David

Milner, Penguin Random House; Penny King, Secretary, and Tony Pull, former Headmaster, St. Edmund's School, Hindhead, Surrey; Gosia Lawik, the London Library; Ann Hearle, Neil Mullineux, and Judith Wilshaw of the Marple Local History Society; Paul Hartley, Professional Support and Conservation Manager Planning Services, Stockport Council; Mark Fletcher, Matrix Archaeology; Garry Miller, Historic Building Consultancy, St. Helens, Lancashire; Judith Ratcliffe, Britten Pears Arts Archive, The Red House, Aldeburgh, Suffolk.

To my family, caught up in this book, like it or not, for as long as you can remember, I can never thank you enough for the sacrifices you have made. It has changed us all; luckily, time spent with Christopher Isherwood changes us for the better.

Notes

GUIDE TO ENDNOTES

For Isherwood's published works, I give page references to the first edition. Before 1939, first editions appeared in England; after 1939, they nearly all appeared in the U.S. until the posthumous diaries and correspondence which appeared in uniform editions. To assist readers using other editions, I give chapter numbers for the books that have chapters. For books by others, I generally quote from the edition Isherwood used, but where I quote from a later edition I give both editions. I use the following abbreviations and acronyms.

FICTION

AC—All the Conspirators (London: Jonathan Cape, 1928)
Memorial—The Memorial: Portrait of a Family (London: Hogarth Press, 1932)
MNCT—Mr. Norris Changes Trains (London: Hogarth Press, 1935; *The Last of Mr. Norris* in U.S.)
SB—Sally Bowles (London: Hogarth Press, 1937)
GB—Goodbye to Berlin (London: Hogarth Press, 1939)
PV—Prater Violet (New York: Random House, 1945)
WE—The World in the Evening (New York: Random House, 1954)
DTV—Down There on a Visit (New York: Simon & Schuster, 1962)
SM—A Single Man (New York: Simon & Schuster, 1964)
MBR—A Meeting by the River (New York: Simon & Schuster, 1967)
Mortmere—The Mortmere Stories with Edward Upward (London: Enitharmon Press, 1994)

PLAYS

DBS—The Dog Beneath the Skin, or Where Is Francis? with W.H. Auden (London: Faber and Faber, 1935)

F6—*The Ascent of F6* with W.H. Auden (London: Faber and Faber, 1936)
OTF—*On the Frontier* with W.H. Auden (London: Faber and Faber, 1938)

MEMOIRS

L&S—*Lions and Shadows: An Education in the Twenties* (London: Hogarth Press, 1938)
K&F—*Kathleen and Frank: The Autobiography of a Family* (New York: Simon & Schuster, 1971)
C&HK—*Christopher and His Kind: 1929–1939* (New York: Farrar, Straus & Giroux, 1976)
MG&HD—*My Guru and His Disciple* (New York: Farrar, Straus & Giroux, 1980)

TRAVEL

JW—*Journey to a War* with W.H. Auden (London: Faber and Faber, 1939)
C&C—*The Condor and the Cows: A South American Travel Diary* (New York: Random House, 1949)

VEDANTA

PI Gita—*Baghavad Gita, The Song of God*, trans. with Swami Prabhavananda (Hollywood: Marcel Rodd Company, 1944)
Patanjali—*How to Know God: The Yoga Aphorisms of Patanjali*, trans. with Swami Prabhavananda (New York: Harper & Brothers, 1953)
VWW—*Vedanta for the Western World*, ed. Isherwood (Hollywood: Marcel Rodd Company, 1945)
VMM—*Vedanta for Modern Man*, ed. Isherwood, (New York: Harper & Brothers, 1951)
Wishing Tree—*The Wishing Tree: Christopher Isherwood on Mystical Religion*, ed. Robert Adjemian (New York: Harper & Row, 1987)
R&HD—*Ramakrishna and His Disciples* (New York: Simon & Schuster, 1965)

LITERARY COLLECTIONS

GESS—*Great English Short Stories*, ed. Isherwood (New York: Dell, 1957)
Exh.—*Exhumations: Stories, Articles and Verse* (New York: Simon & Schuster, 1966)

PUBLISHED DIARIES

October—with Don Bachardy (Los Angeles: Twelve Trees Press, 1980)
D1—*Diaries, Volume One: 1939–1960*, ed. Katherine Bucknell (New York and London: HarperCollins/Methuen, 1996)

LY—*Lost Years: A Memoir 1945–1951*, ed. Katherine Bucknell (New York and London: HarperCollins/Chatto & Windus, 2000)

D2—*Diaries, Volume Two: The Sixties 1960–1969*, ed. Katherine Bucknell (New York and London: HarperCollins/Chatto & Windus, 2010)

D3—*Diaries, Volume Three: Liberation 1970–1983*, ed. Katherine Bucknell (New York and London: HarperCollins/Chatto & Windus, 2012)

PUBLISHED LETTERS

Repton Letters—*The Repton Letters*, ed. George Ramsden (Settrington, York: Stone Trough Books, 1997)

K&C—*Kathleen and Christopher: Christopher Isherwood's Letters to His Mother*, ed. Lisa Coletta, (Minneapolis: University of Minnesota Press, 2005)

F&I—*Letters Between Forster and Isherwood on Homosexuality and Literature*, ed. Richard Zeikowitz (New York and Basingstoke: Palgrave Macmillan, 2008)

Animals—*The Animals: Love Letters Between Christopher Isherwood and Don Bachardy*, ed. Katherine Bucknell (London and New York: Chatto & Windus/Farrar, Straus & Giroux, 2013)

LECTURES AND INTERVIEWS

IonW—*Isherwood on Writing*, ed. James J. Berg (Minneapolis: University of Minnesota Press, 2007)

Conversations—*Conversations with Christopher Isherwood*, ed. James J. Berg and Chris Freeman (Jackson: University Press of Mississippi, 2001)

ARCHIVES

CI—The main Isherwood archive is the Christopher Isherwood Papers at the Huntington Library, San Marino, California. I give call numbers starting with CI for items in this collection, and for some longer items, page numbers. Other Huntington call numbers refer to material that did not come to the library from the Isherwood Estate. Uncertain dates are in square brackets. I sometimes include details of an address to assist in identifying undated letters or supply information of note.

Bancroft—Bancroft Library, University of California, Berkeley.

Beinecke—Beinecke Rare Book and Manuscript Library, Yale University, New Haven

Berg—Henry W. and Albert A. Berg Collection, New York Public Library

BL—British Library, London

Butler—Rare Book and Manuscript Library, Butler Library, Columbia University, New York

Gotlieb—Howard Gotlieb Archival Research Center, Boston University

HRC—Harry Ransom Center, Austin, Texas

Houghton—Houghton Library, Harvard University, Cambridge, MA

McFarlin—McFarlin Library, University of Oklahoma, Tulsa

Morgan—Morgan Library and Museum, New York
Weston—Weston Library, Special Collections, Bodleian Library, Oxford University

BY OTHERS

KBI diary—Kathleen Bradshaw Isherwood diaries, Christopher Isherwood Papers, Huntington Library and, for the years 1911–1959, Harry Ransom Center

Memory Book—Kathleen Bradshaw Isherwood, Memory Books for 1914 and 1915, Christopher Isherwood Papers, Hungtington

"History of Marple and Wyberslegh and the Bradshaw Isherwoods"—Kathleen Bradshaw Isherwood, private hands

SA—Edward Upward, *The Spiral Ascent* (London: William Heinemann, 1977), containing *In the Thirties* (1962), *The Rotten Elements* (1969), *No Home but the Struggle* (1977)

Don Stayed—Don Bachardy, unpublished memoir written during the 1990s based on earlier diaries

Stealing the Show—Don Bachardy, unpublished memoir written 2014

INDIVIDUAL INITIALS

CI—Christopher Isherwood
CWBI—Christopher William Bradshaw Isherwood in youth
KBI—Kathleen Bradshaw Isherwood
KMS—Kathleen Machell-Smith, as she was before her marriage
FBI—Francis (Frank) Bradshaw Isherwood
RGBI—Richard Graham Bradshaw Isherwood
WHA—Wystan Hugh Auden
EU—Edward Upward
PM—Patrick (Paddy) Monkhouse
EF—Eric Falk
SS—Stephen Spender
JL—John Lehmann
EMF—Edward Morgan Forster
BV—Berthold Viertel
BB—Benjamin Britten
LK—Lincoln Kirstein
SP—Swami Prabhavananda
DS and AB—Dodie Smith and Alec Beesley
WC—William (Bill) Caskey
TW—Tennessee Williams
GV—Gore Vidal
DB—Don Bachardy
DH—David Hockney
AP—Anthony Page

PROLOGUE

1. *D1*, bridging passage, January 1939, p. 8.
2. *PV*, pp. 124–5, 125–6.
3. *D1*, February 14, 1960, p. 845.
4. Wilson, "Isherwood's Lucid Eye," *New Republic*, May 17, 1939, p. 51.

I: SON OF THE BRITISH ARMY, HEIR TO THE ESTATE

1. KBI diary, July 27, 1927, HRC.
2. KBI diary, June 2, 1903, CI 606; *K&F*, Chap. 11, pp. 263, 254.
3. "Influences," "A Writer and His World," U.C. Santa Barbara, 1960, in *IonW*, pp. 44–5.
4. KBI, "History of Marple and Wybersleghe Halls and the Bradshaw Isherwoods," includes her watercolors and floor plan. See also "Wybersley Hall, High Lane, Stockport," Historic Building Record, Matrix Archaeology, Manchester, October 2004; Report No. 2004-1 1; *K&F*, Chap. 11, p. 263.
5. KBI diary, June 8, 1911, HRC.
6. KBI diary, August 1, 1904, CI 607, quoted in *K&F*, Chap. 11, p. 270.
7. KBI diary, August 1 and 27, 1904, CI 607; see also *K&F*, Chap. 11, pp. 270, 272.
8. At Wyberslegh, KBI and FBI employed a married couple to shop, cook, clean, polish the silver, wait on table and help with the garden. Sometimes local women came in to help. In Ireland, they had two maids, a cook and a soldier servant. Marple Hall had a staff of at least five women indoors and two men outdoors.
9. KBI diary, August 27 and September 2, 1904, CI 607; see also *K&F*, Chap. 11, p. 272.
10. "Our Regiments: York and Lancaster," *Illustrated Sporting and Dramatic News*, May 5, 1900, p. 371.
11. FBI to KMS, January 22, 1900, from Venter's Spruit, Tugela River, quoted in *K&F*, Chap. 5, p. 92; FBI to KMS, February 10, 1900, from Spearman's Hill, *K&F*, Chap. 5, p. 99. FBI fought in the last three of four attempts to lift the siege. The fourth, successful, attempt was the Battle of Tugela Heights.
12. *K&F*, Chap. 1, p. 19; *Hero-Father, Demon-Mother*, p. 78, CI 1082; *K&F*, Chap. 6, pp. 113, 114.
13. *Hero-Father, Demon-Mother*, p. 19, CI 1082.
14. *K&F*, Chap. 8, p. 184.
15. *K&F*, Chap. 6, p. 121.
16. *D1*, July 12, 1940, pp. 103–4.
17. *K&F*, Chap. 18, p. 492.
18. CI later recalled that FBI "loved Chopin and Debussy" and that "he composed songs," *Hero-Father, Demon-Mother*, p. 6, CI 1082.
19. See Scott's memoir, *My Years of Indiscretion* (1924); they tried the Fletcher cure, the cold-water cure, physical exercise systems, fasting, herbal teas to clear toxins, osteopathy, the Bates method. The plan for a Vedanta society was triggered by a meeting with Swami Abhedananda.
20. *K&F*, Chap. 7, p. 154.
21. See *K&F*, Chap. 8, p. 191, for Frederick's prostate. He acknowledged CWBI's birth only indirectly in a letter to Emily, KBI diary, September 6, 1904, CI 607, quoted in *K&F*, Chap. 12, p. 276. Before he died, Frederick intended to reinstate KBI, but he ran out of time, and the money went to four female Abney cousins.
22. *K&F*, Chap. 7, p. 133.
23. FBI to KMS, February 12, 1903, and KBI diary, March 13, 1903, quoted in *K&F*, Chap. 10, pp. 244, 250.
24. *K&F*, Chap. 5, p. 96.
25. *K&F*, Chap. 12, pp. 273, 274.
26. KBI diary, September 29, 1904, CI 607.
27. KBI diary, October 29, 1904, CI 607.
28. *K&F*, Chap. 12, p. 276.

29. KBI diary, August 31, 1904, CI 607.
30. KBI diary, July 1, 1906, quoted in "The Baby's Progress," CI 591. Fictionalized by CI in *The Memorial*, where Eric Vernon recalls of his mother: "Lily had claimed all his love, since the days when she had come into the nursery in evening dress with spangles [...]" (*Memorial*, Book II, Chap. 4, p. 149)
31. "If I ask Baby where his Mama is he says Ta ta Puff." Anne Avis to KBI, September 26, 1905, MSS Tristram Papers, Huntington. "Puff" was the train which had carried Kathleen away.
32. *K&F*, Chap. 12, p. 278.
33. Anne Avis to KBI, October 6, 1905, MSS Tristram Papers, Huntington.
34. KBI diary, July 23 and August 7, 1906, CI 610.
35. Anne Avis to KBI, October 20, 1905, MSS Tristram Papers, Huntington.
36. *K&F*, Chap. 1, p. 15.
37. *K&F*, Chap. 1, p. 15; KBI diary, December 25, 1904, CI 607.
38. *K&F*, Chap. 12, pp. 278–9.
39. FBI to KBI, February 10, 1900, quoted in *K&F*, Chap. 5, p. 99.
40. Mamie Tristram to KBI, August 1905, MSS Tristram Papers, Huntington.
41. KBI diary, April 17, 1916, HRC.
42. *K&F*, Chap. 11, p. 256; "Country Homes—Gardens Old & New: Marple Hall, Cheshire, The Seat of Mr. John Henry Bradshaw Isherwood," *Country Life*, March 1, 1919, with eight large photographs.
43. *K&F*, Chap. 11, pp. 256–7; the diary of Charles Bellairs, 1838, copied by KBI into her "History of Marple and Wyberslegh Halls and the Bradshaw Isherwoods"; *Country Life*, March 1919; KBI diary, various entries.
44. The Gobelins tapestries, c.1710, were part of a series of eight designed by Charles Le Brun representing the four seasons and the courtly pastimes of Louis XV. The pair at Marple Hall depicted the dark seasons and their comforts; there was no "Spring" or "Summer." They are now at the Art Institute of Chicago.
45. *K&F*, Chap. 11, p. 258; *Hero-Father, Demon-Mother*, p. 18, CI 1082.
46. *Hero-Father, Demon-Mother*, pp. 18, 54, CI 1082. The pond dried up in the 1930s.
47. *K&F*, Chap. 13, pp. 305, 306–7.
48. *K&F*, Chap. 12, p. 280.
49. Moll was Elizabeth Brabyns Bradshaw Isherwood; *K&F*, Chap. 13, pp. 310–11. Her portrait, with "a sour harsh-featured face," hung opposite the front stairs. The summer Christopher turned three, Kathleen copied Moll's portrait for her book about Marple Hall and Wyberslegh Hall and asked the maids to move the portrait for better light. But "strange knockings and creaking noises were heard in the house," according to the maids, so Kathleen was forced to finish her drawing with the portrait hung back in its place.
50. *K&F*, Chap. 13, pp. 311, 313.
51. *K&F*, Chap. 13, pp. 310–17. KBI's diary account was based on reports from Nanny, Jack Isherwood, and others; in analysing it, CI concluded that what happened "was either a paranormal event or a hoax." He told the story to friends over the years, developing its effect. He never mentioned Charles Coyne the gardener, an obvious suspect, with his small, powerful physique, his probable knowledge of the ivy outside the nursery windows and likely access to a ladder.
52. KBI diary, August 8, 1913, HRC; *K&F*, Chap. 13, pp. 321–2.
53. *K&F*, Chap. 12, p. 321.
54. KBI later dismissed the hauntings as the romantic exaggerations of Nanny and Jack Isherwood because she was embarrassed by the piece about Marple Hall that appeared in *Country Life* in 1919. The author was Lady Newton of nearby Lyme Hall, the only greater house in the neighborhood. KBI was beguiled by Lady Newton's social status into divulging too much, and the article caused a local sensation. The *Hyde Reporter* ran excerpts and CWBI and his younger brother were gossiped about. (See KBI diary, January 14 and 22, March 17, 1919, HRC; *Hyde Reporter*, March 15, 1919, p. 5) CI's allusions to the Marple ghost stories in *The Memorial* would have been painful to KBI but unrecognized outside the family. (See *Memorial*, Book 11, Chap. 1, pp. 70–1)

55. KBI diary, October 1, 1907, CI 612; FBI to KBI quoted in *K&F*, Chap. 14, pp. 329–30.
56. *Hero-Father, Demon-Mother*, p. 20, CI 1082.
57. KBI diary, May 29, 1908, CI 613.
58. KBI diary, March 3, 1908, CI 613, quoted in *K&F*, Chap. 14, 334.
59. KBI diary, October 24, 1908, CI 613.
60. KBI diary, April 28, 1909, CI 614.
61. KBI diary, February 17, 1909, CI 614.
62. KBI diary, June 11, 1909, CI 614.
63. KBI diary, November 6, 1909, CI 614.
64. Initialled CW and KBI, with watercolor decoration, pasted inside a gray folder labeled "The History of Marple" in KBI's hand and also including her illustrations of historical events at the house and sketches of CWBI, Berg.
65. Labeled "The Adventures of a Daddie and a Mummie" in KBI's hand, wrongly dated November 1908, for 1909, Berg.
66. KBI diary, July 27, August 2, 4, 1910, CI 615.
67. KBI diary, August 12, 1910, CI 615.
68. KBI diary, August 22, 23, 1910, CI 615.
69. KBI diary, September 15, 1911, HRC.
70. *K&F*, Chap. 15, p. 364.
71. *K&F*, Chap. 14, p. 350.
72. KBI diary, November 4, 1910, CI 615.
73. Virginia Woolf, "Mr. Bennet and Mrs. Brown," lecture delivered in Cambridge, May 18, 1924, and published in *The Captain's Death Bed and Other Essays* (London: Hogarth Press, 1950), p. 91. See Samuel Hynes, *The Edwardian Turn of Mind*, Chap. 9, "Human Character Changes," pp. 325–6.
74. KBI diary, December 3, 1910, CI 615.
75. KBI diary, December 14, 1910, CI 615.
76. RGBI was conceived January 8 and born at 38 weeks, according to KBI's records of her periods and other remarks in her diaries for 1910 and 1911.
77. *K&F*, Chap. 14, pp. 349–50, 350.
78. KBI diary, February 17, 18, 19, 1911, HRC.
79. KBI diary, March 14, 1911, HRC.
80. Inscribed in large, child's handwriting between lightly ruled lines: "Christopher from Arthur Forbes. August 26, 1910." (Huntington) Arthur's father was killed at Ypres, like Frank. Arthur was educated at Winchester and Sandhurst, and served in the Cameronians, becoming Lt. Col. Walter Arthur Hastings Forbes. He married, had children, and served as a game warden in Sudan, retired 1955, died 1987.
81. *K&F*, Chap. 13, pp. 307–8, where CI quotes from *The Roly-Poly Pudding* (London: Frederick Warne & Co., 1908).
82. "Book I. History of Arthur Forbes. Chapter 1," CI box 159.
83. KBI diary, July 21, 1932, HRC.
84. KBI diary, April 4, 1911, HRC; *K&F*, Chap. 15, p. 372.
85. KBI diary, June 20, 1911, HRC.
86. KBI diary, July 1, 22, 1911, HRC.
87. KBI diary, May 24, 1911, HRC.
88. KBI diary, May 9, 1911, HRC.
89. KBI diary, December 5, 1910, CI 615.
90. Circa 1911, pasted into sketchbook, Morgan.
91. *D3*, note to April 11, 1970, p. 50.
92. "The Old Dudley Art Society," *The Times*, March 18, 1911; "Old Dudley Society Jubilee, Fine Watercolours," *Evening Standard*, March 20, 1911, p. 4.
93. KBI diary, May 17, 1911, HRC.
94. KBI diary, September 7, 1911, HRC.
95. KBI diary, August 27, 1911, HRC.
96. KBI diary, September 21, 1911, HRC.
97. On the cover of the *Illustrated London News* was a drawing of Tree bearded and long-haired as Macbeth, his eyes rolling in dread, his hand on the hilt of his sword, about

to enter Duncan's chamber and murder him so he can become king. The caption was the Weird Sisters' prophecy from Act I, scene 3, that flattered Macbeth and tempted him to become a regicide: "Thane of Glamis! Thane of Cawdor! King!" *Illustrated London News*, 16 September 1911.
98. SS had "smirked and sneered when Wystan was awarded the King's Gold Medal for poetry and had to go to the palace to receive it," CI recalled in his diary. It was the medal for 1936 which WHA collected on November 23, 1937, *D3*, July 4, 1983, p. 688.
99. Initialled CBI, Morgan.
100. KBI diary, October 1, 1911, HRC; KBI to Mrs. Joseph Pennell, December 30, 1934, HRC.
101. KBI diary, October 8, 1911, HRC.
102. In letters, FBI called RGBI "ill tempered" (FBI to KBI, January 27, 1914, CI 543) and joked to CWBI, "Richard is very busy breaking up all his toys" (FBI to CWBI, May 3, 1914, CI 562). When told that Nanny was disappointed about RGBI's third birthday being overlooked, he wrote: "I am afraid he will always have to play second fiddle to Christopher at Marple at any rate ... But I don't think he is the sort which will much mind." (FBI to KBI, October 10, 1914, in KBI Memory Book, 1914, CI 619.)
103. KBI diary, October 6, 9, 1911, HRC.
104. CWBI to KBI, October 1911, CI 1192.
105. KBI diary, October 25, 29, 1911, HRC.
106. KBI diary, November 16, 1911, HRC.
107. KBI diary, December 5, 1911, HRC; *K&F*, Chap. 15, p. 364.
108. *K&F*, Chap. 15, p. 372.
109. KBI diary, January 8 and February 11, 1912, HRC; "Notes from My Every Day Diary of Expeditions We Took During Our Stay in Ireland. Roden House Limerick 1912," CI 617; *K&F*, p. 366.
110. KBI diary, February 29, March 1, 1912, HRC.
111. KBI diary, April 4, 1912, HRC.
112. *Antony and Cleopatra*, 5.2, in *Cassell's Illustrated Shakespeare*, ed. and annoted by Charles and Mary Cowden Clarke, Vol. 3, *Tragedies*, p. 669.
113. *K&F*, Chap. 14, p. 353.
114. KBI diary, May 3, 1912, HRC.
115. KBI diary, February 24, 1912, HRC.
116. KBI diary, September 11, 1912, HRC.
117. *The History of My Friends*, "Book III, 1912–1913, Jack Armstrong," CI box 159.
118. *D3*, November 6, 1973, p. 402; *The Diaries of Kenneth Tynan*, ed. John Lahr (London: Bloomsbury, 2001), April 14, 1977, p. 370. As an adult in California, CI recorded in his diaries his friendship with his housekeeper, Dorothy Miller, and her successors and wrote with interest about gardeners, builders, painters, and others he employed. But of the many who had served him and his family during his English childhood, he named in *K&F* only Nanny and Coyne. Anne Pott arrived in her twenties, first as parlormaid and eventually running Marple Hall. There was always a cook, sometimes a kitchen maid, and two or three other housemaids. Robert Dobson, the coachman, lived with his wife Ellen and five children in servants' quarters near the house until the 1890s, when he acquired his own family home in Stockport. Ellen Dobson sometimes helped at Marple Hall and at Wyberslegh, and CWBI knew some of their children well. He knew Coyne the gardener's children even better.
119. KBI diary, August 10, 8, 12, 1912, HRC.
120. KBI diary, August 31, 1912, HRC; *K&F*, Chap. 15, p. 376.
121. *The Black Sash: South Africa's Fight for Democracy* (1956) and *Where Rivers Meet* (1960).
122. KBI and RGBI started one and found it creepily obsessed with fear.
123. KBI diary, August 26, 1912, HRC.
124. KBI diary, September 28, 1912, HRC.
125. *K&F*, Chap. 15, p. 376.
126. KBI diary, October 27, 1908, CI 613.
127. *K&F*, Chap. 15, p. 381.

128. KBI diary, December 25, 1912, HRC.
129. KBI diary, January 5, February 23, 1913, HRC; Paul Bunyan, *The Pilgrim's Progress* (London, 1678), Chap. 1; *The Book of Common Prayer* [...] *Church of England*.
130. KBI diary, July 18, 1913, HRC; "The Spanish Armada," p. 137, and "William the Conqueror," p. 46, in Kipling and Fletcher, *The History of England* (Oxford: Clarendon Press, 1911). Kathleen called it Kipling's *Child's History of England*, perhaps referring to *A School History of England*, another 1911 edition from the Clarendon Press.
131. Mary Mercer to KBI, October, 23, 1912, pasted into "The Baby's Progress," CI 591.
132. KBI diary, March 20, 1913, HRC.
133. KBI saw Bernhardt perform a snippet of *Elizabeth Reine d'Angleterre*, October 14, 1912, and would likely have told her theater-crazed son all about it when she returned from London to Limerick the next day, *Memoirs of Pine House*, p. 12, CI 1098. *Memoirs of Pine House* was a forerunner of *Lions and Shadows*. CI worked on it at the end of 1931 and beginning of 1932 in Berlin.
134. *Memoirs of Pine House*, p. 12, CI 1098; *K&F*, Chap. 15, p. 373.
135. KBI diary, February 12, May 19, 1913, HRC.
136. *The History of My Friends*, "1912–1913 Eddie Townshend," CI box 159.
137. *K&F*, Chap. 15, p. 381.
138. Unnumbered page, typed 1966 or 1967, CI 1082.
139. *A Day at the Seaside* was advertised in *The Times* as part of a frequently changing variety program; it was shown in London from 1909 onward. (See KBI diary, December 5, 1910, CI 615.) The family, including Emily, went to a cinema near Sandhurst to watch the coronation footage; see British Pathé, Gaumont Graphic News Reel, on YouTube (KBI diary, June 26, 1911).
140. *K&F*, Chap. 15, p. 376. He also saw Paul J. Rainy's documentary *African Hunt*, and was soon acting "imaginary hunts out in the Technical-grounds" with Eddie Townshend (KBI diary, June 7, 12, 1913, HRC).
141. KBI diary, February 21, 1914, HRC.
142. "A Berlin Diary (Autumn 1930)," *GB*, p. 13.
143. "Camera Studies," CI 3109.
144. CI to SS, n.d., Bancroft; CI diary, August 20, 1938, p. 40 verso, CI 2751.
145. *K&F*, Chap. 15, p. 402.
146. Family tree enclosed in a letter, FBI to KBI, May 1914, CI 548.
147. KBI diary, December 25, 1913, HRC.
148. KBI diary, December 29, 1913, HRC. Kent the carpenter had begun to make a playbox to pack belongings and a tailor visited to alter CWBI's Eton suit, widely worn by boarding-school boys.
149. *The Talisman* (Edinburgh/London: Constable/Hurst Robinson, 1825), Chap. 2.
150. *LY*, pp. 57–8, note.
151. *The Talisman*, Chap. 4.
152. CWBI drawing, "Blondel," Morgan. The rescue story is told, for instance, in Eleanor Anne Porden's epic poem of 1822 *Coeur de Lion, or The Third Crusade*.
153. *K&F*, Chap. 15, p. 372.
154. "Plays of the Month," *The Theatre, A Monthly Review of the Drama, Music, and the Fine Arts*, ed. Addison Bright, Series 4, Vol. 23, January–June 1894, pp. 222–3, review of opening performance at Terry's, London, February 21, 1894.
155. "Frank very good as the school master, Mr. Gordon as the new boy," reported KBI, and "Mr. Dobbs as the bully caused fits of laughter!" ("Notes from every-day diary of expeditions we took during our stay in IRELAND," April 16, 1914, pp. 80–1, CI 618); see also KBI diary, April 14, 1914, HRC.
156. "I remember him acting in regimental theatricals. The play was Charley's Aunt," wrote CI in *Hero-Father, Demon-Mother*, CI 1082, pp. 1–2. But there is no evidence FBI did so. This farce involving cross-dressing and three sets of lovers mismatched then reunited has a character called Frank and was first produced in Bury St. Edmunds in February 1892, commissioned by the local hunt for their annual social events (the "Hunt Bespeak), so KBI might easily have seen it there even before it became popular.

744 / Notes to Part 1

157. KBI diary, April 22, 1914, HRC; Cf. "Maurice recited a poem and danced a hornpipe," *Memorial*, Book II, Chap. 4, p. 165.
158. "The Baby's Progress," p. 25, CI 591; *Hero-Father, Demon-Mother*, pp. 77–8, CI 1082.
159. KBI diary, April 30, 1914, HRC; "Christopher recognized it from having seen pictures of Bleriot's." (KBI diary, May 4, 1910, CI 615) When the Frenchman Louis Blériot became the first person to fly the English Channel on July 26, 1909, KBI had gone to see Blériot's plane on display at Selfridge's department store in London and described it so vividly that CI later believed he had seen it himself. (See KBI diary, July 26 and 28, 1909, CI 614, and *Hero-Father, Demon-Mother*, p. 80, CI 1082)
160. *Hero-Father, Demon-Mother*, p. 79, CI 1072.
161. KBI diary, May 1, 1914, HRC.
162. CWBI quoted in KBI diary, May 4, 6, 1914, HRC; Rosamira Bulley, "A Prep School Reminiscence," *W.H. Auden: A Tribute* (London: Weidenfeld & Nicolson Ltd, 1974), p. 31.
163. KBI diary, May 9, 1914, HRC; FBI to CWBI, on Roden House letterhead, n.d., CI 563; FBI to CWBI, May 3, 1914, CI 562.
164. *Memoirs of Pine House*, pp. 3, 9, 3–4, CI 1098.
165. "1914–1916 Russell Roberts," CI box 159.
166. *Memoirs of Pine House*, pp. 5–6, CI 1098.
167. *L&S*, Chap. 5, p. 184.
168. KBI diary, May 1, 1914, HRC.
169. *Memoirs of Pine House*, pp. 1–3, CI 1098.
170. *K&F*, Chap. 14, pp. 357–8; *Memoirs of Pine House*, p. 13, CI 1098.
171. *Memoirs of Pine House*, p. 15, CI 1098.
172. *K&F*, Chap. 15, p. 399, CI was firm in this view even though two years later, in summer term 1916, he had come third out of fifty boys in the same event. (KBI diary, May 30, 1916, HRC)
173. *K&F*, Chap. 15, p. 398; *Hero-Father, Demon-Mother*, p. 77, CI 1082; *K&F*, Chap. 15, p. 397.
174. KBI diary, August 1, 1914, HRC.
175. KBI diary, August 4, 1914, HRC.
176. *K&F*, Chap. 15, p. 403. In an earlier draft, CI described his father's voice a little differently: "it sounds controlled, calm but full of tension." (*Hero-Father, Demon-Mother*, p. 86, CI 1082)
177. KBI diary, August 9, 1914, HRC.
178. KBI diary, August 10, 1914, HRC; *Hero-Father, Demon-Mother*, p. 86, CI 1082; *K&F*, Afterword, p. 504.
179. KBI diary, August 14, 1914, HRC.
180. KBI diary, August 15, 1914, HRC.
181. FBI to KBI, August 14, 15, 17, 19, 1914, quoted in *K&F*, Chap. 16, pp. 406, 407.
182. KBI diary, August 18, 1914, HRC.
183. KBI diary, August 26, 1914, HRC.
184. FBI to CWBI [before August 27, 1914], "2/York & Lanc Regt / 16th Infantry Brigade / 6th Division," CI 565; FBI to KBI, November 15, 14, KBI Memory Book, CI 619.
185. KBI diary, September 10, 1914, HRC.
186. The lodging house was "Glan Tivy." CWBI walked the quarter-mile to see them after school Saturday and again on Sunday after chapel. They went for drives and saw soldiers camped at Frensham "mostly in scarlet jackets—*when* they had any sort of uniform having run out of karki [*sic*] . . . many recruits in no uniform—we saw the 9th batt of the York & Lancaster's camp & there were many onlookers—" (KBI diary, September 30, 1914, HRC)
187. FBI to CWBI, September 27, 1914, Memory Book, CI 619.
188. KBI diary, September 28, October 26, 1914, HRC.
189. KBI diary, October 27, November 12, 1914, HRC.
190. FBI to CWBI, November 7, 1914, Memory Book, CI 619.
191. FBI to KBI, October 22, Memory Book, 1914, CI 619.

192. FBI to KBI, November 21, 1914, Memory Book, CI 619; KBI diary, November 25, 26, 28, 1914, HRC.
193. KBI Memory Book, 1914, CI 619.
194. FBI to KBI [before Christmas, 1914], Memory Book, CI 619.
195. *North Cheshire Herald*, in Memory Book, 1914, CI 619.
196. In a draft for *K&F*, CI averred that he could not remember FBI doing anything military: "When I try to picture him giving orders to his men or riding a horse at the head of a column, I can't." He could remember FBI winning running races and playing football, but recalled, "My Father never insisted on my doing the exercises, too. Indeed, I can't remember any attempt on his part to make an athlete out of me . . ." (*Hero-Father, Demon-Mother*, typed notes, pp. 1–2, CI 1082) However, KBI's diaries make clear that CWBI had often seen his father parade to church with his men and attended other regimental events, also that it was FBI who arranged CWBI's first regular exercise, the drilling classes which included elementary training as a soldier. Moreover, from the Front, FBI urged CWBI to "get as good as you can" at cricket, "and that will make it more interesting," because "'it is a fine healthy game and you have to play it' as Doctor Candy said." (FBI to CWBI, May 12, 1914, CI 564)
197. FBI to KBI, December 3, 1914, and FBI to KBI December 31, 1914, Memory Book, CI 619.
198. FBI to CWBI, December 28, 1914, CI 567.
199. FBI to KBI [November 1914?], Memory Book, CI 619; FBI to KBI, March 28, 1915, Memory Book, CI 620.
200. KBI diary, January 2, 4, 1915, HRC.
201. FBI to KBI, January 21, 1915, Memory Book, CI 620. CI's first known poem, evincing already his wish to engage with world events and his gift for atmosphere, has not been found.
202. DB to Bucknell in conversation, 2017. It was a family favorite. Granny Emily wrote in her copy the date on which she finished reading it for the third time; CI had her copy in his library (now in the Huntington). FBI to KBI, February 4, 1915, Memory Book, CI 620; KBI diary, January 19, 1915.
203. *Our Magic: The Art in Magic, the Theory of Magic, the Practice of Magic* (London: George Routledge & Sons / New York: E.P. Dutton, 1911), Part I, Chap. 2, p. 5. They were known for framing their illusions in dramatic sketches performed by magicians and actors, and they sometimes used moving pictures.
204. *Hero-Father, Demon-Mother*, p. 79, CI 1082. Goldston's, in Green Street, was run by the London stage magician Will Goldston, a friend of Harry Houdini. KBI and CWBI discovered it in January 1915 (KBI diary, January 19, 1915, HRC).
205. Hoffmann, *Modern Magic* (London: George Routledge & Sons, 1876), repeatedly reissued, Chap. 1.
206. *Modern Magic*, Chap. 8.
207. *L&S*, Chap. 6, p. 259.
208. FBI to KBI, January 13, 1915, Memory Book, CI 620.
209. KBI diary, February 25, 28, 1915, HRC.
210. FBI to KBI, March 8, 1915, Memory Book, CI 620.
211. KBI diary, memoranda pages and March 17, 20, 1915, HRC.
212. KBI diary, March 21, 22, 1915, HRC.
213. FBI to KBI, March 21, 1915, Memory Book, CI 620.
214. FBI to KBI, March 19, 1915, Memory Book, CI 620.
215. FBI to KBI, March 15, 1915, and FBI to KBI, April 9, 1915, Memory Book, CI 620.
216. *Hero-Father, Demon-Mother*, p. 70, CI 1082.
217. *K&F*, Afterword, p. 505.
218. FBI to KBI, March 25, 1915, and FBI to KBI, April 5, 1915, Memory Book, CI 620.
219. KBI diary, March 31, 1915, HRC.
220. KBI diary, April 7, 1915, HRC.
221. KBI diary, April 2, 1915, HRC; FBI to KBI, April 5, 1915, Memory Book, CI 620.

222. KBI diary, April 10, 1915, HRC.
223. KBI diary, April 20, 1915, HRC.
224. FBI to CWBI, April 11, 1915, CI 569.
225. KBI diary, April 28, 1915, HRC.
226. FBI to KBI, April 26, 1915, Memory Book, CI 620.
227. FBI to KBI, April 27, 1915, and FBI to KBI, April 29, 1915, Memory Book, CI 620.
228. KBI diary, May 1, 1915, HRC.
229. KBI diary, May 4, 1915, HRC.
230. KBI diary, May 9, 1915, HRC.
231. Colonel H.C. Wylly, *The York and Lancaster Regiment: 1758-1919* (London and Frome: Butler & Tanner, 1930), quoted in *K&F*, Chap. 16, p. 461.
232. KBI diary, May 11, 12, 1915, HRC.
233. KBI diary, May 23, 1915, HRC.
234. "Eric" to KBI, quoted in KBI diary, June 6, 1915, and KBI diary, June 5, 1915, HRC.
235. Paraphrased by KBI in her diary, June 19, 1915; KBI diary, June 20, 21, 1915, HRC.
236. KBI diary, June 24, 1915, HRC; letter pasted into Memory Book, CI 620. FBI's death certificate is in German; it was transcribed and translated in the letter with an error resulting from the fact that the original certificate is a pre-printed form with FBI's details filled in by hand. Item 6, *Inhalt der Erkennungsmarke* (contents of identity disk), is filled in as "siehe 5 C of E" (see 5 Church of England). The instruction to *see item 5* should not have been included in the letter to KBI. Item 5, *Truppenteil* (unit), is filled in as "Y. & L. Rgt." (York and Lancaster Regiment). When researching *Kathleen and Frank*, CI misread *siehe* as *siche* (not a word), generating a time-consuming puzzle. The certificate is in the archives of the International Committee of the Red Cross in Geneva.
237. "Our Army's Terrible Ordeal," *Observer*, May 16, 1915, CI 620.
238. PI Gita, Chap. II, "The Yoga of Knowledge," pp. 40 and 42.
239. KBI diary, June 29, 1915, HRC; *K&F*, Afterword, p. 503.
240. KBI diary, July 6, 1, 2, 3, 1915, HRC.
241. Anne Pott, Robert and Ellen Dobson, and Frank's old nanny, now Mrs. Annie Kelsall; newspaper account in Memory Book, CI 620.
242. KBI diary, July 7, 1915, HRC.
243. KBI diary, July 9, 15, 1915, HRC; Intro. to "Stories," *Exh.*, p. 170.
244. KBI diary, July 27, 29, 1915, HRC.
245. *Memorial*, Book II, Chap. 4, pp. 151-2.
246. In *WE*, CI distanced the emotion at several removes—in a fictional letter about an imaginary novel referring to a play, *Macbeth*. Thus, with elaborate indirection, insulating emotion with layers of writing, CI suggested—perhaps exaggerating—how it had felt to him as a boy: that his mother used her grief to manipulate him, to pull him from his untroubled emotional world into her darker one. His authoress character, Elizabeth Rydal, says the mother in the novel she is writing "longs to break down the barrier between them, to get through to him and make him share what she feels, somehow, even if she has to hurt him." (*WE*, Part 2, Chap. 2, p. 66)
247. CWBI collected the Centenary Edition published in London by Chapman and Hall in 1910 and 1911. Many are now in the Huntington with his bookplate and notes (some by KBI) of when he finished reading them. See KBI diary, July 27, 1915, HRC: "chose an edition of Dickens for C. to collect. Got a very nice reprint of the old called 'The Centenary.'"
248. *The Adventures of Oliver Twist, or The Parish Boy's Progress* (1838), Chaps 2, 5, 8, 9, pp. 15, 35, 65-6, 70, 76, 77.
249. KBI diary, August 18, 19, 1915, HRC.
250. KBI diary, September 7, 1915, HRC.

2: SACRED ORPHAN

1. *K&F*, Afterword, pp. 501-2.
2. *Hero-Father, Demon-Mother*, p. 84, CI 1082.

3. KBI diary, April 12–13, 1916, HRC. KBI called it "his parody of 'Horatius.'" She thought it was published in the St. Edmund's *Chronicle*, but it has not been found there, and her copy—which she made herself and bound—is lost.
4. *Memorial*, Book II, Chap. 4, p. 150.
5. London Correspondent for the Sydney *Daily Telegraph*, Dominion, Vol. 9, Issue 2701, February 22, 1916, p. 3; DB conversation with Bucknell, January 2014.
6. KBI diary, May 5, 1916, HRC.
7. KBI diary, August 4, 7, 1916, HRC.
8. "Late Note," *The Eagle House Magazine*, Summer 1916, p. 33.
9. Jack Reid married happily and had four children. CI remained in touch with him and consulted him repeatedly while researching *K&F*.
10. "Two Brothers," *Oxford Outlook*, 7:109–12, May 1925, pp. 109–10.
11. "Two Brothers," autograph fair copy, March 30, 1924, CI 1067.
12. *Oxford Outlook*, 7:109–12, May 1925, p. 109.
13. *SM*, p. 13.
14. CI 1067.
15. KBI diary, August 16, 19, 1916, HRC.
16. KBI diary, August 23, 1916, HRC; *October*, pp. 75–6.
17. KBI diary, September 5, 7, 1916, HRC.
18. CWBI diary, January 6, 8, 1917, McFarlin, microfilm copy BL.
19. Newbolt, *Tales of the Great War* (London: Longmans, Green & Co., 1916), pp. I, vii, vi.
20. CWBI diary, January 3, 1917, McFarlin/BL.
21. CWBI diary, February 7, 1917, McFarlin/BL.
22. CWBI diary, January 27, February 28, March 13, 1917, McFarlin/BL; *K&F*, Chap. 15, p. 399. KBI several times recorded that playing in the hay with country friends was unbearably exciting for him.
23. *LY*, pp. 56–7.
24. *C&HK*, Chap. 2, p. 31.
25. CWBI diary, November 24, 1917; "Mr Bagnall said that everyone who could should go & watch the Boxing. Went accordingly & spent most of the time there." January 23, 1918; CWBI lost matches, January 19 and February 14, 1918, McFarlin/BL; *LY*, pp. 57–8, note.
26. "W.H. Auden," *Poets at Work: The Paris Review Interviews*, ed. George Plimpton (New York: Viking Press, 1977; Penguin, 1989), p. 287; CWBI diary, January 20, 1918, McFarlin/BL.
27. "To the Reader," *L&S*.
28. *L&S*, Chap. 5, pp. 181, 182.
29. *LY*, pp. 57–8, note. He attributed his uncertainty to the fact that, on his side, the sexual part of their friendship called for a return in fantasy to his prepubescent self, and this screened what was actually happening: "Detailed memories of sex with Auden—which went on intermittently from 1926 to 1938—are strangely dim, perhaps because Christopher had to make a mental blackout, switching himself back from a grown-up man to a twelve year old, before getting into bed with him." (*LY*, p. 58)
30. CI diary, April 17, 1936, p. 16, CI 2751.
31. "As It Seemed to Us" (1965), *Forewords and Afterwords* (New York: Random House, 1969; Vintage, 1974), p. 500.
32. WHA, "The Prolific and the Devourer," *The Complete Works of W.H. Auden, Prose Volume II, 1939–1948*, ed. Edward Mendelson (Princeton University Press, 2002), Appendix I, p. 414.
33. "As It Seemed to Us," *Forewords and Afterwords*, p. 501.
34. CWBI diary, January 21, 1917, McFarlin/BL. He tried Harrods, then went to the publishers.
35. Part IV, in WHA and Louis MacNeice, *Letters from Iceland* (London: Faber and Faber, 1936), p. 205.
36. *Memoirs of Pine House*, p. 8, CI 1098.
37. Harold Llewellyn Smith, "At St. Edmund's 1915–1920," in *W.H. Auden: A Tribute*, p. 35; *Letters from Iceland*, p. 206.

38. CWBI diary, January 29, February 4, 11, May 21, 1917, McFarlin/BL.
39. "Stories," *Exh.*, pp. 170–1; "Gems of Belgian Architecture," *Exh.*, p. 177; "Stories," *Exh.*, p. 170.
40. Even after learning his father had more likely died on May 8, CI marked the 9th. In 1940, Uncle Henry, gravely ill, was expected to die May 9 but recovered. In 1966, Uncle Henry's wife, Muriel, died on May 9. In 1977, CI wondered if he, too, would die on that date: "*May 9*. The 'triple anniversary.' Shall I ever make it quadruple?" *D3*, p. 543.
41. The story does not mention, though CI knew, that the Number 9 card depicts the belfry and cathedral of St. Bavo in Ghent, which houses *The Adoration of the Lamb*, the altarpiece by the brothers Hubert and Jan Van Eyck, widely considered the finest example of early Flemish painting. Hubert, the elder brother, designed and began the work; he died in 1426, leaving Jan to finish it alone. In other words, the Number 9 card referred in real life to the death of an elder brother artist figure.
42. *Exh.*, front free endpapers.
43. "Stories," *Exh.*, pp. 169, 170. KBI recorded a summer afternoon near school when "C managed to get quite a lot of cigarette cards off passing soldiers! & nearly completed his Shakespeare set." KBI diary, July 9, 1916, HRC.
44. KBI diary, April 6, 1913, HRC.
45. "As It Seemed to Us," *Forewords and Afterwords*, p. 505.
46. KBI diary, June 2, 1917, HRC.
47. "Letter to Lord Byron" Part IV, in *Letters from Iceland*, p. 205; "As It Seemed to Us," *Forewords and Afterwords*, p. 505; "Letter to Lord Byron," *Letters from Iceland*, p. 206; CWBI diary, October 20, November 28, 1917, McFarlin/BL. Footer was football.
48. "As It Seemed to Us," *Forewords and Afterwords*, 505.
49. *L&S*, Chap. 5, p. 184.
50. *Letters from Iceland*, p. 206.
51. KBI diary, June 14, 28, August 2, 5, 1916, HRC. CI remembered that Granny Isherwood "hummed to herself, not a song exactly but a kind of anxiety noise." *Hero-Father, Demon-Mother*, p. 19, CI 1082.
52. KBI diary, August 14, 1917, HRC.
53. KBI diary, August 16, 1917, HRC.
54. *Historical Records of the 40th (2nd Somerset) Regiment, now 1st Battalion The Prince of Wales's Volunteers (South Lancashire Regiment) from Its Formation in 1717 to 1893*.
55. Smythies objected constantly as the work progressed, asking Gaudier-Brzeska why he didn't use callipers to measure the parts of the head. Gaudier-Brzeska kept the top of the skull open and spat into it loudly and regularly, claiming the plaster was too dry. See the letters about the sittings by Gaudier-Brzeska and his sister Zofia quoted in Paul O'Keefe, *Gaudier-Brzeska: An Absolute Case of Genius*, pp. 118–19. See also Roberta Jeanne Marie Olson, *Record of the Art Museum, Princeton University*, Vol. 33, No. 1 (1974), pp. 1–36.
56. CWBI diary, August 26, 27, 1917, McFarlin/BL.
57. Charlesworth was another family name, the husband of a first cousin of Kathleen, Helen Greene, Uncle Walter's youngest daughter.
58. *Memorial*, Book III, Chap. 2, p. 260. In portraying the Charlesworth–Lily friendship, CI sharply rejected the many jaunts to old buildings that CWBI enjoyed with KBI as an adolescent and which he wrote about in his 1917 diary with a meticulous attention to detail that foretold his professionalism as a travel writer. KBI had once helped Emily to write a guidebook about the similar jaunts taken by mother and daughter, *Our Rambles in Old London* (1895), and CI alluded witheringly to the book in his description of "The Little Society" to which Major Charlesworth and Lily belong: "earnest, curious, simple people, making their rambles into a little cult." (Book I, Chap. 2, p. 22)
59. KBI diary, October 3, 1915, HRC. The next holidays, the dentist would have to fill six of CWBI's teeth.
60. KBI diary, May 17, 1916, HRC.
61. KBI diary, September 30, 1917, HRC; CWBI diary, January 30, 1918, McFarlin/BL.

62. "Coming to London," in *Coming to London*, ed. JL (London: Phoenix House, 1957); repr. *Exh.*, p. 150; KBI diary, October 20, 1917, HRC.
63. CWBI diary, October 17, 30, November 24, 1917, McFarlin/BL.
64. CWBI diary, December 15, 1917, McFarlin/BL. "We had two seats allotted us in Box 36 second tier with very good view." (KBI diary, December 15, 1917, HRC)
65. Ecclesiastes, Chap. XLIV, closing with verse 14. See "Wynne's Diary," December 15, 1917, by Winifred Llewhellin Jackson (1879–1931), https://wynnesdiary.com/herbert-jackson-winifred-llewhellin/ Everyone in the rotunda sang "For All the Saints," which she described as "most terribly upsetting."
66. KBI diary, December 15, 1917, HRC.
67. CWBI diary, December 26, 1917, McFarlin/BL.
68. KBI diary, January 5, 1918, HRC.
69. CWBI diary, January 4, 5, 1918, McFarlin/BL; KBI diary, January 5, 1918, HRC.
70. CWBI diary, note on January 10, 1918, McFarlin/BL.
71. KBI to Mary (Moey) Bradshaw Isherwood, quoted in Peter Parker, *Christopher Isherwood: A Life* (London: Picador, 2004), p. 49.
72. CWBI diary, February 23, March 15, 1918, McFarlin/BL.
73. The poem, dated June 25, 1918, was rediscovered and transcribed by RGBI c.1970–1. RGBI to CI: "And now in her '18 diary I came across one of your poems, an Ode to Wyberslegh, and which M copied out." CI 1450. KBI's fair copy is lost.
74. KBI diary, June 14, 1918, HRC.
75. CWBI diary, June 28, 1918, McFarlin/BL.
76. CWBI diary, July 3, 7, May 13, 29, 1918, McFarlin/BL.
77. CWBI diary, July 13, August 20, 1918, McFarlin/BL. "C went to look out fitting quotations to head the chapters of a Romance that he & Llewellyn Smith are making up together." KBI diary, August 19, 1918, HRC.
78. "At St. Edmund's 1915–1920," *W.H. Auden: A Tribute*, p. 36. Llewellyn Smith also said, "It was to have been in the manner of Harrison Ainsworth, to whose works Wystan was at the time addicted." But, of course, CWBI was also addicted to Ainsworth.
79. "Phantasy and Reality in Poetry," lecture to the Philadelphia Association for Psychoanalysis, March 1971, *Auden Studies 3: In Solitude for Company, W.H. Auden after 1940*, ed. Katherine Bucknell and Nicholas Jenkins (Oxford University Press, 1995), p. 187. See also W.H. Auden, *New Year Letter* (London: Faber and Faber, 1941), Part III, ll. 1096–1152.
80. "Poet and Politician," review of Alvah Bessie, *Men in Battle*, *Common Sense*, January 1940, in W.H. Auden, *Prose, Volume II*, p. 40; "As It Seemed to Us," *Forewords and Afterwords*, 508; "A Literary Transference," *Southern Review*, repr. *Prose, Volume II*, pp. 42–3.
81. CWBI diary, July 19, 20, 21, 1918, McFarlin/BL. The *St. Edmund's Chronicle* records that Auden passed with honors in autumn 1919 and summer 1920.
82. CWBI diary, August 21, 1918, McFarlin/BL.
83. KBI diary, August 24, 1918, HRC; CWBI diary, August 24, 1918, McFarlin/BL; KBI diary, August 24, 1918, HRC.
84. KBI copied "Choosing a School" into a book presented to John Isherwood, CWBI's grandfather, on his birthday, quoted in Parker, *Christopher Isherwood: A Life*, pp. 54–5; KBI diary, September 2, 10, 1918, HRC.
85. CWBI diary, May 15, 1918; see also July 14, 1918, McFarlin/BL.
86. *K&F*, Chap. 11, p. 257. Some details from Charles Bellairs's diary, transcribed in KBI, "History of Marple and Wyberslegh Halls and the Bradshaw Isherwoods."
87. CWBI diary, March 28, April 3, 1918, McFarlin/BL; *Hero-Father, Demon-Mother*, p. 86, CI 1082.
88. CWBI diary, April 23, 1918, McFarlin/BL.
89. CWBI diary, August 8, 1918.
90. CWBI diary, July 5, 1918, McFarlin/BL; KBI diary, November 11, 14, 1918, HRC.
91. KBI diary, December 5, 19, 1918, HRC.
92. KBI diary, January 20, 1919, HRC.
93. Untitled novel about Rugtonstead, 3 chaps, labeled by CI "Just after leaving Repton, Jan. 1923", Chap. 1, pp. 4, 15, CI 1144. The name combined Rugby, PM's school,

Eton, the most famous British public school, and Berkhamsted, where Uncle Charlie Fry had been headmaster and where Charles Greene, a cousin, had succeeded him.
94. KBI diary, January 27, 28, 1919, HRC; RGBI to CI, August 28, 1973, CI 1468.
95. Rugtonstead novel, 1923, Chap. 1, p. 8, CI 1144.
96. See PM to CWBI: "I don't altogether damn the fagging system: if that is what you mean by 'white slave traffic.'" June 29, 1923, CI 1832.
97. KBI diary, April 26, 1919; untitled novel about Rugtonstead begun summer term 1922, p. 12, CI 1143. He described the trench coats again in his 1923 Rugtonstead novel, CI 1144. The trench coat was invented in 1850 and became widely used in the trenches during WWI.
98. Rugtonstead novel, 1922, p. 18, CI 1143.
99. KBI diary, January 27, 1919, HRC; GV, "Art, Sex and Isherwood," Review of *Christopher and His Kind*, *New York Review of Books*, December 9, 1976.
100. KBI diary, February 6, April 2, HRC.
101. KBI diary, February 6, 1920, HRC.
102. KBI diary, January 31, February 1, 1919, HRC; RGBI to CI, November 8, 1977, CI 1503.
103. *Memorial*, Book I, Chap. 1, p. 17.
104. *L&S*, Chap. 4, pp. 173–4; *C&HK*, Chap. 6, p. 105.
105. In real life, Micky Scott died in a flying accident (KBI diary, April 16, 1925, HRC). CI used the first name of Micky's elder brother Gerald for the Ramsbotham who dies in the car crash.
106. KBI saw the memorial when attending church at All Saints, and she found it "pleasing," but "I should have preferred less ornamentation, & think also it was a pity the military rank is not given for those who lost their lives." (KBI diary, August 8, 1920, HRC) CWBI had accompanied KBI to an exhibition of war memorial tablets at the V&A Museum, so he knew exactly what she liked; on the same day, they lunched at the Ladies Park Club, and KBI had a long talk with her friend (possibly cousin) Lily Belgrave, from whom CI perhaps borrowed the name Lily (KBI diary, September 21, 1919, HRC). The allusion to Virginia Woolf's Lily Briscoe, a painter obsessed with the dead like KBI, had the allure of being cruelly ironical.
107. KBI diary, September 14, 1928, HRC.
108. Henry Bradshaw Bagshawe Isherwood to KBI, quoted in KBI diary, August 17, 1919, HRC.
109. KBI diary, April 15, 1919, HRC. KBI thought that her father's bladder and prostate problems resulted from his not being circumcised as a child; she had wanted her infant sons circumcised but let FBI decide. She now consulted a family friend in London, a Dr. Ross, who evidently told her there was no need to subject CWBI to something so painful, though she was characteristically unable to be clear about this in her diary (KBI diary, February 13, 1919, HRC).
110. KBI diary, August 2, 1919, HRC.
111. KBI diary, August 5, 6, 7, 1919, HRC.
112. KBI diary, August 8, 11, 1919, HRC.
113. KBI diary, August 13, 1919, HRC.
114. KBI diary, October 3, December 3, 1919, HRC.
115. *D1*, October 16, 1939, pp. 47–8.
116. Rugtonstead novel, 1922, p. 7, CI 1143.
117. CWBI to KBI, 30 January 1921, *Repton Letters*, pp. 8–9.
118. Preface, *Scenes from European History: A Companion to English History for the Middle Forms of School* (London: Edward Arnold, 1911). His *Outlines of European History* (1916) ran to five editions.
119. *PV*, p. 17.
120. *L&S*, Chap. 1, p. 9; *Memorial*, Book II, Chap. 4, pp. 149, 150.
121. Intro. to "The Speckled Band," first published in *Exh.*, p. 88. In "The Baby's Progress," KBI records that CWBI was nine when he became interested in "thrilling detective stories," p. 24, CI 591.
122. *L&S*, Chap. 1, p. 10; G.B. Smith to CI, May 12, 1923, CI 2018.

123. The real-life Chalmers also wrote poems. He went on to Worcester College, Oxford.
124. *L&S*, Chap. 1, pp. 18–19; CWBI to KBI, November 2, 1921, *Repton Letters*, p. 40; CWBI to KBI, December 16, 1921, pasted into "The Baby's Progress," CI 591.
125. Rugtonstead novel, 1922, p. 15, CI 1143.
126. Photo printed in *Repton Letters*, p. 28; *L&S*, Chap. 1, p. 20.
127. CWBI to KBI, February 1, 1921, *Repton Letters*, p. 10.
128. *L&S*, Chap. 1, p. 16.
129. See Anthony Seldon and David Walsh, *Public Schools and the Great War: The Generation Lost* (Barnsley: Pen and Sword Military, 2013), pp. 96–8.
130. CWBI to KBI, February 6, March 16, November 2, 1921, *Repton Letters*, pp. 12, 17, 40.
131. CWBI to KBI, November 27, 1922, *Repton Letters*, p. 67; *The Reptonian*, December 1922, XLVI, 333, p. 55;*L&S*, Chap. 1, p. 44; *The Reptonian*, December 1922, XLVI, 333, p. 53; *L&S*, Chap. 1, p. 43.
132. Masefield quoted in CWBI to KBI, May 29, 1921, *Repton Letters*, p. 25. The book was about the appalling hardship British sailors endured anonymously, and he knew that KBI would be moved, as he himself was moved, by the idea they would both have connected to FBI, that true patriotism was "a hard life, an unknown grave."
133. *L&S*, Chap. 1, pp. 22, 24–5; CWBI to KBI, December 16, 1921, pasted into "The Baby's Progress" with telegram from Corpus Christi College, CI 591.
134. CWBI to KBI, July 3, 15 May 1921, *Repton Letters*, pp. 26, 20.
135. CI diary, November 19, 1937, p. 27, CI 2751. Ronald Hope Kelsall (1905–1931), The Hall, Repton, and Sandhurst. CI used the name "Ronny" in drafts for various narratives and in a published work, "Paul" in *Down There on a Visit*.
136. CWBI to KBI, October 1, 1922, *Repton Letters*, p. 64; Rugtonstead novel, 1923, Chap. 2, pp. 31–2, CI 1144; *L&S* Chap. 1, p. 42; "Oh for Repton and its rows! I shall never be beaten again, unless I get horsewhipped by an infuriated father." CI to EF, June 16, 1923, HRC; *L&S*, Chap. 1, p. 43. Alistair Darling appeared under his real surname; he was killed in WWII, after *Lions and Shadows* was published. Brian Finney, *Christopher Isherwood: A Critical Biography* (London: Faber and Faber, 1979), implies CI told him on September 5, 1976, that he had not been beaten at Repton, p. 37.
137. *SA*, Vol. 3, p. 612.
138. Rugtonstead novel, 1922, p. 43, CI 1143. The prefect is called "Traynor"—Tresham's "trainer" in school life.
139. "The Old Game," fair copy dated February 22–24, 1924, CI 1125.
140. KBI diary, January 2, 1921, HRC.
141. Rugtonstead novel, 1922, p. 6, CI 1143.
142. CWBI to KBI, January 29, 1922, October 13, 1921, *Repton Letters*, p. 47, 37; *The Reptonian*, December 1921, XLV, 327, pp. 162–3. "You will appreciate the strong Tennysonian atmosphere," CWBI told KBI about "Merlin's Garden" in the October 13 letter. Brian Finney noted echoes of Wordsworth in the adolescent poems (see *Christopher Isherwood: A Critical Biography*, p. 39). Also, CWBI had been reading Japanese poetry, likely in *The Master-Singers of Japan, Being Verse Translations from the Japanese Poets* (London: J. Murray, 1910), trans. Clara A. Walsh, and Arthur Waley's *Japanese Poetry: The 'Uta'* (Oxford, 1919).
143. At CWBI's request, Uncle Jack gave him Arthur Quiller-Couch's *Oxford Book of Ballads* for Christmas, and CWBI copied out favorite passages for Emily. CWBI's adventurous and eclectic taste offers interesting parallels with WHA, laying common ground for their reaquaintance in 1925, when they bonded over recollections of prep school and then WHA's poems.
144. CWBI to KBI, December 16, 1921, pasted into "The Baby's Progress," CI 591; *The Reptonian*, February 1922, XLV, 328, p. 200. "Snowflakes," published in *The Reptonian*, July 1922, signed "Cacoëthes," evoked, nine years before WHA wrote "The Wanderer," the same lonely fate:

> Where a man lies, on clamorous shingle,
> And a weed-woven wrack—
> No sun sets his cold veins a-tingle,
> No prayer wins him back.
>
> His strange eyes are closed by their falling,
> That had guessed too much.
> He might wake at the sea-bird's far calling
> Nor feel such soft touch ...

145. Intro., *Chivalry in English Literature* (Cambridge, MA: Harvard University, 1912), p. 6; Shakespeare, *The Two Gentlemen of Verona*, 3.2.
146. "To a Partner," *The Reptonian*, March 1922, XLV, 329, p. 222, signed Cacoëthes; "Gallinamania," *The Reptonian*, July 1922, pp. 290–1, unsigned, identified by George Ramsden. CWBI's first appearance in print at Repton was in an unofficial humor magazine, *The Phoenix*, produced only once, in July 1921. His contribution, "The Hang-Yu Mysteries," was a parody of Sax Rohmer's detective novels featuring the villain Dr. Fu Manchu and the Holmes and Watson knockoffs, Sir Denis Nayland Smith and Dr. Petrie. See CI to Alan Clodd, August 21, 1955, Add MS89043, BL. For an excerpt, see Brian Finney, *Christopher Isherwood: A Critical Biography*, p. 40.
147. *LY*, p. 89; PM to CI, August 20, 1925, CI 1851; *LY*, pp. 89–90.
148. Allan Monkhouse, *My Daughter Helen* (London: Jonathan Cape, 1922), p. 39. Monkhouse may have known that KBI's father left her fortune to her female Abney cousins.
149. *My Daughter Helen*, pp. 56, 45–6, 42, 62–3.
150. Allan Monkhouse to CI, March 1, 1927, CI 1817; CI to JL, April 23, 1943, Beinecke; CWBI to EF, late June or July, 1923, from Le Vert Logis, Rouen, HRC.
151. CWBI praised Monkhouse's 1927 novel *Alfred the Great* by letter and emulated it in *All the Conspirators*. Both novels are about the battle between the generations in close-knit, middle-class families of declining fortune; both have an artist-invalid at their center. KBI wrote of *Alfred the Great*: "Very clever study of his own family wonder how they like it." KBI diary, April 18, 1927, HRC.
152. Circa 1924–1926, CL 1818.
153. "A Merry Tragical Lover's Complaint by Christopher B" enclosed in letter PM to CWBI, August 28, 1923, CI 1835.
154. PM to CI, August 20, 1925, CI 1851; *LY*, pp. 90–1.
155. KBI diary, October 10, November 20, 1919, HRC.
156. KBI diary, June 23, 1921, HRC. See Norman Sherry, *The Life of Graham Greene, Volume 1, 1904–1939* (London: Jonathan Cape, 1989), Chaps 2 and 3, pp. 93–4 and 119. Greene suffered from bipolar disorder throughout his life, but after six months living with the unshockable Kenneth Richmond, depressive and alcoholic himself, and with Richmond's beautiful wife, whom Greene adored, he succeeded in returning to Berkhamsted as a day boy and went on to read history at Balliol College, Oxford.
157. KBI diary, July 16, 1921, HRC.
158. KBI diary, September 21, 1921, HRC.
159. CWBI to KBI, September 28, 1921; "I know nothing about the pay—but, as we should certainly live together, *anything* would be a help." CWBI to KBI, October 2, 1921, *Repton Letters*, pp. 32, 30.
160. KBI diary, January 3, 1921, HRC.
161. CWBI to KBI, March 24, 1921, *Repton Letters*, p. 19.
162. KBI diary, April 14, 1921, HRC.
163. KBI diary, August 10, 1920, HRC.
164. KBI diary, August 8, 9, 22, 1921, HRC.
165. KBI diary, August 30, 1922, HRC; CWBI to KBI, 2 July 1922, *Repton Letters*, p. 57.
166. CWBI to KBI, June 16, 1922, *Repton Letters*, p. 53.
167. CWBI to KBI, August 7, 1922, *Repton Letters*, p. 61.
168. *L&S*, Chap. 1, pp. 27, 30.
169. *L&S*, Chap. 1, p. 33; *The Prelude* (1850), Book 6, ll. 525–7.

170. *L&S*, Chap. 1, pp. 35, 40.
171. CWBI to KBI, September 24, 1922, *Repton Letters*, p. 63.
172. Rugtonstead novel, 1923, Chap. 3, p. 34, CI 1144.
173. PM to CWBI, October 5, 1922, CWBI 1820.
174. PM to CWBI, October 10, 1922, CI 1821.
175. CWBI to KBI, November 24, 1922, *Repton Letters*, p. 67.
176. CWBI to KBI, July 13, 1922, *Repton Letters*, p. 60.
177. CWBI to KBI, December 19, 1922, pasted into "The Baby's Progress," CI 591; KBI diary, December 19, 21, 1922, HRC.
178. *L&S*, Chap. 1, pp. 46–7, 48.
179. "The Hero," *Oxford Outlook*, 7:153–69, June 1925, see pp. 163, 169. See also CI's fair copy dated March 26, 1924, paired with "Two Brothers" in manuscript notebook, CI 1067. In the fair copy, Thompson comforts Wayne with FBI's favorite word for courage: "I think you were damned plucky to go into that water at all," but CI changed "plucky" to "gutful" (p. 166), concealing the sentimental link to FBI with a raw, deliberately ugly word.
180. Newbolt, *Tales of the Great War*, p. vii.
181. In the fair copy, Thompson is older than Wayne, repeating the father-son pattern.
182. *Poems*, ed. Siegfried Sassoon (London: Chatto & Windus, 1920), p. vii.
183. *Day at Night* with James Day, TV interview, 1974; see also *K&F*, Afterword, p. 504; "A Last Lecture," *IonW*, p. 139.
184. PM to CI, March 20, 1925, CI 1849; PM to CI, July 17, 1925, CI 1850.
185. "It is this story that has convinced me that Christopher has genius." EU, "Imaginary Diary of a Poet," November 23, 1924, Add MS 89002/1/1, BL.
186. PM to CI, February 1, 1925, CI 1848.
187. Rugtonstead novel, 1923, Chap. 1, pp. 1–2, 8, 4, 1, 2, CI 1144.
188. CI diary, August 20, 1938, CI 2751.
189. KBI diary, January 15, 16, February 2, 1, April 7, 1923, HRC.
190. KBI diary, February 25, March 14, 19, 26, 1923, HRC.
191. One of the last things CWBI copied into the commonplace book he began at Repton was Hilaire Belloc's short poem "On Hygiene": "Of old, when folk lay sick and truly tired / The doctors gave them physic, and they died. / But here's a happier age, for now we know / Both how to make them sick and keep them so." (McFarlin/BL)
192. KBI diary, May 8, 14, 1923, HRC; PM to CWBI, June 4, 1923, CI 1830; KBI diary, May 29, 1923, HRC.
193. PM to CWBI, June 29, 1923, CI 1832.
194. PM to CWBI, May 9, 1923, CI 1828; CWBI to EF, May 30, 1923, HRC.
195. KBI diary, February 10, 1923, HRC; CWBI to EF, August 26, 1921, HRC. For his seventeenth birthday, CWBI had seen a double feature, *Dr. Jekyll and Mr. Hyde* and *The Kid*, projecting fantasies that preoccupied him for the rest of his life—the uncontrollable doppelgänger in *Dr. Jekyll and Mr. Hyde*, the adorable orphan boy and his protector, the tramp, in *The Kid*. After the screening, he was ill (KBI diary, August 26, 27, 1921, HRC).
196. CWBI to EU, March 22, 1923, BL.
197. Movie scrapbook, "Newspaper Cuttings" embossed in gold on front cover, Huntington.
198. CWBI to EF, May 8, 23, 1923, HRC; KBI diary, July 15, October 7, 1923, HRC; CWBI to EF, July 20, 1923, HRC.
199. "Verses," *Exh.*, pp. 3, 4; Katharine Tynan, "Long and Short Flights," *The Bookman*, Vol. 65, November 1923, p. 122.
200. CWBI to EF, May 8, 1922; CWBI to EF, May 30, 1923; CWBI to EF, June 16, 1923, HRC.
201. G.B. Smith to CWBI, May 12, 1923, CI 2018; G.B. Smith to CWBI, May 12, 1923, CI 2018.
202. G.B. Smith to CWBI, February 3, 1923–January 26, 1929, CI 2017–2027.
203. G.B. Smith to CWBI, May 12, 1923, CI 2018; see also CWBI to EF, July 20, 1923, HRC.
204. KBI diary, July 28, 30, August 4, 1923, HRC.

205. *L&S*, Chap. 2, pp. 74, 79, 74–5; EU, "Imaginary Diary of a Poet," January 18, 1925, BL.
206. C.E. Montague, "A Note," *Fiery Particles* (London: Chatto & Windus, 1923; Phoenix Library, 1930), p. vii.
207. *L&S*, Chap. 2, p. 75.

3: FAILED HISTORY SCHOLAR, PUBLISHED NOVELIST

1. KBI diary, October 13, 1923, HRC.
2. *L&S*, Chap. 2, pp. 49, 50; see "Introductory Dialogue," in *Mortmere Stories*, and see *SA*, p. 671.
3. *L&S*, Chap. 2, p. 65.
4. *L&S*, Chap. 2, p. 68.
5. *L&S*, Chap. 2, p. 69.
6. *L&S*, Chap. 2, p. 70.
7. *L&S*, Chap. 2, p. 72.
8. *L&S*, Chap. 3, p. 101. This was the cousin who shot himself, in 1926. See, for example, *The Ghost Hunters*, stories about a real estate agent specializing in haunted houses and his female sidekick, a clairvoyant, printed in the *Royal Magazine*, December 1905–April 1906. The memoir was *Some Personalities* (London: J. Murray, 1921). EU referred to him as an uncle, as was a custom with elder cousins at the time.
9. *L&S*, Chap. 3, pp. 113, 114, 113.
10. CI's stories included "The Javanese Sapphires," in which—accessing his snake phobia—the sapphires are swallowed by a black python hidden in a perambulator pushed by a suspicious nurse, "The Greatness of Andy Shanks," "The Adventures of Fooby Bevan," "The Garage in Drover's Hollow." For surviving material, see *Mortmere*.
11. "The World War,"*Mortmere*, p. 121.
12. "They had altered the ending—rightly, I now think—and taken out the Destructive Desmond episode—wrongly, I still think." *C&HK*, Chap. 12, p. 231.
13. CI persuaded JL to publish it in *New Writing*, but EU withdrew it at the last moment. CI called it "one of the most magnificent pieces of narrative prose produced since the war," CI to JL, April 28, 1936, HRC.
14. *L&S*, Chap. 2, pp. 72, 72–3; *SA*, p. 11.
15. *L&S*, Chap. 2, pp. 51, 53; "Imaginary Diary of a Poet," November 23, 1924, BL; *L&S*, Chap. 2, p. 53. The source of the Watcher in Spanish might illuminate the meaning, but CI deliberately threw down a literary scavenger hunt: "the phrase came, I believe, from a line in a poem about: 'The Watcher in Spanish cape . . .' " Perhaps they were riffing on Ben Jonson's satirical verse play *The Alchemist*, in which characters one after another disguise themselves as a Spanish count, in Spanish suit with ruff and Spanish cloak, to win the "rich" widow. Perhaps it was American war poet Alan Seeger's "Paris," with its bohemian poseurs in the Latin Quarter: "And painters with big, serious eyes go rapt in dreams, fantastic shapes / In corduroys and Spanish capes and locks uncut and flowing ties." Perhaps it was the demonic alter ego dogging the narrator in John Buchan's short story, "The Watcher by the Threshold." See *L&S*, Chap. 2, p. 53; Alan Seeger, "Paris II," *Poems* (New York: Charles Scribner & Sons, 1916; London: Constable & Company Ltd, 1917), p. 48; *The Watcher by the Threshold and Other Tales* (Edinburgh and London: William Blackwood & Sons, 1902; 1916 Shilling Edition), p. 159.
16. *L&S*, Chap. 2, p. 54; PM to CI, November 25, 1923, CI 1836.
17. "When I quit writing verse England may not have gained a great novelist but, boy, she certainly lost a truly minor poet!" (CI to Alan Clodd, September 4, 1967) CI refused permission for Clodd, a book collector, to publish his valedictory poem "Recessional from Cambridge" in a pamphlet with EU's "Tale of a Scholar" because he didn't want the poem "featured as something important [. . .] these trifles should only appear in some large book about the period." (CI to Clodd, April 9, 1968) Add MS 89043, BL.
18. *L&S*, Chap. 2, p. 85.

Notes to Part 3 / 755

19. *L&S*, Chap. 2, p. 88; KBI diary, March 20, 1924, HRC.
20. "In Defence of the Cinema," *Cambridge Gownsman*, May 10, 1924, Vol. 3, No. 3, p. 1; for *Hollywood*, see *Cambridge Gownsman*, p. 11, and Carl Sandburg and Arnie Bernstein (eds) in *The Movies Are: Carl Sandburg's Film Reviews and Essays, 1920–1928*, pp. 175–6. CI went to Marple for John Isherwood's funeral May 13, and returned to Cambridge May 14, possibly in time for the film.
21. Film scrapbook, Huntington; *Cambridge Mercury*, February 6, 1924, p. 29.
22. See *Cambridge Gownsman*, February 16, 1924, p. 32; February 23, 1924, pp. 1–2; May 10, 1924, p. 12. The ban was lifted in October 1924, only to be reimposed on January 31, 1925, because undergraduates were being caught there with women. *A Prodigal Knight* came in for a drubbing, and so did *Bluebeard's Eighth Wife*; CI could find nothing to admire about Gloria Swanson.
23. "Film Flashes," *Cambridge Gownsman*, October 25, 1924, p. 19, and November 1, 1924, p. 19.
24. KBI diary, January 4, 1924, HRC; *L&S*, Chap. 2, pp. 60, 89.
25. *Day at Night* with James Day, TV interview, 1974.
26. *K&F*, Chap. 5, p. 78; "India-rubber," *Nine of Hearts* (London: Constable & Co., 1923), p. 145; "Still Life," *The Inner Circle* (London: Constable & Co., 1925), p. 182. In both stories, the first name of the FBI character is "Ralph." Years earlier, FBI had fumed to KMS that one of Mayne's books, not yet published, attributed to him "affected" speech and taste in music and named him "Cis." (FBI to KMS, April 18, 1900, quoted in *K&F*, Chap. 5, p. 107.)
27. *L&S*, Chap. 2, pp. 83, 84.
28. *L&S*, Chap. 3, pp. 96–7; EU, "Imaginary Diary of a Poet," BL; *L&S*, Chap. 3, pp. 97–8.
29. *October*, p. 46.
30. EU, "Imaginary Diary of a Poet," November 26, 1924, BL.
31. EU, "Imaginary Diary of a Poet," October 21, 1924, BL; *L&S*, Chap. 3, pp. 121–2.
32. *L&S*, Chap. 3, p. 122; EU, "Imaginary Diary of a Poet," October 16, 1924, BL; *The Waste Land*," ll. 114–15.
33. *SA*, pp. 684–5.
34. EU, "Imaginary Diary of a Poet," November 4, 1924, BL. They had participated in a reading of *Timon of Athens* at the Gravediggers Society.
35. EU, "Imaginary Diary of a Poet," November 1, 2, 1924, BL.
36. *L&S*, Chap. 2, p. 66; see also EU's diary.
37. EU, "Imaginary Diary of a Poet," October 10, 1924, BL. Orpen (1904–1972) was in Latham House with Upward at Repton and later worked at the Imperial Tobacco Company.
38. EU, "Imaginary Diary of a Poet," October 21, 1924, January 16, 25, March 4, 1925, BL.
39. EU, "Imaginary Diary of a Poet," November 10, 1924, BL.
40. EU, "Imaginary Diary of a Poet," November 18, 21, 23, 1924, BL.
41. EU, "Imaginary Diary of a Poet," November 24, 1924, BL; Frank Harris, *Oscar Wilde: His Life and Confessions* (New York: Brentano's, 1916 / Dodo Press, n.d.), Chap. 27, p. 209; EU, "Imaginary Diary of a Poet," November 24, 1924, BL.
42. Harris, *Oscar Wilde*, Chap. 12, pp. 124, 125, and Chap. 16, p. 189.
43. EU, "Imaginary Diary of a Poet," November 25, 30, December 2, 1924, BL.
44. *C&HK*, Chap. 1, p. 3; EU, "Imaginary Diary of a Poet," November 25, December 7, 8, 1924, BL; *SA*, p. 689.
45. *L&S*, Chap. 3, pp. 116–17.
46. EU, "Imaginary Diary of a Poet," December 5, 1924, BL.
47. David Francis to CI, December 10, 1924, on stationery of 24 South Eaton Place, SW1. CI sent Francis's letters to EU in an undated letter, 1930: "Here they are. Perhaps the most sacred and beautiful things, next to De Profundis, in our English tongue. Poor Davy—if he could see the ruins of his darling, now." (Add MS 72688, BL)
48. *SA*, pp. 690–1; EU, "Imaginary Diary of a Poet," January 14, 1925, BL, EU's deletion.

49. Early novel, *Lions and Shadows*, typescript, pp. 470, 471, 474, McFarlin.
50. *D1*, March 24, 1955, p. 483.
51. EMF's translation, in *Aspects of the Novel*, Clark Lectures, Cambridge 1927 (London: Edward Arnold, 1927; repr. Pelican Books, 1984), Chap. 5, p. 98; Gide, *The Counterfeiters*, Part II, Chap. 3; *L&S*, Chap. 4, p. 168.
52. EU, "Imaginary Diary of a Poet," January 18, 1925, BL.
53. EU, "Imaginary Diary of a Poet," January 25, 1925, BL.
54. KBI diary, March 31, 1925, HRC; *L&S*, Chap. 3, p. 118.
55. EU, "Imaginary Diary of a Poet," March 4, 1925, BL; *L&S*, Chap. 3, p. 123.
56. *L&S*, Chap. 3, p. 125.
57. EU, "Imaginary Diary of a Poet," July 25, 1925, BL; *L&S*, Chap. 3, pp. 129–30, 130.
58. KBI diary, June 2, 1925, HRC.
59. *L&S*, Chap. 3, pp. 134, 135.
60. "The Recessional from Cambridge," Stanza 11, CI 1131.
61. CI to EU, July 1, 1925, Add MS 72688, BL.
62. EU, "Imaginary Diary of a Poet," April 1925, BL.
63. EU, "Imaginary Diary of a Poet," entry headed "July 25" (1925), BL.
64. *L&S*, Chap. 6, p. 249.
65. *L&S*, Chap. 6, pp. 247–8. He seems to have been channeling D.H. Lawrence's heterosexual narrative in *The Lost Girl*, a favorite novel ("Novels I Like," CI 1095). Alvina Houghton, rejecting marriage proposals and tumbling down the social strata as she searches for the sensual fulfillment she eventually finds with an Italian peasant turned actor, hits an early turning point through her intimacy with the traveling theater manager Mr. May: "She liked being *déclassé*. She liked feeling an outsider. At last she seemed to stand her own ground. [. . .] She was off the map: and she liked it." (D.H. Lawrence, *The Lost Girl*, 1920, Chap. 7)
66. KBI diary, August 3, 5, 1925, HRC.
67. Reported by Parker in *Christopher Isherwood: A Life*, p. 116.
68. *L&S*, Chap. 4, p. 136.
69. KBI diary, September 15, 1925, HRC.
70. *L&S*, Chap. 4, p. 138. Sylvain Edouard A. Mangeot, 1913–1978.
71. *L&S*, Chap. 4, pp. 139, 145.
72. Charles Dickens, *Nicholas Nickleby*, Chap. 23.
73. BB diary, August 6, 1933, *Letters from a Life: Selected Letters and Diaries of Benjamin Britten, Volume One, 1923–1939*, ed. Donald Mitchell and Philip Reed (London: Faber and Faber, 1991), p. 305; BB diary, in Barcelona, March 6, 1934, p. 320, and April 26, 1936, p. 425.
74. "They are all very good & one of them positively brilliant," he told his parents. BB to Mr. and Mrs. R.V. Britten, June 22, 1933, *Letters from a Life*, p. 314.
75. *L&S*, Chap. 4, p. 15; *Memorial*, Book II, Chap. 4, p. 166. "The truth was she had fallen in love, not with an individual, but with a family," *Howards End* (London: Edward Arnold, 1910), Chap. 4; "(for she was in love with them all, in love with this world)," *To the Lighthouse* (London: Hogarth Press, 1927), Chap. 4.
76. *L&S*, Chap. 4, p. 153.
77. *C&HK*, Chap. 6, p. 101; *L&S*, Chap. 4, p. 151.
78. WHA, "Journal / April 1929," begun in Berlin, Berg.
79. *L&S*, Chap. 4, p. 173.
80. Wilson, *The Death of Society* (London: W. Collins, Sons/New York: George H. Doran, 1921), Chap. VIII, p. 108. Half a century later, when he reread it, CI commented, "Why on earth did I ever like it? It's one of the most bogus books I ever opened." *D3*, March 8, 1971, p. 154.
81. *L&S*, Chap. 4, p. 139; *C&HK*, Chap. 6, p. 101.
82. DS diary, September 21, 1954, quoted in Parker, *Christopher Isherwood: A Life*, p. 219, with a letter from Fowke Mangeot, "He certainly alienated my mother." (August 7, 1993).
83. EU mentions arrangements in letters evidently written in the summer of 1929. EU to CI, two undated, the third July 11, 1929, CI 2391, CI 2392, CI 2393.

84. *L&S*, Chap. 4, pp. 147–9.
85. August 1949, unpublished typescript of *LY*, CI 4171.
86. *L&S*, Chap. 5, pp. 183–4.
87. *L&S*, Chap. 5, pp. 184–5.
88. *L&S*, Chap. 5, p. 190.
89. *L&S*, Chap. 5, pp. 190–1.
90. He made the list in a manuscript notebook in 1947; see Edward Mendelson, *Later Auden* (New York: Farrar, Straus & Giroux, 1999), p. 266 (notebook in the Lockwood Memorial Library, State University of New York at Buffalo).
91. "Some Notes on Auden's Early Poetry"; repr. *Exh.*, pp. 17–22.
92. Published anonymously in *Oxford Poetry*, 1927, ed. C. Day Lewis and W.H. Auden, p. 48.
93. *L&S*, Chap. 5, pp. 188–9, 190.
94. "Tradition and the Individual Talent," *The Egoist*, Vol. 6, Nos. 4 and 5, September and December 1919; repr. *The Sacred Wood* (1920).
95. Huntington, Rare Books, 616208. The motto plays on the idea stated at the end of Herodotus's *Histories* by the Persian king Cyrus that "soft lands breed soft men"; it was devised by Henry Hart, headmaster 1880–1900, who turned Sedbergh into a school of sporting excellence. (Herodotus, Book IX, "The Wisdom of Cyrus") Researched by Andrew Maynard and Armand D'Angour, see http://www.armanddangour.com/2014/01/dura-virum-nutrix/
96. "I chose this lean country," l. 24, WHA, *Juvenilia, Poems 1922–1928*, ed. Katherine Bucknell (London: Faber and Faber, 1994), p. 210.
97. *AC*, Chap. 4, p. 61.
98. *AC*, Chap. 15, p. 217.
99. *Prufrock and Other Observations* (London: Egoist Press, 1917), ll. 15, 6.
100. *AC*, Chap. 17, pp. 233, 234–5, 235, 238. One of CWBI's own childhood coats had an astrakhan collar and matching cap; RGBI later wore the same coat.
101. CI 1138; *L&S*, Chap. 4, pp. 173–4.
102. *AC*, Chap. 1, p. 11.
103. EU, "Imaginary Diary of a Poet," April 5, September 18, 1926, Add MS 89002/1/1, BL.
104. Intro., *AC*, 1957 Methuen edition, p. 7.
105. *L&S*, Chap. 5, pp. 206, 207. As described in *L&S*, the new novel had two neurotic heroes, "two halves or aspects of the same person," one who imagines and one who acts, another variation on the twins in "Two Brothers." (*L&S*, Chap. 5, p. 211)
106. CI, 1937 pocket diary, McFarlin, and *C&HK*, Chap. 13, p. 258, where he explains he abandoned the title when Kenneth Roberts published a 1937 bestseller, *Northwest Passage*. CI to KBI, December 15, 1945, Beinecke.
107. *The Counterfeiters*, Part III, Chaps 18, 19.
108. *L&S*, Chap. 5, p. 194.
109. KBI diary, September 30, October 7, 15, 18, 1926, HRC.
110. KBI diary, August 6, 1928, HRC.
111. KBI diary, November 16, 1926, HRC.
112. *L&S*, Chap. 5, p. 224; Ian Scott-Kilvert, 1917–1989.
113. *L&S*, Chap. 5, p. 222.
114. KBI diary, January 19, 20, 1927, HRC.
115. KBI diary, June 5, 7, 1927, HRC.
116. *L&S*, Chap. 6, pp. 256–7.
117. CI to John Maunder, June 18, 1937, John Layard Papers, University of California, San Diego. WHA and CI's play *F6* was running in London which evidently reminded Maunder of the friendship.
118. Maunder to John Layard, from Bethlehem Royal Hospital, Eden Park, Kent, September 30, 1937, Layard Papers; KBI diary, October 12, 15, 1937, HRC.
119. *L&S*, Chap. 6, p. 257.
120. *The Artist to His Circle: A Novel*, typed fair copy, dedicated to Roger Burford, Add MS 80774, BL; KBI diary, September 19, 20, 1927, HRC.

121. *AC*, Chap. 18, pp. 240, 242.
122. *L&S*, Chap. 6, p. 261; "This was the noblest Roman of them all. / All the conspirators save only he / Did that they did in envy of great Caesar." *Julius Caesar*, 5.5.
123. "At the Bay," *Westminster Gazette*, February, 4, 11, 18, 1922; repr. *The Garden Party and Other Stories* (London: Constable & Co., 1922; Penguin Modern Classics, 1989), pp. 59–60.
124. *New Country*, ed. Michael Roberts (London: Hogarth Press, 1933); repr. *Exh*.
125. *L&S*, Chap. 6, p. 272; KBI diary, January 5, 1928, HRC.
126. KBI diary, March 25, 1947, HRC; CI diary, May 16, 18, 1928, p. 1, CI 1147.
127. *L&S*, Chap. 6, p. 263.
128. KBI diary, April 5, 17, 1928, HRC.
129. *L&S*, Chap. 6, p. 269.
130. *Times Literary Supplement*, June 14, 1928, p. 452; *L&S*, Chap. 7, p. 275; Fausset, "Books of the Day: New Novels—A Domestic Vortex," *Manchester Guardian*, May 25, 1928, p. 7; "Books I Have Liked Best Since the War—A Symposium," *Sunday Times*, November 12, 1933, p. 3.
131. CI diary, May 21, 1928, pp. 4, 5, CI 1147; CI to EU, [May 1928?], Elsastrasse 42, Bremen, Add MS 72688, BL.
132. *L&S*, Chap. 7, p. 281.
133. *L&S*, Chap. 7, p. 282.
134. *L&S*, Chap. 5, p. 217, and Chap. 7, p. 302.
135. Maugham, *Of Human Bondage* (London: William Heinemann, 1915; Vintage, 2000), Chap. 53, p. 297, and Chap. 55, p. 304; *Day at Night* with James Day, TV interview, 1974; Gore Vidal, *Palimpsest: A Memoir* (London: André Deutsch, 1995), pp. 186–7.
136. *L&S*, Chap. 7, p. 288.
137. *L&S*, Chap. 7, p. 290. Davis (1910–1942), from Great Malvern near Worcester, had been captain of cricket, head of house, and won the classics prize at his public school; he won two more scholarships to King's as well as the surgical prize. He died of malaria in a Rhodesian leper colony where he was government medical officer. See Royal College of Surgeons of England, *Plarr's Lives of the Fellows*, and KBI diary, November 2, 1928, HRC.
138. KBI diary, November 6, 1928, HRC; *Memorial*, Book IV, Chap. 3, p. 263.
139. *L&S*, Chap. 7, pp. 296–7.
140. "Some preliminary Ideas About My Novel," p. 1, CI 1099; *L&S*, Chap. 7, p. 297.
141. KBI diary, December 20, 1928, HRC.
142. *Paid on Both Sides* in *Poems* (London: Faber and Faber, 1930), p. 34.
143. *L&S*, Chap. 7, p. 299; WHA to Patience, fiancée of William (Bill) McElwee, December 1928, Add MS 59618, BL.
144. John Layard, "Homer Lane," in "The Autobiography of a Failure," pp. 1, 2, shared by James Greene and now in Layard Papers, U.C. San Diego, MSCL MSS84, box 59, fol. 6.
145. *L&S*, Chap. 7, p. 300. Such teachings harmonized with CI's favorite stories by D.H. Lawrence, for instance *St. Mawr*, as well as *Fantasia of the Unconscious*, which he mentioned.
146. *L&S*, Chap. 7, p. 307.
147. KBI diary, March 8, 1929, HRC.

4: BERLIN, SEX, POLITICS, AND FAME

1. WHA, "Journal / April 1929—" Berg; *C&HK*, Chap. 1, p. 3.
2. WHA, "Journal / April 1929—" Berg: "Christopher had Paul and I got drunk, partly as a counterblast to the knowledge that C did not want Paul particularly . . . Became intimate with John."
3. *C&HK*, Chap. 2, p. 16.
4. WHA, "Journal / April 1929—" Berg; see EU, *Christopher Isherwood* (London: Enitharmon Press, 1996), pp. 15–16.
5. WHA, "Journal / April 1929—" Berg; XVIII, *Poems* (1930), p. 62.
6. WHA, "Journal / April 1929—" Berg; KBI diary, March 14, 22, 1929, HRC.
7. WHA, "Journal / April 1929—" Berg.

8. *L&S*, Chap. 5, pp. 195, 121.
9. WHA, "Journal / April 1929—" Berg.
10. One character, Charles Franklyn, also appears in CI's abandoned early novel *Lions and Shadows*. Franklyn buys kisses from a younger boy who mocks his hesitant approach: "You're one of those sentimental lechers. Comes of going to see 'Peter Pan' and 'White Cargo' on consecutive nights." After some banter, the younger boy says, "you must be more explicit. You want to bugger me, I gather?" and takes Franklyn to his room, demanding to know what method of buggery he wants: "they're heaps. Dutch Jug. Spanish Screw. French Screw. Double Cross. Cork Squeeze. Twist Push. Bristol Suck. Belgian Itch. Armenian . . ." 11 pp in CI's autograph, n.d., Add MS 72702, BL.
11. "Preliminary Statement," WHA and CI, *Plays and Other Dramatic Writings, 1928–1938, The Complete Works of Auden*, ed. Edward Mendelson (Princeton University Press, 1988), Appendix 1, p. 459.
12. CI diary, March 15, 1936, CI 2751, where CI also listed who wrote what in the play; *C&HK*, Chap. 12, p. 241.
13. KBI diary, May 3, 1929, HRC.
14. *K&F*, Chap. 18, pp. 492–3.
15. *C&HK*, Chap. 3, p. 37.
16. KBI diary, May 15, 23, 1929, HRC.
17. The tapestries were purchased by a London dealer for 600 guineas each and sold on to William Randolph Hearst in 1930. The Hearst Foundation gave the tapestries to the Art Institute of Chicago in 1954. The portrait of John Donne and Anne More was sold to a descendant in Ohio, Doris Done Johnson, purchased by her husband Earl Johnson, according to KBI's note on a photograph of the painting. (McFarlin) Also sold were portraits of Thomas Coventry, Lord Privy Seal during the reign of James I; the Earl of Essex; and Lord John Crewe, 1st Baron Crewe of Crewe, Sheriff of Cheshire in 1764 and afterwards MP for Stafford and later for Cheshire, whose name was used in *The Dog Beneath the Skin*.
18. Letter in Agatha Christie Ltd archives; see www.marple.website She came with her sister who lived nearby.
19. KBI diary, August 2, July 22, 1929, HRC.
20. *MNCT*, Chap. 4, pp. 59, 66, and Chap. 5, pp. 84–5.
21. Jean Ross remembered a visit with CI to Aleister Crowley's flat when the bailiff began to remove Crowley's furniture; see Parker, *Christopher Isherwood: A Life*, p. 208.
22. *C&HK*, Chap. 4, pp. 73–4, and Tom Cullen, *The Man Who Was Norris: The Life of Gerald Hamilton* (Sawtry, Cambridgeshire: Dedalus, 2014).
23. *D1*, July 12, 1940, p. 103; Gerald Hamilton, *Mr Norris and I: An Autobiographical Sketch* (London: Allan Wingate Ltd, 1956), p. 13.
24. *D1*, July 12, 1940, p. 103; *Hero-Father, Demon-Mother*, p. 21, CI 1082; Parker, *Christopher Isherwood: A Life*, p. 471, note.
25. *D1*, July 12, 1940, p. 103.
26. CI to JL, January 30, 1935, Beinecke; CI to KBI, March 12, 1935, *K&C*, p. 11.
27. *The Personal History of David Copperfield* (1850), Chap. 11.
28. *Martin Chuzzlewit* (1844), Book VII, Chap. XVII; also commemorated was Arthur W. F. Norris, portrait painter, a Repton art master who painted Isherwood's portrait (Collection of Michael Estorick, London).
29. CI to KBI, March 12, 1935, *K&C*, p. 12.
30. *David Copperfield*, Chap. 11; Proust, *Within a Budding Grove* (1919; Vintage, 1996), trans. C.K. Scott Moncrieff & Terence Kilmartin, revised by D.J. Enright, Part II, p. 383. See KBI diary, March 19, 1930, HRC: "C in to lunch. Proust . . ."
31. *MNCT*, Chap. 4, p. 55.
32. See Robert Beachy, "The Eulenberg Scandal and the Politics of Outing," *Gay Berlin: Birthplace of a Popular Identity* (New York: Alfred Knopf, 2014), p. 123.
33. KBI diary, August 23, 1934, HRC; CI to KBI, March 12, 1935, *K&C*, p. 11.
34. *MNCT*, Chap. 16, p. 277.
35. *Birmingham Daily Gazette*, March 6, 1935; *Plymouth Gazette*, March 8, 1935; William Soutar, *Dundee Evening Telegraph*, March 16, 1935.

36. *Nottingham Journal*, August 9, 1935; W.E. Williams, "Style and Purpose in Literature," *Listener*, Vol. 14, No. 341, July 24, 1935, p. 169.
37. "New Novels," *New Statesman and Nation*, March 2, 1935, p. 284. American reviews praised CI's ability to make "the unbeautiful fascinating" as the *Saturday Review* put it. (Ben Ray Redman, "Problem for the Book Reviewer," *Saturday Review*, May 11, 1935, p. 18) "The book is a superlative characterization," enthused the reviewer for the *New York Times*, "as an individual he is pretty slimy, despite certain fantastic charm." ("A Rare Character, *The Last of Mr. Norris*," *New York Times*, May 12, 1935)
38. "A Berlin Diary (Autumn 1930)," *GB*, p. 13.
39. He was perhaps again inspired by EMF's handling of middle-class possessions in *Howards End*, where the inherited furniture of the Schlegel sisters illuminates their emotions as they are forced to leave the family home at Wickham Place.
40. KBI diary, September 25, 1946, HRC: "Christ among the Doctors in the Temple The risen Christ in the garden & the women bringing their caskets... Milton's Mother, & all the other pieces—"
41. "A Berlin Diary (Autumn 1930)," *GB*, p.14.
42. http://www.marple-uk.com/sale1.htm
43. "A Berlin Diary (Autumn 1930)," *GB*, pp. 14–15.
44. KBI diary, November 28, December 21, 1921, HRC.
45. Recorded in the memoranda pages of her diaries.
46. "A Berlin Diary (Autumn 1930)," *GB*, pp. 15–17.
47. *C&HK*, Chap. 1, pp. 10–11.
48. De Lichtenberg "had many more incidents with Mrs. Lanigan," CI diary, May 17, 1928, CI 1147.
49. *C&HK*, Chap. 1, pp. 11–12.
50. *DTV*, p. 71, quoted in *C&HK*, Chap. 2, p. 23.
51. *C&HK*, Chap. 2, pp. 23–4.
52. *C&HK*, Chap. 2, p. 25.
53. *C&HK*, Chap. 2, p. 29.
54. *C&HK*, Chap. 2, p. 33.
55. CI to John Layard, January 5, 1930, John Layard Papers, UC San Diego.
56. CI to John Layard, January 5, 1930, Layard Papers. Robert Beachy calls WHA and CI generous for paying ten marks per encounter. A contemporary study suggests the going rate was fifty pfennigs to ten marks and more (see *Gay Berlin*, p. 202 *passim*). In his journal, WHA records Gerhart Meyer saying, "Give me ten marks and I sleep with you tonight." WHA "Journal / April 1929—", Berg.
57. At first, the character was called Otto Kulak, and CI submitted the story for publication under the title "The Kulaks" toward the end of 1935. Early in 1936, he realized this would suggest they were wealthy Russian peasants, class enemies of poorer peasants, scourged by the Bolsheviks. He wrote to JL, "About The Kulaks: it occurs to me that maybe, if the book is to be read at all in Russia, the title conveys quite a wrong impression." CI to JL, January 16, 1936, HRC.
58. KBI diary, December 21, 24, 1929, April 19, 1927, HRC.
59. KBI diary, March 14, 1930, HRC.
60. KBI diary, March 24, 1930, and see February 11, 1930, HRC.
61. *C&HK*, Chap. 3, p. 38.
62. KBI diary, March 28, 1930, HRC.
63. KBI diary, April 1, 1930, HRC; *C&HK*, Chap. 3, p. 39.
64. *C&HK*, Chap. 3, p. 39; KBI diary, May 8, 1930, HRC.
65. EU read the opening of a novel by RGBI and told CI: "It is very significant and extraordinarily exciting. He should join the Mortmere group." (EU to CI, summer or autumn 1931, CI 2410) KBI described the piece as a "history of his own personality." (KBI diary, October 29, 1931, HRC)
66. "On Ruegen Island (Summer 1931)," *GB*, p. 138.
67. "On Ruegen Island (Summer 1931)," *GB*, pp. 127–8.
68. "On Ruegen Island (Summer 1931)," *GB*, pp. 14, 144.
69. *C&HK*, Chap. 12, p. 248.

70. *C&HK*, Chap. 3, pp. 44–5. Robson-Scott's mother died when he was ten; a brother was accidentally shot by another brother and Robson-Scott found the body; another brother died of flu after enlisting to fight in WWI. Robson-Scott's project of self-cure had begun with psychoanalysis by Freud's disciple Ernest Jones and included abasement to several boyfriends in Berlin. See Parker, *Christopher Isherwood*, p. 239.
71. *C&HK*, Chap. 3, p. 46.
72. *C&HK*, Chap. 3, p. 49.
73. *C&HK*, Chap. 3, p. 51.
74. "Translator's Preface," *The Intimate Journals of Charles Baudelaire*," trans. CI, Intro. by WHA (Hollywood: Marcel Rodd Company, 1947), repr. *Exh.*, pp. 28, 30.
75. *C&HK*, Chap. 3, p. 50; "The Nowaks," *GB*, p. 167.
76. "The Nowaks," *GB*, p. 191.
77. "The Nowaks," *GB*, pp. 197–8.
78. FBI to CWBI, October 4, 1914, KBI Memory Book, CI 619; "The Nowaks," *GB*, pp. 200–1.
79. Interview with Paul Bailey, "Christopher and His Kind," BBC Radio 3, March 28, 1977, transcribed by Xenobe Purvis.
80. *C&HK*, Chap. 3, p. 54.
81. "The Nowaks," *GB*, pp. 210–15.
82. EU to CI, May 22, 1935, from 16 Telford Court, Streatham Hill, CI 2449; Grigson, "Books of the Day," *Morning Post*, May 5, 1936, p. 16; Day Lewis included EU in his praise, "An Experiment in Publishing," *Listener*, Vol. 15, No. 32, Supplement, VIII, May 6, 1936, p. 8. EU's piece was the first chapter of his novel *Journey to the Border* (1938), under its earlier title, *The Border-Line*. CI was also paired with EU by I.A. Pavey, "The Poverty Line," *Sunday Times*, May 10, 1936, p. 11. The *Christian Science Monitor* focused on CI, calling it: "the mark of the born novelist—to suggest a whole world by a few lines of conversation and description, to leave a slight sharp flavor of personal observation and yet to suggest that the character described has a life beyond this observation." (V.S.P., "Highbrow Leftist Stories," Review of *New Writing*, *Christian Science Monitor* Weekly Magazine Section, June 24, 1936, p. 11); the *Oxford Mail* praised CI's "brilliant description of Berlin slum life" and named him "one of the brightest hopes of English fiction—" quoted in KBI diary, May 5, 1936, HRC, original item not found.
83. KBI diary, May 21, 1936, February 15, 1937, HRC.
84. "A Berlin Diary (Autumn 1930)," *GB*, p. 28.
85. "A Berlin Diary (Autumn 1930)," *GB*, p. 13.
86. Eliot, *Prufrock and Other Observations*, "Preludes I," ll. 4–10, "Prufrock," ll. 4–6.
87. "A Berlin Diary (Autumn 1930)," *GB*, p. 13; "Prufrock," ll. 70–2, "Preludes II," ll. 8–10.
88. Eliot, "Preludes III," ll. 27, 38; "A Berlin Diary (Autumn 1930)," *GB*, pp. 13–14.
89. https://www.nobelprize.org/prizes/literature/1930/lewis/facts/; *New York Times*, November 6, 1930, p. 27.
90. "A Camera Man," *Life and Letters*, Vol. II, May 1929, pp. 336–43; repr. as "Sinclair Lewis" in *Abinger Harvest* (London: Edwin Arnold Ltd, 1936; Harvest, 1966), see pp. 129–30.
91. "A Berlin Diary (Autumn 1930)," *GB*, p. 13.
92. See Mark Schorer, *Sinclair Lewis: An American Life* (McGraw-Hill, 1961), p. 546; "A Camera Man," repr. as "Sinclair Lewis" in *Abinger Harvest*, p. 136.
93. DB conversation with Bucknell, August 4, 2015. CI was friendly, though, with Lewis's biographer Mark Schorer.
94. *C&HK*, Chap. 6, p. 105.
95. SS told KBI it was "a masterpiece" (KBI diary, January 6, 1931, HRC); "an utter masterpiece" (WHA to Anne Bristow, February 3, 1931, Beinecke); "consistently good" (EU to CI, before March 1931, CI 2436 [wrongly dated 1932]). *C&HK*, Chap. 5, pp. 80–1.
96. Rejections were from Davies, Secker, and Duckworth, CI to SS, "Monday" from Nollendorfstrasse [summer 1931?], Bancroft. John Sutherland says it was also turned down by Faber, *Stephen Spender: The Authorized Biography* (New York: Viking, 2004), p. 128. *C&HK*, Chap. 5, pp. 81–2.

97. *C&HK*, Chap. 5, p. 82; CI to SS, July 8, 1931, from Kleiststrasse 9, Bancroft; WHA to CI, "Sunday" [September 1930?], CI 2970.
98. CI to SS, August 12, 1931, from Kleiststrasse 9; CI to SS, August, 1931, from Nollendorfstrasse 17, Bancroft.
99. SS, *World Within World* (London: Hamish Hamilton, 1951), p. 174; SS, Preface, *Letters to Christopher: Stephen Spender's Letters to Christopher Isherwood 1929-1939*, ed. Lee Bartlett (Santa Barbara: Black Sparrow Press, 1980), p. 10; *C&HK*, pp. 121-2; and see SS, *Poems* (1934).
100. Roger Pippett, "Books of the Week," *Daily Herald*, March 3, 1932, p. 13; "New Books and Reprints," *Times Literary Supplement*, April 14, 1932, p. 272.
101. CI to SS, "Thursday night" from Nollendorfstrasse [late 1931?], and CI to SS, "Wednesday evening" from Nollendorfstrasse [late September 1931?], Bancroft; CI to EU, "March First" from Nollendorfstrasse [1932?], Add MS 89002/3/5, BL.
102. CI to SS, "Wednesday evening" from Nollendorfstrasse [late September 1931?], Bancroft; SS, *World Within World*, p. 126.
103. EU to CI [autumn 1931?], from Edfu, Romford: "provided they pay you properly and don't require you to make statements about the communists I suppose no harm will be done. Whatever happens write nothing about politics—otherwise we shall never be able to meet again." (CI 2410)
104. "The Youth Movement in the New Germany," *Action*, Vol. 1, No. 10, December 10, 1931, p. 18.
105. In *Lady Chatterley's Lover*, which was available in Paris from 1929, D.H. Lawrence tells how Constance Reid, the future Lady Chatterley, had her first love affair with a German boy among the Wandervögel when she was only fifteen and later immersed herself among Cambridge intellectuals wearing open-necked flannel shirts; "The Youth Movement in the New Germany," *Action*, December 10, 1931, p. 18; CI to SS, "Sunday" from Nollendorfstrasse, late 1931, after SS sent him the copy, Bancroft.
106. *SB*, pp. 10-12.
107. *SB*, p. 18.
108. *SB*, p. 33.
109. *SB*, p. 23.
110. CI to JL, January 2, 1937, 99 rue de la Source, Bruxelles, HRC.
111. See Parker, *Christopher Isherwood*, p. 205, letter from Sarah Caudwell, November 25, 1993.
112. SS to JL, October 4, 1936, quoted in Parker, *Christopher Isherwood*, p. 205.
113. CI to SS, "Monday" [summer 1931?] from Nollendorfstrasse, Bancroft. Kantorowicz was press officer for the International Brigades in the Spanish Civil War and wrote *Spanish Civil War Diary* about his experiences. His "A Madrid Diary" appeared in *New Writing* in 1938.
114. She nearly died, according to Parker, who says the doctor left a swab inside (*Christopher Isherwood: A Life*, p. 220). The telephone number for a "(Klinik) Norden" in CI's 1933 appointment book may be relevant. (McFarlin)
115. TW to Donald Windham, July 18, 1943, and August 2, 1943, in *Tennessee Williams' Letters to Donald Windham, 1940-1965*, ed. Donald Windham (1976), repr. University of Georgia Press, 1996, pp. 89, 95. See also TW to Windham, July 28, 1943, pp. 93-4.
116. *C&HK*, Chap. 7, p. 108.
117. Parker, *Christopher Isherwood: A Life*, p. 181.
118. See Parker, *Christopher Isherwood: A Life*, p. 227. Rhoda Doris (Sally) Coole (1906-1980) later worked at the British Council and became a publisher and indexer. She often claimed to be the model for Sally Bowles (see, for instance, SS, December 1, 1952, Rio de Janeiro, Brazil in *Journals 1939-1983* (London: Faber and Faber, 1985)). More likely she was a model for the Helen / Karin figure who became Dorothy in "Waldemar," the third part of *DTV*.
119. CWBI to KBI, September 28, 1921, *Repton Letters*, p. 32.
120. CI to JL, January 16, 1936, HRC.
121. *SB*, p. 76; Parker, *Christopher Isherwood: A Life*, p. 220.
122. *SB*, pp. 78-9.
123. *SB*, pp. 148-9.

124. Neddermeyer, 1915–2004; *C&HK*, Chap. 5, p. 90.
125. *C&HK*, Chap. 5, p. 92; CI to SS, June 7, 1932 from Mohrin l/Neumark Villa Pressman, Bancroft.
126. EU to CI, "Monday" from Edfu, Romford, CI 2426; EU to CI, April 1, 1932, CI 2429. See also KBI diary, March 24, 1932, HRC.
127. KBI diary, February 3, 1929, HRC; *World Within World*, p. 132.
128. *A History of Russian Literature from the Earliest Times to the Death of Dostoevsky (1881)* (London: G. Routledge, 1927) and *Contemporary Russian Literature 1881–1925* (London: G. Routledge, 1926). Both are inscribed "Christopher Isherwood February 1928" and later belonged to EU (Huntington). The English translation of "The Sons of Our Sons" was by Babette Deutsch and Ariamh Yarmolinsky. CI recalled that WHA wrote two lines from Ehrenburg's poem beside their signatures in the guest book of an Amsterdam canal tour boat in 1929: "Read about us and marvel! / You did not live in our time—be sorry!" *C&HK*, Chap. 1, p. 10.
129. "As far as I know Lenin said nothing about buggery. Possibly there wasn't any in Russia. The position of buggery in a communist state will depend largely on the number of buggers who are communists. In any case persecution of buggers is anti-Leninist. But Gide will not be approved." EU to CI, "Sunday" from Edfu [1931?], CI 2424; *C&HK*, Chap. 2, p. 18; CI to SS, "Sunday" from Nollendorfstrasse, late autumn 1931, Bancroft.
130. As described in 1939 by an American intelligence officer, National Archives, Kew, KV2 1401 (20, p. 5). See also CIA Memorandum, https://www.cia.gov/library/readingroom/docs/DOC_0005632259.pdf
131. See Babette Gross, *Willi Münzenberg: A Political Biography*, trans. Marian Jackson (East Lansing: Michigan State University Press, 1974), p. 162.
132. Cockburn, *A Discord of Trumpets: An Autobiography 1932–1940* (New York: Simon & Schuster, 1956), p. 232. See also Arthur Koestler, *The Invisible Writing, The Second Volume of an Autobiography* (1954), Chaps 17, 18.
133. The main building was In den Zelten 10, the annex was 9a; Gross, *Willi Münzenberg*, p. 186; by contrast to the communists, the Nazis blamed homosexuals along with Jews and leftists for the defeat in WWI and announced they would "stamp out homosexuality because 'Germany must be virile if we are to fight for survival.'" *C&HK*, Chap. 2, p. 18; see also Chap. 7.
134. CI to SS from Nollendorfstrasse 17, November 14, 1932, Bancroft. In his 1933 appointment book, CI recorded an address for Gibarti, Wilhelmstrasse 48. Babette Gross places the IAH offices at Unter den Linden.
135. "The Initiates," *The God That Failed*, ed. Richard Crossman (London: Harper & Brothers, 1949; Chicago: Regnery Gateway, 1983), p. 63; *MNCT*, Chap. 6, p. 96.
136. *MNCT*, Chap. 5, p. 75, and Chap. 6, p. 100.
137. *MNCT*, Chap. 5, pp. 78–9.
138. *Hard Times* (1854), Book 2, Chap. 4, "Men and Brothers"; *MNCT*, Chap. 5, pp. 75–7.
139. Dmitrij Svjatopolk Mirsky, *Lenin* (London: Holme Press, 1931), pp. 99–100. CI borrowed the newly published biography from SS in the autumn of 1931.
140. *MNCT*, Chap. 5, p. 77.
141. *MNCT*, Chap. 16, p. 265; CI's *Communist Manifesto*, Huntington.
142. "The Landauers," *GB*, pp. 226, 232.
143. "The Landauers," *GB*, pp. 233–4.
144. "The Landauers," *GB*, pp. 233, 238.
145. *C&HK*, Chap. 4, p. 64; Gisa Soloweitschik letter to Peter Parker, January 15, 1993, quoted in *Christopher Isherwood: A Life*, p. 214.
146. *C&HK*, Chap. 4, p. 64; "The Landauers," *GB*, pp. 250–1; Sarah Caudwell, "Reply to Berlin," *New Statesman*, October 3, 1986, pp. 28–9.
147. "The Landauers," *GB*, pp. 246, 248.
148. "The Landauers," *GB*, p. 265; CI to SS, from Nollendorfstrasse, "Thursday," November 3, 1932, Bancroft.
149. "The Landauers," *GB*, pp. 271, 274.
150. "The Landauers," *GB*, p. 282.
151. *World Within World*, p. 131; *C&HK*, Chap. 4, p. 67.
152. CI diary, September 7, 1935, CI 2751.

153. "The Landauers," *GB*, pp. 240–1.
154. *World Within World*, p. 13.
155. "A Berlin Diary (Winter 1932–3)," *GB*, pp. 288–9, 293, 296, 299, 304, 305.
156. CI to SS, from Nollendorfstrasse, November 14, 1932; CI to SS, "Thursday" from Nollendorfstrasse, November 3, 1932, Bancroft; "A Berlin Diary (Winter 1932–3)," *GB*, p. 308.
157. "A Berlin Diary (Winter 1932–3)," *GB*, pp. 308–9. Werner von Alvensleben (1912–1989) taught art in England under the name Michael Werner and published cookbooks as Peter Purbright. He was a half-brother of the journalist and author Prince Hubertus zu Löwenstein, who mentions him in *Towards the Further Shore: An Autobiography* (London: Victor Gollancz, 1968), pp. 15, 85.
158. "A Berlin Diary (Winter 1932–3)," *GB*, p. 309. CI told William Plomer that the demonstration was deliberately staged in a communist neighborhood, "by way of annoying the Proletariat," and therefore required heavy police protection. He described an agent provocateur, not mentioned in the book, "being manhandled by the crowd, and that was really nasty. He just got away." CI to Plomer, January 25, 1933, from Nollendorfstrasse 17, William Plomer Manuscripts, Durham University Library, Archives and Special Collections.
159. CI to SS, November 14, 1932, from Nollendorfstrasse, Bancroft; "The City and the Plain," *C&C*, February 19, 1948, p. 191; CI to SS, November 14, 1932, Bancroft.
160. "A Berlin Diary (Winter 1932–3)," *GB*, pp. 309–10.
161. "A Berlin Diary (Winter 1932–3)," *GB*, p. 311.
162. Parker, *Christopher Isherwood: A Life*, p. 256.
163. *C&HK*, Chap. 7, p. 129; Bucknell conversation with DB.
164. CI to SS, Sunday [April, 1933?], Berlin, Bancroft.
165. CI diary, May 23, 1933, p. 10, CI 2749; *MNCT*, Chap. 11, pp. 175–6.
166. CI diary, May 22, 24, 1933, pp. 8, 9, 12, CI 2749.
167. CI diary, May 1933, n.d., p. 19 verso; May 28, 1933, p. 15, CI 2749.
168. To his account of a nighttime crossing from the mainland he added elements from Romantic landscape painting with the Journey of the Magi and the Nativity—"the straggling trees which take on forms like a procession of camels. One star burnt very low above the earth, like a portent." Elsewhere he wrote "the boys coming down with their lanterns on the rocks formed a group like a detail from Descent from the Cross," and "The hut at night with the lantern light shining through the branches and the figures within round the lantern makes one think of a nativity." May 1933, pp. 30, 23, 27; September 6, 1933, p. 54, CI 2749.
169. CI diary, June 6, 1933, p. 20, CI 2749.
170. CI diary, June 6, 1933, p. 20, CI 2749; *Günther's Erlebnisse* published in Berlin, 1932, trans. of CI's transcription, Angelica von Hase; *MNCT*, Chap. 4, p. 69.
171. CI diary, June 14, 1933, pp. 26–7. Eldorado, the popular gay bar. See Mel Gordon, "Inventory: Everyone Once in Berlin! A Semiotics of the Weimar Streetwalker" in *Cabinet Magazine*, Winter 2008–9; *MNCT*, Chap. 3, p. 46; *Die Freundin* was published 1923–34; Schableth (illeg.) not identified.
172. CI diary, July 8, 1933, p. 39, CI 2749.
173. CI to EMF, July 8, 1933, in *F&I*, p. 23; CI to SS, June 23, 1933, Bancroft.
174. CI diary, June 23, 1933, p. 31, CI 2749; *The Tempest*, 2.2.
175. CI diary, August 17, 28, 1933, pp. 50–1, 54, CI 2749.
176. CI diary, September 7, 1933, p. 56, CI 2749; *C&HK*, Chap. 1, p. 3.
177. CI to SS, "Saturday," from Mohrin l/Neumark Villa Pressman, Bancroft; *D1*, October 16, 1939, p. 48.
178. CI to SS, June 2, 1933, c/o Thomas Cook, Athens, Bancroft.
179. *C&HK*, Chap. 7, p. 125; "In the evening, like an award, came Ms letter about the legacy." (CI diary, July 12, 1933, p. 4, CI 2749) Agatha Trevor died March 28, 1933; conceivably he learned of her intention in April when he was home in London, but KBI noted the amount of the legacy (£300) in her diary only on September 5, when, after CI pressed for more information, she telephoned the Trevor lawyer and also learned that the money might not be paid for another three or four months.
180. CI diary, September 7, 1933, p. 56, CI 2749.

181. National Archives, KV-2-2178.
182. CI diary, October 6, 1933, p. 58, CI 2749.
183. C&HK, Chap. 9, p. 150.
184. "From a Viertel Daybook," *New York Times*, October 28, 1934, Section 9, p. 5; British Board of Film Censors, Observations of Scenarios, 1934 (January to December), p. 260, BBFC -1-3-305, British Film Institute Reuben Library.
185. Stevenson is portrayed in *PV* as the story editor Sandy Ashmeade. Ashmeade had already appeared briefly in *L&S*. Viertel and CI secretly called Stevenson "Umbrella," and in *PV* Ashmeade carries "a slim umbrella, perfectly rolled." (*PV*, p. 23.) This was a hilarious and intuitive real-life prophecy of Stevenson's future success as the director of Walt Disney's *Mary Poppins* (1964), about the English nanny who uses her umbrella to fly.
186. KBI diary, December 8, 1933, HRC; CI diary, December 17, 1933, CI 2750.
187. CI diary, December 23, 1933, CI 2570.
188. C&HK, Chap. 9, p. 158.
189. C&HK, Chap. 9, p. 158; CI diary, December 27, 1933, CI 2750.
190. KBI diary, January 5, 1934, HRC.
191. C&HK, Chap. 9, pp. 160, 162.
192. See Katharina Prager, *Berthold Viertel, Eine Biografie die Wiener Moderne* (Vienna: Böhlau Verlag, 2018), p. 264; C&HK, Chap. 9, p. 163.
193. KBI diary, January 8, 17, 1934, HRC; CI to Robson-Scott, January 6, 1934, and "Thursday" probably January 11, 1934, HRC.
194. KBI diary, November 28, 1933, January 30, February 1, 1934. HRC.
195. C&HK, Chap. 9, pp. 168–9.
196. CI diary, May 23, 1934, CI 2750.
197. CI to BV, April 5, 1934, and January 1, 1935, Deutsches Literature Archiv, Marbach.
198. CI diary, May 23, 1934, CI 2750; C&HK, Chap. 10, pp. 184–6.
199. Viertel, "From a Viertel Daybook," *New York Times*, October 28, 1934, Section 9, p. 5.
200. C&HK, Chap. 10, p. 186. "He said at the time that this was to save trouble in signing legal documents, but in fact it was a last little smack at Kathleen and her hyphens." *Hero-Father, Demon-Mother*, p. 11, CI 1082.
201. C&HK, Chap. 10, p. 181.
202. C&HK, Chap. 9, p. 155.
203. Through such new techniques, CI thought the theme was "modernized but not at all desentimentalized." (C&HK, Chap. 9, p. 155)
204. C&HK, Chap. 9, p. 170–1.
205. KBI diary, August 27, 1934, HRC.
206. Andre Sennwald, "The Screen: 'Little Friend,' The Sensitive Drama of a Girl, at the Roxy—'Have a Heart,' at the Mayfair," *New York Times*, October 20, 1934 p. 0.
207. EMF to CI, January 16, 1935, F&I, p. 40.
208. Published in the *Listener*, August 28, 1935, and the *Ploughshare*, April–May 1935, repr. *Exh.*, pp. 208–15, 215–18.
209. First printed as "Chorus for a Play," *New Signatures*, ed. Michael Roberts (London: Hogarth Press, 1932), and collected later as "The Wanderer"; see Edward Mendelson, *Early Auden* (New York: Viking, 1981), p. 44.
210. "Now, old father, that you know our will, / That for your estate we do your body kill," *The Poet's Tongue: An Anthology*, chosen by WHA and John Garrett (London: G. Bell & Sons Ltd, 1935), p. 199. See also p. 195, where the fool lists the items he leaves. In courting a bride, the suitors rely on the English custom of primogeniture: "I am my father's eldest son, / And heir of all his land, / And in a short time, I hope, / It will fall into my hands," p. 205.
211. C&HK, Chap. 2, p. 28. See Edward Mendelson, Intro. to WHA, *Plays and Other Dramatic Writings 1928–1938*, p. xxi.
212. "Possible scenes for play," CI diary, November 18, 1934, CI 2750; C&HK, Chap. 11; Edward Mendelson, "The Dog Beneath the Skin, History, Authorship, Texts, and Editions," *Plays and Other Dramatic Writings, 1928–1938*, p. 553; the rest of the title was suggested by Rupert Doone, who directed.
213. *DBS*, 3.5, p. 174.

214. CWBI diary, April 21, 1918, McFarlin; for *Peter Pan*, KBI diary, January 24, 1917, HRC.
215. *DBS*, 3.5, p. 173; CI to SS, June 16, 1935, from Amsterdam, Bancroft.
216. As Edward Mendelson put it, "fitted out with a baronetcy and revolutionary principles." *Early Auden, Later Auden: A Critical Biography* (Princeton University Press, 2017), p. 249.
217. The woman from the village is Mildred Luce, named for CI's grandmother's family. For an account of the complex evolution of *The Fronny*, *The Chase*, *The Dog Beneath the Skin* and the earlier, unpublished WHA–CI play, *The Enemies of a Bishop, or, Die When I Say When: A Morality in Four Acts*, see Mendelson, *Early Auden, Later Auden*, pp. 248–55.
218. CI diary, May 22, 1935, CI 2750; *C&HK*, Chap. 11, pp. 209–10; SS, *World Within World*, p. 104. In his novel *The Temple*, SS attributes this cure to his WHA character, boosting WHA's myth, not CI's.
219. Stekel, *Peculiarities of Behavior: Wandering Mania, Dipsomania, Cleptomania, Pyromania and Allied Impulsive Acts* (London: Williams, Norgate Ltd, 1925), Vol. 2, p. 11; WHA, "Journal / April 1929," Berg; WHA, *The Orators: An English Study* (London: Faber and Faber, 1932), Book II, p. 75.
220. CI diary, May 22, June 21, 1935, CI 2750.
221. CI diary, June 21, May 22, 1935, and see also May 6, 1936, "the assassination," CI 2750.
222. CI diary, September 1, 1935, CI 2751.
223. CI diary, January 3, 1936, CI 2751.
224. *Paul Is Alone*, CI 1041.
225. Frederick Rolfe, Baron Corvo, *The Desire and Pursuit of the Whole: A Romance of Modern Venice* (London: Cassell & Co. Ltd, 1934), p. 9, and see also pp. 19–20; *A Farewell to Arms*, Chaps 30–1.
226. CI diary, May 5, 1936, CI 2751.
227. CI diary, May 29, 1936, CI 2751.
228. CI to KBI, March 18, 1935, *K&C*, p. 13.
229. CI diary, June 26, 1936, CI 2751.
230. KBI diary, June 30, July 4, 1936, HRC.
231. KBI diary, July 9, 1936, HRC.
232. CI to EMF, August 8, 1936, *F&I*, p. 59; KBI diary, August 18, 1936, HRC.
233. KBI diary, July 4, 27, 1936, HRC.
234. KBI diary, August 7, 1936, HRC.
235. KBI diary, August 11, 1936; see also August 19, HRC.
236. KBI diary, August 11, 1936; see also August 19, 21, HRC.
237. *C&HK*, Chap. 13, p. 256.
238. KBI diary, August 27, September 3, 17, 1936, HRC.
239. *L&S*, Chap. 2, pp. 75–6; Humphrey Spender, diary, January 20, 1936, quoted by Matthew Spender in *Sintra Diary*, p. 29, published in Italian 2012 and Spanish 2017, unpublished English original shared by M. Spender.
240. CI thought Eliot's "careful, academic verse" at odds with his "doggerel couplets." "The Book Chronicle," *Listener*, June 26, 1935, p. 1110, unsigned, by CI.
241. CI day-to-day book, 1937, McFarlin; March 15, 1937, *Letters from a Life*, ed. Mitchell and Reed, p. 483, and Marjorie Fass to Daphne Oliver, December 1937, quoted in Mitchell's Intro., p. 19.
242. *New Statesman*, March 6, 1937, p. 368, unsigned; *New English Weekly*, March 11, 1937, p. 433; Ralph Thompson, *Books of the Times*, reviewing the published play, March 9, 1937; Peter Monro Jack, "A Disturbing Drama by W.H. Auden," *New York Times*, May 30, 1937.
243. KBI diary, April 10, 1937, HRC. The portrait was exhibited at Thomas Agnew & Sons, Old Bond Street, June–July 1937, and is now in a private collection; for an illustration see Peter T.J. Rumley, *William Coldstream: Catalogue Raisonné* (Bristol: Sansom & Company, 2018), p. 25.
244. *C&HK*, Chap. 13, p. 274.
245. *C&HK*, Chap. 13, p. 278.

246. KBI diary, May 12, 1937; December 11, 1936; May 12, 1937, HRC.
247. *C&HK*, Chap. 14, p. 285; *MNCT*, Chap. 5, pp. 243–4.
248. CI to Robson-Scott, "Wednesday Evening," [probably May 19], 1937, HRC.
249. *C&HK*, Chap. 14, pp. 286–7.
250. CI diary, July 26, 1937, CI 2751.
251. *OTF*, 2.1, p. 68; CI diary, November 19, 1937, CI 2751.
252. KBI diary, November 20, 1937, HRC.
253. *OTF*, 2.1, p. 68; CI diary, November 20, 1937, CI 2751.
254. CI diary, November 20, 22, 1937, CI 2751.
255. James, "The Pupil" (1891), collected in *The Lesson of the Master: The Marriages, The Pupil, Brooksmith, The Solution, Sir Edmund Orme* (London: Macmillan, 1892), Chap. 1, p. 123, Chap. 4, p. 142.
256. CI diary, November 27, December 15, 1937, CI 2751. In order to spirit Scott-Kilvert away to Paris, CI submitted to a test of fire with Mrs. Lang, Scott-Kilvert's mother, who invited him to dinner. To KBI's surprise, he purchased "a new dinner jacket & suit complete (trousers with 2 narrow lines of braid) shirt collar, tie, silk socks, & patent leather shoes at £13.0.0." KBI observed of her leftist, bohemian son that he no longer ever attended this kind of old-fashioned, formal dinner and "had no need for evening clothes." It was "a great concession" in her eyes. (KBI diary, December 2, 3, 1937, HRC)
257. *C&HK*, Chap. 14, pp. 291–2, and Judith Adamson, *Charlotte Haldane: Woman Writer in a Man's World* (Basingstoke: Palgrave Macmillan, 1998), Chap. 7, pp. 112–31; KBI diary, December 15, 1937, HRC.
258. CI diary, November 29, 1937, CI 2751.
259. WHA, Verse "Commentary" to the Sonnet Sequence "In Time of War," *JW*, p. 292.
260. BB diary, January 18, 1938, quoted in Donald Mitchell, *Britten and Auden in the Thirties* (London/Boston: Faber and Faber, 1981), p. 128, note 9; KBI diary, January 18, 19, 1938, HRC.
261. *Harper's Bazaar*, October 1938, repr. *Exh.*; cable to KBI from Hankow, April 21, 1938, in *K&C*, p. 12.
262. *JW*, pp. 28, 27, March 8, 1938, p. 50.
263. CI to Olive Mangeot, March 10, 1938, Berg.
264. *JW*, March 4, 1938, p. 50.
265. *JW*, March 17, 1938, p. 59.
266. *JW*, March 9, 15, 1938, pp. 53, 70–1.
267. *JW*, p. 74; CI diary, November 11, 1935, CI 2751.
268. *JW*, 104; "Waldemar," *DTV*, p. 173; CI diary, November 24, 1934, CI 2750; *K&F*, Chap. 15, p. 397.
269. KBI diary, December 1, 1912, HRC; *JW*, Chap. 5, p. 120.
270. *C&HK*, Chap. 15, p. 312; *D1*, bridging passage, January 1939, p. 6.
271. *JW*, Chap. 9, pp. 207, 210, 226.
272. WHA and CI, "Meeting the Japanese: Two English Writers Report," August 16, 1938, *New Masses*, p. 10.
273. *D1*, bridging passage, January 1939, p. 4.
274. *C&HK*, Chap. 15, p. 303.
275. CI diary, August 20, 1938, CI 2751; "Detailed memories of sex with Auden—which went on intermittently from 1926 to 1938 ..." *LY*, p. 58; CI diary, August 20, 1938, CI 2751.
276. CI diary, August 20, 1938, CI 2751.
277. The poem begins, "Who is that funny-looking young man so squat with a top-heavy head"; WHA wrote it in CI's copy of D.H. Lawrence's *Birds, Beasts and Flowers* (1931) and dated it "Dover Sept 3, 1937." CI quoted lines in *C&HK*, Chap. 15, pp. 303–4, and the poem was published in full in Brian Finney, *Christopher Isherwood: A Critical Biography*, pp. 287–9.
278. CI diary, August 20, 1938, CI 2751; CI used the phrase again in his work journal when he was writing *DTV*, March 25, 1960, p. 120, CI 1158.
279. CI diary, July 1938, p. 39 verso, CI 2751.

280. CI diary, July 30, 1938, CI 2751.
281. CI diary, August 23, 1938, CI 2751.
282. CI diary, September 8, 1938, CI 2751.
283. CI diary, September 24, 1938, CI 2751.
284. CI diary, September 26, 28, 1938, CI 2751.
285. CI diary, September 30, 24, 1938, CI 2751.
286. Alan Pryce-Jones, *Devoid of Shyness, From the Journal 1926–1939* (Settrington, York: Stone Trough Books, 2015), p. 194. Dated "February 1938," but WHA and CI left for China on January 19, so the dinner must have been earlier, possibly at Cyril Connolly's, January 2, or at SS's before the China farewell party, KBI diary, January 2, 18, 1938, HRC.
287. *The Diary of Virginia Woolf, Volume 5, 1936–1941*, ed. Anne Olivier Bell and Andrew McNeillie (London: Hogarth Press, 1984), February 21, 1937, November 1, 1938, pp. 59, 185.
288. CI day-to-day book, October 22, 1937, "Lunch with Morgan and Maugham," McFarlin; *Tellers of Tales: 100 Short Stories from the United States, England, France, Russia and Germany*, selected and with an introduction by W. Somerset Maugham (New York: Doubleday, Doran & Company, Inc., 1939).
289. "The New Vernacular," *Enemies of Promise* (London: Routledge & Kegan Paul, 1938; repr. André Deutsch), Chap. 8, pp. 82, 87. CI admired Orwell's first novel *Burmese Days* (1934) and twice advised JL to get Orwell to contribute to *New Writing*. *GB* has obvious parallels with Orwell's memoir *Down and Out in Paris and London* (1933).
290. The limited run began November 14, 1938, and, apart from one harsh review, was well received. It had been postponed for the China trip, then CI and WHA rewrote much of the play on the way home. There was one Sunday performance in London, February 12, 1939, at the Globe Theatre, but CI and WHA had left for the U.S. and did not see it. See *Plays and Other Dramatic Writings*, p. 654, and Edward Mendelson's Intro., p. xxviii. See also *IonW*, pp. 89, 171, 184–6.
291. CI to JL, December 13, 1938, Apt 6, 29 Rue de Stassart, Brussels, Beinecke.
292. Berkeley to BB, n.d., quoted in *Letters from a Life*, ed. Mitchell and Reed, p. 607, note 2. BB arrived January 6, 1939. Another BB friend disapproved of CI's "unwise interest in prostitutes male & female." (Marjorie Fass to Daphne Oliver, December 1937, quoted in Mitchell's Intro., p. 19)
293. *D1*, bridging passage, January 1939, p. 4.
294. From a typescript preserved by Tom Driberg and, subsequently, Alan Clodd, printed by permission of the Estate of WHA; *LY*, p. 93.
295. EMF to CI, June 7, 1939, *F&I*, pp. 81–2; CI to EMF, July 3, 1939, *F&I*, p. 83.
296. CI to JL, May 13, 1940, Beinecke; see also March 8, 1939, permitting Hewit to collect his income tax refund, and April 16, 1940, requesting JL to give Hewit further royalties.
297. *Another Time* (London: Faber and Faber, 1940), pp. 30, 47.
298. "A Berlin Diary (Winter 1932–3)," *GB*, pp. 316–17. Rudi was probably based on a boy nicknamed the Pathfinder with whom William Robson-Scott had been involved. "The Pathfinder has already been photographed thirty-seven times," CI to SS, November 14, 1932, from Nollendorfstrasse, Bancroft.
299. "A Berlin Diary (Winter 1932–3)," *GB*, pp. 316–17; *Another Time*, p. 47.
300. *D1*, bridging passage, January 1939, pp. 5–7.

5: HOLLYWOOD SCREENWRITER AND HINDU MONK

1. CI to SS, February 26, 1939, Bancroft; *D1*, March 18, 1939, p. 9.
2. In the *New Republic*: "German Literature in England," April 5, 1939; *The Professor* by Rex Warner, March 8, 1939; *Pale Horse, Pale Rider* by Katherine Anne Porter, April 19, 1939; *Night Rider* by Robert Penn Warren, May 31, 1939. In the *Kenyon Review*, review of *The Grapes of Wrath*, John Steinbeck, Vol. 1, No. 4 (Autumn, 1939), pp. 450–3. With WHA: "Young British Writers on the Way Up," *Vogue*, August 15, 1939: Orwell,

        Ralph Bates, Arthur Calder-Marshall, Graham Greene, Spender, Rex Warner, Edward Upward, Henry Green, William Plomer, James Stern; there were no women.
3. CI to JL, July 7, 1939, Beinecke; "The Head of a Leader" was also reprinted in *Exh*.
4. JL to CI, August 23, 1939, Beinecke, "Your books have been selling very well recently, and in particular, there has been a boom in the Scandinavian countries, I am not quite sure why. We have just sold the Danish rights in GOODBYE TO BERLIN."
5. *New Statesman and Nation*, March 11, 1939, pp. 362.
6. "concerned more with people than with policies," (*Dundee Evening Telegraph*, March 4, 1939); L.P. Hartley called CI "an artist to his finger-tips." ("New Novels: Old Orders Changing," *Observer*, April 16, 1939, p. 7); Edwin Muir could not praise highly enough CI's power of observation. ("New Novels," *Listener*, March 16, 1939, p. 597)
7. Kenneth Muir called it "six fragments of an unwritten novel" in "Berlin Before Hitler: Four Successes in Different Styles," "Novel of the Week," *Yorkshire Post*, March 8, 1939. Arthur Foss also lamented the epic CI had not written. ("Echoes of the September Crisis: Life in Disturbed Europe," *Times Literary Supplement*, March 25, 1939, xiii) But "nothing is lost by publication of these brilliant fragments; indeed the method gains for the book an undiminishing vitality from first to last through fresh inspirations." (March 8, 1939, *Edinburgh Evening News*)
8. *GB*, p. 7.
9. CI to JL, March 8, 1939, Beinecke; CI to KBI, March 26, 1939, *K&C*, p. 130. In other U.S. reviews, Edith Walton failed to recognize the connection between CI's focus on the overlooked and Hitler's success: "He limits himself to the frothy scum of Berlin society." ("Berlin on the Brink, Latest Works of Fiction," *New York Times*, March 19, 1939, p. 24) Basil Davenport praised CI's "universal sympathy": "He does not condemn the painted boys; he presents them. He does not condemn the brutal Storm Troopers who begin to appear in the last diary; he presents them," but Davenport thought "this impartial sensitivity has in it a certain defect of its own." ("Atmosphere of Decay," *Saturday Review*, April 15, 1939)
10. Edmund Wilson, "Isherwood's Lucid Eye," *New Republic*, May 17, 1939, p. 51.
11. CI to KBI, March 26, 10, 1939, *K&C*, pp. 130, 129.
12. CI to EMF, April 29, 1939, *F&I*, p. 78.
13. *D1*, bridging passage, April 1939, p. 14.
14. *LY*, p. 60; *D1*, bridging passage, April 1939, p. 14; CI to KBI, June 18, 1939, *K&C*, pp. 139–40; CI to SS, July 8, 1939, Bancroft.
15. Bucknell conversation with DB, June 5, 2018. DB added, spring 2021, "if queer at all" in TS of this book.
16. *D1*, bridging passage, May 1939, p. 20.
17. CI to KBI, May 23, 1939, *K&C*, p. 136.
18. *C&HK*, Chap. 6, p. 102; CI's day-to-day books from 1933 and 1937 show that he and Wood met for lunch, tea, dinner, and theater in London. On November 13, 1933, CI wrote: "Chris √√: X }{ 7:30." (McFarlin); *D1*, bridging passage, May 1939, p. 24.
19. CI to SS, 8 July 1939, Bancroft.
20. *C&HK*, Chap. 9, p. 156. Viertel moved his family to Hollywood when he signed with Fox. He directed two silents for Fox, *The One Woman Idea* (1929) and *Seven Faces* (1929), then two sound films, *Man Trouble* (1930) and *The Spy* (1931), for Twentieth Century–Fox. For Warner, he co-directed with William Dieterle *Die heilige Flamme* (*The Sacred Flame*, 1931), and for Paramount he directed *The Magnificent Lie* (1932), *The Wiser Sex* (1932), *The Man from Yesterday* (1932), and *The Cheat* (1931, George Abbot was the only credited director). When he returned to Europe in 1932, he directed a film adaptation of Hans Fallada's novel *Kleiner Mann—was nun?* (*Little Man, What Now?* in U.S., 1934) for Europa-Film in Berlin. He returned to Santa Monica when Hitler came to power, and then accepted work with Gaumont-British in London. After *Little Friend* he directed *The Passing of the Third Floor Back* (1935) and *Rhodes of Africa* (1936) for Gaumont. He also had a distinguished stage-directing career and wrote poetry and prose. See Katharina Prager, *Berthold Viertel, Eine Biografie die Wiener Moderne*.
21. *D1*, bridging passage, November 1939, pp. 53–4.

22. Salka Viertel and Garbo became friends when they appeared together in the German-language version of *Anna Christie* (1930).
23. "I Am Waiting," *New Yorker*, October 21, 1939, repr. *Exh.*, p. 219. The *New Yorker* moved the setting from provincial England to Connecticut because England had entered the war in September while America was still on the sidelines "waiting." But CI, celebrated for conveying atmosphere of time and place, had only briefly set foot in Connecticut and the change was for the worse
24. *D1*, bridging passage, May 1939, pp. 26, 27, 28, 29, 30; CI, *Essentials of Vedanta* (Hollywood: Vedanta Press, 1969).
25. *MG&HD*, Chap. 2, p. 23; *D1*, August 4, 1939, p. 43; *MG&HD*, Chap. 3, p. 39.
26. *D1*, August 4, 5, 1939, pp. 44–5.
27. *MG&HD*, Chap. 2, pp. 25–6.
28. *D1*, November 13, 1940, p. 127.
29. *D1*, January 17, 1940, p. 82
30. CI to JL, April 16, 1940, Beinecke.
31. *D1*, March 6, 31, 1940, pp. 93–4.
32. *D1*, July 29, 1940, p. 114.
33. *D1*, bridging passage, August 1939, p. 43.
34. CI to EU, August 6, 1939, Add MS 72688, BL; *Daily Worker*, March 29, 1939, p. 7; repr. *W.H. Auden: The Critical Heritage*, ed. John Haffenden (London: Routledge, Kegan & Paul, 1983), p. 291 (original item not found).
35. CI to EU, August 6, 1939, BL.
36. CI 104; CI to EU, August 6, 1939, BL.
37. *DTV*, p. 231.
38. WHA to CI, July 18, 1943, CI 2994.
39. *D1*, bridging passage, December 1939, p. 55; Tom Driberg, writing as William Hickey.
40. *Horizon: A Review of Literature and Art*, Vol. 2, No. 2, February 1940, pp. 68–9.
41. "People and Things," *Spectator*, April 19, 1940, p. 555; see *Daily Mail*, May 27, 1941; questions asked by Sir Jocelyn Lucas MP of the parliamentary secretary to the Ministry of Labour, June 13, 1940. See Humphrey Carpenter, *W.H. Auden: A Biography* (London: George Allen & Unwin, 1981; Boston, Houghton Mifflin, 1982), pp. 291–2, and Kathleen Bell, "A Change of Heart," in *Auden Studies 1: "The Map of All My Youth": Early Works, Friends and Influences*, ed. Katherine Bucknell and Nicholas Jenkins (Oxford University Press, 1990), pp. 97–8.
42. CI to SS, February 17, 1940, Bancroft.
43. CI to JL, January 11, 1940, Beinecke.
44. *D1*, December 1939, bridging passage, pp. 55–6.
45. *D1*, January 20, 1940, p. 83. The gossip columnist for the *Daily Express* asked CI's permission to print the verse, which was circulating in London. It was eventually published in the *New Statesman and Nation*, February 17, 1940, p. 204, signed "Viper."
46. EMF to CI, September 1, October 31, 1939, *F&I*, pp. 87, 90.
47. *D1*, January 20, 1940, p. 84.
48. On his way from England to California via New York in July 1948, CI collected the typescript, advising LK that he needed it for his novel: "the microfilm would be too difficult to use." (CI to LK, July 3, 1948, HM 81695, Huntington.) Also, "Can you tell me the name and address of the person who is in charge of the manuscripts at Yale, including my journal? I want to write him a letter, in case I die, leaving instructions about what to do with the microfilm. Just a precaution." (CI to LK, October 29. 1948, HM 81691, Huntington)
49. DB to CI, October 18, 1966, *Animals*, p. 229; *MG&HD*, Chap. 13, p. 204. During the 1970s, CI came to feel that his account of himself in the wartime diaries—as a pacifist, a Hindu, a homosexual, and a debutant American—was too apologetic and, in terms of his sexuality, too guarded (*LY*, pp. 72–3). But he did not destroy the diaries or alter them.
50. *D1*, August 7, 1940, p. 116.
51. *D1*, August 1, 1940, p. 115.
52. *D1*, August 7, 1940, p. 116.

Notes to Part 5 / 771

53. *D1*, August 9, 1940, p. 116.
54. *D1*, bridging passage, September 1940, p. 120, and September 7, 1940, p. 121.
55. CI recorded the day as Holy Mother's birthday, perhaps because Jaggadhatri Puja fell on November 8 that year. The goddess Jaggadhatri is an aspect of the goddess Durga with whom Ramakrishna's wife, Sarada Devi, is identified.
56. *D1*, November 8, 1940, p. 125.
57. *D1*, bridging passage, January 1941, p. 143.
58. *D1*, bridging passage, March 1941, p. 151.
59. *D1*, August 7, 1940, p. 116; WHA to CI, on stationery of 7 Middagh Street, Brooklyn [1941, probably before March 21], CI 2991.
60. *D1*, August 13, 1940, p. 118.
61. CI had visited Peter Watson's rue du Bac apartment before the war, for KBI added the address to her list for 1939, but he made no record of meeting Fouts before 1940.
62. *D1*, bridging passage, August 1940, p. 118; bequest note, CI 877. Fouts sold the painting to private collectors long before he died, and it was later donated to the Museum of Modern Art in New York.
63. *D1*, bridging passage, October 1940, p. 123.
64. *D1*, bridging passage, March 1941, p. 148.
65. *D1*, bridging passage, June 1941, p. 155.
66. CI work journal, August 16, 1960, p. 125, CI 1158; Fouts notebook, CI 876; *D1*, bridging passage, June 1941, p. 156.
67. *D1*, bridging passage, July 1941, pp. 164–5, 169, 170.
68. CI to JL, June 24, July 3, 1941, Beinecke.
69. "The Day at La Verne (In the Friends' Service Committee Seminar)," "Report on Today," *New Writing*, ed. JL, No. 14, July–September, 1942, pp. 12–14.
70. *D1*, bridging passage, July 1941, pp. 170–1.
71. *D1*, July 16, 1941, p. 175.
72. *D1*, bridging passage, August 1941, p. 180. Fouts was classed 4E, not prepared to serve in the military even in noncombatant role, but prepared to do civilian public service.
73. *D1*, bridging passage, July 1941, p. 171.
74. WHA told Kallman in a Christmas letter, "On account of you, I have been, in intention, and almost in act, a murderer." See Mendelson, *Early Auden, Later Auden*, pp. 495 and ff.
75. *D1*, bridging passage, August–September 1941, p. 181; KBI diary, September 10, 1941.
76. *D1*, bridging passage, August–September 1941, p. 181.
77. *D1*, bridging passage, October 1941, p. 185.
78. *D1*, bridging passage, October 1941, pp. 193, 188.
79. *D1*, July 1, 1942, p. 230.
80. The phrase was uttered by a refugee who had to clean the room of two others and was disgusted by their personal habits: "Such people are not fit for the school of tragedy." *D1*, June 24, 1942, p. 229.
81. *D1*, bridging passage, October 1941, p. 187. The class was taught by a Swiss scholar, Dora Willson.
82. In *WE* he was to name Sarah Pennington's Haverford house Tawelfan, Welsh for the Quiet Place; it was the name he had used for the family home in Wales of the doomed neurotic hero, the Truly Weak Man, Tommy Llewellyn in his abandoned 1920s novel *The North-West Passage*, *L&S*, Chap. 5, pp. 206–7, 210.
83. *D1*, January 16, 1942, p. 206; CI to BB, February 18, 1942, Britten Pears Arts Archive.
84. *D1*, January 3, 1942, pp. 202–3.
85. EMF to CI, November, 10, 1941, and CI to EMF, January 11, 1942, *F&I*, pp. 98, 101; "The inner life had paid," EMF, *Howards End*, Chap. 37.
86. *D1*, March 18, 20, 1939, pp. 11–12.
87. *D1*, February 9, 1942, p. 209.
88. *D1*, March 20, 1939, p. 12.
89. *D1*, February 13, 15, 16, 1942, pp. 209–10.
90. *D1*, bridging passage, February 1942, p. 211.

91. *MG&HD*, Chap. 7, p. 93.
92. *D1*, April 22, 1942, p. 217.
93. *D1*, April 22, 1942, p. 218.
94. "Take It or Leave It," *New Yorker*, October 24, 1942; repr. *Exh.*, pp. 231, 235.
95. "R.L.S." First published in *Tomorrow*, 1950–51; repr. *Exh.*, p. 52.
96. "Henry Jekyll's Full Statement of the Case," *Strange Case of Dr. Jekyll and Mr. Hyde*, quoted in "R.L.S.," *Exh.*, 52.
97. "R.L.S.," *Exh.*, p. 52.
98. *D1*, September 15, 1943, p. 315; CI to DS, March 22, 1957, Gotlieb.
99. Intro. to "Stories" in *Exh.*, p. 175.
100. *D3*, June 27, 1981, p. 677.
101. *D1*, July 6, 1942, p. 231.
102. *D1*, bridging passage, July 1939, p. 33; CI to JL, July 5, 1942, Beinecke.
103. *D1*, bridging passage, July 1942, p. 231.
104. *D1*, bridging passage, July 1942, p. 234; see Jeremy Lewis, *Shades of Greene: One Generation of an English Family* (London: Jonathan Cape, 2010), pp. 255–6, 19–21. Later, Greene became known as a pro-communist journalist reporting on China, Vietnam, and Cuba.
105. *D1*, bridging passage, July 1942, p. 234.
106. *D1*, bridging passage, July 1942, pp. 232–3, 235.
107. *D1*, September 23, 1942, pp. 241–3.
108. *D1*, bridging passage, August 1942, p. 238.
109. *D1*, September 25, 28, 23, 1942, pp. 240, 245, 250, 240. He expected to be sent to firefighting camp, but the process was slow and confusing. A friend at Los Prietos camp wrote asking why he hadn't turned up, so he telegrammed the camp director, who assured him he shouldn't attend until he received his paperwork.
110. *D1*, September 27, 29, 1942, p. 250.
111. PI Gita, p. 2.
112. "The Sorrow of Arjuna," PI Gita, Chap. I, p. 35.
113. "The Gita and War" appeared in the Vedanta Society magazine, *Vedanta and the West*, September–October 1944, was collected in *VMM*, and included in a shortened version as Appendix 2 in later printings of the PI Gita. CI reprinted it again in *Exh.*, see p. 104.
114. "The Yoga of Knowledge," PI Gita, Chap. 2, p. 47.
115. "The Gita and War," *Exh.*, pp. 104–5.
116. "The Gita and War," *Exh.*, pp. 104, 111. CI wrote the Gita article for the Vedanta Society magazine February 17 and 23, submitted it March 6, and worked on it again on July 27–8, 1944.
117. "The Gita and War," *Exh.*, p. 106; "The Yoga of Knowledge," PI Gita, Chap. 2, p. 43; quoted in "The Gita and War," *Exh.*, pp. 108, 43.
118. "The Gita and War," *Exh.*, p. 108. CI no longer believed that social work could improve the lot of humankind, and he was to explain this often in coming years: "I do not believe that it can produce any permanent material improvement in this world; but it is spiritually constructive, and that is all that finally matters. Right action is the language of spiritual progress." CI, Intro. to *VWW*, p. 13.
119. "Socially, the caste-system is graded [...] but spiritually, there are no such distinctions," CI wrote in "The Gita and War." "Everyone," says Krishna, "can attain the highest sainthood by following the prescribed path of his own caste duty." (*Exh.*, p. 108.) This new emphasis harmonized with the Christian-Tolstoyan ideal of spiritual vocation that CI described in "The Problem of the Religious Novel" in the mid-1940s and which he was to reiterate in his Santa Barbara lectures in 1960–1.
120. "The Gita and War," *Exh.*, pp. 111, 109, 110.
121. *D1*, October 12, 1942, p. 252.
122. *D1*, November 22, 1943, pp. 328–9.
123. "The Sorrow of Arjuna," PI Gita, Chap. 1, p. 32, quoted in *D1*, November 22, 1943, p. 329.
124. *MG&HD*, Chap. 10, p. 149.
125. WHA, *Juvenilia, Poems 1922–1928*, p. 210.

126. "It is time that I wrote my will; / I choose upstanding men / That climb the streams until / The fountain leap, and at dawn / Drop their cast at the side / Of dripping stone; I declare / They shall inherit my pride . . ." W.B. Yeats, "The Tower," III.
127. *L&S*, Chap. 5, p. 193, and quoted in "Stories," *Exh.*, p. 169.
128. CI to LK, August 10, 1943, HM 81676, Huntington.
129. *D1*, December 9, 1943, pp. 329–30.
130. "Books: Universal Cult," *Time*, February 12, 1945, p. 96.
131. *D1*, November 30, 1942, p. 259; *D1*, December 30, 1942, p. 261.
132. "The Wishing Tree," *Vedanta and the West* magazine, November–December 1943, repr. *VWW*, and *Exh.*, pp. 239–40; *D1*, December 31, 1942, p. 262.
133. Pravrajika Brahmaprana, "She Touched God: Sister Lalita's Association with Swami Vivekananda," *Prabuddha Bharata*, magazine of the Ramakrishna Order, March 2011, available on the website of the Vedanta Society of Southern California.
134. *MG&HD*, Chap. 8, p. 102; *D1*, February 1943, p. 266: CI to Caroline Norment, quoted in *D1*, bridging passage, April 1943, p. 285.
135. *D1*, bridging passage, February 1943, pp. 267–8.
136. *D1*, bridging passage, February 1943, p. 269.
137. *D1*, bridging passage, March 1941, p. 150; CI to RGBI, September 30, 1943, Beinecke. By coincidence, Montagu was the man who had hired Homer Lane to come to England and run the Little Commonwealth in Dorset. He was nearly eighty when he and Amiya married.
138. *MG&HD*, Chap. 8, p. 102.
139. *D1*, bridging passage, January 1943, p. 263; *D1*, February 3, 1942, p. 264.
140. *D1*, January 29, 1943, pp. 263–4.
141. *D1*, February 3, 4, 1943, pp. 265–6.
142. *MG&HD*, Chap. 8, p. 101.
143. *D1*, February 5, 1943, p. 270; *MG&HD*, Chap. 8, 102; *D1*, February 8, 1943, p. 270.
144. CI to RGBI, February 15, 1943, Beinecke.
145. CI to RGBI, February 15, 1943, Beinecke.
146. *D1*, February 11, 1943, p. 271.
147. CI to LK, March 29, 1943, HM 81667, Huntington. He told LK that "since being here, I realize why I haven't written for so long—a curious sense of guilt, which has now quite lifted." He did not—yet—feel shut in by "that fearful sense of claustrophobia which, throughout the most lyrical passages of the rest of my adult life, used to make me mutter to myself: don't worry, we won't stay here long, we'll get out of this somehow."
148. CI to LK, April 11, 1943, HM 81668, Huntington. CI was more restrained to Caroline Norment and readers of his wartime diary: "There is ritual, of course, in the worship: ritual which has been practiced in India for tens of centuries; out of which, I imagine, the Catholic mass evolved. There are many points of resemblance." (CI to Norment, April 24, 1943, quoted in *D1*, bridging passage, April 1943, p. 285)
149. CI to EMF, June 21, 1943; EMF to CI, October 23, 1943; EMF to CI, January 16, 1935; CI to EMF, November 27, 1943, *F&I*, pp. 112, 114, 40, 116.
150. *D1*, May 4, 14, 1943, pp. 288, 291.
151. *D1*, May 22, 1943, p. 293; CI to Caroline Norment, April 24, 1943, quoted in *D1*, bridging passage, April 1943, p. 286; *D1*, March 18, 1943, p. 275; CI to Norment, April 24, 1943, quoted in *D1*, bridging passage, pp. 286–7.
152. *D1*, March 26, May 1, 1943, pp. 275, 287.
153. TW, *Notebooks*, ed. Margaret Bradham Thornton (New Haven: Yale University Press, 2006), March 21, 1943, p. 357.
154. TW to Donald Windham, May 12, 1943, in *Tennessee Williams' Letters to Donald Windham*, p. 63; *D1*, May 13, 1943, p. 290. Windham called the cast a cataract.
155. TW, *Notebooks*, May 23, 1943, p. 369.
156. TW to Sandy Campbell, May 29, 1943, *Tennessee Williams' Letters to Donald Windham*, pp. 71–2. He told the same story to James Laughlin, *The Selected Letters of Tennessee Williams, Volume I, 1920–1945*, ed. Albert J. Devlin and Nancy M. Tischler (New York: New Directions, 2000), Letter 270, about May 29, 1943, p. 456.

157. CI to LK, May 30, 1943, HM 81672 Huntington. The friend, David Greggory, was out west doing radio publicity work. (*Notebooks*, p. 370, note 573) TW dropped by the monastery on at least one other evening. (CI day-to-day diary, June 24, 1943)
158. TW to CI [June 1943?], on stationery of Metro-Goldwyn-Mayer; CI to TW, June 10, 1943, HRC.
159. *D1*, June 7, 21, 1943, p. 298.
160. *D1*, July 16, 19, 1943, pp. 303, 305.
161. *MG&HD*, Chap. 5, p. 65.
162. *D1*, July 23, August 6, pp. 306, 308.
163. *D1*, August 18, 1943, pp. 311–12.
164. *The Luck of Friendship: The Letters of Tennessee Williams and James Laughlin*, ed. Peggy L. Fox and Thomas Keith (New York: W.W. Norton and Co., 2018), Letter 17, p. 25.
165. TW to CI [soon after June 10, 1943], HRC. The novel was *Marriage Is a Private Affair*. *The Glass Menagerie* won the New York Drama Critics Circle Award for Best American Play.
166. *D1*, bridging passage, August 1943, p. 313; *LY*, p. 5, and *MG&HD*, Chap. 9, p. 138.
167. CI wrote "The dumb man" in his day-to-day diary at the time. He later wrote "the man was deaf and dumb." (*LY*, p. 5)
168. CI to TW, June 10, 1943, HRC.
169. CI quoted by Maupin, "The First Couple: Don Bachardy and Christopher Isherwood," *Village Voice*, Vol. 30, No. 16, July 2, 1985, repr. *Conversations*, p. 192; Edmund White, "Preface," *D3*, p. xiii; Bachardy, *Don Stayed*, p. 228.
170. Photo by William Caskey, 1946, printed in TW, *Notebooks*, p. 369; *Don Stayed*, p. 250.
171. *D3*, August 7, 1971, p. 184; it was a 1905 edition with illustrations by Jessie Wheeler Wilcox. CI once debunked the collection as a "superpotboiler [. . .] about the way grown-ups would like children to feel," ("R.L.S.," *Tomorrow*, repr. *Exh.*, p. 50), but this had nothing to do with how he felt about TW; TW, *Memoirs*, p. 77.
172. *D1*, August 20, 23, 1943, pp. 312, 313.
173. *D1*, September 20, 1943, p. 318.
174. BV to CI, quoted in *D1*, bridging passage, September 21, 1943, pp. 318–19.
175. CI to BV, September 23, 1943, Deutsches Literatur Archiv, Marbach, quoted in *D1*, bridging passage, September 1943, pp. 319–20.
176. *D1*, April 3, 1944, p. 340. Evidently, CI offered financial help instead, for Brecht apologized for pressuring him and wrote (in German): "Your offer to help me I acknowledge as a great kindness. Fortunately and fortuitously, I do not need money at present." Bertolt Brecht to CI, May 1944, trans. Angelica von Hase, CI 646.
177. *D1*, September 15, 1943, p. 316.
178. *D1*, September 24, 1943, pp. 321–2.
179. Martin Duberman, *The Worlds of Lincoln Kirstein* (New York: Alfred Knopf, 2007; Northwestern University Press, 2008), p. 385. Duberman tells that the printed books were stored in a warehouse hit by a German bomb and most were destroyed. CI to LK, November 18, 1944: "I can't agree with you about yourself as a prose-writer. There is nothing to stop your becoming one of the best we have, if you care to." (HM 81685, Huntington)
180. *D1*, September 30, 1943, p. 322; CI to Richard "Twig" Romney, September 30, 1943, Beinecke.
181. *D1*, August 31, 1943, p. 314.
182. *D1*, October 1, 9, 1943, pp. 323, 324, 325.
183. *D1*, October 9, 1943, p. 325; "I never have before [. . .] now I want to before I see the movie, for which Huxley wrote the dialogue." (CI to Richard "Twig" Romney, September 30, 1943, Beinecke); CWBI to KBI, February 6, 1921, *Repton Letters*, p. 12; *D1*, October 9, 1943, p. 325; Charlotte Brontë as "Currer Bell," *Jane Eyre* (London: Smith, Elder & Co., 1847), Chap. 34.
184. *Jane Eyre*, Chap. 34; *D1*, October 9, 1943, p. 325.
185. *PV*, pp. 122, 126.
186. CI reread *Kim* July 25, 1942; despite objecting to Kipling's values of empire and caste, CI kept his 1919 edition in his library.

187. *PV*, p. 126.
188. *D1*, November 19, 143, p. 328.
189. *D1*, bridging passage, March 1944, pp. 336–7.
190. *D1*, April 14, 1944, p. 343; *D1*, May 14, 1944, p. 345; *D1*, July 8, 1944, p. 353.
191. *D1*, April 24, 1944, p. 344.
192. "Hemingway, Death, and the Devil," *Decision*, January 1, 1941, p. 58.
193. *D1*, bridging passage, February 1943, p. 269.
194. *LY*, pp. 61–3; CI recorded in *LY* (p. 63) Dr. Josef Kolisch's opinion that the median bar operation "had been entirely unnecessary," and he reiterated, "But, as a ritual penalty, it had served its psychological purpose."
195. It didn't sell. Huxley's agent reported that the studios feared the medical establishment, portrayed as charlatans.
196. The 1911 play *Das Mirakel* was by Karl Vollmöller.
197. Huxley and CI treatment, printed in Intro. to *Jacob's Hands*, ed. David Bradshaw (London: Bloomsbury, 1998), pp. xix, xviii.
198. *D1*, November 5, 1939, pp. 49–50.
199. See Radha Rajagopal Sloss, *Lives in the Shadow with J. Krishnamurti* (London: Bloomsbury, 1991).
200. KBI diary, March 31, April 2, June 26, 1928, and August 2, 1932, HRC.
201. *D1*, April 13, 14, 1944, p. 343; *MG&HD*, Chap. 9, p. 125.
202. *D1*, June 22, 30, 1944, pp. 351, 352.
203. *D1*, bridging passage, June 1941, p. 159.
204. *D1*, bridging passage, September 1942, p. 245.
205. *D1*, June 30, July 4, 1944, p. 352.
206. *D1*, July 30, 1944, p. 356.
207. *D1*, August 28, 1944, pp. 359–60; *MG&HD*, Chap. 12, p. 178. In *LY* (p. 6), CI recalled having sex with Young during this period, but did not support the memory with details.
208. *D1*, November 11, 1944, p. 375; CI to KBI, October 15, 1939, *K&C*, p. 154.
209. *D1*, November 30, 1944, p. 377; *LY*, p. 16, and day-to-day diary, January 31, 1945; *D1*, November 30, 1944, p. 377; *LY*, 1944, p. 7.
210. *D1*, December 3, 1944, p. 377.
211. *LY*, p. 7, and *MG&HD*, Chap. 12, p. 188; *D1*, November 30, 1944, p. 377.
212. *PV*, p. 44.
213. Promoted by Willi Münzenberg in *The Brown Book of the Reichstag Fire Trial and Hitler Terror*, published in Paris in August 1933, mostly written by Otto Katz. German political refugees flocked to Münzenberg, bringing documentary evidence used in the book about the fire, the persecution of Jews, and the concentration camps. *The Brown Book* became an international bestseller, and was smuggled into Germany disguised as epic poems by Goethe and Schiller. See Gross, *Willi Münzenberg: A Political Biography*, trans. Marian Jackson, pp. 247, 250, 252, 270, and Koestler, *The Invisible Writing*, Chap. 18, pp. 255 and ff. See also *The Reichstag Fire Trial, 1933–2008: The Production of Law and History*, by John Mage and Michael E. Tigar, https://monthlyreview.org/2009/03/01/the-reichstag-fire-trial-1933-2008-the-production-of-law-and-history/; Benjamin Hett, *Burning the Reichstag*, https://www.smithsonianmag.com/history/true-story-reichstag-fire-and-nazis-rise-power-180962240/#IhjrAl8JsmpoLsjH.99; William L. Shirer, *The Rise and Fall of the Third Reich* (1960), http://www.exberliner.com/features/the-reichstag-fire/
214. *PV*, p. 45.
215. Van der Lubbe famously would not look up while being cross-examined until he heard the command of the police chief the Left suspected was his Nazi handler. As CI tells it: "Then, suddenly, with the harsh authority of an animal trainer, Helldorf barks out: 'Head up, man! Quick!'" (*PV*, p. 46); CI 2750.
216. *PV*, p. 47.
217. CI recalled in *C&HK* that his friend John Van Druten, "a master of pastiche and parody," invented the imaginary film plot for him, but, as so often, he may have been downplaying his own contribution, for among the many possible models, the most

suggestive is Eugène Sue's *The Mysteries of Paris*, about a highborn love child abandoned as an orphan among thieves, which he had seen adapted as a silent film in Limerick way back in 1913. (*C&HK*, Chap. 9, p. 151; KBI diary, August 2, 1913, HRC) Other possible models include Hans Christian Andersen's *The Little Match Girl* (1845), Twain's *The Prince and the Pauper* (1881), and Shaw's *Pygmalion* (1913).
218. *PV*, pp. 49, 50.
219. CI diary, September 1, 1935, CI 2751.
220. *PV*, p. 125.
221. *PV*, p. 98.
222. CI to SS, October 12, 19, 1934, Bancroft; see Sutherland, *Stephen Spender: The Authorized Biography*, pp. 170–4.
223. *PV*, pp. 95–6, 117, 119–20.
224. CI to RGBI, April 1943, Beinecke.
225. Text inside refers to "now in June . . ."
226. CI to Plomer, Sunday [February 1933?], from Nollendorfstrasse 17, Durham University Library, Archives and Special Collections; *The Communist Party of Germany Lives and Fights [The banned literature distributed under the Hitler Terror]* (London: Modern Books Ltd, 1934), p. 31, CI 2750.
227. *Androcles and the Lion: A Fable Play* (1912); CI's edition (London: Constable & Co., 1920) includes Shaw's "Preface on the Prospects of Christianity," pp. 47, 50, Huntington.
228. CI to BV, September 23, 1943, Deutsches Literatur Archiv, Marbach.
229. *PV*, p. 18.
230. Watts, "Zen and the Cultivation of the Far East," *The Spirit of Zen* (1936; repr. John Murray, 1948), p. 124.
231. *C&HK*, Chap. 9, pp. 153–4.
232. *PV*, pp. 101–2. The title *Prater Violet* plays on Pater Viertel.
233. CI to BV, October 22, 1944, Deutsches Literatur Archiv, Marbach; *PV*, p. 40.
234. BV to CI, October 26, 1944, CI 2638; BV to CI, November 8, 1944, CI 2639.
235. WHA to CI, January 10, 1945, CI 3001.
236. *D1*, November 19, 1943, p. 328; *D1*, April 17, 1944, pp. 343–4; *MG&HD*, Chap. 11, p. 158.
237. Huxley to CI, January 7, 1945, CI 998; Heard to CI, February 16, 1946, CI 976.
238. Trilling, "Fiction in Review," *Nation*, 161, November 17, 1945, pp. 530–2.
239. EU to CI, June 10, 1955, CI 2478.
240. It was CI's first novel with his new British publisher, Methuen, to whom he had contracted for three novels, moving on from the Hogarth Press. Methuen considered *PV* too short to count as one of the novels, though worthy of publication as a stand-alone story.

6: AMERICAN APOSTATE

1. *D3*, November 26, 1970, p. 120.
2. *D2*, July 26, 1971, p. 177, and CI to DB, March 11, 1963, *Animals*, p. 126. In CI's library at his death was Jung, *Memories, Dreams, Reflections*, trans. Richard and Clara Winston (New York: Pantheon, 1963), see Prologue, p. 3.
3. *LY*, p. 24.
4. *LY*, pp. 32–3.
5. *LY*, pp. 51, 36; lines from "Ode to the New Year" printed by permission of the Estate of WHA.
6. CI's letter appeared December 17, 1945.
7. W. Somerset Maugham, *The Razor's Edge* (London: William Heinemann, 1944; Vintage, 2000), p. 321. Fouts's friend Michael Wishart wrote that Fouts "claimed to be the model for Sophie, the hopelessly self-destructive opiumaniac drunken girl in Somerset Maugham's *The Razor's Edge*." See *High Diver: An Autobiography* (London: Blond and Briggs, 1977; Quartet, 1978), p. 54.

8. CI to LK, May 1, 1944, HM 81680 Huntington.
9. "The Problem of the Religious Novel," *Vedanta and the West* (Vedanta Society magazine) [between 1945 and 1950]; repr. *VMM* and repr. *Exh.*, pp. 117, 120.
10. *LY*, p. 38.
11. *LY*, p. 19.
12. *LY*, p. 44.
13. *SM*, p. 147.
14. *LY*, pp. 45, 48.
15. *SM*, p. 148.
16. *SM*, p. 149.
17. *MG&HD*, Chap. 13, p. 191.
18. *LY*, p. 42.
19. *LY*, p. 43.
20. *LY*, pp. 52–3.
21. *LY*, p. 61.
22. *LY*, pp. 64, 59.
23. CI and KBI, "1912–1913. Book III. Jack Armstrong," *The History of My Friends*, CI box 159.
24. *LY*, p. 56.
25. *LY*, p. 56.
26. *LY*, p. 54.
27. *LY*, p. 75.
28. *LY*, p. 54.
29. *LY*, pp. 48, 55.
30. See "Books: Fables of Beasts and Men," *Time* magazine, November 5, 1945, p. 33; *LY*, p. 49. CI was interviewed by Philip Scheuer for the *Los Angeles Times*, January 13, 1946. He mentioned it repeatedly to his London publisher (CI to JL, November 25, 1942, January 9, 1943, February 19, 1945), Beinecke. In a 1951 interview with Harvey Breit, he again referred to the trilogy, *PV*, the refugees, and the Greek island. (See the *New York Times* Sunday Book Supplement, December 16, 1951, p. 217.)
31. The poet Kenneth Rexroth encouraged Laughlin, his close friend as well as his publisher: "I found remaindered Christopher Isherwood's book and said this is a permanent classic, you can have this on a back list forever. [...] I think Christopher Isherwood is a very, very fine writer. Very polished and at the same time very witty and ironic. [...] I told Laughlin once, if you want to know the intellectual climate of Weimar Germany there are two books you can pick up by Christopher Isherwood: They are *it*." (Brad Morrow interview, *Conjunctions* 1, Inaugural Double Issue, Fall 1981)
32. CI to JL, July 22, 1934, Beinecke.
33. CI replaced T.S. Eliot's introduction with one by WHA, as well as adding his own preface which included a reference to something new he shared with Baudelaire, "Acedia, 'the malady of monks,' that deadly weakness of the will which is the root of all evil." (*Exh.*, p. 29) The new edition was published by Marcel Rodd, ready as with pornography to brave the law since CI was unable to confirm whether he had rights in the translation. KBI could not find CI's contract, but managed to establish that the original publisher, the Blackamore Press, no longer existed. (CI to KBI, March 7, 1946, Beinecke)
34. Alfred Kazin, "Christopher Isherwood, Novelist, His Berlin Stories, Comment Brilliantly on the Dissolution of the German Psyche," *New York Times*, February 17, 1946, p. 1; "Family Shows Great Changes in Britain, Too," *The Memorial: Portrait of a Family*," Associated Press, *Washington Post*, December 4, 1946, p. C6; John Woodburn, "Artlessness Perfected," on *The Memorial, Saturday Review*, December 14, 1946, p. 15. One review was crammed with mistakes, Harrison Smith, *Saturday Review*, March 9, 1946. A year later, in 1947, came reviews of *L&S*.
35. *LY*, pp. 49, 66.
36. *LY*, p. 70; CI to KBI, May 3, 1946, Beinecke.
37. *LY*, pp. 70, 73, 70.

38. *LY*, pp. 71–2.
39. Claire Nicolas, *Vogue*, U.K., April 1947, p. 71. The *Vogue* profile began underneath a photograph of CI taken in Fouts's apartment, before the move, by George Platt Lynes. Lynes stayed at the Entrada Drive apartment in the spring of 1946 and photographed CI and WC in the apartment and "amongst the big wooden piles on the beach near the Lighthouse Café." (*LY*, p. 65) CI later told Lynes that these were the only photos extant of him in love. (CI to Lynes, April 8, 1946, Beinecke)
40. *LY*, pp. 72, 71.
41. Story outline, treatment and scene-by-scene breakdown, CI 95, CI 96, CI 97.
42. CI to KBI, July 11, 1946, Beinecke; *LY*, p. 81.
43. See *Misalliance, Candida, St. Joan, Major Barbara, Pygmalion, Man and Superman*, and Shaw's essay, "The Quintessence of Ibsenism," where he writes about "the unwomanly woman." At the time of his death, CI had Van Druten's copy of the Ibsen essay in his library. CI's early pornographic play, *Herds of Lions*, had parodied *Misalliance*; Van Druten's 1919 edition was likewise in his library. Some volumes of CI's Shaw collection had belonged to his father, FBI.
44. *LY*, p. 40.
45. CI to EMF, March 26, 1946, *F&I*, p. 138.
46. CI to LK, March 29, 1945, HM 81688, Huntington.
47. *LY*, pp. 77, 40, 81. CI also made a will before traveling.
48. "Coming to London," repr. *Exh.*, see pp. 150, 154, and Intro. to "Places," *Exh.*, p. 143. *Harper's Bazaar* rejected the piece, but JL included it in a collection also called *Coming to London*.
49. *Exh.*, p. 143; CI's day-to-day diary for January 22, when he arrived at JL's, mentioned only JL. He recorded a list of names for January 24 when there was a lunch party and a cocktail party. He decided nevertheless that a few of his nearest friends—EMF, Buckingham, Plomer, Ackerley—must have greeted him on his first night.
50. *LY*, p. 83. In the 1930s, CI had taken a behind-the-scenes position on JL's magazine, *New Writing*, finding contributors and advising, but never committing to any staff role. In the issues for Autumn 1938 and Spring 1939, JL's name as editor appears on the title page and underneath, "With the assistance of Christopher Isherwood / Stephen Spender." When JL became a publisher at the Hogarth Press, CI read and opined on many writers for him, but he always avoided any official commitment that might place him in the limelight or become overly time-consuming.
51. *LY*, p. 95.
52. CI to LK, February 23, 1947, HM 81691, Huntington; JL, *The Ample Proposition: Autobiography III* (London: Eyre & Spottiswoode, 1966), p. 29, quoted in *LY*, p. 86; *LY*, pp. 85–6.
53. *LY*, p. 92.
54. *LY*, p. 107.
55. Correspondence with JL and with KBI shows CI left his U.K. finances to their care, including his income tax, a responsibility that suited KBI. Though he had struggled for funds on first arriving in the U.S., CI had determined not to take any money for himself out of his U.K. bank and instructed only distributions to others.
56. *LY*, p. 98.
57. CI to JL, July 22, 1934, Beinecke.
58. KBI diary, January 22, 25, 26, February 3, 1947, HRC.
59. *LY*, p. 87.
60. In her diary, KBI twice mentioned James Parkinson, the London doctor who discovered Parkinson's disease. KBI diary, December 2, 1942, February 9, 1943, HRC.
61. KBI diary, August 29, September 9, 1939, HRC.
62. KBI diary, January 21, February 26, April 22, 1940, HRC; CI to KBI quoted in memoranda pages at back, HRC.
63. KBI diary, June 27, 1940, HRC; EMF, "These 'Lost Leaders,'" *Spectator*, July 5, 1940, p. 12.
64. KBI diary, March 15, 1940, HRC.
65. Quoted in KBI diary, July 13, 1940, HRC; *D1*, July 12, 1940, p. 103.

66. KBI diary, July 13, 1940, HRC.
67. KBI diary, July 19, 1940, HRC; Henry's personal effects included his library; after the war, Jack sold 400 books to a Manchester bookdealer for £40 (KBI diary, October 20, 1945, HRC).
68. The £31,787-0-9 pounds which KBI recorded as gross personal property is mysterious; possibly Henry had debts that used it up. The legacies totaled less than £2000.
69. Both letters quoted in KBI diary, November 3, July 17, 1940, HRC.
70. KBI diary, November 9, 1940. There was a big stamp duty on this document once RGBI signed it in early 1941, and of course, it would likely have to be redone since it did not reflect his wishes or CI's. See KBI diary January 30, June 24, 1941.
71. KBI diary, February 26, 1941, HRC.
72. KBI diary, July 5, August 29, 30, 31, July 12, 1941, HRC.
73. KBI diary, August 2, 1941, HRC.
74. KBI diary, October 29, 1941, HRC.
75. KBI diary, March 22, 1942, HRC.
76. KBI diary, November 28, 1943, HRC.
77. KBI diary, January 24, 25, 1944, HRC. Advertised in the *Journal of Mental Science* mid-century; made by Mssrs Gabail Ltd London.
78. KBI diary, February 16, 1943, HRC.
79. KBI diary, November 18, 1944, HRC.
80. KBI diary, October 29, 1943, HRC. Van Druten got CI involved (CI to KBI, July 13, 1940, Beinecke).
81. KBI visited twice a week until Elizabeth could walk again, paid the hospital charges, and pursued insurance compensation on Elizabeth's behalf (KBI diary, November 6, 1944, January 3, 1945, HRC).
82. KBI diary, January 25, 1945, HRC.
83. KBI diary, May 2, 1945, HRC.
84. KBI diary, August 13, 1945, HRC.
85. KBI diary, January 6, February 18, June 17, 1946, HRC. Due to the paper shortage, KBI had no 1946 diary until well into the year; she made entries in the endpapers of her 1945 diary and later copied and augmented them in the 1946 diary.
86. *Hero-Father, Demon-Mother*, p. 17, CI 1082.
87. KBI diary, May 4, April 30, 1946, HRC.
88. She listened twice. KBI diary, October 18, 1946, HRC.
89. KBI diary, January 29, 1947, HRC.
90. KBI diary, January 28, 1947, HRC.
91. KBI diary, March 24, 1947, HRC.
92. *LY*, p. 111. In *LY*, CI incorrectly recalled that he had told his mother he was sterile only in the lawyers' office on March 24, "which was extra unkind." This was an example of judging his younger self too harshly. KBI was in fact hearing about his surgery for the second time.
93. KBI diary, August 4, 8, 25, 1939, October 22, 25, 1941, HRC.
94. KBI diary, February 3, 1947, HRC.
95. *C&HK*, Chap. 3, p. 41.
96. RGBI to JL, January 7, 1947, Beinecke; KBI diary, April 13, 1947, HRC.
97. "Ports of Call," the Mexican travel piece, appeared in *Harper's Bazaar*, June 1947, with photos by Louise Dahl-Wolfe; "Los Angeles" appeared in *Art on the American Horizon*, a special issue of *Horizon*, October 1947, repr. *Exh.*, pp. 156–62.
98. *LY*, p. 88.
99. KBI diary, February 27, 1947, HRC.
100. *LY*, pp. 90–1; KBI diary, March 30, 1947, HRC.
101. Good Friday, April 4, 1947, CI 2750.
102. *LY*, pp. 117, 118.
103. *LY*, pp. 120–1.
104. CI interview with Robert Robinson, *The Look of the Week*, BBC, May 14, 1967.
105. *LY*, pp. 122–3.
106. *LY*, p. 119.

107. *LY*, pp. 126, 125; *Don Stayed*, p. 275.
108. See for example, interview with George Plimpton, "The Story Behind a Nonfiction Novel," *New York Times*, January 16, 1966, http://www.nytimes.com/books/97/12/28/home/capote-interview.html.
109. CI destroyed his copies of the photographs in 1957 or 1958 because the poses made him uneasy but later wrote that French "must have known exactly what he was doing, for the figures in many of his paintings of that period are posed in just the same style." (*LY*, p. 128 and note 1)
110. *LY*, pp. 129–30.
111. *LY*, p. 138.
112. *LY*, p. 139.
113. LK wrote about the stolen masterworks for *Art News*, *Nation*, and *Town & Country* ("The Quest for the Golden Lamb," September 1945). See Martin Duberman, *The Worlds of Lincoln Kirstein*, pp. 402–3 and note 4, 668–9.
114. Duberman, *The Worlds of Lincoln Kirstein*, p. 361.
115. CI to EMF, Tuesday [October 1932?], *F&I*, p. 18; *C&HK*, Chap. 10, pp. 172–3.
116. *LY*, pp. 139, 194.
117. *Daily Worker*, March 29, 1939, p. 7; repr. *W.H. Auden: The Critical Heritage*, ed. Haffenden, p. 291.
118. CI interview with Stanley Poss, summer 1960, "A Conversation on Tape," *London Magazine*, New Series I, June 1961, pp. 41–58; repr. in *Conversations*, p. 16.
119. *C&C*, p. 3; "Lima and Arequipa," *C&C*, December 18, 1947, pp. 124–5.
120. "Some Thoughts in Buenos Aires," *C&C*, March 23, 1948, pp. 212–13, 217.
121. "The Voyage Out," *C&C*, September 10, 23, 1947, pp. 8–9, 14.
122. "Up the River," *C&C*, September 28, 1947, p. 22.
123. "Up the River," *C&C*, September 29, 1947, pp. 24, 27.
124. "The great point he makes is that the Indians are still a nation—the Inca nation." ("The Road to Ecuador," *C&C*, November 5, 1947, p. 71)
125. "The Road to Ecuador," *C&C*, November 8, 9, 10, 1947, pp. 74, 78, 80.
126. "Oil in the Jungle," *C&C*, November 13, 1947, p. 82; CI to EU, November 13, 1947, Add MS 72688, BL.
127. "Into Peru," *C&C*, November 28, 1947, p. 107.
128. "Into Peru," *C&C*, November 30, 1947, p. 109.
129. TS, p. 4, Edinburgh University Library.
130. "Oil in the Jungle," *C&C*, November 13, 1947, p. 84.
131. "Oil in the Jungle," *C&C*, November 17, 18, 1947, pp. 92, 96–7.
132. CI to LK, January 8, 1948, HM 81693, Huntington.
133. "Lima & Arequipa," *C&C*, December 18, 28, 1947, pp. 123, 127.
134. "On the Plateau," *C&C*, January 5, 1948, p. 147; "Note to the Reader," *C&C*, p. 5.
135. CI to LK, November 20, [1947], HM 81692, Huntington.
136. "On the Plateau," *C&C*, January 13, 15, 1948, pp. 145, 147.
137. "On the Plateau," *C&C*, January 18, 1948, pp. 154–5.
138. "Titicaca and La Paz," *C&C*, February 3, 1948, pp. 171, 173.
139. "The City and the Plains," *C&C*, February 17, 1948, pp. 185, 186.
140. "The City and the Plains," *C&C*, February 19, 1948, p. 190.
141. *338171, T.E. Lawrence of Arabia* (London: Victor Gollancz, 1963).
142. "The City and the Plains," *C&C*, March 3, 1948, p. 199.
143. *Another Time*, p. 46. Meaningfully, WHA positioned the sonnet as Poem XX just before "Musée des Beaux Arts," Poem XXI, launched by reading the proofs for CI's then newest novel *GB*.
144. "Some Thoughts in Buenos Aires," *C&C*, March 23, 1948, pp. 204–5.
145. "Up the Magdalena River" written in Bogotá in October appeared in *Penguin New Writing*; "Oil in the Jungle" was written during November in Quito for the *Geographical Magazine*. "The Road to Ecuador" appeared in *Holiday*, an article on Quito in *Vogue*. "On the Plateau" was published in *Horizon*, and a shorter version of "The Voyage Out" appeared in *Zero*, titled "A Departure."
146. CI to LK, April 29, 1948, additions by WC, HM 81734, Huntington.

147. GV, 1994 Preface to revised and unexpurgated edition of *The City and the Pillar* (New York: E.P. Dutton, 1948; repr. Abacus, 1998), p. 3.
148. CI to LK, December 17, 1947, HM 81732, Huntington.
149. CI to GV, December 19, 1947, Houghton.
150. *D1*, April 27, 1948, p. 401, and August 15, 1955, p. 521.
151. CI to LK, January 8, 1948, HM 81693, Huntington; *LY*, p. 140, note 1.
152. CI to LK, June 2, 1948, HM 81693, Huntington.
153. *D1*, April 27, 28, 1948, p. 402, and see *LY*, p. 142.
154. In CI's workroom in Santa Monica, there still hangs a sketch, evidently by Jared French who perhaps gave it to CI, of Fouts in his bed in the Rue du Bac apartment. Fouts is shown lying underneath another of the paintings Peter Watson bought him, a monumental nude seen from the back with two attendant figures. The painting in the sketch is most likely Pavel Tchelitchew's *Bathers*, an oil study for *Phenomena*.
155. CI to LK, June 2, 1948, HM 81735, Huntington.
156. EMF to CI, June 25, 1948, *F&I*, p. 144.
157. TW to Carson McCullers, July 5, 1948, *The Selected Letters of Tennessee Williams, Volume II, 1945–1957*, ed. Albert J. Devlin and Nancy M. Tischler (New York: New Directions, 2004), p. 201; *Palimpsest*, p. 190. EMF had asked CI to send him a copy of *PV* two years earlier, in April 1946, and they had seen each other many times since then, in England and in the U.S., so it is unlikely that they had not already discussed the novel.
158. EMF to CI, April 1, 1946, and EMF to CI, June 25, 1948, *F&I*, pp. 140, 144.
159. See EMF to CI, January 14, 1952, *F&I*, p. 149.
160. CI to LK, October 29, 1948, HM 81696, Huntington.
161. *D1*, bridging passage, autumn 1948, p. 406.
162. CI to LK, October 29, 1948, HM 81696, Huntington.
163. "The Great Sinner," CI 8.
164. CI to JL, October 13, 1949, Beinecke.
165. CI to LK, October 29, 1948, HM 81696, Huntington; *LY*, p. 176.
166. *LY*, p. 187.
167. And with a photographic montage that WC designed for the cover.
168. CI to JL, April 7, 1949, Beinecke.
169. CI 115, p. 108; *LY*, pp. 198, 175, note 1.
170. June 15 was the day Goebbels revoked her German citizenship. WHA dedicated his next volume of poems to his new wife—*Look, Stranger!* (London: Faber and Faber, 1936).
171. *D1*, bridging passage, January 1939, p. 8; *C&HK*, Chap. 11, p. 208.
172. *D1*, July 8, 1940, pp. 99–100.
173. *LY*, p. 170; Thomas Mann to Klaus Mann, November 12, 1948, *The Letters of Thomas Mann, 1899–1955*, Vol. II, Selected and trans. Richard and Clara Winston (London: Secker & Warburg, 1970), p. 565.
174. "Klaus Mann," *Klaus Mann—zum Gedächtnis* (printed privately, 1950), repr. *Exh.*, p. 136.
175. *D1*, March 1, 1949, p. 409.
176. *LY*, p. 183.
177. *D1*, February 20, 1949, p. 408; *LY*, p. 180.
178. *D1*, May 22, 1949, p. 412.
179. Information from Alvin Novak.
180. *LY*, pp. 197–8, and day-to-day diary.
181. CI to LK, October 1, 15, 1952, HM 81709 and HM 81710, Huntington.
182. CI to Richard "Twig" Romney, December 11, 1943, Beinecke.
183. *LY*, p. 183.
184. *LY*, pp. 195, 223, 199.
185. *LY*, p. 210; *D1*, November 15, 1949, p. 415.
186. *D1*, November 18, 1949, p. 416; *LY*, p. 211; *D1*, August 22, 1951, p. 439.
187. *LY*, p. 214.
188. *LY*, p. 212; *D1*, November 22, 1949, p. 417.
189. *LY*, pp. 183–5.

190. *LY*, pp. 186, 264, 186–7.
191. *D1*, December 6, p. 418.
192. *D1*, December 4, p. 418.
193. *LY*, pp. 216–17.
194. *LY*, pp. 220–1.
195. *D1*, January 2, 1950, p. 420. Cf. "The Lesson of the Master" and *The Sacred Fount*.
196. *LY*, p. 222, footnote.
197. A young medical student, a Californian "man of science" like Dr. Jekyll, is possessed by a sexy Marine Corps veteran, who was driven to suicide in the very same rented room by his lover, a rich man's wife. The veteran uses the body of the medical student to take revenge. Pacific Coast weather and surf supplied romantic intensity, as in *Wuthering Heights*.
198. *D1*, June 30. 1950, p. 425. "A 'C.O.' Tells His Absorbing Story," *New York Herald Tribune*, Book Review, July 23, 1950, p. 6. CI printed in *Exh.* his preface to a later edition published with another book, *Prison Etiquette*.
199. *Tomorrow*, October 1950, pp. 57, 56; *LY*, p. 247; Bradbury to Digby Diehl, May 30, 1973, FAC 1383, Huntington.
200. *LY*, p. 250.
201. *D1*, August 19, 1950, pp. 429–30.
202. *LY*, p. 253.
203. *LY*, pp. 256–7.
204. *LY*, p. 272.
205. *LY*, p. 240.
206. *LY*, pp. 273–4.
207. *D1*, December 11, 1950, p. 433.
208. *LY*, p. 274.
209. "The Day's Journey," December 21, 1950, with some notes in Charlton's writing, CI 58.
210. "Young American Writers," *Observer*, May 13, 1951, p. 7. The writers were Peter Viertel, William Goyen, Speed Lamkin, Truman Capote, Donald Windham, Gore Vidal, Carson McCullers, Tennessee Williams, Norman Mailer, Paul Bowles, Jean Stafford, Paul Goodman, Ray Bradbury, Robert Penn Warren, Willard Motley, Irwin Shaw, Budd Schulberg, Richard Wright, John Hersey, Gerald Sykes, David Davidson, James Jones, Mary McCarthy, William Saroyan, Thomas Merton, Eudora Welty, Nelson Algren, Calder Willingham, John Hawkes, Shirley Jackson, Frederick Buechner, and as the protytpe for the stoic, Ernest Hemingway.
211. CI to EU, January 24, 1951, Add MS 72688, BL.
212. *D1*, November 30, 1950, p. 432, and see *LY*, pp. 232, 283.
213. *D1*, May 28, 1951, p. 436. See also *D1*, August 22, 1951, p. 437.
214. *LY*, p. 285.
215. *LY*, p. 284.
216. Work journal, May 29, 1951 p. 68, CI 1158, where CI originally recorded Lamkin's comments.
217. CI to EU, August 20, 1947, enclosing synopsis of *The School of Tragedy*, 7 pp., Add MS 72688, BL.
218. LK to CI, June 25, 1951, CI 1569.
219. *D1*, August 22, 23, 29, 1951, pp. 438, 439.
220. "What Vedanta Means to Me," *Vedanta and the West*, May/June 1951; repr. *Wishing Tree*, pp. 56–61; "Migration to Mars," *Observer*, September 16, 1951, p. 7.
221. WC to CI, October 24, 1951, CI 667.
222. WC to CI, "Wednesday" [late autumn 1951?], CI 670; WC to CI, "Wednesday," November 14, 1951. CI sent WC press clippings, and WC also followed the production in the *New York Times*, *Variety*, and Walter Winchell's syndicated gossip column. WC evidently thought of himself and CI as a couple: "By all means go to Corsica and anywhere else that sounds luxurious and strange only be sure to take a rain check on all such excursions for me. Or don't you think rich young barons would be as interested if they knew you weren't a single man?"

223. WC to CI, November 21, 1951, CI 669.
224. CI, Intro., *The Berlin of Sally Bowles*, containing *Mr. Norris Changes Trains* and *Goodbye to Berlin* (London: Hogarth Press, 1975), pp. 3-4.
225. CI, "Author Meets Himself: 'I Am a Camera,'" *New York Herald Tribune*, November 25, 1951, Section 4, p. 3.
226. Walter F. Kerr, "The Theaters," *New York Herald Tribune*, November 29, 1951, p. 18.
227. CI's 1954 introduction to *The Berlin Stories* and his 1975 introduction to *The Berlin of Sally Bowles* are both based on the *New York Herald Tribune* piece.
228. CI, "Author Meets Himself: 'I Am a Camera,'" *New York Herald Tribune*, November 25, 1951, Section 4, p. 3. Paul Sorel reported to WC that Van Druten "has declared there can be only one boss at rehearsals." WC to CI, November 1, 1951, CI 669. Perhaps there was friction between Van Druten and CI, though Sorel may have been stirring the pot. Years later, CI recalled that he used to "put on a bit of an act [...] for John during rehearsals of *I Am a Camera*," seeing it as his job to "radiate satisfaction and confidence." (*D2*, February 26, 1969, p. 546)
229. CI to LK, December 30, 1951, HM 81704, Huntington.
230. *D1*, November 8, 1951, p. 441.
231. *MG&HD*, Chap. 13, p. 204.
232. "California Story," repr. as "The Shore," *Exh.*, p. 162.
233. Then at 1430 Broadway, since rebuilt.
234. "Bad Little Good Girl: Julie Harris Makes a Stage Triumph as a Sentimental Strumpet," *Life*, December 24, 1951, photos by Gjon Mili. CI to LK, December 30, 1951, "thank you so much for sending the divine Julie Harris photos from LIFE." (HM 81704, Huntington)
235. David Astor, Terence Kilmartin, Raimund Pretzel who wrote under the pseudonym Sebastian Haffner.
236. CI, "Back to Berlin," *Observer*, March 23, 1952, p. 2.
237. KBI diary, January 16, 1952, in the back of her 1951 diary, HRC.
238. CI, "Back to Berlin," *Observer*, March 23, 1952, p. 2; see also CI draft "Berlin: February 1952," CI 1020.
239. Day-to-day diary, February 14, 1952.
240. In his *Observer* piece, CI said poverty had forced Frl. Thurau to move to a smaller flat, but ten years later he told a correspondent: "During the War, Nollendorfstrasse 17 was hit by a bomb and Frl. Thurau moved next door or a couple of doors away; it was there that I visited her after the War." (CI to Howard L. Nelson, November 5, 1962, Penn State University Library)
241. "Back to Berlin," *Observer*, March 23, 1952, p. 2.
242. "A Berlin Diary (Autumn 1930)," *GB*, p. 15; CI, "Back to Berlin," *Observer*, March 23, 1952, p. 2.
243. "Back to Berlin," *Observer*, March 23, 1952, p. 2.
244. CI to Gerald Hamilton, May 20, 1952, HRC. In London, he discussed the piece with the literary editor Terence Kilmartin and the novelist and *Observer* critic Philip Toynbee. Cf. draft CI 1020.
245. "I missed him in Berlin despite all my efforts to contact him there," CI told JL a few years later when JL forwarded a letter making clear that Wolff was "married, has an injured hand from the War, and knows that he is 'Otto' in 'Goodbye to Berlin!'" (CI to JL, August 12, 1957, Beinecke)
246. "Back to Berlin," *Observer*, March 23, 1952, p. 2.
247. Heinz Neddermeyer to CI, CI 1870; KBI diary, June 6, August 2, October 5, 1946, HRC.
248. KBI diary, August 1, 1939, HRC; CI to JL, February 13, 1947, Beinecke.
249. Among them, CI introduced the American novelist Calder Willingham to British readers as "one of the very best young comic writers" in a review of *End as a Man*, Willingham's controversial first novel set in a Southern U.S. military academy like the Citadel. (*Observer*, January 27, 1952, p. 7)
250. *D1*, February 10, November 26, 1956, pp. 580, 665. The exhibition was at the Hanover Gallery, London. See also "Francis Bacon Unseen," Bacon's interview with Julian Jebb, filmed 1965 for the BBC but not broadcast at the time.

251. D1, March 4, 1952, pp. 442–3.
252. D1, March 20, 24, 1952, pp. 443, 445.
253. For Wright's account of the friendship, see Thomas E. Wright, *Growing Up with Legends: A Literary Memoir* (Westport, CT: Praeger, 1998), a lively and factually unreliable narrative.
254. CI to LK, March 31, 1952, HM 81706, Huntington.
255. D1, May 12, 13, 1952, p. 447.
256. D1, May 25, June 30, 1952, pp. 449, 450. Costidy and Wright went to Monroe, Louisiana, to meet Wright's parents; eventually, Costidy left his gay life and married.
257. D1, May 6, 1951, p. 435; CI to AB, October 5, 1952, Gotlieb.
258. CI to Gerald Sykes, August 22, 1953, Gerald Sykes Papers, Butler.
259. D1, September 13, 1952, p. 451.
260. D1, November 30, December 1, 1952, January 6, 1953, pp. 451–2.
261. D1, January 27, 1953, p. 453.
262. D1, March 6, 1953, p. 454.

7: THE IDEAL COMPANION: DON BACHARDY

1. DB conversations with Bucknell, September 28–9, 2013, Berlin.
2. DB conversation with Bucknell, January 15, 2014, Santa Monica.
3. DB, *Stealing the Show*, pp. 14–15.
4. DB conversation with Bucknell, c.2015, Monument Valley.
5. *Don Stayed*, p. 2.
6. *Don Stayed*, p. 2; DB conversation with Bucknell, September 29, 2013; DB on film, dir. Guido Santi and Tina Mascara, *Chris and Don: A Love Story* (2007).
7. CI to DS and AB, December 7, 1952, Gotlieb.
8. DB conversation with Bucknell, September 26, 2013, London.
9. D2, February 14, 1965, p. 354.
10. Always a special day for DB and Ted because it was their mother's birthday.
11. *Stealing the Show*, pp. 7, 5.
12. CI to DS and AB, March 10, 1953, Gotlieb.
13. *Don Stayed*, p. 21.
14. D1, March 24, 1952, p. 445.
15. WC to CI, July 13, 1979, CI 687.
16. DB conversation with Bucknell, November 1, 2015, Santa Monica.
17. D1, March 6, 1953, p. 454.
18. *Stealing the Show*, p. 11; DB telephone conversation with Bucknell, April 28, 2016.
19. *Stealing the Show*, p. 11.
20. *Stealing the Show*, p. 7.
21. http://time.com/4199924/vagrancy-law-history/ ; see Risa Goluboff, *Vagrant Nation: Police Power, Constitutional Change, and the Making of the 1960s* (Oxford University Press, 2016). California also had a sexual psychopath law that allowed indefinite medical detention of homosexuals; usually this was used only against people who had sex with children.
22. *Don Stayed*, p. 15
23. DB telephone conversation with Bucknell, April 28, 2016.
24. *Don Stayed*, pp. 28–9.
25. *Don Stayed*, pp. 41–2.
26. "Katherine Mansfield," review of Sylvia Beckman, *Katherine Mansfield: A Critical Study* (Wellesley College/Yale University Press, 1951), *Tomorrow*, Vol. X, No. 11 (July 1951); repr. in *Exh.*, pp. 64, 65.
27. "Katherine Mansfield," *Exh.*, pp. 66, 67, 72.
28. CI to EU, December 5, 1949, Add MS 72688, BL.
29. CI to Peter Grant, June 18, 1939, Lehmann Papers, Princeton University.
30. "December 1919," *Journal of Katherine Mansfield*, ed. John Middleton Murry (London: Constable, 1927; repr. Persephone Books, 2012), pp. 133–4.
31. CI work journal, June 1, 1951, p. 69, CI 1158.

32. CI to EU, January 24, 1951, Add MS 72688, BL.
33. Work journal, May 24, 1951, p. 75, CI 1158.
34. *WE*, Part II, Chap. 4, pp. 124, 127, 142.
35. *WE*, Part II, Chap. 4, p. 128.
36. One poem, "The Common Cormorant," had been included anonymously in WHA's 1938 anthology *The Poet's Tongue*.
37. CI did not especially enjoy DS's *The Hundred and One Dalmations* (1956) even though he had known the Dalmatians, Folly and Buzzle, who, in 1943, produced the litter of fifteen puppies that inspired the story. *The Hundred and One Dalmatians* had too many words to attract him, and the dogs, for him, were too thoroughly anthropomorphized. He confessed to DS, "I do think it is brilliant, a real tour de force. I just don't care passionately for this kind of story. Beatrix Potter isn't really an exception for me, because what I love in her books are the illustrations—the narratives just provide captions for them." He did like DS's villain: "Cruella de Vil I wanted much more of." (CI to DS, January 12, 1957, Gotlieb)
38. Walt Whitman, "Song of Myself," Section 32, *Complete Poetry and Selected Prose and Letters*, ed. Emory Holloway (London: Nonesuch Press, 1938), p. 56. CI had this edition at his death. (Huntington)
39. *K&F*, Chap. 14, p. 357.
40. *MG&HD*, Chap. 14, p. 209.
41. "Note to Producers," *I Am a Camera* (New York: Dramatists Play Service Inc., 1952), p. 5 (CI's copy, Huntington); CI to DS and AB, March 10, 1953, Gotlieb.
42. CI to LK, February 16, 1945, HM 81687, Huntington.
43. *WE*, Part II, Chap. 2, p. 65.
44. Valerie Grove, *Dear Dodie: The Life of Dodie Smith* (London: Chatto & Windus, 1996), p.148, where Grove quotes from Smith's unpublished journal, Gotlieb.
45. *WE*, Part II, Chap. 7, pp. 236–7; EMF, *Aspects of the Novel*, Chap. 3, p. 69.
46. *WE*, Part III, Chap. 2, p. 286.
47. Gerda tells Stephen that she has come to believe in what Sarah Pennington believes, "Because it is *she* who believes, and not another." (*WE*, Part III, Chap. 2, p. 285) CI sometimes described his own belief in God in the same way, for instance, in a 1943 letter: "I believe in the belief of others [...] the Swami—believes in God so entirely, so simply, so calmly, so intelligently and so lovingly, that I am bound to say that, in all my quite large experience of human beings, disbelief has never produced a representative one quarter as convincing." (CI to Hoosag Gregory, quoted in *D1*, bridging passage, April 1943, p. 284)
48. CI explained in his 1951 introduction to *VMM* that Vedanta had little chance of being accepted by "organized Christianity": "I can see only one little door through which Vedanta might squeeze into Christendom, and that is the Society of Friends. The Quaker doctrine of the Inward Light is in general agreement with the principles of Vedanta." (*VMM*, pp. xii–xiii) The Quaker door is the very door through which he squeezed Vedanta into *WE*.
49. See Grove, *Dear Dodie*, pp. 85–6. DB in conversation with Bucknell affirmed AB was completely straight. In *WE*, CI tested the Beesleys by imagining a sex life for Stephen Monk that they found embarrassing. DS wrote in her journal that there was an "overpowering" amount of sex in the draft she read. (Grove, *Dear Dodie*, p. 210) The Beesleys weren't interested in sex, but CI was—not only in having it but also in understanding its workings and effects.
50. *WE*, Part II, Chap. 7, pp. 232–3. CI also had in mind the marriage in Katherine Mansfield's 1921 story "Marriage à la Mode," about a suburban commuter marriage destroyed by outside relationships. Mansfield didn't explicitly mention sex in her story, and CI put into *WE* the couplings that Mansfield only implied (as in the 1920s when he reimagined her delicate story "At the Bay" from a horny, male point of view). He was to choose "Marriage à la Mode" for his 1957 anthology *GESS*.
51. *Madeleine* was published privately in 1947 and commercially in 1951 with until-then unpublished passages from Gide's intimate journal. CI read all three books in January 1953, the month he finally eked out his first draft of *WE*.

52. Gide's Immoralist implicates his friends by confessing his crimes to them, but Stephen Monk, in a meaningful contrast, implicates only himself; moreover, he confesses to being good rather than evil, stating in the last paragraph of the novel, "I really do forgive myself." (*WE*, Part III, Chap. 3, p. 301)
53. CI work journal, July 9, 1950, p. 40, CI 1158.
54. *C&HK*, Chap. 2, p. 17. CI's friend Klaus Mann knew Gide and wrote a biography of him published in 1943, likely affecting CI's views.
55. *L&S*, Chap. 3, p. 97; "The Voyage Out," *C&C*, September 23, 1947, p. 12; "Journal of a Trip to Asia," October 10, 1957, p. 3, unpublished, CI 1076.
56. *C&HK*, Chap. 2, p. 17.
57. *Corydon*, Dialogue 1 (published privately 1911, 1920; Éditions Gallimard, 1925; Gay Men's Press, 1983), trans. Richard Howard.
58. CI to LK, February 11, 1953, HM 81711, Huntington.
59. *WE*, Part I, Chap. 3, p. 38.
60. In 1965, Isherwood was to highlight a different subtext, saying that *Welt am Abend* should actually be translated as *Evening World*, and that his title, *The World in the Evening*, was a different phrase, "from John Donne." ("The World in the Evening," lecture, L.A., May 11, 1965, *IonW*, p. 294) The phrase is from Donne's "The Progress of the Soul," a long religious poem which describes the journey of a "deathless soul" in a changing world that moves "to his agèd evening / From infant morn, through manly noon." In this sense, the novel describes the journey of Stephen Monk's soul: the political revolution of the 1930s has failed, and Stephen undergoes an inward and personal spiritual revolution instead. The old codes, associated with Münzenberg's communist propaganda machine, are no longer relevant.
61. *WE*, Part III, Chap. 3, p. 118. Elizabeth Rydal's name alludes to William Wordsworth's home, Rydal Mount in Cumbria, where Wordsworth turned away from politics after becoming disillusioned with the French Revolution. Gerda is criticizing English Romanticism from Wordsworth to Bloomsbury, and, by implication, CI's wartime sojourns with Chris Wood in Laguna and the like. Stephen Monk defends Elizabeth Rydal's work by explaining that the private feelings portrayed are intended to stand for the agonies of the world—"she tried to reproduce them in miniature, the essence of them"—CI's own approach. (*WE*, Part III, Chap. 3, p. 119)
62. Synopsis enclosed in CI to EU, August 20, 1947, Add MS 72688, BL.
63. *WE*, Part III, Chap. 1, p. 281.
64. *D1*, May 9, 1942, p. 223.
65. "Reserved for Notes on Part Two," work journal, p. 55, CI 1158.
66. *WE*, Part II, Chap. 3, p. 110.
67. "Notes on 'Camp,'" *Partisan Review*, Vol. 31, No. 4, 1964, pp. 515–30, collected in *Against Interpretation* (New York: Farrar, Straus & Giroux, 1966; repr. Vintage, 2001), p. 275; *WE*, Part II, Chap. 3, p. 111; "A sensibility is almost, but not quite, ineffable," Sontag explained. "Any sensibility which can be crammed into the mold of a system, or handled with the rough tools of proof, is no longer a sensibility at all. It has hardened into an idea . . ." ("Notes on 'Camp,'" p. 276)
68. CI to LK, March 29, 1945, HM 81688, Huntington, and CI to LK, "how truly I enjoyed all our times in New York, such fun as I so seldom have, sounding the whole gamut of camp from high to low." (December 30, 1951, HM 81704, Huntington)
69. *Don Stayed*, pp. 45–6.
70. CI to KBI, July 18, 1939, *K&C*, p.144.
71. *Don Stayed*, pp. 52–3.
72. DB telephone conversation with Bucknell, October 28, 2022. CI left no record of what he knew. Hurst also became friendly with Donald Neville-Willing, who managed the George Washington Hotel where WHA and CI lived in New York in 1939; see Christopher Robbins, *The Empress of Ireland* (London: Gardners Books, 2004).
73. *Don Stayed*, p. 54; photos, Monument Valley, May 7, 1953, CI 3162.
74. *Don Stayed*, p. 55.
75. Quoted by Cathy Horyn, *New York Times*, Style Section, April 4, 1999.

76. The novel was republished as *Fast and Loose* (1955). The portrait of Carol Culvers draws on Lamkin's friendship with Marion Davies, and Denny Fouts is portrayed as Danny Hunts. There is a brief scene about camp.
77. *Don Stayed*, pp. 40, 41. Her accent got Marguerite a job as dialogue coach to Elizabeth Taylor on the film of TW's *Cat on a Hot Tin Roof* (1958).
78. "I now see that Stephen is a bisexual. (The degree to which this notion scares me only proves that I'm on the right track.)" (Work journal, July 9, 1950, p. 38, CI 1158)
79. Hyndman joined the International Brigade and went to fight in Spain, where he became a pacifist, deserted, and was imprisoned. SS spent much of his own time in Spain working to get Hyndman released. He told the story in *World Within World*, where Hyndman is disguised as Jimmy Younger. CI used the same name—Jimmy Younger—in *C&HK*.
80. SS joined the party early in 1937. See *Daily Worker*, February 19, 1937, "I Join the Communist Party"; repr. *The Thirties and After: Poetry, Politics, People, 1933–1975* (London: Palgrave Macmillan, 1978), pp. 80–2.
81. *Tomorrow*, April 1951; repr. *Exh.*, pp. 55, 56, 58.
82. WHA to SS, June 20, 1951, "Eleven Letters from Auden to Spender," in *Auden Studies I*, ed. Bucknell and Jenkins, pp. 84–5.
83. "The Hunted Profile," *Sunday Times*, April 8, 1951; repr. as "Stephen Spender," *Evening Colonnade* (London: David Bruce & Watson, 1973), p. 360. See also Matthew Spender, *A House in St John's Wood: In Search of My Parents* (Glasgow: William Collins, 2015), pp. 10–11.
84. SS to CI, September 14, 1934, CI 2070. This passage was cut in *Letters to Christopher: Stephen Spender's Letters to Christopher Isherwood, 1929–1939*, see p. 66. SS and Gardiner began the affair in Vienna while Hyndman was in the hospital there having his appendix out. Gardiner inspired the chapter about "Julia" in Lillian Hellman's 1973 book *Pentimento*, the basis for the movie *Julia* (1977).
85. In the same letter, CI also wrote, "these much-advertised normalities and abnormalities are, in nearly all cases, so entirely a question of place, time, opportunity, environment, temperature, income, class, latitude, longitude, altitude and gratitude, and as Wystan says, knowing that I am I, I just accept my present position until something comes along and jerks me out of it." CI to SS, October 19, 1934, Bancroft.
86. SS to Humphrey Carpenter, May 8, 1980, Butler. In the same letter, SS told Carpenter he had not had a sexual relationship with WHA, but Matthew Spender reported thirty-five years later, when all concerned were dead, that his father had been seduced by WHA, his first sexual partner (*A House in St John's Wood*, p. 16). If SS lied, it may have been to protect his wife's feelings.
87. CI to SS, March 27, [1951?], Bancroft. In a joke scene dropped from *The World in the Evening*, Monk gets drunk with Charles Kennedy and Bob Wood and sees the room "whirling" around him as they press him to admit to his homosexual past. Methuen Archive/Penguin Random House Archive and Library, Rushden, Northamptonshire.
88. Cyril Connolly, "Vale" in "A Georgian Boyhood," *Enemies of Promise* (London: Routledge, 1938; repr. 1996), p. 271.
89. *C&HK*, Chap. 13, p. 272.
90. *LY*, pp. 140–1, note. CI reread *The Rock Pool* in 1947 and "loved it," telling Connolly, "I think it is a little masterpiece: the classic description of that milieu." (CI to CC, December 20, 1947, McFarlin) In the meantime, he had become closer to Connolly's first wife, Jean Bakewell, on whom Connolly drew for his drunken, inescapable character "Ruby." CI later acknowledged that he "affectionately caricatured" Jean Bakewell as the similarly named "Ruthie" in *Down There on a Visit* (*C&HK*, Chap. 13, p. 270). CI also played with Jean's name and personality in creating "Jane" Armstrong in *The World in the Evening*. For Connolly's sexuality and love affairs, see Jeremy Lewis, *Cyril Connolly: A Life* (London: Jonathan Cape, 1997), Chaps 10, 11.
91. CI to Alan Clodd, August 21, 1955, Add MS 890433, BL.
92. "A New List of Characters," work journal, December 13, 1949, p. 20, CI 1158.

93. CI to Harry Heckford, March 21, 1967, CI 1310.
94. *Don Stayed*, pp. 72–3.
95. *MG&HD*, Chap. 14, pp. 209–10.
96. CI work journal, August 18, 1953, p. 91, CI 1158.
97. *D1*, August 25, 1953, p. 458; *MG&HD*, Chap. 14, p. 211.
98. *D1*, August 25, 1953, p. 458; *MG&HD*, Chap. 14, p. 211.
99. *Don Stayed*, pp. 89–90.
100. CI to SS, February 5, 1954, Bancroft; *Don Stayed*, p. 90.
101. CI to SS, February 5, 1954, Bancroft; *Don Stayed*, p. 91.
102. *Don Stayed*, p. 92.
103. *D1*, September 22, 1953, p. 458.
104. Robert Linscott to CI, September 17, 1953, CI 1665. In a subsequent letter, September 24, 1953, Linscott reluctantly gave specific examples of American slang with which, in his view, CI was not surefooted. (CI 1655)
105. J. Alan White to L.A.G. Strong, September 11, 1953, Methuen Archive/Penguin Random House Archive and Library.
106. L.A.G. Strong, Reader's Report, CI 2593.
107. J. Alan White to Spenser Curtis Brown, September 30, 1953, Methuen Archive/Penguin Random House Archive and Library.
108. CI to LK, October 12, 1953, HM 81712, Huntington.
109. In a diary used in 1947, CI refers to a draft made in Santa Monica in 1946 (see April 4, 1947, p. 58, and June 9, 1947, p. 69, CI 2751).
110. *D1*, December 17, 1953, pp. 463–4; FBI to CWBI, December 28, 14, CI 567.
111. Sutra 15, "Non-attachment is self-mastery; it is freedom from desire of what is seen or heard." (*Patanjali*, see p. 30)
112. *Don Stayed*, p. 126.
113. DB often tells this story.
114. *Don Stayed*, pp. 114, 117, 120–1.
115. *Don Stayed*, pp. 139–41.
116. George Platt Lynes quoted in *Don Stayed*, pp. 153–4, 155. Lynes had declared bankruptcy in 1951 after an ill-advised move to L. A. which ended his success as a New York fashion photographer. Afterwards, he made money selling his male nudes to Alfred Kinsey. See *When We Were Three: The Travel Albums of George Platt Lynes, Monroe Wheeler, Glenway Wescott 1925–1935*, texts by Anatole Pohorilenko and James Crump (Santa Fe: Arena Editions, 1998), pp. 291–2.
117. *Don Stayed*, pp. 155–6, 158.
118. CI to LK, January 26, 1954, HM 81716, Huntington; CI to SS, February 5, 1954, Bancroft.
119. "*People's World* 6-15-49 reports one Christopher Isherwood protests the case against the Los Angeles Communists," CI 1316.
120. "U.S. House Un-American Activities Comm. Report, 1951-52," p. 2, "COPY 1/20/54 Isherwood, Christopher," CI 1316.
121. *D2*, September 7, 1969, p. 590.
122. CI to Loew's Incorporated, Culver City, January 21, 1954, CI 1316.
123. WHA told the press that SS had not passed on the message; John Sutherland says SS passed on the message but that WHA didn't want to return the call because Burgess was always drunk (*Stephen Spender: The Authorized Biography*, pp. 359–60). James Smith quotes reports from Italy that WHA, himself drunk during the police interview, admitted to Italian police that SS may have passed on the message (*British Writers and MI5 Surveillance 1930–1960*, Cambridge University Press, 2012, p. 67). Smith also quotes the item in the *Manchester Guardian*, June 11, 1951, reporting on Burgess's telephone call with comments by WHA and SS (p. 62).
124. JL to SS, June 10, 1951, quoted in Sutherland, *Stephen Spender: The Authorized Biography*, p. 360. The man was Goronwy Rees, who recruited for the KGB for a few years.
125. Office Memorandum from SAC Los Angeles to Director, FBI, July 18, 1951, unclassified 2/22/ 82, photocopies from Michael Holzman.

126. In Berlin, he was correspondent for *Inprecor*, the international communist monthly magazine, and for *Argentinisches Tageblatt*, a German-language paper published in Buenos Aires which was banned in Germany by the Nazis. He also edited a German economic weekly *Wirtschaftlicher Ratgeber*. In Buenos Aires, he published *Economic Survey*, a weekly newsletter in Spanish and English. Members of the Rothschild family paid for his advice, and it was a Rothschild who funded the London magazine Katz tried to start with the assistance of Guy Burgess.
127. National Archives, KV-2-2178.
128. June 26, 1951, Note to British Embassy, Washington, National Archives, KV-2-2178.
129. When Hitler seized power, Münzenberg escaped on a borrowed passport and reestablished his propaganda network in Paris, promoting a united front against Hitler and, eventually, against Stalin. He was increasingly threatened by Stalin's purges. After the Nazis invaded France, Münzenberg was interned and then found dead in a forest with a rope around his neck. The police reported suicide; more likely, Münzenberg, trying to escape to Switzerland, was assassinated by a Soviet agent or by the Gestapo. See Gross, *Willi Münzenberg*, pp. 324–6; Arthur Koestler, "The Initiates," *The God That Failed*, ed. Crossman, p. 63, and *The Invisible Writing*, Chap. 18; Stephen Koch, *Double Lives: Stalin, Willi Münzenberg and the Seduction of the Intellectuals* (HarperCollins, 1996), Chap. 1, p. 342, note 23.
130. Gross, *Willi Münzenberg*, p. 311.
131. Salka Viertel, *The Kindness of Strangers: A Theatrical Life, Vienna, Berlin, Hollywood* (New York: Holt, Rinehart & Winston, 1969), pp. 213, 101.
132. See Koch, *Double Lives*, Chap. 3, p. 355, note 16, and Chap. 5, p. 365, note 40.
133. Office Memorandum, To Director of FBI from SAC, Los Angeles, IA 65-5312, photocopies from Michael Holzman.
134. CI work journal, May 22, June 5, July 11, 1955, and May 12, June 23, 1957, pp. 94, 95, 96, 100, CI 1158.
135. *Don Stayed*, p. 249.
136. *Don Stayed*, p. 215.
137. *Don Stayed*, pp. 182, 167.
138. Patrick F. Quinn, Fiction Chronicle, *Hudson Review*, Fall, 1954, 7.3, p. 460.
139. Patricia Hodgart, "New Novels," *Manchester Guardian*, June 29, 1954, p. 6; Edwin Muir, *Observer*, June 20, 1954, p. 9; *Time*, June 7, 1954, p. 60; *New York Times Book Review*, June 6, 1954, pp. 6, 16.
140. Harrison Smith, *Washington Post and Times Herald*, June 6, 1954, found it morally confused; Howard Mumford Jones, *Saturday Review*, June 5, 1954, p. 15, called it too complicated; the *Irish Times* missed CI's "flair for comedy," June 26, 1954, p. 8; *New Statesman and Nation*, June 19, 1954, p. 803; Angus Wilson, "The New and Old Isherwood," *Encounter*, August 1954, pp. 62–8.
141. "Vanity Fair, Latter Day Version," *New York Herald Tribune*, June 6, 1954, Book Review, p. 1; Thom Gunn, *London Magazine*, October 1, 1954, pp. 81–5; John Wain, *Spectator*, June 18, 1954, p. 20; J.B. Ludwig, *New Republic*, also seemed to understand what CI was trying for, July 5, 1954, pp. 19–20.
142. *Observer*, July 11, 1954.
143. *Don Stayed*, pp. 174–5; *D1*, July 20, 1954, p. 465.
144. J. McLaren-Ross, *Punch*, August 25, 1954, pp. 260–2.
145. *D1*, September 8, 1954, p. 467.
146. *MG&HD*, Chap. 14, p. 209.
147. CI to SS, July 22, 1954, Bancroft.
148. John Collins to CI, May 26, [1954?], CI 747.
149. CI to SS, July 22, 1954, Bancroft.
150. *D1*, September 9, 1954, p. 467.
151. *Don Stayed*, pp. 185–6.
152. CI day-to-day diary, July 24, 30, 1954, and L.V. Laurion MD, Beverly Hills, to Brooke Mohun, August 3, 1954, CI 1815.

153. Curtis Harrington, *Nice Guys Don't Work in Hollywood: The Adventures of an Aesthete in the Movie Business* (Chicago: Drag City Incorporated, 2013), p. 77; CI to Harrington, October 8, 1955, Margaret Herrick Library, Academy of Motion Picture Arts and Sciences, Beverly Hills; *D1*, October 20, 1956, p. 654. The film was *Jean-Christophe*, for Jerry Wald.
154. CI to Harrington, "Yes, indeed, I'm still interested in doing the film. When you return, we'll talk." January 7, 1953, Margaret Herrick Library.
155. CI to Harrington, October 8, 1955, Margaret Herrick Library.
156. CI to SS, July 22, 1954, Bancroft; *Don Stayed*, pp. 195, 200; CI day-to-day diary, September 7, 1954.
157. CI to SS, July 22, 1954, Bancroft.
158. *Don Stayed*, pp. 215–16, 217.
159. *D1*, December 11, 1954, p. 472.
160. *D1*, September 20, 1954, p. 468.
161. *D1*, September 20, 1954, pp. 468–9.
162. *Don Stayed*, pp. 219–20.
163. When WHA was working on *Calendar of the Year* for the GPO Film Unit, KBI attended a New Year's Eve party at William and Nancy Coldstream's flat and demonstrated the Sir Roger de Coverley repeatedly, followed by "an interlude of games & talk & refreshments." (KBI diary, January 9, 1936, HRC)
164. *Don Stayed*, p. 230.
165. CI day-to-day diary, November 14, 1954; *Don Stayed*, p. 237; TW to Audrey Wood, November 23, 1954, *The Selected Letters of Tennessee Williams, Volume II*, p. 554.
166. TW to Elia Kazan, November 31, 1954, quoted in John Lahr, *Tennessee Williams, Mad Pilgrimage of the Flesh* (London: Bloomsbury, 2014), p. 304.
167. *Cat on a Hot Tin Roof*, Act 2 (Penguin, 2009), p. 65.
168. Lahr, *Tennessee Williams, Mad Pilgrimage of the Flesh*, p. 312; TW to Brooks Atkinson, March 25, 1955, *The Selected Letters of Tennessee Williams, Volume II*, p. 569; Kazan to TW, April 22, 1960, *Kazan On Directing* (2009), p. 136, quoted in Lahr.
169. *Don Stayed*, p. 234.
170. *D1*, March 8, 1955, p. 479.
171. *D1*, April 13, 1956, p. 604.
172. *Don Stayed*, p. 241.
173. *Don Stayed*, pp. 251, 232–3.
174. *Don Stayed*, p. 254.
175. *D1*, November 2, 1954, p. 469; *October*, pp. 25–6.
176. "How I came to write the first draft . . ." CI 1039; *D1*, December 16, 1954, p. 475.
177. EU to CI, June 10, 1955, CI 2478.
178. "Draft of a Prologue to Down There on a Visit," p. 1, CI 1058; Cf. "Waking up begins with saying *am* and *now*. That which has awoken then lies for a while staring up at the ceiling and down into iself until it has recognized *I*, and therefrom deduced *I am, I am now*." (*SM*, p. 9)
179. CI day-to-day diary, November 3, 1958.
180. "Girls dashing down from their apartments to drag some gorgeous endangered young drunk upstairs to safety and breakfast served in bed like a miracle of joy." (*SM*, p. 114)
181. *D1*, December 11, 12, 1954, pp. 472–3.
182. Intro. to *GESS*, p. 10.
183. In his 1941 book review, "Hemingway, Death and the Devil" (for Klaus Mann's *Decision*), CI had proposed that Hemingway's three post-World War I novels were "a kind of metaphysical trilogy," implying a comparison with Dante's metaphysical trilogy *The Divine Comedy* as well as with his own abandoned epic *The Lost*. Hemingway's trilogy was "about the 'Lost Generation'" so damaged by the war that they are in fact "dead." A pair of lovers, CI had argued, appear in each book with different names, condemned to "a limbo beyond Death, in which earthbound spirits must wander, 'desiring without hope,' as Dante says, and awaiting the pain of rebirth." But the lovers in *For Whom the Bell Tolls*, Robert Jordan and Maria (of holy name, but no surname), "experience the mystic revelation; the earth moves from beneath them." They pass beyond death into eternity. It does not matter that Robert's "body bleeds to death on the hillside, cast

away like an unwanted knapsack." This is how a Vedantist might leave his or her body. ("Hemingway, Death, and the Devil," *Decision*, January 1, 1941, pp. 58–60)
184. *Don Stayed*, pp. 264–5, and conversations with Bucknell.
185. *D1*, December 14, 1954, pp. 473–4.
186. Work journal, August 21, 1955, p. 58; January 27, 1957, p. 97; October 6, 1958, p. 109; September 27, 1958, p. 106, CI 1158.
187. *Don Stayed*, p. 264.
188. *Don Stayed*, p. 268.
189. *D1*, January 13, 1955, p. 476.
190. Maria Huxley to Edward Sackville-West, quoted in Sybille Bedford, *Aldous Huxley: A Biography, Volume 2, 1939–1963* (London: Chatto & Windus, 1977), p. 22.
191. *D1*, March 1, 1955, p. 478.
192. Quoted in Bedford, *Aldous Huxley, A Biography*, Vol. 2, p. 185.
193. Maria Huxley to Sybille Bedford, January 1, 1945, quoted in Bedford, *Aldous Huxley, A Biography*, Vol. 2, p. 50.
194. *D1*, February 7, 1944, p. 334.
195. CI to KBI, November 27, 1939, *K&C*, p. 157.
196. *D1*, January 6, 1940, p. 74.
197. Early in 1944, Huxley asked CI to read the manuscript for *Time Must Have a Stop*. "He has very good judgement," Huxley had told Maria, and Maria told CI that Huxley had never before sought a second opinion in this way. (Maria Huxley to CI, January 30, 1944, CI 1008) See also Nicholas Murray, *Aldous Huxley: An English Intellectual* (Boston: Little, Brown, 2002; Abacus, 2003), p. 346.
198. After *Jacob's Hands* was rejected, Huxley told CI, "It appears that the reason for the hitherto universal rejection of it is fear of the doctors." (*Letters of Aldous Huxley*, ed. Grover Smith, 1969, p. 510, quoted in Murray, *Aldous Huxley*, p. 351)
199. Bedford, *Aldous Huxley, A Biography*, Vol. 2, p. 59.
200. *D1*, bridging passage, May 1941, pp. 152–3.
201. *D1*, February 25, 1955, p. 476.
202. CI to SS, April 3, 1935, from Classensgade 65, Copenhagen, Bancroft.
203. Work journal, August 1955, CI 1158. See also CI to EU, August 20, 1955, enclosing "rough outline," Add MS 72688, BL.
204. CI to EU, May 20, 1955, Add MS 72688, BL.
205. Charles Higham interview, "Isherwood on Hollywood," *London Magazine*, April 1968; repr. *Conversations*, p. 50; Mike Connolly, "Rambling Reporter," *Hollywood Reporter*, October 12, 1955, and "Christopher Isherwood Will Script Cinema 16o's Buddha," *Hollywood Reporter*, August 4, 1958. CI was evidently unaware that the project had begun as a CIA Asian anti-communist initiative. See Laura Harrington, "The Greatest Movie Never Made: The Life of the Buddha as Cold War Politics," *Religion and American Culture*, Vol. 30, issue 3, Fall 2020, pp. 397–425.
206. *Don Stayed*, pp. 287, 309.
207. *D1*, March 4, 1955, 478.
208. The studio friendships were genuine only up to a point, and CI was successful at concealing his sexuality. When Larry Weingarten's wife, Jessie Marmorston, became CI's doctor, a crush flared on her side and she prepared to make a pass at him. "Drove Jessie home, she started giving me such a build up that I had to tell her a bit about myself. She claimed she'd known from the very beginning." (*D1*, May 2, 1955, pp. 494)
209. *Don Stayed*, p. 203.
210. *D1*, March 25, 1955, p. 484.
211. *Don Stayed*, p. 304.
212. *D1*, March 15, 23, April 28, 1955, pp. 480, 482, 493.
213. *D1*, May 2, 1955, p. 494.
214. *D1*, May 20, 1955, p. 499.
215. *Don Stayed*, p. 321.
216. GV, *Palimpsest*, pp. 186–7.
217. *D1*, April 27, 1948, p. 401, July 18, 1955, p. 514.
218. *D1*, June 9, 1955, p. 506.
219. *D1*, July 15, 1955, p. 513; *Don Stayed*, p. 305.

220. *D1*, July 15, 1955, p. 513.
221. *D1*, Jul. 26, August 8, September 6, 1955, pp. 515, 519, 529.
222. CI to EU, September 7, 1955, Add MS 72688, BL.
223. *Don Stayed*, p. 221. Cold-water bathing was a lifelong love for CI, and he had never objected to the cold baths first thing in the morning at his preparatory boarding school. In his 1932 *Memoirs of Pine House*, he recalled that a large tin bath for each boy was kept in a corner of the dormitory. In the mornings, these were filled "with buckets of cold water," and the boys got into them straight from their warm beds. (*Memoirs of Pine House*, p. 8, CI 1098)
224. *D1*, September 29, 1955, p. 533.
225. *D1*, October 8, 1955, p. 535.
226. *D1*, December 30, 1955, January 28, 1956, pp. 562, 569; "Isherwood on Hollywood," *Conversations*, p. 49.
227. *D1*, June 22, 1955, p. 509.
228. *D1*, October 20, 1955, p. 537.
229. *D1*, October 30, 1955, p. 541.
230. *D1*, November 14, 1955, p. 550.
231. "A Visit to Anselm Oakes," *Exh.*, p. 250. CI had come across this kind of cynicism in J.K. Huysmans' 1891 novel *Là-Bas*, which he read in 1954. *Là-Bas* is usually translated as *The Damned*, but the literal translation is *Down There*, the phrase CI used in his title. Huysmans' narrator, Durtal, is writing a biography of the wickedest man in France, Gilles de Rais, Joan of Arc's comrade-in-arms, who, in a later period of his life, raped and murdered hundreds of children. Immersing himself in his research, Durtal has an affair with a succubus and attends a black mass, yet, like Crowley, he is emotionally unaffected, unsure whether he believes in or cares about anything.
232. *D1*, February 20, 1958, p. 738.
233. *D1*, April 3, 1955, pp. 486–7.
234. *D1*, August 6, 1955, pp. 518–19; December 1, 1954, p. 47.
235. *D1*, February 25, 1956, pp. 588–9. CI was to take mescaline again at least twice more, but without vital interest.
236. DB draft letter to CI, March 26, 1961, *Animals*, p. 73.
237. *D1*, November 8, 1956, p. 661, and see November 4, 1956, p. 660.
238. *D1*, November 6, 1955, p. 547.
239. CI interviewed by W.I. Scobie, "The Art of Fiction," *Paris Review*, No. 49, Issue 57, Spring 1974.
240. See Michael Wishart, *High Diver*, pp. 56, 59–60, and Bernard Perlin in Michael Schreiber, *One Man Show: The Life and Art of Bernard Perlin* (Berlin: Bruno Gmünder, 2016), p. 151. CI told EMF that Fouts had a heart murmur, CI to EMF, March 16, 1944, *F&I*, p. 124.
241. *D1*, November 15, 1955, p. 550.
242. *D1*, December 30, 1955, January 5, 10, 1956, pp. 562–3, 564.
243. *D1*, January 10, 20, 1956, pp. 564–5, 567.
244. DB conversation with Bucknell, January 4, 2017.
245. *K&F*, Chap. 11, p. 255; he didn't visit Haworth Parsonage until near the end of his life, with DH. *D1*, February 1, 1956, p. 570.
246. *D1*, February 1, 3, 4, 1956, pp. 570, 571, 572, 576.
247. *D1*, February 4, 1956, p. 576; Georges Bizet, *Carmen*, Act 2, finale. CI believed his "insecurity and immaturity"—identifying him with DB's age group—were his only protection against spiritual death.
248. *D1*, February 5, 7, March 9, 1956, pp. 576, 578, 593. DB proved "a success."
249. CI to EU, July 28, 1956, Add MS 72688, BL.
250. CI to DS and AB, May 12, 1956, Gotlieb.
251. *LY*, p. 100.
252. EU, "Sketch for a Marxist Interpretation of Literature," *The Mind in Chains: Socialism and the Cultural Revolution*, ed. Cecil Day Lewis (London: Frederick Muller, 1937), pp. 52, 8.
253. *New Directions in Prose and Poetry*, No. 11, 1949, ed. James Laughlin; repr. Penguin Modern Classics, p. 33.
254. KBI diary, July 26, 1929, HRC; *D3*, October 14, 1974, p. 458.

255. *L&S*, Chap. 7, p. 273.
256. EU, *Christopher Isherwood*, p. 12. Before he left, CI inscribed one of the copies in French: "à Edward Upward ce livre peu digne de son esprit subtil et dédaigneux. / Le Soir de Wagram." ("To Edward Upward this book unworthy of his subtle and disdainful spirit. / The Eve of Wagram.") Wagram was a decisive victory for Napoleon, whom they had studied together in their history lessons at Repton, and CI was wishing EU a decisive victory on the eve of his writing battle. So negative, though, was EU's attitude after CI's departure to success that he recalled Wagram as a defeat: "We both knew that making a satisfactory start would be a battle for me, but why did he choose to compare it to Wagram, a battle which Napoleon did not win? I suspect he was being ironical, foreseeing that once again I was going to fail."
257. *In the Thirties*, SA, p. 32
258. CI to EU, December 5, 1949, Add MS 72688, BL.
259. CI to EU, March 13, 1950, Add MS 72688. BL; SS "Worshippers from Afar," *The God That Failed*, p. 237; EU conversation with Bucknell, July 19, 1988.
260. CI to EU, October 11, 1958, Add MS 72688, BL.
261. CI to EU, December 19, 1958, Add MS 72688, BL.
262. *AC* (New York: New Directions, 1958); repr. *Exh.*, p. 93.
263. "The Life of the Party," *New Statesman*, July 29, 1977, p. 150.
264. *D1*, April 24, 1956, p. 61; CI saw Paul Robeson and Flora Robson perform it in London in 1933 (KBI diary, April 13, 1933, HRC).
265. *D1*, April 19, 1956, p. 609.
266. *D1*, April 3, 1956, p. 600.
267. *D1*, May 11, 1956 p. 615.
268. *D1*, November 10, 1956, p. 661.
269. *D1*, June 17, 1956, p. 621.
270. CI Prologue, Gerald Hamilton, *Mr Norris and I . . .* (London: Alan Wingate, 1956), p. 11.
271. *D1*, May 11, July 5, 1956, pp. 614, 626–7.
272. *D1*, June 17, 24, 1956, pp. 622, 623.
273. *D1*, November 4, 1956, p. 660.
274. *D1*, January 13, February 12, 14, 1957, pp. 675, 680, 681.
275. *D1*, February 21, March 4, 11, May 9, 1957, pp. 682–3, 684, 685, 686, 697.
276. Mike Connolly, "Rambling Reporter," *Hollywood Reporter*, April 25, 1957.
277. *D1*, July 21, 1956, p. 632.
278. *D1*, May 3, 6, 8, 10, April 30, 1957, pp. 695, 696, 697, 694.
279. *D1*, September 3, 1957, p. 720.
280. *Chéri* (1920; Vintage edition, 2001), trans. Roger Senhouse, p. 3.
281. *D1*, June 20, July 16, 17, August 15, 1957, pp. 705, 710, 711, 715.
282. Gavin Lambert, *Mainly About Lindsay Anderson* (New York: Knopf, 2000), pp. 132–3, 143.
283. CI to DS, August 17, 1959, Gotlieb.
284. Lambert, *Mainly About Lindsay Anderson*, pp. 219, 218, 216, 218.
285. Scene 33, p. 31, CI 114.
286. *D2*, April 9, 1968, p. 507.
287. Murray telephone conversation with Bucknell, January 2, 2016. The community was for WWII refugees still living in camps around Naples.
288. Adapted from Giuseppe Fina, *My Brother Cain*, CI 89.
289. Murray telephone conversation with Bucknell, January 2, 2016.
290. *D1*, October 8, 1957, p. 732.
291. *LY*, pp. 201-2.
292. *LY*, p. 201; Igor Stravinsky and Robert Craft, *Dialogues and a Diary* (New York: Doubleday, p. 1963), p. 40. It remains unclear how much Craft edited his transcription. Craft stated that conversations published before 1958 were mostly by Stravinsky but also that Stravinsky's English was too imperfect to sustain a conversation. See, for example, Craft, *Stravinsky: Glimpses of a Life* (London: Lime Tree, 1992), p. 61. Stravinsky had read *GB* before meeting CI. Like others, he described CI as "boyish: his looks, his laugh, his candor," and remarked the power of his mind: "Christopher's intelligence can clear a path of lucidity through the fuzziest of subjects, and his merciless eye can

pierce every disguise of hypocrisy and cant." (*Dialogues and a Diary*, pp. 38, 40) Craft's description of CI at first meeting includes the striking sentence, "His manner is casual, vagabondish, lovelorn." (Craft, "Diaries, August 10, 1949," in Stravinsky and Craft, *Retrospectives and Conclusions* (New York: Knopf, 1969), Part II, p. 154) *Retrospectives and Conclusions* is dedicated to CI, who later recalled that Craft developed "a crush" on him and that he, CI, "had tried to give Craft some discreet encouragement. But Craft didn't, wouldn't, couldn't respond." When CI's reconstructed diary was published as *LY*, passages suggesting Craft was gay were cut at Craft's request. See CI 4171. DB recalled Craft once surprising him with a surreptitious lover's kiss on the mouth. (DB telephone conversation with Bucknell, March 25, 1998)

293. *LY*, p. 203.
294. *D1*, June 18, 1957, p. 704.
295. *LY*, p. 201.
296. CI Intro. to SP, *Religion in Practice* (London: George Allen & Unwin, 1968), p. 16; Stravinsky and Craft, *Expositions and Developments* (London: Faber and Faber, 2009), pp. 147–8.
297. After Stravinsky's death, CI mentally placed him in "a trio with Prabhavananda and Forster." (*LY*, p. 202)
298. "Journal of a Trip to Asia with Don Bachardy in the Autumn and Winter of 1957," see note on title page and October 14, 15, 1957, pp. 9–10, 13, 14, CI 1076; *C&HK*, Chap. 15, p. 311.
299. "Journal of a Trip to Asia ..." October 14, 1957, pp. 11, 12–13, 12, see also p. 16, CI 1076.
300. Yukio Mishima to CI, February 14, 1958, CI 1813.
301. *D3*, November 25, 1970, p. 119.
302. CI to Jo and Ben Masselink, November 10, 1957, CI 1075.
303. CI to John Van Druten, November 10, 1957, CI 1075.
304. CI to SP, December 5, 1957 (carbon) CI 1035, and Vedanta Society Archives.
305. CI to SP, December 5, 1957, CI 1035.
306. DB telephone conversation with Bucknell, March 3, 2017.
307. *D3*, November 8, 1978, p. 600.
308. "Journal of a Trip to Asia ..." October 9, 1957, p. 3, CI 1076.
309. CI to SP, December 5, 1957, CI 1035.
310. *MG&HD*, Chap. 17, pp. 263–4.
311. Preface to *R&HD*.
312. *D2*, December 26, 1963, p. 311.
313. *MG&HD*, Chap. 16, pp. 247, 248, 248–9.
314. CI to SP, December 27, 1957, p. 2, CI 1035, and Vedanta Society Archives.
315. *MG&HD*, Chap. 2, p. 31; Intro., *Religion in Practice*, p. 19.
316. *MG&HD*, Chap. 2, p. 32; Intro., *Religion in Practice*, p. 20.
317. *MG&HD*, Chap. 2, p. 32; *K&F*, "Afterword," pp. 503, 504.
318. Intro., *Religion in Practice*, p. 21.
319. *D1*, May 25, 1958, pp. 754, 753.
320. *MG&HD*, Chap. 2, p. 33.
321. The scenery in the dream, he explained, "was vaguely Japanese and may have been 'borrowed' from Nara," i.e., one of the sacred places to which CI and DB had recently "moved around" during their visit to Japan. (*MG&HD*, Chap. 2, p. 33)
322. *D1*, May 25, 1958, pp. 753–4; CI later explained, "the Atman in himself was bowing down to the Atman in me in order to remind me of what I truly was. Brahmananda [...] had not only bowed down but also blessed me as an individual soul, thus reassuring me that he loved and accepted me even with all my present imperfections." (*MG&HD*, Chap. 15, p. 230, where the dream is dated December 11, 1957, evidently a typo for December 31)
323. *D1*, July 18, 1959, p. 820.
324. *D1*, February 2, 1958, p. 733; CI to DS and AB, February 8, 1958, Gotlieb; *D1*, February 2, 1958, p. 733.
325. *D1*, March 4, 1959, p. 803.
326. *D1*, April 30, May 4, 11, 1958, pp. 749, 750.

327. D1, March 13, 21, 18, April 12, 1958, pp. 741, 743, 746; CI to DS, September 10, 1958, Gotlieb.
328. D2, July 1965, p. 369.
329. Lambert, *Mainly About Lindsay Anderson*, p. 219; D1, August 11, 1958, October 24, 1959, pp. 768–9, 831.
330. D1, June 25, 1958, p. 761.
331. See Kent Chapman, "The End of Everything," *Spectrum*, U.C. Santa Barbara student magazine, and D1, July 11, 1957, p. 710. Chapman threw away a novella about Vivekananda (correspondence with Bucknell).
332. D1, July 11, August 1, September 3, 10, 1958, June 6, 1959, pp. 763, 765, 774, 777, 815.
333. D1, September 26, 1958, pp. 779–80.
334. D1, October 13, 1958, p. 783.
335. D1, February 8, September 18, 1959, pp. 800, 827.
336. D1, June 21, November 19, 1958, January 8, 1959, pp. 759, 789, 796.
337. D1, March 11, 1959, p. 804.
338. CI to DS, October 18, 1959, Gotlieb.
339. D1, May 24, 1959, and October 7, 1958, pp. 814, 732.
340. D1, June 24, 1959, p. 817.
341. D1, September 2, 1959, p. 823.
342. D1, October 2, 1959, p. 829; KBI, "Notes from My Every Day Diary of Expeditions We Took During Our Stay in Ireland," January 7, 1912, CI 617.
343. CI to DS and AB, October 18, 1959, Gotlieb.
344. D1, October 30, 1959, p. 832.
345. D1, November 11, 1959, p. 834.
346. D1, February 17, May 30, 1960, pp. 846, 858.
347. D1, January 29, 1960, p. 843.
348. D1, February 8, 1960, p. 845.
349. D1, April 9, March 20, 1960, pp. 852, 849.
350. D1, May 30, 1960, p. 857.
351. D1, March 21, 1960, p. 849.
352. D1, June 26, 1961, p. 871, and see also July 11, 1961, p. 880. An outline and a draft script in four parts survive. Three parts draw closely on Plato. CI evidently added the fourth part in 1961 under the influence of Pirandello. CI 100, CI 101.
353. *The Story-teller: A Session with Charles Laughton* (1962), produced by Bill Miller, Capitol Records TBO 1650. The album notes say "Translated by Christopher Isherwood," but more likely CI adapted it from Benjamin Jowett's translation, in his library at his death.
354. D1, June 26, July 4, 1960, pp. 871, 876; September 2, 1959, p. 824; July 21, 1960, p. 885.
355. D1, July 5, 1960, p. 877.
356. D1, July 14, 1960, p. 882; DB conversation with Bucknell, April 19, 2018.
357. D1, August 22, 23, June 20, August 10, 1960, pp. 898–9, 868, 894.
358. D1, June 5, 1960, p. 860, and see June 12, 1960, p. 862.
359. D1, June 16, 1960, p. 863.
360. CI mentioned the proposed biography in letters to JL and SS in the early 1940s. His pieces "On Swami Vivekananda," "On the Writings of Swami Vivekananda," and "Vivekananda and Sarah Bernhardt," appeared in the Vedanta Society magazine, *Vedanta and the West*; the second was collected in *VWW* and all three in *Wishing Tree*. Vivekananda was the first Vedanta author CI gave DB to read. (DB conversation with Bucknell, April 2017)
361. D1, June 28, 1960, p. 873.
362. D2, September 17, December 29, 1960, pp. 7, 37.
363. D2, October 2, December 13, 1960, and March 27, 1961, pp. 14, 33, 56.
364. The transcript of the first lecture was prepared for publication in *Encounter*, and CI himself corrected the proofs, but the magazine publication never happened, see *IonW*, p. 41.
365. *IonW*, p. 48.

366. *IonW*, p. 43. See William Penn's Preface to Fox's journal, "A Character Sketch," Everyman Edition of *The Journal of George Fox* (London/New York: J.M. Dent & Sons/E.P. Dutton, 1924), p. xvii (CI's copy, Huntington). See also CI to JL, March or April 1947 from Wyberslegh, "Incidentally, I'm also reading The Journal of George Fox, in case you want me to do that introduction." (Beinecke)
367. CI once commented on a portrait of Bradshaw: it "shows a long-faced serious looking man with a large sensible nose and mild eyes; it is possible to read into it a certain likeness to Frank." (*Hero-Father, Demon-Mother*, p. 29, CI 1082) Like CI's antiheroes FBI and EMF, Bradshaw was installed in an upside-down pantheon: "The Anti-Ancestor can never be glorified officially: the only valid tributes to him are the insults of his enemies." CI supplied details of these insults for his lecture audience. In the register of baptisms at Stockport Parish Church, an anonymous hand wrote "traitor" next to Bradshaw's name. After the Restoration, Bradshaw's bones were dug up from their place of honor in Westminster Abbey and "hung in chains from the gallows along with those of Cromwell and Fairfax." (*IonW*, p. 43) Through such insults, argued CI, the Anti-Ancestor "achieves his highest political honour." (*K&F*, Chap. 13, p. 304)
368. *K&F*, Chap. 13, p. 304.
369. D2, November 19, 1960, pp. 27–8.
370. *SM*, p. 88, and see *The Englishman*, CI 1061.
371. D2, November 2, 1960, p. 23; *Numbers* (1967; Grove Press, 1984), pp. 163, 162.
372. D2, October 28, 1960, p. 23. DB did the posters for TW for free, note to Bucknell.
373. D2, December 4, November 15, 1960, pp. 31, 26.
374. D2, December 31, 1960, p. 38.
375. D2, January 23, 1961, p. 44; DB conversation with Bucknell, July 22, 2017.

8: EXISTENTIAL ISHERWOOD: THE OUTSIDER

1. Work journal, January 20, March 15, 1959, p. 114, CI 1158.
2. Work journal, March 17, 1959, pp. 114–15, CI 1158.
3. CI to Harry Heckford, March 21, 1967, CI 1310.
4. Translators' Foreword, *Patanjali*, pp. 10, 7; Sutra 19, pp. 47–8; Sutra 18, p. 46. "Sutra" means thread: "Composed in a period when there were no books, these terse sentences were designed to be easily memorized; they form only the bare connective thread of a philosophical exposition." (*MG&HD*, Chap. 13, p. 194) CI and SP expanded and paraphrased their translations and added a commentary to make them accessible.
5. *La Chute* (1956; *The Fall*, Penguin Modern Classics, 2013), trans. Robin Buss, p. 10.
6. *LY*, pp. 140, note 1, 176, note 1; draft for *DTV*, p. 68, CI 1056.
7. CI to DS and AB, October 18, 1959, Gotlieb.
8. *The Widening Circle* (London: William Heinemann Ltd, 1957), p. 4.
9. D1, August 22, 1956, p. 640.
10. *The Widening Circle*, p. 228.
11. "Mr. Lancaster," *DTV*, p. 57.
12. "Ambrose," *DTV*, p. 132.
13. "Waldemar," *DTV*, p. 156.
14. "Paul," *DTV*, pp. 317–18.
15. "Mr. Lancaster," *DTV*, p. 13.
16. Work journal, September 21, 1960, p. 126, CI 1158; *C&HK*, Chap. 1, p. 3.
17. Work journal, September 21, 1960, p. 126, CI 1158.
18. D1, June 17, 1960, p. 865.
19. "Mr. Lancaster," *DTV*, p. 12.
20. Repr. *Exh.*, p. 92.
21. "Mr. Lancaster," *DTV*, pp. 38, 23, 12. KBI possessed a photo of Uncle Charlie Fry just like the photo of Mr. Lancaster's father in the story, McFarlin.
22. As a teenager, CI had been dragooned by Uncle Henry into moving a large portrait of a Mrs. Lancaster from a bedroom to be rehung in the library. (KBI diary, March 5, 1941, and see February 25, 1946, HRC)

Notes to Part 8 / 797

23. "Mr. Lancaster," *DTV*, pp. 36–7, 40.
24. "Mr. Lancaster," *DTV*, p. 52. The episode parodies the conclusion to Virginia Woolf's *To the Lighthouse* in which the painter Lily Briscoe has a vision inspired by the ghost of Mrs. Ramsey that is, in one sense, Lily's answer to another Victorian paterfamilias, Mr. Ramsay. Lily watches Mr. Ramsay reach the lighthouse in his sailboat with his children James and Cam, who have sworn to resist his tyranny. Then she turns back to her painting: "With a sudden intensity, as if she saw it clear for a second, she drew a line there, in the centre. It was done; it was finished. Yes, she thought, laying down her brush in extreme fatigue, I have had my vision." (Woolf, *To the Lighthouse*, Chap. 14) The episode also used details from CI's diary account of the December 1954 Mexican fishing expedition with the Masselinks. (See *D1*, December 12, 1954, p. 473)
25. DB conversation with Bucknell, January 4, 2017, and see *D1*, April 11, 1959, p. 809.
26. Robert Linscott was retiring, and in mid-March 1957, CI committed to Simon & Schuster with a big advance. Then his new editor suddenly died, and CI decided not to take any money until he had completed *DTV*. (See *D1*, March 15, 1957, and August 2, 1957, pp. 686, 714)
27. JL, *London Magazine*, October 1959, Vol. 6. No. 10, p. 7.
28. WHA to CI, "Wednesday" [spring 1944], CI 2995.
29. *LY*, p. 223, note.
30. "Ambrose," *DTV*, p. 100; CI told EMF that Glaspell's book "starts off so genuine," but by the end, it becomes "merely a *description* of some of the effects that the authoress would like to produce, and can't." (CI to EMF, July 22, 1933, *F&I*, p. 26) He chose the name "Ambrose" for his romantic wandering English lord certain that he could write something better.
31. "Ambrose," *DTV*, p. 88. For the painting of Christ walking on water, see George du Roy's "miracle" in the climactic chapter of Guy de Maupassant, *Bel Ami*. In August 1959, while working on "Ambrose," CI spent an afternoon copying out passages from *Diary of a Thief* in which Jean Genet used religious diction to sanctify his poverty, his loneliness, his sexuality, and his crimes.
32. *The Tempest*, 4.1.
33. *Patanjali*, Sutra 18, p. 46.
34. "Ambrose," *DTV*, pp. 129–30.
35. *The Tempest*, 2.1; "Ambrose," *DTV*, p. 76; *The Tempest*, 4.1; "Ambrose," *DTV*, pp. 116, 119, 117.
36. Bucknell conversation with DB, April 10, 2017.
37. *C&HK*, Chap. 8, p. 138; CI to SS, June 23, 1933, Bancroft.
38. Joseph Conrad, *Victory: An Island Tale* (London: Methuen, 1915; Penguin Classics, 2015), Part IV, Chap. 11, pp. 319, 323.
39. W. Somerset Maugham, *The Narrow Corner* (London: William Heinemann, 1932; Vintage, 2001), Chap. 11, p. 40. CI found Maugham's air of having been everywhere, his air "of boredom," to be "strangely reassuring": "He knows the ropes. He can tell you what to expect from any situation." (CI, Intro. to "The Book-bag," *GESS*, p. 295) Maugham's writerly poise, his feeling for closure, promised that any emotion, no matter how extreme, could be resolved in a well-told tale. Being a medical doctor as well as a writer, Maugham epitomized the anonymous professional whom GV recalled CI liked to play.
40. Work journal, May 19, 1959, p. 116, CI 1158.
41. "Ambrose," *DTV*, pp. 124, 125.
42. EU to CI [spring /early summer 1933], CI 2442.
43. "Ambrose," *DTV*, pp. 133–4; draft of *In the Thirties*, p. 25, CI 2277. See also *SA*, p. 19.
44. CI to EU, October 11, 1958, Add MS 72688, BL.
45. "Ambrose," *DTV*, pp. 117, 131; CI to SS, from Nollendorfstrasse 17, Bancroft.
46. Work journal, November 13, 1958, p. 113, CI 1158; "A Last Lecture," Santa Barbara, 1960, *IonW*, p. 139.
47. Work journal, August 15, September 15, 1959, p. 117, CI 1158. Just as the visit of Maria Constantinescu never happened, "the Englishman called Geoffrey is largely fictitious," CI later explained. (*C&HK*, Chap. 8, p. 138) He created Geoffrey in order to bring to the island a member of the group that had persecuted Ambrose; the

character is partly based on an Englishman called MacGregor, homosexual not straight, who arrived on Turville-Petre's island in June 1933; he was an anti-communist and objected ferociously to Turville-Petre's anarchism. Both drank retsina all day.
48. "Ambrose," *DTV*, p. 114; *C&HK*, Chap. 7, pp. 128–9; "Ambrose," *DTV*, p. 114.
49. *D1*, April 7, 1960, p. 851; SS to CI, April 16, 1960, copied by CI into his work journal, April 17, 1960, p. 121, CI 1158; *D1*, January 16, 1956, p. 566.
50. EU quoted in *D1*, May 11, 1960, p. 854.
51. Evelyn Waugh, *Put Out More Flags* (London: Chapman & Hall, 1942), pp. 38, 47, 48, 86, 50.
52. When Howard read *Put Out More Flags*, he wrote to Toni Altmann, "Evelyn Waugh has made an absolutely vicious attack on me in his new novel *Put Out More Flags*." (*Portrait of a Failure*, ed. Marie-Jaqueline Lancaster, London: Anthony Blond Ltd, 1968, p. 428) Waugh acknowleged Howard as his model: "The characters in my novels often wrongly identified with Harold Acton were to a great extent drawn from him." (*A Little Learning*, p. 204, quoted in *The Diaries of Evelyn Waugh*, ed. Michael Davie, 1976; Penguin, 1979, p. 161) Davie states that Howard "largely inspired the character Ambrose Silk," p. 801.
53. Epilogue, *Put Out More Flags*, p. 253. Howard and Toni Altmann had stayed with Francis Turville-Petre on St. Nicholas a few months before CI arrived there; two years later, the four intersected in Amsterdam and considered settling together in Portugal. CI described their dinners and drinking sprees in Amsterdam in several diary entries, which he later embellished in *C&HK*. As with Turville-Petre, CI was fascinated by Howard's devotion to pleasure and his showy use of drugs—cocaine, heroin, hashish (see September 11, 1935, CI 2751, and *C&HK*, Chap. 11, pp. 216–18).
54. LK to CI, September 18, 1944, CI 1545.
55. "Ambrose," *DTV*, pp. 132, 135.
56. "Waldemar," *DTV*, pp. 140–1. Also, "The Others are all the headmasters of the schools I went to, all the clergymen I have ever known, all the reactionary politicians, newspaper editors, journalists, and most women over forty." (*DTV*, p. 141)
57. CI diary, July 28, 1938, p. 33, CI 2751, and CI notebook, CI 1078.
58. One model was Sally Coole. Another was a friend with whom he felt he had much in common, Iris Wright: "The story is really about Iris Wright—i.e. H. and myself." (CI diary, July, 24, 1938, p. 33, CI 2751) Wright, a year younger than he, lived in Berlin in 1933 and worked in the film business in London, for Alexander Korda, during 1936.
59. Work journal, March 25, 26–7, 1960, p. 120, CI 1158.
60. "Waldemar," *DTV*, p. 143; work journal, November 26, 1960, p. 128, CI 1158.
61. "Waldemar," *DTV*, pp. 185, 186, 187, 188.
62. "Karin & Helen," pp. 2–3, CI 1077.
63. "Waldemar," *DTV*, pp. 178, 179.
64. Work journal, March 25, 1960, p. 120, CI 1158; "Waldemar," *DTV*, p. 162.
65. "Waldemar," *DTV*, pp. 170, 175, 177.
66. "Waldemar," *DTV*, p. 175; National Archives, KV-2-2178, KV-2-2179.
67. "Waldemar," *DTV*, p. 142.
68. Work journal, June 15, 1960, p. 121, CI 1158.
69. Work journal, June 15, 1960, p. 122, CI 1158; "Paul," *DTV*, p. 194; work journal, July 27, 1960, p. 122, CI 1158.
70. "Paul," *DTV*, pp. 315, 315–16.
71. GV, *The Judgment of Paris* (reissued, London: William Heinemann, 1968), Chap. 12, p. 321; "Pages from an Abandoned Journal," and "Three Stratagems," *A Thirsty Evil* (London: William Heinemann, 1956; repr. Abacus, 2009), pp. 10, 12.
72. Capote yarned about a sixteen-year-old Fouts eloping with a passing cosmetics tycoon in a 1936 Duesenberg car and making his way to Europe within a month. Fouts was already twenty-two by 1936. There *was* a cosmetics tycoon in his life, George Gallowhur, Swedish by background, educated at Princeton, who invented a sun lotion and later an insect repellent and was accustomed to crisscrossing the Atlantic on private yachts as well as ocean liners.

73. Glenway Wescott to CI, December 25, 1948, CI 2655.
74. Peter Watson to Waldemar Hansen, October 27, 1948, quoted in Michael Shelden, *Friends of Promise* (1989; repr. Faber and Faber, 2009), p. 181. The letter continues, "Later I found he joined the Hitler Jugend in Germany and was a boy friend of Richthofen." This would have been the Prussian WWI flying ace, Wolfram Freiherr von Richthofen, who was later the youngest field marshal in Hitler's army, and who was a cousin of the more skilled WWI flying ace, Manfred von Richthofen, known as the Red Baron. Glenway Wescott recalled that Fouts "got chucked into a Nazi concentration camp, and obscurely escaped, which appealed to people's imaginations." (*Continual Lessons: The Journals of Glenway Wescott 1937–1955*, ed. Robert Phelps with Jerry Roscoe, New York: HarperCollins, 1990, p. 59) Brian Howard and the poet and artist David Gascoyne believed these stories (see Gascoyne, *Collected Journals, 1936–1942*, London: Skoob, 1991, pp. 238–9), but nowhere does CI record anything about Fouts in Germany. Were the stories partly fantasy? Fouts had long been fascinated by German military might as embodied in the von Richthofens. In 1925, Baron von Richthofen's remains were moved from France to Germany and reburied with extraordinary military honors, and Fouts—then only twelve years old—had followed the coverage and participated in a *Time* letters column debate about "the puerile squeamishness of most Americans," as one Karl Busch had written, and the supposed strength of Germans. (*Time*, June 7, 1926, p. 2) In his letter, the adolescent, tender-hearted Fouts protested the cruelty of a German film director who had forced two horses off a cliff "for the sake of making moving pictures of their agony." (*Time*, June 21, 1926, p. 2)
75. Peter Watson to Waldemar Hansen, October 27, 1948, in Shelden, *Friends of Promise*, p. 181.
76. *D1*, November 7, 1940, p. 125.
77. *LY*, p. 7, note 1.
78. "Paul," *DTV*, p. 236.
79. *The Razor's Edge*, Part 7, Chap. 6, pp. 340–1.
80. "A Writer and Religion," *IonW*, pp. 114, 118–19; CI to TW, June 10, 1943, HRC.
81. Lecture 4, "What Is the Nerve of Interest in the Novel," *IonW*, p. 76; CI had established this view of the novel in 1945, see CI to LK, February 16, 1945, HM 81687, Huntington.
82. As quoted by CI, "A Writer and Religion," *IonW*, p. 120; "The Problem of the Religious Novel," *Exh.*, pp. 117–18; "A Writer and Religion," *IonW*, p. 121.
83. Project Gutenberg, trans. by Louise and Aylmer Maude, Chap. 8; "A Writer and Religion," *IonW*, p. 129.
84. "A Writer and Religion," *IonW*, p. 123; "What Is the Nerve of Interest in the Novel," *IonW*, pp. 65, 82–3.
85. CI Intro. to "The Speckled Band," *Exh.*, pp. 88–9. The Conan Doyle Estate refused permission for CI to include "The Speckled Band" in *GESS* because they didn't like CI's ahead-of-trend suggestion that Holmes was comical or ridiculous. Holmes and Moriarty wrestling on the ledge above Reichenbach Falls is depicted in an illustration by Sydney Paget. By popular demand, Conan Doyle brought Holmes back to life after the fall.
86. "What Is the Nerve of Interest in the Novel," *IonW*, p. 83.
87. "What Is the Nerve of Interest in the Novel," *IonW*, p. 65; Taittiriya Upanishad, 3.6.1; see also *R&HD*, Chap. 9, p. 103.
88. "Paul," *DTV*, p. 239; "Dr. Lanyon's Narrative," *Strange Case of Dr. Jekyll and Mr. Hyde* (1886; Project Gutenberg). See also "Henry Jekyll's Full Statement of the Case."
89. "Paul," *DTV*, pp. 237–8; "What Is the Nerve of Interest in the Novel," *IonW*, pp. 80, 80–1; *GESS*, p. 206.
90. "Paul," *DTV*, pp. 192, 195, 205–6.
91. *D1*, May 18, 1960, p. 856. CI met Monroe mostly at the Selznicks' and Frank Taylor's; one night, he and DB sat up talking and drinking with Monroe, Arthur Miller, and Simone Signoret at the Beverly Hills Hotel. (DB telephone conversation with Bucknell, October 25, 2020)
92. "A Writer and Religion," *IonW*, p. 121.

93. *D1*, bridging passage, June 1941, pp. 155, 154.
94. "Paul," *DTV*, pp. 249, 265–6, 295, 247.
95. Work journal, June 9, 1960, p. 121, CI 1158.
96. "The Writer and Vedanta," November 11, 1961, *Wishing Tree*, pp. 162–3.
97. *R&HD*, Chap. 8, p. 94.
98. *D3*, July 9, 1972, p. 243. Bower—under the pseudonym Antony Bourne—had joined the public attack on CI, Huxley, and Heard during the war; he labeled them "the mystic axis" in *Horizon*, emphasizing their disagreements and mocking SP's English. (See Antony Bourne, "Where Shall John Go? III—USA," *Horizon*, January 1944, pp. 13–23, and Bill Roehrick's reply, defending SP as "one of the greatest living mystics"—"Where Shall John Go" pp. 204–7)
99. Goodwin to CI, quoted in *LY*, pp. 172–3, note 2.
100. "Paul," *DTV*, p. 317.
101. *Lafcadio's Adventures*, trans. Dorothy Bussy (New York: Alfred Knopf, 1925; repr. 1927), Book II, Chap. 6, p. 86.
102. *D2*, January 24, February 6, 1961, pp. 45, 46.
103. DB conversation with Bucknell, April 19, 2018.
104. *D2*, February 13, April 2, 1961, pp. 47, 57.
105. *D2*, February 28, 1951, p. 51.
106. *D2*, March 19, 23, 1961, pp. 54; *Animals*, pp. 69, 70.
107. *D2*, April 13, 1961, p. 58; DB to CI, March 13, 1961, *Animals*, p. 63; *D2*, April 16, 1961, p. 60.
108. *D2*, May 15, 1962, p. 65.
109. *D2*, June 9, 6, 10, 1961, pp. 69, 66, 71.
110. *D2*, June 10, July 14, 1961, pp. 70, 84.
111. *D1*, May 21, 1959, p. 814; CI interview with Denis Hart, "Here on a Visit," *Guardian*, September 22, 1961, p. 11
112. WHA to CI, March 4, 1960, CI 3017.
113. WHA to CI, March 10, 1960, CI 3018; *D2*, June 15, 1961, p. 72; WHA to CI, August 8, 1961, CI 3020; WHA and Chester Kallman, "Genesis of a Libretto," repr. *Libretti, 1939–1973, The Complete Works of W.H. Auden*, ed. Edward Mendelson (Princeton University Press, 1993), p. 246; W.B. Yeats, "The Choice," *The Winding Stair and Other Poems* (1933).
114. *D2*, July 4, 1961, p. 78; DB telephone conversation with Bucknell, March 18, 2019; *D2*, July 9, 1961, p. 80; *D2*, June 25, 1961, p. 77; Truman Capote to Andrew Lyndon, July 4, 1961, New York Public Library, quoted in *Too Brief a Treat*, ed. Gerald Clark (New York: Random House, 2004; Vintage, 2005), p. 321.
115. *D2*, June 20, July 4, 22, June 15, 1961, pp. 75, 78, 87, 72.
116. *D2*, August 10, September 29, 1961, pp. 100, 117.
117. *D2*, July 27, 28, October 19, 1961, pp. 89, 90, 92, 93, 124.
118. *D2*, July 28, 1961, p. 91.
119. *D2*, September 6, 7, 8, 15, 1961, added to the diary on September 18, after CI returned to London, pp. 108, 109, 110, 112–13.
120. *D2*, August 4, 1961, p. 96; see also August 8, 1961, p. 98.
121. *D2*, October 6, 1961, p. 119.
122. *D1*, October 12, 1956, pp. 652–3.
123. Miller was another admirer of Ramakrishna, Vivekananda, and SP. In *The Air-Conditioned Nightmare*, his 1945 collection about exploring America by car, Miller wrote that the outstanding experience of the journey was "the reading of Romain Rolland's two volumes on Ramakrishna and Vivekananda." He added, "The most masterful individual, the only person I met whom I could truly call 'a great soul,' was a quiet Hindu swami in Hollywood." (New Directions Paperback, 1970, p. 18) The teachings of Ramakrishna, Vivekananda, and SP (not named) form a counterpoint to the war and to Miller's disillusion with the U.S.
124. Colin Wilson, *The Outsider* (London: Victor Gollancz, 1956; Pan, 1963), Chap. 2, p. 48; *D2*, October 29, 1961, p. 128.
125. *D2*, November 5, 1961, p. 132.

126. D2, November 8, 1961, p. 134.
127. D2, November 12, 1961, pp. 134–5; CI to DB, November 27, 1961, *Animals*, p. 110; CI 100; *SM*, pp. 105, 109, 170, 154, 155.
128. DB to CI, December 11, 1961, *Animals*, p. 113; D2, December 9, 1961, p. 143.
129. Rasponi quoted by DB to CI, November 6, 1961, *Animals*, p. 96; DB to CI, November 25, 1961, *Animals*, p. 108.
130. D2, December 16, 1961, January 2, 6, 12, 23, 24, 28, 1962, pp. 146, 147, 152, 153, 154, 156. Warhol had drawn shoe advertisements for fashion magazines in the 1950s, and his early portraits often showed only hands or feet.
131. D2, January 23, 28, 28, 1962, pp. 156, 157–8.
132. D2, February 12, 23, March 25, 1962, pp. 158–9, 168, 170.
133. D2, February 14, 1962, p. 160; DB to CI, February 5, 1962, *Animals*, p. 118; D2, February 12, 1962, p. 160; WHA quoted in D2, February 14, 1962, p. 166; LK to CI, February 13, 1962, CI 1597; Coulette (a model for Grant Lefanu in *ASM*) quoted in D2, February 14, 1962, p. 166; D2, March 5, 1961, p. 170.
134. Sykes, "Compulsively Detached," *New York Times*, March 18, 1962, p. 4; Peden, "Odyssey to Inner Beings," *Saturday Review*, March 24, 1962, pp. 25–6; D2, March 25, 1962, p. 171. The *Time* review, "Dilettante of the Depths," appeared March 23, 1962.
135. Mitgang, *Books of the Times*, March 23, 1962, p. 31; Gouverneur Paulding, "Journey to Many Places—and to Nowhere," *New York Herald Tribune*, March 11, 1962, "Books," p. 14; D2, March 18, 1962, p. 170. Some provincial reviewers were repulsed by "the increasingly nauseating reek of homosexuality," as the reviewer for the *Oxford Times* called it. (C.H.H. "Descent to the Depths," *Oxford Times*, March 23, 1962)
136. "The Inferno of Herr Issyvoo," *Sunday Times*, March 11, 1962, magazine section, p. 33.
137. Shrapnel, "Hell Is Where the Heart Is," *Manchester Guardian*, March 9, 1962, p. 7; Mayne, "Herr Issyvoo Changes Trains," *New Statesman*, March 9, 1962, p. 337.
138. Wilson, "Views of the Damned," *Observer*, March 4, 1962; SS, "Isherwood's Heroes," *New Republic*, April 16, 1962, p. 25.
139. EMF to CI, March 25, 1962; CI to EMF, April 6, 1962, *F&I*, pp. 160–1, 161–2.
140. Amis, "A Bit Glassy," *Spectator*, March 9, 1962, p. 309.
141. D2, March 28, April 19, 1962, pp. 172, 179. K.W. Gransden's positive but dull March 9 review in the *Times Literary Supplement* triggered two vicious attacks in the Letters column. J. W. Quinton savaged CI's handling of the Munich agreement, his pacifism, and his dislike of authority (April 6, 1962); Storm Jameson accused CI of sentimentality, pseudo-mysticism, and puerile sexual attitudes (April 13, 1962). The *Hudson Review* (Summer 1962) was positive. Dachine Rainer in *Anarchy* (August) was very positive. *Ramparts* (September) was negative, attacking CI for not being a real leftist. *Commentary* (October) was mixed; *Encounter* (November) quite positive. The Mid-Century Book Society made the novel a July 1962 selection.
142. D2, April 7, 1962, p. 175; CI to DB, March 18, 1961, *Animals*, p. 66.
143. D2, April 7, 8, 11, 1962, pp. 176, 177.
144. D2, April 16, 1962, p. 178.
145. D2, April 30, 1962, p. 184.
146. D2, March 25, 1962, p. 171; work journal, March 25, 1962, p. 131, CI 1158.
147. "The secret title of this novel is Une Vie," CI wrote in his work journal, March 25, 1962, CI 1158. He had been reading Willa Cather—*My Mortal Enemy*, *A Lost Lady*, *The Song of the Lark*, *The Professor's House*—and thought of writing a "simple story about a character, a single person and her life. It's a sort of tradition that goes back to Turgenev and Maupassant, at least the story called *Une Vie*." ("The Autobiography of My Books," "*Down There on a Visit*, *A Single Man*," May 18, 1965, *IonW*, p. 227)
148. Work journal, March 25, 1962, p. 131, CI 1158.
149. CI liked and admired Tree's screenwriter son, Ivan Moffat, for his intelligence and talent and his glamorous girlfriends, and he identified with him as a romantic adventurer. As CI was germinating *The Englishwoman*, Moffat and his second wife, Kate Smith, were thinking about returning to Europe like Tree. "He feels Hollywood is done for," CI recorded in his diary. "And indeed America, too." (D2, April 8, 1962, p. 177)
150. D2, February 12, 1962, p. 162.

151. CI to Roger Klein at Harper & Row, August 20, 1963, Butler.
152. Andersen, *Stories and Tales*, trans. H.W. Dulcken (London, 1864), p. 293. CI had used the tale to frame the story of the communist couple Gerda and Peter Mannheim in *WE*, and the name of the heroine, Gerda, for his own character.
153. Work journal, March 27, September 19, 1962, pp. 132–3, CI 1158; *D2*, May 9, 1962, p. 186.
154. *D2*, October 28, 1961, p. 126.
155. *D2*, August 22, 26, 26, 1962, pp. 217, 219.
156. *D2*, September 18, 1962, p. 223; work journal, September 19, 1962, p. 134, CI 1158.
157. Work journal, September 19, 1962, p. 134, CI 1158; *PV*, p. 123.
158. Work journal, September 19, 24, 1962, p. 134, CI 1158.
159. *D1*, June 13, 16, 1959, p. 816.
160. "Afterwards," p. 1, CI 1015.
161. *SM*, p. 27.
162. "Afterwards," p. 52, CI 1015.
163. Work journal, November 27, p. 135, CI 1158.
164. Work journal, November 27, p. 135, CI 1158; "Afterwards," pp. 52–3, CI 1015.
165. *D1*, August 7, 1959, p. 822; EMF to CI, *F&I*, p. 159.
166. "Two Brothers," autograph fair copy, CI 1067.
167. *SM*, p. 13.
168. *SM*, p. 182.
169. *SM*, p. 163, cf. "the wave of love" that engulfs Elizabeth Rydal and Stephen Monk in *WE* (Part II, Chap. 4, pp. 127–8) and which suggests the feelings that swept CI away in the early months of his relationship with DB.
170. *D2*, June 2, 1962, p. 194.
171. Swami Vivekananda, "The Real Nature of Man," in *Jnana Yoga, The Complete Works of Swami Vivekananda*, Vol. 2 (Calcutta: Advaita Ashrama), *D2*, May 4, 1962, p. 185; *D2*, June 7, July 10, 1962, pp. 195, 205.
172. *D2*, July 10, 1962, p. 206.
173. *D2*, June 25, July 2, 1962, pp. 200, 204.
174. *D2*, August 7, 15, 26, 1962, pp. 212, 215, 219.
175. *D2*, September 18, 1962, p. 222; Seldis, "In the Galleries: Portrait Artist's Display Star-Studded," *Los Angeles Times*, September 21, 1962, Part IV, p. 7.
176. John Zeigel phoned to say that his lover had been killed in a car crash, resonating freakishly with what CI was already writing; *D2*, November 29, 1962, p. 246.
177. Work journal, November 27, 1962, pp. 135, 135–6, CI 1158; *The Diary of Virginia Woolf, Volume 5, 1936–1941*, February 21, 1937, p. 59.
178. Work journal, November 27, 1962, p. 139, CI 1158; Woolf, *Mrs. Dalloway* (London: Hogarth Press, 1925; Harvest, 1953); p. 250; *D2*, November 29, 1962, p. 246.
179. Work journal, November 27, 1962, p. 136, CI 1158; *D2*, October 28, 1962, p. 235.
180. Georg Groddeck, *The Book of the It*, trans. V.M.E. Collins (1923; New American Library, Mentor Book, 1961), Letter II, pp. 18, 19, Letter XXXI, pp. 225, 227.
181. "*Tat tvam asi*," *The Book of the It*, Letter XIII, p. 103. CI saw a distinction between the It and the Atman, noting that he could not call his new novel *It Is Alone*: "It couldn't be It, I said to myself because It is the Atman." (*D2*, November 11, 1963, p. 296); *The Book of the It*, Letter II, p. 20; *SM*, pp. 183–4; see also CI to EMF, November 27, 1943, *F&I*, p. 116.
182. *The Book of the It*, Letter XXX, p. 224; *SM*, pp. 10, 180.
183. "To Help Along the Line: An Interview with Christopher Isherwood," Sarah Smith and Marcus Smith, *New Orleans Review*, Vol. 4, No. 4 (1975), pp. 307–10, repr., *Conversations*, see p. 138.
184. *Man's Presumptuous Brain: An Evolutionary Interpretation of Psychosomatic Disease* (London: Longman, Green & Co., 1960), p. 35; *SM*, pp. 9, 13, 185–6.
185. *D2*, October 28, 1962, p. 235.
186. *The Englishman*, p. 23, CI 1061.
187. *D2*, June 27, 23, August 26, November 16, 30, 1962, pp. 202, 200, 218, 247.
188. *D2*, December 20, 1962, p. 252.
189. *D2*, December 26, 1962, p. 253.

190. DB conversation with Bucknell, April 26, 2008; *D2*, January 3, 1963, p. 256.
191. *D2*, January 8, 1963, p. 257.
192. *D2*, December 4, 1962, January 21, February 9, 1963, pp. 248, 260, 265.
193. Work journal, February 3, 1963, p. 136, CI 1158.
194. DB conversation with Bucknell, *c.*2013, with his portraits of Bill Brown; CI to DB, March 11, 1963, *Animals*, p. 127; *D2*, March 6, 1963, p. 269.
195. CI to DB, March 11, 1963, *Animals*, pp. 125–6.
196. CI to DB, March 11, 1963, *Animals*, p. 126; *D2*, March 20, 1963, p. 269.
197. *D2*, April 14, 1963, p. 273.
198. Intro., Cecil Beaton, *Images* (London: Weidenfeld & Nicolson, 1963), excerpted in *Vogue*, September 1963, pp. 207–10.
199. DB to CI, April 30, 1968, *Animals*, p. 133; CI to DB, May 1, 1963, *Animals*, p. 134; *D2*, May 3, 1963, p. 274.
200. *D2*, May 3, 10, 1963, pp. 274–5.
201. *D2*, May 10, 1963, pp. 275, 276; CI to DB, May 10, 1963, *Animals*, p. 136; *D2*, May 10, 1963, p. 277.
202. CI to DB, May 18, 1963, *Animals*, p. 137; *D2*, May 18, 1963, pp. 276, 277.
203. *D2*, June 2, 6, 1963, p. 277.
204. *D2*, August 2, 16, 1963, pp. 283, 285.
205. *D2*, August 9, 1963, p. 284.
206. *D2*, August 20, 1963, p. 286; *D1*, March 22, 1956, pp. 596–7.
207. *D2*, September 19, November 1, 11, 1963, pp. 289, 293, 296.
208. *D2*, August 2, September 19, 1963, pp. 289, 283.
209. EU to CI, August 4, 1963, CI 2510; EU to CI, August 17, 1963, CI 2512.
210. GV to CI, n.d., Edgewater, Barrytown, NY, CI 2622; GV to CI, May 1962, CI 2620.
211. CI to GV, August 30, 1960, Houghton; CI to GV, October 22, 1964, Houghton.
212. Work journal, October 8, 1963, p. 137, CI 1158; *SM*, p. 145.
213. CI to GV, August 12, 1967, Houghton; CI to GV, August 21, 1967, Houghton.
214. *D2*, September 19, 26, October 31, 1963, pp. 289, 290, 291.
215. *D2*, November 5, April 1, 1963, pp. 294, 271.
216. *SM*, p. 57.
217. *SM*, pp. 70, 71–2, 71.
218. *D2*, November 30, 1963, pp. 297, 298.
219. *D2*, December 16, 1963, p. 299.
220. *D2*, December 22, 28, 26, 1963, pp. 303, 313, 311. CI carried a pocket diary and incorporated his notes into his main diary when he got home.
221. *MG&HD*, Chap. 17, p. 269.
222. *D2*, December 24, 25, 28, 1963, pp. 306, 309, 313.
223. *D2*, December 29, 1963, p. 315; *MG&HD*, Chap. 17, p. 271.
224. *D2*, January 3, 1964, December 31, 1963, January 1, 1964, pp. 327, 319, 320.
225. *MG&HD*, Chap. 17, p. 274, Chap. 13, pp. 196, 196–7; *D2*, January 1, 1964, p. 322.
226. *D2*, January 2, 1964, p. 325.
227. *D2*, January 3, 1964, p. 327; CI to EMF, December 13, 1963, *F&I*, p. 163.
228. CI reported on the health of the two American monks as he reported on his own health and SP's; sannyas couldn't be administered to anyone unwell. Critchfield fell ill, though he recovered just in time for the ceremony. Yale, on the other hand, remained well; he had, for the time being, complete control over his "It." "The greatest possible demonstration of India-love is not to get sick here," wrote CI. (*D2*, December 25, 1963, p. 308) In the religious life, everything had symbolic power, and CI was a master decoder. The continual struggle for the upper hand among the monks reflected the continual struggle within each monk to gain mastery of himself—to repress, to sublimate, to renounce. The spiritual life was intensely competitive, too, as CI recorded with grudging excitement.
229. *D2*, January 5, 6, 1964, p. 329.
230. *D2*, January 7, 1964, p. 331–2.
231. *MG&HD*, Chap. 18, p. 285.
232. *D2*, March 13, 1964, p. 337; *LY*, pp. 175–6, note 1.

233. *D2*, March 29, 1964, p. 338.
234. *D2*, September 7, 1964, p. 341; DB conversation with Bucknell, January 20, 2013.
235. DB conversation with Bucknell, January 20, 2013; CI 65.
236. *D2*, September 7, 1964, p. 341, and see Tony Richardson, *The Long-Distance Runner: A Memoir* (London: Faber and Faber, 1993), p. 202.
237. *D2*, October 28, 1964, p. 344; CI to DB, October 14, 1966, *Animals*, pp. 225–6; Richardson, *The Long-Distance Runner*, p. 65; *D2*, January 1, 1967, p. 437.
238. *D2*, March 13, May 26, 1964, pp. 337, 339.
239. DB to CI, June 16, 1964, *Animals*, p. 153, and DB conversation with Bucknell, April 29, 2019.
240. *D2*, September 26, 1964, p. 343.
241. *D2*, October 30, 1964, p. 346.
242. *D2*, November 23, 1964, p. 349.
243. WHA to CI, February 5, 1964, telegram, CI 3026; *D2*, February 11, 1964, p. 335; see also WHA to CI, "Monday," CI 3029, and WHA to CI, n.d., CI 3030.
244. *D2*, March 6, 1967, p. 443.
245. *D2*, March 15, 1964, p. 338; Truman Capote to CI, June 18, 1964, CI 666; SS wrote it was Isherwood's "best book since *Goodbye to Berlin*"—but not better than, SS to CI, July 8, 1964, CI 2181, and see also SS to CI, January 27, 1964, CI 2178; JL to CI, May 17, 1964: "You're funny in a new way, a sour, sardonic, merciless way, and it seems to me just to suit the person you've become." (CI 1642)
246. Bill Jones to CI, February 27, 1964, CI 1530; Paul Cadmus to CI, October 19, 1964, CI 664; Erika Mann to CI, February 3, 1965, CI 1771; John Rechy to CI, December 23, 1971, CI 1936.
247. Pryce-Jones, "Masterful Use of a Close-Up Lens," Book Week, *New York Herald Tribune*, August 30, 1964, p. 5; Hardwick, "Sex and the Single Man," *New York Review of Books*, August 20, 1964, p. 4; Daiches, "Life Without Jim," *New York Times*, August 30, 1964, p.16; *Time*, September 4, 1964, p. 76; Burgess, "Why, This Is Hell," *Listener*, October 1, 1964. Burgess later included *SM* in his influential *Ninety-Nine Novels: The Best in English Since 1939—A Personal Choice* (Allison & Busby, 1984). See also Stanley Kauffmann, "Death in Venice, Cal.," *New Republic*, September 5, 1964; Emile Capouya, "Twilight Man with Sorrow," *Saturday Review*, September 5, 1964; Thomas Hinde, "George and Jim," *Times Literary Supplement*, September 10, 1964; Norman Shrapnel, "Suffering Without Self-pity," *Guardian*, September 11, 1964; Francis Hope, "Promising Youngster," *Observer*, September 13, 1964; Michael Ratcliffe, "Down There for Good," *Sunday Times*, September 13, 1964.
248. *D2*, November 23, 1964, p. 349.

9: THE ANIMALS' GOLDEN AGE

1. *D2*, January 7, 1965, p. 350; DB to CI, January 12, 1965, *Animals*, p. 163; DB to CI, March 3, 1965, *Animals*, p. 182.
2. *D2*, February 7, 1965, p. 352.
3. CI to LK, November 21, 1959, HM 81723, Huntington.
4. *D2*, February 14, 22, 1965, pp. 354, 355.
5. *D2*, February 14, 1965, p. 354; "How I Began A Meeting by the River," CI 1096.
6. *D2*, March 20, 1965, p. 358; "How I Began a Meeting by the River," CI 1096.
7. "Take It or Leave It" and "R.L.S." *Exh.*, pp. 235, 52–3. CI had commemorated her by using the surname Drummond for Stephen Monk's abandoned male lover in *WE*.
8. *D2*, December 22, 1963, pp. 303–4; Thornton Wilder, Foreword, *The Ides of March* (New York: Harper & Bros, 1948); CI to JL, April 7, 1949, Beinecke.
9. CI to DB, January 26, 1964, *Animals*, p. 140.
10. *D2*, March 20, April 2, 1965, pp. 359, 360.
11. DB to CI, May 27, 1965, *Animals*, p. 195; DB to CI, June 2, 1965, *Animals*, pp. 197–8.
12. DB to CI, June 17, 1965, *Animals*, pp. 203–4.
13. *D2*, June 22, 1965, p. 367; "July 29, 1965, A MEETING BY THE RIVER: Notes made for revision of first draft, after talking with Vidya, etc.," CI 1097.

14. D2, July 24, 27, 24 1965, pp. 371, 372, 371.
15. "July 29, 1965, A MEETING BY THE RIVER," CI 1097.
16. D2, August 10, 1965, p. 373.
17. DH conversation with Bucknell, c.2010.
18. DH, September 2010, quoted in Christopher Simon Sykes, *Hockney: The Biography, A Rake's Progress, Volume I, 1937–1975* (London: Century, 2011), p. 159.
19. See Sykes, *Hockney: The Biography*, pp. 163, 165.
20. D2, October 2, 1965, p. 376.
21. D2, October 22, 1965, pp. 376, 377.
22. D2, October 25, 1965, pp. 377–8; D2, September 1, 1966, p. 406.
23. D2, November 1, 1965, p. 378.
24. D2, November 14, 1965, p. 380.
25. D2, December 21, 1965, p. 385.
26. D2, November 18, 1965, p. 381.
27. D2, December 1, 1965, p. 383; D2, January 4, 1966, p. 386.
28. D2, April 17, 1966, pp. 392–3; *The Spirit of Zen*, p. 69; CI to LK, February 16, 1945, HM 81687, Huntington.
29. *MBR*, Chap. 9, p. 190.
30. EMF, *A Passage to India* (London and New York: Edward Arnold & Co., Harcourt Brace & Co., 1924), Part III, Chap. 32, pp. 284–5, 285, 287–8.
31. EU, "Imaginary Diary of a Poet" BL.
32. D2, May 31, 1966, p. 395; CI to DB, June 21, 1965, *Animals*, p. 205.
33. "Personality Cult," *Hindustan Standard*, Sunday magazine, July 4, 1965, p. 2; "Our Man in Nirvana," *Statesman*, Sunday magazine, June 13, 1965, p. 2; "Those Who Made Him Their Pattern to Live and Die," *Amrita Bazar Patrika*, Sunday magazine, July 11, 1965, p. 3; "Religion and Social Service," *Times of India*, Sunday Edition, June 13, 1965, p. 11.
34. *R&HD*, p. 1; "An elephant is true because it exists," Jung had stated when establishing the existence of the idea of the Virgin Birth: "It is a phenomenon." (C.G. Jung, "The Autonomy of the Unconscious Mind," 1937 Terry Lectures at Yale, published as *Psychology and Religion*, Yale University Press, 1938, Chap. 1, p. 3); and see, for instance, Stanton Coblentz, "Mysticism of a Hindu," *Los Angeles Times*, June 20, 1965, B, p. 27; "he was a phenomenon of a type not often encountered."
35. Watts, "One for All, All for One," *San Francisco Examiner*, July 4, 1965, p. 141; Nancy Wilson Ross, *New York Times Book Review*, November 14, 1965, pp. 22, 24.
36. Muggeridge, "Swamis Go West," *Observer*, April 11, 1965; Mortimer, "Krishnapher's Phenomenon," *Sunday Times*, April 18, 1965, p. 27. CI acknowledged debts above others to *The Gospel of Sri Ramakrishna* by M (Mahendar Nath Gupta) and *Sri Ramakrishna the Great Master* by Swami Saradananda (*R&HD*, p. 1). Kermode, "The Old Amalaki," *New York Review of Books*, June 17, 1965; repr., *Continuities* (1968) see pp. 53, 55. Kermode's review was so savage that Gavin Lambert wrote a letter to the editors saying that assigning books to unsympathetic reviewers was part of a campaign to slap down homosexual writers and to "Get Isherwood" for being a homosexual and a Hindu. Smith, *Listener*, April 22, 1965, pp. 607–8.
37. Frank Littler, *Chicago Tribune*, "Books Today," May 30, 1965, p. 134; John Douglas Pringle, "God-intoxicated 'Indian Saint,'" *Sydney Morning Herald*, July 17, 1965, p. 15; see also *Chicago Tribune*, May 30, 1965, p. 134; "Holy Casebook," *The Times*, May 13, 1965, p. 15; Ross, *New York Times Book Review*, November 14, 1965, pp. 22, 24.
38. Watts, "One for All, All for One," *San Francisco Examiner*, "Book Week," July 4, 1965, p. 3.
39. D2, June 4, 1966, p. 396.
40. D3, May 18, 1971, pp. 170–1.
41. D2, July 18, 1966, p. 401; D2, December 17, 1968, January 8, 1969, pp. 534, 536.
42. D2, October 8, 14, 1966, pp. 413, 415.
43. *Hero-Father, Demon-Mother*, pp. 8–9, CI 1082.
44. *Hero-Father, Demon-Mother*, p. 7, CI 1082.
45. CI to DB, October 24, 1966, *Animals*, p. 241.
46. D2, October 29, 1966, p. 421.

47. *D2*, November 23, 1966, p. 423.
48. *D2*, November 30, 23, 1966, pp. 425, 424.
49. *D2*, November 30, 1966, p. 425; typed on the back of draft pages for *K&F* and dated December 2, 1966, CI 1082.
50. D.J. Bartel, "Interview with Christopher Isherwood," August 26, 1979, *Gramercy Review*, Double Issue, Vol. III, No. 4/Vol. IV, No. 1, Autumn 1979/Winter 1980, p. 3.
51. *Hero-Father, Demon-Mother*, p. 70, CI 1082.
52. AP conversations with Bucknell, 2017–18. "Lulu, she had explained, was based on her grandmother, an innocent young woman who exerted overpowering attraction for men—a fact which caused Wedekind enormous jealousy. The play dealt with the fantasies invented about her by her admirers." (In fact, it was Kadidja's mother.)
53. *D2*, January 22, May 2, 1967, pp. 441, 446.
54. Day-to-day diary, July 12, 1965; Jung, "Prologue," *Memories, Dreams, Reflections*," p. 3.
55. *D2*, January 21, September 25, October 21, 1967, pp. 439, 440, 474, 476.
56. *D2*, February 13, 1967, p. 442.
57. *D2*, April 7, June 22, 15, 1967, pp. 445, 452, 448.
58. *D2*, June 15, 1967, p. 447; CI to DB, June 2, 1967, *Animals*, p. 271; AP, *Page by Page*, unpublished memoir; AP conversations with Bucknell, 2017–18.
59. CI to DB, June 1, 1967, *Animals*, p. 270; Baldick, *Daily Telegraph*, June 1, 1967, p. 21; Paul Barker, "The Way Up and the Way Down," *The Times*, June 1, 1967, p. 7, compared it to *Les Liaisons Dangereuses*, also an epistolary novel, which CI indeed greatly admired; Peter Grosvenor called it "skilful and humorous," *Daily Express*, June 1, 1967, p. 9; John Wain, "The Other-Worldly Eye," *Observer*, June 4, 1967, p. 23, agreed: "the relationship between the brothers does draw to a real crisis in which both their lives undergo a change."
60. Kauffman, "Passages to India," *New Republic*, April 15, 1967, p. 22; Wordsworth, "The Swami and the Publisher," *Guardian*, June 2, 1967, p. 2.
61. Sykes, "Tom Spilled the Beans," *New York Times Book Review*, June 25, 1967, p. 103; John Gross, an Englishman writing for the *New York Review of Books*, objected that "the underlying religious assumptions are insufficiently dramatized," "A Question of Upbringing," May 18, 1967; Derwent May in the *Listener* liked the "brilliantly complicated clash" between the brothers, but missed the atmosphere of the Ganges and the monastery that CI had elected to leave out, "Fiction: Self-Deceivers Ever," June 22, 1967, p. 829. Some reviewers admitted their relief that the novel did not try to convert, among them Stanley Kauffmann in the *New Republic*. For *Time*, see "Brothers and Others," April 21, 1967, p. 71.
62. *D2*, July 19, 1967, p. 457; *D3*, August 5, 1972, p. 262; *D2*, August 8, 1967, pp. 461–2.
63. *D2*, July 8, 11, 1967, pp. 454, 455.
64. *D2*, August 29, November 25, 1967, pp. 465, 486.
65. Stromberg couldn't assemble his cast, so the Dickens project never happened; "Selections from the Bhagavad Gita," Caedmon Records TC 1249; CI had agreed to speak in WHA's place at the American Academy, but gave the speech to Glenway Wescott to deliver.
66. *D2*, April 1, 1968, pp. 502, 501.
67. DH to DB, April 4, 1968, CI 4361.
68. "Christopher Isherwood at 824 3rd Street, Santa Monica," (1968), *72 Drawings by David Hockney* (London: Jonathan Cape, 1971), Drawing 41, and DH conversation with Bucknell, 2012; Schlesinger recalled that when DH sketched from life "he would ask you to pose," Schlesinger conversation with Bucknell, November 4, 2016; CI day-to-day diary, April 20, 1968.
69. *D2*, April 7, 22, 24, 1968, pp. 503, 509, 510.
70. DB to CI, April 23, 1968, *Animals*, p. 282; DB to CI, April 30, 1968, *Animals*, p. 283; *D2*, May 3, 1968, p. 512; DB to CI, May 2, 1968, *Animals*, p. 287.
71. AP, *Page by Page*.
72. *D2*, May 6, 1968, p. 512.
73. DB to CI, May 8, 1968, *Animals*, p. 290; *D2*, May 13, 18, 1968, pp. 513, 514.
74. *D2*, August 4, 1967, p. 461; May 18, 26, 1968, pp. 515, 517.

75. *D2*, April 1, 4, June 10, 1968, pp. 502, 503, 518.
76. *D2*, September 2, 1967, p. 469; September 2, 1968, p. 525; April 24, 1968, p. 510.
77. *D2*, July 5, August 9, 1968, pp. 520, 521.
78. *D2*, August 9, 1968, p. 520; August 31, 1967, p. 467.
79. *D2*, September 2, 1968, p. 524.
80. "First Draft of the Opening of Hero-Father," September 14, 1968, CI 1082; *D2*, September 14, 1968, p. 527.
81. "First Draft of the Opening of Hero-Father," September 14, 1968, CI 1082.
82. *D2*, October 16, 1968, p. 531.
83. *Man, Myth, and Magic: An Illustrated Encyclopaedia of the Supernatural*, ed. Richard Cavendish (Leeds: BPC Publishing Ltd, 1972), Issue 105, pp. 2930–5; published separately as CI, *Essentials of Vedanta* (Hollywood: Vedanta Press, 1969).
84. DB to CI, October 9, 1968; DB to CI, October 10, 1968; CI to DB, October 15, 1968; CI to DB, October 18, 1968; CI to DB, October 16, 1968, *Animals*, pp. 303, 306, 310, 324, 314.
85. DB to CI, October 11, 1968; CI to DB, October 15, 1968, *Animals*, pp. 309, 309–10.
86. CI to DB, "Tuesday (deep) Mourning", October 29, 1968, *Animals*, p. 353.
87. DB to CI, October 30, 1968, *Animals*, p. 356.
88. AP, *Page by Page*.
89. DB to AP, "Sunday" continued as "Thursday" [probably November 9 and 16, 1968]; DB to AP, December 9, 1968, possession of AP.
90. DB to AP, December 9, 1968; DB to AP, January 14, 1969, possession of AP.
91. *D2*, January 25, February 17, 1969, pp. 542, 544.
92. *D2*, February 21, 26, 28, 1969, pp. 544, 545, 547.
93. *D2*, February 17, 26, 1969, pp. 544, 546.
94. *D2*, March 19, 1969, p. 549. *Los Angeles Times* drama critic Dan Sullivan called the play "an illustrated lecture ... pleasant but not involving" and identified Batson as "a find," March 21, 1969, pp. 1, 20. A month later, Sullivan mentioned the play in the "Calendar," praising the acting under a headline "It May Be Preachy But It's Shaw," *Los Angeles Times*, April 20, 1969. Later notices in local papers were good. DB had a drawing of CI in the program alongside a Feliks Topolski drawing of Shaw.
95. *D2*, March 19, 6, 1969, pp. 549, 548.
96. *D2*, March 29, 1969, pp. 550, 551.
97. DB to AP, May 13, 1969, possession AP.
98. Quoted by Sykes in *Hockney: The Biography*, Vol. 1, p. 232. Foster's heirs sold it to a dealer, who sold it to a Texan billionaire; from the Texan it went to another dealer, and then to the Swiss financier Gilbert de Botton. When de Botton divorced his first wife, Jacqueline Burgauer, later Mrs. Mark Leland, she received the painting.
99. "Goodbye to Berlin: 100 Jahre Schwulenbewegung" ("100 Years of the Gay Movement"), at the Akademie der Künste from May 17 to August 17, 1997 in cooperation with the Schwules Museum, co-curated by Andreas Sternweiler (Schwules Museum) and Hans Gerhard Hannesen (AdK). The catalogue (nearly 400 pages, published by Verlag Rosa Winkel) had the Isherwood–Bachardy painting on the cover. Wolfgang Theis, co-founder with Sternweiler of the Schwules Museum, masterminded the inclusion of the Hockney painting in the exhibition.
100. *D2*, May 31, July 17, August 20, 1969, pp. 561, 570, 573.
101. *D2*, August 25, 28, 1969, pp. 578, 580.
102. *D2*, September 5, 1969, pp. 585–6; *D3*, November 26, 1970, p. 120.
103. *D2*, September 5, 1969, p. 588.
104. DB to CI, August 21, 1969, *Animals*, p. 409.
105. CI and DB, "I, Claudius," October 30, 1969, pp. 62, 66, CI 55.
106. AP, *Page by Page*.
107. CI to AP, September 27, 1969, possession AP; *D2*, December 24, 1969, p. 596; *D3*, March 12, 1969, March 21, April 1, 1970, pp. 18, 28, 39. In 1973, AP was in L.A. and tried to see DB and CI. "What he actually wants, as of now, is the German version of the Wedekind Lulu plays, edited by Wedekind's daughter. But I'm certain I sent the book back to him years ago." (*D3*, June 26, 1973, p. 373) CI's outline for the Lulu

plays is at the Huntington, CI 41, with his copy of Carl Richard Mueller's translation.
108. DB to AP, July 18, 1970, possession of AP.
109. *D2*, April 2, 1969, p. 552; DB to AP, May 13, 1969, possession AP.
110. Unsigned review in Henry J. Seldis and William Wilson's column, "Art Walk: A Critical Guide to the Galleries," *Los Angeles Times*, March 13, 1970, Part IV, p. 8; *D3*, June 21, 1970, p. 88.
111. *D3*, June 8, 15, April 28, 1970, pp. 84, 85, 73.
112. *D3*, March 25, 1970, p. 31; CI to DB, April 2, 1970, *Animals*, p. 424; *D3*, March 25, 1970, p. 32, note.
113. *D3*, March 28, 1970, p. 34.
114. *D3*, April 1, 29, 1970, pp. 38, 77.
115. *D3*, May 28, 30, 1970, pp. 80, 81; Hockney to CI, October 24, 1971, CI 986; Sykes, *Hockney: The Biography*, Vol. 1, pp. 249–50.
116. *D3*, May 31, 1970, p. 83. The Gay-In was May 30, 1970. *Close-Up*, an eight-part series, was broadcast in the KNBC News slot, 6:30 p.m., February 18–27, 1970. See "Wednesday's T.V. Programs," *Los Angeles Times*, February 18, 1970, p. 15. The hour-long special, *Out of the Shadows*, used footage from the series, including CI's interview, and was broadcast June 26, 1970; see *San Bernardino County Sun*, June 26, 1970, p. 14. The minister from the homosexual church was probably Troy Perry, but the TV footage has not been found.
117. "The Homosexuals," CBS, March 7, 1967; YouTube, my transcription.
118. *D3*, July 30, 1970, April 23, 1971, December 31, 1975, pp. 97, 162, 489; the *Advocate* piece appeared December 17, 1975.
119. *D3*, December 30, 1970, p. 129; *D2*, July 5, 12, 1969, pp. 566, 568.
120. *D2*, October 21, 1969, p. 592; *D3*, February 21, 1971, p. 147.
121. CI wrote the instructions in his diary on August 31, identified as the Gayatri mantra by Pravrajika Vrajaprana.
122. *D3*, September 1, 1970, p. 106.
123. *D3*, December 4, 1970, September 23, 1972, pp. 125, 282.
124. *D3*, October 22, 1972, June 14, 1973, September 23, 1972, pp. 287, 369, 282.
125. *D3*, September 11, 1970, p. 110.
126. *D3*, August 17, 1972, December 25, 1973, pp. 269, 412.
127. *D3*, December 6, 1973, p. 407. In February 1974, SP touched CI with the relics at vespers before the Ramakrishna puja: "I was quite overwhelmed and began to cry." In April, CI visited SP in his room where SP began to talk about Rama, the avatar of Vishnu and perfect model of humanity who was the hero of the Rāmāyana: "The whole room was filled with joy. Tears of joy ran down my cheeks. I forget everything he said." (*D3*, February 25, April 14, 1974, pp. 422, 431)
128. *D3*, April 22, 1973, June 16, August 23, 1974, pp. 354, 440, 448.
129. *D3*, February 11, 1974, p. 420.
130. *D3*, November 26, 1970, p. 119.
131. *D3*, September 18, 1970, pp. 111, 112.
132. *D3*, December 11, 1970, p. 126; DB conversation with Bucknell, August 18, 2019; *D3*, December 11, 1970, February 22, 1971, pp. 126, 149.
133. *D3*, December 28, 1970, pp. 128–9; *K&F*, Chap. 15, p. 380; *D3*, December 30, 1970, p. 129; *D2*, November 14, 1961, p. 137.
134. *D3*, January 13, 1971, p. 132; Arthur Bell, "Christopher Isherwood: No Parades," *New York Times Book Review*, March 25, 1973, p. 12. Evidently Bell taped the interview February 3, 1972, for the *Village Voice* and drew on it later for the *New York Times* piece. *D3*, July 27, 1971, p. 178. In his diary, CI tracked the legal situation for homosexuals as it developed in the U.S. from state to state, recording the changes in penal codes during the early 1970s. In 1975, he wrote out the names of every California state senator who voted against Assembly Bill 489 to remove criminal penalties for adultery, oral sex, and sodomy between consenting adults in California, even though it passed.
135. *D3*, July 6, 1973, p. 241, and see July 3, 1972, p. 239.
136. "Kathleen's account of her efforts to find out what happened to Frank," CI wrote, "nearly makes me cry whenever I read it." *D3*, July 23, 1970, p. 93.

137. *D3*, September 1, 1970, p. 108.
138. *D3*, September 20, 1970, February 1, 1971, April 9, 1975, September 13, 1978, pp. 112, 135, 476, 577.
139. The show with Ruscha opened at the Hansen-Fuller Gallery, December 1, 1970; Wilson, "'Drawings '71 at San Pedro Gallery," *Los Angeles Times*, March 22, 1971, Part IV, p. 14.
140. *D3*, June 3, February 10, 1971, pp. 175, 140.
141. *D3*, March 19, May 13, 1971, pp. 156, 166.
142. *D3*, July 12, 1972, p. 245.
143. *D3*, June 24, December 8, 1972, pp. 237–8, 294.
144. *D3*, December 3, 8, 1972, pp. 293, 294.
145. *D3*, December 25, 1973, pp. 412, xxi; DB conversation with Bucknell, 2007; *D3*, October 5, April 7, 1975, pp. 484, 474.
146. *D3*, September 23, 1971, p. 201.
147. *D3*, October 1, 1971, p. 202; Peter Schlesinger to CI and DB, postcard from Rhodes, Greece, CI 1953; *D3*, October 1, 1971, p. 203; Peter Schlesinger to CI and DB, from London, on stationery of Hotel Grande-Bretagne, Athens, crossed out, CI 1954. See also *D3*, October 21, 1971, pp. 206–7.
148. DH to CI and DB, October 24, 1971, CI 986.
149. DH to CI and DB, October 24, 1971, CI 986; *D3*, November 11, 1971, p. 210. Jack Larson told DH's biographer that DH blamed CI for the breakup and that he was "secretly angry with Isherwood for having advised him to give his younger lover his wings." (Sykes, *Hockney: The Biography*, Vol. 1, p. 263.) Larson may have wished to hurt DB and to tarnish CI's image after he was dead because, like GV, he was unhappy when CI's diaries were published with passages about himself and Bridges which he considered unflattering.
150. DH to CI and DB, October 24, 1971, CI 986.
151. C.P. Snow, "Family Figures," *Financial Times*, October 21, 1971, p. 34; *The Economist*, November 6, 1971, p. xiv; Fuller, "The Making of Herr Issyvoo," *Listener*, October 21, 1971, p. 545; Bayley, "The Author's Parents," *Guardian*, October 28, 1971, p. 9. See also Michael Ratcliffe in the *Sunday Times*, October 21, 1971, p. 12.
152. *D3*, October 27, 1971, p. 208; Wilson, "Issyvoo and His Parents," *Observer*, October 24, 1971, p. 36. Arthur Calder Marshall, *TLS*, October 22, 1971, p. 1338, was even duller.
153. Wilson, "Detached Retina," *Spectator*, November 27, 1971, pp. 767, 768. Jonathan Raban wrote in the *New Statesman*: "It is a book whose own meticulously impersonal narration contrives to tell, by implication, how a narrator—someone whose sole vocation is to watch and tell—may be born and become, in the end, his own hero." ("A Born Narrator," *New Statesman*, October 22, 1971, p. 546) Raban was also writing about himself. The Oscar-winning screenwriter Frederic Raphael, citing the climacteric of Sartre's existentialism, pointed out that heredity was currently unfashionable but appreciated the book's literary qualities against his own better judgment: "Curiously, this largely historical work restores one's confidence in the traditional novel, in the value of the particular." ("Familiar Faces" *Sunday Times*, October 24, 1971, p. 36)
154. *D3*, December 4, 1971, August 13, 1972, pp. 213, 267.
155. *New Yorker*, January 22, 1972, p. 100. The *Washington Post* ran C.P. Snow's piece as "'Kathleen and Frank': True-to-Life 'Forsyte Saga,'" January 22, 1972, B6; *New York Times Book Review* and *Life* magazine also hired British reviewers. Robert Kirsch made a curiously personal attack, praising CI's parents and the book but scolding CI as "the taunting, sarcastic, brittle person his writing has shown him to be." ("Writer Confronts His Past, Debunks Childhood Myths," "The Book Report," *Los Angeles Times*, January 18, 1972, Part IV, p. 3)
156. Blythe, "An Oblique Autobiography and a Lesson on How to Handle the Family Records," *New York Times Book Review*, January 23, 1972, pp. 3, 10. It was not just KBI who had inspired CI; WHA, reviewing for the *New York Review of Books*, pointed this out: "Of the two, Frank was the odd character." ("The Diary of a Diary," *New York Review of Books*, January 27, 1972)
157. *D3*, February 7, 1972, p. 221; Bell's interview, written up a year later in the *New York Times*, is the one in which CI expressed his wish that he had formally come out sooner.

158. CI quoted by Thomas Lask, "Isherwood Looks at an English Era," *New York Times*, February 25, 1972, p. 26.
159. CI quoted by Bell, "Christopher Isherwood: No Parades," *New York Times Book Review*, March 25, 1973, p. 14.
160. *D2*, January 15, 1969, p. 539; *D3*, January 3, August 17, 1970, pp. 3, 101.
161. *D3*, December 11, 1970, November 5, 1972, pp. 127, 289.
162. *D3*, March 29, 1973, February 25, 1974, pp. 350, 422.
163. "'River' Billed at the Mark Taper," *Los Angeles Times*, Calendar, April 23, 1972, p. 38; *D3*, April 30, 1972, p. 231; Dan Sullivan, "'Meeting by the River' for NTN," *Los Angeles Times*, May 3, 1972, Part IV, p. 17; Viola Hegyi Swisher, "In Los Angeles," *After Dark*, July 1972, p. 15. See also Sam Eisenstein, *Coast* (July) quoted in *D3*, July 9, 1973, p. 243.
164. *D3*, December 23, 1972, p. 298. Mike Montel directed the New Phoenix Theater Company using the staging devised by Bridges. Jerry Tallmer for the *New York Post* called the play "witty, intelligent, provocative drama [...] invigorating [...] with its overtones of E.M. Forster," ("One Saint in Two Acts," *New York Post*, December 19, 1972); Richard Shepard for the *New York Times* wrote "wordy" but "worth more work and refinement." ("Stage: A Series Begins," *New York Times*, December 20, 1972) Reviews quoted in *D3*, December 22, 1972, p. 296.
165. *D3*, August 19, 1971, pp. 192–3.
166. *D3*, November 23, 1972, p. 292; *D3*, p. 314, summary of the trip written after returning on February 15, 1973.
167. *D3*, summary, January 27, February 2, 1973, pp. 319, 324.
168. *D3*, summary, February 10, 1973, p. 335.
169. *D3*, summary, February 9, 1973, p. 333.
170. *D3*, summary, February 14, 1973, p. 341.
171. *D3*, August 14, 1973, pp. 380, 381; broadcast, Friday and Saturday, November 30 and December 1, 1973; Sam Irvin, *Little Shoppe of Horrors* magazine, #38, cites reviews from *Los Angeles Times*, *New York Daily News*, *Dallas Times Herald*, *Christian Science Monitor*, *San Diego Union*, *San Francisco Chronicle*, *Variety*, *Hollywood Reporter*, p. 103; see the *Advocate*, December 5, 1973, quoted in Irvin, *Little Shoppe of Horrors*, #38, p. 102; *D3*, June 16, 1974, p. 439.
172. *D3*, summary, February 7, September 14, 1973, pp. 329, 387.
173. *D3*, September 14, 25, 1973, pp. 387–8, 392–3.
174. The BBC telephoned CI "at a time when most of California was still asleep." Christopher Ford, "Christopher's Jungle Book, Christopher Isherwood Discusses His Autobiography with Christopher Ford," *Guardian*, March 30, 1977; the BBC tape, for *World at One*, does not survive.
175. *JW*, pp. 114, 128; *D3*, September 30, 1973, p. 393.
176. *D3*, October 9, 29, 1973, pp. 395, 398.
177. *L&S*, Chap. 7, p. 312; *D3*, October 29, 1973, p. 398.
178. *D3*, November 2, 6, 1973, pp. 400, 402.
179. *D3*, April 14, August 11, 1974, pp. 430, 447.
180. *D3*, July 30, August 31, October 14, 1974, pp. 446, 450, 458.
181. *D3*, April 8, 1975, pp. 476, 475.
182. *D3*, April 23, 1974, pp. 433, 432.
183. *D3*, August 7, 1972, p. 263.
184. EMF, *Aspects of the Novel*, Chap. 5, pp. 98–9, 101.
185. *D3*, December 3, 1972, p. 293.
186. *D3*, May 24, 1973, p. 361.
187. *D3*, July 12, 15, 1973, pp. 374, 376 (Candy Darling was the New York drag queen made famous in Andy Warhol films).
188. *D3*, July 15, 1973, p. 377; William Wilson, "Bachardy Images at Barnsdall Park," *Los Angeles Times*, July 13, 1973, Part IV, p. 10, quoted in *D3*, July 15, 1973, p. 377.
189. The NPG has portraits of Ackerley, EMF, and DS done in 1961; John Osborne done in 1968; Thom Gunn, 1996; and, by commission, James Ivory, Ismail Merchant, and Ruth Prawer Jhabvala, also 1996. Charles Saumarez Smith, head of the NPG 1994–2002, acquired most of these.
190. *D3*, December 8, 1973, August 31, 1974, pp. 408–9, 451.

191. Henry J. Seldis, "Art Walk," *Los Angeles Times*, November 15, 1974, Part IV, p. 86; *D3*, November 15, 1974, p. 461.
192. DB conversation with Bucknell, 2015.
193. Ford, "Christopher's Jungle Book," *Guardian*, March 30, 1977, p. 10.
194. *D3*, August 17, 1976, p. 522.
195. *D3*, November 28, 1976, p. 530.
196. *D3*, December 23, 1976, p. 530.
197. *Publishers Weekly*, "Nonfiction," November 1, 1976, p. 67, and Penelope Mesic, "Young Christopher Isherwood and the Company He Kept," *Chicago Tribune Book World*, 7, December 12, 1976, p. 1, and *D3*, November 21, 1976, p. 529.
198. Leonard, "Books of the Times: Isherwood Revises Record," *New York Times*, December 9, 1976, p. 45; Stansky, "Christopher and His Kind," *New York Times*, November 28, 1976, pp. 31–4.
199. Snow, "Ego Trip," *Financial Times*, April 1, 1977, p. 14; West, "A Symphony of Squalor," *Sunday Telegraph*, April 3, 1977, p. 15; Annan, "The Issyvoo Years," *TLS*, Memoirs, April 1, 1977, pp. 401-2.
200. Toynbee, "Herr Issyvoo Comes Clean," *Observer*, April 3, 1977, p. 26; Bayley, "Thinking About Erich," *Guardian*, March 31, 1977, p. 14. On the revisionism, Michael Ratcliffe was playful: "All right, the reader concedes, you were *not* a camera," and called it CI's "best book for some years." ("Herr Issyvoo in His Element," *The Times*, "New Books," March 31, 1977, p. 17) Peter Conrad wrote a long compare-and-contrast of CI and WHA, scolding them both for rewriting their earlier work; his astute, densely assembled observations show how carefully he had followed both careers. ("The Trouble with Christopher," Spring Books, *Spectator*, April 2, 1977, pp. 20–1) Frank Kermode also objected to the idea that CI's early fiction was untrue and pointed out the new fictional shaping that CI employed in *C&HK*. ("In the Best Sense, Silly," Books, *Listener*, March 31, 1977, p. 419)
201. SS, "Issyvoo's Conversion," *New York Review of Books*, August 14, 1980, pp. 18-21.
202. CI to Heinz Neddermeyer, draft, in German, October 19, 1978, CI 1317; *D3*, November 22, 1978, p. 602; Neddermeyer to CI, November 14, 1978, CI 1875; CI to Neddermeyer, November 22, 1978, in German, CI 1318, my translation; DB conversation with Bucknell, 2019.
203. GV, "Art, Sex and Isherwood," *New York Review of Books*, December 9, 1976.
204. EU, "The Resolute Anti-Hero," *New Statesman*, April 1, 1977, pp. 434–5.
205. CI interview with Leslie Hanscom, "The Boys in Berlin," *Guardian*, January 4, 1977.
206. *D3*, October 16, 1976, March 16, 1977, pp. 527, 539.
207. *D3*, June 8, 1977, p. 543.
208. *D3*, October 23, 1977, p. 554.
209. *D3*, December 25, 1977, January 22, 1978, pp. 558, 560.
210. *D3*, September 25, 1977, p. 550; Seldis and Wilson, "Art Walk: A Critical Guide to the Galleries," *Los Angeles Times*, September 30, 1977, Part IV, p. 10, this section signed WW.
211. In March 1971, CI picked up DB at his parents' house, and they had DB invite CI inside to watch TV with them, "a symbol of reconciliation," as CI wrote in his diary. By then, he and DB had been living together for eighteen years. The four had shared a cafeteria meal earlier the same year, at Clifton's in Century City, and they continued to meet there and at Mexican and Chinese restaurants four or five times a year. They never ate together at home.
212. *D3*, December 17, 1977, p. 557.
213. *D3*, October 9, November 20, 1978, pp. 587, 602.
214. *D3*, April 16, 1978, p. 567.
215. *D3*, August 27, October 4, 1978, pp. 570, 585–6.
216. *D3*, November 26, 28, 1978, February 6, 1980, pp. 603, 626.
217. *D3*, June 10, 1975, p. 479.
218. "'Meeting' Arrives Early on Broadway," *New York Times*, March 13, 1979, p. C7; DB telephone conversation with Bucknell, 2019.
219. Eder, "Stage: 'A Meeting by the River,'" *New York Times*, March 29, 1979; Jacques le Sourd, "'A Meeting by the River' deals with religious sect," *Journal News*, March 29, 1979, p. 8. A Catholic priest reviewing four religious plays on Broadway that spring

noted, "at least it takes religion seriously." Rev. Robert E. Lauder, "Plays That Probe the Roots of Faith," *New York Times*, May 20, 1979.
220. DB conversation with Bucknell, 2013; Carol Lawson, "Two cultures clash in new play by Isherwood," *New York Times*, January 26, 1979, p. C2; DB conversation with Bucknell, 2019; and see also James Ivory, "Isherwood," *Sight and Sound*, April 1986, p. 94.
221. James, *The Varieties of Religious Experience: A Study in Human Nature* (London/New York: Longman, Green & Co, 1902; Penguin Classics, 1985), p. 107. James attributed the phrase to the "mind-cure movement," promoting optimistic thinking for healing and empowerment, for instance Mary Baker Eddy's Christian Science.
222. *D3*, May 26, 1979, p. 610.
223. *D3*, July 4, November 11, 1979, pp. 612, 623.
224. *D3*, September 17, 1979, p. 618. He had a similar reception at Marin College, north of San Francisco, where he was accompanied by Armistead Maupin and Maupin's friend and manager Ken Maley.
225. *October*, pp. 11, 42.
226. *D3*, February 17, June 8, 1980, pp. 627, 634.
227. Hogan, "Isherwood's Guru," World of Books, *San Francisco Chronicle*, June 9, 1980, p. 41. Atlas, "Books of the Times," *New York Times*, August 27, 1980.
228. Toynbee, "Sacred and Profane Love," *Observer*, July 13, 1980, p. 28.
229. Ratcliffe, "Issyvoo's American Self," *The Times*, July 10, 1980, p. 11; Binding, "The Way of the Vedanta," *TLS*, July 18, 1980, p. 800; "Christopher Isherwood: Flirting with Faith," *The Economist*, July 12, 1980, p. 97; JL, "Lotus Living," *Sunday Telegraph*, July 13, 1980, p. 14. The *Daily Mail* prized the gossip value, as signaled by the review title, "The Day That Garbo Met a Guru," Ann Leslie, July 10, 1980, p. 7. Francis Huxley, a nephew of Aldous, admired CI's "appreciation of every kind of relationship" and considered that SP "emerges as quite the sweetest of men, utterly devoid of egotism, who loved Isherwood for not hiding anything from himself, and who in turn amply repays this love by not hiding from us." ("Through the Dreamhouse Door: Francis Huxley Reviews Two Accounts of States of Mind," *Guardian*, July 10, 1980, p. 8) Anthony Curtis also accepted CI on his own terms, "Christopher and His Masters," *Financial Times*, July 19, 1980, p.8.
230. SS, "Issyvoo's Conversion," *New York Review of Books*, August 14, 1980.
231. White, "A Sensual Man with a Spiritual Quest," *New York Times Book Review*, June 1, 1980, p. 39; Hollinghurst, "Masks," *New Stateman*, August 29, 1980, p. 20.
232. Ricks, "From a Hollywood Cloister," *Sunday Times*, July 13, 1980, p. 43.
233. *D3*, September 13, November 3, 1978, July 20, 1980, pp. 577, 597, 638; Maupin, *Logical Family: A Memoir* (New York: Harper, 2017), pp. 254, 260.
234. *D3*, July 21, August 24, 1980, pp. 638, 644.
235. *D3*, July 17, 1979, pp. 613–14.
236. *D3*, July 17, August 7, July 17, 1980, pp. 636, 642, 637.
237. Muchnic, "The Galleries," *Los Angeles Times*, March 7, 1980, Part VI, p. 8; *D3*, July 30, 1972, p. 257.
238. *D3*, January 24, 1981, p. 665; Voeller started the Mariposa Foundation that year to study human sexuality and sexually transmitted diseases and to collect materials relating to the history of the gay and lesbian movement. The portraits were called the Mariposa Portraits; while in Manhattan, DB drew Barbara Gittings, Charles Bryden, Elaine Noble, and Franklin Kameny. The portraits are now part of the Human Sexuality Collecton at Cornell University.
239. *D3*, October 19, 22, November 2, 1980, pp. 653–4, 657.
240. *D3*, April 19, 24, 1981, pp. 671, 672.
241. *D3*, June 27, 1981, pp. 676–7.
242. *D3*, October 16, 1981, p. 680; January 1, 1982, p. 680.
243. *D3*, January 3, 24, 1981, pp. 664, 665.
244. DB diary, September 21, December 6, 9, 2, 1985, January 3, 1986; Intro., *Last Drawings of Christopher Isherwood* (London: Faber and Faber, 1990), pp. xii, xiii, xv, xiv, xvii, xviii.

Index

ABC (television network), 654, 700–1
Abiquiú (New Mexico), 424, 425
Abney family, 136
Academy Awards, 446, 465, 466, 622, 676, 700
Ackerley, J.R., 253, 293, 480, 586, 588, 661
ACLU *see* American Civil Liberties Union
Acquired Immune Deficiency Syndrome *see* AIDS
Action (magazine), 234–5
Acton, Harold, 564
Adam's Rib (film; 1923), 164
Adjemian, Bob, 720
Adventure in Baltimore (film; 1949), 381–2, 395, 414
"Adventures of Daddie & Mummie, The" (with Kathleen Isherwood; 1909), 31–2
Adventures of the Black Girl in Her Search for God, The (Shaw), adaptation, 658–9, 665, 673, 674–5
Advocate (magazine), 687, 703
"Afterwards" (unpublished story), 603–5
AIDS (Acquired Immune Deficiency Syndrome), 9, 725, 728
Aigues-Mortes (France), 683
Ainsworth, (William) Harrison, 112, 115, 546; *The Tower of London*, 95; *Windsor Castle*, 109
Álamos (Mexico), 495
Albee, Edward, 673, 683
Albert Hall (London), 108
Albert I, King of the Belgians, 121
Alcibiades, 419, 590
Aldeburgh (Suffolk), 711; Festival, 412
Aldershot army camp (Hampshire), 30, 59, 107, 294
Alertonic (vitamin and mineral supplement), 673, 679
Alexander, Peter, 693, 694, 720
All the Conspirators (1928): autobiographical aspects, 187–8, 189; characterization, 123, 137, 187, 188, 189, 194–5; dedication, 513; influences on, 188–9, 456–7; plot and themes, 187–8, 189, 194–5, 265, 269, 457; publication and editions, 158, 190, 195–6, 512, 513, 561; reception and reviews, 197, 233; title, 187, 194, 195, 458; writing of, 187–90, 192, 193, 194–5

Allen, Alan, Dr., 597, 633, 634, 646, 666
Alleyn's School (London), 510
Altaussee (Austria), 400
Altmann, Toni, 362, 564, 566
Alvensleben, Werner von, 250
Amalfi coast (Italy), 506
"Ambrose" (1962), 254, 550–1, 554, 557–65, 568, 582, 594, 596, 603
Ambrose, St., 557
American Academy and Institute of Arts and Letters, 665
American Ballet Caravan (traveling company), 400
American Civil Liberties Union (ACLU), 641, 675
American Trader, SS, 3
Amis, Kingsley, 596
Amiya *see* Sandwich, Amiya, Countess of
Amsterdam, 211, 248–9, 262, 263, 362, 416, 552, 721; Rijksmuseum, 417
Anders als die Andern (film; 1919), 220
Andersen, Hans Christian, 546; "The Snow Queen," 502, 600
Anderson, Hedli, 283–4
Anderson, Maxwell, 288
Andrews, John, 131, 280, 507
Angelo, Waldo, 421
Angkor Wat (Cambodia), 525
Annan, Gabriele, 713
Annecy (France), 142, 191
Anouilh, Jean, *Mademoiselle Colombe*, 475
Anschluss (Austria; 1938), 285, 303, 360
Aramis, SS, 284
Ardmore (Pennsylvania), 323, 326
Arequipa (Peru), 407
Argo, Leif, 421
Arles (France), 683
Armendáriz, Pedro, 499
Armentières (France), 68, 78–9, 82
Armistice Day (1918), 116–17, 163
Armstrong, Bob, 47, 52–3, 378
Armstrong, Jack, 47, 52, 378
Arnold, Edwin, *The Light of Asia*, 342
Arthur Murray Dance Studios, 471
Artist to His Circle, An see All the Conspirators
Arts and Monuments Commission, 400

Arup Chaitanya *see* Critchfield, Kenny
Arvin, Newton, 398
Ascent of F6, The (with W.H. Auden; 1936), 99, 209, 276–7, 280, 409
Ascot Park (speedway circuit), 694
Asher, Betty, 682
Ashford, Daisy, *The Young Visiters*, 162
Ashton, Frederick, 39
Ashton, Major (military colleague of Frank Isherwood), 40, 41
Ashton, Nicky, 41
Asperger's syndrome, 139
Aswell, Mary Louise, 397
Athens, 253, 255, 257, 258, 724
Atlas, James, 721
atomic and nuclear weapons, 369, 382, 424, 480, 488, 584
Auden, Constance, 99, 100
Auden, George, 99–100, 114, 126
Auden, John, 97, 103, 207
Auden, Wystan Hugh: family background and early life, 99–100, 114; at St. Edmund's School, 97–101, 103–5, 111–13, 333, 612; first meets CI, 97; early development of friendship with CI, 97–9, 112–13, 333; at Gresham's School, 132, 184, 185; at Christ Church, Oxford, 184, 198; renewed friendship with CI, 161, 184–7, 191; and CI's relations with Mangeot family, 181–2; visits CI on Isle of Wight (summer 1926), 185–7, 190; publication of first poetry collection, 186–7, 198; in Berlin, 200, 201, 202, 205–9, 219, 233; in Rothehütte, 210; travels to Amsterdam with CI (summer 1929), 211; and CI's translation of Baudelaire, 226; holiday on Ruegen Island with CI (summer 1931), 223, 232–3, 399; teaching job at Downs School, 261; and Heinz Neddermeyer's proposed entry into Britain, 261; collaboration with CI on *The Dog Beneath the Skin*, 268–70; marriage to Erika Mann (June 1935), 416; writing and productions of *The Ascent of F6* and *On the Frontier*, 99, 276–7, 280–1, 288, 294; and Spanish Civil War, 276, 282, 507; awarded King's Gold Medal for Poetry, 42, 283; travels to China with CI (1938), 204, 282–8, 290–1, 303, 308, 523, 525, 704; returns to England via New York, 288–9; writing of *Journey to a War*, 282–3, 294–5; final months in Europe, 294–7, 372; decision to emigrate to U.S., 2, 4, 294–5, 296–7, 310–11, 564; crosses Atlantic with CI, 1, 297, 416; in New York, 298–9, 301, 430, 435, 475; and Gerald Heard, 300, 301, 306, 312, 318; relationship with Chester Kallman, 306, 318; trip to California with Kallman (summer 1939), 306–7; reaction in Britain to emigration, 308–11, 383, 386–7, 563, 596; second visit to California (summer 1940), 311–12; CI visits on East Coast (August–September 1941), 318–19; house-share on Middagh Street, Brooklyn, 318–19; teaches at Swarthmore College, Pennsylvania, 319, 326, 368; reads draft of *Prater Violet*, 368; during CI's 1947 visit to New York, 396; on Fire Island, 398–9; in Paris (spring 1948), 411; and Burgess and Maclean defection, 480; and first performances of *I Am a Camera*, 434, 435; during CI's 1953–4 trip to New York, 475–6; and CI's relationship with Don Bachardy, 475–6; lecture tours in California (1954; 1963), 483, 489, 617; and *Down There on a Visit*, 565, 569, 579, 582, 594; in England (summer 1961), 582–5, 586; proposed musical about Sally Bowles, 583–4; at Bachardy's debut New York show (January 1962), 592; in Kirchstetten (Austria), 636; preaches at Westminster Abbey (autumn 1966), 655; awarded Gold Medal by American Academy and Institute of Arts and Letters, 665; and death of E.M. Forster, 683; last conversation with CI, 702; death, 702, 704–5, 711; Spender's proposed biography, 706; commemoration events, 707, 727
Character & characteristics: appearance, 97–8, 184, 185–6; awards, 42, 283, 665; characteristics of friendship with CI, 42, 48, 98–9, 112–13, 184–7, 271, 289, 290–1, 306–7, 308, 333, 435, 592, 683, 705; dancing, 489; game-playing, 307; grubbiness, 112, 184; imagination, 112, 306; intelligence, 98; landscape interests, 100, 112; literary importance, 7, 184, 198, 199, 283, 712–13; love of bad weather, 100; mining interests, 98, 112; musical interests, 100; names, 114, 569; nannying qualities, 592; portraits, 618, 636, 675, 681, 709; portrayal in CI's works, 98, 125, 199, 201, 207, 565, 569, 612, 694, 705; psychological interests, 610; relations with mother, 99, 100, 184, 318; relations with Stephen Spender, 467, 636; religion, 99, 306, 312, 435, 637; scientific interests, 98; sexuality, 201, 206–7, 267, 311, 637; smoking, 306; solitariness, 112; views on CI's works, 161, 368, 582, 594, 636, 637
Works: "1929," 207; "Brussels in Winter," 296; "The Capital," 296; *The Chase*, 268, 269; "Commentary," 283; *The Dance of Death*, 267–8, 340; *Elegy for Young Lovers*, 582, 584; *The Fronny*, 267, 268, 340; "Letter to Lord Byron," 100, 101, 104, 283; *Letters from Iceland*, 283; "London to Hong Kong," 283; *Look, Stranger!* 283; "Musée des Beaux Arts," 296; "The Novelist," 409; "Ode to the New Year," 295, 372; *The Orators*, 161, 232, 270, 283; *Paid on Both Sides*, 113, 201, 276, 333; *Paul Bunyan*, 711; *The Play of Daniel*, 592; *Poems* (1928), 186–7, 198, 333; *Poems* (1930), 283; *The Poet's Tongue*, 267; *The Rake's Progress*, 432, 522; *The Sea and the Mirror*, 557; "Spain," 283, 563; "In Time of War," 283; "The Wanderer," 267; *see also The Ascent of F6*; *The Dog Beneath the Skin, or Where is Francis?*; *The Enemies of a Bishop, or Die When I Say When*; *Journey to a War*; *On the Frontier*
Aufderheide, Charles, 418
Austen, Howard, 502, 592, 633, 702
Austen, Jane, 128
Australia, 677, 678, 687

Austria, 359–60, 400; Bachardy visits, 636; CI visits, 253, 654–5; *see also* Vienna
Austrian Anschluss (1938), 285, 303, 360
Austrian Civil War (1934), 362–3
"Autobiography of My Books, The" (lectures; 1963), 618, 659
Avedon, Richard, 433, 716
Avis, Anne (Nanny/Nurse), 20–33, 36, 41–6, 50, 56, 58, 66, 76–80, 83, 84, 87, 105, 107, 123, 138, 151, 152, 180, 194, 304, 377, 385–6, 392, 422, 442, 612, 729
Avon (paperback publishers), 703

Babes in the Wood (pantomime), *109*
Bachardy, Don: family background, 446–7, 451–2, 453; birth, 452; childhood and schooling, 446, 449, 453, 454; teenage years, 445–6, 449–50, 451–3; and brother's mental health and breakdowns, 449, 451, 500, 540; student at UCLA and Los Angeles City College, 447, 453, 473, 483, 500–1; first meets CI, 3, 447–51; early development of relationship with CI, 3, 453–5, 458–9, 464–6, 470, 471, 482, 515–16; and writing of *The World in the Evening*, 454–5, 457–8, 470, 707; road trip to Arizona, New Mexico, Utah and Nevada with CI (May 1953), 464–5; moves into Marguerite and Harry Brown's apartment, 466; trip to San Francisco with CI (summer 1953), 471–2; moves into apartment on Olive Drive, West Hollywood with CI, 472–3; trip to New York with CI (December 1953–January 1954), 474–7; photographed nude by George Platt Lynes, 476–7, 543; moves to house on Mesa Road, Santa Monica with CI, 483; life at Mesa Road, 483–4, 502–3; parties and socializing in California (1954–60), 483–4, 486–7, 491–2, 493, 500, 501, 521; and publication of *The World in the Evening*, 485; begins taking art classes, 487, 547; draft board interview and tests, 488; trip to Key West (November 1954), 346, 489–91; road trip to Mexico (December 1954–January 1955), 492–6; twenty-first birthday, 476–7, 501–2; moves to Zuma Beach with CI, 503; European tour with CI (October 1955–March 1956), 143, 503, 504–11; in Tangier en route, 504–5, 614, 618; takes hashish, 505, 506, 614, 618; returns to United States with CI, 510, 514; life at Sycamore Road with CI, 510, 514–18, 534–6, 537, 612; hospitalized with hepatitis, 510, 514; psychological counseling, 514; studies at Chouinard Art Institute, 514, 518, 534, 537; early development of interest in Vedanta, 516, 517–18; works on proposed television series with CI and Gavin Lambert, 520–1; solo trip to New York (June–July 1957), 518–19; tour of Far East and India with CI (October–December 1957), 519, 523–30; returns to California via London, 530, 557; development of open relationship with CI, 534–6, 540–1, 542–3, 580, 606–7, 614–22, 639, 679, 695–7; affair with Paul Millard, 535, 537–8, 540, 542, 543, 549, 591, 604; first drawing jobs, 537; sale of Sycamore Road house and purchase of property on Adelaide Drive, 537; vacation in New York and Europe with CI (summer 1959), 538; life at Adelaide Drive with CI, 538–9, 540–3, 547, 634, 635; affair with Tony Richardson, 543, 548, 622; drawings for *A Taste of Honey* production, 543, 548, 587; and *Down There on a Visit*, 554, 555, 556, 581; leaves to study art in London, 548–9, 590; in London (January 1961–December 1962), 550, 580, 581, 599, 647; CI joins in England (summer 1961), 580, 581–7; holiday at Richardson's in south of France, 587–8; first show at Redfern Gallery, 582, 585–6, 587, 588, 592, 652; in New York for debut show (December 1961–January 1962), 591–3, 594; returns to California, 593–4, 596–7; and *A Single Man*, 602, 604, 606, 608–9, 612, 622; growing interest in Vedanta, 606–7, 613, 646, 689; house renovations and construction of studio at Adelaide Drive, 597, 607–8, 679; West Coast debut show, 597, 608; initiated by Swami Prabhavananda, 613, 614, 689; affair with George Kramer, 615–16, 620–2, 664; CI meets in New York on return from India (January 1964), 633; thirtieth birthday, 635; trip to Europe with Lee Garlington (summer 1964), 635, 636; extended stay in New York following October 1964 Banfer Gallery show, 636, 637, 639–40, 644, 646; commissions for Lincoln Kirstein in New York, 636, 639, 640, 644, 647, 654; visits California (Christmas and New Year 1964–5; April–May 1965), 639, 644; returns to California (July 1965), 644–5; and *A Meeting by the River*, 645, 646; parties and socializing in California (1965–86), 647–8, 660, 664–5, 693–4; January 1966 Rex Evans Gallery show, 647, 652; trip to New York (February–April 1966), 652, 654; end of friendship with Kirstein, 654; in New York for *Cabaret* opening (November 1966), 657, 658; celebrates fifteenth anniversary with CI, 664; trips to London (May–June and October–November 1968), 665–9, 671–3; affair with Anthony Page, 666–8, 671–4, 676–7, 678, 679–81, 697; collaboration with CI on stage adaptation of *A Meeting by the River*, 667, 670, 672, 673, 679–80, 681; writes screenplay for *Cabaret* with CI, 676; first sale of drawing to public gallery, 673–4, 681; trip to England (April–May 1969), 676–7; writes screenplay for *I, Claudius* with CI, 677–9, 694; in Tahiti and Australia (July–August 1969), 677–8; Irving Blum Gallery show (March 1970), 681–2, 708; 1970–1 group shows, 693, 694; collaboration with CI on *Frankenstein* screenplay, 694–6, 701, 702–3; stage productions of *A Meeting by the River*, 700–1, 718–19, 724; trip to Europe with CI (January–March 1973), 701–3; travels to New York to deliver CI's Brandeis Medal acceptance speech, 707; Los Angeles Municipal Art Gallery (Barnsdall Park) show (summer 1973), 708–9; Nicholas Wilder

Bachardy (cont.)
  Gallery show (November 1974), 709–10; enlarges studio at Adelaide Drive, 710; collaboration with CI on proposed film adaptation of *The Beautiful and Damned*, 710; trip to England and Scotland with CI (summer 1976), 710–11; in Tangier with Gavin Lambert, 711; death of Prabhavananda, 711; and publication of *Christopher and His Kind*, 712, 714; officially adopted by CI, 716; Nicholas Wilder Gallery show (September 1977), 716; death of father, 716–17; affair with Bill Franklin, 717–18; trips to New York with CI for Broadway production of *A Meeting by the River* (January–March 1979), 718–19, 724; collaboration with CI on illustrated diary, 720–1, 725; first Corcoran Gallery show (March 1980), 724; trip to New York with CI for Robert Miller Gallery show (September 1980), 725; and CI's hernia operation and cancer diagnosis, 726–7; travels to New York with CI for Auden symposium (October 1983), 727–8; and CI's final illness, 728–9; and CI's death, 729; and publication of CI's diaries, 620, 649
  Character & characteristics: Animal identities with CI, 23, 39, 47, 458–9, 538, 617; appearance, 445, 487; artistic talent and reputation, 446, 487, 537, 548, 555, 582, 640, 680, 682, 694, 709–10; ballet interests, 450; cars and driving, 483, 607, 614, 695–6; clothes, 445, 474; dancing, 471; diary-keeping, 523; dislike of making plans, 707; eating and doll-making, 621; driving, 445–6, 536–7, 549; eyes, 445; finances, 518, 587, 676; foreign language skills, 453; gym-going, 487, 646; height, 445; home movie-making, 489, 491, 526; independence, 473, 519, 540, 548, 597, 606; moviegoing and film interests, 446, 452, 483–4, 489, 500; name, 452; nicknames, 23, 47, 155, 458–9; portraits, 539, 665–6, 669, 672, 677, 683, 721; portrayal in CI's works, 457–8, 555, 603, 604; sexuality, 445–6, 452–3, 488; similarities to CI's mother, 544; spirituality, 614, 646; working methods, 585–6, 707–8, 720–1
  Drawings & paintings: of J.R. Ackerley, 586; of Peter Alexander, 694; of Betty Asher, 682; of W.H. Auden, 586, 636, 675, 681, 709; of Francis Bacon, 588, 682; of James Baldwin, 636; of Cecil Beaton, 582; of Alec Beesley, 586; of Larry Bell, 682; of Billy Al Bengston, 682; of Leslie Caron, 636; of Oleg Cassini, 597, 607; of CI, 562, 586, 588, 593, 636, 645, 720, 728, 729; of Salvador Dalí, 682; of Candy Darling, 708; of Shelagh Delaney, 587; of Richard Diebenkorn, 682; for *Down There on a Visit*, 588; of Gregory Evans, 708; of Albert Finney, 586, 592; of Glenn Ford, 636; of E.M. Forster, 586, 636; of Henry Geldzahler, 682; of John Gielgud, 586, 636; of Paulette Goddard, 636; of Kenneth Haigh, 672–3; of Earl and Countess of Harewood, 675–6; of Victor Henry, 672; of David Hockney, 682; of Brooke Hopper, 682; for *The Hotel in Amsterdam*, 668, 672–3; of Aldous Huxley, 636; of Robert Irwin, 682; of Jasper Johns, 682, 708; of Chester Kallman, 586; of Curt Klebaum, 721; of Charles Laughton, 542; of Vivien Leigh, 586, 636; of Margaret Leighton, 586; of Lotte Lenya, 586; of Roy Lichtenstein, 682, 708; for *Little Moon of Alban*, 548; of Anita Loos, 593; of Myrna Loy, 592; of Norman Mailer, 593; of Robert Mapplethorpe, 725; for Mariposa Foundation, 725, 726; for May Company, 537; for New York City Ballet, 636, 639, 640, 644, 654; of Paul Newman, 593; of Merle Oberon, 597; for *October*, 720–1; of John Osborne, 667; for *Period of Adjustment*, 548; of Patrick Procktor, 647; of Lee Radziwill, 597; of Nancy Reagan, 708; of John Rechy, 547; of Tony Richardson, 587; of Jerome Robbins, 593; of Amiya, Countess of Sandwich, 588; of David Selznick, 608; of Simone Signoret, 636; of Norton Simon, 708; of Dodie Smith, 586; of Stephen Spender, 636; of Igor Stravinsky, 582, 636, 708; of Vera Stravinsky, 636; of Barbra Streisand, 636; for *A Taste of Honey*, 543, 548, 587; of Virgil Thomson, 636, 708; for *Time Present*, 666, 668; of Gore Vidal, 636; of Andy Warhol, 682, 708; of Nicholas Wilder, 682; of Natalie Wood, 636; of Joanne Woodward, 593
  Exhibitions & shows: Banfer Gallery, New York, 636; Chouinard Art Institute, Los Angeles, 537; Corcoran Gallery, Los Angeles, 724, 727; Dootson-Calderhead Gallery, Seattle, 710; group shows, 693, 694, 708; Irving Blum Gallery, Los Angeles, 681–2, 708; Los Angeles Municipal Art Gallery (Barnsdall Park), 708–9, 724; National Gay Archives, 726; Nicholas Wilder Gallery, Los Angeles, 708, 709–10, 716; Phoenix, 616, 617; Redfern Gallery, London, 582, 585–6, 587, 588, 592, 652; Redlands College, Houston, 724; Rex Evans Gallery, Los Angeles, 597, 608, 647, 652; Robert Miller Gallery, New York, 725; Sagittarius Gallery, New York, 591, 592; San Francisco, 636; Santa Barbara, 597, 615, 616; Stanford University, 597, 616
Bachardy, Glade (DB's mother), 446, 447, 451–2, 500, 501, 516, 596, 717
Bachardy, Jess (DB's father), 446–7, 449, 451, 452, 453, 500, 608, 716–17
Bachardy, Joe (DB's uncle), 453
Bachardy, Julia (DB's aunt), 453
Bachardy, Laura Elenore Lednisky (DB's grandmother), 453
Bachardy, Stephan (DB's grandfather), 453
Bachardy, Ted (DB's brother): appearance and character, 445–6, 452; birth and childhood, 452, 453; teenage years, 445–6, 449–50, 451–3; mental health and breakdowns, 449, 450, 451, 452, 453, 500, 540, 596; early encounters and relationship with CI, 421, 447, 448–9; CI and DB visit at state mental hospital, 453; social life in California, 491, 596; short prison sentence for shoplifting, 596; later life, 717

Bachardy, Ted (DB's uncle), 453
"Back to Berlin" (1952), 437-9
Bacon, Francis (painter), 440, 508, 545, 588, 603, 614, 662, 682, 693, 701-2, 716
Bacon, Francis, (writer), 161
BAFTAs (awards), 622
Bagnall, Reginald Oscar Gartside, 103-4, 109, 111
Bagshawe, Muriel *see* Bradshaw Isherwood-Bagshawe, (Beatrice) Muriel
Bakewell, Jean *see* Connolly, Jean
Balanchine, George, 322, 397, 400, 640, 654
Balcon, Michael, 259, 260, 364
Balcon, S.C., 259, 260, 364
Baldick, Robert, 662
Baldwin, James, 636, 693
Balfour, Arthur Balfour, 1st Earl of, 108
Bali (Indonesia), 524, 525
Ballet Rambert, 280
Balzac, Honoré de, 239, 430; *La comédie humaine*, 239; *Splendeurs et misères des courtisanes*, 214
Bandits of Orgosolo (film treatment), 521
Banja Luka (Bosnia and Herzegovina), 23
Bankhead, Tallulah, 301
Barbellion, W.N.P., *Diary of a Disappointed Man*, 166
Barlow, Betty, 133-4
Barnes, Alfred, 321
Barr, Richard, 673
Barranquilla (Colombia), 403
Barrett Browning, Elizabeth, 23
Barrie, James Matthew (J. M.), *Peter Pan*, 95, 269
Barrie, Michael, 581, 663
Batson, Susan, 675
Battleship Potemkin (film; 1925), 241
Baudelaire, Charles, 143, 161, 166, 409; *Les Fleurs du Mal*, 142; *The Intimate Journals*, 226, 379
Baux, Les (France), 683
Baxter, Keith, 718-19
Bayley, John, 697, 713
BBC, 317, 327; *Omnibus* (television program), 673; radio, 293, 480, 704
Beach at Falesá, The (film treatment), 581, 643
Beach Boys (band), 660
Beamsmoor (Cheshire), 105, 106
Beatles (band), 660
Beaton, Cecil, 521, 536, 548, 582, 586, 591, 617, 618; *Images*, 618; *The Wandering Years*, 586
Beautiful and Damned, The (film treatment), 710
Beckerman, Sidney, 676
Becket, Thomas, 276
Bedlam (Bethlem Royal Hospital, Kent), 194
Bee-Eye Enterprises, 608
Beesley, Alec, 181, 311, 342, 357, 375, 457, 461, 474, 508, 536, 586, 698
Beethoven, Ludwig van, 175, 422, 516
Belcher, Muriel, 440
Belfrage, Cedric, 163
Belgian Radio Symphony Orchestra, 295
Belgrade, 253
Bell, Arthur, 698, 699
Bell, Larry, 682, 693
Bell, Ruby, 418
Bell and Howell (movie camera), 489
Bella Vista (Argentina), Ramakrishna Ashrama, 409
Bellairs, Fanny, 56
Below the Equator (film treatment), 423-4

Belur Math (India), 516, 518, 523, 526-8, 529, 531, 627-33, 641, 642, 643, 654, 711, 718
Bengston, Billy Al, 647, 682, 693-4, 708
Benson, E.F., 156; *David Blaize*, 128
Benton Way Group, 418-20, 437, 441, 591
Berezina, Battle of (1812), 507
Bergman, Ingrid, 302
Berkeley (California): Vedanta Center, 711; *see also* University of California, Berkeley
Berkeley, Lennox, 295
Berkhamsted School (Hertfordshire), 132, 138-9
Berlant, Tony, 693
Berlin, 201, 203-9, 210, 218-21, 223-32, 235-40, 436-8, 515, 584; portrayal in CI's works, 3-4, 8, 125, 204, 205-6, 211, 226-30, 234, 244-52, 255-6, 360, 432, 515, 578-9
Berlin (landmarks and places): Admiralstrasse, 228; Bertheim's (department store), 246; British Press Club, 437; Bülowplatz, 247, 250, 251; Charlottenburg, 251; Cosy Corner (Noster's Restaurant zur Hütte), 34, 205, 219, 220, 227, 255; In den Zelten, 218, 220, 699; Hallesches Tor, 205, 225-6, 437; Hirschfield Museum, 205-6; Hotel am Zoo, 436; Institute for Sexual Science, 205, 218, 220, 240, 242, 252-3, 304, 462, 699, 713; Kaiser Wilhelm Memorial Church, 436-7; Kleiststrasse, 233, 296; Kottbusser Tor, 228, 229; Kurfürstendamm, 436-7; Mommsen Gymnasium, 248; N. Israel (department store), 246; Nollendorfstrasse, 216, 229-30, 252, 404, 437; Opernplatz, 252, 444, 562; Potsdamerplatz, 291; Simeonstrasse, 225-6, 437; Sportspalatz, 250; Tauentzienstrasse, 218, 437; Tiergarten, 218, 437; Unter den Linden, 221; Weissensee, 439
Berlin Airlift (1948-9), 438
Berlin am Morgen (newspaper), 462
"Berlin Diary, A (Autumn 1930)" (1937), 204, 225-6, 229-30, 237
"Berlin Diary, A (Winter 1932-3)" (1938), 204, 250, 295-6
Berlin Stories, The (1945), 379
Berlin Wall, 584
Bermuda, 440-1, 450
Bernhardt, Sarah, 15, 51, 91, 103, 137
Berwyn (Pennsylvania), 326
Besant, Annie, 355
Besley, Elizabeth, 386, 392, 442
Best Man, The (film; 1964), 622
Bethnal Green (London), 234
Bettyhill (Sutherland), 217-18
Beverly Hills (California), 326; Beverly Hills Hotel, 490, 491; Beverly-Wilshire Hotel, 643; Brown Derby (restaurant), 314, 338, 343; Greystone Mansion, 636
Bhagavad Gita, vii, 65, 83-4, 330-1, 729; translation (with Prabhavananda; 1944), 313, 330-4, 342, 356, 373, 391, 395, 631, 665
Biddulph, Jack, 38
Big Sur (California), 635
Bill, George, 419
Binding, Paul, 722
Birmingham, 99, 277
Birmingham University, 99

818 / Index

Bizet, Georges, *Carmen*, 509
"Black and White Ball" (New York; 1966), 657, 658
Blake, William, 161
Blanc-Roos, René, 324, 325
Blavatsky, Madame, 73
Bleuler, Eugen, 190
Blitzkrieg (1940), 311, 312, 334, 383–4, 392
Blomshield, John, 239
Bloomsbury Group, 8, 328, 539, 596
Blum, Irving, 681–2, 708
Blunt, Anthony, 295, 384, 479, 480–1
Blythe (California), 465
Blythe, Ronald, 698
Boca Grande (Florida), 571
Boer War *see* Second Boer War (1899–1902)
Bogotá, 403–4, 407
Bok, Curtis, 326
Bok, Derek, 326, 337
Bolton, Guy, *Sally*, 238
Boman, Eric, 684, 697, 718
book burning (Germany; 1933), 252–3, 444, 562
Bopp, Bill, 614–15, 616
Bora Bora (French Polynesia), 677
Borrow, George, 39, 128
Boston Globe (newspaper), 698
Bosworth Hall (Leicestershire), 219
Bouché, R.R., 548
Boulogne (France), 82
Bowen, Marjorie, 306; *Black Magic*, 95, 145, 239, 505
Bower, Tony, 277, 314, 316, 323, 327, 329, 396, 578–9
Bowie, David, 725
Bowles, Jane, 319
Bowles, Paul, 238, 319, 504–5, 673; *The Sheltering Sky*, 495
boxing, 96–7
Boyer, Charles, 301
Brabyns Hall (Cheshire), 26, 67, 70, 91, 93, 122, 386, 388, 427
Brackett, Charles, 643
Bradbury, Ray: *The Martian Chronicles*, 424, 433; *The Silver Locusts*, 433
Bradley, Alan, 586, 624, 655
Bradley, Dan, 655, 702, 719–20
Bradley, Edna, 586, 624
Bradley, Evelyn, 655, 702, 719–20
Bradley, Tom, 727
Bradshaw, Henry, 19, 22, 29, 546
Bradshaw, John (17th-century judge), 13, 25, 130, 367, 545–6
Bradshaw, John (CI's great-great-grandfather), 116
Bradshaw, William (army friend of Frank Isherwood), 19
Bradshaw, William (father of Henry Bradshaw), 19
Bradshaw Bowles, C.E., 238
Bradshaw Hall (Derbyshire), 238
Bradshaw Isherwood-Bagshawe, (Beatrice) Muriel, 28–9, 31, 121, 140, 141, 387
Bradshaw Isherwood-Bagshawe, Henry (CI's uncle): appearance and character, 16, 29, 141; education and early life, 16, 25; career, 16, 25; rheumatic fever, 16, 188; religious conversion, 16, 17, 546; homosexuality, 16, 93, 209; and CI's parents' marriage, 17; and Marple Hall Estate, 25, 141, 180, 206, 210; marriage, 28–9; married life, 29, 31, 140, 141; during World War I, 71, 72, 82, 87–8, 93, 109; and CI's school holidays from St. Edmund's and Repton, 87–8, 93, 121; allowance paid to CI, 141, 210, 226, 387; later life, 209–10, 252; and *Mr. Norris Changes Trains*, 211, 212–14, 215, 388; death and will, 29, 30, 141, 387–8; CI's relations with and views on, 16, 22, 29, 73, 93, 141, 180, 209–11, 212–13, 359, 387
Brahmananda, 336, 518, 526, 528–9, 530–1, 630, 632, 688
Brainard, Joe, 644
Bramshott Camp (Hampshire), 108
Brandeis University (Massachusetts), 707
Brando, Marlon, 427, 518
Brandywine Farm (Pennsylvania), 463
Brecht, Bertolt, 268, 347–8, 360, 362, 365, 478, 589, 625; *The Caucasian Chalk Circle*, 348; *Der Jasager*, 640; *A Penny for the Poor* (*Dreigroschenroman*), 347
Breen, Joseph, 499
Bremen (Germany), 197–8, 205, 235, 253, 551, 555
Bridges, Jim, 646, 647, 652, 665, 673; and stage adaptation of *A Meeting by the River*, 669–70, 672, 673, 679, 700–1
Brighton, 282, 367
British Museum, 123, 140, 308
British Union of Fascists, 234
British War Relief Fund, 392
Britten, Benjamin, 181, 276, 284, 289, 294, 295, 319, 321, 322–3, 384, 421, 705, 711; *Albert Herring*, 412; *Paul Bunyan*, 711; *Peter Grimes*, 321, 412
Brompton Cemetery (London), 169
Brontë, Charlotte, 128, 649; *Jane Eyre*, 350
Brontë, Emily, 128, 160, 166, 649; *Wuthering Heights*, 350, 508–9, 538, 656
Brooke, Rupert, 145
Brooks, Louise, 220, 239, 659
Brosman (Santa Monica doctor), 727
Brown, Bill, 614, 620, 636, 647
Brown, Harry, 466, 473, 474, 475, 501
Brown, Marguerite *see* Littman, Marguerite
Browne, Thomas, 160
Brownie (camera), 54, 231
Brownies, The (comic strip), 54
Browning, Herbert Brook, 150, 166, 179–80
Browning, Robert, 23, 124, 134, 145, 166
Brunton, Maud, 386
Brussels, 273, 275, 278, 294–7, 372, 384
Bryn Mawr College (Pennsylvania), 319, 321
Buchan, John, *Greenmantle*, 95
Büchse der Pandora, Die (film; 1929), 220
Buckingham, Bob, 341, 661, 683
Buckingham, May, 341, 661, 683
Buckingham Palace, 42, 117
Buckingham Street (London), 59, 107, 139
Buckle, Richard, 654, 674, 675–6
Budapest, 253

Buddha and Buddhism, 303, 342, 499, 586, 650, 660
Buenos Aires, 408-9, 481
Bühler, Jean, 131, 280, 282
Bülowplatz shootings (1931), 247
Buñuel, Luis, *Los Olividados*, 448, 498, 549
Bunyan, John, *Pilgrim's Progress*, 50, 428
Burbank (California), 483, 503
Burczinzky, Hank, 421
Burford, Roger, 163, 177, 179, 192, 196
Burgess, Anthony, 638
Burgess, Guy, 294-5, 384, 479-81
Burns, Phil, 442, 535, 621
Burroughs Corporation (data-processing company), 614
Burton, Richard, 581, 643
Burton, William, Dr., (Marple doctor), 122
Bury St. Edmunds (Suffolk), 15, 20, 30
Bus Stop (film; 1956), 521
Buster Brown (cartoon character), 40-1, 269
Butler, Eleanor, 24
Buxton (Derbyshire), 538
Buzzard, Richard, 291
Bynner, Witter, 425
Byron, George Byron, 6th Baron, 127, 165, 621, 695; "Manfred," 142

Cabaret (film; 1972), 4, 664, 676, 699-700
Cabaret (musical), 4, 657-8
Cadmus, Fidelma *see* Kirstein, Fidelma
Cadmus, Paul, 322, 323, 396, 398, 637
Caesar, Julius, 195, 642-3
Café Royal (London), 293, 301
Cage of Gold, The (film treatment) *see* Diane (film)
Cairncross, John, 479
Cairo, 284
Calcutta, 525-6; City College, 528, 529; Cossipore Garden House, 335, 525; Great Eastern Hotel, 525-6; Ramakrishna Mission Institute of Culture, 628-30; Star Theatre, 629; University College, 529; *see also* Belur Math
Caldwell, Evelyn *see* Hooker, Evelyn
Calendar of the Year (film; 1936), 489
California State University, Long Beach, 588, 687
California State University, Los Angeles, 707; *see also* Los Angeles State College
"California Story" (1952), 435
Camarillo (California), state mental hospital, 451, 453, 500
Cambridge, 66, 159, 277, 412, 661, 682; Arts Theatre, 294; Garret Hostel Bridge, 159, 167; Rendezvous (cinema and dance hall), 164; Silver Street, 159; St. Bene't's Church, 171; University Arms (hotel), 18
Cambridge Five (spy ring), 479-81
Cambridge Gownsman (Cambridge University weekly periodical), 163-4
Cambridge Mercury (Cambridge University magazine), 163, 164
Cambridge University, 1, 14, 16, 99, 126, 281, 321; clubs and societies, 162, 163, 164, 168, 169, 170, 173, 179; scholarship exams, 130, 142, 145; *see also* Corpus Christi College; Emmanuel College; King's College

Camelot (musical), 581
camp (aesthetic), 464, 504
Campbell, Alan, 594
Campbell, Douglas, 675
Campbell, Sandy, 398
Camus, Albert, 552-3, 589
Canary Islands, 263-7, 432
Canberra, 678
Cannes (France), 417, 587
Canton (China), 284
Canyon de Chelly (Arizona), 465
Cap Ferrat (France), Villa Mauresque, 507, 588
Capa, Robert, 285
Cape, Jonathan, 195, 232
Cape Wrath (Scotland), 197
Capote, Truman, 7, 397-8, 411, 412, 434, 585, 636, 664, 693, 718; "Black and White Ball" (1966), 657, 658; *Answered Prayers*, 570; *Breakfast at Tiffany's*, 398; *In Cold Blood*, 379, 398, 636; *The House of Flowers*, 500; *Other Voices, Other Rooms*, 398, 411
Capri (Italy), 506
Carcassonne (France), 683
Caron, Leslie, 521, 636
Carpenter, Edward, 206, 723
Carroll, Lewis: *Alice's Adventures in Wonderland*, 160; *Through the Looking Glass*, 68
Cartagena (Colombia), 401, 403
Caskey, Catherine, 401
Caskey, William (Bill): background and early life, 3, 376-7; appearance and character, 3, 374, 376-7, 379, 413; CI first meets, 374-5, 450-1; CI leaves monastery and moves into apartment with, 375; development of relationship with CI, 3, 374-81, 396, 406, 417-18, 420-1, 458, 515; career as photographer, 381, 397, 399, 415, 435, 696; moves into Viertels' garage apartment with CI, 380-1; trip to Mexico City with CI (Christmas and New Year 1946-7), 382; in New York and Massachusetts with CI (summer 1947), 396-7, 398-400; trip to South America with CI (September 1947-March 1948), 397, 400-9; and *The Condor and the Cows*, 397, 401, 402, 406, 415; sails to Europe with CI, 409-10; in Paris and England (spring 1948), 410-12; returns to New York, 413; rejoins CI in California and moves into house on East Rustic Road, 414; life at East Rustic Road, 414, 417-18, 421, 425, 426, 597, 612; tensions in relationship with CI, 417-18, 420-1, 424, 427, 430-1, 441, 443, 457; temporary split from CI, 421; in Florida and Kentucky, 421, 424; returns to CI in Santa Monica, 424; arrest for drunk driving, 425-6, 427; moves to Laguna with CI, 427-8; life at Monterey Street, Laguna, 428, 429, 430-1, 432; in merchant navy, 431, 433, 441, 442, 443; on leave in California, 441, 443, 454, 471; break up with CI, 454, 471; and CI's relationship with Bachardy, 454, 471, 491; and *The World in the Evening*, 455, 461, 464, 491; CI's later contact and relations with, 471, 491; later life and career, 696; death, 724; portrayal in CI's works, 52, 378, 402, 455, 461, 624

Caserole restaurant (Chelsea, London), 662
Cassini, Oleg, 597, 607
Castleton (Derbyshire), 538
Catherine de Medici, 477, 499
Catullus, 642-3
Caudwell, Sarah, 246, 385
Cavendish Hotel (London), 508
Cavett, Dick, 698, 718
CBS (television network), 685-6
Cerf, Bennett, 3, 299, 397
Ceuta (Spanish Morocco), 267
Cezanne, Paul, 34
Chalia (Greece), 253
Chamberlain, Neville, 293
Chamonix (France), 142, 143, 191
Champion, Marge and Gower, 465
Champlain, SS, 1, 3, 297, 416
Chaney, Lon, 153
Chaplin, Charlie, 152, 396, 416, 420
Chapman, Kent, 534-5
Charing Cross Station (London), 59, 68
Charities Organisation Society, 229
Charles I, King, 25, 216, 545-6
Charles II, King, 93
Charlton, Jim, 413-14, 420, 421, 422, 433, 440, 441, 442, 448, 463, 538, 581, 604, 614, 615, 617, 618-19, 678
Charterhouse School (Surrey), 111, 114, 130
Chaucer, Geoffrey, 135
Chefchaouen (Spanish Morocco), 267
Cheim, John, 725
Chekhov, Anton, 182, 199, 460; *The Three Sisters*, 662
Cheltenham (Gloucestershire), 385
Cheng-chow (China), 286
Chenil Gallery (London), 181
Cherry, Budd, 635-6
Cherry Grove (Fire Island, New York), 398-9
Cheshire Regiment, 15
Chester Square (London), 661
Chetanananda, Swami, 711; anthology on meditation, 689
Chiang, Madame (Soong Mei-ling), 285
Chiang Kai-shek, 285
Chicago, 631, 632, 712
Chicago Tribune Book World, 712
China, 204, 282-8, 290-1, 293, 303, 308-9, 480, 525, 704
Chisholm, Hugh, 291
"Chivalry in English Literature" (1922), 135
"Choosing a School" (poem), 114
Chou En-lai, 285
Chouinard Art Institute (Los Angeles), 514, 518, 534, 537
Christ Church, Oxford, 183, 184, 564, 702
Christian, Bob, 635
Christian Science, 532, 619
Christie, Dame Agatha, 210
Christmas Carol, A (Dickens), proposed television adaptation, 665
Christopher and His Kind: 1929-1939 (1976): characterization, 205, 366, 568, 659; influences on, 371, 703; publication, 710, 711-12; quotations and extracts, 97, 171-2, 181, 182, 205-6, 210, 217, 219, 222, 224-5, 228, 232-3, 240, 241, 245, 248, 257, 258, 261, 262, 263, 264, 265, 266, 274, 278, 279, 287, 289, 366, 400, 416, 523, 555, 559, 562; reception and reviews, 712-15, 720, 722, 723; themes, 8, 97, 204, 205-6, 242, 260, 394, 618, 705-6; title, 705, 710; writing of, 659, 703, 705-6, 710
Christopher Garland (unpublished novel), 175-6
"Christopher Isherwood Day" (May 21, 1983), 727
Churchill, Winston, 533-4
CIA (U.S. Central Intelligence Agency), 198, 437, 467
cigarette cards, collecting, 85, 101-3
Circus Days (film; 1923), 153
Clayton, Jack, *The Great Gatsby*, 710
Clemson, Colonel (Frank Isherwood's commanding officer), 70, 79
Cleopatra, 46, 168, 642-3
Cleopatra (film; 1963), 643
Cleveland (Ohio), 452
Clifton, Al, 350
Coast (magazine), 700
coats of arms *see* crests and coats of arms
Cobbold, Mirabel, 48-9, 53, 59, 108, 236, 238, 398, 560; writings, 49
Cockburn, Claud, 242, 385
Cocteau, Jean, 448
Cohn, Harry, 647
Col des Aravis (France), 142, 191, 404
Colacello, Bob, 725
Colbert, Claudette, 301
Colchester (Essex), 74
Coldstream, William, 277, 549
Colefax, Sibyl, Lady, 294
Coleridge, Samuel Taylor, 142
Colette: *Chéri*, 519, 635, 662; *Gigi*, 435, 521
Collier, John, 372
Collins, Wilkie, *The Woman in White*, 371
Colombo (Ceylon), 284
Colony Room Club (London), 440
Columbia Pictures (film company), 647
Columbia University (New York), 728
"Coming to London" (1947), 107, 383
Communist Manifesto, 244
Communist Party of Germany Lives and Fights, The (pamphlet), 364-5
Condor and the Cows, The (1949), 397, 401-10, 415, 481, 483
Congress for Cultural Freedom, 437
Connolly, Cyril, 294, 314, 317, 377, 395, 467, 468-9, 563, 586; on CI's and Auden's emigration, 309-10, 386; reviews of CI's works, 215, 595; *Enemies of Promise*, 468-9, 539; *The Rock Pool*, 461, 469, 610
Connolly, Jean, 314, 316, 469, 576, 578
Conrad, Joseph, 128, 248, 503, 524, 595, 596; *Nostromo*, 403, 406, 409; *Romance* (with Ford Madox Ford), 19; *Victory*, 524-5, 557, 559; *Youth*, 554-5
Conway, Steve, 372
Coogan, Jackie, 152-3, 154, 165, 699
Cooke, Colonel (Frank Isherwood's commanding officer), 40
Cooke, Mrs. (wife of Colonel Cooke), 37, 109-10, 294

Coole, Sally, 238
Coombs, Don, 420
Cooper, Prentice, 401–2
Cooper family (Wyberslegh Hall Farm), 105, 196, 386
Cooperative College Workshop (Haverford, Pennsylvania), 319–22
Copacabana (Bolivia), 408
Cope, Private (Frank Isherwood's soldier-servant), 115
Copenhagen, 267, 268, 286, 692
Copland, Aaron, 238
Coppola, Francis Ford, 710
Corbin, Ella *see* Sandwich, Amiya, Countess of
Corcoran, Jim, 724, 727
Coronel, Battle of the (1914), 95–6
Corpus Christi College, Cambridge, 55, 154, 158–77
Corwen (Wales), 84, 85, 102
"Costidy, Sam," 440–1, 450
Costigan, James, *Little Moon of Alban*, 548
Cotton, Mr. and Mrs. (Marple Hall caretakers), 389, 390–1
Coulette, Henri, 594
Country Life (magazine), 25
Covent Garden (London), 165, 676; Royal Opera House, 35, 39
Coventry, 661, 683
Covered Wagon, The (film; 1923), 164–5
Covid-19 epidemic, 285
Coward, Noël, *Design for Living*, 535
Cox, Joseph, 178
Cox, Palmer, 54
Cox & Co. (bank), 81, 109
Coyne, Alan, 53, 55, 56, 106, 108, 116, 122, 226, 392
Coyne, Charles, 26, 27, 53
Coyne, Edwin, 56, 106, 392
Coyne, Ernest, 105
Crabbe, George, "Peter Grimes," 104, 135, 321
Craft, Robert, 183, 311, 432
Crainquebille (film; 1922), 153
Cresswell Place (South Kensington, London), 180
crests and coats of arms, 111, 114–15
Criccieth (Wales), 194
Crichton-Miller, Hugh, 191, 192
cricket, 61, 62, 111–12, 587
Cricklewood (London), film studios, 179
Critchfield, Kenny (Arup Chaitanya), 631, 632–3
Cromwell, Oliver, 25
Crowley, Aleister, 212, 505
Cruikshank, George, 109
Cruze, James: *The Covered Wagon*, 164–5; *Hollywood*, 164
Cuevas de Vera, Countess Tota, 399, 408, 434
Cukor, George, 533, 615, 685; *My Fair Lady*, 617, 694
Culver City (California), 483
Cumming, Alan, 658
Cunard, Nancy, *Authors Take Sides on the Spanish Civil War*, 283
Curaçao, 401
Curtis Brown (literary agency), 232, 234, 323, 582, 583
Cusco (Peru), 407

Daiches, David, 638
Daily Express (newspaper), 309, 480, 662
Daily Herald (newspaper), 233
Daily Mail (newspaper), 309
Daily Telegraph (newspaper), 662, 692
Daily Worker (newspaper), 307
Daladier, Édouard, 293
Dalí, Salvador, 682
Dan Bank Farm (Cheshire), 389
Dangerfield, George, 615
Dante Alighieri, 135, 441, 497, 498, 551, 552, 595, 599
Darling, Alistair, 131–2, 152, 184
Darling, Candy, 708
David, Vince, 596
Davidson, Gordon, 659
Davidson, Michael, 184
Davies, Marion, 377, 446
Davis (nanny), 20
Davis, Bob, 618–19
Davis, George (doctor), 200
Davis, George (literary editor), 288, 298, 319, 397
Davis, Ron, 693, 724
"Day at La Verne, The" (1941), 317
Day at the Seaside, A (film; 1910), 53
"Day in Paradise, A" (1935), 266–7
Day Lewis, Cecil, 7, 229, 280
Day's Journey, The (film treatment), 428–9, 492, 601
de Lichtenberg, Bill, 196–7, 200, 217, 218
de Lisio, Mike, 396
Dean, James, 483, 524
Death Valley (California), 497
Decision (magazine), 417
DeLand, Donnabell (DB aunt), 451, 452
DeLand, Waldo (DB grandfather), 451, 452
Delaney, Shelagh, 587; *A Taste of Honey*, 543, 548, 587
DeMille, Cecil B.: *Adam's Rib*, 164; *The Sign of the Cross*, 364–5, 626
Dench, Dame Judi, 203, 664
Derby, Edward Stanley, 17th Earl of, 108
Detroit (Michigan), 202, 664
Devant, David, 73, 126
Devine, George, 659
Dexamyl (drug), 543, 706, 717
di Capua, Michael, 710, 718
Diane (film; 1956), 477, 478, 483, 488, 499, 501, 502–4
Diane de Poitiers, 477, 499
Diary of a Lost Girl (film; 1929), 220, 239
Dick Cavett Show, The (television program), 698, 718
Dickens, Charles, 187, 213, 227, 265, 723; *Barnaby Rudge*, 296; *A Christmas Carol*, 665; *David Copperfield*, 72–3, 213, 214, 215, 264, 456, 498; *Dombey and Sons*, 272; *Great Expectations*, 109; *Hard Times*, 243; *Martin Chuzzlewit*, 122, 213; *Nicholas Nickleby*, 105, 180; *Oliver Twist*, 86–7, 152–3, 235, 427, 498, 646; *A Tale of Two Cities*, 324, 703
Diebenkorn, Richard, 682, 709
Dietrich, Marlene, 464
Dimitrov, Georgi, 361

Disley (Cheshire), 11; Bentside Road, 655; Church, 19; Disley Hall Farm, 196; Meadowbank Farm, 94, 136, 395; Ploughboy pub, 586–7, 624
Djakarta, 524
Djibouti, 284
Dobson, Robert, 27, 76, 83, 116
Dodds, E.R., 310
Dog Beneath the Skin, The; or Where is Francis? (with W.H. Auden; 1935), 41, 82, 83, 96, 161, 268–70, 458
dog tags (identity disks), 82–3, 270
Dolfuss, Engelbert, 363
Donadio, Candida, 710
Donald, Henry, 285
Donne, John: portrait, 25, 210, 665; "Death, be not proud," 619
Donoghue, Mary Agnes, 694
Doone, Rupert, 270, 294, 440
Dostoevsky, Fyodor, 414, 531, 551, 589, 594; *The Brothers Karamazov*, 78, 200, 460, 524, 573, 650; *Crime and Punishment*, 414; *The Gambler*, 413, 414; *The Idiot*, 264
Douglas, Lord Alfred (Bosie), 206, 454
Douglas, Norman, *South Wind*, 154–5
Dover (Kent), 290, 291, 312
Down There on a Visit (1962): autobiographical aspects, 38, 553–6, 565–6, 568–9; characterization, 38, 308, 316, 439, 482, 495, 498, 507, 553–80; dedication, 581; influences on, 448, 492, 498, 525, 550–4, 557, 588; plot and themes, 5, 125, 198, 254, 261–2, 315–16, 394, 432, 448, 482, 492–3, 498–9, 505, 506, 508, 550–1, 553–80, 599; publication, 556, 562, 582, 588, 593, 594; quotations and extracts, 286, 553, 565–9, 575, 577; reception and reviews, 585, 594–6, 622; structure and form, 198, 254, 261–2, 272, 550–1, 582; title, 498; writing of, 5, 198, 204, 253–4, 482, 497–9, 511, 515, 516, 543, 544, 550–4, 565, 581, 585, 641, 659; *see also* "Ambrose"; "Mr. Lancaster"; "Paul"; "Waldemar"
Downs School (Herefordshire), 261
Downton Abbey (television series), 697
Doyle, Arthur Conan, 34, 95, 161, 574; Sherlock Holmes stories, 39, 95, 125–6, 144, 154, 199, 574
Doyle, Peter, 206
"Drawings '71" (exhibition; 1971), 694
"Dream-Garden, The" (1921), 134
Driberg, Tom, 309
Drinkwater, John, 128
Drosia (Greece), 253
Drummond, Kate, 642
Drutman, Irving, 396
Duberman, Martin, *The Worlds of Lincoln Kirstein*, 349, 400
Dublin, 45
Duke, Joan Toogood, 387
Duke, Shirley, 387
Dulwich (London), 385, 510–11
Dumas, Alexandre, 34, 128
Dunkirk evacuation (1940), 334
Dunne, Irene, 499

Dupuytren's contracture (disease of fingers), 674, 695, 696
Duquette, Elizabeth (Beegle), 501
Duquette, Tony, 501
Duras, Marguerite, *Le Marin de Gibraltar*, 635
Dürer, Albrecht, 159

Earles, Bob, 648
Earth (film; 1930), 241
Easiest Thing in the World, The (film treatment), 415–16
East of Eden (film; 1955), 483
Eastman, George, 54
Easton, Harvey, 612
Ebb, Fred, 657
Ebeling, Gretl, 320, 337
Economist, The (magazine), 697, 722
Edale (Derbyshire), 114
Eder, Richard, 719
Edinburgh, 642, 710
Edward VIII, King (*later* Duke of Windsor), 278
Eerde Castle (Netherlands), 355
Ehrenburg, Ilya, "Sons of Our Sons," 241, 283
Eick, Götz von (Peter Van Eyck), 237
Eisenstein, Sergei, 478; *Battleship Potemkin*, 241; *October: Ten Days that Shook the World*, 241
Eisler, Hanns, 347, 478
Eleanor of Aquitaine, 676
elections (Germany): (1930), 225, 239; (1933), 244, 360
elections (United States): (1960), 622; (1968), 669
Elephant Man, The (film; 1980), 725
Eliot, T.S., 167, 185, 186, 226, 333, 618, 712; "The Love Song of J. Alfred Prufrock," 187, 230; *Murder in the Cathedral*, 276; "Preludes," 230; *The Waste Land*, 167, 241, 299
Elizabeth I, Queen, portrait, 25, 210
Elizabeth II, Queen, 676; coronation, 114; marriage, 114
Ellis, Havelock, *Studies in the Psychology of Sex*, 206
Emily Ermengarde (proposed television show), 520–1, 541
Emmanuel College, Cambridge, 66, 130
Empire cinema (Leicester Square, London), 504
Encounter (magazine), 199, 298, 437, 467, 484, 562
End of St. Petersburg, The (film; 1927), 241
Enemies of a Bishop, The, or Die When I Say When (with W.H. Auden; unpublished play), 208–9
Englishman, The see *A Single Man*
Englishwoman, The see *A Single Man*
Ensenada (Mexico), 301, 414, 440, 454, 535, 540
Epstein, Barbara, 710
"Escales" (1938), 284
Esquire (magazine), 594
Essentials of Vedanta (1969), 671
Essex-Crosby, Mr. and Mrs. (Marple Hall caretakers), 391, 392
Eton College, 564
Eulenburg-Hertefeld, Prince Philipp zu, 214
Evans, Gregory, 7–8, 718
Evans, Rex, 597, 681, 682
"Evening at the Bay, An" (1928), 195
Evening Standard (newspaper), 40
Exhumations: Stories, Articles and Verse (1966), 102–3, 634, 640, 642

Faber and Faber (publishers), 282
Fabian, Olga, 437
fagging system (public schools), 117–19, 128, 131–2
Fairbanks, Harold, 417, 433
"Faithful, The" (1921), 134
Faithfull, Marianne, 662
Falk, Eric, 143, 150, 152, 153, 154, 180, 582
Falkenburg, Jinx, 397
Falklands, Battle of the (1914), 95–6
Fanfreluche (Corpus Christi College magazine), 163
Farrar, Straus & Giroux (publishers), 710
Faulkner, William, 543
February Uprising (Austria; 1934), 362–3
Field, Gus, 430, 474
Fielding, Henry, *Tom Jones*, 622
Film Society (London), 179, 181, 241
Financial Times (newspaper), 697
Finney, Albert, 586, 587, 592, 622
Finney, Brian, 706
Firbank, Ronald, 398
Fire Island (New York), 398–9, 411, 518
First World War *see* World War I
Fisher, Geoffrey, 114, 117, 119, 124, 128–9, 130, 145
Fisher, George, 183–4
Fisher, Stanley, 184
Fitts, George (Swami Krishnananda), 336, 358, 628, 629
Fitzgerald, F. Scott, 495; *The Beautiful and Damned*, 710; *The Great Gatsby*, 494, 710; *Tender is the Night*, 494
Flaubert, Gustave, 143; *Madame Bovary*, 460
Fleming, Ian, 287
Fleming, Peter, 287–8
Fletcher, C.R.L., *A History of England*, 51
Florence, 32, 507
Fodor, Ladislas, 413
Foote, Dick, 532, 583
For Whom the Bell Tolls (film; 1943), 352–3
Forbes, Agnes, 32, 33
Forbes, Arthur, 32–3, 37, 48, 52, 213
Forbes-Robertson, Johnston, 53
Ford, Ford Madox, 19, 424
Ford, Glenn, 499, 636
Ford, John, 465
Ford, Ruth, 237
Ford, Tom, *A Single Man*, 550
Ford Foundation, 437
Ford Republic (reform school; Michigan), 202
Forest, Jean, 153, 699
Forester, C.S., 392
Forever Amber (film; 1947), 446
Forever and a Day (film; 1943), 392
Forster, E.M., 253, 256, 266, 283, 294, 295, 384, 458, 480, 523, 545, 566, 584, 586, 595, 605, 636, 693, 707–8, 723; and CI and Auden's emigration, 310, 387, 568; friendship and socializing with CI, 121, 232, 271, 274, 292, 321–2, 341, 396, 412–13, 508, 588; influence on CI, 8, 121, 188–9, 197, 200, 232, 233, 300, 440, 460–1, 596, 609, 641, 651–2; later life and death, 661, 683; portrayal in CI's works, 568; relationship with Bob Buckingham, 341, 661, 683; views on CI's works, 232, 266, 412–13, 595–6, 605; *Aspects of the Novel*, 175, 460–1, 539; "A Camera Man" (essay on Sinclair Lewis), 230–1; *Howards End*, 121, 181, 188–9, 322, 539, 687; *The Longest Journey*, 189, 508; *Maurice*, 413; *A Passage to India*, 341, 508, 523, 587, 651–2; *A Room with a View*, 185; "The Temple," 651
Forsyte Saga, The (television series), 697
Fortescue-Brickdale, Eleanor, 123
Fosse, Bob, 700
Foster, John, 677
Foster, Peter Le Neve, 163
Fouts, Denham (Denny): background and early life, 314, 571; appearance and character, 314–15, 324, 412, 571; relationship with Peter Watson, 314, 315, 571; and Gerald Heard, 315, 571–2, 576–7; CI first meets, 314–16, 571; attends Quaker La Verne Seminar with CI, 316–18, 719; begins writing novel, 316; wartime public service, 318, 327, 348; during CI's time as monk at Vedanta monastery, 348, 349, 352, 356, 359; medical student at UCLA, 358; and CI's relationship with Bill Caskey, 374, 375, 379–80, 411–12; and John Goodwin, 396, 579; in Paris, 411–12; last meetings with CI, 380, 411–12; death, 507, 571, 578, 579; CI visits grave with Bachardy, 507; characteristics of friendship with CI, 315–16, 318, 325, 357, 373, 380, 507; portrayal in CI's works, 315–16, 507, 570–2, 576–7, 578, 579; portrayal in works of Vidal, Capote and Maugham, 570, 572
Fox (film company) *see* 20th Century-Fox
Fox, George, 546, 589
Fox, Johnny, 165
France, Anatole, 128; *The Crainquebille Affair*, 153
Francis, Arlene, 698
Francis, David, 170, 173
Francis, Sam, 647, 724
Francis I, King of France, 499
Franco, Francisco, 198
Franco-Prussian War (1870–71), 83
Frankenstein: The True Story (television film; 1973), 694–6, 701, 702–3
Frankenthaler, Helen, 647
Franklin, Bill, 717–18
Frazer, James, *The Golden Bough*, 340
French, Jared, 398
French, John French, 1st Viscount (*later* 1st Earl of Ypres), 108
French, Margaret, 398
French, Robin, 672, 676, 679, 701
Freshwater Bay (Isle of Wight), 177–9, 185–7, 193–5, 197, 199, 210
Freud, Sigmund, 144, 167, 555, 609–10; *Introductory Lectures on Psychoanalysis*, 144
Freundin, Die (magazine), 255, 256
Frezenberg Ridge, Battle of (1915), 80–1, 82
Frimley Green (Surrey), 30–2, 41, 107, 661
From, Isadore (Eddie), 418
From, Sam, 419, 591
From the Manger to the Cross (film; 1912), 54
Fry, Basil, 197, 555
Fry, Charles, 87–8, 132, 139, 197, 555
Fry, Julia Greene, 87–8, 139, 197
Fry, Roger, 34–5

824 / Index

Fryer, Jonathan, 706
Fuller, Roy, 697
Furbank, Philip Nicholas, 683

Gabbitas & Thring (tutoring agency), 191
"Galilee Man" (archaeological artefact), 219
"Gallinamania" (1922), 135
Gallup (New Mexico), 465
Galsworthy, John, *The Forsyte Saga*, 697
Gandhi, Mohandas, 663
Gannett Newspapers, 719
Garbo, Greta, 302, 305, 337, 342, 355, 380, 416, 483, 618; *Two-Faced Woman*, 323
Gardena (California), 694
Gardiner, Muriel, 467
Gardner, Ava, 415
Garland, Judy, 700
Garland of Questions and Answers, A (Prabhavananda), translation, 689
Garnett, David, 298–9; *Lady into Fox*, 55
Garrett, Eileen, 456, 521
Gaudier-Brzeska, Henri, 106
Gauguin, Paul, 34
Gaumont Lime Grove studios (London), 163
Gaumont-British (film company), 259, 263, 266, 301, 338
Gay Activists Alliance, 698
Gay Advocates, 720
Gay Liberation Front, 685
gay liberation movement, 9, 419–20, 469, 685, 686–7, 690–3, 698, 714, 720, 725
Gay Pride parades, 687
Gay-In (Los Angeles; 1970), 685
Geldzahler, Henry, 682
"Gems of Belgian Architecture" (1927), 101–2, 103, 113, 219, 333
George IV, King, as Prince Regent, 198
George V, King, 108, 123; coronation, 38, 53
George VI, King: award of King's Gold Medal for Poetry to Auden, 42, 283; coronation, 277, 278
Ghosh, Abanindra Nath *see* Prabhavananda, Swami
Ghosh, Asit, 336, 368
Ghosh, Girish, 629–30
Gibarti, Louis, 241, 242–3
Gibbs, Christopher, 683
Gibraltar, 504
Gide, André, 461–2, 513, 531, 693, 698, 707–8; *Les Caves du Vatican (Lafcadio's Adventures)*, 579–80; *Corydon*, 462; *Les Faux-Monnayeurs (The Counterfeiters)*, 175, 190, 368, 455; *L'Immoraliste (The Immoralist)*, 461–2, 495; *Journals*, 594; *Madeleine, ou Et nunc manet in te (Madeleine, or And Now He Is in You)*, 461–2; *La Porte étroite (Strait is the Gate)*, 461–2
Gielgud, John, 397, 582, 586, 636, 702; *The Tempest*, 557
Gigi (film; 1958), 521
Gilbert, Clement Scott, 679
Gilbert and Sullivan, 268
Gingold, Hermione, 520, 521
Ginsberg, Allen, 693
Giorgi, Elsie, Dr., 715, 718, 726, 729
Giroux, Robert, 710
Giselle (ballet), 228
Gish, Dorothy, 53

Gish, Lillian, 53
Gisli the Outlaw (Icelandic saga), 333
"Gita and War, The" (1944), 330–1, 391
Glaspell, Susan, *Ambrose Holt and Family*, 557
Glendale (California), 316, 452
Glendora (California), 318
Glossop (Derbyshire), 538
Glück, Erika, 237
Glyndebourne Festival (opera festival), 582
Gmeyner, Anna, 262
Goddard, Paulette, 636
Godfather, The (film; 1972), 700
Goebbels, Joseph, 252, 360, 361, 444
Goering, Hermann, 252, 360, 361
gold standard, Britain leaves (1931), 226
Golden Globes (awards), 622
Golders Green Cemetery (London), 169
Goldsmith, Joel, 532, 553
Goldsmith, Oliver, 128
Goldwyn, Samuel, 163, 302, 364, 388, 477, 478, 479, 533
Gollancz, Victor, 129
Goodbye to Berlin (1939): autobiographical aspects, 4, 38, 224–5, 239–40, 245, 247; characterization, 4, 38, 49, 59, 203, 217, 223–5, 226–8, 229–30, 235–40, 245–6, 248–9, 250–1, 343, 437, 494, 713–14; plot and themes, 8, 204, 215–17, 223–5, 226–8, 229–30, 231–2, 234, 239–40, 244–52, 295–6; publication and editions, 3, 204, 295–6, 298–9, 379; quotations and extracts, 215, 230, 231, 239–40, 248, 250–1, 252; reception and reviews, 3–4, 229–30, 298–9, 343, 646; structure and form, 204, 215, 223, 244, 299, 379; style and influences, 230, 248; writing of, 204, 215, 250, 259, 272, 394; *see also* "A Berlin Diary (Autumn 1930)"; "A Berlin Diary (Winter 1932–3)"; *Cabaret*; *I Am a Camera*; "The Landauers"; "The Nowaks"; "On Ruegen Island (Summer 1931)"; *Sally Bowles*
Goode, Joe, 647, 693–4, 708
Goodman, Paul, 419
Goodwin, John, 396, 518, 579
Gordon (expatriate hoteliers in Mexico), 495
Gordon, Charles George, 587
Gorfain, A.D., Dr., 353, 394
Goulding, Harry, 465
Gowan, Adam, *Characteristic Passages from the Hundred Best English Prose Writers*, 119
Gowland, Peter, 648
GPO Film Unit, 276, 489
Graham, Robert, 647
Gran Canaria, 263–5, 267
Granada (Spain), 267
Granard, Arthur Forbes, 1st Earl of, 32
Grant, Alexander, 39
Grantchester (Cambridgeshire), 167
Granville-Barker, Harley, 59
Grateful Dead (rock band), 660
Grave Diggers (Cambridge University society), 168
Graves, Robert: *Claudius the God*, 677; *Goodbye to All That*, 539; *I, Claudius*, 677–9, 694
Great English Short Stories (anthology; 1957), 494, 516, 575–6

Great Gatsby, The (film; 1974), 710
Great Sinner, The (film; 1949), 413–15
Great War *see* World War I (1914–18)
Greece, 253–8; *see also* Athens
Greene, Charles, 132, 138–9
Greene, Edward, 274
Greene, Felix, 316–17, 327, 391
Greene, Graham, 138–9, 148, 274, 379
Greene, Sir Walter, 15, 18, 100
Greene, Sir William Graham, 43, 139, 274
Gregory, Horace, 484
Grenoble (France), 143
Gresham's School (Norfolk), 132, 184, 185
Grettir's Saga (Icelandic saga), 333
Grey, Joel, 657, 658, 700
Grigson, Geoffrey, 228–9
Grimm Brothers, 160
Groddeck, Georg, 609–10, 615, 660; *The Book of the It*, 609, 610, 611–12, 646
Groix (ship), 409
Gross, Alfred, 357
Gross, Babette, 242, 481
Grosz, George, 436
Group Theatre (theater company), 268, 270, 276, 294, 440
Gruber, Franz, "Silent Night," 654–5
Guardian (newspaper), 663, 697; *see also* Manchester Guardian
Guaymas (Mexico), 493–4
Guggenheim, Peggy, 507
Gunn, Thom, 484, 502, 693
Gunter Grove (Chelsea, London), 261
Günther's Erlebnisse (Aus dem Tagebuch eines Flagellanten), 255
Guptarakse, Niti, 153
Gurian, Manning, 591, 592, 594
Gypsy Rose Lee, 319

Haddon Hall (Derbyshire), 106
Hagedorn House (Nantucket, Massachusetts), 398
Hagenbuehler, Hanns, 421
Haggard, (Henry) Rider, 306; *Ayesha*, 95
Haigh, Kenneth, 672–3
Haight, Genevieve Watson, 546
Hair (musical), 675
Haldane, Charlotte, 282
Hall, Michael, 581
Halsey, Ed, 580–1
Hamburg, 224, 463
Hamilton, Gerald, 212, 242, 262, 273, 274, 278–9, 295, 308–9, 385, 465, 481; as model for Arthur Norris, 203, 211–12, 213, 264, 279, 388, 515, 713; *Mr. Norris and I...*515
Hamlet (film; 1913), 53
Hammerstein, Oscar and Dorothy, 499–500
Hankow (China), 284–6
Hansen, Erwin, 240, 253, 254, 257, 558
Hardwick, Elizabeth, 638
Hardwick, George Clifford, 131, 152
Hardy, Thomas, 128
Harewood, George Lascelles, 7th Earl of, 676–7
Harewood, Patricia Lascelles, Countess of, 676–7
Harewood House (Yorkshire), 676
Harper's Bazaar (magazine), 284, 288, 369, 382, 395, 397, 435, 597, 682

Harrington, Curtis, 486–7
Harris, Bill, 351–2, 356, 358–9, 423, 682
Harris, Julie, 136, 435, 542, 591, 592, 593, 594; *East of Eden*, 483; *I Am a Camera*, 203, 433, 434, 435; *Little Moon of Alban*, 548; *Mademoiselle Colombe*, 475
Harrison, Rex, 665, 694
Harrity, Marguerite *see* Littman, Marguerite
Harrity, Rory, 592
Harrods (department store, London), 59
Hartford (Connecticut), 434–5
Hartford, Huntington, 430, 432, 482
Hartley, Neil, 655, 659, 661, 666, 667, 678, 683
Harvey, Anthony, 676
Harwich (Essex), 261–2, 566
hashish, 504–5, 506, 614, 618
Hastings (Marple doctor), 390, 391
Haverford (Pennsylvania), 318, 319–22, 396, 455, 534, 642
Haverford College (Pennsylvania), 319, 324
Hawes, Dee, 664
Haworth, Jill, 657
Haworth Parsonage (Yorkshire), 508–9
Haydn, Joseph, 181
Hayfield (Derbyshire), 114
Hayward, Leland, 682
Heard, Gerald: appearance and character, 300, 303; background and early career, 300; CI first meets, 300; friendship with W.H. Auden, 300, 303, 306, 312, 318; relationship with Chris Wood, 301, 315, 326, 328; relocation to California, 300, 301, 309; spiritual quest, study of Vedanta and disciple of Swami Prabhavananda, 300, 303–5, 307, 312, 334, 601, 689, 690; introduces CI to Prabhavananda, 304, 648; split with Prabhavananda, 313–14, 315; and Denny Fouts, 315, 571–2, 576–7; at Quaker La Verne Seminar (summer 1941), 316–18, 329; moves to Laguna Beach with Wood, 326, 327; establishment of Trabuco College, 315, 327–9, 576; life at Laguna Beach, 328, 335, 342; donates Trabuco College site to Vedanta Society, 417; critical of CI's lifestyle, 430, 432–3; interest in parapsychology, 456; life in Pacific Palisades, 470; and CI's relationship with Don Bachardy, 470; drug-taking experiments, 505–6; *A Meeting by the River* dedicated to, 648; later life and death, 581, 640, 663; portrayal in CI's works, 308, 329, 576–7, 581; portrayal in Aldous Huxley's works, 625; views on CI's works, 369, 581, 637; writings, 308
Heckford, Harry, 661
Heflin, Lee, 685
"Hemingway, Death, and the Devil" (1941), 353
Hemingway, Ernest, 494, 495, 589; *A Farewell to Arms*, 271–2; *For Whom the Bell Tolls*, 352–3; *The Old Man and the Sea*, 369, 494; *The Sun Also Rises (Fiesta)*, 492, 494, 495, 533, 710; *To Have and Have Not*, 494
Hendon airfield (Middlesex), 59
Henri II, King of France, 477, 499
Henry II, King, 676
Henry VII, King, 216

Henry VIII, King, 112
Henry, Victor, 672
Henty, G.A., 34
Henze, Hans Werner, *Elegy for Young Lovers*, 582, 584
Hepburn, Audrey, 435, 694
Hepburn, Katharine, 676
Herd of Lions (unpublished play), 208
Hernández de Alba, Gregorio, 404
"Hero, The" (1924), 146–7, 148–9, 170, 606
Hewit, Jack, 294–5, 384, 479, 480–1, 482
Hichens, Robert, *The Garden of Allah*, 338
High Valley Theater Company (California), 354–5
Hill, Frida (*later* Isherwood), 120, 150, 720
Hillcox, John Lenville, *In Chancery, or, Browne with an E*, 33–4, 50
Hilton, James, 392
Hinde, John, 383
Hindenburg, Paul von, 360, 361
Hindhead (Surrey), 56, 69, 107; *see also* St. Edmund's School (Hindhead)
Hines family (Sycamore Road, Santa Monica), 537
Hiroshima, atomic bombing (1945), 369
Hirschfeld, Magnus, Dr., 205, 218, 220, 242, 444, 462, 677, 713; *see also* Institute for Sexual Science
History of My Friends, The (with Kathleen Isherwood; 1910–11), 37, 47, 49, 51, 52, 53, 61, 131, 237, 378
Hitchcock, Alfred, 392; *The Man Who Knew Too Much*, 266; *Young and Innocent*, 266
Hitler, Adolf, 214, 239, 240, 248, 252, 285, 292, 293, 359–61, 392; portrayal in CI's works, 362, 363, 365
Hockney, David, 7, 539, 646–8, 664–6, 682, 683–5, 693, 696–7, 701–2, 710–11, 716, 718, 724; exhibitions, 677, 680–1, 684; *Christopher Isherwood and Don Bachardy*, 539, 665–6, 672, 677, 683, 721; "A Hollywood Collection," 647; *Portrait of an Artist (Pool with Two Figures)*, 684; *A Visit with Christopher and Don, Santa Monica Canyon*, 721
Hoffmann, Professor (Angelo Lewis), *Modern Magic*, 73, 87
Hofmann, Hans, 647
Hogan, William, 721
Hogarth Press, 3, 233, 349, 439
Hohnsbeen, John, 434
Hölderlin, Friedrich, 271
Hollinghurst, Alan, 693, 723
Hollywood (film; 1923), 164
Hollywood Authors Club, 706
Hollywood Reporter (magazine), 504, 655
Hollywood Ten (blacklisted film-makers), 477–8, 479
Hollywood Vedanta Center *see* Vedanta Place
Home Rule (Ireland), 55–6, 64, 529
Homer, *Odyssey*, 565, 646
homosexuality: W.H. Auden's, 201, 206–7, 267, 311, 637; Don Bachardy's, 445–6, 450–1, 488; CI's, 4, 8, 9, 96–7, 124, 132–4, 170–1, 178–9, 204, 206–7, 257, 260, 305, 311, 378, 420, 450–1, 472–3, 692–3; CI's uncle's, 16, 93, 209; CI's views on, 57, 98–9, 138, 170–1, 178–9, 206, 406–7, 410–11, 637, 640–1, 698–9; in CI's works, 8, 9, 74, 133, 169, 178–9, 200, 201, 204, 205–6, 214, 419–20, 444, 462, 463–4, 468–9, 485–6, 550, 558, 566, 599, 603–5, 623–4, 625–6, 637, 643, 692, 694, 698–9, 712–13, 714–15; Dr. Kinsey's studies of, 632; and kleptomania, 270; legal status, 4, 241, 242, 311, 422–3, 452; Los Angeles homosexual community, 418–20, 438, 441, 444, 591; media coverage, 685–6, 691, 712; and the military, 376; in Nazi Germany, 252–3, 256, 260, 279; psychological studies of, 418–19, 691–2; public opinion on, 685–6; and public schools, 118, 132–3, 468–9; in Soviet Russia, 241; and Vedanta, 305, 527–8, 686–7, 720; in Gore Vidal's works, 410–11, 559, 570, 623; in Evelyn Waugh's works, 563–4; in Weimar Berlin, 201, 208, 219–20, 255–6; *see also* gay liberation movement
"Homosexuals, The" (television news report; 1967), 685–6, 691
Hong Kong, 284, 524
Honolulu (Hawaii), 523, 525, 678
Hooker, Edward, 442, 443, 444, 451, 466, 472, 474, 691, 707
Hooker, Evelyn (*earlier* Caldwell), 418–19, 441–2, 443, 444, 450, 451, 472, 474, 488, 514, 685, 691–2, 707
Hope, Sir Anthony, *The Dolly Dialogues*, 239
Hopper, Brooke, 682, 708
Hopper, Dennis, 682
Horizon (magazine), 199, 309, 310, 383, 386, 395, 413
"Horror in the Tower, The" (1994), 161
Horse Guards (London), 81
Hour Before Dawn, The (film; 1944), 334, 338, 391–2
House & Garden (magazine), 397
House Un-American Activities Committee, 477–8
Houseman, John, 673, 679
Howard, Brian, 362, 385, 564, 566, 592
Howe, James Wong, 489
Hoyningen-Huene, George, 615, 621
Hudson, Fanny, 91, 122, 386, 388
Hudson, Rock, 635
Hugenberg, Alfred, 252
Hugh Town (Scilly Isles), 188–9
Hugo, Victor, 128, 143, 322
Hull (Yorkshire), 390, 391, 442
Hungarian Revolution (1956), 515
Hungerford Bridge (London), 68
Huntington Hartford Foundation (writers' colony), 430, 431, 432, 441, 480, 482; advisory board, 430, 441
Hurst, Brian Desmond, 465
Huston, John, 635
Huxley, Aldous: appearance and character, 300, 365; background and early career, 300; friendship and socializing with CI, 7, 420, 456, 496–7, 512, 522; relocation to U.S., 309, 496; in California, 300, 305, 327, 329, 342, 496; spiritual life and disciple of Prabhavananda, 300, 321, 326, 329, 334, 347, 348, 354–5, 496, 497, 689; and CI and Prabhavananda's Bhagavad Gita translation,

332, 334; screenwriting work, 350, 354, 423–4, 497; critical of CI's lifestyle, 420, 433; interest in parapsychology and psychedelic drug culture, 456, 497, 506; death of first wife, 496–7; second marriage, 516, 589; house destroyed in brush fire, 589, 648; CI visits with Colin Wilson and Henry Miller, 589; and *A Single Man*, 589, 625–6; final illness, 612, 625; death, 627; memorial volume, 633; views on CI's works, 332, 369; *The Doors of Perception*, 497, 506; *After Many a Summer*, 539, 625–6; *Brave New World*, 300; *Island*, 589; *The Perennial Philosophy*, 334; *Time Must Have a Stop*, 573
Huxley, Julian, 321
Huxley, Laura (née Archera), 512, 589
Huxley, Maria, 305, 326, 327, 342, 354–5, 456, 506
Hyndman, Tony, 273, 291, 362, 363, 466

I, Claudius (film treatment), 677–9, 694
I Am a Camera (film; 1955), 4, 372, 504
I Am a Camera (Van Druten; play), 4, 430–1, 433–6, 437, 441, 443, 447, 459–60, 485, 532, 553, 592, 657, 676
"I Am Waiting" (1939), 302–3
IAH *see* Internationale Arbeiter-Hilfe (International Workers' Aid)
Ibsen, Henrik, 128; *Ghosts*, 456; *Peer Gynt*, 237; *Rosmersholm*, 381–2
Icelandic sagas, 101, 113, 333, 612
identity disks (military), 82–3, 270
Illustrated London News (magazine), 42, 574
Images (Beaton; 1963), introduction, 618
Importance of Being Earnest, The (film; 1952), 454
"In the Passage" (1923), 154
Inadmissable Evidence (film; 1968), 668, 672
India, CI visits, 525–30, 531, 624, 627–33, 641, 642
Indian independence movement, 529, 663
Indio (California), 342
Infinite Way (spiritual movement), 532, 553
"Influences" (lecture; 1960), 545–6
Inge, William, 594; *Bus Stop*, 521
Ingram, Rex, *Scaramouche*, 164
Ingres, Jean-Auguste-Dominique, 682, 694
Institute for Sexual Science (Berlin), 218, 220, 240, 242, 252–3, 304, 444, 462, 562, 713
Institute of Contemporary Arts (London), 439
International Festival of Fantastic and Science-Fiction Film (1976), 703
International String Quartet, 180, 522
Internationale Arbeiter-Hilfe (International Workers' Aid; IAH), 241–3, 250
Inverchapel, Archibald Clark Kerr, 1st Baron, 480
Inverness (Scotland), 196, 710
Ipiales (Colombia), 404
Irish Times (newspaper), 484
Irvine Hospital (Ayrshire), 82
Irving, Henry, 104
Irwin, Robert, 682
Ischia (Italy), 506
Isherwood, Christopher William Bradshaw: family background, 11–13, 15–17, 19, 24, 25, 56, 99, 136, 238, 545–6; birth, 11, 13–14, 19; christening, 6, 19; infancy and early

childhood, 18, 19–59, 269, 287; early childhood family holidays, 31, 36; earliest writings, 31–2, 34, 37, 47, 72, 109–10, 237, 252, 378; childhood illnesses, 33, 46, 59, 72, 74–6, 77, 78, 79–80, 88, 93, 114, 116, 167, 188, 428, 726; first masturbation fantasy, 36, 71; early schooling, 38–9, 45–6, 51, 52, 57; early theater-going and Shakespeare seasons, 39–40, 44, 51, 58, 59, 72–3, 91, 238; birth of brother Richard, 30, 36, 42–3; in Limerick during father's posting, 45–59, 92, 292, 378, 471; first terms at St. Edmund's preparatory boarding school, 55, 56, 59–64, 74–7, 146, 292, 459; early school holidays from St. Edmund's, 64–5, 71–4, 428; and outbreak of World War I, 64–6; early months of war, 66–80, 475, 601; father's disappearance and death, 2, 51, 65, 80–8, 90–1, 92, 102, 498; later years at St. Edmund's, 89–91, 96–117, 146, 333, 378; later school holidays from St. Edmund's, 91, 93–5, 105–6, 108–10, 110–11, 112; early sexual experiences, 96–7, 98–9, 378; first meets Wystan Auden, 97; early development of friendship with Auden, 97–9, 112–13, 333; scholarship exam for Charterhouse School, 111, 114, 130; admission to Repton School, 113–14, 117; leaves St. Edmund's, 111, 117; at Repton, 50, 55, 117–38, 142–55; adolescent illnesses, 119, 167; school holidays from Repton, 119–20, 131, 136–8, 142–3; joins Officers' Training Corps, 55, 122–3, 132, 154; circumcised, 122–3; mooted career as librarian, 123, 140, 175; confirmation in Anglican Church, 50, 124; first meets Edward Upward, 124, 126–7; Cambridge University scholarship exams, 130, 142; publications in *The Reptonian* magazine, 134–5; and mother's move to St. Mary Abbot's Terrace, Kensington, 140, 150; walking tour in France with Upward (August 1922), 142–4, 404; preparation for Cambridge, 145–51, 154–7; leaves Repton, 142, 149; language-learning trip to Rouen (1923), 151–2, 153–4, 156; poem published in *Public School Verse* anthology, 153–4; writing of *Lions and Shadows* (novel), 156–7, 173–5; at Cambridge, 8, 140, 158–77, 206, 547; collaborations with Upward, 159–62, 171; film extra and reviewer, 163–5; passes first-year examinations, 165; decides to pursue literary career, 165–6, 173–6; buys motorbike, 166; death of grandmother, 169–70, 171; fails second-year Tripos and leaves Cambridge, 158, 176–7, 203, 430; attempts to get work as screenwriter, 176, 177, 179; visits Isle of Wight (summer 1925), 177–9; twenty-first birthday, 179–80; buys first car, 179–80; secretary to André Mangeot, 158, 180–3, 191, 458, 522; renewed friendship with Auden, 161, 184–7, 191; visits Isle of Wight (summer 1926), 185–7, 190; holidays in Scilly Isles and France with Upward (summer 1926), 188–90; writing of *All the Conspirators*, 187–90, 192, 193, 194–5; tutoring jobs, 158, 191–2;

Isherwood (*cont.*)
briefly takes room in Redcliffe Road, Chelsea, 192–3, 195; visits Isle of Wight (early summer 1927), 512; road trip to Scotland with Bill de Lichtenberg (April 1928), 196–7, 217, 218; publication of *All the Conspirators*, 158, 190, 195–6, 197, 512, 561; first trip to Germany, 158, 197–8, 205, 235, 555; introduced to Stephen Spender, 198–9; medical student, 194, 199–200, 201, 202, 274; writing of *The Memorial*, 200–1, 204, 218, 226–7; first visit to Berlin (March 1929), 202, 203–4, 205–9; rift in relations with mother, 209, 210, 211, 221–3; holiday in France with Mangeots (March–April 1929), 209; and sale of Marple Hall furniture, 210–11; travels to Harz Mountains, Berlin and Amsterdam (summer 1929), 210–11; first and last complete sexual experience with a woman, 217–18; returns to Berlin to stay (November 1929), 218; life in Berlin, 218–21, 223–32, 235–40, 241–4, 462, 699; trip to England (February–May 1930), 221–3; and brother's arrest and court case, 222–3; relationship with Walter Wolff, 203, 221, 223–5; moves in with Wolff family, 225–8; moves to Kottbusser Tor, 228–9; moves to Nollendorfstrasse, 229–30, 234, 252, 404; trip to London (March 1931), 232; reconciliation with mother, 232; *The Memorial* rejected for publication, 232; holiday on Ruegen Island (early summer 1931), 223, 232–3, 399; *The Memorial* accepted for publication, 233–4; writing of *Memoirs of Pine House*, 234; publication of *The Memorial*, 233–4; article for *Action* magazine, 234–5; first meets Heinz Neddermeyer, 240–1; development of relationship with Neddermeyer, 131, 223, 240, 255, 258, 291–2, 300, 322; trip to London (summer 1932), 237–8; dictates work to brother, 237–8, 454; translation work for International Workers' Aid (IAH), 241–4; prepares to leave Berlin, 252–3; flight from Berlin with Neddermeyer, 204, 253; in Greece, 253–8, 557, 559; writing of Berlin novels, 204, 254–6, 259–60, 263–5, 272; tensions in relationship with Neddermeyer, 256–7, 258; returns to England via France, 257–8; in London (late-1933–early-1934), 258–62; first meets Berthold Viertel, 258; works on film script of *Little Friend* for Viertel, 258–66, 340, 361, 366, 367–8, 432, 456; Neddermeyer denied entry into Britain, 260, 261–2, 277, 507–8, 566; efforts to be reunited in safe haven with Neddermeyer, 82, 204, 262–3, 271, 272–6, 277–8, 362, 401, 473; in Canary Islands, 263–7, 432; tour through North Africa and Spain (autumn 1934), 267; in Copenhagen, 267, 268, 286; collaboration with Auden on *The Dog Beneath the Skin*, 268–70, 458; writing and abandonment of *Paul Is Alone*, 270–2, 307, 558, 571; in Portugal, 99, 272–4, 275, 298, 362; in Belgium, 274–5, 286; writing and productions of *The Ascent of F6* and *On the Frontier*, 99, 209, 276–7, 280–1, 288, 294; ill following botched wisdom tooth extraction, 277–8, 352, 353; in Luxembourg, 277–8; Neddermeyer's arrest and imprisonment in Germany, 204, 278–80, 281; relationship with Ian Scott-Kilvert, 280–2, 291; travels to China with Auden (1938), 204, 282–8, 290–1, 293, 303, 308, 480, 523, 525, 704; publication of *Lions and Shadows*, 283, 511; returns to London via New York, 288–9, 291; first meets Harvey Young, 288, 291, 293; writing and publication of *Journey to a War*, 282–3, 292–3, 294–5, 307, 401, 704; decision to emigrate to U.S., 2–3, 4–5, 294–5, 296–7, 309–11, 564, 566, 569; final months in Europe, 294–7, 372, 384; crosses Atlantic (January 1939), 1–3, 297; arrival in New York, 3, 143, 416, 504; in Manhattan (January–May 1939), 298–300, 396; publication of *Goodbye to Berlin*, 3–4, 204, 295–6, 298–9; development of relationship with Young, 298, 300, 305; travels to California with Young, 301, 568–9; obtains employment visa, 301; first months in Los Angeles, 301–8; works on anti-Nazi film treatment with Viertel, 301–2, 361–2; secures studio contract with MGM, 302, 305, 387; introduced to Swami Prabhavananda by Gerald Heard, 303–6, 648; early teaching and training by Prabhavananda, 2–3, 304–8, 312–13; death of Uncle Henry, 387–8; inherits Marple Hall Estate and passes it on to Richard, 388–9; visited by Auden (summer 1939), 306–7; reaction in Britain to emigration, 308–11, 383, 386–7, 563, 596; second visit by Auden (summer 1940), 311–12, 314; two minor mystical experiences, 312–13; initiated as disciple of Prabhavananda, 313–14, 329, 382, 434; first meets Denny Fouts, 314–16, 517; splits from Harvey Young, 315, 356–7, 418, 497; moves to apartment in Laurel Canyon, 315; attends Quaker La Verne Seminar with Fouts (summer 1941), 316–18, 319, 327, 329, 577; visits Auden on East Coast (August–September 1941), 318–19; works at refugee hostel in Haverford, Pennsylvania (October 1941–July 1942), 318, 319, 326, 463, 534, 642; applications to draft board, 325–6, 329, 334, 348; returns to California, 326–7; stays at Laguna Beach and visits Heard's Trabuco College, 327–9; revises wartime diaries, 328–9; translation of Bhagavad Gita with Prabhavananda, 313, 330–4, 342, 356, 373, 391, 395, 631, 665; works on film adaptation of Somerset Maugham's *The Hour Before Dawn*, 334, 338, 391–2; lives as monk at Vedanta monastery (February 1943–August 1945), 3, 329, 334–69, 371–5, 650; writing of *Prater Violet*, 204, 263, 272, 340, 357, 359, 363, 364, 367–9; challenge of celibate life, 342–7, 348–9, 351–2, 358–9, 420; ten-day break from monastery (August 1943), 345–8, 352; argument with Bertolt Brecht, 347–8, 360, 362, 365, 589, 625; travels to Vedanta centers in San Francisco, Portland and

Seattle (late 1943), 349–51; suffers from hemorrhoid, 352–3; plans for leaving monastery, 356–8; screenwriting work for Warner Brothers, 371–2, 519; catches gonorrhea, 372–3; first meets Bill Caskey, 374–5, 450–1; leaves monastery and moves into apartment with Caskey, 375, 376; development of relationship with Caskey, 3, 374–81, 396, 406, 417–18, 421–2, 458, 515; operation for blocked urethra, 353–4, 393–4; moves into Viertels' garage apartment with Caskey, 380–1; becomes U.S. citizen, 312, 382–3, 386, 434; jaunt to Mexico City with Caskey (Christmas and New Year 1946–7), 382; visits England (January–April 1947), 383–5, 393–6; returns to U.S., 396; in New York and Massachusetts (summer 1947), 396–400, 434; trip to South America (September 1947–March 1948), 397, 400–9, 422, 481; sails to Europe, 409–10; in Paris and England (spring 1948), 410–13; returns to California and moves into house on East Rustic Road, 413–14; works on screenplay for *The Great Sinner*, 413–15; life at East Rustic Road, 414, 417–18, 421–4, 425, 426, 597, 600, 612; elected to National Institute of Arts and Letters, 415; tensions in relationship with Caskey, 417–18, 420–1, 424, 427, 430–1, 441, 443, 457; temporary split from Caskey, 421; first encounters Ted Bachardy, 421, 447, 448–9; arrested during raid on bar (December 1949), 422–3; Caskey returns to Santa Monica, 424; trip to New Mexico with Peggy Kiskadden (August 1950), 424–5; and Caskey's arrest for drunk driving, 425–6, 427; visits World War II paraplegic veterans, 426–7; moves to Laguna with Caskey, 427–8; life at Monterey Street, Laguna, 428–33, 601; questioned by FBI on connections with Guy Burgess, 480–2; travels to East Coast for performances of *I Am a Camera* (October–December 1951), 433–6; sails to Europe, 436; in England and Berlin (January–March 1952), 436–40, 578–9; reunited with Neddermeyer, 439, 585; returns to United States, 438; in New York (March 1952), 438, 440; holiday in Bermuda with "Sam Costidy" (March 1952), 440–1, 450; returns to California, 441; moves to garden house in Brentwood, 441–3, 454; and garage fire at Brentwood house, 443–4, 448; first meets Don Bachardy, 3, 447–51; early development of relationship with Bachardy, 3, 453–5, 458–9, 464–6, 470, 482, 515–16; life at the Brentwood garden house, 454–5, 458–9, 464, 487, 691; road trip to Arizona, New Mexico, Utah and Nevada with Bachardy (May 1953), 464–5; and Spender's 1953 lecture tour of United States, 466, 470; trip to San Francisco with Bachardy (summer 1953), 471–2; evicted from Brentwood garden house, 472–3; 474–5; moves into apartment on Olive Drive, West Hollywood with Bachardy, 473; suffers from pyloric spasms, 474, 488–9, 567, 633; trip to New York with Bachardy (December 1953–January 1954), 474–7; questioned on supposed Communist Party links, 477–83, 488; further script-writing contract with MGM, 477, 483, 499; and writing and production of *Diane*, 477, 478, 483, 488, 489, 499, 501, 502–4; moves to house on Mesa Road, Santa Monica with Bachardy, 483; life at Mesa Road, 483–4, 502–3; parties and socializing in California (1954–60), 483–4, 491–2, 493, 499–500, 501, 502, 521, 540, 576; publication of *The World in the Evening*, 473–4, 483, 484–6, 488, 504; fight with Curtis Harrington, 486–7; trip to Key West (November 1954), 346, 489–91, 654; road trip to Mexico (December 1954–January 1955), 492–5, 497; and Bachardy's twenty-first birthday, 501–2; moves to Zuma Beach with Bachardy, 503; European tour with Bachardy (October 1955–March 1956), 143, 503, 504–11; in Tangier on route, 504–5, 614, 618; visits Upward in London, 510–14; returns to United States, 510, 514; buys house in Sycamore Road, Santa Monica, 510; life at Sycamore Road with Bachardy, 510, 514–18, 534–6, 537, 612; hospitalized with hepatitis, 434, 510, 514, 516, 517, 525; begins work on Ramakrishna biography, 516, 523, 525; lectures at Sarada Convent, Santa Barbara (March 1957), 517–18; and Bachardy's solo trip to New York (June–July 1957), 518–19; works on proposed television series with Gavin Lambert, 520–1; tour of Far East and India with Bachardy (October–December 1957), 523–30, 531; returns to California via London, 530–2, 557; learns of death of John Van Druten, 531–2; and mother's stroke, 532; development of open relationship with Bachardy, 534–6, 540–1, 542–3, 580, 606–7, 614–22, 639, 679, 695–7; and Bachardy's affair with Paul Millard, 535, 537–8, 540, 542, 543, 549, 591, 604; teaches at Los Angeles State College, 537, 539, 594, 596, 606, 663, 707; sale of Sycamore Road house and purchase of property on Adelaide Drive, 537; vacation in New York and Europe with Bachardy (summer 1959), 538, 544, 605; life at Adelaide Drive with Bachardy, 538–9, 540–3, 547, 634, 635; affair with Paul Kennedy, 540, 585, 604; proposed Socrates project with Charles Laughton, 541, 544, 590, 600; suffers slipped disk following fall, 543; death of mother, 543–4, 586; lectures at University of California, Santa Barbara, 12, 148, 440, 540, 545–7, 572–3, 574–6, 599, 615, 651, 707; Bachardy leaves to study art in London, 548–9, 550, 590; life in California during Bachardy's time in London, 580–1, 588–91, 594, 599–600; joins Bachardy in England (summer 1961), 580, 581–7, 647; last meeting with Neddermeyer, 439, 584–5; holiday at Tony Richardson's in south of France, 587–8; parties and socializing in California (1961–4), 589, 594, 606, 614–15, 620, 621, 622, 634, 635–6, 667; in New York for Bachardy's debut exhibition, 591–3;

Isherwood (*cont.*)
returns by train to California, 593; publication of *Down There on a Visit*, 556, 562, 582, 588, 593, 594–6; prostate infection, 596–7; writing of *A Single Man*, 590–1, 597–606, 608–12, 615–16, 620, 622–7, 659; house renovations and construction of Bachardy's studio at Adelaide Drive, 597, 607–8, 679; death of Laughton, 590, 612–14; and Bachardy's affair with George Kramer, 615–16, 620–2, 664; in San Francisco for Regents' Lectureship at Berkeley, 608, 618–19, 659; completion of Ramakrishna biography, 624, 627; death of Aldous Huxley, 625, 627; in India for Vivekananda centenary celebrations (December 1963–January 1964), 624, 625, 627–33, 641, 642; returns to California via Rome and New York, 633, 642; collection of material for *Exhumations*, 634, 640, 642; works on screenplays of *The Loved One* and *The Sailor from Gibraltar*, 633, 634, 635, 640; and Bachardy's thirtieth birthday, 635–6; parties and socializing in California (1964–86), 643, 646–8, 652, 660, 664–5, 693–4; publication of *A Single Man*, 624, 627, 637–8; visits Bachardy in New York (February 1965), 640; Regents' Professorship at UCLA, 640, 641; publication of *Ramakrishna and His Disciples*, 632, 635, 652–3, 721–2; writing of *A Meeting by the River*, 641–6, 648, 650–1, 652; research and writing of *Kathleen and Frank*, 15, 18, 52, 70, 648–50, 655–7, 658, 659–60, 661–2, 670–1, 673, 682, 684; Regents' Professorship at UC Riverside, 652; end of friendship with Lincoln Kirstein, 654; trip to Austria for "Silent Night" television project (September 1966), 654–5; returns to California via England, 655–7; avoids seeing productions of *Cabaret*, 658–9; adaptation of Shaw's *The Adventures of the Black Girl in Her Search for God*, 658–9, 665, 673, 674–5; proposed adaptation of Wedekind's Lulu plays, 659, 662, 664, 680–1; hears Maharishi Mahesh Yogi speak, 660–1; trip to England (spring 1967), 661–2; publication of *A Meeting by the River*, 654, 662–3; celebrates fifteenth anniversary with Bachardy, 664; ill health and breakdown during Bachardy's 1968 trips to London and affair with Anthony Page, 666–9, 671, 672–3, 697; stage adaptation of *A Meeting by the River*, 669–71, 672, 673, 679–80, 681, 682, 684; Dupuytren's contracture diagnosis, 674, 695, 696; writes screenplay for *Cabaret* with Bachardy, 676; writes screenplay for *I, Claudius* with Bachardy, 677–9, 694; in Tahiti and Australia (July–August 1969), 677–8, 687; trip to London (January–March 1970), 680–1, 682–3; last visits to Forster, 683; holiday in south of France with Tony Richardson, 683–4; collaboration with Bachardy on *Frankenstein* screenplay, 694–6, 701, 702–3; operation on hand, 696; publication of *Kathleen and Frank*, 148, 693, 696, 697–9, 706;
stage productions of *A Meeting by the River*, 700–1, 718–19, 724; trip to Europe with Bachardy (January–March 1973), 701–3; and proposed publication of correspondence with John Lehmann, 703–4; death of Auden, 702, 704–5, 711; writing of *Christopher and His Kind*, 659, 703, 705–6, 710; and Bachardy's summer 1973 Barnsdall Park show, 708, 709; collaboration with Bachardy on proposed film adaptation of *The Beautiful and Damned*, 710; trip to England and Scotland with Bachardy (summer 1976), 710–11; in Tangier with Gavin Lambert, 711; death of Prabhavananda, 711; publication of *Christopher and His Kind*, 710, 711–15, 720, 722, 723; injures knee in fall, 715–16, 717; officially adopts Bachardy, 716; writing of *My Guru and His Disciple*, 711, 716–17, 718, 719, 720; and Bachardy's affair with Bill Franklin, 717–18; trips to New York for Broadway production of *A Meeting by the River* (January–March 1979), 718–19, 724; death of brother Richard, 719–20; collaboration with Bachardy on illustrated diary, 720–1, 725; publication of *My Guru and His Disciple*, 713–14, 720, 721–3; starts writing *Scenes from an Emigration*, 723–4, 726, 727; death of Caskey, 724; trip to New York with Bachardy for Robert Miller Gallery show (September 1980), 725; works on film adaptation of "Paul," 725, 726; injured during burglary at Adelaide Drive, 725–6; hernia operation, 726–7; cancer diagnosis, 489, 727; receives PEN and Robert Kirsch awards, 727; travels to New York for Auden symposium (October 1983), 727–8; final illness, 728–9; death, 83, 489, 729

Character & characteristics: albums, commonplace books and scrapbooks, 54–5, 114–15, 119, 134, 152–3, 164, 178; Animal identities with Bachardy, 23, 39, 47, 458–9, 514, 617; anxiety, 2, 31, 33, 90, 146; appearance, 14, 89, 127, 294, 447; astrological sign, 451; aviation interests, 59; back problems, 488, 543, 634; bicycling, 84–5, 105, 131; birthday, 11, 266; blood donations, 434–5; book collection, 122, 275, 394–5, 397, 415; cars and driving, 180, 301, 429, 448, 449, 536–7, 607, 621, 695; catalogue of books, 122, 123; charisma, 1, 133, 294; cinema-going and love of films, 34, 41, 49–50, 53–4, 152–3, 163–5, 179, 699; circumcision, 122–3, 353, 354; classlessness, 47–8; clothes, 22, 38, 59, 118–19, 127, 150, 171, 220, 284, 286–7, 380–1, 447, 503; collecting, 55, 85, 101–3, 114–15, 139, 185, 254; compulsiveness, 668; conversationalist, 483–4; dancing, 471, 489; diary- and journal-keeping, 5, 7, 94–7, 110, 117, 144, 166–7, 234, 253–4, 311, 328–9, 370–1, 394, 396, 484, 497, 523, 620, 656; dislike of change, 649; drawings, 42, 58, 111, 720; drinking, 407, 420, 506, 520, 522, 547, 620, 661, 662, 725–6; drug-taking experiments, 505–6; exhibitionism, 36, 373, 377, 427, 547, 658; fame, 4, 7, 283, 284, 373–4, 379, 393, 402, 484–5; father figures, 2,

16, 141, 304, 367, 475, 661; fear of loss of identity, 83, 350, 434, 506, 693; foreign language skills, 180, 203, 313, 438; friendships with women, 135-6, 294, 302, 337; fun-loving, 93, 120; game-playing, 24, 307, 377, 430, 458, 464; handwriting, 94, 397, 655; height, 447; heraldry interests, 111, 114-15; historical analysis, 124-8, 477; imagination, 5-6, 44, 56, 286-7, 305; inner strength, 519; intermittent impotence, 354, 517, 518, 571, 581; intuition, 90, 366, 397; jogging, 671, 673, 717; lecture style, 545; leg problems, 72, 74-5, 77, 81, 100, 114, 201, 233, 426, 428, 436, 715-16, 726; lifetime achievement awards, 706, 707, 727; literary importance, 7, 8-9, 119, 283, 294, 299, 393, 653, 723; magic and conjuring interests, 56, 73-4, 87, 126, 505, 626; meditation, 154, 300, 304-5, 313, 320, 322, 344-5, 520, 660-1, 670, 687-8, 716; motor-cycling, 166; musical interests, 100, 379, 522; names, 6, 19, 71, 149, 265; neurosis, 158, 167; nicknames, 6, 23, 39, 155, 458-9; nightmares, 38-9, 45, 253, 367, 443-4, 503; pacifism, 2, 130, 147, 287, 307, 330-1, 340-1, 391-2, 464, 643, 663; photographic interests, 49, 54-5, 231; politics, 128-30, 225, 234-5, 241, 244, 307-8, 481-2, 692; portraits, 277, 323, 475, 539, 582, 586, 588, 593, 615, 645, 665-6, 669, 672, 677, 683, 721, 728, 729; prose stylist, 8-9, 119, 184, 294, 299; pseudonyms, 134, 159, 203; restlessness, 5, 530-1; role-playing, 23, 24, 38; roller-skating, 150, 156, 173; school sports, 62-3, 96-7, 103, 108-9, 111-12, 134; search for better life, 4-5; search for permanent loving relationship, 1-2, 322, 351, 454, 534-5, 617; self-criticism, 5, 6, 698; sexuality, 4, 8, 9, 35-6, 96-7, 124, 132-4, 170-1, 178-9, 204, 206-7, 218, 257, 260, 305, 311, 378, 420, 450-1, 472-3, 692-3; singing voice, 117; smoking, 119, 290, 313-14, 421; snake phobia, 38-9, 46, 168; sociability, 150, 168, 323, 324; speaking voice, 178, 313, 384; spirituality, 5, 50-1, 124, 303-4, 312-13, 320, 322, 329, 407-8, 471, 530-1, 601, 660-1, 687-8; supernatural interests, 26-8, 95, 109-10, 145, 421-2, 456, 457, 505; swimming, 103, 111, 420, 503; talkativeness, 118, 294; teeth problems, 277-8, 352, 353, 634; traveling interests and love of far away places, 50, 142-3, 400-1, 530-1, 677; vertigo, 102, 407; wit, 97, 135, 304, 369; yearning for power to heal, 199

Finances: *All the Conspirators* income, 196; allowance from Uncle Henry, 141, 210, 226, 387; business merger with Bachardy, 608; *Cabaret* income, 658, 676; car accident and insurance costs, 536-7, 621; *The Condor and the Cows* income, 483; debts, 257; *Down There on a Visit* income, 590, 607; family inheritances, 141, 387-8, 580, 590, 607, 719-20; film-extra earnings, 163; *Goodbye to Berlin* income, 295, 385; *I Am a Camera* income, 441, 532, 676; *Judgement Day in Pittsburgh* income, 382, 395, 414; lecturing income, 545; legal settlement with Curtis Harrington, 487; loan from Chris Wood, 301; MGM contracts, 387; overdrafts, 225-6; parents' education funds, 109; savings, 473, 510, 695; screenplay-writing for David Selznick income, 533; secretarial salary from Mangeot family, 181; support from mother, 273-5; teaching income, 537, 606; television projects income, 654, 655; trust fund and legacy from godmother, 18, 257, 607, 719-20; wartime bank interest, 384-5; will, 518; *The World in the Evening* income, 473, 483

Views on: Wystan Auden, 98-9, 289, 290-1, 307; being in love, 280, 450; British Empire, 90, 116, 587, 624; Albert Camus, 551-2; Catholicism, 407; chivalric way of life, 42, 57-8, 115, 135; Christianity, 124; Communism, 241; courage, 148; death, 2, 83, 92-3, 148, 715, 726, 728; doctors, 199; T.S. Eliot, 276; fagging system, 118-19; E.M. Forster, 121, 232; friendship, 37, 49, 50, 52-3, 55, 57, 271, 521; ghosts, 26-8, 95, 457; André Gide, 462; heroes and heroism, 146-9, 190, 367, 545-6; his family background, 12, 22, 25, 545-6, 590-1; historical study, 124, 145, 164; homosexuality, 57, 98-9, 138, 178-9, 206, 406-7, 410-11, 637, 640-1, 698-9; kleptomania, 270-1; T.E. Lawrence, 409; loneliness, 429-30; Somerset Maugham, 373; New York, 298, 397, 593, 640; patriotism, 129-30; poetry and poets, 134, 168, 184; Protestantism, 407; purification, 522-3; Puritanism, 25, 324-5, 546; racism, 90; Ramakrishna, 409, 652; sainthood, 167; social class, 17, 44, 47-8, 90, 116; Stephen Spender, 198, 466-7, 636-7; sport and competitive games, 96-7; Igor Stravinsky, 522-3; Truly Strong and Truly Weak men, 190, 276, 485; United States, 300, 309, 311, 429, 435; Edward Upward, 162, 510-11, 513; war, 129-30, 275, 286, 287, 330-1, 533-4, 643; warriors and fighting men, 42, 57-8, 65, 97, 98-9, 545-6; Oscar Wilde, 8, 170-1, 246

Works (Essays & articles): see "Back to Berlin"; "California Story"; "Coming to London"; "The Day at La Verne"; *Essentials of Vedanta*; "The Gita and War"; "Hemingway, Death, and the Devil"; *Images* (Beaton), introduction; "Katherine Mansfield"; "The Problem of the Religious Novel"; "R.L.S."; "Young American Writers"

Works (Fiction): see "Afterwards"; *All the Conspirators*; "Ambrose"; "A Berlin Diary (Autumn 1930)"; "A Berlin Diary (Winter 1932-3)"; *Christopher Garland*; "A Day in Paradise"; *Down There on a Visit*; "An Evening at the Bay"; "Gems of Belgian Architecture"; *Goodbye to Berlin*; "The Hero"; "The Horror in the Tower"; "I Am Waiting"; "The Landauers"; *Lions and Shadows*; *A Meeting by the River*; *The Memorial*; *The Mortmere Stories*; "Mr. Lancaster"; *Mr. Norris Changes Trains*; *The North-West Passage*; "The Nowaks"; "The Old Game"; "On Ruegen Island (Summer 1931)"; "Paul"; *Paul Is Alone*; *Prater Violet*;

Isherwood (*cont.*)
"Rugtonstead" novels; *Sally Bowles*; *The School of Tragedy*; *A Single Man*; *The Summer at the House*; "Take It or Leave It"; "The Turn Round the World"; "Two Brothers"; "A Visit to Anselm Oakes"; "Waldemar"; "The Wishing Tree"; *The World in the Evening*; "The World War"
Works (*Juvenilia*): see "The Adventures of Daddie & Mummie"; "Chivalry in English Literature"; "Choosing a School"; "The Dream-Garden"; "The Faithful"; "Gallinamania"; *The History of My Friends*; "In the Passage"; "A Lay of Modern Germany"; *La Lettre*; "Mapperley Plains"; "Ode to Wyberslegh"; "One Man's God"; The Wrong God"
Works (*Lectures & talks*): see "The Autobiography of My Books"; "Influences"; "What Is the Nerve of Interest in the Novel"; "A Writer and a Minority"; "A Writer and His World"; "A Writer and Religion"; "The Writer and Vedanta"
Works (*Literary collections & omnibus editions*): see *The Berlin Stories*; *Exhumations*; *Great English Short Stories*
Works (*Memoirs & diaries*): see *Christopher and His Kind*; *Kathleen and Frank*; *Lions and Shadows*; *Lost Years*; *Memoirs of Pine House*; *My Guru and His Disciple*; *October*; *Scenes from an Emigration*
Works (*Plays & play adaptations*): see *The Adventures of the Black Girl in Her Search for God*; *The Ascent of F6*; *The Dog Beneath the Skin, or Where is Francis?*; *The Enemies of a Bishop, or Die When I Say When*; *Herd of Lions*; *La Lettre*; Lulu plays; *A Meeting by the River*; *The Monsters*; *On the Frontier*
Works (*Poetry*): see "Choosing a School"; "The Dream-Garden"; "The Faithful"; "A Lay of Modern Germany"; "Mapperley Plains"; "Ode to Wyberslegh"; "The Recessional from Cambridge"; "Souvenir des Vacances"
Works (*Screenplays & film treatments*): see *Bandits of Orgosolo*; *The Beach at Falesá*; *The Beautiful and Damned*; *Below the Equator*; *Cabaret*; *The Day's Journey*; *Diane*; *The Easiest Thing in the World*; *Forever and a Day*; *Frankenstein: The True Story*; *The Great Sinner*; *The Hour Before Dawn*; *I, Claudius*; *Jacob's Hands*; *Jean-Christophe*; *Judgement Day in Pittsburgh*; *Little Friend*; *The Loved One*; *Mary Magdalene*; *The Miracle*; *The Mummy, or The Lady from the Land of the Dead*; *The Nazi*; "Paul"; *Rage in Heaven*; *Reflections in a Golden Eye*; *Rosmersholm*; *The Sailor from Gibraltar*; *Up at the Villa*; *The Vacant Room*; *The Wayfarer*; *The Woman in White*; *A Woman's Face*
Works (*Television shows*): see *The Beautiful and Damned*; *A Christmas Carol*; *Emily Ermengarde*; *Frankenstein: The True Story*; *The Legend of Silent Night*
Works (*Translations*): see Baudelaire, Charles, *The Intimate Journals*; Bhagavad Gita; Brecht, Bertolt, *A Penny for the Poor*

(*Dreigroschenroman*); *A Garland of Questions and Answers*; Patanjali, *How to Know God*; Shankara, *Vivekachudamani*
Works (*Travel*): see "Back to Berlin"; "California Story"; "Coming to London"; *The Condor and the Cows*; "Escales"; *Journey to a War*
Works (*Vedanta & religion*): see Bhagavad Gita translation; Chetanananda, Swami, anthology on meditation; "The Day at La Verne"; *Essentials of Vedanta*; *A Garland of Questions and Answers* translation; "The Gita and War"; *Narada Bhakti Sutras* introduction; Patanjali, *How to Know God: The Yoga Aphorisms of Patanjali* translation; "The Problem of the Religious Novel"; *Ramakrishna and His Disciples*; *Religion in Practice* introduction; Shivananda, Swami, foreword for biography; *Vedanta for the Western World*; *Vedanta for Modern Man*; *What Religion Is: In the Words of Vivekananda* introduction; "What Vedanta Means to Me"; "The Wishing Tree"; "A Writer and Religion"; "The Writer and Vedanta"

Isherwood, Elizabeth (née Luce; CI's grandmother), 16, 95, 105, 140, 141
Isherwood, Esther (CI's aunt) *see* Toogood, Esther
Isherwood, Francis Bradshaw (Frank; CI's father): family background, 11–12, 16–17, 56; appearance and character, 14, 17, 102; education and early life, 14, 16; relations with brother Henry, 16, 28–9, 30, 71; early military career, 12, 14–15, 17, 19, 29–30, 40, 41; marriage, 15–19, 23, 193; artistic, theatrical and musical interests, 24, 32, 33–5, 40, 41, 50, 58, 94, 100, 165–6, 194, 545, 554, 702; and birth of CI, 11, 13–14, 19; family life and children's upbringing, 13–14, 18, 20, 24, 29–30, 32, 33–6, 40–1, 51–2, 91, 92; and CI's schooling, 33, 36, 52, 56, 57, 60, 62, 76–7; compiles *Toy-Drawer Times* newspaper for CI, 34, 51, 252; and birth of son Richard, 30, 40, 42–3; posting to Limerick, 36, 40, 41, 43–4, 45–59, 529; and outbreak of World war I, 64–6; early months of war, 66–80, 96, 227, 475; disappearance and death, 2, 51, 65, 80–8, 90–1, 92, 102, 498; memorialization, 84, 121, 286, 715; sword returned, 115; continued impact on CI's life and work, 92, 102, 115, 122–3, 148, 194–5, 227, 246, 251–2, 269–70, 367, 442, 518, 532, 545–6, 606, 660, 678, 702; and *Kathleen and Frank*, 656–7, 660, 661, 671
Isherwood, Frida (née Hill), 120, 150, 720
Isherwood, Henry (CI's uncle) *see* Bradshaw Isherwood-Bagshawe, Henry
Isherwood, John Bradshaw (Jack; CI's uncle), 17, 27, 74, 81, 83, 108, 109, 113, 114, 116, 120, 139–40, 150, 151, 387, 388, 389, 393, 720
Isherwood, John Henry Bradshaw (CI's grandfather), 11, 13, 16, 17, 27, 29, 67, 88, 102, 109, 115–16, 140, 166, 266
Isherwood, Kathleen Bradshaw (née Machell-Smith; CI's mother): family background, 15–16, 24; childhood and early life, 13, 15, 18, 74; marriage, 15–19, 23, 193; relations with husband's family, 17, 18, 28–9, 140–1;

birth of CI, 11, 13–14, 19; early family life, 13–14, 18, 19–59, 99, 428; foreign travel with husband, 23, 24, 28, 31; early writing collaborations with CI, 31–2, 37, 47, 109, 131, 237, 378; second pregnancy and birth of son Richard, 30, 35, 36, 40, 42–3; in Limerick during husband's posting, 45–59, 92; and CI's schooling at St. Edmund's, 56, 59–60, 62, 63, 74–6, 103, 105, 107, 111; and outbreak of World War I, 64–6; early months of war, 66–80, 601; husband's disappearance and death, 2, 51, 80–8, 102, 498; first months of widowhood, 84–8; and husband's memorialization, 84, 121, 715; later war years, 88, 91, 93, 94, 95, 103, 105–11, 116–17; and CI's education at Repton, 111, 113–14, 116–17, 119, 128, 131, 134; crack in relationship with CI, 120; and CI's circumcision, 122, 353; and CI's possible career as librarian, 123, 140; and CI's confirmation in Anglican Church, 124; and Richard's schooling, 138–9, 150–1, 191, 555; and Richard's developmental disorder, 139, 155–6, 191, 221, 555; moves to St. Mary Abbot's Terrace, Kensington, 139–40, 217; family life in London, 140, 150–1, 180, 190–1, 192–3, 195; and CI's undergraduate career at Cambridge, 130, 145, 158, 163, 165–6; death of mother, 169–70, 171; and CI's failure of second-year exams and withdrawal from Cambridge, 158, 176, 177; and beginnings of CI's literary career, 175, 179, 193, 194, 196, 200, 201; French holiday with Richard (September 1926), 191; and CI's tutoring jobs, 191; visits CI on Isle of Wight (early summer 1927), 193; hears Krishnamurti speak, 355–6; trip to Scotland (early summer 1928), 196; moves to Pembroke Gardens, Kensington, 196, 197, 442; and CI's brief time at medical school, 194, 200, 201; and sale of Marple Hall furniture, 209, 210–11; rift in relations with CI, 209, 210, 211, 221–3; and Richard's arrest and court case, 222–3; charity work, 229; reconciliation with CI, 232; and CI's legacy from godmother, 257; and CI's Berlin novels, 259; and CI's relationship with Heinz Neddermeyer, 261, 263, 273–4, 275, 278, 439; visits CI in Portugal (summer 1936), 273; sends money to CI in Belgium, 273–5; at screening of *Little Friend*, 266; at 1936 New Year's party, 489; and CI's illness following tooth extraction, 277; watches George VI's coronation, 278; at National Book Fair (1937), 280; and CI's trip to China with Auden, 284; during World War II, 382, 386–93, 394; and CI's naturalizaton as U.S. citizen, 386–7; and Uncle Henry's death and legacies, 387–9, 394; and Richard's nervous collapse following incident at Marple Hall, 389–91; and CI's time as monk at Vedanta monastery, 391–2; and CI's 1947, 1948 and 1952 visits to England, 385–6, 393–6, 412, 439–40, 555; reaction to CI's bladder operation and subsequent sterility, 393–4; and CI's 1956 and 1959 visits to England, 509–10, 538, 544; suffers stroke, 532, 538; death, 543–4, 586; cremation and burial of ashes, 544, 586; will, 580, 590, 607; and *Kathleen and Frank*, 655–7, 662, 670–1, 698 *Character & characteristics*: after-death communication interests, 109–10; appearance, 12–13, 509; artistic interests, 17; Don Bachardy's similarities with, 544; birthday, 720; compulsiveness, 668; dancing, 38; diary-keeping, 6, 20, 94, 655–6; female friendships, 23–4, 38, 47; finances, 18, 109, 115–16, 136, 140–1, 217, 273–5, 387, 388, 393, 439; handwriting, 655; horror of "progress," 649; intelligence, 13; literary interests, 24, 393; nicknames, 23, 47; portrayal in CI's works, 120–1, 123, 194, 211, 216, 217, 440, 521, 598, 720; religion, 47, 50–1; role-playing, 24–5, 38; sexual life, 18–19, 35–6; shyness, 47–8; sketches and watercolors, 105–6, 191; snobbery, 47–8, 393, 649; tenacity, 111; views on sons' sexuality, 222–3; views on war and militarism, 275, 391–2; vivaciousness, 13; writings, 105–6, 115, 116, 191, 229, 238

Isherwood, Mary Bradshaw (Moey; CI's aunt), 17, 22, 67, 74, 76, 110, 182, 188

Isherwood, Richard Graham Bradshaw (CI's brother): birth, 30, 42–3, 377; christening and names, 43, 139; infancy and early childhood, 18, 43, 45–6, 56, 66, 67–8, 74, 76, 77–8, 80, 84, 87, 105, 107, 118, 120; appearance and character, 74, 105, 139, 156, 222–3, 385, 509, 538, 586; schooling, 109, 138–9, 150–2, 155–6, 191–2, 555; developmental disorder, 2, 105, 139, 152, 156, 191, 221, 555; family life in London, 140, 150–1, 180, 191; fails university entrance exams, 191–2, 221; arrest and court case, 222; sexuality, 222–3; writings, 223; social life in London, 223; CI dictates work to, 237–8, 454; and CI's planned move to Chelsea, 261; at screening of *Little Friend*, 266; during World War II, 386–93; briefly employed in farm work, 386, 389, 390, 391; and death of Uncle Henry, 387; CI passes on Marple Hall Estate to, 387–9; as proprietor of Marple Hall, 388–91, 392–3, 510; concerns about succession, 390–1, 393; suffers nervous collapse following incident at Marple Hall, 389–91; and CI's time as monk at Vedanta monastery, 339; and CI's 1947, 1952, 1956 and 1959 visits to England, 385, 393, 439–40, 509–10, 538; and mother's stroke, 532; death of mother, 544, 586; and 1961 visit to England, 586; and Bradley family, 586, 655, 702; and CI's 1966, 1967, 1970 and 1973 visits to England, 655, 656, 661–2, 682, 702; and CI's researches for *Kathleen and Frank*, 655, 656, 661–2; death, 719, 720; will, 719–20

Isherwood, Thomas (CI's cousin), 720

Isle of Wight, 36, 75–80, 81, 177–9, 185–7, 193–5, 197, 199, 210, 291, 428, 512, 601

Israel, Wilfrid, 203, 246, 247, 248, 714

Ivory, James, 701

Jacobs, Christopher, 168, 172
Jacobs, W.W., 168
Jacob's Hands (film treatment), 354
Jaffe, Sam, 719
Jagger, Mick, 662, 683; *Ned Kelly*, 677, 678
James, Henry, 165, 393, 423, 589, 600; "The Beast in the Jungle," 106; *The Bostonians*, 415; "The Pupil," 281; *The Turn of the Screw*, 701; *What Maisie Knew*, 264
James, William, 589; *Varieties of Religious Experience*, 315–16, 719
James II, King, 45
Jamestown (Rhode Island), 318
Jane Eyre (film; 1943), 350
Japan, 283, 288, 369, 523–4, 631
Jayrambati (India), 528
Jean-Christophe (film treatment), 516, 518, 519–20, 521
Jebb, Julian, 594
Jenkins, Terry, 541, 542
Jermyn Street Baths (London), 276
Joël, Annie, 246
Johns, Jasper, 682, 708
Johnson, Lamont, 659
Johnson, Lyndon B., 669
Johnson, Philip, 654
Jonathan Cape (publishers), 195, 232
Jones, Bill, 635, 637
Jones, Jennifer (*later* Selznick), 136, 500, 533, 594, 646, 652
Jorgensen, Christine, 685
Journey to a War (with W.H. Auden; 1939), 4, 282–8, 291, 292–3, 294–5, 307, 401, 704
Joyce, James, 601, 712; *Ulysses*, 189, 609
Judgement Day in Pittsburgh (film treatment), 381–2, 395, 414
Judkyn, John, 463
jujitsu, 366
Julius Caesar, 195, 642–3
Jung, Carl, 191, 377, 555, 617, 652, 653, 659–60, 703; *Memories, Dreams, Reflections*, 371

Kafka, Franz, 492
Kallman, Chester, 306, 318, 396, 399, 411, 475, 476, 506, 522, 582–5, 586, 702; *Elegy for Young Lovers*, 582, 584
Kalpataru Day (January 1), 335
Kamarpukur (India), 528
Kameny, Franklin, 692
Kander, John, 657
Kantorowicz, Alfred, 237
Karachi (Pakistan), 633
Kasmin, John, 665, 677
"Katherine Mansfield" (1951), 455–6
Kathleen and Frank: The Autobiography of a Family (1971): characterization, 20, 21–2, 23, 657–8, 659–60; influences on, 370–1, 649–50, 659–60; publication, 148, 693, 696, 697, 706; quotations and extracts, 20, 21–2, 23, 24–5, 26, 27–8, 29, 34, 35, 37, 38, 44, 46, 48, 49–50, 52–3, 56, 58, 59, 63, 65, 76–7, 81, 84, 89, 90, 96, 115, 166, 346; reception and reviews, 697–9; research and writing of, 15, 18, 52, 70, 648–50, 655–7, 658, 659–60, 661–2, 670–1, 673, 682, 684; sales, 698; structure and form, 649, 659; themes, 15, 26, 27, 38–9, 51, 53, 56, 65, 71, 86, 440, 545, 649, 659–60, 692; title, 648, 649
Katz, Otto, 481–2
Katz, Rudolf (Rolf), 251, 258, 262, 263, 300, 367, 401, 408, 480–1, 568–9
Kauffmann, Stanley, 662
Kazan, Elia: *Cat on a Hot Tin Roof*, 490–1; *East of Eden*, 483; *A Streetcar Named Desire*, 427, 490
Kellog, Spencer, 358
Kelsall, Ronald (Ronny), 131, 152
Kennedy, Bill, 424
Kennedy, Helen (Sudhira), 337, 342, 352–3, 358, 715
Kennedy, Jaqueline, 597
Kennedy, John F., 584; assassination, 627
Kennedy, Margaret, 259, 266
Kennedy, Paul, 540, 581, 604, 612
Kennedy, Robert, assassination, 669
Kermode, Frank, 653
Kern, Jerome, *Sally*, 238
Kerr, Deborah, 702
Key West (Florida), 346, 489–91, 654
Keystone Cops, 53
KH3 (anti-aging pills), 673, 679, 712
Khartoum, Siege of (1884–5), 587
Khrushchev, Nikita, 584
Kid, The (film; 1921), 152
Kight, Morris, 685, 690
Kilhefner, Don, 690–1
Kinema Club (Cambridge University), 162, 163, 164, 179
King, Martin Luther, 663; assassination, 669
King's College, Cambridge, 125, 412, 441, 682
King's College, London, 199–200, 201
King's Gold Medal for Poetry, 42, 283
Kinnear (aviation company), 452
Kinsey, Alfred, *Sexual Behavior in the Human Male*, 632
Kipling, Rudyard, 90, 134; *A History of England*, 51; *Kim*, 351; "Rikki-Tikki-Tavi," 39
Kirchstetten (Austria), 636
Kirstein, Fidelma (née Cadmus), 322, 396, 400
Kirstein, Lincoln: background, appearance and character, 322, 644; career, 322, 400; sexuality, 322, 643; marriage, 322; CI first meets, 322; relationship with Pete Martinez, 323, 349; development of friendship with CI, 7, 311, 322–3, 325, 458, 464, 654; wartime military service, 564; and CI's time as monk at Vedanta monastery, 339; during CI's 1947 visit to New York, 396, 398–400; and CI's trip to South America, 400; and Speed Lamkin, 430, 432; and first performances of *I Am a Camera*, 434; and *The World in the Evening*, 432, 463, 469, 474; during CI's 1953–4 trip to New York, 475–6; and CI's relationship with Don Bachardy, 475–6; Bachardy visits in New York, 518; during CI's 1959 and 1961–2 trips to New York, 592, 605; and *Down There on a Visit*, 594; drawing commissions for Bachardy in New York, 636, 639, 640, 644, 647, 654; selection of poems for anthology and proposed collaboration with CI, 640, 644; and *A Meeting by the River*, 650; ending

of friendship with CI and Bachardy, 654;
  mental breakdown, 654; later life, 654;
  Rhymes (& More) Rhymes of a PFC, 640, 644
Kiskadden, Margaret (Peggy); *earlier* Rodakiewicz),
  181, 326, 329, 332, 338, 342, 352, 358, 391,
  397, 416, 424–5
Kiskadden, William (Bill), 181, 326, 352, 489
Kitty (horse), 47, 66, 76, 79
Klabund (Alfred Henschke), *The Circle of Chalk*,
  348
Klebaum, Curt, 721
Klimt, Gustav, 636
Klosters (Switzerland), 702
Knopf, Alfred, 302
Knopf, Eddie, 302, 477, 482, 483, 488, 499, 501
Knox, Ronnie, 635, 658, 661
Knoxville (Tennessee), 718, 719
Kodak Brownie (camera), 54, 231
Koestler, Arthur, 258
Kokoschka, Oskar, 710
Kolisch, Josef, Dr., 305, 356, 426, 589
Korda, Alexander, 280
Korean War (1950–53), 488, 521
Kramer, George, 615–16, 620–2, 664
Kramer, Terry Allen, 718
Krishnamurti, 24, 354–5, 520, 641
Krishnananda, Swami *see* Fitts, George
Ktiponisi *see* St. Nicholas (Greece)
Kurella, Tania *see* Stern, Tania
Küsel, Otto, 208

La Guaira (Venezuela), 401
La Paz (Bolivia), 408
L.A. State *see* Los Angeles State College
La Verne Seminar (Society of Friends; summer
  1941), 316–18, 319, 327, 329, 577
Ladbroke Grove (Notting Hill, London), 666–7
Ladies of Llangollen (Eleanor Butler and Sarah
  Ponsonby), 24
Ladysmith, Siege of (1900), 15
Laguna Beach (California), 326, 413, 421, 601;
  Monterey Street, 427–8; Rockledge Road,
  327, 328, 335, 342
Lahr, John, 490
Laing, Olivia, 693
Lalita, Sister (Carrie Mead Wyckoff) *see* Sister
  Lalita
Lamb, Charles and Mary, *Tales from Shakespeare*,
  39, 41
Lambert, Gavin, 311, 520–1, 533, 543, 581, 597,
  606, 614, 620, 622, 643, 652, 665, 685, 702;
  The Slide Area, 520
Lamkin, Speed, 430–1, 432, 441, 466, 476, 501,
  535; *The Easter Egg Hunt*, 466, 547
Lampel, Peter Martin, *Revolte im Erziehungshaus*,
  208, 255, 256
Lancaster, Burt, 491
Lanchester, Elsa, 521, 541, 542, 613
Landauer, Walter, 248–9
"Landauers, The" (1938), 204, 244–6, 249
Landor, Walter Savage, 198
landslides (Santa Monica), 674
Lane, Homer, 201–2, 206, 208, 209, 219, 300, 354
Lange, Hope, 521
Lanigan, Mrs., 217–18
Lanigan, Wallace, 217
Lardner, Ring, 477
Larson, Jack, 646, 647, 652, 665, 679
Las Palmas (Gran Canaria), 263–5, 267
Las Vegas, 465
Lasky, Melvin, 437
Lathwood, Jo *see* Masselink, Jo
Laughlin, James, 345, 346, 349, 379
Laughton, Charles, 541–2, 544–5, 555, 605, 643;
  proposed Socrates project with CI, 541, 544,
  590, 600; death, 590, 612–14; *King Lear*, 541;
  The Sign of the Cross, 364
Laval, Jay, 374, 424, 425, 495
Law, Arthur, *The New Boy*, 58, 60, 61
Lawrence, D.H., 425, 512, 575–6, 693; *Birds,
  Beasts and Flowers*, 290; "The Blind Man,"
  575–6; *Lady Chatterley's Lover*, 235, 605; *The
  Plumed Serpent*, 425; *St. Mawr*, 300, 425, 575;
  Women in Love, 224
Lawrence, Frieda, 425
Lawrence, Jerry, 448, 540, 614, 670
Lawrence, T.E. (of Arabia), 276, 409, 427, 589;
  The Mint, 408–9
"Lay of Modern Germany, A" (1915), 90, 147
Layard, John, 193–4, 201, 202, 205, 207, 209, 219,
  220, 223, 270, 300, 514, 705; *Stone Men of
  Malekula*, 340
Le Havre (France), 409
Leadbeater, Charles Webster, 355
Lear, Edward, 458
Leary, Timothy, 660
Ledbury (Herefordshire), 418
Left Review (journal), 283
Legend of Silent Night, The (television show),
  654–5
Lehane, Brendan, 692
Lehmann, John, 263, 291, 299–300, 310, 317, 349,
  362, 383, 384, 394, 413, 480, 508, 605, 637,
  722; at Hogarth Press, 233, 237, 349; and *The
  Memorial*, 233; and *Sally Bowles*, 236, 237,
  239; and *Down There on a Visit*, 556, 594;
  lectures in California, 675, 697; proposed
  publication of correspondence with CI,
  703–4
Lehmann, Rosamond, 480
Leigh, Vivien, 586, 636
Leighton, Margaret, 586, 702
Lenin, Vladimir, 168, 241, 244
Leningrad, 241
Lenya, Lotte, 586, 657
Leonard, John, 712–13
Leopold, Michael, 423, 600
Lerman, Leo, 398, 434
Lerner and Loewe: *Camelot*, 581; *My Fair Lady*,
  617, 694
LeSueur, Joe, 644
Lettre, La (1913), 51–2
Lewenstein, Oscar, 583
Lewis, Hayden, 376, 448
Lewis, Leopold, *The Bells*, 104
Lewis, Sinclair, 230–2
Lichtenstein, Roy, 681, 682, 708
Life (magazine), 379, 435
Life and Letters (journal), 230–1
Lima (Peru), 401–2, 406, 410

Limerick (Ireland), 36, 45–59, 64–5, 92, 378, 471, 529; Cathedral, 47, 50, 56, 65; Gaiety cinema, 49, 53–4, 65; Roden House, 45, 46, 48, 65, 538, 539
Lin Yutang, 342
Linscott, Robert (Bob), 473, 474
Lion in Winter, The (film; 1968), 676
Lions and Shadows (unpublished novel), 156–7, 173–5, 454–5, 467, 598, 641
Lions and Shadows: An Education in the Twenties (1938): characterization, 98, 104, 125, 126–7, 128, 129, 137, 180, 181, 182, 183, 184, 192, 193–4, 196, 198, 200, 201, 207, 511, 512, 521, 694; dedication, 262; influences on, 125; plot and themes, 128, 129, 142, 143, 145–6, 159, 161–2, 175, 176, 178–9, 184, 192, 193–4, 196, 199, 206, 705; publication, 283, 511; quotations and extracts, 104, 128, 129, 130, 132, 145–6, 159–60, 160, 162, 165, 166, 167, 172–3, 175, 176–7, 178–9, 179–80, 181, 182, 184–6, 188–9, 190, 192, 195–6, 197, 199, 200, 201, 202, 207, 512; title, 156–7, 190; writing of, 98, 125, 156–7, 272, 275
Lisbon, 263, 273
List, Herbert, 504
Listener (magazine), 293, 638, 697
Little, Penny, 693–4
Little Commonwealth (reform school; Dorset), 202, 208
Little Friend (film; 1934), 258–66, 340, 361, 367, 432, 456
Littman, Marguerite (*earlier* Brown), 466, 473, 474, 501, 592, 639, 661, 666, 677
Littman, Mark, 661, 666
Living Authors (radio program), 393
Llangollen, Ladies of (Eleanor Butler and Sarah Ponsonby), 24
Llano (California), 342, 496
Llewellyn Smith, Harold, 112
Locke, Charlie, 519
Lockheed (aircraft manufacturer), 446
Lodge, Carter, 342, 359, 532, 583, 608
London Hippodrome, 53
London Magazine, 484, 556, 594
London Zoo, 59
Long Beach (California), 348; California State University, 588, 687; Veterans Hospital, 426, 427
Loos, Anita, 355, 593, 594; *Gigi*, 435
Los Angeles, 301, 326–7; Atwater, 445–6; Barnsdall Park, 708–9, 724; Benton Way, 418; Biltmore Theater, 443, 543; Brooks Steam Baths, 539; Bublitchki (restaurant), 448; Bullock's (department store), 446; Café Gala (nightclub), 338; California Hospital, 696; Cedars of Lebanon Hospital, 613, 625; Ceeje's (restaurant), 708; Center Theater Annex, 675; Chasen's (restaurant), 622, 667; Chateau Marmont, 520; Ciro's (nightclub), 448–9; Corcoran Gallery, 724, 727; Curson Avenue, Hollywood, 541; Deronda Drive, Hollywood, 589; Forest Lawn (cemetery), 613; Gemini Artists' Studios, 647, 710; Grauman's Chinese Theater, 446; Green Valley Road, 315; Griffith Park, 449, 685; Harold Way, Hollywood, 451; Hollywood High School, 336; Irving Blum Gallery, 682, 708; Ivar Avenue, 335–7, 358; John Marshall High School, 453; La Cienega Boulevard, 359, 648; London Bookshop, 356; Mark Taper Forum, 658, 673, 679, 700–1; Miramar Hotel, 424, 549, 684; Mocambo (nightclub), 448; Mount Sinai Hospital, 691; Nicholas Wilder Gallery, 647, 648, 708, 709–10, 716, 721, 724; Ocean Park, 614, 620; Olive Drive, West Hollywood, 473; Pacific Palisades, 416, 470; Palos Verdes, 312; Pershing Square Turkish bath, 348; Players Ring (theater), 448; Rex Evans Gallery, 597, 608, 647, 652, 681; Rose Gardens Apartments, 301; Saltair Avenue, Brentwood, 441–4, 454; San Pedro Municipal Gallery, 694; San Vicente Boulevard, 673; Silver Lake, 348, 418; Spalding Avenue, Hollywood, 464; Sunset Boulevard, 313, 327, 338, 448; Sycamore Trail, 301; Washington Irving Junior High School, 446; Will Rogers State Beach, 445; *see also* Beverly Hills; Burbank; Culver City; Glendale; Pasadena; Santa Monica
Los Angeles City College, 453, 473, 483, 500, 597
Los Angeles County Honor Farm (correctional facility), 596
Los Angeles County Museum of Art, 549
Los Angeles Drama Critics Awards, 675
Los Angeles Municipal Art Gallery (Barnsdall Park), 708–9, 724
Los Angeles State College, 537, 539, 590, 594, 596, 606, 663, 707
Los Angeles Times (newspaper), 608, 657, 681, 682, 694, 700, 708–9, 709–10, 716, 724; Robert Kirsch Award, 727
Lost, The see *Goodbye to Berlin*
Lost Horizon (film; 1937), 719
Lost Years: A Memoir 1945–1951 (2000): influences on, 371; quotations and extracts, 57, 96, 97, 354, 371–2, 374, 377, 378, 380, 381, 383, 399, 401, 418, 420, 426, 427–8, 431; themes, 57, 96, 97, 370–1, 419; writing of, 370–1, 659
Lothar, Ernst, *Kleine Freundin*, 258–9, 264, 265, 266
Louvain (Belgium), 72
Loved One, The (film; 1965), 633, 634, 635, 636, 639, 640, 655
Lowenthal, Richard, 437
Loyola University (New Orleans), 707
Lubitsch, Ernst, 481
Lucca (Italy), 507
Luce, John, 95–6
Luce, Marjorie *see* Reid, Marjorie (Madgie)
Luce, Mary, 133
Luce, Thomas, 16
Luckinbill, Laurence, 701
Lüdecke, Wenzel, 437
Lulu plays (Wedekind), adaptation, 659, 662, 664, 680–1
Luther, Martin, 587
Luxembourg, 277–8, 314
Lyme Hall (Cheshire), 388
Lyme Regis (Dorset), 31, 107
Lyndon, Andrew, 434, 585
Lynes, George Platt, 322, 476–7, 543, 571

Macaulay, Thomas Babington, *Lay of Ancient Rome*, 90
Machell-Smith, Emily (CI's grandmother): appearance and character, 15–16, 22, 51; and CI's parents' marriage, 15–16, 17, 18, 24; and birth of CI, 11; and CI's infancy and early childhood, 19, 30, 31, 36, 269; dogs, 269; London flat, 59, 68, 107, 120, 139; during World War I, 67, 78, 80, 84, 85, 88, 107, 109–10; later life, 120, 122, 134, 139–40, 145; death and funeral, 169–70, 171; portrayal in CI's works, 521, 720; *Our Rambles in Old London*, 191
Machell-Smith, Frederick (CI's grandfather), 15, 17–18, 22, 23, 169
Machell-Smith, Kathleen *see* Isherwood, Kathleen
Machu Picchu (Peru), 407
Mackenzie, Compton, 156
MacLaren-Ross, Julian, "I Am a Chimera," 485
Maclean, Donald, 479–80
MacNeice, Louis, 7, 283, 411
Mad Dog of Europe, The (proposed film), 301–2; see also *The Nazi*
Madame Tussaud's (wax-works museum), 59
Maddox, Freddy, 654, 669
Madeira, 263
Mademoiselle (magazine), 397
Madrid, 267
Maesmor Hall (Wales), 84
magic lanterns, 49, 50
Magnani, Anna, 491, 618
Maharishi Mahesh Yogi, 660
Mailer, Norman, 426, 593; *The Naked and the Dead*, 426
Malibu (California), 375, 448, 503
Malory, Thomas, 135
Malvern (Pennsylvania), 321
Man, Myth and Magic (encyclopedia), 671
Man Who Knew Too Much, The (film; 1935), 266
Manchester, 109, 386, 389, 395, 586
Manchester Academy of Fine Arts, 94
Manchester Guardian (newspaper), 93, 156, 197, 395, 484, 595; see also *Guardian*
Manchester Society of Women Painters, 94
"Manet and the Post-Impressionists" (exhibition; 1910), 34–5
Mangeot, André, 180–3, 191, 458, 521, 522
Mangeot, Fowke, 180–1
Mangeot, Olive, 136, 180–3, 192, 209, 261, 278, 285, 385, 521, 598
Mangeot, Sylvain, 180–3, 209, 458
Mann, Danny, 654–5
Mann, Erika, 416, 637
Mann, Heinrich, 478
Mann, Katja, 416
Mann, Klaus, 397, 416–17
Mann, Thomas, 416, 417, 478, 589
Mansfield, Katherine, 160, 165, 166–7, 238–9, 455–6, 458, 523, 557; "At the Bay," 195, 503, 610
"Mapperley Plains" (1923), 154, 157
Mapplethorpe, Robert, 725
Mar del Plata (Argentina), 408–9
Mariposa Foundation, 725, 726
Marlborough College (Wiltshire), 92, 314

Marlowe, Christopher, *Doctor Faustus*, 239
Marmorston, Jessie, Dr., 488–9, 501, 517, 519
Marple (Cheshire), 11, 74, 112, 116, 389; All Saints Church, 115, 116, 121; St. Martin's School, 109
Marple (Pennsylvania), 320–1
Marple Hall Estate (Cheshire), 13, 24–8, 32, 37, 42, 53, 67, 69, 71, 93, 106, 112, 115–16, 140, 141, 180, 392–3, 394, 510, 568, 656–7; CI inherits and passes on to Richard, 387–91; sale of furniture, 210–11, 216
Marple Hall Grammar School, 656
Marre, Albert, 718–19
Marseilles, 209, 258, 284
Marshall Plan, 437
Martin, Agnes, 647
Martinez, Pete (Jésus José Martínez Berlanga), 323–4, 325, 348–9, 396, 400, 401; *For My Brother*, 349
Marx, Karl, 168, 251, 268
Mary, Queen consort, 108
Mary Magdalene (film treatment), 533
Masefield, John, 134; *Sea Life in Nelson's Time*, 130
Maskelyne, John, 73, 87, 126
Mason, James, 702
Masselink, Jo and Ben, 493–6, 497, 524, 603, 614, 618, 660, 664, 677
Massey, Raymond, 613
Masteroff, Joe, 657
masturbation, 36, 71, 132, 206, 290, 291, 602, 632
Matisse, Henri, 34
Maugham, W. Somerset, 199, 294, 334, 403, 507, 524, 588, 693, 723; *The Hour Before Dawn*, 334, 338, 391–2; *Of Human Bondage*, 199, 225; *The Magician*, 505, 588; *The Narrow Corner*, 557, 559, 588; *The Razor's Edge*, 373, 570, 572, 573, 588, 663; *Up at the Villa*, 371
Maunder, John (Jack), 193–4, 199
Maupassant, Guy de, 143; *Une Vie*, 598
Maupin, Armistead, 346, 693, 723; *Tales of the City*, 723
May Company (department store chain), 537
Mayne, Ethel Colburn, 41, 165–6, 175, 190, 302, 455, 458
Mayne, Richard, 595
McCallum, David, 702
McCarthyism, 163, 415, 452, 477, 485
McCracken, John, 647, 693
McCrary, Tex, 397
McCullers, Carson, 319, 412; *Reflections in a Golden Eye*, 635
McDermott, Keith, 718
McKinnon, Russell, 548, 580, 608
McPherson, Aimee Semple, 415–16
meditation, 154, 300, 303, 304–5, 313, 320, 322, 344–5, 520, 660–1, 670, 687–8, 716
Medley, Robert, 184, 185, 294, 440, 683
Meeting by the River, A (1967): autobiographical aspects, 450, 643, 650–1; characterization, 24, 137, 450, 469–70, 634, 641, 643–6, 648, 652, 716; dedication, 648; influences on, 633, 641–3, 650–1; plot and themes, 450, 469–70, 572, 633, 643–6, 650–1; publication, 654, 662; quotations and extracts, 651; reception and reviews,

Meeting by the River (cont.)
652–3, 662–3; stage adaptation, 669–71, 672, 673, 679–80, 681, 682, 684, 700–1, 718–19, 724; structure and form, 641; title, 641; writing of, 641–6, 648, 650–1, 652
Meiki (China), 287–8
Melville, Herman, 322, 393, 398, 574; *Moby-Dick*, 574, 651
Memoirs of Pine House (unfinished), 51–2, 60–1, 62–3, 87, 100, 234, 293, 296
Memorial, The: Portrait of a Family (1932): characterization, 85–6, 106, 120–1, 123, 137, 169, 181, 182, 200–1, 468, 568; influences on, 200, 226, 233, 670; plot and themes, 85–6, 90–1, 94, 110, 120–1, 140, 190, 200–1, 204, 207, 258, 265, 468, 564–5, 626; publication, 232, 233, 379; quotations and extracts, 90–1, 106, 125–6, 181, 182; reception and reviews, 232, 233–4, 379; structure and form, 201; writing of, 200–1, 204, 218, 226–7
Men, The (film; 1950), 427
Mendelson, Edward, 706
Mercer, Mary, 45
Merchant, Ismail, 701
Mercury Theatre (Notting Hill, London), 276, 278
Meredith, George, 128
Merlo, Frank, 434, 435, 489, 518, 592
Merrill, George, 206
mescaline (drug), 497, 506
Methuen (publishers), 385, 473, 485, 582, 588, 633, 703
Metro-Goldwyn-Mayer *see* MGM
Mexico City, 382, 494, 495, 552
Meyer, Elizabeth, 323
Meyer, Gerhart, 207
MGM (Metro-Goldwyn-Mayer), 266, 302, 305, 343, 413, 417, 477, 483, 502, 521, 634
MI5 (British Security Service), 481, 569
Middlesex Regiment, 80
Middleton, Thomas, *Women Beware Women*, 676
Midnight Cowboy (film; 1969), 701
Milan, 507, 557
Milk, Harvey, 692
Millard, Paul, 535, 537–8, 540, 542, 543, 549, 591, 604
Miller, David, 499, 501
Miller, Henry, 589; *Tropic of Cancer*, 605
Miller, Robert, 725
Miller's Dale (Derbyshire), 538
Milne, A.A., *The Red House Mystery*, 144
Milton, John, 124, 216
Ministry of Information, 334
Minneapolis, 712
Minnelli, Liza, 4, 203, 700
Minnelli, Vincente, *Kismet*, 501
Miracle, The (film treatment), 354
Mirrlees, Hope, *The Counterplot*, 174–5, 455, 557
Mirsky, D.S.: *Contemporary Russian Literature*, 241; *A History of Russian Literature*, 241; *Lenin*, 244
Mishima, Yukio, 524
Mitchell, J.J., 644
Mitchison, Naomi Mitchison, *The Corn King and the Spring Queen*, 339, 340
Mitgang, Herbert, 594–5

Moffat, Ivan, 420, 594
Mohr, Joseph, "Silent Night," 654–5
Mohrin (Germany), 131, 240, 257
"Moll of Brabyns" (ghost), 26–7, 28
Moltke, Kuno von, 214
Monat, Der (magazine), 437
Monkhouse, Allan, 93–4, 136, 137, 166, 396; *The Conquering Hero*, 147; *My Daughter Helen*, 136–7
Monkhouse, Dorothy, 94, 136
Monkhouse, Elizabeth (Mitty), 136, 395–6
Monkhouse, Florence, 94
Monkhouse, Johnny, 136
Monkhouse, Patrick (Paddy), 93–4, 136–8, 144, 145, 147, 148–9, 150, 151, 152, 154, 162, 184, 377, 395–6, 458, 469, 643, 646
Monkhouse, Rachel (*later* Natzio), 133, 136, 137, 183, 196, 389–90
Monroe, Marilyn, 414, 446, 521, 576, 583
Monsters, The (with Don Bachardy; unfinished play), 536
Mont Blanc, 142–3, 189, 191, 404
Montagu, Ivor, 179
Montague, C.E., 156–7
Monte Carlo, 226
Montecito (California), 358, 645; Sarada Convent, 358, 518–19
Monument Valley (Utah), 465
Moody, Robert, 274, 291
Moore, George, 573, 650
Moore, Roger, 499
Moorea (French Polynesia), 677
Moorehead, Agnes, 702
Morand, Eugène, *Les Cathédrales*, 91
More, Anne, portrait, 25, 210, 665
Moreau, Jeanne, 635, 699
Morgan Brown, Cyril, 56, 59, 61–4, 76, 90, 100–1, 112, 113, 150, 184, 459
Morgan Brown, John, 56
Morgan Brown, Rosamira (Rosa), 56, 75, 76, 89, 90, 98, 100, 107, 117, 150
Morris, Jan, 693
Morris, William, 135
Mortimer, Raymond, 653
Mortmere Stories, The (with Edward Upward; 1994), 39, 159–62, 167, 171, 505, 511, 634
Moscow, 241
Moses, Ed, 647, 682, 693
Mosley, Oswald, 234
Mount Vernon (Virginia), 569
"Mr. Lancaster" (1962), 198, 253–4, 510, 551, 554–6
Mr. Norris Changes Trains (1935): autobiographical aspects, 243, 264–5; characterization, 29, 73, 203, 211–14, 238, 242–4, 254, 254–5, 279, 388, 515; film rights, 301; plot and themes, 8, 204, 211–15, 234, 242–4, 254, 255–6, 259–60, 462; publication and editions, 215, 379; quotations and extracts, 211, 243–4, 254, 255–6; reception and reviews, 214, 215, 388; style and form, 264–5, 379; writing of, 204, 254–6, 259–60, 263–5, 394, 432
Muchnic, Suzanne, 724
Muggeridge, Malcolm, 653
Muir, Edwin, 484

Müller, Hermann, 239
Müller, Max, 653
Müller, Willi, 250
mummers' plays, 267, 268, 558
Mummy, The, or The Lady from the Land of the Dead (film treatment), 701
Muni, Paul, 301
Munich, 507
Munich Crisis (1938), 292–3, 303, 396, 551, 566–7, 568, 584
Münzenberg, Willi, 241–3, 364, 462–3, 481, 482, 626
Murray, Arthur, 471
Murray, Don, 521
Musil, Robert, *Der Mann ohne Eigenschaften*, 290
Mussolini, Benito, 212, 293
My Fair Lady (film; 1964), 617, 694
My Guru and His Disciple (1980): characterization, 323, 568; publication, 720, 721; quotations and extracts, 304, 336, 338, 344, 356, 358, 368–9, 376, 435, 470–1, 527–9, 530, 628, 629; reception and reviews, 713–14, 721–3; sales, 723; themes, 304, 338, 470–1, 580; title, 718; writing of, 711, 716–17, 718

Nadeau, Nicky, 421
Nadelman, Elie, 399
Naeve, Lowell, *A Field of Broken Stones*, 424
Nagasaki, atomic bombing (1945), 369
Nanny *see* Avis, Anne (Nanny)
Nantucket (Massachusetts), 398, 434
Naples, 506
Napoleonic Wars (1803–15), 198, 507
Narada Bhakti Sutras (Prabhavananda), introduction, 689
Narendrapur (India), 629
Nation (magazine), 369
National Book Fair (London), 280
National Council for Civil Liberties, 641
National Gay Archives, 726
National Gay Students Liberation Conference (San Francisco; 1970), 686–7
National Gay Task Force, 725
National Institute of Arts and Letters, 413, 593; CI elected to, 415
National Portrait Gallery (NPG; London), 673–4, 677, 681, 709, 710
Natural History Museum (London), 59
Natzio, Eustace, 389–90
Nauman, Bruce, 647
Nazi, The (film treatment), 301–2, 361–2
Nazism and Nazis, 204, 214, 225, 244, 251–2, 256, 274, 301–2, 359–61, 400, 416, 444, 523, 562; CI's nightmares about, 253, 367, 443–4; portrayal in CI's works, 247–8, 250–2, 360–6, 367, 432, 565–7, 626
NBC (television network), 685, 703, 710
Ned Kelly (film; 1970), 677, 678
Neddermeyer, Gerda, 439, 515, 585, 714
Neddermeyer, Heinz: CI first meets, 240–1; development of relationship with CI, 131, 223, 240, 255, 258, 291–2, 300, 322; flight from Berlin with CI, 204, 253; in Greece, 253–8, 557, 559; tensions in relationship with CI, 256–7, 258; returns to Berlin, 257–8; denied entry to Britain, 260, 261–2, 277, 507–8, 566; CI's efforts to be reunited in safe haven with, 82, 204, 262–3, 271, 272–6, 277–8, 362, 401, 473; in Canary Islands, 263–7; tour through North Africa and Spain, 267; in Copenhagen, 267, 268; in Portugal, 272–4, 275, 362; called for military service in Germany and further immigration problems, 273–8, 488; in Belgium and Paris, 274–7, 286; in Luxembourg, 277–8, 314; arrest and imprisonment in Germany, 1, 204, 278–81, 291, 363; term of hard labor and military service, 279, 280, 291–2; marriage and family, 301, 439, 515, 584–5; postwar life, 439, 515, 585; reunited with CI in Berlin, 439, 585; family's proposed emigration to U.S., 515, 567; last meeting with CI, 439, 584–5; and publication of *Christopher and His Kind*, 714; portrayal in CI's works, 439, 508, 565–8, 714
Neddermeyer, Peter Christian, 301, 439, 515, 585, 714
Needles (California), 593
Nether Hall (Suffolk), 15, 18
Neumann, Elisabeth (Liesl), 397
New Directions (publishers), 379
New English Weekly (magazine), 277
New Journalism, 379
New Orleans, 376, 707
New Republic (magazine), 3–4, 298, 344, 595, 662
New Statesman (magazine), 246, 277, 299, 484, 513, 595
New Verse (magazine), 185, 283
New World Writing (journal), 431
New Writing (magazine), 3, 204, 228, 237, 283, 298, 310
New York, 3, 143, 288–9, 298–300, 322–3, 396–400, 433–4, 438, 440, 474–7, 500, 504, 518–19, 538, 543, 548, 591–3, 633, 639–40, 657–8, 710, 712, 718–19, 725, 727–8; André Emmerich Gallery, 677; Banfer Gallery, 636; Bethune Street, 434; Bowery, 288; Broadhurst Theater, 657; Broadway Theater, 658; Christopher Street, 687, 712; Coney Island, 288; East 52nd Street, 396; Empire State Building, 475; Empire Theater, 435; the Factory, 682, 725; George Washington Hotel, 298, 475; Guggenheim Museum, 636; Harlem, 288; Imperial Theater, 657; Middagh Street, Brooklyn, 318–19; Museum of Modern Art, 322, 400, 571; New York State Theater, 640; Oscar Wilde Memorial Bookshop, 712; Palace Theater, 719; Park Central Hotel, 396; Plaza Hotel, 476, 657; Robert Miller Gallery, 725; Sagittarius Gallery, 591, 592; Sardi's (restaurant), 592; St. Regis Hotel, 500; Statue of Liberty, 475; Studio 54 (nightclub), 718; Yorkville, 298
New York City Ballet, 322, 397, 475, 640; Bachardy's drawings for, 636, 639, 640, 644, 654
New York Drama Critics' Circle Award, 658
New York Herald Tribune, 434, 484, 592, 595, 638
New York Review of Books, 638, 710, 714–15, 722
New York Times, 266, 277, 379, 594, 638, 657, 663, 698, 699, 712, 718, 719, 721

New York Times Book Review, 484, 594–5, 652–3, 698, 722–3
New Yorker (magazine), 324, 641, 698
New Zealand, 239, 456, 678
Newbolt, Henry: *Tales of the Great War*, 95–6, 146, 148, 624; "Vitaï Lampada," 587
Newman, Barnett, 681
Newman, Lennie, 424, 425
Newman, Paul, 593
Newsweek (magazine), 700
Newton, Caroline, 318, 326
Newton, Thomas Legh, 2nd Baron, 388
Nichol (tutor to Richard Isherwood), 191–2
Nichols, Robert, 134
Nicolson, Harold, 234, 309, 386, 436
Nid du Duc, Le (France), 683–4
Nîmes (France), 683
Nobel Prize in Literature, 130–1, 232, 494, 516, 534, 552, 704
Noeske, Willi, 258
Noland, Kenneth, 647
Norland Place (pre-preparatory school; London), 150
Norment, Caroline, 319, 342, 461
Northolt aerodrome (Middlesex), 436
North-West Passage, The (unfinished novel), 190
Northwood House School (Kent), 151, 155–6, 191
Nottingham Journal (newspaper), 215
Novak, Alvin, 419
"Nowaks, The" (1936), 204, 221, 223, 226, 227–9, 237, 244–5, 294, 368, 437
NPG *see* National Portrait Gallery (London)
nuclear weapons *see* atomic and nuclear weapons
Nutcracker, The (ballet), 475

Oakes, The (Yorkshire), 28, 31, 87, 140
Oakland (California), 471
Obendorf (Austria), 655
Oberon, Merle, 597
Observer (newspaper), 83, 429, 433, 436, 484, 595, 683, 698, 721–2
Ocampo, Victoria, 408–9
Occidental College (California), 483, 706
O'Connor, Isabelle (DB grandmother), 451
October (with Don Bachardy; 1980), 720–1, 725
October: Ten Days that Shook the World (film; 1927), 241
"Ode to Wyberslegh" (1918), 111
Oderberg, Dr. (psychiatrist), 620
Odetta (singer), 471
Odysseus, 565, 646
Oedipus, 643
Offenbach, Jacques, *The Tales of Hoffmann*, 236
O'Hara, Frank, 644
Ojai (California), 354–5
O'Keeffe, Georgia, 424, 425
Oklahoma Dust Bowl, 316
Old Dudley Art Society (London), 34, 40, 43
"Old Game, The" (1924), 133, 148, 179, 598
Old Vic Theatre (London), 277
Oldenburg, Claes, 681
Olitski, Jules, 647
Oliver Twist (film; 1922), 152–3, 154
Olvidados, Los (film; 1950), 448, 498, 549

Omnibus (television program), 673
"On Ruegen Island (Summer 1931)" (1939), 204, 223–5, 232, 399
On the Frontier (with W.H. Auden; 1938), 277, 280–1, 294
One, Incorporated (advocacy group), 640–1
"One Man's God" (1923), 154
O'Neill, Eugene, 376; *All God's Chillun Got Wings*, 376
O'Neill, Oona, 396, 416
Orpen, Christopher, 168–9
Orwell, George, 294
Osborne, John, 587, 622, 667; *The Hotel in Amsterdam*, 668, 672–3; *Inadmissable Evidence*, 668, 672; *Look Back in Anger*, 672; *Luther*, 587; *Time Present*, 666, 668, 672
Oscar Levant Show, The (television show), 533–4, 565
Osmond, Humphry, 506
Ostend (Belgium), 274–5
Out of the Shadows (television program), 685
Owen, Wilfred, 148, 160
Owens, Rod, 448
Oxford Outlook (magazine), 148, 149
Oxford University: entrance exams, 130, 192; extension lectures, 24, 85; *see also* Christ Church

Pabst, Georg Wilhelm, 220, 239
Page, Anthony, 659, 662, 664, 667; affair with Don Bachardy, 666–8, 671–4, 676–7, 678, 679–81, 697; and stage adaptation of *A Meeting by the River*, 673, 679–80, 681; *The Hotel in Amsterdam*, 668, 672–3; *Inadmissable Evidence*, 668, 672; *Look Back in Anger*, 672; *Time Present*, 666, 668, 672; *Women Beware Women*, 676
Pagett, Nicola, 702
Palerang (Australia), 678
Paley, Bill, 533
Palm Springs (California), 421, 664, 689
Palomar, Mount (California), 414
Pandora's Box (film; 1929), 220
Paoli (Pennsylvania), 321, 463
Paramount (film company), 301, 334, 357
Paris, 142, 189, 258, 262–3, 275, 277, 380, 410–13, 504, 507; Les Deux Magots, 410; Hotel Quai Voltaire, 280, 282, 507; Meudon, 258, 260, 263; Ritz Hotel, 412; Rue du Bac, 411
Parker, Dorothy, 594
Parker, Louis, 72
Pasadena (California), 335, 452; Art Museum, 636
Passaic (New Jersey), 453
Passing of the Third Floor Back, The (film; 1935), 263
Patanjali, *How to Know God: The Yoga Aphorisms of Patanjali* translation (with Prabhavananda; 1953), 417, 429, 433, 440, 441, 475, 552, 558
"Paul" (1962), 272, 308, 315–16, 550–1, 554, 569–80, 581; film adaptation, 725, 726
Paul Is Alone (unfinished novel), 270–2, 290, 307, 351, 558, 571
Paul the Apostle, St., 572
Paulding, Gouverneur, 595

Pavan, Marisa, 499, 504
Pavitrananda, Swami, 648
Paxton, Larry, 619
Peak Forest Canal Company, 116
Pearl Harbor, Japanese attack (1941), 320, 325, 455, 534
Pearn, Inez, 467
Pears, Peter, 319, 321, 323, 384, 421
Pearson, George, 163, 179; *Reveille*, 163, 179
Peat Society (archaeological group), 106
Peck, George, 177–9, 226, 291, 300
Peck, Gregory, 414, 415
Peden, William, 594
Pell, Angela, 93, 101, 133
Pell, Barbara, 93, 133
Pembridge Square (Notting Hill, London), 237
Pembroke Gardens (Kensington, London), 196, 232, 258, 389, 394, 442
PEN literary awards, 727
Penmaenmawr (Wales), 31, 55, 120, 386, 389, 394
Perils of Pauline, The (film serial), 53
Petrarch, 135
Pfeiffer, Virginia, 589, 660
Philadelphia, 321, 435, 475, 491, 500, 592
Philby, Kim, 479
Phippenny, Robert, 486
Phipps, Bill, 613
Phoenix (Arizona), 616, 617
Picasso, Pablo, 34, 314, 315; *Girl Reading*, 315
Pidgeon, Walter and Ruth, 500
Pilates, Joseph, 397
Pilbeam, Nova, 266
Pirandello, Luigi, *Six Characters in Search of an Author*, 549, 590
Pisa, 507
Pitman School of Shorthand, 221
Pitt Club (Cambridge University), 173
Pizarro, Francisco, 406
Place in the Sun, A (film; 1951), 466
Plante, David, 683
Plato, 577, 600, 641, 679; *Apology*, 541; *Crito*, 541; *Gorgias*, 541; *Phaedrus*, 541; *Republic*, 541, 577; *Symposium*, 419, 541, 590
Play of Daniel, The (medieval drama), 592
Playfair, Nigel, 237
Plomer, William, 232, 274, 364, 508
Plumer, Herbert Plumer, 1st Viscount, 121
Poe, Edgar Allan, 160, 161, 424; *Tales of Mystery*, 119
Point Dume (California), 375
Point Mugu State Beach (California), 450
Polidori, John, 695
Pollard (employer of Richard Isherwood), 221, 222
Pompeii, 506
Ponsonby, Sarah, 24
Popish Plot (1678–81), 93
Popov, Blagoy, 361
Port Huron (Michigan), 451
Port Said (Egypt), 284
Port Tewfik (Egypt), 284
Porter, Paul, 420
Portland (Oregon), 349, 350, 530
Portugal, 99, 263, 272–4, 275, 298, 362
post-impressionism, 34–5

Pott, Anne, 27, 83, 95
Potter, Beatrix, 44, 62, 380, 458, 459, 546, 549; *The Roly-Poly Pudding*, 37, 86, 159, 213, 380, 498
Pound, Ezra, *Des Imagistes*, 160
Powell, Anthony, 310, 386
Powis Terrace (Notting Hill, London), 701
Prabhavananda, Swami: background and early life, 528–30, 633; appearance and character, 304, 314, 529; foundation of Vedanta Society of Southern California, 300, 335–6, 529–30, 688–9; Gerald Heard and Aldous Huxley as disciples, 300, 303–4, 313–14, 506, 689, 690; CI introduced to, 303–6; early teaching and training of CI, 2–3, 304–8, 312–13, 601; and CI's sexuality, 305, 527–8, 686–7, 722; CI initiated as disciple, 313–14, 329, 382, 434; and Denny Fouts, 315; translation collaborations with CI, 313, 317, 330–4, 342, 356, 373, 376, 381, 417, 552, 558, 665, 689; and CI's time living as monk at Ivar Avenue, 329, 338–9, 344, 349, 351, 356–9; and CI's decision to leave monastery, 376; CI's later contact and meetings with, 417, 420, 426, 432–3, 451, 517–18, 536, 589–90, 620, 631, 635, 649–50, 661, 687–90; at Trabuco monastery, 417, 432–3, 443, 589–90, 620, 687; Auden's views on, 435; and CI's relationship with Don Bachardy, 470, 516, 536, 589–90, 631; CI dreams about, 470–1, 475, 530–1, 726; views on drugs, 506; and Bachardy's interest in Vedanta, 516, 517–81, 606, 646, 689; and CI's biography of Ramakrishna, 516, 525, 526, 624, 635; and CI's research trip to India, 528; and death of CI's mother, 543; initiation of Bachardy, 613, 614, 689; in India with CI for Vivekananda centenary celebrations, 624, 627–33; and publication of CI's *A Meeting by the River*, 648, 652, 653–4; declining health, 690, 711; and succession at Hollywood Vedanta Center, 689, 711; death, 711; characteristics of friendship with CI, 2, 148, 304, 313–14, 338–9, 344, 350, 359, 470–1, 475, 517, 536, 601, 629–31, 687–90, 711; *A Garland of Questions and Answers*, 689; *Narada Bhakti Sutras*, 689; *Religion in Practice*, 522, 529; see also *My Guru and His Disciple*
Prague, 248, 253
Prater Violet (1945): autobiographical aspects, 1–2, 260, 300–1, 362, 363, 365–7; characterization, 1–2, 125, 325, 340, 351, 361–2, 364, 366–8; dedication, 325; as first part of proposed trilogy, 379; plot and themes, 1–2, 33, 285–6, 348, 350–1, 359–69, 498, 602; publication, 369, 392, 485; quotations and extracts, 1–2, 285–6, 348, 350–1, 361, 362, 363, 364; reception and reviews, 368, 369, 412–13, 485, 556, 596; structure and style, 359–60; title, 360; writing of, 204, 263, 272, 340, 357, 359, 363, 364, 367–8
Pratt, Dallas, 463
Prema Chaitanya *see* Yale, John
Price, Ken, 647, 693, 694
Prince, Harold, 657
Prince, William, 434, 435–6

Princeton University, 416
Pritchett, Victor Sawdon (V. S.), 484
"Problem of the Religious Novel, The" (1945/50), 373, 572, 573
Procktor, Patrick, 647, 648, 655, 659, 667, 680, 681, 709
Protetch, David, Dr., 592, 593
Proust, Marcel, 214, 269, 372, 398, 410, 463, 594
Provincetown (Massachusetts), 398
Prussian Landtag referendum (1931), 247
Pryce-Jones, Alan, 294, 638
psychoanalysis, 139, 144, 207, 405, 610
Public School Looks at the World, A (Repton magazine), 128–9
Public School Verse 1921–1922 (anthology), 153–4
Publishers' Weekly (magazine), 712
Pudovkin, Vsevolod, *The End of St. Petersburg*, 241
Puerto Cabello (Venezuela), 401
Punch (magazine), 176, 485
Purden (doctor with York and Lancaster Regiment), 75, 76
Purdie, Nettie May, 122–3, 353, 715
Pushkin, Alexander, 4, 299

Quakers (Society of Friends), 316, 320–1, 323, 355, 423, 466, 546, 663; La Verne Seminar, 316–18, 319, 327, 329, 577
Queen Elizabeth, HMS, 413, 436, 438, 440
Queen's Hall (London), 100, 181
Queenstown (Ireland), 66
Quito (Ecuador), 400–1, 404–5, 406–7, 677
Quo Vadis? (film; 1913), 53–4

Rabin, Reverend (tutor to Richard Isherwood), 221
Radinghem-en-Weppes (France), 68
Radziwill, Princess Lee, 597
Rage in Heaven (film; 1941), 302, 305
Rajagopal, Desikacharya, 355
Rajagopal, Rosalind, 355
Ramakrishna, 300, 335, 336, 409, 417, 443, 516, 518, 526–9, 575, 578, 589, 625, 628, 646, 653, 688, 721; *The Gospel of Sri Ramakrishna*, 471
Ramakrishna and His Disciples (1965), 516, 523, 525, 527–8, 531, 575, 578, 590, 597, 624–5, 627, 632, 635, 652–3, 721–2
Random House (publishers), 3, 299, 397, 473, 556
Rasponi, Count Lanfranco, 591
Rassine, Alexis, 508
Ratcliffe, Michael, 722
Rattigan, Terence, 393
Ravagli, Angelo, 425
Ray, Nicholas, 520
Reading (Berkshire), 41, 178, 179
Reagan, Nancy, 500, 708
Reagan, Ronald, 500
Rebel Without a Cause (film; 1955), 520
"Recessional from Cambridge, The" (1925), 177
Rechy, John, 311, 547–8, 581, 637, 693, 706
Redcliffe Road (Chelsea, London), 192, 195
Reddish House (Wiltshire), 586
Redfern Gallery (London), 582, 588, 592, 652
Redgrave, Vanessa, 635
Redlands College (Texas), 724

Reece Mews (South Kensington, London), 701–2
Reflections in a Golden Eye (film treatment), 635
Reform Club (London), 384, 413
Regester, Bob, 655, 659, 661, 662, 666, 667, 683
Reichsbanner (anti-Nazi movement), 250
Reichstag Fire and Trial (1933), 360–2, 363, 364, 365, 626
Reid, Bob, 91–2, 605
Reid, Jack, 76, 91–2, 123, 355, 605
Reid, Marjorie (Madgie; née Luce), 63, 76, 91–2, 95, 123, 191, 355
Reinhardt, Gottfried, 302, 354, 413
Reinhardt, Max, 236, 302, 354
Reinhardt, Wolfgang, 354, 371, 381
Reis, Meta, 395
Religion in Practice (Prabhavananda), introduction, 522, 529
Renoir, Jean, 613
Repton School (Derbyshire), 50, 55, 113–14, 117–38, 142–9, 155
Reptonian, The (magazine), 134, 135, 143
Reuters (news agency), 704
Reveille (film; 1924), 163, 179
Revesby Play, The (mummers' play), 267, 558
Revolte im Erziehungshaus (film; 1930), 208
rheumatic fever, 16, 17, 79–80, 173, 188, 209, 726
Richard I (the Lionheart), King, 58, 71
Richards, I.A., 167–8, 184, 291, 469; *Practical Criticism*, 167
Richardson, Ralph, 702
Richardson, Tony, 7, 469, 583, 587–8, 622, 635, 643, 644, 655, 659, 667, 671, 672, 677, 678, 683–4; affair with Don Bachardy, 543, 548, 622; *The Long-Distance Runner*, 635; *The Loved One*, 633, 634, 635, 636, 639, 640, 655; *Luther*, 587; *Ned Kelly*, 677, 678; *The Sailor from Gibraltar*, 635; *A Taste of Honey*, 543, 548, 587
Richmond (London), 180, 291
Richmond, Kenneth, 139
Ricks, Christopher, 723
Riesengebirge (Poland), 220
Rigby, Harry, 718
Riley, James Whitcomb, 100
Rivers, Larry, 644
Riviera Beach (California), 375
RKO (film company), 381, 395
"R.L.S." (1950–51), 324–5, 429, 642
Robbins, Jerome, 593
Roberts, Russell, 52–3
Robeson, Paul, 282
Robin of Locksley (Robin Hood), 71
Robson-Scott, William, 224, 225, 262, 279, 385
Rochester (New York), 220, 712
Rockefeller, Nelson, 400
Rodakiewicz, Henwar, 326
Rodakiewicz, Margaret (Peggy) *see* Kiskadden, Margaret (Peggy)
Rodd, Marcel, 356
Roditi, Edouard, 437
Roehm, Ernst, 260, 361
Roerick, Bill, 396
Rohmer, Sax, 306
Rolfe, Frederick, *The Desire and Pursuit of the Whole*, 271–2

Rolland, Romain: *Jean-Christophe*, 516, 518, 519–20, 521; *The Life of Ramakrishna*, 516, 653
Rolling Stones (band), 683
Roman Empire, 642–3
Rome, 506–7, 578, 579, 628–30, 633, 642, 702
Romford (Essex), 126, 150
Rondeaux, Madeleine, 461, 462
Rooney, Mickey, 699
Roosevelt, Franklin D., 315, 400
Rose Tattoo, The (film; 1955), 489–92, 501, 654
Rosemary's Baby (film; 1968), 701
Rosenberg, Meta, 395
Rosmersholm (film treatment), 381
Ross, Jean: background and early life, 236; career, 236–7, 258; relationships, 237, 385; in Berlin, 237, 246; friendship with CI, 136, 236, 237, 258, 302; as model for Sally Bowles, 59, 203, 236–7, 238, 246; in London, 258, 261
Ross, Nancy Wilson, 653
Ross, Robbie, 171
Rote Fahne, Die (newspaper), 250
Rothehütte (Germany), 210
Rotterdam, 263
Rouen (France), 142, 143, 151–2, 153–5, 156
Rousseau, Jean-Jacques, *Confessions*, 594
Rowe, John, 404, 407
Royal Army Medical Corps, 99
Royal Ballet, 39, 683
Royal College of Needlework, 108
Royal Court Theatre (London), 543, 587, 659, 662, 666, 667, 668, 672, 673, 679
Royal Shakespeare Company, 676
Rueda, Victor, 421
Ruegen Island (Germany), 223–4, 232–3, 399
Rugby School (Warwickshire), 138, 144, 222
"Rugtonstead" novels (unpublished), 117–18, 124, 127, 132, 133–4, 143–4, 149, 156
Ruscha, Ed, 682, 693, 694
Ruskin, John, *Sesame and Lilies*, 23–4
Russell, Bertrand Russell, 3rd Earl, 321, 355
Russell-Roberts, Edmund Godfrey, 61

Sachs, David, 419
Saigon, 284, 291, 308
Sailor from Gibraltar, The (film; 1967), 635
Salinger, Cecil, 273–5, 277–8, 549
Sally (musical), 238
Sally Bowles (1937), 4, 204, 235–40, 246, 272, 283, 345, 430–1; see also *Cabaret*; *I Am a Camera*
Salome (opera), 35
Salzburg (Austria), 400, 655
Sammlung, Die (magazine), 416
Samuel French (publishers), 508
Samuels, Lesser, 334, 381–2, 395, 415, 424, 521
San Diego, 327, 711–12
San Fernando Valley State College (California), 673
San Francisco, 313, 335, 349, 350, 431, 433, 471–2, 489, 530, 618–19, 636, 686, 694, 720, 721
San Francisco Chronicle (newspaper), 721
San Francisco Examiner (newspaper), 652
San Gimignano (Italy), 507
Sanctuary (film; 1961), 543

Sandhurst (Berkshire), Royal Military College, 14, 36, 92
Sandwich, Amiya, Countess of (*earlier* Ella Corbin), 342, 358, 397, 543–4, 588
Sandwich, George Montagu, 9th Earl of, 337
Sant, Ivor, 55, 60
Santa Ana (California), jail, 426
Santa Barbara (California), 597, 615, 616, 620, 621, 645; Sarada Convent, 358, 517–18; Vedanta temple, 577–8, 631; *see also* Montecito; University of California, Santa Barbara
Santa Fe (New Mexico), 425, 426, 522
Santa Monica (California): Adelaide Drive, 344, 537, 538–9, 541, 607–8, 649, 674, 710, 724; Café Jay, 374, 424; Civic Auditorium, 660; East Rustic Road, 414, 421–4, 425, 426, 510, 597, 674; El Kanan (hotel), 413; Entrada Drive, 352, 375, 379–80, 608; Friendship (bar), 34, 374, 380, 493; Mabery Road, 344, 380–1, 479; Machell-Smith, Emily (CI's grandmother), 380; Mesa Road, 483–4, 502, 510; Muscle Beach, 413; Ocean Avenue, 345, 413, 674; Pier, 433, 441, 486, 507; the Pits, 377; Rustic Canyon, 430, 483; Santa Monica Hospital, 353; St. John's Hospital, 726, 728; State Beach, 375, 377, 483, 614; Sycamore Road, 510, 516–17, 537, 603; Ted's Grill, 608; 3rd Street, 664, 665; Tumble Inn, 646; Variety (bar), 422; West Channel Road, 375
Santa Paula, SS, 401
Santayana, George, 433
São Pedro (Portugal), 272–4
Sarada Devi, 313, 518, 526, 528–9, 688
Saradananda, Swami, *Sri Ramakrishna, The Great Master*, 516
Sarah Lawrence College (New York), 399, 546
Sardinia, 521
Sargent, John Singer, 640
Sarrazin, Michael, 702, 703
Sartre, Jean-Paul, 552, 589; *No Exit*, 552
Sassoon, Siegfried, 134
Sassoon, Victor, 284
Saturday Review of Books, 379, 484, 594
Saul of Tarsus, 572
Sausalito (California), 471
Savoy Hill House (London), 180
Savoy Hotel (London), 163
Scappoose (Oregon), 349
Scaramouche (film; 1923), 164
Scenes from an Emigration (unfinished memoir), 125, 721–3, 723–4, 726, 727
Schary, Dore, 483, 488
Schenck, Joseph, 477
Schenck, Marvin, 477–9, 483, 488
Schenck, Nicholas, 477
Schiele, Egon, 636, 710, 716
Schleicher, Kurt von, 251, 252
Schlesinger, John, 689; *Midnight Cowboy*, 701
Schlesinger, Peter, 664–5, 669, 672, 680, 681, 683–4, 685, 696–7, 718
Schoenberg, Arnold, 478
Schofield, William, 135
Scholz, Gerda *see* Neddermeyer, Gerda

School of Tragedy, The see *The World in the Evening*
Schorer, Mark, 484, 521, 545, 594, 608
Schreiber, Taft, 613
Schulberg, Budd, 478
Science Fiction and Fantasy Writers of America, Nebula Awards, 703
Science Research Association, 631
Scientific-Humanitarian Committee, 219, 677
Scilly Isles, 188–9
Scobie, William, 687
Scofield, Paul, 672
Scott, Cyril, 17
Scott, Gerald, 94
Scott, Ian Michael (Micky), 94, 109, 113, 118, 120, 196
Scott, Walter, 112, 115, 135, 187, 306, 343, 574; *Guy Mannering*, 285; *Ivanhoe*, 71; *Peveril of the Peak*, 93; *The Talisman*, 57–8, 71
Scott-Kilvert, Ian, 192, 280–2, 384, 507
Screenwriters' Film Society (Los Angeles), 622
Searle, Alan, 507, 588
Seascape with Figures see *All the Conspirators*
Seattle: Dootson-Calderhead Gallery, 710; Vedanta center, 349
Second Boer War (1899–1902), 12, 14–15, 19, 30, 105
Second World War see World War II
Sedbergh School (Cumbria), 186
Seldis, Henry, 608, 709–10
Selznick, David, 500, 533, 534, 594, 608, 646
Selznick, Jennifer see Jones, Jennifer
Semarang (Indonesia), 524
Seymour, Jane, 702
Shadwell (London), 221
Shakespeare, William, 124, 135, 161, 168, 189, 541, 574; *Antony and Cleopatra*, 46, 168; *As You Like It*, 51, 136; *Coriolanus*, 554–5; *Hamlet*, 51, 53, 331, 362, 539; *Henry V*, 60; *Julius Caesar*, 195; *King Lear*, 541; *Macbeth*, 41–2, 44, 51, 109, 135, 256; *The Merry Wives of Windsor*, 109; *A Midsummer Night's Dream*, 39–40, 58, 59, 84, 182, 205, 702; *Othello*, 44; sonnets, 147; *The Tempest*, 256, 557–8, 559, 613
Shanghai, 212, 284, 288
Shankara, 376, 529; *Vivekachudamani (Crest Jewel of Discrimination)*, 376, 381, 689
Shaw (Emmanuel College porter), 66, 130
Shaw, George Bernard, 128, 145, 393, 589, 701; *The Adventures of the Black Girl in Her Search for God*, 658–9, 665, 673, 674–5; *Androcles and the Lion*, 364, 365; *Misalliance*, 208; "Preface on the Prospects of Christianity," 365; *Pygmalion*, 694
Sheinberg, Sidney, 701
Shelley, Mary, *Frankenstein*, 694
Shelley, Percy Bysshe, 145, 176, 409; *The Cenci*, 144–5; "Mont Blanc," 142
Shell-Mera oil camp (Ecuador), 405–6, 422
Shepherd, Amos, 421
Shere (Surrey), 150
Sherwood Forest, 71, 87
Shivananda, Swami, 417; foreword for biography (1949), 417
Shrapnel, Norman, 595
Sidebotham, Herbert, 391

Sidmouth (Devon), 107
Sidney, Philip, 135
Sienkiewicz, Henryk, *Quo Vadis?* 53
Sign of the Cross, The (film; 1932), 364–5, 626
Signoret, Simone, 636
Sikra Kulingram (India), 630
"Silent Night" (Christmas carol), 654–5
Silverstein, Michael, 691–2
Silvia (Colombia), 404
Simeons, A.T.W., 611, 660; *Man's Presumptuous Brain*, 611
Simon, Norton, 708
Simon & Schuster (publishers), 556, 588, 593, 607
Simpson, Wallis, 278
Sinatra, Frank, 379
Single Man, A (1964): autobiographical aspects, 38, 537, 540, 602, 606, 612, 614, 615; characterization, 38, 92–3, 123, 126, 419, 534–5, 537, 540, 546, 550, 587, 590, 597–602, 603, 604, 606, 608–13, 615–16, 622, 623–4, 699; dedication, 622; influences on, 462, 492, 598, 601, 609–12, 625–6; literary importance, 8, 638; plot and themes, 8, 92–3, 147, 148, 190, 374–5, 414, 419, 422, 464, 492–3, 537, 550, 590–1, 597–606, 608–12, 615–16, 623–4, 625–6, 637, 649; publication, 624, 627, 637–8; quotations and extracts, 374, 375, 493, 586; reception and reviews, 622–3, 637–8, 720; structure and form, 492–3, 609, 641; title, 597, 602, 622; writing of, 590–1, 597–606, 608–12, 615–16, 620, 622–4, 659
Single Man, A (film; 2009), 550
Sino-Japanese War (1937–45), 283, 284–5, 287–8
Sintra (Portugal), 99, 273, 275
Sister Lalita (Carrie Mead Wyckoff), 335–7, 530
Slade School of Fine Art (London), 549, 591, 665
Slater, Montagu, 412
Sleep, Wayne, 39, 683
Sleeping Beauty (ballet), 640
Slum Angel, The (variety show playlet), 44
Smedley, Agnes, 285
Smight, Jack, 701, 703
Smith, Dodie, 136, 181, 311, 342, 357, 375, 457, 458, 460, 461, 470, 474, 508, 520, 536, 586, 681, 698; *I Capture the Castle*, 357
Smith, Geoffrey Burrell, 124–30, 142, 145, 154–5, 177, 186, 220; *Scenes from European History*, 125, 724
Smith, Stevie, 653
Smolen, Jay, 594
Smyth (Repton pupil), 168
Smythies, Raymond, 105–6, 169
Snake Pass (Derbyshire), 538
Snape Maltings (Suffolk), 711
Snow, Charles Percy, 697, 713
Snow, Edgar, 416
Snow White and the Seven Dwarfs (film; 1937), 446
Society of David (gay liberation group), 690
Society of Friends see Quakers
Socrates, 419, 541, 544, 590, 600, 641, 660
Soldati, Mario, 507
Soller, Kyle, 681
Soloweitschik, Gisa, 203, 245–6
Something for Everyone (film; 1970), 699
Somme, Battle of the (1916), 92–3

Sontag, Susan, 464, 710
Sophocles, 642; *Oedipus at Colonus*, 342, 643
Sorel, Paul, 328, 335, 342, 397
Sorley, Charles, 134
South Africa, 12, 14–15, 19, 49; *see also* Second Boer War (1899–1902)
Southern, Terry, 634
Southwark (London), 184
"Souvenir des Vacances" (1926), 185
Spa (Belgium), 275
Spanish Civil War (1936–39), 198, 276, 282, 283, 286, 353, 466, 507
Spectator (magazine), 309, 386, 387, 484, 596, 698
Spee, Maximilian von, 95–6
Spender, Humphrey, 224, 275
Spender, Natasha, 467, 480, 508
Spender, Stephen: background and early life, 466; appearance, character and sexuality, 198, 466, 467–8, 643; at Oxford, 198–9; publication of Auden's *Poems* (1928), 186–7, 198; CI visits in Hamburg (summer 1930), 224; in Berlin, 232, 236, 241, 270, 467; holidays on Ruegen Island with CI (1931; 1932), 223–4, 232–3, 399; and publication of *The Memorial*, 232, 233; disagreement with CI over *Goodbye to Berlin*, 245, 248, 249; relationship with Tony Hyndman, 273, 363, 466; in Portugal with Hyndman, 273, 362; and Spanish Civil War, 198, 282, 466; first marriage, 467; and Heinz Neddermeyer's arrest by Gestapo, 278; editorship of *Horizon* and *Encounter*, 199, 309–10, 437, 467, 484, 562, 601; and CI's and Auden's emigration, 309–10, 383; during World War II, 383–4; second marriage and family, 467, 508; and CI's 1947 visit to England, 383–4, 467; teaches at Sarah Lawrence College, 399; on Fire Island (summer 1947), 399; and Burgess and Maclean defection, 480; lecture tour of United States (1953), 466, 470; and CI's relationship with Don Bachardy, 508; during CI and Bachardy's 1956 trip to London, 562–3; suspected CIA agent, 198, 437, 467; and Bachardy's art studies in London, 549; in Manchester for television show with CI (June 1961), 586; at Bachardy's 1964 Banfer Gallery Show, 636; in California for lecture tour (autumn 1964), 636–7; during CI and Bachardy's 1973 trip to London, 701; and *Christopher and His Kind*, 706; knighthood, 42; characteristics of friendship with CI, 42, 113, 198–9, 233, 249, 271, 309–10, 348, 377, 383–4, 399, 467–8, 563, 636–7; literary importance, 7, 199; portrayal in CI's works, 125, 198, 225, 271, 458, 466–70, 694; views on CI's works, 245, 248, 595, 596, 637, 697–8, 713–14, 722; *Citizens in War – and After*, 383–4; *The God that Failed*, 512–13; *Poems* (1933), 233; *The Temple*, 232, 233; translations, 271; *Vienna*, 363; *World Within World*, 245, 248, 249, 466–7, 513, 706
Spens, William, 154, 176–7
Spenser, Edmund, 135
Spock, Benjamin, 663
Squire's Mount (Hampstead, London), 581–2

St. Edmund's School (Hindhead), 55, 56, 59–64, 74–7, 89–91, 96–117, 146, 184, 208, 292, 377, 459
St. Edmund's School Chronicle, 103
St. Just, Maria Britneva, Lady, 559
St. Just, Peter Grenfell, 2nd Baron, 559
St. Martin-in-the-Fields Church (London), 117
St. Mary Abbot's Terrace (Kensington, London), 140, 150, 183, 192, 193, 196, 217
St. Nicholas (Ktiponisi; Greece), 253–7, 557, 559
St. Tropez (France), 209
Stagecoach (film; 1939), 465
Stalin, Joseph, 481, 513
Standen (art teacher to Frank Isherwood), 702
Stanford University, 597, 616, 647, 713
Stansky, Peter, 713
Starcke, Walter, 397
Starhemberg, Prince Ernst, 363
Steinbeck, John, *East of Eden*, 483
Stekel, Wilhelm, 270
Stern, James, 273, 323, 396, 397, 415
Stern, Tania (née Kurella), 273, 323, 396, 397, 415
Stevenson, Robert, 259
Stevenson, Robert Louis, 24, 34, 429, 512, 649, 651, 677–8; "The Beach of Falesá," 581, 643; *A Child's Garden of Verses*, 346–7; "The Lantern Bearers," 574; "Requiem," 678; *Strange Case of Dr. Jekyll and Mr. Hyde*, 324–5, 424, 575, 642; *Treasure Island*, 95
Stewart, Donald Ogden, 392
Stickel family (Sycamore Road, Santa Monica), 537, 603
Stockport (Cheshire), 15, 94, 131, 393, 394
Stoll, Oswald, 177, 179
Stoll Pictures (film company), 177, 179
Stonewall Riot (1969), 685, 687
Strange Ones, The (film; 1950), 448
Strasberg, Paula, 414, 421
Stratford (Connecticut), Shakespeare Festival Theater, 640, 644
Stratford-on-Avon (Warwickshire), 541
Straus, Roger, 710
Strauss, Richard, *Salome*, 35
Stravinsky, Igor, 181, 183, 304, 311, 420, 521–3, 582, 592, 633, 636, 708; *Agon*, 522; *Canticum Sacrum*, 522; *The Rake's Progress*, 432, 522; *Le Sacre du printemps*, 522
Stravinsky, Vera, 311, 521–2, 592, 636
Streetcar Named Desire, A (film; 1951), 427, 490
Streisand, Barbra, 636
Strensall (Yorkshire), 29, 55
Strickland, Agnes, *Lives of the Queens of England*, 221
Stromberg, Hunt Jr., 665, 694, 701, 703
Strong, Leonard, 474
Strong, Roy, 673–4
Sturgess (drill instructor), 36
Stuurman, Douwe, 547
Sü-chow (China), 286
Sudetenland, 292, 293
Sudhira *see* Kennedy, Helen
Suez Port (Egypt), 284
Sullivan, Maxine, 288
Summer at the House, The (unfinished novel), 182, 188

Sun Shines Bright, The (film; 1953), 465
Sunday Telegraph (newspaper), 697
Sunday Times (newspaper), 197, 467, 595
Surmanagar (India), 528–9
surrealism, 159, 511
Suzhou (China), 286
Swahananda, Swami, 711, 720
Swan Lake (ballet), 450
Swarthmore College (Pennsylvania), 319, 368
Swingler, Randall, 307
Sydney, 678
Sykes (Repton pupil), 144
Sykes, Christopher Simon, 647
Sykes, Gerald, 594, 663
Symonds, Charles, 123, 210, 388, 389, 391
Symonds, William, 116
syphilis, 218, 219, 226, 254, 457
Szczesny, Bethold (Bubi), 205, 206–7, 208, 210–11, 219, 220, 300, 399, 401, 408

Tagenbuch einer Verlorenen (Diary of a Lost Girl) (film; 1929), 220, 239
Tahiti, 262, 400, 677, 678
"Take It or Leave It" (1942), 324–5, 641–2
Tanev, Vasil, 361
Tangier, 465, 504–5, 614, 618, 711
Tao Te Ching (Chinese text), 561
Taos (New Mexico), 425
Taste of Honey, A (film; 1961), 587
Tavistock Clinic for Nervous Diseases (London), 191
Taylor, Elizabeth, 643
Taylor, Frank, 416, 417, 427, 430, 458, 469, 583, 643
Taylor, Nan, 416, 427
Tchaikovsky, Pyotr: *The Nutcracker*, 475; *Sleeping Beauty*, 640; *Swan Lake*, 450
Temple, Shirley, 382
Tempo (television program), 675
Tenerife, 265
Tenniel, John, 68
tennis, 55, 123, 133, 134, 181, 602
Tennyson, Alfred Tennyson, 1st Baron, 134, 291; *Idylls of the King*, 123; "Tithonus," 625
Ter-Arutunian, Rouben, 639, 654
Tetouan (Spanish Morocco), 267
Theosophy, 24, 73, 333, 355
Thompson, Dorothy, 230
Thomson, Virgil, 636, 644, 708
Threlkeld (Cumbria), 280
Thurau, Meta, 203, 212, 217, 229, 234, 251, 404, 437–8
Thurston (Suffolk), 15
Tibetan Book of the Dead, 303
Time (magazine), 334, 374, 379, 416, 480, 484, 594, 638, 663, 700
Times, The (newspaper), 40, 82, 145, 592, 662, 722
Times Literary Supplement, 197, 233, 722
Today Show, The (television program), 698
Tokyo, 288, 523–4, 631; Imperial Hotel, 523
Toller, Ernst, 298
Tolstoy, Leo: *Father Sergius*, 573–4; *War and Peace*, 200, 507, 670
Tom Jones (film; 1963), 622, 667
Tomorrow (magazine), 424, 429, 455–6, 466
Tony Awards, 435, 657

Toogood, Esther (née Bradshaw Isherwood; CI's aunt), 17, 28, 94–5, 182, 387, 389
Toogood, Joan, 28, 55, 94–5, 121
Toogood, Joseph Hooker, 17
Toogood, Timothy, 28, 55, 94–5, 121, 366, 553
Tooker, George, 396, 398
Torgler, Ernst, 361
Toronto, 712
Torrington (Devon), 156
Tower of London, 216
Town & Country (magazine), 397
Townshend, Eddie, 50, 52, 53, 154
Toynbee, Philip, 713–14, 721–2
Trabuco (California), 327; Trabuco College, 327–9, 336, 417; Vedanta Society monastery, 417, 421, 430, 432–3, 441, 443, 471, 620
Trancas (California), 448
Trebaol, Edouard, 153
Tree, Herbert Beerbohm, 354; *David Copperfield*, 72–3, 213; *Macbeth*, 42–3; *A Midsummer Night's Dream*, 39
Tree, Iris, 136, 181, 354–5, 420, 433, 486–7, 507, 598, 666
Trevor, Agatha Greene, 18, 84, 156, 257, 607, 719
Trevor, Raymond, 156
Trier (Germany), 278, 279
Trilling, Diana, 369
Tristram, Harold, 24
Tristram, Leonard, 24, 355–6, 641
Tristram, Mable (Mamie), 23–4, 355–6
Trollope, Anthony, *Framley Parsonage*, 285
Trott, Byron, 658
Trumbo, Dalton, 477
tuberculosis, 160, 227, 228, 247, 355, 426, 456
"Turn Round the World, The" (1935), 266–7
Turner, Lana, 345, 499, 503–4
Turner, Reggie, 171
Turner, W.J., 393
Turville-Petre, Francis, 218–20, 240–1, 253, 254–5, 256, 257, 267, 269–70, 284, 315, 394, 559, 699
TV and Radio Times (magazine), 700
Twain, Mark, 128
20th Century-Fox (film company), 301, 350, 466, 477, 543
Twickenham Studios (London), 635
"Two Brothers" (1924), 92–3, 102, 146, 148–9, 605–6
Two-Faced Woman (film; 1941), 323
Twombly, Cy, 647
Tynan, Katharine, 154
Tynan, Kenneth, 48

UCLA *see* University of California, Los Angeles
UCSB *see* University of California, Santa Barbara
Ullman, Franz von, 236
"Underhill, Ben," 581, 618–19
Universal (film company), 701, 702
University of California, Berkeley, CI lectures, 545, 606, 608, 618–19, 640, 659
University of California, Los Angeles (UCLA), 358, 418, 447, 453, 466, 483, 500–1, 540, 549, 650, 664, 675, 715; CI's extension lectures, 545, 580; CI's Regents' Professorship, 640, 641

University of California, Riverside, CI's Regents' Professorship, 652
University of California, Santa Barbara (UCSB), CI lectures, 12, 148, 440, 540, 545–7, 572–3, 574–6, 599, 615, 651, 707
University of Southern California (USC), 336, 631, 707
Up at the Villa (film treatment), 371
Upward, Allen, 127–8, 160
Upward, Christopher, 510, 511
Upward, Edward: family background and early life, 126, 127–8; appearance and character, 127–8, 142, 162, 168, 225, 511–12; at Repton School, 126–8, 134, 142; CI first meets, 124, 126–7; walking tour in France with CI, 142–3, 404; at Cambridge, 8, 55, 144, 159–63, 166–73, 175, 184, 206, 499, 547, 560–1; collaborations with CI, 159–62, 171; and CI's sexuality, 168, 177–8, 241; leaves Cambridge, 176; post-Cambridge friendship with CI, 177–8, 234, 271; visits CI on Isle of Wight (1925), 512; and Olive Mangeot, 183; holidays in Scilly Isles and France with CI (1926), 188–90; and CI's *All the Conspirators*, 188–90, 512, 513; visits CI in Berlin, 225, 241; politics and involvement in Communist Party, 225, 234, 241, 307, 511, 513; and CI's Berlin novels, 259; and CI and Auden's *Journey to War*, 307; and CI and Auden's emigration, 310; marriage and family, 385, 510–11; and CI's 1947 and 1956 visits to England, 385, 510–11; and CI's *Down There on a Visit*, 560–1, 563, 581, 582; and CI's *A Single Man*, 622; and CI's *A Meeting by the River*, 648; later life and career, 161, 510–14; characteristics of friendship with CI, 42, 124, 150, 159, 162, 167, 168, 171–3, 178, 186, 189, 234, 271, 307, 512, 513–14; literary importance, 7, 161, 186, 513; portrayal in CI's works, 125, 126–7, 128, 189, 511, 512, 560–1, 612, 694; views on CI's works, 148, 170, 175, 228, 369, 492, 563, 622, 714, 715; *In the Thirties*, 511, 512, 513, 560; "The Little Hotel," 161; "The Railway Accident," 161, 511; "Sketch for a Marxist Interpretation of Literature," 511; *The Spiral Ascent*, 128, 132, 162, 167–8, 512, 513; see also *The Mortmere Stories*
Upward, Harold, 126, 127
Upward, Hilda, 510–11, 513
Upward, Louisa, 127
Upward, Mervyn, 129
Ure, Mary, 567
USC *see* University of Southern California

Vacant Room, The (film treatment), 424, 521
Vailly (France), 68
Val d'Isère (France), 143
Valbonne (France), 567
Valencia (Spain), 282, 283
van der Lubbe, Marinus, 361
Van Druten, John, 322, 334, 342, 396–7, 426, 454, 460, 531–2, 541; portrayal in CI's works, 460–1; *I Am a Camera*, 4, 430–1, 433–6, 437, 443, 447, 459–60, 485, 532, 553, 592, 657, 676; *The Widening Circle*, 553, 723–4

Van Eyck, Peter (Götz von Eick), 237
Van Gogh, Vincent, 34
Van Meegeren, Han, 417
Van Nuys (California), Birmingham Hospital, 426, 427
Van Vechten, Carl, 425, 475
Vancouver, 288
Variety (magazine), 504, 655, 657
Vaughan, Keith, 385, 581–2, 614
Vedanta: importance to CI, 2–3, 124, 303–4, 310, 339–41, 375–6, 510, 517, 520, 530–1, 536, 544, 551, 631, 632–3, 646, 687–90, 723; tenets and practices, 300, 303–5, 313–14, 339, 344–5, 462, 498–9, 516, 518, 520, 526, 553, 610, 645
Vedanta and the West (magazine), 313, 334, 335, 356, 391, 429, 433, 624, 631
Vedanta for the Western World (1945), 356
Vedanta for Modern Man (1951), 429
Vedanta Place (Hollywood Vedanta Center): CI lives as monk at, 3, 329, 334–69, 371–5, 650; establishment and running of, 335–7, 688–9, 711
Vedanta Society of Southern California: foundation, 300, 335–6, 530; magazine, 313, 334, 335, 356, 391, 429, 433, 624, 631–2; properties, 335–7, 358, 417
Veidt, Conrad, 220
Veiller, Bayard, *The Thirteenth Chair*, 109
venereal disease, 122, 205, 372–3
Venice, 143, 507, 567; Film Festival, 622; Santa Maria della Salute, 143
Venice (California), 693, 708
Ventnor (Isle of Wight), 36, 75–80, 81, 193, 428, 601
Ventura (California), 356, 641
Verlorenhoek (Belgium), 80
Verne, Jules, 403
Vernon family, 568–9
Versailles, Treaty of (1919), 225
Vesey, Desmond, 347
Victoria Station (London), 284
Vidal, Gore, 7, 119, 199, 410–13, 434, 463, 502, 559, 592, 622, 633, 636, 682, 686, 693, 702, 712, 714–15; *The Best Man*, 622; *The City and the Pillar*, 410, 411, 413; *The Judgment of Paris*, 570; *Myra Breckinridge*, 624; "Pages from an Abandoned Journal," 570; *Palimpsest*, 412–13; *Romulus*, 592; *Williwaw*, 411
Vidor, Florence, 500
Vidyatmananda, Swami *see* Yale, John
Vienna, 253, 265, 290, 359, 363, 479, 584, 636, 664, 704
"Viennese Expressionism 1910–1924" (exhibition; 1963), 636
Viertel, Berthold: early life, 481; CI first meets, 258; CI works on script of *Little Friend* for, 258–66, 366, 432; and CI's sexuality, 260, 262; relationship with Beatrix Lehmann, 263; family life in California, 301, 345; Hollywood career, 301; CI works on anti-Nazi film treatment with 301–2, 361–2; in New York, 323, 380, 397; CI socializes with in California, 339, 340, 342, 347–8, 355; and CI's life at Vedanta monastery, 338, 347–8;

Viertel (cont.)
    and CI's argument with Bertolt Brecht,
    347–8, 365, 589; reads draft of *Prater Violet*,
    367–8; returns to Europe, 380; CI and Bill
    Caskey live in garage apartment in Santa
    Monica, 380–1; death, 479; portrayal in CI's
    works, 340, 360, 361–2, 366–7, 368; *Little
    Friend*, 258–66, 340, 361, 367, 432, 456; *The
    Passing of the Third Floor Back*, 263
Viertel, Peter, 380, 478, 702; *The Canyon*, 380
Viertel, Salka, 302, 342, 345, 355, 372, 416, 489,
    506, 702; CI and Bill Caskey live in garage
    apartment in Santa Monica, 380–1; political
    activities and blacklisting, 477–9, 481
Viertel, Tommy, 380
Viertel, Virginia (Jigee), 380, 478, 479
Vietnam War (1955–75), 488, 669; protest
    movement, 478, 663
Village Voice (newspaper), 698, 699
Villon, François, 161
Vincent Square (London), 191
"Visit to Anselm Oakes, A" (1966), 505, 506
Vitsahokananda, Swami, 526
Vivaldi, Antonio, 181
Vivekananda, 335, 518, 526, 528–9, 530, 544, 688,
    711, 727; centenary celebrations, 624, 628,
    631–3; "The Real Nature of Man," 606; *What
    Religion Is: In the Words of Vivekananda*, 544
Voeller, Bruce, 725
Vogue (magazine), 298, 380–1, 396, 398, 597,
    682, 698
Voight, Jon, 701
von Linde, Dr. (plastic surgeon), 593
Vortrupp (anti-Nazi youth group), 250

Wagner, Richard, 100
Wain, John, 484
"Waldemar" (1962), 261–2, 550–1, 554,
    565–9, 585
Waldorf Hotel (London), 436
Waley, Arthur, *Monkey* translation, 342
Wallace, Mike, 685–6, 691
Walpole, Hugh, 156, 197
Walters, Barbara, 698
Wandervögel movement, 234–5, 272
Wanne-Eickel (Germany), 585
War and Peace (film; 1956), 507
War Graves Commission, 121
War Office (London), 81
Ward, Simon, 718–19
Warhol, Andy, 593, 682, 708, 718, 725
Warner, Jack, 371–2
Warner, Sylvia Townsend, 282
Warner Brothers (film company), 301, 371–2,
    483, 519
Warner Hot Springs (California), 413
Warren, Robert Penn, 416
Warshaw, Howard, 487, 547, 548
Washington, D.C., 400
Washington, George, 568–9
Washington Post (newspaper), 379, 484
Waterloo Station (London), 59, 60, 74, 107, 117,
    355
Waterston, Sam, 701

Watson, Peter, 310, 314, 315, 508, 571
Watson-Gandy, Tony, 579
Watts, Alan, 652, 653, 660; *The Spirit of Zen*, 366,
    650
Waugh, Alec, *The Loom of Youth*, 127, 132
Waugh, Evelyn, 563–5; *Black Mischief*, 561;
    Brideshead Revisited, 547–8, 564; *Decline and
    Fall*, 561; *A Handful of Dust*, 677; *The Loved
    One*, 633; *Put Out More Flags*, 563–4; *Vile
    Bodies*, 561
Wayfarer, The (film treatment), 499
Weatherby, Meredith (Tex), 524
Weatherford, Jim, 681
Wedekind, Frank, Lulu plays, 220, 659, 662,
    664, 680–1
Wedekind, Kadidja, 659, 664, 680–1
Wedekind, Pamela, 249
Week, The (newspaper), 385
Weigel, Helene, 347
Weingarten, Larry, 488–9
Welles, Orson, 288
Wellesley, Arthur Wellesley, 1st Duke of, 36
Wellington College (Berkshire), 36, 111
Wells (Somerset), 110–11
Wells, H.G., 34, 128, 429, 546; *The Time Machine*,
    303
Welt am Abend, Die (newspaper), 241–2, 462
Wescott, Glenway, 311, 396, 434, 571
West, Dominic, 681
West, Rebecca, 713
Western Samoa, 677–8
Westminster Abbey, 59, 278, 655
Westminster Gazette (newspaper), 239
Westminster Hospital, 199
"What Is the Nerve of Interest in the Novel"
    (lecture; 1960), 440, 545, 574–5, 575–6
What Religion Is: In the Words of Vivekananda (Yale),
    introduction, 544
"What Vedanta Means to Me" (1951), 433
Wheeler, Monroe, 396, 571
White, Alan, 385, 473–4, 582
White, Edmund, 346, 693, 722–3
Whitechapel Galley (London), 680–1, 684
Whiting, Leonard, 702
Whitman, Walt, 57, 98, 161, 206, 300, 535, 723;
    Leaves of Grass, 459, 540–1
Whitman–Radclyffe Foundation, 693
Wick (Caithness), 196
Wilberforce, Samuel, Bishop of Oxford, 287
Wild Party, The (film; 1975), 701
Wilde, Constance, 171
Wilde, Oscar, 176, 206, 212, 701, 723; CI's views
    on, 8, 170–1, 246; Frank Harris's biography
    of, 169, 170–1; *Lady Windermere's Fan*, 521;
    The Picture of Dorian Gray, 324, 412, 424, 694;
    De Profundis, 170, 171, 454; *The Importance of
    Being Earnest*, 454; *Salome*, 35
Wilder, Nicholas, 647–8, 682, 708, 709, 716, 718,
    721, 724, 725
Wilder, Thornton, *The Ides of March*, 642–3
"Wiley, Frank," 599–600
Wilkinson (father and son pre-preparatory
    schoolmasters), 150, 151
Williams, Esther, 491

Williams, Rose, 491
Williams, Sybil, 581
Williams, Tennessee, 7, 343–4, 345–7, 349, 412–13, 434, 435, 489–92, 518, 548, 559, 572, 592, 594, 667; *Cat on a Hot Tin Roof*, 489–91, 500; *The Glass Menagerie*, 345; *The Night of the Iguana*, 592; "One Arm," 669; *Period of Adjustment*, 548; *The Rose Tattoo*, 435, 489, 490, 491, 501, 654; *A Streetcar Named Desire*, 427, 490
Williamson, Nicol, 680
Wilson, Angus, 484, 595, 596, 598–9, 698; *Hemlock and After*, 419
Wilson, Colin, 588–9, 598–9, 625, 698; *The Outsider*, 589, 598
Wilson, Edmund, review of *Goodbye to Berlin*, 3–4, 299
Wilson, Romer, *The Death of Society*, 182
Wilson, Sandy, 583
Wilson, William, 694, 708–9, 716
Wimbledon (London), 20; Common, 20, 200
Windham, Donald, 398
Windsor, Edward, Duke of (*earlier* King Edward VIII), 278
Winters, Marian, 592, 594
Wintle, Hector, 128, 150, 152, 154, 156, 188, 194, 199; *The Final Victory*, 199
"Wishing Tree, The" (1943), 335
Wittenberg, Henry, 717
Wizard of Oz, The (film; 1939), 266
Wolff family: CI lives with in Berlin, 225–8; portrayal in CI's works, 203, 221, 226–9
Wolff, Walter, 204, 221, 223–5, 232, 256, 300, 437, 438, 567
Woman in White, The (film; 1948), 371
Woman's Face, A (film; 1941), 302
Wonner, Paul, 614, 616, 617, 620, 636, 647
Wood, Audrey, 490
Wood, Chris, 301, 315, 326, 327, 328, 335, 338, 342, 397, 399, 594
Wood, Natalie, 636
Woodcock, Patrick, 582
Woodfall Productions (film company), 655
Woodward, Joanne, 593
Woolf, Leonard, 3, 233
Woolf, Virginia, 8, 34–5, 337, 417, 458, 588, 609, 611, 693; publication of CI's works, 3, 233; views on CI, 294; *Jacob's Room*, 189, 610; *Mrs. Dalloway*, 402, 601, 609; *To the Lighthouse*, 181, 524, 610; *The Voyage Out*, 402
Wordsworth, Christopher, 663
Wordsworth, William, 143; *The Prelude*, 142
Workers' Educational Association, 129
World in the Evening, The (1954): autobiographical aspects, 5, 38, 427, 455–6, 458, 460–1; characterization, 38, 52, 123, 137, 320, 337, 384, 455–8, 460–2, 463, 466–70, 511, 564, 598; influences on, 455, 457, 461–2; literary importance, 464; plot and themes, 5, 86, 190, 427, 431–2, 444, 455–8, 460–4, 468–70, 490, 603; proposed play version, 536; publication and editions, 473–4, 483, 484, 485; reception and reviews, 464, 473–4, 484–6, 488, 504, 595; title, 457, 462; writing of, 5, 320, 371, 379, 396, 397, 415, 423, 427, 429, 432, 441, 443, 454–5, 459, 466, 470, 474, 707
World League for Sexual Reform, 253
"World War, The" (1927), 161
World War I (1914–18), 64–88, 91–4, 95–6, 99, 100, 103–4, 106–10, 116–17, 193, 494
World War II (1939–45), 309–11, 317, 369, 372, 375, 382, 383–4, 386–93, 437–8, 463, 464, 523, 533–4; Blitzkrieg, 311, 312, 334, 383–4, 389, 392; Pearl Harbor attack, 320, 325, 455, 534
Worsley, Cuthbert, 310
Worth (Repton pupil), 152
wrestling, 96–7, 99, 324, 377–8
Wright, Frank Lloyd, 413, 613
Wright, Frank Lloyd Jr., 613
Wright, Nicholas, 673
Wright, Tom, 441
"Writer and a Minority, A" (talk; 1965), 640–1
"Writer and His World, A" (lecture; 1960), 545, 707
"Writer and Religion, A" (lecture; 1960), 572–3, 574, 576
"Writer and Vedanta, The" (lecture; 1961), 577–8
"Wrong God, The" (1923), 154
Wuhan (China), 285
Wybergslegh Hall (Cheshire): history, 11–12; location and descriptions, 11–12, 20, 29, 105, 110, 385, 586, 702; ownership and occupation, 11–12, 19, 88, 140–1, 386, 389–90
Wyckoff, Carrie Mead *see* Sister Lalita
Wynne, Brian, 52
Wystan, St., 113–14

Xauen (Spanish Morocco), 267

Yacoubi, Ahmed, 504–5
Yale, John (Prema Chaitanya; Swami Vidyatmananda), 627, 630, 631–3, 634, 643, 645, 648; *What Religion Is: In the Words of Vivekananda*, 544; *A Yankee and the Swamis*, 632
Yale University, 277, 311
Yarnall, Mr. and Mrs., 319
Yarnall, William, 319
Yeats, W.B., 134, 333, 342, 584
Yokohama, 288
York, 29; Minster, 29
York, Michael, 699, 700
York and Lancaster Regiment, 11, 19, 29, 36, 41, 68, 77, 79, 80–1, 92, 96, 300
Yosemite (California), 535
Young, Filson, *Tales from Wagner*, 100
Young, Harvey: background, appearance and character, 291, 300; CI first meets, 288, 291, 293; development of relationship with CI, 298, 300, 305; travels to California with CI, 301, 568–9; life in Los Angeles with CI, 301; break up of relationship with CI, 315, 356–7, 418, 497; and Vedanta, 356–7, 358; marriage and later life, 300, 534, 720; and publication of *My Guru and His Disciple*, 720; portrayal in CI's works, 568–9

"Young American Writers" (1951), 429–30
Young and Innocent (film; 1937), 266
Young Visiters (Cambridge University club), 162, 168
"Young Writers of the Thirties" (exhibition; 1976), 710
Yow, Jenson, 434
Ypres (Belgium), 79, 80, 82, 83, 91, 95, 96, 286; Menin Gate memorial, 121, 286, 715
Ypres, John French, 1st Earl of, 108

Zeigel, John, 580–1
Zeiler (Los Angeles doctor), 372
Zeininger, Russ, 420, 421
Zhangzhou (China), 286
Zimbalist, Sam, 416
Zinnemann, Fred, 416, 427
Zinnemann, Renée, 416
Zonnebeke (Belgium), 80
Zortman, Bruce, 621
Zuma Beach (California), 503

Illustration Credits

1. "The Baby's Progress," CI 591, Christopher Isherwood Papers, Huntington Library, San Marino, California
2. "The Baby's Progress," CI 591, Christopher Isherwood Papers, Huntington
3. Christopher Isherwood Papers, Huntington
4. Christopher Isherwood Papers, Huntington
5. Marple Local History Society
6. Marple Local History Society
7. "The Baby's Progress," CI 591, Huntington
8. Marple Local History Society
9. CI 3124, Huntington
10. Christopher Isherwood Papers, Huntington
11. "Camera Studies" album, CI 3109, Huntington
12. *W.H. Auden: A Tribute*, ed. Stephen Spender (London: Weidenfeld & Nicolson, 1974) p. 20
13. *W.H. Auden: A Tribute*, p. 21
14. Freshwater album, CI 3110, Huntington
15. *The Repton Letters*, Christopher Isherwood, edited by George Ramsden (Settrington: Stone Trough Books, 1997), p. 27
16. *Georgian Stories*, ed. Arthur Waugh (London: G.B. Putnam's Sons, 1928), opp. p. 242
17. Isherwood album, CI 3109, Huntington
18. Isherwood album, CI 3111, Huntington
19. Stephen Spender, by permission of his estate / Licensed by Bridgeman Images; Isherwood album, CI 3113, Huntington
20. Isherwood album, CI 3115, Huntington
21. Stephen Spender, by permission of his estate / Licensed by Bridgeman Images; Isherwood album CI 3115, Huntington
22. Christopher Isherwood Papers, Huntington
23. Stephen Spender, by permission of his estate / Licensed by Bridgeman Images; Christopher Isherwood Papers, Huntington
24. Isherwood film cuttings book, Christopher Isherwood Papers, Huntington
25. Isherwood album, CI 3113, Huntington
26. Isherwood album, CI 3114, Huntington
27. Christopher Isherwood Papers, Huntington
28. Christopher Isherwood Papers, Huntington
29. George Kramer, Christopher Isherwood Papers, Huntington
30. Courtesy of the Vedanta Society of Southern California
31. Courtesy of the Vedanta Society of Southern California
32. Christopher Isherwood Papers, Huntington
33. Attributed to Alec Beesley, by permission of the Estate of Dodie Smith, Christopher Isherwood Papers, Huntington

34 William Caskey, Christopher Isherwood Papers, Huntington
35 William Caskey, Christopher Isherwood Papers, Huntington
36 William Caskey, Christopher Isherwood Papers, Huntington
37 William Caskey, Christopher Isherwood Papers, Huntington
38 William Caskey, Christopher Isherwood Papers, Huntington
39 Don Bachardy, home movie still, Christopher Isherwood Papers, Huntington
40 William Caskey, Christopher Isherwood Papers, Huntington
41 William Caskey, Christopher Isherwood Papers, Huntington
42 William Caskey, Christopher Isherwood Papers, Huntington
43 Carl Van Vechten © Van Vechten Trust, Library of Congress
44 Christopher Isherwood Papers, Huntington
45 Christopher Isherwood Papers, Huntington
46 Christopher Isherwood, Christopher Isherwood Papers, Huntington
47 Ted Bachardy, Don Bachardy Collection
48 Attributed to Richard Avedon, Christopher Isherwood Papers, Huntington
49 Courtesy Everett Collection Inc / Alamy Stock Photo
50 Don Bachardy, Christopher Isherwood Papers, Huntington
51 © Michael Childers, Christopher Isherwood Papers, Huntington
52 Kelvin Brodie for London *Sunday Times*, *Chris and Don: A Love Story*, © Zeitgeist Films 2007 / Courtesy Everett Collection
53 Don Bachardy, Bachardy Archive
54 Don Bachardy, Julian Machin
55 Stephen Stewart, CI 3874, Huntington, and ONE National Gay & Lesbian Archives, USC Libraries, University of Southern California
56 Alice Springs / Helmut Newton Foundation / Trunk Archive; CI 3787, Huntington